1500

New profits from old buildings

by Raynor M. Warner,
Sibyl McCormac Groff
and Ranne P. Warner
with Sandi Weiss

editor: Frank Stella

Private enterprise
approaches
to making
preservation pay

New profits from old buildings

An INFORM Book

McGraw-Hill Book Company
New York St. Louis San Francisco
Auckland Bogotá Düsseldorf Johannesburg
London Madrid Mexico Montreal
New Delhi Panama Paris São Paulo
Singapore Sydney Tokyo Toronto

INFORM Publications

Studies
At Work in Copper: Occupational Health and Safety in Copper Smelting
Energy Futures: Industry and the New Technologies
Promised Lands
   Volume 1: Subdivisions in Deserts and Mountains
   Volume 2. Subdivisions in Florida's Wetlands
   Volume 3. Subdivisions and the Law
New Profits from Old Buildings: Private Enterprise Approaches to Making
   Preservation Pay (Originally published as *Business and Preservation:*
   A Survey of Business Conservation of Buildings and Neighborhoods)

Handbooks and Summaries
A Clear View: Guide to Industrial Pollution Control
What You Should Know Before Buying A Lot: Consumer Guide to Subdivisions
Planner's Guide to Subdivisions
Business and Preservation, Summary Report
Energy Futures Abstract
Promised Lands 1 & 2, Summary Report
Promised Lands 3, Summary Report

To obtain any of these publications, or information on a subscription to all INFORM publications including its newsletter, communicate with INFORM, 25 Broad St., New York, NY 10004, (212) 425-3550.

INFORM is a nonprofit, tax-exempt organization, established in 1973, which conducts research on the impact of American corporations on the environment, employees, and consumers. INFORM publishes books, condensed reports, and newsletters. These seek to clarify and define the nature of some of today's most serious corporate social problems. They describe and evaluate programs and practices that industries could adopt to improve future social performance. INFORM's program is supported by subscriptions and contributions from foundations, corporations, financial institutions, universities, government agencies, and concerned individuals.

Library of Congress Cataloging in Publication Data

ISBN 0–07–068315–8

1234567890 HDHD 765432109

This project is supported by a grant from the National Endowment for the Arts in Washington, D.C., a federal agency.

All photographs unless otherwise credited were provided by the company profiled.

Originally produced for INFORM by the Publishing Center for Cultural Resources, New York City.

Warner, Raynor M
  New profits from old buildings.

Published in 1978 under title: Business and preservation.
  "An Inform book."
  Includes index.
  1. Architecture — United States — Conservation and restoration — Business community participation. 2. Buildings — United States — Remodeling for other use. I. Groff, Sibyl McC., joint author. II. Warner, Ranne P., joint author. III. Stella, Frank, 1945-   IV. Title.
NA110.W37   1979   363   79-2286
ISBN 0-07-068315-8

Contents

Preface

This book could not have been written ten years ago, and it would not have been written five years ago. It expresses a truth become tolerable. By the time it goes into its second printing, what is now tolerable may have become self-evident. We are so quick to adapt to changed circumstances that we may not recognize how much has changed and how rapidly. The peril is that, having adapted, we may fail to see that the tide of events still swells, and that what has become easy is already insufficient.

Therefore, it may be well to note why urban and industrial preservation is beginning to seem a necessary response to economic reality, and also why it has not been so in past decades. Recycling buildings may be as much an expression of the 1980s as disposable clothing and planned obsolescence were of the 1950s and 1960s. We are no more pious than our predecessors; we are responding to a different normalcy. Let us review the record and then ask whether mere adaptation to the obtrusive present is enough to prepare us for the future.

I was born while the nation was keeping cool with Coolidge. Construction costs had been constant for fifty years. A building could be put up for the same dollars in 1926 as in 1876. There was no need to explain in 1926 what kind of dollars you were spending. For half a century, "nominal" dollars had equaled "real dollars" for houses or factories. Indeed, inflation for all goods and services averaged less than one-half percent per year for forty years until World War I. That was my father's experience.

My grandfather had learned economics during a long deflationary boom during which most of the downtown area in my hometown was built. St. Paul, Minnesota, like Chicago and most other places built around railroad depots, tripled its size in the 1880s, while construction costs declined steadily. Logs jammed the rivers on the way to the mills, wheat glutted the elevators, labor was cheap, and there were plenty of eager replacements coming ashore. Land? Some land was still $2 an acre along James J. Hill's shiny new rails. (Most was more, but still very cheap by present standards.)

Although Frederick Jackson Turner told us that the frontier was closing in 1893, more land was homesteaded after that date than before it, and the frontier could be defined as the edge of the unused, plentiful and cheap. The common experience of my parents and grandparents was profusion and steady prices. On the micro-economic level, there were privation and hard work, bleached bones on the prairie, and squalor in the immigrant slums, but speaking in macro-economic terms (as we are wont to do in short introductions like this) there was plenty for Cal to be cool about.

The Depression came as an abrupt deflationary shock. Bond holders in corporations which stayed solvent made fortunes, but as the NRA told us, the rest of the nation suffered from glut: too much unemployed labor, and too many goods. The War of 1941 produced a recovery from that Depression. Its shortages were perceived as sufficiently abnormal to permit those at home a little easy heroism in self-denial. Profusion was still our natural setting, and we feared a post-war depression because we did not know what to do with profusion. Wartime self-restraint was an economic necessity because government expenditure, financed by debt and taxes, accompanied a program of government employment on a scale which made the WPA seem trifling. The money, of course, went for what might be called single-purpose goods, more quickly depreciable than usual, and the work was perilous but (again speaking from the perspective of macro-economics) we had always been an unusually wasteful people, and we were just wasting more than usual.

After the War, there was no Depression, but there was, after a while, a second amazingly profusive aberration in our economic history: the capital glut which seemed to condition the normalcy of the middle classes of my generation. Our parents and grandparents grew up with cheap labor and steady prices. We grew up with the cheapest capital in the history of American capitalism. The postwar boom had such enormous momentum that a businessman selling stock could sell a dollar of current earnings (and, of course, the hope of capital gains) to a new shareholder for twice as much in 1958 as he could in 1948, and five years later, buyers of common stock on the New York Stock Exchange were willing to pay twice as much—again—for a dollar of current earnings.

During the 1950s, the large corporations were still paying rates of interest for borrowed money less than a third of those prevailing today.* That meant, of course, that even though construction costs had begun to escalate in the late 1920s, it was easy to take in partners (new equity owners) for the purpose of building new plants. It is possible, although the figures are slippery, that the decline of the cost of capital just about offset the increase of the cost of construction between 1926 and 1966.

What has all this to do with this book? The discovery of preservation is natural to my generation because we live in a time of steadily rising costs and expensive capital. We owe our predecessors some graceful acknowl-edgment that their normalcy is no longer accessible to us. We are, therefore, free to adapt to circumstances which have now prevailed long enough for them to become normalcy to us.

There are examples in this book of action which anticipates necessity by so wide a space as to be remarkable. Why remarkable? A businessman operating to protect his shareholders cannot go too far ahead of what appears likely to be required of him lest he be caught by changes of economic climate or of governmental requirements which turn a good plan into an embarrassing anachronism.

Yet, the only greater danger than planning too far in advance is refusing to plan far enough. As the corporate managers described in this book looked about at the inventory of buildings which they could include in their plans, they had to make computations about alternative ways of housing their plants. They knew what an existing building would cost, and they could get respectable estimates of what conversion would cost. All they could know about new facilities was that they would go up in cost the longer their construction was delayed.

Computations produced more preservation, I'll bet, than sentiment did. And having written more books and articles about architectural history than I like to count, and having given more lectures about historic

---

*Computing the effect of money cost, of interest, upon construction is a dicey business. But if one could imagine zero interest cost—a Swiss instance, perhaps—that would differ from the 12 percent construction loans of 1974 atop what we *now* think to be an underlying inflation rate of 6 percent and differ again from 5 percent construction loans atop a 3 percent inflation rate of earlier years.

buildings than I can remember, I am fully prepared to put my faith in computation as the better hope for the future than moral suasion or aesthetic admonition.

When it makes economic sense to reuse an existing plant, there is presented an opportunity to do the job well. When among one's choices for reuse there are ugly buildings and handsome buildings, at nearly the same price, one will be likely to use a handsome one, as several case studies in this book demonstrate. Solving an aesthetic and economic puzzle simultaneously is fun, like Chinese checkers. And there are good reasons for doing so.

There are very few corporate managers who are indifferent to the multiple constituencies who surround them: stockholders, workers, customers, bankers, suppliers, and journalists. When the economics are close to right, it is pleasant to have something good to report.

Businessmen occupy places of power quite briefly, and they know it. The long progression up the corporate Jungle Gym consumes decades, for most people, and when the summit is reached, the person who becomes boss looks about to make a mark while he may; and for interesting ways to make that mark. This is as true in a corporation as it was in the feudality or the Renaissance church, in Pharaoh's Egypt, or in any People's Republic. And throughout human society, a sound economic decision may be to create something beautiful, or save something beautiful, which may be associated with the boss for many years. It may be his best way of proclaiming his survival as well as his taste.

I do not mean to discredit this impulse. It is hardly derogatory to classify anyone with Lorenzo de'Medici, Urban II, Cheops, the Earl of Carlisle, Louis XIV, or Pericles. What this book adds to the earnest work of architectural historians, and to the education which has refined the taste of those who hold economic power, is a series of examples of sound business arguments for the cause of old buildings.

There are, of course, less numerical arguments to be made. We could speak of used buildings as constructed natural resources, to be regarded with as much, or even more, reverence as natural resources. We would emphasize the fact that the environment for most people is an urban environment, not a bucolic or sylvan one. Bombed-out and brutalized neighborhoods are inhabited by more people than bosky dells, and we should use public policy to make it easier, not harder, for the individual local choices of businessmen to serve these people.

Finally, I must express a personal apprehension which I cannot support with any elaborate statistical base. The largest unknown cost of future construction is energy or, to be more precise, oil. We have adjusted to a large single price increase in oil and are adjusting to the syphoning off of consumer disposal income from industrial countries toward producing countries. But there are good economists who say that we are growing more slowly, as an economy, than in the past.

Slower growth coupled with intractable unemployment (possibly occasioned by the gap between the requirements of high technology and the attainments of popular education, possibly by deeper causes related to the nature of human services actually required by modern, mechanized society) constitute heavy weights on a society already burdened by a need to buy much of its energy from others. An economy which has an oil leak,

x

out of which flows consumer purchasing power, *and* which grows slowly, cannot afford waste.

This book suggests that we are beginning to learn how to diminish our waste of old buildings: to return our empty bottles. We are going to have to learn these lessons and a lot more. The corporate managers who created these test cases can take satisfaction in having led the way through what was desirable in the present toward what will be necessary in the future.

Roger G. Kennedy
Vice President
The Ford Foundation

Acknowledgments

The authors and editor of this INFORM study would like to express their gratitude to the scores of friends, advisors, preservationists, community leaders, and businesspeople whose cooperation helped make the project possible. We are particularly indebted to INFORM's director, Joanna Underwood, for her attention, support, and enthusiasm. We'd also like to thank Jean Halloran, INFORM's editorial director, for her dedication to the task of completing this book, as well as for the confidence she showed in us, and the fresh perspective and thoughtful analysis she brought to the review of our efforts.

We would like to express our appreciation to Garry Tanner for his research efforts, particularly in the area of residential revitalization; to Michael Friedman for his research on Bird & Son, Tremont Nail, and Harbridge House; and to copyeditor Dan Smullyan for his patient contribution to making our text more lucid. Special thanks to typists Mary Ferguson, Bob Szwed, John Klingberg, and Marsha Archer, both for their care in creating the comprehensible from the chaotic, and for their editorial suggestions and comments. We are grateful for the help of Sheron Milliner, Dick Griffin, and Nancy Stella for preparing the glossary and footnotes; and beyond these specific contributions, we deeply appreciate the moral support of the entire INFORM staff.

The authors and editor would like to express their appreciation to the members of the advisory board: especially to Roger Webb, President of Architectural Heritage Foundation in Boston who, along with providing expert guidance, also donated office space to carry out much of the research and writing; to Martin Cleary, Vice President, Teachers Insurance and Annuity Association; to Professor James Marston Fitch of the Columbia University School of Architecture; to Ronald Lee Fleming, Executive Director of Vision, Inc.; to Dun Gifford, a real estate developer in Boston; to Roger Lang, Director of Restoration and Renovation Services, Perry, Dean, Stahl and Rogers; to Theodore H. M. Prudon, restoration architect (whose analysis and advice were especially helpful), Ezra D. Ehrencrantz & Associates; to Lynda Simmons, Vice President, Phipps Houses; and to Arthur Ziegler, President, Pittsburgh History and Landmarks Foundation.

Many others assisted this study in a variety of ways. We are particularly grateful to Gideon Chagy, Vice President, Business Committee for the Arts; Robertson Collins, Board member, National Trust for Historic Preservation; and Kip Forbes, Editor, *19th Century* magazine, for their advice and assistance. Special thanks for help in the area of residential revitalization must go to Stephen Allen, Program Specialist, Urban Reinvestment Task Force; Jim Cook, Director, Neighborhood Housing Services of Jamaica; Robert Corletta, President, National Center for Urban Ethnic Affairs; and Helen Murray, Redlining Reinvestment Specialist, National Training and Information Center.

We'd also like to thank the staff of the National Trust; especially, Jess Barnett, John Frisbee, Richard Haupt, Russell Keune, Michael Leventhal, Pat Martin, J. E. Moody, and Tom Slade.

Architectural Heritage's staff deserve credit for their assistance and support. Special thanks to Andrew Burns, F. Aldrich Edwards, and Patricia Swygert. For their assistance and advice we'd also like to thank AIA staff members, Mark Maves and Maurice Payne.

Many local preservationists and friends helped us with information about their projects and also with generous hospitality as we visited their cities and towns. We are especially indebted to: Leopold Adler II, Chip and Amanda Allen, Kenneth Anderson, Robert Berner, Peter Brink, Chris Carson, Henry Cauthen, Jr., John W. Cheek, Stephanie Churchill, Dana Crawford, Karen and Fred Diamond, Carl Feiss, Jack Finglass, Junius Fishburne, John Flowers, Richard Freeman, James W. Garrison, Sam Gowan, Rick and Margaret Green, Dorothy Hall, Kay and Bill James, William Kelso, Judy Kitchen, Ruth La Compte, Truett Latimer, Weiming Lu, Bruce and Jill MacDougale, Elaine Mayo, Langdon Morris, Nancy Negley, Deborah Neu, Susan and John Owens, John Parry, Boone and Cathy Powell, Martha Robinson, Alicia Rudolph, Nadine Russell, Janet Seapker, David Sherman, Nancy Shirk, Joseph Stettinius, José and Yvonne Tacoronte, Michele and Dennis Walters, Mary and Vernon Weston, Jay Williams and family, Joe Williams, J. Reid Williamson, Merrill Wilson, and Samuel Wilson. To any whom we may have missed, our apologies and thanks as well.

We would like to thank the National Endowment for the Arts, the Rockefeller Family Fund, the Chase Manhattan Bank, the Ford Foundation, and the J. M. Kaplan Fund for their most generous support which, over the past two years, has enabled us to proceed with this work.

Introduction

The United States has historically been a country endowed with natural resources in such abundance as to inspire profligacy. Land, energy, water, minerals, timber: all of these have been used, until very recently, with little regard for their supply. When converted to other forms—when hauled, hammered, bolted, and transformed to create buildings—we generally ceased thinking of these items as resources at all. Buildings became products, to be used until other products—less worn, more stylish, or better located—were constructed.

Nevertheless, over the decades America's buildings have become extraordinary storehouses of our natural resources, of wood, stone, mortar, and steel, as well as of the energy used to assemble them. At the same time, they have become repositories of cultural and social resources. Human effort, imagination, and creativity are embodied in everything from simply and functionally designed homes to ornately decorated public edifices. Our social structure is embodied in buildings from county courthouses to downtown storefronts. Buildings are the physical shells which have formed neighborhoods, shaped social contacts, and molded patterns of doing business to such a degree that to alter them today tears our economic and social fabric.

Today, we are gradually coming to realize the value and importance of our physical, social, and cultural resources. With many of our prime forests cut down, the highest quality iron reserves mined, and most accessible oil fields pumped dry, raw-material costs are rising. With the vast waves of immigration over and the sons and daughters of immigrants demanding a better standard of living, the era of cheap labor has passed. And with the migration of millions of people from rural areas to megalopolis, particularly to its mass-produced suburbs, much of the former character and identity of neighborhoods has been lost.

These trends have led some groups, individuals, and businesses—including the 71 businesses profiled in this study—to a new appreciation of old buildings, and thus to work for their preservation. Some companies have recycled buildings, others have worked to renew neighborhoods and older business districts, and still others have made donations to projects working toward these ends, as well as to more traditional historic-preservation activities. The case studies presented in this book provide useful examples for other businesses interested in building and community preservation, and for citizens groups interested in obtaining support for these causes.

Appreciation of the worth of old buildings is by no means universal, however. Indeed, for most of this century, countervailing social and economic forces have held sway. Older cities and towns have been steadily losing businesses and population. In twenty years, New York, Chicago, Pittsburgh, Philadelphia, Boston, and Detroit's share of the top 500 companies has decreased from 250 to 140.[1] Between 1968 and 1978, New York City will have lost 111 of the nation's top 1,100 corporations, though its suburbs will have gained 60.[2] As businesses left cities, so did jobs. New York City lost

650,000 jobs between 1969 and 1976.[3] Detroit's workforce has declined by 26 percent in the last five years.[4] The loss of jobs has meant the escalation of unemployment and welfare costs, as well as the lethal combination of a shrinking tax base and rising taxes: in short, a climate increasingly hazardous to both businesses and communities.

Because of such losses, older neighborhoods and commercial districts in both cities and towns, as well as important older buildings, have increasingly stood underutilized, their very existence threatened. New York City in mid-1977 had upwards of 10,000 abandoned buildings.[5] Its Chrysler Building, an Art Deco landmark, will be only 50 percent occupied by January 1, 1978. The Prudential Building in downtown Buffalo, a masterpiece of early skyscraper construction, can find no business tenants. Similar situations exist across the country.

The suburbs, to which many city dwellers chose to pick up and flee, are now beginning to face problems similar to those their residents hoped they had left behind: crime, rising real estate prices and taxes, and in some places, aging housing stock. Building moratoriums and more stringent zoning laws have created a scarcity of land for new construction. Both the remaining open land and the existing housing stock in urban and suburban areas are resources which are requiring increasingly careful use and preservation.

Until the last fifteen years, just a few preservation groups scattered around the U.S. had much interest in saving old buildings. Their interest was focused on the historic, aesthetic, or architectural significance of a structure. The number of such groups has grown as the threat to such buildings has grown. In 1966, there were 2,500 preservation groups; as of mid-1977, there were over 6,000. Battles have been waged to save New York City's Grand Central Station; and others are underway across the country. Preservation groups are fighting to save South Hall, a National Register landmark on the campus of the University of Wisconsin, River Falls; and the Harvey House in Barstow, California, a turn-of-the-century grand hotel built in the Spanish style.

Added to the voices of these historic-preservation organizations have been those—especially since the sixties—of community groups and government agencies concerned about deteriorating or abandoned urban housing in once sound neighborhoods. Brooklyn's Bedford Stuyvesant Restoration Corporation and Rochester's WEDGE have been actively involved in improving their neighborhoods for about ten years. In 1965, the federal government created the Department of Housing and Urban Development to deal with these issues.

The Bicentennial has helped too, bringing increased awareness of America's heritage.

Yet private industry in this country, which has perhaps the largest impact on real estate, has been slow in developing an interest in using old buildings or in seeing the need to support their continued use. American corporations, through direct ownership, control approximately $650 billion in domestic real property assets.* This does not include property controlled through leasing or other influences, nor does it include property owned or leased by smaller business institutions. Until recently, much of the business community believed that preservation was regressive. While building the *new* was seen as progressive and good for business image, rebuilding the *old* was not.

The climate established by political, legal, social, and economic forces did not favor the widespread preservation and reuse of buildings, especially by business. Tax incentives were provided for demolishing an old structure and building a new one in its place. Banks regarded older buildings and neighborhoods not as challenges but as high risks. Government renewal programs of the 1950s cleared vast areas of built-on land for new buildings, many of which were never built. Public and government opinion took little account of the uniqueness or economic value of older buildings, or of their contribution to the scale, identity, and visual richness of the environment.

If preservation is to become widespread, the participation and support of private industry will be essential. Data on the corporate involvement is sparse, but what indicators there are suggest possible new trends. Figures on the total extent of current recycling of old buildings by companies for their own business purposes—as headquarters, plants, or offices—are not available. However, a few recent developments point to increased activity. Each year, the McGraw-Hill Information Systems Company publishes the *Dodge Manual for Building Construction and Pricing Scheduling*. In its 1977 issue, a special section was included for the first time on "remodeling and renovation," referring to it as a "popular segment of the construction industry."[6] *Buildings* magazine, a publication for the construction and building management industries, publishes a special issue on "modernization" each year. For the past few years, it has surveyed its readers to determine the size of this growing market. Although the magazine's survey includes both private- and public-sector work, the total modernization market for 1976 was estimated at $10 billion, up $2 billion from the previous year.[7] Of this figure, more than 50 percent was attributable to commercial-business expenditures.

Because business-sponsored neighborhood revitalization is an even newer phenomenon, meaningful figures on the overall corporate contribution to such projects are even less readily available.

The level of business's involvement in preservation activities presents a mixed picture. A study carried out by the Business Committee for the Arts, a nonprofit organization established in 1967 to promote business support for the arts, indicated that arts support increased overall from $144 million to $221 million between 1973 and 1976, but that preservation's share of these contributions slipped from 5 percent in 1973 to 3 percent in 1976.[8]

*Howard Stevenson of the Harvard Graduate School of Business Administration faculty is currently preparing a paper on corporate investments in real estate. He places total corporate ownership of real estate at 18 percent of total corporate assets, based on historical costs (actual past costs). The most recent figures, as published in U.S. Bureau of Census, *Statistical Abstract of the United States 1976,* Washington, D.C., indicate that active corporate assets are currently $3.6 trillion.

Perhaps, over the coming decade, of sheer necessity, the business sector will increasingly turn to reusing buildings and to rebuilding the neighborhoods and communities around them. At present, however, substantive information about what businesses have already attempted and achieved in these fields could greatly extend industry's overall awareness of preservation as an alternative. It could help to define the problems and benefits that have accrued to both the companies and communities involved, as well as to the broader rural and urban environment. While business efforts around the U.S. may only undertake preservation on a building by building or block by block basis, what, after all, are cities and towns physically, but aggregations of buildings and blocks?

The INFORM Study INFORM has sought to fill the existing information gap on business involvement in preservation. In two years of research, several hundred projects across the country were identified. The projects profiled illustrate the ways in which business has either made use of existing buildings or given support to others for their preservation. These projects involve preservation by profit-oriented, privately and publicly owned commercial, industrial, and service organizations of old buildings, industrial facilities, neighborhoods, and commercial districts. Some of the buildings rebuilt and reused were of architectural and historic significance; others had purely economic, social, and ecological values.

A total of 71 of the projects best exemplifying the range of efforts and the kinds of experience business has had in this field were selected for examination in some detail. Companies whose primary line of business is development were excluded, in order to highlight the potential for involvement of businesses of all types. These 71 project profiles make up the bulk of this report. They are presented in three separate chapters by project type:

- *Building Recycling*—discussing the adaptive reuse of old buildings for new business purposes; continued use of significant buildings for extended business life; and the combination of new and old buildings for image and efficiency.

- *Community Revitalization*—presenting some of the ways business has participated in breathing new life into residential neighborhoods; highlighting several business development and support efforts to create new economic vitality in older commercial areas.

- *General Preservation Support*—discussing the variety of ways in which business has contributed to the preservation of historic buildings and sites.

Each case study begins with a brief summary highlighting the project's most important aspects. Following the summary are discussions of: the sequence of events leading up to the company's decision to become involved in the project; the project execution; the costs involved; the problems encountered in the work itself and in dealings with community groups or government agencies, if these problems arose; the short-term and long-term benefits obtained; and a brief description of the company involved. At the end of each case study, at least one contact at the company and sometimes other contacts at related preservation or community groups are noted, should further information on the work be of interest to the reader.

The 71 companies profiled include international industrial giants, such as Exxon, R. J. Reynolds Industries, and General Mills, as well as small specialty firms like Hitchcock Chair of Riverton, Connecticut, or Pinaire Lithographing of Louisville, Kentucky. They represent a broad range of business activity: there are heavy manufacturing firms, oil companies, public utilities, consumer-oriented industries, banks, insurance companies, and service companies. Each firm had different reasons for embarking on its project: a need for space; a desire to help improve the value and quality of its city or town, the neighborhood surrounding its plant or headquarters; a special cultural or aesthetic interest in seeing a valuable old structure have continued life; or a request for assistance by a local preservation or community organization.

In addition to the 71 case studies, 71 company projects are listed and described briefly in the Appendix.

The portrait of resource reuse contained in these pages reveals the considerable ingenuity, planning, and skills that businesses have recently begun to devote to preservation. It suggests the tremendous potential value that such activity offers to companies and to communities, as well as to the nation's rural and urban environments.

These cases should certainly inspire a closer, more serious look at preservation possibilities by the still many thousands of businesses and corporations that continue to stampede for increasingly expensive and scarce "new turf," remaining oblivious to a resource now too valuable to ignore. The range of problems and benefits accruing to the firms profiled here should assist other companies plan projects of their own.

Benefits   The projects profiled in this study suggest that many economic, aesthetic, and public-relations benefits have accrued to the companies involved.

Economics.   The recycling and continued use of existing buildings can usually be justified on economic grounds alone. The shell of an office or factory building, including the foundation, supporting structure, and outer enclosure, represents a substantial cost in construction dollars and time. The cost of demolition and new construction, both from a dollars-and-cents and an energy standpoint, is often high. While there are no universal rules, INFORM found that at most of the seventeen reuse projects profiled, the costs ran from 30 percent to 40 percent less than replacement new construction. Lawyers Co-operative, a Rochester publishing company, spent about $15 per square foot to convert a nineteenth-century mill complex to office space. This represented a considerable saving over the approximately $45-per-square-foot cost of similar new construction. Adaptive reuse exceeded the cost of new construction in only three of seventeen cases.

Construction time, as well as cost, depends on the scope of work required, the number and extent of changes from the original, the number of unforeseen problems, and the skill of the architects and contractors executing the work. An accurate restoration of a historic building, even if only the exterior, costs a great deal of time and money. Skilled labor is expensive, and repair and reproduction of intricate detail takes time. The exact duplication of the Hotel Utah's exterior terra cotta and the recreation of the atmosphere in its turn-of-the-century public rooms cost $40,000 per room and took three years. Most business recycling projects, however, need not require such major restoration work.

Based on the projects studied by INFORM, operating costs in recycled buildings average no higher than in new construction. Operable windows, thick masonry walls, high ceilings, and proper orientation, often characteristics of older structures, actually made some of the buildings more efficient in warm weather, although some were less efficient during the winter heating months. Heating costs were substantially higher for Connecticut Savings Bank's Cheshire branch, located in an old mansion, than they would have been in a comparable new building. This occurred because the branch did not wish to replace the old windows and interfere with the building's appearance. Loose, poorly sealed windows often need to be tightened. To be truly energy efficient, many must be replaced with dual-pane insulating glass or covered with storm windows. New insulation, of course, is a necessity in most recycling projects, since many older buildings are poorly insulated. In general, however, with the addition of proper insulation and modern heating and other mechanical systems, old buildings can be as economical to operate as new ones.

One final advantage to a company's recycling an older building can be good employee relations and retention of a trained workforce. Levi Strauss' renovation of its Mission District plant in San Francisco enabled many employees to stay on who would not have been able to commute had the compay decided to move to a suburban location.

Where a corporation is reusing a building for its own business purposes, the economic advantages accrue mainly to the firm itself. However, where business supports community revitalization, cost and time savings most directly benefit community residents and governments. In most such cases, homes and local businesses can be occupied more quickly, and dislocation problems are usually not as severe as they would be if the areas were totally razed and built over. Dislocation of residents proved to be a problem in only two of the thirteen residential-revitalization cases studied. Underutilized or abandoned buildings, often defaulting in their tax obligations, are returned to tax-paying status without an appreciable increase in the cost of city services. The Brooklyn Union Gas Company has helped buyers obtain financing to purchase and renovate abandoned houses and storefronts in several sections of Brooklyn with just this effect.

The companies who participated in residential-revitalization projects often benefited directly as well, as in the case of South Shore Bank in Chicago. After three years of working with residents of its deteriorating service area to improve housing, stabilize business, and increase public understanding of banking services, the bank reversed a seven-year decline in deposits and recorded a 25 percent increase. Other companies studied hoped to register indirect gains by improving the quality of life in their city or neighborhood. Tasty Baking is hoping to accomplish exactly this by supporting a program to renovate and sell (at a slight loss) houses in the Philadelphia neighborhood in which it is located.

Even if a company does not undertake an entire building or community revitalization and simply makes a donation to preservation activities, it can and usually does accrue some financial benefit through tax write-offs. Only two of the companies studied were actually willing to indicate the amount of such benefits. One of them, Union Camp, realized a $26,000 tax deduction for its donation of the Tower Hill Plantation to the National Trust for Historic Preservation.

Aesthetics. Aesthetic benefits, while more difficult to categorize, also accrue to company employees and society at large. A look at any American city or town today affirms that new construction, often standardized to reduce cost, tends to produce a bland similarity of spaces and appearance. Several companies, on the other hand, have noted that recycling buildings is good for employee morale and has brought a favorable response from the community. Employees of Digital Equipment Corporation like the option of designing their own office space in a former textile-mill complex. SEDCO's conversion of an old school in Dallas to corporate offices has brought the company acclaim from local historical and architectural groups.

New additions can harmonize with older buildings through the use of modern materials, techniques, and details. In the six such cases profiled, an effort was made to develop stylistically compatible new designs. Older residential areas often contain architectural diamonds in the rough, like Brooklyn Union's brownstones in Brooklyn or Lakewood Bank's Dallas project which contained prairie-style homes inspired and in one case designed by Frank Lloyd Wright.

Landmark industrial, community, or residential buildings are an invaluable part of the past. The twenty companies profiled in the "general support" section realized the importance of preserving this legacy. Hercules, a chemical company, donated $50,000 to help restore the Grand Opera House in Wilmington, Delaware. Its contribution encouraged other businesses to donate funds and helped bring the century-old Grand back to productive use.

Company Public Relations. Probably the most consistently cited benefit among all of the projects surveyed is that of enhanced image.

Preservation activities can provide a sophisticated advertising vehicle whereby awareness of both the company and its products is increased. Older buildings usually reflect quality, stability, and continuity in the community. This may, in fact, be one major reason why 11 of the 29 recycled-building cases surveyed involved the conversion of older buildings by banks. The First New Haven National Bank's renovation of an eighteenth-century house as its Westbrook branch brought the bank extensive local publicity. In addition, new accounts and deposits in the branch exceeded projections. The experience was similar for the Connecticut Savings Bank, which turned another eighteenth-century house into one of its branches.

On the other hand, recycled buildings need not project a conservative image or rely on nostalgia for acceptance. With much of modern architecture resulting in look-alike anonymity, the unique identity an old building provides is often a positive business benefit in itself. McGraw-Hill is pleased with both the location and individuality of its Publications Company's Western Regions Office located in a converted ice cream factory. Although the company is only a tenant, the building was renamed the McGraw-Hill Building.

Support of community revitalization also brings public-relations benefits. Most such projects have resulted in extensive local publicity. Some have brought industry recognition, and state and national attention as well. Frederic Rider, the Brooklyn Union official in charge of the company's residential-redevelopment activities, has been interviewed by newspapers across the country. Trend Publications received the 1976 Annual Governor's Award in the Arts for its conversion of an old cigar factory in Tampa, Florida, into a commercial center.

Similarly, business donations can produce image and public-relations benefits. The contribution of money, property, materials, and services to preservation efforts has done so in seventeen of twenty cases. Bird & Son was praised by former Vice President Rockefeller, cited in the *Congressional Record*, and recognized by the Bicentennial Commission for its matching-grants awards to preservation groups.

Problems   In the 71 cases in this survey INFORM found three general problem areas to be associated with business-sponsored preservation activities: problems in obtaining adequate capital, uncertainties and delays resulting from the unconventional nature of the projects, and employee apprehensiveness about recycling and revitalizing. These problems relate largely to recycling buildings and revitalizing neighborhoods, and do not apply to charitable contributions to preservation. While preservation groups are frequently hard pressed to raise money, the giving of donations does not involve many problems for companies. The problems found were real enough, but in most cases not insoluble. As preservation projects proliferate, construction problems will lessen and financial backing should become easier to obtain. If commercial and residential revitalization projects are successful, apprehension should decrease.

Availability of Capital. The novel and—for now—somewhat uncommon nature of many preservation projects leads to greater technical and financial uncertainty than is generally encountered in new construction. Difficulties in obtaining mortgages and loans because of banks' perceptions of greater risk were found to cause delays and/or to require changes in the plans of 9 of 22 community-revitalization projects. The more ambitious the project, the more prevalent the problem seemed to be. The Jefferson Company's $20 million project to redevelop the neglected Minneapolis river front was delayed nearly three years while the company searched for bank financing. The company finally obtained partial financing, and was able to proceed with the first phase of the project.

Uncertainties in Construction. Contractors and architects are often hesitant to provide firm bids and guaranteed completion dates on recycling projects. Structural problems, initially hidden from view, are at times exposed as work progresses, resulting in extensive delays and/or cost overruns. Replacing the existing plumbing in Cleveland's Cuyahoga Building, an unexpected part of the renovation of the structure, resulted in a $300,000 overrun in the Sohio case. Obtaining variances for zoning or code violations can also cause delays and cost money.

Such uncertainities could, of course, be reduced by employing architects and contractors with previous experience in recycling, and by thoroughly inspecting a building before making a reuse decision. Nevertheless, there is no way to eliminate all risks involved.

Community, Employee, and Management Apprehension. Employees and management alike often have not been exposed to the good qualities of recycled buildings. Managers of public companies are also reluctant to invest in properties that might not appear profitable to stockholders. In addition, communities and sometimes, ironically, preservation groups are hesitant to allow a business to reuse a historic building for fear that the use might destroy the landmark's original character. Many Philadelphians resisted Design Research's efforts to convert an old mansion to its Philadelphia branch, until local efforts to find an alternate use failed.

Similar reservations exist within neighborhoods and commercial districts. Some residents fear the heavy hand of business support; ostensibly, control might outweigh the benefits of revitalization. General Mills' Stevens Court project in Minneapolis, which purchases and renovates small apartment buildings and rents them to local residents, initially encountered fear of company control and the evils of the company town among some Minneapolis residents.

Public Sector Policies and Programs   Government recognition of the need to support preservation is increasing, and on several levels, efforts are beginning to be made to encourage the recycling of old buildings for commercial, business, and residential use. On the federal level, diverse regulations, programs, and tax policies are being reviewed. On the state and local levels, a reevaluation is taking place of building codes, zoning ordinances, and property taxes which affect business decisions about reusing old buildings.

Federal. Federal support for preservation has been evolving slowly since the beginning of the century. The first piece of preservation legislation passed was the Antiquities Act of 1906, which provided for the protection of historic and prehistoric sites on federal lands and for the designation of national monuments. In 1916, the National Park Service was created as a bureau of the Department of the Interior. (The Department of the Interior still supplies most federal support for historic-preservation activities.) However, it was not until passage of the Historic Sites Act of 1935 that a national policy for preserving historic sites, buildings, and objects for public use was established. Under this Act, the Historic American Buildings Survey (HABS), originally established under the Works Progress Administration in 1933, became a permanent body recording the country's architectural heritage. (In 1969, the Historic American Engineering Record [HAER] was set up to supplement the HABS by recording and documenting industrial buildings and engineering artifacts, such as bridges.) The National Historic Landmarks Program, which identifies, lists, and maintains nationally important properties, also evolved from the 1935 Act.

In 1966, another major piece of legislation was passed, the National Historic Preservation Act (NHPA). The NHPA expanded the kinds of property eligible for federal notice, and officially created the National Register of Historic Places. Besides properties of national significance, the Register was to include districts, sites, buildings, and objects of state and local significance. Published biennially, the Register serves as the primary catalog of significant historic properties in the United States. Although only approximately 20 percent complete, it contains more than 12,000 entries. The NHPA also established a matching-grants program for survey, acquisition, and restoration of historic properties. These funds are administered by the National Park Service and allocated in each state by a State Historic Preservation Officer appointed by the Governor. Still another provision of the NHPA created the Advisory Council on Historic Preservation to advise the federal government on preservation matters, to coordinate federal, state, and local programs, as well as public and private preservation activities, and to insure that federal funds are not used to the detriment of historic properties.

In 1969, Congress passed the National Environmental Policy Act (NEPA), which included preservation of historic and cultural assets as a major goal. A section of the NEPA requires that Environmental Impact Statements (EIS) be prepared for federal actions that may significantly affect the quality of the environment. In May, 1971, a presidential directive, Executive Order 11593, was issued to encourage federal agencies to support the preservation of federally owned historic properties and to assure that federal plans and programs contribute to preserving and enhancing historic properties even when they are not under federal ownership.*

Since its inception in 1949, the National Trust for Historic Preservation has been one of the key organizations in the preservation field. It was chartered by Congress as a private, nonprofit organization to promote preservation through educational, technical, service, and advisory programs. The Trust administers small grants and revolving loan funds, and maintains and leases historic buildings. Although not equipped with any regulatory powers, the organization has provided leadership, and serves as a valuable information clearing house, producing a variety of publications on preservation subjects. The work of the Trust is funded by federal support, by the dues of its 115,000 members, and by private contributions. Recently, in an attempt to stimulate corporate awareness and support for preservation, the Trust created a Corporate Associates Program, which has enlisted more than 100 corporate members at a minimum annual membership fee of $1,000. The National Trust has a current budget of $5.8 million.

Federal preservation regulations only partially protect historic properties from direct federal or federally assisted intervention, and they do not apply at all to private-sector action. For example, properties listed in or eligible for listing in the National Register of Historic Places are only guaranteed review if threatened with destruction by a federally financed project. Even then, they are only assured a delay to permit Advisory Council review and recommendations. Protection from totally private intervention is provided only if a local landmark or historic-district ordinance assures it.

There are some federal programs and policies that may be used by business to obtain financial assistance for building reuse. These include a variety of grants, loans, and tax incentives. As indicated above, businesses using or supporting properties included in or eligible for inclusion in the National Register may obtain National Park Service matching grants for acquisition and restoration under the National Historic Preservation Act of 1966. Matching grants provide a maximum of 50 percent of project funds. Approximately 3,000 projects have received grant aid to date. Funding for the grants increased from $2 million in 1967 to $40 million for fiscal 1978. Authorizations of $100 million for fiscal 1978 and 1979, and $150 million for fiscal 1980 and 1981, have already been made, but may not be fully funded. The Land and Water Conservation Act, passed in 1976, authorized the creation of the National Historic Preservation Fund, which distributes monies the government receives from off-shore oil leases and mineral rights. One of the companies studied by INFORM, Harbridge House, Inc., with corporate headquarters in a nineteenth-century mansion in Boston's Back Bay historic district, applied for a $73,000 grant of this

*A more complete description of this Executive Order can be found in *A Guide to Federal Programs*, published in 1974 by the National Trust for Historic Preservation and updated in 1976.

type in 1976 to restore its facade. Park Service allocations to Massachusetts were not sufficient to finance the project at that time.

Other federal funding programs that may be applicable to business preservation projects include low-interest loans and grants-in-aid under the Department of Agriculture, the Commerce Department's Economic Development Administration (EDA), the Small Business Administration (SBA), and the Department of Housing and Urban Development (HUD). The Department of Agriculture programs are primarily directed toward private business development in rural areas and would include renovation projects if they reinforce employment. The EDA's programs are directed at improving employment through state and local public-works projects, especially in high-unemployment and redevelopment areas.

In 1976, the EDA-administered Local Capital Development and Investment Program channeled $3.2 billion into state and local public-works projects, including preservation efforts. Current efforts are underway to extend the Program and increase its preservation-related application.

Preservation work is more labor intensive than new construction. Kenneth Tapman, legal counsel for the Advisory Council on Historic Preservation, testified before the House Subcommittee on Economic Development in February, 1977, that "50 percent more jobs [per $1 million spent were] produced by restoration and renovation than by new construction."[9] This finding could increase EDA funding for preservation in the future.

The Small Business Administration (SBA) administers several loan programs and offers loan guarantees that can assist commercial revitalization and reuse of older buildings. Section 502 of the Small Business Investment Act of 1958, as amended, authorizes the SBA to "make loans to state and local development companies for use in assisting specific small businesses . . . to construct, modernize or expand their plants."[10] The Lowell Development and Financial Corporation, a local Massachusetts development company discussed in this study, was established under SBA guidelines. In September, 1976, the SBA initiated a neighborhood-revitalization program to expand the "502" concept in urban areas. Old Town Mall in Baltimore was the first neighborhood commercial-revitalization project to receive substantial assistance from the SBA's Section 502 lending program. More than eighty stores built in the 1800s on Baltimore's East Side were redeveloped under a renovation/ preservation theme. The SBA loaned approximately $2 million to businesses to purchase and renovate these buildings. Urban-renewal funds and private investment completed the coalition. The project has been so successful that the City of Baltimore has expanded the concept to apply to a dozen other neighborhoods.

The Department of Housing and Urban Development (HUD) has several programs designed to assist the commercial and residential revitalization of city buildings. Under Section 312 of the National Housing Act of 1964, loans for repairs and improvements are available to bring privately owned property up to current building-code standards. More than $80 million is budgeted in fiscal 1977 for the rehabilitation-loan program.

Under Title I of the Housing and Community Development Act of 1974, a number of HUD categorical grant programs were replaced. Money is now given directly to communities in the form of Community Development Block Grants. Funding for the Block Grant program amounts to $3.15 billion in 1977. These funds can be spent on the rehabilitation of commercial properties as part of a total neighborhood-rehabilitation program. The community can also transfer the funds to local development corporations for commercial rehabilitation. The money may be used to acquire and rehabilitate older buildings, provide low-interest loans or grants for renovation, and finance preservation planning. In addition, Community Development Block Grants can be used to obtain National Park Service matching restoration grants.

The Tax Reform Act of 1976 offered increased tax incentives to businesses renovating and reusing landmark buildings. Section 2124 of this Act permits a five-year amortization of certain owner-incurred expenses resulting from the rehabilitation of a qualified depreciable property. Such property must be listed in the National Register or be designated significant by state or local statute (subject to approval by the Secretary of the Interior). The Act disallows a deduction for demolition and the undepreciated costs of such a property, and if the property is still demolished, it disallows accelerated depreciation for any new structures built on that site. A business or developer which buys a historic property to renovate and preserve, even if it is adapted for new use, may be able to take accelerated depreciation if renovations meet standards specified by the Secretary of the Interior.

The first rehabilitation to be approved under the 1976 Act may be the new corporate headquarters for the Schlegel Corporation, to be located in a converted historic house in Rochester, New York.*

State and Local. Most state and local regulations and programs that apply to preservation deal specifically with building renovation and reuse. In the area of corporate donations to preservation activities, however, the Commonwealth of Pennsylvania allows a charitable deduction up to a total of 89.5 cents on every $1. Since Pennsylvania's law became effective in March, 1977, the Tasty Baking Company has taken such deductions for its contribution to the Allegheny West Community Development Project, an effort to improve the neighborhood adjacent to the company's plant.

State and local registers and historic districts also provide a degree of protection for buildings designated as important. Boston's regulations require city approval of any exterior alteration or any change of use that conflicts with current residential zoning for buildings in its historic districts.

Some states provide funds for preservation projects. The State of Washington has authorized $1.7 million for preservation grants

*The news of this corporate adaptive use came too late to include here as a complete case study, but a short description and a source for further information can be found in the Appendix.

between 1975 and 1979. These funds are allocated through local governments for properties on both the state and National Registers. (State-registered properties receive preference.) Money is provided for code-requirement improvements, structural stabilization, and documented restoration. Matching grants up to a 50 pecent maximum are available for work on privately owned buildings. Publicly owned buildings are eligible for grants of up to 100 percent of costs.*

Building codes can either aid or complicate rehabilitation projects. While codes have traditionally been locally determined and enforced, there is a trend today toward uniform statewide application. The Basic Building Code published by the Building Officials and Code, International (BOCA) and the Uniform Building Code are widely used as models for these regulations. When an old building is recycled for a new use, it must meet current code standards. Because such standards are usually written explicitly for new construction, they are often difficult to comply with in recycling. An amendment to the BOCA Code, Section 318.0, dealing with special historic buildings and districts, may help to alleviate this problem. It specifies that in designated historic structures, certified architects and engineers may vary established code regulations if their designs meet the basic tenets of health, safety, and welfare. Although there are still difficulties in defining a "historic building" and in determining adequate and enforceable performance standards for life-safety compliance, code problems previously confronted in converting old buildings to new uses may be less serious in the future.

Local zoning ordinances regulate density, height and bulk limitations, and land use. Residential, commercial, industrial, recreation and entertainment, and historic districts are but a few of the typical uses zoned by most municipalities. Although a large aggregation of historic buildings may promote the establishment of special historic districts, many historic buildings and others worthy of preservation are located in other parts of town. Local landmark or historic commissions and planning organizations are usually responsible for identifying and protecting these structures.

There are two major zoning issues that affect business reuse and revitalization of older buildings and areas. First, if a building with recycling potential is located in a district defined for a use other than that proposed in the recycling, a zoning variance may be required. For example, large, late-nineteenth-century homes in established residential districts often cannot be affordably maintained as residences. Some alternative use must be found, or the buildings will have to be demolished. Businesses such as small publishers, law firms, insurance agencies, and banks may be able to efficiently reuse these structures if zoning variances are permitted. While there are no guarantees that variances will be obtainable, in the cases researched by INFORM, no examples were found where change-of-use presented a difficult zoning-variance problem. In fact,

*Further information about state preservation programs can be found in *A Guide to State Programs*, published by the National Trust for Historic Preservation in 1972 and revised in 1976.

some local regulatory bodies appear to be encouraging this activity. In Savannah, the Morris Newspaper Corporation has adapted a historic house for its offices with strong support from the city. As public awareness of recycling projects is increased, business reuse of buildings in non-business zones is likely to become more common.

The second zoning issue affecting business reuse of old buildings and areas is more complicated. Many important buildings are located in neighborhoods that are zoned for greater density than the old buildings provide. Although they have historic and social value, and there are strong reasons for their retention, under the philosophy of "highest and best use," these landmarks are often not able to justify their existence economically. More profitable structures can be built to the maximum allowable density level. In larger cities like New York and Chicago, a concept known as Transfer of Development Rights (TDR) has been developed to deal with this problem.* TDR refers to the transfer of developable density from one site to another. The owner of a historic building may sell the extra density rights currently unused at the site to increase occupancy levels on another piece of property. The proceeds can then be applied to the old building's maintenance and support. TDR can help historic buildings to survive even if they are not fulfilling the highest and most profitable use allowable for the site. The same concept is also being applied to open-space areas. None of the projects in the INFORM study utilized this conservation tool, but it will undoubtedly be applied in larger cities in the future.

Property taxes can also hinder preservation. Local property taxes are often assessed on the potential value of a site, rather than on the actual economic value generated. This policy obviously discourages preservation of old buildings, since the owner must pay the same high taxes on the old structure as he would have to pay if a new, higher-revenue-producing building were located on the site. However, such policies can backfire. In recent years, economic realities have restricted the amount of new construction possible. Older, underutilized buildings have often been razed for potential new development that never took place, leaving the city's fiscal burdens not reduced, but exacerbated.

Some cities and states have introduced tax abatements and other incentives to attempt to encourage building reuse and commercial and neighborhood revitalization. New York City has several abatement programs to promote residential and commercial re-habilitation. Section J-51-2.5 of New York City's Administrative Code was originally implemented in 1955 to encourage owners of multiple-unit dwellings to bring their properties up to building-code requirements. As of January, 1976, it provides up to a twelve-year exemption from any increase in assessed valuation and an abatement of property taxes up to 90 percent of the cost of rehabilitating a residential or commercial building for residential use.

A concept known as tax increment financing has been established

---

*This concept is presented in detail by John J. Costonis, in his book, *Space Adrift*, published by the National Trust for Historic Preservation.

in several cities to promote neighborhood or district revitalization. Sacramento, California, was the first city to adopt the concept in an effort to restore economic vitality to Old Sacramento, its historic business center. Tax increment financing attempts to encourage private rehabilitation efforts by freezing the existing property-tax levels in a renewal area. In this way, owners are not penalized by higher taxes for improving their properties, a common disincentive to rehabilitation. As investment and improvement take place in the area, some increases are made in the property valuation, but the increment is set aside in a special city fund, to be reinvested only in the area. Bonds, secured by the increment, are also sold to support extensive improvements like new street lighting, sidewalks, and landscaping. Through this approach, the whole area may be rapidly renewed, benefiting both the private and public sectors.

While public and private support of preservation has been slow to develop, advances are gradually being made. Perhaps with an increased public awareness that preservation is more than just the exact restoration of historic structures, government and business alike will come to agree with James Biddle, President of the National Trust, who said:

Progress doesn't always have to be something new. Progress is taking the best advantage of the assets you have. Preservation is progress.[11]

Footnotes

1. Michael Sterne, "Corporate Moves: New York Region Holds Its Own," *New York Times*, 21 August 1977, sec. 11 (Long Island Weekly), p. 8.
2. *Ibid.* p. 1.
3. INFORM interview with Frank Corbin, Deputy Director, Economic Development Administration, New York City, August, 1977.
4. Gurney Breckenfeld, "It's Up to the Cities to Save Themselves," *Fortune*, March, 1977, p. 195.
5. Urban Homesteading Assistance Board, *Urban Homesteading Assistance Board Annual Report*, (New York: Urban Homesteading Assistance Board, 1976).
6. McGraw-Hill Information Systems and Wood and Tower, Inc., *Dodge Manual for Building Construction and Pricing Scheduling*, (New York: McGraw-Hill, 1976), p. 1.
7. "More is Better: Strong Modernization Market Continues," *Buildings*, 1976, p. 56.
8. Business Committee for the Arts, *Business Support of the Arts—1976*, (New York: Business Committee for the Arts, 1976).
9. "EDA Funding Reviewed," *Preservation News*, March, 1977, pp. 1, 12.
10. *U.S. Small Business Administration Loans to Local Development Companies*, (Washington, D.C.: U.S. Small Business Administration, n.d.).
11. Alan Otten, "Politics & People—Spare that Building," *Wall Street Journal*, 8 January 1976.

Restoration, renovation, rehabilitation, remodeling, retrofitting; all involve saving and extending the useful life of an existing building. Recycling, as this activity is called, includes: *adaptive reuse*, converting an existing building from its originally intended (or currently defined) purpose to a new one; *continued use*, consciously extending the useful life of important older buildings for the purpose originally intended; and *new additions*, adding compatible new construction onto older structures, or building new structures which "fit" within an established historic context.

Adaptive Reuse INFORM has examined seventeen recycling projects in the adaptive-reuse category. Among the leading practitioners of this form of recycling are banks. Five cases deal with historic houses which have been turned into bank branches, such as the Victorian residence of a former cattle baron in Sacramento, converted into a San Diego Federal branch. Other kinds of businesses met their own divergent space needs through the adaptation of a variety of structures. Three cases involve townhouses now serving as distinctive office spaces. Morris Newspaper's offices, for example, are located in one of Savannah's ten oldest buildings. Two cases involve vintage homes which were successfully converted to retail space. One of them, Design Research's Philadelphia store, is actually a city-registered landmark. Three conversions involve old industrial buildings made into office space: an ice cream factory converted into McGraw-Hill Publications' Western Regions Office; a textile mill used by Digital Equipment Corporation to meet its office and production needs; and a factory complex reused as the home offices of Lawyers Co-operative. The remaining four cases involve conversion of a school building, a hotel, a nondescript storefront, and a courthouse to commercial or office space.

In almost every case, the exteriors of the buildings have been rehabilitated or maintained in their original state, while the interiors have been adapted to fit the new use. In many projects, the interior adaptation has also attempted to respect the original design, including the restoration and incorporation of important decorative elements and original room configurations.

Companies and financial institutions that have decided to adaptively reuse old buildings give a variety of reasons for their decision. In thirteen of the seventeen cases profiled by INFORM, the firms wanted and believed they received enhanced public images. This was particularly important to the First New Haven National Bank, which was moving into a new market in Westbrook, Connecticut. However, it seemed to be equally important to a firm like Lawyers Co-operative, a law publisher long established in Rochester.

Economic considerations were another strong reason given for recycling. Space in an adapted older structure is often less expensive than that acquired through new construction. This was true for Digital in Maynard, Massachusetts, which obtained office and manufacturing space for $15 per square foot as opposed to the $25 to $30 per square foot it would have had to pay for new construction; and for Wachovia Bank, where recycling proved to be 20 percent cheaper than new construction. Costs varied according to the degree of renovation, the nature of the business, the availability of materials, and regional pay scales. Among the cases studied by INFORM, the per-square-foot cost of renovation ranged from a low of $15 in the Lawyers Co-operative and Digital cases to a high of $110 in the San Diego Federal Savings and Loan case. Adaptive reuse was reported to be as much as two-thirds less expensive than new construction. In only three cases—San Diego Federal, Design Research, and Commonwealth Bank and Trust—did the cost of rehabilitation exceed the estimated cost of new construction designed for similar use.

Location was also often a key factor in the decision to reuse existing buildings. The study includes nine cases of companies who were looking for a new location for a branch or other facility in an established area. They found that construction of a new building would generally necessitate demolition of an existing structure. Demolition is often expensive, and the approvals required are not easily obtained. Thus, the adaptive reuse of structures already existing in good locations became a logical alternative. Connecticut Savings Bank found a location for its Cheshire branch in a badly neglected old house on a main commercial street. Instead of demolishing the building, the bank restored the exterior and renovated the interior, turning the old home into a productive branch and helping maintain the character of the area.

INFORM also profiled six cases of companies which were established in an area and needed to expand their facilities. Building on adjacent sites often proved to be the most feasible plan. Harbridge House, a Boston-based consulting firm, purchased a house adjacent to its Back Bay offices (also located in old houses), and is using it for additional office space. The reused houses provide the cheapest office space of any of the company's locations.

In almost every building-recycling project studied by INFORM, aesthetic considerations played a significant role. Often the force behind the project was a concerned executive to whom aesthetics were important. This top-level individual often had participated in local preservation and community activities. While companies tend to stress economic or "image enhancement" grounds as justification for their projects, aesthetics and that special interest of a high-level official seemed to have triggered the initial consideration and study of reuse as an option in almost every case. One example is Morris Newspaper's President Charles Morris. A Trustee of Historic Savannah, Morris wanted a historic building to house his offices in that city.

Although not a major motivating factor, five of the companies INFORM studied felt that reusing older buildings resulted in improved employee morale. The employees of Digital Equipment Corporation like the option they have of personalizing their office space in the company's converted textile mill.

The problems encountered in adaptive reuse varied according to the nature of the building and the purpose for which it was to be renovated. Among the problems cited, technical difficulties were most common, but they were reported by only four of the seventeen companies studied. For example, the National Bank of the Commonwealth, in converting the Indiana County Courthouse to bank offices, found that the thickness of the building's walls limited floor-plan designs and created difficulties in installing heating and air-conditioning systems.

Continued Use   INFORM has also profiled the efforts of six businesses to continue to use significant old buildings. Continued use, while not requiring as extensive alteration as adaptive reuse, can still at times involve major rehabilitation.

Just as with adaptive reuse projects, businesses decide to continue to use existing buildings primarily for economic and aesthetic reasons. Most of the examples of continued use studied by INFORM involve company-owned buildings. The companies, including nail producers, banks, chair manufacturers, lumber companies, and clothing manufacturers, have made major investments in buildings, and over the years have reduced the debts on them. Property taxes are usually low as well, since the assessed valuation is in most cases less than for comparable new buildings.

A comparison of costs for renovation versus new construction reveals that renovation is often the cheaper alternative. This was true in almost all the cases studied by INFORM, and was specifically cited by two companies as a reason for continued use. According to its architects, Alamo National Bank got a $30 million bargain from a $5 million renovation.

A further reason for continuing to use an old building is that good public and employee relations often result. All six companies received favorable publicity and recognition for their efforts. Levi Strauss was praised by the Mayor of San Francisco for renovating and preserving its 71-year-old clothing factory located in the city's Mission District. The company's employees had roots in the neighborhood, and needed to be near homes and children. Many would have found it difficult to commute to a suburban location since they did not own automobiles.

Several companies, through association with a particular building, had achieved an image and identity which they did not want to alter. The Hitchcock Chair Company is located in the same building as the original nineteenth-century "manufactory." Hitchcock's President John T. Kenney revived both the process and the building more than eighty years after the original company ceased operations.

One company, Sohio, cited energy conservation as a factor motivating its commitment to lease 40,000 of the Cuyahoga Building's 63,000 square feet. According to the company, renovation and continued use saved the energy that would have been expended in demolition and new construction, as well as that used in the production of building materials.

Finally, aesthetic considerations played a role in the decision to continue to use five buildings. Three projects are even tourist attractions, providing a source of additional revenue. Tremont Nail's nineteenth-century nail factory attracts many customers to the company's gift shop.

None of the companies studied encountered major internal difficulties in their continued-use projects. The original buildings were structurally sound and accommodated the space and functional needs of the businesses and residents involved. Mechanical and life-safety systems could usually be upgraded at a lower cost than would have been required if they were being built from scratch. Alamo National Bank redesigned and enlarged the service area in its San Antonio headquarters, but only had to refurbish rather than totally replace the electrical and mechanical systems.

Where problems did occur, they were generally the result of some external factor, such as location, rather than the nature of the building itself. Most older buildings are located in dense, central-city areas. At projects in Cleveland and San Francisco, this created difficulties with employee and customer accessibility, parking, and security. Other problems connected with continued-use projects were unique to the individual situation, like the inconvenience Pope & Talbot's renovation efforts caused residents of historic homes in Port Gamble. Port Gamble is a company lumbering town in the State of Washington. Residents have been badgered by over-eager tourists wanting to see the interiors of their restored homes.

New Additions Often, a business will want to remain or locate in an old building whose present size and condition fails to suit its needs; or, it may want to locate in a historic area with explicit design restrictions. The result in many cases has been to pick another location and start over. However, as an alternative, some companies have undertaken construction of compatible new additions and enlargements. While the benefits of such efforts are obvious—demolition or abandonment of the older building is often avoided, and the economic stability and well-being of the area is maintained—the designing of new additions in order to "fit" within an established historic context is a controversial subject. Among the points of debate are: the degree of alteration of historic structures which should be permitted; the elements that constitute compatible design; and the extent to which cost and functional considerations should be allowed to take precedence over historical accuracy and aesthetics. Given the many design restrictions placed on older areas, the scarcity of prime building land, and the faltering economic vitality of many existing "downtowns," the need for harmonious combinations of new and old buildings is a growing and important concern.

The six projects in this category studied by INFORM all involve new intervention which has attempted to respect older surroundings. They include hotels, insurance-company offices, banks, and department-store complexes. The six cases illustrate three basic design approaches:

1. *Recreation*—copying the design of the past with today's materials and labor; exemplified by Charleston Associates and Deseret Management. Critics claim that this approach is anachronistic, lacks originality, and may deceive the untrained observer into believing that the new is actually not new. Many others, however, see no problems with recreation.

2. *Tokenism*—incorporating an artifact or piece of the old building as a historic symbol within new construction; exemplified by Zions Cooperative and Penn Mutual. There is some controversy over this approach too, since all but a small part of the original building is lost. Furthermore, tokenism generally creates sculptures of portions of buildings never intended for that purpose. However, the alternative is often complete destruction.

3. *Compatible contemporary additions*—building in today's idiom, but relating the new building to adjacent older buildings through design elements such as scale, proportion, configuration, pattern, materials, color, and texture; exemplified by the Boston Five Cents Savings Bank

and the Bank of California. This approach, clearly the most challenging to architects, also involves the most subjective judgments. What is good compatible contemporary architecture? How can compatibility be measured? Should it be measured? Does striving for compatibility stifle creativity and originality? Will it yield a bland environment containing stripped-down contemporary copies of historic counterparts?

For these questions, all well worth considering, there are no concrete answers. However, the City of Savannah has made an attempt at creating some measurable standards for evaluating new development within historic areas. Its findings, published in a *Historic Preservation Plan*, include sixteen criteria by which to judge the relationship between new and old buildings:

Height	Relationship of color
Proportion of buildings' front facades	Relationship of architectural details
Proportion of openings within that facade	Relationship of roof shapes
Rhythm of solids to voids in front facades	Walls of continuity
Rhythm of spacing of buildings on streets	Relationship of landscaping
Rhythm of entrance and/or	Ground cover
porch projections	Scale
Relationship of materials	Directional expression
Relationship of textures	of front elevation[1]

Most business decisions concerning whether or not to construct a new building that is sympathetic to its historic surroundings are not made on a strictly economic basis. Accommodating the craftsmanship and detail which characterize older buildings can be a costly and time-consuming proposition. Quality in architecture, as in most other things, costs money. It is almost impossible to devise any tangible scale of measurement for the business benefits derived. Deseret Management decided on an addition which was an exact replica of the old Hotel Utah at a cost of about $40,000 per room, much more than a modern addition would have cost. Indeed, it appears that several of these projects were undertaken because companies feared the negative consequences of not doing so, rather than because any positive economic benefit was to be gained. In two cases, Penn Mutual and Zions Cooperative, pressure from local preservation groups saved at least part of the original historic structures.

While economics are usually a secondary consideration in creating compatible new additions, Salt Lake City has gained special economic benefits from the Zions Cooperative and Deseret Management projects. The city has become a center of restoration expertise, and its architects and craftsmen have assisted in other projects around the country.

The companies studied by INFORM cited costs and delays as the major difficulties associated with the construction of new additions. These seemed to correlate with the degree of compatibility of recreation the company desired. The Bank of California's attention to detail, careful workmanship, and unique design brought the cost of building a new addition to its old banking hall to $90 per square foot, a relatively high figure. The exact duplication of terra cotta exteriors and the recreation of turn-of-the-century-style public spaces helped delay the opening of the Hotel Utah's new addition for about a year. Technical difficulties, including the use of unfamiliar building material, such as the terra cotta at the Hotel Utah, arose in four projects, but in all instances were overcome.

An additional problem arose after completion in three cases. Public reaction to the new addition and to the philosophy behind it was divided, and the projects became the focus of controversy among architecture critics.

Footnotes

1. *Historic Preservation Plan for the Central Area General Neighborhood Renewal Area, Savannah, Georgia,* (Washington, D.C.: U.S. Department of Housing and Urban Development, n.d.), pp. 12-18.

Commonwealth Bank and Trust Company

Adaptive Reuse

Summary Commonwealth Bank and Trust Company purchased the historic Squire Hays Homestead in Williamsport, Pennsylvania, to save it from demolition, and relocated and renovated it for use as a branch office which opened in 1975. The branch has been very successful; the renovation provided a unique way of establishing the bank in a new market.

Background In 1973, the construction of Robert Hall Village, a shopping-center complex, threatened the demolition of the Squire Hays Homestead, one of the oldest surviving structures in Lycoming County. The Homestead, standing in the middle of the complex's proposed parking lot, was scheduled to be torn down. Commonwealth Bank and Trust, under President Glenn Fenstermacher, had decided to locate a branch in Williamsport and was looking for a way to promote itself in a new community. The bank thought the Squire Hays Homestead would serve both these ends.

The Squire Hays Homestead was built in 1806 by John Hays to replace a log house, the original home of the Hays family. Constructed entirely of stone and wood from the surrounding countryside, the house was originally two stories, with two doors on the first floor. After the Civil War, a two-story addition was made, and in 1885, a porch was added to the front of the house.

Execution The house was moved across the road from its original site, an effort requiring considerable time and patience; and its architecture and history were researched with the help of the Lycoming County Historical Society and Museum. The restoration architect, Richard Merrill Sweitzer, A.I.A., returned the exterior of the house to its post-Civil War appearance, removing the 1885 porch. He added drive-in banking windows, custom built to blend in with the original bay windows, and a vault extension covered with stone taken from the foundation of another vintage building that had been demolished.

The house has seven rooms. On the first floor, in what was the kitchen/dining area, a wall was removed to make more room for the bank manager's office and bank lobby. Other rooms are used for banking and office space. Two were set aside as period rooms, and another as a meeting room. The period rooms were furnished with colonial pieces from the Lycoming County Museum, and with other items of special interest from the early 1800s. The offices are furnished with antique office furniture where possible. Objects and documents were supplied by the people of Lycoming County; some of these donations are now being collected and placed in a *Memory Book* by the bank. In addition, the bank was instrumental in having the home placed on the Pennsylvania Inventory of Historic Places in 1974.

Costs While Commonwealth Bank and Trust indicated that the costs of renovating this building were higher than those for building a new branch, it would not release any specific financial figures.

Problems The major cause for concern during the course of the renovation was the initial relocation. Due to the extreme age of the stone building, the move across the street required great care, and as a result took many months. It was, nevertheless, completed without incident.

Squire Hays Homestead being moved to its new location.

Benefits The restoration has generated much favorable publicity for the bank, which also uses the Squire Hays Homestead in its advertising. Squire Hays Homestead hand-cast coins and metal plates are given away for new accounts over $50.

The renovation and the branch's excellent location, near a prime traffic area, both contributed to its success. The community's economy has benefited from the jobs and tax revenues created by the new addition, as well as from the preservation of a part of its heritage. The Squire Hays branch was a stop on the Christmas, 1976, Williamsport tour of Historic Homes.

The Company In 1965, Commonwealth Bank and Trust was formed by the merger of the Tioga County Savings and Trust Company, the First National Bank of Galeton, the First National Bank of Lawrenceville, and the Farmer's and Trader's National Bank of Westfield. Commonwealth serves a five-county area, and has seventeen branches besides its home office in Muncy, Pennsylvania. The bank employs 189 people and had assets of $152 million as of 1976.

Other Preservation Activities. Commonwealth Bank and Trust has recently renovated its branch office in Renovo, Pennsylvania. The building, in continuous use as a bank since the turn of the century, has marble floors and rich woodwork.

For further information contact:
Linda S. Williams
Marketing Assistant
Commonwealth Bank and Trust
Company
61 Main Street
Wellsboro, Pennsylvania 19601

The renovated farmhouse, now a branch office of the Commonwealth Bank and Trust Co.

Summary In December, 1973, the Connecticut Savings Bank opened its Cheshire branch office in the historic Governor Foote House on South Main Street. Built in 1769, the house is a superb example of colonial Connecticut architecture and an important component of historic Cheshire. In return for this contribution to preservation, the bank has received business benefits, as well as much local and even national public acclaim. Bank President Paul Johnson states: "business growth in the new branch is far above projected expectations and better than any other branch in our system."[1] He believes that the building is responsible for much of the branch's popularity.

Background In 1973, the bank was looking for a site in Cheshire for a new branch office. The Governor Foote House was ideally suited to its needs; it was on the main commercial street, but had enough adjacent land to accommodate a drive-in window and bank parking. In recent years, however, the Foote House had been neglected by its owner and, according to local historian, Dr. Robert Craig, was in a "deplorable state."[2] The three-story frame house retains many of its original clapboards still held in place with hand-crafted nails. It also has many of its original shutters.

The house was the birthplace of Samuel Augustus Foote who served both in Congress and as the Governor of Connecticut. It remained a residence until the end of the nineteenth century, when it became a private girls' school Its eighteenth-century interiors were altered at that time to accommodate its function as a school. Later, the house was converted back into a residence, and was the home of a former journalist with the *Cheshire Herald*. It is still one of the finest and best-preserved examples of early colonial architecture in the Cheshire area.

On Cheshire's South Main Street, as on the main streets of many older towns, residential and commercial development have been intertwined. South Main Street is zoned for commercial use on one side and for residential use on the other. The Foote House is on the residential side. However, the residential zoning permitted banks to establish branches in the area, subject to approval by the town's Planning and Zoning Board. Recently, the property directly across the street was scheduled to be the new location of a fast-food restaurant. While local residents blocked this change, future growth was bound to pose further threats. Just up the street from the Foote House, one of the large older homes was gutted by fire, and has since been converted to office use. Dr. Craig feared that the Foote House was in such a state of disrepair that it would soon be razed for another gas station. He evaluates the bank's use of the building and site: "Either the bank made it a 'taxpayer' or the old shack was going to fall down."[3] Two letters published in the

Cheshire Herald—and in part, reprinted here—illustrate the diversity of opinion concerning the bank's proposed reuse. One, by an Assistant Commissioner in the state Department of Environmental Protection, praised the bank's plan. The other, by a freshman at Southern Connecticut State College in New Haven, took an opposing view.

One of the most environmentally sound actions which a bank could take in Cheshire has now been started by CSB. The purchase and renovation of an existing historic structure, i.e., the Foote house in Cheshire, for a branch bank, is a significant action. It has no disturbing effect on open space land as a new structure would; it has the character of the community as a base in its architecture, and it improves a building which was becoming a blight to the town.

Other financial institutions which operate in Cheshire should note as a sound example the action of CSB. [4]

In my opinion the Clinton Branch Bank [a previous renovation by CSB] was tastelessly put together and permanently ruined. I do not know the historical background of the house, as on the outside there was no sign or plaque containing its history, but we can be sure it is not as historically significant as our Foote House. The outside of this house (which isn't even one half the size of the Foote House) had evidences of being at one time a fairly nice looking home. But with all the new fixtures and shutters bolted to the structure, its Colonial charm was somehow lost. . . . What I am trying to say to the bank is this: I hope they realize that restoration means more than just redoing the outside appearance of something, it means taking time and care to fix things and not just tear out and replace them. And it means taking this care in both the outside and inside. They are equally important aspects to consider when undertaking such an important project as the Foote House, and can not be taken lightly. [5]

Execution The bank, in fact, did restore the exterior of the Foote House to its original state, and managed to retain many key features of the interior, while accommodating modern banking needs. The original exterior clapboards were hand sanded and then stained a brownish grey, and the shutters were restored and stained a dark brown. The roof was re-shingled with cedar shingles, and the modern double

The Governor Foote House before restoration. Bank President Paul Johnson escorts visitors.

The same building after restoration. (Interdesign)

front door was replaced with an authentic eighteenth-century single door found in Newport, Rhode Island. In the interior, the first floor was opened up to produce a more convenient banking space. Those partitions which were removed were mostly nineteenth-century additions. The central fireplace was left exposed in the middle of the open space, acting as a divider for banking activities and as the focal point of the interior. Because much of the original interior finish was missing, new wood trim, appropriate to the original period of the house, was used, and even the tellers' counters were paneled. Modern flooring on the ground level was replaced with wide oak floorboards salvaged from another period house in Durham, Connecticut. The second floor, used as office space, was generally refurbished without any structural alteration.

The building is equipped with all the conveniences and security of a completely new facility: a computer system links the branch to all records stored in the main office; and a modern vault facility, with eighteen-inch-thick walls to meet Federal Deposit Insurance Corporation requirements, has been incorporated in a new addition to the rear of the house. The renovated building contains 3,800 square feet of usable space; the ground floor is used for customer banking needs, and the second floor for office suites. A parking lot, accommodating 24 cars, has been designed at the rear of the building, and is hidden from the main street by landscaping. The drive-in window is separate from the building, and utilizes an automated TV teller system. The cost of this convenience is greater than an integrated drive-up system, but the unit helps preserve the character of the house. Frederick Biebesheimer and Jonathan Isleib of Interdesign, Inc., were responsible for the conversion design and restoration.

Lighting and mechanical systems sometimes cause problems in renovation projects where preservation of an original character is desired. Modern

Plan of first floor illustrating arrangement of main banking activities. (Interdesign)

Main Floor

banking needs and local code requirements prohibited the use of period oil lamps, and modern fluorescent fixtures were not in keeping with eighteenth-century design. Interdesign chose recessed incandescent lighting which unobtrusively provides adequate light for the workspace and enhances architectural detail. A completely new gas-fired, ducted heating system and electric central air conditioning have been installed. The seven-and-a-half-ton air-handling unit is located in the basement, and ground-level heating and cooling is provided by registers in the floor. For the upper level, the ducts are brought up vertically to the attic and then branch out and blow down to condition the rooms below. This solution eliminated any exposed ducts or dropped ceilings. New plumbing and wiring were also installed. According to Interdesign, there were no specific building-code or structural problems. The construction took six months.

Costs The bank paid approximately $65,000 for the house. Interdesign puts the renovation cost at $147,000, and the mechanical and electrical work at $43,000, for a total project cost, excluding furnishings and bank equipment, of approximately $255,000, or $35 per square foot for the total 5,600 square feet.

Operating costs for heating/ventilation and air conditioning average about $650 per month, according to Branch Manager, Carol Oesterlin.[6] This is approximately 11 cents per square foot per month. No storm windows were used because the designers felt that they would detract from the original character of the windows. Heating the house is thus somewhat more expensive than it would otherwise be.

Benefits The benefits accrued to the town of Cheshire have been discussed. The business benefits to the bank are important. According to Mrs. Oesterlin, "Customers are mentioning what a fine job we did with the restoration all the time. For many of them it would appear to be the main reason they come in."[7] The three-year projected deposits for the branch were estimated at $14 million. Actual deposits have been $15.4 million. Bank President Paul Johnson attributes most of this increase to the restoration. The bank has received widespread favorable publicity for the project, including an article in the National Trust's April, 1976, *Preservation News*.

The central chimney and fireplace divide the banking floor into the teller and office areas. (Charles M. Pratt)

The Company The Connecticut Savings Bank was chartered in 1857, and is today the fourth largest savings institution in the state. Assets rose from $505 million in 1975 to $586 million in 1976. Fifteen branch offices serve New Haven and its surrounding communities. Several are in older buildings.

Other Preservation Activities. The bank's main office in New Haven is located in a Greek-temple-like structure built in 1907. This building has been fully restored by the bank and Interdesign. The exterior marble was water cleaned; the old barrel-vaulted, coffered ceiling was uncovered and restored (it had been hidden behind a lowered ceiling for many years); and new lighting and mechanical systems were introduced. The bank has linked this older building to a new administrative building on an adjacent piece of land. Although joining a classical temple—meant to be seen from all sides—to anything is a difficult problem, the resulting solution of a neutral black "hyphen" between the two buildings is quite effective. The bank received a plaque from the New Haven Preservation Trust declaring the temple building a historic landmark.

For further information contact:
Paul Johnson
President and Chief Executive Officer
Connecticut Savings Bank
47 Church Street
New Haven, Connecticut 06510

Footnotes

1. INFORM interview with Paul Johnson, President, Chief Executive Officer, Connecticut Savings Bank, May, 1976.
2. INFORM interview with Dr. Robert Craig, Historian, March, 1977.
3. *Ibid.*
4. Carroll J. Hughes, "A Bank Plans For Restoring Foote House: The Case For It," *Cheshire Herald*, 2 November 1972, p. 21.
5. Donald Menzies, "A Bank Plans For Restoring Foote House: The Case Against It," *Cheshire Herald*, 2 November 1972, p. 21.
6. INFORM interview with Carol Oesterlin, Manager, Connecticut Savings Bank, Cheshire branch, May, 1976.
7. *Ibid.*

The barrel-vaulted interior of the bank's restored main office.

Summary In October, 1975, Design Research, a retail chain specializing in contemporary furnishings, fabrics, and accessories, opened its eleventh store in the historic Van Rensselaer Mansion on Philadelphia's Rittenhouse Square. Prior to the company's adaptive reuse, the building—once the home of one of the city's wealthiest and most prominent families—was unoccupied and threatened with demolition because it was an unprofitable structure on a very valuable piece of urban real estate. Design Research has a twenty-year lease on the 17,000 square feet of space in the Van Rensselaer Mansion. It pays more than $130,000 per year to use the building, and has spent more than $1.2 million on the adaptation/ renovation. Design Research's reuse scheme, resulting in the removal of most of the original interior to achieve more efficient selling space, generated considerable public controversy. Although the project has not been a financial success to date, the company still feels it was worthwhile and may reuse other buildings in the future.

Background The Van Rensselaer Mansion was built in 1897 for Sara Drexel Fell, a member of the wealthy Drexel family, which owned most of the property around Rittenhouse Square. After the death of her husband, John R. Fell, Sara married Alexander Van Rensselaer, and her mansion has been known ever since by the Van Rensselaer name.*

The three-story building, designed in the Renaissance Revival style by the Boston architectural firm of Peabody and Stearns, possesses an exterior of finely carved granite. A two-story, pavilion-like wing is joined on the north side. The central feature of the interior is a stained-glass, domed

*Information on the history of this building has come from a student paper by Hava J. Gelblum titled "1801-1803 Walnut St.— Past & Present," which was written on December 1, 1975 for Art History 446 at the University of Pennsylvania.

skylight which is visible from the first floor through a semicircular three-story space. The major living/ entertaining rooms were on the first floor, including a grand dining room in the wing. This room has been named the Pope's Room because of the framed, painted portraits of religious leaders which are affixed to the ceiling. The second floor contained the primary sleeping quarters, and the third floor was for guests and servants. Kitchen and storage facilities were located in the basement.

The Van Rensselaer Mansion was owned and used by the family until the 1940s, when it was sold to the Penn Athletic Club. In 1964, the Club was forced to sell because of declining membership and high maintenance costs. However, the Presbyterian Ministers Fund, an insurance company for the clergy, bought the property and leased it to the Club until 1972. After

The Van Rensselaer Mansion.

The stained glass, domed skylight in its new setting. (Tom Crane)

the Club left, the Fund was unable to find a new tenant, and the building remained empty for the next two years. The Presbyterian Ministers Fund reportedly contemplated demolishing the structure.

In 1973, Design Research Chairman Peter Sprague and President Phillip Doub were looking for a location in Philadelphia for a branch store. The Van Rensselaer Mansion was of immediate interest. Although the building's interior was in need of refurbishing, Rittenhouse Square was a fashionable location, close to some of Philadelphia's finest stores, and an established and growing residential neighborhood. The Van Rensselaer Mansion is a city landmark, and Sprague and Doub believed that its image would help the store. Design Research has several other stores located in older buildings. The two men had also "fallen in love"[1] with the Mansion, and were interested in its preservation. Design Research's architects, Architectural Resources Cambridge, Inc., examined the building and developed preliminary plans. In January, 1974, the company signed a twenty-year lease with the Presbyterian Ministers Fund.

The architects—Architectural Resources Cambridge, Inc.—created four selling floors from three. Cut-outs and two-story spaces provide a flow of space and view from one floor to the next. (Architectural Resources Cambridge, Inc.)

Execution Because the Mansion is a registered Philadelphia landmark, no exterior alterations could be made. All reuse plans had to be reviewed by the Philadelphia Historical Commission. The residential interiors were elegant, but their formality and organization restricted flexible use. To transform the old home into a workable store displaying and selling contemporary furnishings and accessories, the three existing floors in the main part of the house were removed, and four new floors were created. This produced slightly over 11,000 square feet of sales space. The old ceiling heights had been nine, seventeen, and eleven feet; the new ones are eight-and-a-half feet. Two-story spaces were strategically located to visually connect one floor to the next

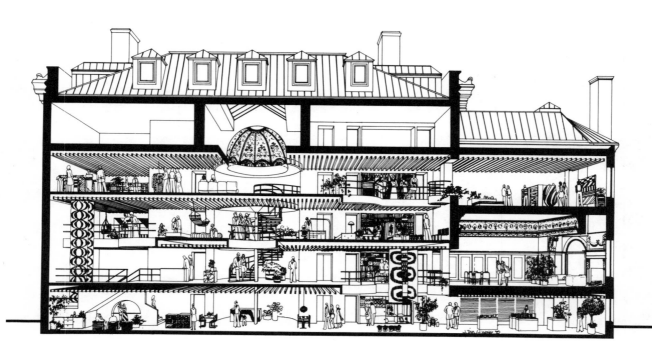

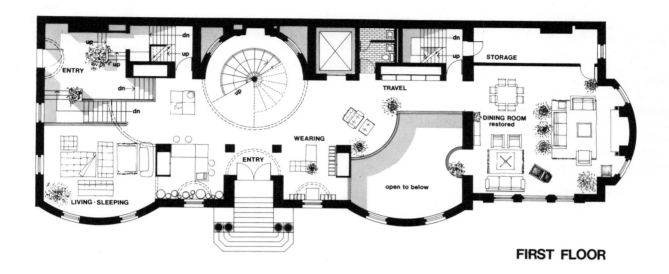

FIRST FLOOR

Floor plan of Design Research's Philadelphia store. Floor area is divided by product line. (Architectural Resources Cambridge, Inc.)

(below)

Philadelphia's design restrictions permitted no alteration of the building's exterior. (Architectural Resources Cambridge, Inc.)

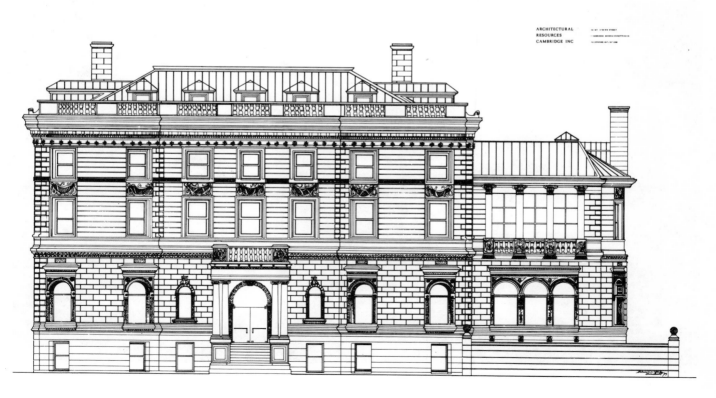

and create a sense of open space. Because much of Design Research's business is the result of impulse-buying, the open flow of light, space, and view is important to the store's marketing efforts. The new interior has white walls, quarry-tile and brightly colored, carpeted floors, and wood slatted ceilings. The latter were used to hide ducts and wires and to display hanging merchandise. The original interior was symmetrically organized around the central three-story space, emphasized by the stained-glass dome. To promote customer circulation, a new spiral staircase was introduced in this space.

After some discussions with the Philadelphia Historical Commission and others, Design Research and its architects agreed to preserve the stained-glass dome, the marble fireplace and flanking stained-glass windows in the entry hall, and the Pope's Room, complete with painted ceiling, and ornate plaster and wood detailing. The Historical Commission approved the company's decision to cut a new entry into one of the basement windows on Walnut Street to meet building/fire-code egress requirements. The renovation took 21 months to complete from the date the lease arrangements were made.

Costs The cost for adapting the space exceeded $1.2 million, or $107 per square foot for 11,200 square feet of selling space. (There are approximately 17,000 gross square feet in the building.) The Presbyterian Ministers Fund loaned Design Research $600,000 of the renovation cost at 9¼ percent interest for twenty years. The annual rent for the twenty-year lease is $64,500, bringing the total annual cost to the company, including debt service, to $130,500, or $11.65 per square foot leased. This compares to a $7.45-per-square-foot average cost for all other Design Research stores. Fixture costs for Design Research stores average a maximum $5 per square foot.

Former dining room of the Van Rensselaer Mansion. (Tom Crane)

Problems Design Research's reuse of the Van Rensselaer Mansion produced two major problems. First, the design plans, specifically the major alteration of the interiors, generated considerable public controversy. When the company submitted its plans to the city in spring, 1974, it met with opposition from the Preservation Committee of the Philadelphia Chapter of the American Institute of Architects, the Philadelphia Historical Commission, and other groups. An article by *Philadelphia Inquirer* architecture critic Thomas Hine referred to Design Research's plans to preserve and reuse the building as: "a sweet and sour kind of recycling . . . battle that's not yet finished."[2] Because of the controversy and required approvals, it took Design Research until the following winter before actual renovations could begin. Opposition continued in June, 1974. Three high school students wrote a letter to Mayor Rizzo protesting the company's plans: "You're the only one left," they wrote. "Please can't you do something to prevent the gutting?"[3] While the city did not want to discourage Design Research from coming to Philadelphia, nor to thwart the company's efforts to try to inject life into the old building, the Mayor could not ignore the controversy. He directed the appropriate city agencies, primarily the Historical Commission, to determine the proper action to take to ensure that the significant interiors were preserved.

The Committee for the Mansion, a group of concerned citizens headed by Roy Warren West, developed an alternative proposal. They suggested that the building be used as a residence for Philadelphia's mayors. The cost to restore the Mansion for this use was placed at $2 million, which was to be raised from private sources. Mayor Rizzo had just spent a considerable sum on his house in the suburbs, so the Committee's proposal may not have received strong city support, but Design Research realized that its plans were in jeopardy. The company offered to swallow its losses—approximately $30,000 at that time—and according to President Phillip Doub, "step aside and assign the lease to any qualified person or company who can use the building without changes."[4]

No qualified person or company came up with the necessary funding, and Design Research moved ahead with its plans. According to Susan Becher, Manager of the Philadelphia store after it opened in October, 1975, "We probably converted about 40 percent of the negative opinions after they saw the finished results. About 85 percent of the people coming in have a positive reaction."[5] Nevertheless, Dr. George Thomas, an architectural professor at Drexel University and a historical consultant for the American Institute of Architects' Preservation Committee, believes that the gutted house will be worthless and unusable in twenty years. "The slick-shick banal modern interior will be dated then,"[6] he says.

The project faces an additional difficulty. According to company owner and Chairman Sprague:

The Philadelphia store is our least profitable store. We could have done four conventional 6,500 square foot mall stores for the same price. Economically, it probably did not make much sense.[7]

The location is good, but it may not be good enough. Sprague indicates that Design Research's presence in the area has lured several competitors to nearby shops. Philadelphia may just not be ready to absorb so much contemporary merchandise. Judy Kasameyer, a resident, says, "Philadelphia is a conservative city. The downtown stores are all hurting because Philadelphians either shop in the suburbs or in New York."[8]

Some of the high-cost problems obviously fall on the building's shoulders; some of the poor business performance may also. According to Susan Becher, "the formality of the building may be its biggest problem. It doesn't feel like a store. It is almost too elegant . . . a sort of museum quality."[9] Peter Sprague feels that people may see the building, be intimidated by it, and "be afraid to come in."[10] Although there are signs in the windows and banners of Marimekko fabric hanging outside, it is not easy to recognize the Mansion as a store.

Benefits In spite of its problems, the Design Research reuse of the Van Rensselaer Mansion has resulted in some significant benefits. The store's design has been widely praised by the public and by many preservationists. In the *Art* column of the *Philadelphia Inquirer*, Thomas Hine wrote:

In an earlier column we complained about plans to gut the building, destroying some truly eccentric and irreplaceable domed spaces and fireplaces.

But the building plans which do involve rebuilding of nearly the entire interior, now propose to preserve intact the building's one outstanding room, its ceiling lined with medallions of the Doges of Venice*, and they increase the dramatic impact of an existing glass dome.

Most importantly, though, Design Research has a 20-year lease. Thus at least one stately house on the Square will be around for another two decades.

Like many of the properties on the Square, this one is owned by an institution which has neither the money nor the inclination to preserve the atmosphere of the city. Fortunately, a tenant was found who does.[11]

The project has also been written about in architectural and interior-design publications. An editorial accompanying an extensive article on the recycling in the April, 1976, issue of *Interiors* stated:

The new Design Research store in Philadelphia, housed in the old Van Rensselaer mansion, is a superb example of how to use today's materials, products and techniques—with a respect equal to that held for the space itself.[12]

In response to criticism of the building's modern interior, Colin Smith of Architectural Resources Cambridge, Inc., the architects for the project, says:

It is a normal part of the design cycle which reflects society's tasks and aspirations at any given point in our history—for better or for worse. An honest design needs to be concerned about that. Being dated in twenty years often leads to being fashionable in

---

*Medallions in the Pope's Room had been mistakenly identified as portraits of the Doges of Venice.

another twenty, and so the process goes.[13]

An editorial in the National Trust's *Preservation News* examined the alternatives:

If Design Research had not been permitted to adapt the building, it may have become another parking lot and the visual quality of that corner of Rittenhouse Square lost forever. Today the building stands, an example of realistic preservation.[14]

Employees like the store, as do most shoppers. Maggie Mayer, Assistant Store Manager in Philadelphia, says, "This is our most beautiful store . . . I love the contrasts of contemporary furnishings in an old building."[15] .

The Company   Design Research, Inc., a retailer of contemporary furnishings, fabrics, and accessories, with eleven branch stores located in Massachusetts, Connecticut, New York, Pennsylvania, and California, was founded in Cambridge, Massachusetts, by architect Benjamin Thompson in 1953. Its first store was in a converted house. As business grew, Thompson and his architectural firm designed a modern concrete and glass shop in Cambridge's Harvard Square. The New York and San Francisco branches are in adaptively reused older buildings. The company is privately held, and no financial figures are available.

For further information contact:

Peter Sprague
Chairman
Design Research, Inc.
2 Campanelli Drive
Braintree, Massachusetts 02184

Colin Smith
Architectural Resources Cambridge, Inc.
102 Mt. Auburn Street
Cambridge, Massachusetts 02138

Footnotes

1. INFORM interview with Peter Sprague, Chairman, Design Research, May, 1977.
2. Thomas Hine, "Playing Cupid Proved Trust-Worthy," *Philadelphia Inquirer*, 3 March 1974.
3. Nessa Forman, "Update: . . . On the Fate of a Mansion," *Sunday Bulletin* (Philadelphia), 18 August 1974, sec. 5, p. 8.
4. Nessa Forman, "Mansion Eyed As Home for Philadelphia Mayors," *Sunday Bulletin* (Philadelphia), 8 September 1974, sec. 1, p. 30.
5. INFORM interview with Susan Becher, Manager, Design Research, Philadelphia branch, May, 1977.
6. Peg Harris, "Store Fits Midcity Mansion to Its Design," *Philadelphia Daily News*, 9 October 1975, p. 28.
7. INFORM interview with Peter Sprague, Chairman, Design Research, May, 1977.
8. INFORM interview with Judy Kasameyer, Philadelphia resident, May, 1977.
9. INFORM interview with Susan Becher, Manager, Design Research, Philadelphia branch, May, 1977.
10. INFORM interview with Peter Sprague, Chairman, Design Research, May, 1977.
11. Thomas Hine, "New Building Ruins a Scene, and That's on the Square," *Philadelphia Inquirer*. 5 May 1974.
12. "Editorial," *Interiors*, April, 1976.
13. INFORM interview with Colin Smith, architect, Architectural Resources Cambridge, Inc., July, 1977.
14. "Editorial: The Enemy Within," *Preservation News*, October, 1976.
15. INFORM interview with Maggie Mayer, Assistant Manager, Design Research, Philadelphia branch, May, 1977.

Summary A rambling nineteenth-century mill complex in Maynard, Massachusetts, is currently being recycled for use by the Digital Equipment Corporation as corporate offices, design and engineering facilities, and a manufacturing center. The buildings, dating from the 1860s, have proved to be easily adaptable to today's needs and inexpensive to renovate. Kenneth Olsen, President of the company, explained the primary reason for Digital's location in the old mill as "cheap space."[1] Other less tangible reasons, relating to the emotional and psychological benefits of working in these surroundings, were summed up in the statement of one of the company's oldest and most loyal employees: "If they moved me to a *new* building, I don't know if I would stay."[2]

Background Maynard is a typical small New England town that grew up around a textile mill. In the beginning, it was just a few small houses for the mill workers. Later, retail shops and public buildings were added. The mill itself was the economic and social hub of the town. In 1871, Maynard was incorporated, and began to function as a separate entity. Its name was taken from the man who had developed it from a sparsely settled farming district to a prosperous, bustling manufacturing center: Amory Maynard, founder of the mill. Residents of Maynard are descended from the many nationalities who came to work in the mill in search of a "better life."

The American Woolen Company ran the mill at one point. It installed a dynamo system to produce electric power for the mill and also sold electric power to the town to light the streets. Except for a brief period during the Great Depression, the mill and the town flourished. However, with the introduction of synthetic cloth materials in the 1940s, the textile industry underwent a dramatic transformation. In 1950, the American Woolen Company closed down permanently, leaving the mill and the town to deteriorate together.

The 1950s and 1960s in Massachusetts and other New England states represent a period of great change. The textile industry was moving south, and the technology and service industries were in their infancy. In 1953, a group of businessmen purchased the mill and formed Maynard Industries. Their plan was to provide leaseable space for many of these growing new firms. In 1957, the Digital Equipment Corporation—then just an idea—purchased a lease for 8,500 square feet of space in the mill. By 1974, it would own and occupy the entire complex.

Execution An article in *Business Week* calls the company's base in Maynard "one of the world's most incongruous high-technology plants, a 1 million sq. ft. Civil War woolen mill that turned out blankets for the Union Army."[3]

There are more than twenty individual buildings in the mill complex, dating from the 1860s through more recent times. Most are joined together to form, in effect, a horizontal highrise, permitting separate departments to function in their own buildings or floors, but allowing easy interdepartmental communication. Administration, research, and engineering take place in the smaller buildings,

This clock tower was once the focal point of Maynard's nineteenth-century woolen mill complex. Today it serves the same function for a new industry.

while the larger ones are used for production.

Like most mill construction, the individual buildings are long, low, and shallow with many window openings. The construction is heavy-timber framing with brick-masonry supporting walls. The column spacing and deep floor beams create large, flexible interior spaces with high ceilings. The load capacity of the floors in the mill complex ranges from 50 pounds per square foot to 200 pounds per square foot. This inconsistency makes using the buildings for manufacturing and production more complicated, since the floor-load requirement for such use is 150 pounds per square foot. Office and engineering use, however, are easily accommodated. Differential settlement over the years has created a noticeable sloping of floors in most buildings, but there is no indication of structural deficiency.

The mill was built along the banks of the Assabet River, and waterpower is still available today for a number of Digital's needs, the most recent, a cooling source for the air-conditioning system.

According to Digital's published *General Guidelines for Mill Renovation,* the company is not renovating the entire mill at once, but instead, as natural moves occur, renovations are made to improve the space. Nevertheless, with over a million square feet to work with, and the company's rapid expansion, a full-time renovation operation is necessary. To do this, Digital primarily uses an in-house team of designers, engineers, and carpenters. Even the renovation materials, like partitions and duct work, are made in the company shop. Outside contractors are brought in for specialized tasks when needed.

The renovation plan is simple and efficient. As a floor becomes ready for renovation, all existing partitions, walls, lighting, and mechanical systems are removed. The brick walls and wood ceilings are sandblasted. The old wood floors are sanded and sealed. In certain areas, floor coverings are used and experimentation with different types of floor coverings is now being conducted to determine an inexpensive but efficient way to reduce noise-level problems. The old windows are replaced with dual-pane insulating glass,

and new wiring, plumbing, heating, and air-conditioning systems are installed.

"Open office" planning is employed on each floor. Low partitioned enclosures allow light and ventilation to enter the space freely through the many windows. According to the Digital *Renovation Guidelines*:

Fundamentally, the Mill has the potential for an ideal working environment because of its general layout, high ceilings, open areas, and expanse of windows. We must realize this potential and not try to panel it or otherwise build within it on the basis of a non-descript modern building.[4]

Heating, ventilating, plumbing, and electrical systems run unobstructed and exposed in the high ceiling space. This minimizes the cost of installation and makes alterations and repairs easier and cheaper. Bright colored partitions and pipes, as well as individual personal decoration such as plants and pictures, add life and an informal atmosphere.

According to the company, there have been no major building-code problems which have caused it to alter its reuse plans. Sprinklers are incorporated in all spaces, and fire- and smoke-detection equipment is also used. Stairs—some of them winding—are of original wood construction, but are located in nonflammable enclosures.

Renovation designer Pat McCormick has provided a "kit of parts"—a variety of layouts, partition types, and color schemes—to be used in all future space alterations. Hired to work on Digital's staff, she has participated in this renovation process from 1975 to 1977. Ms. McCormick is particularly interested in the psychological effects of working environments on workers. She describes how her kit is used: "Managers and department personnel are like kids with a tinker toy set . . . moving the parts around to shape their own environments."[5]

Other than the installation of the new windows, few changes have been made in the exterior of the buildings. Because the complex is so large, and because it is industrial in character, changes can take place without altering the overall visual integrity or

impact of the architecture. For example, rooftop mechanical equipment has been added to some buildings, but blends with all the other stacks and appendages to avoid being visually disturbing. Research is currently being conducted to evaluate the benefits of utilizing roof-mounted solar collectors to produce hot water for hygienic and industrial use. The addition of these collectors should not detract from the overall appearance of the mill complex.

Costs The exact price Digital paid for the mill is unknown. A stock transfer in exchange for mill assets was made in 1974. The previous owners had paid approximately $200,000 for the complex in 1953. All financing for the renovation work comes from within the company. Depreciation is computed on a straight-line basis over 33 years.

Digital estimates the cost of renovating the mill, including the purchase price, at approximately $15 per square foot ($5.50 per square foot for renovation, $5.50 per square foot for "fit up," and $4.00 per square foot for amortization). According to its real estate people, comparable new construction, for the same purpose, costs, conservatively, $25 to $30 per square foot. Thus, the renovated space costs 40 percent to 50 percent less. In addition, renovated space can be occupied in less than three months, while it takes anywhere from one-and-a-half to two years to complete a new building.

Problems The difficulties arising from Digital's association with the mill have been primarily external problems for the town of Maynard. The demand on services and the traffic and parking problems have been significant. A new sewage-treatment facility had to be built, and the company's use of the town water supply has reduced the pressure to a trickle during peak-consumption periods. New roads are contemplated to ease the traffic burden, and the police force has had to be increased to control the 6,000 cars going in and out of town each day. Maynard currently has a population of 9,901, with approximately 10 percent of its residents employed by Digital. This figure represents only about 15 percent of the 7,000 employees working in the Maynard facilities, meaning that over 5,000 people commute to the town every workday. Needless to say, traffic congestion could easily consume Maynard's microscopic 5.2-square-mile area if proper planning is not carried out. Digital is working on this problem in cooperation with local and state government planners.

Another problem resulting specifically from the renovation of the mill buildings is excessive internal noise. Old mill buildings, unless expensively adapted by adding new concrete floors or sound insulation in the ceilings, are going to be noisy. Digital has hired acoustical consultants to try to find a solution.

Benefits The primary benefit to the company is the lower cost of space. Although maintenance and security costs are higher, the overall cost of operating the mill is less than similar new construction. This is primarily due to lower real estate taxes on the existing facility. The costs for lighting and power are roughly the same as in a new building, but efforts to encourage user-controlled lighting should help reduce electrical-energy consumption in the future. While heating the space is more expensive, due to the perimeter exposed, the high ceilings, and the many windows, cooling costs can be reduced because windows may be opened to introduce outside ventilation.

Functionally, the mill provides a great degree of internal flexibility.

Interior of the mill after renovation.

The mill complex containing more than a million square feet.

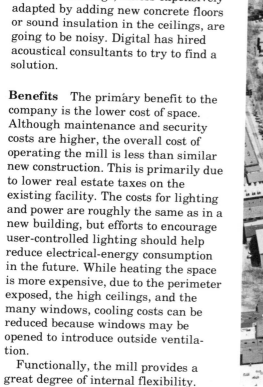

Alterations are quickly, easily, and inexpensively made. The goal of the renovation is to provide an efficient and pleasant working environment in the shortest possible time. Parts and components are designed to permit future changes in even a shorter period of time.

The feeling of participation and pride in working in an unusual but pleasant environment has improved employee morale at Digital. Librarian Karen Feingold refers to a "sense of history" and an "informal atmosphere"[6] when describing the mill and her experience working in it. Her library space has recently been refurbished and it rivals many a public library in its pleasant reading environment. Mary Jane Forbes, Assistant to Vice President Gordon Bell, describes Digital's employees as "individuals"[7] operating, in large part, on their own initiative. According to Ms. Forbes, the mill is a perfect environment for this kind of creative work.

Gordon Bell, Vice President, Engineering, has been in the mill for fifteen years. In addition to his engineering responsibilities, he has taken on the job of "landlord of the mill." Wearing this hat, he is responsible for all the space allocations and renovations of the structure. His goals are to reduce the mean time that it takes a particular department to move to a new location within the mill; and to increase the mean time between moves by making the space adaptable to growth and change. According to Bell, the mill has performed very well in helping to realize these goals.

The location, within an easy commute from a number of residential communities, helps provide an available and contented company work force, free from many of the problems that plague a more densely urban working population.

Some Maynard residents are critical of the impact of Digital on the town, primarily because of the traffic congestion problems, but others seem to take it in stride. Ralph Sheridan, the 78-year-old President of the Maynard Historical Society, was born and raised in the town, as was his father. Every member of his family has worked in the mill at some time. When asked about the image of the old mill in the town, Sheridan concludes:

I believe most of us who have worked in it and looked at it all our lives see a great deal of beauty in the mill. They don't build buildings like that today! Just look at that clock tower and at some of the interesting ways that they used bricks. It is an asset to the town.[8]

The Company The Digital Equipment Corporation designs, sells, and services computers and other items and systems using digital techniques. For the year ending June 30, 1977, the company had revenues of $1.1 billion, an increase of 49.5 percent over the previous year's revenues of $736 million. Over the same period, net income rose 47.5 percent from $73.4 million to $108.4 million. Digital's products are used worldwide in a variety of applications and programs, including scientific research, computation, communications, education, data analysis, industrial-control systems, and medical-systems instrumentation. The company employs over 19,000 people, and occupies more than 3 million square feet of floor space in fourteen plants throughout the world. In Massachusetts alone, it employs more than 11,000 people and is located in six communities across the state.

Because of its extremely rapid growth, Digital has had difficulty meeting space needs quickly. It has reused a variety of existing buildings: an old armory building, storefronts on mainstreets, and even more modern facilities recently vacated by RCA in Marlboro, Massachusetts. In each case, the primary reasons for reusing the existing buildings were the location, the employment picture, and the economic viability (the costs and time considerations). The armory is located in Springfield, Massachusetts, and is situated in the middle of a ghetto. It has proved to be a "great success," according to President Olsen. "Ninety-five percent of the people we hired were unemployed."[9] The former RCA plant was simply an irresistible bargain. Digital was able to acquire the 730,000-square-foot building for $12.8 million or approximately $17 per square foot. This is less than half of what it would have cost to build the same facility new. Furthermore, the building took a fraction of the time to prepare for use.

For further information, contact:
Gordon Bell
Vice President
Digital Equipment Corporation
146 Main Street
Maynard, Massachusetts 01754

Footnotes

1. INFORM interview with Kenneth Olsen, President, Digital Equipment Corporation, September, 1976.
2. INFORM interview with employee, Digital Equipment Corporation, May, 1976.
3. "Mini Computers Challenge the Big Machines," *Business Week,* April 26, 1976, p. 63.
4. Memorandum: *General Guidelines on Mill Renovation,* from Gordon Bell and Al Sharon, Digital Equipment Corporation executives, November 11, 1974.
5. INFORM interview with Pat McCormick, Designer, Digital Equipment Corporation, September, 1976.
6. INFORM interview with Karen Feingold, Librarian, Digital Equipment Corporation, April, 1976.
7. INFORM interview with Mary Jane Forbes, Assistant to Vice President, Engineering, Digital Equipment Corporation, April, 1976.
8. INFORM interview with Ralph Sheridan, President, Maynard Historical Society, January, 1977.
9. Lawrence Collins, "A Critical Look At Massachusetts," *Boston Sunday Globe,* 30 November 1975, pp. 64-65.

Summary Between 1969 and 1972, C. J. Feldmann, owner and manager of a retail clothing operation in Des Moines, Iowa, purchased and renovated two late-nineteenth-century mansions for use as fashion shops. He wanted to preserve these older homes and provide an intimate sales space in a central-city location, adjacent to downtown but without its traffic and parking problems; a space different from the large commercial floor areas common to most present-day retail establishments. While the location and space have cost him some additional expense in maintaining security, the distinctive atmosphere has proved attractive to customers, giving him a competitive edge in a very tough market. The cost of the renovations averaged approximately $22 per square foot (including the price of the land and buildings) and compares favorably to $40 per square foot for comparable new construction in the area.

Background The Feldmann family has been in the retailing business since 1887. In 1952, C. J. "Pete" Feldmann entered the business, and between that year and 1969, his shops expanded to shopping centers, first in Minnesota and later in Des Moines. In 1969, Feldmann wanted to get away from the gigantism of the shopping center and move back to the central-city area. He purchased number 1915 Grand Avenue in Des Moines for $200,000—"essentially the price of the land,"[1] says Feldmann—and began to restore it for use as a store.

The house was the former Finkbine mansion, a three-story stone and brick structure, built in 1895. The Finkbines had been in the construction, lumber, and hardware business in Des Moines during the last century (State Senator Robert Finkbine personally supervised the construction of the Iowa state capitol in the late 1870s). The Finkbines spared no expense in building their home. Eclectic in style, it possesses many neo-classic and Romanesque details and was decorated with beveled glass windows and handsomely carved wooden interiors. Architecturally, it was a museum piece worth preserving.

In 1972, Feldmann also purchased the Polk family home across the street. Constructed in the early 1880s for Mr. and Mrs. Jefferson Polk, this home was known as Herndon Hall, after Mrs. Polk's maiden name, and was designed by a celebrated architect of the day, T. A. Roberts of Newark, New Jersey. An example of the Victorian style of architecture, it contains a massive central staircase, nine large fireplaces, stained glass, beautiful rare-wood interior paneling, frescoed plaster ceilings, and a large ballroom on the third floor. Mr. Polk was a leading Des Moines citizen during the latter half of the nineteenth century, and participated in the founding of the Equitable Life Insurance Company of Iowa, the Des Moines Waterworks, a steam-railway company, and the Interurban Electric Railway Company.

Although originally located in a residential area, both of these fine homes are now adjacent to the downtown commercial district. They most recently served as offices for small insurance and printing companies. The land itself is valuable, but when it was acquired by Feldmann, the buildings had been appraised at next to nothing because local lending institutions were not familiar with evaluating old buildings for potential new uses. In fact, when Feldmann bought the Finkbine mansion, the building had a negative value of $5,000, the cost of demolition. Feldmann wanted to expand his fashion line but preferred not to build carbon-copy "boxes" in the suburbs to house it. He explained his reasons for buying and renovating the old houses: *I believe for a city to be healthy, it has to have a central area that is healthy. The land is valuable, but business traditionally does not look on buildings of this age as worth being restored... We didn't try to create museums. We attempted to take a landmark and make out of it a living thing for this generation.*[2]

Execution The Finkbine mansion contains approximately 10,000 square feet and the Polk house about 15,000. Feldmann started out doing a pure restoration of the Finkbine mansion, but soon found this impractical for modern retail use because of the expense and functional requirements. Accordingly, he changed his efforts to preservation and compatible modernization.

Both renovations included new wiring and lighting. Previous tenants had installed fluorescent fixtures but Feldmann had them removed and replaced with antique fixtures and more compatible modern lighting. Smoke and heat alarm systems were also installed to comply with the local building code. A code variance had to be obtained to avoid installing sprinklers which would have ruined the beautiful old ceilings and woodwork. The Des Moines Board of Review granted this variance provided that the smoke and heat alarm system were substituted. The third floor in the Polk house only had one means of egress, so Feldmann had to have another set of stairs constructed. An interior staircase was installed unobtrusively. Central air conditioning was not feasible because of the number of small rooms and because a duct system would have destroyed the woodwork and ceilings. For these reasons, individual window units are used. Woodwork was restored and refinished, and rooms were repainted and covered with new wallpaper where appropriate. Other renovations included the surfacing of outside parking areas and minor landscaping.

In most cases, old buildings are adapted to fit new uses by altering the interiors to meet new functional needs. In this case, the use has been adapted to fit the old building and is actually enhanced by it. Clothing is displayed in the existing residential rooms and is hung from the woodwork. The stairs are also used as a progressive display case for merchandise.

The Polk mansion's opulent exterior is depicted in an early photograph.

The original floor plans show large rooms radiating from a central stairhall and chimney.

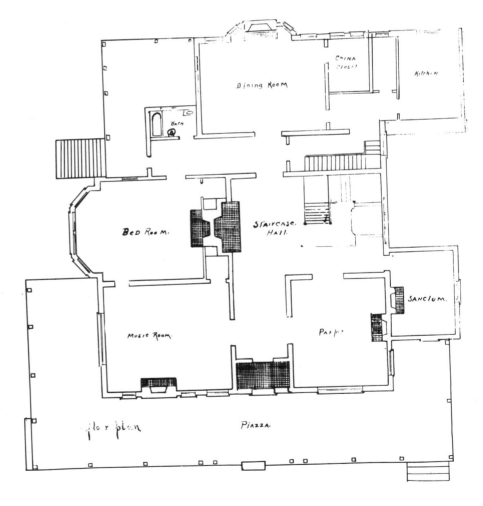

Costs Feldmann paid $200,000 for the Finkbine mansion and land, and spent approximately $60,000 for renovation, for a total of $260,000 or approximately $26 per square foot for the 10,000 square-foot house. The building was valued at a negative $5,000, so essentially it was thrown in for the price of the land. The Polk mansion was appraised at zero value, and Feldmann paid $175,000 for the land with the building included. While no figures are available on the specific renovation costs, Feldmann says that he has spent about $290,000 total to date on Herndon Hall. This would put renovations at approximately $115,000. Prorated over the total 15,000 square feet, the cost for building and land is about $20 per square foot. According to Feldmann, new construction in the area costs about $40 per square

foot, and one would be hard pressed to call it comparable. The Polk mansion was again appraised in January, 1977, for $525,000: land, $266,500; building $258,500.

Problems The primary reason for Feldmann's selection and use of the old homes was the different kind of sales space they offered. A variety of small spaces would provide a more personal shopping experience. Unfortunately, these kinds of spaces require more personnel to supply the same degree of service as conventional retail stores. They also require a greater attention to security. A large number of small spaces with plenty of places to hide is an ideal environment for shoplifting. To overcome this problem, Feldmann has had to hire more personnel and install an electronic tag security system.

In 1976, because of financial difficulties, Feldmann sold the Finkbine mansion for $370,000. While the new owners—a construction company— were primarily interested in the land, which was adjacent to their corporate headquarters, they have preserved the building and are using it for additional office space. Although he feels that his decision to reuse the old houses was a good one, Feldmann is concerned by the high cost of doing business in them and by the lack of financial support for old buildings provided by local financial institutions. As lenders become aware of the potential value in the reuse of old buildings, the latter problem may be reduced.

Benefits From a business standpoint, Feldmann feels that the old buildings enabled him to maintain his position in a glutted market. In the last five years, the number of retail clothing stores in Des Moines has grown from 47 to more than 198. Feldmann has been able to hold his position in this fragmented market, and the old houses have provided unique display areas.

Feldmann has also received a great deal of publicity for his preservation and restoration efforts. The Iowa Antique Association presented him with a brass plaque inscribed: "In appreciation for the restoration of Herndon Hall."[3] In 1977, the State Historical Department of Iowa recommended that Herndon Hall be included in the National Register of Historic Places. At present, the application is pending.

The Company Feldmann's Phase 2 is a privately held family business. No financial figures are available.

For further information contact:
C. J. Feldmann
President
Feldmann's Phase 2
2000 Grand Avenue
Des Moines, Iowa 50309

Footnotes

1. INFORM interview with C. J. Feldmann, President, Feldmann's Phase 2, March, 1977.
2. Patricia Cooney, "The Restoration of Two Mansions," *Des Moines Tribune*, 25 May 1973, p. 17.
3. *Ibid.*

The First New Haven National Bank

Summary On December 7, 1974, the historic 1750s Redfield House became the 24th office of the First New Haven National Bank. The house, located in the small Connecticut shoreline town of Westbrook, is a classic example of mid-eighteenth-century house design. It had been occupied but severely neglected for many years. Deterioration was so extensive that almost no one thought the building could be saved, much less reused as a functioning bank branch. The cost to adapt the building was $146,000, or $36 per square foot.

Background The bank had decided to locate a branch office in Westbrook back in the early 1970s, and in 1972 bought the Redfield property. It was an excellent location, situated near the center of town on the old Post Road. The bank originally planned to raze the old two-story frame house, with its steeply pitched gabled roof, and "build a small, efficient and architecturally attractive branch that would provide full service commercial banking in a hometown environment."[1] A delay in plans for the next two years saved the building.

In 1972, Assistant Vice President Bruce D. Stuckey was placed in charge of planning and coordinating the construction of new branches. He, a designer friend, Tim Rosenham, and architect Al Davis had experience with residential restoration and thought that the old Redfield House could be used as the new Westbrook branch. Bank officers were skeptical; the building was in very bad condition, and they believed that it would cost too much to restore and adapt. A professional engineering firm was hired by Mr. Stuckey to examine the feasibility of reusing the structure; the study found the building to be structurally unsound, and concluded that commercial use would require complete reconstruction. Bruce Stuckey still had his doubts; he felt that the engineering firm was not familiar with restoration practices. He convinced his superiors that: 1. the building was potentially useful as a branch; 2. it would be less expensive to restore this building than to build a new one on the same site; 3. saving the structure would be appreciated by the community and would greatly enhance the bank's hometown image. Doubts about the practicality of the project turned to increased support and enthusiasm as the work progressed.

Execution The exterior of the building was restored to its original state. The masonry foundation was repointed as was the central chimney. The roof was re-shingled with cedar shakes; the clapboarding was repaired—or where necessary replaced—and stained a dark brown. The original windows were repaired, and the paneled front door was recreated. A new addition, executed in a compatible but contemporary design, was built at the rear of the building. The addition, not visible from the street, houses the new vault. A driveway circles the building, accommodating drive-up service. Parking is in the rear.

In the interior of the house, the walls of the main rooms on the first floor were removed, creating a large space for banking/teller service. The original central chimney and fireplaces act as a pivot point, dividing the space and directing the flow of customer movement to the tellers' counter on one side or to a town historical-society display of local community crafts or historical objects on the other. To further open up the space and to provide an education in eighteenth-century framing and masonry techniques, the upper-story flooring has been removed exposing the structural skeleton and allowing a view up to the peak of the gabled roof. A staircase built in front of the central chimney permits access to a small catwalk on the second floor from which it is possible to look down on the mortised and numbered framing members. (When houses like this were originally constructed, timbers were numbered with Roman numerals to assist in assembly.) This catwalk leads to an employee kitchen/lounge/conference area on the second story of the new rear addition. The entire main banking area is lighted by fluorescent lighting suspended from the gabled roof. All new plumbing, wiring, heating, and air-conditioning systems have been installed.

Costs According to the bank, the cost of the restoration and adaptation was $146,000, or $36 per square foot, for the completed job (including banking equipment, furniture, signs, and landscaping).

Problems The major problems came initially in trying to convince bank executives of the desirability of restoring an old building that engineers deemed beyond repair. The structure proved to be sound.

Benefits Benefits were realized by the bank, the town of Westbrook, and the nearby communities. The bank got a new branch office at approximately 75 percent of the cost of new construction. According to Bruce Stuckey:

The Westbrook branch before renovation. (James Meehan)

The Westbrook branch after renovation. (James Meehan)

We have paid as much as $90 per square foot in the past for our branches and my estimates for new construction in Westbrook came in at about $47 per square foot. We completed our project for $36 per square foot and held extras to less than 2 percent realizing a savings of about $25,000.[2]

Articles in local newspapers and periodicals publicized the restoration and probably served to increase support and patronage for the bank. New accounts and deposits have exceeded expectations. In addition, a very good example of mid-eighteenth-century architecture has been preserved and reincorporated into the economy of the town.

A most important business benefit was the resulting enthusiasm among the branch's staff. Mr. Christopher Soulias, the Manager of the bank, is extremely proud of his "new" old building and says it is a "hometown bank with a hometown way of looking at things."[3] Bruce Stuckey is equally pleased: "As a result of Chris's competence and enthusiasm, the branch has been a complete success for us."[4]

The Company Founded in 1792, the First New Haven National Bank is today the eighth largest bank in the State of Connecticut. Assets increased from $327 million in 1975 to $357 million in 1976. Thirty branches, most of new construction, are located primarily in New Haven County.

For further information contact:
Bruce D. Stuckey
Assistant Vice President
The First New Haven National Bank
One Church Street
New Haven, Connecticut 06502

Footnotes

1. The First New Haven National Bank, *The Redfield House and the First New Haven National Bank* (brochure distributed at Westbrook branch's opening, The First New Haven National Bank, December 7, 1974), p. 1.
2. INFORM interview with Bruce D. Stuckey, Assistant Vice President, The First New Haven National Bank, May, 1976.
3. INFORM interview with Christopher Soulias, Manager, Westbrook branch, The First New Haven National Bank, May, 1976.
4. INFORM interview with Bruce D. Stuckey, Assistant Vice President, The First New Haven National Bank, May, 1976.

The interior space has been opened exposing the timber framing and central chimney. Banking activities take place on the ground floor. (James Meehan)

An extension was added on the rear of the building housing the vault and offices. Parking is accommodated in the rear, hidden from the street.

Harbridge House, Inc.

Summary   Harbridge House, Inc., an international consulting firm, has its Boston home offices in "the finest surviving mansion of those originally fronting on the Public Garden."[1] The original structure, completed in 1861, was one of the first houses erected in the Back Bay after it was reclaimed from the Charles River by land-filling begun in 1857. Harbridge House bought the building in 1967. According to Harry Hague, one of the founders of the company: "It is by far the cheapest cost-per-square-foot space to occupy of our offices anywhere in the world; and it provides the best of all possible images . . . of stability, durability, and tradition."[2] The cost for Harbridge House's 46,000-square-foot Back Bay office complex was just under $1 million.

Background   In the early 1960s, Harbridge House had outgrown its Back Bay headquarters and was looking for room to expand. When numbers 10 and 11 Arlington Street came up for sale, the company bought these attached nineteenth-century rowhouses and set up operations there. In 1967, Harbridge House purchased the former mansion of the J. Montgomery Sears family, number 12 Arlington Street, which the Sears had combined with number 1 Commonwealth Avenue, just around the corner, in 1893.

Number 12 Arlington Street is a five-story building, faced with brownstone, and crowned with a mansard roof. Typical of the Second Empire style of architecture, it was designed by Boston architect Arthur Gilman, who helped design the Old Boston City Hall.

The building is located in the Back Bay Historic District which was listed in the National Register of Historic Places in 1973. Boston's strict municipal regulations for historic districts require approval of any change of use that conflicts with current residential zoning, and of any exterior alteration of a building.

The interiors of number 12 Arlington Street, although not protected by historic-district restrictions, are of superb architectural quality. There is lavishly carved hardwood detail throughout the main two floors, along with ornate plaster moldings, medallions, and cornices. When number 12 Arlington was combined with number 1 Commonwealth in 1893, two huge rooms, one on the first floor and one on the second, were created. Architectural details suggest that these rooms served as a music room and formal dining room, respectively; there is also a large ballroom over the kitchen. These large rooms, with exceptionally high ceilings—twelve to fourteen feet—and elaborate detail, make conversion to office space especially difficult: division into smaller spaces would destroy the proportions and detail of the rooms, and the high columns represent a large amount of unusable space. City zoning regulations affecting change of use were not a problem. The building had previously been owned and occupied by the Ursuline religious order so that precedent for a change from residential to institutional/office use had already been established.

A former elegant parlor now a conference room.

Execution No single plan guided the renovation work at Harbridge House's number 12 Arlington Street location. Mr. Hague set forth the basic guidelines for the work: the architectural integrity of the first two floors of the building was to be respected and restored, but the upper three floors could be rearranged to suit the firm's particular needs. The exterior of the building remained in its original state.*

The main foyer of the building was carpeted; walls were repainted with original colors; and woodwork was restored on the first two floors. These floors serve as reception, conference, library, and office facilities. Above the second floor, little if any major work was done except for general painting and cleanup; the upper three floors are used for offices. Existing heating, plumbing, and electrical systems were retained. In numbers 10 and 11 Arlington Street more extensive renovation has taken place, with new wiring and other services installed, but the basic room layouts have remained the same.

In 1977, Harbridge House retained the architectural firm of Perry, Dean, Stahl and Rogers to devise more specific and efficient space/renovation plans for all the buildings.

*In 1976, the company applied to the Massachusetts Historical Commission, under the National Park Service's Historic Preservation Grants Program, for matching funds for exterior restoration of the building, but the application was turned down due to the Commission's lack of funds at that time.

Costs The total cost of acquiring and renovating the three structures has thus far been just under $1 million, or $21 per square foot. More money will be spent to improve the buildings following the recommendations of the architects, but comparable new-construction costs in the same location would probably be more than double the total costs to date.

Problems The existing steam heating system at number 12 has created zoning-control difficulties. In order to maintain a comfortable temperature on the lower floors, the upper floors must be very hot. According to a company official, it is not surprising to find air conditioners in use during the winter on the top floors. Conditions might be improved by upgrading the current heating system to provide separate zoning on each floor.

Space and staff circulation also pose problems. Small rooms impair the traffic flow between offices. Proper planning may improve this situation.

Benefits The primary benefits to Harbridge House from re-using these former residences are the desirable location and the exceptionally inexpensive cost of space. A secondary advantage to the company is the pride officers and employees take in the buildings and the image they present.

The Company Harbridge House, founded in 1950 by three Harvard Business School faculty members, is a management consulting organization. With offices in five U.S. cities and three European countries, it provides a range of services including: socioeconomic studies, management consulting, organization and management development, and systems training. Harbridge House is a subsidiary of the Allstate Insurance Company, Inc. It would not make available any company financial information.

For further information contact:
Kristin L. Servison
Assistant Manager, Personnel and Administrative Services
Harbridge House, Inc.
11 Arlington Street
Boston, Massachusetts 02116

Footnotes

1. Nancy Smith, "Architectural Notes, 12 Arlington Street, Boston (unpublished paper presented to the Boston chapter of the Victorian Society, n.d.), p. 1.
2. INFORM interview with Harry Hague, member, Board of Directors, Harbridge House, May, 1976.

Number 12 Arlington Street, and numbers 10 and 11 next door, the headquarters of Harbridge House in Boston. These Second-Empire-style buildings were once grand city residences.

Summary In 1971, Lawyers Co-operative, located in a vintage mill complex in downtown Rochester, needed additional space for its expanded operations. The company, one of the nation's leading law publishers, asked its architects, Handler/Grosso, to determine whether it would be practical to recycle the existing structures. The architects' feasibility study showed that renovating the 125,000 square feet of the existing buildings would cost approximately $15 per square foot as compared to $45 per square foot for demolition and new construction. Completed in one year, the Lawyers Co-operative recycling, the first major rehabilitation project in downtown Rochester, has served as an instructive example. The success of the first project inspired Lawyers Co-operative to recycle another building in the complex, as well as to create a new park adjacent to its headquarters.

Background Lawyers Co-operative is located in six brick buildings along the Genesee River. In 1901, the company occupied the Aqueduct Building, the oldest structure in the complex, a former shoe factory dating from about 1880. As business increased, Lawyers Co-operative gradually expanded to the adjacent buildings: a warehouse dating from 1890; a smaller pre-1900 industrial building; and a 1950 addition to the 1880s mill. Two other buildings, yet to be renovated, complete the complex. Floor space for the four renovated buildings measures approximately 125,000 square feet.

Through the years, the company continued to grow. In 1965, it also leased additional space outside the complex to house administrative offices, and two years later, it expanded into suburban Rochester, adding a new manufacturing plant for printing and binding. In 1971, management asked Handler/Grosso, architects, to study the feasibility of recycling their historic building complex to meet their space requirements.

Execution Handler/Grosso found the buildings to be structurally sound and in excellent condition, and concluded that renovation would be economically feasible. The company decided to proceed.

The recycling of the buildings took one year, and was done in stages so that production would not be disrupted. The exterior masonry was cleaned, using dry grit, and waterproofed—except where ivy-covered—with a silicone coating. Some of the finer architectural details, the brick-arched floors, cast-iron columns, and wrought-iron beams, typical of nineteenth-century mill construction, were left exposed. Many interior walls were cleaned, highlighting the brick. Windows were replaced, and air conditioning was installed throughout the complex. All new heating, wiring, and plumbing systems were added. The newly retrofitted buildings now serve as administrative and editorial offices. All manufacturing previously done in the complex has been transferred to the suburban Rochester facility.

Interior with exposed and painted original brickwork.

The crowning feat of the renovation was the construction of an Italianate tower, topped by a statue of Mercury 163 feet above street level, on an existing elevator shaft. A familiar landmark, the 21-foot, 700-pound copper-plated statue, dating from 1881, had been atop the nearby Peerless Tobacco Works. It had been kept in storage by the City of Rochester since Peerless's demolition in 1950.

Relying on this experience, the company has recently retrofitted another smaller building in its complex and is now leasing the space. Handler/Grosso revitalized the 1890 structure, exposing the brickwork, installing new plumbing, heating, air-conditioning and electric systems, as well as new windows, a new elevator, and an acoustical ceiling. This renovation took ten months.

Adjacent to its buildings, along the Genesee River, Lawyers Co-operative created a pleasant public park. Designed by Carol R. Johnson and Associates, the park effectively links the complex with the rest of downtown, and provides increased green space for Rochester's citizens.

Costs The cost of recycling the vintage buildings was much lower than the cost of new construction: about $15 per square foot as compared to about $45 per square foot. Handler/Grosso provided a breakdown on the comparative costs (see below).

The renovation cost an estimated $1.8 million. Development of the park cost about $250,000.

Problems The temperature of the condensate from the steam used to heat the renovated buildings had to be lowered before it was returned to the city's sewers. To solve this problem, condensate-cooling pipes were installed below the sidewalks. In winter, the pipes serve to melt the abundant snow, while at the same time lowering the condensate temperature.

Benefits Richard Handler, of Handler/Grosso, enthusiastically assessed the results of the rehabilitation:

At a cost of less than one-half of a new building, this office building provides functional area equal to any new building with the elements of charm and historic continuity for the company as well as historic significance for the community.[1]

In addition to the cost savings, rehabilitation, unlike new construction, made it unnecessary for the company to reshuffle its operations and employees. The newly decorated, bright, and spacious interiors also enhance the working environment. Employees take pride in their offices and in Mercury, a Rochester landmark for years.

The new park is popular with both employees and city residents; it has even led to the establishment of a bocce league among the employees. In addition, some local citizens have telephoned the company to express their appreciation. The company has received a good deal of favorable publicity in local newspapers and magazines.

Following the Lawyers Co-operative example, other businesses have chosen to remain and retrofit rather than flee to the suburbs. Rochester Telephone Company has recently completed a new mini-park, and Handler/Grosso is renovating a vintage former Federal Building (c.1890) as the City Hall.

In June, 1975, Handler/Grosso received a Design Award from the Rochester Chapter of the American Institute of Architects for the Mercury statue and tower. The Award read, "Chosen for its imaginative contribution to the city of a meaningful landmark and its sensitive relationship to existing buildings."[2]

The Company The Lawyers Co-operative Publishing Company, the second largest publisher of law books and related materials in the country, was founded in 1882. Its publications include legal text and reference books, and *Case and Comment*, a magazine for lawyers. In 1964, Lawyers Co-operative acquired the Research Institute of America, which publishes information on business management, including security and tax matters, training, automation, and economics. Lawyers Co-operative is privately held, and no financial figures are available.

For further information contact:
Thomas Ryan
Facilities Planner
The Lawyers Co-operative
Publishing Co.
Aqueduct Building
Rochester, N.Y. 14603

Architects/Engineers:
Handler/Grosso
2209 Monroe Avenue
Rochester, N.Y. 14618

Footnotes

1. Written communication from Richard Handler, partner, Handler/Grosso, to IN-FORM, February, 1977.
2. Sally Walsh, "Eight Buildings Cited in Design Awards," *Rochester Democrat & Chronicle*, 20 June 1975, p. 15C.

	Retrofitting		New
land value	$ 300,000		$ 300,000
value of existing shell	1,250,000		—
cost to demolish	—		100,000
total square foot need	125,000		125,000
		new construction	
renovation costs, including:	1,800,000	costs, including:	6,250,000
mechanical systems	700,000		700,000
floor finish	150,000		150,000
window replacement	100,000		—
		time for new	
time for renovation	1 year	construction	1½ years

The recycled Lawyers Cooperative buildings.

McGraw-Hill, Inc.

Summary Since 1971, McGraw-Hill Publications, a subsidiary of McGraw-Hill, Inc., a large and diversified international publishing and communications company, has operated its U.S. Western Regions office from a 1920s ice cream factory located in the heart of the downtown San Francisco business district. Although the company leases only about one-half of the 65,000-square-foot space, it has renovated the structure to meet its specific needs, as well as to provide additional space for subleasing. These subleases help offset the cost of building improvements. They also allow a measure of security for future expansion. Including the cost of improvements, the cost to McGraw-Hill for the master lease is approximately 50 percent of what it would be for comparable space in one of the area's new high-rise office buildings. In addition, the company is not just a name on a large lobby directory, but the principal tenant in a unique building.

Background Since 1912, McGraw-Hill has had offices in San Francisco in several locations; in 1970, the Publications Company was once again looking for new space. Thomas Carmody, a Vice President in charge of its Western Regions office, is confined to a wheelchair. His primary requirements for new space were that it be free of architectural barriers and be accessible to the handicapped, unlike so many of the new buildings he had worked in or looked at. In addition, business required that the office be located in the central downtown district. After examining buildings in the area, Carmody found:

In many of these new office buildings, designed for the most modern of conveniences, I have to enter the building like a "piece of baggage" from the service alley and up the freight elevator. I cannot negotiate the many steps and escalators that are often the only means of gaining access to the building and to such amenities as plazas and commercial mall areas . . . the main selling attractions of most of these newer buildings.[1]

One day, Ron Kaufman, a local developer, asked Carmody to look at the recently renovated Fibreboard Headquarters Building at 55 Francisco Street. This fifty-year-old corrugated-box plant had been converted into offices for the Fibreboard Corporation (see Appendix) and additional leaseable space for other tenants. Carmody and representatives from the company's Real Estate and General Services Division in New York visited the Fibreboard conversion and liked what they saw. The only problem was that the location was not quite right; it was a few blocks away from the desired area.

Kaufman then found the old Foremost Ice Cream Factory, built in the 1920s, in just the right location for McGraw-Hill. He approached Carmody and the New York staff with a proposal to sign a master lease for 24,000 square feet of this space and to spend a considerable sum of money improving the building's interior and exterior. Foremost had made some mechanical improvements, including the installation of air conditioning, but the part that McGraw-Hill would lease was virtually "raw space" and required all new finishes. Windows had to be replaced, and in the eyes of the company, the exterior needed some modernization. Carmody and his staff were less than enthusiastic about space in the new high rises they had visited, but the idea of recycling an old ice cream factory for their new offices excited them. According to Carmody, "This was a project that we all felt we were taking an active part in creating, and the entire staff is very proud of the results."[2]

A new front unifies two old industrial buildings now the San Francisco offices of McGraw-Hill. (Cine Kersha Photography)

Execution The building contains approximately 65,000 square feet: four floors of 12,000 square feet each, 5,000 square feet on the roof, including a penthouse of about 1,000 square feet, and approximately 12,000 square feet of street-level commercial space. McGraw-Hill leased 24,000 square feet, of which 12,000 was subleased to other tenants. The lease extended for twenty years with a termination clause available to McGraw-Hill after ten.

Although McGraw-Hill was to spend a sizable sum of its own money improving the space and the exterior, the lease arrangements were financially beneficial to the company. The building owner pays for all taxes, utilities, and maintenance. This arrangement results in the space costing McGraw-Hill approximately 50 percent of what it would cost in a new building, excluding the cost of improvements, and about 75 percent after these costs are included. In addition, if the owner receives higher rent from other tenants in the future, which can be attributable to McGraw-Hill's improvements, the company receives a percentage of the rent increase as a reduction in its rent. Although McGraw-Hill had to absorb most of the 20 percent tax increase due to exterior improvements, it was able to recoup this added expense from the other tenants in the building.

Actually, the ice cream factory was not one building, but two separate structures attached to each other. There is a difference in floor levels of from three to three-and-a-half feet. This could have been a formidable architectural barrier, but Carmody's conversion design circumvented this problem by utilizing a system of ramps. Other design features specifically for the handicapped included: wider door openings to accommodate wheelchairs, grip bars, elevator controls which can be reached from a sitting position, and toilet facilities specifically designed to accommodate the handicapped. A special parking spot was included on the ground level to permit Mr. Carmody to enter the building conveniently from his car.

McGraw-Hill's staff designed the office interiors, which involved some partitioning of the open industrial space and refurbishing of existing offices. The exterior of the buildings was unified by installing new matching operable windows, and spandrel and column coverings. In addition, a roof terrace, with a trellis designed to equalize the height of the roof lines, was built, providing employees with an outdoor space for relaxation. A small covered kitchen area was installed on the roof to provide refreshments.

Other tenants rent office and banking space in the building, but McGraw-Hill positioned its logo over the entry doors, making the structure, in effect, the McGraw-Hill Building, an identifiable address in the city.

Costs The company did not disclose the exact lease rate per square foot in its building, but it did indicate that the cost to McGraw-Hill is below the average $12-per-square-foot market rate for comparable space in new office buildings in the area.

According to Lou Gallo, General Manager-Real Estate for the company, McGraw-Hill spent approximately $415,000 for the improvements on the building. Of this, about $240,000 went for exterior alterations; the balance was used for interior renovations of the company's own space, tenant space, elevators and lobby, and the new penthouse garden. Since occupying the building in 1971, McGraw-Hill has spent another $50,000 on additional improvements. This equals a total investment of about $19 per square foot for the 24,000 square feet leased by McGraw-Hill, to be amortized over twenty years.

No figures are available on operating costs, but according to Lou Gallo, the 425 Battery Street building is "very efficient to operate and comparable to offices in newer buildings."[3]

Problems In the original proposal, the additional space that McGraw-Hill was to sublease was to provide enough income above expenses to offset the cost of the exterior improvements. Because the space was made available during a very soft office market—there was a glut of new office buildings in downtown San Francisco at that time—it did not rent as quickly as expected. The building took two years to fully lease, and this delay increased McGraw-Hill's total cost.

Benefits Even with this additional cost, the company's decision to lease space in an older renovated building has provided it with excellent space at a cost lower than that in new office construction. Space could be shaped to suit McGraw-Hill's requirements, and the location conforms well to the company's needs. Employees are proud of the new home they helped to design. Mr. Carmody says:

It is like a little oasis in a high rise forest and we feel like we are special people. It has been a profitable venture for McGraw-Hill, and we have our own building with our own name on it. We are not just one of the many hundreds of tenants in someone else's monument.[4]

The Company McGraw-Hill, Inc., is a diversified communications company, which publishes business, trade, and educational publications for national and international markets. The company also produces audio-visual materials and owns four television stations in the United States. Its regional offices are located across the United States and around the world. The company's total operating revenue for 1976 was $590 million, up from 1975 operating revenues of $536 million. Net income rose from $33 million in 1975 to $40.4 million in 1976.

For further information contact:
Thomas H. Carmody
Vice President, Western Regions
McGraw-Hill Publications
425 Battery Street
San Francisco, California 94111

Footnotes

1. INFORM interview with Thomas Carmody, Vice President, Western Regions, McGraw-Hill Publications, August, 1975.
2. *Ibid.*
3. INFORM interview with Lou Gallo, Jr., General Manager, Real Estate, McGraw-Hill, Inc., August, 1975.
4. INFORM interview with Thomas Carmody, Vice President, Western Regions, McGraw-Hill Publications, August, 1975.

Morris Newspaper Corporation

Summary The Morris Newspaper Corporation decided to locate its corporate headquarters in a historic Federal-style house in the heart of the financial district in Savannah, Georgia. Under Charles H. Morris, President and former publisher of the *Savannah Morning News and Evening Press*, who founded the firm in 1970, Morris Newspaper expanded rapidly. By 1971, it was faced with finding a new location for its headquarters. Mr. Morris gives his reasons for choosing to renovate an old building:

Our direction was influenced through my interest in Savannah for more than a decade, and through my activities as a Trustee of Historic Savannah. We decided to look for a historic building that might meet our corporate space needs and my interest in Savannah's past.[1]

The renovation of the 8,000-square-foot structure cost approximately $30 per square foot.

Background The Oliver Sturges House was built in 1813 facing Reynold's Square. It is among the ten oldest buildings in Savannah and is both architecturally and historically significant. The site on which the building stands was included in the plans drawn up by General Oglethorpe when he first laid out the town of Savannah in 1733. Oglethorpe designed the street patterns around the squares that Savannah is famous for today. The Sturges House site was originally reserved for the Christ Church, and a parsonage was built on it shortly after 1733. When John Wesley came to Savannah from England in 1736, he lived in this parsonage for almost two years. It was here that he was said to have experienced his second conversion which led to the development of Methodism.

The parsonage occupied the site until after the Revolutionary War, when it was leveled in the great fire of 1796. Shortly thereafter, Oliver Sturges and a partner bought the lot from the church, and the two men built their houses on it. In 1816, Oliver Sturges helped form the Steam Boat Company of Georgia and later the Steam Ship Company of Savannah, which commissioned the construction of a 320-ton steam vessel that would make the first

The corporate offices of the Morris Newspaper chain are now located in the old Oliver Sturges House on the site where John Wesley once lived and preached. (Richard Meeks)

trans-Atlantic steam crossing. It is believed that many of the plans for the historic voyage of the S.S. Savannah took shape in meetings held in the Oliver Sturges House.

Originally, the brick house consisted of two stories over a semi-basement. An octagonal boardroom was added to the rear in 1819, and its interior detail reflects the increasing affluence of its owner. The moldings and plasterwork are more ornate than in any room in the original house. A third story was added sometime between 1850 and 1860. This addition is especially evident in the exterior because of the change in brick color. The brick was

probably imported from Pennsylvania or Baltimore and was laid in a Flemish bond. The house had several other owners after Sturges, and during the twentieth century, became a boarding house and rapidly deteriorated. Threatened with destruction, it was purchased in 1964 by the Historic Savannah Foundation.

The Historic Savannah Foundation was established in 1955 to foster the preservation of Savannah's historic townscape. To accomplish this task, the Foundation operates and maintains historic properties; supports a revolving redevelopment fund which acquires endangered properties and resells them

for restoration; and conducts an educational program to acquaint people with the importance of preserving Savannah's historic buildings. The revolving redevelopment fund owned the Sturges House for six years before Charles Morris offered to purchase and restore the structure for use as his company's offices. His offer was accepted, and construction began in fall, 1971.

The building stood empty and rundown for many years until the Historic Savannah Foundation, Inc., purchased it for resale to a buyer who would restore it.

Execution Morris hired architects Robert Gunn and Eric Meyerhoff to execute the restoration and conversion. Historian Walter Hartridge provided research to guide the restoration. All of the rooms on the first two floors were returned to their original configuration, and the original heart-pine floors were restored. Moldings and other plaster details were measured and photographed, and replicas were made where necessary with castings from the remaining original segments. All the original mantelpieces were restored except for one in the octagonal boardroom which had to be replaced with a replica. The variety of colors used on the first two floors came from the group of "Historic Savannah" colors developed by Ann Osteen, a restoration consultant. The rooms on these restored floors are used for offices for Mr. Morris, Mr. William B. Hill, Vice President, and their secretaries. The boardroom is used as a conference room, and there is a library on the second floor.

The third floor, which has been converted to general office space, is decorated in contemporary style. In the basement, the original kitchen of the house, the floor was lowered to provide adequate headroom, and the stone-rubble masonry was left exposed in the new offices that were created there. This rubble was originally ballast from some of the many merchant ships that sailed in and out of Savannah, and was used in building many of the city's old foundations and walls. All masonry had to be repointed with new mortar, and in some cases, where severe bowing had occurred, reinforcement was necessary. Heavy turnbuckles were used to pull the walls back to their proper position. Reinforcing rods had already been used on the upper levels to stabilize the house after the earthquake that jolted Savannah in the 1890s.

All new plumbing and wiring was installed. Heating and cooling are supplied electrically, and duct work has been concealed in walls and between floors. Work was completed in September, 1973.

Costs The total usable area in the converted building is approximately 8,000 square feet. Renovations cost about $250,000 or roughly $30 per square foot. This figure is roughly equivalent to the cost of comparable new construction at the time.

Problems The company experienced difficulties in matching the moldings and other plaster details, and old doors. In digging out the basement to create additional office space, workmen had to go below the original foundation and below the sewer line. Additional foundation reinforcing was necessary, and as a precaution, a pump has been installed to handle any potential sewage overflow.

Benefits The major benefits to the company have been in the area of corporate image. When the building was dedicated, more than 3,000 people lined up to visit it. It has received many awards, including a special Award of Merit from the Georgia Land Development Association. The building has been recorded by the Historic American Buildings Survey and is in the National Register of Historic Places.

The Company Morris Newspaper Corporation owns fifteen newspapers in Florida, Georgia, Tennessee, Kansas, New York, and California. It has eight employees in the Savannah offices. Since Morris is a privately held company, financial figures were not available.

For further information contact:
Charles H. Morris
President
Morris Newspaper Corporation
27 Abercorn Street
Savannah, Georgia 31401

Footnotes

1. "Preserving the Past While Growing into the Future," *Provident Review*, May 14, 1977, p. 12.

Summary In 1973, the National Bank of the Commonwealth signed a fifty-year lease with the County of Indiana, Pennsylvania, for use of the historic Indiana County Courthouse. The building, which dates back to the 1870s, had been vacant since the construction of a new courthouse in 1970. The bank needed space to house executive offices and central support facilities for its growing fourteen-branch network. It agreed to restore the exterior of the building as a part of the bargain. This restoration and interior renovation cost $500,000. The bank pays the County a monthly rent of $1,000 for the 12,500 square feet of usable space, less than half the cost of comparable space in the area's new buildings.

Background The county courthouse has played an important role in American history. It was not just the legal and political center of the community, but often the social center, as well. In addition to functioning as a repository of county records of all kinds, from titles and deeds to birth, marriage, and death certificates, the courthouse was the place where licenses were issued, taxes were collected, and ballots were counted. These activities generated a stream of daily visitors, as did the courtroom hearings themselves.

Architecturally, county courthouses usually reflect the dignity and prominence that their function dictates. The three-story Indiana County Courthouse is no exception. Designed in 1870 by architect James W. Drum, the structure:

is a magnificent example of the Second Empire Style. Because the building received its impetus from the New Louvre in Paris, a contemporary structure, it was considered an example of the then "modern movement." The style was prominent in domestic architecture from the 1850's through government and commercial structures during the period of Grant's Administration. . . . The simple rectangular form with its mansard roof, and Renaissance moldings, lintels and columns, is distinguished by a large clock tower that rises above and dominates the structure. The simplicity of the form is reinforced by the combination of materials. The use of brick and stone recalls the Georgian tradition and contributes to the building's stately appearance, while the cast iron capitals on the stone columns exemplify the beginning of industrial architectural components.[1]

In 1970, Drum's building stopped serving its original purpose. County offices were moved to new, more spacious quarters. The old building stood abandoned and neglected for the next three years. The peeling paint, rotted and missing woodwork, and age-soiled masonry soon turned a once distinguished landmark into an eyesore. In 1973, the National Bank of the Commonwealth needed to expand its central office facilities in the town of Indiana. The vacant courthouse stood just across the street from the bank's existing offices, and a Vice President suggested moving into the old building. Edward B. Bennett, Jr., President of the bank, liked and personally championed the proposal.

Execution In early 1973, the bank entered into a fifty-year preservation lease agreement with Indiana County. The agreement stipulated that the bank would pay a monthly rent of $1,000, and would finance the restoration of the exterior of the building and all interior improvements and maintenance. Ownership would remain in public hands with the County responsible for paying the property tax. An escalator clause allows the County to increase the annual rent if taxes increase. The primary concern during the restoration was maintaining the architectural integrity of the century-old structure, while providing a pleasant work area for bank officers and staff. Work began in spring, 1973. The exterior was sand-blasted to clean the surface, and the masonry was re-pointed and sealed to retard future deterioration. Rotted and missing decorative detail was replaced, and all detail, including the cupola dome, was refinished. The four-faced clock in the tower was also restored and put in working order.

The first two floors of the interior were completely refurbished: walls re-plastered and painted; marble floors and woodwork refinished; new lighting and heating systems installed; and offices carpeted and finished. Although the interior was redesigned to accommodate modern office functions, according to Bob Wagner, the bank's Marketing Director, "much of the old interior remains; we couldn't knock down the walls even if we wanted to."[2] Approximately fifty people work in the building. The architect for the restoration/renovation was William E. Kerr, A.I.A. of Pittsburgh, and the contractor was Pevarnik Brothers of Latrobe, Pennsylvania. The courtyard was totally relandscaped by Raymond Blanchard, Enterprises.

Costs The cost for the restoration and renovation was $500,000. The bank also pays the County a monthly rental of $1,000 and all maintenance and operating expenses, which average $15,000 per year. The $500,000, amortized over the fifty-year lease period, amounts to $10,000 per year, making the total annual payment approximately $37,000, or equivalent to $3 per square foot. This compared to $7 to $8 per square foot for comparable space in new buildings in the area in 1976.

Problems Because of the thickness of the interior and exterior walls, floor-plan options were limited, and the installation of the heating/air-conditioning system was unusually difficult.

Benefits The community benefited by the preservation of a publicly owned landmark, and county income was increased through the rent payments. In the words of Bob Wagner, "What had become an eyesore was transformed into an attractive center-of-town focal point all are proud of, and the lease agreement has turned a county liability into an asset."[3] The County was also relieved of the maintenance costs on the building and spared the eventual expense of demolition. The building is now included in both the Pennsylvania Register of Historic Sites and Landmarks and the National Register of Historic Places.

The bank benefited by the addition of much-needed office space at a reasonable cost. According to the President of the bank, Edward Bennett: "We've been delighted with it. It is built like a fort and works well for our needs. Although it can't be measured, the restoration has had a very positive effect on our business. On opening day more than 4,000 people came through, and we have had many letters of praise from people we don't even know."[4] The bank opens its large hall for community art and cultural affairs.

In 1975, the bank was presented one of twenty Business in the Arts Awards sponsored by the Business Committee for the Arts and *Esquire* magazine. The Pennsylvania Federation of Garden Clubs has twice honored the bank with statewide awards, and the Pittsburgh Chapter of the American Institute of Architects cited the project as the best reclamation effort in the Pittsburgh area completed within the past five years.

The Company The National Bank of the Commonwealth serves approximately 200,000 people in five western Pennsylvania counties, including: Cambria, Clearfield, Indiana, Jefferson, and Westmoreland. It has fourteen full-service offices and two drive-in facilities located in twelve towns. Assets rose from $138 million in 1975 to $161 million in 1976. Net income increased from $944,600 in 1975 to $1.13 million in 1976

For further information contact:
Robert Wagner
Marketing Director
National Bank of the Commonwealth
P.O. Box 400
Indiana, Pennsylvania 15701

Footnotes

1. Edward B. Bennett, Jr., "Pennsylvania Register of Historic Sites and Landmarks and Museum Commission Nomination Form," December 17, 1973, p. 3.
2. INFORM interview with Robert Wagner, Marketing Director, National Bank of the Commonwealth, June, 1977.
3. *Ibid*.
4. INFORM interview with Edward B. Bennett, Jr., President, National Bank of the Commonwealth, June, 1977.

The Indiana County Courthouse.

Summary In 1968, the Pfaltzgraff Company, a stoneware manufacturer and a division of the Susquehanna Broadcasting Company, purchased the mid-Victorian Lebach House on East Market Street in York, Pennsylvania. The house, located in York's historic center, has been completely restored and adapted for use as the company's offices. The renovation cost $73,000, or $42 per square foot.

Background The Lebach House derives its name from its second owners, Joseph and Jacob Lebach, who purchased it in 1867. Thought to have been constructed in the mid-1850s, the house functioned as a single-family residence until sometime between 1867 and 1883, when a two-story addition facing the street was made, converting it to multi-family use. Between 1883 and 1900, several rooms were added to the rear of the house.

The two-story, mid-Victorian structure is laid in Flemish Bond brickwork. The window lintels are rococo, a more elaborate style than the austere Greek Revival architecture in vogue during the earlier part of the nineteenth century. The ornamental ironwork over each of the doorways was cast at York's Variety Iron Works, a foundry which has served York since the time of the Civil War.

The house, continuously owned by the Lebach family for almost a hundred years, underwent some striking changes in this century. In 1940, it became a retail store called the Fabric Shop, selling yard goods and women's apparel. In 1955, Sophia and Bella Lebach, descendants of Jacob and Joseph, opened a gift shop and mail-order caramel business in the original section of the house. This business continued until Pfaltzgraff's purchase of the property in 1968.

Pfaltzgraff's reasons for recycling the Lebach House were both pragmatic and social; it needed additional space and wanted to help preserve the area's historic architecture. Specifically, the project would provide: additional studio space for the company's growing Product Development staff; a design workshop and modeling studio; and an adequate showroom for company products. It would also serve to enhance the appearance of the house and that of the neighborhood.

Execution Planning and design work for the Lebach House project, as with all company renovation efforts, was executed by Pfaltzgraff's own design staff. Maurice G. Mountain, Design Director, was responsible for developing the plans. He was assisted by C. William Dize, A.I.A., an outside advisor.

Initially, the company found the rooms to be small and awkwardly arranged. The house had been neglected; and the elements had not been kind: the roof leaked, and much of the interior had been destroyed by water damage. One of the later additions had settled unevenly, and according to Maurice Mountain, "Listed so badly that it made you feel dizzy."[1] This addition was removed, but others were reused, including one that originally had been an outhouse. Where the brick walls needed structural reinforcement, steel tie-rods were inserted through the building at the second-floor level and fastened on the outside with retaining plates to hold the brick in place.

In redesigning the interior, Mountain sketched out several alternative floor arrangements to suit the needs of the Product Development staff. The final selection was made on the basis of efficiency of traffic patterns and space requirements. Non-structural interior walls were removed and replaced to conform to the new plans. Completely new plumbing, heating, and electrical systems were installed. Window-unit air conditioners were used on the first floor since there was no room for a central ducted system. However, a central system was used on the second floor where ducts could be concealed in the attic.

The building's exterior was restored to its original state. Paint was removed from the brickwork by sandblasting. Later porch additions on the rear were also removed. The old roof was replaced, and the windows, wood trim, and shutters were restored. Some window openings which had been enlarged over the years were returned to their original size and configuration. All renovation and restoration was executed by Harold Hogg, the general contractor. The grounds were landscaped with new shrubbery and brick-paved walks by Burns & Longwell, landscape architects, and Shiloh Nurseries, landscape contractors.

Approximately twenty employees use the building's 1,700-square-foot space. The project took approximately nine months from conceptual planning to actual occupancy.

Costs The total restoration and recycling of the Lebach House cost the company $73,000, including $48,000 for construction and exterior restoration; $19,000 for interior decoration, furnishings, and finishing; and $6,000 for landscaping. The company purchased the house and land for $32,500 in 1968.

Problems Pfaltzgraff described the following difficulties encountered in undertaking this project:.

Our organization is not structured to undertake this type of project on a full-time basis. It was necessary to proceed with normal work activities in addition to this project. Original design of the house was conceived in another era and was not easily changed to include the modern accommodations needed or the specialized functions that were planned to be performed.[2]

A few specific problems were encountered in trying to meet standards established by the Pennsylvania Department of Labor and Industry. All plans for renovations and new construction of office and industrial facilities must receive the Department's approval prior to implementation. Fire-safety requirements, such as two second-floor exits, door swings, and approved doorknobs, locks, and other safety hardware, were problems. An existing fire escape solved the second-floor exit problem. Doors were rehung to swing in the direction of the exit ways, and a compromise was reached eliminating the necessity of installing the new safety hardware. This hardware is not in keeping with the style and scale of older buildings, and the company wanted to reuse the original period knobs and locks instead of the approved modern ones. The compromise solution was to fix the old locks in the open position and install automatic door closers, keeping the doors shut by pressure rather than by locking.

The rear of the Lebach House before restoration. (Maurice Mountain, Jr.)

Exterior of the house after cleaning and repointing. (Maurice Mountain, Jr.)

Benefits In addition to providing a functional and pleasant place to work, the recycled Labach House is close to Susquehanna's corporate headquarters and convenient for all employees. Cleared land in the area, large enough to accommodate a new building, is nonexistent. Reusing an existing structure permitted occupancy at a reasonable cost in a short period of time.

Improvement of the surrounding area is another significant plus. The neighborhood has been enhanced, and according to the company, "an otherwise unproductive building has been turned into a center for creative productivity."[3] As a result of the success of this project, the company is currently renovating several other old buildings in the area, including a warehouse and two nineteenth-century residences, for use as additional office space.

The Company The Pfaltzgraff Company, a division of the Susquehanna Broadcasting Company, has been manufacturing stoneware products in York since 1811. These nationally distributed products, with designs in early American and country patterns, are used for cooking and serving food, as well as for decorative purposes. Susquehanna Broadcasting is a privately owned company, and financial information is not available.

Other Preservation Activities. Susquehanna Broadcasting, through the efforts of its President, Louis J. Appell, and some of its management personnel, has also been involved in many preservation projects in York, including the maintenance of the historic Bonham House, owned and operated by the York County Historical Society. This house/museum is located between the Lebach House and Susquehanna's corporate headquarters, a new structure designed to relate to the surrounding historic architecture. In addition, Susquehanna employees have contributed time and talent to the proposed reuse of two movie theaters as a performing arts center, and to the continuing use of York's major downtown hotel.

For further information contact:
Louis J. Appel, Jr.
President
Susquehanna Broadcasting
Company
P.O. Box 2026
York, Pennsylvania 17405

Footnotes

1. INFORM interview with Maurice Mountain, Design Director, The Pfaltzgraff Co., June, 1977.
2. Written communication from Dawn D. Russo, Executive Secretary, Susquehanna Broadcasting Company, to INFORM, February 25, 1977.
3. *Ibid.*

Summary On December 31, 1973, the San Diego Federal Savings and Loan Association opened its branch offices in Sacramento, California, in a Victorian mansion, the Heilbron House. Excellent central location, distinct individuality and high visibility, and a desire to preserve an important part of Sacramento's heritage, all contributed to San Diego Federal's decision to purchase and adaptively restore the 1881 structure. The cost for the project was $851,000, or approximately $110 per square foot, including the land.

Background In 1880, August Heilbron, a German immigrant who became one of California's leading cattle breeders, commissioned Nathaniel Dudley Goodell, a distinguished eastern architect, to design and build a house. Goodell had recently completed a beautiful mansion for a Sacramento businessman, Albert Gallatin; this mansion later served as the official residence for California governors. Today it is a state-maintained museum.

The Heilbron House was designed as a compact but beautifully detailed Victorian residence complete with a rich bracketed cornice and high mansard roof. Symmetrical bay windows on the front facade frame an entrance portico supported by Corinthian columns. The entire first floor rests on a basement foundation setting it eight feet off the ground. This was done as a precaution against Sacramento River floods, a frequent occurrence at that time. High ceilings on the first two floors, together with this eight-foot base, give the building a soaring and stately presence. All window openings are decorated with richly carved and detailed wood trim. An ornamental grand front stair, with turned balusters and contoured railings, reinforces the elegant entrance. An ornamental iron fence encircles the property.

In the interior, before its conversion, the basement contained servant quarters, storage rooms, and a summer kitchen. The first floor was the entertaining area and consisted of two formal parlors, the dining room, library, kitchen, and pantry. The master bedroom and bath were on the second floor in addition to other bedrooms and a nursery. The top mansard floor contained other sleeping quarters and a large water tank which maintained water pressure for the bathroom fixtures below. On the main floors, carved plaster moldings and ceiling ornamentations together with hand-rubbed woodwork provided rich interior detail. Five marble-manteled fireplaces furnished warmth on winter days. The Heilbron House was ready for occupancy in 1881 and cost $10,000 to build.

The Heilbron family lived in the house until 1953. It was then sold and converted to a restaurant which operated until 1971. Gordon C. Luce, President and Chief Executive Officer of San Diego Federal, had served as head of the state's Business and Transportation Agency in Sacramento from 1967 to 1969. During that time, he had eaten many times in the restaurant in the Heilbron House. When San Diego Federal was granted a branch office in downtown Sacramento in the early 1970s, Luce and the bank's Board of Directors purchased the Heilbron House to preserve it and create from it a new and distinctive business address in the city. According to Luce:

We wanted a site where we could build something that would stand alone. A place that would stand for building homes, adding to them, and refurbishing them. . . . We looked at the "Mall," but everything had a feeling of sameness.

We purchased this grand old Victorian home because of its historical significance and determined at the outset to maintain its grace and charm in the conversion to a financial institution. Our goal—in addition to providing an efficient savings and loan institution—is to preserve the building so its heritage can be enjoyed by the entire community.[1]

Execution The architectural firm of William C. Krommenhoek and Associates and interior designer Brenda Mason were responsible for the restoration/conversion. The exterior of the house remains essentially unchanged and has been carefully restored by the architects. Missing or deteriorated woodwork has been duplicated or repaired, and the exterior has been repainted. A Victorian-style gazebo was designed to provide drive-up window service and is located on a landscaped piece of property adjacent to the house.

In the interior, steel reinforcing provides additional support for the house's new use as a savings and loan office. The basic integrity of the main rooms has been retained, but walls had to be opened up to accommodate the banking facilities. Plaster detail has been carefully preserved, and, in many cases was reinstalled after the steel was in place. Three of the five marble fireplaces have been retained as well as the grand staircase. Antiques, period fabrics, and wall coverings mix with more contemporary office furnishings and equipment. Private loan offices and other administrative functions are located on the second floor. The total area used for business purposes is 7,748 square feet, resulting in an efficiency factor comparable to new construction.

Cost The purchase price for the land and building was $225,000. About $626,000 more was spent on the restoration and conversion, including all fixtures and furnishings. The $80 cost per square foot for renovation, according to the company, is comparable to the cost of constructing and furnishing a new branch-office.

Benefits Chief Executive Officer Gordon Luce evaluates the project:

We believe that restoration of handsome historic landmarks such as these by the private sector is in the interest of the communities we serve and, at the same time, makes good business sense.[2]

The Sacramento community deposited more than $9 million in new savings in that office during the first year alone. During the first week of the bank's operations in the Heilbron House more than 6,000 visitors came to see the results.

Many special commendations from a variety of sources have been given to San Diego Federal for its restoration of the Heilbron House, including: the California Historical Society, the California State Assembly, the Sacramento Board of Supervisors, the Sacramento Old City Association, and the Sacramento Chapter of the American Association of University Women.

The Company San Diego Federal Savings and Loan is the oldest federally chartered savings and loan association in the state of California, dating from 1885. It had branches in 48 locations around the state and total assets of more than $1.3 billion as of 1976.

Other Preservation Activities. Following the successful results of the Heilbron House restoration and the favorable public response to it, San Diego Federal recently undertook another conversion, this time of the historic Los Altos, California, train depot into its 26th branch office. This early-1900s structure was the hub of the Los Altos community and played an important part in California transportation history.

For further information contact:
Nancy A. Peterson
Assistant Vice President, Public Affairs
San Diego Federal Savings and Loan
600 B Street
San Diego, California 92183

The former Heilbron House, now the San Diego Federal Sacramento branch.

Footnotes

1. Paul Mapes, "Old Mansion: Wall-to-Wall Memory At New S and L Office," *Sacramento Union*, 8 January 1974.
2. San Diego Federal Savings and Loan Association, "San Diego Federal Savings Will Restore and Preserve the Old Los Altos Station as its Newest Savings and Loan Office," *News from San Diego Federal*, May, 1975, pp. 1-2.

Summary   SEDCO, Inc., a major international offshore-drilling, pipeline-construction, and engineering company, has corporate offices in an 1888 "Texas Victorian" school. Reputed to be the first brick school built in Dallas, the Cumberland Hill School was up for sale in the 1960s, and almost everyone expected that it would soon be razed for new development.[1] However, William P. Clements, Jr., SEDCO's Chairman of the Board, liked the building; his relatives had taught there, and he thought its uniqueness and location gave it commercial potential. In 1969, Clements purchased the property and convinced SEDCO to renovate it. The total cost of purchase and renovation was more than $2.5 million, or approximately $64 per square foot.

Background   The Cumberland Hill School once served an affluent Dallas community. The original building was constructed in a square configuration with four classrooms on each floor rotating about a central stair space in pinwheel fashion. Through the years, the neighborhood changed, becoming a melting pot of immigrant nationalities, and so did the school. Wings were added increasing the number of classrooms to meet the growing student population. The early additions conformed to the style of the original structure, employing the same "Dallas Stiff Mud" brick, a light buff-colored brick native to the area. In 1919, however, a square section was added to the north end of the school using different brick and different construction techniques.

As the neighborhood became more heavily commercial, enrollment declined, and in 1959, the building became a vocational training school. In 1961, the school board put the building up for sale, but it was not sold until 1969, when William P. Clements, Jr., made an offer of nearly $1.4 million.

The Cumberland Hill School site was ripe for redevelopment. It was located on a major artery in the central business district and was near the new Fairmont Hotel. Although Clements was determined to save the building, he had no specific use in mind when he purchased it. One early idea was to convert it into a boutique shopping complex, but Clements felt that if it were good enough for that use, it might also be good for SEDCO's own offices. At that time, that company's Dallas headquarters was spread out over three floors of the First National Bank Building, and it was in the process of looking for a home of its own. The young architectural team of Rodger Burson and James Hendricks—now Burson, Hendricks, and Walls—was hired to explore the possibilities of renovating the sound but neglected school building.

The Cumberland Hill School after SEDCO's renovation. (Burson, Hendricks & Walls, Architects)

Execution According to James Hendricks:

Until we saw the old picture of the original building, we didn't fully realize what was wrong with the building we had. It was that flat roof. We sketched the building with a pitched roof and cupola and it was right. The parapet had destroyed what was a beautiful building. The building had deteriorated each time it was remodeled and enlarged.[2]

The architects set out to unify and restore the original character of the old school while adapting it to serve the functions of a contemporary office building. They did not plan a pure

School before renovation and re-creation of pitched roof. (Burson, Hendricks & Walls, Architects)

On-site parking is accommodated and extensive landscaping creates a park-like setting. (Burson, Hendricks & Walls, Architects)

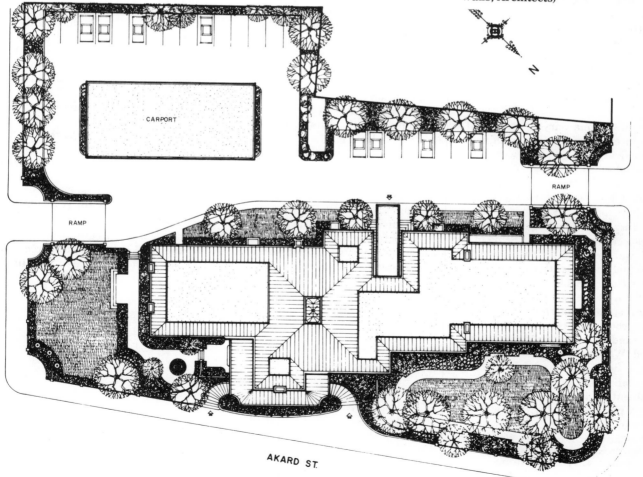

restoration, but rather attempted to recreate the "spirit" of the original.

The two-story structure, which also has a basement, was constructed with brick supporting walls and wood framing. Its total gross area is 40,000 square feet. In the renovation, all exterior masonry walls were saved, and new windows, porches, and entrances were installed. A new steel roof structure was superimposed on the existing flat roof to accommodate the recreated pewter-finish sheet-metal pitched roof and cupola. The entire facade is painted yellow ochre, the color of the original Dallas Stiff Mud bricks. Painting was necessary to waterproof the exterior, as well as to unify the various additions which had used different color brick. The window and door trim is white, while the railings and porch columns are black iron.

To level the original wood floors, which had settled unevenly over the years, steel beams were installed under all wood floor joists, and a concrete topping was poured on the existing floors. The floor loads were carried directly by the masonry supporting walls; additional structural reinforcing was only necessary where the original masonry had been punctured for openings.* The foundation was in excellent condition and rested directly on solid rock.

All interior masonry walls, as well as some interior details, were retained in the renovation. Also saved were a few of the old school's wooden doors, complete with initials carved by mischievous students. The interior was completely redone in a Victorian manner, including wood paneling, and new stairs, ceilings, and floors. Some of the brick walls were left exposed, and old globe and chain lighting fixtures from Dallas Hall at Southern Methodist University were reused. A 45-foot-high central space, opening into the cupola above, contains a reception area and the grand staircase. An elevator was added. Waiting rooms, executive offices, general office and office-pool areas, and a dining facility in the basement fill the remaining space.

New plumbing and wiring, and a new two-duct heating, ventilating, and

*According to architect Larry Walls, several unreinforced openings were discovered after plaster was removed during demolition.[3]

air-conditioning system were installed throughout the building. Mixing boxes, blending the hot and cold air, and individual thermostat controls are located in each office. The original ceiling heights, 15 feet floor to floor, were lowered in some areas to accommodate the mechanical system, but never below the existing window heights. In the executive offices, the high ceilings were retained, and the heating, ventilation, and air-conditioning were designed to feed from below, through the floor.

The site was completely landscaped with new brick retaining walls, ornamental iron fencing, walkways, drives, and parking facilities. It contains a rich variety of plants which make it a green oasis in downtown Dallas.

The post-renovation ratio of 38,000 net square feet of usable space to 40,000 gross square feet in the building provides approximately a 95 percent efficiency factor, better than in most new construction. Renovations were completed in only eleven months through the use of a "fastrack" system of design and construction. Under this system, demolition and construction begins before all plans have been completed. Interior demolition began as soon as measured drawings and demolition plans were executed. Design and working drawings followed, and many of the drawings were actually completed on the site during construction. A number of the tradesmen who worked on the project had actually studied in the building when it was a vocational school. According to architect Larry Walls: "They took great pride in the place."[4] The efficiency of the operation was also improved by the use of a construction-management company, Earl L. Jones & Associates.

Costs The land was purchased outright by Mr. Clements in 1969 for $1.36 million. Disregarding the value of the building, this is equal to approximately $20 per square foot for the one-and-a-half acre site. The cost of the renovation, excluding landscaping and furnishings, was about $1.2 million for the entire 40,000-square foot structure or $30 per square foot. This is comparable to the cost of new construction in the area in 1971. Operating costs are not available.

Benefits SEDCO has improved its corporate image through its reuse of the Cumberland Hill School. William P. Clements, Jr. describes the renovation's effects:

SEDCO will identify with this building as we could never do with just another modern glass-walled building. Everyone in town will be aware of this building, and know it's the SEDCO building.[5]

In 1971, SEDCO was awarded an official historical marker by the Texas State Historical Survey Committee. The company also received top honors from the Texas Society of Architects and an Award of Merit from the American Association for State and Local History. The latter award, given for the year 1971, cited the SEDCO conversion as a "handsome and functional building and a richer legacy to Dallas almost certainly than a new structure could have been."[6]

The more than ninety employees who use the building also find it an efficient and pleasant environment. One functional benefit was the reduced noise level due to the high ceilings.

The Company Founded in 1947 by William P. Clements, Jr., as an oil-drilling contractor, SEDCO over the years has expanded from land drilling to offshore drilling, pipeline construction, manufacturing, research, and consulting. SEDCO's sales increased from $229 million in 1975 to $337 million in 1976. Net income for 1976 was $44 million, up from 1975's figure of $37.5 million. Within the last five years, the company has more than tripled its income. However, offshore drilling is a volatile and unpredictable industry, and SEDCO is currently working on diversification projects, such as floating production facilities and deep-ocean mining.

Growth and expansion since 1971 have caused SEDCO to seek more space for its Dallas operations. While the Cumberland Hill School still serves as corporate headquarters, the company is developing the land immediately behind it. An eight-story, 130,000-square-foot concrete and glass office building is now under construction, and another thirteen-story tower is planned. SEDCO will occupy about 50 percent of the space in the new eight-story tower and will lease the rest. The new buildings provide a background for the old school and will be related to it through similar landscaping. Other than a concern for scale, no attempt has been made to relate the new with the old via materials or architectural design. Burson, Hendricks, and Walls are also the architects for this complex.

For further information contact:
Edwin J. Smith, Jr.
Manager, Insurance Department
SEDCO, Inc.
Cumberland Hill
1901 North Akard
Dallas, Texas 75201

Footnotes

1. Dorothie Erwin, "Victorian Flavor: Old Cumberland School to be Office," *Dallas Morning News*, 23 May 1970, section AA.
2. *Ibid.*
3. INFORM interview with Larry Walls, architect, Burson, Hendricks and Walls, March, 1977.
4. *Ibid.*
5. Erwin, *op. cit.*
6. "Dallas-Based Firm Preserves Historic School," *History News*, September, 1972, p. 188.

Executive office after renovation. (Burson, Hendricks & Walls, Architects)

Major structural walls were retained, and former classroom spaces were subdivided for office use. (Burson, Hendricks & Walls, Architects)

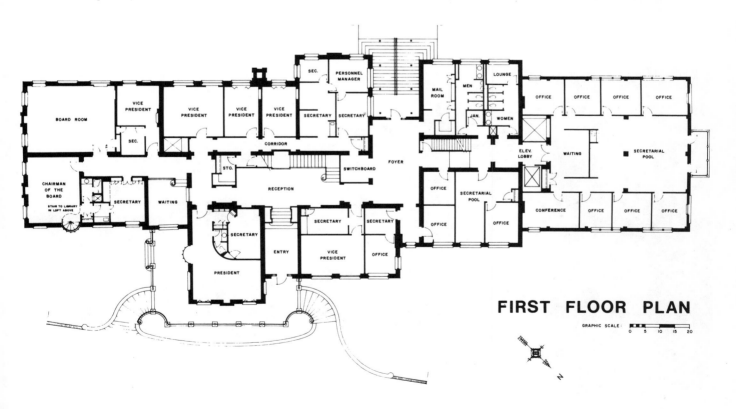

FIRST FLOOR PLAN

GRAPHIC SCALE: 0 5 10 15 20

Summary In January, 1965, the U.S. National Bank of Oregon opened a branch office in the vintage United States Hotel in Jacksonville, a gold rush boom town gone bust. Ironically, the town's decline had produced the unexpected benefit of preserving much of its original nineteenth-century flavor. In the early 1960s, a local group, seeing the value of maintaining and capitalizing on Jacksonville's history, purchased the hotel and sought federal funds to renovate other existing buildings. The hotel, completed in 1880, was the keystone in this effort. The bank agreed to prepay $25,000—covering the first ten years of its lease—for 2,300 square feet of space in the old building. In 1965, it paid approximately $76,000, or $33 per square foot, to remodel the space. In addition, the hotel's owners renovated the building to meet minimal building-code standards at a cost of more than $100,000. Although the town ultimately rejected federal urban-renewal financing, reuse of the hotel encouraged additional renovations, and Jacksonville is becoming a popular tourist attraction.

Background In 1851, Jacksonville was a bustling boom town; gold had been discovered in the area, and the town's population of 1,200 residents was prosperous and proud. But the mother lode soon ran out, and the economy shifted to agriculture. A more serious decline began in 1883, when the railroad bypassed Jacksonville, putting it off the beaten track. By the early 1960s, the population had dropped to less than 1,000. However, the decline had unexpected advantages; Jacksonville remained almost perfectly preserved, reflecting much of the physical character of the gold rush days. For this reason, in 1964, the town was declared a National Historic Landmark.

The United States Hotel, completed in 1880, quickly became an important part of the community. This two-story Western-style brick building includes a wooden porch and balcony. President Rutherford B. Hayes stayed in it in 1881. The hotel remained in operation until 1915 when the town took ownership because of tax arrears. It served as a museum until 1949. The hotel was used intermittently by local groups but continued to deteriorate, and in the early 1960s the town condemned it.

Jacksonville Properties for Historic Preservation, led by Robertson Collins, a local businessman and currently a trustee of the National Trust for Historic Preservation, was formed in 1963 to explore ways to save the vintage hotel. The group learned that the U.S. National Bank of Oregon was planning to open a branch office in Jacksonville. Aware that the bank had several branch offices in historic buildings, the group asked it to lease ground-floor space in the old hotel. The bank agreed, and signed a twenty-year lease. It also prepaid $25,000, its rent for ten years, which enabled Jacksonville Properties for Historic Preservation to obtain additional financing.

In 1964, the federal Urban Renewal Administration conducted engineering studies for an extensive urban-renewal project to renovate and restore the buildings in Jacksonville's core area. This project would have restored the entire district and capitalized on the town's historic character to attract tourists. The hotel's reuse and the efforts of Jacksonville Properties for Historic Preservation were important factors in obtaining federal attention.

The former United States Hotel now houses the Jacksonville branch of the U.S. National Bank of Oregon. (Graphics West Photo)

Execution The two-story brick building needed a great deal of work. Jacksonville Properties for Historic Preservation reconstructed the wooden porch, installed a new roof, and added steel supporting columns, concealed in the original brick of the exterior walls. The brick was repointed, and new plumbing, wiring, air conditioning, and fire-protection equipment were also installed. These renovations were required to bring the building up to current building codes and to keep it from further deterioration.

The bank hired architect Walter Pappas, A.I.A., general contractor Jack Batzer, and interior decorator Lila Colwell, A.I.D., to recreate an authentic nineteenth-century interior. "More than 16,000 man hours of research were done to provide a decor of the 1850s for the Jacksonville Branch, and the result is one of the most unique banking institutions on the West Coast."[1] Burlap wall coverings and custom-reproduced wallpaper cover the walls. Eight branch chandeliers with glass shades were reproduced from old sketches. Oak teller cages were duplicated from period ones. The furnishings include gold scales from 1840, yew wood chairs (c. 1840), a wall clock (c. 1876), antique inkwells, and brass spitoons. In addition, the bank contributed to the renovation of the ballroom, on the second floor, which is leased for social events, and distributed a free brochure describing Jacksonville's historic buildings.

Costs The total cost for renovating the building to bring it up to code requirements was well over $100,000. It was paid by the owners, Jacksonville Properties For Historic Preservation. The bank's cost for remodeling its 2,300 square feet of space is itemized as follows:*

General Construction	$38,500
Counters and Tellers' fixtures	20,000
Office Furniture	5,000
Vault Door and Night Depository	6,500
Alarm	1,500
Miscellaneous	4,500
TOTAL:	$76,000

*These costs are twelve years old; comparable work today would be much more expensive.

The hotel's recycled interior. (Graphics West Photo)

Problems The reuse of the United States Hotel was to be a catalyst for a large-scale renewal effort. However, according to a spokesman for Jacksonville Properties for Historic Preservation, Jacksonville citizens rejected the urban-renewal project in a local referendum, out of fear of federal intervention.[2]

Benefits Because of a well conceived public relations campaign for the opening of the Jacksonville branch, the bank has been featured in numerous Oregon newspapers, including the *Portland Oregonian* and the *Ashland Daily Tidings*, as well as in the *Western Banker*, the *Pacific Banker & Business*, and *Sunset* magazines.

In addition to saving and reusing the old hotel, the bank's decision to locate in Jacksonville became the catalyst for the renovation of other historic buildings in the town. These efforts are gradually turning the town into a popular tourist attraction. In 1976, the Jacksonville Museum attracted almost 86,000 visitors.

The bank has also provided mortgages for the revitalization of residential areas and other historic buildings. The town now has grown to 2,000, but further expansion is presently restricted due to a sewer moratorium. The assessed valuation of the town has increased from $2.7 million in 1965 to $22 million in 1976.

The Company The U.S. National Bank of Oregon is a wholly owned subsidiary of U.S. Bancorp, which provides financial services. U.S. Bancorp had assets of $3.1 billion in 1975 and of $3.3 billion in 1976. For the same period, net income rose 18 percent, from about $25 million to $29.6 million. The U.S. National Bank of Oregon has 150 offices throughout Oregon.

For further information contact:
James W. Parry
Assistant Vice President
Bank Properties Division
United States National
Bank of Oregon
P.O. Box 4412
Portland, Oregon 97208

Footnotes

1. "A Modern Bank Steps into the Past," *Medford Mail Tribune*, 17 January 1965, sec. B, p. 1.
2. INFORM interview with official, Jacksonville Properties for Historic Preservation, August, 1977.

Summary In 1974, the Wachovia Bank and Trust Company, a leading North Carolina bank, recycled a storefront dating from 1918 for use as a branch office in downtown Chapel Hill. Although not an individually significant structure, this building was an integral part of the small-town streetscape, and was protected by city ordinances. The bank's recycling effort won it considerable praise and a number of awards. The 3,300-square-foot project cost $140,000, 20 percent less than the cost of new construction, and took about one year to complete.

Background In 1972, the Wachovia Bank and Trust Company requested permission to locate a branch office on Franklin Street, a major artery of downtown Chapel Hill, home of the main campus of the University of North Carolina. Since Chapel Hill's small-town character is considered a valuable asset and is regulated and protected by city ordinances, there was great reluctance on the part of many residents to welcome a modern bank facility to Franklin Street. In 1972, the City of Chapel Hill had barred the construction of a six-story bank building proposed by one of Wachovia's competitors.

When Wachovia received approval to establish an office, it sent Lloyd Abbott, the Chief Facilities Officer of its General Services Department, to Chapel Hill to seek guidance on a building design from the Planning Board and city Appearance Commission. The Appearance Commission approved the bank's suggestion of a contemporary building, but one in harmony with the unique atmosphere of Franklin Street. The solution was to recycle the interior of an existing building, converting it into a modern banking facility, while preserving the original exterior facade to maintain continuity with the surrounding area. The building chosen had been used for several purposes since its construction in 1918. It housed, at one time, an electrical-appliance company, at another, a university cafeteria.

Execution Wachovia hired John D. Latimer and Associates of Durham, North Carolina, and Roger C. Clark of the North Carolina State University School of Design to furnish the architectural design. Two problems immediately arose: eliminating the tunnel-like effect caused by windowless interior walls, and preserving the continuous street-scape design. The building's exterior featured a brick flat arch, previously covered by aluminum siding, which ran along under the roof line and linked the structure to nearby storefronts. According to architect Clark, "We saw Franklin Street as a kind of brick wall that really should be saved."[1]

The original facade was retained, but does not function as the entrance to the building. Instead, the flat arch opens on a second facade made of white stucco and grey tinted glass set off by black window frames. A glass door to the bank is located there. Two structural bays behind the original facade were removed, and the roof was cut back so that the area in front of the new

entrance is opened to the sky. Glass was installed above the stucco wall over the door, and the interior ceiling of the bank slopes dramatically to meet the top of the glass. This introduces natural light into the building.

The entrance to the bank on Franklin Street was specifically designed with pedestrians in mind. The night deposit box and Teller II, an automated banking service, both have been set in white stucco in the facade itself. This effect is explained:

[The] night deposit box has become an integral part of the design, reaching out from the new in one corner to touch the old, "marrying" the two as architect Clark puts it.[2]

The inside of the 3,300-square-foot bank is like any other modern bank facility, with teller counters to one side and customer counters on the other. Bank officers' desks are in the rear. There is no drive-in window, since the bank is downtown and is readily accessible to pedestrians.

Wachovia's Chapel Hill branch. (Jim Thornton)

Costs The work on the building took one year to complete and cost the Wachovia Bank and Trust Company $140,000—$16,000 for architectural fees and $124,000 for general construction—or approximately $42 per square foot. This includes the cost of the vault, but not of other banking equipment.

According to the company, recycling represented a 20 percent savings over the cost of new construction.

Benefits The Wachovia Bank Building provides architectural continuity with the rest of Franklin Street, which chiefly consists of smaller buildings, the University Methodist Church, and part of the campus of the University of North Carolina.

Charles H. Wartman, the bank's Manager, says that after being in the building for a year, "The employees love to work there because it's so light and airy."[3] He couldn't directly attribute new deposits to the appearance of the building, but indicated that the bank is doing well.

Wachovia's building received high praise from the American Institute of Architects' South Atlantic Regional Convention, in Savannah, Georgia, in 1974, as "a fine example of recycling which appropriately blends with its surroundings."[4] The Chapel Hill Appearance Commission also awarded it a Certificate of Commendation. The bank has been featured in articles in several magazines and newspapers, including the *Raleigh News-Observer* and *Architecture Plus* magazine.

The Company Founded in 1879, the Wachovia Bank merged in 1911 with the Wachovia Loan and Trust Company to create the Wachovia Bank and Trust Company. Wachovia is an English version of the name *Wachau* which the Moravians, who acquired the land in 1753, applied to the area around Piedmont, North Carolina. The bank currently has 186 offices throughout North Carolina. Wachovia ranked 33rd among the nation's banks, with $2.85 billion in deposits, $3.5 billion in assets, and $30 million in earnings for the year ending December 31, 1976.

For further information contact:
Tonya Widemon
Writer, Public Relations
Wachovia Bank and Trust Co.
P.O. Box 3099
Winston-Salem, North Carolina
27102

Footnotes

1. Ernie Wood, "A Small Town Streetscape Saved," *Raleigh News-Observer*, 29 September 1974, p. 5-V.
2. *Ibid.*
3. *Ibid.*
4. *Ibid.*

The branch's modern interior. (Jim Thornton)

Summary In 1974, Zions First National Bank moved its Heber City, Utah, branch into the Abram Hatch House, which was built about 1892 for a prominent local religious, civic, and business leader. Early in 1972, the bank had rejected a remodeling plan for the building as too expensive, and had considered razing the structure or moving it to another location so that a new branch could be constructed on the site. In summer, 1972, after a Historic American Buildings Survey team study of the house, the bank reevaluated its earlier scheme and decided to execute an "adaptive restoration." It would retain the character of the house and much of its interior design, while at the same time, converting the 4,100 square feet of space to accommodate a modern commercial operation. According to Don Bingham, the project's architect, costs were comparable to other new branch offices constructed during this time.

The Abram Hatch House. (Busath Photography)

Background Abram Hatch was sent to Heber City by Brigham Young in 1867 to establish himself as community and religious leader. He also built and operated a store, and was responsible for the construction of several other buildings in town. Among them was a fine residence, built in the early 1890s to accommodate his family and his official functions. Only the best native materials and craftsmen were used in construction. The walls of the house are light, salmon-colored, trimmed sandstone quarried outside of Heber City, and the elaborately shaped roof is shingled in red cedar. The large, 50-foot by 64-foot, one-and-a-half-story structure features a symmetrical facade decorated with delicate spindled and carved wood. Although the neighborhood where the house is located was residential in the 1890s, it is today part of Heber City's central business district.

The Hatch family occupied the house until the 1930s. After that, there were several other owners, but except for a few modifications to convert it into apartments, the building remained essentially in its original state.

The local office of the Zions First National Bank had outgrown its facility in the early 1970s, and was looking at possible sites for a new building. The Hatch House site was considered most desirable. A remodeling plan was explored in early 1972, but the bank believed that it would be too costly an alternative, and it was rejected. Thought was then given to moving the old house to another site to make room for a new building.

In summer, 1972, a team from the Historic American Buildings Survey completely documented the Hatch House and studied its history. The bank was encouraged and impressed by this survey and reevaluated its former decision. That fall, at the urging of President Roy W. Simmons and with the encouragement of the Utah Historical Society, the bank decided to adaptively reuse and preserve the structure.

Execution The adaptive-reuse plan was coordinated by Don Bingham, an architect with Montmorency, Hayes and Talbot, Architects, Inc., of Salt Lake City. Minimum repair was required on the exterior stone work. The addition on the rear was removed, returning the building to its original configuration, and some of the stone from this addition was reused to reconstruct a window in one of the bays, which had been enlarged at some point to make a doorway. A new cedar-shingle roof was installed, and all the wood trim and porches were refurbished, retaining as much of the original detail as possible. Sam Moss, of the Perce-Young Construction Company and job foreman for the project, utilized old photographs of the building to duplicate the carvings and turnings. New dowels, spindles, and other elements were reconstructed to exactly match their missing or deteriorated counterparts, and all wood trim was repainted. The site was also redesigned to accommodate new driveways, walkways, and landscaping. A drive-in facility utilizes one of the bay windows, fitted with bullet-resistant glass, as a view station connected to remote units by underground pneumatic tubes.

The rooms on the main floor have been adapted to accommodate banking needs. The parlor, sitting room, and central stair hall were opened up by the removal of several interior walls, creating a large public banking area. Where these walls were structurally supporting, steel and concrete columns have been installed to carry the loads. Teller counters, designed and built by Fetzer's, Inc., of Salt Lake City to match the woodwork of the house, have been placed in this space. Modern recessed incandescent lighting and restored chandeliers provide illumination. The bank vault now occupies the former two first-floor bedrooms. Eighteen-inch, reinforced, concrete walls, ceilings, and floor, together with the original sandstone outer walls of the house, form a secure "box" for the vault. The additional load is supported on concrete piers from the basement grade below.

The rooms on the other side of the hall have not been altered, and serve as conference and office space. A small elevator has been installed at the rear of the hall. The rooms on the second floor, used for lounge space, toilets, storage, and future offices, remain essentially in their original configuration.

All surfaces in the building have been repainted or refinished. The original Brigham Oak graining—a method of painting the surface to look like oak-grained wood—has been duplicated on woodwork throughout the main floor. All the brass door knobs, locks, and hinges were removed, repolished, and replaced.

New mechanical systems were installed in the unused attic and enlarged basement crawl spaces, and all plumbing and wiring has been replaced.

Costs According to the architect, the project costs were comparable to those for new branch offices constructed during the same period. Operating costs are also comparable to those of new construction. The bank did not disclose cost figures.

Benefits The bank is proud of its Heber City office and claims that business has exceeded expectations. The location is excellent, and the adaptation of the historic building has generated much public goodwill. Several local publications have written articles about it. In 1974, the Hatch House was included in the National Register of Historic Places.

The Company Zions First National Bank was founded in 1873 by Brigham Young. Originally known as Zion's Savings Bank and Trust, it was Utah's first state-chartered savings bank. The bank is now held by Zions Utah Bancorporation, a holding company which had total assets of $798.2 million in 1976. Zions First National Bank has 42 branch offices throughout the State of Utah.

For further information contact:
Clair Norton
Branch Manager
Zions First National Bank
81 East Center Street
Heber City, Utah 84032

Don Bingham, A.I.A.
Montmorency, Hayes and Talbot, Architects, Inc.
2398 West North Temple Street
Salt Lake City, Utah 84116

Several interior walls were removed to provide space for banking use. Teller counters were designed to match the house's woodwork. (Busath Photography)

Alamo National Bank

Summary In January, 1975, the Alamo National Bank began the recycling of its existing 23-story, 1930s landmark building in downtown San Antonio. The bank's decision to stay and renovate was based on several considerations, including the inexpensive space and prime location the building would provide, and the position of the building in the historic fabric of the city. The remodeling cost $5 million, or $38 per square foot, and according to one of the project's architects, Chris Carson, "We could afford to do it because the building was already here. If you replaced this building today, you'd have to spend upwards of $25 million to $30 million."[1] The project was completed fourteen months later in February, 1976.

Background The 23-story tower was built in 1930 at a cost of $2.5 million. It was designed by the Chicago architectural firm of Graham, Anderson, Probst and White. (The firm also designed Chicago's landmark Wrigley Building.) The tower was designed in the Art Deco style, clad in earth-tone brick masonry, and decorated with terra cotta and bronze. The bank has continuously occupied four floors, leasing the remaining nineteen for other office use. Such original materials as travertine floors, marble wainscoting, solid brass and bronze fittings, and a grand lobby which soars to forty feet, "made the bank a landmark in San Antonio,"[2] states William Flannery, Alamo National's Chairman of the Board.

Functional needs, additional customer services, and the bank's growth all required expansion in 1975. About 35,000 square feet of additional space was needed. The tower's location on San Antonio's main commercial thoroughfare as well as its distinctive aesthetic character were both important factors in the bank's decision to remodel.

Execution The bank decided that all contracts for the remodeling work would go to San Antonio firms to keep the money in the city. Accordingly, Ford, Powell and Carson Architects and Planners, Inc., of San Antonio, designed the recycling plan to accommodate new functional and space requirements, while blending the changes with the existing character and materials of the building. The Bartlett Locke, Jr., Construction Company was the general contractor and worked with consulting engineers Fred T. Goetting and Associates, and W. E. Simpson Company, Inc. Orville Carr and Associates, in conjunction with the architects, was responsible for the interior design.

The first eight floors, designed to accommodate banking needs, received the major alterations, but the electrical and mechanical systems and the windows were refurbished throughout the entire building. On the main banking floor, at street level, the mezzanine area was enlarged, and the service area was redesigned. A large spiral staircase, enclosed by a glass-and-bronze handrail, was built surrounding a three-story center well to connect the new mezzanine area with the main banking floor and the safe-deposit area on the lower level. New teller paying/receiving counters have been installed between existing columns on the main level, and are sheathed in bronze and marble. The most dramatic visual change has been the addition of a Tiffany-like lighted ceiling consisting of five-foot-square bronze coffers containing a grid of bronze light diffusers.

The accounting, bookkeeping, and administrative offices, as well as community rooms, a boardroom, and a new employees' snack bar are located on floors three through seven. These floors are designed on the open-plan office concept, featuring flexible work stations, acoustic screens, and new lighting systems.

To conserve energy, save money, and update the existing wood-frame double-sash windows in the building, a bronze-glazed, snap-on aluminum frame was applied directly over the existing wood frames. The 1,100 windows are all operable, and can be cleaned from the inside. The cost was approximately $300,000, or approximately $270 per window. According to Bradford R. Breuer, a Vice President at Alamo National, "What we have done is to remodel to meet all existing building codes. In essence, we've built a new building without 'building a new building.'"[3]

On the exterior, new bronze-tinted glass panels were installed at street level to provide an easy view of banking activities. These windows also create a spacious atmosphere in the bank's lobby. The walk-in front of the building has been paved with brick in a herringbone pattern, and trees in recessed plant wells have been included.

The Alamo National Building. (Zintgraff Photographers)

Costs   The renovation cost $5 million, or according to a report by the architects, about $38 per square foot for the 85,000 square feet renovated. This is well below the $70 per square foot cost for comparable new construction. Architect Chris Carson says that the "Alamo Bank got a $25 million bargain in usable space out of a $5 million investment in repair and renovation."[4] (see graph.)

Problems   During the recycling, the bank temporarily located movable banking facilities in a former furniture building across the street, while the vaults and other fixed items remained in the old structure. This resulted in some inconveniences during the fourteen months of construction.

Benefits   The bank was able to consolidate specific service departments, which previously were scattered throughout the building and even in other buildings. This has resulted in a more efficient operation. The renovation extended the life of the building at least another forty years and offered space to the bank at a great savings.

The bank has received much praise and attention for the recycling. Texas Governor Dolph Briscoe was present at the dedication ceremonies and congratulated all who made the project possible. Richard Teniente, Mayor Pro Tem of San Antonio, also at the reopening ceremonies, congratulated the bank for setting a good example for downtown revitalization. A local editorial stated:

Key to the center of the city is the community's financial structure and the major banks are the hub of that structure. Alamo National's upgrading is visible encouragement to a new wave of downtown interest at a time when San Antonio's heart is being examined with a keener interest than usual. Major investment by any institution and particularly by a major bank is important because it helps buoy the kind of momentum needed to stimulate other investment for renewal.[5]

**The remodeled main banking floor.
(Zintgraff Photographers)**

The Company   Founded in 1891, the Alamo National Bank is the third largest bank in San Antonio. Its assets declined from $334 million in 1975 to $326 million in 1976.

For further information contact:
Bradford R. Breuer
Vice President
Alamo National Bank
Saint Mary's at Commerce
P.O. Box 900
San Antonio, Texas 78293

Footnotes

1. Deborah Weser, "Bank Completes Renovation Plan," *San Antonio Express News* 29 February 1976.
2. Morris Willson, "Face Lift Plans Related," *San Antonio Light*, 21 January 1975.
3. "Alamo National to Open," *San Antonio Light*, 22 February 1976, p. 24C.
4. Weser, *op. cit.*, p. 4-G.
5. "Editorial: Alamo National's Forward Steps Help Encourage More Renewal," *San Antonio Express,* 23 January 1975, p. 18A.

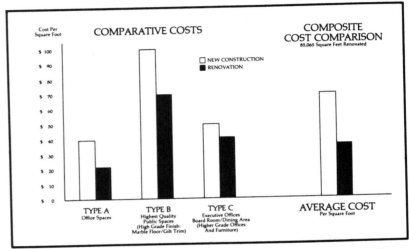

Architect's comparison of recycling costs and typical new construction. (Architectural Recycling, Ford, Powell, and Carson, Architects and Planners)

Summary The Hitchcock Chair Company has revived production of Hitchcock furniture, following nineteenth-century practices, and has even utilized the historic 1826 factory in Riverton, Connecticut, where until 1849, Lambert Hitchcock maintained his "Chair and Cabinet Furniture Manufactory." Since beginning the endeavor in 1946, John T. Kenney, owner of the present company, has built this furniture-making concern into a profitable and flourishing business. The Hitchcock Chair Company has also used an 1830 Gothic Revival church as a museum exhibiting Lambert Hitchcock's wares. Because of the company's efforts, jobs, a measure of prosperity, and an increasing number of tourists have been attracted to the picturesque town of Riverton, in northwestern Connecticut.

Background Lambert Hitchcock was born on May 28, 1795, in Cheshire, Connecticut. After an apprenticeship to a local cabinetmaker, Hitchcock set off for the northwestern part of the state in 1818. He settled in a tiny community at the fork of the Farmington River, because it possessed abundant water-power and trees.

Hitchcock's business, producing chair parts with a saw and lathe, must have prospered, because a new brick factory employing about 100 people was completed in 1826. This three-story structure still has its original weathervane and cupola. Some of Hitchcock's "fancy" chairs resembled country versions of chairs appearing in Hepplewhite and Sheraton's pattern books, while others of his chairs resembled Duncan Phyfe's. The chairs were made in different styles, such as "pillow" and "bolster," and had seats of rush, cane or wood.

An article describes Hitchcock's "manufactory":

The chairs were assembled in the factory, often called the "works," as well as in the homes, in a kind of family manner. Men did all the woodworking: sawing, turning, bending, shaping, and "driving-up" parts into frames. Then children rubbed on a priming coat of red paint so that a patina similar to Duncan Phyfe's real rosewood was obtained when black paint was grained over it. Several variations of graining were used. . . . Women did most of the ornamenting. They stripped fine lines with quills; brushed gold bands on the front of the legs: cut stencil designs out of the best available paper and laid them on tacky surfaces . . . . With bare fingers or a piece of velvet they rubbed the varicolored powders through the open stencil pattern. The finished product was then varnished all over.[1]

Hitchcock chairs wholesaled for from 40 cents to $3 for the top of the line. For a few years, the business flourished, and these chairs were sent all over the eastern United States. But in 1829, a cash squeeze, due to late customer payments, forced Hitchcock to declare bankruptcy, although the manufactory was able to continue operations under trustees. Hitchcock resolved his financial crisis with help from his brother-in-law, Arba Alford, and the two

formed a new partnership, "Hitchcock, Alford & Co." They expanded their furniture production lines to include chests, tables, and mirrors, as sales increased in the growing Western market. The partnership grew; they bought a nearby factory in 1839, and stepped up production to 40,000 items a year. In 1844, Hitchcock and Alford leased another factory in Unionville, whose location on a canal gave access to additional markets. Unfortunately, four years later, the railroad replaced the canal system as the primary means of shipping goods. Since none of their manufactories were near railroads, the business was doomed. In 1849, the company was dissolved, and Hitchcock's former partner and his brother created the A. & A. Alford Company, which continued the manufactory in Hitchcocks-ville. In 1852, Lambert Hitchcock died; in 1865, the town's name was changed to Riverton.

Production of Hitchcock-style chairs ceased in 1864, when the Alfords sold the factory to a producer of ivory-tipped wooden pocket rulers, which continued operations until 1901. The factory was used for various purposes during the following years until finally, it was abandoned. The windows were blocked up, and the site of the manufactory of Hitchcock chairs seemed doomed to decay.

Execution In spring, 1946, while on a fishing trip, John T. Kenney of West Hartford noted the boarded-up Hitchcock Chair factory and a state marker describing Lambert Hitchcock's manufactory. Although he was a shoe salesman with little expertise in furniture, Kenney decided to revive the old factory and make furniture reproductions in the Hitchcock style. He leased the factory from its owners for $300 a year with an option to buy it for $10,000 after two years. On October 17, 1946, the Hitchcock Chair Company again became operational with Kenney serving as President and Treasurer and his woodworking colleague, Richard Coombs, acting as Vice President and Assistant Treasurer. Working capital amounted to about $25,000. For two and a half years, they worked retrofitting the old factory and researching Hitchcock's furniture-making techniques. With assets of $375.63, the team finally obtained a $7,000 bank loan in March, 1949.

Since then, the Hitchcock Chair Company has prospered by creating reproductions of "fancy furniture" for a growing market. Today, its seven retail stores in Connecticut, Massachusetts, and New York gross over $15 million. The product line has been expanded to include bookcases, chests, mirrors, tables, and benches. However, Hitchcock-style chairs are still the biggest seller. They are handcrafted in thirty different standard colors and designs, as well as in limited editions. Production is carried on in the original factory and two modern plants.

The present company employs about 150 people, who rotate their jobs in order to become familiar with various aspects of furniture making. Production techniques used at the restored factory are virtually the same as in Lambert Hitchcock's time. Automation is utilized only in the production of individual chair parts. According to G. Stafford Broughton, Hitchcock Vice President, "On a single lathe today, we get 1,200 to 1,600 turnings. The best a skilled craftsman could turn out on a lathe in the old days was about 120 pieces."[2] Approximately 3,000 chairs a week are produced at the factory. In Hitchcock's time, about 30,000 a year were turned out.

Tourists can visit the factory, observe the craftsmen at work, and hear them describe their tasks: turning a leg, rushing a seat, or applying stencils on the furniture. More than one-half of the Hitchcock factory is now a retail store, where pieces can often be bought at a discount.

Kenney has also reused the Old Union Church in the town as a museum. A short walk from the Hitchcock Factory, this Gothic Revival church was built with the assistance of Lambert Hitchcock, and it was there that he was married. Antique pieces of Hitchcock furniture and vintage woodworking tools provide an appropriate setting for the study of Hitchcock's life and work. About 30,000 visitors tour the museum each year. There is no charge.

Costs The company did not release figures on the cost of the retrofitting. However, it did release the following figures on the Hitchcock Museum:

Cost of purchase	$30,000
Renovation	$50,000
Annual Operating Costs	$50,000

Benefits The Hitchcock Chair Company, having profitably adapted nineteenth-century furniture techniques to twentieth-century requirements, is today providing jobs and increased tourism, thus improving the local economy. In addition, the company has expanded its business ventures in the town of Riverton and further helped to preserve the character of this New England village by purchasing and renovating eight vintage houses which it leases as antique, dress, and clock shops and a restaurant.

The Company The Hitchcock Chair Company is privately held. No financial figures are available.

For further information contact:
Thomas Glennon
President
Hitchcock Chair Company
Riverton, Connecticut 06065

Ellen Glennon
Director
Hitchcock Museum
Riverton, Connecticut 06065

Sue White
Vice President
Advantage Associates
60 Washington Street
Hartford, Connecticut 06106

Footnotes

1. "Lambert Hitchcock of Hitchcocks-ville, Connecticut," *Bulletin of the Antiquarian and Landmarks Society, Inc., of Connecticut,* July, 1966, p. 3.
2. Virginia Bohlin, "Hitchcock: Some Day These Products Will Be Antiques," *Boston Sunday Globe* (New England), 20 February 1977, p. 53.

The restored old Hitchcock Chair Factory.

Summary From 1968 to 1970, Levi Strauss & Co., the famous maker of blue jeans, completely renovated its wood-frame Valencia Street manufacturing plant, built in 1906. The cost of this renovation was $1 million. The plant now serves not only the company, but the community as well: its cafeteria is being used after hours as a center for community meetings and also as a classroom where the company's Spanish- and Chinese-speaking employees may study English. Using company land near the plant, Levi Strauss also made improvements of value to the community. It helped renovate a rundown playgound located directly in front of the plant. It also built an employee parking lot which is used as a basketball court after hours by neighborhood residents.

Background Levi Strauss opened the Valencia Street factory, a three-story timber-frame structure, shortly after the San Francisco earthquake in 1906. It has been producing blue jeans there ever since. The 83,000-square-foot plant is located in the Mission District of San Francisco, once a suburban area but now part of the deteriorating inner city. Levi Strauss is one of the area's major employers, drawing almost 350 workers from the surrounding neighborhoods.

By the late 1960s, the plant was becoming a burden to the company; it was old, unattractive, and almost obsolete. Levi Strauss considered moving to an industrial area in South San Francisco, ten miles from its present location. However, an informal survey of employee reaction found that most people working at the plant had very close ties with the neighborhood. Many employees didn't own cars, and either walked or took the bus to work each morning. Many female employees especially needed to be near their homes and children.

Levi Strauss is a major participant in the JOBs (Just One Break) program of the National Alliance of Businessmen, a program intended to help individuals who are having trouble finding employment on their own. According to the company, its awareness of local job-related problems made it reluctant to disrupt the lives of its employees, or to make the inner-city job situation any worse.

Furthermore, although most of its factories are located outside California, the company wanted to maintain a plant in San Francisco, the city where Levi Strauss opened his first store in 1850.

Execution In late 1967, Levi Strauss asked architect Howard A. Friedman, F.A.I.A., to improve the looks and efficiency of the Valencia Street plant. The plan proposed by Friedman and his staff, in addition to consisting of a general renovation, included construction of a Western-style porch to run the length of the front of the building, giving it the look of an old hotel.

Renovation work began on the first floor in 1968, under general contractors Maloney and O'Hare. It proceeded one floor at a time until the work was completed in 1970. In this way, the company was able to keep the plant in full operation throughout the renovation.

The major construction work included erecting a series of stair towers at the four corners of the building. After these were finished, all interior stairs were removed. The interior was then altered to accommodate the conveniences of a modern plant, including air conditioning. New washrooms were added, and the sewing operation was consolidated from three floors to one. Hardwood floors were refinished, but the old timber structure was found to have stood up well. The exterior required little work: the building was painted bright white and yellow, and the Western-style front porch, once erected, was furnished with benches and checker tables.

The first floor of the refurbished factory contains the company's administrative offices, a warehouse, and the shipping department. The second floor is the location of all manufacturing facilities which produce Levi's denim and corduroy jeans. The third floor houses several staff operations moved from the company's downtown office building, including research and development, a product-testing laboratory, an experimental sewing factory, and the styling and design department, as well as a cafeteria dining room. The latter is made available to neighborhood and civic groups for meetings and banquets, and also serves employees as an after-work classroom where English is taught.

After the renovation was completed, Levi Strauss had to decide what to do with the land surrounding the factory. In front was a playground which had fallen into disuse and disrepair. After consulting the San Francisco Recreation and Parks Department and community leaders to determine the best use for the land, the company decided to restore this playground. It had a mini-park built that was designed by Howard Friedman. The City of San Francisco agreed to contribute shrubbery and landscaping as well as the services of a park director. On additional company land, since many plant employees needed parking facilities, a parking lot was constructed. It is used after hours as a basketball court for neighborhood youth.

Costs The renovation of the Valencia Street factory cost Levi Strauss & Co. almost $1 million.

Benefits The newly renovated plant has been praised by community residents and even by commuters. San Francisco Planning Director Allan

Jacobs wrote to Levi Strauss: "I hope that others will follow your example in staying in San Francisco and in doing such tasteful rehabilitation of fine old properties."[1] Mayor Joseph Alioto said that the remodeled plant "gives testimony to the recognition by a leading corporate manufacturer of the problems of the neighboring community and participation in the solution."[2]

The Company In 1850, Levi Strauss, a Bavarian dry-goods merchant, arrived in San Francisco with a roll of canvas tent material. Discovering gold miners' need for good-quality, tough-wearing pants, he asked a local tailor to make several pairs of pants from his tent material. These were sold almost immediately, and the miners wanted more of "Levi's Pants." Strauss opened a shop in San Francisco, and began to produce waist-high overalls in the canvas material, and sometime later, in denim.

Today Levi Strauss & Co. produces a variety of clothes. In 1976, it had sales of $1.2 billion, up from 1975 sales of $1.01 billion. Income rose from $64.7 million in 1975 to $104.8 million in 1976.

Several pairs of Levi Strauss's original canvas jeans are now in the Smithsonian Institution, part of its Americana collection.

For further information contact:
Elise Rychlewski
Assistant Director, History Room,
Public Relations Department
Levi Strauss & Co.
2 Embarcadero Center
San Francisco, California 94106

Footnotes

1. Walter A. Hass, Jr., "Levi's Old/New Pants Factory," *Historic Preservation* (Washington, D.C.: Preservation Press, National Trust for Historic Preservation, n.d.), p. 17.
2. *Ibid.*, p. 14.

The renovated 1906 factory.

Summary Pope & Talbot, one of the country's oldest forest-products companies, has restored most of the buildings in the town of Port Gamble, Washington, where it has operated continuously since it was founded in 1853. The company has renovated about thirty residential and commercial buildings since the late 1960s at a cost of about $250,000. Port Gamble is a living, working company town, a historic community, and a unique example of preservation.

Background During the heyday of the gold rush, in the 1850s, Andrew J. Pope and Captain William C. Talbot left Maine and migrated west to make their fortunes. When they got to California, they put their lumber backgrounds to good use, and developed a thriving wood-products business tied directly to the gold boom. Shortly thereafter, Captain Talbot set off for Puget Sound to find timberlands and a sawmill site. He chose Port Gamble, and in 1853, Pope & Talbot built a sawmill there. This sawmill, which has been modernized several times, is still processing lumber, and has the distinction of being the oldest continuously operating sawmill in North America.

As business grew, so did Port Gamble. Houses were built for the employees, and a few shops were constructed to service their needs. Port Gamble, with a population of about 250, is still a company town today. All 35 buildings are owned by Pope & Talbot and rented to its employees. About 35 percent of the Port Gamble plant's 225 employees live there.

Although the buildings were maintained through the years, the mostly Victorian-style edifices suffered heavy wear and tear. In the 1960s, the company had to decide whether to restore or demolish the existing buildings.

Pope & Talbot President Guy Pope, his wife, and several other company officials realized that Port Gamble provided a unique example of a living and working historic community. Furthermore, the mostly Victorian architecture (several buildings are copies of New England prototypes) was of widespread interest. Lumber processed from the company's timberlands was utilized in the original construction of the buildings.

Restoration of the town seemed an appropriate way to commemorate the company's 125th anniversary and the Bicentennial. Management also decided to collect all records and historical documents spread around the company's offices in the Pacific Northwest and to establish an archives in Port Gamble.

Execution Renovation began in 1969. Since the interiors had been modernized and maintained, exteriors were the central focus. Many of the houses were scraped and painted their original colors. Among the popular colors are: mustard, light grey, white and dark red. Where necessary, woodwork was replaced by company carpenters. To date, five houses, two commercial buildings, and St. Paul's Church have been restored to their original condition. One of the houses, the Gothic Revival Thompson House (c. 1859), is the oldest continuously occupied house in the state. Another, the Walker Ames House, was built in 1887 as the manager's residence, and is an excellent example of the Queen Anne shingle style. About fifteen years ago, previous tenants

Port Gamble homes restored by Pope & Talbot.

completely renewed the rich interior, which includes fine handcrafted woodwork, stained glass, and a fireplace still boasting its original tiles. The wooden, two-story General Store (c. 1853) originally served as a trading post. The store now houses the newly collected company archives in its basement, as well as the Port Gamble Historic Museum. The Museum's exhibits and artifacts depict the past, present, and future of Pope & Talbot and the lumber business in the Pacific Northwest. The restored Romanesque Revival St. Paul's Episcopal Church (c. 1870) is a copy of the Congregational Church in East Machias, Maine. Also repainted was the Masonic Temple (c. 1870), the oldest masonic temple in the state.

The improvements to the town continue. Recently, about twenty workmen's row houses, dating from the turn of the century, have been renovated and repainted, and the chimneys on the town's buildings are being repaired where necessary.

The streetscape of Port Gamble has been improved by placing electric and telephone lines underground and installing reproductions of turn-of-the-century gas streetlights.

Pope & Talbot has prepared a promotional pamphlet called *Port Gamble—America's Oldest Continuously Operating Forest Products Community* which describes the town's historic structures. Although tourists may walk around and identify the various historic sites, none of the houses are open to the public.

Costs   The company has spent about $250,000 on the renovation and improvements to Port Gamble. These funds have been generated internally.

Problems   The increasing flow of tourists has caused some problems for town residents. They complain of eager visitors ringing their bells and wanting to see the interiors of their houses. Some tourists complain about the lack of restaurants, although the company has provided picnic facilities.

The Port Gamble church, designed after a church in Maine.

Benefits   Pope & Talbot's efforts have resulted in better employee relations. According to the company, residents take great pride in their unique town. The project has also generated favorable publicity; Port Gamble has been the subject of articles in such publications as *Sunset* magazine, the *Christian Science Monitor*, the *New York Times*, *Progressive Architecture*, and the *Seattle Times* as well as other regional newspapers. An increasing number of visitors to the nearby Olympic Mountains, a prime tourist attraction, are now stopping at Port Gamble. The Port Gamble Historic Museum, opened in July, 1976, has been another attraction. The company reports that the number of tourists doubled between 1976 and 1977.

The Company   Pope & Talbot has manufacturing operations in Oregon, Washington, and British Columbia. The company had revenues of $94.3 million in 1976 and a net income of $3.6 million. The revenues reflect a 35 percent increase over 1975 sales of $69.4 million. However, the net income for 1976 was down from a 1975 figure of $3.99 million, primarily due to losses on a discontinued operation. Sales break down as follows: lumber, 59.2 percent; pulp chips, 12.4 percent; specialty plywood, 12.3 percent; logs and timber, 8.1 percent; veneer, 4.3 percent; and other, 3.7 percent.

For further information contact:
Holly R. Hutchins
Director
Corporate Communications
Pope & Talbot, Inc.
P.O. Box 8171
Portland, Oregon 97207

Summary In September, 1976, the Engineering Department of the Standard Oil Company of Ohio (Sohio) moved into the 83-year-old Cuyahoga Building on Superior Avenue and Public Square in downtown Cleveland. This historic landmark, designed by Daniel H. Burnham, is one of the few remaining examples of the Chicago skyscraper school of architecture. In 1976, the building was renovated by its owners, Broadview Management (a subsidiary of the Broadview Savings and Loan Company) and private interests. Sohio is the largest tenant. It has leased 40,000 of the building's 63,000 square feet for seven years at an annual cost of $7 per square foot. The desirable location, plus Sohio's confidence that the structure could be successfully and comfortably renovated to accommodate its engineering staff were the major reasons behind the decision to rent the space.

Background Sohio, founded by John D. Rockefeller and located in Cleveland since 1870, has its headquarters in the Midland Building, a Classical Revival structure built in 1929. By 1976, the company had outgrown its space in the Midland Building and sought additional office space in the nearby Cuyahoga Building. Built in 1893, the Cuyahoga was developed by two of Cleveland's most prominent business leaders, Myron T. Herrick and James Parmalee. Herrick was a banker and statesman, a Governor of Ohio, an advisor to President William McKinley, and an Ambassador to France. Parmalee was Herrick's business partner.

The eight-story Cuyahoga Building was designed by Daniel H. Burnham, and was the first steel-frame structure in Cleveland. Burnham was one of the leading architects at the turn of the century. Among his other credits were the World's Columbian Exposition in Chicago in 1893 and the Western Reserve Building (see Higbee) in Cleveland, where he also developed a plan of wide vistas, malls, and a spacious center of municipal and office buildings for the downtown area.

The Cuyahoga Building is faced with brown brick and has a sandstone and terra cotta trim. Stylistically, it contains neo-classical elements such as horizontal divisions clearly defining the base, middle, and top portions of the building. Romanesque arches are interspersed between three-part, projecting bay windows, and these features are grouped in vertical strips that correspond to the dimensions of the structural-steel supports. The central entrance on Superior Avenue is a two-story archway surrounded with terra cotta ornamentation. The archway contains a delicate, lace-like iron grillwork above the doors. According to the National Register Nomination Form for the building:

As an urban design element it [the Cuyahoga Building] effectively complements the Romanesque facade of the Society National Bank, also by Burnham and Root [Burnham's partner], on the north side of the Public Square, and the Romanesque Cleveland Arcade in the middle of the same block on Superior.[1]

All three buildings are in the National Register of Historic Places.

In 1904, the Williamson Building, an eighteen-story structure designed by George B. Post, was erected next to the Cuyahoga Building. In 1944, the two buildings were joined and connected by an arcade and stairway. The Cuyahoga Building had been vacant since 1967, when it was purchased in 1971 by the Broadview Savings and Loan Company and private interests who also own the Williamson Building. No renovations were planned until 1973. That year, Richard Kortier, President of Broadview Management and Vice President of Broadview Savings, who had just joined the firm, contacted several contractors. He recognized the demand for additional office space in the Public Square area, and felt that the Cuyahoga Building had excellent renovation potential.

The restored Cuyahoga Building. The Williamson Building is on the right. (Broadview Management Corporation)

Execution Kortier hired Drake Construction, a firm experienced in renovation, as the general contractors; and Myron Manders, of Bialosky and Manders, as the supervising architect. According to architect Manders, the objective of the renovation was "to preserve the historical richness of the exterior and to provide modern usable interior office space."[2] The business objective was to extend the building's useful and profitable life, while upgrading an area where the owners have additional property investments. To accomplish these objectives a "backward plan" was developed, which first determined the cash flow the renovated building could generate, and then decided what renovation work this cash flow would support. Commonly, developers first determine the cost of the renovation work, and then decide whether the market will accept the rents required. If net revenues do not provide an adequate return on investment, then a new renovation scheme must be developed. Leonard Nyman, Secretary-Treasurer of Drake Construction, states, "Why waste the cost of designing the building twice? A six-month delay when inflation is 10 percent can be pretty costly."[3]

The owners determined that an acceptable return on the building's rents after conversion could be achieved if $1.5 million were invested in renovation work and amortized over fifteen years. A six-month schedule was established. All subcontractors bidding on the job knew that there was a $400-a-day penalty for each day over the schedule. This approach matched the renovation work and the money available. It also rigidly budgeted and conserved time.

The building's interior was gutted, and new mechanical, plumbing, and electrical systems, as well as new elevators, were installed. A new steam/hot-water heating and cooling system was installed which has lowered energy costs by 25 percent.

The exterior was cleaned by sandblasting; the masonry was repointed; and all the wood window frames were covered with baked-enamel, aluminum frames and operable sashes that matched the originals. One-eighth-inch insulating glass was used in the new windows. The public lobby was restored to its original 1890s decor. The owners plan to restore the street-level retail space to its original style in 1978.

Work began on April 1, 1976, and by August, 1976, the Sohio Engineering Department moved into four of its five 8,000-square-foot floors. The Sohio facilities include an engineering library, a computer terminal area, reception and meeting rooms, and offices.

By September, 1977, all retail space on the ground level had been rented, and the building's owners were negotiating with interested tenants for the available top two floors at rents of $8.50 per square foot. The owners pay all taxes, operating expenses, and debt service for the building, but tenants are required to pay a proportionate share of all increases in taxes and operating costs. Tenants finished individual spaces to their own specifications.

Costs The cost for renovation of the total 63,000 square feet was $1.8 million or $28.50 per square foot. An additional $300,000 expenditure over the original $1.5 million budget was required to replace the plumbing system, which was found to be inadequate during renovation. Renovation costs were financed with a $1.8 million mortgage payable over fifteen years at a 10 percent interest rate. When the building is fully leased, tenant income will cover all building operating expenses and debt service. It will also provide the owners with a 6 percent return on their investment.

Sohio pays approximately $7 per square foot for 40,000 square feet of space, and has spent nearly $25,000 making improvements of its own. This rent compares to about $10 per square foot for space in new buildings in the area.

Main entrance to Cuyahoga Building. Archway has elaborate terra cotta ornamentation with iron filagree screen. (Broadview Management Corporation)

Problems Although the renovation proceeded nearly on schedule, when the mechanical and structural systems were exposed, it was found that the existing plumbing could not be reused. The pipes had to be replaced at a cost of nearly $300,000.

Benefits Broadview Management has brought a vacant, unprofitable building back to life and is receiving a reasonable return on its investment. According to Richard Kortier, "I wish we had ten more floors on Public Square like those in the 63,000-square-foot Cuyahoga Building. Public Square office space will be at a premium."[4]

Sohio, because of this recycling effort, has been able to gain the additional office space it needed close to its home offices. John Graham, Engineering Manager for the company, says:

We looked at a number of potential office sites before we selected the Cuyahoga Building. We were certain it could be modernized nicely and we were pleased with its proximity to the Midland building and the departments we serve. We've got the best of both worlds, the inside is as attractive and comfortable as any new building in the city, and the outside retains the character of an era that was exciting in Cleveland's history. Recycling soundly constructed older buildings, especially of a landmark like this one, is a form of energy conservation one should not overlook.[5]

The Company Standard Oil of Ohio, a diversified oil company, became independent in 1911 when the original Standard Oil Company was broken up. Today, Sohio's products include gasoline and other petroleum products, plastics, chemicals, and fertilizers. The company also has holdings in uranium, motels, and the food-service industry. Sohio's sales rose from a figure of $2.5 billion in 1975 to a figure of $2.9 billion in 1976. Net income increased from $126.5 million to $136.9 miHion over the same period.

For further information contact:
Samuel B. Baker
Public Affairs Associate
The Standard Oil Company of Ohio
Midland Building
Cleveland, Ohio 44115

Richard G. Kortier
President
Broadview Management Company
320 Williamson Building
Cleveland, Ohio 44114

Footnotes

1. "National Register of Historic Places, Inventory, Nomination Form" 10-300 (Washington, D.C.: U.S. Department of the Interior, National Park Service, December 31, 1974), sec. 6.
2. Gene Bluhm, "Restoring the Grandeur of the Past . . . the Cuyahoga Building," *Properties*, September, 1976, p. 90.
3. *Ibid.*, p. 92.
4. *Ibid.*, p. 97.
5. Standard Oil Company of Ohio, *Sohio News Service*, September 13, 1976, pp. 2-3.

Tremont Nail Company

Summary The Tremont Nail Company, dating from the early nineteenth century, is reputed to be the country's oldest nail manufacturer. Located in Wareham, Massachusetts, it is one of only three cut-nail manufacturers in America today. The company's factory complex, composed of nine nineteenth-century buildings, has been in continuous operation since 1848, when the main factory building was erected. The National Register of Historic Places' nominating form describes the complex:

Architecturally, the original factory building . . . and the other nineteenth and early twentieth century buildings comprise a significant industrial complex. Industrially, the nineteenth century processes which are still used to produce cut nails . . . illustrate well the human skill oriented processes of manufacture which characterize nineteenth century production.[1]

The Tremont Nail Factory has been listed in the National Register of Historic Places since October, 1976.

Background Tremont Nail was established in 1819 in Tremont, a suburb of Wareham, Massachusetts. In 1848, the company moved into buildings previously owned by the Parker Mills Nail Company in Wareham. It has been continuously operating there ever since. Seven out of the nine buildings in the complex are still used in the cut-nail manufacturing process.

The main factory building, located on the Wankinco River and originally powered by a waterwheel, is a large, shingled, rectangular structure. The original building is 240 feet long and 90 feet wide; an extension at the rear measures 50 feet by 50 feet. The factory's medium-pitched, ridged, green-shingled roof is topped by a wooden cupola. Sash windows line the facade of the building, and are supplemented in the two-story rear addition by smaller-paned windows.

The interior of the main building is an open area filled with machinery. Its walls and ceiling are constructed of unfinished lumber. Situated in the center of the room is the original brick tempering forge, which with the help of pot-bellied stoves, heats the building in winter.

Other buildings, all dating from about 1900, include a clapboard office building built in the Federal style, two workers houses, and three sheds. Two nineteenth-century shingle buildings, the store and the carpenter's shop, complete the complex.

Cut nails differ from wire nails in having four distinct sides and blunt tips. These features prevent chipping and splitting when working with cinderblock or concrete, and provide greater holding power. The production of cut nails is an intricate process. After being blasted with shot to remove rust and scale, sheets of steel are cut into strips whose width is determined by the size of the nail to be produced. The strips are then fed by hand into a nail-cutting machine, run by a wood and canvas belt-pulley system, which cuts and heads the nail with one stroke.

Actual production is carried out by highly skilled workmen, including a master mechanic and a nail maker. It takes years of experience to learn the process of nail making:

A good operator can produce 4,000-5,000 pounds of nails a day from his battery of four nail machines. But the key man is the "nailer" who fine tunes the machines, grinds the blades and sets the dies that determine the shape and quality of the nails.[2]

Today, there are only three nail makers at Tremont, and no one in training. The skill is not being passed along, and in fact, nail-cutting machines are no longer being produced.

The cut-nail business is closely tied to the housing market. Originally used for the installation of hardwood flooring, cut nails were very much in demand. However, with the increased use of automatic nailing machines which use wire nails, the market for the cut flooring nail is declining. Apart from flooring and masonry, cut nails are used in boat building, foundry work, the restoration of older houses, and for decoration.

In 1969, the company celebrated its 150th birthday. Efficiency has enabled the factory to operate today almost as it did during the Civil War. Recently, the price of wire nails has risen to equal that of cut nails, which should help Tremont Nail remain competitive.

Execution The continued use of the old factory complex has not presented any unusual maintenance problems. The main factory building, where most of the production takes place, is a sturdy structure. The company has recently replaced the wooden-shake roof with asphalt tile, and the roof itself is replaced every 25 to 30 years. The trim on the buildings is painted every 3 years.

Recently, to make way for machinery, several roof supports were removed. Several months later the roof began to sag in that area. To remedy this, Tremont Nail replaced the supports using cut-down telephone poles.

The buildings have also at times been hit hard by hurricanes, resulting in water damage from the nearby Wankinco River. Once, in 1938, the entire roof was ripped off. The company replaced the roof, but apart from that, continued functioning as usual.

In the past, Tremont Nail sponsored tours of its factory during the summer months, since Wareham's seaside location attracts tourists to the area. However, due to the lack of space, and safety considerations, the tours have been discontinued for the present.

Costs The new steel-shot cleaning system (see "Problems") cost Tremont Nail nearly a quarter of a million dollars. Other figures were not available.

Problems   Although structurally
sound, the building was not designed
with twentieth-century safety regulations in mind. Tremont Nail has had
particular difficulty meeting new
health regulations established by the
Occupational Safety and Health Administration (OSHA), which sets am-
bient noise levels and other safety
standards. To solve some of these
problems, the company requires workers to wear goggles and ear-protection
devices specified by OSHA regulations.

In addition, the company has instituted a new method of cleaning the
sheet steel. Previously, the metal was
cleaned by dipping it in hot sulphuric
acid, which was then discharged into
the nearby Wankinco River. Now, due
to Environmental Protection Agency
regulations, the steel is cleaned by
bombarding it with steel shot, a non-
polluting method. This effort has
brought Tremont Nail a citation from
the Massachusetts Pollution Control
Agency.

Benefits   Continued use of the old
factory complex has generated considerable publicity. James Kenyon, Jr.,
President of Tremont Nail, estimates
that from 1971 to 1976, there were
fifteen to twenty unsolicited articles
about the company. Most recently,
Tremont Nail was featured in a report
by CBS news, inspired by a 1976
front-page story in the *Wall Street
Journal*. This exposure has helped the
company a great deal, especially in the
do-it-yourself market. According to
Kenyon:

*When I first came here, I'm not sure the
old buildings helped our image, but
now I'd say that they surely do. . . .
Some people say we're a backwoods
company, but our product is good and
people know that.*[3]

Kenyon believes that the old buildings
signify reliability and friendly, personal service to Tremont's customers.

The Company   In 1973, sales for this
privately held company reached a record $2 million, and afterwards, de-
creased to $1.5 million. In 1976, sales
rose to $1.65 million, and 1977's pro-
jected sales are back to the $2 million
mark.

Other Preservation Activities. In 1969,
Tremont Nail redesigned its nineteenth-century cooper's shop, which
originally manufactured the kegs
in which the cut nails were shipped,
as an "Old Fashioned Country
Store." The store sells peanut butter,
pot-bellied stoves, oil lamps, nail kegs,
and sassafras. It features antiques and
cut-nail jewelry, along with a regular
display of cut nails.
For further information contact:
James Kenyon, Jr.
President
Tremont Nail Company
21 Elm Street
Wareham, Massachusetts 02571

Footnotes

1. Andrea M. Gilmore and Christine Bould-
   ing, "National Register of Historic Places,
   Inventory, Nomination Form," 10-300
   (U.S. Department of the Interior, National Park Service, July, 1976), p. 3.
2. Richard Martin, "Old Plant Bangs Out
   Old-Fashioned Nails and Tries to Stay
   Old," *Wall Street Journal*, 17 May 1976,
   p. 1.
3. *Ibid.*, p. 19.

**Tremont Nail's nineteenth-century main
factory building.**

The Bank of California

Summary By the 1960s, the Bank of California had outgrown its landmark, Corinthian-columned, classic banking hall located in the heart of San Francisco's financial district. The first major building constructed after the earthquake of 1906, this structure is considered one of the city's prime examples of Classical Revival architecture. The bank's Board of Directors considered razing the structure to build a more lucrative new building, but, instead, decided to build a new tower addition which would complement and enhance the existing banking hall. The resulting design has received widespread praise for its response to the older building. The restoration and new construction cost more than $22 million.

Background The Bank of California opened its doors in San Francisco on July 5, 1864. By 1867, it occupied the site of its present main office at 400 California Street. Outgrowing this facility by 1905, the bank demolished the building to build a new one, and, by January, 1906, had moved to temporary quarters nearby. On April 18, 1906, a massive earthquake and subsequent fire left San Francisco in ruins. Almost 500 blocks of the city, including the financial, wholesale, and retail districts, were destroyed. Within six weeks, as the city began its rebuilding efforts, the bank received authorization to begin work on its new building. By September, 1908, the new building, 112 feet long, 80 feet wide, and with 60-foot ceilings, was completed and occupied.

In the 1950s, the bank expanded and added branch offices up and down the Pacific Coast. By the 1960s, it was a $1 billion institution with 48 offices. The bank had long since outgrown its classic headquarters, and its staff was spread out in offices in adjacent buildings. A new building was clearly needed. Although some consideration was given to the financial benefits of razing the existing landmark and building a large, leasable office building on the site, the directors decided otherwise. Instead, a new tower addition would be built incorporating the old building. President Charles De Bretteville explained the bank's decision:

The new 314-foot tower is approximately four times the height of the old building, but relates to it in scale and detail. (Ted Mahieu)

The endeavor of the Bank was to uphold the architectural traditions that have helped San Francisco earn a worldwide reputation for beauty. As a bank with roots in the earliest San Francisco and the West, we felt an obligation to ourselves and the city to preserve our historic building, the first major structure after the 1906 earthquake.[1]

Execution   After several years of research by bank personnel and the San Francisco architectural team of Anshen and Allen, a design attempting to integrate the old and new was developed. The old banking hall would be completely preserved and remodeled, including restoration of exterior and interior detail and incorporation of new electrical and mechanical systems. A new skyscraper, related in proportion, line, and detail would be built next to the older temple-like structure, adding over 240,000 square feet of floor space. To retain the unity and prominence of the original, powerfully symmetrical building, the new tower is set back ten feet from the property line; it is asymmetrical in design and appears to be growing out of the wall of the original building. The interiors are linked by interconnecting lobby passageways.

Although the new tower is 314 feet tall, or approximately four times the height of the old building, it produces a visual and proportional harmony without overpowering the smaller structure. To contrast and set off the banking hall's monumental form with its tall portico, strongly vertical entrance, and enclosure of columns, the tower has a broad, low horizontal entrance with a good deal of glass.

The decorative reeds or fluting of the tower's precast concrete facade match the fluting of the original Corinthian columns and the curved granite cornices of the old building. The original color scheme of light grey granite and dark bronze grills is also repeated on the new tower.

The established setbacks from public streets, the desired setback for the entry, and the height constraint required a daring and relatively expensive design to create the necessary usable floor area to make the project economically feasible. The new building is cantilevered up to 30 feet over the banking hall gaining more than 3,100 square feet of usable space per floor (82 percent of the total floor space). Additional space was created by sinking the new building three levels below ground to a depth of 54 feet below the sidewalk; 45 feet below the high-water tide level of San Francisco Bay and 40 feet below the existing water table. In order to accomplish this, a unique foundation was constructed. A 2-foot-thick concrete wall was poured 80 feet deep—four times deeper than normal for local foundations—around the entire site, and an 8-foot thick concrete mat was poured at the bottom. This formed a floating raft-like foundation. The project was completed in December, 1968, six years after its inception.

Costs   Approximately $2.8 million, or $140 per square foot, was spent on the restoration and remodeling of the banking hall. The new headquarters tower cost $19.7 million, or $90 per square foot. Together, the two buildings have a gross floor area of 300,000 square feet.

Problems   Time and expense were the major difficulties involved in this project. The high quality, compatible detail, and careful workmanship specified by the architects and client were costly and time-consuming. Unlike many standard curtain-wall facades that can be purchased virtually prefabricated and affixed to steel frames, the precast fluted spandrels had to be custom-designed and custom-made. The unusual foundation and cantilevering necessary to satisfy the building's space needs also required additional expense and time.

Benefits   The bank has received praise for its efforts to preserve the old building and to design the tower in a compatible manner. In a report, *The Preservation of Landmarks in San Francisco*, published by the San Francisco Department of City Planning, the success of this project was affirmed: "These efforts substantially support the goal of the city having character and depth in its physical environment."[2]

The Company   The Bank of California ranks 39th among the banks in the United States. It was the first incorporated commercial bank in the West, and, through a unique national charter, it is the only tri-state bank in the country. A wholly owned subsidiary of BanCal Tri-State Corporation, the bank provides services throughout the world. The parent company had assets of about $3 billion in 1976, compared with 1975's assets of $3.1 billion. Net income declined from $3.3 million in 1975 to $2.7 million in 1976.

For further information contact:
Diana Fedorchak
Director of Public Relations
The Bank of California
400 California Street
San Francisco, California 94145

Footnotes

1. The Bank of California, *400 California Street . . . A Century Plus Five*, n.d., p. 66.
2. *Ibid.*, p. 94.

Summary In 1966, the Boston Five
Cents Savings Bank held an architectural design competition for a new
addition to its 1920s, eight-story neo-
classic headquarters on School Street
in Boston's central business district.
The design problem was not only to
functionally and aesthetically complement the existing bank building, but
also to relate the new addition to
Boston's historic urban core. To the
east, stood the Old South Meeting
House, an important landmark built in
1729; to the north, was the Old Corner
Book Store, recently restored with financial support from the Boston Globe
(see Appendix); and to the west, was the
Old Boston City Hall, a nineteenth-
century landmark. Further complicating the design task, a proposed street
realignment by the Boston Redevelopment Authority would create a new
triangular public "square" and a
wedge-shaped redevelopment site adjacent to the bank. Kallmann & McKinnell, architects of Boston's new City
Hall, won the competition. As evaluated by the jury, their design, a
contemporary, glass and concrete, colonnaded structure, "handsomely related to the square, the church, and
the other existing buildings."[1] The
45,000-square-foot addition was completed in 1967. The bank spent $3.3
million on its construction; it contributed another $96,000 for the design
and construction of the triangular
plaza.

Background The Boston Redevelopment Authority (BRA) is Boston's
planning and renewal agency. It has
made innovative efforts to improve the
city and encourage new development
within an overall framework that consciously respects existing historic architecture.

In the mid-1960s, the BRA proposed
a realignment of School Street to ease
traffic flow through the central business district. This project would create
two triangular pieces of land: one, to be
left open as a public plaza, and the
other, to be privately developed. The
plaza, in the historic heart of the city,
was to open up and set off two important landmarks on Boston's Freedom
Trail: the Old Corner Book Store, one of
the city's oldest buildings, built in

**The public plaza in front of the new
building. (Ezra Stoller © ESTO.)**

1718, and the Old South Meeting House, where the Boston Tea Party was planned, built in 1729. The plaza was also designed to offer the pedestrian a stopping place along Washington Street, the main shopping street in town.

The developable triangular plot abutted the Boston Five Cents Savings Bank building on its east side, and contained 9,350 gross square feet of buildable land. Before the BRA could implement its realignment/plaza plans, it had to find a buyer for this land. The bank had been contemplating expansion and saw the odd-shaped building plot as a way to reorient its main entrance from School Street toward Washington Street to capitalize on the heavier pedestrian traffic flow. Constructing an addition to the present building would also permit uninterrupted service and allow future expansion in the same location.

The existing bank building, neoclassical in design, was constructed in the 1920s. It contains: a colonnaded base, the former banking hall, a middle section of offices with paired windows corresponding to the column spacing, and a crowning, broad cornice. Pilasters on the corners extend the height of the building and define the outer edges.

(on facing page)
The new building's fan-like form opens out to the street, the public plaza, and the historic buildings that surround it. (Ezra Stoller © ESTO.)

(below)
Competition drawing of the new addition, the bank, and the Old South Meeting House. (Kallmann, McKinnell & Wood, Architects, Inc.)

Execution Robert M. Morgan, then Chairman of the bank, had also served as Chairman of the Government Center Commission, which had redeveloped an extensive portion of Boston's downtown area. He had been closely involved with the process of selecting and working with the architects for the new City Hall.* He believed that an architectural competition would result in the best possible design for the new bank addition. Four architectural firms were invited to participate; the design competition proposal read as follows:

Though not large or complex, the new building must satisfy conditions that are unusual, difficult, perhaps contradictory. Clearly both BRA and the Bank are concerned about the exterior

*Morgan was later responsible for putting together the financial support to back the adaptive reuse of the Old Boston City Hall for office use.

NORTH ELEVATION

manifestation of the building and the treatment of its setting, and therefore the combination of plaza and facade should be of major concern to the designer. In addition the Bank, as client, has a real business function to perform that requires a noble interior space, so there is the opportunity to fuse the expression of the inside with the outside. Yet the conditions are stringent: to come to terms with colonial tradition while extending a building conceived in a quite anti-colonial spirit and scale, and to cope with a site whose distorted and curtailed form is the byproduct of a traffic adjustment.[2]

The BRA required:

[that] the new building facade on the open space be throughout at least as high as the ridge of Old South, 65 feet above its street . . . also . . . a setback along the curve frontage such that the sidewalk of the new building will be at least 12 feet wide throughout.[3]

The selection jury consisted of: Pietro Belluschi, F.A.I.A., G. Holmes Perkins, F.A.I.A., both distinguished architects, and bank Chairman Robert Morgan.

The winner, Kallmann & McKinnell, was selected from drawings and models. Their design was praised for its impressive, interestingly lighted banking room, and the relationship of this structure to the street. The jury stated that:

the visual and operational relation to the old bank is so outstandingly handled that this feature, uniting the old and the new, could be made a major asset in the operation of the Bank. The exterior with its simple colonnade is handsomely related to the square, the Church, and the other existing building.[4]

The corner, wedge-shaped site dictated the basic fan form of the new contemporary addition. Large radiating beams and columns placed outside the building enclosure free the interior space, providing internal flexibility, and create a covered walkway adjacent to the sidewalk. The spacing of the exterior columns echoes the column and window configuration of the old building. The glass skin, set back seven feet from these columns, encourages views both into the building and out from within. From almost all points inside, one can see the Old South

Church, the Old Corner Book Store, and the new plaza. In this way, the plaza becomes an "urban living room" with the new and the old buildings forming its perimeter furnishings.

In keeping with the spirit of the old, as well as with BRA restrictions, the height of the new addition is approximately the same as the ridge height of Old South Church. The addition also is capped by a wide cornice similar to that of the original bank building. The predominantly concrete addition is also compatible in color with the earlier structure's grey limestone.

In the interior, the new building's four stories match the floor levels of the original building. The decoration is contemporary, with granite finishes used throughout on the street level. Fluorescent strip lighting follows the radiating beams, emphasizing the fan-like form.

Costs The total cost for the building's 45,000 square feet was $3.3 million, or approximately $73 per square foot. The bank also contributed $96,000 to the design and construction of the public plaza in front of the new building in lieu of, and exceeding, the city's requirement that 1 percent of the cost of construction for all new buildings be donated for public art.

Problems The only difficulty encountered was the relatively high cost of construction. Much of it was the result of the extensive granite interior finishes and other furnishings specifically requested by the client, not the building's basic design.

Benefits Boston received a new public space and a new building that complements the landmarks surrounding it. The bank's image was enhanced, and in 1975, it received the Harleston Parker Award of the Boston Society of Architects for excellence in architectural design. The building has been praised by several architectural publications, as well as several books on Boston landmarks.

The Company The Boston Five Cents Savings Bank, founded in 1854, has long been one of New England's largest mutual savings banks. It has fourteen offices throughout Boston. Total assets increased from $899 million in 1975 to $964 million in 1976.

For further information contact:
John Vernon
Manager, Purchasing Department
Boston Five Cents Savings Bank
10 School Street
Boston, Massachusetts 02108

Footnotes

1. Pietro Belluschi, Robert M. Morgan, G. Holmes Perkins, Chairman, "Report of Jury: The Boston Five Cents Savings Bank," (mimeographed, The Boston Five Cents Savings Bank, September 14, 1966), p. 2.
2. The Boston Five Cents Savings Bank, "Competition to Select an Architect for a Proposal to Redevelop a Parcel at School and Washington Streets in Boston" (mimeographed, The Boston Five Cents Savings Bank, June, 1966), pp. 2-3.
3. *Ibid.*, p. 2.
4. Belluschi, Morgan, Perkins, *op. cit.*, p. 2.

Summary   In October, 1970, the
Mills Hyatt House opened its doors as
Charleston's "newest-oldest" hotel. The
240-bedroom luxury hotel is a finely
executed reproduction of the original
Mills House, an 1853 hotel built on the
same site. Charleston Associates, a
limited partnership, purchased the old
building in 1968 with the idea of
restoring it. This plan was scrapped,
however, when architectural consultants found the structure unsafe. Instead, an alternative plan to faithfully
recreate the older building in an enlarged version was adopted. The new
hotel cost $5.8 million to construct and
furnish. Today, this hotel, managed by
the Hyatt Corporation, serves an important business and preservation role
in historic Charleston's core.

Background   The oldest portion of
the original Mills House was constructed on the site by silversmith John
Paul Grimke before 1791. The property
became a hotel in 1801. Otis Mills, a
New Englander, came to Charleston in
the 1820s and made a fortune in the
grain business. He invested his earnings in real estate, and bought and
leased the hotel in 1836. Mills took
over the operation of the hotel himself
in 1852, renovating and enlarging the
structure. According to some reports, it
was the finest building in Charleston,
with both running water and steam
heat. Samuel Gaillard Stoney,
a Charleston historian, described the
building as representing the "apex of
Charleston's Victorian style."[1] Distinguished guests such as General Robert E.
Lee, Stephen A. Douglas, and President
Theodore Roosevelt are reported to have
lodged in the hotel.

During this century, the hotel
changed owners and names several
times, and in 1954, it became known as

the St. John Hotel. Active overnight
business was on the decline in the
1960s, and the St. John became a
residential hotel. The Baptist College
of Charleston even leased it for temporary dormitory space in 1965. Although still an elegant building, the
years were taking their toll, when in
1967, Richard H. Jenrette, a New York
investment banker, became interested
in the structure. He saw the possibilities of a renovated hotel as an
integral part of Charleston's restored
historic district. After discussing the
building with several Charleston
friends, including Frances Edmunds,
Director of the Historic Charleston
Foundation, Jenrette took an option on
the building. He became full owner in
1968.

Richard H. Jenrette is a partner in
the New York City-based investment
banking firm of Donaldson, Lufkin and
Jenrette. Although he was not able to
interest representatives of the finan-

The Mills-Hyatt House. (Al Satterwhite)

cial community in the Mills House project, he did secure interim financing from the Ford Foundation and put together a limited partnership, called Charleston Associates, to syndicate interested investors.

Jenrette hired architectural consultants to study the feasibility of renovating the old hotel. The building was found to be structurally unsound: pilings would have to be placed under it and this could not be accomplished without razing the present structure. A plan was proposed to reconstruct the old hotel on the same site but in an enlarged version that would make it economically feasible.

Execution The original five-story hotel contained 150 rooms. The new seven-story version would contain 240 rooms, but be only ten feet taller than the original because ceiling heights would be reduced. The architectural firm of Curtis and Davis, with offices in New York, New Orleans, and London, was retained to carry out the reconstruction. This firm was responsible for the design of the new Royal Orleans Hotel, in the French Quarter of New Orleans, the model for the new Mills House concept. Simons, Lapham, Mitchell and Small, a Charleston architectural firm, was retained as consultants on the design's historical appropriateness.

Before the reconstruction could take place, Jenrette had to secure the endorsement of the local historic-preservation groups. The hotel site was in the Historic Charleston downtown district, and any new construction had to conform with the character of the surrounding buildings. Both the Historic Charleston Foundation and the Preservation Society of Charleston gave approval.

Construction began in summer, 1968, and took about sixteen months to complete. The exterior walls of the old Mills House were made of brick with a stuccoed cement facing. The new exterior walls are made of concrete block, faced with brick, and covered with stucco to exactly duplicate the old surface. The new windows exactly match the old; even the pediment detail has been recast in fiberglass from molds made from the original building. The antique iron grillwork on the Meeting Street facade was salvaged from the building and reused on the new Meeting Street facade. A copy made from a mold of this original ironwork has been installed on the Queen Street side as well. Although originally there was never such a detail on the Queen Street facade, it was believed that its placement there would help provide visual relief from the essentially solid wall of windows. Roof cornices and bracket details were also exactly duplicated. The general contractor was Ruscon Construction Company of Charleston.

A new one-story wing on the rear south side of the building has been added. This accommodates a restaurant and kitchen on the ground level and a swimming pool and sun deck on top. Flagstones, preserved from old Charleston sidewalks dating back to the late 1790s, have been reused in front of the hotel. A replica of a formal nineteenth-century Charleston garden with a cast-iron fountain is situated on the south side of the building. Both the new wing and the garden are shielded from the street by an arcaded gallery. The garden provides a pleasant view from the restaurant and main lobby/lounge area. The landscape architect was Loutrel Briggs of Charleston.

In the interior, the original ceiling heights of the first two floors have been retained, but on the upper floors, the ceilings were lowered to keep the overall building height as low as possible. An attempt was made to duplicate the detail and atmosphere of the lobby and the two main rooms on the first floor. One room serves as a cocktail lounge and the other as the main waiting lounge. The front two rooms on the second floor, also duplicates of the original rooms, are now used for large group meetings and social events. Hand-molded, decorative pediments, medallions, friezes, and cornices—all representing a nearly lost art—were executed on these first two floors by A. Lewis Keyser of High Point, North Carolina, and Clarence Ketner, an associate.

A period chandelier from Belle Meade, a plantation in Nashville, Tennessee, now hangs in the main registration lobby. An English Regency zebrawood table serves as a center table in the lobby. Georgian mirrors, Greek Revival sofas, Chippendale chairs, antique Chinese vases, and much more help to give this recreated "old hotel" an authentic feeling. The New England Society has even loaned a portrait of Otis Mills, which now hangs in the hotel parlor. Anthony Hail, A.I.D., an interior designer from San Francisco, was responsible for the furnishings and interior decoration. He was assisted by John Dickenson, A.I.D., also of San Francisco, and H. Chambers and Company, decorators from Baltimore. Mr. Hail had earlier assisted in the restoration of the White House.

The average room rate is $39 per day, and occupancy has averaged 85 percent. In the spring, during the tourist season, the hotel is virtually 100 percent filled.

Costs The total project cost was approximately $6 million: land, $150,000; construction, $4 million; furnishings, $1 million; and initial year operating expenses, $600,000. The total construction cost prorated per room was $20,000 in 1969/1970—quite low when compared to industry standards, and even low when compared to adaptive-reuse hotel conversions like the Stanford Court in San Francisco, which cost $22,344 per room in 1972. Mills Hyatt's low cost is primarily attributable to the location. According to Mr. Jenrette, "Charleston's building costs were quite low at that time."[2]

Problems When the hotel first opened, there were a few lean years. Jenrette and other partners in Charleston Associates had to invest an additional $600,000 to keep the hotel afloat. "This is a common problem with new hotels,"[3] claims Jenrette. Today, the hotel is enjoying a better cash flow.

Setting up the management and the financing presented more problems. Jenrette and Charleston Associates were not in the hotel business, and had to secure a qualified management team to operate the hotel. At first, Hotel Corporation of America (HCA) agreed to do it, a key factor in Jenrette's decision to go through with the project. However, this was not a period of great financial stability, and HCA withdrew during the planning stages. After approaching a few other hotel companies, Jenrette was finally able to interest the Hyatt Corporation, which was beginning to receive national acclaim for its Hyatt Regency in Atlanta. Although the Mills House did not have breathtaking open spaces like the Regency, it had a historic atmosphere and an excellent location. Hyatt recognized these qualities as valuable business assets.

Mortgage rates were very high at the time. The four-year Ford Foundation loan was for interim financing only. It was high-risk money at 12 percent interest. Because of the difficulty in securing a management contract and the negative cash-flow picture during the first few years of operations, it was difficult to interest permanent lenders at a favorable interest rate. After several other temporary loans, Charleston Associates was finally able to obtain longer-term financing from Aetna Business Credit, and the Washington Mutual Savings and Loan in Seattle, Washington.

There were many technical problems in executing the reconstruction, but all were surmountable because skilled designers and craftsmen were utilized.

Another, more controversial problem involves the philosophy of recreating images of the past rather than building in today's idiom. Many believe that it is deceptive to disguise a modern building in antique trappings. For this reason, the Mills Hyatt House has received some criticism from architects and architectural critics.

Benefits The success of this project as a popular and profitable hotel has helped to improve Charleston's economic base. The Mills Hyatt House is the largest private employer in the city's downtown area. It has received local and national press coverage and praise for the quality of its reproduction and for its compatibility within the local historic context.

The Company Charleston Associates was formed specifically for the purchase of the Mills House. No financial information is available.

For further information contact:
Richard H. Jenrette
Donaldson, Lufkin & Jenrette, Inc.
140 Broadway
New York, New York 10004

Footnotes

1. "Hope For A Hotel," *Preservation Progress,* January, 1968, p. 6.
2. INFORM interview with Richard H. Jenrette, partner, Charleston Associates, May, 1977.
3. *Ibid.*

The new lobby and public meeting rooms emulate the grand rooms in the old building. (Al Satterwhite)

Summary In 1973, Deseret Management Corporation, a profit-oriented branch of the Church of Jesus Christ of Latter Day Saints (Mormons), decided to renovate the Hotel Utah, which it owns, and to build a new 160-room addition. The 1911 building, an example of the "Grand Hotel" style of architecture, is rich in classical ornamentation both inside and out. In the renovated and new portions of the structure, the company chose to meticulously duplicate the terra cotta facade and decoration of the original. Deseret spent approximately $40,000 per room on the project.

Background The opulent Classical Revival Hotel Utah, designed by architects John Parkinson and Edwin Bergstrom of Los Angeles, was opened in the heart of Salt Lake City in 1911. The gleaming, white glazed-brick and terra cotta facade boasts many decorative embellishments, such as festoons, lions' heads, and medallions, all made of terra cotta by the firm of Gladding, McBean & Co. of Lincoln, California. Terra cotta was a popular building material in this country from about 1880 to 1930, before other materials and technologies replaced it. It was durable, and particularly resistant to fire and weather.

The ten-story hotel reflects the richness of the era in which it was built. In the lobby, grey marble columns with composite capitals support cornices filled with decorative plaster motifs. The latter are highlighted with gold leaf. Delicate iron railings adorn the balcony overlooking the elegant lobby. The lobby is crowned by a leaded, blue and green stained-glass interior skylight designed in geometric patterns. Guest rooms are spacious. In 1911, *Hotel Monthly*, a trade publication, heralded this new, luxurious hotel:

No other hotel anywhere in the world has a more interesting or beautiful setting, or more self-contained features for the pleasure and comfort of the guests, than the new Hotel Utah.[1]

The Hotel Utah is located across from the ten-acre Temple Square and the Gothic Revival Mormon Temple, with its renowned Tabernacle Choir and landscaped gardens. It is near the Utah State Capitol, Brigham Young's

residence, the Beehive House, the shopping mall of the recently expanded Zions Cooperative Mercantile Institution (see profile), and the new $20 million Salt Palace convention and sports center.

In recent years, however, in spite of the hotel's prime location, and the fact that it has been well maintained—it was modernized in 1967—occupancy levels declined because of competition from outlying motels and general lack of interest in the downtown area.

In 1973, a feasibility study was undertaken by the firm of Harris, Kerr, Forster & Co. and Robert A. Fowler Associated Architects of Salt Lake City to determine the future of the hotel. Since Deseret Management respected the architecture of the old building, it never seriously considered demolition or construction of a non-compatible modern addition. But based on the study, the company decided to renovate the hotel, both inside and out, and to add the 160-room extension that was to replicate exactly the exterior of the original building.

Execution Work began on the Hotel Utah in March, 1974; it was completed in mid-1977. The hotel remained open during the entire construction period. The architects, Robert A. Fowler and Edward Joe Ruben of Robert A. Fowler Associated Architects, planned the new wing and restored the facade using the original architectural plans and drawings. In addition, the original drawings and molds for the terra cotta were located at Gladding, McBean & Co. in Lincoln, California.

The interior of the original hotel was completely renovated. The richly ornamented lobby was cleaned and repainted. All new wiring, new plumbing, and a heat-pump heating/air-conditioning system were installed. The kitchen was modernized, and all of the hotel's bedrooms and 100 bathrooms were refurbished. Heinz Janders of San Francisco was the interior designer and decorator for both the renovation and the new addition.

In the 160-room addition, Janders attempted to coordinate the ambiance and style of the new public rooms with the old hotel. The new ballroom is designed in the Victorian style and has damask curtains, a red and gold pat-

The new addition and the old Hotel Utah.

terned carpet, and Belgian crystal chandeliers. New consoles (ornamental brackets), beneath the ceiling cornice which extends around the ballroom, were duplicated from existing consoles in the vintage hotel and reproduced in plaster. Wood panels around this room were hand grained as in the old hotel. The ballroom's 15,000 square feet can accommodate 1,200 people for banquets and 1,800 for receptions.

The new addition includes a 10,000-square-foot exhibit hall to attract the convention and corporate trade, and a new roof restaurant.

Terra Cotta. One of the most interesting aspects of the construction of the new addition and the restoration of the old facade involves the duplication and installation of the terra cotta. When the old facade was cleaned, using hot water and detergent, the terra cotta was found to have held up quite well. It was in much better condition than the wooden sashes, metal trim, roofing, and cast iron, which had to be replaced or reworked.

The architects solicited bids for both terra cotta and precast concrete substitutes to be used in building the new addition and in replacing lost details in the old facade. The production contract

was awarded to Gladding, McBean & Co., the firm that had done the original terra cotta work for the hotel. (The precast concrete bid was nearly $200,000 higher and was not guaranteed.) The installation contract went to Earl Child Masonry of Salt Lake City.

Even for a master mason, the installation of the terra cotta was a monumental undertaking. Child said that this job was "the biggest challenge I've ever had in the masonry business."[2] Installation techniques had changed since 1911; then, the terra cotta was put in place first, and backing brick was laid, tying it into the clay-tile interior wall; today with the development of concrete-block unit construction, the procedure is reversed. The terra cotta facing units were tied to the concrete-block wall with stainless steel wires and dowels. The cavity between the terra cotta and the concrete-block wall was then reinforced and filled in with a concrete grout consisting of three-eighths-inch rock, sand, and cement. This could only be accomplished four inches at a time. An earlier attempt at pumping in the grout indicated that the terra cotta units shifted too much. It was therefore necessary to pour the grout gently from coal buckets, and then pack it into the cavity by hand.

The actual installation was not the only problem; once the 12,000 terra cotta units were received from Gladding, McBean, Child had to organize them into 400 different configurations. Still another challenge was lifting and placing the terra cotta units on the new addition. The lions' heads weighed 425 pounds each, and the festoons 500 pounds each. According to Child:

There was not a craftsman on the job who wasn't challenged. For example, if the terra cotta was not in line, the craftsman had to stay with it until it was set. Thus, on every piece of terra cotta, the mason had to make his own decision when it was set well enough for him to let it go. However, just when the mason would become familiar with the setting process for one shape of terra cotta unit, it would be time to use a different type unit requiring different work procedures.[3]

In addition to increasing the capacity of the hotel, Deseret has made a concerted effort in the last three years to attract more tourist and convention business. The present marketing staff promotes the hotel through such devices as trade luncheons and advertising in trade-convention and airline publications. The annual budget for national advertising is $30,000.

The opulent lobby of the original hotel.

Costs Deseret would not release figures on the total cost of the renovation, addition, and refurbishing. However, the company estimated the cost of the project at about $40,000 per room. Judging from the quality of the work, as reflected in the replacement and duplication of the terra cotta and the hand-crafted decorations, it could be easily estimated that this was a multi-million-dollar undertaking.

The financing was generated internally by Deseret. The company is presently considering converting some of its short-term obligations into long-term debt.

Problems Stuart G. Cross, Executive Vice President and Managing Director of the Hotel Utah, said in an interview that the main problem experienced was the difficulty in carrying on an efficient hotel operation in the midst of construction. Occupancy was down, while staff were maintained, a combination which cut profits and increased costs. In addition, construction took a year longer than planned.

Benefits Occupancy levels are running at about 60 percent of new capacity. Before the restoration/addition, the old hotel—with fewer rooms—was running at roughly the same percentage. As a result of the new addition and the advertising campaigns, conventioneers now account for 35 percent of the guests, as opposed to 20 percent before renovation.

The restoration/re-creation work on Hotel Utah has been featured in many publications, such as *Hotel & Motel Management*. The new terra cotta techniques have brought additional publicity in *Masonry* and the *International Union of Brick Layers and Allied Craftsmen Journal*.

Because of the success of this and other complex and extensive projects, like Zions Cooperative Mercantile Institution, Salt Lake City is gaining a wide reputation for quality workmanship in restoration techniques. Its architects and craftsmen have assisted in projects across the country, including the Wilmington, Delaware, Grand Opera House (see Hercules).

The Company The Deseret Management Corporation, owner of the Hotel Utah, is a holding company of the Church of Jesus Christ of Latter Day Saints. This profit-oriented division of the Mormon Church includes among its operations bookstores, farms, and TV and radio stations. Deseret is privately owned; no financial figures are available.

For further information contact:
Stuart G. Cross
Executive Vice President and Managing Director
Hotel Utah
Main at South Temple
Salt Lake City, Utah 84111

Footnotes

1. *Hotel Monthly*, November, 1911, p. 36.
2. "The Enduring Elegance of Masonry," *Masonry*, March, 1977, p. 7.
3. *Ibid.*, p.26.

Summary   In mid-1974, Penn Mutual Life Insurance Company re-erected a four-story Egyptian Revival marble facade on its original site on Walnut Street in Philadelphia. The company incorporated this historic artifact, designed in 1835, as part of the facade of its new 21-story, $22 million, office-building addition facing Independence Hall. Penn Mutual spent several hundred thousand dollars to save and reuse the facade. In 1977, the company received an American Institute of Architects Honor Award for the new building.

Background   When the Pennsylvania Fire Insurance Company expanded in 1902, it duplicated the facade of its original building, forming a unified front. The original or eastern half, designed by John Haviland and erected in 1838, is a fine example of the Egyptian Revival style popular in this country during the 1830s. The western half, a replica of the Haviland design, was created in 1902 by architect Theophilus P. Chandler. Chandler united the two fronts with a crowning cornice featuring a hawk relief of the Egyptian god Horus, and the Pennsylvania Fire Insurance Company name carved in Vermont marble. John Haviland was an architect of some renown, having designed many of the nation's well-known prisons. Among his buildings are the Tombs in New York, state penitentiaries in New Jersey, Missouri, and Rhode Island, and the U.S. Mint in Philadelphia.

By 1970, Penn Mutual, which had owned the property for many years, was contemplating expansion of its adjacent facilities. The original Penn Mutual Building, a ten-story structure on the western corner of the block, had been erected in 1913. A nineteen-story addition had been built to the east in 1931. Penn Mutual and its architects, Mitchell/Giurgola Architects of Philadelphia and New York, proposed a scheme for a new 21-story, 440,000-square-foot addition that would abut the 1931 structure. The Haviland/Chandler Egyptian Revival building would have to be demolished to accommodate this plan. Local opposition to the demolition encouraged Penn Mutual to incorporate the old facade in the new design. Because of the historic context, the new design proposals had to be submitted to both the Philadelphia Historical Commission—which until 1970 had included Penn Mutual's Chairman—and the Philadelphia Art Commission for review and approval. The Historical Commission regretted the demolition of the old building, but commended the retention of the facade.

The old facade was one of the two remaining examples of Egyptian-influenced design in Philadelphia, a city once believed to have had the largest number of Egyptian Revival buildings in America. This stylistic treatment incorporates decorative Egyptian motifs like papyrus leaves, bundled reeds, and bird forms.

Execution   According to the architects: "The new building relates in mass to the existing office structure and completes a symmetrical backdrop for Independence Hall on axis with the Mall."[1] The eastern facade includes a poured-in-place concrete screen which shades the glass on that side. This screen also carries one-half of the load of the seventy-foot framing trusses which extend to the concrete service core on the west. These large span trusses create a totally column-free and flexible office space, and match floor levels with the existing 1931 structure. The south facade consists of double-pane, insulating, reflective glass, and the north facade is of similar grey-tinted glass. The north facade provides a neutral backdrop for Independence Hall and the Mall which face it. Glass-walled elevators on this face carry visitors up to a public observation deck and a 10,000-square-foot exhibit hall on the top level of the building. The Egyptian Revival facade was designed into the north facade as a free-standing sculptural screen marking the entrance to the building and creating a transition between the human scale of the street, and the high-rise tower to the rear.

Thomas Hine, writing in the *Philadelphia Inquirer*, describes the building: "It is a both-and building— both steel structure and concrete structure, both historic preservation and new development, both background and assertion." [2]

The project took three-and-a-half years to complete. In April, 1971, the Albert Cosenza Co., Philadelphia stone specialists, began dismantling the old facade. Some 400 blocks of Vermont marble, weighing as much as 1,000 pounds each, were numbered and stored for reconstruction. In August, 1974, the facade was returned to its original position in a new role, that of public art.

Costs   Although local newspapers have written that the preservation and reuse of the Egyptian Revival facade cost Penn Mutual $130,000, Geoffrey Irvine, Staff Engineer with the company indicates that the cost was considerably more.[3] The exact figure is difficult to itemize. Besides dismantling, storing, and re-erecting the facade, a new reinforced concrete backup wall and foundation had to be designed and built to support it. Engineering, architectural, and construction fees for the facade were included in the overall $22 million cost for the new addition. These expenditures fulfilled Philadelphia's required public art contribution. This statute stipulates that 1 percent of total construction costs, for any new construction or renovation project on redevelopment property, be spent to purchase public art for the city.

Problems   There were no specific problems directly related to reusing the facade, other than some of the technical difficulties encountered in the actual dismantling and re-erection. Although most public reaction to the project has been positive, some architectural critics feel that Penn Mutual has been given too much praise. They would rather have seen the old building kept intact than become a sculpture.[4]

Benefits According to Romaldo Giurgola, one of the principals in the architectural firm, "The Egyptian Revival facade allows Penn Mutual and the city to retain an original example of great architecture of the past as well as maintain a cultural heritage of another generation."[5] The Philadelphia Art Commission termed the preservation of the Haviland/Chandler facade "a great teaching example of combining modern building with historic and traditional landmarks."[6] The project received much praise in the press. Nessa Forman, writing in the Art column of the *Sunday Bulletin*, said: "Penn Mutual deserves kudos for its preservation approach. The facade, when all is said and done, is the only part of the building worth saving."[7] Paul Goldberger, of the *New York Times*, stated that the inclusion of the Egyptian Revival facade is:

a brilliant design decision—not in terms of preservation, for the old building was hardly preserved, but in terms of its meaning for urban architecture. For the thin elegant facade is a reminder that even real building fronts often serve a stage-set role. The relationship between this one and the glass and concrete tower is a comfortable one and, as an added bonus, the space behind the false front—that is, between the old facade and the new building—is full of dramatic tension and excitement.[8]

Original facade and new addition from ground level. (Rollin R. La France)

(below)
The original facade forms a free-standing sculpture screen. (Rollin R. La France)

(on facing page)
Penn Mutual tower with preserved facade at lower left. (Rollin R. La France)

In 1977, the American Institute of Architects selected the new Penn Mutual Tower as one of eleven recipients of its "Top Building Projects—Honor Awards" for new buildings. The Award's jury commented:

This office tower addition to an older area in Philadelphia sensitively retains the remnants of the original . . . facades integrating them with the new high rise structures behind them. Broken massing and window penetrations recall, at a different scale, the previous architectural endeavors. The complementary use of color and materials, in conjunction with the scale, provides a sensitive addition to the historic area.[9]

The Company Penn Mutual, Pennsylvania's largest insurance company, was founded in Philadelphia in 1847. It offers a variety of life insurance plans, pension programs, and other financial services for individuals, families, and business and professional groups. More than 1,900 people are employed in the Philadelphia office.

Penn Mutual is the seventeenth largest insurance company in the nation in terms of assets. Assets rose from $2.9 billion in 1975 to $3.07 billion in 1976. Net investment income increased from $168.5 million to $179.5 million over the same period.

Other Preservation Activities. Penn Mutual also preserved two original marble fireplaces from the Haviland/ Chandler building. One of these has been donated to the Philadelphia Museum of Art.

In 1818, architect John Haviland made what was our nation's first attempt at restoration by a master craftsman. He reproduced some paneling for use in Independence Hall's assembly room, copying the designs of the paneling in Congress Hall. In 1963, historians discovered the original designs for the Independence Hall paneling, and the Haviland additions were removed and stored in a National Park Service warehouse. They were to be discarded in 1973, when Penn Mutual offered to install them in the exhibit space on top of its new tower.

In addition, the company, together with other Philadelphia corporations, contributed $100,000—which brought federal matching funds—to refurbish the subway station at Fifth and Market Streets.

For further information contact:
William A. Burbaum
Media Relations Manager
The Penn Mutual Life Insurance
Company
Independence Square
Philadelphia, Pennsylvania 19172

Footnotes

1. INFORM interview with Mitchell/ Giurgola, Architects, May, 1977.
2. Thomas Hine, "Penn Mutual Building: View Changes the Face," *Philadelphia Inquirer*, 28 February 1975, p. 1-B.
3. INFORM interview with Geoffrey Irvine, Staff Engineer, Penn Mutual Life Insurance Company, May, 1977.
4. Hine, *op. cit.*
5. *Downtown Record*, 4 March 1971.
6. The Penn Mutual Life Insurance Company, "Penn Mutual Tower's Unique Egyptian Facade," (Background Information Sheet, The Penn Mutual Life Insurance Company, n.d.).
7. Nessa Forman, "On the Survival of a Facade," *Sunday Bulletin* (Philadelphia), 18 August 1974.
8. Paul Goldberger, "Innovative Firm Puts Its Imprint on Philadelphia," *New York Times*, 6 May 1976.
9. American Institute of Architects, *Press Release*, May 13, 1977.

Summary   Zions Cooperative Mercantile Institution (ZCMI), reputed to be America's first department store, was founded in 1868 in Salt Lake City, Utah. Brigham Young, the pioneer Mormon leader, conceived of the store as a community-owned establishment which could sell goods "as low as they can be sold, and let the profits be divided among the people at large."[1] In 1976, in conjunction with Zions Securities Corporation, this expanding operation completed construction of a 2 million-square-foot ZCMI Center, claimed by the company to be "the only downtown covered supermall in Western America and the largest of its kind in the nation."[2] The contemporary facade of this new multi-use complex incorporates the classically ornate cast-iron front of the former store, commemorating ZCMI's heritage, and pleasing local preservationists who fought for its retention.

Background   More than twenty years ago, ZCMI realized it needed to expand its downtown store. Initial plans called for expansion into the basement and first three floors of an adjacent, new office building erected to house the Utah office of the Kennecott Copper Corporation. However, difficulties arose in aligning the floors of the old buildings with the floors of the new one. In addition, fire protection, heating, and air conditioning presented obstacles. The plan was scrapped, and the company decided instead to acquire property and expand south of the store. This plan called for dismantling the present store and constructing a completely new facility. A feasibility study determined that a new downtown shopping mall might encompass most or all of the ten-acre block in which the store was located. The planning, study, acquisition, and execution took almost twenty years.

The new ZCMI Center utilizes approximately 75 percent of the ten-acre block. During construction, ZCMI continued operations in its old building, while the surrounding property was demolished and rebuilt to the new design. Original plans did not provide for the preservation of the old store's cast-iron front. However, as word of ZCMI's intentions spread, a movement started within the community to save it. Actually, this front was a combination of three separate facades. The center portion had been completed in May, 1876, the south section in April, 1880, and the north section in April, 1892. The center and south sections were cast-iron, while the north section was wood covered with molded sheet metal to approximate the design of the cast iron. The facade is a three-tiered composition of neoclassical design incorporating Corinthianesque columns supporting slightly arched lintels and

The restored facade incorporated in the new mall.

crowned with a triangular pediment. The cast-iron construction was based on a technique developed in the mid-1800s by New York architect James Bogardus to achieve the effect of carved stone.

Without ZCMI's knowledge or support, a local organization was formed to develop a preservation publicity program. Postage-meter-stamp ads and other printed materials stated "ZCMI's Main Street Facade Is Irreplaceable! Help Save It!" ZCMI architects, after some coaxing, decided to retain the old facade and incorporate it into the new design. At first, only the two cast-iron portions were to be used, but it was finally decided to save the entire front.

Execution   According to Steven T. Baird, a local architect hired by ZCMI to oversee the restoration project:

This is the first time a cast iron facade has been restored and we had to relearn an old craft. We simply went back to the original system used and put it to the test.[3]

Hand-carved wood patterns were made locally from the pieces removed from the two cast-iron sections, and new parts were cast for the north section. Each column consists of approximately 140 pieces. When the original front was disassembled, every piece was cleaned and marked for reassembly. The restored front was fastened to a special steel framework and inserted in an exterior wall of the new shopping mall. It is used as a display feature or free-standing sculptural grille. The new wall has been recessed approximately sixteen feet, leaving a space between it and the old facade. At night, lighting behind the old facade produces an interesting play of shadows. A ceiling surface has been constructed between the old front and the new wall. It is covered with pressed sheet metal similar to that used on many ceilings in the old store. The entire facade has been given a 23-carat gold-leaf finish emphasizing its jewel-like quality. Alfred A. Lippold, the painting contractor, has worked on many restorations in the Salt Lake area, including the Beehive House and the Hotel Utah (see Deseret Management). Mr. Lippold estimates that his gold-leaf work will last at least thirty years.

State Brass, the Rummel Pattern Company, and the Metals Manufacturing Company, all in the Salt Lake area, executed the ZCMI restoration.

Costs   The company states that it has spent in excess of $500,000 for the restoration and installation of the cast-iron front. Cost figures for construction of the new 2-million-square-foot complex were not available.

Problems   According to Wendell E. Adams, a Vice President of the company, "The major problems have been those of economics, engineering, architectural design and more than a small element of public relations finesse."[4] The gold-leaf finish, of course, contributed significantly to the high cost, as did the recreation of one section in cast iron. Additional architectural and engineering costs resulted from the extra design work involved in adapting the new facade to receive the old one, and in making the entire construction safe and stable.

Benefits   According to Wendell Adams,

The real benefits of this restoration are several. First it is a beautiful building with a combination of the very modern along with a delightful retention of our nostalgic heritage. It has delighted those who were vocal for saving the front and has pleased the rest of the community who had not given much priority to the problem of worrying about the past. All concerned, both within and outside the company, are delighted with this beautiful solution to a special problem.[5]

Although the company did not consider this when the decision was made to restore the facade, much new business has been brought to the "restoration industry" in Utah. Salt Lake City has now built a reputation for quality craftsmanship in metals restoration and replication. New processes involving the recasting of original designs in aluminum are being implemented. As a result, hundreds of thousands of dollars in new business are expected to come to Utah. Since the ZCMI project architect Steven Baird has developed a special skill in cast-iron restoration and has been called on to work on a number of other cast-iron restorations including the Wilmington Opera House (see Hercules) in Wilmington, Delaware.

The Company   Net sales for the company in 1976 were $82 million, an increase of 19 percent, over a comparable 1975 figure of $68.7 million. Net income for each year was about the same, $2.9 million. In addition to its new facilities in the ZCMI Center, the company has operations in five other locations in and around Salt Lake City.

For further information contact:
Wendell E. Adams
Vice President—Director
Personnel & Services
Zions Cooperative Mercantile
Institution
15 South Main Street
Salt Lake City, Utah 84137

Footnotes

1. Zions Cooperative Mercantile Institution, *ZCMI: Pioneering Still* (Advertising brochure, Salt Lake City: Zions Cooperative Mercantile Institution, 1976), p.2.
2. *Ibid.*
3. R. Scott Henderson, "Shopping the ZCMI Center," *Utah Holiday*, 18 October 1976, p. 47.
4. Letter from Mr. Wendell E. Adams, Vice President, Director, Personnel and Services, ZCMI, to INFORM, February 14, 1977, p. 3.
5. *Ibid.*

Community Revitalization

A persistent national problem since the late 1940s has been the slow deterioration of urban neighborhoods. Ironically, a series of decisions by government and business appear to have inadvertently stimulated the process. The Housing Act of 1949, which poured massive amounts of federal money into America's cities, often produced ill-conceived and ineffective urban-renewal efforts. In many cases, these resulted in the leveling of sound but deteriorating housing stock, and the destruction of poor, but sometimes still viable neighborhoods. The programs created monolithic apartment complexes like Pruitt-Igoe in St. Louis. Pruitt-Igoe suffered from such low occupancy and high crime rates that much of it has already been demolished. Federal programs also subsidized an extensive highway system which bisected cities or bypassed them entirely while speeding the flight of the middle class to the suburbs. Mass transit was neglected; inner-city crime increased; downtown commercial areas declined; and business sought more secure and less expensive locations outside the city. Redlining by banks and unrealistic insurance premiums often made staying in the city impossible even for those who wished to do so. Cities lost jobs and population, and became increasingly polarized between the very rich and the very poor.

In the 1960s, the equation began to change. Riots, which shook cities to their foundations, brought a reexamination of priorities. Urban pioneers, like Jane Jacobs, championed the scale and diversity of city neighborhoods and opposed massive urban renewal.

In the early 1970s, suburbanites began to discover that they shared some of the cities' problems. Suburban crime was increasing; real estate prices and taxes were rising. At the same time, the energy crisis made suburban life more expensive and less convenient.

Even so, the attraction of the suburbs remains strong. In recent years, businesses have participated in and often led the flight from the cities. Between 1969 and 1976, New York City lost 650,000 jobs.[1] It is projected that by the end of 1978, only 127 of the nation's 1,100 largest companies will be headquartered in New York City, as opposed to the 238 that were there in 1968.[2] Of the companies that remained in the cities in the early 1970s, many prepared to leave if the prognosis grew much worse. Some businesses, however, perhaps because, like the utilities, they had little choice about their location or because they felt their present location had valuable advantages, chose to face urban problems head on. A few tried—on a limited scale—to save existing housing, preserve sound neighborhoods, and restore downtown commercial areas.

Residential Revitalization   INFORM has examined thirteen companies which have attempted some form of housing and neighborhood redevelopment projects, twelve in deteriorating urban areas and a thirteenth in a relatively healthy suburb. Among them are five banks, three food manufacturers, one insurance company, a utility, and a consortium of businesses and foundations. These companies have supplied money and expertise, formed development banks, and joined local residents and activists to fight urban decay.

In twelve of the thirteen cases studied, INFORM found that the company's location was a key reason for undertaking the venture. Connecticut Mutual encouraged formation of a community organization to improve conditions in Asylum Hill, the Hartford neighborhood in which its headquarters are located. The company also provides short-term home-improvement loans at low interest rates to employees of local firms and of the City of Hartford who wish to move to Asylum Hill. In Minneapolis, General Mills' former home city, the company has joined a local developer to renovate the deteriorating Stevens Square area, and upgrade housing while keeping rents within reach of community residents.

In seven of the cases INFORM studied, business participants received favorable publicity as a result of their efforts. Brooklyn Union's financial support, advertising, and leverage with local banks have helped renovation projects throughout Brooklyn. The company has received an award for its advertising from the American Gas Association, and Frederic Rider, the company Vice President directing the "Cinderella" projects, has been interviewed by national publications.

Six projects have brought an economic return to their sponsors. The South Shore National Bank has successfully increased its assets as a result of helping its blighted Chicago service area return to economic health. The bank's management undertook a variety of programs, including special high-risk loans to local residents, the organization and support of renovation projects within the community, and the education of local residents about banking operations and services.

Five companies reported that their efforts, which concentrated mainly on improving the housing stock, have brought increased commercial interest to the project areas. Better city services and increased job opportunities have resulted in three cases. As a community organizes and improves, the backing of an important company can make city officials become more receptive to its requests. This occurred in both the Connecticut Mutual case and the Tasty Baking project. Real estate values increased in nine of the cases profiled.

Helping neighborhoods can be good for employee morale too. In two cases, companies reported that employees appreciated attempts to improve the areas in which they worked. In the Connecticut Mutual case, a direct benefit to company employees was inexpensive housing.

A final motivating factor may have been tax benefits obtained through contributions of money, materials, facilities, or employee time. Although the companies surveyed usually did not divulge tax benefits gained from their efforts, at least one company, Tasty Baking, reported that it took special tax deductions related to its neighborhood-rehabilitation efforts.

Urban revitalization is no simple matter; needless to say, the thirteen companies studied by INFORM experienced many problems in the course of their projects. Five were plagued by escalating costs. In the General Mills case, a dispute over the company's use of nonunion labor brought the threat of a national boycott of its products by the AFL-CIO. General Mills capitulated, but the cost to its Stevens Court project in Minneapolis destroyed any hopes of an economic return for the company, and increased rents 25 percent to 40 percent. Three projects suffered from bureaucratic delays. Ralston Purina's project, a three-phased program, was scheduled to be completed in five years. It is now in its second phase, nine years after inception. The primary problem has been the slowness of federal approvals and cash commitments.

In three cases, local organizations have overextended themselves, forcing both reorganization and cutbacks. ACTION-Housing, a community group supported by 21 major businesses in Pittsburgh, tried to fill a cash-flow gap left by government and other large lenders, and subsequently found itself with a number of debtors who could not repay their loans. The organization, in turn, could not repay the businesses who had provided the money for the loan program. Today, ACTION-Housing is in the process of trying to change its funding from loans to grants.

Dislocation of community residents was cited as a problem in only two cases. However, most of the revitalization programs studied by INFORM are in their early stages, and dislocation may become a greater problem in the future. In the Lakewood Bank case, a zoning change and the renovation and reconversion of older multiple-unit housing back to single-family homes forced relocation of former residents.

A wide variety of government programs affect neighborhood revitalization. Many have been tried as vehicles of support, some successfully, some not.* The federally sponsored Neighborhood Housing Services (NHS) program has been among the most successful. Conceived in Pittsburgh in 1968, the NHS is a partnership of local residents, government, banks, and businesses, which: helps residents of deteriorating areas comply with building- and health-code standards; provides counseling; obtains commitments from local banks to make loans to credit-worthy applicants; offers financial rehabilitation assistance through a high-risk loan fund; supplies technical help and supervises renovation work; educates residents about home maintenance; and obtains city cooperation in improving public facilities. The NHS-Jamaica, located in New York City's Borough of Queens and actively supported by Citibank, is helping stabilize and improve the Baisley Park section through just such a program. An NHS in Philadelphia is assisting Tasty Baking and the Allegheny West Community Development Project improve that part of the city.

The success of the NHS resulted in the establishment of the Urban Reinvestment Task Force in 1974 to promote the NHS idea nationally. The Task Force includes representatives of the Federal Home Loan Bank, the Department of Housing and Urban Development, the Federal Deposit Insurance Corporation, the Federal Reserve System, and the Comptroller of the Currency. It provides counseling to interested local groups who wish to establish an NHS, and commits dollars—usually between $50,000 and $100,000 depending on the size of the project and the area—for the creation of a high-risk revolving fund. Today, there are fifty NHS's, operational or in the planning stage, around the country. HUD funding for the Task Force amounted to $5 million in 1977.

The Housing and Community Development Act of 1974 (which replaced the urban-renewal grants, Model Cities, and other diverse federal programs) authorizes Community Development Block Grants to cities and towns for a wide variety of programs, including neighborhood revitalization. These Block Grants allow a greater autonomy to local government than the old urban-renewal grants, which were earmarked for specific projects.

The Home Mortgage Disclosure Act of 1975 requires all federally chartered and insured financial institutions to report their lending

*For further information on local programs consult: *Neighborhood Preservation*, published by the U.S. Department of Housing and Urban Development in 1975; *Neighborhood Conservation*, published by the National Endowment for the Arts in 1975; *Neighborhood Reinvestment*, published by the National Center for Urban Ethnic Affairs in 1977; and *A Guide to Federal Programs for Historic Preservation*, published by the National Trust for Historic Preservation in 1974, with a supplement in 1976.

practices by census tract, making it simpler to monitor redlining. These institutions must include information on the type of unit receiving loans, and on the kind of loan: first-mortgage, refinancing, or home-improvement. However, no information on the number of rejections, or the income, age, race, or sex of the borrowers is required.

The Carter administration has established a task force to study neighborhood revitalization and the creation of an urban-development bank, which would encourage both commercial and residential development in cities.

A HUD-proposed $1.2 billion "action grants" program, according to HUD Secretary Patricia Harris, "will stimulate new and increased private investment in cities of greatest need."[3] The program would furnish such cities with extra money over a three-year period for the purpose of attracting private investment to inner-city neighborhoods. At present, the proposal is tied up in interdepartmental jurisdictional disputes and a Senate-House conference committee.

The National Neighborhood Policy Act, also as yet unpassed, would create a National Commission on Neighborhoods, composed of at least one-third neighborhood representatives, to analyze government and business activities, as well as investment patterns in neighborhoods. It is scheduled for reintroduction before Congress in the near future.

Numerous regulations affect neighborhood revitalization on the state and local level. Lending-practice disclosure requirements, which augment the Federal Home Mortgage Disclosure Act by requiring information on the number of rejections, are in effect in several states, including Illinois and California. However, many rejections never reach a formal written stage, and some opponents of redlining believe that banks should be required to undertake an affirmative-action plan to solicit loans in inner-city areas as they do in the suburbs. This would make disclosure statistics more significant. New York City also provides a number of incentives for neighborhood revitalization, such as section J-51-2.5 of the Administrative Code of the City of New York, which provides tax incentives for recycling residential and commercial buildings for residential use. This directive provides up to a twelve-year exemption on increases in assessed valuation and an abatement of property taxes of up to 90 percent of the cost of rehabilitation for such renovations.

Commercial Redevelopment The causes of commercial decline are the same as those affecting residential neighborhoods. For various reasons, a number of businesses have decided to become involved in large-scale commercial-redevelopment projects in older downtown areas. INFORM has studied nine such projects, ranging in scope from Bethlehem Steel's financing of a $40,000 planning study on how to revitalize downtown Bethlehem, to the Higbee Company's projected $100 million project to rebuild a seven-acre section of Cleveland's river front. Eight of the nine projects involve the renovation and usually the reuse of older buildings in a way which capitalizes on their uniqueness and character (the ninth involves a historic village). Many of these projects rely on "nostalgia" or the contrast between restored exteriors and adapted interiors to attract customers or tenants. The vintage structures are solidly built, often with greater attention to detail than contemporary buildings. Their high quality is frequently a strong selling point.

The companies profiled represent diverse sectors of American business. They include banks, department stores, bus lines, heavy industry, and communications companies. All are medium to large corporations with the staying power to see through innovative and large-scale projects. None of them is primarily a developer, although five have formed special development subsidiaries. While most of the projects studied are ventures undertaken by individual companies, one is supported by a consortium of ten local financial institutions which have united to help redevelop downtown Lowell, Massachusetts, in cooperation with local, state, and federal programs. All efforts are directed toward turning downtown Lowell into a vital commercial area, preserving and capitalizing on its nineteenth-century industrial character.

Four cases involve redevelopment in large cities, two deal with small cities, and two more are being carried out in small towns. Four companies are trying to redevelop waterfront areas.

The goal of all but one of the projects studied is to revitalize downtown business areas which have suffered decline. The most prevalent reason for undertaking such projects was a concern on the part of the business for its home community. Seven of the projects are in the cities where the company itself is headquartered. Textron, a diversified manufacturing company located in Providence, for example, has undertaken a $46 million redevelopment in downtown Providence, including renovation of the Union Station and Biltmore Hotel.

Six projects were at least partly prompted by a desire for income or savings from leasing or using commercial or office space. In rehabilitating an old cigar factory in a Hispanic area of Tampa, Trend, a magazine publisher, created space for its own offices. It also provided space for a restaurant, specialty shops, and for vendors in a weekend Nostalgia Market.

Three projects, including Higbee's, stemmed from a particular personal interest in the community on the part of a member of management. Higbee's Chairman Herbert Strawbridge, as head of a major Cleveland department store, felt that his company had a substantial stake in the city's future and should try to reverse the pattern of decay in the downtown area. Higbee's Settlers' Landing project is the result.

Although all the companies received press coverage for their efforts, four specifically referred to the public relations benefits they have gained. Trend Publications received Florida's Annual Governor's Award in the Arts for its Tampa project.

Many factors influenced the success of the various projects, including location; the unique character of the architecture and its convertibility; the mix of new uses; the size of the project; its marketability; the availability and cost of financing; the ability to attract public dollars and support; and the depth and staying power of the developer.

The projects studied have met with varying degrees of success. Five have brought increased commercial interest in the redeveloped areas. In Corning, New York, for example, a 15 percent vacancy rate on Main Street has been eliminated due to the efforts of the Corning Glass-sponsored Market Street Restoration Program. The Program encourages store owners to renovate their facades in keeping with the town's nineteenth-century character and provides free designs to those wishing to participate. The Program also attempts to encourage tourists to visit the town and promotes preservation activities.

In five cases, commercial redevelopment has helped attract government funding, leading to joint public-private revitalization efforts. Commitments of $350,000 from ten Lowell-area financial institutions, and plans for a $2 million private bond issue to fund commercial renovation, helped attract $26 million in combined local, state, and federal commitments to revitalize that city's downtown area.

Although many of these nine projects are still in progress, four have already resulted in a return on investment for the companies involved. Inland Steel's project in Washington, D.C., has adapted an old foundry and constructed a new building in keeping with the nineteenth-century surroundings. Inland's buildings now house a restaurant and shopping arcade in what was formerly a neglected industrial property.

The most common problem INFORM found in these projects was a lower return on investment than anticipated. This seemed to be at least partly the result of the relative newness of the concept of commercial redevelopment. Many large and small businesses, as well as lenders, have adopted a "wait and see" attitude, leading to low occupancy rates, high turnover, and inadequate capital. Progress in leasing in both the Higbee and Trend projects has been slower than anticipated. Trend's cigar-factory renovation has been hindered by its inability to attract larger numbers of shoppers to an inner-city location isolated from Tampa's other shopping areas. Four firms have had to alter plans and extend schedules to accommodate cash-flow difficulties. The Jefferson Company's difficulties in finding tenants and long-term financing caused a three-year interval between the announcement of its project and the actual start of construction.

Inconvenient locations have hampered success in two cases, and structural and technical problems have created difficulties for two others.

Footnotes

1. INFORM interview with Frank Corbin, Deputy Director, Economic Development Administration, New York City, August, 1977.
2. Michael Sterne, "Corporate Moves: New York Region Holds Its Own," *New York Times*, 21 August 1977, sec. 11 (Long Island Weekly), p. 1.
3. "An Erosion of Aid to the Cities," *Business Week,* August 15, 1977, p. 36.

ACTION–Housing, Inc.

Residential Revitalization

Summary The Allegheny Council to Improve Our Neighborhoods, or ACTION-Housing, Inc., was established in the late 1950s. Its aim was to revitalize Pittsburgh's housing and neighborhoods and to help achieve this goal, ACTION-Housing established a revolving loan fund, called the Pittsburgh Development Fund (PDF). The Fund provided intermediate equity capital, and/or seed money, for the construction of privately or federally financed housing for moderate-income families. The PDF was terminated in 1976, but its successor, known as the ACTION-Housing Development Fund, is supported by grants from major corporations and foundations in Pittsburgh. It will become active in 1978. During the fourteen years of its existence, the PDF had accumulated more than $1.2 million from 24 companies, and had made loans of $4.1 million. The initial funds were turned over four times, assisting creation of more than 3,000 units of new and rehabilitated housing. Rehabilitation, as a tool for neighborhood renewal, accounted for 13 percent of the PDF's work.

Background In 1957, the Allegheny Conference on Community Development, a leading Pittsburgh nonprofit business and civic group, sponsored a study to determine Pittsburgh's and Allegheny County's housing needs. Based on the study's recommendations, ACTION-Housing, Inc., was formed. It was designed to provide encouragement, consultation, and economic support to those wishing to initiate private development of new and rehabilitated moderate-income housing. Its area of operation included some of Pittsburgh's most deteriorated neighborhoods.

Execution ACTION-Housing quickly discovered that many qualified but underfinanced private developers could not obtain the funds to initiate much-needed housing development. Private developers needed money at reasonable rates early in the development process. However, short-term loans were expensive, if they could be obtained at all. To deal with this problem, ACTION-Housing created the Pittsburgh Development Fund (PDF), a revolving loan fund designed to provide short-term loans at market rates. As the loans were repaid—usually after construction financing was secured—the money would once again become available to other borrowers.

The PDF's goals were set forth as follows:

1. Involving the business community as an active partner in improving Pittsburgh's housing stock.

2. Providing initial short-term financing to builders and others, either for the construction of new housing, or for the modernization of older houses and neighborhoods, thus speeding regeneration.

3. Providing large-scale demonstrations of new housing materials, design, technology, and production.

4. Acquiring land available only upon total cash purchase for resale in whole or in part to developers, thereby also acting as a "land bank."

Action-Housing reviewed these concepts with three Mellon Foundations which subsequently made grants of $350,000 to establish the Fund. The grants, however, were made conditional on the PDF's receipt of additional major financial support from local business and industrial interests. If no such support was forthcoming, the entire proposal was to be abandoned. The group approached the Westinghouse Electric Corporation, Jones and Laughlin Steel Corporation, and the United States Steel Corporation, the three largest private employers in Pittsburgh. It was estimated that one out of every six houses in Allegheny County was occupied by an employee of one of these three firms.

The three giant corporations, together with many other Pittsburgh businesses, supported the PDF through grants and loans. The Fund initially sought $2 million, but it was activated after $1.4 million was raised. Grants initially accounted for about 12 percent of the total, while the balance was made up of loans, a concept encouraged by ACTION-Housing because of its businesslike approach and its value as a model to other cities. The loan subscriptions ranged from $10,000 to $250,000, and returned 4 percent interest to the subscribers if the money was used by a private developer. For the developers, the loans resembled a line of credit at a bank. They were made at the prevailing interest rate, and the difference between this rate and the 4 percent due the subscribers was used to meet the PDF's administrative costs. To encourage reuse of financial resources, loans to developers were not to exceed five years.

The PDF specifically implemented its objectives by:

1. Lending up to:
   a. 90 percent of the cost of the raw land;
   b. 70 percent of the cost of land improvements, streets, and utilities; and
   c. 70 percent of equity capital on completed developments for a short term (five years).

2. Requiring repayment of loans at the going rate of interest on a completed-unit basis.

3. Supplying a land-bank program for builders, holding land until needed for timely construction.

4. Providing preliminary site planning and architectural study.

5. Acquiring large tracts of land for cash to assure lowest cost and economic large-scale development.

6. Avoiding excess interest, bonuses, or service charges for land and land improvements, permitting a reasonable relationship of land to total dwelling cost.

7. Reviewing the builder's architectural planning. Sales and rental prices are similarly subject to prior agreement and review to assure reflection of cost savings to the consumer.

8. Providing the builder with public-oriented aid and support in zoning, planning, financing, and general community problems.

9. Providing aid and guidance in formulating advertising and sales programs.

10. Serving as a conduit between government and builder; business and builder; and consumer and builder.[1]

The rehabilitation of Cora Street, a typical example of a neighborhood-improvement project executed with the PDF's assistance, was described in a case-study ACTION-Housing publication:

Cora Street . . . lies in the very heart of the poorest area of Brushton, classified as a poverty neighborhood by the Mayor's Committee on Human Resources of the Federal Office of Economic Opportunity. However, Cora Street happens to be outside that portion of Homewood-Brushton designated an official urban renewal district. . . .

The Cora Street houses acquired for rehabilitation were 22 single-family, two-story row houses more than 60 years old, ten located on one side of the street, twelve directly opposite on the other side. . . . The row dwellings are small and compact and the relative isolation and nondescript character of the street together with its location in one of the poorest areas of the city make it a difficult candidate for any kind of improvement. One realtor in the area said of it: "It is a sore spot, a cancerous spot; you name it and it takes place in that area."

This difficulty was one of the motivations for ACTION-Housing. . . . Slums are never pleasant or congenial places, and facing them realistically in the form of Cora Street made for a more widely applicable demonstration program. . . . As Mr. Loshbough [Executive Director of ACTION-Housing] has observed: "If rehabilitation can be carried out successfully here, it can be done anywhere."

The 22 Cora Street brick row houses purchased by ACTION-Housing each contained a living room, two bedrooms, a kitchen, bathroom and basement. Their condition varied considerably.

In order to bring such a project into being, considerable funds are needed.

Not only must fiscal soundness and integrity be demonstrated to FHA when applying for mortgage insurance, but ACTION-Housing had to risk hand money (amounting to $6,000), fees for preliminary work by the architect, a real estate commission, legal fees, and ultimately one third (in excess of $70,000) of the purchase and construction costs in a participation construction loan with the lender. Except for the construction loan participation, this is called in the trade "front money," and without ACTION-Housing's Development Fund to provide it, the program could not have proceeded.

ACTION-Housing obtained 100% financing of the final mortgage under the Demonstration Program of Section 233 of the Housing Act of 1961, as amended in 1965 pursuant to Section 221 (d) (3). As a result, all of the "front money" the organization expended in the project development could be returned to its Development Fund. In addition, the Fund served, together with Mellon Bank, to provide all the interim financing required until completion of construction when federal funds (FNMA) provided the permanent mortgage at 3% interest rate. The Cora Street rehabilitation was carried out without other subsidy except for a foundation grant for landscaping.[2]

Unfortunately, the corporate loan program had to be discontinued in 1976 due to difficulties in making interest payments on time (see "Problems," below). The ACTION-Housing Development Fund, which is replacing the terminated PDF, will operate only on grants.

Costs The total value of the ACTION-Housing Development Fund today is $133,164, of which 22 percent has been contributed by businesses. Administration costs approximately $15,000 per year depending on the Fund's activity. The administrative staff consists of three to five paid employees and seven volunteer Finance Committee Members.

The Pittsburgh Development Fund provided loans for the rehabilitation of 22 brick row houses on Cora Street. (John L. Alexandrowicz)

Problems In 1976, the original Pittsburgh Development Fund was terminated, and a new fund was established. The business loan-subscription program had not been successful. The reasons stem from the difficulties in promptly paying off interest to the corporations. Most of the housing projects were subsidized through inadequately financed government programs. The PDF tried to offset cash-flow problems by making operating loans to the projects. However, by trying to keep the projects afloat when the government did not, it utilized income that should have been used for interest payments to note holders. When it became apparent that the funding structure was not going to improve, the PDF's cash assets were liquidated, and a new fund, called the ACTION-Housing Development Fund, was established. This Fund is supported entirely from grants. The process of lending money to private developers has not changed, and the requirements and goals are the same. Interest collected on the loans will be completely returned to the Fund. Corporations, previously offering loans, have been encouraged to convert their contributions into outright grants. Staff is currently reviewing proposals for use of the new Fund, and anticipates that it will become active during 1978.

Benefits Corporate participation in the revolving loan program has helped create more than 3,000 units of new and rehabilitated housing in Pittsburgh.

Companies Participating Companies Participating in the Pittsburgh Development Fund were:

Note Holders

Allegheny Ludlum Steel Corp.
The Alcoa Foundation
Columbia Gas of Pennsylvania
Consolidated Coal Company
Duquesne Light Company
Koppers Foundation
The Levinson Steel Company
Mine Safety Appliances Company, Charitable Trust
The Peoples Natural Gas Co.
Pittsburgh Coke and Chemical Co.

Rockwell Manufacturing Co.
United States Steel Corp.
Western Pennsylvania National Bank
Westinghouse Air Brake Company
Westinghouse Electric Corp.
Edwin L. Wiegand Company

Grantors

Commonwealth Trust Company
Crane Company
Equitable Gas Company
Jones & Laughlin Steel Corporation
Mellon National Bank and Trust Company
Pittsburgh National Bank
The Pittsburgh Plate Glass Foundation
Retail Merchants Association
The Union National Bank of Pittsburgh
West Penn Power Company

Companies Making Grants to the ACTION-Housing Development Fund are:

The Alcoa Foundation	$ 57,374
Columbia Gas of Pennsylvania	5,737
Consolidated Coal Company	5,737
The Hillman Foundation	8,606
Koppers Foundation	28,688
Mine Safety Appliance Co., Charitable Trust	9,254
The Peoples Natural Gas Company	14,344
Edwin L. Wiegand Company	3,424
Total Grants	$133,164

For further information contact:
Sally Mizerak
Director
Education & Community Affairs
ACTION-Housing, Inc.
Number Two Gateway Center
Pittsburgh, Pennsylvania 15222

Footnotes

1. ACTION-Housing, Inc., "The Pittsburgh Development Fund of ACTION-Housing, Inc.," (mimeographed, ACTION-Housing, Inc., n.d.), pp. 5-7.
2. Arthur P. Ziegler, Jr., *Cora Street: A Pioneering Demonstration in Rehabilitating Aging but Structurally Sound Housing*, (Pittsburgh: ACTION-Housing, Inc., 1969), pp. 9-10.

Cora Street after renovation. (Mark Perrott)

Summary In January, 1975, based on a company task-force recommendation, the Bank of America, the major subsidiary of BankAmerica Corporation, created the City Improvement and Restoration Program (CIRP) to seek out financing opportunities to assist community-revitalization efforts in the State of California. The CIRP's five-man staff advises municipalities on funding sources, including city bonds, tax revenues, Community Development Block Grant funds, and federal revenue-sharing monies, as well as on the availability of the bank's own loans. The CIRP's monies also support home-improvement loans at below the market interest.

In order to further improve California cities, the CIRP announced the formation in 1977 of a second subsidiary to revitalize housing stock. This new subsidiary, Bank of America City Improvement and Restoration Program Corporation (BACIRP), will purchase and rehabilitate abandoned properties and offer them for sale. East Oakland was chosen as its first target area.

Background In 1973, the Bank of America became concerned about the impact of massive suburbanization on urban neighborhoods and business districts located in its home state of California. It was particularly interested in the metropolitan areas of San Francisco and Los Angeles, which house about two-thirds of the state's population. Many districts had seen declining personal income, business, and residential values, and were experiencing financial disinvestment.

In 1974, BankAmerica's President A. W. Clausen appointed a task force to collect data and to formulate a role for the bank in urban revitalization. Communities in the state were analyzed to determine their revitalization needs and to define appropriate banking services which could assist them. Four areas required immediate attention: "rehabilitation of existing housing stock, mortgage financing of older homes, construction of low-cost and senior citizen housing, and open space acquisition."[1]

Execution In 1975, the City Improvement and Restoration Program (CIRP) was created to actualize the bank's commitment to urban revitalization. The supervisory committee, composed of senior management, was headed by K. S. Smeby, Senior Vice President, Administration. The committee evaluates proposed projects, provides expertise in structuring them, and monitors their progress. The CIRP adopted a package of plans, each to be tested before wide implementation.

Under CIRP's auspices the following programs have been established:

Victorian Period Homes—Purchase and Restoration, San Francisco. In February, 1975, the Bank of America became involved in the restoration of ten Victorian homes in San Francisco's Western Addition. The unoccupied homes were previously owned by the San Francisco Redevelopment Agency. These were to be removed from the site of a redevelopment project. The Agency paid the relocation costs. It is coordinating rehabilitation plans, specifications, and code-requirement approval with the city and with the bank's Appraisal Department. The Bank of America allocated $500,000 for mortgages and restoration. A total of $350,000 has been loaned thus far, under flexible terms, to seven homeowners renovating these houses.

Community Development Program. This CIRP-backed Program assists municipalities in obtaining and administering government monies for housing rehabilitation. Under this Program, the bank makes loans to homeowners in areas designated by the cooperating city or county. Federal Community Development Block Grant funds deposited by the participating government provide collateral enabling the bank to lend money at interest rates below the prevailing market rate. Loans amounted to over $1 million in 1976. The housing-stock rehabilitated has ranged from 25 to 100 years old. The CIRP administers the loans in cooperation with 3 counties and 22 cities.

The Community Development Program calls for a clear separation of duties between the bank and the city.

The bank performs its customary credit evaluation of the applicant; then the city evaluates an applicant with community preservation and development objectives in mind. If the city decides the loan should be made in spite of the applicant's lack of qualifications for normal credit consideration, it directs the bank to do so. All loans are secured by a non-interest-bearing deposit account in which the city places a share of its Community Development funds.

Since the deposit account is non-interest-bearing, the bank is relieved of all but 3 percent of the amount it ordinarily pays for using Federal-Reserve-administered funds in support of public agency projects. Thus, the effective rate to the borrower can be as low as 3.75 percent when supported by a 100 percent deposit from the city.

Residential Assistance Program, San Francisco. In San Francisco, the BankAmerica Investment Securities Division, the CIRP, the county, and the city are cooperating to develop a city-financed housing-rehabilitation program which would offer loans at below current interest rates.

In November, 1976, the City and County of San Francisco sold bonds to capitalize the Residential Assistance Program, a rehabilitation loan fund. The Bank of America has made a

Victorian house restored with Bank of America's help. (Sirlin Studios)

commitment to bid for up to $20 million in rehabilitation-assistance bonds over a five-year period, and has already purchased $2.5 million of these bonds, the entire initial offering. As security for the bonds, the city pledged the accumulated proceeds from rehabilitation-loan payments, the deeds of trust it receives when making rehabilitation loans, and a bad-debt reserve established from the sale of the bonds.

A temporary roadblock in implementing the Residential Assistance Program was removed when the state appellate court ruled favorably on the constitutionality of public loans from a municipality to individuals. An Internal Revenue Service ruling on taxation of the interest income earned by financial institutions on bonds issued by a municipality is pending.

Although the Program is not yet operational due to city administrative delays, Residential Assistance loans will be made to all qualified property owners in certain target areas. They will cover minimum building code-enforcement work, minor building violations, or obsolescence of plumbing, wiring and other mechanical systems. The Program will provide up to $17,500 per unit, with a maximum indebtedness of 90 percent of after-rehabilitation value. The loans will be repaid over a period of twenty years, or three-fourths of the economic life of a building, whichever is less. The interest rate to borrowers depends on the interest rate on city bonds on the date of purchase. If the Internal Revenue Service decides that a bank's income from the purchase of city bonds is tax free, interest charges to the city can be reduced, and loans to property owners can be made at below market rates. The average life of a Residential Assistance loan is expected to be eight to ten years.

Applicants unqualified under conventional lending standards are eligible for hardship loans of up to $3,500 per building. These interest-free loans will cover code-enforcement repairs, and will carry a lien against the property, with no repayments due until sale or transfer to a new owner, or after twenty years.

BankAmerica City Improvement and Restoration Program. After receiving approval from the Federal Reserve Board in January, 1977, the BankAmerica City Improvement and Restoration Program (BACIRP) began to purchase vacant single-family homes in a declining area in the eastern part of Oakland, California. Upon completion of rehabilitation work by local contractors, the properties will be sold through local real estate brokers. The moderately priced homes will be sold to low- and middle-income, credit-worthy applicants.

A. W. Clausen, President of BankAmerica Corporation, explained that the new subsidiary will operate "essentially at a break-even level." He added, "No profits will accrue to BankAmerica Corp."[2] Any profits that are made will be used for expansion of the Program. The BACIRP is capitalized with $150,000 for operating expenses and $150,000 for a revolving line of credit. Based on the level of success here and on Federal Reserve approval, the bank will consider expanding this Program to other California cities. Since the BACIRP is in its infancy, details on its activities and results are not yet available. The bank states that because of the efforts of speculators and problems dealing with foreclosed HUD properties, real estate prices in Oakland had escalated before the bank got clearance for the BACIRP. The bank is delaying implementation of the proposed Program since many houses in the targeted area are being independently renovated.

Before the CIRP was established, the bank had undertaken the following revitalization projects:

Rehabilitation, Chico. The Bank of America, through its Chico, California, branch, committed $102,000 in 1973 to the Chico Housing Improvement Program (CHIP) for rehabilitation of senior-citizen and low-income dwellings. The bank loans were earmarked for the purchase of building materials for homeowners to make limited renovations of their residences. The CHIP also received $22,000 from federal revenue-sharing funds to cover its operating costs and to create a high-risk loan pool.

The CHIP is sponsored by the bank, the city, and California State University, Chico. Its seven-member Board of Directors is composed of local citizens, including a loan officer of the Chico branch of the Bank of America. Thus far, 32 homes have been rehabilitated using loans made at market interest rates and loans from the city's high-risk loan pool.

To stretch the available funds, the CHIP organized a system of free labor. Chico State University students, the University's Industrial Technology Department, and Vista Volunteers have provided free assistance to low-income and disabled homeowners, but homeowners themselves have been expected to participate as fully as possible.

The CHIP distributes information about home improvements, and advises homeowners of the sources of financial assistance. The improvements made under its auspices are limited to structural corrections, such as wiring, roofing, foundations, and plumbing.

Neighborhood Rehabilitation, Berkeley. In 1974, Bank of America Vice President Leo Sullivan helped the City of Berkeley, California, plan and develop a pilot program to assist individual homeowners in the rehabilitation of some fifty-year-old housing stock.

Berkeley established a Municipal Loan Pool with $550,000 in city funds. The Pool is administered by a loan committee, which is assisted by the Manager of the bank's Berkeley branch. The committee reviews home-improvement-loan applications from homeowners who are normally unqualified for conventional mortgages. The loans cover code-enforcement repairs, the elimination of substandard conditions, and room additions.

The city provides the cost estimate, counsels the homeowner in applying for an improvement loan, and supplies community services to the residents of the target area. To date, loans amounting to $350,000 have been made. The average loan has been about $8,000. There have been no defaults.

Costs Operating budgets for the CIRP are funded annually through the bank's Urban Affairs Department. The Program's current staff includes the department head, two officers, a research assistant, and a secretary. The CIRP relies very heavily on existing bank personnel and resources to meet its objectives. Its loan totals are carried under appropriate existing loan categories. Since they are not segregated from other bank resources, a breakdown of Program costs is not available.

Problems Two programs supported by the Bank of America have not yet been implemented as of mid-1977. The Residential Assistance Program is not yet underway, in part because of City of San Francisco administrative delays. The BACIRP has had difficulties obtaining foreclosed HUD properties. Real estate prices in Oakland have also risen faster than the bank anticipated.

Benefits The Bank of America is deeply involved in California's economy, and its prosperity depends on the health of the state. It feels that its economic self-interest is directly served by preserving the soundness of neighborhoods. The bank also maintains goodwill by helping communities with neighborhood revitalization.

The Company The Bank of America, the major subsidiary of BankAmerica Corporation, is the largest commercial bank in the world and the largest savings institution in the country. Branch offices in California number over 1,060. Net interest income of the holding company was $1.61 billion in 1976, up 7.5 percent from $1.50 billion in the previous fiscal year. Net income rose 11.2 percent from $302.8 million in 1975 to $336.8 million in 1976.

Other Preservation Activities/Trust for Public Land. The Trust for Public Land (TPL), a San Francisco-based nonprofit organization, works to preserve open-space areas for public use. Its primary effort involves locating and purchasing land parcels around the United States that are suitable for recreation or conservation. TPL holds them until they can be purchased by an already interested government agency or until the TPL can find an appropriate purchaser and work out resale and land conservation terms.

Since 1973, the Bank of America has annually committed a $10 million credit line to this organization. The TPL's other contributed support comes from foundations and individuals. The "TPL's method of acquisition offers tax benefits to the seller and substantial cash savings to the acquiring city or other agency."[3] In the past four years, the TPL has arranged and accomplished transfer of 33 properties in seven states totaling over 10,000 acres, and saved public agencies approximately $4 million.[4]

The TPL also sponsors the National Urban Land Program, whose purpose is to create land trust/conservancies in urban centers. Unused city lots are obtained and turned over to residents to be cultivated for vegetable gardens or planted with grass and trees for use as public parks. Some parcels are placed in a land bank for future use.

A Bank of America specialist in land appraisal and acquisition began assisting the TPL with this Program in January, 1976. Other corporations, private individuals, and lending institutions have made donations to it of land parcels with an estimated total value of $110,000.

Beaudry Street House, Los Angeles. In 1975, the Bank of America financed the relocation of Beaudry Street House in Los Angeles. The house was moved from the site of a bank data-processing center to Heritage Square, a public park for landmark homes dating from the period 1860 to 1910. The Bank of America Foundation also donated $30,000 to construct a permanent foundation for the house.

For further information contact:
James S. Young
City Improvement Coordinator
Kyhl S. Smeby
Senior Vice-President, Administration
City Improvement and Restoration Program
Bank of America
Bank of America World Headquarters
Suite 2135
555 California Street
San Francisco, California 94104

Footnotes

1. Bank of America, *The Community and the Bank: A Report on 1975 Social Policy Activities* (San Francisco: Bank of America, 1975), p. 9.
2. "Bank America Plans Unit to Buy, Restore Urban-Area Housing," *Wall Street Journal*, 10 November 1976.
3. Bank of America, "City Improvement and Restoration Program, Information Packet," (mimeographed, Bank of America, February, 1977), p. 8.
4. *Ibid.*

Summary   In 1966, the Brooklyn Union Gas Company joined the "Back to Brooklyn" movement, an effort by Brooklyn businesses and residents to arrest the urban decay beginning to encompass downtown Brooklyn. Realizing its stake in the stability of its market, Brooklyn Union initiated the Cinderella Program to encourage renovation rather than demolition of sound housing. The company purchased and renovated a dilapidated and abandoned brownstone at 211 Berkeley Place in Park Slope. This restoration, named Cinderella I, was to demonstrate that brownstone renovation was economically feasible, and was made the focal point of an extensive advertising campaign to involve middle-income families in brownstone renovation in downtown Brooklyn.

The success of Cinderella I has led to other renovations. Brooklyn Union selects projects in marginal areas, which are carried out by a local contractor or community group, and are financed by a local bank. These sites are then given the Cinderella designation, and Brooklyn Union supplies the renovated site with improvements, such as gas lights and patio furniture, and publicity. To date, the company has spent $400,000 on the program, which now includes fifteen projects around the borough.

Cinderella project: before.

Background   Brooklyn was New York City's first suburb. In the nineteenth and early twentieth century, many wealthy Manhattanites, in search of a more residential atmosphere, moved to Brooklyn Heights, Cobble Hill, Boerum Hill, Park Slope, and other affluent brownstone communities. Most of the brownstones in Brooklyn are well built and beautifully designed. Many are Victorian in style, with three or four floors, large rooms, sliding wooden doors, stained glass, decorative plaster moldings, high ceilings, and parquet floors.

During the 1940s, the racial composition of downtown Brooklyn began to change. Middle-income families were emigrating to the borough's newly developed outlying areas and to Queens and Long Island. Absentee landlords neglected their buildings, and many were abandoned; businesses closed, and banks refused new mortgages. The downtown communities rapidly deteriorated. Neighborhoods which had been home to the wealthy one hundred years before had badly decayed by the mid-1960s.

These changes worried Brooklyn Union, whose headquarters has been located in Brooklyn Heights since its founding in 1895. Brooklyn Union, unlike many corporations, could not move to a more affluent area. Its

investments—gas pipelines—lie beneath the surface of every Brooklyn street. Frederic H. J. Rider, Assistant Vice President for Public Relations at Brooklyn Union, and coordinator of the Cinderella Program, summarized the situation:

Our future growth hinges on the future of our service area. It's that simple. We realized years ago that the everyday problems of our business are a part of a much larger social problem. The only way to help our own situation was to try to pump some life and money back into Brooklyn neighborhoods before the entire borough becomes a ghetto.[1]

Brooklyn Union was determined to try to encourage a return of middle-income people who had moved to the suburbs during the previous decades. With more money in circulation, old businesses would remain, and new ones would move into the area, bolstering the downtown economy. It hoped that the renovation project at 211 Berkeley Place would be a catalyst for economic renewal.

Execution   In 1966, Brooklyn Union purchased an abandoned mid-nineteenth-century brownstone at 211 Berkeley Place with the intention of filming its transformation from an eyesore into an elegant residence. The work on Cinderella I, as the project was called, began in 1966 under architect Edwin B. Taylor, with the Dover Construction Company acting as general contractors. The renovation took one year to complete. A local interior decorator, Evelyn Ortner, herself a brownstone enthusiast, designed the interiors and selected the furnishings.

The brownstone was converted into two duplex apartments. This necessitated some redesign of its 4,000-square-foot interior. A basement kitchen was reused as a laundry room, and a bathroom in the master bedroom was removed to create more space. The renovation utilized the best talents and materials available. All woodwork and plasterwork were restored. The house was furnished with a combination of contemporary and Victorian furniture in an attempt to maintain, within practical limits, the house's original flavor. Brooklyn Union purchased the abandoned brownstone for $15,000 and renovated it for $50,000, for a total cost of $65,000, or $16.25 per square foot. After the renovation, the house was opened to the public for one year, and 4,000 people visited it. It was later sold for $63,000.

In 1972, Brooklyn Union became involved in a project that was to become Cinderella II. During that year, Everett Ortner, founder of the Park Slope Betterment Committee, and President of Back to the City, Inc., asked Brooklyn Union's help in renovating several abandoned brownstones on a Prospect Place block which Frederic Rider has called "the worst block in Brooklyn."[2] In addition to the abandoned and neglected brownstones, there were three abandoned storefronts on the other side of the street. Brooklyn Union felt these stores would make ideal renovation projects, since they had been abandoned for over twenty years and had become a haven for drug addicts and other unwanted elements in the neighborhood.

The company purchased the three stores for $10,000, and sold them to Asen Brothers and Lester Brooks, builders and contractors, who renovated them as residences at a cost of between $35,000 and $38,000 per store. Brooklyn Union repaved the backyards, supplied gravel for the patios, and provided gas lights and gas barbecue grills. The company also purchased interior furnishings for these "colonial townhouses" from Abraham & Strauss, Brooklyn's largest downtown department store. Financing for the renovation was obtained from the Greater New York Savings Bank, which paid for one-half of the promotional campaign for Cinderella II. Asen Brothers sold the first two townhouses for $45,000 and $48,000. The last house was re-purchased by Brooklyn Union and opened to visitors for one year; it was later resold for $65,000. Brooklyn Union has shown a continuing interest in this block, donating gas lights and advising people who wish to renovate properties on it.

In 1975, the Bedford Stuyvesant Restoration Corporation renovated five adjoining apartment buildings in the Bedford Stuyvesant section of Brooklyn. The organization asked Brooklyn Union's assistance in cleaning up the vacant and trash-filled lot between the

buildings, which had been gutted by fire. Brooklyn Union spent $25,000 in cleaning out the lot and renovating it as a brick-paved, gas-lit central courtyard. The five-building restoration was designated Cinderella III.

Later in 1975, a two-story brownstone at 93 Prospect Place became Cinderella IV. The partially renovated building had been abandoned after several mishaps, and after an adjoining store was torn down, leaving a vacant lot between it and an abandoned supermarket. Brooklyn Union financed the renovation, with Mara Management Corporation acting as general contractors. The supermarket became a branch of Brooklyn Union and the brownstone became the company's Brownstone Information Center. The vacant lot became a gas-lit, brick-paved courtyard, complete with fountain. The Center provides information on local bank mortgages, local electricians, contractors, and all aspects of home renovation to Brooklyn residents and those who wish to move there. Recently, the Center began compiling and distributing a community calendar and newsletter.

Cinderella V is being undertaken by John Melvin Associates in 1977, and is perhaps the most strategically important project thus far in the Program. It is located on St. Felix Street, near the

Brooklyn Academy of Music which draws thousands of people to downtown Brooklyn each year. Ten abandoned houses on St. Felix Street are slated for renovation by the end of the year; six have already been completed under the Cinderella name. Financing for the construction was obtained from the Williamsburg Savings Bank, whose banking headquarters are around the corner. Brooklyn Union is supplying decorative shrubbery, trees, and gas lights for the **street**.

While Cinderellas VI through XV have not yet been completed, Brooklyn Union has sought to become involved in every Brooklyn community. Several of these projects are located in some of the borough's most deteriorated areas, and most are being carried out by neighborhood-improvement organizations. In East New York, for example, 27 homes are being renovated by the city's Small Home Improvements Program; in Sunset Park, a local developer is converting a factory into 10 apartment units. The most recent project, the old Cathedral Club on Flatbush Avenue, is being renovated by a Haitian Society. In 1978, the company plans to begin several projects in Woodside, Queens, part of its service area.

Brooklyn Union's main contribution to these renovations has been its exten-

Cinderella project: after. The old stores were converted into town-houses.

126

sive advertising of each project. To date, full-page ads have been run in 170 major newspapers across the country. This advertising, of course, creates good publicity for the company; but it also often helps the individual project gain credibility, particularly with local lenders. In addition to its advertisements, Brooklyn Union sponsors films outlining the renovation process, and promoting brownstones in Brooklyn. The films are distributed free to interested community groups. Titles have included: *My, My Brooklyn, Cinderella of Prospect Place, Brownstone Brooklyn, To Brooklyn with Love from Geraldine Fitzgerald*. The company plans an upcoming film that will deal with the first four Cinderella projects, and hopes to sponsor one film each year in the future. Brooklyn Union also sponsors the annual Brownstone Fair and Promenade Art Show held every October. In 1976, 25,000 people turned out for the event. In addition, the company holds Brownstone seminars at its main office, explaining the history of the Program and the advantages of brownstone living.

Costs   In addition to advertising expenditures, Brooklyn Union Gas spent $400,000 on Cinderellas I through IV. The costs included: the purchase price of the house on Berkeley Place, $15,000, and the cost of renovation, $50,000; the purchase price of the three stores on Prospect Place, $10,000; and the creation of the courtyard in Cinderella III, $25,000. Information on other specific costs was not available. Brooklyn Union plans to allocate $70,000 a year to the Cinderella Program, as well as a substantial amount for advertising. For accounting purposes, the company's expenditures have thus far been considered part of operating expenses, and amount to approximately 1/2 cent per meter per month.

Problems   The greatest problem facing Brooklyn Union, or anyone interested in renovating in the downtown area, is financing. Banks often judge a house solely on the area in which it is located, not the soundness of the structure itself, or the purchaser's ability to pay. This "redlining" has made it very difficult to finance houses in some neighborhoods. However, due to the efforts of Brooklyn Union Gas and Frederic Rider, several local banks have provided mortgage money.

Benefits   According to a Brooklyn Union official, the company's sales have increased because of the new customers attracted to Brooklyn,[3] and the company has gained a good deal of favorable publicity. One of the company's Cinderella ads won an award from the American Gas Association for the best advertisement by a utility in 1976. Company Assistant Vice President for Public Relations Frederic Rider was recently interviewed for an article scheduled to appear in 22 major newspapers across the country. The success of the Program has also solidified the company's commitment to Brooklyn (it had contemplated a move to Queens).

Brooklyn Union feels its Program has been much more successful in changing the attitudes and climate of downtown Brooklyn than could have been anticipated:

We simply wanted to demonstrate . . . what could be done with a hammer, some paint and imagination. We had no idea that we were starting a boom, let alone a renaissance. To our great delight we discovered that improvement in a community is far more contagious than deterioration.[4]

Property values have risen since the Program began. Two years after the completion of Cinderella I, twenty new families had moved into Berkeley Place, and in the past decade, the values of some of the houses have risen from $15,000 to $90,000.

Since the inception of the Cinderella Program, the communities in the downtown area have begun to take a serious interest in renovation, and Brooklyn Union is being approached by many organizations who wish to have their project given the Cinderella des-

ignation. One example of Cinderella's impact is a dry-cleaning store located around the corner from Cinderella IV. The owners had just about given up trying to survive the surrounding decay, but Brooklyn Union's efforts prompted them to stay and modernize. The store has been renamed the Cinderella Cleaners.

The Cinderella Program has helped inspire house tours of the various neighborhoods, and has helped attract new business and craftsmen to the area. It has also aided the growth of the Victorian Society and the Back to the City movement, which are now nationwide organizations.

The Company   Brooklyn Union Gas has been located on Court and Montague Streets in Brooklyn Heights since its founding in 1895. The company today distributes natural gas to an estimated 4 million people in the boroughs of Brooklyn, Queens, and Staten Island. Revenues rose from $267 million in 1975 to $312 million in 1976. Net income increased from $17.8 million to $18.6 million over the same period. Revenues break down as follows: 59 percent residences with gas heating, 22 percent other residences, 16 percent commercial and industrial, and 2 percent temperature-control heating.

For further information contact:
Frederic Rider
Assistant Vice President for Public Relations

Alan Smith
Manager of Public Relations and Advertising

Alfred Jennings
Community Relations Supervisor
The Brooklyn Union Gas Company
195 Montague Street
Brooklyn, New York 11201

Footnotes

1. "Brooklyn Union's Cinderella Luring People Back to the City," *Gas Line*, 1976, vol. 2, no. 2, p. 14.
2. INFORM interview with F. H. J. Rider, Assistant Vice President for Public Relations, The Brooklyn Union Gas Company, June, 1977.
3. *Ibid.*
4. *Gas Line, op. cit.*, p. 14.

Summary Chemical Bank, one of New York City's major financial institutions, has played a vital role in the rehabilitation of a badly deteriorated tenement on Manhattan's Lower East Side. Residents of East 11th Street, assisted by local housing activists, acquired an abandoned, city-owned building at address 519, and set out to rehabilitate it themselves; a concept known as "sweat equity." The project also included the installation of a solar collection system to heat domestic hot water and a two-kilowatt windmill to partially meet power needs. The bank, through its Urban Affairs Department, provided loans for seed money to cover architectural, legal, and developmental costs, as well as bridge loans to relieve cash-flow problems which occurred during the reconstruction process. The East 11th Street rehabilitation was part of a diverse program of inner-city projects supported by Chemical Bank.

Background Policy for all the bank's social-action programs is determined by the Urban Affairs Advisory Committee, which is composed of senior management from its major departments. After a study of inner-city needs and possible strategies, the Committee, under Chairman Norborne Berkeley, Jr., Chemical's President, established the Urban Affairs Department in 1971. According to the bank:

The reality underlying this thinking is that Chemical's success as a business depends on the health of the markets it serves. If New York and other urban centers crumble under the impact of problems like slum housing, crime, drug abuse, poor education and unemployment, the bank's business and the quality of its employees will also erode.[1]

Chemical's Urban Housing Unit, a division of the Urban Affairs Department, administers a $100 million allocation of credit for use in low- and moderate-income housing and community development projects. Juan Villaneuva, a former administrator in the New York City Housing and Development Administration, was hired in May, 1975, to head the Unit, and he has been liaison to the East 11th Street Housing Movement.

Number 519 East 11th Street was built in the first decade of the twentieth century. The five-story brick building is functional in design, with the exception of brick window decoration, two intricate cornices at the roofline, and sculpted masks and cherubs.

Throughout the first half of the century, it served as a tenement for Italian, Ukrainian, Polish, and Jewish immigrants. In the 1960s, poor blacks and Puerto Ricans moved in. "I couldn't believe the conditions," said Robert Nazario, who helped organize the tenants several years ago. "Junkies were using the roof as a shooting gallery."[2] The residents were prey to constant criminal activity, and the children had no place to play other than streets heaped with rotting garbage and debris.

By spring, 1972, thirteen fires had ravaged 519 East 11th Street, finally driving the tenants out. When the building was abandoned by its owner, the city took possession because of property tax arrears.

Abandonment is the end of the line for most tenement buildings, and in 1972, it looked as if 519 would be counted among them.* Demolition for safety reasons seemed certain.

*According to the Urban Homesteading Assistance Board, approximately 150,000 units in 10,000 buildings were abandoned in New York City by 1976, and an average of two or three buildings are added to this number each day.[3]

Execution In August, 1973, a group of low-income neighborhood residents, supported by professional housing activists from Interfaith Adopt-a-Building, a church-supported, non-profit organization, asked the city if it could supply them with a suitable building for renovation and occupation. Many of the residents had no high school education, little command of English, and little work experience. The city's Department of Real Estate, which had jurisdiction over a large stock of abandoned buildings acquired from landlords delinquent in paying property taxes, sold number 519 to the group for $1,800.

The group—by this point constituted as the East 11th Street Housing Movement—negotiated a $177,494 loan with the New York City Housing and Development Administration (HDA) through the "sweat equity" portion of the now-defunct Municipal Loan Program. The terms of the loan called for a thirty-year renovation mortgage at 7 1/2 percent interest.

Instead of a substantial downpayment to purchase already renovated apartment units, future residents were required to contribute their "sweat," doing most of the rehabilitation work themselves.

Interior of 519 East 11th Street in the process of rehabilitation. (East 11th Street Housing Movement)

In winter, 1974, Interfaith Adopt-a-Building received a $20,000 "seed money" loan from Chemical Bank's Urban Affairs Department to cover the architectural, legal, and developmental (cost estimating, construction supervision, loan packaging) costs of its projects, including 519 East 11th Street.

The Office of Cooperative Conversion of the city's Housing and Development Administration has a range of programs which use the sweat-equity concept. At 519, the Sweat Equity Training Program was employed. The fifty members of the Movement were paid $3 per hour, using federal Comprehensive Employment and Training Act (CETA) Funds, to carry out all aspects of the rehabilitation except electrical wiring. Partial supervision and some tools were provided by union and nonunion tradesmen. The tradesmen were paid a total of $2,000. Each member of the Movement worked a forty-hour week, of which eight hours were unpaid as sweat equity on the project. The Office of Cooperative Conversion estimates that 6,758 sweat-equity hours over a period of one-and-a-half years were invested in the building. This amounts to a savings of $20,274.

Renovation work began in spring, 1974. The interior of the building was cleared of debris and gutted of all interior fixtures. Entirely new interior walls, floors, plumbing, and wiring were installed; and windows, doors, ceilings, and 300 beams were replaced.

Cash-flow difficulties arose soon after the loan closing in October, 1974. Renovations were funded after the need was verified by city inspectors, but Municipal Loan Program allocations were too slow to satisfy creditors who supplied the homesteaders with materials. These delays endangered the project's credit standing. The HDA, which administered the Municipal Loan Program, routinely took between six and eight weeks to process checks. Michael Freedberg, director of the East 11th Street project, could see that he needed some kind of short-term financing to cover the costs between allocations, so he again turned to Chemical's Urban Affairs Department for help. The bank provided a "bridge" loan of $5,000, with ninety-day repayment terms, using the group's vouchers, backed by the city, as security. On five

subsequent occasions, bridge loans were made, each of about $5,000.

More recently, the problem has been cost overruns, a result of inflation, financing delays, and unforeseen reconstruction problems. The Hayden Foundation supplied a grant of $15,000 to cover the overruns.

The rehabilitation of 519 East 11th Street was completed in March, 1977, and the building was inspected by the New York City Office of Housing Rehabilitation, a department of the Housing and Development Administration. All eleven apartments and two storefronts have been renovated. The eleven families moved in while the work was still in progress, and pay $42 per room, per month. This income covers the mortgage, operational costs, and maintenance.

Currently, Michael Freedberg is supervising three more sweat-equity rehabilitation projects in adjacent buildings on East 11th Street. Chemical Bank is providing seed money for two of them.

Energy. Under the supervision of architect Travis Price, a member of the Movement, three types of energy-conservation measures were employed in the rehabilitated building. These included: extra insulation, a solar collector, and a windmill. Refitting the entire building with the highest grade of insulation plus the installation of storm windows cost about $11,000. The solar collector was financed by a $43,000 grant from the federal Community Services Administration. Installed on the roof, it heats and circulates hot water through pipes to a heat exchanger and storage tank in the basement. The system consists of thirty glass-covered solar collecting units, which have the capacity to supply 80 percent of the building's hot-water needs. A two-kilowatt windmill, designed and installed under a $13,622 grant from the Community Services Administration, is also located on the roof. It generates enough electricity to operate twenty 100-watt lightbulbs when it is operating at full capacity.

The solar hot water system and effective use of insulation have cut the BTU requirements of the building by 70 percent (20 percent through the use of the solar hot water system and 50 percent through effective insulation). The annual energy bill for a building

this size would be about $8,000 to $9,000. The savings achieved by this lower energy use is about $5,600.

Costs Doug Ades, Vice President of Chemical's Urban Affairs Department, estimated the cost of new apartment construction to be between $35,000 and $45,000 per unit.[4] Commercial costs for a gut rehabilitation similar to the one at 519 East 11th Street are over $25,000 per unit. With sweat equity, rehabilitation of the East 11th Street project cost $13,657 per unit.

Problems Initial difficulties at 519 East 11th Street stemmed largely from the project's innovative nature. Residents had no experience in construction and little overall work experience. This caused organizational problems. There was a high turnover in workers as well. About half the original members of the cooperative dropped out in the early stages.

The city's administrative practices are slow and cumbersome. Individuals or groups applying for the right to homestead on city properties have frequently run into a wall of bureaucratic red tape, and have become discouraged from following through. The level of discouragement rose here appreciably during periods when city-committed assistance was delayed and work could not proceed.

Benefits The initiative and persistence of the East 11th Street Movement, the assistance of Chemical Bank, and other public and private agencies have helped turn around a block in the process of complete deterioration. The 519 project, though delayed by the inexperience of its work force and municipal red tape, has created a viable residential property.

Efficient insulation and innovative energy systems have reduced operating costs substantially for the building's residents and brought extensive publicity. The building was the focus of a series of tours by business leaders conducted by several environmental groups.

The 519 project also illustrates the benefits of sweat equity. Lower rehabilitation costs make sweat equity an affordable method of housing the poor without long-term subsidy. No other program can do this. "Adequate subsidies," the Urban Homesteading Assistance Board points out, "simply do not exist to align these extremely high costs of new construction and commercial rehabilitation with the income of the poor."[5] Robert Schur, Executive Director of the Association of Neighborhood Housing Developers and former Deputy Commissioner of the New York City Housing and Development Administration, adds, "Anything below luxury housing is not do-able, economically."[6]

Community residents gained job skills while working on the rehabilitation, which increased their employment potential. The expertise gained on the project is currently being used to help three other buildings on the block follow the same sweat equity process.

The financial community and the neighborhood also benefit from the sweat-equity program. Chemical Bank has demonstrated that supporting housing cooperatives in a poor, minority community, as it did on East 11th Street, is a practical step which strengthens the urban environment in which the bank operates. Over the years, the revitalized community should be a regular customer for the bank's financial services. Goodwill has been generated in the community; a very visible process of community stabilization has begun, and from the bank's point of view, a pool of potential depositors has been created there.

After a period of ten years, during which property taxes are abated, the once-abandoned buildings are returned to the city tax rolls. Furthermore, the $6,000 cost of demolition is avoided. People who at one time were consumers of city social services become taxpaying citizens through job training and placement.

Exterior view of 519 East 11th Street after renovation. (Richard Griffin)

The Company   Chemical Bank, the major subsidiary of Chemical New York Corporation, is the sixth largest bank in the United States. It has about 220 branches in the New York area. In 1976, revenues for the holding company amounted to $577 million with a net income of $92.6 million. Comparable figures for 1975 were $645.4 million and $95.9 million.

Other Preservation Activities/Branch 139, Bedford Stuyvesant. In 1967, Chemical opened a branch in the newly renovated Sheffield House, headquarters of the Bedford-Stuyvesant Restoration Corporation. The area was in very bad condition, but had a 28 percent rate of owner-occupancy—much higher than similar areas in either Harlem or the South Bronx—and many of its houses were solidly built brownstones. The work of the Bedford-Stuyvesant Restoration Corporation has reassured the bank that its commitment is secure. Restoration, as it is called, has developed housing, encouraged industry to settle in the area, and has established both for-profit and nonprofit businesses.

Street Banking. Chemical set up the first street-banking unit in Harlem in 1969 to deliver financial services to individuals and organizations who have not routinely used them: in many cases, people who are just beginning to raise themselves and their communities out of poverty and require project funding on an interim basis. Today, the program has been expanded to several other inner-city areas, including the East Village and the Lower East Side. The street bankers make daily visits to residents, businesses, government organizations, schools, day-care centers, and health facilities to familiarize the community with various banking services, such as checking-and savings accounts, loan programs, and payroll management.

The Urban Homesteading Assistance Board. The Urban Homesteading Assistance Board is the city-wide organization established by the Cathedral of St. John the Divine in 1975 to help urban homesteaders successfully manage the process of rehabilitating abandoned buildings. The Board has tried to fill the gap left by city agencies which were forced to cut back their efforts due to budget restraints.

Chemical Bank, Bankers Trust, Morgan Guaranty, Chase Manhattan, and Manufacturers Hanover Trust made grants to the organization totaling $56,900. Most of this funding went to individual buildings or to programs with which the Board is involved.

Interfaith Adopt-a-Building. Adopt-a-Building is the Lower East Side church-supported community organization which established the East 11th Street Housing Movement. Adopt-a-Building has served as an intermediary between tenant groups and the legal system, the financial community, and real estate interests.

Chemical has been closely involved with Adopt-a-Building since 1969. The bank has provided the following grants for the East 11th Street project: in 1972, $2,500 for general support; in 1974, $5,000 to establish professional bookkeeping procedures; in 1975, $2,500 for administration, $5,000 for general support, and a $15,000 loan; and in 1976, $1,000 for general support. Chemical's staff has also contributed its financial and technical expertise.

For further information contact:
Barbara Fiorito
Vice President for Urban Affairs
Chemical Bank
20 Pine Street
New York, New York 10005

Michael Freedberg
East 11th Street Housing Movement
519 East 11th Street
New York, New York 10003

Footnotes

1. Chemical Bank Corporation, *Banking on New York*, (New York: Chemical Bank Corporation, 1976), p. 3.
2. Jim Kaplan, "When Tenants Take Over," *New York Sunday News Magazine*, 19 March 1976, p. 40.
3. Urban Homesteading Assistance Board, *Urban Homesteading Assistance Board Annual Report*, (New York: Urban Homesteading Assistance Board, 1976).
4. INFORM interview with Douglas Ades, Vice President, Urban Affairs Department, Chemical Bank, May, 1977.
5. Urban Homesteading Board, *op. cit.*, p. 2.
6. INFORM interview with Robert Schur, Executive Director, Association of Neighborhood Housing Developers, May, 1977.

Summary In 1972, in an effort to diversify its holdings and increase cash flow, Chicago Bridge and Iron (CBI), a leading fabricator of heavy-gauge-steel industrial storage facilities, purchased Fairlington, a 340-acre apartment development in Arlington, Va. That same year, CBI formed a real estate subsidiary, CBI-Fairmac, to manage these developments and recycle the Fairlington complex as 3,439 condominium townhouse and apartment units.

Although the Fairlington conversion experienced early losses as costs exceeded initial selling prices, it has subsequently proven to be extremely profitable. Built in 1942, the complex is just fifteen minutes from Washington, D.C., one of the strongest residential markets in the country. The units were constructed of top-quality materials and have been well maintained, providing a solid base for the renovation work. Because CBI purchased the existing buildings and land at an initial cost of $15,000 per unit,[1] it is able to invest up to $21,000 per unit in renovation work and still maintain a 14 percent pre-tax profit margin.[2]

Fairlington villages are a series of small clusters, many of which surround small parks. (Eduardo E. Latour)

Background Fairlington was built in the early 1940s for Pentagon executives who came to Washington after the U.S. entry into World War II. President Roosevelt commissioned the 3,439-unit project and allowed Houston architect Kenneth Franzheim his pick of skilled workers and scarce building materials. A generous budget, allowing an average cost of $10,300 per unit, permitted the installation of slate roofing, heavy hardwood doors, plaster walls, and brick and stone exteriors.

Franzheim also employed advanced planning techniques. Instead of a grid design, units were clustered in a variety of patterns, predominantly around private courtyards. Although there is a basic regularity to the overall design, the architect varied rooflines and entranceways, alternating long rows of houses with short ones and juxtaposing groups of units against each other. With only ten units per acre, there was ample room for large lawns and scattered trees. Built in a neo-Georgian style, with small porches and colonial-style windows and shutters, the units were clustered in a series of seven villages.

After the War, the government sold the complex to two Texas businessmen, who operated it as rental units from 1947 to 1959. In 1959, the Texans dissolved their partnership by flipping a coin. One retained the ownership of

Fairlington, worth an estimated $15 million and the other took the $4 million the project had in the bank. Leland Fikes, the winner, became sole owner of the complex and named one of his executives, Walter J. Hodges, General Manager. Fikes died in 1966, and two years later, his estate sold Fairlington to Hartford Fire Insurance. Hodges and another executive, J. D. Lee, became minority stockholders. In 1972, Hartford Fire, now part of ITT, sold the project to Chicago Bridge and Iron.

CBI's purchase was based on an appraisal of Fairlington as a rental project. In its cost analysis, the company allocated $15,000 per unit for building and land: a $51.6 million initial investment. A subsidiary, CBI-Fairmac, was formed with Hodges as President and Lee as Executive Vice President and Treasurer.

Under Hodges' management, Fairlington had been well maintained, and a sense of community spirit had been created. However, after thirty years, bathrooms and kitchens needed modern fixtures and appliances; exteriors needed a face-lift; and there was substantial underutilized space in the basements of all the units. Hodges believed that to obtain the greatest financial return from the modernization, the units should be renovated in phases and sold as condominiums.

Execution Since 1972, the Fairlington condominium conversion has been developed in phases by villages. Each village contains over 300 townhouse and apartment units. Existing tenants in a section under renovation are given ninety-day notices to vacate, and if they desire, can move to other rental units in the project.

In the conversion, each unit is renovated as follows:

- All mechanical systems are replaced, including wiring and plumbing, and individual gas-fired heating and cooling units are installed. (Originally, the buildings were heated with steam from large boiler units located in each village. Technical obsolescence of these systems made it impossible to reuse them.)

- Kitchens and baths are totally refurbished with new appliances, fixtures, tile, vanities, and cabinets.

- Slate roofs are insulated, and double-glazed windows are installed to reduce energy consumption.

- Tunnels which originally connected all units are sealed off, and the basements are finished to create recreation rooms, dens, baths, and laundries. This adds an average of 500 square feet of living space to each unit.

- Exterior masonry is cleaned and re-pointed; flashing and downspouts are replaced; all exterior trim is re-painted; and new door and window hardware is installed.

- Exterior amenities are created through landscaping and the addition of fenced patios and decks.

All electrical lines are being placed underground, and colonial-style fixtures are being substituted for light poles. Parking areas are being expanded, sidewalks and streets are being repaired and resurfaced, and storm-drainage systems are being enlarged to handle the increased runoff. Extensive recreational facilities are also being provided. Each village has its own Olympic-sized swimming pool (and children's wading pool), bath-house, paddle-tennis courts, tennis courts, basketball courts, and children's play area.

After conversion, most villages contain a selection of ten models ranging from 712 square feet to 2,145 square feet. The smallest models are on one floor and have one bedroom, while larger houses have three bedrooms, three baths, and a den. The most popular model, which accounts for 60 percent of the total complex, is a 1,500-square-foot triplex with two bedrooms, two baths, and a den. The smallest units in the project are priced as low as $38,500, while the most expensive reach $70,000. Financing plans have been arranged which allow down payments as low as 5 percent of the purchase price.

A low-key sales strategy has been adopted. Salespeople are paid straight salaries, and prospective buyers are encouraged to tour the grounds and models unescorted. In Village I, existing tenants bought 73 percent of the townhouses, while in Village II, the figure was down to 62 percent. As the purchase prices have risen, less than 50 percent of the former tenants have been able to purchase the renovated units. The average Fairlington homeowner has an annual income of $32,000.[3]

The development has a good reputation, and 45 percent of its sales come from referrals. Community activities, such as art shows and house tours, also provide useful marketing tools. Fairlington has an annual advertising and promotion budget of $475,000, with 55 percent allotted to newspapers, 40 percent to television, and 5 percent to radio.[4]

By mid-1977, 2,750 units had been completed and sold. At a production rate of 25 units per week, the remaining 700 units were expected to be complete by the end of 1977, and the total project sold out by early 1978.

Costs To cover the costs of the renovation, the project's $17 million five-year loan was refinanced to $24 million at a half percentage point over prime. As the condominiums are sold, the company pays 115 percent of the money it has borrowed on each unit, gradually reducing the principle on the entire loan. Other funds for the renovation program are provided from cash generated by condominium sales.

In 1976, the company spent about $21,000 to renovate each unit and the surrounding grounds. The budget for an average unit breaks down as follows:[5]

Construction costs		$17,000
Permits	$ 400	
Plumbing	3,200	
Electrical	1,600	
Heating/air conditioning	1,100	
Ventilation	1,100	
Insulation/weatherproofing	150	
Masonry	350	
Cleaning	250	
Finishing costs:		
Lower bath/laundry	1,200	
Upper bath	860	
Kitchen	2,200	
Bedrooms/hallway	900	
Living and dining room	1,090	
Basement	1,900	
Patio/fencing	700	
Site improvements, including landscaping and recreational facilities		2,000
Construction field overhead		2,000
Total Renovation Costs/ average unit.		$21,000
Other costs per unit average:		
Land and existing unit	$15,000	
Warranty work and customer service	400	
Sales and marketing	3,000	
Financing and closing cost	3,200	
Administrative overhead	1,200	
Subtotal/other costs		$22,800
TOTAL Cost/Average Unit		$43,800

According to Hodges, since 1972, the average purchase price has risen from $36,000 to $51,000 per unit, allowing CBI-Fairmac a $7,200 pre-tax profit or a 14 percent pre-tax margin on each sale.[6]

Problems Cost controls have been developed through bitter experience. Since contractors were uncertain about the extent of renovation the units required most submitted high bids to protect themselves. Hodges first tried to control renovation costs by forming his own construction operation. However, his crews were inexperienced, and a few trained men had to teach and supervise a work force that eventually grew to 700. The in-house construction firm produced less than one house per day. In the first two years, renovation costs averaged $20,000 per unit. Total unit costs reached $41,000, and the cost of borrowing money shot up. The average price of the first 400 sales was only $36,000 resulting in a $5,000 loss per unit and a $2 million reduction in working capital in 1973.[7]

In order to increase efficiency and lower unit costs, Hodges radically altered his operation in 1974. The Fairlington Construction Company was disbanded, and the most skilled and industrious workers were asked to form their own independent subcontracting firms to work on a piecework basis. With the best workers receiving the highest wages and overtime, production jumped from less than one house a day to three and then to over four. Improved cost control and better accounting systems also helped reduce renovation costs by 25 percent.

In addition to construction problems, Hodges faced problems with Arlington County officials. In 1972, Virginia's condominium law and much of the county building code were not applicable to renovation work. Extensive meetings with county officials were required to establish guidelines for the construction work and the sales program.

Other problems were encountered in coordinating the construction activities with tenant relocation. Those rental units which were not ready to be renovated were hard to keep occupied. In some cases, tenants failed to receive adequate information about construction schedules. They tended to move out in anticipation of the renovation work, reducing the project's annual income.

Benefits After overcoming the initial construction management and pricing problems, Fairlington has become a major financial success for CBI. Due to the constant turnover of government personnel, the Washington, D.C., area has represented an exceptionally strong housing market during the 1970s. The price of houses has increased steadily along with the market demand. CBI-Fairmac will continue its management contract to maintain the condominium project for the new owners, and will receive brokerage commissions for the resale of condominiums.

The project has won many awards, including the first in a new category created in 1974 by the local chapter of the National Association of Home Builders: Revitalization of Community and Excellence in Restoration.

The Fairlington conversion has created construction jobs for the Arlington community, and has resulted in 3,439 units of modern housing at prices nearly 25 percent less than competitive new construction in the area. The Fairlington units retail at approximately $34 per square foot, compared with an estimated $45 per square foot cost for similar new housing.[8]

The Company Chicago Bridge and Iron Company (CBI) is a leading fabricator of heavy-gauge steel-plate structures. It was founded in 1889, and is headquartered in Oak Brook, Illinois. CBI owns a 92 percent interest in CBI-Fairmac, with the remaining 8 percent held by the subsidiary's two top officers, Walter Hodges and J. D. Lee.

Net income for the parent company increased 36 percent in 1976 to nearly $56 million, or $5.73 per share on total sales of $577 million. Corresponding figures for 1975 were $41 million and $564 million. CBI-Fairmac contributed about 50 cents per share, or $4.86 million, to CBI's net earnings in 1976, approximately 9 percent of the parent company's net income.

For further information contact:
Walter J. Hodges
President
CBI-Fairmac Corporation
3118 South Abington Street
Arlington, Virginia 22206

Footnotes

1. Michael Robinson, "Is This the Hottest Condo Conversion in the Country?," *House & Home*, August, 1975, p. 51.
2. Robinson, *op. cit.*, p. 51, updated by INFORM interview with W. J. Hodges, President, CBI-Fairmac Corporation, May, 1977.
3. INFORM interview with W. J. Hodges, President, CBI-Fairmac Corporation, May, 1977.
4. Robinson, *op. cit.*, p. 53.
5. Robinson, *op. cit.*, updated by INFORM interview with W. J. Hodges, President, CBI-Fairmac Corporation, May, 1977.
6. INFORM interview with W. J. Hodges, President, CBI-Fairmac Corporation, May, 1977.
7. Robinson, *op. cit.*, p. 51.
8. John Sower, "Financing and Developing Large Commercial Preservation Projects," *Economic Benefits of Preserving Old Buildings* (Washington, D.C.: Preservation Press, National Trust for Historic Preservation, 1976), p. 137.

Citibank

Summary In response to the turmoil of the late 1960s, New York's Citibank assigned several of its officers the task of improving banking services and community relations in inner-city neighborhoods. One of these officers, Norman Hunte, was assigned to Jamaica, Queens. In the early 1970s, he was alarmed by the accelerating deterioration of the area and worked closely with local neighborhood groups to stabilize it. Residents of Baisley Park, a section of Jamaica, were concerned about their degenerating neighborhood and the lack of financial commitment by the local banks. They organized, and together with Hunte, rallied community, financial, and government support, resulting in the formation of a Neighborhood Housing Services (NHS) in Jamaica in 1974. NHS-Jamaica, part of a growing national movement, is a nonprofit organization which counsels neighborhood residents on financial and housing matters, stimulates lending by financial institutions in neighborhoods showing early signs of deterioration, and establishes a high-risk loan pool for home-improvement loans. Hunte serves as Treasurer of NHS-Jamaica and is on the organization's Board of Directors. With his encouragement, as well as that of other interested bankers, financial institutions in Jamaica have committed over $1.2 million in conventional home-improvement and mortgage loans.

Background In the early 1970s, Jamaica was experiencing the classic problems of urban decay: absentee ownership was increasing; more and more houses were being abandoned or poorly maintained; and there was a growing inability among homeowners to obtain mortgages and home-improvement loans.

Several local organizations were formed to deal with these problems, including Baisley Neighbors in Housing, a group which helped tenants with problems caused by absentee landlords and tried to persuade banks to grant loans and mortgages. Some residents of Baisley Park (population 8,200) also sought advice from Norman Hunte and Sherman Brown, Hunte's counterpart at Chase Manhattan Bank.

Norman Hunte, Assistant Vice President for the Street Banking Unit at Citibank, has a long history of community involvement, especially in Jamaica. In 1968, he recognized a growing juvenile crime problem, at least partially brought on by high teenage unemployment, and instituted a summer employment program, backed by Citibank, among gang members. Beginning in 1972, Hunte worked from a storefront office, counseling residents of South Queens, the section of the borough in which Jamaica is located, in all aspects of financial management.

Because of his long experience, Hunte was asked by Citibank to head its Street Banking Unit in 1973 in its first location, South Jamaica. The Street Banking Unit makes consumer loans to people who are turned down at the bank's branches. In 1976, it made 521 loans to 3 percent of those who applied. It provides financial assistance to independent businesses, and assists people in getting professional help with social problems, such as compulsive gambling.

Hunte and Sherman Brown urged community leaders, the Office of Jamacia Planning and Development, and other financial institutions to establish an organization to seek solutions. At their urging, Citibank helped finance a visit to Pittsburgh by about ten Baisley Park residents in 1973. These residents went to investigate NHS-Pittsburgh, the first Neighborhood Housing Services in the nation, formed in 1968.

NHS-Pittsburgh, located in a section known as the Central North Side, was established through the efforts of interested residents and public officials, who sought and finally obtained the financial backing of local banks. The Central North Side (population 7,900; 46.5 percent black) underwent significant disinvestment and decline during the 1960s. Its turn-of-the-century row houses, 23 percent owner-occupied, were in need of major renovation. However, financing from the city's banks was not forthcoming. NHS-Pittsburgh, still in operation today, provides financial assistance through a high-risk revolving loan fund; obtains the backing of banks to grant loans; helps residents comply with building- and health-code standards; supervises all contracted rehabilitation work; establishes a maintenance program; offers financial and home-repair counseling; and plans neighborhood capital improvements. By 1974, over 350 homes had been renovated using loans from the high-risk revolving loan fund. With 80 percent of the housing in the area brought up to code, property values gradually increased. The success of NHS-Pittsburgh has provided an example for other neighborhoods; almost forty other cities have developed programs based on the Pittsburgh model.

The staff of NHS-Pittsburgh pinpointed four elements of critical importance to the formation of NHS-Jamaica:

1. A target area of residents who wish to preserve their home and community.

2. A firm commitment from the financial industry to make all bankable loans for the target area, and to pay for the administrative cost of an NHS office.

3. Availability of a revolving loan fund for non-bankable loans within the target area.

4. City support to ensure enforcement of minimal code compliance and improvement of public services.[1]

Baisley Park, a predominantly black neighborhood, needed the program and seemed to offer a good chance for success. Of its 2,100 dwellings, 1,650 were one- and two-family homes, with 67 percent owner-occupied, a relatively high level. About half the housing was built prior to 1939, but much of the rest was of comparatively recent construction: 28 percent between 1940 and 1959, and 21 percent since 1960. The average price of a house was about $20,000. Many homes had flower gardens and well-tended yards, and the area had shaded streets, a park, a pond, and several playgrounds. Its community leaders were active and capable.

However, there were some alarming developments too. Absentee ownership of housing increased from 26 percent to 33 percent between 1960 and 1970. Only 51 percent of the residents remained in the same house between 1965 and 1970, compared to 64 percent between 1955 and 1960. Vacant properties were becoming a problem: eleven houses and eight commercial buildings were burned out, sealed, or abandoned by 1970, further discouraging residents from making repairs. Mortgages and home-improvement loans were hard to obtain, and the quality of public services was diminishing.

A detailed map of Baisley Park. (Neighborhood Housing Services—Jamaica)

LAND USE

SINGLE AND TWO FAMILY DETACHED

SINGLE FAMILY ATTACHED

THREE AND FOUR FAMILY

RETAIL

VACANT LAND

INSTITUTIONAL

OPEN SPACE

Execution In 1974, after a year devoted to preliminary research and securing financial support, NHS-Jamaica was formed. A Board of Directors was chosen from among the active community and business participants. Sherman Brown of Chase Manhattan was elected President of the NHS-Jamaica Board. Norman Hunte became a Board member and the organization's Treasurer. To assure local control of the Board, eight of its fifteen members are community residents.

Hunte and Brown approached many financial institutions before they successfully managed to obtain enough firm commitments to finance NHS-Jamaica's operating expenses. In addition to the financial backing of their own banks—Citibank, $10,000 and Chase Manhattan, $12,500—they received contributions from Bankers Trust, $4,000, Manufacturers Hanover Trust, $2,500, the First Federal Savings and Loan Association, $1,000, and The Savings Bank Association, $20,000. Whenever possible, NHS-Jamaica tried to get a multi-year commitment from these institutions.

Some of the above financial institutions also contributed office equipment, supplies, meeting rooms, funds for special summer projects, clerical assistance, accounting services, salaried community workers, and legal planning advice.

In September, 1974, the Board of NHS-Jamaica hired James Cook to direct the program. Cook, who left a position as Associate Director of NHS-Pittsburgh to come to Jamaica, hired two additional staff members: an Assistant Director, and an Administrative Assistant/Secretary. NHS-Jamaica then became operational.

While temporary headquarters were set up in the Office of Planning in Jamaica, Cook convinced the Board that to more fully understand the needs and problems of the target area's residents, the NHS-Jamaica office should be located in Baisley Park. NHS-Jamaica bought a dilapidated house in Baisley Park for $5,000, and renovated it for $16,000. In summer, 1975, the house became the organization's headquarters.

Cook spoke to community groups about NHS-Jamaica and distributed flyers describing its services. Hunte and Brown helped secure commitments from Citibank, Chase, and other local financial institutions to make conventional home-improvement and mortgage loans to all qualified applicants. Since the inception of NHS-Jamaica, financial institutions have made loans totaling over $1.2 million. The organization aims for a three-to-one ratio of conventional loans to high-risk loans.

Through its contacts with city officials, NHS-Jamaica also attempts to improve the quality of community services, such as garbage removal and street maintenance, in Baisley Park.

NHS-Jamaica has four principal programs:

The High Risk Revolving Loan Fund. This Fund makes long-term, low-interest loans to high-risk homeowners for home improvements to meet minimal building-code standards. In 1975, it received grants from the following foundations: The Rockefeller Brothers Fund, $60,000; The Taconic Foundation, $25,000; the New York Community Trust, $10,000; and the Klingenstein Foundation, $10,000. In addition, an $85,000 matching fund was established by the Urban Reinvestment Task Force, which is made up of representatives of the federal financial regulatory agencies and the Secretary of the U.S. Department of Housing and Urban Development. The Task Force's main objective is to further the establishment of the NHS nationally.

A loan committee, composed of three local residents and two representatives of the business community, reviews each application, approves loans, and sets interest rates and monthly payments based on the applicant's ability to pay. Interest rates are flexible, ranging from 0 percent to 8 percent, with the average loan made at 3 percent. Repayment terms run from five to fifteen years, depending on the borrower's ability to pay.

After guiding the applicant through the qualifying stage, NHS-Jamaica's staff examine the property and secure the services of a reputable contractor; explain the process; monitor the progress of the renovation; and provide follow-up services.

Between the inception of the program in 1975 and April, 1977, 68 high-risk loans for home improvements were approved, representing a total outlay of $150,000. These loans averaged $2,900, with a $5,000 ceiling. The average recipient has resided in Baisley Park for over ten years and is employed. Senior citizens on pensions and Social Security received 25 percent of the loans.

The following case helps illustrate the program:

Mr. P, 39, single and disabled, lived with his 74-year-old, widowed mother in a single-family home. Together they received Social Security and Supplemental Security Income, amounting to $406.16 per month. They had no mortgage, a small savings account, and monthly housing expenses which permitted no financial flexibility. A year before the implementation of NHS, their converted boiler ceased to function. Mr. P contacted various public agencies for assistance, but was refused. After reading a news article describing the NHS program, Mr. P applied for a loan. Within five days a High Risk Loan was granted to cover the cost of replacing the boiler and repairing the heating system, at a rate and term suited to Mr. P's ability to repay. Encouraged, he applied $500 in personal savings toward the cost of repairs.[2]

To date, Cook has been satisfied with the results of the High Risk Revolving Loan Fund. There have been no foreclosures or write-offs. By monitoring the loans and carefully selecting the recipients, Cook and his staff are able to keep abreast of delinquencies.

Financial Counseling. The NHS has found that stabilizing the finances of individual families helps stabilize the overall community. The staff, aided by Hunte and Brown, either assist applicants with debt consolidation and credit counseling, or refer them to the proper community service agency. Currently, between 35 and 50 people per month take advantage of this counseling service.

NHS-Jamaica offered an example of a Baisley Park resident who has come to them for aid:

Mr. C, 63, had four dependents and was recently married. He was the owner of a two-family home with a mortgage from a savings and loan association. Laid off from his job as a trucker, he was unable to secure another job because of heart trouble, age, and tension. He supported his family on unemployment benefits until they ran out; mortgage payments fell behind, and eventually Mr. C was foreclosed by the savings and loan association. He approached NHS-Jamaica, which contacted the savings and loan association and negotiated a delay of the foreclosure action. The staff helped Mr. C untangle his financial problems, and helped secure part-time work for both Mr. C and his wife. The organization also provided financing to bring the mortgage up to date, and contracted to have repairs made on the property.[3]

Home Maintenance Education. The NHS recognizes that preventive maintenance is the most cost-effective form of neighborhood conservation. NHS-Jamaica, in cooperation with the Queens branch of the New York Urban League, which also provides facilities, and York College's Division of Adult and Continuing Education, initiated a Home Maintenance Training Program to teach community residents basic techniques in carpentry, plumbing, and electrical wiring. Some students of the Program have been put to work rehabilitating a foreclosed property obtained from HUD. An additional course has been developed to train community youths to do minor home repairs for older residents.

The original home maintenance course has increased from one to three sessions per week, and is of twelve weeks duration. An advanced course has been added to meet growing demand. The Program is partly financed by a $32,000 grant from the Urban Reinvestment Task Force. About 150 community residents have taken advantage of this Program.

Urban Homesteading. About fifty properties in Baisley Park have been the subject of foreclosure by the Federal Housing Administration (FHA). Since 1976, Cook has been negotiating with FHA and city officials to establish an urban-homesteading program in the neighborhood, which would be partially financed under Section 312 of the Federal Housing Act of 1964, and administered by the city's Housing and Development Administration (HDA).

Baisley Park streetscape. (Neighborhood Housing Services—Jamaica)

Debris-filled yards. Neighborhood Housing Services—Jamaica tries to deal with deterioration before it becomes widespread. (Neighborhood Housing Services—Jamaica)

Under Section 312, loans at 3 percent interest, and up to a maximum of $3,450, would be available to homeowners who wish to renovate. The staff of NHS-Jamaica have been counseling several potential homesteaders.

NHS-Jamaica studies estimate that renovation of each house will cost about $10,000. Since urban homesteaders do not receive clear title to a property for three years, banks will not grant conventional loans. Therefore, Cook hopes to finance the approximate $6,550 differential between Section 312's maximum loan and the cost of renovation through NHS-Jamaica's High Risk Revolving Loan Fund. With the assistance of the project's staff, two urban homesteaders have already obtained contractors for renovation. However, construction is being delayed until the HDA gives clearance to the renovation. Cook is optimistic that the program will soon be operational.

Costs NHS-Jamaica's budget for 1976 was $54,254, of which $45,374 was used to pay salaries and fringe benefits for the staff of three. Operating expenses, including office rental, repair, and maintenance, supplies, utilities, insurance, legal expenses, credit membership, printing costs, and travel, totaled $8,880. The budget for 1977 is $60,000 and is subject to monthly review by the Board.

Citibank commits $10,000 per year toward the project's operating expenses and has a three-year renewable commitment. The bank also donates administrative services, such as Hunte's time and expertise. Donations by financial institutions pay all operating costs. In 1975, foundation grants, totaling $125,000, and an $85,000 grant from the federal Urban Reinvestment Task Force served the High Risk Revolving Loan Fund.

Problems An increased work load and a limited budget have strained NHS-Jamaica's resources. Cook and his staff also feel that New York City government should become more directly involved in Baisley Park by upgrading services and enforcing building-code standards for single-family units.

Benefits Financial support of NHS-Jamaica has proven to be a sensible and profitable business investment. As indicated above, lending institutions have made $1.2 million in conventional home-improvement loans in the area since the project's inception in 1975. About 250 homes have been renovated using bank loans and the High Risk Revolving Loan Fund.

Since the average value of homes in Baisley Park has increased, more property tax revenues will be coming to the city. Home values now range from $20,000 to $35,000, up from a $20,000 average. Another sign of the community's improving economics is that for the first time in seven years, a new house is being built.

Through the help of Norman Hunte, Citibank has gained new customers, increased visibility, and goodwill from the residents of Baisley Park. NHS-Jamaica and Citibank have been featured in numerous articles in the *New York Times*, the *New York Post*, and the *New York Daily News*.

The Company Citibank, the largest bank in New York and the second largest in the world, is part of the holding company, Citicorp. Citibank has about 270 branch offices in the New York metropolitan area.

The holding company's net interest income for 1976 amounted to $1.78 billion, an increase of 10.5 percent over 1975's $1.61 billion. Net income for the same period rose 15 percent from $349.9 million to $401.4 million.

Other Preservation Activities/Bedford-Stuyvesant Restoration Corporation. Citibank has provided $50,000 in operating capital for 1976 to the Bedford-Stuyvesant Restoration Corporation. Bedford-Stuyvesant, a section of Brooklyn, is one of the largest and poorest black communities in the nation. The bank's president, William I. Spencer, has led fund-raising efforts for the Restoration Corporation.

Economic Development Center. Citibank also assists New Yorkers through its Economic Development Center (EDC), established in 1971. The EDC makes loans in three kinds of situations:

1. To minority entrepreneurs for help in purchasing, expanding, or starting a business.

2. To businesses that may not be minority-owned, but will create or increase employment for New Yorkers.

3. To nonprofit groups and firms whose activities result in a measurable improvement of the environment.[3]

To these businesses, Citibank provides technical assistance in the form of financial counseling and sales analysis, and if necessary, refers the businesses to other agencies.

South Street Seaport. Citibank pledged a five-year, $100,000 grant to the South Street Seaport Museum in 1976, to be used for the renovation and maintenance of piers 15 and 16. The two piers are at the center of the Seaport, which today is a popular shopping and sightseeing attraction, as well as a reminder of the Port of New York's history.

For further information contact:
Norman Hunte
Assistant Vice President, Urban Community Affairs
Citibank
399 Park Avenue
New York, New York 10022
James Cook
Director
NHS-Jamaica
152-13 118th Avenue
Jamaica, New York 11434

Footnotes

1. Neighborhood Housing Services of Jamaica, Inc., *Neighborhood Housing Services of Jamaica, Inc., First Annual Report*, (New York: Neighborhood Housing Services of Jamaica, Inc., May 31, 1976), pp. 3-4.
2. *Ibid.*, p. 11.
3. *Ibid.*, p. 12.

Summary In 1971, the multi-billion-dollar Connecticut Mutual Life Insurance Co., concerned by the deterioration of Asylum Hill, its home area just west of downtown Hartford, encouraged other local businesses to undertake a study of the Hill's problems and needs. In 1972, the study resulted in the formation of Asylum Hill, Inc., a nonprofit organization which attempts to improve the neighborhood and attract employees of local companies to live as well as work there. As a further incentive to promote owner-occupancy in Asylum Hill, in summer, 1975, Connecticut Mutual Life created a $150,000 revolving loan pool through which its employees and the employees of the nearby St. Francis Hospital could obtain short-term loans to purchase and renovate houses at a 6 percent interest rate, well below the going market rate. The company hired the Connecticut Housing Investment Fund (CHIF), a nonprofit organization which specializes in assisting families in purchasing homes, to screen and counsel applicants and arrange financing. So far, thirteen families have taken advantage of the program. In March, 1977, Connecticut Mutual lowered the interest rate to 3 percent and extended these benefits to city employees and employees of the other major contributors to Asylum Hill, Inc.

Background Connecticut Mutual has maintained its headquarters in Asylum Hill since 1926. At the turn of the century, the streets were lined with large late-Victorian houses, and the residents included Hartford's most successful businessmen and citizens (Mark Twain once live there). But, as in many other inner-city neighborhoods, the flight to the suburbs had taken its toll. Crime and deteriorating houses were becoming major problems. The population, which today consists mostly of students, the elderly, transient younger people, and welfare recipients, is racially mixed: approximately 50 percent white, 30 percent black, and 20 percent Hispanic.

The area is a mixture of modern office buildings, Victorian and more modern houses, and older apartment buildings. The housing stock is about one-third one- and two-family residences and two-thirds four-family dwellings or apartments. Many period houses were demolished in order to build apartments. However, many of the Victorian-style houses which remain possess fine architectural details and such decorative amenities as stained-glass windows and magnificent interior woodwork.

More than 25,000 people work in Asylum Hill, though just 9,000 live there; Connecticut Mutual itself has 1,400 workers in its home office.

Connecticut Housing Investment Fund. The Connecticut Housing Investment Fund (CHIF), which administers the revolving loan pool, is a nonprofit organization founded in 1965 to promote open housing in the Hartford suburbs. Headquartered in Hartford and funded by corporate, foundation, and individual contributions, its operations have expanded into broader areas of housing needs as well as other locations. It now has offices in Waterbury, Stamford, and New Haven. The CHIF's operations include engaging in service contracts with many corporations to assist relocated employees in finding adequate housing, and arranging second mortgages for home buyers who cannot meet all the financial requirements for the purchase of a house. The CHIF also provides free advice on real estate, credit, mortgages, and renovation to prospective home buyers. In February, 1975, the CHIF created a Back to the City Program which encourages and counsels middle-income families contemplating buying houses in Hartford. It helped 64 families relocate there in 1975 and 1976.

Execution
Asylum Hill, Inc. Connecticut Mutual's management recognized the problems and potential of Asylum Hill in 1971. The company, supported by its corporate neighbors, Aetna Life and Casualty, the Hartford Insurance Group, and the Society for Savings, initiated a fact-finding study of Asylum Hill's needs and problems, outlined a plan of action, and sought additional local backing. As a result of this study, Asylum Hill, Inc., was founded in February, 1972. Its initial budget of $118,000 included provision for a full-time director. By 1976, the budget had expanded to $144,000.*

The first priority of this nonprofit, neighborhood-improvement association was to stabilize the area to attract potential home buyers. Since crime was a major concern, high-intensity streetlights were installed with the aid of the city, and citizen and canine patrols were established. In addition, traffic patterns were changed by creating one-way streets and cul-de-sacs to decrease traffic flow through the neighborhood. To strengthen community spirit and attract middle-class interest, Asylum Hill, Inc., sponsors an annual Octoberfest, an outdoor festival including arts and crafts displays, entertainment, food, and walking tours of the area. Asylum Hill, Inc., also fosters the establishment of civic organizations. Several organizations—West Hill Organization, Central Asylum Hill Association, Laurel Gardens and Sigourney Square Civic Association—have been formed. Their programs include: social events for children and adults; zoning and code-enforcement courses at a local educational institution; summer musical programs in the park; lawn-care advice; an annual plant sale; and gardening plots on some

*The major contributors in 1976 were:

Aetna Life & Casualty	$55,000
The Hartford Insurance Group	36,650
Connecticut Mutual Life	23,000
Society For Savings	23,000
Hartford Home Savings & Loan	2,000
Veeder Industries	1,750
Mechanics Savings Bank	1,350
Connecticut Bank & Trust	600
St. Joseph Cathedral	500
State Bank for Savings	260
Total	$144,110

of Aetna's property. Asylum Hill, Inc., coordinates these diverse activities, serves as a resource center, and publishes a local newspaper, *The Hill Ink*, distributed free to area residents.

Establishment of Revolving Loan Pool. Connecticut Mutual realized that for the neighborhood to improve further, more middle-income people had to move there. In 1975, the company created a $150,000 revolving loan fund, as an incentive enabling potential home buyers to purchase and renovate houses. The interest charge was first set at 6 percent, well below the prevailing market price; and later, in March, 1977, it was lowered to 3 percent, about one-third the market rate. The average cost of a house in the area is $20,000 to $30,000, with renovation costing $10,000 to $15,000. The average short-term loan is about $45,000, including purchase price and renovation, and has a duration of about six months. Once renovation is completed, the owner obtains a conventional long-term mortgage and repays the interim loan. There is usually no difficulty in securing a long-term mortgage.

Connecticut Mutual hired the CHIF to administer the program in October, 1975. The CHIF screens and counsels potential home buyers, and arranges a short-term loan when a house is selected. Fees for its services range from $50 to $350 per case depending on staff time and final disposition. The CHIF also assists in arranging permanent mortgages from local banks when rehabilitation is completed.

Connecticut Mutual is responsible for the promotion of the program. In summer, 1975, the company began a detailed promotional campaign on Asylum Hill, consisting of articles in its house publications and local newspapers, slide shows and dinners for interested employees, and walking tours of the area.

Another objective was outlined by Connecticut Mutual's President, Edward B. Bates:

We not only hope to stimulate interest in buying homes but also hope to stimulate interest in similar action programs by other companies in the area.[1]

In April, 1976, Aetna Life & Casualty

Company established a revolving low-interest, short-term loan fund. The Connecticut Bank and Trust Company is also providing mortgages to employees with interest rates below those of the prevailing market. In another section of Hartford, Trinity College, Hartford Hospital, and the Institute of Living have recently announced similar programs for their employees.

Since the inception of Connecticut Mutual's revolving loan pool, about 13 families have taken advantage of the loan program, and 52 families have moved to the area.

In order to increase participation and expand the pool of eligible borrowers, Connecticut Mutual lowered the interest rate on its loans to 3 percent and extended borrowing privileges to all city employees and employees of the

other major contributors to Asylum Hill, Inc. (Aetna Life & Casualty, the Hartford Insurance Group, and the Society for Savings). Jill Diskan of the CHIF reports that since the interest rate was lowered, inquiries have increased from 12 to 35 per month. In this period, twelve houses have been sold through the CHIF, with six buyers utilizing Connecticut Mutual's revolving pool.

A house in Asylum Hill, before renovation with Connecticut Mutual's help.

Costs Connecticut Mutual contributed $150,000 to create the short-term revolving fund. When this amount is committed, Connecticut Mutual has indicated its intent to contribute more. In addition, the company pays the CHIF for its administration of the program, and Connecticut Mutual employees help promote it. Figures for these costs are not available. In 1976, the company's annual contribution to Asylum Hill, Inc., was $23,000.

Problems Connecticut Mutual says that there are no existing problems. However, it anticipates the displacement of local residents and escalating real estate prices within the foreseeable future.

Benefits Because of the publicity on Asylum Hill, real estate prices have increased 10 percent since the inception of the program in late 1972. Although this is not a significant increase, it represents a reversal of the 10 percent annual decrease in property values prior to the program's inception, and indicates that Asylum Hill's real estate is stabilizing. The number of local real estate agents has increased from one to four since Connecticut Mutual became involved in the community.

In mid-1976, a Neighborhood Housing Services (see Citibank) was established in the Sigourney Square section of Asylum Hill. In its first year, it made about forty home loans.

In another sign of Asylum Hill's changing character, a private developer recently purchased property near Connecticut Mutual's headquarters and plans to build a childcare center there. This facility, scheduled for completion in fall, 1977, will accommodate 100 children.

Connecticut Mutual has created good will among its employees, and also has influenced other corporations to establish similar loan programs. Mrs. Lurayn Haines, the second Connecticut Mutual employee to relocate there stated:

I like cities. I plan to stay with the company so I figured why not live close to it? . . . And let's face it, the price is a bargain.[2]

In March, 1977, the company received the CHIF's second annual Corporate Responsibility in Housing Award. The citation stated:

This year we honor Connecticut Mutual Life Insurance Company for its creative approach to employee housing needs, an approach which also emphasizes corporate involvement in the community. . . . Connecticut Mutual Life's is an excellent example to the corporate and business community. It provides a stimulus for others to begin thinking about corporate responsibility in satisfying employee housing needs and to define the corporate role in the neighborhood, community, and region in which offices are located.[3]

The Company Connecticut Mutual, founded in 1846, is the oldest life insurance company in Connecticut and the sixth oldest in the United States. Principally a life insurance company, its product line also includes guaranteed, variable, and accumulation annuity plans, individual pension and profit-sharing plans, and disability-income plans. Connecticut Mutual ranked tenth among American mutual companies, with assets of $3.95 billion in 1976, up from 1975's figure of $3.67 billion. Net investment income also rose from $198 million in 1975 to $212 million in 1976.

For further information contact:
Terry M. D'Italia
Associate Consultant, Communications Division
Connecticut Mutual Life Insurance Company
140 Garden Street
Hartford, Connecticut 06115
Jill Diskan
Director
Back to the City
Connecticut Home Improvement Fund
121 Tremont Street
Hartford, Connecticut 06105
Jack D. Middleton
Executive Director
Asylum Hill, Inc.
121 Sigourney Street
Hartford, Connecticut 06105

Footnotes

1. "Housing Owner Plan Signed," *Hartford Times*, 16 October 1975.
2. Terry D'Italia, "Collins Considers Asylum Hill Home," *CML News*, 15 April 1976.
3. Connecticut Housing Investment Fund, *Second Annual Connecticut Housing Investment Fund Corporate Social Responsibility in Housing Award and the 10 Plus 3 Anniversary of Connecticut Housing Investment Fund, Dinner Program,* (Hartford: Connecticut Housing Investment Fund, March 2, 1977), p. 1.

Eastman Kodak Company

Summary Eastman Kodak has long taken an active interest in the well being of Rochester, its home community. In 1968, the company, in response to requests for help from WEDGE, a local community action group, became involved in the effort to revitalize Brown Square, a rapidly deteriorating area adjacent to company headquarters. Kodak contributed $150,000 to build a new neighborhood park. Kodak and other local businesses are contributing personnel, money, and ideas to help revitalize the neighborhood. These donations, together with the efforts of local community groups, are improving the Brown Square area.

Background In the early 1800s, Matthew and Francis Brown developed a millrace along the Genesee Falls, utilizing its water to generate power. This area became one of the first industrial sections in Rochester. The Browns built their homes and designed a park—later deeded to the city—adjacent to the falls and the mill. The area became known as Brown Square.

Through the years, the composition of the neighborhood which grew up in this 216-acre area changed. The number of buildings run by absentee landlords increased; junkyards flourished; a railroad track bisected the area; businesses were left vacant; and buildings decayed.

However, there are still many houses—mostly single-family units dating from the nineteenth and twentieth centuries—that are well maintained or at least structurally sound. The neighborhood has many tree-lined streets, well-maintained yards, and a strong community spirit.

Brown Square's population of about 1,100 people is approximately 55 percent white, primarily of Italian extraction; 29 percent Hispanic, and 16 percent black. Of the Italians, 90 percent are homeowners and 29 percent are retired. However, overall less than 35 percent of the households are owner-occupied. Unemployment fluctuates, but as of mid-1977, it was high.

In 1967, the City of Rochester requested U.S. Department of Housing and Urban Development (HUD) sponsorship of an urban-renewal plan for Brown Square. But this project did not materialize due to lack of federal funding. Since help from HUD was not forthcoming, parishioners of nearby downtown churches decided to mobilize the residents of the area to try to improve their own living conditions. They enlisted a local resident, Mrs. Jenette Major, to organize the community. As a result of these initiatives, WEDGE, a neighborhood action group dedicated to improving the physical surroundings and fostering economic growth in Brown Square, was founded in 1967.

Award-winning house in the "Fix-Up '76" Program.

Execution In 1968, when WEDGE decided to open an operations office, it approached its corporate neighbor, Eastman Kodak, for a loan to purchase a building. Kodak agreed to supply the money if WEDGE would apply to the Community Chest for membership as a social agency and for operating funds. Both requests were made and granted, and Kodak donated the money WEDGE needed to buy the building.

Between 1968 and 1973, WEDGE organized meetings and social events to unify the neighborhood, and solicited residents' suggestions for improving the area. Based on these suggestions and on the research of Gruen Associates, a professional planning firm whose work on the project was underwritten by Kodak, a master plan, Total Community Renewal in Brown Square, was conceived.

Following the plan, in June, 1973, WEDGE set up the Brown Square Development Corporation (BSDC). The BSDC has four main objectives:

1. Providing for the construction of new housing and community facilities, the renovation of existing housing, and the creation of a viable urban service center.

2. Fostering private and public investment in Brown Square.

3. Encouraging orderly land development.

4. Assembling technical assistance from individuals and organizations for redeveloping Brown Square.[1]

The fourteen-member BSDC Board of Directors draws on all fields of expertise in the Rochester area. Three Board members are from WEDGE, two from businesses in Brown Square; two from its churches; two from industry; and five from Rochester's legal, financial, accounting, real estate, and construction sectors. Kodak presently has two employees on the Board. A member of WEDGE must serve as Chairman or Vice Chairman. There is a full-time Director. The 1977 BSDC budget is about $56,000, entirely raised from private sources, including Kodak. The company also donates in-kind services.

Since the BSDC's inception, its staff and Board members, along with local residents, have conducted several surveys. An exploratory economic analysis examined possible reuses of existing commercial, industrial, and residental structures. A diagnostic family survey collected information on area households and computerized it for future use. Property maps were prepared in detail. A structural-qualifications survey examined the existing housing stock and recommended needed repairs. In a sample section, more detailed inspections and cost estimates for repairs were made.

In late 1976, another Kodak employee, who is a BSDC Board Member, surveyed existing and required community service agencies in the Brown Square area in an attempt to centralize the agencies in one location.

Based on these surveys, the BSDC is currently considering several projects:

1. Setting up a revolving fund for buying and rehabilitating houses, which would allow houses to be rented with an option to buy.

2. Establishing a Neighborhood Housing Services agency (see Citibank and Tasty Baking). However, to qualify for this program, the area must cover one square mile. The Brown Square area is too small, so the BSDC is considering broadening its base to include the adjacent Edgerton area.

3. Building about 120 single-family rental units, to be financed by developers and local banks and managed by the BSDC.

In 1976, the BSDC, WEDGE, and the American Jewish Society for Service, a New York-based organization, sponsored FIX-UP '76, a seven-week summer project in which twelve young people, aged 16 to 21, from all over the country, donated their services along with the Director of the American Jewish Society for Service, his wife, and two of the Society's camp counselors to renovate and repaint about 25 Brown Square houses. Materials were paid for through a $5,000 donation from Rochester's Department of Community Development, the BSDC, and WEDGE.

The BSDC and WEDGE publicized the project. Members from both groups then selected the houses that would be renovated. Kodak provided two employees to teach basic repair skills and supervise the project. Residents of the houses selected chose the colors for repainting, and the young workers repaired gutters and roofs, and painted the houses inside and out. According to Charles Fitzgibbon of Kodak, a great sense of camaraderie developed between the summer work group and the local residents. Their efforts resulted in additional home improvements by other area residents.[2]

The BSDC has also been instrumental in removing the junkyards which were numerous in the neighborhood. In 1974, at the BSDC's urging, the zoning was changed from commercial to residential on the 67 acres where the yards were located. A court order required the removal of the last remaining yard by June, 1977.

In 1976, the BSDC obtained funding for improving the commercial area on Lyell Avenue. Storefronts are now being rehabilitated, and more parking space and better street lighting are being added under Rochester's Community Development Block Grant Program. In June, 1976, a neighborhood newsletter, the *Brown Square News*, began to be published. It appears quarterly and is available to area residents at no cost.

In 1976, the BSDC initiated an awards program for property improvements in the area. Six awards were given each year, in 1976 and 1977, for residential, commercial, and industrial improvements, as well as for the best compatible new construction.

In keeping with the spirit of the Brown brothers' park, established in the 1820s, Kodak announced, in summer, 1976, plans for construction of a new Brown Square Bicentennial Park. Kodak contributed $150,000 with the City of Rochester adding another $75,000. Design services were contributed by the architectural firm of Joe Y Ko. The 4.2-acre park, completed in summer, 1977, includes an open meadow, walkways, bocce courts, a fountain plaza, picnic facilities, and gardens as well as a late-nineteenth-century freight station that will be adaptively reused for park offices, maintenance services, and public facilities.

Costs Kodak did not provide a breakdown of its financial contribution to Brown Square. However, the company contributed $150,000 to rebuild Brown Square Park. Kodak employees have also donated time and technical assistance to the BSDC.

Problems Publicity on Brown Square has made absentee landlords seek higher prices for their real estate. There is also a problem with neighborhood continuity, since many of Brown Square's residents are elderly. Homes in the area are difficult to sell, and the heirs of deceased residents often must rent to transients who sometimes fail to maintain the property.

Benefits The Brown Square neighborhood is improving. Many houses have been and are being renovated. Community stability has been reinforced by the BSDC and WEDGE, which provide avenues for local citizens to obtain information and assistance on financial and housing needs.

Revitalization efforts have increased commercial interest in Brown Square. A foundry is being converted into a restaurant, and a cast-iron commercial structure is being renovated to accommodate specialty stores. A local public broadcasting station has relocated in the area and built new headquarters on land donated by Kodak.

The Company Kodak, the world's largest producer of photographic products, had sales of $5.4 billion for fiscal 1976, representing a 10 percent increase over the 1975 figure of $4.9 billion. For the comparable period, net income rose 6 percent from $613.7 million to $650.6 million. Sales are broken down as follows: photographic equipment, U.S. and Canadian, 50 percent; international, 31 percent; chemicals, 19 percent. Kodak is also an important producer of plastics and man-made fibers.

Other Preservation Activities. Hospitals, medical and musical schools, and other educational institutions, not only in Rochester, but also in Europe and other parts of the United States, have been the beneficiaries of Kodak's contributions. Kodak's preservation support in Rochester includes:

1. Contributions to the establishment of the independent International Museum of Photography at George Eastman's fifty-room, early-twentieth-century mansion.

2. Donations to finance the restoration of George Eastman's birthplace. The 1854 Greek Revival house was moved from its former location in upstate New York and relocated on the property of Eastman's later home in Rochester.

3. A $1.7 million donation, in 1971, to renovate the Eastman Theatre, dating from 1922, reputed to be one of the finest theaters acoustically in the world.

4. Contributions to the Landmark Society of Western New York.

Kodak also spent about $30 million to update its own facilities and landscape them. As part of the program, the company has incorporated several old factory buildings into its corporate headquarters. This required creating a uniform facade and remodeling the interior.

For further information contact:
Charles Fitzgibbon
Director of State and Local Affairs
Eastman Kodak Company
343 State Street
Rochester, New York 14650

Robert J. Ferraro
Director
Brown Square Development Corporation
507 North Plymouth Avenue
Rochester, New York 14608

Footnotes

1. "Brown Square Development Corporation," *Brown Square News*, June, 1976.
2. INFORM interview with Charles Fitzgibbon, Director, State and Local Affairs, Eastman Kodak Company, December, 1976.

Summary In July, 1974, General Mills announced its intention to help reverse the process of physical deterioration and economic downslide in its home city of Minneapolis. Its plan was to purchase, renovate, and revitalize a fifty-block residential neighborhood, known as Stevens Square, located in a sound but rapidly deteriorating section of the city. For this purpose, General Mills formed a profit-making subsidiary with an established local real estate developer called Stevens Court, Inc. The project utilized community residents and local subcontractors, wherever possible. In October, 1975, the company was threatened with a national boycott of its products by the AFL-CIO because it was paying nonunion wages and using nonunion construction personnel at Stevens Court. The union's demands were subsequently met, but the original profit-making goals and the rent structure of the renovated units had to be greatly altered.

Background In 1958, General Mills moved to a new suburban office complex in Golden Valley, west of downtown Minneapolis. The reasons cited for the move were: the physical inadequacies of its downtown building, including overcrowding, limited meeting space, lack of room for expansion, and inefficient office layouts; and the traffic, parking, and congestion problems employees experienced coming to work downtown. The company felt that only a new building, in a suburban location, designed specifically for its needs could overcome these shortcomings.

Nevertheless, showing a continued interest in and allegiance to its home city, General Mills has continued to contribute to education, the arts, and civic activities in Minneapolis. Its foundation dispenses more than $3 million in grants annually.

General Mills believed that it could accomplish more for Minneapolis through normal profit-oriented business activities than through traditional channels of civic support. As a result, in 1974, it decided to form a for-profit subsidiary to renovate a fifty-block residential neighborhood in the Stevens Square area, a few blocks from the downtown Minneapolis central business district. In the initial press conference describing General Mills' involvement in Stevens Court, Inc., Cyrus Johnson, Vice President for Social Action, said:

I believe that doing what is in society's interest can and should be profitable. I believe that a company that attempts to improve its city and its society is entitled to a profit. We have to lay the idea to rest that social responsibility is incompatible with profit. We have to begin to seek out new areas of activity where there is a happy confluence of profit and principle.[1]

Execution In its regular consumer-products business, General Mills has grown by developing new products in areas of existing company expertise. In areas where it has no prior experience, growth is usually achieved through merger with or acquisition of successful companies. Possessing no internal residential real estate experience, General Mills selected as its partner in the venture Jim Larson, who had been working in the Stevens Square area for over eight years. Larson had already renovated approximately 85 apartment units in the area and was eager to do more, should financing become available.

Jim Larson and his staff were made responsible for selecting, purchasing, renovating, renting, maintaining, and managing all properties developed by the company. General Mills acted as the "banker" for the Stevens Court real estate development enterprise, but with more control and personal involvement in the operation and outcome than is customary for one acting in that capacity.

Initially, Stevens Court, Inc., planned to buy about 1,000 apartment units within a fifty-block area, approximately 40 percent of the apartments in the Stevens Square neighborhood. General Mills selected Stevens Square because improvement would not require total demolition of the existing housing stock. The buildings were sound, renewable brick structures dating from the early 1900s and the resident population was committed to improving conditions.

After renovations, rents were to range from $125 to $127 per month, only $10 to $15 per month higher than pre-renovation rents. New plumbing, wiring, appliances, bathrooms and kitchens, walls, ceilings, and the refinishing of hardwood floors and original woodwork were to be included in the work. This resulted in roughly a $3,000-per-unit expenditure for renovation in addition to a $6,000 per-unit acquisition cost. Neighborhood residents were to provide labor for the project, and if possible, subcontractors and suppliers were also to have local affiliations. Almost all construction work was to be done by nonunion crews.

The neighborhood population mix—

approximately 60 percent elderly and 40 percent young, working, and students—was to remain the same. A key feature of the proposal was that Larson's organization would establish permanent residence in Steven's Square and play an important role in the neighborhood's social and political life, as well as in the construction and maintenance of the renovated apartments. According to the plan, Stevens Court, Inc., would help residents find jobs, and participate in health-care programs. It would also facilitate communication in the neighborhood through close contact between staff and residents, build information kiosks, and perhaps hire a protection agency to supplement the local police force.

In the three years since General Mills' involvement began, 457 units have been purchased and 300 have been renovated. Jim Larson reports that property values have not escalated, and he can still acquire distressed or abandoned buildings for around $6,000 per unit.

Costs   Initially, General Mills invested just under $400,000 for a 51 percent interest in Stevens Court, Inc. Jim Larson and his partner owned the remaining 49 percent. By early 1975, General Mills owned 65 percent of the operation, while Larson owned the remaining 35 percent.

Although Stevens Court, Inc., was established as a profit-making venture, all profits for the first ten years were expected to be reinvested in additional buildings and further improvements. After ten years, General Mills anticipated a return on its investment of 5 percent to 10 percent, a rate substantially below that required on the parent company's other new capital expenditures. As Cyrus Johnson points out: "It is very important for the public to know that in a strict financial sense, General Mills could make better investments. But, socially, we seriously doubt we could."[2]

Problems   At first, some Stevens Square residents were suspicious that General Mills might be out to milk the community for exorbitant profits, or to gain title to large tracts of land for future speculation or development. Father Greg Welch of St. Stephen's Roman Catholic Church, located in the neighborhood, stated:

This is an exciting pilot project in renovation of present housing by a private institution. But it will be a huge gathering of land in a single given area under single ownership and that kind of power says "danger."[3]

Charlie Ellis, a 27-year-old seminary student who lives in the area, commented that he has:

more confidence in Larson and Waage [a partner] than in General Mills. Big money is big money. I'm suspicious of it. I agree that it's important for corporations to be involved in neighborhood renovation. But they can't forget that residents must have some sense of control over their destiny.[4]

Stevens Square neighborhood and two buildings renovated by Stevens Court, Inc.

In October, 1975, after about 200 apartments had been purchased and renovations had been underway for sixteen months, the project ran into difficulty with the unions. The members of the buildings trades unions and their parent organization, the AFL-CIO, threatened to stage a national boycott of General Mills' products unless the company discontinued involvement in the Stevens Court renovations or complied with union labor rates and restrictions on all the work performed. According to the company, the unions were upset because Stevens Court, Inc., was using nonunion workers to carry out the renovations, and paying them less than union scale.

General Mills presented its case in "A Message to the Twin Cities Community," published in the *Minneapolis Tribune* on October 1, 1975. In this message, the company threatened to discontinue its efforts unless a mutually satisfactory agreement could be reached with the unions. However, General Mills did not wish to abandon the people and property of Stevens Court, nor its new concept of corporate community involvement. As a result, it finally agreed to the union demands and replaced nonunion workers with card-carrying crews under union subcontractors and at union wage scales. The boycott threat was dropped, but twenty area residents employed in the renovation work had to be let go.*

*Since that time, the unions claimed that General Mills was still using nonunion workers for some operations.

Dan Gustafson, President of the Minneapolis Building and Construction Trades Union Council, claims that the union was concerned about the undercutting of the union wage scale, not about the hiring of non-card-carrying residents. Gustafson also suggested that if General Mills was truly concerned with helping the city, it could have "put the $3 million it gives annually through its foundation into the Stevens Court project, hired union workers, and really made some impact on unemployment as well as housing."[5] He added that if General Mills had remained in the city, instead of moving to the suburbs, "it would have kept its money where its mouth is."[6] Gustafson cited the Honeywell Corporation as an example of a company concerned with the revitalization of the city.**

**Honeywell has stayed in its downtown location and has contributed to the city's employment base as well as to the neighborhood surrounding its plant. Through its neighborhood-improvement program, the company purchases rundown properties, rehabilitates them, and resells them to community residents at or below cost.

Buildings owned by Stevens Court, Inc., and possible future acquisitions (as of October, 1976).

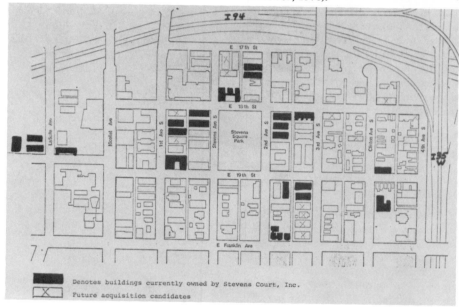

During renovation.

After renovation.

As of mid-1977, almost two years after the threatened boycott, Stevens Court, Inc., is still in business. However, any potential profits for General Mills or Jim Larson are virtually gone. According to Larson, General Mills' contribution must now be considered totally philanthropic. Due to the increased cost of labor, building materials, energy, and taxes, renovation costs as well as rents have increased considerably over the original estimates. "An apartment that formerly rented for from $150 to $175 had to be raised to $210 to $220,"[7] says Larson.

Benefits   As a result of General Mills' efforts, 300 units have been upgraded in an important central-city residential area. This neighborhood, which had started to decline, is receiving renewed attention from local citizens' groups and the city government. City services have increased, and street and park improvements have been made. Finally, according to the company, the renovation of buildings in Stevens Square has helped increase community spirit and pride.

The Stevens Square Community Organization (SSCO), a group of residents from the area, stated:

We are confident that this General Mills interest [in the restoration and rehabilitation of sound existing structures] is compatible with the interests of the neighborhood, and that rents will continue to remain within the realm of current residents' ability to live here.[8]

A representative of the SSCO said:

In the past, American corporations have not been responsive to the needs of the communities they affect. If General Mills does indeed operate as they have described, it will be a welcome change. The S.S.C.O. hopes the company will respond to this challenge.[9]

Eight months after General Mills began its involvement in the revitalization of the area, John McNamara, another member of SSCO who lives in a rehabilitated apartment, said:

Our neighborhood is beginning to form a strong image. . . . I think we're well on our way to becoming a stable, viable community.[10]

The Company   In 1886, C. C. Washburn built his first flour mill on the banks of the Mississippi in Minneapolis, forming the Washburn Crosby Company. In 1921, the company created a food authority, Betty Crocker, to represent its expanding line of food products, and in 1923, it introduced Wheaties. In 1928, several leading milling companies merged with the Washburn Crosby Company to form General Mills, Inc. The first product introduced by this new corporation was Bisquick, the nation's first prepared cake mix. Since that time, General Mills has grown and expanded its operations until today it is a large, diversified, international company. In 1976, sales increased to $2.9 billion, up from a 1975 figure of $2.3 billion. Net income rose from $76.2 million in 1975 to $117 million in 1976. General Mills employs more than 52,000 people; 3,600 of these in the Minneapolis area.

For further information contact:
Cyrus Johnson
Vice President for Social Action
General Mills, Inc.
9200 Wayzata Boulevard
Minneapolis, Minnesota 55440

Footnotes

1. General Mills, Inc., "Press Conference for Stevens Court Project," *News Release*, July 25, 1974, p. 3.
2. *Ibid.*, p. 4.
3. Ron Ostman, "Stevens Renovations Will Hold Closed Meetings," *The Paper*, 2 October 1974.
4. Terry Wolkerstorfer, "General Mills Backing Renovation," *Minneapolis Star*, 26 July 1974.
5. INFORM interview with Dan Gustafson, President, Minneapolis Building and Construction Trades Union Council, November, 1976.
6. *Ibid.*
7. INFORM interview with Jim Larson, President, Stevens Court, Inc., November, 1976.
8. Bill Grimberg and Doug Madson, "Stevens Square Residents Testing Selves, General Mills," *Common Ground*, November, 1974, p. 30.
9. *Ibid.*
10. Carol Matlack, "For-profit Rehab: Can Investors Save Neighborhoods," *Common Ground*, Summer, 1975.

Summary In 1972, Lakewood Bank and Trust Company of Dallas, Texas, established a $1 million loan fund to finance the purchase and renovation of the homes along Swiss Avenue, a deteriorating section of Old East Dallas, its home area. Lakewood Bank made additional loan commitments of $1 million each in 1974 and 1975 to renovate homes in the Hollywood Heights and Belmont Extension areas of Old East Dallas. Expanding its involvement, the bank announced a $2 million loan program in September, 1976, in cooperation with the Federal National Mortgage Association to provide financing for the purchase and renovation of single-family owner-occupied homes in Munger Place. These programs have helped check the spread of urban blight in Old East Dallas.

Background Lakewood Bank and Trust is located four miles from Dallas's center in Old East Dallas, which was one of the first sections of the city to be developed. Most of the homes were built between 1890 and 1940, when the area was the residence of the city's political and cultural elite. Many homes, especially the older ones in the Munger Place and Swiss Avenue sections, are large and well built, reflecting a wide range of architectural styles.

The homes along Swiss Avenue, dating from 1905 to 1925, are slightly newer and more luxurious than those in Munger Place. The architecture is mixed: Spanish-style and Classical Revival houses, interspersed with some examples of the "prairie style," including one designed by Frank Lloyd Wright. The latter style, characterized by low horizontal roof lines, overhanging eaves, and massive porch columns, was created in the 1890s by Wright, and remained popular through the early twentieth century.

Many homes in the Hollywood Heights and Belmont Extension areas are less than 45 years old. Those in Hollywood Heights are two-story brick structures, designed in the Tudor style, with steep pitched roofs and decorative stone, brick, and stained-glass detail. Most homes in this area were built in the 1930s and are single-family units. The sixty-square-block area is 90 per-

cent owner-occupied and has 600 homes. The Belmont Extension area, located northwest of Lakewood Bank, is composed of one-, two-, and three-story wooden-frame structures. The architecture is largely mixed; many homes are built in the cottage style, with front porches and dormers in the attic. Apartment houses and two-family brick buildings are interspersed with the smaller dwellings. There are 550 homes in the fifty-square-block area. While the houses in Hollywood Heights and the Belmont Extension are not as large as those on Swiss Avenue or Munger Place, they are newer and have been better maintained. The average house in Hollywood Heights and the Belmont Extension "as is" is worth between $20,000 and $25,000.

Most of the homes in the ten-square-block Munger Place area are in great need of repair. They sell for about $20,000 "as is," and require $35,000 to $40,000 to recondition. Rotting wood needs to be replaced; the house must be painted inside and out; siding replaced; and new plumbing, heating, and electrical systems installed.

The homes on Swiss Avenue were carefully maintained until the mid-1950s, when many residents began leaving for the newly developed suburbs. In response to this outward flow of homeowners, the City of Dallas rezoned the 2,000 homes in Old East Dallas for multi-family use in 1965. Many old homes were converted into boarding houses; some were divided into apartments; and two structures were demolished to make way for more lucrative high-rise construction. The predominantly owner-occupied (75 percent) area became 80 percent renter-occupied. Absentee landlords allowed their buildings to decay, while waiting for developers to purchase their properties for demolition and new construction. Rents were cheaper in these dilapidated boarding houses, attracting a more transient population. Crime increased. Those attempting to maintain their homes found it difficult to obtain home-improvement loans for major repairs. Nevertheless, a few older families were determined to maintain their homes in spite of the deteriorating conditions.

In 1971, the residents of Swiss Avenue and other parts of Old East Dallas

decided to do something about the encroaching decay. They formed a small group and sought advice from neighboring districts, the National Trust for Historic Preservation, the State Historic Preservation Officer, the Texas Historical Commission, and Jacob Morrison, author of *Historic Preservation Law*. Acting on what they learned, the group incorporated as the Historic Preservation League in 1973. The Historic Preservation League learned from the Urban Design Division of the Dallas City Planning Department that further demolition could be prevented by having Swiss Avenue designated a historic district. However, to obtain this designation for the neighborhood, the League needed the support of local residents, owners, businesses, and financial institutions.

After much effort and many slide presentations, the League won its battle, and in September, 1973, Swiss Avenue was designated a historic district, under the landmark ordinance of the City of Dallas. That same year, after Swiss Avenue's redesignation and rezoning for single-family use, the National Trust awarded an $800 matching grant to help the League pay legal fees accumulated in the fight against construction of a high-rise apartment complex in the district.

Execution The concern of Swiss Avenue's residents, the neighborhood's designation as a historic district, and the soundness of many of the buildings greatly facilitated revitalization. In 1972, Lakewood Bank and Trust, concerned by the swift decline of the neighborhood which was the source of almost all of its business, made a commitment to lend $1 million for the purchase and renovation of 200 homes on Swiss Avenue. This innovative gesture provided needed financing which had been nonexistent during the years of decline.

Target areas for loans were chosen by bank officials and community leaders. Special departments were created at the bank for processing the loans and securing second mortgages, since Lakewood is a commercial bank and normally does not handle many such transactions. The loan program itself is directed by the bank's Senior Vice President for Community Affairs, Artie Barnett, who is also on the Historic Preservation League's Advisory Board. Each new program was announced at a gathering of interested citizens and the news media.

The mortgage loans furnished by Lakewood finance 80 percent of the cost of a house (90 percent with Prime Mortgage Insurance). These conventional loans extend for twenty years, with an interest rate of 9¼ percent. Loans are made on the condition that the homes will be owner-occupied and improved to meet city safety regulations. Since the establishment of the $1 million loan fund, financing on Swiss Avenue has become comparatively easy to obtain. Approximately one year after Lakewood's successful involvement with the neighborhood, ninety homes had been renovated. In 1973, ten financial institutions also became interested in supplying mortgage loans in the area at terms of 8¾ percent for 25 years. In 1974, Swiss Avenue was listed in the National Register of Historic Places.

In 1974 and 1975, Lakewood made two commitments of $1 million each in the Belmont Extension and Hollywood Heights areas for similar loan programs. Seventy-five conventional loans, totaling $2 million, have been made.

In September, 1976, Lakewood Bank and Trust initiated a $1 million Munger Place mortgage loan fund, and with an additional $1 million from the Federal National Mortgage Association (FNMA), succeeded in making available $2 million in funds for purchase and renovation. This is the first instance of the FNMA's involvement with only one local bank.

The Historic Preservation League has also established a revolving fund to buy homes in Munger Place and resell them through local realtors. So far 22 homes have been bought by the League. In addition, the League is trying to obtain historic-district status for Munger Place. Following Lakewood's lead, other banks have begun making loans in the area.

In the one year the program has been in effect, almost 30 percent of the 200 houses in Munger Place have been renovated, and thirty loans totaling $900,000 have been made by Lakewood. Though progress is being made, it will take three to five years before the revitalization of Munger Place reaches a level comparable to that of Swiss Avenue. In the five years that Lakewood has been financing these two high-risk projects, there has not been one foreclosure.

Lakewood is now planning to establish a $5 million loan fund to further encourage residential and commercial redevelopment in Junius Heights and other sections of Old East Dallas. The bank also helped finance a Historic Preservation League booklet entitled, *Buying a Home in Historic Old East Dallas.*

Costs Over the past two years, Lakewood Bank and Trust has spent approximately $50,000 on the revitalization of Old East Dallas. This amount includes the cost of opinion surveys, public relations, and luncheons for community leaders. Lakewood feels that the income from new loans, as well as new business generated from the public relations surrounding the programs, offset the costs.

Problems In some cases, it was necessary to help relocate families when multi-family dwellings were sold by their owners.

Benefits Since the beginning of the Swiss Avenue loan fund and related projects, real estate values in the area have skyrocketed. Homes along Swiss Avenue have doubled and even tripled in value. One home, which was purchased for $28,000, was resold after renovation for $239,000. With minor repairs and some home improvements, the prices of homes in Hollywood Heights and the Belmont Extension increased from between $20,000 and $25,000 to between $30,000 and $35,000. In Munger Place, unrenovated homes that were sold "as is" for $12,000 before the neighboring Swiss Avenue renovations are now sold for $20,000.

Lakewood Bank and Trust has benefited from the neighborhood stabilization and improved economic base of its prime market. In addition, its involvement with the revitalization effort has brought much publicity, and as a result, new business. In 1976, Lakewood received an award from the Dallas Chapter of the American Institute of Architects for the work in Old East Dallas. This Citation of Honor was presented by Downing Thomas, Chapter President, who said of the renovations:

Lakewood's significant contribution made in the revitalization and environmental improvement of the East Dallas area can be measured in terms of rising property values, new construction, historic restoration, influx of new families and above all increased community pride.[1]

The community has benefited from these renovations as well. Decay has been checked in the project areas, and the tax base has been increased, resulting in more city services, such as street improvements and new parks.

The Company Lakewood Bank and Trust began serving the Dallas area in 1941. Since then, it has expanded throughout Dallas and North Texas. Its assets for 1976 were $119.3 million, as compared with $99.9 million in 1975. Net income for 1976 was $1.01 million versus $.7 million in 1975.

Other Preservation Activities
Lakewood is currently the major participant in a home-improvement loan pool involving five other financial institutions. The project is intended to help low- and moderate-income families, and is guaranteed by the City of Dallas.

For further information contact:
A. L. Artie Barnett
Senior Vice President
Lakewood Bank and Trust Company
Gaston and LaVista Streets
P.O. Box 140000
Dallas, Texas 75214

Virginia Savage Talkington
Chairman of the Historic Dallas Fund
Historic Preservation League
5600 Swiss Avenue
Dallas, Texas 75214

House in Old East Dallas before renovation.

The same house after renovation.

Footnotes

1. Lakewood Bank and Trust Company, *Lakewood Bank and Trust Company Annual Report* (Dallas: Lakewood Bank and Trust Company, 1976), p. 4.

Ralston Purina Company

Summary In 1968, Ralston Purina, a leading producer of consumer food products and animal feeds, set up a wholly owned subsidiary, the LaSalle Park Redevelopment Corporation, to redevelop a 140-acre area of blighted urban real estate adjacent to its St. Louis corporate headquarters complex, Checkerboard Square. The program sought to create a self-sufficient, balanced community of residential, commercial, and industrial inhabitants. Originally, the company planned a great deal more new construction than rehabilitation of older structures, but pressure from local preservationists has resulted in something of a change in emphasis. Governmental delays have caused actual construction and rehabilitation to proceed much more slowly than expected. However, this unique project is the first renewal plan of its type and magnitude to involve federal, state, and local government programs, as well as the participation of a major industrial corporation. Ralston Purina has already invested nearly $2 million in the project, and expects to spend at least another $1.5 million before its completion.

Background Pierre Laclede founded St. Louis in 1764, setting up his fur-trading operations along the Mississippi near the spot where the famous Gateway Arch is located today. The LaSalle Park area is situated southwest of the Arch. It was first settled by Laclede's French followers; later inhabitants came from Germany, Ireland, Italy, and other European countries. At the turn of the century, a Lebanese population settled there. The Lebanese church, St. Raymond's Catholic Church, has since then been a symbol of neighborhood identity and cohesiveness. Even after many of the Lebanese moved away from the area, they continued to return to the church in its old quarters, a converted four-family brick flat. Today, persistent fund-raising efforts by the congregation have financed a new church building which has become the harbinger of the neighborhood's renewal.

The LaSalle Park area has always been a white working-class neighborhood. However, since World War II, many businesses have moved out. (Even Ralston Purina contemplated relocating its operations to the suburbs.) Houses have been neglected, abandoned, and vandalized, and most of the more successful residents have moved away, leaving primarily the poor.

The same range of problems as was afflicting this aging neighborhood was occurring in other parts of St. Louis, and by the early 1950s, the city was faced with a need for major urban renewal. Its initial reaction, like that of many other cities, was to wipe away the blight and start anew. Throughout the city, the nineteenth-century housing stock—primarily low-rise units on small lots or row houses—was demolished. Utilizing government funds, new medium-rise apartment buildings were constructed with the hope of attracting a racially and economically mixed population. But, because the whites, who were more mobile, continued to flee the city, the new projects soon became almost totally occupied by poor blacks.

A much publicized St. Louis public-housing project—Pruitt-Igoe—which attempted to provide housing on a large scale, failed, and in fact, this failure became a valuable lesson to renewal planners in many U.S. cities. Completed in 1954, Pruitt-Igoe consisted of 33 eleven-story block buildings containing 2,762 units. The design of the buildings on large, open, unprotected sites, and their unsatisfactory layout and poor construction led to safety hazards and deterioration so severe that many of the buildings have already been abandoned and demolished.

In the LaSalle Park area, the city's efforts at selective clearance resulted in land parcels too small to make total redevelopment feasible. This further detracted from the appearance and safety of the neighborhood, creating

Exterior view of the first home being completely rehabilitated by Ralston Purina Company's LaSalle Park Redevelopment Corporation. Resurfacing of streets and sidewalks has not yet been completed.

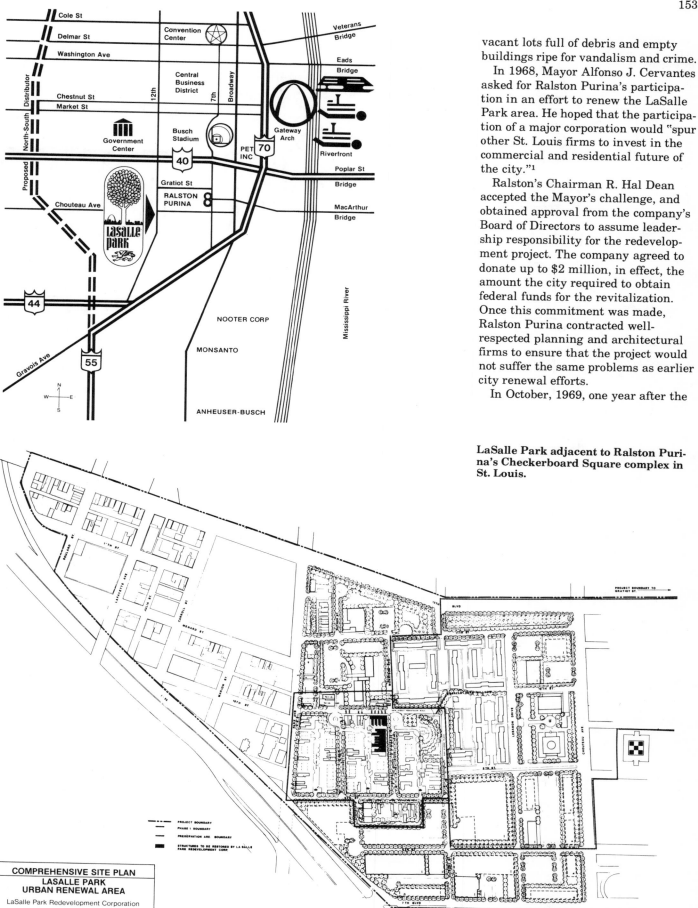

vacant lots full of debris and empty buildings ripe for vandalism and crime.

In 1968, Mayor Alfonso J. Cervantes asked for Ralston Purina's participation in an effort to renew the LaSalle Park area. He hoped that the participation of a major corporation would "spur other St. Louis firms to invest in the commercial and residential future of the city."[1]

Ralston's Chairman R. Hal Dean accepted the Mayor's challenge, and obtained approval from the company's Board of Directors to assume leadership responsibility for the redevelopment project. The company agreed to donate up to $2 million, in effect, the amount the city required to obtain federal funds for the revitalization. Once this commitment was made, Ralston Purina contracted well-respected planning and architectural firms to ensure that the project would not suffer the same problems as earlier city renewal efforts.

In October, 1969, one year after the

LaSalle Park adjacent to Ralston Purina's Checkerboard Square complex in St. Louis.

COMPREHENSIVE SITE PLAN
LASALLE PARK
URBAN RENEWAL AREA
LaSalle Park Redevelopment Corporation
Architects: Murphy, Downey, Wofford & Richman

154

Numbered buildings are to be preserved. Broken lines indicate proposed new housing.

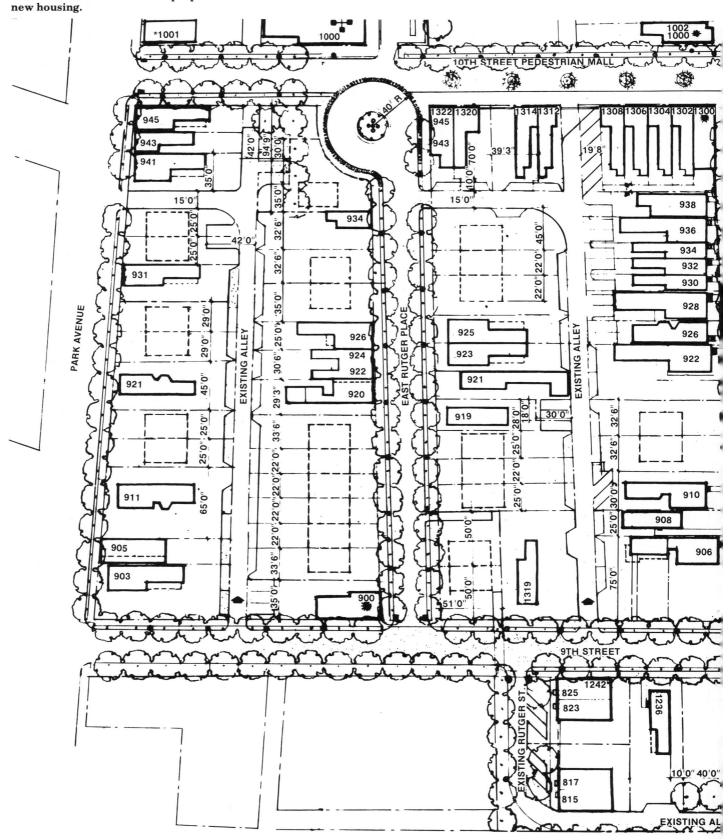

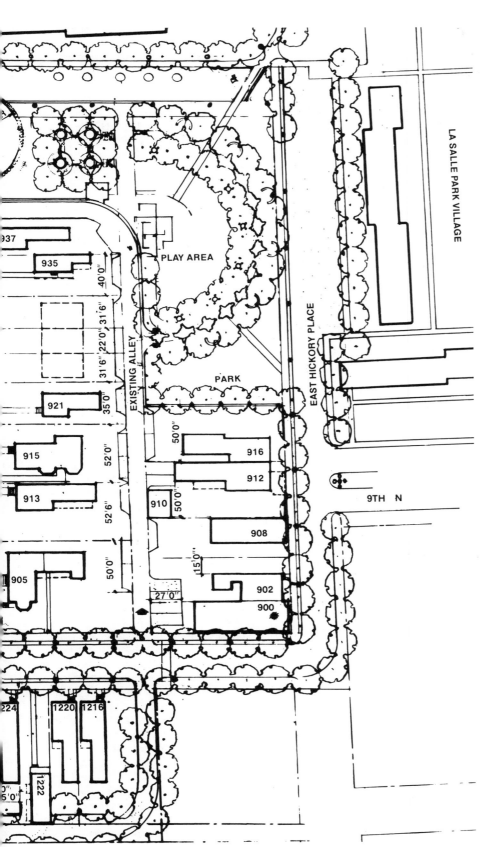

Mayor approached Ralston Purina, the company announced its redevelopment plan, a $30 million proposal to create a "newtown-intown."[2] The plan had to be approved by city and federal agencies, but it was designed to be implemented by the LaSalle Park Redevelopment Corporation, a subsidiary of Ralston Purina. While the company would supply personnel for this new subsidiary, as well as financial and legal management services, new construction and renovation was to be financed by a variety of federal programs. In 1969, it was estimated that the project—to be completed in three phases—would take about five years. The work in each phase consisted of the following:

Phase I
- Construction of 9 acres of new residential development, including 148 townhouse apartment units
- Construction of 2 acres of commercial development
- Construction of 6 acres of light industrial development
- Allocation of 3 acres for the new St. Raymond's Church complex
- Reservation of 24 acres for Ralston Purina's use

Phase II & III
- Development of the balance of the renewal area for:
  200 new townhouses
  400 apartments for the elderly
  rehabilitation of a small number of selected residential structures
- Development of additional commercial and industrial facilities
- Retention of all existing churches, social, and recreational facilities.

According to the St. Louis Land Clearance for Redevelopment Authority, the city's overall urban-renewal agency, all but 75 of LaSalle Park's 875 residences were in substandard condition as of 1969. There were 450 families and 200 single residents in the area. The total LaSalle Park project called for more than 1,500 new or rehabilitated housing units.

The proposal also called for tax incentives provided by the Missouri Urban Redevelopment Act to encourage additional commercial and light industrial development. Local institutions established in LaSalle Park would be preserved, and land would be set aside for their expansion.

Execution

Phase I. The project progressed gradually from proposal to dedication:

In February, 1971—sixteen months after the initial announcement, following much work with the planners, residents, and city agencies, a plan for "about 700 low rise dwelling units"[3] was submitted to the St. Louis Board of Aldermen and the U.S. Department of Housing and Urban Development (HUD).

In May, 1972—two-and-a-half years after the initial announcement, and after much planning, the company announced the approval of Phase I, involving demolition of buildings and new construction in 44 acres of the LaSalle Park urban-renewal area, by the St. Louis Land Clearance for Redevelopment Authority. Ralston Purina was also selected to develop the balance of the 140-acre area, pending the availability of federal and local funding.* The housing would be financed under the "Turnkey I" federal homeowner-opportunity program for low-and moderate-income families. In accordance with this program, Ralston Purina would sell the completed residences to the St. Louis Housing Authority which, in turn, would be reimbursed by federal funds.

In February, 1974—nineteen months later—Ralston Purina announced that the federal government had finally reserved funds for the construction of the 148 garden apartment and townhouse units in the initial phase of the project.

In April, 1975—ten months later—the official ground-breaking ceremony took place for 16 two-story buildings containing 30 two-bedroom units, 78 three-bedroom units, and 40 four-bedroom units. The St. Louis Housing Authority anticipated that the average rental would range from $115 to $130 per month, with the average gross income of residents between $6,000 and $10,000. The first units would be available for occupancy within twelve months.

Finally, in September, 1976—another seventeen months later—the dedication ceremonies were held. The new housing is now fully occupied.

*Five months earlier, in January, 1972, the federal government made $4 million available to the city to start the project.

By mid-1977, the LaSalle Park Redevelopment Corporation was working on Phase II and Phase III of its project. This was more than nine years after the project, which was originally scheduled to take a total of only five years, was conceived. But during the nine years, the corporation had learned a great deal about working with a neighborhood, a city and its many agencies, and about dealing with the complex, slow-moving federal bureaucracy.

Ralston Purina also learned how to work with local public-interest groups concerned with specific causes like the preservation of old buildings. The City of St. Louis and its Land Clearance for Redevelopment Authority (LCRA) had paid little attention to the architectural value of the many buildings they were eliminating in the name of renewal, and this strategy was not initially questioned by Purina. A 1971 "Architectural Survey of LaSalle Park" carried out by Heritage/St. Louis, a local preservation organization, indicated that about eight buildings still standing at that time could be considered "most significant architecturally." Another approximately ninety buildings in the area could be considered "architecturally significant," and another approximately 160 buildings were labeled as being of "some architectural interest for the neighborhood."[4] Among these buildings were seven houses in the St. John Nepomuk District which had been included in the National Register. As of 1975, when the ground breaking commenced on LaSalle Park Village, as the new construction in Phase I was called, almost ninety buildings in all three categories had been demolished.

Local preservationists were understandably disturbed. Carolyn Toft, now preservation planner of the Landmarks Association of St. Louis, Inc., had few kind words for the project in its early days, claiming that LCRA, the city, and the company were anything but sensitive to the opportunities for reusing existing buildings. However, since federal funds were being used to complete the project, the local agencies were required to justify the removal of historic buildings to obtain full funding. Ms. Toft notified the Advisory Council on Historic Preservation that

preservation was being completely ignored, and the Council sent the City of St. Louis a letter requesting compliance.

Later, Ms. Toft was appointed the Historic Preservation Officer for the St. Louis Community Development Agency, a body established in 1974 to administer Community Development Block Grants made by HUD. In this position, she worked with the city and Ralston Purina to draft a $2 million Community Development Block Grant funding program which included preservation as a key element of the development strategy. The program insured the preservation and renovation of architecturally important buildings still remaining in the Phase II and Phase III sections of the project.

Working closely with community groups, Ralston Purina redirected its plan for the residential development in Phase II. The company will invest over $500,000 to rehabilitate 13 of the 57 architecturally significant structures remaining in a three-block, six-acre parcel. It will offer them for sale to area families "at cost" and, if necessary, at a slight loss. According to Fred H. Perabo, Manager of the Ralston Purina Real Estate Division and President of the LaSalle Park Redevelopment Corporation, "Our investment is designed as a catalyst to demonstrate the possibilities in the area and will hopefully encourage other citizens to buy and renovate the remaining homes."[5]

The remaining houses in Phase II are being offered at cost to families who will renovate them. By mid-1977, over 70 percent of these had been sold, and buyers had expressed interest in Phase III houses. Renovation guidelines have been established to insure that the architectural integrity of the nineteenth-century buildings is preserved. Once the renovation work is complete, additional new housing will be built. A pedestrian mall, period lighting fixtures, a small park, and off-street parking for each dwelling are also planned for the area. New utility lines will be installed below ground.

In addition, the company has donated the historic Lucy Dolusic House to the Landmarks Association. The group will restore the exterior and sell the house to a family who will renovate the interior. Ralston Purina has also

New townhouse apartments.

donated $2,500 to the Landmarks Association for a revolving fund which will be used in the restoration.

Costs It is estimated that over $30 million in new investment, from both public and private sources, will be required to complete the LaSalle Park project. By 1977, nearly $12 million had been invested in Phase I, and renovation work in Phase II was underway. By mid-1977, Ralston Purina's share of this investment included:

Direct Contributions

• $1.2 million—a cash contribution to the City of St. Louis to help the city meet a $2 million goal enabling it to obtain $4 million in federal funds for the urban-renewal program. Ralston Purina's money was used for land acquisition, clearance, feasibility studies, and street improvements.*

• $500,000—an estimated amount spent on surveys, studies, reports, and staff time.

Additional Investment (Most of this money will be recovered as the project is completed.)

• $700,000—the cost of the land purchased from the LCRA for Phase I. Of the 44 acres purchased, the firm will retain 24 for its own expansion needs; 12 have been developed and sold for the new housing and the new church; and the remaining acres are to be developed for commercial and light industrial use.

• $750,000 to $1 million—required to purchase the remaining acreage in Phase II and III.

• $500,000—required to restore and renovate the thirteen houses in the Phase II preservation area. These houses will be sold at cost.

Problems The most significant problem for this corporation posed by participating in neighborhood renewal projects involving local, state, and federal programs has been the long time period necessary for the review and

*Since the inception of Phase I, the urban-renewal programs have been replaced by a program of Community Development Block Grants which no longer require the city to supply funds to obtain federal money.

approval mechanism to work. This has required more staff time than was anticipated and has increased Ralston Purina's costs.

Benefits LaSalle Park Redevelopment Corporation's President Fred Perabo described the benefits to Ralston Purina:

We have purchased property for our own use; the area has improved aesthetically, as well as from a safety standpoint; and our own investment in the area has been strengthened. A public relations "profit" has resulted. [6]

Chairman R. Hal Dean also gave an assessment of the project:

Now we can see that a once dying neighborhood has become a vital community, a place where people can live, work and prosper. [7]

Ralston's officer in charge of corporate social responsibility, John P. Bard, added:

The management of our company has gained credibility in the social responsibility arena. . . . As far as conclusions go, I believe that large corporations should and must seek ways to support efforts to improve our cities. Taking an active role can be more important, and more productive, than simply a dollar investment. A corporation can and should become a part of the community in which it operates. Clearly there are risks, but well conceived approaches and programs can be rewarding. [8]

In 1975, *Business and Society Review* awarded Ralston Purina recognition for improving urban life. The company was one of 13 winners selected from 45 applicants for a Corporate Responsibility Awards Program.

The company, city, and developer all learned that urban re-development requires—and benefits from—a respect for, and use of existing older buildings as well as the construction of new ones.

The Company Established in 1894 in a small feed store along the St. Louis Mississippi Riverfront, Ralston Purina has grown into the largest producer of commercial feeds for livestock and poultry in the world. Sales rose from $3.15 billion in 1975 to $3.39 billion in 1976. Net income in 1976 was $83 million, a decline from 1975's $99.5 million. Ralston Purina is also a leading producer of pet foods and consumer food products, such as cereals. Its corporate symbol, the Checkerboard, and its products are known throughout the world.

For further information contact:
Fred H. Perabo
President, LaSalle Park Redevelopment Corporation
Ralston Purina Company
Checkerboard Square
St. Louis, Missouri 63188

Footnotes

1. Ralston Purina Company, *News from Checkerboard Square*, October 31, 1969, p. 3.
2. *Ibid.*, p. 1.
3. Ralston Purina Company, *News from Checkerboard Square*, February 25, 1971, p. 1.
4. "Architectural Survey of LaSalle Park Area, St. Louis," (unpublished survey conducted by Heritage/St. Louis, May 7, 1971).
5. INFORM interview with Fred H. Perabo, Manager, Ralston Purina Real Estate Division; President, LaSalle Park Redevelopment Corporation, January 25, 1977.
6. *Ibid.*
7. Ralston Purina Company, *News from Checkerboard Square*, September 26, 1976.
8. INFORM interview with John P. Bard, officer, Corporate Responsibility, Ralston Purina Company, May, 1977.

LaSalle Park Preservation Area Marketing Office.

Summary In 1972, the former management of the South Shore National Bank decided to turn its back on its inner-city neighborhood and relocate in downtown Chicago. Area residents fought the move and in a landmark decision, the Comptroller of the U.S. Currency thwarted the bank's management. Local groups then approached Ronald Grzywinski, a banker and student of urban problems who had studied the possibilities and methods of setting up a neighborhood-development bank. He took over the bank in August, 1973, aided by a recent Federal Reserve ruling that allowed a bank holding company to establish a subsidiary that is both profit- and community-oriented. Under the new management, whose primary investment objective is neighborhood revitalization, depositors have been attracted to the bank; close cooperation has been established with community organizations, and some of the housing and commercial buildings have been partially rehabilitated. Both the bank's assets and the housing stock are appreciating.

Background South Shore (population 80,000), a turn-of-the-century area of broad, tree-lined streets, is located along Lake Michigan only fifteen minutes from Chicago's central downtown "Loop." The housing stock is diversified and includes early-twentieth-century mansions, large tracts of red-brick two-story middle-income residences, stucco and brick homes built by the affluent Irish in the 1920s and 1930s, and numerous bungalows dating from the same period. The area also possesses pockets of high-density walk-up rental buildings with six to thirty flats. Modern high-rise apartments line the lakefront. Although more than 75 percent of the dwellings are rental units, more than 75 percent of the geographic area is covered by single-family, owner-occupied houses. South Shore has three commercial strips.

Like many other urban areas in recent years, South Shore was a victim of the flight to the suburbs and a changing neighborhood population. A stable middle-class neighborhood rapidly deteriorated. Absentee landlords neglected buildings or abandoned them outright. Chicago's generous

grace period for nonpayment of property taxes—ten years—aggravated the situation. Federal Housing Administration loans were foreclosed, accelerating the demise of sound housing; and businesses fled the area. In 1960, only 1 percent of the residents were black. By 1970, 88 percent of the former residents had left the neighborhood, and it was 77 percent black.

The management of South Shore National Bank, the area's major financial institution, saw deposits steadily decrease from $72 million in 1967 to $47.8 million in 1972. In the same period, the bank's assets dropped from $78 million to $54.8 million. Management made little effort to relate to the community and its problems, and the general level of banking services declined. The building itself became dirty and unkempt.

In 1972, the bank announced that it would move to a new location in the Loop. However, before it could do so, it had to get the approval of the Comptroller of the Currency of the United States. The South Shore Commission, a local citizens' group, rallied and fought the bank's plan to abandon the neighborhood. In a landmark decision the Comptroller ruled:

South Shore National Bank has failed to show persuasive reason at this time for abandoning its present service area and leaving the South Shore community without a strong, established and adequately capitalized commercial bank.[1]

Following the decision, the South Shore Commission sought buyers for the bank. The Commission approached Ronald Grzywinski of nearby Hyde Park, former President of the Hyde Park Bank and Trust Company. Grzywinski and his associates, Mary Houghton and Milton Davis, had previously implemented progressive neighborhood-development financing, such as loans to minority businesses. In 1972, Grzywinski had just completed a three-year study at the Adlai Stevenson Institute and Center for Community Change. His research had convinced him that neighborhood banks should be the catalyst for neighborhood revitalization. Using a substantial pool of capital, knowledge of the social and economic conditions in their areas, and

locally trained personnel, neighborhood banks could profitably help stem the wave of decay. Grzywinski thought that:

A true development bank should be an innovative institution which continuously infuses capital, long-term credit, and technical assistance into social and economic improvement projects. It should possess the capacity to initiate development projects when other initiators are unavailable.[2]

Up to this time, commercial banks were legally able only to render financial services. However, the Federal Reserve had recently decided that banks could establish holding companies with community-oriented subsidiaries whose prime objective would be high-risk development. These subsidiaries would invest in and assist lower-income areas. Highly profitable, middle-income-oriented activities would be explicitly excluded. As a result, in 1972, Grzywinski and his colleagues formed the Illinois Neighborhood Development Corporation (INDC). After reviewing the financial statements of the South Shore National Bank and conferring with neighborhood residents, INDC proceeded to raise $3.2 million for acquisition of the bank. Nearly $1 million came from selling stock units of $160,000 each to six investors: foundations, individuals, and churches in the Chicago area. The remaining $2.2 million was obtained from a loan made by the American National Bank, located in Chicago's Loop.

Execution In August, 1973, the Illinois Neighborhood Development Corporation officially acquired the South Shore National Bank. The new management team, Ronald Grzywinski, Milton Davis, and Mary Houghton, wanted to restore the image of the bank both figuratively and literally. To assure continuity and improve morale, former employees of the bank were retained. Salaries were reviewed and raised, and the banking hall and exterior were refurbished. Mary Houghton describes the transformation that took place:

[At first] I was ashamed to say that I worked there, it was grubby and depressing. . . . People had been saying the bank must be in trouble, any place that looked as lousy as this one had to be in trouble. Then we fixed up the place and people began saying the bank must be doing real well, and that meant South Shore was doing better because not only were we staying here, but we looked prosperous.[3]

The new management team spent a good deal of time in the lobby, talking to present and potential customers over coffee. They went to neighborhood meetings to find out residents' wants and needs, to attract customers, and to restore the image of the bank. These efforts paid off. Deposits increased from $40.6 million to $48.1 million between 1973 and 1976.

The new management strengthened the organization of the bank and increased the staff. The Conventional Loan Divison, which administers business and personal loans and mortgages for those customers who meet credit requirements, made loans totaling $26.1 million in 1976. The percentage of the bank's portfolio loaned to the community increased from 25 percent to 33 percent, the latter being a much higher figure than at other Chicago banks. At the end of 1976, mortgage loans totaling $8.5 million were outstanding, an 18 percent increase over the previous year. Of this amount, $1.6 million was committed to seventy single-family and condominium mortgages in the South Shore community.

South Shore's most visionary banking innovation was the establishment of the Neighborhood Development Center (NDC). This profit-oriented di-

Two typical houses in Chicago's South Shore area.

vision screens and administers loans and mortgages to high-risk applicants, assists neighborhood residents who need special banking services, and helps implement revitalization projects in the community. The Center is financed by development deposits—minimum $1,000—from outside the South Shore neighborhood. While these depositors receive the same interest rates that other banks pay, South Shore makes it clear that a large portion of the revenues from such deposits will be used to improve the neighborhood and help borrowers who cannot meet conventional banking standards.

The NDC, headed by Mary Houghton, made $2.9 million in loans in 1976. These break down as follows:

New Development Loans: 1976[4]

Type of Loan

Small Business	$ 582,964
Community Organizations	115,689
Mortgage	1,416,065
Education	246,518
Home Improvement	321,835
Development/Personal	245,734
Total	$2,928,805

Of the NDC's mortgage and home improvement loans, 54 percent went for the purchase or renovation of properties in the South Shore community.

NDC deposits increased from less than $3 million in 1974 to nearly $8 million at the end of 1976. Additional NDC funds accounted for one-third of the total increase in the bank's deposits for 1976. Although the NDC is profit-oriented, margins are not as great as those of conventional divisions. This is due in part to the great expenditure of staff time high-risk loans require. The NDC funds are subject to separate audit.

The NDC provides other services for the community: it publishes a newsletter, *The Bread Rapper*, that tells of the bank's activities and gives consumer advice. It sponsors conferences on various aspects of banking that provide a better understanding of financial matters. The NDC also publishes a pamphlet, *Guide to Banking Services*, which familiarizes customers with banking practices.

Besides its financial commitments to South Shore, the staff of the NDC devotes much of its time to developing, and sometimes supporting, new projects with residents and local groups. To formalize this working relationship with the community, a nineteen-member Resident Advisory Board has been established, consisting of representatives of the nine local councils and other community organizations. Meetings of the Board are held bimonthly.

The Resident Advisory Board has been instrumental in creating the South Shore Area Development Corporation, whose objective is attracting business to the area. This independent nonprofit organization administers Small Business Administration (SBA) loans of up to $500,000 at 6⅝ percent interest for periods of up to 25 years. One of only a few such organizations in the country, the Development Corporation, in its first year, granted one loan for $275,000. As of mid-1977, two additional loans were under review.

At the end of 1976, the Resident Advisory Board also was responsible for the establishment of the South Shore Community Trust which will solicit and administer funds for commercial and rehabilitation pursuits. The Trust hopes eventually to distribute revenue to nonprofit organizations.

In addition to those projects already mentioned, South Shore Bank has been involved with and encouraged several other community organizations. The South Shore Block Club Coalition for United Action is rehabilitating nine postwar abandoned houses which it obtained from HUD. The bank's staff has lent its expertise. The project is utilizing a $30,000 Model Cities Administration grant.

Another neighborhood group is attempting to rescue a turn-of-the-century Spanish-style country club and golf course, which has been neglected since being taken over by the Chicago Park District. In cooperation with the Resident Advisory Board and the Neighborhood Development Center, this group is exploring different ways to make the club—now designated the South Shore Center—viable.

In the future, the bank plans to establish profitable development subsidiaries to rehabilitate multi-unit buildings and improve the area's commercial districts. It also wants to set up a nonprofit subsidiary to seek government and foundation funding for community service organizations.

The bank also sponsors a street-side banker who works in one of the most deprived parts of the community, known as Parkside, attempting to discover the needs of the area's people and to familiarize potential customers with the bank's services. This bank representative, whose salary is paid by a foundation, has been responsible for soliciting and processing several home-improvement loans. Commenting on his job, the street-side banker says:

At first we really weren't trusted, but lately that's changed. In one month we made seven home improvement loans; we've applied for a grant to landscape three empty lots as parks.[5]

Costs The INDC paid $3.2 million to purchase South Shore National Bank.

Problems Mary Houghton states:

The major problems are to run a profitable bank in an urban area with high transiency and a low-income segment while also pulling off neighborhood revitalization. The bank was moderately profitable in 1976, will hopefully improve on that performance in 1977, but it is a difficult management task.[6]

Benefits Between 1974 and 1976, the average single-family dwelling in South Shore has appreciated about 18 percent, from $22,500 to $26,500. Furthermore, because of the bank's efforts, developers and other banking institutions are investing in the area. Assisted by bank financing, the South Shore Villa, an older apartment building, has been renovated to provide 39 condominium units. Renewal Effort Service Corporation (RESCORP), a consortium of sixty Chicago savings and loan associations, rehabilitated 148 units in five apartment buildings. All the apartments have been rented. Since RESCORP found this undertaking profitable, it is currently renovating 154 additional apartments in six buildings. Commercial confidence is increasing: Walgreen's, a drugstore chain, is renovating one store and adding to another. Jewel Company, a supermarket chain, is planning to build a new 44,000-square-foot store, its second largest in the Chicago area. A letter written by Edwin W. Booth, Executive Director of the Cummins Engine Foundation and a member of the Board of the Illinois Neighborhood Development Corporation, clearly states the accomplishments and hopes of the South Shore National Bank:

The South Shore National Bank is an important experiment whose implications reach well beyond Chicago's South Shore Community. . . . It is beginning to show that neighborhood redevelopment can also be a source of superior profit performance. If successful, the Bank should set new performance standards, helping other financial institutions recognize that their own self-interests can best be served by similar actions.[7]

The Company Between 1975 and 1976, South Shore National Bank's assets rose from just under $42 million to over $54 million. Operating income rose over the same period from over $3.5 million to more than $4 million.

The Neighborhood Development Center audit for 1976 showed $66,953 in income, up from $29,292 the year before. Expenses also rose from $154,978 to $184,093.

For further information contact:
Mary Houghton
Vice President
South Shore National Bank of Chicago
71st and Jeffrey Boulevard
Chicago, Illinois 60649

Footnotes

1. South Shore National Bank of Chicago, *The Rebuilding of an American Neighborhood*, (Chicago: South Shore National Bank of Chicago, n.d.).
2. "Memorandum: Bank Companies as Neighborhood Development Corporation" from Ronald Grzywinski, Chairman of the Board, South Shore National Bank of Chicago, January 30, 1976, p. 3.
3. Judith Barnard, "Money Matters," *Chicago*, February, 1977, p. 100.
4. South Shore National Bank of Chicago, *1976 Annual Report and Neighborhood Development Audit* (Chicago: South Shore National Bank of Chicago, 1976), p. 23.
5. Barnard, *op. cit.*, p.104.
6. Letter from Mary Houghton, Vice President, South Shore National Bank of Chicago, to INFORM, July 11, 1977.
7. South Shore National Bank, *1976 Annual Report*, p.3.

Tasty Baking Company

Summary   In May, 1968, Paul R. Kaiser, President and Chairman of the Board of the Tasty Baking Company, started considering ways to arrest the urban decay beginning to afflict the neighborhoods adjacent to the company's Hunting Park Avenue headquarters in North Philadelphia. After meetings with a City Councilman, an expert on urban renewal, the head of a local industrial real estate firm, and a group of community leaders, it became apparent to Mr. Kaiser that there was little chance of government support to help stop the deterioration of the Allegheny West area. He decided, with the approval of the company's Board of Directors, to involve the Tasty Baking Company in improving conditions in the surrounding neighborhoods. This resulted in the establishment of the Allegheny West Community Development Project (AWCDP), a nonprofit organization.

Since its inception in 1968, the Project has rehabilitated 55 abandoned "shell" buildings, and now plans to rehabilitate approximately 50 each year. The AWCDP has been involved in every phase of community life, from assisting home buyers in obtaining mortgages and home improvement loans to supporting day-care centers, schools, neighborhood groups, and block associations. To date, Tasty Baking has spent $933,627 on the AWCDP. Other corporations have followed Tasty's example by contributing funds. The company itself, committed to its Allegheny West location, will spend $3 million to expand its own facilities there.

Background   After the decision was made to create the AWCDP, the area from the industrial complex along Hunting Park Avenue on the north to Clearfield Street on the south, and between 22nd Street and Ridge Avenue on the east and west respectively—was surveyed by the Jackson Cross Company, a Philadelphia industrial real estate firm. The area covers a total of ten city blocks north and south and six city blocks east and west. The survey examined the overall conditions there and particularly assessed the state of the exterior of the houses.

Allegheny West is almost purely residential, with the exception of some industrial facilities at the north end. It has a population of about 23,000, and approximately 6,300 single-family two-story row houses, which were built between 1900 and 1925. The housing quality of Allegheny West is erratic, with blocks of well-kept homes next to blocks riddled with poorly kept or boarded-up and abandoned houses. Most of the once numerous corner stores have been abandoned, and many yards are littered with broken glass and trash. The decay is even more extensive in the southern section, a tightly packed area with seemingly endless blocks of row houses; only two playgrounds, one playing field, and one park serve a population more than 43 percent of which is nineteen years of age or younger.

Prior to 1960, Allegheny West was what is commonly called a community in transition. Though it was not far from slum areas of the core city, south of Lehigh Avenue, it had been able to maintain its stability. Many of its residents were of Irish and Italian descent, 15 percent and 13 percent respectively, and there was a large community of eastern European Jews. Of the homes there, 83 percent were owner-occupied. However, during the decade of the 1960s, Allegheny West experienced a traumatic ethnic and socio-economic shift. By 1970, only 74 percent of its homes were owner-occupied (still far above Philadelphia's average of 60 percent). The neighborhood had gone from a middle-class/ working-class area to working-class and poor. Unemployment had risen from 5 percent to 7.2 percent. The percentage of families below poverty

level (16 percent) and the percentage receiving public welfare assistance (40 percent) in 1970, were both above the city's average. Of children under nineteen, 94 percent were black. Older buildings were abandoned, but rarely demolished. Overcrowding became a problem, since average family size grew, and little addition or improvement had been made to the existing housing stock since 1960.

Apparently, migration to Allegheny West was occurring from the slum areas to the south, and was beginning to bring its characteristic problems. Crimes against persons and property were increasing, and small industries were moving out of the area due to vandalism and the higher cost of security. The average level of education dropped to below the high school level, and the number of welfare recipients continued to increase. In 1960, more than one-third of the working force held white collar or professional jobs; by 1970, white collar workers constituted less than one-quarter of the jobholders. While the percentage of blue collar workers remained constant at 45 percent, that of unskilled laborers rose from 18 percent to 32 percent. It was after these changes in the character of the area that the Allegheny West Community Development Project came into being.

Tasty Baking Company came to the Allegheny West area in 1923. In that year, the company, which was rapidly expanding, left its original Philadelphia plant on Sedgely Avenue to move to its present facility at 2801 Hunting Park Avenue, a six-story structure covering approximately three-and-a-half acres and housing 1,900 of Tasty Baking Company's 2,200 employees. One of the reasons for the move in 1923 was the readily available labor supply in the surrounding residential areas of East Falls, Roxborough, and Allegheny West. Allegheny West alone supplied almost one-half of the work force.

Tasty Baking undertook the AWCDP with two goals in mind: the first was to preserve the equity of its stockholders, including 80 percent of the company's employees who take advantage of a stock-purchase plan; the second was to help serve and preserve the community of Allegheny West.

Execution For six months in 1968, exploratory meetings were held between Mr. Kaiser, local community leaders, and company employees examining the interdependence of the community and company. Mr. Kaiser first announced that a community-controlled organization would be formed by Tasty Baking with the task of improving a target neighborhood. This concept was abandoned before the project began, however, when Tasty Baking decided it was important to maintain initial control over the AWCDP and to take advantage of favorable tax deductions.

In 1968, the AWCDP was formed with the Greater Philadelphia Foundation, the nonprofit affiliate of the Greater Philadelphia Chamber of Commerce, acting as the vehicle for the renewal effort until the AWCDP became more familiar with the local community organizations. The goal of the AWCDP was to improve and renovate all derelict housing in Allegheny West as a way of "assisting community maintenance and improvement." Mr. Kaiser explained, "Tasty Baking's interest is primarily housing, although we realize the importance of education and jobs."[1] The company wished to boost real estate values and to attract home buyers to the area. Tasty committed $40,000 a year for three years, which was used to hire the AWCDP staff: a director and secretary housed in an office in the Tasty plant. There are now five full-time staff members: the Project Director, Phillip Price, who is a lawyer; a technical advisor, a former builder with teaching experience in architectural design and construction; an executive secretary; a secretary-bookkeeper; and a neighborhood representative. In 1969, the AWCDP began to assist those community organizations already in existence—the Adelphos Civic Association and the R-A-H Civic Association (Ridge Avenue, Allegheny Avenue and Hunting Park Association)—by providing financial, legal, and technical help where needed so that the residents could determine the Project's ultimate course of action. Although its primary interest is housing, more than 25 percent of staff time is devoted to individual counseling and assisting with the organization of community groups. From 1968 to 1977, Tasty spent a total of $933,627 (see table). At present, the AWCDP's Board of Directors consists of seven local businessmen, including Tasty's Chairman, Paul Kaiser, three community residents, and a member of the Philadelphia City Council.

Housing. Since late 1970, the AWCDP has rehabilitated more than 55 "shell" houses as single-family residences.

Rehabilitation work began slowly, since the Project Director had little experience in housing. It took nine months to work out a satisfactory mortgaging agreement with the Philadelphia National Bank, and one year for the first house to be rehabilitated and sold. In 1970, a technical advisor was hired to supervise all rehabilitation work. He decided that each house should be completely redesigned according to modern standards, with all structural faults corrected. Additional rooms and closets were to be added where necessary; plumbing, electrical, and heating systems revamped; all doors and windows replaced; a modern kitchen with new appliances installed—in most instances donated by co-sponsor, Sears, Roebuck and Company; the exterior of each house painted or sided; and the buyer given a guaranteed roof. The AWCDP has employed local labor so far, and most repairs of defects, however minor, are made by the Project for three years after sale.

The average purchase price for a shell is $600. The rehabilitation cost for a typical 1,240-square-foot three-bedroom row house is $13,900 or $11.20 per square foot. A new building with exactly the same facilities and square footage would cost twice as much: approximately $27,170, or $22 a square foot. The renovated house includes wall-to-wall carpeting, a washer-dryer, a full bath, a stove, and a refrigerator.

The AWCDP sells each house at a loss—the present average loss is $4,000—under a 25-year mortgage provided by an installment sale. For the first three years, the Project has title to the house and thereby retains the risk of loss. If a family defaults in the first three years, they are evicted and the property resold. Mortgages are obtained from four commercial banks: the Philadelphia National Bank, Fidelity Bank, Girard Bank, and Central Penn National Bank. From the Project's inception, there have only been three foreclosures after the 3-year period. The monthly payments include settlement costs, water and sewer rents, insurance, and real estate taxes.[2] The homes are usually sold quickly upon referral of applicants by community leaders, and their availability is publicized by word of mouth and poster advertising throughout Allegheny West.

Decaying row house in Allegheny West.

House renovated by Allegheny West Community Development Project.

In April, 1970, the AWCDP began Operation Facelift, which offered free advice about home maintenance and improvement in the form of Service Bulletins and other literature. The initial mailing brought responses from about 1,000 area households, about one in six. Anyone responding to it became a member of the "Development Team," and was sent a membership card, entitling him or her to discounts on home-maintenance supplies from five retail stores in the area, free advice on any home-improvement problem, Service Bulletins, and information about community matters. The Service Bulletins prepared for the members of the Development Team dealt with topics like roofing, plumbing, electrical work, painting and paneling, ceiling and floor tiles, and prices and contractors. All Bulletins were eventually consolidated into the *Allegheny West Community Handbook*, which has had two separate editions, and has been distributed to more than 2,500 households in the area.

In 1972, the AWCDP began the "Merit Award" program, which recognizes efforts made at home improvement by individuals either with or without the Project's help. By the end of the year, over 120 homeowners received these awards. They have encouraged increased neighborhood involvement and boosted residents' morale. Beginning in 1973, the Project also made available a team of mechanics to do home-remodeling work at a substantial savings.

Because of the AWCDP's success, in 1976, a Neighborhood Housing Services (NHS) unit was established in Allegheny West. NHS is a national program designed to help maintain and renew inner-city areas. Under the leaderhsip of Executive Director Julia Robinson and President Donald McGill, the NHS-Allegheny West has provided a source of private conventional loans for mortgages and home improvement, and helped obtain improved city services for the area. The local NHS is financed by approximately thirty banks as well as by a grant from the William Penn Foundation.

Education. The AWCDP has supplied assistance to several educational and child-care institutions. It provided the money to purchase juice and cookies for one year for twenty pre-school children at the day-care center located in the Berean Baptist Church. After that year, a Tasty employee and the head of a foundation took over the responsibility. The Project helped the center obtain a use certificate from the Philadelphia Zoning Board of Adjustment, so the center could receive regular medical and technical assistance from the city. In addition, it supervised renovation of the basement area which is used for the child-care center. Funds for the work came from members of Berean Baptist Church.

The AWCDP also supervised and coordinated the incorporation of an organization called Black Interested Parents, Inc. Under this incorporated structure, a group of working mothers became eligible to receive funds for operation of a pre-school child-care center. The AWCDP acted as negotiator for the John Greenleaf Whittier Elementary School in its effort to obtain financial support from the Philadelphia National Bank for what is now the Philadelphia National Bank-Whittier Reading Improvement Center. Finally, Tasty personnel donate several hours each week to the Thomas May Pierce School to tutor elementary school students in math and reading.

Jobs. Tasty and other local large industries have attempted to aid area residents by giving them preference in job consideration. In addition, Tasty and The Budd Company have instituted summer-job programs for teenagers to work on community improvements. At the end of each summer, the participating teenagers, working under the supervision of Tasty employees, receive certificates for "outstanding support to the community," signed by company Chairman Kaiser.

Community Affairs. The AWCDP has helped the local groups in their fight against the sources of problems in their respective neighborhoods. On several occasions, from 1969 to 1975, Phillip Price, the Director of the AWCDP, successfully represented R-A-H and Adelphos, local community organizations, at Liquor Control Board hearings; in 1974, he assisted community groups in their fight to have a long-time and very profitable State Liquor Store removed from its present site, 300 feet away from an elementary school.

In 1970, the AWCDP requested additional street lighting from the city to deter street crime. This request led to the allocation for lighting of over $48,000. That same year, the Project helped coordinate the efforts of the Ringgold Square Improvement Committee, and donated $3,628 to turn a run-down lot in the center of 61 houses into a park. Work on the park began in spring, 1970; co-sponsor, Morris, Wheeler & Co., Inc., donated steel railing for it, and Tasty Baking arranged the donation, from a paving contractor, of materials and labor to repair the broken surfacing tiles. The city cooperated by providing the labor to do the remaining work. Phillip Price provides general legal services to the community, while the Project's builder provides architectural services.

In 1973, the AWCDP was the subject of an in-depth study conducted by the Institute for Environmental Studies of the University of Pennsylvania for the U.S. Department of Housing and Urban Development. The Project was selected as a unique example of a privately financed neighborhood conservation effort.

The study focuses on two main questions: "the actual and potential impact of the AWCDP on the Allegheny West area, and the immediate causes of decay and abandonment in the neighborhoods where these problems are in their early stages."[3]

A voluminous account of the inception of the AWCDP, Tasty Baking Company's part in it, and its progress up through 1972, the study describes the economic changes that have shaken Allegheny West, the structure of the AWCDP, and the real estate market and its impact on the housing quality and economics of the area. It found that though whites are moving out of the area, many black residents and small businessmen are optimistic about the change taking place within their neighborhoods.

The interviewers also found that only 35 percent of area residents had heard of the work that Tasty Baking was doing, and that even fewer people recognized the AWCDP's activities. A quarter of those interviewed had heard of Operation Facelift, and three-quarters of those who knew of Tasty's housing activities described them as very helpful. In the ensuing five years, both the visibility and effectiveness of the AWCDP have increased dramatically.

Costs   In addition to the $933,627, donated by Tasty Baking to the AWCDP from the time of its inception in 1968 through 1976, the company planned to contribute another $300,000 in 1977. Tasty's annual allocation of $40,000 constituted the Project's entire operating budget until September, 1970, when Mr. Kaiser began meeting with heads of other locally based corporations to obtain funds for the coming years. Eight other firms are now contributing regularly and account for between 10 percent and 20 percent of all contributions made in any one year.

Beyond Paul Kaiser's involvement, other Tasty Baking employees have worked with the Project since its inception: the Treasurer, Controller, Assistant Treasurer, Art Director, Public Relations Manager, and Personnel Director. Tasty has also provided office space, as well as telephones, duplicating facilities, and stationery to the AWCDP.

Problems   The AWCDP has found major problems in reeducating some residents of Allegheny West. Many people did not know or understand and had to be instructed in how to maintain their newly renovated homes. The AWCDP also devoted much time helping existing community groups become better organized to increase their effectiveness in dealing with the city.

Approximately 15 percent of the new residents in the renovated homes default within the initial three-year period. Some of these people have refused to move, at times resulting in complicated legal battles.

Many new residents have also had problems adjusting to their new homes. The first renovated structure was sold to a minister in 1970, who made the home available to a needy family. This family had several children, and had previously lived in a one-room apartment. After several months of living in their new home, the family moved back to their apartment; coping with a full-size house was too drastic a change.

Benefits   Federal and state tax benefits are available to contributors to the AWCDP. Since the latter part of 1968, the Commonwealth of Pennsylvania has granted tax credits under the Neighborhood Assistance Act to corporations which spend money on improving impoverished neighborhoods. This Act has provided corporate contributors with credits against corporate net reserve taxes of up to 50 percent of monies donated to the Project.

The combined federal and state tax situation is encouraging. Prior to March 19, 1977, approximately 77 cents out of every corporate dollar contributed to the AWCDP was deductible against income for federal or state tax purposes. Since March 19, 1977, for "special program priorities," of which the AWCDP is one, the Commonwealth grants a tax credit of 70 percent. Each contributing company can now deduct 89½ cents of every dollar given.

If a company doing business in Pennsylvania earns more than $25,000, and contributes $10,000 under the recently liberalized Neighborhood Assistance Act, tax credits reduce the actual cash outlay as follows:

Contribution to The Allegheny West Foundation	$10,000
Less State and Federal Income Taxes (9½ percent—Corporate Net Income Tax Rate—of $10,000 and 48 percent of remainder—$9,050, respectively)	5,294
Net Cost before Credit	4,706
Pennsylvania Tax Credit (70 percent) $7,000	
Less Federal Income Tax (48 percent of $7,000) 3,360	
Net Credit After Taxes	3,640
Net Cost of Contribution	1,066

Tasty's leverage in the business community has greatly aided the AWCDP in dealing with local merchants, contractors, and financial institutions, as well as in obtaining increased services from the city. The Project has attracted more and better medical services to the area; several doctors have opened practices there.

Due to Tasty's efforts, many corporations have joined the AWCDP's war on deterioration. The success of the Project has confirmed the company's decision to remain in Allegheny West and continue to upgrade the area. As a natural outgrowth of this policy, Tasty recently purchased a large vacant industrial building and the surrounding land for $1 million and will spend $1.8 million to improve the complex for additional corporate facilities.

The AWCDP should, in time, realize its intention of rehabilitating all derelict property in Allegheny West. Although in the beginning, the rate of abandonment was very high, abandonment has ceased in recent years. Private investment, in the form of small-scale speculation and investor interest, is now reappearing. In 1970, a shell property sold for $350; today it sells for over $2,600. The AWCDP's managers estimate that a continuation of the current rate of rehabilitation of fifty houses a year, coupled with the vital program of the Neighborhood Housing Services, and the addition of new large-scale employers to the area, will in four years bring about a takeover by the private real estate sector. At that point, the stabilization of Allegheny West will be a fact.

The Company The Tasty Baking Company was founded in Philadelphia in 1914 by Phillip J. Baur, a baker, and Herbert C. Morris, a salesman. The first product was a pre-sliced and iced individually wrapped cake, a revolutionary item at a time when almost all cake was baked at home. The product caught on, and Tasty Baking expanded. In the 1930s, it introduced rectangular fruit pies that further increased sales. In 1965, Tasty Baking started diversifying into other product lines: toys, graphic arts, and cookies. The main baking plant is located in North Philadelphia, and houses 1,900 of the company's 2,200 employees.

Total sales were $157.4 million in 1976, up from $146.2 million in 1975; the earnings for 1976 were $6.66 million, up from $6.45 million the previous year.

An excerpt from the company's 1976 Annual Report reflects Tasty's concern about social issues:

In the area of social responsibility, our neighborhood approach to urban renewal, begun in 1968, has come of age. It is now receiving community development funds from the City of Philadelphia. To us, this is compelling evidence that government agrees the best way to halt inner city decay is through projects similar to our three-way Allegheny West partnership among business, government, and the citizens themselves.[4]

Other Preservation Activities. At the Franklin Institute's new Science Park, Tasty Baking has reconstructed two row houses, one deteriorated and one rehabilitated, to show what the AWCDP, in cooperation with the residents of the area and local government, has accomplished. A film and illustrative material accompany the exhibit and show the process and cost of rehabilitation.

For further information contact:
Phillip Price, Jr.
Secretary and Director
The Allegheny West Foundation
2801 Hunting Park Avenue
Philadelphia, Pennsylvania 19129

Footnotes

1. Institute for Environmental Studies, University of Pennsylvnia, "The Allegheny West Community Development Project: An Experiment in Privately Financed Neighborhood Conservation," (mimeographed, prepared for the U.S. Department of Housing and Urban Development, 1973), chap. 3, p. 12.
2. Allegheny West Community Development Project, *A Unique Approach to Urban Development*, (Philadelphia: Allegheny West Community Development Project, n.d.), pp. 5–6.
3. Institute for Environmental Studies, *op. cit.*, chap. 1, p. 2.
4. Tasty Baking Company, *Tasty Baking Company 1976 Annual Report* (Philadelphia: Tasty Baking Company, 1976), p. 3.

Cash Contributions to Allegheny West Community Development Project
1969–1976

1968–1969

Tasty Baking Company		$ 37,200.

1970

Tasty Baking Company		$ 54,028.*
Cassidy/Richlar, Inc.	$ 1,667	
Morris, Wheeler & Co., Inc.	3,333.	
Penn Fishing Tackle Mfg. Co.	833.	
Rosenau Brothers, Inc. (Foundation)	1,000.	
Sears, Roebuck & Co.	6,667	
Steel Heddle Mfg. Co.	500.	
Other		$ 14,000.
Total		$ 68,028.

*$3,000. of this amount was from Tasty Baking Company's Foundation.

1971

Tasty Baking Company		$ 42,873.
Crown Printing Company	$ 50.	
Penn Fishing Tackle Mfg. Co.	2,500.	
The Pep Boys—Manny, Moe & Jack	500.	
Philadelphia Electric Company	5,000.	
Rosenau Brothers, Inc. (Foundation)	3,000.	
Other		$ 11,050.
Total		$ 53,923.

1972
Tasty Baking Company $120,792.

Helen D. G. Beatty Trust	$ 1,500.
The Budd Company	1,000.
Container Corporation of America Foundation	1,000.
Morris, Wheeler & Co., Inc.	10,000.
Penn Fishing Tackle Mfg. Co.	2,500.
Philadelphia Electric Company	10,000.
Rosenau Brothers, Inc. (Foundation)	500.
Sears, Roebuck & Co.	7,000.
Strauss Foundation	1,000.

Other $ 34,500.
Total $155,292.

1973
Tasty Baking Company $107,550.

Helen D. G. Beatty Trust	$ 1,000.
The Budd Company	1,500.
Container Corporation of America Foundation	1,000.
Philadelphia Electric Company	10,000.
Philadelphia National Bank	1,500.
Rosenau Brothers, Inc. (Foundation)	1,000.
Strauss Foundation	1,500.

Other $ 17,500.
Total $125,050.

1974
Tasty Baking Company $147,500.

Container Corporation of America	$ 1,000.
The Fidelity Bank	500.
Girard Bank	500.
Morris, Wheeler & Co., Inc.	5,000.
Penn Fishing Tackle Mfg. Co.	2,500.
Philadelphia Electric Company	10,000.
Royal Electric Supply Co.	1,000.
Steel Heddle Mfg. Co.	500.

Other $ 21,000.
Total $168,500.

1975
Tasty Baking Company $202,500.

Alexander & Alexander, Inc.	$ 100.
The Budd Company	6,000.
Container Corporation of America	1,500.
Morris, Wheeler & Co., Inc.	5,000.
Philadelphia Electric Company	10,000.
Steel Heddle Mfg. Co.	8,000.
Van Tents, Inc.	100.

Other $ 30,700.
Total $233,200.

1976
Tasty Baking Company $221,184

The Fidelity Bank	$ 200.
The Budd Company	8,000.
F.M.C. Corporation (Foundation)	750.
Van Tents Inc.	100.
Steel Heddle Mfg. Co.	10,000.

Other $ 19,050.
Total $240,234.

American Broadcasting Companies, Inc.

Commercial Redevelopment

Summary In July, 1974, American Broadcasting Companies, Inc. (ABC), acquired the Historic Towne of Smithville in southern New Jersey for $8 million. This historic village complex contains restaurants, shops, and a museum village. ABC's purchase was the first instance of a publicly held company's buying a historic village. To date, ABC has spent $1.5 million to renovate the Towne.

Background A rambling stagecoach inn, whose original section dates from about 1787, was the nucleus for the development of the flourishing Historic Towne of Smithville complex. In 1949, Mr. and Mrs. Fred Noyes purchased this rundown historic inn, and renovated it, establishing a restaurant. Through the years, they moved additional vintage buildings from southern New Jersey to the thirty-acre site, and renovated these structures as restaurants and shops. New compatible buildings were constructed as Smithville became an increasingly popular tourist attraction.

In recent years, the Noyeses had been developing a separate Living Village as part of the Historic Towne, again utilizing historic New Jersey buildings from the late eighteenth and nineteenth centuries. Several structures were renovated and furnished with authentic period pieces. Now known as the Old Village, this is an additional attraction of the Towne which also provides theater, concerts, lectures, and craft shows.

Several years ago, wanting more leisure time, the Noyeses decided to sell the Historic Towne.

Execution ABC was approached by a broker, and purchased the Historic Towne of Smithville from the Noyeses in July, 1974, for $8 million, to be paid over a four- to five-year period.

After the purchase by ABC, Mr. and Mrs. Noyes stayed with the operation until they retired in November, 1975. During the transition period, ABC invested about $1.5 million to complete the Old Village. All 33 buildings were renovated, including private houses, a fire house, a blacksmith shop, and Liederkranz Hall, a social hall. The houses are appropriately furnished with authentic period pieces. The completely landscaped Village, depicting life in a typical southern New Jersey community from the 1820s to 1850s, was opened to the public in spring, 1975. Today, each house has a resident artisan demonstrating local crafts, such as glass blowing, wood carving, weaving, spinning, apple-doll making, leathercraft, and pottery.

Although the Historic Towne of Smithville is less profitable than ABC's television operations, television, radio, and press promotion in the contiguous Delaware Valley area is expected to increase margins.

Costs To date, ABC has spent a total of more than $9.5 million for the purchase and renovation of Historic Smithville.

Benefits Besides being profitable, the Historic Towne of Smithville is an asset to other divisions of ABC. In January, 1976, ABC televised a two-hour Bicentennial show utilizing various historic sites throughout the country, including the Towne. This of course served to publicize the Smithville venture as well.

Historic Smithville employs about 800 people in the summer and 350 in the winter. With ABC's advertising and promotional help, receipts at the Old Village have tripled.

The Company American Broadcasting Companies, Inc., is an entertainment conglomerate whose operations include television and radio networks, theaters, and special-attraction parks. In 1954, Leonard Golden, the founder of ABC and currently its Chairman, helped finance California's Disneyland, and in the same year, ABC bought Silver Springs, Florida, a special-attraction park. Through the years, it has expanded this property to include not only subtropical and underwater features, but also an Early American Museum featuring displays of horse-drawn vehicles and cars. In 1957, ABC purchased another Florida entertainment park, Weeki Wachee, where young women costumed as mermaids perform in an underwater amphitheater. These two wholly owned theme parks have been highly profitable. However, a wildlife park in Largo, Maryland, has proven less successful.

In 1976, ABC's revenues amounted to $1.3 billion, representing an 18 percent increase over 1975's $1.1 billion. Net income rose from $17 million to $71.4 million over the same period. With increased profit margins, earnings per share improved to $4.05 in 1976, versus 99 cents the year before.

For further information contact:
Michael Winter
Director of Marketing
American Broadcasting Companies, Inc.
1330 Avenue of the Americas
New York, NY 10019

Frank Lyons
President and General Manager
Historic Towne of Smithville
Rte. 9
Smithville, NJ 08201

The Smithville Inn (c. 1787), the nucleus of Historic Smithville.

Summary Bethlehem Steel, the second largest steel producer in the country, has taken an active role in preservation causes, particularly in its hometown of Bethlehem, Pennsylvania. The company has been a major contributor to Historic Bethlehem, Inc. (HBI), a voluntary nonprofit community organization founded in 1964 to preserve and restore Bethlehem's eighteenth-century Moravian community. In 1975, its support for HBI included a donation of $100,000 in Lehigh Valley Industrial Park Bonds plus $50,000 in accumulated interest. The following year, it sponsored a study by the Urban Land Institute on the redevelopment of downtown Bethlehem's commercial area, which is adjacent to Historic Bethlehem. Implementation of a redevelopment program for this commercial area began in 1977.

Background Bethlehem, Pennsylvania was founded in 1741 by a group of German-speaking Protestants known as Moravians. By 1747, the town had 32 industries in operation and a variety of businesses, trades, and crafts fostered by the hard-working Moravians. This wealth of economic activity made the town almost self-sufficient. But the nineteenth century brought some drastic changes to Bethlehem. New technologies made most of the early industries outmoded, and the buildings which had housed them were either torn down or put to new uses.

By the twentieth century, only a few buildings of historic importance remained. These were surrounded by an automobile junkyard. When the few remnants were threatened by a flood in the mid-1960s, it became clear that decisive action would have to be taken, or they would be lost.

Execution Flood-control measures were instituted, and the citizens of Bethlehem rallied to save what was left of the colonial industrial area; Historic Bethlehem, Inc., was founded in 1964. Bethlehem Steel donated $125,000 at the new organization's inception to help pay for administrative expenses and archeological surveys. Assisted by Bethlehem Steel and other individuals and businesses, HBI has expanded rapidly. To date, five buildings have either been restored or totally reconstructed. In addition, five sites of historic value have been identified, and parts of the foundations of four former structures have been located.

The first building restored by HBI was the Tannery, built in 1761. The structure had been an industrial facility until 1873, when it was converted to tenement housing, and later, to a laundry. The restoration, begun in 1971 and completed at a cost of $250,000, has provided HBI with its main exhibit area, including displays on tanning, spinning, weaving, and pottery. The reconstruction of the Spring House, a log structure whose prototype had been built in 1764, was completed in 1971 at a cost of $43,000. In 1972, HBI restored the 1762 Waterworks. It was intact but required extensive interior and exterior improvements which took four years and $125,000 to accomplish. HBI also restored the Goundie House, built by a prosperous brewer in 1810. The house, opened in 1976, contains a museum shop and several period rooms, including a kitchen. In 1976, HBI also made structural improvements costing $23,000 on the Grist Miller's House, a 1782 building with an 1832 brick addition.

HBI has located and surveyed the sites of many of the other buildings in the colonial industrial complex, including the Bark Shed and Oil Mill. The organization conducts walking tours of the area with guides often dressed in eighteenth-century Moravian fashions.

In 1975, Bethlehem Steel donated $100,000 in Lehigh Valley Industrial Park Bonds to HBI. These bonds, which had been issued in 1963 to finance construction of buildings and support facilities for the industrial park, paid 5 percent interest annually and matured in March, 1975. Instead of redeeming the bonds, Bethlehem Steel, in an innovative gesture of support, donated them to HBI. HBI also received the accumulated interest on the bonds—amounting to $50,000—which Bethlehem Steel had not collected through the years. HBI's budget in 1977 was $119,000.

Many Bethlehem Steel employees, including high-level management officials, have been and continue to be active in HBI.

Study on the Revitalization of the Downtown Business District. In spring, 1976, Bethlehem Steel financed a $40,000 study of ways to revitalize and redevelop downtown Bethlehem. The published study was conducted by the Urban Land Institute, an independent Washington-based research group established in 1936 to examine land-use trends and to help identify the best and most efficient development methods.

Due to suburban competition, the Bethlehem Plaza Mall, a new shopping center, was finding it difficult to attract department stores, and leasing was proceeding slowly. The Urban Land Institute's study suggested that downtown Bethlehem would benefit more from taking into account the tourism inspired by HBI's colonial industrial area than from the addition of large shopping and office areas. The study found that many of the stores along Main Street were of Victorian vintage. It emphasized utilizing their unique nature to attract business, and suggested developing specialty stores, such as ice cream parlors, antique stores, and craft shops, rather than large supermarket complexes. A mall-like atmosphere would be encouraged by two large pedestrian walkways lined with benches and trees. Each store owner would be responsible for his own frontage, but each structure would have to conform to standards set by the city to maintain a unity of atmosphere. This would create a Main Street more effectively linked to the adjacent HBI industrial area. The restoration would also attract shoppers and tourists to the Bethlehem Plaza Mall through development of a "hinge block" at the end of Main Street. This link to the new mall would contain a variety of sites of interest, including the restored colonial Sun Inn, and a new performing arts center and garage.

The Sun Inn, a colonial inn built in 1758, would be both a tourist attraction—"George Washington slept here"—and a functioning inn. The proposed 450-seat performing arts center would help the area attract business. A parking facility, which opened in December, 1976, is located adjacent to the Bethlehem Plaza Mall, and shops between the garage and the mall serve as a link between performing-arts patrons and mall shoppers.

In order to implement the Urban Land Institute's proposals, the study suggested the formation of the Committee for Center City Greater Bethlehem (CGB), a nonprofit corporation. This organization, composed of concerned citizens and a staff executive, would help identify community problems, serve as a catalyst in spurring community action, provide nonpartisan leadership to projects undertaken, and secure cooperation from city or state government agencies. The CGB would require an annual budget of $125,000 and would need a five-year pledge commitment to ensure its effectiveness.

Hotel Bethlehem. In response to the Urban Land Institute's study, Bethlehem Steel is also currently investigating the possibility of further improving the Hotel Bethlehem, of which it is part owner. The Hotel has been a main tourist attraction and convention center since its construction in 1921. The company has renovated and improved parts of the building over the years: in 1963, the exterior was completely renovated at a cost of $300,000; in 1966, a parking garage was added; the Continental Dining Room was completed in 1969; and the interior was refurbished in 1973.

Costs In addition to its initial $125,000 donation and the $150,000 in Lehigh Valley Park Bonds and interest, Bethlehem Steel supports HBI fund-raising campaigns. It also paid for the Urban Land Institute's $40,000 study. The company has made additional expenditures on renovations and improvements of the Hotel Bethlehem. But the figures on its costs in this area were not available, nor was information on tax benefits gained by Bethlehem Steel through its donations to HBI.

Benefits Bethlehem Steel's donations to HBI have allowed the organization to renovate or reconstruct the Tannery, Goundie House, the Waterworks, Spring House, and the Grist Miller's House, helping make the complex a major local tourist attraction, and bringing economic benefits to the City of Bethlehem. According to Dennis Scholl, an official of the Bethlehem Chamber of Commerce, HBI's restorations and reconstructions attract about 20,000 visitors per year.[1]

The implementation of the Urban Land Institute's study could help revitalize downtown Bethlehem's commercial area. The expansion of HBI and the development of downtown Bethlehem may draw more people to the area and could increase business for the Hotel Bethlehem and other commercial establishments. The company's contributions are also an important factor in generating goodwill in its home city.

The Company Bethlehem Steel is the second largest steel maker in the United States, processing 15 percent of the nation's raw steel. Its turn-of-the-century Bethlehem facility is the largest structural-steel-producing plant in the country. Bethlehem Steel is also the principal employer in the Lehigh Valley, employing almost 20,000 people from Bethlehem and the surrounding area.

In 1976, company revenues were $5.3 billion, a 5.5 percent increase over the previous year's $5.03 billion. However, net income declined 30.6 percent from $242 million in 1975 to $168 million in 1976. Bethlehem Steel's principal markets are: construction, 22 percent; transportation, 29.5 percent; service centers and processors, 20 percent; machinery, 10.2 percent; and other, 18 percent.

Other Preservation Activities. Bethlehem Steel contributed $30,000 for the renovation and relocation of the Johnstown Flood Museum, commemorating one of the country's worst natural disasters, which took place in 1889.

The company has also donated funds for the re-creation of a historic oil boom town, Gladys City, Texas. This town became famous in January, 1901, when two men made a strike which produced twice as much oil as all the wells in Pennsylvania. It was here that four major oil companies, Mobil, Exxon, Gulf, and Texaco, began. The museum-city, now open to the public, includes clapboard houses of the 1880s, oil derricks, wooden tanks, and oil-field-equipment display areas. Future plans call for relocating an existing monument and museum to the re-creation site.

In addition, Bethlehem Steel has donated a steel door to cover the mouth of a pre-Civil War Underground Railway tunnel at the Orchard Street Church in Baltimore, Maryland, used to aid slaves from the South to reach the free North. The church, built in 1828, is a major part of the historic section of Baltimore, and its restoration is a local Bicentennial effort. The company also helped produce "The Underground Tunnel," an audio-visual presentation on the tunnel and its history.

For further information contact:
J. V. Robertson
Manager of Community Affairs
Bethlehem Steel Corporation
Martin Tower
Bethlehem, Pennsylvania 18016

(on facing page)
An 1810 house, restored by Historic Bethlehem, Inc. (Historic Bethlehem, Inc.)

(below on facing page)
The Tannery (c. 1761). (Historic Bethlehem, Inc.)

Footnotes

1. INFORM interview with Dennis Scholl, Director of Convention and Visitors Bureau, Bethlehem Area Chamber of Commerce, September, 1977.

Corning Glass Works

Summary In Corning, New York, Corning Glass Works is contributing to urban revitalization by providing the leadership and financial support to help restore and preserve the original nineteenth-century character of a four-block downtown commercial street. Market Street's basically sound buildings suffered from neglect and disfiguration over many years. In 1972 they were, further, hit by a devastating flood. That same year, to help reverse the fortunes of the area, the Market Street Restoration Program was developed with seed money from the Corning Glass Works Foundation. A team of professional consultants conducted studies to map out appropriate restoration and revitalization plans. These plans were coordinated with major urban-renewal plans developed in 1970 for an eight-square-block area directly east of Market Street.

In 1974, the Market Street Restoration Agency, a private, nonprofit corporation, fully supported by grants from the Corning Glass Works Foundation, was established to assist local businesses in revitalizing the street. So far, more than 75 percent of the store owners on Market Street have participated in the Program. Corning Glass has contributed close to $3 million to the Market Street project and to area urban renewal over the past five years. The company's reasons are clear: to support the community in which its employees live and work; and to make the town a more desirable environment which will attract and keep good employees.

Background The town of Corning is located on the banks of the Chemung River in a beautiful valley in Steuben County. It is near both the recreation and resort area of the Finger Lakes and the intersection of Routes 15, 17, and 81, major east-west and north-south traffic arteries in western New York State. This central location and the existence of the Corning Glass Center and Museum, which contains one of the finest glass collections in the world, have helped make Corning the third largest tourist site in the state: it attracts more than 750,000 people a year. Until recently, however, most tourists only passed through the town on their way to the Glass Center.

The Corning Glass Works has been headquartered in Corning since 1868, and it is the largest employer in the area.

Downtown Corning's Market Street is a typical American "Main Street," a four-block commercial street with an assortment of two- and three-story structures built between 1880 and 1910. Like many older downtown commercial districts across the country, Market Street has suffered from the growth of the suburbs and a loss of business to surrounding shopping centers.

Market Street store owners initially resisted this loss of business by trying to "modernize" their stores with new facades and larger, more contemporary signs. But these efforts failed to attract customers, and many merchants were forced to close down and move out.

In 1970, an urban-renewal plan, financed in part by the Corning Glass Works Foundation, and coordinated by James Sheaffer, Executive Director of the Corning Urban Renewal Agency, was developed for an eight-square-block downtown area. Geddes, Brecher, Qualls, and Cunningham, architects and urban design consultants from Princeton, New Jersey, and Philadelphia, Pennsylvania, were hired to conduct studies and develop the renewal plans. They were assisted by Davis A. Chiodo, an architect and Manager of Product and Business Development for the Corning Glass Works. The studies resulted in proposals for a new city hall, a new public library, a new civic center/ice rink, a new 125-room hotel, and residential and commercial complexes. Market Street was to become a pedestrian retail/commercial mall.

The idea of restoring Market Street to its turn-of-the-century character did not arise from the urban renewal plans. It came later in 1971 and 1972 when Thomas S. Buechner, President of the Corning Glass Works Foundation, began to promote the idea, perhaps partially inspired by the efforts in the late 1960s of two women from the local historical society, Virginia Wright and Jean Wozinski, who had tried to interest Market Street merchants in restoring their buildings. Buechner had been the Director of the Brooklyn Museum prior to joining Corning as President of Steuben Glass and Chairman of the Foundation's Board of Trustees. He convinced many local merchants and the Corning Urban Renewal Agency of the business benefits of restoring and maintaining the scale and unified style of architecture along Market Street.

Market Street in Corning, New York consists of four blocks of two-, three-, and four-story commercial buildings dating from the turn of the century. (Corning Glass Foundation)

Facades along Corning's Main Street. (Market Street Restoration Agency)

Execution A Restoration Committee was established which included Buechner, Sheaffer, Chiodo, Mayor Joseph J. Nasser, and eighteen other Corning citizens. Geddes, Brecher, Qualls, and Cunningham suggested that John Milner and the National Heritage Corporation, a firm specializing in restoration architecture, be retained to study and plan the Market Street Restoration Program. A seed grant from the Corning Glass Works Foundation would support the project in the planning stage. The Program's objectives were:

1. To reestablish Market Street as a unique commercial center.

2. To establish within an attractive environment a downtown that reflects the quality of life in the community; the quality of its people, organizations, business, and industry.

3. To preserve structures that possess a rare uniformity of architectural style and character as a downtown attraction for the thousands of visitors who annually tour the Corning Glass Center and other area attractions.[1]

The overall plan dealt with such issues as: traffic and pedestrian flow, parking, improved lighting and signs, and landscaping, as well as building rehabilitation. Rehabilitation guidelines, shaped by the local historical society's extensive research of old photographs of Market Street, were published and distributed to insure appropriate facade treatment. Facades were to be restored to their original design where possible or to new designs that would harmonize with the scale of the building, the configuration of windows and doors, and the nature and color of the predominant building material.* The Program aimed at re-establishing the small, pleasant scale of a nineteenth-century shopping street, and at developing a "sense of a special unified space."[2] In addition to the rehabilitation guidelines, sign guidelines and

*Prior to the restoration concept, the Corning Glass Works had contributed to the modern "cover-ups" on two of these old storefronts. The company produced a glass-ceramic wall panel material that had been tested on a store and a bank along Market Street.

design recommendations for public-space developments were also set forth.

Although the Restoration Program was conceived in 1972, it did not get into full swing until 1974. A major disaster hindered restoration progress, although in the long run, it may have stimulated greater citizen participation and support. Hurricane Agnes, struck Corning in the summer of 1972, and the Chemung River flooded the town. More than 60 percent of it was under water. The Corning Glass Works, the state government, and the federal government all pitched in to help Corning recover. Local residents united behind an effort to rebuild the town and preserve its remaining heritage.

Corning Glass Works played an active as well as supportive role in the revitalization of Market Street. The company owned several buildings on the street and took the lead by rehabilitating a nineteenth-century mill turned recreation center to house its offices and archives. Corning Glass also renovated the first floor of the old Baron Steuben Hotel as a series of shops, while the second floor served as a temporary home for the Rockwell-Corning Museum, a collection of art of the American West; other floors will provide office space. In addition to company and town activities, public funds in the form of a HUD "open space grant" of $500,000 provided new brick sidewalks and trees for the street.

In 1974, the Market Street Restoration Agency was established to coordinate rehabilitation of storefronts on the street and to oversee the entire revitalization effort. This private, nonprofit organization is being directed by Norman Mintz, who was trained in Columbia University's Historic Preservation Program. Mintz's task has demanded diplomatic as well as design skills. He has had to convince some store owners that their new aluminum and plastic fronts were "inappropriate." Not all merchants agree that restoration, rather than modernization, is best. "It is as much an education job as it is a design job,"[3] says Mintz. Mintz and his wife, Melanie, have also been working with schools in the area to create an awareness of architecture and to introduce students to the benefits of preserving old buildings.

Since 1974, about 25 percent of the buildings along Market Street have been rehabilitated, and over 75 percent of the merchants and landlords have participated in the Program in some way. The Market Street Restoration Agency provides free design plans and working drawings, but does not fund the actual costs of rehabilitation. These costs are paid by the store owners, and range from $250 to $4,500. "The most important thing to remember," says Mintz, "is that we are not trying to create a Disneyland of cute recreations of somebody's concept of the past. We are just trying to design new storefronts that respect the design of the original buildings."[4] As a result, not all storefronts or signs are in the Victorian style; contemporary designs that harmonize with the character of the original architecture are also used.

Norman Mintz has also been responsible for promoting Market Street. He works closely with the Market Street Association (MSA), a merchants' organization, coordinating radio and newspaper advertising under the MSA logo, and creating special events to attract local residents and some of the more than 750,000 tourists who visit the Corning Glass Center each year. In June, 1976, a summer festival celebrating the town's rebuilding efforts and the nation's Bicentennial brought more than 50,000 people to Market Street.

Costs The Corning Glass Works, through its Foundation, has provided more than $250,000 for the revitalization of Market Street since the idea was first conceived. Approximately $100,000 of this was spent on the initial studies and plans. The balance has supported the Market Street Restoration Agency whose budget is about $60,000 per year.

Since 1970, the company has also contributed about $2.8 million more to the overall urban-renewal effort in downtown Corning. Of this, $128,000 was used for the initial planning studies; $144,000 paid for the architectural fees for the new city hall and firehouse; $500,000 helped build the ice skating rink; and $1.6 million was used to design and build the new Corning Public Library. The company has also donated $31,232 to fund restoration/conversion studies for the old city hall, a Victorian brick structure vacated when the new city hall was completed. Plans are now under consideration to reuse the old building to house the Rockwell Corning Museum, featuring a superb collection of Western American art on loan from Mr. and Mrs. Robert Rockwell of Corning.

Problems According to George Douglas, Director of Community Affairs for the company, Corning Glass Works is "the largest company with its World Headquarters in a town this small in the United States."[5] This presents problems both for the company and for the town; while the company could take a more active role to speed the Market Street revitalization project, it feels that a democratic process is more desirable. Of course, the effort may take more time to produce visible results.

Contemporary storefronts are compatible in design, materials, color, and signs with the original buildings. (Kellogg Studio)

Benefits Since Corning Glass has acted as a catalyst for the revitalization of downtown Corning, its private capital has helped to attract public capital. More than $7 million has gone into the renewal program from state and federal sources, more than doubling the company's contribution.

Market Street itself has been a widely touted success. All stores on the street are now occupied as compared to a 15 percent vacancy rate in 1974. The scale of Market Street has been maintained and has strongly influenced the kind of new architecture in the renewal area. Norman Mintz has been asked to speak in many parts of the country, and the Market Street Restoration Program has been a model for other commercial-district revitalization programs. A recent article on the rebirth of Corning states: "These accomplishments . . . cast a whole new light on how urbane our outlying communities could end up being."[6]

Besides seeing its community environment improve, Corning Glass has also received its share of favorable publicity for its efforts and has developed community goodwill. According to Urban Renewal Director Jim Sheaffer: "The high quality of the product is definitely related to the fact that the Corning Glass Works is in Corning, New York."[7]

The Company Corning Glass Works, an international producer of glass, glass-ceramic, and related products, was established in 1851 and has been located in Corning, New York, since 1868. The company has offices, plants, and subsidiary and associated companies in 25 countries. Corning's net sales for 1976 were $1.02 billion, up from 1975's $938.9 million. The company's net income in 1976 was $83.7 million, the highest in its history, more than double 1975's $31.1 million.

Other Preservation Activities. The Corning Glass Works Foundation, incorporated in 1952, has usually supported projects in areas where the parent company has plants, although some programs have been national and international in scope. Preservation grants in the past five years have included donations for: the restoration of the Old Slater Mill and Museum expansion, Pawtucket, Rhode Island; the restoration of the Patterson Inn, Corning, New York; the creation of a storefront museum for the Corning-Painted Post, New York, Historical Society; the restoration of City Square and historic homes, Bradford, Pennsylvania; the downtown restoration project, Greenville, Ohio; the conversion of old theater buildings to performing arts centers in Elmira, New York, Providence, Rhode Island, and Louisville, Kentucky; the renovation of the Martins Mill (covered) Bridge, Greencastle, Pennsylvania; general support for the Historic Homes Foundation, Louisville, Kentucky; and co-sponsorship of a New York State preservation conference.

For further information contact:
Norman Mintz
Project Director
Market Street Restoration Agency
2 West Market Street
Corning, New York 14830

Footnotes

1. *Market Street Restored*, (Corning, New York: City of Corning, n.d.).
2. *Ibid.*
3. INFORM interview with Norman Mintz, Project Director, Market Street Restoration Agency, February, 1977.
4. *Ibid.*
5. INFORM interview with George Douglas, Director, Community Affairs, Corning Glass Works, April, 1977.
6. "The Home Towns Come Back," *Architectural Record*, December, 1976.
7. INFORM interview with Jim Sheaffer, Executive Director, Corning Urban Renewal Agency, February, 1977.

Summary   In 1973, Higbee's, a Cleveland department store, formed a real estate subsidiary, the Higbee Development Corporation, to redevelop a 6.9-acre site in downtown Cleveland. The redevelopment project combines the recycling of existing buildings with new construction in an area along the Cuyahoga River called Settlers' Landing. Modeled after Ghirardelli Square in San Francisco, the project will contain retail shops, restaurants, entertainment facilities, a hotel, and office buildings. Work is proceeding in stages. By mid-1977, the company had converted a former trucking terminal into a contemporary discotheque and restaurant, renovated the historic Western Reserve Building as modern office space, and adapted a former hemp mill as office space for architects, artisans, and other professionals. To date, Higbee's has invested almost $7 million in the project. Although progress has been slower than anticipated, the company has been recognized in the community for its pioneering work in saving the historically important river front. Its efforts have encouraged additional investment and interest in the area.

Background   Historians believe that Moses Cleaveland—the city's founder—and his band of surveyors first landed at the Settlers' Landing site in 1796. The city was orginally named Cleaveland, but the Ohio legislature changed the spelling to Cleveland in 1831. With the opening of the Ohio Canal, the city, located at the mouth of the Cuyahoga River on Lake Erie, prospered as a shipping and warehouse center. Later, after the railroads were built, it became an industrial center.

Cleveland experienced tremendous growth during the last half of the nineteenth century. Its population increased from 17,000 in 1850 to 361,000 in 1900. Today the Cleveland metropolitan area has 2 million residents. Until 1900, the financial and commercial center of the city remained compact, clustered on either side of Superior Street, which stretches along the river front surrounding Settlers' Landing. In the late nineteenth century, great industrialists, such as Samuel Mather and John D. Rockefeller, built high-rise office buildings and massive warehouses in the area.

By the turn of the century, downtown Cleveland was suffering from increasing congestion, and water and air pollution. At about that time, the configuration of downtown was substantially altered by Chicago architect Daniel Burnham. Burnham's plan emphasized the Public Square as the central point of the city. By creating wide boulevards, he oriented future commercial development toward the east, away from the river front. As a result, during the last seventy years, the river front and the surrounding commercial areas have been increasingly underutilized, abandoned, or destroyed.

In recent decades, as in other major urban areas, pollution, increased crime, and racial conflicts stifled new investment. In the late 1960s, the Cuyahoga River became famous when the surface sludge spontaneously caught fire. As head of a major downtown department store with a substantial stake in the central-city's vitality, Higbee's Chairman, Herbert Strawbridge, decided to help reverse downtown deterioration.

Execution   Strawbridge felt that the river front, the birthplace of the city, was the appropriate place to begin. At the time, a local businessman was attempting to convert the area into an auto junkyard. In late 1972, Higbee's acquired four acres at the western end of Superior Street along the Cuyahoga River; and in July, 1973, the Higbee Development Corporation was formed to revitalize the property.

The acreage includes approximately 600 feet of river front and encompasses all the land to West Ninth Street, stretching from the Superior Viaduct Bridge to St. Clair. The company owns all the real estate in the parcel, except for two large warehouse buildings near St. Clair, which are owned by the International Seaway Trading Company. A railway track of the Pennsylvania Railroad crosses the property and is actively used. The Western Reserve Building, erected in 1891 and 1892 by wealthy industrialist Samuel Mather and designed by Chicago architect Daniel H. Burnham, is the most important building on the site. Located on a triangular plot at the corner of West Ninth and Superior, the building is one of three Burnham structures in Cleveland, and the one most characteristic of the Chicago style of architecture. It is eight stories tall, made of brick, and has a series of irregularly spaced bays on the exterior with a simple curved, corbelled-brick cornice, similar to Burnham's Chicago masterpiece, the Monadnock Building. The exterior walls are masonry load-bearing, and interior supports are cast and wrought iron. The floors are supported by tiled arches. From the elaborately paneled offices on the top floor of the Western Reserve, Mather conducted his diverse business operations, which included United States Steel, American Ship Building, and iron-ore and coal-mining interests, as well as many educational and philanthropic activities.

Other buildings on the site include a former truck-loading terminal, a warehouse building near the river front, and a row of warehouse structures on West Ninth Street. One of the latter group has an ornamental cast-iron facade only 25 feet wide. The remainder of the hillside site is open space, intersected by railroad tracks and the Old River Road. Two important structures have been lost in recent years. A fire in 1974 destroyed the National Furniture Warehouse, a building adjacent to the Western Reserve on West Ninth Street which had excellent renovation potential. The Bethel Hotel (1870), built by wealthy Cleveland families as a hotel for sailors, was determined to be structurally unsound and demolished in late 1975.

On July 3, 1973, Higbee's announced that it would commit $17 million to redevelop the four-acre parcel (later increased to nearly seven acres). Although the property was then overgrown with weeds and littered with debris, company Chairman Herbert Strawbridge saw the river front with its barges, mechanical bridges, and industrial structures as a unique setting for an imaginative development similar to San Francisco's Ghirardelli Square. Higbee's helped develop several suburban shopping centers, and Strawbridge decided that the company should become the developer for Settlers' Landing in order to control the project and effectively manage the risks.

He hired Lawrence Halprin & Associates, the San Francisco urban planners who had worked on Ghirardelli Square, to prepare the development scheme. Gruen and Gruen Plus Associates of San Francisco was retained to conduct the sociological and economic feasibility studies.

As a first step, the property was cleared of weeds and debris. The City of Cleveland placed markers on the river front noting the place where Moses Cleaveland first landed and the spot where Lorenzo Carter built the first cabin. Throughout 1973 and 1974, Halprin's firm planned a development concept for the site. However, as work progressed, it became clear that completion of the entire project would take five to ten years. In addition, for the effort to be successful, local residents would have to rediscover and use the river front area. The likelihood of this happening was increased by implementation of an extensive pollution-control program for the Cuyahoga River.

In early 1975, Higbee's decided to create immediate visibility for the project by converting a vacant trucking terminal on the lower portion of the

site into a discotheque. On June 13, 1975, 55 days after the start of construction, Cleaveland Crate and Trucking Company opened for business. The discotheque featured an automated bar and disc jockey stand in the cab of a diesel truck. Cleaveland Crate and Trucking was initially a huge success, attracting large crowds of young professionals. Although its popularity soon waned (see "Problems"), the endeavor demonstrated that a sizable market existed for river-front entertainment activities.

Halprin finished his development plan for the entire project in summer, 1975. His strategy was to create a constituency for river-front businesses by building in a captive market, the office workers who would eat, drink, and shop in the complex; and by providing enough excitement and unique attractions to bring local citizens and tourists into the area both day and night. Renovation of the Western Reserve Building as a modern office facility was to be the keystone of the project. In addition, new ten- to twelve-story office buildings with retail shops on the street level were to be built, providing the commercial anchor for the total development. These office buildings would incorporate the facades of the existing warehouse structures on West Ninth Street. A small luxury hotel was planned for a site near St. Clair Street, while the upper portion of the property was to be nearly covered by a multi-level, glass-enclosed walkway extending over the railroad track and containing a variety of shops and restaurants. A park, including a boat dock offering excursion rides, and a museum were to be located on the river front. The museum would house a local collection of Salvador Dali's paintings, the largest single, privately owned collection of the artist's work. The plan provided for 1,500 parking spaces on three levels below the glass-enclosed walkway.

Although the Halprin scheme was visually exciting, its price tag of nearly $70 million was not. The total project was too large for Higbee's to assume at once. In addition, the amount of income-producing property under the plan was too small to support the investment required to create the large open spaces and parking facilities. In order to manage the risks involved, the

company decided to complete the development in phases. Because of its historical and architectural importance, the Western Reserve Building was to be renovated first. This work could be completed with internally generated funds, and would not require additional borrowing. Work began in fall, 1975.

Restoration of the Western Reserve's exterior included the re-creation of the original arched doorway with cast concrete. After World War II, the exterior had been modernized, and the original carved pink-sandstone arch had been defaced and covered with imitation marble. Pollution had badly discolored the brick building, and windows were broken and rotted. Exterior brick was cleaned by sandblasting, and repointed. Windows were replaced with new bronze-colored aluminum ones. New brick sidewalks were installed, along with cast-iron street lamps.

The "modernization" work of the late 1940s had also obliterated the ornate Italian-marble main lobby. Except for the impressive cast-iron staircase—with marble treads and ornamental cast-iron risers—and the elaborately paneled offices of Samuel Mather, there was little interior detail left in the building. Modern lighting, wiring, plumbing, heating, air conditioning, life-safety systems, fluorescent lighting in new dropped ceilings, and new automatic elevators have been installed. The new lobby, a series of domed vaults covered with brick tiles, was developed from research of period designs. Heavy steel and leaded-glass gates of a spider-web design were installed for first-floor retail and restaurant tenants. Additional space was created for restrooms, fire stairs, and heating and air-conditioning ducts by filling in a light well at the north end of the building. Two sections of the site were graded and hard surfaced, providing 104 parking spaces.

On September 3, 1976, restoration work on the Western Reserve was completed, and shortly thereafter, the building's first tenant, Parker B. Advertising moved in. Seven of the eight floors—approximately 52,500 net leasable square feet—were converted to modern office space, but the leasing program has moved slowly. By July, 1977, the building was 28 percent leased with five tenants occupying

15,950 feet. The largest single tenant, United Airlines, occupies 4,000 square feet. Samuel Mather's office on the top floor will be restored when a tenant is found for the entire floor. Rents range from $9 to $10 per square foot, which is competitive with prime downtown office space.

Also available for lease are 9,300 square feet on the street and basement levels designed for use as a rathskeller and restaurant, and an additional 900 square feet adjacent to the main door on the street level which is suitable for retail use.

During 1976, as work on the Western Reserve Building was being completed,

Exterior of the Western Reserve Building restored in 1976.

Aerial view of downtown Cleveland showing boundaries of the Settlers' Landing development.

Higbee's explored a variety of ambitious development proposals for the second phase of the project:

1. *A high-rise office building with a large single tenant.* Higbee's tried to persuade a large Cleveland industrial company to locate its corporate headquarters in Settlers' Landing and co-develop a major high-rise office building of 650,000 to 850,000 square feet along West Ninth Street.

2. *A series of smaller office buildings.* Major tenants were sought to pre-lease a series of smaller multi-tenant office buildings ranging in size from 200,000 to 400,000 square feet to be built along West Ninth Street.

3. *Condominium apartments and townhouses.* A series of river-front condominium units was designed. However, cost estimates dictated selling prices of $165,000 to $300,000 per unit.

4. *A retail/restaurant/entertaiment complex.* A local architectural firm, Hoag-Wismar, which had also worked on the Western Reserve Building, prepared a plan for 100,000 square feet of restaurant and retail space in a series of buildings clustered along the river front. The structures would be historically accurate replicas of early nineteenth-century buildings.

By early 1977, however, having found no market support for these large-scale development proposals, Higbee's decided that a slower, more cautious approach would be appropriate until the Western Reserve Building was fully leased. Still, the company was anxious to preserve the project's momentum. It decided that another building, a former hemp-rope mill, could be renovated and profitably rented to architects, artisans, and similar professionals. Although architecturally undistinguished, the three-story brick building—actually a series of three buildings—had a good view of the river and was structurally sound. During spring and summer, 1977, a local architectural firm, Todd-Schmidt, was retained to prepare conceptual plans for renovating the building. The

exterior was sandblasted, windows were enlarged on the upper floors, and a new interior staircase was added. New plumbing, electrical wiring, air conditioning, and life-safety systems were installed. Interior spaces were left with exposed beams and brick walls. By mid-summer, 1977, approximately two-thirds of the 20,000 square feet had been leased to architects, a weaver, an opera company, and a furniture maker. Only space on the third floor and in the old boxcar shed was still vacant. Depending on tenant improvements, rents range from $4 to $6 per square foot.

Before the end of 1977, Higbee's plans to remodel the Cleaveland Crate and Trucking Company, placing more emphasis on the food business. It will upgrade and expand the lunch and dinner menus, increase the size of the cocktail lounge, and change the disco entertainment to a lower-key format. Cini, Grissom, restaurant consultants, have been retained to help Higbee's develop this new concept.

Costs   In July, 1973, Higbee's committed $17 million to redevelop the four acres of the Settlers' Landing project. Since that time, the project has increased to nearly seven acres, and a development plan has been devised which if implemented could cost $100 million. By mid-1977, the company's investment totaled approximately $7 million. The costs break down as follows:

Acquisition (nearly seven acres and eight structures)	$2,500,000
Renovation of the Western Reserve	3,360,000
Cleaveland Crate and Trucking Company	675,000
Renovation of the River-view Building	225,000
Fees, operating costs, parking	125,000
	$6,885,000

There are no mortgages or long-term debts held against the property. Funds for the project's first phase have been provided from Higbee's regular business operations. Since only a small percentage of the total project is complete and rented, the current income has yet to provide the company with a return on its investment.

Problems   Creating a commercial base to support the retail, restaurant, and entertainment complex originally envisioned for Settlers' Landing has been a major barrier frustrating the project's progress. Renovation of the Western Reserve Building was the first attempt to establish such a base, but the work was completed without a major anchor tenant. The leasing of the building to smaller tenants has been slow, since many firms have been reluctant to move into a nearly empty building several blocks from downtown shopping, restaurants, and other office buildings. In addition, because there are few offices in the area, it has been difficult to attract ground-floor retail tenants and a restaurant.

Although Higbee's spent nearly $56 per square foot to restore the Western Reserve Building, the work has prompted controversy. Some local architectural critics and preservationists have questioned whether the building's historic or architectural value warrants such lavish treatment. The lobby's brick-veneer domes, alcoves, and arches have been characterized as "early wine cellar," and criticized as "corny" and "inappropriate."[1] Although the exterior brick has been sealed against further deterioration the surface is badly pitted from earlier sandblasting.

Progress has also been slowed by the loss of two major buildings. The National Furniture Warehouse Building, which was destroyed by fire in 1974, could have been converted into office space complementing the Western Reserve and providing a larger nucleus for the project. Demolition of the Bethel Hotel left the Western Reserve isolated on the site. Financing for new construction is not available.

Efforts to build the entertainment segment of Settlers' Landing have been similarly hampered. The Cleaveland Crate and Trucking Company's initial success was based on the fact that it was the first discotheque in Cleveland. The idea was soon copied in suburban locations, and the initial clientele declined as people were attracted to competing discos closer to their homes. In six months, gross sales fell off sharply, and the less profitable restaurant business became more important. Higbee's now plans to upgrade and expand the restaurant facilities to attract a higher-income clientele.

As of mid-1977, the future of the Dali Museum is uncertain, since the donation of the artist's work is in doubt. Finally, if Higbee's is to complete its land holdings within the Settlers' Landing project, it must still purchase the two International Seaway Buildings sometime in the future.

Benefits   Although after four years, the company has yet to achieve a financial return on its investment in Settlers' Landing, the project is becoming a catalyst for further development. Diagonally across Superior Street from the Western Reserve Building, the State of Ohio is building a 600,000-square-foot building which will bring 2,000 office workers a day into the area. Standard Oil of Ohio has also recently announced plans to erect a new high-rise headquarters office building behind the Terminal Tower near Settlers' Landing.

In May, 1977, a study by the Cleveland Landmarks Commission recommended revitalization of the Warehouse District, a more than fifty-acre area which surrounds Settlers' Landing and includes numerous landmark buildings. Adjacent to Settlers' Landing, on the river front along the Old River Road, enterprising entrepreneurs are opening a variety of shops in old warehouses. The stores offer high-quality gifts, antiques, gourmet kitchenware, and furniture. Another developer is converting a former power station located across the Cuyahoga River from the project into an entertainment complex and a series of shops.

Higbee's regards Settlers' Landing as both a business venture and part of its social responsibility to downtown Cleveland. As a result of its leadership, other companies are also making commitments to the downtown area. In May, 1977, Higbee's along with Chessie System, TRW, Eaton, Cleveland Stadium Company, the Stouffer Corporation, and E. J. O'Neill agreed to purchase the Sheraton-Cleveland Hotel on the Public Square. This once grand hotel will receive a $10 million renovation, and will be operated by Stouffer.

The Company   Founded in 1860 by two Ohio entrepreneurs, John G. Hower and Edwin C. Higbee, the Higbee Company has grown from a small retail clothing store to a large independent department-store chain. It operates 25 stores throughout northern Ohio, as well as women's specialty shops and shoe stores. In 1976, the company's total income reached $173 million, up 5.3 percent from the 1975 figure of $164.3 million. Net income for 1976 dropped 15.2 percent to $3.5 million from the previous year's $4.1 million. Assets at the beginning of 1977 totaled $118 million. The company has 5,700 full-time employees and 1,500 seasonal staff. The stock is closely held by under 3,000 shareholders and is traded on the over-the-counter market.

Settlers' Landing is the only project of the Higbee Development Corporation. However, Higbee's has investments in several suburban shopping malls, and owns a 117-acre farm in Summit County, Ohio, which was purchased as a potential development site for a shopping center.

For further information contact:
Herbert Strawbridge
Chairman
The Higbee Company
Public Square
Cleveland, Ohio 44113

Footnotes

1. Jim Wood, "A Vote Against Reserve Building," *Sunday Plain-Dealer* (Cleveland), 14 November 1976, sec. 5, p. 2.

Summary   In 1970, Inland Steel, the sixth largest steel producer in the United States, created the Inland Steel Development Corporation (ISDC), a wholly owned subsidiary. The ISDC has recently developed several preservation-related projects. Work began on the Foundry, a modern commercial complex in Washington, D.C. which includes an old foundry, in 1970. A second project, initiated in 1973, was the conversion into apartments of the old Cairo Hotel built in 1894 and still the tallest private building in Washington. Renovation of the Foundry building cost $1.3 million, while the Cairo project cost $4.3 million. Both projects have helped revitalize the areas in which they are located, and brought additional economic benefits to the company.

Background   According to Inland Steel, the ISDC is committed to urban revitalization, emphasizing high-quality commercial and residential development as a means of bringing people and business back to the cities. The Washington area is also a lucrative real estate market.

Inland's Foundry project was initiated in Georgetown, a historic section of Washington established in the early eighteenth century. The community possesses a large and well-preserved supply of eighteenth- and nineteenth-century buildings.

Although there have always been some blighted and unsightly areas, especially along the river front, much of Georgetown has remained an exclusive residential community for Washington's wealthy. Today, it contains an active retail district of fine shops, restaurants, and entertainment facilities.

The Progressive Citizens Association of Georgetown, a group of residents who became interested in preservation in the 1940s, worked diligently to maintain the community's architectural heritage. Because of its efforts, Congress passed a bill in 1950 requiring that all building and demolition permits for the area be submitted for review to a committee of architects appointed by the Fine Arts Commission of Washington, D.C. Shortly thereafter, Historic Georgetown, Inc., was formed and has served as a citizen-based catalyst for a variety of preservation projects, including the restoration of the old Chesapeake and Ohio Canal which runs through Georgetown.

In 1970, the developers of Canal Square, a shopping and office complex incorporating new design with renovated and adapted nineteenth-century industrial buildings along the edge of the Canal, approached Inland Steel. They proposed to co-develop twelve acres of underutilized industrial property lying between the Canal and the Potomac River. The ISDC hired an architectural firm from Berkeley, California, ELS Design Group, and the Real Estate Research Corporation from Chicago to study the feasibility of the project from both the design and marketing standpoints.

Execution   In fall, 1970, the ISDC purchased seven of the available twelve acres. The company's plan, later known as Georgetown Harbor, encompassed property from the Chesapeake and Ohio Canal south to the Potomac, and included offices, shops, restaurants, a luxury inn, a conference center, recreational facilities, and public spaces. The Canal Square developers became minority stockholders (they were later completely bought out), and the group's architect, Arthur Cotton Moore, became involved with the planning and design.

Moore had successfully mixed new construction with historic preservation in the Canal Square project a few blocks from the Inland site. Besides being a respected architect, he was a resident of Georgetown, which would make him extremely valuable in implementing the ISDC's plan within the regulations imposed by the preservation-oriented Georgetown community. The ISDC hired both ELS and Moore to work cooperatively on designing the first building. Another design firm, Sasaki Associates of Watertown, Massachusetts, was hired to work on landscaping and to design a public plaza along the Canal. Washington architect Vlastimil Koubek prepared the construction documents and supervised the work. Tishman Construction Company was the Construction Manager.

The total project was to be developed in three major phases. The first, begun in 1970, included construction of a building containing offices, shops, and restaurants directly south of the Canal, and rehabilitation of an existing building. The undeveloped site contained a two-story brick building used as office space, an auto repair shop, and a storage building, as well as a former foundry which had been used to produce arms and implements during the Civil War. The office and storage buildings were not of significant economic or architectural value and were demolished. However, the Foundry, built in the 1850s, was a fine example of early Georgetown industrial architecture. Moore and ELS urged the ISDC to save the structure and incorporate it into the design of the new complex.

The reuse of the Foundry required considerable effort and expense. The two-and-a-half story, 88-foot long building was raised from its foundation, and large steel beams were placed under the main supporting walls. To facilitate excavation work for a new underground garage, the building was rolled on rails off the site. Once the initial construction work was complete, it was rolled to its present location, where the exterior was restored, a new roof, skylight, and windows were installed, and the brick masonry, previously covered with aluminum paint, was cleaned and repaired. The original interior had been completely altered over the building's life and contained nothing worth preserving. It has been completely redesigned to accommodate a two-level restaurant and bar.

This act of preservation helped mute some of the local criticism of the new development. Nevertheless, the Fine

The old Foundry building was carefully jacked up and moved on railroad tracks to its new location on the development site. (Georgetown Photo Center)

The Foundry complex. The C&O Canal is in the foreground. (Steve Altman Photography)

Arts Committee initially did not approve the plans for the complex. The community was concerned that the development would increase traffic congestion in an already car-crowded Georgetown, that the new building proposed for the site would not fit within the traditional Georgetown architecture of small, residential brick buildings, and that public access to and use of the Canal would be curtailed.

To help alleviate the traffic-congestion problem, a 300-car parking garage was designed under the new building. The basic form and facade of the new building was designed to relate to its existing context. The exterior cladding is brick in keeping with the older surrounding architecture. Current zoning allowed a structure up to six stories or ninety feet tall on the site. The new design called for six stories, but an actual height of only about sixty feet. The height was minimized by stepping back some of the upper floors, producing outdoor landscaped terraces overlooking the Canal.

Five of the new building's levels are above ground. One is mostly below grade, but is partially visible because the site slopes to the south. A retail shopping mall occupies the ground level and one level below. It is connected by an interior "piazza" containing a reflecting pool and grand staircase. The five upper floors are leased as offices. Elevators to all levels are accessible from the piazza.

The building is cut back along the canal edge creating a public plaza. The ISDC rents a strip of land along the Canal from the National Park Service, and has spent more than $50,000 landscaping and improving the canal-front area.

Both the new building and the placement of the Foundry respect Georgetown's historic form. Their facades establish a building line related to the street edge, just as the traditional rowhouses do on many of the community's streets. On the uppermost floors, the new building's facade is sloped back, reminiscent of the pitched-gable roofs of the early Federal-style houses. The Foundry's small scale and pitched roof also help to reduce the mass of the new building behind it.

Costs Inland Steel spent $135,000 to move the Foundry. Restoration of the building's masonry cost approximately $60,000, while the new roof and other work cost $50,000. The ISDC spent an additional $1 million for restaurant fixtures and finishes, bringing the total cost for the Foundry reuse, including new landscaping, to $1.3 million. The cost for the remaining 366,000 square feet of the complex was about $12 million, or equivalent to $33 per square foot.

Problems The only significant difficulties encountered were those involving design approvals by the Fine Arts Commission and objections from the community. After considerable negotiation, the project was able to move forward.

Benefits A portion of the Canal has been improved and made more accessible to the public through the Company's efforts. A blighted section of Georgetown has been refurbished and returned to active, revenue-producing use. New business has been attracted to the area. The office floors are fully leased, and the retail space is 90 percent rented. According to William Marlin, writing in the February, 1977, *Architectural Record*:

Because the new building in town, even for the most suspicious, is fitting in very well, offering a spritely mix of activities, going about its business in a polite pleasant fashion, and (the real test) showing respect for its elders . . . the new neighbor on Thomas Jefferson Street has not only accommodated the history of Georgetown, it is making some.[1]

The Cairo Hotel

Background In 1894, Thomas Franklin Schneider designed and built the Cairo Hotel, the first steel-framed skyscraper in Washington, D.C. His 156-foot, thirteen-story building was and still is taller than any other privately owned building in the capital. The brick- and stone-clad structure is eclectic in style, with classical, Romanesque, and Art Nouveau elements. Many called it:

"Schneider's Folly" because they were convinced that its steel frame, a novelty at the time, would never hold all that stone and brick in place. One neighbor moved out of his house and into a hotel and tried to make Schneider pick up the bill—until the building passed the wind tests.[2]

Fearing that the city might soon be filled with skyscrapers like New York and Chicago, Congress passed a law in 1910 limiting all buildings in Washington to a height of 130 feet, 26 feet less than the Cairo. This law is still in effect today.

The building, located east of the Dupont Circle area of Washington, remained an elegant residential hotel well into the twentieth century. In its heyday, it contained a restaurant, ballroom, drugstore, billiard room, bowling alley, bakery, and a rooftop tropical garden. The Schneider family owned the Cairo until the 1950s when the old hotel was finally sold, and served as a transient residence until it was boarded up in 1972.

Execution Inland Steel purchased the property in 1973, and then converted it into apartments utilizing the Federal Housing Administration's (FHA) 221 d (4) Program. Under this Program, upon completion of a project, permanent financing was available for up to 90 percent of the renewed property's FHA-appraised value for forty years at 7 percent interest. Market rents could be charged in the renovated building. The ISDC raised equity capital by forming a limited partnership with a syndicate of high-income individuals.[3] The cost of construction was financed through another of the parent company's subsidiaries, Inland Steel Finance Company.

CAIRO APARTMENTS
INFORMATION CENTER
HOURS
FRI: 10:00 AM to 8:00 PM
AYS 10:00 AM to 6:00 PM
S 12:00 AM to 6:00 PM
BY APPOINTMENT
232-4020

Arthur Cotton Moore was selected as the architect for the renovation. His design converted 350 small hotel rooms and several larger public areas—a total of 130,000 square feet of space—into 162 apartments and eight two-story townhouse units.

The hotel's exterior was cleaned and preserved, and new windows were installed. A contemporary front door, echoing but not imitating the style of the original, provides a transition to the modern contrasting interior.

Very little has been saved of the old hotel's lush interior decoration. The lobby's original marble fountains, mosaic tiles, richly carved plasterwork, and elegant Victorian furnishings have all been removed. Only a few traces of plaster detail remain. The high ceilings are still there, but the rooms in the new apartments are quite small, resulting in very different proportional relationships. The new rooms are contemporary, with rough-cut cedar used to replace the original window casings and baseboards. At least one wall in each apartment is exposed brick. Many of the apartments still retain the original ornamental fireplaces, and a few have niches and balconies from the grand public function rooms that were partitioned to accommodate the renovation scheme.

The alteration which made the project financially feasible was Moore's decision to remove the roof from the original back lobby and east ballroom.[4] This left an open well or atrium in the middle of the building, allowing light and ventilation into the interior, and creating garden spaces for townhouse units. The completed two-story townhouses utilize the old basement level as their first floor, and open on to the atrium.

Efficiency apartments rent for $240 to $291 per month; one-bedroom units for $315 to $375; two-bedroom units for $430 to $493; and townhouses for $500 to $555. All utilities are included.

Costs Inland purchased the building for $500,000, and spent $3.8 million on the renovation. The resulting cost per square foot was approximately $33, or an average of $25,000 per unit.

Problems During the construction, some of the clay-tile, arched floor supports were found to be defective and had to be replaced with steel-reinforced concrete. This delayed the project's completion and increased total costs. A decision to install an all-electric system for cooking and heating caused additional problems. Between 1972 and 1976, while the building was being renovated, the cost of electricity in Washington more than tripled. The Cairo's electric bill increased from $52,000 to $150,000, drastically altering the original operating expense projections. Both problems resulted in rents substantially above those initially planned and reduced the level of the return.

Benefits In addition to the preservation benefits from saving the Cairo and returning it to the tax rolls, the area in which it is located has received an economic boost. Business has improved for local merchants, and property values are rising.

The Company Inland Steel is engaged in the production, fabrication, and sale of steel and related products, as well as the mining of iron ore, coal, and limestone. Inland's net sales in 1976 were over $2.6 billion, an increase from a 1975 figure of $2.1 billion. Net income rose from $83.3 million to $104 million over the same period. In addition to Inland Steel Development Corporation's real estate development activities, Inland has subsidiaries engaged in the design and production of mobile homes and prefabricated housing units, and the development, construction, and management of commercial and residential real estate, including government-assisted housing.

Other Preservation Activities. The ISDC has also converted the 75-year-old Woodley apartment building in northwest Washington into 73 condominium units.

For further information contact:
Paul H. Upchurch
Vice President and General Manager
Inland Steel Development
Corporation
1055 Thomas Jefferson Street, N.W.
Washington, D.C. 20007

Footnotes

1. William Marlin, "Georgetown's Nice New Neighbor," *Architectural Record*, February, 1977, p. 95.
2. Sarah Booth Conroy, "Moving in Where Legend Leaves Off," *Washington Post*, 11 April 1976, p. H3.
3. John Sower, "Financing and Developing Large Commercial Preservation Project," *Economic Benefits of Preserving Old Buildings*, (Washington, D.C.: Preservation Press, The National Trust for Historic Preservation, 1976), p. 136.
4. Conroy, *op. cit.*, p. H1.

The Jefferson Company

Summary In summer, 1977, the Jefferson Company, the third largest bus line in the United States, began renovation work on St. Anthony Main, a multi-use development located on the east bank of the Mississippi River near downtown Minneapolis. When complete, the project, which covers almost two city blocks, will contain nearly 200,000 square feet of space. Its ten buildings will house retail stores, restaurants, a theater and entertainment complex, apartments, and perhaps a luxury inn. New construction may also be added. The first phase, scheduled for completion by fall, 1977, involves renovation of a 40,000-square-foot former mattress factory to accommodate three restaurants and 11,000 square feet of specialty stores. Jefferson's investment in this initial phase totals approximately $3.1 million, including all land and building acquisition costs. Although the project has moved more slowly than anticipated, when it becomes operational, it is expected to be an important catalyst in the revitalization of the long-neglected Minneapolis river front.

St. Anthony Main Street project prior to renovation work in early 1977. The Pillsbury A mill is in the background. (Minneapolis Star)

Background The St. Anthony Main development consists of nearly two square blocks on the site where Minneapolis was first settled in 1838. St. Anthony, as the town was originally called, merged with Minneapolis in 1874. The river front was developed primarily as an industrial center. However, as industries along the river declined, the area deteriorated and became increasingly inaccessible.

In recent years, several comprehensive plans have been proposed for reclaiming all 200 acres of the river front and three river islands, and reusing them as a public park. Approximately $7 million in federal, state, and local funds have been committed for the first phase of the work which covers a

Salisbury Mattress Factory

Upton Block

Limestone Building

Pracna Restaurant

S.E. Main St.

20-acre area on the river's east bank surrounding the St. Anthony Main project. South East Main Street, which runs in front of the project, was to be recobbled, new landscaping and lighting fixtures were to be added, and an observation deck was to be built by summer, 1978. Future plans call for open air facilities for the performing arts, hiking trails, a recreated waterfall, and a river-front museum across from the St. Anthony Main project.

The prime mover behind the St. Anthony Main project is Louis Zelle, President of both the Jefferson Company and the firm's real estate development subsidiary, the MTS Company. A civic-minded businessman, Zelle has previously served on the building committees for the Guthrie Theater for the Performing Arts and the Orchestra Hall in Minneapolis and as Chairman of the Minnesota State Arts Council.

The total St. Anthony Main site contains about 180,000 square feet of land and ten buildings, some of which have been in the Zelle family since 1900. The oldest building on the site, the Upton Block was built of light-colored brick in 1854 by the Upton Brothers as their general store. The offices and newsroom of the first Minneapolis newspaper, the *Minnesota Republican*, were

upstairs in this building. The Limestone Building next to the Upton Block served as municipal offices for St. Anthony's mayor and housed the town's fire department. In 1879, the Union Iron Works Foundry was added behind the two buildings. Next to this complex is an 1898 Victorian commercial building, which is the only building in the project not owned by the Jefferson Company. In 1974, the latter structure was converted into a restaurant and bar called Pracna-on-Main, which has been very successful, averaging about a thousand meals a day. Above the Pracna on the same block is the three-story Truman Building, a 1918 industrial building. A one-story structure formerly used as the bus company's gas station is next door.

In addition, the site contains the Salisbury Mattress Factory, which is actually six buildings. The rear section was built in three parts in 1860 and 1880 as a warehouse for nearby flour mills. The main building, erected in 1906, was also a warehouse, and has the same heavy timber construction as the Butler Building, a downtown Minneapolis warehouse that has been recycled into a retail and office complex. The Mattress Factory complex includes an 1898 warehouse and a turn-of-the-century foundry.

Execution In April, 1974, the Jefferson Company announced plans to redevelop 200,000 square feet of existing building space, and add over 800,000 square feet of new construction in order to create an extensive multi-use complex on the two-block St. Anthony Main site. The project was to include 424 apartments and condominiums, 171,000 square feet of office space, and 180,000 square feet of commercial, retail, and entertainment space. In addition, the plan called for construction of a new hotel on the nearby Pillsbury A Mill property.

In announcing these preliminary plans, Zelle expressed determination to involve the people of Minneapolis in the project: "The project is being designed for people. We want people's help in putting it together."[1] Throughout the planning stages, Zelle has actively sought advice from local preservation and community groups, including the Riverfront Advisory Council and the Heritage Preservation Commission.

Zelle hired Benjamin Thompson of Cambridge, Massachusetts, architect for Boston's Faneuil Hall Market interiors, to prepare the master plan and architectural drawings for the project. However, money became very tight during the recession of 1974 and 1975,

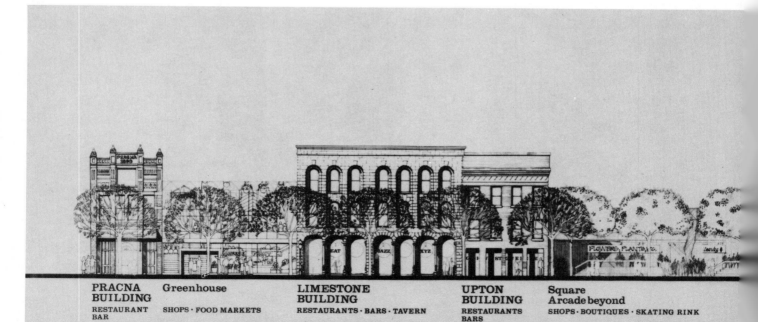

PRACNA BUILDING	Greenhouse	LIMESTONE BUILDING	UPTON BUILDING	Square Arcade beyond
RESTAURANT BAR	SHOPS · FOOD MARKETS	RESTAURANTS · BARS · TAVERN	RESTAURANTS BARS	SHOPS · BOUTIQUES · SKATING RINK

IRONWORKS BUILDING beyond
RESTAURANT · BAR

and Zelle could not find the necessary long-term financing to start construction. In addition, it took longer than expected to secure tenants for the complex. As a result, construction was delayed until spring, 1977, when the project's first phase received a $1.2 million long-term mortgage commitment from the locally based Northwestern National Life Insurance Company.

The original master plan was reworked several times, and by 1977, the total project was scaled down considerably. The revised design called for little new construction, emphasizing instead the reuse of existing buildings. The section of the Salisbury Mattress Factory facing Main Street, known as Salisbury A, was selected for renovation in the project's initial phase. Conversion of this 40,000 square-foot building into space for restaurant and retail use could be accomplished at a reasonable cost.

Major tenants in the Salisbury A building will be three restaurants occupying 20,000 square feet of the total 31,000 net leasable square feet. The remaining 11,000 square feet on the first and second floors will contain retail shops offering specialty clothing, jewelry, foods, and plants. A store offering quality home furnishings and gourmet cookware is being sought for the first floor.

Interior renovation work includes exposing and cleaning brick walls and heavy timber supports, refinishing wood floors, and installing new electrical and plumbing systems throughout the building. A new energy-conserving heat-pump system has also been installed to supply heating, cooling, and ventilation with separate controls for each tenant. Tenants will finish individual shops to their own specifications.

The exterior brick will be cleaned, and new windows will be installed. A covered deck is to be built around the exterior on the ground level, and an outdoor courtyard will be created between the buildings. A new entrance way and elevator will be built on 2nd Avenue S.E. where the A building joins the back wing, known as the B and C buildings. Automobile access to 2nd Avenue S.E. will be limited, and the street will be landscaped.

Commercial tenants in the Salisbury A building will pay rents based on a percentage of sales above a required minimum. In addition to this base rental rate, each tenant will pay a pro-rata share of common operating costs: heat, air conditioning, electricity, security, garbage removal, maintenance of common areas, and real estate taxes. An additional fee will be assessed for advertising and marketing. Minimum rentals in the Salisbury A will start at $8 per square foot.

The B and C buildings will be converted when additional long-term financing is obtained. Final plans for these buildings have not been established, but at least one floor is to house an open market area with a series of small shops offering foods and specialty items. Renovation work will be similar to that in the A building.

Development plans for other buildings in the St. Anthony Main complex are uncertain. The warehouse next to the Salisbury buildings may be recycled as either a luxury inn with sixty rooms, facilities for small meetings, a cocktail lounge, and a gourmet restaurant, or as rental apartments. In the

Architectural rendering of the completely renovated St. Anthony Main Street project. (Benjamin Thompson Associates)

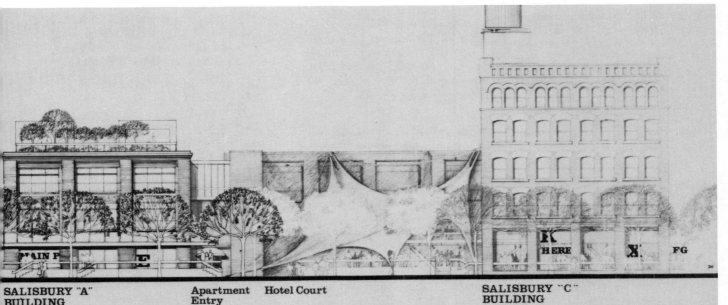

SALISBURY "A"
BUILDING
SHOPS·
PENTHOUSE APARTMENTS ABOVE

Apartment
Entry

Hotel Court

RESTAURANT

SALISBURY "C"
BUILDING
HOTEL·RESTAURANT·TAVERN
PENTHOUSE APARTMENTS ABOVE

next block, a theater and entertainment complex is contemplated for the Upton, Limestone, and Foundry buildings. Condominium apartments have been discussed for the Truman Building, where the addition of two new floors to the existing three floors could create nine to twelve large luxury units ranging in size from 3,500 to 5,500 square feet. Prices for the units would start at $150,000. Additional new townhouses with a garden court are also under consideration for a site in front of the Truman Building. Zelle feels strongly that the project needs a residential base. Future development projects will proceed as financing becomes available and market demand dictates.

Costs By mid-1977, the Jefferson Company had invested approximately $1.5 million to acquire land for the project other than that already held by the Zelle family. Total renovation costs for the Salisbury A Building, including fees, interest, overhead, and tenant improvements, but not land and acquisition costs, are $1.6 million. Construction financing has been provided by a local bank. In addition, a $1.2 million mortgage has been secured from the Northwestern National Life Insurance Company at 10 percent interest. Total costs for the project are estimated at $20 million. However, since the development plans are not final, these estimates are no more than guesses.

Problems The inability to find long-term financing for the project and the difficulty in finding retail and restaurant leases delayed the start of construction for nearly three years, from 1974 when the project was announced, until 1977. Completion of the total project may require as much as ten years. In addition, the initial construction cost estimates were greater than could be justified economically, and architectural plans had to be revised accordingly.

There has been some deterioration in the foundation of the Upton Block buildings. If these problems are excessive, renovation of the structures may not be justifiable economically.

Although the project is centrally positioned between the downtown Minneapolis business district and the University of Minnesota campus, it is not within walking distance of either, particularly in harsh Minnesota winters. Nevertheless, the initial success of the Pracna restaurant has demonstrated that the river-front area has unique appeal. Whether enough people will come to the area to support the St. Anthony Main project remains to be seen.

Minneapolis is a car-oriented community, and additional parking must be provided to assure the project's completion and long-term success. There is surface parking on the Jefferson property for 150 cars, adequate only for the Salisbury A building. The city has discussed building a parking ramp on property adjoining the project, but as yet no appropriations have been made.

Benefits Since the St. Anthony Main project was not yet operational by mid-1977, the company has yet to achieve a financial return. However, initial leasing activity indicates that in the long term, the development should be profitable. For the citizens of Minneapolis, the project will be the first major commercial investment on the river front in recent years. If successful, it will bring economic and social vitality to this important natural amenity. For Louis Zelle, completion of the project will mean the rebirth of an area where his family started in business over 125 years ago.

The Company The Jefferson Company was founded in 1922 by Louis Zelle's father, Edgar Zelle. Peter Rauen, Zelle's great grandfather, started a dry-goods store on the east bank of the Mississippi near St. Anthony Main in the 1850s. Except for Greyhound's 40 percent interest in Jefferson Bus Lines, the major subsidiary of the Jefferson Company, the firm is privately held. As a result, no data on total sales, income, or assets is available.

The MTS Company, a wholly owned subsidiary of the Jefferson Company headquartered in Minneapolis, is the developer of the St. Anthony Main project. The company has real estate holdings on the interstate highway in Owatonna, and other properties in Albert Lea and downtown Rochester, Minnesota, as well as in Bethany, Missouri. It also owns hotels in Owatonna and Albert Lea.

Other Preservation Activities. In September, 1976, the Jefferson Company announced it would develop the First Street Depot in downtown Rochester, Minnesota, as a retail, restaurant, and entertainment complex at an estimated cost of $785,000. The Victorian-style building, formerly the Chicago-Northwestern railway depot and freight house, is now a company bus station. By mid-1977, Jefferson was still seeking a new location for the bus terminal and a liquor license for the restaurant. Benjamin Thompson Associates is the project architect.

For further information contact:
Louis Zelle
President
The Jefferson Company
1206 Currie Avenue
Minneapolis, Minnesota 55403

Footnotes

1. The Jefferson Company, *News Release,* April 26, 1974.

Lowell Development and Financial Corporation

Summary The Lowell Development and Financial Corporation (LDFC) is a consortium of financial institutions in the greater Lowell, Massachusetts, area that have joined together to promote the development and expansion of business activities and organizations through rehabilitation and restoration of the city's historic central business district. The LDFC provides low-cost loans to encourage building owners and tenants to renovate and restore their properties in harmony with the State Heritage Park and the proposed Urban National Cultural Park. Established in December, 1975, the LDFC has accumulated more than $350,000 which it lends at 4 percent to 5½ percent for this purpose, and it expects to raise a total of $2 million over the next three years. The program is acting as a catalyst for local, state, and federal programs to help revitalize Lowell's central business district.

Design suggestions for the same building by Lowell's Division of Planning and Development. (Lowell Division of Planning and Development)

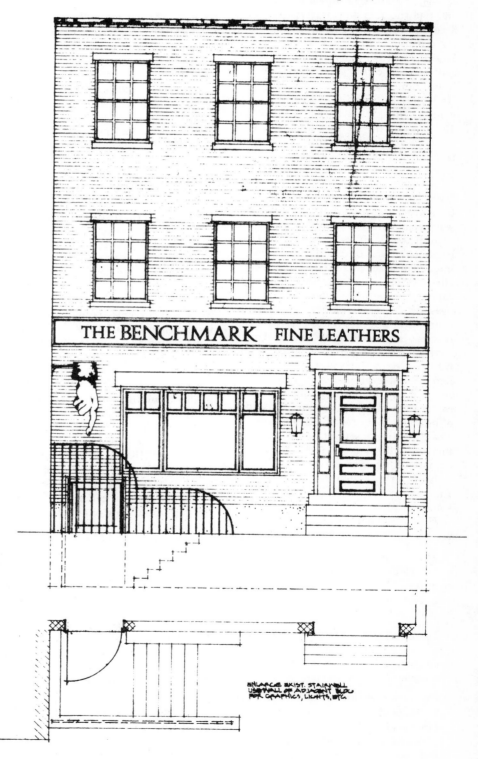

THE BENCHMARK FINE LEATHERS

Lowell's Division of Planning and Development provides free design service to local businesses who want to rehabilitate the facades of their buildings. Photo of Kimball Sign Building before renovation. (Lowell Division of Planning and Development)

Background Lowell, located on the Merrimack River thirty miles northwest of Boston, was founded in 1822. It was one of the first planned industrial communities in the United States, and today is known as the birthplace of the American Industrial Revolution. The city had the abundant waterpower and access to cheap transportation ideal for the growing textile industry. By 1850, Lowell was the largest cotton textile center in the country; thousands of immigrants settled there to staff the "mile of mills" that lined the Merrimack. This prosperity lasted until the 1920s, when the New England textile industry started to collapse. At that time, the industry moved south leaving workers and mills behind.

As with many other New England towns, the departure of Lowell's industry caused a decline. Factory buildings were abandoned or underutilized.

In the early 1970s, however, the city began to realize that perhaps its most important asset was its past: the derelict mill buildings, machinery, and canal systems that, to many, were just eyesores. Through a Model Cities program several local groups showed an interest in preserving this asset. They developed the idea of making Lowell into an Urban National Cultural Park and a State Heritage Park. This was the first time that an urban-park concept had ever been proposed. A group of interested city residents and outside consultants set out to formulate more specific plans. The concept was explored further by private groups aided by grants from the National Endowment for the Arts and other sources.

The following revitalization objectives were established:

- The use of the city as a learning laboratory utilizing the existing buildings, manufacturing machinery, and engineering artifacts to illustrate industrial history.

- The improvement of the environment by rehabilitating existing buildings and support facilities to reinforce this unique historical theme.

- An increased respect for the cultural heritage of Lowell's people to reinforce pride in the diverse nationalities and backgrounds of former mill workers.

- The preservation and enhancement of these historic resources as a strategy for economic revitalization to encourage tourism and associated industries.[1]

Local, state, and federal governments are contributing to this project. The city adopted the cultural-park theme as the centerpiece of its planning efforts. By 1977, Lowell had already invested more than $1.6 million in downtown street improvements to reinforce the area's nineteenth-century flavor. Building owners in the central business district can use the free design service provided by the city's Division of Planning and Development if they wish to restore or renovate their facades. The canal system and surrounding area, as well as the central business district, have been designated local historic districts.

On the state level, $9.1 million has been committed to the development of the Lowell State Heritage Park aimed at preserving and developing the recreational potential of Lowell's canal system and riverbanks. Another $10 million is currently being used for improvements in the city, including landscaping and pedestrian amenities adjacent to the canals and in the historic districts.

Federal support has come through grants from the National Park Service for renovations of historic buildings and in-depth studies. Both local historic districts are listed in the National Register of Historic Places. According to a recent report, "over $26 million in local, state and federal monies is already expended or committed in projects either integral or supportive of the Cultural Park."[2] The same report proposes a future federal commitment of $40 million in capital improvements for building restoration and exhibits, and a yearly operating budget of over $1 million to establish and administer the Lowell National Cultural Park.

George L. Duncan, Executive Vice President of the First Bank and Trust Company in nearby Chelmsford, Massachusetts, and a resident of Lowell, recognized a problem early in the planning for Lowell's urban revitalization: local financial institutions were reluctant to lend money for major restorations, renovations, and even for new construction in the central busi-

ness district; and potential borrowers were also hesitant to seek loans to renovate their businesses in an area of depreciating real estate values and poor retail trade.

Duncan had observed the successful economic results of Boston's and nearby Newburyport's restoration and preservation efforts, and believed in the concept of the Lowell Cultural Park. In 1975, he set out to establish the Lowell Development and Financial Corporation (LDFC) to provide building owners and tenants with low-interest loans to renovate and restore their properties in accordance with the concept. LDFC's purpose was to provide attractive and consistent design in the downtown area, and at the same time, to improve business, raise property values, encourage investment, and build community pride.

Execution The Lowell Development and Financial Corporation, chartered in December, 1975, by the Massachusetts legislature, has been set up under guidelines established by the U.S. Small Business Administration (SBA) for the creation of state and local development corporations. A local development corporation, defined in Section 502 of the Small Business Investment Act of 1958, may be established under applicable state corporation law "to improve the local economy by encouraging community effort to assist small businesses, and to provide the necessary financing."[3] Often, a local banker will help to form a local development company to bring together resources of business, industry, local, state, and the federal government to jointly develop the economic potential of the community. Local residents or business people must own and control the corporation, which may be either profit or nonprofit, but must have at least 25 stockholders.

In its first effort, LDFC has sold more than $350,000 in $50 non-dividend shares to ten local banks in the Lowell area; its ultimate goal is $2 million. This money is being loaned to small businesses in the central business district for facade and interior renovations. Renovation work must be consistent with design guidelines established in accordance with the State Heritage

Park and the proposed Urban National Cultural Park. A nineteenth-century theme is recommended and, as noted, the city's Division of Planning and Development provides a free design service to ensure consistency.

The LDFC charges 4 percent to 5.5 percent interest on these loans to cover losses on defaulting loans and to allow the corporation to break even. The funds are available under three programs:

	Building Owners Facade & Interior Renovation Program	Building Owners Facade Program	Tenant/Lessee Facade Program
Maximum Amount of Loan	$33,000 or 30 percent of entire facade and interior improvements, whichever is greater	$12,000 or 75 percent of facade improvements, whichever is greater	$12,000 or 75 percent of facade improvements, whichever is greater
Rate of Interest	4 percent	4 percent	5½ percent
Maximum Terms	25 years or same length of first mortgage, whichever is greater	10 years or same length of first mortgage, whichever is greater	10 years or the remaining term of the lease, whichever is greater
Other Source of Funding	For all of the above programs up to a maximum of $4,000, there is funding for 25 percent of the costs of approved facade improvements available from the Division of Planning and Development for those buildings in the historic district. This is an outright grant which does not have to be repaid.		
Bank Financing Available if Needed	First mortgage	First mortgage or improvement loan	Leasehold improvement loan

By mid-1977, the LDFC program was operational. To date, four projects have been completed including a delicatessen, a beauty salon, a taxicab company, and a jewelry store. Six other projects are scheduled for completion by the end of 1977.

The A&L Taxi Company is an interesting example. Lucian Petren, the owner, rented space on Bridge Street, and for more than ten years, watched the abandoned building across the street deteriorate and blight the neighborhood. When the property came up for sale for the tax title, he bought it and began renovating it using materials to which he had been accustomed, like plastic coverings and neon signs. He was approached by the LDFC and told that he could get a $30,000 loan at 4 percent interest if he followed the city's design guidelines. In addition, he would be able to receive an outright grant of $4,000 for facade improvements. Since the 4 percent rate was considerably lower than the 9 percent he was getting from the banks, he signed up. Petren removed the plastic and signs that he had erected and re-renovated using brick and black and gold trim signs. The recent project is not meant to be a pure restoration, but it complements the existing architecture. In addition to his taxi operation, Petren leases space to other businesses and plans to build a new building on adjacent property, also in keeping with the nineteenth-century theme. According to Petren, "I had the opportunity to move out, but I believe the town is going to pick up. People have to work hand-in-hand to do it."[4]

Since the LDFC is structured as an SBA-recognized development corporation, it is also eligible to obtain SBA loans and loan guarantees which can total up to $500,000 per project. Once the initial $350,000 has been committed, the LDFC intends to broaden the scope of its activities to include even high-risk development—possible under a variety of SBA programs—bringing together banks and borrowers to achieve the preservation goals established for the downtown redevelopment.

The Petren building after renovation. (Lowell Division of Planning and Development)

Costs LDFC's overhead is minimal; administrative services are donated by its members. Figures for these costs were not available.

Problems The problems to date have been administrative and logistic. In the beginning, it was difficult to get the ten banks, the local business community, and the political structure to agree on a theme and direction. It has also taken time to encourage local participants to contribute by buying shares. In addition, processing applications, a service which is currently donated, places some administrative burden on corporation officers. Nevertheless, according to George Duncan, "The entire operation is functioning smoothly and the results are much better than we originally anticipated."[5]

Benefits This type of business involvement forms an interested coalition, spreads the risk, and increases the impact of preservation activities. It also elicits local, state, and federal funds through matching grants and loans, which increase the program's scope and effectiveness. "For every dollar invested by the LDFC," says Duncan, "three additional dollars are invested in the downtown from other sources. This kind of leverage can be a key factor in improving the economic and visual vitality of the downtown."[6]

The Company The following financial institutions have purchased shares in the LDFC:

B. F. Butler Co-operative
10 Hurd Street
Lowell, Massachusetts 01852

Lowell Institution for Savings
18 Shattuck Street
Lowell, Massachusetts 01852

Middlesex Bank
174 Central Street
Lowell, Massachusetts 01852

Lowell Bank and Trust Company
489 Merrimack Street
Lowell, Massachusetts 01852

Union National Bank
61 Merrimack Street
Lowell, Massachusetts 01852

The Lowell Five-Cent Savings Bank
34 John Street, PO Box 440
Lowell, Massachusetts 01852

First Bank and Trust Company
44 Central Square
Chelmsford, Massachusetts 01824

First Federal Savings & Loan
15 Hurd Street
Lowell, Massachusetts 01852

Lowell Co-operative Bank
18 Hurd Street
Lowell, Massachusetts 01852

Central Savings Bank
50 Central Street
Lowell, Massachusetts 01852

For further information contact:
George L. Duncan
President
Lowell Development and
    Financial Corporation
722 East Merrimack Street
Lowell, Massachusetts 01852

Footnotes

1. *Report of the Lowell Historic Canal District Commission to the Ninety-Fifth Congress of the United States of America,* January 3, 1977, p. 20.
2. *Ibid.,* p. 23.
3. U.S. Small Business Administration, *Urban Neighborhood Revitalization,* (Washington, D.C.: U.S. Small Business Administration, n.d.), p. 4.
4. INFORM interview with Lucian Petren, Owner, A&L Taxi Company, June, 1977.
5. INFORM interview with George L. Duncan, President, Lowell Development and Financial Corporation, June, 1977.
6. *Ibid.*

Summary Textron, a diversified manufacturing company, is the largest equity participant in one major renovation project and the developer of another in downtown Providence, Rhode Island, its home city. By mid-1977, Textron and three other local businesses had purchased the defunct Biltmore Hotel, and had begun renovations to transform it into a first-class 360-room facility. The city had also named Textron to renovate and develop the Providence Union Station complex, and negotiations were underway to obtain clear title to the land and buildings. The Union Station project will require ten years to complete. Over $60 million in public and private funds will be invested in the planned revitalization of seventy-acres of Providence's downtown area. Textron's projects will require over $46 million. Although the company's return on investment in these two reuse projects will probably be less than in its regular business ventures, the effort is expected to bring new vitality to the downtown area, thereby attracting further new investment.

Plot plan for Kennedy Plaza area in downtown Providence showing location of Biltmore Hotel and Union Station. (William McKenzie Woodward)

The Biltmore Hotel on Kennedy Plaza in downtown Providence. (Warren Jagger)

Background Providence (population 170,000) is Rhode Island's capital and business and financial center, as well as its largest city. Nearly 82 percent of the state's 923,000 residents live in its metropolitan area. A nineteenth-century textile and manufacturing center, Providence declined with its industries after World War II, and began to lose population to the suburbs. During the 1950s, Interstate 95 bisected the city, destroying nearly forty acres of mid-nineteenth-century neighborhoods. Urban renewal and Model Cities programs have also wiped out important commercial and mill buildings in and around the city. Since there has been relatively little new high-rise construction in the last ten years, most of the important nineteenth-century central business district still exists, but suffers from neglect.

Large-scale work to revitalize the Providence business district did not begin until the early 1970s. In 1973, Professor Gerald Howes and his transportation-planning students at the Rhode Island School of Design completed a study titled *Interface: Providence,* which assessed the city's accessibility and vitality, as well as the impact of the automobile on it. The following year, the Providence Citizens Lobby, which grew out of a series of forums prompted by the study, was formed to promote a revitalization program for downtown. At about the same time, newly-elected Mayor Vincent Cianci, Jr. filled the post of City Planner, which had been vacant for twelve years.

In 1975, the Providence business community formed its own group to assist in the revitalization effort. Led by Mr. G. William Miller, Chairman of

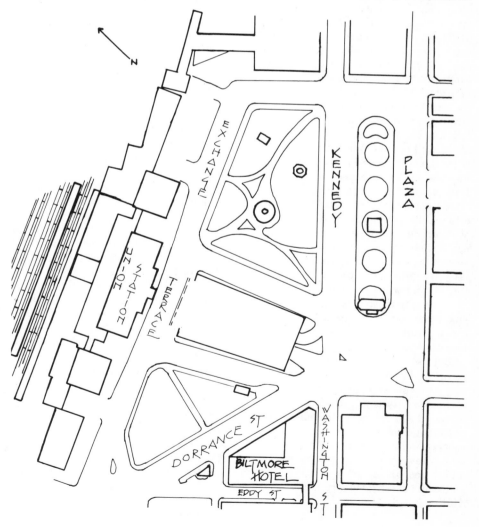

Textron, eight prominent firms—four local businesses and four banks—formed the 21st Providence Group.

During this same period, the Chamber of Commerce formed the Providence Foundation, a nonprofit corporation funded by thirty business, religious, philanthropic, and educational organizations to encourage citizens, businesses, and government officials to work together to attract new downtown investment. Through the Providence Foundation, the city's business community has helped develop the necessary planning and marketing feasibility studies to determine the course of future redevelopment. The Foundation's first project was a City Options Program, funded in conjunction with a grant from the National Endowment for the Arts and the City of Providence, which identified possibilities for future downtown development, and selected individual target areas. The Foundation is working closely with business and local and state government leaders to implement projects identified in the City Options Program. In 1975, the Foundation helped to fund a feasibility study for the adaptive reuse of the Providence Union Station, an underutilized four-building complex, as a transportation, office, and retail/entertainment center. Once the study was complete, the Foundation obtained federal Economic Development Administration grants to start the renovation work. Other projects include feasibility studies on renovating the Arcade, a nineteenth-century shopping mall, and the conversion of the Ocean State Theater, a recently refurbished rococo movie theater, into a performing-arts center. The Foundation is also attempting to persuade the state to locate a $24 million court complex in Providence's central business district.

Redevelopment will begin in the Kennedy Plaza/Burnside Park area, a major downtown open space near City Hall. The City Hall's exterior has already been cleaned, and renovation of the interior is underway. Textron, in cooperation with several other local firms, has agreed to help renovate two structures on this plaza: the Biltmore Hotel and the Providence Union Station.

Execution *The Biltmore Hotel.* The Biltmore Hotel was completed in 1922 at a cost of $7 million. It was partially financed by $2.5 million in preferred stock sold to local businesses by the Providence Chamber of Commerce. The hotel, designed by the New York architectural firm of Warren and Wetmore—architects for New York's Grand Central Station—employed highly advanced design techniques. The completely fireproof, nineteen-story structure with 500 guest rooms was Providence's second skyscraper. The Biltmore's simple, almost "modern" exterior contrasted sharply with its classically inspired interior public spaces. The ceiling of the main two-story lobby is covered with elaborate geometric coffering richly detailed with classical motifs. Public function rooms and a grand ballroom on the top two floors possess similar elaborate decorative detail. Throughout it history, the Biltmore has been the gathering place for Rhode Island's social, business, and government leaders. However, in the late 1960s, the hotel fell on hard times, and it finally closed in January, 1975.

Recognizing the destructive effect of a highly visible empty building and the need for a first-class hotel downtown, members of the 21st Providence Group formed a limited partnership to restore the Biltmore to active use. It purchased the hotel building in September, 1976. The general partners, Textron, the Outlet Company, a local retail store, the *Providence Journal*, a local newspaper, and the Business Development Company of Rhode Island, a nonprofit business development firm which loans money to local businesses, all developed subsidiaries to participate in the project. This consortium retained Hotels of Distinction, Inc., a hotel-management company which currently operates the Copley Plaza in Boston, to supervise the renovation and manage the hotel. The Boston architectural firm of Shepley, Bulfinch, Richardson and Abbot, and Providence architects Sturgis, Daughn and Salisbury, and Morris Nathanson Design have been retained for the project.

After examining several reuse options for the building, the new owners decided to restore the Biltmore as a first-class hotel catering to business travelers and corporate meetings. The public rooms will be elegant, the guest rooms, spacious. Relatively few exterior changes are planned, with the possible exception of a new glass elevator on the outside which will serve the public function rooms on the lower floors and the restaurant and the ballroom on the upper two stories. Interior renovation work will respect the character of existing detail. One major change will be the removal of the marble staircase in the main lobby to create a three-story entrance lobby with a registration desk on the ground level. Many of the original 500 rooms will be enlarged, reducing the total to 360. The smallest rooms will contain 225 square feet; the largest, 550 square feet. Most of the existing tubs and tile work will be saved, but other plumbing and lighting fixtures will be replaced. All new room furniture, carpeting, and draperies will be installed. On the top floor, several windows will be enlarged to provide restaurant patrons with a panoramic view of the State House and the Union Station.

Since the new owners acquired the property, work has moved forward on an exacting schedule:

September to October, 1976—Financial feasibility studies were completed for a variety of potential uses, and the hotel option chosen as the most attractive.

November, 1976, to April, 1977—Architectural drawings and specifications were prepared.

May, 1977—Demolition and renovation work began.

June, 1978—Grand opening scheduled, 56 years after the original opening party.

Providence Union Station. Completed in 1898 by the New York, New Haven & Hartford Railroad, the Union Station is built on a low man-made hill. The platforms are reached from the main terminal through underground passageways. The complex originally consisted of five buildings, laid out symmetrically, with the main passenger terminal in the center connected by colonnades to flanking buildings. A fire in 1941 destroyed the easternmost building. The station, built of yellow mottled brick with red sandstone trim, was designed to harmonize with the Renaissance-inspired architecture of the City Hall and the State Capitol. The original plans called for a boulevard running under the complex, connecting it with the State Capitol and the City Hall. This boulevard was never executed. The space between the rear of the station and the foot of the capitol terrace, planned as a park, is now used as a parking lot. In addition, compounding the design problems, the

Aerial view of Union Station prior to renovation in 1977. Elevated parking deck is in the foreground with railroad tracks behind. (Dennis P. Albert)

Artist's rendering of the Union Station complex after renovation with elevated parking deck removed.

city had built an elevated parking deck in front of the main terminal obscuring the view of the building from Kennedy Plaza, the prime open space in the area.

As train travel diminished during the 1950s, the station suffered from neglect and lack of maintenance. Many described it as a "Chinese Wall" cutting through the city center. However, recent efforts to improve service in the Northeast Rail Corridor have increased use of the terminal facilities. Under the Amtrak Improvement Act, federal funds are now available to renovate stations as transportation centers. In early 1977, the Federal Railway Administration allocated $13.2 million to repair the central terminal building, improve vehicular access to the complex, and add nearly 1,200 new parking spaces (480 in a new parking garage) around the station. Of the total new investment in the station, $6.4 million will be used to upgrade the central terminal. Improvements planned for the building include: installation of new mechanical systems; replacement of the porte cochere (an iron and glass structure extending from the main terminal's entrance over the adjacent driveway), removed in 1954; and addition of new escalators and direct access passageways to rail platforms. The city will also remove the elevated parking deck in front of the main terminal.

The city named Textron as the commercial developer for the Union Station in February, 1977. Redeveloping the complex and the 55-acre surrounding area is expected to take ten years. The renovation and adaptive reuse of the station itself is the keystone of the project. Textron is obligated to go forward with the station-complex renovation if a series of conditions are met, including improvement of the Kennedy Plaza area by the city.

Major elements in the company's redevelopment plan include the following:

1. Within the next three years, subject to a number of conditions, Textron will renovate the four-building, 120,000-square-foot Union Station complex located on 4.3 acres. Amtrak will be the major tenant in the center building, with the remaining space rented for government offices, retail shops, and a restaurant.

2. Textron will explore the feasibility of constructing a 400,000-square-foot high-rise office building on land adjacent to the station complex. The company would use about 100,000 square feet for its headquarters, doubling its present space. The remaining space would be leased to other tenants. Completion of the office tower would follow the station-complex renovation by several years.

3. If the station complex renovation and the office tower are successful, Textron will explore the feasibility of building a 200,000-square-foot retail center in the vicinity.

4. Textron will undertake long-range planning for use of the remaining land between the State House grounds and the Union Station. This land, currently used as parking lots, could be developed for park, recreational, commercial, and residential purposes, including luxury condominiums.

As of mid-1977, attempts were being made to resolve the intricate ownership problems so that the city could gain unchallenged title to the railroad property and sell it to Textron. Textron is interviewing architects to plan the station renovation. If the title problems can be cleared, financing arranged, and the necessary leases signed, construction work could begin during winter, 1978.

Costs *The Biltmore Hotel.* Textron and its partners purchased the hotel for $925,000 in September, 1976, and plan to invest another $10.5 million in the renovation. This represents a new investment of $31,740 per room, approximately half the expenditure required to build a new hotel of similar size, though not of similar quality. It would be impossible to duplicate the quality in some of the public function rooms at almost any price today. If the hotel maintains a 65 percent occupancy level at a $34 average room rate, it will break even. While the venture is not expected to show a tremendous return, Textron and its other partners do not expect the hotel to show continuing losses.

The Rhode Island Historical Commission has nominated the Biltmore Hotel to the National Register of Historic Places. If the nomination is accepted, and the renovation plans are approved by the National Park Service, the building will be eligible for accelerated depreciation benefits under the Tax Reform Act of 1976. The current equity investment in the hotel is $1.75 million, of which Textron has supplied $1 million. The partners hope to raise a total equity of $2.5 million and obtain a first mortgage from a consortium of five local banks for $6.5 million. These banks have agreed to provide the construction funds for the renovation and to grant a 25-year mortgage at less than conventional rates when the work is complete. The remaining $2.5 million will come from the U.S. Economic Development Administration which will provide a 25-year second mortgage at 7⅜ percent interest.

Providence Union Station. Textron estimated that a $35.5 million investment will be required to complete the first three phases of the station project, including:

1. $7.5 million for the renovation of the four-building station complex. Since Textron expects to purchase the buildings from the city for a nominal price, nearly all the funds will be used for improving the facility. Textron expects to invest $1 million to $2 million, with the remaining funds coming from government grants or loans and conventional financing from local banks. As in the Biltmore renovation, other local businesses may join Textron as equity participants.

2. $20 million for a new high-rise office tower. This figure represents a cost of approximately $50 per square foot for the new construction.

3. $8 million for a 200,000-square-foot retail complex.

Problems Both the Biltmore Hotel and the Union Station are high-risk development projects which require a developer with substantial financial strength and staying power. In both projects, there is great uncertainty about the required total renovation cost and whether the necessary market exists for the hotel, restaurants, shops, and office space. Although the hotel has already been granted preferred tax status for ten years, both projects must receive long-term property-tax concessions. Similar ventures in other cities have been successful, but there is no guarantee that they will work in Providence.

In the Union Station project, Textron and the city are having difficulties obtaining clear title to the property. The company has invested substantial legal and administrative personnel time in ownership negotiations. If a clear title for the station complex cannot be achieved, the project may be killed and Textron will lose its investment. Textron also still has to negotiate a satisfactory arrangement with Amtrak for use of the main building and be satisfied that the remaining 55 acres can be developed in a satisfactory and harmonious manner.

Benefits The long-term benefits of these projects to both the City of Providence and Textron are not entirely related to each project's "bottom line." According to John B. Henderson, Textron's Senior Vice President—Policy Planning, who is guiding the company's involvement in the Biltmore and the Union Station, the completion of the two renovations should serve as a catalyst to attract further new investment into the downtown from both the public and private sectors. Textron would like to build a major high-rise building to house its corporate headquarters and believes that when revitalized, the Union Station area would be an extremely attractive site. If the number of people using the downtown can be increased markedly, then the dependent retail, cultural, and entertainment sectors can grow as well. By making the downtown a better working environment, the company is in a better position to retain and attract top-quality employees.[1]

A major advantage of the renovation over new construction is the reduced time and money required to complete it. If completed on schedule, the Biltmore will be operating only nineteen months after purchase: less than half the time (and cost) required to build a new hotel.

The Company Founded in 1923 in Providence as the Franklin Rayon Company, Textron today is a highly diversified multi-national corporation with 181 plants and 64,000 employees (3,200 in Rhode Island). In 1976, sales reached $2.6 billion up from 1975's figure of $2.45 billion. Net income over the same period rose from $95.9 million to $121 million. Textron's products include helicopters, zippers, snowmobiles, greeting cards, and metal machinery, as well as fire and casualty insurance.

For further information contact:
John Henderson
Senior Vice President
Textron, Inc.
40 Westminster Street
Providence, Rhode Island 02903

Ron Marsella
Executive Director
Providence Foundation
10 Dorrance Street
Providence, Rhode Island 02903

Footnotes

1. "Project Seen Benefiting Both Textron and City," *Providence Evening Bulletin*, 10 February 1977.

Trend Publications

Summary Trend Publications, the largest publisher of business periodicals in the South, is developing a former cigar factory in Ybor City, the Latin section of Tampa, Florida, into a multi-use commercial center, named Ybor Square. Trend purchased the 90,000-square-foot complex of three buildings in 1972. Since that time, it has created modern offices for itself on the top floor of one building; an arcade of specialty shops and a restaurant on the ground floor of the same building; and a Nostalgia Market, where vendors sell antiques and collectibles from small open cubicles, in another former factory building. The development is attracting both local shoppers and tourists to an area rich in Hispanic ethnic history. The retail shops opened in late 1974, and by 1978, the complex is expected to be operating in the black.

Background V. M. Ybor, a cigar manufacturer, originally moved his factory from Cuba to Key West. In 1885, he founded Ybor City after purchasing forty acres outside Tampa. There, he built another cigar factory and later invested $500,000 to create a model city for his workers. In the 1890s, Cubans, fleeing the harsh treatment of the Spanish, flocked to Ybor City, and it became a center for cigar making. Cuban patriot Jose Marti spoke on the steps of the Ybor Cigar Factory in 1893 to rally American support for Cuba's fight against Spain. In 1898, Teddy Roosevelt and his Rough Riders stopped in Ybor City on their way to Cuba. Once larger than downtown Tampa, Ybor City is now part of that city.

In recent years, the urban-renewal bulldozer has destroyed much of the early factory-worker housing in Ybor City. In its place now stand the functional buildings of the Hillsborough Community College. However, most of the historic commercial structures in the area have been saved, although some show signs of severe neglect.

The three buildings of the original Ybor Cigar Factory, once the largest cigar factory in the world, are located between 8th and 9th Avenues and 13th and 14th Streets near the Community College. These Victorian brick and timber commercial structures contain 90,000 square feet of space on one-and-a-half acres of land. They adjoin each other in a U-shape configuration around a Spanish-style central courtyard. Interior beams are heart pine, as are the wide floor boards. The latter are commonly four inches thick. The complex is listed in the National Register of Historic Places and is a Florida Monument.

The original Factory Building, erected in 1886, is three stories tall, with the exception of a one-story north wing. Tobacco was graded on the first floor, and the fine Havana types were stored in the basement humidor along with the finished cigars. On the two upper floors, more than 500 workers hand rolled cigars while a reader, known as "El Lector," entertained, educated, and propagandized from his elevated box. Each worker paid a quarter per week for the reader's services. Arriving tobacco ships were sighted from the cupola on the top of the Factory. Adjacent to the Factory, a three-story Stemmery Building, where the tobacco-leaf stems were removed, was added in 1902. At the same time, a warehouse was constructed across the courtyard from the Factory. This one-story structure with 24-foot ceilings was served by a small-gauge railroad which delivered tobacco from the harbor. A garden patio connects the Stemmery and the Factory.

In 1955, the American Tobacco Company sold the buildings—acquired in an earlier transaction—to the Havatampa Corporation, which continued to make cigars there until the mid-1960s. The buildings became obsolete with the introduction of modern mechanized cigar-production techniques, and they were sold to Trend Publications in December, 1972.

Execution By 1972, Trend Publications had outgrown its Tampa offices, and was looking for a site for expansion. Behind the peeling paint of the severely neglected old buildings, Trend President Harris H. Mullen envisioned a unique corporate home, a combination office, retail, and entertainment complex that would house artists, writers, antique dealers, galleries, and boutiques, attracting both local residents and tourists. The integrity of the historic buildings was to be maintained, while the interiors were updated with modern facilities. Trend established a real estate division to develop the complex.

Relying on his own intuition, not feasibility studies, Mullen's first project was to create new offices for Trend Publications. Architects Friedman and McKenna of Tampa were retained to develop drawings for the conversion. However, as the planning process stretched into the second year, Mullen recognized that if the total project were to be successful, he must demonstrate that there was a market for his idea. In summer, 1974, the first floor of the Factory Building was cleaned out, and 28 individual wire cubicles were built, each containing 200 square feet of storage space. The cubicles were rented on a monthly basis to individual collectors, antique dealers, and artisans. Every Saturday and Sunday since October, 1974, these vendors have sold their wares in the courtyard and from the cubicles. This Nostalgia Market has become a major event in Ybor City, attracting several thousand spectators and collectors. All the cubicles are rented, and there is a waiting list for space. Each dealer pays $62.50 per month.

By July, 1975, Trend's new offices on the third floor of the Stemmery Building were complete, and the company had moved in. A new glass-enclosed elevator was built on the exterior of the wing between the Factory Building and the Stemmery. The interior brick in the wing was cleaned, and a new three-story staircase was installed, providing a modern entrance way to the firm's offices. To create Trend's 12,000 square feet of contemporary office space, interior designers Dean-Redman of Tampa exposed and sandblasted interior brick and timber, and sanded and refinished the pine floors. The building materials provide the major elements of interest in the offices. Modern furnishings and paintings decorate the major rooms, which are defined by partial walls and flow easily into each other. There are several meeting rooms, individual offices for executives, and plenty of light and open space for editors and layout artists.

By October, 1975, the interior brick and timber on the first floor of the Stemmery Building had also been cleaned, and a mini-shopping mall had been created there. This was accomplished by placing a series of ten-foot partitions between the supporting posts. The fourteen specialty shops in the Stemmery Arcade offer a variety of merchandise, including candles, antiques, candy, jewelry, stamps, children's toys and clothes, plants, Cuban coffee and sandwiches, and, of course, hand-rolled cigars. Each shop contains approximately 380 square feet of space. By mid-1977, all the shops were occupied, although only about half were original tenants. Arcade tenants pay about $9 per square foot per year for shop space, plus a percentage of gross sales over a specified minimum. Gross sales for the Stemmery Arcade shops average approximately $20,000 per year, and some of the more successful enterprises are expected to pay percentage rentals in 1978. Utilities and services are prorated for tenants.

The Stemmery Arcade also contains the Rough Riders Restaurant, a bar and grill, run by a local entrepreneur, which serves delicatessen fare. The restaurant has steadily built its clientele, and now attracts 250 for lunch daily. By fall, 1977, renovation work on the second floor of the Stemmery will be complete, and the Rough Riders will expand into 4,000 additional square feet. Also on the second floor, a large open display space is planned, where dealers and individuals can sell antiques.

The central courtyard was landscaped to create an entrance way for the complex and in 1976, vintage Ybor City streetlights were installed. Throughout the year, arts and crafts festivals, antique shows, and photography exhibits are held in the courtyard. Local performing groups entertain the shoppers in the outdoor theater each weekend.

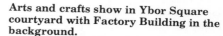

Aerial view of Ybor Square complex.

Arts and crafts show in Ybor Square courtyard with Factory Building in the background.

Future development of Ybor Square will continue in stages as market demand permits. With renovation work in the Stemmery complete, Mullen plans to upgrade the cubicles on the first floor of the Factory to more sophisticated shops similar to those in the Stemmery Arcade, and perhaps build additional cubicles on the second and third floors. The garden patio between the Factory and the Stemmery will be landscaped. Development plans for the warehouse are still uncertain. At one point, Mullen considered building a 256-seat theater in it, and creating additional floors for apartments. Townhouses on the second and third floors of the Factory have also been contemplated. The theater idea has been abandoned, but Mullen would still like to build some residential units in the project, if it can be done profitably.

In 1976, Trend's total income from the Ybor Square rentals was approximately $80,000.

Costs Trend would not disclose the amount of its investment in Ybor Square. The company paid cash for the land and the three buildings in 1972, acquiring them for substantially less than the $250,000 asking price.[1] Renovation work in the Stemmery cost approximately $20 per square foot. Construction costs were financed by a local bank at a floating rate 3 percent over prime. The construction loan was recently refinanced with an $800,000 long-term mortgage.

Trend spends approximately $20,000 per year promoting the complex, including $10,000 for media advertising. While the project income has yet to cover the yearly expenses, Mullen expects Ybor Square to be operating in the black by 1978.

Problems Although Ybor Square has been developed nearly as originally planned, the timetable for completion has been lengthened from two or three years to six or eight. Trend began construction work on the project in early 1974, just as the country entered its most severe recession since the 1930s. During the same period, the company was starting its new magazine, *The South*, and its own financial resources were strained. Money was very tight, and the construction loan, floating at 3 percent above prime, reached 15 percent at one point.

Another problem has been attracting a clientele to Ybor Square. The complex is small compared to the regional shopping centers, and inconveniently located. In addition, local prejudices about inner-city neighborhoods have had to be overcome. There were also problems during the initial phase of the Stemmery Arcade, since many merchants were first-time shop owners. Half the original tenants are no longer there, and a series of new ones had to be found.

Benefits Although Ybor Square has been slow to pay its own way, during the first five years the depreciation deductions and losses did provide some tax savings for the company. Mullen projects profitable long-term development. Recent appraisals indicate that the market value of the property is appreciating faster than operational losses.

For Harris Mullen, the chief benefit of Ybor Square has been the satisfaction of seeing his vision become reality. At the same time, Trend employees have gained a very special working environment. For Ybor City, the development has brought new visitors, new revenues, and new life to an area that had been deteriorating for several decades.

Florida Governor Reubin Askew recognized Trend's development at Ybor Square and its many cultural programs by naming it the 1976 recipient of the Annual Governor's Award in the Arts.

The Company Trend Publications is the South's largest publisher of business periodicals, textbooks, books, and pamphlets about the region. Its two major publications are *Florida Trend*, a monthly magazine with a circulation of 30,000 featuring articles on Florida business and finance; and *The South*, a monthly magazine with a circulation of 50,000 featuring articles of general interest about the South.

Harris Mullen is the publisher and major stockholder of Trend, which he founded in Tampa in 1957. The company employs 28 people and maintains headquarters at Ybor Square, as well as branch sales offices in Atlanta and Fort Lauderdale. All stock is privately held, and financial information is not available.

For further information contact:
Harris Mullen
Publisher
Trend Publications
P.O. Box 2350
Tampa, Florida 33601

Footnotes

1. Robert Fraser, "Monumental Faith," *St. Petersburg Times*, 10 December 1972, p. 5-H.

Once viewed as a genteel pursuit for aristocratic matrons, preservation today has meaning for everyone from inner-city residents to jazz buffs. Residents of Boston, New York, Richmond, San Francisco, and cities and towns across the country are discovering that they too have roots. Today, there are over 6,000 local historical societies in the United States.

Yet, business support for preservation, in such forms as outright donations of money, goods, or services has always been limited and indeed, by some measures, may even be decreasing. A 1976 survey by the Business Committee for the Arts, a nonprofit organization interested in stimulating corporate giving, found that business contributions to the arts increased overall from $144 million to $221 million between 1973 and 1976, and the number of times "historical and cultural restorations" were cited as recipients by participating companies increased from 10 percent in 1973 to 32 percent in 1976. Nevertheless, the amount of each charitable dollar contributed to preservation actually declined from 5 cents to 3 cents over the same period,[1] representing a decline from $7.2 million in 1973 to $6.63 million in 1976.

INFORM's study indicates that business would have much to gain by reversing this apparent trend. For the twenty companies profiled, the donation of money, property, materials, and publicity to preservation causes has always produced a return: either literally, in tax write-offs of business expenses or charitable tax deductions; or figuratively, in enhancing the company's image.

The firms profiled here represent a cross section of American business. They include large and small companies from the steel, tobacco, oil, and printing industries, as well as consumer-oriented businesses and public utilities.

These firms have donated funds to support a wide variety of projects: an archeological dig in Virginia, a photographic survey of U.S. county courthouses, an architectural analysis of important buildings in Mississippi, and the restorations of a grist mill in New Jersey, an opera house in Wilmington, Delaware, and a Moravian village in North Carolina. The companies have contributed property, including historic houses in Louisiana and Virginia, an 1883 office building in Troy, New York, and surplus gas stations in various cities and towns. They have given publicity support in several forms, ranging from Flanigan's underwriting of short films on historic local structures to Pinaire's production of four-color posters on preservation themes.

INFORM found that the motives behind contributions to preservation projects were frequently quite complex. In thirteen cases, location was a determining factor. R. J. Reynolds Industries' long association with Winston-Salem, for example, helped prompt its donations to Old Salem, Inc., a nonprofit group dedicated to the preservation of that city's Moravian heritage.

Nine of the companies studied reported that they were motivated by a sense of social responsibility, either on a local or national scale.* This "enlightened self-interest" encouraged Atlantic Richfield's gift of abandoned gas stations to community groups, providing the groups with

*Although not directly related to INFORM's study, a survey of 309 corporate chairmen and presidents conducted by The Conference Board of New York found self-interest (defined as public service necessary for the long-range survival of the corporation as an institution) was the second leading motive for corporate public-service activity.[2]

General Preservation Support

meeting places and relieving the company of abandoned properties which earned no income.

In six cases, INFORM found executive interest in preservation to have played a major role in the company's decision to contribute. Reynolds Metals, for example, preserved several stone canal locks in Richmond partly because a company Vice President saw the benefits of a revitalized river front to both the company and the city, and persuaded management to save them.

Among the companies studied, the indirect public-relations and economic benefits gained by contributing to preservation were found to have varied. Seventeen of the twenty businesses received significant favorable publicity of one sort or another. Flanigan's, to give one example, was cited by the City of Rochester, the State of New York, and the Business Committee for the Arts for its work on behalf of preservation in upstate New York. This furniture company sponsored films, distributed reprints of articles on preservation, helped develop articles on the same subject, and sponsored an essay contest on area landmarks. Bird & Son has been cited in the *Congressional Record* as well as by national columnists Bob Considine and Don Oakley for its national matching-grants awards to preservation groups.

Most companies studied by INFORM were reluctant to reveal tax benefits gained from contributions to preservation. However, Union Camp did disclose that it took a $26,000 tax deduction from its gift of the Tower Hill Plantation and ten surrounding acres to the National Trust for Historic Preservation. It had acquired the Plantation and surrounding woodlands in 1960 as part of a routine expansion of its holdings. The company instituted a program of donations of ecologically or historically important lands in 1975.

Sometimes, companies deducted the cost of their donations as part of their operating expenses, as Pinaire Lithographing did in the design and production of its two preservation posters.

In general, the contribution process has gone smoothly, with few problems encountered by the companies involved in preservation support. While those problems that arose were usually peculiar to the individual case, one which was common to several projects turned out to be administration. Two companies established their own support mechanisms without realizing that administering a nationally oriented program can be a full-time job. Bird & Son, a building-materials manufacturer, discovered this to be true in distributing a series of grants to preservation groups across the country.

All the contributions described here were handled by the companies themselves. However, some companies have established foundations to administer donations. This mechanism is especially appropriate for businesses whose earnings fluctuate dramatically, since it insures funding continuity even in bad financial years.

As of mid-1977, there were about 1,500 company-sponsored foundations in the United States. Although the Tax Reform Act of 1969 imposed a 4 percent levy on recipients of foundation grants and required more detailed financial disclosure from foundations, the number of foundations has not noticeably decreased.

The most important piece of federal legislation affecting business support of preservation is the Federal Revenue Act of 1935. Under this law, a corporation may donate up to 5 percent of its pre-tax income to charitable causes and deduct contributions as an expense for income-tax purposes. (An amendment to the Act later extended the same benefit to banks.) Companies may also deduct business expenses—including charitable contributions of facilities, employee time, products, services, and advertising—from taxable income. Nevertheless, the Commission on Private Philanthropy, a privately sponsored group consisting of representatives from business, community groups, and government, issued a report in 1975 which found that the average corporate charitable contribution has been about 1 percent of pre-tax net income in recent years. The Commission, chaired by John H. Filer, Chairman of Aetna Life & Casualty, reported that half of the annual $1 billion contribution by business to philanthropic causes is generated by the 1,000 largest corporations. It estimated that perhaps another $1 billion is given in other ways, such as donations of in-kind services, use of facilities, investments in urban revitalization, and support of job-training programs for the underprivileged or handicapped. The Commission's primary recommendation was that "corporations set as a minimum goal, to be reached no later than 1980, the giving to charitable purposes of 2% of pre-tax income."[3] Not everyone, of course, favors what amounts to public subsidy of corporate and private giving via tax benefits. However, the Commission, which generally favored this approach, recommended a "disappearing floor" for tax deductions only when donations amount to 1 percent or 2 percent of pre-tax income; a 10 percent tax credit if donations exceed an established level; and a 2 percent "philanthropy needs" tax which corporations or the federal government could distribute to charitable causes. Others feel that a social audit of business expenditures should be instituted. They prefer a fixed-percentage tax of corporate income for charitable causes.

The Business Committee for the Arts (BCA), founded in 1967 and backed by corporations, is also trying to stimulate company giving. It counsels both cultural institutions and businesses about effective programs, and presents annual awards in cooperation with *Forbes* magazine (they were formerly given in conjunction with *Esquire*) to businesses for contributions to the nation's cultural life. Of the companies profiled in this book Exxon, Reynolds Metals, Atlantic Richfield, Eastman Kodak, Flanigan's, and Seagram's have received such awards.

Business support of preservation has a significance beyond its direct and indirect benefits to company and community. It also helps shape broader public attitudes. As James Biddle, President of the National Trust, pointed out in *Preservation News*:

Actively promoting historic preservation or merely suggesting that old buildings are culturally significant, has a lasting effect on American attitudes. Just as "new, modern and improved" were key adjectives in advertising copy in the 1950's and 60's, so "enduring, antique, old-fashioned" and even "renewed" are the top sellers of the mid-1970's.[4]

210

Footnotes

1. Business Committee for the Arts, *Business Support for the Arts—1976* (New York: Business Committee for the Arts, 1976).
2. James F. Harris and Anne Klepper, *Corporate Philanthropic Public Service Activities, 1976* (New York: The Conference Board, 1976), p. 17.
3. Commission on Private Philanthropy and Public Needs, *Giving in America—Toward a Stronger Voluntary Sector* (Washington, D.C.: Library of Congress, 1975).
4. *Preservation News,* November, 1976, p. 5.

Summary In 1972, Busch Properties, Inc., a wholly owned subsidiary of Anheuser-Busch, Inc., contributed more than $150,000 to support archeological surveys conducted at Kingsmill on the James, a new residential community near Williamsburg, Virginia. This money, given directly to the Virginia Historic Landmarks Commission, supports efforts to identify and document early settlement on the property as far back as prehistoric times. Busch Properties is developing the 2,900-acre site under a master plan that will accommodate up to 5,000 homes and still leave more than 40 percent of the land as greenbelts and open spaces. The results of the survey have caused the developer to revise many of the original plans to avoid encroaching on newly uncovered historic sites. These changes have cost additional time and money, but have helped provide a good public image and a unique marketing approach for the new community.

Background In the late 1960s, Anheuser-Busch wanted a new location in the mid-Atlantic region of the United States for its diverse operations including a brewery. The company was invited to the Williamsburg area by the leadership of the Colonial Williamsburg Foundation, which is responsible for the direction, administration, and support of Colonial Williamsburg. Anheuser-Busch was interested in the area because of its proximity to the major metropolitan markets of Richmond, Norfolk, Newport News, and Hampton, Virginia, as well as Washington, D.C., and because of its rail, truck, and ship-transport accessibility. Anheuser-Busch acquired approximately 3,600 acres of land—most of it from Colonial Williamsburg—for the site of its ninth brewery, for Busch Gardens, a family entertainment attraction featuring exhibits, rides, and wildlife, for the Kingsmill on the James residential development, and for a Busch corporate-center complex.

When Colonial Williamsburg sold the property to Busch, it stipulated in the purchase agreement that a review committee, consisting of Foundation and community representatives, was to be established to ensure that Kingsmill would be developed in harmony with the present character of Colonial Williamsburg and its environs. With the help of well-respected planners such as Carl Feiss, Grady Clay, and Conrad Wirth, tight environmental and aesthetic controls regulating land use and building design were developed and implemented. Kingsmill was not to compete with Colonial Williamsburg, but was to preserve the historic character of the land. By controlling and overseeing the development of the Kingsmill property adjacent to its new brewery, Anheuser-Busch could ensure maintenance of the high quality, character, value, and use of its immediate neighborhood. The company hired the well-known planning and landscape-design firm, Sasaki, Daw-

The remains of the eighteenth-century Kingsmill Plantation.

son, and Demay, which in conjunction with local planners and community representatives, developed a master plan for the site. Ecologically sensitive areas were identified, and major construction, with the exception of unobtrusive pedestrian and bicycle trails, was prohibited.

It was widely known that the remains of historic sites existed on the property. However, these sites, except for the extant outbuildings of the Kingsmill Plantation, were not considered in the original master plan. Their archeological value was overlooked until a major discovery was made. Early in 1972, Dr. William H. Kelso, an archeologist with the Virginia Historic Landmarks Commission (VHLC), discovered an old well eroding away from the steep banks of the James River on the Busch property. He obtained a $10,000 grant from Anheuser-Busch to excavate and survey the well. Wells are excellent archeological resources, since they contain a preserved time line of layers of sediment and discarded objects that clearly illustrate the history of settlement. The artifacts found in this well, dating back to the early 1700s, prompted Busch Properties to offer $150,000 to the VHLC to survey other parts of the Kingsmill property. Kelso and a team of assistants have been working on the project ever since, and the company has continued its support beyond the original grant.

Execution Since 1972, more than 34 sites have been surveyed at Kingsmill by the VHLC. Under the direction of Dr. Kelso, teams of students from the Department of Archeology at William and Mary, as well as from other colleges and universities, together with several state archeologists, have traced the historic settlement of the Kingsmill property back to the early seventeenth century, just after Jamestown was colonized in 1607. In addition, the Department of Anthropology at William and Mary, supported by grants from Busch Properties, has surveyed fourteen prehistoric sites, some dating from as far back as 3000 B.C. Oysters, abundant in the James River, attracted early Indian settlement. Shell middens, or waste pits, indicated the presence of campsites. Artifacts, such as stone tools and projectile points, were also found, as were the outlines of one-room oval dwellings.

Major historic sites that have been excavated include:

- Littletown, the early-seventeenth-century plantation of Colonel Thomas Pettus. Pettus was a prominent landowner and public official. The site includes the remains of the mansion house, several outbuildings, and a well. Among the artifacts recovered from this site are a bottle seal bearing the initials of Pettus, a copper tobacco-can lid, and a Spanish silver coin.

- The Bray Plantation, the eighteenth-century residence of James Bray II, a burgess and justice of the peace from James City County. The remains of the mansion house together with five other buildings and a well were found. Artifacts from this site include a number of family wine-bottle seals; a pewter spoon bearing the name of David Menetrie, a Williamsburg brick mason; a sheet-brass lion's paw; and a sealed bottle more than 200 years old and still half-filled with milk.

- The Kingsmill Plantation, an eighteenth-century structure, and one of the grandest in the colonial Tidewater region. This was the most elaborate site surveyed and included the foundation of the mansion house flanked by two extant outbuildings. The site also yielded the remains of an earlier seventeeth-century building which contained one of the most valuable Kingsmill artifacts: a seventeenth-century pipe bowl bearing a carving of a small ship. The remains of a nineteenth-century dwelling were also found. This site yielded high-quality ceramics and cutlery.

The artifacts found at these and other sites have been publicly exhibited in the nearby Anheuser-Busch Hospitality Center. Several excavation sites have been preserved as parks within the development area, but are only open to residents of Kingsmill and guests.

While William Kelso first recognized the hidden value of the land and the means of preserving it, a number of other people contributed greatly to the effort's success. Among them were Walter E. Diggs, Jr., then President of Busch Properties, who recognized both the responsibilities and benefits of such a project, and Junius R. Fishburne, Jr., then Executive Director of the VHLC. The VHLC has encouraged corporate participation in several important preservation projects in the Commonwealth of Virginia (see Reynolds Metals, Ethyl, and Union Camp).

Costs
Direct

- $10,000 for the excavation and documentation of the Harrop Well "kick off" project urged by Dr. William Kelso.

- $150,000 for the initial contract with the Virginia Historic Landmarks Commission to conduct the archeological survey.

- $10,000 for archeological surveys of the prehistory of Kingsmill conducted by the College of William and Mary.

Indirect
Figures for the cost of the time and effort spent revising original plans for the development, and the donation of personnel and equipment to help with survey excavations were unavailable.

Problems The most difficult problems for Anheuser-Busch were the costs caused by delays and plan revisions necessitated by the discovery of significant archeological sites. These meant that the designs for road and building-site placements had to be redrawn.

Benefits Anheuser-Busch and Busch Properties have received extensive favorable publicity for their archeological efforts at Kingsmill. Although Busch bought the property primarily because of its location and the resulting "spin off" benefits of being situated in a major historic tourist area, the archeological project was an additional bonus, creating community goodwill and attracting people to the site. Several of the Kingsmill homesites were sold as a direct result of articles written about the archeological activities. Kingsmill is no longer just a development in a unique environment. It incorporates a rich legacy of art and artifact that no competitive new residential community can offer. Materials and information found in the surveys are incorporated in advertising and promotional campaigns. (The Kings-

mill logo was developed from a seal found on an early-eighteenth-century wine bottle found in one of the excavations.) The local economy has been bolstered by the additional business and employment generated by the new brewery and Busch Gardens. Anheuser-Busch also pays approximately 25 percent of the county's taxes. In a report to the community in February, 1976, Anheuser-Busch noted that its combined Williamsburg operations had a direct impact on the local economy of just under $80 million in 1975. The approach of the Kingsmill development has stimulated other improvements such as cleanup of the James River in the area. Flood, erosion, and pollution control are also receiving more attention from local and state agencies.

Moreover, in documenting and pre-

Brass harness ornament was unearthed at an area called the Littletown Quarter. Several outbuildings at the site were associated with the Bray Plantation. The winged lion was the Bray family crest. The artifact is 5⅝ inches high.

Map of Kingsmill on the James with major archeological sites.

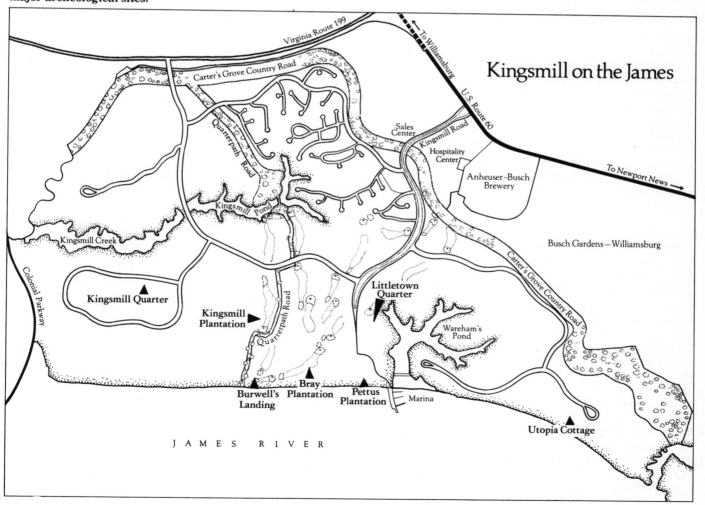

serving a part of U.S. history, the project has proved valuable to the Commonwealth of Virginia and to all those interested in a greater understanding of the country's past. The Commonwealth's educational institutions have used the excavations as a training ground for archeological scholars and as a source of data on Virginia's early rural history. In a report on his findings at Kingsmill, Theodore R. Reinhart of William and Mary's Department of Anthropology praised corporate support for this project:

The concern for the preservation of the historic and prehistoric resources and data of the Kingsmill property demonstrated by Anheuser-Busch, Inc., and Busch Properties, Inc., serves as an outstanding example for all developers and business organizations at a time when American archeology faces an acute "crisis" of its own.[1]

The Company Busch Properties was established in 1970 as a land-development subsidiary of Anheuser-Busch. In addition to the Kingsmill residential community, Busch Properties is developing 155 acres of land in Columbus, Ohio, as a business center for office, warehouse, and light industrial use. This project, known as Busch Corporate Center-Columbus, will provide new facilities for more than 57 companies and institutions. A second Busch corporate-center development is now underway at Williamsburg adjacent to Kingsmill on the James.

Anheuser-Busch began its brewery operations in St. Louis in 1852, when Adolphus Busch joined in partnership with his father-in-law, Eberhard Anheuser. Today, it is the world's largest brewer, with ten breweries throughout the country and an annual production capacity of more than 42 million barrels of beer. The company also produces industrial products such as baker's yeast, and owns and operates two Busch Gardens. Anheuser-Busch ranked 127th in the 1976 list of *Fortune* 500 companies. The company's net sales were $1.6 billion in 1976 and $1.4 billion in 1975. Net income came to $84.7 million in 1975 and $55.4 million in 1976.

Other Preservation Activities. Anheuser-Busch has also preserved its original brewery facilities in St. Louis which date from the founding of the company in 1852; this complex includes three historic landmark buildings listed in the National Register of Historic Places: Stables (1885), the Brew House (1891-1892), and the adapted Executive Office, formerly the Lyon Elementary School (1868). The company has also supported preservation through donations of money and property. In Clinton, Missouri, for example, an old Anheuser-Busch beer depot was turned over to the local historical society for use as its headquarters.

For further information contact:
Richard G. Knight
General Manager
Busch Properties, Inc.
100 Kingsmill Road
Williamsburg, Virginia 23185

Dr. William H. Kelso
Virginia Historic Landmarks
  Commission
221 Governor Street
Richmond, Virginia 23219

Footnotes

1. Theodore R. Reinhart, "The Prehistory of Kingsmill," (unpublished report, College of William and Mary, Department of Anthropology, October, 1974).

This 1860s schoolhouse, shown here in earlier years, is now the Main Office Building for Anheuser-Busch in St. Louis. (Boehl & Koenig)

Atlantic Richfield Company

Summary In 1973, Atlantic Richfield, one of the largest integrated U.S. oil companies, developed a Service Station Conversion Program to dispose of surplus gas stations, and help improve the environment. Under this Program, the company funds the recycling of the gas stations and donates them to communities. Plans call for five conversions in 1977. To date, Atlantic Richfield has spent approximately $250,000 on the Program.

Background In recent years, because of changing traffic patterns and relocation of the population, Atlantic Richfield realized that many of its gas stations were not profitable and closed them. These abandoned gas stations became graffiti-covered eyesores, strewn with garbage. To alleviate the problem, Atlantic Richfield decided to explore ways of utilizing these properties. Some of the stations had been put up for sale, but their deteriorated condition made them undesirable.

Execution In 1973, the company proposed a plan to convert its abandoned gas stations to community use. Atlantic Richfield first ascertains from local government officials which community groups or organizations might be interested in the property, then confers with them to determine what plans they envision. Upon approval, the company offers its advice and spends from $5,000 to $10,000 on the conversion. Refurbishing, which the company oversees, takes from two to six months, depending on the size of the project and the weather. The property is then usually donated to the community.

From 1973 through 1976, the project resulted in twelve conversions; five more are projected for 1977. A few examples illustrate the Program:

• In North Plains, Oregon, a remodeled gas station is now the Senior Citizens Community Center. Behind the Center, members cultivate a vegetable garden.

• In Long Beach, California, a former service station has been converted into a mini-auto clinic. Under the auspices of the Inner City Ministries (ICM), unemployed adults and high school students are taught automobile mechanics. ICM is responsible for maintenance and leases the old gas station from Atlantic Richfield for $1 a year. ICM trainees have made further improvements in the building, which is also used for concerts and other civic functions.

In most cases, Atlantic Richfield has found local government authorities or community groups receptive to its Program. Only one municipality has refused the offer, because the station in question was located in a proposed redevelopment area.

Costs Through 1976, Atlantic Richfield had spent about $250,000 on the Service Station Conversion Program. Since each gas station conversion is handled differently and involves several departments, a company official said that it was too complicated to provide a breakdown of financial figures.

Typical surplus gas stations: #1) Before. #2) After.

Problems The pilot project indicated that most community groups prefer to tear down the station and build a mini-park, garden, or new building. However, as new-construction costs continue to soar, more gas stations may be adaptively reused.

Benefits Atlantic Richfield is improving the quality of the areas where it has undertaken gas station conversions by providing a useful structure in place of an abandoned eyesore. The company is able to dispose of its surplus gas stations, and receives tax benefits for its contributions. The Program also helps create community goodwill.

The Company In 1976, Atlantic Richfield, a major integrated oil company, saw revenues increase 16 percent from $7.3 billion to $8.5 billion, and net income rise 28 percent from $450.4 million to $575.2 million. The company's sales break down as follows: domestic petroleum 87 percent, foreign petroleum 4 percent, and chemicals 9 percent. In January, 1977, the company acquired the Anaconda Company, a copper and aluminum producer.

Other Preservation Activities. In 1974, the company donated its former headquarters in Philadelphia to the Philadelphia College of Art. This contribution of a 21-story landmark building resulted in a $7 million tax deduction.

The Atlantic Richfield Foundation has also contributed to the following preservation efforts:

1. Donation of $15,000 in 1975 to the Grays Ferry Community Council in Philadelphia toward the adaptive reuse of a vintage church as a community center.

2. Donation of $5,000 in 1974 and 1975 to the Trinity Square Repertory Company in Providence, Rhode Island for conversion of an old movie theater into a playhouse.

3. Donation of $25,000 in 1977 toward a survey of noteworthy Victorian structures in Cape May, New Jersey, a turn-of-the-century seaside resort. Measured drawings were prepared, and photographs were taken during the summer of 1977 by a local group. The study will be published and will include a section on how to restore Victorian structures. Matching funds for the study were provided by the National Endowment for the Arts.

For further information contact:
Gene Owings
Senior Representative
Special Projects Development
Atlantic Richfield Company
515 South Flower Street
Los Angeles, California 90051

Bird & Son, Inc.

Summary In 1975, Bird & Son, Inc., one of the nation's largest producers of building materials, awarded $100,000 in preservation matching grants. Projects involving historic homes and houses of worship received about 40 percent of the funds, but almost all types of structures and landscapes were represented, including a six-story wooden elephant constructed in 1881. The company received nationwide publicity as a result of its Historic Grant Program, and in 1975, became the first member of the National Trust's Corporate Associates Program. In 1976, Bird & Son followed up its Program with a donation of $125,000 to the National Trust for Historic Preservation for production of a film on preservation. In 1977, in cooperation with the National Trust, it contributed $140,000 in support of a program to revitalize U.S. "Main Streets."

Background Bird & Son was founded in 1795. Its long association with American institutions is both a source of pride and publicity for the firm. Thus, when Bird's President Ralph E. Heim directed that the firm develop a public-service program for the nation's Bicentennial, some kind of preservation effort seemed appropriate.

According to Program Administrator D. Stuart Laughlin, Bird wanted to "give something back to the country in which we grew."[1] In addition, the company wanted a program which would provide maximum public exposure. Bird sought the assistance of the Society for the Preservation of New England Antiquities (SPNEA), the National Trust for Historic Preservation, and the Boston-based public-relations firm of Newsome & Co., Inc.

Once the decision to support preservation had been made, Bird first had to determine whether to turn the program over to some outside concern, or to keep the entire operation in-house. Donating money to an outside group, such as the National Trust, has the advantage of avoiding the bureaucratic complications usually attendant with program administration. On the other hand, a large contribution to an outside organization has the drawback of being a one-shot affair; the publicity it generates comes at a high price and can be

short-lived. An in-house project, for the same price, might produce both more sustained coverage and a closer association of the company with the service.

Bird opted for the in-house alternative, but still had to determine the program which would best suit its objectives. For a large building materials manufacturer, the first alternative was obvious: to donate its own products to preservation projects. However, it rejected this alternative, because, as Laughlin explains, "We thought that giving away our own roofing and other products would appear too crass and commercial. We wanted to get away from that kind of thing."[2] Consequently, the company shifted its emphasis from product give-aways to simple cash grants. It then had to face the problem of how best to award the money.

Execution An early suggestion was that Bird donate $1,000 to the most attractive historic house in each state; this proposal opened the door to myriad problems. Long consultation with SPNEA and the National Trust finally produced a plan which also won the approval of Newsome & Co., the public-relations firm. Under this proposal, Bird would award $100,000 to preservation projects on a regional basis. Panels of experts would judge the projects and select the winners. All funds would be available only as matching grants.

Bird officials claimed three major objectives for their program. First, and most obvious, their goal was to make money available for restoring and preserving America's historic landmarks. Second, they hoped to stimulate a "greater general awareness of the nation's historic sites, as well as of the financial needs of organizations attempting to preserve those sites."[3] Finally, they wanted to "develop a model

Lucy, a six-story "white elephant" located in Margate, New Jersey.

program in the field of historic preservation on which future efforts by corporate sponsors could be based."[4]

Actual planning for the Program began in June, 1974. At this time, Bird distributed a broadside to over 5,000 organizations throughout the country stating that matching funds up to $5,000 ($100,000 was allocated for the entire Program) would be provided for "any project designed to visibly improve the exterior of historic properties . . . to make them more accessible, understandable, or environmentally compatible to the public they serve."[5] The company established the following guidelines for eligibility:

1. Any nonprofit incorporated group in America can apply for up to $5,000, providing they can present matching capabilities.
2. The chosen site must be registered, or under consideration for registration, by the National Register of Historic Places.
3. There should be public access to the property.
4. The proposal should refer to an exterior-improvement project that had not yet been started (as of December, 1974), but could logically be completed by January, 1976.
5. Only one proposal per organization would be accepted.

After nearly five months of deliberation, Bird & Son's Historic Grant Program was announced on November 21, 1974, at separate press conferences in New York and Boston.

To begin an application, Bird required a letter of intent describing the project and plans for obtaining matching funds. If review of this preliminary material was favorable, then the submitting group would receive an official application. The firm set a March 31, 1975, deadline for receipt of completed applications.

In order to ensure success, Bird instructed Newsome & Co. to publicize the nature and progress of the Program. Meanwhile, with the aid of the National Trust, regional judgings were organized. Six panels of three persons each would participate in the initial screening according to geographic region. The company sought highly qualified people from many fields, including history, preservation, architecture,

conservation, education, and business, to serve as judges. The judges would recommend projects on the basis of overall merit, which Bird defined as "community interest and support of the project [a prime reason for the matching funds stipulation], a realistic assessment of costs, and a responsible plan of execution."[6] These recommendations were, in turn, passed to a national screening board for final review. Members of this group included historian Alistair Cooke, James Biddle, President of the National Trust, and William Murtagh, Keeper of the National Register of Historic Places. Regional panelists met during late April and early May, 1975, in Boston, Philadelphia, Charleston, Chicago, New Orleans, and Portland, Oregon.

Response to the Program was overwhelming: Program staffers acknowledged over 4,000 inquiries; 811 formal applications, requesting more than $3.2 million in grants were received from all 50 states and the District of Columbia. To lessen the difficulty of selecting winners, Bird officials, in consultation with preservation authorities, sent letters to all groups that had received preliminary approval, asking if they would accept partial grants so that other projects could be recognized. They agreed, and final awards were announced at a press conference on June 3, 1975, in the courtyard of Washington's historic Decatur House, headquarters of the National Trust. Bird & Son subsequently presented checks to 115 organizations.

The following examples illustrate the variety of projects that received grants: $600 went to the Brush Creek Bicentennial Commission to refurbish a unique Octagonal Schoolhouse in Sinking Springs, Ohio, dating from 1831; $500 was given to the Save Lucy Committee, Inc., to help preserve Lucy, a six-story wood and tin elephant, constructed in 1881, in Margate, New Jersey; $500 went to the Cullman City Commission to maintain the Clarkson Covered Bridge in Clarkson, Alabama; and $1,500 was donated to Historic Hannibal, Inc., to restore Main Street in Hannibal, Missouri, Mark Twain's boyhood home and the setting for several of his novels.

Costs

- $100,000 for individual matching grants distributed among 115 projects.
- $50,000 (approximately) for company administration of the Historic Grant Program.

Problems The Program's most serious drawbacks for Bird & Son were logistical. No one knew exactly what kind of reaction the Program would elicit. Certainly few anticipated the enormous number of inquiries and applications that were forthcoming. The project was "frightfully time-consuming,"[7] says Laughlin. While much of the difficulty certainly stemmed from the fact that methodology was being tested for the first time and modified as circumstances required, Laughlin believes that the administration of such a comprehensive nationwide program is inherently costly. "I had intended to spend only part-time on the project," he says, "but as the months wore on I found myself devoting almost all my energies to it."[8] When company executives evaluated the Program to determine a future course of action, it was felt that the grants could continue only if Bird employed a full-time administrator. "And at that time, we weren't prepared to do that,"[9] notes Laughlin.

According to Laughlin, "The main concern with the project was that it was too little in a well where there is no bottom. We wanted to do something to create a greater awareness of the need for preservation."[10] Bird has had only limited success in developing a model program of corporate donation to preservation. As Laughlin explains, "Every company wants to be original. This was our program, and we took credit for it. Companies are usually hesitant about following someone else's lead."[11]

Benefits From a preservationist's point of view, the Program represented a major step forward in corporate involvement. Stan Smith of the SPNEA, who worked closely with Bird & Son in the Program's development, reports that the company was highly responsive to suggestions and criticisms. The grants themselves, although too small in most cases to cover the total costs of restoration projects, nevertheless did serve as catalysts and incentives for further work within the communities receiving them.

From Bird & Son's perspective, the major benefit of the Program was clearly the favorable exposure it produced. Among the accolades received were a personal letter from Vice President Nelson Rockefeller praising Bird's commitment, a certificate of official recognition from the American Revolution Bicentennial Administration, and a special citation read into the *Congressional Record* by Congressman John Moakley:

I think in a time of spiraling inflation and high unemployment that Congress would not look very happily on any kind of restoration project, and I think a private sector has to involve itself. . . . I just hope this action of theirs [Bird's] is contagious and that other corporations take a note out of their book.[12]
—*John Joseph Moakley*
 U.S. Congressman
 9th District, Massachusetts

In addition, the Program received massive coverage by both print and electronic media in all fifty states: from syndicated articles by Bob Considine and Don Oakley to numerous television appearances by Heim, nationally syndicated wire stories, countless local articles, and feature pieces in a number of specialty publications.

The Company Bird & Son, Inc., is one of the nation's leading building-materials manufacturers. Established in 1795, the company had sales in 1976 of $236 million, a 23 percent increase over 1975's sales of $191 million. Over the same period net income declined from $18.1 million to $16 million. Its three main divisions employ over 3,600 people in thirty plants and offices located in fourteen states.

Other Preservation Activities. In June, 1975, Bird became the first Corporate Associate of the National Trust for Historic Preservation. The Corporate Associates Program seeks corporate support for preservation through a minimum $1,000 annual contribution to the National Trust. In addition to this donation, Bird also sent all companies on the *Fortune* 500 list a pamphlet describing Bird's historic grant program and a letter from Heim asking for a donation to the National Trust.

The Octagonal Schoolhouse in Sinking Springs, Ohio.

Over 100 companies have since become Corporate Associates.

In 1976, the company sponsored—at a cost of $125,000—a film on historic preservation, entitled *A Place in Time*. The film, made by John Karol of Apertura, Inc., will be nationally distributed through the National Trust.

In 1977, Bird contributed $140,000 to the National Trust's Main Street Project, a three-year program designed to encourage small municipalities to revitalize their central business districts. This project focuses on three model demonstration communities selected from among 69 in a ten-state competition. Professional consultants will prepare master plans utilizing historic-preservation techniques. A handbook, film, and workshops will be developed.

SPNEA's Stan Smith believes that Bird could also make a lasting contribution to preservation in another way:

Bird & Son is one of America's leading building materials manufacturers, and nothing is more crucial to preservation work than the proper materials. If you've ever looked around, you know that the materials available today are simply ill-suited to the task. I have already consulted with Bird & Son on some product development ideas of designing high quality materials for use in preservation projects. I believe that there is a real market for such products. The tremendous response to the grants program proved that.[13]

Officials at the company are considering his suggestion.

For further information contact:
D. Stuart Laughlin, Jr.
Administrator, Historic Grant
  Program
Bird & Son, Inc.
Washington Street
East Walpole, Massachusetts 02032

Footnotes

1. INFORM interview with D. Stuart Laughlin, Administrator, Historic Grant Program, Bird & Son, Inc., April, 1976.
2. *Ibid.*
3. Bird & Son, Inc., "The Bird & Son Historic Grant Program, Information Sheet," (mimeographed, Bird & Son, Inc., n.d.), p. 1.
4. *Ibid.*
5. *Ibid.*
6. *Ibid.*
7. INFORM interview with D. Stuart Laughlin, Administrator, Historic Grant Program, Bird & Son, Inc., April, 1976.
8. *Ibid.*
9. *Ibid.*
10. INFORM interview with D. Stuart Laughlin, Administrator, Historic Grant Program, Bird & Son, Inc., May, 1977.
11. INFORM interview with D. Stuart Laughlin, Administrator, Historic Grant Program, Bird & Son, Inc., April, 1976.
12. John Joseph Moakley, *Congressional Record*, (Washington, D.C.: U.S. Government Printing Office, July 15, 1975), E3811.
13. INFORM interview with Stan Smith, official, Society for the Preservation of New England Antiquities, April, 1977.

Summary In fall, 1973, CertainTeed Corporation, a manufacturer of building materials located in Valley Forge, Pennsylvania, developed its Building Restoration Program, which donates roofing products to historic buildings around the country. Since the Program was implemented in spring, 1974, CertainTeed has given its materials to over 23 projects, and plans to continue the contributions. The Program has been an excellent source of public-relations material for the company.

Background CertainTeed began its Building Restoration Program as a public-relations activity and to help preserve historic structures which reflect the social, political, and/or economic development of the United States. The Program was designed to help projects that needed the materials, but lacked the funds to pay for them.

Execution Each year, in response to articles and editorials in local newspapers, historical-society publications, and magazines such as *House Beautiful* and *House and Garden*, CertainTeed is contacted by up to 500 historical societies wishing to submit projects for consideration in the Program. These applications receive a color pamphlet outlining the Program and submission procedures, as well as before-and-after photographs of buildings already re-roofed with CertainTeed's help. Review sessions are held every four months to choose additional sites.

The 1860s Honolulu House in Marshall, Michigan, reroofed with shingles donated by CertainTeed.

Each building, which must be owned by a nonprofit organization, is evaluated for its historic and/or architectural attributes as they reflect the growth of the United States. Geographic location is considered to assure equitable regional distribution. The building's condition and the financial stability of the operating organization are also factors in the review of applications. The selection of new sites is administered by CertainTeed's public-relations firm, Lewis and Gilman, Inc., of Philadelphia. The entire procedure from application to donation can take up to eighteen months.

Upon approval and establishment of a re-roofing date, CertainTeed donates its asphalt roofing shingles. Contributions range from 12 to 110 squares (one square equals a hundred square feet). The recipient selects the kind of shingle, usually CertainTeed's best product, which looks like a wooden shake and does not distort the historic integrity of the structure. Fiberglass-base shingles, which carry the highest fire rating available, are also occasionally selected.

Although CertainTeed only donates and does not install the materials, it will make available technical experts if guidance is needed. On request, it will also suggest local roofing contractors from whom bids can be solicited. Operating organizations may either pick up the shingles from their local outlet on a credit billing system, or from a CertainTeed dealer, if one is nearby.

Many organizations have used the value of the roofing to obtain matching grants from local, state, or federal sources.

To date, 23 sites have been selected to receive materials. Those which have already been re-roofed include: Thomas Edison's birthplace (1841) in Milan, Ohio; Poe Cottage (1812), Bronx, New York; Fort Mifflin, a British fort built in 1772 in Philadelphia; and Honolulu House (1860) in Marshall, Michigan, the only example of Hawaiian architecture extant on the mainland. Many of the sites are in the National Register of Historic Places.

Costs   Information on the cost of the program and possible tax benefits gained by the donation of the materials was not available.

Benefits   The gifts create goodwill between the historical societies and the company. In addition, CertainTeed has received extensive local and national exposure through radio broadcasts and magazine and newspaper articles. The historic structures also provide a showcase for its products.

The Company   CertainTeed is a leading manufacturer of building products, including fiberglass insulation, polyvinyl-chloride and asbestos-cement pipe, asphalt roofing, and other items used in construction and underground utilities systems. CertainTeed had 1976 sales of $665 million, representing a 20 percent increase over 1975 sales of $553 million. Net income rose 88 percent over the same period, from $19.5 million to $36.6 million.

Other Preservation Activities. CertainTeed is currently sponsoring an exhibit demonstrating changes in housing technology at the National Museum of History and Technology of the Smithsonian Institution in Washington, D.C. The exhibit includes reconstructions of a "balloon frame" house developed during the mid-nineteenth century, and Hart House, a seventeenth-century home.

For further information contact:
Tom Newton
Director of Community Relations
CertainTeed Corporation
Shelter Materials Group
P.O. Box 860
Valley Forge, Pennsylvania 19482

Walter Rowen
Account Executive
Public Relations Division
Lewis and Gilman, Inc.
1700 Market Street
Philadelphia, Pennsylvania 19103

Summary   In 1973, the Ethyl Corporation, a chemicals manufacturer, undertook the restoration of an 1861 foundry building in Richmond, Virginia. The building had been part of the Tredegar Iron Works, which was called the "Arsenal of the South" during the Civil War. Although Ethyl has not yet completed the restoration, and at present, has no specific plans for the structure, the project has already brought the company national and local recognition.

The Tredegar restoration and Reynolds' Kanawha Canal restoration, a few hundred yards downriver (see Reynolds Metals), mark the initial attempts to improve Richmond's James River waterfront.

Background   Chartered in 1837 and located on the James River in Richmond, Virginia, the Tredegar Iron Works received its first U.S. government contract for artillery shells in 1839. By 1848, Joseph Reid Anderson, a West Point graduate, had purchased a controlling interest in the company. Under Anderson, Tredegar started producing iron rails and locomotives for the growing railroads. At the outset of the Civil War, the plant returned to munitions production, this time for the Confederacy. Tredegar provided 1,100 cannons and millions of projectiles, and may have built the first iron submarine. The company also supplied the iron plating used to clad the Merrimac-Virginia, the famous ship that fought the North's Monitor in the first battle of iron warships off Hampton Roads, Virginia.

After the Civil War, Tredegar returned to peacetime production, including spikes, angle bars, railroad-car wheels, practice shot for the Union, industrial castings, and horseshoes. However, munitions were still manufactured in wartime, from the Spanish American War to the Korean War.

By the early 1950s, the Tredegar buildings were beginning to show signs of age and deterioration. Steel had replaced iron, and a large part of Tredegar's market disappeared. The plant remained in operation until 1957, although a fire destroyed two of its large machine shops in 1952. After the sale of the historic property to the

Albermarle Paper Manufacturing Company (which later became the Ethyl Corporation), Tredegar's owners, descendants of Joseph Reid Anderson, moved operations to Chesterfield County, Virginia. The old Iron Works buildings were abandoned, and, according to the National Register:

Vacant and fire ridden, the several structures that housed the mills and

foundries in various stages of ruin, and a majority of the large rooms stand open or partially open to the sky.[1]

The old Foundry which Ethyl hoped to restore was in a badly deteriorated condition. After the collapse of one of its trusses, its slate roof had been removed to prevent the great weight from causing the building's walls to crumble.

The 1861 Tredegar Foundry Building in the process of restoration. (Al Cothran Studio)

A recent photo of the partially restored building. (Al Cothran Studio)

224

Execution The impetus for Ethyl's restoration of the 1861 Foundry was provided by Hurricane Agnes in 1972. After the flood caused by the hurricane, a city inspector called the company's attention to the advanced state of decay of the Tredegar buildings. Ethyl decided it was time to take a stand, and commissioned Property Manager Roy E. Johnson to study the Foundry's history and condition. After consultation with the Virginia Historic Landmarks Commission, the company decided:

Several of the buildings were, in addition to being in execrable condition, of uninteresting early 20th century construction. Other older ones had been so battered by hard use and the elements that they were beyond saving. But the jewel of the complex, a vast foundry building erected in 1861 was definitely restorable as well as another antebellum structure used for pattern storage. The decision was to save the latter two, and raze the rest though leaving buttresses and arches of exceptional interest.[2]

The building under restoration is the principal building, or Foundry. The 61-foot by 125-foot red-brick structure was built in 1861 to help Tredegar meet its tremendous wartime work load. Although the building had a strictly functional use, it includes decorative brick corbeling, fancy gable ends, and iron detailing.

Ethyl hoped the Tredegar restoration would turn the area into one of Virginia's most desirable pieces of real estate:

This restoration project will enhance both the appearance and the historic value of the area, as well as add a new dimension to the cultural value of downtown Richmond.[3]

The restoration of the Foundry included major brick-masonry work. The 21-inch-thick walls were stabilized, and in some cases, completely rebuilt. Ethyl has also constructed a replica of the original chimney stack which ventilated the large air furnaces used to melt iron for casting. The original chimney was dismantled earlier in this century. The roof too had to be fully reconstructed, since the original had been removed to prevent the walls from crumbling. The trusses supporting the roof were duplicated using castings from the originals. Taylor and Parrish were the restoration contractors; Garrett Brothers did the brick-masonry restoration and reconstruction; and Carneal and Johnston were the architects. All firms are from Richmond. The project was designed to take approximately one year, but has taken much longer because the initial plans did not include restoration of chimney and air furnaces. To date, the project remains unfinished.

Costs The company did not release any figures for the cost of restoring the Tredegar Iron Works' main building.

Problems Because the original trusses did not comply with the Richmond Building Codes, the Building Department initially rejected the company's plans to duplicate them. Ethyl and its consultants reminded the Department that the trusses had supported the roof until deterioration necessitated their removal. A grandfather clause in the Building Codes, establishing historic precedence, permitted their restoration.

Benefits Ethyl as yet has not made specific plans for the restored building, so company rewards for the effort are conjectural. However, a valuable piece of architecture has been saved, pleasing preservationists. Junius R. Fishburne, Executive Director of the Virginia Historic Landmarks Commission, praised the project:

I think Ethyl Corporation should be commended for what it's doing. Not many companies are willing to do this type of thing. The easiest and cheapest thing would be to just bulldoze it.[4]

In addition, in August, 1976, the American Society for Metals selected the Tredegar Iron Works as one of its National Historic Landmarks. The National Register of Historic Places accepted the Ethyl Corporation's nomination of the Tredegar Iron Works in 1973. James Wamsley, writing in *Commonwealth*, described the site:

In ruins . . . the old Tredegar represents not only a 19th century industrial complex, but also a contemporary expression of the picturesque spirit which thrived on romantic ruins. The walls which once supported the broad roof spans are now free standing arcades and their Romanesque manner conjures up the images of a far earlier age. The old Tredegar works have a tremendous potential as a part of Richmond's redeveloped riverfront.[5]

The Company In 1962, the Albermarle Paper Manufacturing Company of Virginia, a paper and chemical producer, purchased Ethyl Corporation, a manufacturer of gasoline additives. Albermarle changed its name to Ethyl Corporation and now produces chemicals, plastic, aluminum products, and energy-related products. Ethyl sold its paper interests in April, 1976. Sales for 1975 were $930 million and increased 19 percent in 1976, to $1.11 billion. Net income for 1975 was $61 million, and was up 13 percent in 1976 to $69 million.

For further information contact:
Charles H. Zeanah
Director—Corporate Public Relations
Ethyl Corporation
330 South Fourth Street
Richmond, Virginia 23219

Footnotes
1. James W. Moody, Jr., "National Register of Historic Places, Inventory, Nomination Form," 10-300, (Washington, D.C.: Department of the Interior, National Park Service, December 18, 1970), p. 5.
2. James S. Wamsley, "Tredegar: Where Pioneer Industrialists Worked Iron, Restoring Begins," *Commonwealth*, May, 1973, p. 45.
3. *Ibid.*, p. 42
4. Laurence Hilliard, "Walls of 'The Works' Haven't Changed Much," *Richmond Times-Dispatch*, 1 April 1973, p. 6.
5. Wamsley, *op. cit.*, pp. 45-46.

Summary Exxon, the world's largest oil company, has contributed to preservation efforts throughout the United States. Its activities have ranged from financing Historic American Buildings Survey (HABS) teams and publishing the results of their studies in Texas and California, to contributing money and expertise to help maintain an old General Store in North Carolina. In addition, Exxon has donated funds to: recycle New York's 1890 Federal Archives Building; maintain the recycled quarters of Boston's Institute of Contemporary Art; and create a park in New York's South Street Seaport. These contributions have helped improve company-community relations, and have strengthened awareness of the vital link between community and corporate prosperity.

Background Exxon is particularly interested in activities which are related to its products—notably, those concerned with energy conservation and the environment—but has supported projects related to education and broad social concerns as well.

Exxon prepares an annual budget for charitable contributions based on advice from all departments and field locations. Whenever possible, contributions are identifiable items in the budget, but budget additions are periodically approved for specific projects proposed to the company. Most projects are either national in scope or are in areas where Exxon has significant operations or concentrations of employees. National projects are usually brought to the attention of the Public Affairs Department in Houston or New York City, while local or regional projects are evaluated by local Exxon officials. Projects near Exxon facilities or involving Exxon employees receive preference.

In most instances, a community advocate for a proposed project has sought out a local or district Exxon official or public-relations representative. For example, in the Benicia case (see below), a member of the local historical society proposed to Exxon's oil-refinery manager that the company fund a study by the Historic American Buildings Survey. Since the required amount of funding was beyond the district office's budget, the manager submitted a proposal to the Public Affairs Department in Houston, which granted the funds.

Several examples of Exxon projects are described below.

Reprint of a 1910 post card of Benicia, California's Main Street. Most of these structures are still standing. (Stumm Photo)

Execution

Funding of the Historic American Buildings Survey Texas Catalogue. Since 1933, the Historic American Buildings Survey (HABS), part of the National Park Service, has been documenting the nation's historic structures through measured drawings, photographs, and research reports. Teams of architects, historians, and draftsmen have studied and documented vintage buildings in diverse locations, and published the results of their findings. To date, about 12,000 structures have been recorded.

In 1974, Exxon donated $8,000 to the State of Texas to finance publication of a Texas survey of over 200 buildings. The resulting catalogue includes drawings, photographs, and text describing the architecture and historical importance of each structure. Selected buildings were photographed inside and out. The most significant entries in the catalogue are illustrated with measured drawings. The catalogue sells for $5, and is available from the Trinity University Press in San Antonio. Exxon is also funding a similar study of historic structures in Arkansas.

Funding a HABS Survey, Benicia, California. In summer, 1976, the significant structures in Benicia, a historic California city, were studied and recorded by a HABS team under a $12,000 grant from Exxon and matching federal funds. Since Benicia is the site of an Exxon oil refinery, the company also volunteered its facilities for the HABS team's headquarters.

In 1847, Benicia was planned as "the Queen City of San Francisco Bay." In the 1850s, it became the site of the first U.S. Arsenal on the West Coast and grew substantially. Originally encompassing 252 acres, the Arsenal covered 2,700 acres by the time it closed in 1962. Many nineteenth-century structures remain there, complemented by Benicia's Victorian houses and commercial buildings.

When the Arsenal closed, the citizens of Benicia organized and raised the funds to convert the site into an industrial park. Today, it includes about 100 factories and distributors.

The HABS team surveyed the town's historically and/or architecturally significant buildings. Following the rec-ommendations of the Benicia Historical Society, several vintage structures were selected for detailed measured drawings and analysis:

1. *The Camel Barns.* These warehouses of native sandstone date from the mid-nineteenth century, and once housed camels imported from the Mediterranean and the Far East in the early 1860s for the U.S. Army's Camel Corps. The animals were used briefly in the arid Southwest but their stubbornness made them unsuitable for service. Some of them were brought to Benicia for auction and berthed in these two barns, which also have the distinction of possessing one of the first elevators designed by Elisha Graves Otis.

2. *The Powder Magazine.* Built of local sandstone, with four-foot-thick walls, the structure dates from 1857, and considering its function, has an interior which is particularly rich in detail. The building has a vaulted ceiling supported by Grecian pillars.

3. *The Clock Tower.* Originally constructed as an arsenal in 1859, this building was California's first federal bastion. It was gutted by fire in 1912, and only two of the three floors and the tower, with its huge Seth Thomas clock, remain.

4. *St. Paul's Episcopal Church.* The Church was built in 1860 of California redwood and has been extensively remodeled through the years.

5. *Benicia State Capitol.* This impressive brick building with Doric columns was originally built in 1853 as the City Hall, and once housed the California legislature before it moved to Sacramento.

In addition to these extensively researched buildings, twenty others were studied and photographed. The HABS team also helped property owners by providing information about the finer details of their structures, such as the origin of the brass and building materials. Plans called for the publication of the Benicia survey in summer, 1977.

Donation to Help Save a General Store in North Carolina. In Valle Crucis, North Carolina, a town of about 25 people, a general store that had been the center of Appalachian life since 1883 was in danger of closing. In its heyday, the Mast Store "sold everything from cradles to caskets,"[1] and was particularly famous for its cured hams. A rambling 8,700-square-foot structure, with chestnut walls and clapboards, the site was considered important enough to be nominated for inclusion in the National Register of Historic Places in 1973.

In 1970, because of the owner's age and because profits were sagging, the Mast Store was sold to two absentee owners, who hired inexperienced managers to run it. Conditions worsened, and finally, in 1975, the decision was made to close the old store.

In an effort to prevent the closing, local residents formed the Friends of the Mast Store. They brought the problem to the attention of one of Exxon's sales representatives, when he called at the Exxon station next to the store. He, in turn, approached the company's Public Relations Manager for the Southeast Region. These two Exxon employees suggested establishing a foundation to raise funds to preserve the historic Mast Store.

The Appalachian Association for the Preservation of Important Places was launched with a $3,000 grant from Exxon. Others have contributed as well. The Appalachian Association is helping the present owner to make the Mast Store profitable and to make improvements in the century-old structure. The Association's Board, consisting of the owner and three other members, must approve any improvements or new undertakings. To date, indoor plumbing has been installed, additional heating units have been added to assist the coal potbellied stove; and the walls and ceiling have been insulated to save energy. One of the previous owners, an experienced businessman, has moved to Valle Crucis and taken over as President of the Mast Store.

Today, the Mast Store is flourishing. The seven-foot cast-iron potbellied stove is the center for the display of groceries, household items, medicines, and clothes. On weekends, country music is played outside. The emphasis remains on serving local customers, but the new Manager/President has

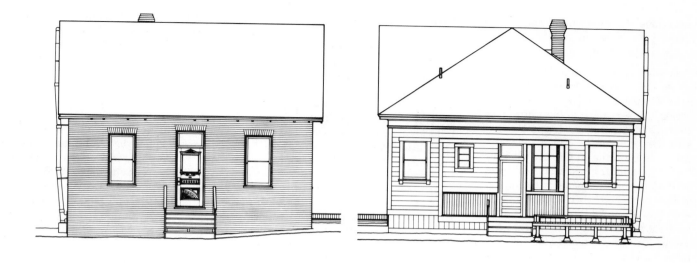

SOUTH ELEVATION

NORTH ELEVATION

0 1 2 3 4 5   10
FEET   1/4"=1'-0"

0   1   2   3
METERS   1:48

MATERIALS·
FOUNDATION· BRICK
WALLS· BRICK AND WOOD SIDING
ROOF· ASPHALT SHINGLES
FASCIA· WOOD

Line drawings from the Benicia Historic American Buildings Survey: (above) the 1870s Carr House, and (below) the interior vaulting of the 1855 Arsenal. (Historic American Buildings Survey)

ISOMETRIC VIEW OF INTERIOR VAULTING

0 1 2 3 4 5   10
FEET   1/4"=1'-0"

0   1   2   3
METERS   1:48

ambitious plans to promote the store by opening a restaurant, a delicatessen, and a crafts center.

Contribution to the New York Landmarks Conservancy. In 1977, Exxon gave $30,000 to the New York Landmarks Conservancy, a nonprofit organization, to study and promote the adaptive reuse of the 1890s Federal Archives Building in Greenwich Village. The building was designed by Willoughby J. Edbrooke, supervising architect of the U.S. Treasury and architect of the Old Federal Post Office in Washington, D.C. The Federal Archives Building is a one-block-square, brick building designed in the Richardsonian-Romanesque style. Its arcaded base is its most distinctive feature. Future plans for the building include a mixture of revenue-producing and community uses, such as housing and a retail arcade. Currently, a number of designs have been submitted and are being considered.

Bicentennial Gift to Boston, Massachusetts, for the Institute of Contemporary Art. In July, 1975, Exxon donated $25,000 for maintenance of the Institute's headquarters in a recycled Romanesque Revival police station built in 1886. The project's architect, Graham Gund of Cambridge, gutted the old interior and designed a modern decor. The vintage police station now boasts a five-story center staircase and interiors displaying outside exhibits as well as the Institute's artwork.

Support of the South Street Seaport Museum Park. Exxon donated $200,000 to build a park at the entrance to the South Street Seaport Museum. Located on a thirty-acre site, this museum depicts the history of the nineteenth-century Port of New York. The completed mini-park was dedicated in April, 1977. Its focal point is a 1913 lighthouse.

Costs Exxon, the largest corporation in the United States, donates more money to charitable causes than any other American corporation. In 1976, the company's contributions totaled $22 million, an increase of 20 percent over 1975.[2] However, this is less than 1 percent of Exxon's pre-tax income. Individual projects are itemized in the "Execution" section. Exxon did not break down its contributions to preservation.

Benefits Exxon, through its support of these various preservation-related projects, believes it is helping to improve employee and community relations, while at the same time, contributing to a greater public awareness of the American heritage.

In a recent company publication, Exxon comments on its charitable contributions:

At Exxon, we feel that it is in the best interest of business to continue to meet public expectations in these areas and to show through its actions that we believe the prosperity of any business is clearly related to the vitality of the community in which it functions.[3]

The Company Exxon, the world's largest oil company, had gross sales of $51.6 billion in 1976 and a net income of $2.6 billion, representing an 8 percent increase in sales and a 5.5 percent increase in earnings over 1975. Its sales breakdown is as follows: 44.1 percent petroleum and natural gas operations in the U.S.; 36 percent foreign exploration and production; 7.9 percent foreign refining and marketing; 8.2 percent chemicals; and 3.8 percent miscellaneous, including nuclear, coal, minerals, and land development.

For further information contact:
Contributions and Program
 Development
Public Affairs Department
Exxon Company, USA
P.O. Box 2180
Houston, Texas 77001

Public Affairs Department
Exxon Corporation
1251 Avenue of the Americas
New York, New York 10020

Footnotes

1. Downs Matthews, "Saving Mast Store," *Exxon USA,* Fourth Quarter, 1975, p. 9.
2. Written communication from Robert E. Kingsley, Senior Advisor, Communications and Cultural Programs, Exxon Corporation, to INFORM, August 12, 1977.
3. Exxon Corporation, "Introduction," *The Other Dimensions of Business: A Report on Exxon's Participation in Areas of Public Interest,* (New York: Exxon Corporation, 1977), p. 1.

Flanigan's

Summary Flanigan's, a furniture retailer in upstate New York, has supported the preservation movement in a variety of ways, ranging from financing the preparation and distribution of films and articles on preservation, to helping establish a local business committee which supports the arts. The company's efforts on behalf of preservation, which since 1974 have entailed a total expenditure of $12,000, have been due essentially to the interest and involvement of its President, Alan Cameros.

Background The association of furniture with the preservation of historic homes and other landmarks is, of course, a natural one. In addition, Alan Cameros has long been a supporter of preservation causes.

Execution Flanigan's has given its support to five particular projects since 1974. They are:

TV—Mini-Documentaries. It sponsored a series of five-minute shorts about the history and preservation needs of some of Rochester's landmarks. These were aired at various times between 1974 and early 1976 on a local public broadcasting station. In addition, the company donated a total of $2,000 to the six landmarks featured in the television series. The landmarks featured were: the Stone Tolan House, the Erie Canal aqueduct over the Genesee River, St. Luke's Church, the Frank Lloyd Wright House, and Rochester's Federal Building.

American Lifestyle Films. These three-minute films, narrated by E.G. Marshall, depict the lives and homes of famous people, such as Thomas Jefferson and Monticello, Brigham Young and the Beehive House, Will Rogers and his ranch, and Andrew Jackson and the Hermitage. Originally financed and produced by Bassett Furniture Industries, the films provide a

A winning entry in Flanigan's Landmark Essay Contest.

1st

Our Neighborhood Cemetery

This cemetery is real'ly old. I visited the cemetery last week. I saw a grave of a baby boy who lived only one day, on a plaque. The plaque was old. This cemetery started before 1821. I saw a plaque that fell down but I could read it. The plaque said death 1821 but I do not know when he was born. Soldiers who died in the Civil War are buried there. On Memorial Day someone puts flags on their graves. It is called the Brighton Cemetery, and it is near East Ave and Winton Road South. The cemetery is very big and I like to walk there.

Kenny LuKacher
Third Grade
Hillel School
age 8
442-1442

brief view of practical preservation efforts. Flanigan's obtained two sets of the ten-part series and has made them available without cost to local schools and organizations. It is also sponsoring the series on commercial television. Distribution began in 1974 and is an ongoing project.

Article Distribution. In 1976, Flanigan's distributed free 6,000 copies of "A Preservationist's Guide," a featured article in *House and Garden*'s "Guide to American Tradition, 1976," a special Bicentennial issue. Written by Billie Harrington, Director of the Landmark Society of Western New York, the article provides information about the Society's projects in a nine-county area around Rochester, as well as about its basic preservation policies and methods of implementation.

Flanigan's has received a number of additional requests for this reprint, which is also being distributed by the National Trust for Historic Preservation and the Preservation League of New York State. The Business Committee for the Arts is using it to assist in soliciting funds for preservation activities.

The Landmark Essay Contest. In 1974, Flanigan's sponsored and organized an essay contest. Promotional ads in local newspapers were headlined: "Rochester has its famous landmarks, too. Why not enter Flanigan's Landmark Contest and tell us about your favorite Rochester area landmark." Contestants were asked to write 100 to 300 words on their candidate. Nine prizes of Flanigan's gift certificates amounting to $1,000 were awarded winners in three categories: grades 3 to 6; grades 7 to 12; and over 18 years of age. Winners and runners-up were guests on local radio and television shows.

Preservation issue of Scene. In 1974, a local monthly emphasizing the arts devoted an entire issue to historic preservation in the area. Underwritten, and largely written by Flanigan's staff, the issue included an introduction by Cameros on the goals of preservation, as well as articles on the adaptive reuse of commercial buildings and stately residences, area landmarks, the relationship of vintage and modern buildings, and an examination of architectural details of area commercial buildings.

In addition to company contributions to the Landmark Society, Flanigan's President Alan Cameros has personally been involved in preservation activities. He is currently on the Society's Board of Directors, and has encouraged Flanigan's employees to volunteer their time and solicit funds for the Society from the local business community.

As a result of his contributions to preservation, Cameros was also invited to join the Business Committee for the Arts, a national organization of business leaders that encourages business and industry to assume a greater share of responsibility for the support, growth, and vitality of the arts. Based on his experience with the national organization, Cameros founded a local prototype in August, 1976. This new organization currently consists of a participating membership of twenty-one local businesses. Cameros served as its first president.

Costs Flanigan's doesn't itemize the cost of its preservation projects. The company stated that each of its six projects cost about $2,000, totaling $12,000 to date. Funds are allocated on an *ad hoc* rather than annual basis.

Benefits Because of its numerous preservation projects, Flanigan's has received awards from both the City of Rochester and the State of New York. A company spokesman said that it was not possible to ascertain any direct effect of these projects on furniture sales. Nonetheless, many customers have remarked favorably on the company's involvement with preservation causes.

Although Flanigan's would not divulge how the costs of its preservation projects were treated for tax purposes, it is likely that such items were written off against advertising expenses or deducted for charitable contributions.

Alan Cameros expressed his philosophy of corporate responsibility:

We feel the responsibility of business goes beyond "making the sale"—a long range view must be taken to preserve the heritage and character of our community itself. Only if Rochester and the surrounding area have the fiscal ability to maintain and care for their resources will the community in its entirety prosper.[1]

The Company Flanigan's dates back to 1925, when William Flanigan started a moving and storage company that later expanded into retail furniture. Bought by Edward Cameros—father of the current President—in 1940, Flanigan's grew under its new management, and currently has four locations: three in the Rochester area and one in Buffalo. Today, Flanigan's is western New York's largest furniture retailer. The privately held company had recent sales amounting to about $9 million.

For further information contact:
Alan L. Cameros
President and Chief Executive Officer
Flanigan's
845 Maple Street
Rochester, New York 14611

Footnotes

1. Alan Cameros, "Preserving the Past: The Past is Alive and Well and Living Just off East Avenue," *Scene*, November, 1974, p. 1.

Summary In 1974, Hercules, a major chemical producer headquartered in Wilmington, Delaware, since 1912, pledged $50,000 toward the restoration of the city's century-old Grand Opera House. The Hercules gift was the first corporate contribution to this restoration, and spearheaded other contributions by the business community. The $5 million effort, completed in 1976, returned the Grand to its original use, and has served as a catalyst for further revitalization of downtown Wilmington.

Background The Masonic Lodges of Delaware laid the cornerstone for the Grand Opera House in 1869. Construction was financed by a $100,000 public subscription, and completed in 1871 under architect Thomas Dixon of Baltimore.

The Grand is one of the finest extant examples of French Second Empire architecture. The brick structure, measuring 211 feet long, by 92 feet wide, by 78 feet high, has a richly decorated cast-iron facade and a mansard slate roof topped by three cupolas. The design of the building both inside and out, incorporates the symbolism of the Masonic Order, based on the numbers three, five, and seven:

The facade was divided in 5 basic sections. The center section became number 3 when the sections were counted from left of center. . . . On the storefront level, each store comprised 3 sections. . . . On the second and third floors, each of the 5 sections included 3 arches and 3 keystones.[1]

Among the noteworthy features in the interior were the drop curtain painted with a romantic Italian scene, which was designed by Russell Smith, an eminent nineteenth-century theatrical designer, and the frescoed ceiling depicting the muses. At the time of its completion, the Grand Opera House boasted the second largest stage in the nation, and its acoustics were considered exceptional.

Through the years, the Grand gained a national reputation as a showcase for such performers as Little Nell, Edwin Booth, Ethel Barrymore, and George M. Cohan. President Ulysses S. Grant attended a "Fair" there in February, 1873. It was also the setting for diverse forms of entertainment, including symphonies, operettas, readings, minstrels, balls, and variety shows.

In 1897, an Edison Vidascope was installed. The Warner Brothers movie chain became manager of the Grand in 1930. Through the years the fabric of the once elegant theater grew shabby. A fire in 1934 destroyed the roof and the three cupolas. To meet fire regulations, in 1943, a false ceiling had to be added beneath the frescoed ceiling. Faced with dwindling receipts, the Grand closed in June, 1967, with the film, *The Game Is Over*.

Drawing of the Grand Opera House in the 1870s.

Execution Local groups attempted to keep the Grand open as a theater. But, gradually, the idea evolved to restore the once elegant building as a performing-arts center. Support was obtained from twelve area organizations representing the symphony, opera, and drama, and from volunteer groups. In 1971, a successful Centennial Gala Evening, marking the landmark's 100th year, brought together interested groups who established volunteer committees, cleaned up the debris, researched the history of the Grand, sponsored entertainment, and publicized the restoration efforts.

Three studies of the Grand were undertaken:

1. To investigate thoroughly the structural integrity of the building and propose new construction enabling the theater and office areas to meet 20th Century safety codes and artistic requirements.

2. To research all facets of the original house to permit authentic restoration of the theater as an historical landmark.

3. To determine the economic feasibility of embarking on a multi-million

dollar restoration project that would lead to a self-supporting center for the performing arts in an area that had not previously benefited from such a facility.

These aims required five years of planning. While the feasibility studies were being completed and the required financing obtained, live performances again began taking place on the stage of the Grand. National, state, and local groups and celebrities filled the hall with the sounds of jazz, symphonies, operas, and modern music. Ballet companies performed, and film classics were screened.

The studies and the eventual restoration cost $5 million. A sixty-member Board of Directors was responsible for raising this money. One of its members was a Hercules officer, and through his efforts the company agreed to pledge $50,000 toward the restoration endeavor. This represented the first major corporate contribution and encouraged gifts from other corporations. Besides corporate community support, funding for the restoration was also provided by individuals, the Greater Wilmington Development Council, the Delaware State Arts Council, the Masonic Hall Company,

the state, county, and city, and the National Endowment for the Arts.

The restoration of the Grand was carried out in two phases. In mid-1974, the exterior was restored as a visual symbol for the project, while the theater remained open. When removing the false storefronts, some of the original cast-iron facade was exposed. In several areas, the cast iron was missing, but it was duplicated and replaced. The mansard roof was re-slated, and the three cupolas and the grillwork were replaced. The rest of the building was cleaned and painted its original white. Most of the exterior restoration was completed by the end of 1974.

On May 1, 1975, the theater was closed so that interior renovation—scheduled for completion within a year—could begin. During this time, 26 different trades worked on the Grand. Plans called for blending the old with the new. The original seating plan, with a capacity of 1,144, was retained, but backstage facilities utilized the most modern theater technology. In addition, a computerized lighting system was installed; one of the first in the country. Right on schedule, the renewed Grand Opera House was rededicated on May 1, 1976.

Missing sections of the Grand's original cast-iron facade were recast and replaced.

Reconstruction of the Grand's interior.

Costs Hercules' pledge of $50,000 was made in 1974, payable in three annual installments in 1975, 1976, and 1977. In addition, the company donated more than $4,000 to the Grand Opera House for the feasibility study's operating budget.

Benefits Hercules was able to take tax deductions for its charitable contributions and its pledge of support, as indicated above, prompted other corporations to donate funds to the Grand. Besides serving as a cultural center for the greater Wilmington area, the restoration and revival of the Grand Opera House has spearheaded other revitalization projects in the inner city, notably a new downtown shopping mall on Market Street, the street on which the Grand is located. In addition, a new federal, state, and city office complex has been built; and a community college which opened downtown in 1974, is rapidly expanding.

The Company Hercules produces a broad range of specialty chemicals. In 1976, the company had sales of $1.6 billion representing a 13 percent increase over the 1975 figure of $1.4 billion. Net income jumped from $32.5 million to $106.8 million. The company's sales break down as follows: specialty chemicals, 45 percent; agricultural and industrial chemicals, 29 percent; plastic materials, 21 percent; and aerospace and defense products, 5 percent. Foreign markets account for about 40 percent of sales.

For further information contact:
John M. Martin
Chairman
Hercules, Inc.
910 Market Street
Wilmington, Delaware 19899

Lawrence J. Wilker
Executive Director
The Grand Opera House
818 Market Street Mall
Wilmington, Delaware 19801

Footnotes

1. Toni Young, *The Grand Experience* (Watkins Glen, New York: The American Life Foundation for the Grand Opera House, Inc., 1976), p. 39.

A copy of the original ceiling fresco reinstalled.

The restored Grand Opera House.

Liggett Group Inc.

Summary In August, 1976, Liggett Group, a major tobacco and consumer-products company headquartered in Durham, North Carolina, donated 71 acres of the 3,400-acre Stagville Plantation, including its house and out-buildings, to the state. This site is listed in the National Register of Historic Places. Now, with partial funding by Liggett, it has become the home of the first state-owned preservation center in the country.

Background The Stagville complex consists of the Bennehan House dating from 1787, four antebellum slave houses, an eighteenth-century barn, and a cottage dating from about 1776. One of the oldest homes in Durham County, the Bennehan House was built by Richard Bennehan who first bought property in the area in 1766. Bennehan was a prosperous plantation owner and merchant, an early trustee of the University of North Carolina, and a commissioner responsible for planning the capital city of Raleigh. His descendants were also successful and civic-minded. By 1890, their land holdings were among the largest in the South.

Liggett Group purchased the Stagville holding in 1954 because of its rich tobacco land, and installed a caretaker on the site. The Historic Preservation Society of Durham, established in 1972, wanted to preserve and utilize the historic property for community use. To accomplish this, the staff of the North Carolina Division of Archives and History conceived the idea of establishing an educational research facility there: the Stagville Center for Preservation Technology.

Execution The Preservation Society and the Division of Archives and History approached Liggett Group and asked for the donation of the property. Liggett consented, and its donation in August, 1976, was the largest gift of its kind ever received by the state.

The North Carolina Division of Archives and History will administer

The Stagville Plantation House. (Stagville Preservation Center)

the Stagville facility. Dr. Larry Tise of the Division describes the Center's purpose:

We hope that the Stagville Center for Preservation Technology will help more people understand and get involved in the practical side of historic preservation. This will not be a place where people just learn from books. The historic property itself will serve as a study laboratory for people—not just professionals, but other interested citizens—to learn by working with artifacts, 18th and 19th century buildings, and real problems in preservation. Professionals will come to the center to exchange opinions and ideas and to study new preservation techniques.[1]

John B. Flowers III, Executive Director of the Stagville Center, has established a curriculum, and classes began in spring, 1977. At present, there are four staff members, but Flowers hopes to add more. Experts in preservation technology will be brought in from all over the country to teach the nuts and bolts of conservation practices. The Center will offer short courses, those leading to a certificate, and in time, a degree offered in conjunction with neighboring universities. The first courses offered in spring, 1977, under the City of Durham's Continuing Education Program were "A Survey of North Carolina Architecture from 1700 to 1939" and "A History of Stagville." North Carolina State University will offer course credit for an archeological survey to be undertaken on the property in summer, 1977. A ten-day preservation seminar is being arranged for the fall.

Flowers is also overseeing the physical development of the Center. The Bennehan House is now restored, and efforts are underway to obtain contributions of period pieces to furnish the rooms now used for meetings and classes. A Board of Directors has been established, consisting of state officials, community leaders, and members of the business coummunity, including the President of Liggett Group.

Costs Information on the initial purchase price paid for Stagville by Liggett Group is not available.

Benefits The gift of Stagville will provide Liggett with a tax deduction of about $250,000. Further tax benefits will derive from the company's additional contributions to help finance the Center for several years (amount undisclosed).

The donation of 71 acres of the Stagville Plantation is furthering better community relations by returning a bit of history to the public domain.

The Company Liggett was initially a tobacco company but started diversifying in 1964 through acquisitions and internal growth. It now markets a wide range of consumer products. Revenues break down as follows: tobacco products, 43.8 percent; spirits and wines, 19.7 percent; pet foods, 25.3 percent; and other products, 11.2 percent. For the year ending December, 1976, this international company had gross sales of $851.9 million and a net income of $36.2 million. This compares with 1975 figures of $813 million and $36.2 million respectively.

Other Preservation Activities. Liggett Group also contributed land to the state of North Carolina for a tobacco museum in Durham which opened in spring, 1977.

For further information contact:
Robert H. Fasick
Vice President and Assistant to the
    President
Liggett Group Inc.
4100 Roxboro Road
Durham, North Carolina 27702
John B. Flowers III, Executive Director
Stagville Preservation Center
Box 15628
North Durham Station
Durham, NC 27704

Footnotes

1. Liggett Group Inc., "Liggett Group Donates Historic Site to North Carolina," *News Release,* August 5, 1976, p. 2.

Summary In 1974, this Mississippi public utility funded the research and publication of two books on the archeological and architectural heritage of Claiborne County. Mississippi Power & Light undertook this project in conjunction with the preparation of a federally mandated Environmental Impact State for a nuclear plant it wished to build. Five buildings in the County have been added to the National Register of Historic Places as a result of the architectural survey, now in its second printing. The nuclear plant is scheduled for completion in 1977.

Two structures included in the Architectural Survey of Claiborne County: a house in Port Gibson (c. 1885) and the Windsor Ruins (c. 1860). (Mississippi Department of Archives and History)

Background In January, 1972, Mississippi Power & Light announced its intention to build a nuclear generating plant in Claiborne County, Mississippi. The Federal Power Commission required an Environmental Impact Statement evaluating the effects of the plant on the local ecology before construction could begin.

In addition, the Mississippi Department of Archives and History recommended that the power company survey the archeological remains and historic buildings not only of the area immediately surrounding the plant site, but of the entire County. Mississippi Power & Light agreed to fund the research and the eventual publication of two books.

Execution Mississippi Power & Light contracted with the Mississippi Department of Archives and History for two two-man teams to conduct the two studies. The research took about eight months. One book, *Architecture in Claiborne County, Mississippi: A Selective Guide,* was the result of the following process. In summer, 1972, the research team, an architectural historian and a historian, examined the records of the local historical society, the courthouse, local newspapers, and private sources to determine what sites in the County were important. These properties were visited and photographed. The resulting 110-page publication surveys the architectural history of Claiborne County; presents pictures of structures that have been demolished; and describes extant structures. This latter group includes:

churches; a synagogue; government, commercial, and educational buildings; plantation houses; vernacular dwellings; and ruins. The *Guide* contains black and white photographs depicting the exteriors, interiors, and architectural details of the historic buildings, and maps giving the exact locations of the entries. It also indicates whether sites are open to the public. The entries are rated in four categories: national significance, major significance, local significance, or valuable parts of the local scene. The criteria for each category is spelled out:

Those with national significance are either important works by nationally famous architects, are included in The National Register of Historic Places *because of their architectural qualities, or are unique examples illustrating the architectural development of the United States. Buildings with major significance are either outstanding examples of the work of important architects or builders, unique or exceptionally fine examples of a particular style or period, or important examples of construction techniques. Those of local significance are important examples of the architectural styles which make the greatest contribution to the overall character of their surroundings, or buildings which best show local developments in style and change of taste. The buildings judged valuable as part of the local scene are not in themselves examples of distinguished architecture, but are, nonetheless, important elements in their environment because of style, material, scale, and increasing age.*[1]

The *Guide* discusses 119 important structures, including 3 of national significance, 29 of major significance, 55 of local significance, and 22 of value to the local scene.

Initially, 1,000 copies of the book were printed. They were distributed through the Mississippi Department of Archives and History for $3.50 a copy. Because of unexpected demand, there was a second printing of 1,000 copies in 1975. These books are being sold at $5.00 per copy. Proceeds go to the Department of Archives and History.

Costs Mississippi Power & Light provided $25,000 for research and publication of the *Guide,* which was published by the Mississippi Department of Archives and History.

Benefits The architectural survey has increased awareness of the diversity of Mississippi's architectural heritage. Because of the interest generated by the *Guide,* five properties have been placed in the National Register of Historic Places. The survey has saved the Mississippi Department of Archives and History considerable time and expense. Robert Bailey, a Department official, said the survey would have taken much more time to complete if it had to await financing by the state. The state also benefits from the proceeds of the sale of the book, which help finance the Department's other publications. The company's involvement in historic preservation has encouraged many employees to take an active role in restoring houses in Claiborne County. In addition, Mississippi Power & Light has gained public-relations benefits by undertaking the two surveys. Articles about the projects have appeared in the *Jackson Daily News,* the *Jackson Clarion Ledger,* and the *Port Gibson Reveille.*

The Company Mississippi Power & Light, a subsidiary of Middle South Utilities, a large public-utility holding company, provides electric service to the western half of Mississippi. Revenues for 1976 amounted to $308.8 million, a 28 percent increase over 1975's figure of $240.1 million. Net income for the same period increased 25 percent, from $20.8 million to $25.7 million. Revenues break down as follows: commercial and industrial, 38 percent; residential, 31 percent; and other, primarily sales to other utilities, 30 percent.

Other Preservation Activities. Mississippi Power & Light also funded an archeological survey of Claiborne County. From June to July, 1972, two archeologists examined the 2,200-acre tract where the proposed nuclear plant would be built. One significant mound site was discovered, and its excavation, later in 1972, was funded by the company. Pieces of ceramic and prehistoric tools were among the artifacts unearthed. From August through October, 1972, the same team carried out a surface analysis of archeological sites in other parts of Claiborne County. They identified 86 sites dating from 7000 B.C. to 1000 A.D. In 1973, the findings were published as the *Archaeological Survey of Claiborne County, Mississippi,* which sold for 50 cents. There was an initial printing of 1,000 copies. A second printing costing about $2,000 was financed by the Mississippi Historical Society and the Mississippi Department of Archives and History. Proceeds of all sales go to these organizations.

For further information contact:
Alex McKeigney
Vice President for Information
 Services
Mississippi Power & Light Co.
Box 1640
Jackson, Mississippi 39205

Gregory B. Free
Restoration/Preservation Specialist
State of Mississippi
Department of Archives and History
P.O. Box 571
Jackson, Mississippi 39205

Footnotes

1. Ed Polk Douglas, *Architecture in Claiborne County, Mississippi: A Selective Guide,* (Jackson: Mississippi Department of Archives and History, 1974), p. 4.

Summary In 1976, Nabisco, the country's largest specialty baker, donated $75,000 to Waterloo Village, New Jersey's only remaining "colonial village." The funds were earmarked for restoration of a 1760s Grist Mill. The company researched and provided colonial recipes that are cooked in the Dutch oven in the recently restored Mill, and donated the Nabisco memorabilia on display there. Nabisco employees are charged a reduced admission fee at Waterloo Village, with the company making up the difference.

Background Located in western New Jersey, Waterloo Village was settled as a farming community by the English about 1740. In 1763, when an iron forge was constructed, Waterloo began to prosper. During the Revolutionary War, the iron produced there was used for gun barrels for the colonial troops. Although the iron forge subsequently stopped production for lack of wood, the town again prospered with the construction of the Morris Canal in 1824. Waterloo, one of the main depots along the Canal, flourished until the rise of the railroad after the Civil War.

The railroad brought the town's growth to an abrupt halt. Waterloo became nearly a ghost town. Then in the late 1960s, Percival Leach and Louis Gualandi gradually bought up most of the existing historic buildings. They recreated the early American village and the nineteenth-century transportation center on the Morris Canal by restoring and furnishing numerous historic structures, including: the Canal House (c. 1760), the Wellington House (c. 1859), and the Old Stage Coach Inn (c. 1740 with an addition c. 1830). Waterloo Village, open to the public, also provides exhibits and demonstrations of early American crafts and trades. The Waterloo Foundation for the Arts, a nonprofit organization partially subsidized by the State of New Jersey, administers the Village. It relies primarily on admission fees to cover its operating costs. Leach and Gualandi have proceeded with restoration of the Village's historic buildings as time and money have permitted.

The Grist Mill was an integral part of the original Village. During the heyday of the Morris Canal, its flour was shipped throughout New Jersey. At the time of restoration, the sturdy stone structure still possessed the grinding stones needed to process the flour, but at some point, the waterwheel had disappeared.

The Grist Mill at Waterloo Village.

Execution   In fall, 1975, Nabisco moved its executive offices from New York City and set up a new world headquarters in East Hanover, New Jersey. At the time the company was searching for a suitable method of observing the nation's Bicentennial. Although numerous projects and events were suggested, Nabisco sought a project which would have lasting value and which, preferably, would be related to the State of New Jersey. Early in 1975, the producers of a Nabisco sales-promotion film shot several scenes on location at Waterloo Village, acquainting company executives with the work of restoration underway there. The Grist Mill seemed an appropriate Bicentennial gift. Nabisco contributed $75,000 for materials, and Leach and Gualandi obtained another $75,000 for labor under the federal government's Comprehensive Employment and Training Act (CETA).

Research for the restoration was not difficult since the mill was still standing. Rotting beams and other structural remains provided evidence of the building's original appearance. The recollections and expertise of an elderly local resident, whose father had operated the Grist Mill, were also helpful. Charles Howell, one of the world's experts on grist mills, and a professional miller, supervised the entire restoration.

After a feasibility study, restoration began with replacement of the eighteenth-century supporting beams, the underprop for the heavy grinding machinery. New beams were cut down and sized from nearby oak trees. The new props measure from 9 feet to 27 feet in length and the heaviest ones weigh over 1,000 pounds. The millstones were treated and returned to working order; a new wooden waterwheel, 10 feet in diameter and 6 feet thick, was constructed. With the waterwheel generating power, and the supporting machinery sound, the Grist Mill was once again operational.

A Dutch oven, used for baking goods in colonial times, was installed to complete the milling operation, and Nabisco researched and prepared colonial recipes. Tourists at Waterloo Village can now view the entire baking process from whole grain to baked goods.

The second floor of the restored Grist Mill contains an exhibit of early farm implements and Nabisco memorabilia, such as paintings done for advertisements and packaging used through Nabisco's history.

Costs   Nabisco spent $75,000 for the restoration of the eighteenth-century Grist Mill, and CETA funds provided another $75,000. Costs of the time spent researching colonial recipes, and the value of the donation of the company's advertising art and memorabilia were not available.

Benefits   Another attraction has been added to historic Waterloo Village while Nabisco has obtained public-relations benefits. A flier distributed at the Grist Mill and a plaque on the building credit the Company for its contribution. The exhibit of Nabisco memorabilia is another advertising vehicle, and company Christmas cards have featured a painting of the Grist Mill. The reduced admission plan has encouraged Nabisco employees to visit Waterloo Village, bringing additional revenue to the site. The company did not disclose information on any tax benefits gained from its $75,000 gift or its other contributions.

The Company   Nabisco had sales of over $2 billion and a net income of $77 million in 1976, an increase over 1975's $1.97 billion in sales and $59 million in net income. Its products include cookies and crackers, pharmaceuticals, toys and games, pet foods, and confectionaries.

For further information, contact:
Glenn Craig
Director of Public Relations
Nabisco, Inc.
River Road and Forest Avenue
East Hanover, New Jersey 07936

Percival H.E. Leach &
    Louis Gualandi
The Historic Village of Waterloo
Stanhope, New Jersey 07874

Summary Niagara Mohawk, the largest public utility in upstate New York, has headquarters in an Art Deco building dating from 1932. Proud of this landmark, the company provides guided tours of it and a descriptive pamphlet. In spring, 1976, Niagara Mohawk assisted the Everson Museum in Syracuse in mounting a major Art Deco exhibition, including photographs and measured drawings of its headquarters. The company has also built an architecturally compatible addition to its building.

Background The modern architectural style called Art Deco had its roots in the *Exposition des Arts Decoratifs et Industriels* held in Paris in 1925. Utilizing modern technology and materials, Art Deco buildings are sleek, streamlined, and incorporate geometric designs. The style also employs many of the period's innovations in lighting techniques, such as reflective lighting, cove lighting, and spotlighting.

In the 1920s, at the suggestion of the Buffalo architectural firm of Bley and Lyman, Niagara Hudson, a predecessor of the present company, built several of its new smaller offices in the then popular Art Deco style.

The structures reflected the company's growth, and served as showcases for many new lighting systems. Niagara Mohawk's headquarters is an imposing building with a facade of black glass and stainless steel. Completed in 1932, it became a central New York attraction. The building resembles a ziggurat, the Assyrian or Babylonian temple-tower, rising from a large base in multiple steps to a central tower. It measures 208 feet by 88 feet at ground level, and extends 114 feet to the tower. Flanked by three steps, the tower is 28 feet high and 20 feet wide; it is graced with a helmeted, winged figure called the Spirit of Light. The statue, made of stainless steel, is believed to be one of the first instances of this metal's use for outdoor sculpture.

Lighting, used to emphasize building structure and detail, was a significant part of the overall design. Helium tubes supplemented incandescent lamps in illuminating the building's exterior. Hidden floodlights highlight the Spirit of Light at night, and when fully lit, the building itself can be seen for miles. In the tower, there are 16,000 pounds of heat-resistant glass with thousands of watts of floodlights. Since World War II, however, reasons of economy and energy conservation have prevented the use of much of the original lighting.

The interior of the building is particularly rich in Art Deco ornamentation. There are four fused-glass murals in the lobby depicting Gas, Illumination, Generation, and Transmission, thereby visually explaining the company's operations. A photograph by Margaret Bourke-White, the famous photographer, depicting the Schoellkopf Station in Niagara Falls was used as the model for the Generation panel. The stainless steel elevator doors are etched with applied geometric designs characteristic of Art Deco. To fully appreciate the building one must walk through the interior and observe the way the lighting changes the visual impression of the decorative ornamentation.

Execution Through the years, the Niagara Mohawk building has been nicknamed Early Jukebox, Steel Wedding Cake, and Aztec Temple. In recent years, however, Art Deco has become recognized as an important architectural style, and the company, in response to the many requests received from architectural and art students to view its building, began conducting tours and distributing a descriptive brochure, *Niagara Mohawk's Art Deco Building.*

In spring, 1976, Niagara Mohawk assisted the Everson Museum of Syracuse in preparing a major exhibit on Art Deco, in which the company's building served as a central example. Niagara Mohawk's employees helped mount the show, and the company provided numerous photographs, a photo essay in mural scale, and measured drawings of its building. In conjunction with the exhibit, Niagara Mohawk arranged special tours of the landmark building.

Niagara Mohawk's Art Deco headquarters in Syracuse.

Costs The utility did not provide cost figures for its work on the Everson Art Deco exhibit, the descriptive brochure, or the guided tours of the building.

Benefits Maintenance of this vintage building and the educational program on its history and merits help create a good public image for Niagara Mohawk. The building has been written about in many publications. Ada Louise Huxtable, the *New York Times* architectural historian, discussed the building in an April, 1974, article on Art Deco architecture. In addition, Niagara Mohawk's headquarters received a citation from the Landmark Preservation Board of the City of Syracuse.

The Company Niagara Mohawk is the major public utility serving upstate New York. Revenues for 1976 amounted to $1.1 billion, reflecting an 11 percent improvement over 1975 revenues of $972 million. However, net income declined from 1975's record results of $114.8 million to $108.4 million. Approximately 82 percent of the company's revenues are derived from the sale of electricity, and the remaining 18 percent from gas. Electric sales break down as follows: residential, 31 percent; commercial, 32 percent; and industrial, 24 percent.

Other Preservation Activities/ Western Division Headquarters in Vintage 1913 Building. The Buffalo headquarters of the company's Western Division are also located in a landmark building with terra cotta decorative details. Completed in 1913, the thirteen-story tower was modeled after the Tower of Light, the central attraction of the Pan-American Exposition held in Buffalo in 1901. The Tower of Light, a Classical Revival structure, elaborately illuminated and decorated, was crowned by the Goddess of Light

statue. Buffalo General Electric Company, one of the present corporation's predecessors, used the Exposition building as a prototype for its headquarters. The extant structure, with a three-tiered tower of classical details, resembles a wedding cake. It is still economical to operate, and is a downtown Buffalo landmark.

Niagara Mohawk News. Niagara Mohawk publishes this magazine eight times a year for its employees. Besides containing articles on the public-utility industry and on company operations and employees, it has included features on upstate history and on historic structures. The *News,* which has a circulation of 17,000, has been published continuously since 1930 (except during the Depression years of 1932 to 1938).

For further information contact:
Jack L. Mowers
Supervisor
Photography
Niagara Mohawk Power Corporation
300 Erie Boulevard West
Syracuse, New York 13202

A view of elevator doors with Art Deco motifs.

A glass mural from a picture by Margaret Bourke White.

Summary Between 1975 and 1976, this offset printer, in Louisville, Kentucky, produced two posters promoting preservation causes and explaining aspects of the printing process. The posters, which cost $4,000 to produce, have received national acclaim, and demonstrate how a business enterprise can promote preservation as well as its product. Because of the success of these posters, the company is currently designing a series of Ethnic Heritage posters to commemorate Louisville's 200th anniversary.

Background In 1975, Pinaire asked its designers to create a poster as a handout for a business exposition in Louisville. The poster was to be visually arresting and reflect the quality of the company's work.

Execution Pinaire's designers, Julius Friedman and Nathan Felde, produced a two-sided color poster. One side depicted four interior details of a vintage house: two stained-glass windows, a Classical Revival newel post and staircase, and some rich Victorian paneling. The poster was headlined "When we build let us think that we build forever." The other side of the poster showed the top of the newel post in several amplified pictures. Its purpose was to explain the technical aspects of pictorial reproduction utilizing dots in various sizes, colors, and positions. The poster was distributed at no cost and was well received.

Because of the first poster's popularity, Pinaire decided to produce a second for the Bicentennial observance. The same designers focused on two important issues of the times: urban problems and historic preservation. One side of the poster, headed "Fight Urban Decay," is illustrated by a fresh tube of toothpaste marked "Preservation" flanked by a glass of water and a toothbrush. The other side is entitled "Preserve for the Future" and stresses the importance of printing in preserving the past and promoting progress in the future. The picture depicts a mason jar containing a Georgian Revival house, an apple, an apple slice, and a knife.

The poster was also used as an ad in a Bicentennial publication on preservation in Louisville prepared by the local Chamber of Commerce. This publication was sold at the National Trust for Historic Preservation's bookstore in Washington, D.C. The Trust received many inquiries about the ad and its availability in poster form. In response to these inquiries, the Trust obtained the Bicentennial poster from Pinaire at a discount, and sold it as two separate $4 posters. Mention of the poster in the Trust's monthly publication, *Preservation News,* resulted in additional sales.

Costs The cost of each poster was about $2,000.

Benefits By allowing printing of these posters and permitting the National Trust to sell them, Pinaire has gained national exposure for preservation, its product, and itself. The company has also been able to deduct the cost of the posters from its advertising expenses. The success of Pinaire's effort has led the company to plan another poster project—this time a series commemorating the 200th anniversary of Louisville.

The Company Pinaire has been in existence for about thirty years. Its offset-printing plant produces quality reproductions of collector prints, advertising brochures, annual reports, and books. Since Pinaire is privately held, financial figures are not available.

For further information contact:
Jack Ernwine
Sales Representative
Pinaire Lithographing Corporation
175 West Jefferson St.
P.O. Box 1060
Louisville, Kentucky 40201

A Pinaire preservation poster.

Republic Steel Corporation

Summary In October, 1974, Republic Steel Corporation donated the Burden Iron Company Office Building, built in 1882, and two acres of land in Troy, New York, to the Hudson-Mohawk Industrial Gateway, a nonprofit educational organization founded in 1972 to study and help preserve local industrial buildings and sites, as well as nineteenth-century industries. The Gateway commissioned an architectural firm to study the structure in 1975, and is currently renovating it as its headquarters. Republic has received tax write-offs and favorable publicity by donating a "white elephant" building to an interested group which recognizes the value of preserving and recycling historic industrial structures.

Background In the early part of the nineteenth century, the area north of Albany at the confluence of the Hudson and Mohawk Rivers, expanded rapidly as an industrial and transportation center. Abundant waterpower, excellent shipping, and later, railroad facilities brought many iron and metal works, textile mills, and manufacturers of scientific surveying instruments to the area.

Henry Burden, a Scottish immigrant and well-known inventor, took over the Troy Iron and Nail Factory in 1848. Powered by Burden's timely inventions, which included the first machine capable of mass producing horseshoes, a unique railroad spike and production process, and the first American improvement in the process of manufacturing wrought iron, the company rapidly expanded. It was the sole supplier of horseshoes to the Union forces during the Civil War. In 1864, the Troy Iron and Nail Factory became Henry Burden and Sons. When Burden died in 1871, the company was employing about 2,000 people, and was one of the largest employers in New York State.

In 1881, the company, now the Burden Iron Company, began building a new headquarters building. New York City architect Robert H. Robertson, who had designed Burden's country house in the then popular Queen Anne style, was commissioned to design the headquarters adjacent to the lower works and the railroad.

This building, eventually donated to the Hudson-Mohawk Industrial Gateway, was designed in a combination Queen Anne/Richardsonian Romanesque style. It measures 86 feet long and 68 feet wide, and is of brick construction, with pressed-brick decorative elements. The gable over the entrance has a pressed-brick arch with a hand-carved stone floral garland beneath it; above the garland, the company name appeared in gilded letters. Two flanking brownstone panels with floral motifs stand over the doorway. The building is crowned by a galvanized iron cupola and four molded, corbelled chimneys. Its original roof was tile. The interior was lavishly paneled with cherry wood, including walls, floors, and ceilings. Most of the labor was provided by employees of the iron works.

The office building's interior prior to renovation. (Hudson-Mohawk Industrial Gateway)

The Burden Iron Company continued to flourish until the deaths of Henry's sons just before World War I. About this time, steel was replacing iron. Since the Burden Company did not produce steel, it gradually declined, until it was liquidated in 1940.

Republic Steel bought the lower works in 1940 and operated a steel blast furnace there until 1972, when it closed and demolished the plant because of declining markets, soaring costs, and antipollution requirements. Between 1940 and 1972, the office building was used as a storage facility and was stripped of most of its cherry wood paneling. After the plant closed, the abandoned office building soon began to decay. Today, the only other buildings remaining are parts of a horseshoe warehouse and factory, and the steel frame of a rolling shed.

Hudson-Mohawk Industrial Gateway. The Hudson-Mohawk Industrial Gateway is a nonprofit educational organization founded in 1972 to study the industrial development of America during the nineteenth century, and to preserve nineteenth-century industries and buildings along the Hudson and Mohawk Rivers. Gateway tries to encourage the continued operation of these industries, preserve their buildings and sites through adaptive reuse, and attract tourists to them. It also counsels companies on the rehabilitation or recycling of buildings.

In 1975, Gateway staff advised the W. & L. E. Gurley Company, manufacturers of scientific and surveying instruments, on the rehabilitation of the company's original 1862 buildings in Troy. In the same year, it provided technical assistance on masonry problems encountered in converting the Cohoes Harmony Mills, a textile mill complex dating from the 1830s to the 1860s, into space usable by smaller manufacturers.

The organization, financed by donations, state grants, memberships, and receipts from tours it conducts, has five employees and a current budget of $60,000. The Gateway also publishes a quarterly newsletter for its 550 members. In 1976, about 1,800 people participated in the Gateway's tours, which are conducted from May through November.

The Burden Iron Company Office Building. (John Peckham)

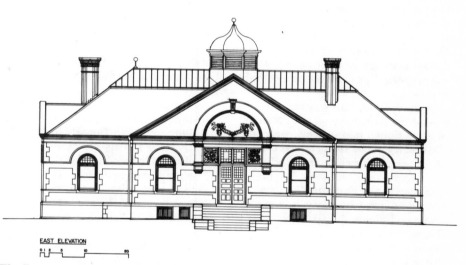

EAST ELEVATION

The Burden Iron Company Office Building. East elevation. (Hudson-Mohawk Industrial Gateway)

The Burden Iron Company Office Building. South elevation. (Hudson-Mohawk Industrial Gateway)

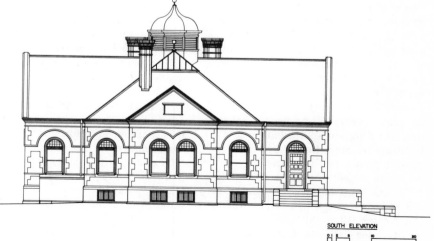

SOUTH ELEVATION

Execution In 1973, the Hudson-Mohawk Industrial Gateway received funds from the National Endowment for the Arts to survey important industrial buildings and sites in the Troy area. The Burden Iron Company Office Building, listed in the National Register of Historic Places in 1972, was among the buildings it surveyed. Gateway realized that the abandoned Burden building, although in need of renovation, would be ideal for its headquarters. The group prepared a feasibility study on the adaptive reuse of the building, and in spring, 1974, asked Republic Steel officials if they would contribute the unused structure. Republic Steel's legal department studied the possibility of donation, and in October of that year, the company gave the building, as well as two acres of land, to Gateway. Republic's real estate department drew up the deed describing property lines and Gateway's rights of access.

In July, 1975, Gateway commissioned the architectural firm Mendel, Mesick, Cohen to prepare a report on the history of the Burden Iron Company, the construction of the office building in 1881 and 1882, the present condition of the building, the measures needed to arrest its decay, and appropriate techniques for adaptive reuse as Gateway's headquarters. One immediate recommendation by the architects was that the asphalt roof, which had replaced the original red tile one, be repaired or replaced. The roof was leaking and causing water damage to the fabric of the building. Ultimately, many changes had to be made. The mortar in some sections of the brickwork, and some of the brick, had to be replaced, as did the old wiring, heating, and plumbing systems. The skylight had to be sealed, and to arrest vandalism and increase security, the doors and windows had to be made secure. The architects' report suggested, as a further security measure, installing an apartment for a full-time resident. Repair and construction—the first phase of the recycling project—began in December, 1976, and was completed in June, 1977.

The second phase will be remodeling the Burden Office Building as headquarters for Gateway. If sufficient funds can be raised, work will begin in late 1977 and be completed by 1979. To date, Gateway has raised $160,000: a $110,000 Historic Preservation Grant from the National Park Service and $50,000 from the City of Troy's Community Development budget.

Although only a few remnants of the cherry wainscoting remain, structurally, the interior is in relatively good shape. The renovated interior will include offices for the staff, a library, an exhibition and reception area, an auditorium, and meeting rooms; and even the paneling may be reproduced. The renovated Burden Office Building will house lectures, social gatherings, and exhibitions, and will serve as the orientation center for numerous tours run by Gateway.

Costs The architects' report, plan, and specifications cost $3,500. Republic would not divulge the value of the building and surrounding property.

Benefits The adaptive reuse of the historic Burden Iron Company Office Building will functionally and symbolically serve the objectives of the Hudson-Mohawk Industrial Gateway. The renovated building will serve as a visual symbol demonstrating that "the fullest future of the area rests in large measure on the successful restructuring of these historic industrial resources in the revitalized fabric of the urban environment."[1] Based on Gateway findings, several other industrial structures have been recycled by businesses.

The residents of Troy will benefit from the increased interest and tourism the complex will create, as well as from the recycling of an abandoned building. In addition, the building's use as an education and exhibition center will enhance the quality of the nearby residential neighborhood.

Republic Steel took a tax deduction for the donation, based on an independent appraisal. The company considers this confidential information and would not reveal the amount.

The company's donation of the Burden Iron Company Office Building to Gateway has been featured in several publications, including the *Troy Times Record,* the *Albany Times-Union,* the *Albany Knickerbocker News,* and *Fortune* magazine.

The Company Republic Steel Corporation, the fourth largest steel company in the U.S., is involved in all aspects of the manufacture of steel. It provides raw materials and a variety of finished products to a broad range of national and international markets. The company's sales break down as follows: autos, 25 percent; distributors, 15 percent; machinery and equipment, 15 percent; construction and contractors' products, 8 percent; forging, 11 percent; and oil and gas, 7 percent. In 1976, Republic had net sales of $2.5 billion and a net income of $65.9 million; comparable 1975 figures were $2.3 billion and $72.2 million.

Other Preservation Activities. On July 2, 1974, the company donated 36 acres of land, including a lake, near the old Burden Iron Company Office Building, to the City of Troy for use as a park. It also gave a 65-ton Whitcomb diesel locomotive, an 87-ton diesel rail crane, and an old-style ladle car, all dating from the 1920s, to the Mohawk & Hudson Chapter of the National Railway Historical Society. The ladle car is presently on loan to Gateway.

For further information contact:
A. F. Connors
Director of Public Relations
Republic Steel Corporation
P.O. Box 6778
Cleveland, Ohio 44101

Tony Opalka
Historical Researcher
Hudson-Mohawk Industrial Gateway
5 First Street
Troy, New York 12180

Footnotes

1. Letter from Tony Opalka, Historical Researcher, Hudson-Mohawk Industrial Gateway, to INFORM, May 12, 1977, p. 1.

Summary Since 1950, R. J. Reynolds Industries has made several grants for the renovation and preservation of Old Salem, a historic Moravian town which is now part of Winston-Salem, Reynolds' home city. A $452,800 grant made in 1976 is financing the reconstruction of the Single Brothers Workshop. The company is helping to preserve some of Old Salem's heritage, and in so doing, has received a good deal of favorable publicity.

Background In the mid-eighteenth century, the Moravians, a German-speaking group of Protestants, immigrated to Pennsylvania. Part of this group eventually settled in Salem, North Carolina, in 1766. The town prospered as a religious community until the mid-1800s, when there was a relaxation of the religious laws excluding non-Moravians.

By the 1940s, many of the buildings of the eighteenth-century town of Salem had either been demolished, modernized and used for commercial purposes, or left to decay. In 1947, a local grocer announced plans to construct a large supermarket in the heart of the historic area. Fearing the total destruction of the last remaining Moravian buildings, local citizens formed a nonprofit organization dedicated to the restoration and preservation of the Moravian town.

Since its inception in 1950, Old Salem, Inc., has restored or reconstructed seven Moravian buildings as exhibit areas: Single Brothers House (1769), Miksch Tobacco Shop (1771), Salem Tavern and Barn (1784), Boys' School (1794), Market Fire House (1803), John Vogler House (1819), and the Winkler Bakery (1800). These buildings are furnished with period pieces and are open to the public. Old Salem, Inc., administers the Winkler Bakery, Salem Tavern, and an old country store, all of which sell German-style food and goods.

Old Salem, Inc., is a multi-faceted organization whose main goal is education. Its tours and lectures, given by hostesses dressed in period costumes, cover all aspects of Moravian life. It also sponsors crafts demonstrations, concerts, archeological digs, and student summer programs, and publishes many descriptive pamphlets and brochures.

Old Salem is a residential community, as well as a historic attraction. Many of its 96 renovated properties are now either owner-occupied or rented to tenants by Old Salem, Inc. The Village is a registered National Landmark.

Execution Executives of R. J. Reynolds have served on Old Salem, Inc.'s Board of Trustees and Executive Committee since the restoration effort began more than 25 years ago. During the 1960s, the company made several grants totaling $414,000 to Old Salem's capital fund program for general restoration and operations. It also donated a substantial sum toward the restoration of the Miksch Tobacco Shop in 1957. Several members of the Reynolds family have personally made large contributions to the project.

Early in 1975, archeological research conducted by the Department of Restoration of Old Salem uncovered the original foundation, bake oven, and surviving building materials from the Single Brothers Workshop. The Workshop was built by the Moravian Single Brethren in 1771. The original building stood behind the Single Brothers House, and measured 71 feet by 31 feet. The one-and-a-half-story log structure rested on a stone foundation. The roof was covered with wooden shakes and boasted three molded-brick chimneys. The center section of the building was of half timber construction with brick infill, and contained a bake oven. In 1771, the Workshop housed a baker, a joiner, a weaver, a blacksmith, and a tailor. In the next century, it became a toy shop and general store. By 1921, the building had fallen into ruin, and the last remains of the wooden structure were demolished to make way for an apartment house. By the 1970s, this too had been abandoned.

In October, 1975, the Campaign Organization of Old Salem approached R. J. Reynolds Industries' Contribution Committee for a grant to remove the remains of the apartment house and reconstruct the Workshop. The proposed grant was submitted to the company's Board of Directors, who voted to approve $452,800 for the reconstruction, beginning with $55,000

to remove the remains of the apartment house still standing on the site.

Old Salem's Department of Restoration researched the project and is supervising the reconstruction. Original eighteenth-century architectural plans and drawings, written in German, were translated and studied to ensure an authentic reproduction of the building.

In the past two years, the site has been cleared, and the stone foundation of the original building has been repaired and reinforced. Oak logs needed for construction were, as of mid-1977, in the process of being secured and trimmed. Once completed, the Workshop, under the direction of the Old Salem Department of Education and Interpretation, will house a Learning Center with an eighteenth-century kitchen and dining room, a Moravian classroom, and a "best room" which will be furnished with period or reproduction pieces. In these areas, visitors will be able to learn about and gain first-hand experience in crafts such as soap making, spinning, and weaving.

Costs R. J. Reynolds Industries has contributed $452,800 for the Single Brothers Workshop reconstruction. Of this amount, $55,000 was donated for site preparation and demolition; $7,800 was set aside for archeological excavation; $315,000 to be contributed in two annual installments will be used for the actual reconstruction; and $75,000 has been reserved for furnishings and educational materials.

Problems Old Salem has found the preparation of the oak logs to be used in the reconstruction both costly and time-consuming, since it is done by hand.

Benefits Completion of this long-desired reconstruction will be an important visual addition to Old Salem Village. The project will also serve as an educational exhibit on the unique heritage of Winston-Salem, Reynolds' home city. Old Salem's efforts have had the positive effect of attracting many people to live and work in the area, providing an increased tax base, and boosting the town's economy. R. J. Reynolds has gained much publicity from the grant. Old Salem is frequently mentioned in the local and national media. It has been featured in articles in such magazines as *Reader's Digest* and *Seventeen*, in local newspapers and in papers as far away as Phoenix, Miami, Atlanta, Wilmington, and Cleveland as well. In 1974, Old Salem received an award from the North Carolina Literary and Historical Society for its significant contribution to the preservation of North Carolina history.

The Company R. J. Reynolds Industries, Inc., is a diversified international corporation and the largest tobacco manufacturer in the United States. Its 1976 sales were $5.75 billion, compared with $4.8 billion in 1975. Its 1975 earnings were $338 million. Its products include tobacco, petroleum, package foods, and aluminum products.

For further information contact:
Mark Gutsche
Assistant Public Relations
    Representative
R. J. Reynolds Industries, Inc.
Winston-Salem, North Carolina 27102

Frances Griffin
Director of Information
Old Salem, Inc.
Drawer F, Salem Station
Winston-Salem, North Carolina 27108

Miksch Tobacco Shop, Old Salem. (Old Salem, Inc.)

Summary   The Reynolds Metals Company, a leading producer of aluminum, has preserved a stretch of the historic James River and Kanawha Canal in downtown Richmond, Virginia, acquired in the purchase of additional facilities. This first canal system built in North America represented a major link between the Atlantic Coast and middle America. The preservation site includes two of the five stone locks that made up the Tidewater Connection linking the Canal and the tidewaters of the James River, and is considered an early American engineering landmark. In all, more than three-and-a-half acres along the James River have been incorporated in Reynolds' restoration and beautification project, which includes signs describing the Canal's history and picnic facilities open to the public.

Background   The history of American interest in navigating the James goes back to the first permanent English settlers who landed at Jamestown in 1607. After only ten days on this continent, and many long months in ocean voyage, they had progressed 125 miles westward up the James until they reached the impassable seven miles of falls at what is today the City of Richmond.

Richmond grew as the commercial hub of the area, because it was the link to the River and transportation to the coast. Waterpower from the River and the Canal supplied many mills which later produced a large portion of the country's flour. Until the middle of the nineteenth century, however, most of the products of these mills could not be shipped to the West without a great deal of trouble and expense.

The James River and Kanawha

Canal were part of the Great Central American Waterway conceived by George Washington as early as the 1740s. Then a surveyor, Washington proposed a connection between the James River and the Ohio and Mississippi Rivers to the west. In 1785, the Virginia Assembly created the James River Company charged with clearing and improving the River, and named Washington its first president, although he served only in an honorary capacity. Initially, two short canals were built, one around the falls at Westham, west of Richmond, and the other from the River into the city itself. At the eastern terminus of the latter canal, in the heart of Richmond, a Great Basin was completed in 1800 to permit boat turning. In 1810, construction on a connection—consisting of thirteen wooden locks—between this basin and the tidewaters of the James was initiated. Later, in the 1840s, these wooden locks were replaced with five granite locks of such exact specifications that they can truly be considered great engineering artifacts. By the 1850s, the complete canal system was open to navigation, from the harbors of the Atlantic Coast to the town of Buchanan, Virginia, some 197 miles away. There, a short overland connection to the Great Kanawha River led to the Ohio and then the Mississippi. The

Each of the five locks of the Tidewater Connection had a lift of 13 feet 8 inches, for a total lift of 68 feet 4 inches from 13th Street to 9th Street.

A schematic of the Tidewater Connection and the Great Basin of the James and Kanawha Canal.

The remains of the James River and Kanawha Canal Company's works cover over 480 miles from Richmond, Virginia to the Ohio River.

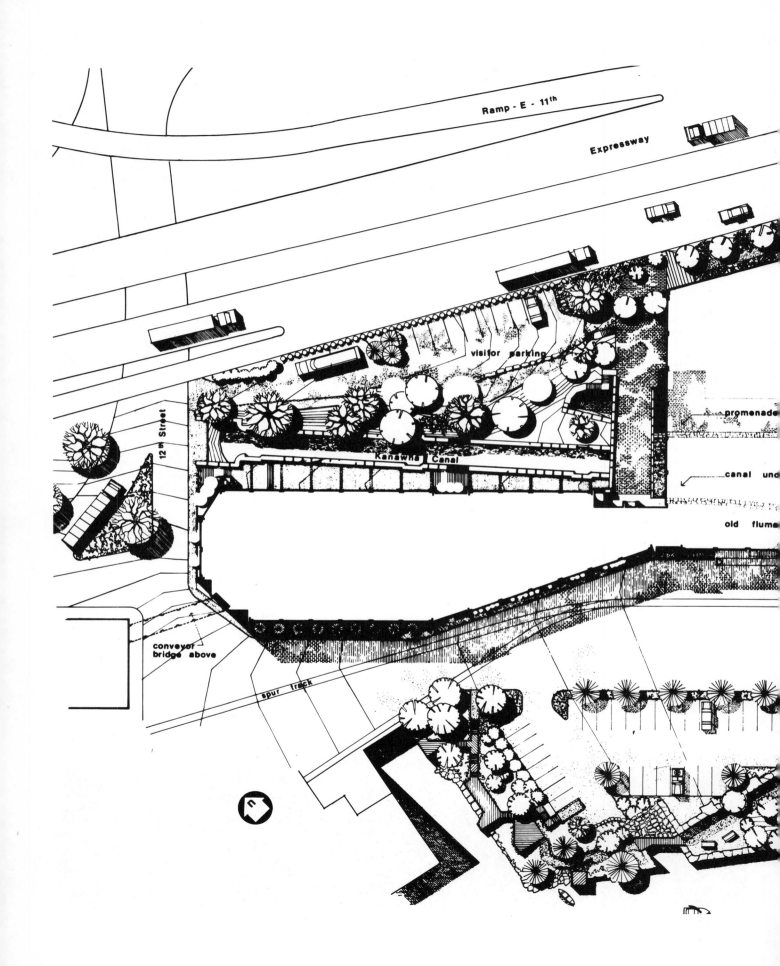

Ramp - E - 11th

Expressway

12th Street

visitor parking

Kanawha Canal

promenade

canal und

old flume

conveyor
bridge above

spur track

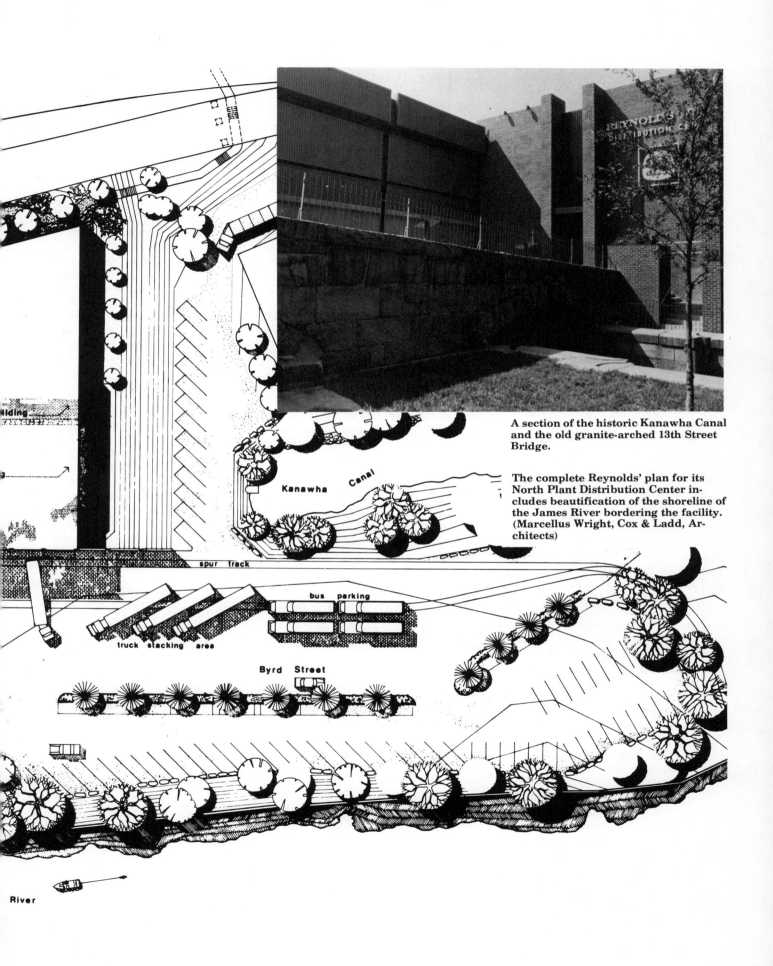

A section of the historic Kanawha Canal and the old granite-arched 13th Street Bridge.

The complete Reynolds' plan for its North Plant Distribution Center includes beautification of the shoreline of the James River bordering the facility. (Marcellus Wright, Cox & Ladd, Architects)

Canal's heyday lasted from the 1850s to the 1860s, when it was severely damaged by Union forces during the Civil War. Competition from newly developed railroads prevented its revival following the War, and it was sold to the Richmond and Allegheny Railway Company in 1880.

In the wake of "progress and development," much of the Canal had been filled in or left to collect trash. Local historians recognized this, and through their efforts, the Canal was included in the National Register of Historic Places in 1970. The Nomination Form for the James River and Kanawha Historic District—from the Great Ship Lock to Bosher's Dam—stated:

The range of local interest in the canal is illustrated, on the one hand, by the plans of Reynolds Metals Company to incorporate the two lower locks of the Tidewater Connection into their new plant, and on the other hand, with the threatened demolition of the upper three locks of the Connection by the Richmond Metropolitan Authority's expressway.[1]

Reynolds purchased an old factory complex along the James River in the 1940s, and adapted it for use by their Packaging Division. In the late 1960s, needing more warehouse space, the company acquired additional property in Richmond. This included two of the Tidewater Connection's granite locks, just east of Reynolds' present facility. At that time, the locks and other original stonework were not an obvious concern, since a building previously constructed on the site covered over much of them. Fortunately, however, the building's architect had anticipated eventual interest in the Canal, and had constructed his building without disturbing the artifacts below. When Reynolds razed this building, it found the preserved stonework, and decided to design the new distribution facility to incorporate it. The 1860s granite-arched 13th Street Bridge was also incorporated in the design, and the new warehouse took its shape from these historic artifacts.

* It has since been reported that the Richmond Metropolitan Authority had numbered, disassembled, and removed the stone locks for reassembly and display at a later date.

Execution   From the beginning, Paul Murphy, Vice President and General Manager of the Packaging Division, was convinced that preserving the Canal would be an asset to the company and the city. He persuaded the company to hire the architectural firm of Marcellus Wright, Cox, Cilimberg & Ladd to design the warehouse building. Reynolds' own staff did the working drawings and site supervision. The granite works were reassembled where necessary, and Mr. Steven Slaughter, a 74-year-old stonemason who had worked on restorations at Williamsburg, was brought in to assist with the work. The Virginia Historic Landmarks Commission lent technical assistance, and advised the company on historical accuracy.

At about the same time, the 100-year-old wooden 9th Street Bridge was being demolished to make way for a new bridge. Reynolds bought the old bridge's wrought-iron railings to use in the Canal project. In addition to the restoration, the company opened the entire project to the public and installed signs describing the Canal's history, as well as restroom facilities and a picnic area. A film on the Canal is also planned. Phase I of the project was completed in 1973, and work continues on further improvements, including restoration of the wooden locks.

Costs   Because the costs of restoring the Canal and locks were incorporated in the total cost of building the new warehouse facility, Reynolds is not able to provide an exact figure for the project's cost.

Problems   The only special problems resulting from Reynolds' plans for restoring the Canal were technical difficulties in actually executing the project. Some of the original granite walls had caved in and had to be reassembled.

Benefits   The benefits to the city and the public are clear. The company has received considerable favorable publicity, and the tourist site enables it to reap additional public-relations benefits. Reynolds, in cooperation with the Metropolitan Richmond Chamber of Commerce, has instituted a "Lunch at the Locks" program, serving lunch to tourist groups. Preservation activities by Reynolds and other companies along the James have encouraged the city to plan major improvements in the riverfront area to make it more accessible to the public. Several new buildings, including the Federal Reserve Bank of Richmond and the First & Merchants National Bank, have recently been constructed there. The Ethyl Corporation, just upriver from Reynolds, is also restoring a historic property, the Tredegar Iron Foundry, which made Civil War armaments.

The Company   Reynolds Metals is the country's second largest producer of primary aluminum and the world's largest producer of aluminum packaging materials. In 1976, it had net sales of over $2 billion and total assets of more than $2.3 billion. More than 325 people work at Reynolds' North Plant facility in Richmond, and approximately fifteen new jobs were added by the company's decision to build the new Distribution Center.

For further information contact:
A. R. D. Perrins
Director, Creative Services
Reynolds Aluminum Packaging
  Division
Reynolds Metals Company
Richmond, Virginia 23261

Footnotes

1. Tucker H. Hill and William Trout, "National Register of Historic Places, Inventory, Nomination Form," 10-300, (Washington, D.C.: U.S. Department of the Interior, National Park Service, June 23, 1971), p. 7.

Safeway Stores, Incorporated

Summary   Safeway, the largest supermarket chain in the nation, made a rather unique contribution to preservation: during the month of September, 1976, it placed a message about the National Trust for Historic Preservation on its milk cartons. About 900,000 of these cartons were distributed in northern California and Nevada. The Washington, D.C.-based National Trust believes this campaign increased awareness of and interest in the organization.

Background   In July, 1975, the National Trust's San Francisco office staff indicated to Safeway that the organization was in need of more exposure on the West Coast. Safeway, which for many years had placed messages on milk cartons for public-service and environmental organizations, such as CARE, the Red Cross, and Johnny Horizon, suggested that the recently opened National Trust Regional Office might want to take advantage of the same service.

Execution   The National Trust provided the copy for the message, and Safeway's ad agency did the layout.

Costs   Each impression for the message cost about ½ cent, and there were three impressions per carton, making Safeway's donation (not including the costs of layout by the company's ad agency) approximately $13,500.

Benefits   The advertisement brought the National Trust many inquiries about membership, although the exact number of new members the organization gained through this exposure is not known: Safeway has received many favorable comments from preservationists.

The Company   Founded in 1915, Safeway became a corporation in 1926. Originally a Western supermarket chain, it has expanded to 29 states and now has outlets in England, Canada, West Germany, and Australia. Stores number about 2,440. Sales reached $970 million in 1975, and topped $1 billion in 1976. In the same period, net income declined from $148 million in 1975 to $105 million in 1976.

For further information contact:
Felicia Del Campo
Manager, Public Relations
Safeway Stores, Incorporated
4th & Jackson Streets
Oakland, California 94660
The National Trust for Historic
  Preservation
740-748 Jackson Place, N.W.
Washington, D.C. 20006

National Trust for Historic Preservation advertisement on Safeway milk carton.

Summary

To celebrate the United States Bicentennial, Joseph E. Seagram & Sons has originated a project documenting the County Courthouse across the country from the inception of the county system to the present. In the development of the country, the Courthouse is undoubtedly the single most important building type.

Specially commissioned photographs by fine photographers will form the core of the archive. Work selected from the body of material and essays on the social and political role of the county seat and the architecture of the courthouse will be assembled in the form of a book and a national exhibition.[1]

The above is an excerpt from a questionnaire and letter sent in February, 1975, to county clerks, state bar associations, historical societies, and any other source that was thought to be interested. Seagram's allocated $250,000 for this study and will finance publication of the book.

Joseph E. Seagram & Sons, Inc., is the largest subsidiary of The Seagram Company, Ltd., the largest producer and distributor of distilled spirits and wines in the world.

Background

At a meeting of Seagram's executives in 1974, Ms. Phyllis Lambert, an architect and the sister of Mr. Edgar Bronfman, the company's Chairman and Chief Executive Officer, was given the job of choosing an appropriate way for the company to mark the Bicentennial.

Ms. Lambert decided that the Bicentennial project should take the form of a survey of a particular type of building in some way symbolic of the growth and development of the country. The choice was the county courthouse, and the means of preservation, photography. Ms. Lambert enlisted the help of Mr. Richard Pare, who teaches photography in Chicago, to prepare a feasibility study and report to Edgar Bronfman.

Execution

Mr. Pare devoted two months to drawing up a proposal. The courthouses of Indiana were the pilot project. After receiving the approval of the Board, Mr. Pare relocated to New York to coordinate and plan the project.

In February, 1975, 5,000 letters and questionnaires were sent to county clerks, state bar associations, historical societies, and state organizations, requesting photographs or postcards and information from an architectural, historic, and social viewpoint on the presently used courthouse, and any predecessors, if such structures were still standing.

Seagram's commissioned 24 photographers to photograph over 1,000 courthouses, roughly one-third the number of existing courthouses in the 48 contiguous states. This group of photographers worked systematically all over the country in an attempt to survey the architecture and the present status of the buildings. Shooting began in spring, 1975, reached a peak of activity that summer, and concluded in January, 1977.

Seagram's located and recorded many remarkable buildings. One—in King William County, Virginia—was the oldest courthouse still in use today, dating from about 1725. Built in Flemish bond brickwork, it is surrounded by a boundary wall.

Also documented was the oldest frame courthouse, which dates from 1749, and is located in Plymouth, Massachusetts. Besides its occasional use as a courthouse, this building now functions as a museum known as the Old Towne House.

Some courthouses were photographed as they were being demolished. Others have fallen victim to the bulldozer since being photographed.

Because the courthouse is often a focal point of the community, it was viewed as more than simply a structure, and was photographed both in detail and in the context of the surrounding area. Extant courthouses that are no longer serving their original function were also included. Over 8,000 pictures of interiors and exteriors, as well as photographs of other pertinent architectural details, have been taken. Not every county or state will be included in the book, though all of the 48 contiguous states are represented in the archive.

A book, drawing on the archive, was published in 1978. It is primarily pictorial, utilizing about 300 photographs. Three essays accompany the pictures: the first, by Henry-Russell Hitchcock and William Seale, on the architecture; the second, by Paul Reardon, Associate Justice (Ret.), Supreme Judicial Court of Massachusetts, on the history of the county system; and the third, by Calvin Trillin of the *New Yorker,* on the genre and folklore of the courthouse and county offices.

Richard Pare negotiated a contract for the publication of the book, which retails for $35. Seagram's will pay for the cost of production, and will share the royalties generated by the sale.

Several exhibitions have taken place, including a major exhibition of 86 prints in St. Louis in March, 1976. A touring exhibit is being planned in collaboration with the American Federation of the Arts and the National Trust for Historic Preservation. Changing exhibits drawn from the archive may be seen in the reception area of Seagram's national headquarters in New York City. Also in New York, 64 photographs in an exhibit called "Courthouse" were on view at the Museum of Modern Art from April to July, 1977.

Costs The Board of Seagram's committed $250,000 for the study; this sum financed the photography and paid all expenses, including travel, photographic materials, and salaries. The company will also finance the book of 300 of the best photographs, paying the editor's salary, the essayists' fees, and the bill for archival materials purchased to accommodate the photographs and information gathered. Indirect expenditures include use of an office at Seagram's headquarters in New York, salary for a secretary, mailings, and administrative services.

Benefits Seagram's undertook this project as its contribution to the Bicentennial in the hope that the photographic documentation of courthouses throughout the United States would encourage more research in similar areas by other groups.

The Company For the fiscal year ending July, 1976, Joseph E. Seagram & Sons had sales of $1.7 billion and a net income of $32.2 million, compared to sales of $1.6 billion and a net income of $29.1 million for the previous year. Seagram's sales account for 20 percent of the distilled-spirits market in the United States. The company also is involved in oil and gas exploration and production through its subsidiary, Texas Pacific Oil Company, Inc.

Other Preservation Activities. The company's headquarters are presently the subject of a preservation effort. In October, 1976, Seagram's applied to New York City for landmark status for its headquarters building on Park Avenue. This bronze-and-glass tower was designed by the well-known architects Mies Van Der Rohe and Philip Johnson, and was completed in 1958. Reputed to be among the finest metal curtain-wall buildings, the Seagrams Tower has served as the prototype for similar structures all over the world.

Seagram's application for official landmark status is the subject of lively discussion among preservationists, since the present New York Landmarks Preservation Law stipulates that a structure must be at least thirty years old before it can be considered. Seagram's decision to seek landmark status is also interesting because owners of buildings usually fight landmark designation. Seagram's request is currently under review.

Phyllis Bronfman Lambert, the originator of the courthouse project, has recently purchased and successfully renovated the vintage Biltmore Hotel in Los Angeles, California.

For further information contact:
Richard Pare
General Editor
Phyllis Lambert
Director
Caroline Sederbaum
Assistant to the Editor
United States Bicentennial Project
Joseph E. Seagram & Sons, Inc.
375 Park Avenue
New York, New York 10022

Footnotes

1. Letter from Richard Pare, General Editor, United States Bicentennial Project, Joseph E. Seagram & Sons, Inc., to county officials, state Bar Associations, historical societies, and other interested parties, February, 1975.

Courthouse (c. 1877) in Lake City, Colorado. (William Clift)

A view of Pittsburgh's Allegheny Courthouse (c. 1880), designed by Henry Hobson Richardson. (Richard Pare)

Summary In 1972, Standard Oil Company (Indiana) donated the historic Destrehan Plantation House, and four acres of the surrounding land, valued at $160,000, to the River Road Historical Society of Destrehan, Louisiana. The company also contributed an initial $12,000 toward renovating the eighteenth-century mansion. The gift has enabled the Historical Society to begin the work of preserving the house. Partly due to the success of this project, the Society is administering another newly restored plantation.

Background The Destrehan Plantation House was built in 1787 for a French sugar and indigo planter named Robert Antoine Robin De Logny. De Logny hired a free mulatto named Charles Pacquet to construct the house according to his specifications. It was completed by slave labor in 1790.

The house contains two stories: the top floor, reachable by two mahogany staircases, contains the main living area, including the dining room and bedrooms; the service areas, added later, are on the lower floor. In 1812, two two-story additions were made on either side of the main house.

The galleries were supported by masonry Tuscan columns, and the roof over them by painted wooden columns. At the time of the house's construction, there were no levees for the Mississippi River, and flooding was a regular occurrence. As a result, the house originally had no lower floor, but was supported by masonry columns. In 1840, when the levee system for the River was completed up to Baton Rouge, the lower floor was enclosed for use as a service area. During the Greek Revival period—about 1840—both sets of columns were replaced by massive Doric columns.

The house has been a local landmark since it was built. In 1973, it was included in the National Register of Historic Places. The nomination form explained a bit of the Destrehan Plantation's uniqueness:

The house is one of the oldest in Louisiana and one of the best documented structures of the colonial period. It represents three major phases of construction and illustrates the changes in architectural style in Louisiana from the original eighteenth century colonial structure to the post colonial addition of the detached wings, to the ante-bellum Greek Revival alterations in the colonnade and interior details.[1]

Upon his death in 1792, Robert De Logny willed the plantation to his daughter, Marie.

Later, Marie married Jean Noel Destrehan. Jean Noel constructed the two additions to either side of the house to accommodate Marie's and his fourteen children, and he officially gave his name to the plantation. It was after Jean Noel died in 1823 that Stephen Henderson purchased the property for $187,294. Pierre Adolph Rost, the adopted son of Stephen Henderson, resided in the plantation house until 1914.

During Rost's occupancy, rumors sprang up around Destrehan that the house grounds were haunted by the long-deceased pirate, Jean Lafitte, who had been a frequent visitor to Destrehan in Henderson's time. This rumor gave rise to the belief that Lafitte may have buried a part of his booty somewhere in the plantation house or grounds.

In 1914, the Mexican Petroleum Company bought the house and grounds for $40,000, and built a refinery on the property. The company subsequently sold the house, refinery, and grounds to the Pan Am Southern Corporation, a predecessor of Standard Oil. Standard Oil furnished the house and maintained it during its 44-year occupancy. Before World War I, the house served as a club for employees who resided on the plantation grounds. Later, it served as the offices of the refinery accounting department. In 1958, Standard Oil closed down its refinery operations in Louisiana and the building was vacated.

During the fourteen years it remained vacant, the plantation house was totally stripped of valuables, both inside and out, by vandals. They believed the story of hidden treasure, but found none. Instead, they took everything removable: shutters, mantelpieces, doors, windows, cisterns, woodwork, pipes, and whatever furnishings remained.

Some local residents, fearing the entire mansion would be destroyed through neglect, formed the River Road Historical Society in 1972. Their aim was to preserve and restore what was left of the old plantation house.

Execution In 1971, Standard Oil had the house and grounds appraised; the house was appraised at $74,000, and the land at $86,000, for a total of $160,000. The next year, at the insistence of the Historical Society, Standard Oil donated to it the mansion and four acres of the surrounding land. However, the newly formed Historical Society was having difficulty in raising the money to begin the restoration. Standard Oil donated $12,000 for a new roof and structural reinforcement, badly needed to halt further interior and exterior deterioration until more money could be raised. In May, 1973, Standard Oil discovered the original plantation bell, mentioned in a 1792 inventory, and mounted it near its original position.

In November, 1972, the River Road Historical Society held its first annual Fall Festival on the plantation grounds in order to help raise $500,000, the estimated cost of complete restoration. The *Torch,* a magazine published by Standard Oil, described a later Fall Festival:

More than 20,000 people attended the event, which was based on the Bicentennial theme. Local artisans made, displayed and sold their works, which were produced in the same manner as they were in the days when the house was being built. Louisiana foods including piquante, jambalaya, gumbo, and "dirty" rice were served by the potful.[2]

By the time of the third annual fair, which brought in $38,000, the first phase of the restoration project was completed. The Society had succeeded in raising $104,000, which was spent in clearing the land around the mansion, restoring the wooden columns, and reinforcing the structure.

Since then, the River Road Historical Society has raised an additional $50,000 toward its goal. The money has been used to paint most of the exterior, and to replace every window and door, as well as the stolen hardware and shutters. In addition, the parlor and dining rooms will be refurbished and repainted, and the floors will be refinished. To date, only one interior room has been completely restored. This room, which was the wine cellar, serves as an antique shop to raise funds for the Society.

The River Road Historical Society has received contributions from other major corporations such as Dupont and Shell Oil. It has also succeeded in placing Destrehan in the National Register of Historic Places, making the project eligible for matching funds at both the state and federal levels. Through the Society's efforts, the mansion is now open to the public, and an estimated 2,000 people visit it each month.

Costs Aside from providing a figure of $12,000, which represented its donation for early restoration work, Standard Oil gave no other financial details on its involvement in the Destrehan project.

Problems The major difficulty in the restoration was replacing all the portable valuables stolen by vandals during the house's fourteen-year vacancy. According to Ann Little, Destrehan's current Administrator, "What nature couldn't do in two centuries, man has done in fourteen years."[3]

Benefits Standard Oil's image has been enhanced by the public-relations material the donation has generated; the Destrehan restoration has been prominently featured in the local media. Information on tax benefits the company gained by donating the property is not available.

The River Road Historical Society was at last able to begin the restoration it had long hoped for. As a result of its success with Destrehan, the Society has recently become administrator of the newly restored San Francisco Plantation in Garyville, Louisiana.

The Company Standard Oil is the leading petroleum-products company in the Midwest, and distributes to all other states under the AMOCO name. The company also markets natural gas, and agricultural and chemical products. In 1976, Standard Oil's revenues were $11.5 billion, an increase of 16 percent over 1975 revenues of $10 billion. Net income, over the same period, rose 11 percent from $787 million to $893 million. Of the company's earnings, 78 percent came from U.S. petroleum and natural gas; 9.2 percent from Canada; and 12.5 percent from overseas.

For further information contact:
S. L. Paffenrath
Staff Writer, Communications Division
Public and Government Affairs
  Department

Standard Oil Company (Indiana)
200 East Randolph Drive
P.O. Box 5910-A
Chicago, Illinois 60680
A. Rush Little
Administrator
Destrehan Plantation House
P.O. Box 5
Destrehan, Louisiana 70047

Footnotes

1. Samuel Wilson, Jr., "National Register of Historic Places, Inventory, Nomination Form," 10-300, (Washington, D.C.: U.S. Department of the Interior, National Park Service, July 14, 1972), p. 4.
2. Rod Taylor, "Destrehan Rides Again," *Amoco Torch,* January/February 1976, p. 23.
3. INFORM interview with Ann R. Little, Administrator, Destrehan Plantation, March, 1977.

The Destrehan Plantation House. (River Road Historical Society)

Union Camp Corporation

Summary In March, 1976, this leading wood-products producer donated the historic Tower Hill Plantation in Virginia with ten acres of land to the National Trust for Historic Preservation. The donation of this property, dating from 1775, was significant for two reasons: it was the first corporate gift of a historic house and property to the National Trust, and it was the first such gift by Union Camp, which had previously given away vast tracts of historically and ecologically important woodlands.

Tower Hill, appraised at $55,000, was donated to the National Trust for use in its asset real property program. The property will be sold subject to protective covenants that will prohibit subdivision of the land and alterations to the house without the Trust's consent.

Background The Tower Hill property marks the second donation made by Union Camp under its Land Legacy Program set up in November, 1975. Two years before, Union Camp had made its largest single land donation ever. It had given its entire holdings in the Great Dismal Swamp of Virginia, involving almost 50,000 acres valued at $12.6 million. This swampland, rich in ecological and historic resources, is now part of the National Wildlife Refuge System of the U.S. Department of the Interior. The contribution was officially completed in January, 1975, and Union Camp received in return a federal tax reduction of approximately $6 million over three years.

The Land Legacy Program was established as an expression of the company's ongoing interest in making donations of land and resources. Alexander Calder, Jr., Chairman of the Board of Union Camp, stated the corporation's preservation philosophy:

There are many companies such as Union Camp whose business activities involve the ownership of large land-holdings. In our case, as a forest products firm, trees are our major natural resource. . . . Thanks to the nation's tax laws, which . . . entitle companies to the normal deductions for charitable contributions, investor-owned corporations are able to . . . participate with conservation agencies to assure the safekeeping of these lands [of unique ecological

and historical significance] for future generations.[1]

The Land Legacy Program's role was to administer company donations. Under it, several of Union Camp's grants have been made through The Nature Conservancy, a nonprofit agency that accepts and makes donations of land and acquires land for government and other conservation bodies. The other four gifts, in addition to the Tower Hill property, made under the Land Legacy Program have included:

Turtle Island, South Carolina (1975)—Located at the mouth of the Savannah River, this 1,700-acre island is the southernmost barrier island in South Carolina. It was given to the South Carolina Wildlife and Marine Resources Department in December, 1975, and is maintained as a wildlife area. Donation of Turtle Island and the Great Dismal Swamp represent a contribution valued at $13 million. This was the first contribution under Union Camp's Land Legacy Program.

Chowan Swamp, North Carolina (1976)—This 3,800-acre tract will eventually become an environmental-studies center for educational and public use under the auspices of the State of North Carolina. The donation was made in April, 1976.

Hall's Knoll, Georgia (1976)—Located about thirty miles from Savannah in Midway, this site was the home of Dr. Lyman Hall, a signer of the Declaration of Independence and the first Governor of Georgia after the Revolutionary War. In July, 1976, the Land Legacy Program donated 88 acres to the Liberty County Historical Society which plans to establish a wildlife sanctuary. In time, trails and markers will indicate the numerous species of plants and trees indigenous to the area. Since Lyman Hall's house was burnt by the British during the Revolutionary War in 1782, the Society will undertake an archaeological dig to determine its exact location.

Crescent Lake, Florida (1976)—In November, 1976, the company contributed 2,850 acres to the Florida Department of Natural Resources Endangered Lands Program. The Department will maintain the land as a wildlife preserve. Appraised at $955,000, this ecologically valuable land abounds in wildlife, including bald eagles.

Execution The second donation under the Land Legacy Program was Tower Hill. In 1968, Union Camp bought the plantation tract and woodlands to which the Blow family had retained title for nearly 200 years. The one-and-a-half-story frame house on a raised brick foundation had originally been built in 1775 as the plantation manager's residence. With its exposed end chimneys, laid in Flemish bond brickwork, Tower Hill House is an excellent example of Virginia architecture of that period. It is a relatively small house with five dormers that have unusual jerkin head roofs.

The four-room house, with two rooms on each floor, was remodeled in the twentieth century. However, its interior still boasts a central staircase with a molded handrail, turned balusters, and square newel posts, and the dining room retains its original chair rail molding. After the larger plantation house burned, this smaller house served as the owner's residence. In recent years, the company rented it to local organizations.

The Tower Hill tract has historic significance; the property was once owned by the Harrison family, which gave the United States two Presidents, Henry Harrison, the 9th President, and Benjamin Harrison, his grandson, the 23rd President.

Union Camp continually analyzes its properties for historic and ecological significance. When the company realized the importance of Tower Hill, it approached the National Trust which gladly accepted the gift. The house is presently on the real estate market.

Benefits When the property is sold, the National Trust will be able to use the funds received for further preservation activities, while the restrictive covenants assure that the historic house's architectural integrity will be protected.

Union Camp earned from this donation a $26,500 reduction in its federal income taxes, in addition to public-relations benefits.

260

The Company Union Camp Corporation, a major natural-resources company, owns about 1.7 million acres of woodlands in Alabama, Florida, Georgia, South Carolina, North Carolina, and Virginia. The company's product lines consist of paper, packaging, building materials, and specialty chemicals. In 1976, for the first time, Union Camp's sales totaled more than $1 billion, representing a 20 percent increase over 1975 sales of $835.9 million. Its net income showed a 34 percent improvement, from $88.7 million to $118.6 million.

Other Preservation Activities. In early 1977, Union Camp offered to pay half the cost of membership in The Nature Conservancy for any of its employees who wished to join.

In line with the company practice of researching its vast holdings for ecological and historic significance, Union Camp recently co-sponsored an archaeological dig that took place on a fifteen-acre site belonging to one of its mills in Michigan. The site was the scene of a battle between British soldiers and Indians and American troops in January, 1813. The dig was conducted in cooperation with the local historical society and resulted in unearthing such items as lead rifle balls and arrowheads.

The company is currently analyzing its holdings in the South to ascertain if any important Civil War events took place on them.

For further information contact:
John G. Gregory
Director of Resource Development
Union Camp Corporation
1600 Valley Road
Wayne, New Jersey 07470

J. E. Moody
Vice President, Real Estate and
    Legal Services
National Trust for Historic
    Preservation
740-748 Jackson Place, N.W.
Washington, DC 20006

Footnotes

1. Union Camp Corporation, "Union Camp Corporation Donates Plantation Homesite of Patriot Lyman Hall, Declaration of Independence Signer [Who] Was Governor of Georgia," *News Release*, July 1, 1976, p. 2.

The Tower Hill Plantation House.

APPENDIX

INFORM identified many more business-supported preservation projects across the United States than are profiled in the body of this book. For those on which some information was available, a short description of the project is included below. The organization of this section mirrors that of the full case studies. It is divided into three sections: recycled buildings, community revitalization, and general preservation support. Where possible, contacts are provided for readers wishing to obtain further information.

Recycled Buildings

Project: Restoration of the Lockerly Plantation House (c. 1839) as a guest complex

Company: American Industrial Clay Company
433 North Broad Street
Elizabeth, New Jersey
07207

In 1963, the American Industrial Clay Company purchased Lockerly Hall, located in Baldwin County, Georgia. The company completely restored the lavish antebellum plantation house for use as a guest house for visiting technicians, scientists, and manufacturers interested in kaolin. Kaolin is a kind of white clay used in the production of ceramics, paper, and textiles. It is mined by the company nearby.

The house, built in 1839 by Daniel Tucker, a local judge, remained a residence until the 1963 sale. The company restored the building, and the late Edward Grossman, company President, placed his private collection of Southern antiques on display there.

Project: Reuse of a Victorian mansion (c. 1886) as corporate offices

Company: Atlantic Coast Life Insurance Company
149 Wentworth Street
Charleston, South Carolina
92401

Contact: Robert Scarborough
Secretary-Treasurer

In 1940, the Atlantic Coast Life Insurance Company purchased the 13,883-square-foot Rogers Mansion located on the edge of Charleston's historic urban core. This ornate four-story Victorian house was originally built for a wealthy merchant by architect Daniel C. Waynes at a cost of approximately $200,000.

Atlantic Coast Life renovated the structure and adjacent stables for $225,000, or $16 per square foot. According to the company, operating costs on the building are high due to high ceilings and maintenance, but the only way "to preserve Charleston is to save the old buildings and keep them on the tax rolls."

Project: Reuse of a vintage residence as corporate offices

Company: Atlantic Mutual Life Insurance
17 West Mcdonough Street
Savannah, Georgia 31401

Contact: Ann Connor
Secretary

In 1954, Frederick Wessells, Jr., President of Atlantic Mutual Life Insurance and several other companies, purchased the Moses Eastman Mansion in Savannah, Georgia, to house the offices of his many businesses. This project was the first adaptive reuse of a vintage residence for office space in Savannah.

The three-story brick and stucco structure, built in 1843 by Eastman, a wealthy merchant, includes a porch with a two-story rounded colonnade. In 1893, a fourth story was added, and the raised basement was converted to use as the first floor. The Mansion remained a residence until 1939 when it became a millinery shop. In 1946, it returned to residential use.

Atlantic Mutual Life discovered that the Mansion required little renovation. All systems were in working order. A vault was added to the raised basement, several walls were removed from the upstairs bedrooms, and the interior was painted. Several outbuildings, including an old garage and outhouse, were demolished to provide parking spaces. The office furnishings are contemporary, although the original lighting fixtures and crystal chandeliers remain. An intricate iron fence, featuring the faces of famous men, surrounds the house.

Today, the first floor houses the Southern Bank and its vaults. The second floor has been kept exactly as it was when Wessells first purchased the house. The library and drawing room remain as period rooms. The third and fourth floors serve as the offices of Wessells' other companies.

Project: Use of a museum building (c. 1861) as a retail clothing store

Company: Bonwit Teller
234 Berkeley Street
Boston, Massachusetts
02116

In 1947, the New England Mutual Life Insurance Company purchased the New England Museum of Natural History building and site which were adjacent to its company offices in Boston's Back Bay. The Museum was moving to new quarters, and was vacating its 1861 classical landmark building. New England Mutual Life contemplated demolition and new commercial construction, but Walter Hoving, then President and owner of Bonwit Teller, a retail clothing chain, agreed to lease the old museum and convert it into a specialty store. Bonwit Teller has been located in the building ever since. High real estate taxes—at an assessed value much greater than the market value of the property—have caused the company some concern, but it is pleased with the prime location and image of the historic structure.

Project: Reuse of an old bookstore as newspaper office

Company: The Boston Globe
Old Corner Bookstore
50 Bromfield Street
Boston, Massachusetts
02108

The Old Corner Bookstore, a brick structure built about 1718 at the corner of School and Washington Streets in the heart of Boston, was originally a private home. It was later adapted as a bookstore by Ticknor and Fields, publishers of Longfellow, Stowe, Emerson, Holmes, Thoreau, Whittier, and many others. In the twentieth century, the bookstore declined. The building was last used as a pizza parlor before its existence was threatened by the urban-renewal bulldozer. In the mid-1960s, Historic Boston, Inc., an *ad hoc* group of concerned citizens, was formed to purchase and restore the building. The group was supported in its efforts by a contribution of more than $100,000 from the *Boston Globe,* the city's major newspaper. The *Globe* also signed a long-term lease for use of the building as the company's in-town office, insuring the project's financial success.

Project: Continued use of a historic hotel

Company: Braniff International Hotels, Inc.
P.O. Box 35001
Dallas, Texas 75235

In October, 1974, Braniff International Hotels, Inc., a subsidiary of Braniff Airways, purchased the Driskill Hotel in Austin, Texas. The 1886 structure long served the city as a center of social and political life. In 1964, President Johnson watched the televised results of his election there, and the hotel served as the White House Press Center whenever the President was at his nearby ranch. In 1966, the building was designated an official state historic site and a Texas Historical Medallion was awarded; however, by 1969, it was closed for financial reasons. A group of local preservationists fought to save the old hotel. After two years, they raised enough money to purchase and renovate the building, through the sale of $500,000 in stock in the Driskill Hotel Corporation. The hotel was reopened in 1973. Braniff purchased the building from the Driskill Hotel Corporation in 1974 and committed at least $350,000 to restore and remodel the lobbies and general ballroom space.

Project: Reuse of three factory buildings for office space

Company: Burroughs Corporation
Burroughs Place
Detroit, Michigan 48232

Contact: Robert Farkas
Manager, Press Relations

The Burroughs Corporation's world headquarters in Detroit consists of three renovated factory buildings. Between 1967 and 1972, the buildings were stripped down to their steel-reinforced concrete frames, and unified by enclosure in concrete, glass, and aluminum walls. The new five-story complex contains more than 600,000 square feet of floor space. The reuse scheme was executed by the architectural firm of Smith and Gardner of Detroit.

Project: Reuse of the Hale Houston House as corporate offices

Company: R.W. Byram Company
706 Guadalupe Street
Austin, Texas 78701

Contact: Chuck Christensen
President

In 1969, R.W. Byram Company, which publishes oil- and gas-industry trade publications, purchased the Hale Houston House at 706 Guadalupe Street in Austin, Texas. The house is on the Bremond block (see Appendix: Texas Classroom Teachers Association), a street which contains six of the city's oldest homes, all listed in the National Register of Historic Places.

The Hale Houston House was built in 1850 by John Bremond, a wealthy merchant. The original section of the house is a one-story Greek Revival structure which includes a central hall, five bay windows, and a gallery with Doric columns. The ceilings are ten feet high, and the interior boasts fine wainscoting. In 1873, Bremond's son, Eugene, added the second story, consisting of three bedrooms and a screened porch. The house today has five fireplaces and one-and-a-half-inch-thick oak flooring.

Byram adapted the building for its offices and constructed a two-story, 2,400-square-foot addition to house its printing offices.

Project: Renovation of the Joseph Foster House as a branch bank

Company: Cape Ann Bank and Trust Company
154 Main Street
Gloucester, Massachusetts 01930

Contact: William F. Bonney
President

In 1972, the Cape Ann Bank and Trust Company purchased the Joseph Foster House in Gloucester, Massachusetts, as a facility for its expanding trust department. The house, built in 1760 by Colonel Joseph Foster had been continuously occupied most recently by a confectionery and a dental office. It had been divided into four apartment units prior to the bank's purchase. The bank's original renovation plan was expanded at the urging of then bank President Kendall to include an accurate restoration of the house. The interior was returned to its original proportions. The original chimney and main entrance sites were found and suitably reproduced. Much of the original wooden paneling was salvaged and reused. The interior doors are all replicas of a door found in the house and believed to be an original. The new interior blends eighteenth-century atmosphere and modern banking conveniences. According to the bank, the restored building is a highly satisfactory facility, as well as a source of community pride and good public relations.

Project: Reuse of pre-earthquake San Francisco office building

Company: The Chartered Bank of London
California Branch
465 California Street
San Francisco, California 94104

In 1976, this British bank, like many American banks in Europe, established operations in a renovated historic building. The bank spent more than $250,000 to restore and adapt the 1905 Merchants Exchange Building in San Francisco. The Exchange, designed by Willis Polk and Julia Morgan, long a San Francisco landmark, is one of the few buildings to survive the earthquake of 1906.

Project: Renovation of 1902 bank building and construction of a compatible contemporary addition

Company: Citizens Savings and Loan Association
700 Market Street
San Francisco, California 94102

Contact: Casey MacKenzie
Community Relations Manager

In 1964, the Citizens Savings and Loan Association completed renovation and new-construction work on its building near the intersection of Market, Kearny, and Geary Streets in San Francisco. The original 1902 structure, built in the French Renaissance style, was one of the few buildings to survive the 1906 earthquake and fire. The original twelve floors were completely refurbished and extended to connect with a new service-tower corner designed to complement the style of the older building. Clark and Beuttler, with associates Charles W. Moore and Alan E. Morgan, were the architects. The cost of the alterations and addition was $2.25 million, or approximately $24 per square foot.

Project: Conversion of a church into a temple of finance

Company: Consolidated American Life Insurance Company
National Headquarters
308 North West Jackson Street
Jackson, Mississippi 39205

Contact: George W. Pickett
President

The First Baptist Church, built in 1843, was one of the few buildings not burned by the Union Army as it pushed through Jackson, Mississippi, during the Civil War. In the early 1900s, the building was converted into a dormitory and classroom facility. Later, it became an apartment house, a church again, and finally, in 1959, the home office of the American Liberty Life Insurance Company (now merged with Consolidated American).

The temple-like structure is today one of only four publicly used buildings still remaining from Jackson's pioneer days.

Project: Renovation of Federal Reserve branch for office use

Company: Crispin Company
22 World Trade Center
Houston, Texas 77001

In 1973, the Crispin Company, an international trading company specializing in steel products, moved its headquarters into an old branch of the Federal Reserve Bank of Dallas. The 1922 structure, located in Houston's central business district, is limestone-faced with terra cotta detail. Architect for the renovation Howard Barnstone highlighted the building's grand main-floor area by using glass walls for office partitions and marble designed to blend with the original decor. The former vault has now become a conference room.

Project: Conversion of industrial buildings to offices

Company: Fibreboard Corporation
55 Francisco Street
San Francisco, California 94133

Contact: Ron Kaufman
The Kaufman Companies
55 Francisco Street
San Francisco, California 94133

In 1970, the Montgomery/North Block was an abandoned and unattractive group of industrial buildings located in the North Waterfront area of San Francisco. Although it was separated from the established downtown by several blocks, developer Ron Kaufman felt that the buildings and the area had recycling potential. Kaufman convinced the Fibreboard Corporation of this potential, and the company agreed to take a fifty-year lease on 100,000 square feet in one of the buildings for use as its world headquarters. The cost for the space was about 30 percent to 40 percent less than the cost of similar space in a new building. Other major businesses, including the Western Contract Furnishers and the Victoria Station restaurant chain, have also leased space in the complex.

Project: Relocation and reuse of two houses as bank branches

Company: Franklin Savings Association
P.O. Box 1723
Austin, Texas 78767

Contact: Charles Betts
President

In 1974, in Austin, Texas, the Franklin Savings Association bought a historic house threatened with demolition, moved it to a new location, restored the exteriors, and adapted the interiors for use as a branch bank. The project cost $150,000 (including banking equipment). In 1976, the Association followed a similar process with another historic home. This relocation and renovation cost $345,000. The bank's efforts have resulted in extensive publicity and savings deposits above expectations.

Project: Modernization of Goodyear's vintage corporate headquarters

Company: Goodyear Tire and Rubber Company
1144 East Market Street
Akron, Ohio 44305

Contact: Howard P. Tolley
Manager, Community Relations

In 1970, Goodyear Tire and Rubber began a multi-million-dollar renovation of its approximately sixty-year-old corporate headquarters, located in a commercial district of Akron, Ohio. The facade of the seven-story building was covered with bronze-tone aluminum, and rows of tinted-glass windows were installed. A new factory gate house and main entrance were also built. Interior additions included construction of a terraced lobby and a seventh-floor cafeteria. A system of moving rubber ramps, instead of conventional elevators, takes employees between floors. Several factory buildings were renovated as well. They were retrofitted with the same bronze-tone aluminum as was used on the corporate headquarters to create a unified look.

The project was completed in 1973. Goodyear estimates that the cost of these renovations was approximately one-half what it would have been for similar new construction.

Project: Reuse of historic inn as a bank branch

Company: Home Federal Savings and Loan Association
419 Main Street
Worcester, Massachusetts 01608

Contact: Charles M. Zettuck
Senior Vice President

In 1974, the Home Federal Savings and Loan Association relocated and restored historic Stearn's Inn in Worcester, Massachusetts, as a branch bank. The two-story frame inn, which originally served as a stagecoach stop on the Boston to New York run, was believed to have been built in 1812. However, during its relocation, architectural evidence suggested the possibility of its dating from about 1750. The taproom of the inn has been set aside for banking operations, but all the other rooms (except the kitchen, which houses the bank's safe-deposit vault) have been restored as accurately as possible, and are open to public tours. A porch, added after 1750, was removed, and the building's exterior was painted ivory white. The original window frames were restored, and the few panes of glass surviving since 1750 were preserved. New paneling in the banking section matches existing paneling in the rest of the rooms, and wallpaper and carpets were chosen in keeping with the period.

Project: Adaptive reuse of a Victorian mansion as corporate offices

Company: Indianapolis Life Insurance Company
North Meridian and 30th Streets
Indianapolis, Indiana 46208

In 1923, Edward B. Raub, founder of Indianapolis Life, purchased the Fairbanks Mansion to house the offices of his new business. The 26-room, Renaissance Revival Mansion, built in 1913 by Charles Warren Fairbanks, a former U.S. Vice President, is constructed of Indiana limestone on a brick and steel foundation. Indianapolis Life's adaptation of the building left the first-floor library intact. The company's offices on the second floor still feature the original decorations, fireplaces, and mirrors. Air conditioning and central heating were installed in the mid-1950s.

Project: Reuse of a nineteenth-century mansion as magazine offices

Company: Industry Media, Inc.
311 Steele Street
Denver, Colorado 80206

Contact: Charles W. Cleworth
President

Industry Media, Inc., publishers of *Plastic Machinery and Equipment Magazine,* is headquartered in a late-nineteenth-century house in Denver. Charles W. Cleworth, President and Publisher, wanted his company to have its own building. He purchased the house and land for $36,000. Renovation of the 2,900-square-foot building (not including a carriage house used for storage), cost $57,000. Calculated with the purchase price, this made a $32-per-square-foot cost for the overall space.

Project: Renovation of the Grove Park Inn

Company: Jack Tar Hotels, Inc.
403 South Akard Street
Box 5235
Dallas, Texas 75202

The Grove Park Inn, completed in July, 1913, was built in Asheville, North Carolina, for E.W. Grove, owner of the pharmaceutical firm manufacturing Bromo-Quinine. Grove wanted the structure built from the stone of nearby Sunset Mountain, and finally entrusted the work to his son-in-law, Fred L. Seely, a former newspaperman. Seely designed and constructed the five-sectioned, terraced structure using lichen- and moss-covered boulders, just as they were taken from the mountain. After almost a year of labor by local artisans and Italian stonemasons, the hotel boasted a great hall, 120 feet long and 80 feet wide, 400 rugs made at Aubusson, France, 700 pieces of furniture, and over 600 solid-copper lighting fixtures. William Jennings Bryan spoke at its opening. Other distinguished visitors included the Franklin Delano Roosevelt family, Henry Ford, John D. Rockefeller, and Woodrow Wilson. During World War II, the State Department used it as an internment center for Axis diplomats, The Philippine government-in-exile was also located in one of the cottages on the sixty-acre tract.

Jack Tar Hotels, Inc., bought the Grove Park Inn on September 28, 1955 and made considerable effort to restore the resort to its original state. The finest of the original furnishings were renewed and retained, and additions were made to facilitate its use as a resort and convention center.

266

Project: Reuse of a Victorian mansion as insurance offices

Company: Kling Brothers Insurance Company
43 W. King Street
York, Pennsylvania 17401

In 1954, Ralph and Earl Kling purchased a neglected sixteen-room Victorian mansion in York, Pennsylvania. The house, built in 1870, features a circular cherry staircase and wooden mantels. The Klings renovated it as an office for their insurance business, and mounted their large Currier & Ives print collection on the walls. Originally, the prints, which the brothers bought from local farmers, were intended only as period decorations for the mansion. However, by 1963, word of the collection had spread. Tour guides of the Pennsylvania Dutch area began to mention it as one of York's attractions. The collection, now open to the public, attracts as many as 200 visitors a day.

Project: Adaptive reuse of a century-old hardware store as newspaper offices

Company: Logan Leader/News Democrat
120 Public Square
Russellville, Kentucky 42276

Contact: Robert Stuart
Publisher

In 1973, the *Logan Leader/News Democrat* purchased a hardware store built in 1876 by the Ryan family, the most affluent family in Russellville, Kentucky. The two-story brick structure housed the Ryan's food and hardware business until sometime after the turn of the century. At that time, it became a tractor dealership. The *Logan Leader* purchased the building for $70,000. The renovations, which cost $90,000, included sandblasting the exterior, the creation of a staircase, and the construction of partitions. The latter were made from the original oak flooring removed from one of the rooms. All new electrical, gas, and water systems were installed, and the floors were refinished.

The renovated Logan Leader Building. (Balthazar Korab)

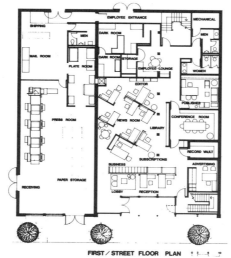

Street-floor plan Logan Leader Building.

FIRST / STREET FLOOR PLAN

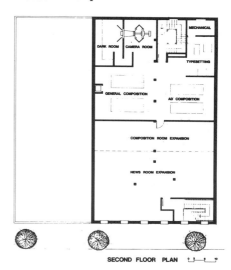

Second-floor plan.

SECOND FLOOR PLAN

Project: Renovation of the Samoa cookhouse and the preservation of a historic lumber town

Company: Louisiana Pacific Company
Samoa Division
Samoa, California 95564

Contact: Lois Lee Bishop
Public Relations Manager

In 1973, Louisiana Pacific Company became the owner of the Hammond mill complex located in Samoa, California, one of the few remaining company towns in the U.S. Samoa has been a lumber town since 1892, when the first mill, built by John Vance, was put into operation. By 1912, the complex was sold to A.B. Hammond, and was known by the Hammond name until its purchase in 1956 by the Georgia Pacific Company. Later, Louisiana Pacific became independent of Georgia Pacific.

Samoa is a 600-acre complex containing 105 homes dating from 1900. It was isolated until several years ago when a new road opened it to tourist trade. Today, the town and its logging museum, a recent addition, are popular attractions, and the renovated eighty-year-old cookhouse has become a popular eating spot.

Project: Continued use of a vintage winery

Company: Paul Masson Vineyards
Brown Vintners
505 Beach Street
San Francisco, California 94133

Contact: Lois A. Leal
Assistant Publicity Manager

At the turn of the century, Paul Masson, son-in-law of the winery's founder, planted a vineyard in the Santa Cruz Mountains near San Jose, California, and built a fortress-like stone winery in the hills. After the earthquake of 1906 left San Jose's St. Patrick's Church in ruins, Masson purchased a twelfth-century Romanesque arch, which was shipped from Spain for use in the church, and included it as part of the winery's facade. The winery was damaged by fire in 1941, but was restored to its original design. The Paul Masson Winery is registered by the State of California as a Historic Landmark.

Project: Renovation of the Willard Carpenter Mansion as Medco's corporate offices

Company: Medco Corporation
405 Carpenter Street
Evansville, Indiana 47703

Contact: Glenn Medcalf
Director of Communications

In 1974, the Medco Corporation, which operates 25 nursing homes, purchased and began renovation of the Willard Carpenter Mansion in Evansville, Indiana, as its corporate headquarters. Carpenter, who made his fortune in merchandising and real estate, built the Mansion in 1848. Subsequently, his home was a stop on the Underground Railway for blacks fleeing the South.

The Mansion is built in the Greek Revival style, the only building of this style extant in Evansville. The two-story structure is made of brick, covered with stucco scored to imitate dressed stone. The original tin cover on the pitched roof was later replaced by asphalt shingles. The main entrance is located behind a small porch, supported by pairs of pillars and pilasters.

In the Medco renovation, the building's exterior was patched and repainted, and as much of the interior as possible was restored. However, the interior design was altered to accommodate functional office requirements. The lower two floors house the executive offices, accounting department, computer room, and meeting rooms.

Project: Conversion of the Brewmaster's House, Zang Brewery, to offices

Company: Mood Music Systems, Inc.
2345 7th Street
Denver, Colorado 80211

Contact: Keene Z. Smith
President

In January, 1972, Keene Z. Smith, President of Mood Music Systems, distributors of jukeboxes and other music systems, purchased the Zang Brewery's Brewmaster's House in Denver. The two-story brick house, built in 1855, is one of the few remaining structures of the old brewery. Mood Music Systems restored the house to its original appearance, installing only modern plumbing and wiring, and a fire escape. The company moved to the ground floor of the building in April, 1973. It leases the upper floor as offices for architects and engineers. Space in the Brewmaster's House rents for $6.50 to $7.50 per square foot, comparable to downtown rentals. According to the company, the carefully restored environment has improved employee morale and seems to have boosted productivity.

The renovated Willard Carpenter Mansion, now Medco's corporate offices.

Project: Reuse of farm buildings as commercial and office space

Company: Nashua Federal Savings and Loan Association
157 Main Street
Nashua, New Hampshire 03060

Contact: Charles F. Rutter
President

In 1976, the Nashua Federal Savings and Loan Association, with the help of Royal/Longstreet, a development firm specializing in bank buildings, restored and adapted as offices a farmhouse and barn dating from the 1730s. The bank's branch office is located in the reconstructed barn, which includes a silo. The office space in the restored farmhouse is leased to other tenants. The project required a $500,000 investment. The branch has attracted more than $2 million in deposits, exceeding the $1 million to $1.5 million originally projected.

Project: Conversion of a railroad station to a newspaper office

Company: The Naugatuck Daily News Corporation
195 Water Street
Naugatuck, Connecticut 06770

Contact: Frederick Hennick
Publisher

In 1964, Rudolph and Frederick Hennick of the *Naugatuck Daily News* purchased the Borough of Naugatuck's vintage railroad station for use as their paper's offices. The 1910 red-brick building cost $1 million; an additional $2 million was spent on improvements. Renovations were carried out by W. J. Megin and Company of Naugatuck, and took one-and-a-half years to complete. Except for replacing the original badly decayed Spanish-tile roof, all efforts were made to preserve the building's original form, while accommodating the facilities of a modern newspaper.

Project: Reuse of an 1813 bank

Company: North Carolina National Bank
Box 120
Charlotte, North Carolina 28201

In 1968, the North Carolina National Bank relocated and readapted as a branch bank a building constructed in 1813 to house the State Bank of North Carolina. The State Bank opened in 1814, with William Polk its first President occupying the structure both as an office and residence. In 1873, the bank sold the building to Christ Church. The structure served as a rectory, and more recently, as a Sunday school. In 1968, the North Carolina National Bank purchased the building and hired Arthur McKimmon II of McKimmon & Rogers, a Raleigh architectural firm, to research and plan for the restoration. The actual restoration was done by Williams Realty, also of Raleigh. The building was moved about 100 feet, and its interior was stripped of all plaster and woodwork. All windows and doors were replaced, and the wood molding, cornices, and wainscoting were reproduced and replaced where necessary. Flooring from demolished historic houses was installed, and the original entrance was restored. The bank provides full banking services, and has added a drive-in window.

Project: Continued use of the Oneida Mansion House

Company: Oneida, Ltd., Silversmiths
Oneida, New York 13421

Contact: Elaine McCoy
Assistant Manager, Public Relations

The Oneida Community Mansion House was built in 1861 by John Humphrey Noyes and his followers. Noyes, a religious leader who taught a perfectionist ideal, founded the Oneida Community in 1848. The 400 Community members lived as one family in their House, the center of all phases of life and work. To support themselves, the members manufactured and sold such useful items as canned goods, traps, bags, and silverware. Although the Community prospered, it abandoned its religious and social goals in 1880, forming a joint stock company to carry on business operations.

Today, the 475-room Mansion serves as an apartment complex and guest house. It also hosts local gatherings.

The three-story brick structure boasts three-arched windows, both gabled and flat roof sections, a balustraded deck, and four-story projecting towers. Built in High Victorian and Second Empire styles, the Mansion has been preserved almost as it was during the days of the Oneida Community (there are several period rooms), with only the addition of a library in an old school room. It is listed in the National Register of Historic Places.

Today, Oneida, Ltd. (formerly the Oneida Community, Ltd.), is the world's largest producer of stainless-steel flatware and a leading producer of silver and silver plate.

Pacific Northwest Bell's switching installation in Jacksonville, Oregon.

Project: Construction of a compatible modern building for switching equipment

Company: Pacific Northwest Bell Telephone
421 S.W. Oak Street
Portland, Oregon 97204

Contact: D. L. Gunderson
Vice President—Oregon

In 1973, Pacific Northwest Bell installed modern electronic switching equipment in a new brick building located in the historic mining town of Jacksonville, Oregon. The building is constructed of structurally reinforced concrete and concrete block veneered with brick. The street facade's arcade is modeled after the design of the nearby Table Rock Saloon, and includes space for a display of early telephone equipment. The building's size, color, and brickwork conform to those of the surrounding structures, and its exterior lighting consists of recreations of the town's original gas streetlights. Professor D. Marion Ross, Architectural Historian of the University of Oregon, was retained as consultant on the project.

The Oneida Community Mansion House.

Project: Renovation of the "oldest food store" in America

Company: Piggly Wiggly
101 Broad Street
Charleston, South Carolina
29401

Contact: F. Marion Brabham

In 1969, Piggly Wiggly, a supermarket chain, purchased a vintage food store on Broad Street in Charleston. The store had been in continuous operation since it was chartered as a grocery in 1847.

Charleston's beautification program establishes strict standards for any new construction or renovation in its historic district. These include the maintenance of a harmonious color scheme, the elimination of inappropriate signs, and the installation of gas streetlights. The renovated structure has nineteenth-century-style window-panes, and features a turn-of-the-century-style snack shop, a tobacco shop, a bakery, a gourmet food shop, and a wine cellar.

The renovation won awards from the Charleston Chamber of Commerce and the Charleston Historical Preservation Society in 1970.

Project: Continued use of an 1881 flour mill

Company: The Pillsbury Company
1162 Pillsbury Building
608 Second Avenue South
Minneapolis, Minnesota
55402

Contact: Robert G. Walker
Assistant Vice President

For the past five years, the Pillsbury Company, a large producer of baking goods, has allocated $50,000 annually for the renovation and upkeep of its A Mill. Completed in 1881, the mill was once the largest and most advanced flour mill in the world. It was originally one of five mills owned by the Pillsbury-Washburn Company. The stone and concrete structure has been in continuous use since 1881, and over the years Pillsbury has maintained the exterior facade. The portion of Minneapolis where the mill is located is being gradually converted into a waterfront "old town." Preservation of the A Mill has been an important contribution to the restoration of this historic area.

Project: Continued use of the oldest hardware store in Maryland

Company: Quynn's Hardware Store
10 and 12 East Patrick
Street
Frederick, Maryland 21701

Contact: Katherine C. Anders
Co-owner

Quynn's Hardware Store has been in continuous operation on the same corner of Patrick Street since 1796, when Frederick, Maryland, was a stop on the Cumberland Trail going west from Washington to the Cumberland Gap. Quynn's sold westbound pioneers flour, sugar loaves, guns, tobacco, and countless other items. It was only in the late 1800s that the store began to specialize in hardware.

Descendants of Allan Quynn, the original proprietor, retained ownership of the store until 1977, when Dr. William G. Quynn sold the property to Mr. William H. B. Anders, Jr. Mr. Anders has maintained the Quynn name and tradition. The store is located in a small two-story structure laid in Flemish bond brickwork. Its facade has hardly changed over the years, except for the replacement of the original frame windows with plate glass, and the addition of an occasional coat of paint. The store has five rooms on the ground floor. Several rooms in the basement and on the upper floor are used for storage.

Project: Reuse of vintage railroad stations as restaurants

Company: The Santa Fe Railroad
80 East Jackson Boulevard
Chicago, Illinois 60604

Contact: Bill Burke
Vice President, Public Relations

In 1972, the Santa Fe Land Improvement Corporation, a subsidiary of the Santa Fe Railroad, leased a two-story vintage railroad station in National City, California. The building was converted into a restaurant called The Depot. The restaurant includes a main dining room on the first floor, two smaller dining rooms, a wine cellar, and a freight room. The latter boasts a bar made of railroad ties. The restaurant, which can accommodate 147 people, is entered through an authentic railroad club car.

The Depot Steak, another restaurant, was opened in a vintage train station in Berkeley, California. The depot's ticket windows now serve as a salad bar, and the interior is lit with railroad chandeliers. The restaurant seats 110 customers in the main area, and 35 at the bar.

Project: Reuse of 109-year-old house as corporate offices

Company: Schlegel Corporation
1555 Jefferson Road
Rochester, New York
14623

Contact: Richard Turner
Chairman and President

In 1974, Schlegel, a leading producer of perimeter and area sealing systems for the construction and automotive industries, was looking for additional office space and for a new location for its corporate headquarters. The Rochester, New York, company began to explore the feasibility of constructing a new headquarters facility, while at the same time investigating the option of relocating in existing buildings. In summer, 1976, Richard Turner, Schlegel's Chairman, learned of the availability of the 109-year-old Hiram Sibley House. It contained the 15,000 square feet needed for the corporate headquarters. Schlegel took an option on the building and commissioned a feasibility study comparing the conversion of the historic house with new construction. By the early fall, the company's Board of Directors had approved the renovation, and work is now in progress. Although it was not a factor in Schlegel's decision, the rehabilitation may qualify for accelerated depreciation under the new federal tax law, making the cost for the renovation lower than originally anticipated.

Project: Restoration of part of the William Aiken House

Company: Southern Railway System
920 15th Street, N.W.
Washington, D.C. 20013

Contact: William F. Geeslin
Assistant Vice President
Public Relations and
Advertising

In 1973, the Southern Railway System restored part of the second floor of the William Aiken House in Charleston, South Carolina. The part of the floor which was not restored had been utilized as a display area for the National Railway Historical Society.

William Aiken, the first President of the South Carolina Canal and Railroad Company, built the three-story brick and white stucco house between 1807 and 1811. He added an East Wing in 1831. In 1863, his son sold the house to Aiken's company, which used the building as its offices. At the turn of the century, Southern Railway acquired the company, and the house became its Charleston offices. The building still serves that function today. In 1977, the company donated space in the house to the National Trust to serve as the Trust's Southern Field Office. The building was designated a National Landmark by the U.S. Department of Interior in 1964.

The second floor renovation took three years and cost approximately $50,000. A drawing room, the main stairway, and another room across from the drawing room were restored to their original appearance, and now serve as offices. The ballroom is now a meeting room. Simons, Lapham, Mitchell and Small were the architects who advised the local contractors on the project.

Restored ceiling and light fixture in the downstairs hallway at Aiken House. (Savannah Chamber of Commerce)

Project: Adaptive reuse of a vintage railroad station

Company: Southern Railway System and the Savannah Chamber of Commerce
Southern Railway System
P.O. Box 2202
227 West Broad Street
Savannah, Georgia 31402

Contact: Savannah Chamber of Commerce
P.O. Box 530
301 West Broad Street
Savannah, Georgia 31401

The Central of Georgia Railroad, a subsidiary of the Southern Railway System, had no further need for its 1860s brick station in Savannah and donated it to the city. In 1973, the Savannah Chamber of Commerce raised $200,000 from local businesses to renovate the building as a visitors center. (Visitors spend more than $500 million annually in Savannah.) The actual renovation cost $300,000, and to make up the difference, the Chamber of Commerce is paying $25,000 annually to the city. Architects Gunn and Meyerhoff designed the adaptation and renovation. The center, which opened in 1975, now includes a theater, an exhibit area, offices, a lounge, and rest-room facilities. Tourist parking is also available. Southern Railway maintains a small railroad museum complete with a restored locomotive in a former station shed.

Project: Restoration of the Stewart Building, erected in 1884

Company: Stewart Title Insurance Company
P.O. Box 1540
Galveston, Texas 77553

The Stewart Building, built by the Stewart Title Insurance Company in 1884 as its corporate headquarters, is a four-story red-brick structure designed in the Neo-Renaissance style. It is located in the Strand National Historic Landmark District of Galveston, a ten-square-block area that was the financial center of Texas during the nineteenth century.

In summer, 1976, Stewart Title, aided by a $20,000 matching grant from the Texas Historical Commission, began restoring the exterior of the building, including the reproduction of a cornice which was destroyed by a hurricane in 1900.

The first two floors of the building serve as company offices. Plans call for adapting the remaining two floors as apartments.

Project: Continued use of Syracuse Savings' landmark headquarters

Company: Syracuse Savings Bank
1 Clinton Square
Syracuse, New York 13203

Contact: Frederick Schwartz
Vice President, Marketing

The headquarters of the Syracuse Savings Bank is located in an 1876 banking hall designed by Joseph Tyman Silsbee and built by master builder John Moore at a cost of $281,000. The six-story building, once the tallest in Syracuse, is constructed of buff- and red-colored sandstone. It was modeled after the Palace of the Doges in Venice, and is a combination of Venetian and Gothic architecture. The building has pointed arches and Gothic moldings. Its interior carvings were executed by Italian stonecutters. The structure's 170-foot tower also boasted the first public elevator in Syracuse.

The building has been renovated several times. Part of the second floor has been removed to increase the height of the ceiling in the first-floor lobby to forty feet. In 1975, the bank began installing air conditioning and a new heating system. To date, it has spent $1.5 million on the renovations, which are still in progress.

Project: Renovation of the Arizona Biltmore Hotel

Company: Talley Industries, Inc.
3500 N. Greenfield Rd.
Mesa, Arizona 85203

In June, 1973, Talley Industries purchased the Arizona Biltmore Hotel in Phoenix. The building, designed by Frank Lloyd Wright, was constructed in 1927. Talley immediately closed the hotel and began installing a sprinkler system in accordance with Phoenix fire codes. However, before the installation was completed, a fire broke out, destroying the roof and damaging some of the hotel furnishings. Talley hired Taliesin Associated Architects of the Frank Lloyd Wright Foundation to design and supervise the reconstruction of the damaged floors as well as the refurnishing and decoration of the main building. The work was carried out under the direction of Mrs. Franz G. Talley, wife of Talley's owner.

The hotel was built of precast concrete blocks, the first time this material was used in the construction of a large public building. It featured a roof made of Arizona copper, and boasted the largest gold-leaf ceiling in the world, located in the main lobby and adjacent areas. Some of the gold leaf had to be replaced due to fire damage. Other renovations involved creating a cocktail lounge and bar in an area previously known as the Sun Room. Talley is also considering erecting a free-standing addition that will contain eighty rooms and a convention meeting room.

Project: Conversion of a nineteenth-century mansion to office space

Company: Terracor Company
529 East South Temple
Salt Lake City, Utah 84103

Contact: Dan Cunningham
Director of Public Relations

In 1969, Terracor, a development company, converted and restored the historic nineteenth-century Brown Mansion in Salt Lake City for use as its headquarters. A University of Utah class, under Owen Olpin, Professor of Law, and lawyer E. Scott Savage, conducted an economic feasibility study. The study revealed that, given current zoning requirements, renovating the existing building would bring greater benefits than new construction on the same site. The existing building contains 25,600 square feet, and the zoning code would have permitted only a 23,973-square-foot new building.

Project: Adaptive reuse of three Victorian mansions as the Association's offices

Company: Texas Classroom Teachers Association
700 Guadalupe Street
Austin, Texas 78701

Contact: C. E. Saunders
Executive Director

In 1958, the Texas Classroom Teachers Association purchased four vintage Victorian buildings originally owned by a wealthy merchant family in Austin. The buildings, which the Association is presently using as its offices, include: the John Bremond Home (c. 1888), the Pierre Bremond Home (c. 1890), the Walter Bremond Home (c. 1886), and a carriage house of the same period. Apart from minor repairs, refurnishing, and the replacement of some of the original fixtures, little alteration of the three homes was made by the Association. However, the carriage house was completely renovated as a residence for the Association's President.

The Bremond buildings had been used by community organizations prior to their purchase, and the John Bremond Home remains a meeting place for the YMCA, the Texas Medical Association, and the Elks Club.

Project: Continued use of 1924 bank building

Company: Union Commerce Bank
917 Euclid Avenue
Cleveland, Ohio 44115

The bank's 1924 building in downtown Cleveland, Ohio, contains one of the world's largest banking halls. Designed by Chicago architects Graham, Anderson, Probst, and White, the hall is sixty feet high and contains 27,000 square feet. In 1974, the bank, encouraged by architect Peter van Dijk, decided to restore rather than remodel the grand hall as part of business's overall commitment to the redevelopment of downtown Cleveland.

274

Project: Continued use of nineteenth-century railroad depot

Company: Union Pacific Railroad
Company
1416 Dodge Street
Omaha, Nebraska 68102

Contact: Barry B. Combs
Director of Public Relations

In 1966, the Union Pacific Railroad Company undertook exterior restoration of the Union Pacific Depot, the oldest Union Pacific property in Cheyenne, Wyoming. Built in 1886 at a cost of $100,000, the Richardsonian Romanesque building was designed by architects Van Brunt and Howe of Kansas City, Missouri. It is constructed of red and grey sandstone blocks of random size, laid on a wood and iron frame. The interior of the building is finished with native red oak and yellow pine. In 1890, a tower clock was added, and in 1922, a one-and-a-half-story restaurant was attached to the Depot's eastern end. Today, the latter addition, known as Hicks Hall, serves as office and meeting space. In 1929, the wooden supports of the building were replaced with steel, and the half story over the east extension was remodeled as a functional third floor. New train sheds were added to the south end in 1937 as part of Union Pacific's $375,000 improvement of the Depot and surrounding yards. A park originally located directly to the north was replaced by a Greyhound Bus Terminal in 1940. The original slate roof was replaced in 1952 with asbestos. In the 1966 restoration, the entire exterior was sandblasted, cleaned, and restored. In 1976, Union Pacific funded the complete remodeling of the second and third floors of the building. The Depot at Cheyenne was nominated for inclusion in the National Register of Historic Places in 1972.

The Union Pacific Depot at Cheyenne, Wyoming.

Project: Reuse of a textile mill for production and company offices

Company: Ursula of Switzerland
31 Mohawk Avenue
Waterford, New York
12188

Contact: Hudson-Mohawk Industrial Gateway
5 First Street
Troy, New York 12180

In 1972, Ursula and Richard Garrow of Ursula of Switzerland, a women's-apparel manufacturer, purchased the Laughlin textile mill, built in 1894. The five-story red-brick structure located in Waterford, New York, includes corbeled brick cornices and a brick tower which houses a water tank.

Thus far, the Garrows have renovated three of the mill's five floors to serve as their manufacturing plant and offices. Windows were replaced, and the roof was repaired, along with other minor refitting. Old textile machinery was removed; the wooden floors were sanded and oiled; and the mechanical systems were improved.

Offices were created and partitions erected to form a design studio, cutting area, sewing and finishing workshop and storage space for finished garments.

Eighty employees currently use the three floors of the mill.

Project: Restoration and conversion of an old hotel into a modern bank

Company: Van Horn State Bank
P.O. Box 728
Van Horn, Texas 79855

Contact: J. E. Billingsley
President

In the mid-1970s, the Van Horn State Bank purchased the rundown El Capitan Hotel in Van Horn, Texas. The bank renovated and restored the building, which now houses the bank, an office of the Border Patrol, a florist, and a jewelry store.

The El Capitan Hotel was opened in 1930 as part of a chain extending from El Paso to San Antonio. In 1963, the building was sold to a developer who planned to convert it into an apartment complex. The developer later abandoned both the idea and the hotel. Vandals tore up the property, removing windows, doors, and plumbing. The Van Horn State Bank purchased the building for $30,000.

The renovation of the two-story concrete and brick structure cost the bank $250,000. It involved 16,000 of the hotel's original 30,000 square feet, and included a total revamping of the wiring and heating systems. The former lobby serves as the bank's service area; an old coffee shop is now the bank's note department; and the basement has been converted into offices for the Border Patrol. The original walk-in cooler now serves as a jail. The two wings of the building house the Wallis Jewelry Store and Stephen's Flower Shop.

Community Revitalization

Project: Community revitalization in Camden

Company: Campbell Soup Company
Campbell Place
Camden, New Jersey
08101

Contact: Gabe Danch
Director, Community Relations

Campbell Soup, the food-products company, is helping revitalize its hometown of Camden, New Jersey. In 1967, the company spearheaded the formation of the Camden Home Improvement Program (CHIP), a nonprofit organization backed by local business. The CHIP bought, renovated, and sold about 550 turn-of-the-century row houses, before it was terminated in 1975 due to the cessation of federal financing for prospective low-income buyers.

At present, Campbell Soup is subsidizing the State Street Housing Corporation, an organization similar to the CHIP, which is purchasing and remodeling about 300 deteriorating houses. The State Street Housing Corporation also arranges mortgages for home buyers with eight Camden banks. Campbell Soup has committed $70,000 to the mortgage pool.

To further commercial redevelopment, the company helped form the Camden Community Loan Plan, which provides financial assistance to minority businesses in conjunction with the federal Small Business Administration. Campbell Soup's staff also counsels these new businesses about management and finance.

Project: Founding of the Community Preservation Corporation

Company: 34 Major Banks
Community Preservation Corporation
641 Lexington Avenue
New York, New York
10022

In 1974, 34 major commercial and savings banks with headquarters in New York City founded the Community Preservation Corporation (CPC). This organization, a nonprofit housing finance corporation, was established to provide a mechanism through which banking and other financial interests could join the government in an effort to preserve New York City's housing stock. Initially concentrating on Crown Heights in Brooklyn and Washington Heights in Manhattan, the CPC began financing the rehabilitation and preservation of one- to four-family homes through short-term and permanent mortgage loans. It also offers first and second mortgages at up to 90 percent of value for periods of up to thirty years. Mortgages are either conventional or insured by the Federal Housing Administration, the New York City Rehabilitation Mortgage Insurance Corporation, or the Veterans Administration.

The 34 members of the CPC have contributed: $400,000 capital to cover operating costs; an $8 million revolving fund for short-term construction financing; and $32 million in permanent financing through the purchase of the CPC's collateral trust notes. The CPC has two offices located in Crown Heights and Washington Heights. Each is staffed with a full-time mortgage officer.

Project: Donation of $3.8 million to the City of Akron for neighborhood revitalization programs

Company: B.F. Goodrich Company
500 South Main Street
Akron, Ohio 44318

Contact: Timothy W. Early
Community Planning Administrator

In 1964, B.F. Goodrich gave Akron, its home since 1870, $300,000 to finance a feasibility study on the revitalization of the city's downtown industrial district, which was beginning to deteriorate. To help implement the study's recommendations, the company donated an additional $3.5 million in June, 1965, to the Opportunity Park Project. This revitalization project called for the creation of a new residential district to include garden, townhouse, and high-rise apartments, new factories, shops, two large parking decks, new churches, a new school, an elevated highway (Akron's first), and an industrial park.

B.F. Goodrich is also spending several million dollars to modernize its headquarters, and is planning to purchase several parcels of land in Akron as part of the revitalization effort.

Project: Residential and commercial redevelopment in Minneapolis

Company: Honeywell Corporation
Honeywell Plaza
Minneapolis, Minnesota 55408

In the early 1970s, Honeywell began a housing-renovation program in the neighborhood around its plant and corporate offices in Minneapolis. The company purchased, renovated, and sold houses in the area to low-income families, with prospective buyers receiving support and assistance from the Model Cities and other federal programs. Honeywell wanted to break even, but actually lost from $2,500 to $5,000 on each project. Since 1971, the company has completed more than fifteen houses, concentrating on the area's worst buildings to stimulate other owners to improve their properties. In 1957, Honeywell converted a former thermostat factory into its corporate headquarters and remained in the city instead of following many other Minneapolis corporations to the suburbs.

Project: Renovation of Newburyport's downtown

Company: Institution for Savings
93 State Street
Newburyport, Massachusetts 01950

Contact: John Pramberg
President

In addition to maintaining its offices in an elegant Victorian building constructed for the bank in the 1870s, the Institution for Savings has been a preservation leader in the historic seaport town of Newburyport, Massachusetts. Utilizing a recent state law called the "leeway bill," allowing banks to invest a portion of their earnings in any projects they wish, the bank has purchased, renovated, and rented several old buildings in the downtown historical area. Its latest project, the adaptive reuse of the Knight Grain Building, an urban redevelopment property in the waterfront area, was completed in 1976.

Project: Commercial renovation in an Iowa town

Company: Pella Rolscreen Company
102 Main Street
Pella, Iowa 50219

Contact: H. S. Kuper
Vice President

Pella, Iowa, a small town settled by pioneers of Dutch descent in 1847, is the home of the Pella Rolscreen Company, a producer of windows and doors. The company has contributed funds for a "Dutch Fronts" project, which provides $500 grants to individual store owners to remodel their storefronts according to an approved design. This helps to preserve the original Dutch character of the town and its architecture, and to improve the physical condition of the main commercial center. Pella Rolscreen provides design and planning services through Des Moines architect William Wagner and interest-free loans of up to $5,000 to store owners who wish to do more complete remodeling.

The company also provides about one-third of the financial support for the local historical society, and has purchased and restored the town railroad station.

Project: Renovation of the Hotel Florence and other buildings in the Pullman Historic District

Company: Pullman Incorporated
200 South Michigan Avenue
Chicago, Illinois 60604

Contact: Barbara Lahnum
Assistant Secretary—Contributions and Stock Plans

In 1963, Pullman, Inc., donated $1,000 to the Historic Pullman Foundation to help renovate the Historic Pullman Center, a former Masonic Lodge. In 1975, the company donated $25,000 to the Foundation for the renovation of the nearby Hotel Florence dating from 1881. Both buildings are located in a part of Chicago called the Pullman District.

The Pullman District was originally a separate company town built in 1880 by George M. Pullman, owner of the Pullman Palace Car Company, a railway-car manufacturer. In the 1890s, an economic crisis depressed business, and Pullman lowered his wages without lowering his rents. This led to the Pullman strike in 1894 and the court-ordered assimilation of the District into the City of Chicago.

The Historic Pullman Foundation was founded in 1973 as a nonprofit organization dedicated to the preservation of the Pullman District's buildings. The area itself has been recognized as a Historic District by the city (1972), state (1969), and federal (1970) governments. The Foundation has succeeded in renovating three buildings to date: the old Masonic Lodge, the Market Hall, and the Hotel Florence.

The Hotel Florence was named after George Pullman's favorite daughter. He himself maintained a private suite in the building. The Queen Anne-style hotel, designed by architect Solon Beman, has 49 guest rooms and a large dining area with a capacity of 100. It has been back in operation as a hotel since July, 1975, and the Pullman Suite has been restored.

Project: Revitalization of Trustees' Garden section of Savannah

Company: Savannah Gas Company
114 Barnard Street
Savannah, Georgia 31401

In 1945, Hansell Hillyer purchased the Savannah Gas Company and, with it, ten acres of some of the worst slums in Savannah. The site, known as Trustees' Garden, was planned by James Oglethorpe, Georgia's founder, and the Trustees of the Colony of Georgia in 1733. It was the first experimental garden in the country. Over the years, Trustees' Garden became a residential community. In 1945 Hillyer was about to tear down the area's deteriorated houses, when his wife convinced him to let her try to restore them. Mrs. Hillyer, with support from the company, soon turned Trustees' Garden into one of the most sought-after residential sections of the city. In 1953, when the use of natural gas eliminated the need for the gas-manufacturing plant on the site, Mrs. Hillyer and the company converted the plant buildings into modern apartments.

Project: Contribution to the Stevens Neighborhood Housing Improvement Program

Company: Seattle Trust and Savings
804 Second Avenue
Seattle, Washington 98104

Contact: Rick Hooper
Stevens Neighborhood Housing Improvement Program
522 19th Avenue E.
Seattle, Washington 98112

The Stevens District Neighborhood Housing Corporation, sponsor of the Stevens District Housing Improvement Program, was established in 1976 to encourage the residents of Seattle's Stevens District to bring their single-family frame homes up to present building-code standards over a five-year period. In December, 1976, Seattle's City Council allocated $100,000 to the Program in Community Development Block Grand funds. The city will also subsidize low-interest loans at 4 percent to 7 percent for those residents in a "high risk" loan category.

As of 1977, Seattle Trust and Savings is paying the salary of the Program's Director, providing office space, and financing publicity. The bank also provides the services of an administrative secretary and loan officers, and technical assistance when needed. The Stevens Neighborhood Housing Improvement Program will process Seattle Trust loans, and both the Program and the bank will process subsidized loans from the city's Rehabilitation Program. In addition, Seattle Trust has initiated an Energy Conservation Loan Program offering home-improvement loans at 8¾ percent interest (compared to a 9½ percent conventional rate) to all homeowners in the Seattle area who are willing to include energy-related improvements in their remodeling.

Project: Neighborhood revitalization in several Vermont towns

Company: Vermont National Bank
100 Main Street
Brattleboro, Vermont 05301

Contact: Jean A. Hubner
Marketing Officer

The Vermont National Bank has been involved in several preservation efforts, including support for town-scape improvement in Bellows Falls, Bennington, and Springfield. In Springfield, the company renovated a vacant A&P store in a blighted area, converting it into a branch bank and a shopping mall. The bank uses about one-third of the building and rents the rest. The branch opened in 1977. The entire project was coordinated with Downtown Springfield Beautification's plans for a landscaped pedestrian mall area.

General Preservation Support

Project: Distribution of Iowa Landmark Calendars

Company: American Federal Savings and Loan
Sixth and Grand Avenues
Des Moines, Iowa 50308

In 1960, American Federal Savings and Loan Association, the largest savings and loan in Iowa, began distributing Landmark Calendars to its patrons. The Calendars contain thirteen (the number may vary) illustrations of Iowa's historic buildings drawn by Des Moines architect William J. Wagner. Sites depicted have included: the Drake University Administration Building, the Langworthy Home, the Frank Lloyd Wright Hotel, the Des Moines Old Federal Building, the Manning Mansion, and the Keokuk Post Office and Federal Court Building.

The Landmark Calendars have been popular with bank patrons: the bank finds it often cannot print enough to meet demand.

Project: Distribution of a guidebook to the "Governor's Mansion"

Company: Banker's Trust Savings and Loan of Mississippi
P.O. Box 918
Jackson, Mississippi 39205

In 1976, Banker's Trust of Mississippi helped fund and distribute *An Historical Guide to the Governor's Mansion.* The Greek Revival structure, a Jackson landmark, was completed in 1841 at a cost of $50,000. The first residents were Governor Tilghman Tucker and his family, who took possession in 1842, and the Mansion was continuously occupied until 1971, when it was declared unsafe. At that time, the State of Mississippi appropriated $1.5 million to restore the building. Architects Charles E. Peterson and Edward Vasson Jones restored both the interior and exterior, and added a modern townhouse. Work was completed in 1975.

The guide book, distributed by Banker's Trust Savings and Loan, included color photographs of the Mansion's interior and exterior and short biographies of its inhabitants. Funds received from the sale of the $3 book (over and above production costs) are donated to the Executive Mansion Commission. The Mansion is also open to the public. As of March, 1977, Banker's Trust is no longer distributing the *Guide,* since it has filed a bankruptcy claim, and has been in receivership since spring, 1976.

Project: Restoration of the Pemberton House

Company: The Coca-Cola Company Incorporated
P.O. Drawer 1734
Atlanta, Georgia 30301

Contact: Beverly Lee Taylor
Historic Columbus Foundation
P.O. Box 5312
Columbus, Georgia 31906

In 1969, the Coca-Cola Company, the largest manufacturer of soft-drink products in the United States, underwrote the Historic Columbus Foundation's restoration of the Pemberton House in Columbus, Georgia. Dr. John Styth Pemberton, inventor of the formula for Coca-Cola, lived in the house from 1855 to 1860, and is believed to have developed the formula there. The Foundation restored the building to its original 1850s form: later additions were removed; the gingerbread facade was taken down, and the home was furnished with mid-Victorian antiques and replicas. The backyard kitchen, removed from the house to prevent fires, was restored as an 1850s apothecary shop. Both buildings are administered by the Historic Columbus Foundation and function as a museum open to the public.

Project: Restoration of the Marland Mansion, a private home in Oklahoma

Company: Continental Oil Company (Conoco)
1000 South Pine Street
Ponca City, Oklahoma 74601

The Marland Mansion was built between 1926 and 1928 by E. W. Marland, a wealthy oil magnate and President of Marland Oil, now part of Conoco. The 55-room stone structure was modeled after the Renaissance Davanzatti Palace in Florence, Italy, and built at a cost of $2.5 million. The Mansion has terrazzo floors, wrought-iron doors, fancy ironwork railings, richly carved wooden paneling, and ornate mosaic ceilings. John Duncan Forsyth, a prominent architect, designed the building, and hired a team of architects to execute the detail work. Over 100 craftsmen were brought in to work on the construction. At its completion, the Mansion was reported to be the largest home in Oklahoma and the largest air-conditioned home west of the Mississippi.

Marland and his family lived in the Mansion until 1941, when he sold it to a Catholic religious order for $66,000. Several religious groups owned the property subsequently. In 1975, the home was purchased by Ponca City, with Conoco donating half the purchase price to the city. The House was vacant at the time of purchase, but has since been refurnished with period furniture, some of which originally belonged to the estate. Opened to the public in April, 1976, the Mansion, now houses seminars and meetings, and on April 23, 1977, hosted the Lieutenant Governor's Ball of Oklahoma. The city plans to turn one of the buildings on the estate's grounds into a petroleum museum.

Project: Awards program for renovations

Company: Esco Corporation
2141 N.W. 25th Avenue
Portland, Oregon 97210

Contact: Nello J. Vanelli
Director of Public Affairs

Since 1969, the Esco Corporation, a steel foundry, has given four awards each year to businesses in and around Portland, Oregon, which "remodel their buildings to enhance the beauty of the area." These plaques and certificates are given to both the owners of the buildings and the architect(s) responsible for the design.

Project: Donation of an eighteenth-century house and funds to the Preservation Society of Charleston

Company: First Federal Savings & Loan Association
of Charleston, South Carolina
34 Broad Street
Charleston, South Carolina 29402

Contact: Howard F. Burkey
President

The First Federal Savings & Loan Association of Charleston donated the Frederick Wolfe House and an adjacent lot to the Preservation Society of Charleston in spring, 1973. The donation was made with the understanding that the house, which stood in the First Federal parking lot, would be moved to the adjacent lot (First Federal donated the $6,400 necessary for the move), and there be renovated as a residence by the Society. The 1796 house, typical of Charleston architecture, is a two-and-a-half-story, wood-frame structure with a two-story piazza containing Doric columns. There are three dormer windows on its pitched roof.

The renovation cost $49,800, and was carried out by the H.A. DeCosta Company under the Preservation Society's supervision. It included the installation of new mechanical systems, wiring, and roofing. Renovation also required metal work, masonry, plumbing, carpentry, weather stripping, painting, and the removal of enclosed portions of the piazza.

Project: Restoration of an 1890s statue and fountain

Company: The First National Bank and Trust Company
Third and High Streets
Hamilton, Ohio 45012

Contact: Richard Shutte
Vice President, Marketing

In 1975, the First National Bank and Trust Company of Hamilton, Ohio, agreed to finance the complete restoration of a statue and drinking fountain which had been out of use since 1928. The statue of Herbe, the Greek nymph of streams and brooks, was installed in front of the First National Bank Building in 1890. The fountain had pumped water into street-side bowls, a large one for horses, a smaller one for dogs, cats, and other animals, and had provided a continuous stream for people. The statue itself was conceived by Bartel Thorvaldsen, whose original is located in Copenhagen, Denmark. Hamilton had recently developed a central water supply, and the statue symbolized this achievement.

The fountain was utilized for 38 years, until the bank began construction of its new central office building. The statue was removed from the front of the bank, and for a time, was used by a former Hamilton police sergeant as a garden ornament. It began to rust, and eventually both arms broke off. Then, in 1975, the statue was rediscovered by the First National Bank and the Hamilton Foundry. The bank paid Theodore Gantz, a sculptor from Cincinnati, to supervise the restoration and recreate the missing pieces. The Hamilton Foundry agreed to cast and replace what was needed. The restoration returned the statue to its original appearance, but water is only piped to the human drinking fountain.

Project: Relocation and renovation of the century-old Bashford House

Company: Food Maker Industries, Inc.
9330 Balboa Avenue
San Diego, California
92123

Contact: Ken Kimsey
Director
Prescott Historical Society
415 W. Gurley Street
Prescott, Arizona 86301

In 1973, Food Maker Industries, owners of the Jack-In-the-Box fast-food chain, purchased the land on which the 100-year-old Bashford House, one of the oldest buildings in Prescott, Arizona, was located. At this time, the Prescott Historical Society, a state museum, and the Sharlot Hall Historical Society, a sister organization, began a fund raising drive to finance moving the house to the museum grounds where renovation as a community meeting house would begin. After three months, $25,000 was collected, including $1,000 donated by Food Maker. The house is now located on the museum grounds and serves as a combination art gallery and community meeting house.

Project: Creation of the Genesee Country Museum

Company: The Genesee Brewing Co.
P.O. Box 762
Rochester, New York 14603

Contact: Mark Holdren
Public Relations Manager

In 1967, the Genesee Brewing Company, led by John D. Wehle, its Board Chairman, and several of his associates, founded the Genesee Country Museum. The Museum is a nonprofit educational organization established to develop the early American Genesee Country Village. It seeks to identify historically significant farm and village structures, and relocate them on the 55-acre Village site in Mumford, New York. The Village's cost, calculated at $3 million over a ten-year development period, was financed almost entirely by charitable contributions from Genesee Brewing, and from the Louis A. Wehle Foundation. The Genesee Brewing Co. is also providing engineering and restoration assistance.

Over thirty early street plans of upstate New York towns were studied by the Museum's staff to ensure an accurate reproduction. Development plans called for a village of forty buildings. To date, over thirty buildings have been moved to the site, including a ten-room inn, a Greek Revival mansion, several office buildings, a farm, a blacksmith shop, a printer's shop, and a store, as well as other shops and residences, all dating from 1799 to 1859. There are also crafts demonstrations. Once moved to the Village, each building is completely restored and furnished.

Genesee Village opened in 1976, and attracted 64,000 tourists in its first five months. The Village has been featured in many newspaper articles and on several TV news shows. In 1977, John L. Wehle received the Rochester Chamber of Commerce's Business in the Arts Civic Award.

Project: Contribution of $1,000 to the Utah Heritage Foundation

Company: Kearn's Tribune Publishing Company
143 South Main Street
Salt Lake City, Utah 84111

Contact: Stephanie Churchill
Director
Utah Heritage Foundation
355 Quince Street
Salt Lake City, Utah 84103

In 1977, Kearn's Tribune Publishing Company contributed $1,000 to the Utah Heritage Foundation. The Foundation, a nonprofit organization, was established in 1966 to identify and preserve Utah's historic buildings. It buys historic homes, and resells them on the condition that they be restored. The Foundation will also move a house threatened with demolition. Its headquarters are located in Salt Lake City in the renovated Thomas Quayle home, a one-story frame structure built in 1884.

Project: Donation of $50,000 to the Community Triangle Project

Company: Mississippi Chemical
P.O. Box 388
Yazoo City, Mississippi
39194

Contact: Jo G. Pritchard
Library Chairman
Ricks Memorial Library
Yazoo City, Mississippi
39194

In 1974, Mississippi Chemical contributed $50,000 in the form of a matching grant toward the Main Street School/ Ricks Memorial Library Community Triangle Project. The other $50,000 was to be donated by local merchants and residents. Mississippi Chemical's President, Tom C. Parry, is helping to spearhead the fund-raising drive. The Community Triangle Project, requiring $600,000 over a three-year period, is attempting to renovate and reuse the 1904 neoclassical Main Street School as a community center and expand the 1900 Beaux Arts-style Ricks Memorial Library. The latter is listed in the National Register of Historic Places. Plans also call for the creation of a landscaped triangle joining the two buildings. The Project is slated for completion late in 1977.

Project: Donation of a nineteenth-century magneto switchboard and building to the Virginia City Historic District Commission

Company: Nevada Bell Telephone
645 E. Plumb Lane
P.O. Box 1911
Reno, Nevada 89502

Contact: James Riley
Public Relations

On June 14, 1975, the manually operated 1882 magneto phone system in Virginia City, Nevada, was replaced with a modern, totally automated switching system, providing dial service. That same year, Nevada Bell donated the original magneto switchboard, building, and land to the Virginia City Historic District Commission. The old telephone building is now open to the public. Nevada Bell's new system is located in a new two-story frame switching station built to blend in with the 1860s Gothic buildings in Virginia City, a gold and silver boom town which is today a popular tourist attraction

Project: Commercials featuring the painting of "Great American Homes"

Company: Sears & Roebuck Company
Sears Tower
Chicago, Illinois 60684

Contact: Glenn Spaerl
Manager, Marketing
Public Relations
Home Improvement
Group

In 1971, Sears began its "Great American Homes Program" to promote its best interior and exterior latex house paint. Under the Program, Sears paints landmark buildings, such as the homes of famous Americans. The projects are filmed for use in Sears commercials.

Most structures are owned by non-profit organizations, are open to the public, and are listed in the National Register of Historic Places. Those chosen so far have included the homes of John Quincy Adams, Mark Twain, Casey Jones, and Betsy Ross.

The buildings are painted their original colors or as close to them as possible. In addition, Sears does any necessary exterior carpentry work. The company receives approximately three applications per week from organizations wishing to have their homes considered. The Program is now in its sixth year.

Project: Donation of the Melrose and Southdown Plantation buildings to historical societies

Company: Valhi, Inc.
1010 Common Street
New Orleans, Louisiana 70112

Contact: The Association of Natchitoches Women for the Preservation of Historic Natchitoches
P.O. Box 2564
Natchitoches, Louisiana 71457

The Terrebonne Historical and Cultural Society
P.O. Box 2095
Houma, Louisiana 70361

In 1971, the Southdown Land Company (now Valhi, Inc.) donated the Melrose Plantation in Louisiana and several acres of land to the Association of Natchitoches Women for the Preservation of Historic Natchitoches. The company had purchased the Plantation and its pecan orchards for $2.2 million the previous year. The donation was made after Southdown had auctioned off the Plantation's furnishings.

The complex, originally called the Yucca Plantation, includes the Yucca House, the African House, the Ghana House, and a barn. It was built in 1776 by a former black slave, who later became a slave owner, Marie Therese Coin Coin Metoyer. The wooden plantation buildings with steep thatched roofs are the only African-style buildings extant from this period. In 1833, Marie's grandson, Louis, constructed the "Big House," now known as the Melrose Plantation House. The House is built in Louisiana French colonial style, with Greek Revival details.

In 1973, the Southdown Land Company donated the Southdown Plantation House to the Terrebonne Historical Society of Houma, Louisiana. The House was built by W.J. Minor, founder of the Southdown Sugar Company, in 1848. The Plantation includes: the main house, constructed mostly of brick, with two rounded Gothic turrets; a two-story structure connected to the main building by several walkways, which is thought to have been part of the slave quarters built in 1848; a stable complex; and a carriage house.

Both the Melrose and Southdown Plantations are listed in the National Register of Historic Places.

Methodology

This book is designed to be a tool for both businesses interested in building reuse and neighborhood preservation, and preservation and community groups interested in soliciting business support for these causes. Through a series of 71 case studies, the achievements of business in preservation are defined and illustrated. An appendix listing of 71 more projects substantiates the scope of the effort. The examples selected were chosen for their variety, scale, and geographic location, as well as for the degree of company cooperation.

The methodology used to identify business participation in preservation involved travel, periodical review, and follow-up interviews. In spring, 1975, the authors made several trips to Washington, D.C., to confer with federal officials, including officers of the U.S. Department of Housing and Urban Development and the Environmental Protection Agency. In addition, the authors met with members of the staff of the National Trust for Historic Preservation. These visits were made in an effort to identify important issues in the area of business contributions to preservation. An advisory board for the project was established to review concepts and offer direction.

In summer 1975, the study authors visited thirty states and talked personally with State Historic Preservation Officers (SHPOs), their staffs, and local preservation and business leaders. (Each state has a Preservation Officer appointed by the Governor to oversee preservation matters.) More than 100 examples of business involvement in preservation were identified from this effort.

In fall, 1975, letters and questionnaires were sent to all the SHPOs not personally contacted that summer, and to State Preservation Coordinators of the American Institute of Architects (AIA). (Two AIA-designated architects coordinate the organization's preservation activities in each state.) The questionnaires generated about fifty additional examples. That same fall, the National Trust for Historic Preservation distributed flyers at its annual conference in Boston. Several people wrote in response to the flyers.

In August, 1976, letters were sent to

Fortune magazine's list of the 500 largest U.S. industrial corporations. Approximately 5 percent of the companies responded to the mailing, producing several interesting projects. Additional companies carrying out preservation projects were identified via a variety of sources, including periodicals, books, and word of mouth.

In January, 1977, INFORM sent a questionnaire to the over 200 companies identified over the previous year and a half as having preservation projects. Approximately 20 percent replied. In all, 71 projects were selected for profiling. Follow-up phone calls to these companies continued throughout spring and summer, 1977.

Other useful sources of information on the projects in this study were: newspapers, including *Preservation News,* the newspaper of the National Trust, the *New York Times,* the *Wall Street Journal*, and local papers; and periodicals, like *Fortune, Business Week,* and *Architectural Record.*

Many publications helped provide an overview of the situation. Several were particularly important in surveying relevant legislation. They include: the National Trust for Historic Preservation's *A Guide to Federal Programs for Historic Preservation,* published in 1974, and supplemented in 1976, and *A Guide to State Programs,* published in 1972, and revised in 1976; the U.S. Department of Housing and Urban Development's *Neighborhood Preservation;* the National Endowment for the Arts' *Neighborhood Conservation*; and the National Center for Urban Ethnic Affairs' *Neighborhood Reinvestment.* Much information about business involvement in preservation support comes from publications of the Business Committee for the Arts, including its 1976 survey, *Business Support for the Arts,* and Gideon Chagy's *The New Patrons of the Arts.* The Filer Commission's Report, *Giving in America,* and the Conference Board's *Annual Survey of Corporate Contributions* were also helpful in their analyses of business contributions to preservation. Frederick L. Rath, Jr., and Merrilyn Rogers O'Connell have produced a useful preservation bibliography entitled *Historic Preservation: A Bibliography on Historical Organization Practices.* Ronald Lee Fleming and Vision,

Inc., of Cambridge, Massachusetts, will soon publish a survey of corporate design in historic areas.

The case-study format was finalized, and most drafting of profiles was completed in winter and spring, 1977. In April, 1977, the project's advisory board reviewed the format and offered suggestions on the shape of the cases and the project. In the months that followed, first drafts were sent for verification of factual material to companies profiled, and often to local preservation groups for review and comment. Changes were incorporated when appropriate.

Chapter introductions were written in summer, 1977, incorporating findings from the case studies, as well as materials from outside sources. Sections on legislation affecting community-revitalization and recycling programs were reviewed by experts in the field.

The information presented in each case study was supplied by the companies involved, their architects or contractors, community groups, or nonprofit organizations. It is the result of friendly questions, and depends for its accuracy on these groups' cooperation.

Glossary

AIA the American Institute of Architects, a national professional organization of architects.

AID American Interior Designers, a national professional organization of interior designers, now part of the American Society of Interior Designers, (ASID).

Art Deco a decorative style stimulated by the Paris Exposition Internationale des Arts Decoratifs et Industrieles Modernes of 1925. Widely used in American architecture and decorative arts of the 1930s, Art Deco was a glorification of technology. It placed emphasis on gleaming steel and sharp angular or zigzag surface forms.

Art Nouveau a decorative style of architecture and applied art developed in France and Belgium at the end of the nineteenth century. Essentially an aesthetic movement, it featured organic, dynamic forms and the luxuriant use of curving designs and whiplash lines.

balloon frame a wood frame in which the vertical members run continuously from the lowest horizontal member to the lower edge of a sloping roof.

balustrade a handrail supported by miniature columns, or other forms, called balusters. In the Georgian and Federal periods, balustrades were often placed on the edge of roofs of houses.

Beaux Arts historic and eclectic design on a monumental scale, featuring elaborate exterior decoration. It originated at the Ecole des Beaux Arts in Paris in the nineteenth century.

bracket an overhanging member projecting from a wall or other body to support a weight acting outside the wall. Brackets also often serve a purely decorative purpose.

cantilever a structural beam which projects horizontally out beyond its supporting member.

Chicago skyscraper style a tall multi-story commercial-building style that flourished particularly in Chicago at the end of the nineteenth century. It was based on the development of steel structural framing in the 1880s.

Classic Revival an architectural movement based on the use of pure Roman and Greek forms. It was popular in England and the United States during the nineteenth century.

Colonial a broad term covering a variety of architectural styles developed during the American Colonial period. Based on English, French, Dutch, and German styles of the seventeenth and eighteenth centuries, Colonial was essentially a transfer of these designs to the New World. Its features vary by region, but can include brickwork, steeply pitched roofs, and half-timbering.

column a supporting pillar, basic to much of classical architecture. A column consists of three parts: a base, a shaft, and a capital.

Doric column the oldest and sturdiest type of column, the Doric is distinguished by a thick shaft with a flat capital.

Ionic column distinguished by its scroll-shaped capital.

Corinthian column characterized by a slender shaft and a capital of carved leaves.

Tuscan column a Roman simplification of the Greek Doric column, usually featuring smooth shafts.

Community Development Block Grant the funds granted to communities for their use and disbursement under Title I of the Housing and Community Development Act of 1974, which replaced many different federal renewal programs. These funds are allocated in a lump sum rather than for individual projects, and allow local governments greater autonomy.

console a decorative projection from a wall designed for support.

corbel a supporting projection for a floor or overhanging member. If the corbel is one of a series, each is stepped progressively further forward from the wall.

cornice a molded, projecting, horizontal member which crowns a structure.

cottage style an eclectic architectural style of small, simple, typically rural residences, usually one or one-and-a-half stories, prominent in the nineteenth century.

cove lighting a method of lighting in which a light source is concealed by a horizontal recess or cornice below it and directs light up at a reflecting ceiling.

cupola a small domed turret, usually centered on the ridge of a roof.

curtain wall a wall supporting only itself. The weight of the roof or floor above is supported by the framework of the building.

dry grit a method of cleaning the exterior of a building by forced air through a directing nozzle using some form of grit (e.g., sand, silica, copper slag). Although this type of cleaning has been used on many of the buildings discussed in this book, it is not recommended for exterior cleaning as it can destroy the building surface, encouraging deterioration.

FAIA Fellow of the American Institute of Architects.

Federal an architectural style in vogue in the United States after the Revolutionary War until about 1830. The English architect Robert Adams was the primary influence on the Federal style, which was characterized by the use of classical forms and details such as columns and pilasters.

flashing sheet copper or another substance used to make an intersection between units weathertight.

Flemish bond a pattern of brickwork in which headers (bricks laid so that the end appears on the wall face) and stretchers (laid so that the side appears) are laid alternately in each row.

frieze the decorated band along the upper part of a wall immediately beneath the cornice.

gallery an intermediate floor projecting out into an enclosed space from one of the enclosing walls.

gazebo a small, fanciful, garden summerhouse.

Georgian an architectural style of eighteenth century England. Georgian emphasized the use of classical symmetry and form. Pilasters, balustrades, and brick were common. It was popular in America from 1720 to 1790.

gingerbread style refers to the elaborate woodwork of Victorian-style houses.

Gothic European medieval architecture of the late twelfth to sixteenth centuries characterized by the use of the pointed arch and ribbed vaults.

Gothic Revival a style which resulted from a conscious attempt to revive medieval forms. It was popular in the United States and Europe from 1820 to 1870, and was distinguished by pointed-arch windows with tracery.

Greek the architecture of ancient Greece, characterized by the use of the column and the lintel as supporting elements, marble as a building material, and symmetrical forms.

Greek Revival a style stimulated by the Greek fight for independence, Greek Revival was marked by a use of Greek and Roman forms. It was popular in England and the United States in the first half of the nineteenth century.

HABS Historic American Buildings Survey, established by the federal government in 1933 to record and document important buildings and sites.

HAER Historic American Engineering Record, founded in 1969 to record and document important industrial and engineering sites and structures.

heart pine mature pine from approximately the center of the tree.

HUD the United States Department of Housing and Urban Development.

jerkin head roof a roof in which the end of the top of the roof is cut short, and a secondary slope is formed.

joist one of a series of parallel horizontal timber beams upon which floor boards or ceiling supports are fastened.

lintel a horizontal piece of stone, timber, or masonry spanning an opening.

mansard roof a roof which slopes on all sides, with the lower slope generally steeper than the upper one. A feature French in origin.

measured drawings drawings to scale of a given structure.

mortise a cut-out hollow in one member, often a timber, meant to receive and hold another corresponding part, or tenon.

National Register of Historic Places the federal inventory of historic buildings, sites, and districts of national, state, or local importance. It is administered by the National Park Service. Nomination must first be approved by the appropriate state historic-preservation officers.

National Trust for Historic Preservation the national organization which furthers preservation activities in the United States. Chartered by Congress in 1949, it is a nonprofit organization backed by federal and private funding.

neoclassical a style which dominated Europe and America in the late eighteenth and early nineteenth centuries. It was characterized by the monumentality of its buildings, and the sparing application of detail and strict symmetry.

Neo-Renaissance a style which came about in the mid-nineteenth century as a reaction to the Gothic Revival. Neo-Renaissance is characterized by a division of the building facade into a base, middle, and top, and the use of carved stone and sculpture.

newel post the posts at the bottom and top of a staircase.

NHS Neighborhood Housing Services, a nonprofit partnership of local residents, government, and financial institutions whose purpose is revitalizing neighborhoods through financial counseling, loan programs, and education.

nogging the filling-in of brick between closely spaced vertical members of a frame wall or partition.

outbuilding a small separate building whose function depends on a main structure.

pediment a surface used ornamentally over doors or windows, usually triangular but sometimes curved.

piazza an open public space surrounded by buildings.

pilaster a shallow column usually projecting from but engaged to a wall.

pressed brick smooth-faced brick molded by mechanical pressure.

Queen Anne an eclectic style of domestic architecture popular in England and America in the nineteenth century. The term is a misnomer since the style is a mixture of Gothic and Renaissance characteristics.

redlining refusal by a financial institution to make loans in a given area regardless of the qualifications of the potential borrower.

Regency a type of architecture popular in England during the regency and reign of George IV. It was a colorful neoclassical style which often combined Oriental motifs with stucco and balconied terraces.

Richardsonian Romanesque a style named after its foremost practitioner, American architect Henry Hobson Richardson (1838 to 1886). Richardson integrated Romanesque elements, such as large rounded arches, into strong solid buildings symbolic of the burgeoning growth of American capitalism. He also emphasized asymmetrical design and rusticated masonry walls.

riser the vertical piece between the horizontal treads of a staircase.

rococo a mid-eighteenth-century style, French in origin, rococo emphasized profuse curved decoration expressed in light colors and fanciful forms.

Romanesque a term generally used to cover European architecture during the time between the Roman and the Gothic styles. Based on Roman forms, rounded arches and semicircular vaulting were typical.

Second Empire a French architectural style, popular in the 1860s and 1870s, which employed neoclassical motifs and mansard roofs primarily on public buildings. It was named after the French Second Empire of Napoleon III (1852 to 1870).

shake a type of hand-split shingle.

shingle-style a style of American architecture, popular in the late nineteenth century, whose foremost proponent was the firm of McKim, Mead and White. The style emphasized the use of shingles on roof and walls, and large open interior spaces.

spandrel a panel covering of an exterior wall in a skeleton frame building between structural supports and window openings.

terra cotta cast and fired clay used for wall facings and architectural ornamentation. It was popular in the United States in the early twentieth century.

terrazzo floors floors consisting of marble chips cast in cement and then ground and polished.

travertine a cream-colored limestone used as a building material.

truss the triangular frame structure used to support a roof or floor.

turnbuckle a device with screw threads at both ends, or a screw thread at one end and a swivel at the other, that is turned to bring ends closer together. It is usually used to tighten rods.

vernacular folk buildings or decorations characteristic of an area.

Victorian a broad term referring to eclectic and revival buildings and decorative arts during the reign of Queen Victoria (1840 to 1901). The main characteristics include low-pitched, bracketed roofs, asymmetrical design, towers, and sometimes round-arched windows.

wainscoting a wood, stone, or masonry overlay of a wall surface, usually less than half the height of the wall.

Index

THE MASTER SERIES LSAT

2004

Thomas H. Martinson

Australia • Canada • Mexico • Singapore • Spain • United Kingdom • United States

About The Thomson Corporation and Peterson's
With revenues of US$7.8 billion, The Thomson Corporation (www.thomson.com) is a leading global provider of integrated information solutions for business, education, and professional customers. Its Learning businesses and brands (www.thomsonlearning.com) serve the needs of individuals, learning institutions, and corporations with products and services for both traditional and distributed learning.

Peterson's, part of The Thomson Corporation, is one of the nation's most respected providers of lifelong learning online resources, software, reference guides, and books. The Education Supersite[SM] at www.petersons.com—the Internet's most heavily traveled education resource—has searchable databases and interactive tools for contacting U.S.-accredited institutions and programs. In addition, Peterson's serves more than 105 million education consumers annually.

For more information, contact Peterson's, 2000 Lenox Drive, Lawrenceville, NJ 08648; 800-338-3282; or find us on the World Wide Web at: www.petersons.com/about.

ISBN (book only): 0-7689-1199-0
ISBN (book with CD-ROM): 0-7689-1198-2

Printed in the United States of America

10 9 8 7 6 5 4 3 2 1   05   04   03

Contents

PART I: LSAT BASICS

Contents

Contents

PART IV: THREE PRACTICE TESTS

PART V: APPENDICES

Before You Begin

HOW WILL THIS BOOK HELP YOU?

Taking the LSAT is a skill. It shares some things in common with other skills, such as playing basketball or singing opera. These are skills that can be improved by coaching, but ultimately improvement also requires practice. This book gives you both.

- "The Top 10 Ways to Raise Your Score" gives you a preview of some of the critical strategies you'll learn. "Track your Progress" is where you'll record your scores on the Diagnostic and Practice tests as you work through the book.

- Part I provides essential general information about taking the LSAT. You'll learn how to register for the test, what kinds of questions to expect, and how the test is scored. You'll also find out how to make the most of whatever time you have to study.

- Part II is a full-length Diagnostic Examination. It can show you where your skills are strong—and where they need some shoring up. Record your score in "Track Your Progress."

- Part III is the coaching program. The chapters in this part analyze each question type and give you powerful strategies for taking the test on its own terms.

- Part IV contains three full-length sample LSATs. Record your scores in "Track Your Progress." Each test is followed by a detailed analysis of each question. The detailed analysis is very important because it helps you learn from your mistakes.

ABOUT THE AUTHOR

Professor Thomas H. Martinson is widely acknowledged to be America's leading authority on test preparation. A graduate of Harvard Law School and a member of the New York State and Washington, D.C., bars, Professor Martinson has published more than three dozen books on test preparation. He is routinely invited to lecture on test preparation and related topics at top colleges and universities throughout the United States and abroad.

THE TOP 10 WAYS TO RAISE YOUR SCORE

When it comes to taking the LSAT, some test-taking skills will do you more good than others.

There are concepts you can learn, techniques you can follow, and tricks you can use that will give you the biggest "bang for your buck." Here's our pick of the Top 10.

1 **Make a study plan and follow it.** The LSAT study plan will help you get the most out of this book in whatever time you have. See Chapter 1.

2 **Learn the directions in advance.** If you already know the directions, you won't have to waste precious test time reading them. You'll be able to jump right in and start answering questions as soon as the test clock starts. See Chapter 2.

3 **If you don't know the answer, always make a guess.** On the LSAT, it's to your advantage to answer every question. If you can make an educated guess by eliminating one or more answer choices, so much the better. See Chapter 2.

4 **In logical reasoning questions, start by finding the conclusion.** Since the conclusion is the main point of the argument, it's the key to answering every question of this type. See Chapter 5.

5 **In logical reasoning questions, use circle diagrams to define relationships.** When a problem asks you to deduce how certain terms are related, a circle diagram can make the relationship clear. See Chapter 5.

6 **In reading comprehension, read for structure, not details.** When you read LSAT passages, don't let the details bog you down. Most of the questions will ask about the structure of the passage rather than specific facts. If you need the facts, they're always there in the passage. See Chapter 6.

7 **In reading comprehension, there are really only six kinds of questions.** Identify the type of question asked and you're halfway to finding the correct answer. See Chapter 6.

8 **For analytical reasoning questions, set up a "bookkeeping" system to summarize the information.** Use your own notational devices or adapt the ones shown in this book. See Chapter 7.

9 **For analytical reasoning questions, treat each question separately.** In these "puzzle" sets, don't use new information supplied in any question to answer any other question in the set. But see Chapter 7 for "What the Smartest Test-Takers know – Breaking News on Puzzles."

10 **For the writing sample, don't try to do too much.** It's better to write a short but balanced and structurally complete essay than one that you have to cut off in the middle because you've run out of time. See Chapter 8.

TRACK YOUR PROGRESS

For each exam:

1 Enter the number of questions that you answered correctly in each section in the appropriate row. Experimental sections are NOT scored.

2 Enter the total number of questions that you answered correctly for that exam in the "TOTAL" row.

3 Enter your score for the exam in the "SCORE" row using the chart below.

4 Enter the appropriate data from the top part of the table into the rows in the second part of the table to keep track of your progress in each of the three content areas.

LSAT SCORE TRACKER

	Diagnostic Examination (Number Correct)	Practice Test 1 (Number Correct)	Practice Test 2 (Number Correct)	Practice Test 3 (Number Correct)
Section 1			Experimental	
Section 2	Experimental			
Section 3				
Section 4		Experimental		Experimental
Section 5				
TOTAL				
SCORE				

Content Areas—Raw Subscores
(Enter data from above)

Logical Reasoning	Sec. 3 + Sec. 4 =	Sec. 1 + Sec. 5 =	Sec. 2 + Sec. 5 =	Sec. 3 + Sec. 5 =
Analytical Reasoning	Sec. 1 =	Sec. 2 =	Sec. 3 =	Sec. 2 =
Reading	Sec. 5 =	Sec. 3 =	Sec. 4 =	Sec. 1 =

PART I

LSAT BASICS

Getting Started

OVERVIEW
- **Preparing for the LSAT**
- **Your LSAT Study Plan**
- **Seeing Your Work Pay Off**

CAN YOU PREPARE FOR THE LSAT?

This is the question of the day. Can you indeed prepare for a test that purports to test your aptitude for success in law school rather than your mastery of any particular subject? Of course you can. The LSAT is long, and some of its questions are tough, but it's not unconquerable.

There are many ways to prepare and many tricks and tips to learn. One of the most important things to learn is to think like the test makers so you can find the answers they have designated as best. Once you learn "LSAT thinking," you'll be more likely to pick the best answer—and up will go your score.

WHAT IS AN LSAT STUDY PLAN?

As you can tell, this book contains a lot of information about the LSAT, and you'll need a plan for getting through it. The right study plan will help you manage your time so that you get the most out of this book whether you have three months, three weeks, or only a few days to prepare. It will help you work efficiently and keep you from getting stressed out.

Choose the Plan That's Right for You

To decide on your study plan, answer these two questions: (1) How long do you have until the test? (2) How much time can you devote to LSAT study?

Here are some suggestions to make your job easier. If you are starting early and the LSAT is two or three months away, go for broke. Complete the book from beginning to end. If the LSAT is a month or less away and you need a more concentrated course, focus on the chapter exercises and Practice Tests.

TIP

HOW CAN YOU TELL IF YOUR WORK IS PAYING OFF?

Start with the tough stuff. To make the most of your study time, study the difficult sections first. If you run out of time later, you can just skim the sections that are easy for you.

No matter what plan you choose, you should start by taking the Diagnostic Examination. After you score it, you'll be able to see where you need to concentrate your efforts. Note your scores in "Track Your Progress."

The next step is to see how you do with the exercises at the end of each chapter. Compare your scores to your results on the Diagnostic Exam. Have you improved? Where do you still need work?

When you're ready, take the Practice Examinations. These are just like the test you'll take, and you should try to simulate test conditions as nearly as you can. After you score a Practice Examination, again note your scores in "Track Your Progress." Make another comparison to the chapter exercises and to the Diagnostic Exam. This will show you how your work is paying off.

All about the LSAT

OVERVIEW

- About the LSAT
- Registering for the LSAT
- Kinds of Questions on the Test
- The Structure of the Test
- The Answer Sheet
- Scoring the Test
- What Smart Test-Takers Know

WHAT IS THE LSAT?

The Law School Admission Test (LSAT) is a half-day-long standardized exam that is required for admission by all law schools approved by the American Bar Association as well as by many Canadian law schools. It consists of six separately timed sections, five of which use multiple-choice questions; the sixth presents an essay topic. The essay portion is not scored.

The LSAT is given four times a year—in February, June, September, and December. Scores are reported to law schools by the Law School Data Assembly Service (LSDAS), which also forwards applicants' transcripts and biographical information.

According to the Law School Admission Council (LSAC), the consortium of law schools that owns and controls the LSAT, the test scores are designed to measure an applicant's ability to "read, understand, and reason" at a level required for success in law school. The LSAT is considered to be an "objective" measure, and that is very important to law school admissions officers. A law school's applicant pool is made up of candidates from many different undergraduate institutions, some with advanced degrees and others without, and each with a unique life history, but all have taken the LSAT. LSAT scores are the one objective measure that an admissions officer has.

For this reason, your LSAT score is very important. Simply stated, if your LSAT score is too low, you will be rejected. That is not to say, however, that a high LSAT score guarantees that you will be accepted. On the contrary, every year, top law schools reject a significant number of applicants with perfect or near-perfect LSAT scores. While it is a very important factor in the admissions process, the LSAT score is not the only factor. Law schools also consider grades, extracurricular activities, work experience, and other aspects of your background.

chapter 2

HOW DO YOU REGISTER FOR THE LSAT?

You must register in advance to take the LSAT; you cannot simply walk in on the day of the test. Registration materials for both the LSAT and the Law School Data Assembly Service are available either from your college's prelaw adviser or by writing to the following address:

> Law School Admissions Services
> Box 2000
> Newtown, PA 18940-1001

You can also get information about the LSAT on line:

> http://www.lsas.org

Regular registration requests must be postmarked approximately six weeks before the test. Late registration is also available.

Special arrangements can be made for the visually and physically disabled, for persons whose religious beliefs forbid taking the test on a Saturday, and for other persons with special needs. The key to making satisfactory arrangements is time. If you want to make any special arrangements for taking the LSAT, communicate immediately with the Law School Admissions Services at the address given above.

Most law schools require LSAT scores by December for admission the following fall. Because you must allow at least six weeks for your score to be reported, you might not receive September scores in time. Therefore, the June test date is recommended.

WHAT KINDS OF QUESTIONS ARE ON THE TEST?

The LSAT uses three different kinds of multiple-choice questions.

① Reading Comprehension

Reading Comprehension questions are based on reading passages that are each approximately 450 words long. You will be asked to demonstrate your understanding of the passage by answering questions about the structure, meaning, and implications of the passage. Your Reading Comprehension section will have 26 to 28 questions.

② Logical Reasoning

Logical Reasoning questions present an argument contained in a short paragraph. You are asked to demonstrate that you understand the argument by choosing an answer that describes the argument, weakens or strengthens it, identifies its premises, or states its conclusions or its implications. Your test will have two Logical Reasoning sections. Each section will have 24 to 26 questions.

③ Analytical Reasoning

Analytical Reasoning questions present a situation and some conditions. You will need to organize the conditions in order to answer the questions. Diagrams of various sorts are almost sure to be helpful. When you talk to other people who are going to take the LSAT, they may refer to this section as the "logical games" or "logical puzzles." The number of questions is 22 to 24.

MYSTERY SECTION

Your LSAT will also include a mystery section. The Mystery Section is a separately timed section that contains questions that will not be scored. These questions are still in the experimental or testing phase.

WRITING SAMPLE

The Writing Sample is technically not a part of the LSAT. It is an essay exercise that was added on. It is not scored, but copies of your essay response are sent to the law schools.

HOW IS THE TEST STRUCTURED?

The order of sections in an LSAT varies. You might have Analytical Reasoning first and Reading Comprehension last or vice versa or Reading Comprehension first and the Mystery Section second or vice versa. Even at the same test administration, different test booklets will have the sections arranged in different orders. Do not be concerned about the order in which the question types are presented; just take them as they come.

The following table shows the structure of a typical LSAT.

ANATOMY OF A TYPICAL LSAT

Section	Number of Questions	Time Allowed
Logical Reasoning 1	24–26	35 min.
Reading Comprehension	27–28	35 min.
Analytical Reasoning	24–25	35 min.
Logical Reasoning 2	24–26	35 min.
Mystery Section	??	35 min.
Writing Sample	One Essay	30 min.

(Note: The order of the sections varies from administration to administration, and the Mystery Section is not necessarily the last section of multiple-choice questions.)

You will not be told which is the Mystery Section, and you will probably not be able to tell. So do your best on all test sections.

WHAT DOES THE ANSWER SHEET LOOK LIKE?

On the LSAT, your test materials come in two parts: a booklet of 30-odd pages containing the test questions and an answer sheet covered with rows of lettered spaces

Get the latest LSAT information on the Web. You can get up-to-the-minute LSAT information on the World Wide Web. The address is http://www.lsas.org.

NOTE

for your responses. The space for marking your answers to a section will look something like this:

15 Ⓐ Ⓑ Ⓒ Ⓓ Ⓔ

The answer sheet is graded by a machine that "reads" the marks you have made. Therefore, it is important to record your answers properly and neatly, completely filling each answer space with a dark pencil mark. Leave no stray marks on the answer sheet. Enter one, and only one, answer per question. Don't worry if the answer sheet has more blanks than your booklet has questions. Leave the extra spaces blank.

Take a look at these examples of properly and improperly recorded answers.

SECTION 1	SECTION 2
1 Ⓐ ● Ⓒ Ⓓ Ⓔ	1 Ⓐ Ⓑ Ⓒ Ⓓ Ⓔ
2 Ⓐ Ⓑ Ⓒ ● Ⓔ	2 Ⓐ Ⓑ Ⓒ Ⓓ Ⓔ
3 Ⓐ ● Ⓒ Ⓓ Ⓔ	3 Ⓐ Ⓑ ● Ⓓ ●
4 Ⓐ Ⓑ Ⓒ ● Ⓔ	4 Ⓐ Ⓑ Ⓒ Ⓓ Ⓔ
5 Ⓐ Ⓑ Ⓒ Ⓓ ●	5 Ⓐ Ⓑ Ⓒ Ⓓ Ⓔ
6 ● Ⓑ Ⓒ Ⓓ Ⓔ	6 Ⓐ Ⓑ Ⓒ Ⓧ Ⓔ
7 Ⓐ Ⓑ ● Ⓓ Ⓔ	7 Ⓐ Ⓑ Ⓒ Ⓓ Ⓔ

NOTE

Why does the LSAT use scaled scores?

Scaled scores allow the test-makers to account for differences from one version of the LSAT to another. Using scaled scores ensures that a score of, say, 165 on one LSAT is equivalent to 165 on another.

All of the answers in Section 1 are properly recorded. Each mark is black and completely fills the answer space, so the scoring machine is sure to read it correctly. In Section 2, the answer to question 1 is too light; the machine might not see it. The answer to question 2 is messy and covers two answer spaces; the machine will record this as an incorrect answer. In question 3, two answers are marked correctly, but there can be only one right answer; again, the machine will record this as an incorrect response. Question 4 will be treated in the same way since it has been left blank. Leaving it blank was a mistake. It should have been answered, even with a guess, because there is no penalty on the LSAT for wrong answers. Questions 6 and 7 have been marked with an "X" and a checkmark, respectively. Both answers will register as incorrect because neither mark totally fills the answer space.

The most common error in answer sheet management is misplacing an entire block of answers. This occurs when a test taker skips a question in the test booklet but fails to skip a corresponding space on the answer sheet. The result is that the intended pattern of response is there, but it is displaced by one or more spaces. Unfortunately, the machine that grades the paper reads what actually is on the answer sheet—not what the test taker intended.

HOW IS THE TEST SCORED?

The scoring system used by the LSAT is very simple: Each correct answer is worth +1 on the raw score; and, unlike some other exams that you may have taken (such as the SAT), there is no adjustment made for incorrect responses. The scoring system simply ignores wrong answers and omitted questions. *In other words, there is no guessing penalty.*

Because each form of the LSAT contains 100 or so questions (with no penalty for guessing), raw scores range from a theoretical minimum of 0 to a theoretical maximum of slightly more than 100. The bell-curve distribution of raw scores can vary slightly from test administration to test administration, so to keep test results comparable over time, scores are reported to law schools on a scale of 120 (the minimum) to 180 (the maximum). The following table gives you some idea of how many correct answers are needed for selected scaled scores.

SAMPLE SCORING TABLE

Correct/Score	Correct/Score	Correct/Score	Correct/Score
98+/180	77/164	56/152	35/138
97/179	76/163	55/151	34/137
96/178	75/163	54/151	33/137
95/177	74/162	53/150	32/136
94/176	73/162	52/150	31/135
93/175	72/161	51/149	30/134
92/174	71/161	50/148	29/133
91/173	70/160	49/148	28/132
90/173	69/159	48/147	27/132
89/172	68/159	47/146	26/131
88/171	67/158	46/145	25/130
87/170	66/158	45/144	24/129
86/170	65/157	44/144	23/128
85/169	64/157	43/143	22/127
84/168	63/156	42/143	21/126
83/168	62/156	41/142	20/125
82/167	61/155	40/142	19/124
81/167	60/154	39/141	18/123
80/166	59/154	38/141	17/122
79/165	58/153	37/140	16/121
78/164	57/152	36/139	15-/120

The Writing Sample is not graded by LSAT and does not affect your LSAT score. Copies of your essay, however, are sent to each law school that you designate to receive an LSAT score report.

The Writing Sample is usually used as a "tie-breaker" or secondary credential of much less importance than the LSAT score. However, a very poor Writing Sample could seriously undermine an otherwise strong application at many schools. While a very strong Writing Sample will not equally redeem an otherwise weak application, it may be the deciding factor when your application is approximately as strong as someone else's.

WHAT SMART TEST-TAKERS KNOW

General Test Smarts

Change is always possible.

Be cautious regarding the test format. Some small adjustments are always possible, and you do not want to be caught off guard. When you are told to begin work on a section, take five or ten seconds to look through the pages of that section. If there are unexpected changes, you can readily adjust your plan of attack.

The LSAT takes concentration.

The LSAT is an arduous task. There is no way that you can maintain your concentration throughout all five of the 35-minute sections. There will be times when your attention begins to flag. Learn to recognize this. For example, if you find that you are reading and rereading the same line without understanding, put down your pencil, close your eyes, take a deep breath or two (or rub your eyes or whatever), and then get back to work.

Obsessing doesn't pay.

You're not going to be able to answer every question with supreme confidence. In fact, you may answer very few questions with confidence. That does not mean, however, that you are not doing well. In fact, answering even 75 percent of the questions correctly will earn you a 160 or so, which is above the 80th percentile.

Pacing

A watch can be an asset.

The proctors in charge of administering the test are supposed to keep you advised of the passing time, for example, by writing on a blackboard how many minutes remain. But you should not rely on their diligence. In the first place, it's easy for a proctor to forget to mark the passing time at exactly the right moment. So when you see the proctor write "5 minutes left," you might have only 4 minutes left or as many as 6 minutes left.

TIP

Set your watch to exam time. At the beginning of each test section, set your watch to 12 o'clock. Then all you have to do is glance quickly at the hands (or the readout of a digital watch) to see how much of the section has passed.

Further, the proctor might mark the correct time at the right moment without your knowledge. When you look up from your work you see "5 minutes left," but when did the proctor write that down? The solution is to have a watch with you. If you have a digital watch with a stopwatch function, you can use that. If your digital watch does not have a stopwatch function, write down the starting time for the section when you begin. Quickly add 35 minutes to that and write down the time you must finish. Circle that number for easy reference.

It's important to find the pace that's right for you.

The scoring mechanism for the LSAT is the simple formula "score = correct answers." No points are awarded for near misses, and no extra points are given for difficult questions. This means you have got to cover as much ground as possible.

On the one hand, you want to respond correctly to as many questions as you can in the 35 minutes; on the other hand, you cannot afford to be so careful that you begin to beat yourself by not answering enough questions to get a good score. There is a trade-off between speed and accuracy, one that only you can find through practice.

To demonstrate the necessity of the trade-off, consider the cases of three hypothetical students: Timmy Toocareful, Carl Careless, and Terry Testwise.

On his exam, Timmy Toocareful attempted only 65 questions, but he was very accurate. Of the 65, Timmy answered 60 correctly, missing only 5. In addition, he guessed at the remaining 35 questions, getting one fifth of those right (as expected) for another 7 points.

Carl Careless used the opposite strategy. He worked very quickly to ensure that he attempted all 100 questions, and he paid the price. Of the 100, he answered only 70 correctly.

Terry Testwise used the proper strategy of working as quickly as possible without unnecessarily sacrificing accuracy. Of the 100 questions, she attempted 85, missing 10. And she guessed at the other 15 questions, hitting one fifth of them (as expected) for another 3 points.

The score reports would show the following:

Timmy Toocareful:	Raw Score 67	Scaled Score 157
Carl Careless:	Raw Score 70	Scaled Score 159
Terry Testwise:	Raw Score 78	Scaled Score 165

Most students are probably prone to err on the side of caution. In this case, Timmy, fearful of answering incorrectly, doesn't attempt enough questions to get his best score. Since there is no penalty for answering incorrectly, don't be overly worried about mistakes. Of course you don't want to be needlessly careless, but it's probably better to go too quickly than too slowly.

ALERT!

Don't spin your wheels. Don't spend too much time on any one question. Give it some thought, take your best shot, and move along.

It pays to keep moving.

All questions are given equal weight. No extra credit is given for a difficult question. So there is no reason to keep working on a question after you have given it your best shot. Instead, once you realize that you are spinning your wheels, make the decision to make a guess and move on to the next question.

If you know the directions in advance, you won't have to waste time reading them.

Your allotted 35 minutes is all the time you get for a section. No additional time is given for reading directions. If you spend 30 seconds reading the directions each time you begin a new section, you could lose a whole question in each section. The solution to this problem is to be thoroughly familiar in advance with the directions for every question type and with the format in which each question type appears. Then, when you get to the exam, you will recognize those formats and already know what is required without having to review any directions.

It's more efficient to code answers in groups.

Most test takers code their response to each question just after they have answered the question. They work in the rhythm: solve, code, solve, code, solve, code, and so on. It is this rhythm that can trip them up if they skip a question. Instead of coding your responses one by one, try coding them in groups. Work problems for a while (noting your choices). Then find an appropriate moment to enter your responses on your answer sheet. You might wait until you have reached the end of a page. As time for a section draws to a close, you should make sure you are current with your coding, so you will probably want to go to the one -by- one method. You don't want to run out of time on a section without the opportunity to enter answers to every question that you have worked. Even if you are coding in groups, there is the ever-present danger of an error. If you find that you have made a mistake, what do you do? You erase the wrong responses and enter the correct ones.

Questions you want to return to can be found more quickly if you flag them.

A mark in the margin of your test booklet will quickly identify questions you want to reconsider if you have time. Develop a shorthand marking system to identify skipped questions, doubtful questions, and answer choices that you're sure can be eliminated. Here's one marking system you might try:

    Correct Answer: Circle the letter of the choice.
    Definitely Eliminated Choice: Put an "X" over the letter.
    Changed Choice: Fill in the circle of the first answer, and circle the new choice.
    Skipped Question: Put a "?" by the number of the question.
    Question to Recheck: Circle the number.

If you find that you have made a mistake, what do you do? You erase the wrong responses and copy the correct ones from your "paper trail."

Guessing Strategies

Because of the multiple-choice format, you have a real advantage over the LSAT. The correct answer is always right there on the page. To be sure, it's surrounded by wrong choices, but it may be possible to eliminate one or more of those other choices as non-answers.

You can toss out dumb answers.

Look at the following Reading Comprehension question:

The author argues that the evidence supporting the new theory is

- **(A)** hypothetical.
- **(B)** biased.
- **(C)** empirical.
- **(D)** speculative.
- **(E)** fragmentary.

You might think that it is impossible to make any progress on a Reading Comprehension question without the reading selection, but you can eliminate three of the five answers in this question as non-answers. Study the question stem. We can infer that the author of the selection has at least implicitly passed judgment on the evidence supporting the new theory. What kind of judgment might someone make about the evidence adduced to support a theory? Choices (A), (C), and (D) all seem extremely unlikely. As for choice (A), while the theory is itself an hypothesis, the evidence supporting the theory would not be hypothetical. As for choice (C), evidence is empirical by definition. So it is unlikely that anyone would argue "This evidence is empirical." And choice (D) can be eliminated for the same reason as choice (A). Admittedly, this leaves you with a choice of (B) or (E), a choice that depends on the content of the reading selection; but at least you have a 50–50 chance of getting the question correct—even without reading the selection.

You absolutely, positively must GUESS.

Because there is no penalty assessed for wrong answers, guessing, even randomly, is necessary to ensure that you get your best score. Two techniques will help you to garner every possible point.

Unlike some other standardized exams you might have taken (such as the SAT), no points are deducted for incorrect answers. Since there is no penalty for taking a guess and since there is always a chance you will hit on the right answer, don't leave any answer space blank. For those questions on which you can eliminate choices, make an educated guess. But even if you don't get to some questions, at least make a random guess on your answer sheet. You can't lose; you can only win.

Strings of three letters are used, but strings of four or more letters are not used.

Although strings of four or more of one letter are theoretically possible, they just don't occur. This is because the test writers break them up. So you will not find a string of four (A)s in a row. If you do, at least one of your four answers will be wrong. Which one is it? There is no way of knowing for sure without checking your work.

There has been one exception to this rule in nearly twenty-five years, and there appears to be no logical explanation for it; so go with the trend—no strings of fours.

LSAT Questions:
A First Look

OVERVIEW

- **What to Expect on the Test**
- **How the LSAT Tests Logical Reasoning**
- **How the LSAT Tests Reading Comprehension**
- **How the LSAT Tests Analytical Reasoning**
- **About the Writing Sample**

WHAT CAN YOU EXPECT ON THE TEST?

The LSAT uses three different types of multiple-choice questions to test your abilities in Logical Reasoning, Reading Comprehension, and Analytical Reasoning. There is also a 30-minute Writing Sample that tests your ability to organize and compose a short essay. This chapter will describe each question type in turn and show you samples. Learning the question types in advance is the best way to prepare for the LSAT. This way, you'll know what to expect, and you won't have any unpleasant surprises on test day.

HOW DOES THE LSAT TEST LOGICAL REASONING?

A typical Logical Reasoning question presents an argument or an explanation that you are asked to analyze. You may be asked to describe the argument, draw further conclusions from it, attack or defend it, or just find the assumptions of the argument. The LSAT contains two Logical Reasoning sections, each with 24 to 26 questions. Here are the directions for this question type and a sample item:

> **Directions:** In this section, the questions ask you to analyze and evaluate the reasoning in short paragraphs or passages. For some questions, all of the answer choices may conceivably be answers to the question asked. You should select the *best* answer to the question; that is, an answer that does not require you to make assumptions that violate commonsense standards by being implausible, redundant, irrelevant, or inconsistent.
>
> After choosing the best answer, blacken the corresponding space on the answer sheet.

chapter 3

1. Wilfred commented, "Of all the musical instruments I have studied, the trombone is the most difficult instrument to play."

   Which of the following statements, if true, would most seriously weaken Wilfred's conclusion?

   (A) The trombone is relatively easy for trumpet players to learn to play.

   (B) Wilfred has not studied trombone as seriously as he has studied other instruments.

   (C) Wilfred finds he can play the violin and the cello with equal facility.

   (D) The trombone is easier to learn as a second instrument than as a first instrument.

   (E) There are several instruments that Wilfred has not studied and that are very difficult to play.

The best answer is (B). The question asks you to identify a possible weakness in the argument. The conclusion of the argument is that the trombone is intrinsically more difficult to play than other instruments. The question asks you to find another explanation for Wilfred's impression. Choice (B) suggests the fault is not in the trombone but in Wilfred. The seeming difficulty of the trombone stems from the fact that Wilfred did not study it as diligently as he has studied other instruments.

HOW DOES THE LSAT TEST READING COMPREHENSION?

As the name implies, LSAT Reading Comprehension questions test your ability to understand the substance and logical structure of a written selection. An LSAT Reading Comprehension section contains four reading passages, each approximately 450 words in length. Each passage is followed by 5–8 questions, for a total of 26–28 questions per section. The questions ask about the main point of the passage, about what the author specifically states, about what can be logically inferred from the passage, and about the author's attitude or tone. Here are the directions for LSAT Reading Comprehension questions and an example of a reading passage. (This sample passage is shorter than an actual LSAT passage and is followed by only two questions rather than the usual six to eight.)

> **Directions:** Below each of the following passages, you will find questions or incomplete statements about the passage. Each statement or question is followed by lettered words or expressions. Select the word or expression that most satisfactorily completes each statement or answers each question in accordance with the meaning of the passage. After you have chosen the best answer, blacken the corresponding space on the answer sheet.

The international software market represents significant business opportunity for U.S. microcomputer software companies, but illegal copying of programs is limiting the growth of sales abroad. If not dealt with quickly, international piracy of software could become one of the
(5)   most serious trade problems faced by the United States.

Software piracy is already the biggest barrier to U.S. software companies entering foreign markets. One reason is that software is extremely easy and inexpensive to duplicate compared to the cost of developing and marketing the software. The actual cost of duplicating
(10)   a software program, which may have a retail value of $400 or more, can be as little as a dollar or two—the main component being the cost of the CD. The cost of counterfeiting software is substantially less than the cost of duplicating watches, books, or blue jeans. Given that the difference between the true value of the original and the cost of the
(15)   counterfeit is so great for software, international piracy has become big business. Unfortunately, many foreign governments view software piracy as an industry in and of itself and look the other way.

U.S. firms stand to lose millions of dollars in new business, and diminished U.S. sales not only harm individual firms but also adversely
(20)   affect the entire U.S. economy.

2. In this passage, the author's primary purpose is to

(A) criticize foreign governments for stealing U.S. computer secrets.

(B) describe the economic hazards software piracy pose to the United States.

(C) demand that software pirates immediately cease their illegal operations.

(D) present a comprehensive proposal to counteract the effects of international software piracy.

(E) disparage the attempts of the U.S. government to control software piracy.

The best answer is (B). This question, typical of the LSAT, asks about the main point of the selection. Choice (A) is incorrect. Though the author implies criticism of foreign governments, their mistake, so far as we are told, is not stealing secrets but tacitly allowing the operation of a software black market. Choice (C) is incorrect since this is not the main point of the selection. You can infer that the author would approve of such a demand, but issuing the demand is not the main point of the selection you just read. Choice (D) can be eliminated for a similar reason. Though the author might elsewhere offer a specific proposal, there is no such proposal in the selection you just read. Choice (E) also is wrong since no such attempts are ever discussed. Finally, notice how well choice (B) describes the main issue. The author's concern is to identify a problem and to discuss its causes.

3. The author's attitude toward international software piracy can best be described as

   (A) concern.

   (B) rage.

   (C) disinterest.

   (D) pride.

   (E) condescension.

The best answer is (A). This question asks about the tone of the passage, and *concern* very neatly captures that tone. You can eliminate choice (B) as an overstatement. Though the author condemns the piracy, the tone is not so violent as to qualify as rage. Choice (C) must surely be incorrect since the author does express concern and, therefore, cannot be disinterested.

HOW DOES THE LSAT TEST ANALYTICAL REASONING?

TIP

Make the best of it.
Note that these directions ask you to choose the best answer. That's why you should always read all the answer choices before you make your final selection.

LSAT Analytical Reasoning questions involve a situation such as people standing in a row, choosing items from a menu, or scheduling vacations. Based on the conditions described, you are asked to draw logical conclusions about the situation. An LSAT Analytical Reasoning section contains 4 to 5 problem sets, with 5 to 7 questions per set for a total of 22 to 24 questions per section. Here are the directions for this question type and two sample items:

> **Directions:** Each group of questions is based on a set of propositions or conditions. Drawing a rough picture or diagram may help in answering some of the questions. Choose the best answer for each question and blacken the corresponding space on your answer sheet.

Questions 4 and 5

Five people, P, Q, R, S, and T, are standing single file in a ticket line. All are facing the ticket window.

Q is the second person behind P.
P is not the second person in the line.
R is somewhere ahead of S.

4. T could occupy all of the following positions in the line EXCEPT

   (A) 1

   (B) 2

   (C) 3

   (D) 4

   (E) 5

The correct answer is (C), as shown by the following reasoning. The initial conditions establish that Q is behind P separated by one person, an arrangement that can be shown as P →? → Q. And because P cannot be the second person in line, only two arrangements are possible for Q and P:

1	2	3	4	5
P		Q		
or		P		Q

With these as the only two possibilities, either Q or P must be third in line, which means no one else can be third. Therefore, T cannot stand in the third position.

NOTE

What other kinds of questions will there be on the LSAT? What you see is what you get. The questions on these pages show you what you'll find.

5. If R is the fourth person in line, which of the following must be true?
    (A) T is the second person in line.
    (B) Q is the second person in line.
    (C) P is the third person in line.
    (D) S is the third person in line.
    (E) Q is the fifth person in line.

The correct answer is (A). Here we are given additional information to use in answering this item. Given that R is the fourth in line, since R is ahead of S, S must be fifth in line.

1	2	3	4	5
			R	S

This forces P and Q into positions 1 and 3:

1	2	3	4	5
P		Q	R	S

Finally, T must be second in line:

1	2	3	4	5
P	T	Q	R	S

WHAT IS THE WRITING SAMPLE?

The LSAT Writing Sample is a 30-minute exercise administered at the end of the test. For the Writing Sample, you are given a situation in which a choice must be made between two possible courses of action. You must write an argument in favor of either one of the two given choices. In each case, either course of action can be taken. The idea of the exercise is to support the course you choose with reasoned arguments and a well-written essay, given the time constraints. You are given a page of lined paper on which to write your essay.

PART II

Answer Sheet

Use a No. 2 pencil only. Be sure each mark is dark and completely fills the intended oval. Completely erase any errors or stray marks. Start with number 1 for each new section. If a section has fewer than 30 questions, leave the extra answer spaces blank.

SECTION 1	SECTION 2	SECTION 3	SECTION 4	SECTION 5
1 Ⓐ Ⓑ Ⓒ Ⓓ Ⓔ	1 Ⓐ Ⓑ Ⓒ Ⓓ Ⓔ	1 Ⓐ Ⓑ Ⓒ Ⓓ Ⓔ	1 Ⓐ Ⓑ Ⓒ Ⓓ Ⓔ	1 Ⓐ Ⓑ Ⓒ Ⓓ Ⓔ
2 Ⓐ Ⓑ Ⓒ Ⓓ Ⓔ	2 Ⓐ Ⓑ Ⓒ Ⓓ Ⓔ	2 Ⓐ Ⓑ Ⓒ Ⓓ Ⓔ	2 Ⓐ Ⓑ Ⓒ Ⓓ Ⓔ	2 Ⓐ Ⓑ Ⓒ Ⓓ Ⓔ
3 Ⓐ Ⓑ Ⓒ Ⓓ Ⓔ	3 Ⓐ Ⓑ Ⓒ Ⓓ Ⓔ	3 Ⓐ Ⓑ Ⓒ Ⓓ Ⓔ	3 Ⓐ Ⓑ Ⓒ Ⓓ Ⓔ	3 Ⓐ Ⓑ Ⓒ Ⓓ Ⓔ
4 Ⓐ Ⓑ Ⓒ Ⓓ Ⓔ	4 Ⓐ Ⓑ Ⓒ Ⓓ Ⓔ	4 Ⓐ Ⓑ Ⓒ Ⓓ Ⓔ	4 Ⓐ Ⓑ Ⓒ Ⓓ Ⓔ	4 Ⓐ Ⓑ Ⓒ Ⓓ Ⓔ
5 Ⓐ Ⓑ Ⓒ Ⓓ Ⓔ	5 Ⓐ Ⓑ Ⓒ Ⓓ Ⓔ	5 Ⓐ Ⓑ Ⓒ Ⓓ Ⓔ	5 Ⓐ Ⓑ Ⓒ Ⓓ Ⓔ	5 Ⓐ Ⓑ Ⓒ Ⓓ Ⓔ
6 Ⓐ Ⓑ Ⓒ Ⓓ Ⓔ	6 Ⓐ Ⓑ Ⓒ Ⓓ Ⓔ	6 Ⓐ Ⓑ Ⓒ Ⓓ Ⓔ	6 Ⓐ Ⓑ Ⓒ Ⓓ Ⓔ	6 Ⓐ Ⓑ Ⓒ Ⓓ Ⓔ
7 Ⓐ Ⓑ Ⓒ Ⓓ Ⓔ	7 Ⓐ Ⓑ Ⓒ Ⓓ Ⓔ	7 Ⓐ Ⓑ Ⓒ Ⓓ Ⓔ	7 Ⓐ Ⓑ Ⓒ Ⓓ Ⓔ	7 Ⓐ Ⓑ Ⓒ Ⓓ Ⓔ
8 Ⓐ Ⓑ Ⓒ Ⓓ Ⓔ	8 Ⓐ Ⓑ Ⓒ Ⓓ Ⓔ	8 Ⓐ Ⓑ Ⓒ Ⓓ Ⓔ	8 Ⓐ Ⓑ Ⓒ Ⓓ Ⓔ	8 Ⓐ Ⓑ Ⓒ Ⓓ Ⓔ
9 Ⓐ Ⓑ Ⓒ Ⓓ Ⓔ	9 Ⓐ Ⓑ Ⓒ Ⓓ Ⓔ	9 Ⓐ Ⓑ Ⓒ Ⓓ Ⓔ	9 Ⓐ Ⓑ Ⓒ Ⓓ Ⓔ	9 Ⓐ Ⓑ Ⓒ Ⓓ Ⓔ
10 Ⓐ Ⓑ Ⓒ Ⓓ Ⓔ	10 Ⓐ Ⓑ Ⓒ Ⓓ Ⓔ	10 Ⓐ Ⓑ Ⓒ Ⓓ Ⓔ	10 Ⓐ Ⓑ Ⓒ Ⓓ Ⓔ	10 Ⓐ Ⓑ Ⓒ Ⓓ Ⓔ
11 Ⓐ Ⓑ Ⓒ Ⓓ Ⓔ	11 Ⓐ Ⓑ Ⓒ Ⓓ Ⓔ	11 Ⓐ Ⓑ Ⓒ Ⓓ Ⓔ	11 Ⓐ Ⓑ Ⓒ Ⓓ Ⓔ	11 Ⓐ Ⓑ Ⓒ Ⓓ Ⓔ
12 Ⓐ Ⓑ Ⓒ Ⓓ Ⓔ	12 Ⓐ Ⓑ Ⓒ Ⓓ Ⓔ	12 Ⓐ Ⓑ Ⓒ Ⓓ Ⓔ	12 Ⓐ Ⓑ Ⓒ Ⓓ Ⓔ	12 Ⓐ Ⓑ Ⓒ Ⓓ Ⓔ
13 Ⓐ Ⓑ Ⓒ Ⓓ Ⓔ	13 Ⓐ Ⓑ Ⓒ Ⓓ Ⓔ	13 Ⓐ Ⓑ Ⓒ Ⓓ Ⓔ	13 Ⓐ Ⓑ Ⓒ Ⓓ Ⓔ	13 Ⓐ Ⓑ Ⓒ Ⓓ Ⓔ
14 Ⓐ Ⓑ Ⓒ Ⓓ Ⓔ	14 Ⓐ Ⓑ Ⓒ Ⓓ Ⓔ	14 Ⓐ Ⓑ Ⓒ Ⓓ Ⓔ	14 Ⓐ Ⓑ Ⓒ Ⓓ Ⓔ	14 Ⓐ Ⓑ Ⓒ Ⓓ Ⓔ
15 Ⓐ Ⓑ Ⓒ Ⓓ Ⓔ	15 Ⓐ Ⓑ Ⓒ Ⓓ Ⓔ	15 Ⓐ Ⓑ Ⓒ Ⓓ Ⓔ	15 Ⓐ Ⓑ Ⓒ Ⓓ Ⓔ	15 Ⓐ Ⓑ Ⓒ Ⓓ Ⓔ
16 Ⓐ Ⓑ Ⓒ Ⓓ Ⓔ	16 Ⓐ Ⓑ Ⓒ Ⓓ Ⓔ	16 Ⓐ Ⓑ Ⓒ Ⓓ Ⓔ	16 Ⓐ Ⓑ Ⓒ Ⓓ Ⓔ	16 Ⓐ Ⓑ Ⓒ Ⓓ Ⓔ
17 Ⓐ Ⓑ Ⓒ Ⓓ Ⓔ	17 Ⓐ Ⓑ Ⓒ Ⓓ Ⓔ	17 Ⓐ Ⓑ Ⓒ Ⓓ Ⓔ	17 Ⓐ Ⓑ Ⓒ Ⓓ Ⓔ	17 Ⓐ Ⓑ Ⓒ Ⓓ Ⓔ
18 Ⓐ Ⓑ Ⓒ Ⓓ Ⓔ	18 Ⓐ Ⓑ Ⓒ Ⓓ Ⓔ	18 Ⓐ Ⓑ Ⓒ Ⓓ Ⓔ	18 Ⓐ Ⓑ Ⓒ Ⓓ Ⓔ	18 Ⓐ Ⓑ Ⓒ Ⓓ Ⓔ
19 Ⓐ Ⓑ Ⓒ Ⓓ Ⓔ	19 Ⓐ Ⓑ Ⓒ Ⓓ Ⓔ	19 Ⓐ Ⓑ Ⓒ Ⓓ Ⓔ	19 Ⓐ Ⓑ Ⓒ Ⓓ Ⓔ	19 Ⓐ Ⓑ Ⓒ Ⓓ Ⓔ
20 Ⓐ Ⓑ Ⓒ Ⓓ Ⓔ	20 Ⓐ Ⓑ Ⓒ Ⓓ Ⓔ	20 Ⓐ Ⓑ Ⓒ Ⓓ Ⓔ	20 Ⓐ Ⓑ Ⓒ Ⓓ Ⓔ	20 Ⓐ Ⓑ Ⓒ Ⓓ Ⓔ
21 Ⓐ Ⓑ Ⓒ Ⓓ Ⓔ	21 Ⓐ Ⓑ Ⓒ Ⓓ Ⓔ	21 Ⓐ Ⓑ Ⓒ Ⓓ Ⓔ	21 Ⓐ Ⓑ Ⓒ Ⓓ Ⓔ	21 Ⓐ Ⓑ Ⓒ Ⓓ Ⓔ
22 Ⓐ Ⓑ Ⓒ Ⓓ Ⓔ	22 Ⓐ Ⓑ Ⓒ Ⓓ Ⓔ	22 Ⓐ Ⓑ Ⓒ Ⓓ Ⓔ	22 Ⓐ Ⓑ Ⓒ Ⓓ Ⓔ	22 Ⓐ Ⓑ Ⓒ Ⓓ Ⓔ
23 Ⓐ Ⓑ Ⓒ Ⓓ Ⓔ	23 Ⓐ Ⓑ Ⓒ Ⓓ Ⓔ	23 Ⓐ Ⓑ Ⓒ Ⓓ Ⓔ	23 Ⓐ Ⓑ Ⓒ Ⓓ Ⓔ	23 Ⓐ Ⓑ Ⓒ Ⓓ Ⓔ
24 Ⓐ Ⓑ Ⓒ Ⓓ Ⓔ	24 Ⓐ Ⓑ Ⓒ Ⓓ Ⓔ	24 Ⓐ Ⓑ Ⓒ Ⓓ Ⓔ	24 Ⓐ Ⓑ Ⓒ Ⓓ Ⓔ	24 Ⓐ Ⓑ Ⓒ Ⓓ Ⓔ
25 Ⓐ Ⓑ Ⓒ Ⓓ Ⓔ	25 Ⓐ Ⓑ Ⓒ Ⓓ Ⓔ	25 Ⓐ Ⓑ Ⓒ Ⓓ Ⓔ	25 Ⓐ Ⓑ Ⓒ Ⓓ Ⓔ	25 Ⓐ Ⓑ Ⓒ Ⓓ Ⓔ
26 Ⓐ Ⓑ Ⓒ Ⓓ Ⓔ	26 Ⓐ Ⓑ Ⓒ Ⓓ Ⓔ	26 Ⓐ Ⓑ Ⓒ Ⓓ Ⓔ	26 Ⓐ Ⓑ Ⓒ Ⓓ Ⓔ	26 Ⓐ Ⓑ Ⓒ Ⓓ Ⓔ
27 Ⓐ Ⓑ Ⓒ Ⓓ Ⓔ	27 Ⓐ Ⓑ Ⓒ Ⓓ Ⓔ	27 Ⓐ Ⓑ Ⓒ Ⓓ Ⓔ	27 Ⓐ Ⓑ Ⓒ Ⓓ Ⓔ	27 Ⓐ Ⓑ Ⓒ Ⓓ Ⓔ
28 Ⓐ Ⓑ Ⓒ Ⓓ Ⓔ	28 Ⓐ Ⓑ Ⓒ Ⓓ Ⓔ	28 Ⓐ Ⓑ Ⓒ Ⓓ Ⓔ	28 Ⓐ Ⓑ Ⓒ Ⓓ Ⓔ	28 Ⓐ Ⓑ Ⓒ Ⓓ Ⓔ
29 Ⓐ Ⓑ Ⓒ Ⓓ Ⓔ	29 Ⓐ Ⓑ Ⓒ Ⓓ Ⓔ	29 Ⓐ Ⓑ Ⓒ Ⓓ Ⓔ	29 Ⓐ Ⓑ Ⓒ Ⓓ Ⓔ	29 Ⓐ Ⓑ Ⓒ Ⓓ Ⓔ
30 Ⓐ Ⓑ Ⓒ Ⓓ Ⓔ	30 Ⓐ Ⓑ Ⓒ Ⓓ Ⓔ	30 Ⓐ Ⓑ Ⓒ Ⓓ Ⓔ	30 Ⓐ Ⓑ Ⓒ Ⓓ Ⓔ	30 Ⓐ Ⓑ Ⓒ Ⓓ Ⓔ

Diagnostic Test

SECTION I

24 Questions • Time—35 Minutes

Directions: Each group of questions is based on a set of propositions or conditions. Drawing a rough picture or diagram may help in answering some of the questions. Choose the *best* answer for each question and blacken the corresponding space on your answer sheet.

Questions 1–6

The programming manager of a television station is scheduling movies for the upcoming week. The station has seven films, J, K, L, M, N, O, and P. Exactly one of the films will be shown each day, and no film will be shown more than once. The films must be shown in accordance with the following programming restrictions:

K must be shown either Monday or Saturday.
O must be shown on Thursday.
P must be shown on Sunday.
J and L must be shown on consecutive days.
J and N must not be shown on consecutive days.

1. If M is shown on Tuesday, which of the following must be true?
   (A) N is shown on Monday.
   (B) N is shown on Wednesday.
   (C) L is shown on Friday.
   (D) J is shown on Saturday.
   (E) K is shown on Saturday.

2. If J and K are shown on consecutive days, which of the following must be true?
   (A) J is shown on Wednesday.
   (B) K is shown on Saturday.
   (C) L is shown on Wednesday.
   (D) M is shown on Saturday.
   (E) N is shown on Friday.

3. If N is shown on Tuesday, which of the following must be true?
   (A) K is shown on Saturday.
   (B) L is shown on Friday.
   (C) M is shown on Wednesday.
   (D) J is shown on Friday.
   (E) N is shown on Thursday.

4. If K is shown on Saturday, which of the following must be true?
   (A) M is shown on Monday.
   (B) N is shown on Tuesday.
   (C) If N and L are shown on consecutive days, J is shown on Wednesday.
   (D) If J and M are shown on consecutive days, L is shown on Wednesday.
   (E) If K and M are shown on consecutive days, L is shown on Tuesday.

5. If J is not shown on Monday, Tuesday, or Wednesday, which of the following must be true?

   (A) If J is shown on Saturday, M is shown on Wednesday.

   (B) If L is shown on Friday, N is shown on Tuesday.

   (C) If M is shown on Tuesday, J is shown on Friday.

   (D) If M is shown on Wednesday, L is shown on Saturday.

   (E) If N is shown on Wednesday, M is shown on Tuesday.

6. If L is shown on Tuesday, which of the following must be true?

   (A) If M is shown on Monday, N is shown on Friday.

   (B) If K is shown on Monday, M is shown on Friday.

   (C) If K is shown on Saturday, J is shown on Wednesday.

   (D) If N is shown on Friday, J is shown on Wednesday.

   (E) If N is shown on Friday, M is shown on Saturday.

Questions 7–12

Nine people, G, H, J, K, L, M, N, O, and P, are taking part in a parade. They will ride in three cars, the cars forming a line. Three people will sit in each car.

  G and H must ride in the same car.
  J must ride in the second car.
  N and P must ride in the same car.
  K and O must not ride in the same car.
  M must ride in the same car with either O or J or both.

7. Which of the following groups of people could ride together in the same car?

   (A) G, J, and N

   (B) J, L, and O

   (C) K, H, and L

   (D) K, N, and O

   (E) O, N, and P

8. Which of the following CANNOT be true?

   (A) K rides in the first car.

   (B) M rides in the first car.

   (C) N rides in the second car.

   (D) O rides in a car two cars behind M's car.

   (E) L rides in a car two cars behind G's car.

9. If P rides in the second car and O rides in the third car, which of the following must be true?

   (A) G rides in the third car.

   (B) L rides in the first car.

   (C) L rides in the third car.

   (D) M rides in the first car.

   (E) M rides in the second car.

10. All of the following people could ride in the same car as G EXCEPT

    (A) J

    (B) K

    (C) L

    (D) N

    (E) O

11. If G and O are riding in the first car, which of the following people must ride in the second car?

    (A) H

    (B) K

    (C) L

    (D) M

    (E) N

12. If P rides in the same car as J, and if M rides in the third car, who must ride in the first car?

(A) H and O

(B) K and N

(C) O and N

(D) H, K, and G

(E) H, L, and O

Questions 13–18

Seven children, J, K, L, M, N, O, and P, are students at a certain grammar school with grades 1 through 7.

One of these children is in each of the seven grades.

N is in the first grade, and P is in the seventh grade.

L is in a higher grade than K.

J is in a higher grade than M.

O is in a grade somewhere between K and M.

13. If there are exactly two grades between J and O, which of the following must be true?

(A) K is in the second grade.

(B) J is in the sixth grade.

(C) M is in a higher grade than K.

(D) L is in a grade between M and O.

(E) K and L are separated by exactly one grade.

14. If J is in the third grade, which of the following must be true?

(A) K is in grade 4, and L is in grade 5.

(B) K is in grade 5, and O is in grade 6.

(C) L is in grade 4, and M is in grade 6.

(D) M is in grade 2, and K is in grade 5.

(E) O is in grade 4, and L is in grade 5.

15. If K is in the second grade, which of the following is a complete and accurate listing of the students who could be in grade 5?

(A) J

(B) J and M

(C) L and M

(D) L, M, and J

(E) O, L, M, and J

16. If J and N are separated by exactly one grade, which of the following must be true?

(A) L is in grade 6.

(B) L is in grade 3.

(C) K is in a lower grade than J.

(D) K is in a lower grade than O.

(E) O is in a grade between J and N.

17. Which of the following CANNOT be true?

(A) O is in the third grade.

(B) O is in the fourth grade.

(C) O is in the fifth grade.

(D) M is in the fourth grade.

(E) M is in the fifth grade.

18. If L is in the grade immediately ahead of J, the number of logically possible orderings of all seven children, from the lowest grade to the highest grade, is

(A) 1

(B) 2

(C) 3

(D) 4

(E) 5

Questions 19–24

Ten sports car enthusiasts, J, K, L, M, N, O, P, Q, R, and T, participate in a sports car rally in which a series of races are held. Five cars participate in each race, finishing first through fifth, with no ties. Exactly two people ride in each car.

P and M always ride together and never finish last.
L and Q never ride in the same car.
N and O always ride in the same car.
R's car always finishes exactly one place ahead of L's.

19. All of the following lists of pairs of participants, in order of finish from first to last, are possible EXCEPT

(A) J, T; R, Q; K, L; M, P; O, N
(B) P, M; R, T; L, K; J, Q; O, N
(C) K, T; R, Q; J, L; P, M; N, O
(D) O, N; P, M; R, J; L, Q; K, T
(E) O, N; P, M; R, Q; L, T; K, J

20. If the car in which L is riding finishes somewhere ahead of the car in which M is riding and somewhere behind the car in which O is riding, which of the following must be true?

(A) R rides in the first-place car.
(B) J rides in the first-place car.
(C) R rides in the second-place car.
(D) Q rides in the second-place car.
(E) Q rides in the fifth-place car.

21. If N's car finishes second and R's car finishes third, which of the following must be true?

(A) M's car finishes first.
(B) Q's car finishes second.
(C) Q's car finishes fourth.
(D) J's car finishes ahead of K's car.
(E) O's car finishes exactly two places ahead of Q's car.

22. If J and T ride together in a car, and if L's car finishes fourth, which of the following must be true?

(A) P's car finishes first.
(B) N's car finishes second.
(C) Q's car finishes third.
(D) M's car finishes fourth.
(E) N's car finishes fifth.

23. If L, O, and T ride in cars finishing second, third, and last, respectively, and if J and R ride in the same car, which of the following must be true?

(A) P's car finishes first.
(B) L's car finishes first.
(C) N's car finishes second.
(D) P's car finishes third.
(E) Q's car finishes last.

24. If P's car finishes third and K and T ride in the same car, Q could be riding in a car that finishes either

(A) first or second.
(B) first or fourth.
(C) first or last.
(D) second or fourth.
(E) second or last.

STOP

END OF SECTION 1. IF YOU HAVE ANY TIME LEFT, GO OVER YOUR WORK IN THIS SECTION ONLY. DO NOT WORK IN ANY OTHER SECTION OF THE TEST.

SECTION 2

28 Questions • Time—35 Minutes

Directions: Below each of the following passages, you will find questions or incomplete statements about the passage. Each statement or question is followed by lettered words or expressions. Select the word or expression that most satisfactorily completes each statement or answers each question in accordance with the meaning of the passage. After you have chosen the *best* answer, blacken the corresponding space on the answer sheet.

Reverse discrimination, minority recruitment, racial quotas and, more generally, affirmative action are phrases that carry powerful emotional charges.
(5) But why should affirmative action, of all government policies, be so controversial? In a sense, affirmative action is like other governmental programs, such as defense, conservation and public schools.
(10) Affirmative action programs are designed to achieve legitimate government objectives such as improved economic efficiency, reduced social tension and general betterment of the public wel-
(15) fare. While it cannot be denied that there is no guarantee that affirmative action will achieve these results, neither can it be denied that there are plausible, even powerful, sociological and economic
(20) arguments pointing to its likely success.

Government programs, however, entail a cost, that is, the expenditure of social or economic resources. Setting aside cases in which the specific user is
(25) charged a fee for service (toll roads and tuition at state institutions), the burdens and benefits of publicly funded or mandated programs are widely shared. When an individual benefits personally
(30) from a government program, it is only because of membership in a larger beneficiary class, for example, a farmer; and most government revenue is obtained through a scheme of general taxation to
(35) which all are subject. Affirmative action programs are exceptions to this general rule, though not, as might at first seem, because the beneficiaries of the programs

are specific individuals. It is still the
(40) case that those who ultimately benefit from affirmative action do so only by virtue of their status as a member of a larger group, a particular minority. Rather, the difference is the location of
(45) the burden. In affirmative action, the burden of "funding" the program is not shared universally, and that is inherent in the nature of the case, as can be seen clearly in the case of affirmative action
(50) in employment. Often job promotions are allocated along a single dimension, seniority; and when an employer promotes a less senior worker from a minority group, the person disadvantaged by
(55) the move is easily identified: the worker with greatest seniority on a combined minority–non-minority list passed over for promotion.

Now we are confronted with two
(60) competing moral sentiments. On the one hand, there is the idea that those who have been unfairly disadvantaged by past discriminatory practices are entitled to some kind of assistance. On the
(65) other, there is the feeling that people ought not to be deprived of what is rightfully theirs, even for the worthwhile service of other humans. In this respect, disability due to past racial discrimina-
(70) tion, at least insofar as there is no connection to the passed-over worker, is like a natural evil. When a villainous person willfully and without provocation strikes and injures another, there is
(75) not only the feeling that the injured person ought to be compensated but

there is consensus that the appropriate party to bear the cost is the one who inflicted the injury. Yet, if the same (80) innocent person stumbled and was injured, it would be surprising to hear someone argue that the villainous person ought to be taxed for the injury simply because the villainous person (85) might have tripped the victim had there been the opportunity. There may very well be agreement that the injured person should be aided with money and personal assistance, and many will give (90) willingly; but there is also agreement that no one individual ought to be singled out and forced to do what must ultimately be considered an act of charity.

1. The passage is primarily concerned with

   (A) comparing affirmative action programs to other government programs.

   (B) arguing that affirmative action programs are morally justified.

   (C) analyzing the basis for moral judgments about affirmative action programs.

   (D) introducing the reader to the importance of affirmative action as a social issue.

   (E) describing the benefits that can be obtained through affirmative action programs.

2. The author mentions toll roads and tuition at state institutions (lines 25–26) in order to

   (A) anticipate a possible objection on counterexamples.

   (B) avoid a contradiction between moral sentiments.

   (C) provide illustrations of common government programs.

   (D) voice doubts about the social and economic value of affirmative action.

   (E) offer examples of government programs that are too costly.

3. With which of the following statements would the author most likely agree?

   (A) Affirmative action programs should be discontinued because they place an unfair burden on non-minority persons who bear the cost of the programs.

   (B) Affirmative action programs may be able to achieve legitimate social and economic goals such as improved efficiency.

   (C) Affirmative action programs are justified because they are the only way of correcting injustices created by past discrimination.

   (D) Affirmative action programs must be redesigned so that society as a whole rather than particular individuals bears the cost of the programs.

   (E) Affirmative action programs should be abandoned because they serve no useful social function and place unfair burdens on particular individuals.

4. The author most likely places the word "funding" in quotation marks (line 46) in order to remind the reader that

   (A) affirmative action programs are costly in terms of government revenues.

   (B) particular individuals may bear a disproportionate share of the burden of affirmative action.

   (C) the cost of most government programs is shared by society at large.

   (D) the beneficiaries of affirmative action are members of larger groups.

   (E) the cost of affirmative action is not only a monetary expenditure.

5. The "villainous person" discussed in line 72 functions primarily as
   (A) an illustration.
   (B) a counterexample.
   (C) an authority.
   (D) an analogy.
   (E) a disclaimer.

6. According to the passage, affirmative action programs are different from most other government programs in the
   (A) legitimacy of the goals the programs are designed to achieve.
   (B) ways in which costs of the programs are distributed.
   (C) methods for allocating the benefits of the programs.
   (D) legal structures that are enacted to achieve the objectives.
   (E) discretion granted to the executive for implementing the programs.

7. It can be inferred that the author believes the reader will regard affirmative action programs as
   (A) posing a moral dilemma.
   (B) based on unsound premises.
   (C) containing self-contradictions.
   (D) creating needless suffering.
   (E) offering a panacea.

8. The primary purpose of the passage is to
   (A) reconcile two conflicting points of view.
   (B) describe and refute a point of view.
   (C) provide a historical context for a problem.
   (D) suggest a new method for studying social problems.
   (E) analyze the structure of an institution.

The number of aged in Sweden is one of the largest in the world, close to 14 percent of the total population, and the need for health and social support for
(5) them has been intensified by improvements in the standard of living. Life expectancy has increased and at the same time there is a greater unwillingness on the part of adult offspring to care
(10) for aged parents living in their households. The percentage of aged persons living with their children a decade ago was approximately 10 in Sweden (3 in Stockholm), contrasted with 20 in Den-
(15) mark, 30 in the United States, 40 in England, 70 in Poland, and 90 in Russia. Sweden placed a moratorium on the construction of new acute beds in favor of long-term beds, but that has foun-
(20) dered because care in a long-stay facility, if done correctly, while less costly than an acute facility, may still be prohibitively expensive.

Payroll is the single most impor-
(25) tant budgetary component in all branches of hospital service, accounting for over 60 percent of total costs; and the staff-bed ratio requirements for the chronic aged are higher than for acute
(30) patients, especially with respect to nursing and rehabilitation personnel. Payroll expenditures have grown sizably as the result of advancing standards of industrial justice which challenge the
(35) validity of the traditional idea that health workers other than doctors should work for lower wages than persons doing comparable work elsewhere in the economy because of the eleemosynary and hu-
(40) manitarian ethic of patient care. The progress of women in securing greater parity with men in income and employment opportunities are especially notable in the health field where women
(45) who comprise roughly three-fourths of the labor force have been concentrated disproportionately in low-paying and low-status jobs.

In nearly all highly developed coun-
(50) tries recently the policy has been to bring the wages of low-income hospital workers into line with those in industry

and manufacturing. Even so, the conditions of employment are unattractive
(55) and staffing remains a problem, especially during off hours, weekends, and
summers when people prefer to be with
their families or on vacation. The magnitude of these problems is greater in
(60) long-stay than in short-stay facilities,
because of the differences in prestige
and responsiveness of patients to intervention.

Paradoxically, the cutbacks in
(65) long-term care spending in Sweden may
have contributed to an improvement in
treatment outcomes. Patients have been
required to take maximum responsibility for their own care, and this has less-
(70) ened dependency and fostered rehabilitation. A similar principle of self-care
applies to the treatment of the mentally
retarded and the aged. In addition to the
patient care benefits, significant econo-
(75) mies can be obtained, demonstrating
that the two objectives are not necessarily incompatible. The medical director of
a large-sized long-term care facility has
found that in the case of the aged over
(80) 80, multiple-patient rooms are better
than single-patient rooms. Older and
mentally disoriented patients are much
quieter when they have roommates, and
because of the tendency of people to help
(85) one another, they require less staff time.
Staff time per patient is directly correlated to the number of beds in the room,
decreasing from 217 minutes for single
room to 99 minutes for four-bed rooms.
(90) Many new long-term hospitals for the
psychogeriatrics of advanced age are
being designed for four to five beds per
room. The reaction to resource scarcity
has resulted in unexpected contribu-
(95) tions to patient welfare.

9. It can be inferred from the passage that
the increasing number of aged requiring
care prompted Sweden to

(A) shift funds from construction of facilities for care of the acutely ill to projects
to build facilities for long-term care.

(B) restructure its tax laws to penalize
families who refused to provide
in-house care for their aging relatives.

(C) attempt to reduce long-term care costs
by depressing salaries of hospital
workers and delaying wage increases.

(D) crowding four or five patients into a
room designed for only one patient in
order to reduce payroll costs.

(E) discontinue construction of long-term
hospitals for the psychogeriatrics of
the aged.

10. All of the following are mentioned in the
passage as difficulties in staffing long-stay
facilities EXCEPT

(A) the low prestige of such jobs.

(B) the relatively low rate of pay.

(C) the character of the patient population.

(D) the inconvenient work schedules.

(E) the large number of weekly hours.

11. It can be inferred from the passage that
pay rates in the health field have historically been lower than those for manufacturing and industry because

(A) jobs in the health field have a lower
status.

(B) service in the health field was considered charitable work.

(C) doctors insisted on receiving higher
salaries than other workers.

(D) labor costs are the greatest category
of expenditures for hospitals.

(E) aged people are not able to pay high
fees for long-term care.

12. It can be inferred from the passage that the staff/bed cost of long-stay care in Sweden is

(A) greater than that for acute care.

(B) increasing less rapidly than that for acute care.

(C) unrelated to the number of persons being cared for.

(D) borne primarily by the individual patient.

(E) less than in other countries such as England and the United States.

13. The author refers to the results of cutbacks in long-term care spending as "paradoxical" because

(A) cutbacks in expenditures ordinarily result in worse care.

(B) the longer a patient lives, the greater is the need for care.

(C) fewer adult offspring are willing to care for aged parents in their own homes.

(D) reduced staffing needs mean fewer positions for hospital workers.

(E) reductions in spending placed a moratorium on new construction.

14. Which of the following, if true, would most strengthen the author's contention that improvements in the standard of living increase the reluctance of adults to care for aged parents?

(A) The United States has a higher standard of living than Sweden.

(B) Stockholm has a substantially higher standard of living than the rest of Sweden.

(C) The number of long-term care beds in England has not increased appreciably in the past five years.

(D) Sweden has fewer aged persons than Denmark.

(E) Sweden has a higher acute to long-term beds ratio than Russia.

Can computers reason? Reasoning requires the individual to take a given set of facts and draw correct conclusions. Unfortunately, errors frequently occur, (5) and we are not talking about simple carelessness as occurs when two numbers are incorrectly added, nor do we mean errors resulting from simple forgetfulness. Rather, we have in mind (10) errors of a logical nature—those resulting from faulty reasoning. Now, or at least soon, computers will be capable of error-free logical reasoning in a variety of areas. The key to avoiding errors is to (15) use a computer program that relies on the last two decades' research in the field of automated theorem proving. AURA (Automated Reasoning Assistant) is the program that best exemplifies this (20) use of the computer.

AURA solves a problem by drawing conclusions from a given set of facts about the problem. The program does not learn, nor is it self-analytical, but it (25) reaches logical conclusions flawlessly. It uses various types of reasoning and, more important, has access to very powerful and sophisticated logical strategies. AURA seldom relies on brute force (30) to find solutions. Instead it solves almost all problems by using sophisticated techniques to find a contradiction. One generally starts with a set of assumptions and adds a statement that (35) the goal is unreachable. For example, if the problem is to test a safety system that automatically shuts down a nuclear reactor when instruments indicate a problem, AURA is told that the system (40) will not shut the reactor down under those circumstances. If AURA finds a contradiction between the statement and the system's design assumptions, then this aspect of the reactor's design has (45) been proved satisfactory. This strategy, known as the set of support strategy, lets AURA concentrate on the problem at hand and avoid the many fruitless steps required to explore the entire (50) theory underlying the problem. Almost never does the program proceed by carrying out an exhaustive search. The chief

use for AURA at this time is for electronic circuit design validation, but a
(55) number of other uses will arise. For example, there already exist "expert systems" that include a component for reasoning. An expert system is a special-purpose program designed to au-
(60) tomate reasoning in a specific area such as medical diagnosis. These expert programs, unlike human experts, do not die. Such systems continue to improve and have an indefinite life span. More-
(65) over, they can be replicated for pennies. A human who can expertly predict where to drill for oil is in great demand. A program that can predict equally well would be invaluable and could be dupli-
(70) cated any number of times.

     Will the computer replace the human being? Certainly not. It seems likely that computer programs will reproduce—that is, design more clever
(75) computer programs and more efficient, more useful components. Reasoning programs will also analyze their own progress, learn from their attempts to solve a problem, and redirect their at-
(80) tack on a problem. Such programs will assist, rather than replace, humans. Their impact will be felt in design, manufacturing, law, medicine, and other areas. Reasoning assistants will enable
(85) human minds to turn to deeper and far more complex ideas. These ideas will be partially formulated and then checked for reasoning flaws by a reasoning program. Many errors will be avoided.

15. According to the passage, the primary purpose of AURA is to

  (A) design new and easily replicated programs.

  (B) function as a safety mechanism in nuclear reactors.

  (C) detect contradictions and other faults in computer programs.

  (D) develop expert human programs for technical fields.

  (E) check human reasoning for possible errors.

16. Which of the following titles best describes the content of the passage?

  (A) "Scientific Applications of Computers"

  (B) "Theories of Artificial Intelligence"

  (C) "Some Suggested Applications for AURA"

  (D) "Using Computers to Assist Human Reasoning"

  (E) "The Dangers of Automated Reasoning Assistants"

17. According to the passage, all of the following are advantages of expert programs EXCEPT

  (A) they have an indefinite life span.

  (B) they cost little to reproduce.

  (C) many copies can be made available.

  (D) they are self-analytical.

  (E) more knowledge can be added to them.

18. The author mentions all of the following as areas for applying AURA EXCEPT

  (A) electronic engineering.

  (B) nuclear engineering.

  (C) mathematic and formal logic.

  (D) medical diagnosis.

  (E) petroleum exploration.

19. If the design of an electronic circuit were tested by AURA, and the conclusion that under certain circumstances a switching device would remain open generated a contradiction, this would lead to the conclusion that

  (A) the circuit was properly designed.

  (B) the switch would remain closed under the circumstances.

  (C) the switch would remain open under the circumstances.

  (D) an error in human reasoning invalidated the design.

  (E) the circuit was incorrectly designed.

20. The author's attitude toward the developments he describes can best be described as

(A) enthusiastic.

(B) reluctant.

(C) cautious.

(D) skeptical.

(E) worried.

21. The author is primarily concerned to

(A) discuss recent developments.

(B) correct a misconception.

(C) propose a theory.

(D) refute an objection.

(E) recommend a solution.

Until Josquin des Prez, 1440–1521, Western music was liturgical, designed as an accompaniment to worship. Like the intricately carved gargoyles perched
(5) atop medieval cathedrals beyond sight of any human, music was composed to please God before anybody else; its dominant theme was reverence. Emotion was there, but it was the grief of Mary stand-
(10) ing at the foot of the Cross, the joy of the faithful hailing Christ's resurrection. Even the secular music of the Middle Ages was tied to predetermined patterns that sometimes seemed to stand in
(15) the way of individual expression.

While keeping one foot firmly planted in the divine world, Josquin stepped with the other into the human. He scored magnificent masses, but also
(20) newly expressive motets such as the lament of David over his son Absalom or the "Deploration d' Ockeghem," a dirge on the death of Ockeghem, the greatest master before Josquin, a motet written
(25) all in black notes, and one of the most profoundly moving scores of the Renaissance. Josquin was the first composer to set psalms to music. But alongside *Benedicite omnia opera Domini Domino*
(30) ("Bless the Lord, all ye works of the Lord") he put *El Grillo* ("The cricket is a good singer who manages long poems")

and *Allegez moi* ("Solace me, sweet pleasant brunette"). Josquin was praised by
(35) Martin Luther, for his music blends respect for tradition with a rebel's willingness to risk the horizon. What Galileo was to science, Josquin was to music. While preserving their allegiance to God,
(40) both asserted a new importance for man.

Why then should Josquin languish in relative obscurity? The answer has to do with the separation of concept from performance in music. In fine art, con-
(45) cept and performance are one; both the art lover and the art historian have thousands of years of paintings, drawings and sculptures to study and enjoy. Similarly with literature: Poetry, fic-
(50) tion, drama, and criticism survive on the printed page or in manuscript for judgment and admiration by succeeding generations. But musical notation on a page is not art, no matter how lofty or excel-
(55) lent the composer's conception; it is, crudely put, a set of directions for producing art. Being highly symbolic, musical notation requires training before it can even be read, let alone performed.
(60) Moreover, because the musical conventions of other days are not ours, translation of a Renaissance score into modern notation brings difficulties of its own. For example, the Renaissance notation
(65) of Josquin's day did not designate the tempo at which the music should be played or sung. It did not indicate all flats or sharps; these were sounded in accordance with musicianly rules, which
(70) were capable of transforming major to minor, minor to major, diatonic to chromatic sound, and thus affect melody, harmony, and musical expression. A Renaissance composition might include
(75) several parts—but it did not indicate which were to be sung, which to be played, nor even whether instruments were to be used at all.

Thus, Renaissance notation per-
(80) mits of several interpretations and an imaginative musician may give an interpretation that is a revelation. But no matter how imaginative, few modern musicians can offer any interpretation

(85) of Renaissance music. The public for it is small, limiting the number of musicians who can afford to learn, rehearse, and perform it. Most of those who attempt it at all are students organized in *collegia* *(90)* *musica* whose memberships have a distressing habit of changing every semester, thus preventing directors from maintaining the year-in, year-out continuity required to achieve excellence *(95)* of performance. Finally, the instruments used in Renaissance times—drummhorns, recorders, rauschpfeifen, shawms, sackbuts, organettos—must be specially procured.

22. The primary purpose of the passage is to

    (A) introduce the reader to Josquin and account for his relative obscurity.

    (B) describe the main features of medieval music and show how Josquin changed them.

    (C) place Josquin's music in an historical context and show its influence on later composers.

    (D) enumerate the features of Josquin's music and supply critical commentary.

    (E) praise the music of Josquin and interest the reader in further study of medieval music.

23. The passage contains information that would help answer all of the following questions EXCEPT which of the following?

    (A) What are the titles of some of Josquin's secular compositions?

    (B) What are the names of some Renaissance musical instruments?

    (C) Who was the greatest composer before Josquin?

    (D) Where might it be possible to hear Renaissance music performed?

    (E) What are the names of some of Josquin's most famous students?

24. The passage implies that all of the following are characteristics of modern musical notation EXCEPT which of the following?

    (A) The tempo at which a composition is to be played is indicated in the notation.

    (B) Whether a note is sharp or flat is indicated in the notation.

    (C) The notation indicates which parts of the music are to be played by which instruments.

    (D) Whether a piece is in a major or minor key is clearly indicated.

    (E) The notion leaves no room for interpretation by the musician.

25. The author would most likely agree with which of the following statements?

    (A) Music is a more perfect art form than painting or sculpture.

    (B) Music can be said to exist only when it is being performed.

    (C) Josquin was the greatest composer of the Middle Ages.

    (D) Renaissance music is superior to music produced in modern times.

    (E) Most people dislike Josquin because they do not understand his music.

26. The passage leads most logically to a proposal to

    (A) establish more *collegia musica*.

    (B) study Josquin's compositional techniques in greater detail.

    (C) include Renaissance music in college studies.

    (D) provide funds for musicians to study and play Josquin.

    (E) translate Josquin's music into modern notation.

27. The author cites all of the following as reasons for Josquin's relative obscurity EXCEPT

(A) the difficulty one encounters in attempting to read his musical notation.

(B) the inability of modern musicians to play instruments of the Renaissance.

(C) the difficulty of procuring unusual instruments needed to play the music.

(D) the lack of public interest in Renaissance music.

(E) problems in finding funding for the study of Renaissance music.

28. The author's attitude toward Galileo can best be described as

(A) admiring.

(B) critical.

(C) accepting.

(D) analytical.

(E) noncommittal.

STOP

END OF SECTION 2. IF YOU HAVE ANY TIME LEFT, GO OVER YOUR WORK IN THIS SECTION ONLY. DO NOT WORK IN ANY OTHER SECTION OF THE TEST.

SECTION 3

25 Questions • Time—35 Minutes

> **Directions:** In this section, the questions ask you to analyze and evaluate the reasoning in short paragraphs or passages. For some questions, all of the answer choices may conceivably be answers to the question asked. You should select the *best* answer to the question; that is, an answer that does not require you to make assumptions that violate commonsense standards by being implausible, redundant, irrelevant, or inconsistent. After you have chosen the *best* answer, blacken the corresponding space on the answer sheet.

1. All of the following conclusions are based upon accurate expense vouchers submitted by employees to department heads of a certain corporation in 2003. Which of them is LEAST likely to be weakened by the discovery of additional 2003 expense vouchers?

   (A) The accounting department had only 15 employees and claimed expenses of at least $500.

   (B) The sales department had at least 25 employees and claimed expenses of at least $35,000.

   (C) The legal department had at least 2 employees and claimed no more than $3,000 in expenses.

   (D) The public relations department had no more than 1 employee and claimed no more than $200 in expenses.

   (E) The production department had no more than 500 employees and claimed no more than $350 in expenses.

2. Mr. Mayor, when is the city government going to stop discriminating against its Hispanic residents in the delivery of critical municipal services?

   The form of the question above is most nearly paralleled by which of the following?

   (A) Mr. Congressman, when is the Congress finally going to realize that defense spending is out of hand?

   (B) Madam Chairperson, do you anticipate the committee will take luncheon recess?

   (C) Dr. Greentree, what do you expect to be the impact of the Governor's proposals on the economically disadvantaged counties of our state?

   (D) Gladys, since you're going to the grocery store anyway, would you mind picking up a quart of milk for me?

   (E) Counselor, does the company you represent find that its affirmative action program is successful in recruiting qualified minority employees?

3. The main ingredient in this bottle of Dr. John's Milk of Magnesia is used by nine out of ten hospitals across the country as an antacid and laxative.

If this advertising claim is true, which of the following statements must also be true?

(A) Nine out of ten hospitals across the country use Dr. John's Milk of Magnesia for some ailments.

(B) Only one out of ten hospitals in the country does not treat acid indigestion and constipation.

(C) Only one out of ten hospitals across the country does not recommend Dr. John's Milk of Magnesia for patients who need a milk of magnesia.

(D) Only one of ten hospitals across the country uses a patent medicine other than Dr. John's Milk of Magnesia as an antacid and laxative.

(E) Nine out of ten hospitals across the country use the main ingredient in Dr. John's Milk of Magnesia as an antacid and laxative.

Questions 4 and 5

(1) All wheeled conveyances that travel on the highway are polluters.

(2) Bicycles are not polluters.

(3) Whenever I drive my car on the highway, it rains.

(4) It is raining.

4. If the above statements are all true, which of the following statements must also be true?

(A) Bicycles do not travel on the highway.

(B) Bicycles travel on the highway only if it is raining.

(C) If my car is not polluting, then it is not raining.

(D) I am now driving on the highway.

(E) My car is not a polluter.

5. The conclusion "my car is not polluting" could be logically deduced from statements (1)–(4) if statement

(A) (1) were changed to "Bicycles are polluters."

(B) (2) were changed to "My car is a polluter."

(C) (3) were changed to "If bicycles were polluters, I would be driving my car on the highway."

(D) (4) were changed to "Rainwater is polluted."

(E) (4) were changed to "It is not raining"

6. Statistics published by the U.S. Department of Transportation show that nearly 80 percent of all traffic fatalities occur at speeds of under 50 miles per hour and within 25 miles of home. Therefore, you are safer in a car if you are driving at a speed over 50 miles per hour and not within a 25-mile radius of your home.

Which of the following, if true, most weakens the conclusion of the argument above?

(A) Teenage drivers are involved in 75 percent of all traffic accidents resulting in fatalities.

(B) Eighty percent of all persons arrested for driving at a speed over the posted speed limit are intoxicated.

(C) Fifty percent of the nation's annual traffic fatalities occur on six weekends that are considered high-risk weekends because they contain holidays.

(D) The Department of Transportation statistics were based on police reports compiled by the 50 states.

(E) Ninety percent of all driving time is registered within a 25-mile radius of the driver's home and at speeds less than 50 miles per hour.

7. Usually when we have had an inch or more of rain in a single day, my backyard immediately has mushrooms and other forms of fungus growing in it. There are no mushrooms or fungus growing in my backyard.

Which of the following would logically complete an argument with the premises given above?

(A) Therefore, there has been no rain here in the past day.

(B) Therefore, there probably has been no rain here in the past day.

(C) Therefore, we have not had more than an inch of rain here in the past day.

(D) Therefore, we probably have not had more than an inch of rain here in the past day.

(E) Therefore, mushroom and fungus will be growing in my backyard tomorrow.

Questions 8 and 9

Can you really have that body you want without a monotonous program of daily exercise? Is there really an exercise routine that will help you to shed that fat quickly and painlessly? Now, a university study shows that this is possible. Surely, you would not want to miss a chance to find out whether you can have that body once again. Try the new Jack Remain's twice-a-week workout—and judge for yourself.

8. Which of the following conclusions can be completely justified assuming that the statements made are true?

(A) Only Jack Remain's program offers the possibility for effortless weight loss.

(B) Exercise experts have developed a program to help people of all ages lose weight.

(C) Following Jack Remain's twice-a-week workout program might help you to lose weight.

(D) If you follow Jack Remain's twice-a-week workout program, you will lose weight.

(E) Most people must exercise in order to lose weight.

9. The method of persuasion used by the advertisement can be described as

(A) providing evidence and allowing the listener to arrive at his or her own conclusions.

(B) presenting the reader with a logical set of premises and inviting the reader to draw a further conclusion.

(C) presenting both sides of an issue while carefully avoiding influencing the reader's decision.

(D) asking that the reader provide evidence to test the truth of the claims made in the advertisement.

(E) attempting to convince the reader that similar claims made by others are false.

10. I recently read a book by an author who insists that everything a person does is economically motivated. Leaders launch wars of conquest in order to capture the wealth of other nations. Scientists do research in order to receive grants or find marketable processes. Students go to college to get better jobs. The author even maintains that people go to museums to become better informed on the off-chance that some day they will be able to turn that knowledge to their advantage. So persuaded was I by the author's evidence that, applying the theory on my own, I was able to conclude that the author had written the book _____ .

Which of the following provides the most logical completion of the above paragraph?

(A) as a labor of love

(B) in order to make money

(C) as a means of reforming the world

(D) as an exercise in scientific research

(E) in response to a creative urge to be a novelist

11. In our investigation of this murder, we are guided by our previous experience with the East End Killer. You will recall that in that case, the victims were also carrying a great deal of money when they were killed but the money was not taken. As in this case, the murder weapon was a pistol. Finally, in that case also, the murders were committed between six in the evening and twelve midnight. So we are probably after someone who looks very much like the East End Killer, who was finally tried, convicted, and executed: 5'11" tall, a mustache, short brown hair, walks with a slight limp.

The author makes which of the following assumptions?

(A) Crimes similar in detail are likely to be committed by perpetrators who are similar in physical appearance.

(B) The East End Killer has apparently escaped from prison and has resumed his criminal activities.

(C) The man first convicted as the East End Killer was actually innocent, and the real East End Killer is still loose.

(D) Serial killers usually do not take money or personal property from their victims.

(E) Serial killers are more likely to use a firearm than a knife or a blunt instrument.

12. (1) Everyone who has not read the report either has no opinion in the matter or holds a wrong opinion about it.

    (2) Everyone who holds no opinion in the matter has not read the report.

    Which of the following best describes the relationship between the two above propositions?

    (A) If (2) is true, (1) may be either false or true.

    (B) If (2) is true, (1) must also be true.

    (C) If (2) is true, (1) is likely to be true.

    (D) If (1) is true, (2) must also be true.

    (E) If (1) is false, (2) must also be false.

13. The idea that women should be police officers is absurd. After all, women are on the average three to five inches shorter than men and weigh 20 to 50 pounds less. It is clear that a woman would be less effective than a man in a situation requiring force.

    Which of the following, if true, would most weaken the above argument?

    (A) Some of the female applicants for the police force are larger than some of the male officers presently on the force.

    (B) Police officers are required to go through an intensive eighteen-month training program.

    (C) Police officers are required to carry pistols and are trained in the use of their weapons.

    (D) There are a significant number of desk jobs in the police force that women could fill.

    (E) Many criminals are women.

14. No sophomores were selected for Rho Rho Phi. Some sophomores are members of the Debating Society. Therefore, some members of the Debating Society were not selected for Rho Rho Phi.

    Which of the following is logically most similar to the argument given above?

    (A) Everyone who exercises in the heat will get ill. I never exercise in the heat, so I will probably never be ill.

    (B) Drivers who wish to avoid expensive automobile repairs will have their cars tuned up regularly. My uncle refuses to have his car tuned up regularly. Therefore, he enjoys paying for major repairs.

    (C) Some books that are beautiful were written in French, and French literature is well respected. Therefore, any book that is beautiful is well respected.

    (D) All pets are excluded from this apartment complex. But many pets are valuable. Therefore, some valuable animals are excluded from this apartment complex.

    (E) St. Paul is a long way from London. Minneapolis is a long way from London. Therefore, St. Paul is a long, long way from Minneapolis.

15. All Burrahobbits are Trollbeaters, and some Burrahobbits are Greeblegrabbers.

    If these statements are true, which of the following must also be true?

    (A) If something is neither a Trollbeater nor a Greeblegrabber, it cannot be a Burrahobbit.

    (B) It is not possible to be a Trollbeater without being a Greeblegrabber.

    (C) An elf must be either a Trollbeater or a Greeblegrabber.

    (D) No Greeblegrabbers are Trollbeaters.

    (E) No Burrahobbits are Trollbeaters.

16. If the batteries in my electric razor are dead, the razor will not function. My razor is not functioning. Therefore, the batteries must be dead.

Which of the following arguments is most similar to that presented above?

(A) If Elroy attends the meeting, Ms. Barker will be elected club president. Ms. Barker was not elected club president; therefore, Elroy did not attend the meeting.

(B) All evidence is admissible unless it is tainted. This evidence is inadmissible. Therefore, it is tainted.

(C) If John committed the crime, his fingerprints will be found at the scene. John's fingerprints were found at the scene; therefore, John committed the crime.

(D) Grant is my uncle. Sophie is Grant's niece. Therefore, Sophie is my sister.

(E) Jonathan will wear his dark glasses if the coast is clear. The coast is clear. Therefore, Jonathan will wear his dark glasses.

17. All general statements are based solely on observed instances of a phenomenon. That the statement has held true up to a certain point in time is no guarantee that it will remain unexceptionless. Therefore, no generalization can be considered free from possible exception.

The logic of the above argument can best be described as

(A) self-defeating.

(B) circular.

(C) ill defined.

(D) valid.

(E) inductive.

Questions 18 and 19

The films of Gonzalez have had a lasting impact on motion pictures in this country. By showing what a Mexican-American woman could accomplish as a director, she paved the way for other, more commercially acceptable movie makers of similar backgrounds. Furthermore, by firmly resisting pressure to abandon the political and social themes that are central to her work, she _____ .

18. Which of the following best completes the paragraph above?

(A) demonstrated the remarkable popularity that politically engaged films can have

(B) set an example of integrity for younger, socially conscious filmmakers

(C) revealed the underlying ethnic and social bias so pervasive in the film industry

(D) weakened the chances for later filmmakers to develop similar themes

(E) overcame the obstacles she faced as a member of an oppressed minority group

19. The passage implies that the films of Gonzalez

(A) deal mainly with feminist issues.

(B) have become widely popular.

(C) are generally regarded with favor by film critics and historians.

(D) portray Mexican Americans in a positive light.

(E) were not extremely profitable.

20. Hospital administrators and medical officials often say that bringing spiralling health-care costs under control will require a reduction in the levels of care expected by many groups in our society, particularly the elderly and the chronically ill. And it is true that recent increases in health-care costs have been caused partly by improved levels of care for these groups. But the basic causes of the uncontrolled growth of health-care costs lie elsewhere. Duplication of the most costly services within regions, inefficient allocation of medical expertise and resources, and excessive salaries for some groups of health-care professionals—these are some of the more fundamental problems that must be addressed.

Which of the following conclusions is most strongly supported by the paragraph above?

(A) Controlling the growth of health-care costs need not involve a significant reduction in the level of services for the elderly and chronically ill.

(B) Duplication and inefficient allocation of medical resources are important factors contributing to the increasing cost of health-care services for the elderly and chronically ill.

(C) To control costs in the health-care sector, it will be necessary to reduce the levels of services provided to certain groups.

(D) People who are elderly and/or chronically ill are forced to pay higher prices in order to receive the same quality of health-care services once purchased at a lower price.

(E) Unless immediate action is taken to slow the rate of inflation in the health-care sector, health-care services will be beyond the means of most elderly and chronically ill people.

21. A recent study ranked American cities according to ten different criteria, including among others, the incidence of crime, cost of living, ease of transportation, and cultural amenities. Since San Francisco ranked third overall and Detroit sixth, we can conclude that Detroit has a more serious crime problem than San Francisco.

Which of the following, if true, most weakens the argument above?

(A) The cost of living is higher in Detroit than in San Francisco.

(B) San Francisco ranked higher than Detroit on seven of the ten criteria.

(C) Both Atlanta and Houston, which have more serious crime problems than Detroit, ranked higher than Detroit on the overall index.

(D) Seattle, which has a more serious crime problem than Boston, also ranked below Boston in seven other categories.

(E) San Francisco and Detroit both have more serious crime problems than Washington, D.C., which ranked first in overall desirability.

22. Adults often assume that the emotional lives of children are radically different from those of adults, while their thinking is basically the same (though less accurate and skillful). In fact, psychologists who have studied children carefully know that the very opposite is true.

Which of the following conclusions can be most reliably drawn from the statements above?

(A) Children react to the world around them in ways that clearly prefigure the adult personalities they will develop.

(B) Children's feelings are much like those of adults, but their ways of reasoning are often very different.

(C) Differences between individuals of the same age are more important than differences between groups of different ages.

(D) Emotional responses and thought patterns are established at a very early age and continue into adulthood.

(E) The reactions of children are the mirror images of those that would be expected of adults in the same situation.

23. Whenever it is sunny, Hector either goes fishing or goes swimming. When Hector goes swimming, Sharon plays tennis. On Saturday, Sharon did not play tennis.

If the statements above are true, then which of the following must also be true?

(A) Hector did not go swimming on Saturday.

(B) It was not sunny on Saturday.

(C) Hector did not go fishing on Saturday.

(D) Sharon did not go fishing on Saturday.

(E) Sharon does not play tennis when it is cloudy.

24. JOHN: I oppose spending more money on the space program. Those tax dollars should be spent right here on Earth rather than being used to construct satellites and spaceships to be sent to the heavens.

JOAN: Well, then you should support the space program, for those dollars are spent right here on Earth, creating jobs for thousands of scientific and technical workers in the aerospace and other industries.

Which of the following best describes Joan's response to John?

(A) It points out that John's position is inherently contradictory.

(B) It attempts to force John into choosing between two horns of a dilemma.

(C) It exploits an ambiguity in a key phrase in John's statement of his position.

(D) It tries to refute John's position by attacking John personally rather than by analyzing the merits of John's claim.

(E) It uncovers a hidden assumption in John's position that is highly questionable.

25. I am perfectly capable of driving home safely from this party. I drank only wine and scrupulously avoided all hard liquor.

The statement above presupposes that

(A) someone who has been drinking hard liquor is drunk.

(B) drinking hard liquor impairs driving more than drinking wine.

(C) the police are less likely to arrest someone who has been drinking wine than someone who has been drinking hard liquor.

(D) only someone who has had no alcohol to drink is fit to drive.

(E) drinking wine will impair driving ability only if the person has also been drinking hard liquor.

STOP

END OF SECTION 3. IF YOU HAVE ANY TIME LEFT, GO OVER YOUR WORK IN THIS SECTION ONLY. DO NOT WORK IN ANY OTHER SECTION OF THE TEST.

SECTION 4

24 Questions • Time—35 Minutes

Directions: In this section, the questions ask you to analyze and evaluate the reasoning in short paragraphs or passages. For some questions, all of the answer choices may conceivably be answers to the question asked. You should select the *best* answer to the question; that is, an answer that does not require you to make assumptions that violate commonsense standards by being implausible, redundant, irrelevant, or inconsistent. After you have chosen the *best* answer, blacken the corresponding space on the answer sheet.

1. Which of the following activities would depend upon an assumption that is inconsistent with the judgment that you cannot argue with taste?

   (A) A special exhibition at a museum

   (B) A beauty contest

   (C) A system of garbage collection and disposal

   (D) A cookbook filled with old New England recipes

   (E) A movie festival

2. If George graduated from the University after 1974, he was required to take Introductory World History.

   The statement above can be logically deduced from which of the following?

   (A) Before 1974, Introductory World History was not a required course at the University.

   (B) Every student who took Introductory World History at the University graduated after 1974.

   (C) No student who graduated from the University before 1974 took Introductory World History.

   (D) All students graduating from the University after 1974 were required to take Introductory World History.

   (E) Before 1974, no student was permitted to graduate from the University without having taken Introductory World History.

3. Largemouth bass are usually found living in shallow waters near the lake banks wherever minnows are found. There are no largemouth bass living on this side of the lake.

   Which of the following would logically complete an argument with the preceding premises given?

   (A) Therefore, there are no minnows on this side of the lake.

   (B) Therefore, there are probably no minnows on this side of the lake.

   (C) Therefore, there will never be any minnows on this side of the lake.

   (D) Largemouth bass are not found in the shallow water of rivers unless minnows are also present.

   (E) Lakes that contain minnows are the only habitat where largemouth bass are found.

4. TOMMY: That telephone always rings when I am in the shower and can't hear it.

   JUANITA: But you must be able to hear it; otherwise you couldn't know that it was ringing.

Juanita's response shows that she presupposes that

(A) the telephone does not ring when Tommy is in the shower.

(B) Tommy's callers never telephone except when he is in the shower.

(C) Tommy's callers sometimes hang up, thinking he is not at home.

(D) Tommy cannot tell that the telephone has rung unless he actually heard it.

(E) the telephone does not always function properly.

5. ADVERTISEMENT: You cannot buy a more potent pain-reliever than RELIEF without a prescription.

Which of the following statements is inconsistent with the claim made by the advertisement?

(A) RELIEF is not the least expensive non-prescription pain-reliever one can buy.

(B) Another non-prescription pain-reliever, TOBINE, is just as powerful as RELIEF.

(C) Some prescription pain-relievers are not as powerful as RELIEF.

(D) An experimental pain reliever more powerful than RELIEF is available to subjects in a study free of charge.

(E) A non-prescription pain-reliever more powerful than any other, including RELIEF, is available for purchase without a prescription.

Questions 6 and 7

A behavioral psychologist interested in animal behavior noticed that dogs who are never physically disciplined (e.g., with a blow from a rolled-up newspaper) never bark at strangers. He concluded that the best way to keep a dog from barking at strange visitors is not to punish the dog physically.

6. The psychologist's conclusion is based on which of the following assumptions?

(A) Striking a dog with a newspaper or other object is an inappropriate method for conditioning canine behavior.

(B) Dogs that are never physically disciplined grow up better adjusted than dogs that have been subjected to such discipline.

(C) There were no instances of an unpunished dog barking at a stranger that had not been observed.

(D) Dogs normally bark only at strangers who have previously been physically abusive or threatening.

(E) Human children who are physically disciplined are more likely to react negatively to strangers than those who are not.

7. Suppose the psychologist decides to pursue his project further, and he studies 25 dogs that are known to bark at strangers. Which of the following possible findings would undermine his original conclusion?

   (A) Some of the owners of the dogs studied did not physically punish the dog when it barked at a stranger.

   (B) Some of the dogs studied were never physically punished.

   (C) The owners of some of the dogs studied believe that a dog that barks at strangers is a good watchdog.

   (D) Some of the dogs barked at people who were not strangers.

   (E) None of the dogs was disciplined by the method of a rolled-up newspaper.

8. Everything a child does is the consequence of some experience he has had before. Therefore, a child psychologist must study the personal history of his patient.

   The author's conclusion logically depends upon the premise that

   (A) everything that a child is doing he has already done before.

   (B) every effect is causally generated by some previous effect.

   (C) the study of a child's personal history is the best way of learning about that child's parents.

   (D) a child will learn progressively more about the world because experience is cumulative.

   (E) it is possible to ensure that a child will grow up to be a mature, responsible adult.

9. It is sometimes argued that we are reaching the limits of the earth's capacity to supply our energy needs with fossil fuels. In the past ten years, however, as a result of technological progress making it possible to extract resources from even marginal wells and mines, yields from oil and coal fields have increased tremendously. There is no reason to believe that there is a limit to the earth's capacity to supply our energy needs.

   Which of the following statements most directly contradicts the conclusion drawn above?

   (A) Even if we exhaust our supplies of fossil fuel, the earth can still be mined for uranium for nuclear fuel.

   (B) The technology needed to extract fossil fuels from marginal sources is very expensive.

   (C) Even given the improvements in technology, oil and coal are not renewable resources; so we will eventually exhaust our supplies of them.

   (D) Most of the land under which marginal oil and coal supplies lie is more suitable to cultivation or pasturing than to production of fossil fuels.

   (E) The fuels that are yielded by marginal sources tend to be high in sulphur and other undesirable elements that aggravate the air pollution problem.

Questions 10–12 refer to the following arguments.

(A) The Bible must be accepted as the revealed word of God, for it is stated several times in the Bible that it is the one, true word of God. And since the Bible is the true word of God, we must accept what it says as true.

(B) It must be possible to do something about the deteriorating condition of the nation's interstate highway system. But the repairs will cost money. Therefore, it is foolish to reduce federal appropriations for highway repair.

(C) The Learner Commission's Report on Pornography concluded that there is a definite link between pornography and sex crimes. But no one should accept that conclusion because the Learner Commission was funded by the Citizens' Committee Against Obscenity, which obviously wanted the report to condemn pornography.

(D) People should give up drinking coffee. Of ten people who died last year at City Hospital from cancer of the pancreas, eight of them drank three or more cups of coffee a day.

(E) Guns are not themselves the cause of crime. Even without firearms, crimes would be committed. Criminals would use knives or other weapons.

10. Which of the above arguments contains circular reasoning?

11. Which of the above arguments contains a generalization that is based on a sample?

12. Which of the above arguments addresses itself to the source of the claim rather than to the merits of the claim itself?

13. Some sociologists believe that religious sects such as the California-based Waiters—who believe the end of the world is imminent and seek to purify their souls by, among other things, abstaining completely from sexual relations—are a product of growing disaffection with modern, industrialized, and urbanized living. As evidence, they cite the fact that there are no other active organizations of the same type that are more than 50 or 60 years old. The evidence, however, fails to support the conclusion for_____ .

Which of the following is the most logical completion of the passage?

(A) the restrictions on sexual relations are such that the only source of new members is outside recruitment, so such sects tend to die out after a generation or two

(B) it is simply not possible to gauge the intensity of religious fervor by the length of time the religious sect remains viable

(C) the Waiters group may actually survive beyond the second generation of its existence

(D) there are other religious sects that emphasize group sexual activity that currently have several hundred members

(E) the Waiters are a California-based organization and have no members in the Northeast, which is even more heavily urban and industrialized than California

14. Any truthful auto mechanic will tell you that your standard 5,000-mile checkup can detect only one fifth of the problems that are likely to go wrong with your car. Therefore, such a checkup is virtually worthless and a waste of time and money.

    Which of the following statements, if true, would strengthen the above conclusion?

    (A) Those problems that the 5,000-mile checkup will turn up are the ten leading causes of major engine failure.

    (B) For a new car, a 5,000-mile checkup is required to protect the owner's warranty.

    (C) During a 5,000-mile checkup, the mechanic also performs routine maintenance that is necessary to the proper functioning of the car.

    (D) During a 5,000-mile checkup of a vehicle, a mechanic can detect incipient problems that might later lead to major difficulties.

    (E) A manufacturer's review of reports based on 5,000-mile checkups shows that the checkups found problems in less than 1/10 or 1 percent of the cars checked.

Questions 15 and 16

In recent years, unions have begun to include in their demands at the collective bargaining table requests for contract provisions that give labor an active voice in determining the goals of a corporation. Although it cannot be denied that labor leaders are highly skilled administrators, it must be recognized that their primary loyalty is and must remain to their membership, not to the corporation. Thus, labor participation in corporate management decisions makes about as much sense as _____ .

15. Which of the following represents the best continuation of the passage?

    (A) allowing inmates to make decisions about prison security

    (B) a senior field officer asking the advice of a junior officer on a question of tactics

    (C) a university's asking the opinion of the student body on the scheduling of courses

    (D) Chicago's mayor inviting the state legislators for a ride on the city's subway system

    (E) the members of a church congregation discussing theology with the minister

16. The author's reasoning leads to the further conclusion that

    (A) the authority of corporate managers would be symbolically undermined if labor leaders were allowed to participate in corporate planning.

    (B) workers have virtually no idea of how to run a large corporation.

    (C) workers would not derive any benefit from hearing the goals of corporate management explained to them at semiannual meetings.

    (D) the efficiency of workers would be lowered if they were to divide their time between production line duties and management responsibilities.

    (E) allowing labor a voice in corporate decisions would involve labor representatives in a conflict of interest.

17. DRUGGIST: Seventy percent of the people questioned stated that they would use Myrdal for relief of occasional headache pain. Only 30 percent of those questioned indicated that they would take Blufferin for such pain.

CUSTOMER: Oh, then more than twice as many people preferred Myrdal to Blufferin.

DRUGGIST: No, 25 percent of those questioned stated they never took any medication.

In what manner may the seeming inconsistency in the druggist's statements be explained?

(A) The 30 percent who indicated they would take Blufferin are contained within the 70 percent of those who indicated they would take Myrdal.

(B) The questioner asked more than 100 people.

(C) The questioner did not accurately record the answers of at least 25 percent of those questioned.

(D) The sampling population was too small to yield results that were statistically significant.

(E) Some of those questioned indicated that they would take both brands of pain relievers.

18. (1) No student who commutes from home to a university dates a student who resides at a university.

(2) Every student who lives at home commutes to his university, and no commuter student ever dates a resident student.

Which of the following best describes the relationship between the two preceding sentences?

(A) If (2) is true, (1) must also be true.

(B) If (2) is true, (1) must be false.

(C) If (2) is true, (1) may be either true or false.

(D) If (1) is true, (2) is unlikely to be false.

(E) If (2) is false, (1) must also be false.

19. All books from the Buckner collection are kept in the Reserve Room.

All books kept in the Reserve Room are priceless.

No book by Hemingway is kept in the Reserve Room.

Every book kept in the Reserve Room is listed in the card catalogue.

If all of the statements given are true, which of the following must also be true?

(A) All priceless books are kept in the Reserve Room.

(B) Every book from the Buckner collection that is listed in the card catalogue is not valuable.

(C) No book by Hemingway is priceless.

(D) The Buckner collection contains no books by Hemingway.

(E) Every book listed in the card catalogue is kept in the Reserve Room.

20. The new car to buy this year is the Goblin. We had 100 randomly selected motorists drive the Goblin and the other two leading subcompact cars. Seventy-five drivers ranked the Goblin first in handling. Sixty-nine rated the Goblin first in styling. From the responses of these 100 drivers, we can show you that they ranked Goblin first overall in our composite category of style, performance, comfort, and drivability.

The persuasive appeal of the advertisement's claim is most weakened by its use of the undefined word

(A) randomly.

(B) handling.

(C) first.

(D) responses.

(E) composite.

21. Recently, the newspaper published the obituary notice of a novelist and poet that had been written by the deceased in anticipation of the event. The last line of the verse advised the reader that the author had expired a day earlier and gave as the cause of death "a deprivation of time."

The explanation of the cause of the author's death is

(A) circular.

(B) speculative.

(C) self-serving.

(D) medically sound.

(E) self-authenticating.

22. Since Ronnie's range is so narrow, he will never be an outstanding vocalist.

The statement above is based on which of the following assumptions?

(A) A person's range is an important indicator of his probable success or failure as a professional musician.

(B) Vocalizing requires a range of at least two and one half octaves.

(C) It is possible for a singer, through study and practice, to expand the vocal range.

(D) Physical characteristics can affect how well one sings.

(E) Very few people have vocal ranges sufficiently broad enough to permit them to be successful vocalists.

Questions 23 and 24

During the 1970s, the number of clandestine CIA agents posted to foreign countries increased 25 percent and the number of CIA employees not assigned to field work increased by 21 percent. In the same period, the number of FBI agents assigned to case investigation rose by 18 percent, but the number of non–case-working agents rose by only 3 percent.

23. The statistics best support which of the following claims?

    (A) More agents are needed to administer the CIA than are needed for the FBI.

    (B) The CIA needs more people to accomplish its mission than does the FBI.

    (C) The proportion of field agents tends to increase more rapidly than the number of non-field agents in both the CIA and the FBI.

    (D) The rate of change in the number of supervisory agents in an intelligence gathering agency or a law-enforcement agency is proportional to the percentage change in the results produced by the agency.

    (E) At the end of the 1960s, the CIA was more efficiently administered than the FBI.

24. In response to the allegation that it was more overstaffed with support and supervisory personnel than the FBI, the CIA could best argue that

    (A) the FBI is less useful than the CIA in gathering intelligence against foreign powers.

    (B) the rate of pay for a CIA non-field agent is less than the rate of pay for a non-investigating FBI agent.

    (C) the number of FBI agents should not rise so rapidly as the number of CIA agents given the longer tenure of an FBI agent.

    (D) a CIA field agent working in a foreign country requires more backup support than does an FBI investigator working domestically.

    (E) the number of CIA agents is determined by the Congress each year when they appropriate funds for the agency, and the Congress is very sensitive to changes in the international political climate.

STOP

END OF SECTION 4. IF YOU HAVE ANY TIME LEFT, GO OVER YOUR WORK IN THIS SECTION ONLY. DO NOT WORK IN ANY OTHER SECTION OF THE TEST.

SECTION 5

28 Questions • Time—35 Minutes

Directions: Below each of the following passages, you will find questions or incomplete statements about the passage. Each statement or question is followed by lettered words or expressions. Select the word or expression that most satisfactorily completes each statement or answers each question in accordance with the meaning of the passage. After you have chosen the *best* answer, blacken the corresponding space on the answer sheet.

There is extraordinary exposure in the United States to the risks of injury and death from motor vehicle accidents. More than 80 percent of all households own
(5) passenger cars or light trucks, and each of these is driven an average of more than 11,000 miles each year. Almost one-half of fatally injured drivers have a blood alcohol concentration (BAC) of 0.1
(10) percent or higher. For the average adult, over five ounces of 80 proof spirits would have to be consumed over a short period of time to attain these levels. A third of drivers who have been drinking, but
(15) fewer than 4 percent of all drivers, demonstrate these levels. Although less than 1 percent of drivers with BACs of 0.1 percent or more are involved in fatal crashes, the probability of their involve-
(20) ment is 27 times higher than for those without alcohol in their blood.

There are a number of different approaches to reducing injuries in which intoxication plays a role. Based on the
(25) observation that excessive consumption correlates with the total alcohol consumption of a country's population, it has been suggested that higher taxes on alcohol would reduce both. While the
(30) heaviest drinkers would be taxed the most, anyone who drinks at all would be penalized by this approach.

To make drinking and driving a criminal offense is an approach directed
(35) only at intoxicated drivers. In some states, the law empowers police to request breath tests of drivers cited for any traffic offense and elevated BAC can

be the basis for arrest. The National
(40) Highway Traffic Safety Administration estimates, however, that even with increased arrests, there are about 700 violations for every arrest. At this level there is little evidence that laws serve as
(45) deterrents to driving while intoxicated. In Britain, motor vehicle fatalities fell 25 percent immediately following implementation of the Road Safety Act in 1967. As Britishers increasingly recog-
(50) nized that they could drink and not be stopped, the effectiveness declined, although in the ensuing three years the fatality rate seldom reached that observed in the seven years prior to the
(55) Act.

Whether penalties for driving with a high BAC or excessive taxation on consumption of alcoholic beverages will deter the excessive drinker responsible
(60) for most fatalities is unclear. In part, the answer depends on the extent to which those with high BACs involved in crashes are capable of controlling their intake in response to economic or penal threat.
(65) Therapeutic programs which range from individual and group counseling and psychotherapy to chemotherapy constitute another approach, but they have not diminished the proportion of acci-
(70) dents in which alcohol was a factor. In the few controlled trials that have been reported there is little evidence that rehabilitation programs for those repeatedly arrested for drunken behavior
(75) have reduced either the recidivism or crash rates. Thus far, there is no firm

evidence that Alcohol Safety Action Project supported programs, in which rehabilitation measures are requested (80) by the court, have decreased recidivism or crash involvement for clients exposed to them, although knowledge and attitudes have improved. One thing is clear, however; unless we deal with automo- (85) bile and highway safety and reduce accidents in which alcoholic intoxication plays a role, many will continue to die.

1. The author is primarily concerned with

   (A) interpreting the results of surveys on traffic fatalities.

   (B) reviewing the effectiveness of attempts to curb drunk driving.

   (C) suggesting reasons for the prevalence of drunk driving in the United States.

   (D) analyzing the causes of the large number of annual traffic fatalities.

   (E) making an international comparison of experience with drunk driving.

2. It can be inferred that the 1967 Road Safety Act in Britain

   (A) changed an existing law to lower the BAC level defining driving while intoxicated.

   (B) made it illegal to drive while intoxicated.

   (C) increased drunk driving arrests.

   (D) placed a tax on the sale of alcoholic drinks.

   (E) required drivers convicted under the law to undergo rehabilitation therapy.

3. The author implies that a BAC of 0.1 percent

   (A) is unreasonably high as a definition of intoxication for purposes of driving.

   (B) penalizes moderate drinkers but allows heavy drinkers to consume without limit.

   (C) will effectively deter more than 90 percent of the people who might drink and drive.

   (D) is well below the BAC of most drivers who are involved in fatal collisions.

   (E) proves a driver has consumed five ounces of 80 proof spirits over a short time.

4. With which of the following statements about making driving while intoxicated a criminal offense versus increasing taxes on alcohol consumption would the author most likely agree?

(A) Making driving while intoxicated a criminal offense is preferable to increased taxes on alcohol because the former is aimed only at those who abuse alcohol by driving while intoxicated.

(B) Increased taxation on alcohol consumption is likely to be more effective in reducing traffic fatalities because taxation covers all consumers and not just those who drive.

(C) Increased taxation on alcohol will constitute less of an interference with personal liberty because of the necessity of blood alcohol tests to determine BACs in drivers suspected of intoxication.

(D) Since neither increased taxation nor enforcement of criminal laws against drunk drivers is likely to have any significant impact, neither measure is warranted.

(E) Because arrests of intoxicated drivers have proved to be expensive and administratively cumbersome, increased taxation on alcohol is the most promising means of reducing traffic fatalities.

5. The author cites the British example in order to

(A) show that the problem of drunk driving is worse in Britain than in the U.S.

(B) prove that stricter enforcement of laws against intoxicated drivers would reduce traffic deaths.

(C) prove that a slight increase in the number of arrests of intoxicated drivers will not deter drunk driving.

(D) suggest that taxation of alcohol consumption may be more effective than criminal laws.

(E) demonstrate the need to lower BAC levels in states that have laws against drunk driving.

6. Which of the following, if true, most WEAKENS the author's statement that the effectiveness of proposals to stop the intoxicated driver depends, in part, on the extent to which the high-BAC driver can control his intake?

(A) Even if the heavy drinkers cannot control intake, criminal laws against driving while intoxicated can deter them from driving while intoxicated.

(B) Rehabilitation programs aimed at drivers convicted of driving while intoxicated have not significantly reduced traffic fatalities.

(C) Many traffic fatalities are caused by factors unrelated to the excessive consumption of alcohol of the driver.

(D) Even though severe penalties may not deter the intoxicated driver, these laws will punish that driver for the harm caused by driving while intoxicated.

(E) Some sort of therapy may be effective in helping the problem drinker to control his intake of alcohol, thereby keeping him off the road.

7. The author's closing remarks can best be described as

(A) ironic.

(B) indifferent.

(C) admonitory.

(D) indecisive.

(E) indignant.

At the present time, 98 percent of the world energy consumption comes from stored sources, such as fossil fuels or nuclear fuel. Only hydroelectric and wood
(5) energy represent completely renewable sources on ordinary time scales. Discovery of large additional fossil fuel reserves, solution of the nuclear safety and waste disposal problems, or the de-
(10) velopment of controlled thermonuclear fusion will provide only a short-term solution to the world's energy crisis. Within about 100 years, the thermal pollution resulting from our increased
(15) energy consumption will make solar energy a necessity at any cost.

Total energy consumption is currently about one part in ten thousand that of the energy we receive from the
(20) sun. However, it is growing at a 5 percent rate, of which about 2 percent represents a population growth and 3 percent a per capita energy increase. If this growth continues, within 100 years our
(25) energy consumption will be about 1 percent of the absorbed solar energy, enough to increase the average temperature of the earth by about one degree centigrade if stored energy continues to be
(30) our predominant source. This will be the point at which there will be significant effects in our climate, including the melting of the polar ice caps, a phenomenon which will raise the level of the oceans
(35) and flood parts of our major cities. There is positive feedback associated with this process, since the polar ice cap contributes to the partial reflectivity of the energy arriving from the sun: As the ice
(40) caps begin to melt, the reflectivity will decrease, thus heating the earth still further.

It is often stated that the growth rate will decline or that energy conser-
(45) vation measures will preclude any long-range problem. Instead, this only postpones the problem by a few years. Conservation by a factor of two together with a maintenance of the 5 percent
(50) growth rate delays the problem by only 14 years. Reduction of the growth rate to 4 percent postpones the problem by only 25 years; in addition, the inequities in standards of living throughout
(55) the world will provide pressure toward an increase in growth rate, particularly if cheap energy is available. The problem of a changing climate will not be evident until perhaps ten years before it
(60) becomes critical due to the nature of an exponential growth rate together with the normal annual weather variations. This may be too short a period to circumvent the problem by converting to
(65) other energy sources, so advance planning is a necessity.

The only practical means of avoiding the problem of thermal pollution appears to be the use of solar energy.
(70) (Schemes to "air-condition" the earth do not appear to be feasible before the twenty-second century.) Using the solar energy before it is dissipated to heat does not increase the earth's energy bal-
(75) ance. The cost of solar energy is extremely favorable now; particularly when compared to the cost of relocating many of our major cities.

8. The author is primarily concerned with

(A) describing a phenomenon and explaining its causes.

(B) outlining a position and supporting it with statistics.

(C) isolating an ambiguity and clarifying it by definition.

(D) presenting a problem and advocating a solution for it.

(E) citing a counterargument and refuting it.

9. According to the passage, all of the following are factors that will tend to increase thermal pollution EXCEPT

(A) Earth's increasing population.

(B) melting of the polar ice caps.

(C) increase in per capita energy consumption.

(D) pressure to redress standard of living inequities by increasing energy consumption.

(E) expected anomalies in weather patterns.

10. The positive feedback mentioned in line 36 means that the melting of the polar ice caps will

(A) reduce per capita energy consumption.

(B) accelerate the transition to solar energy.

(C) intensify the effects of thermal pollution.

(D) necessitate a shift to alternative energy sources.

(E) result in the inundations of major cities.

11. The author mentions the possibility of energy conservation (lines 44–51) in order to

(A) preempt and refute a possible objection to the argument.

(B) directly support the central thesis of the passage.

(C) minimize the significance of a contradiction in the passage.

(D) prove that such measures are ineffective and counterproductive.

(E) supply the reader with additional background information.

12. It can be inferred that the "air-condition" of the earth (line 70) refers to proposals to

(A) distribute frigid air from the polar ice caps to coastal cities as the temperature increases due to thermal pollution.

(B) dissipate the surplus of the release of stored solar energy over absorbed solar energy into space.

(C) conserve completely renewable energy sources by requiring that industry replace these resources.

(D) avoid further thermal pollution by converting to solar energy as opposed to conventional and nuclear sources.

(E) utilize hydroelectric and wood energy to replace non-conventional energy sources such as nuclear energy.

13. The tone of the passage is best described as one of

(A) unmitigated outrage.

(B) cautious optimism.

(C) reckless abandon.

(D) smug self-assurance.

(E) pronounced alarm.

14. Which of the following would be the most logical topic for the author to address in a succeeding paragraph?

(A) The problems of nuclear safety and waste disposal

(B) A history of the development of solar energy

(C) The availability and cost of solar energy technology

(D) The practical effects of flooding of coastal cities

(E) The feasibility of geothermal energy

It would be enormously convenient to
have a single, generally accepted index
of the economic and social welfare of the
people of the United States. A glance at
(5) it would tell us how much better or
worse off we had become each year, and
we would judge the desirability of any
proposed action by asking whether it
would raise or lower this index. Some
(10) recent discussion implies that such an
index could be constructed. Articles in
the popular press even criticize the Gross
Domestic Production (GDP) because it
is not such a complete index of welfare,
(15) ignoring, on the one hand, that it was
never intended to be, and suggesting, on
the other, that with appropriate changes
it could be converted into one.

The output available to satisfy our
(20) wants and needs is one important determinant of welfare. Whatever want, need,
or social problem engages our attention,
we ordinarily can more easily find resources to deal with it when output is
(25) large and growing than when it is not.
GDP measures output fairly well, but to
evaluate welfare we would need additional measures which would be far more
difficult to construct. We would need an
(30) index of real costs incurred in production, because we are better off if we get
the same output at less cost. Use of just
hours-worked for welfare evaluation
would unreasonably imply that to in-
(35) crease total hours by raising the hours of
eight women from 60 to 65 a week imposes no more burden then raising the
hours of eight men from 40 to 45 a week,
or even than hiring one involuntarily
(40) unemployed person for 40 hours a week.
A measure of real costs of labor would
also have to consider working conditions. Most of us spend almost half our
waking hours on the job and our welfare
(45) is vitally affected by the circumstances
in which we spend those hours.

To measure welfare we would need
a measure of changes in the need our
output must satisfy. One aspect, popu-
(50) lation change, is now handled by converting output to a per capita basis on
the assumption that, other things equal,

twice as many people need twice as many
goods and services to be equally well off.
(55) But an index of needs would also account for differences in the requirements
for living as the population becomes
more urbanized and suburbanized; for
the changes in national defense require-
(60) ments; and for changes in the effect of
weather in our needs. The index would
have to tell us the cost of meeting our
needs in a base year compared with the
cost of meeting them equally well under
(65) the circumstances prevailing in every
other year.

Measures of "needs" shade into
measure of the human and physical environment in which we live. We all are
(70) enormously affected by the people around
us. Can we go where we like without fear
of attack? We are also affected by the
physical environment—purity of water
and air, accessibility of park land and
(75) other conditions. To measure this requires accurate data, but such data are
generally deficient. Moreover, weighting is required: to combine robberies
and murders in a crime index; to com-
(80) bine pollution of the Potomac and pollution of Lake Erie into a water pollution
index; and then to combine crime and
water pollution into some general index.
But there is no basis for weighting these
(85) beyond individual preference.

There are further problems. To
measure welfare we would need an index of the "goodness" of the distribution
of income. There is surely consensus
(90) that given the same total income and
output, a distribution with fewer families in poverty would be the better, but
what is the ideal distribution? Even if
we could construct indexes of output,
(95) real costs, needs, state of the environment, we could not compute a welfare
index because we have no system of
weights to combine them.

15. The author is primarily concerned with
    (A) refuting arguments for a position.
    (B) making a proposal and defending it.
    (C) attacking the sincerity of an opponent.
    (D) showing defects in a proposal.
    (E) reviewing literature relevant to a problem.

16. The author implies that hours-worked is not an appropriate measure of real cost because it
    (A) ignores the conditions under which the output is generated.
    (B) fails to take into consideration the environmental costs of production.
    (C) overemphasizes the output of real goods as opposed to services.
    (D) is not an effective method for reducing unemployment.
    (E) was never intended to be a general measure of welfare.

17. It can be inferred from the passage that the most important reason a single index of welfare cannot be designed is
    (A) the cost associated with producing the index would be prohibitive.
    (B) considerable empirical research would have to be done regarding output and needs.
    (C) any weighting of various measures into a general index would be inherently subjective and arbitrary.
    (D) production of the relevant data would require time; thus, the index would be only a reflection of past welfare.
    (E) accurate statistics on crime and pollution are not yet available.

18. The author regards the idea of a general index of welfare as
    (A) an unrealistic dream.
    (B) a scientific reality.
    (C) an important contribution.
    (D) a future necessity.
    (E) a desirable change.

19. According to the passage, the GDP is
    (A) a fairly accurate measure of output.
    (B) a reliable estimate of needs.
    (C) an accurate forecaster of welfare.
    (D) a precise measure of welfare.
    (E) a potential measure of general welfare.

20. According to the passage, an adequate measure of need must take into account all of the following EXCEPT
    (A) changing size of the population.
    (B) changing effects on people of the weather.
    (C) differences in needs of urban and suburban populations.
    (D) changing requirements for governmental programs such as defense.
    (E) accessibility of park land and other amenities.

21. The passage is most likely
    (A) an address to a symposium on public policy decisions.
    (B) a chapter in a general introduction to statistics.
    (C) a pamphlet on government programs to aid the poor.
    (D) the introduction to a treatise on the foundations of government.
    (E) a speech by a university president to a graduating class.

Our current system of unemployment compensation has increased nearly all sources of adult unemployment; seasonal and cyclical variations in the demand (5) for labor, weak labor force attachment, and unnecessarily long durations of unemployment. First, for those who are already unemployed, the system greatly reduces the cost of extending the period (10) of unemployment. Second, for all types of unsteady work—seasonal, cyclical, and casual—it raises the net wage to the employee, relative to the cost of the employer.

(15)   As for the first, consider a worker who earns $500 per month or $6,000 per year if she experiences no unemployment. If she is unemployed for one month, she loses $500 in gross earnings but only (20) $116 in net income. How does this occur? A reduction of $500 in annual earnings reduces her federal, payroll and state tax liability by $134. Unemployment compensation consists of 50 percent of (25) her wage or $250. Her net income therefore falls from $366 if she is employed, to $250 paid as unemployment compensation. Moreover, part of the higher income from employment is offset by the (30) cost of transportation to work and other expenses associated with employment; and in some industries, the cost of unemployment is reduced further or even made negative by the supplementary (35) unemployment benefits paid by employers under collective bargaining agreements. The overall effect is to increase the duration of a typical spell of unemployment and to increase the frequency (40) with which individuals lose jobs and become unemployed.

The more general effect of unemployment compensation is to increase the seasonal and cyclical fluctuations in (45) the demand for labor and the relative number of short-lived casual jobs. A worker who accepts such work knows she will be laid off when the season ends. If there were no unemployment compen- (50) sation, workers could be induced to accept such unstable jobs only if the wage rate were sufficiently higher in those jobs than in the more stable alternative. The higher cost of labor, then, would (55) induce employers to reduce the instability of employment by smoothing production through increased variation in inventories and delivery lags, by additional development of off-season work (60) and by the introduction of new production techniques, e.g., new methods of outdoor work in bad weather.

Employers contribute to the state unemployment compensation fund on (65) the basis of the unemployment experience of their own previous employees. Within limits, the more benefits that those former employees draw, the higher is the employer's tax rate. The theory of (70) experience rating is clear. If an employer paid the full cost of the unemployment benefits that his former employees received, unemployment compensation would provide no incentive to an excess (75) use of unstable employment. In practice, however, experience rating is limited by a maximum rate of employer contribution. For any firm which pays the maximum rate, there is no cost for (80) additional unemployment and no gain from a small reduction in unemployment.

The challenge at this time is to restructure the unemployment system (85) in a way that strengthens its good features while reducing the harmful disincentive effects. Some gains can be achieved by removing the ceiling on the employer's rate of contribution and by (90) lowering the minimum rate to zero. Employers would then pay the full price of unemployment insurance benefits and this would encourage employers to stabilize employment and production. Fur- (95) ther improvement could be achieved if unemployment insurance benefits were taxed in the same way as other earnings. This would eliminate the anomalous situations in which a worker's net (100) income is actually reduced when he returns to work.

22. The author's primary concern is to

    (A) defend the system of unemployment compensation against criticism.

    (B) advocate expanding the benefits and scope of coverage of unemployment compensation.

    (C) point to weaknesses inherent in government programs that subsidize individuals.

    (D) suggest reforms to eliminate inefficiencies in unemployment compensation.

    (E) propose methods of increasing the effectiveness of government programs to reduce unemployment.

23. The author cites the example of a worker earning $500 per month in order to

    (A) show the disincentive created by unemployment compensation for that worker to return to work.

    (B) demonstrate that employers do not bear the full cost of worker compensation.

    (C) prove that unemployed workers would not be able to survive without unemployment compensation.

    (D) explain why employers prefer to hire seasonal workers instead of permanent workers for short-term jobs.

    (E) condemn workers who prefer to live on unemployment compensation to taking a job.

24. The author recommends which of the following changes be made to the unemployment compensation system?

    (A) Eliminating taxes on benefits paid to workers

    (B) Shortening the time during which a worker can draw benefits

    (C) Removing any cap on the maximum rate of employer contribution

    (D) Providing workers with job retraining as a condition of benefits

    (E) Requiring unemployed workers to accept public works positions

25. The author mentions all of the following as ways by which employers might reduce seasonal and cyclical unemployment EXCEPT

    (A) developing new techniques of production not affected by weather.

    (B) slowing delivery schedules to provide work during slow seasons.

    (C) adopting a system of supplementary benefits for workers laid off in slow periods.

    (D) manipulating inventory supplies to require year-round rather than short-term employment.

    (E) finding new jobs to be done by workers during the off-season.

26. With which of the following statements about experience rating would the author most likely agree?

    (A) Experience rating is theoretically sound, but its effectiveness in practice is undermined by maximum contribution ceilings.

    (B) Experience rating is an inefficient method of computing employer contribution because an employer has no control over the length of an employee's unemployment.

    (C) Experience rating is theoretically invalid and should be replaced by a system in which the employee contributes the full amount of benefits he will later receive.

    (D) Experience rating is basically fair, but its performance could be improved by requiring large firms to pay more than small firms.

    (E) Experience rating requires an employer to pay a contribution that is completely unrelated to the amount his employees draw in unemployment compensation benefits.

27. The author makes which of the following criticisms of the unemployment compensation system?

    (A) It places an unfair burden on firms whose production is cyclical or seasonal.

    (B) It encourages out-of-work employees to extend the length of time they are unemployed.

    (C) It constitutes a drain on state treasuries that must subsidize unemployment compensation funds.

    (D) It provides a source of income for employees who have no income or only reduced income from employment.

    (E) The experience rating system means that employers responsible for higher-than-average turnover in staff pay higher-than-average premiums.

28. It can be inferred that the author regards the unemployment compensation system as

    (A) socially necessary.

    (B) economically efficient.

    (C) inherently wasteful.

    (D) completely unnecessary.

    (E) seriously outdated.

STOP

END OF SECTION 1. IF YOU HAVE ANY TIME LEFT, GO OVER YOUR WORK IN THIS SECTION ONLY. DO NOT WORK IN ANY OTHER SECTION OF THE TEST.

WRITING SAMPLE

Time—30 minutes

ASHLEY REEVE has just inherited $50,000. Ashley wants to invest the $50,000 in a business that she can operate herself. She is considering two possibilities, a fast-food franchise and a clothing store. Write an argument in favor of one of the two proposals. The following criteria should be considered:

—Ashley recently received her M.B.A. and wants a business that will give her an opportunity to apply her theoretical knowledge in a practical setting.

—Ashley has considerable student loans and no substantial assets, so the $50,000 must cover the start-up costs of the business.

Ashley is considering buying a Hearty Burger franchise. Hearty Burger is a regional company with 5 company-owned stores and 20 franchise stores. The cost of the franchise is $10,000, and the estimated cost of the physical plant is another $25,000, depending on whether the franchisee buys or leases a building and on the extent of renovation required. A franchisee must attend a two-week "Hearty Burger Orientation" and is required to purchase all supplies from the company's commissary. The main company does regional advertising and special promotional campaigns and supplies franchisees with everything they need to run their restaurants, including cooking equipment, employee time sheets, tax forms, cooking procedure booklets, and technical assistance. Ashley is also considering purchasing an existing clothing store. The owner of the store, which has been in operation for more than fifty years, is retiring and is willing to sell the store with all its fixtures and stock for $40,000. In recent years, the store has not been very profitable, but the current owner apparently failed to keep abreast of style changes. Ashley anticipates that there is a large student market in the area that has not yet been tapped. She is concerned, however, about the terms of the lease on the store. The current lease will expire in eight months. The owner intends to co-op the building. Ashley will be given the opportunity to buy the commercial space, provided she has the funds available. Otherwise, she will be forced to relocate.

ANSWER KEY

Section 1

1.	B	6.	A	11.	D	16.	A	21.	A
2.	C	7.	E	12.	D	17.	C	22.	C
3.	C	8.	D	13.	B	18.	B	23.	E
4.	E	9.	C	14.	D	19.	D	24.	B
5.	E	10.	D	15.	D	20.	C		

Section 2

1.	C	7.	A	13.	A	19.	B	25.	B
2.	A	8.	E	14.	B	20.	A	26.	D
3.	B	9.	A	15.	E	21.	A	27.	B
4.	E	10.	E	16.	D	22.	A	28.	A
5.	D	11.	B	17.	D	23.	E		
6.	B	12.	A	18.	C	24.	E		

Section 3

1.	B	6.	E	11.	A	16.	C	21.	C
2.	A	7.	D	12.	A	17.	A	22.	B
3.	E	8.	C	13.	A	18.	B	23.	A
4.	A	9.	D	14.	D	19.	E	24.	C
5.	E	10.	B	15.	A	20.	A	25.	B

Section 4

1.	B	6.	C	11.	D	16.	E	21.	A
2.	D	7.	B	12.	C	17.	E	22.	D
3.	B	8.	B	13.	A	18.	A	23.	C
4.	D	9.	C	14.	E	19.	D	24.	D
5.	E	10.	A	15.	A	20.	E		

Section 5

1.	B	7.	C	13.	B	19.	A	25.	C
2.	B	8.	D	14.	C	20.	E	26.	A
3.	A	9.	E	15.	D	21.	A	27.	B
4.	A	10.	C	16.	A	22.	D	28.	A
5.	C	11.	A	17.	C	23.	A		
6.	A	12.	B	18.	A	24.	C		

EXPLANATORY ANSWERS

Section 1

Questions 1–6

Here we have a linear ordering set. Even though the ordering is temporal, it can be represented spatially like a calendar. We begin by summarizing the given information:

$$K = (Mon. \text{ or } Sat.)$$
$$O = Th.$$
$$P = Sun.$$
$$J = L$$
$$J \neq N$$

1. **The correct answer is (B).** We begin by entering the additional information:

   Mon. Tu. Wed. Th. Fri. Sat. Sun.

   K   M   N   O   J/L J/L P

   The only open question, as shown by the diagram, is of J or L, which is shown on Friday and Saturday. With M shown on Tuesday and O and P on Thursday and Sunday, J and L must be shown on Friday and Saturday, though not necessarily respectively. Then, K must be shown on Monday, which means N must be shown on Wednesday. As the diagram shows, only choice (B) is necessarily true. Choices (C) and (D) are possibly, though not necessarily, true. Choices (A) and (E) are definitely untrue.

2. **The correct answer is (C).** We begin by processing the additional stipulations:

   Mon. Tu. Wed. Th. Fri. Sat. Sun.

   K   J   L   O   M/N M/N P

   If J and K are shown on consecutive days, then to respect the requirement that J and L also be shown on consecutive days, we have a group of either KJL or LJK. With Thursday and Sunday already

scheduled, however, this group must be aired on Monday through Wednesday. This means K must be Monday, J Tuesday, and L Wednesday. As a result, M and N will be scheduled Friday and Saturday, though we cannot establish which one will be shown on which day. Thus, choices (D) and (E) are only possible, not necessary. Choices (A) and (B) are both impossible. Choice (C), however, makes a necessarily true statement.

3. **The correct answer is (C).** We begin by processing the additional information:

   Mon. Tu. Wed. Th. Fri. Sat. Sun.

   K   N   M   O   J/L J/L P

   With N scheduled for Tuesday, this forces the programming manager to air J and L on Friday and Saturday, though which is shown on which day is not established. Then, K must be aired on Monday, which means that M is aired on Wednesday.

4. **The correct answer is (E).** We begin by processing the additional information:

   Mon. Tu. Wed. Th. Fri. Sat. Sun.

              O   K   P

   This is not sufficient to establish either choices (A) or (B). We must then look to the remaining answer choices and process the extra information supplied therein. As for choice (C), knowing that N and L are aired on consecutive days establishes only that N, L, and J are aired consecutively: NLJ or JLN; but this does not determine which film is shown on Wednesday. As for choice (D), knowing that J is aired either immediately before or immediately after M sets up a LJM or a JLM sequence. Choice (E) is the correct answer. If K and M are shown on consecutive days, then M is shown on

Friday. We are left with J and L, which must be shown on consecutive days, and N, which must not be shown on a day before or after J. There are only two possible schedules for this three-film sequence that must be aired Monday, Tuesday, and Wednesday: JLN or NLJ. Either way we schedule the films, L is scheduled on Tuesday.

5. **The correct answer is (E).** For this question, we must use not only the additional stipulation provided in the stem of the question but also the additional information provided in the answer choices as well. If J is not shown on Monday, Tuesday, or Wednesday, we know:

Mon. Tu. Wed. Th. Fri. Sat. Sun.

K   O J/L J/L P

because K must be shown on either Monday or Saturday. Tuesday and Wednesday must be dedicated to M and N, though not necessarily in that order. As for choices (A) and (B), fixing the JL combination for Friday and Saturday is not going to affect the showing of films on Tuesday and Wednesday. As for choices (C) and (D), scheduling M and N will not affect the order of J and L. Choice (E), however, is correct. If N is shown on Wednesday, then M must be scheduled for Tuesday.

6. **The correct answer is (A).** Here we have a similar problem. We must test each statement using all the information available. The stem establishes:

Mon. Tu. Wed. Th. Fri. Sat. Sun.

L   O   P

As for choice (A), knowing that M is shown on Monday allows us to determine that L is shown on Tuesday, K on Saturday, and N on Friday:

Mon. Tu. Wed. Th. Fri. Sat. Sun.

M L J O N K P

So choice (A) is correct. As for choice (B), if K is shown on Monday, we deduce:

Mon. Tu. Wed. Th. Fri. Sat. Sun.

K L J O   P

And we know that M and N must be shown on Friday and Saturday, but we do not know their order. So choice (B) is not necessarily true. As for choice (C), if K is shown on Saturday, this leaves both Monday and Wednesday open for J, so choice (C) is not necessarily true. So the correct answer is choice (A) only.

Finally, test choices (D) and (E):

Mon. Tu. Wed. Th. Fri. Sat. Sun.

   L   O N   P

Since K could be shown on either Monday or Saturday, J could be shown on either Monday or Wednesday, and M could be shown on Monday, Wednesday, or Saturday.

Questions 7–12

Here we have a selection problem. The three-cars aspect introduces what seems to be an element of spatial ordering, but in actuality, this aspect does nothing more than specify that three groups will be selected. We could as easily have dispensed with spatial ordering in favor of another device, say, three tables at a banquet, the blue table, the green table, and the red table. We begin by summarizing the information for ready reference:

$$G = H$$
$$J = 2$$
$$N = P$$
$$K \neq O$$
$$M = (J) \vee (O) \vee (J \& O)$$

7. **The correct answer is (E).** With this question we just check each answer choice against the restrictions given in the initial conditions. Using the requirement

that G = H, we eliminate both choices (A) and (C). Then, using the requirement that N = P, we eliminate choice (D). Choice (B) can be eliminated because we have both J and O together with L, but that means M cannot be riding with J or O, as required. Finally, choice (E) is consistent with all the restrictions. We can show this by example: First (GHL), second (JMK), and third (ONP). But as a matter of test practice, we would not do so. Once we have eliminated choice (A) through choice (D) for good reasons, we would assume that the test writers had correctly drafted the problem and that choice (E) could be proved correct by example. Trying to construct such an example will not further the issue of the correct answer: It must, by elimination, be choice (E).

8. **The correct answer is (D).** For this question, we must again check our choices against the restrictions given, but here we will have to dig a little deeper. As a matter of tactics, we would look at choices (A), (B), and (C) first, since they are simpler than choices (D) and (E). On the surface, there appears no good reason why those three could not be true. This is not to say that they are possible; rather, since there is no obvious reason for them to be impossible, we look for another, obvious answer. We find it in choice (D). This asserts that O and M ride in cars 1 and 3, in that order. But this is not possible, for this places M in a car without O or J. (Remember that J must ride in car 2.) Choice (E) is possible, for L is under no such restriction. So, as a matter of tactics, we preview the choices, looking for a good reason to select one. The point is, there might be some exotic reason why choice (B) or choice (A) is impossible, such as when K is in the first car, and M is in the third, G cannot be in the

second. But for a train of reasoning of this sort to be the key to the correct answer would make a very difficult problem indeed. With a set such as this, we do not expect to see such a difficult problem. So we look for a more obvious answer.

9. **The correct answer is (C).** We begin by using the additional information. With O in the third car and P in the second, we deduce:

1	2	3
G	J	O
H	P	M
K	N	L

for P requires N in the second car.

This means M must go with O in the third. Now, for G and H to go together, they must be in the first car. And K must go in the first car as well—not with O in the third car. This means that L will ride in the third car. Our diagram shows that choice (C) is necessarily true, while choices (A), (B), (D), and (E) are all false.

10. **The correct answer is (D).** Here we are looking for a reason to disqualify one of the individuals listed from riding with G. We know that G and H must go together, so what might disqualify another individual from riding in the same car? Again, rather than look for very subtle tricks, we look for an obvious disqualification. N and P must ride together, so N cannot ride with G, for that would put a total of four persons in the same car. Thus, choice (D) is correct. As for choice (A), we could have J, G, and H in the second car. As for choice (B), we could have G, K, and H in the first or third cars. Similarly with L, since L is under no restriction at all. Finally, choice (E) is also possible; with G, O, and H together, we can put M into the second car, so that M rides with J.

11. **The correct answer is (D).** We begin by processing the additional information. With G and O in the first car, we have H in the first car as well, so choice (A) is incorrect. With that first car full, M must ride in the second car with J, proving choice (D) is the correct answer. As for choice (E), this is false, since N and P together would preclude us from placing M with J. Finally, either K or L could ride with J and M in the second car, but that is only possibly and not necessarily true.

12. **The correct answer is (D).** Processing the additional information, we have:

1	2	3
G	J	M
H	N	O
K	P	L

With P in the second car, N must also ride in the second car. And this means that O must accompany M in the third car. This requires that G and H go in the first car, and that they be accompanied by K, who must not ride with O. So L must ride in the remaining spot in the third car. This proves that the correct answer is (D).

Questions 13–18

Here we have a linear ordering problem, a type now very familiar. We begin by summarizing the information:

> N = 1 and P = 7
>
> L > K
>
> J > M
>
> K > O > M or K < O < M

13. **The correct answer is (B).** We begin by processing the additional information. For J and O to be separated by exactly two grades, it must be that they are in grades 2 and 5 or grades 3 and 6, though not necessarily in that order:

1	2	3	4	5	6	7
N	J			O		P
N	O			J		P
N		O			J	P
N		J			O	P

We can eliminate all but the third possibility. The first arrangement is not possible because we cannot honor the requirement J > M. The second is not possible because we cannot place O between K and M. The fourth is not possible for the same reason. Using only the third possibility, we know further:

	1	2	3	4	5	6	7
	N	K	O	M	L	J	P
or:	N	K	O	L	M	J	P
or:	N	M	O	K	L	J	P

This proves choice (B) is necessarily true. The diagram further shows that choices (A), (C), (D), and (E) are only possibly, though not necessarily, true.

14. **The correct answer is (D).** We begin by processing the additional information:

1	2	3	4	5	6	7
N	M	J	O	K	L	P

With J in grade 3, M must be in grade 2. And we know that L must be higher than K and, further, that O must go between K and M. This means that O, K, and L must be in grades 4, 5, and 6, respectively. The diagram shows that choice (D) is necessarily true and that each of the remaining choices is necessarily false.

15. **The correct answer is (D).** Enter the new information on a diagram:

1	2	3	4	5	6	7
N	K					P

Next, since K is in grade 2, the three students, O, M, and J, must be arranged in that order. So the only question is where to put L:

1	2	3	4	5	6	7
N	K	L	O	M	J	P
N	K	O	L	M	J	P
N	K	O	M	L	J	P
N	K	O	M	J	L	P

So L, M, or J could be in the fifth grade—but not O.

16. **The correct answer is (A).** We begin by processing the additional information:

1	2	3	4	5	6	7
N	M	J	O	K	L	P

We separate J from M by one grade by placing J in grade 3, which means that M, to be in a lower grade, must be in grade 2. Next, we reason that for L to be in a grade higher than K's and yet allowing that O must be between K and M, we have O, K, and L in grades 4 through 6, respectively. The diagram, therefore, proves that choice (A) is correct, while each of the other choices is necessarily false.

17. **The correct answer is (C).** Looking back over the work we have already done, we learned in our discussion of question 13 that O can be in grade 3 and that M can be in grade 4 or grade 5. Our discussion of question 14 shows that O can be in grade 4. So choices (A), (B), (D), and (E) are all possible. Choice (C), however, is not possible. If O is in the fifth grade, we cannot place either K or M above O without violating one or the other restriction that L > K and that J > M.

18. **The correct answer is (B).** We begin by processing the additional information:

1	2	3	4	5	6	7
N	K/M	O	K/M	J	L	P

For L to be in the grade ahead of J, they must be in grades 6 and 5, respectively; otherwise, it will not be possible to get O between K and M, since both K and M must be in grades lower than those of L and J, respectively. Then, we must put O between K and M, but there is no reason to place K in grade 2 and M in grade 4, as opposed to K in 4 and M in 2. So there are two possible arrangements, as shown by the diagram.

Questions 19–24

This is an ordering problem in which individuals are aligned two by two. We begin by summarizing the information:

(P & M) ≠ last

L ≠ Q

N = O

R → L

19. **The correct answer is (D).** With this question, we simply apply the initial conditions to each choice. All choices meet the requirement regarding P and M. Further, all choices meet the requirement on N and O. Finally, all choices meet the requirement on R and L. Choice (D), however, fails to meet the requirement that L and Q never ride together. The remaining choices respect this requirement. Choice (D), therefore, is not a possible order.

20. **The correct answer is (C).** We begin by processing the additional information. We know that R and L finish so that R is one place ahead of L. This means

that the order for this question must be O, R, and L. But with M following L, this means our O, R, L, and M order must be 1 through 4, respectively, for M never finishes last:

```
1    2    3    4    5
ON   R    L    MP
```

There do not appear to be any further deductions of an obvious nature, so we check our choices against the diagram. We can see that choice (A) is definitely false, that choice (B) is definitely false, that choice (D) is only possibly true, and that choice (E) is only possibly true. Choice (C), however, is necessarily true, as shown by the diagram.

21. **The correct answer is (A).** We begin by processing the additional information:

```
1    2    3    4    5
PM   NO   R    L
```

If N finishes second, then O must also finish second. And if R finishes third, then L must finish fourth. Since P and M must finish together in any place but fifth, P and M must finish first. This seems to be as far as we can go, so we look to the choices. Choice (A) is confirmed by our diagram. Choice (B) is shown by the diagram to be false. Choices (C) and (E) are incorrect for similar reasons. Q does not ride with L, so Q cannot finish in fourth place. Finally, choice (D) is possibly, though not necessarily, true.

22. **The correct answer is (C).** We begin by processing the additional information:

```
1    2    3    4    5
               R    L
```

We have three pairs of participants who must ride together: P and M, N and O, and, by stipulation, J and T. Of course, P and M cannot finish last, but they may

finish first or second. This means there are several ways of distributing our pairs. There is, however, one further deduction. Since our pairs, in whatever order they finish, occupy cars 1, 2, and 5 and since Q cannot ride with L, Q must ride in the third-place car and K in the fourth-place car.

23. **The correct answer is (E).** We begin by processing the additional information:

```
1    2    3    4    5
JR   KL   NO   MP   QT
```

With L in second place, R must finish first. This leaves only place 4 for the pair P and M. Then we know further that N finishes with O in place 3 and by stipulation that J rides with R and finishes first. Q cannot ride with L, so Q rides with T and finishes last, and K rides with L in the second-place car. Thus, the diagram confirms that choice (E) is correct and that the other choices are incorrect.

24. **The correct answer is (B).** For the final time, we begin by processing the additional information:

```
1    2    3    4    5
               MP
or:  R    L         R    L
```

We see that R and L must finish first and second or fourth and fifth, respectively. Since Q cannot ride with L and since the non-L car not occupied by a pair of participants is the R car, Q must ride with R. This means that Q finishes either first or fourth.

Section 2

1. **The correct answer is (C).** This is a main idea question. The author begins by posing the question: Why are affirmative action programs so controversial? The author then argues that affirmative

action is unlike ordinary government programs in the way it allocates the burden of the program. Because of this, the passage concludes, we are torn between supporting the programs (because they have legitimate goals) and condemning the programs (because of the way the cost is allocated). Choice (C) neatly describes this development. The author analyzes the structure of the moral dilemma. Choice (A) is incorrect since the comparison is but a subpart of the overall development and is used in the service of the larger analysis. Choice (B) is incorrect since the author reaches no such clear-cut decision. Rather, we are left with the question posed by the dilemma. Choice (D) is incorrect since the author presupposes in the presentation that the reader already understands the importance of the issue. Finally, choice (E) is incorrect since the advantages of the programs are mentioned only in passing.

2. **The correct answer is (A).** This is a logical structure question. In the second paragraph, the author will describe the general structure of government programs in order to set up the contrast with affirmative action. The discussion begins with "Setting aside…," indicating the author recognizes such cases and does not wish to discuss them in detail. Tolls and tuition are exceptions to the general rule, so the author explicitly sets them aside in order to preempt a possible objection to his analysis based on claimed counterexamples. Choice (B) is incorrect since the overall point of the passage is to discuss this dilemma, but the main point of the passage will not answer the question about the logical substructure of the argument. Choice (C) is incorrect since tolls and tuition are not ordinary government programs. Choice (D) is incorrect since the author never raises such doubts.

Finally, choice (E) misses the point of the examples. The point is not that they are costly but rather that the cost is borne by the specific user.

3. **The correct answer is (B).** This is an application question. In the first paragraph, the author states affirmative action is designed to achieve social and economic objectives. Although the claim is qualified, the author seems to believe that those arguments are in favor of affirmative action. So choice (B) is clearly supported by the text. Choice (A) is not supported by the text since the author leaves us with a question; the issue is not resolved. Choice (C) can be eliminated on the same ground. The author neither embraces nor rejects affirmative action. Choice (D) goes beyond the scope of the argument. While the author might wish that this were possible, nothing in the passage indicates such restructuring is possible. Indeed, in paragraph 3, the author remarks that the "funding" problem seems to be inherent. Finally, choice (E) can be eliminated on the same ground as choice (A). Though the author recognizes the unfairness of affirmative action, he also believes that the programs are valuable.

4. **The correct answer is (E).** In paragraph 2, the author mentions that government programs entail both social and economic costs. Then, the cost of the specific example, the passed-over worker, is not a government expenditure in the sense that money is laid out to purchase something. So the author is using the term "funding" in a non-standard way and wishes to call readers' attention to this. Choice (E) parallels this explanation. Choice (A) is incorrect since it is inconsistent with the reasoning just provided. Choice (B) is incorrect, for though the

author may believe that individuals bear a disproportionate share of the burden, this is not a response to the question asked. Choice (C) is incorrect for the same reason: It is a true but non-responsive statement. Finally, choice (D) fails for the same reason. Though the author notes that affirmative action programs are similar to other government programs in this respect, this is not an explanation for the author's placing "funding" in quotation marks.

5. **The correct answer is (D).** This is a logical structure question. In the final paragraph, the author analyzes a similar situation. This technique is called arguing from analogy. The strength of the argument depends on our seeing the similarity and accepting the conclusion of the one argument (the "villainous person") as applicable to the other argument (affirmative action). Choice (A) is perhaps the second-best response, but the author is not offering an illustration (e.g., an example of affirmative action). To be sure, the author is attempting to prove a point, but attempting to prove a conclusion is not equivalent to illustrating a contention. Choice (B) is incorrect since the author adduces the situation to support his contention. Choice (C) is incorrect since the author cites no authority. Finally, choice (E) can be eliminated since the author uses the case of the villainous person to support, not to weaken, the case.

6. **The correct answer is (B).** This is an explicit idea question. In paragraph 1, the author mentions that affirmative action is like other government programs in that it is designed to achieve certain social and economic goals. So choice (A) cites a similarity rather than a difference. Choice (C) can also be eliminated.

In paragraph 3, the author states that the relevant difference is not the method of allocating benefits. The salient difference is set forth in the same paragraph, and it is the difference described by choice (B). Choices (D) and (E) are simply not mentioned anywhere in the selection.

7. **The correct answer is (A).** This is an inference question. In the first paragraph, the author asks why affirmative action is so controversial. In the final paragraph, the answer is revealed: the moral dilemma. The wording of the passage, for example, "we are confronted with…," indicates that the author expects his reader will share this tension. So the passage is addressed to those who think affirmative action has value but who also believe it is unfair to non-minority persons. As for choice (B), the author believes that affirmative action is based on sound premises, achieving a legitimate social goal, but that the world is built so that we encounter this conflict. As for choice (C), it is not the programs themselves that contain contradictions. Rather, it is our value structure that creates the conflict. As for choice (D), the author believes the reader will regard the programs as creating suffering but not that the suffering is needless. It may very well be the cost that must be paid. Choice (E) is easily eliminated since the author expresses reservations about the programs.

8. **The correct answer is (E).** This is a main idea question but one that asks about the main idea in the abstract. The discussion thus far makes clear the justification for choice (E). The author has a sense of this moral dilemma—which, it is expected, will be shared by readers—and wants to explain why we experience this as conflict. As for choice (A), though the author develops a dilemma, the text does

not suggest that it is possible to slip between the horns of the dilemma. As for choice (B), the author offers no refutation, so we will eliminate this as incorrect. As for choice (C), any historical references are purely incidental to the overall development of the thesis. And as for choice (D), though the analysis of affirmative action may suggest to the reader a method of analyzing other social problems, the focus of the passage is a particular problem—not methodology.

9. **The correct answer is (A).** This is an inference question. The material we need is in the first paragraph. There the author discusses the high percentage of aged persons living in Sweden and notes that relatively few live with family. The author then states that Sweden placed a moratorium on the construction of acute beds in favor of long-term beds. From the order of presentation, we may infer that the one caused the other. So choice (A) is inferable from the text. Choice (B) is incorrect since no mention is made of tax laws. Choice (C) is incorrect and represents a confused reading of the second paragraph. Wages in the health field are depressed because of historical circumstances, not government policy. Choice (D) is incorrect and is a confused reading of the final paragraph. The text states that rooms are now designed to accommodate more patients, not that more patients are being crowded into small rooms. Choice (E) is incorrect and is a misreading of the first paragraph. The moratorium halted the building of acute-care beds, not long-term beds.

10. **The correct answer is (E).** This is an explicit idea question. Choices (A), (B), (C), and (D) are all mentioned in paragraph 3 as contributing to staffing problems. Choice (E), however, is not

mentioned. Though the author cites irregular hours as a problem, long hours are never mentioned as contributing to the staffing problem.

11. **The correct answer is (B).** This is an inference question. In the second paragraph, the author notes that wages in the health sector (aside from those of doctors) have traditionally been lower than those for comparable work in non-health-care sectors because of a traditional presumption that health care is eleemosynary, or charitable, work. Choice (B) nicely captures this idea. Choice (A) is incorrect since it fails to make this connection. Moreover, it will not do to argue that, generally speaking, low-paying jobs have a lower status. In the first place, that does not respond to the question, which asks about the health field. In the second, that low status and low pay are correlated does not mean that one necessarily causes the other. As for choice (C), though the passage states that doctors earned acceptable salaries, the passage does not suggest that other workers were paid low wages because of this. It was traditional bias against health-care workers other than doctors, who are professionals, which accounted for the low compensation. Choice (D) is incorrect, for while it makes a true statement, the statement is not responsive to the question. Finally, choice (E) is not suggested by the text.

12. **The correct answer is (A).** This is an inference question. At the beginning of paragraph 2, the author notes that staff costs are the most important budgetary component of health care and, further, that this is higher for chronic aged than for acute patients. Since the author uses long-term care and care for the chronic aged almost interchangeably, we may

infer that most long-term care is for the aged. So we conclude that the staff cost for long-term care generally is greater than for acute care. This is stated by choice (A). Every other answer choice can be eliminated. Choice (B) must be incorrect, for to the extent that staffing requirements are greater for long-term than for acute care, the general inflationary trend in labor costs will cause the cost of long-term care to rise more rapidly than that of acute care. Choice (C) can be eliminated because the last paragraph establishes that there is a connection. Choice (D) cannot be inferred since no mention is ever made of methods of payment. Finally, choice (E) is not supported by the passage. Though we have information about relative numbers of aged living with family, that will not generate a conclusion about relative cost.

13. **The correct answer is (A).** This is an inference question. The author states in the final paragraph that cutbacks in funding actually lead to better care. This is labelled paradoxical. This can only be paradoxical if cutbacks in funding ordinarily result in a decline in the quality of care and increases improve quality. This is answer choice (A). As for choice (B), though this may be true (and that is a question we need not answer), this will not answer the question posed. As for choice (C), though this is clearly stated in the passage, it does not explain why the cutback in funding led, paradoxically, to an improvement in care. Choice (D) can be eliminated for it, too, does not explain the paradox. Finally, choice (E) is a confused reading of the first paragraph. The moratorium was placed on construction of acute-care beds; then, later, there was a cutback in funding for long-term care.

14. **The correct answer is (B).** This is an application question of some difficulty. The author states that rising standards of living have decreased the willingness of young adults to care for aging parents in their own homes. The percentage in Sweden is 10 percent as compared with 20 to 30 and even higher percentages in other countries. There is also the intriguing note that it is only 3 percent in Stockholm. Why the large difference between Sweden as a whole and Stockholm? If it were the case that the standard of living is higher in Stockholm than in Sweden as a country, this would add support to the author's explanation. This is articulated in choice (B). As for choice (A), if the U.S. has a higher standard of living, this would undermine the author's point. That would suggest a higher percentage of aged not cared for in homes, yet the numbers show a higher percentage of aged living with family in the U.S. Choice (C) is incorrect for it is only remotely connected, if at all, with the cause for the percentages under consideration. Choice (D) will not do the trick, for we are interested in percentage of aged living with family, not in the absolute number of aged. Finally, choice (E) must fail for the same reason that choice (C) fails: it is only remotely, if at all, connected to the question of why aged parents are not cared for in family homes.

15. **The correct answer is (E).** This is an explicit idea question. According to the passage, automated theorem proving, of which AURA is the best example, is used to check human reasoning. So choice (E) is the best response to the question. Choice (A) is incorrect, since though this is a feature of programs such as "expert" programs, it is not the primary purpose of a system such as AURA. Choice (B)

fails for the same reason; this is one of many possible applications. Choice (C) is incorrect since the function of AURA is to check human reasoning. To the extent that it can be used to analyze other computer programs, an issue we need not resolve, that is not the ultimate or primary purpose. The passage is quite clear on this score. The purpose of AURA is to aid human beings in solving problems by checking logic. Finally, choice (D) is just one of several possible applications.

16. **The correct answer is (D).** This is a main idea question, cast in the form of a "best title" question. The best title will be neither too broad nor too narrow—that is, just right. Choice (A) is too broad. The author is discussing one limited aspect of computer use. Choice (B) too is wide of the mark. Though AURA programs may have some implications for theories of artificial intelligence, the author does not discuss them. Choice (C) is surely the second best answer, but it is too narrow on two counts. First, AURA is just an example of how computers might be used to assist human reasoning. So choice (D) is better in this respect. Second, even allowing that AURA is the best example of this possibility, the discussion of AURA is broader than just possible applications. The author sketches some basic theoretical concepts of AURA as well. Choice (E) is wide of the mark since the author seems to endorse the use of AURA.

17. **The correct answer is (D).** This is an explicit idea question. Choices (A), (B), (C), and (E) are all mentioned as advantages of expert programs in paragraph 3. The only reference to self-analytical programs is in paragraph 2. There the author states that AURA is not self-analytical.

18. **The correct answer is (C).** This is an explicit idea question. Choices (A) and

(E) are mentioned in paragraph 3. Choices (B) and (D) are mentioned in paragraph 2.

19. **The correct answer is (B).** This is a fairly interesting application question. In the second paragraph, the author describes the theory of the AURA program. The computer is given the design of the system and then told that the goal cannot be reached given the design. Then, if the computer finds a contradiction in that information, this means the goal will be achieved by the design. In other words, we have a sort of indirect proof. We take the set of premises and the negation of the conclusion we hope to prove. If a contradiction can be found in the premises and negation of the conclusion, then the conclusion itself is proved. Applying this to our question, if the assertion that the switch remains open generates a contradiction, then the opposite conclusion is proved: The switch should be closed. And that answer is choice (B). Choice (A) is too broad a conclusion. The contradiction does not prove the system was well designed, only that the result described by choice (B) will occur. That may or may not be the desired result. Choice (C) is incorrect for it is contradicted by our analysis. Choices (D) and (E) make the same error as choice (A), just in the opposite direction.

20. **The correct answer is (A).** This is a tone question. The author obviously thinks very highly of the development he is describing. The only adjective in the array of choices consistent with this attitude is choice (A). Every other choice has certain negative connotations. But no reservations are expressed by the author.

21. **The correct answer is (A).** This is a main idea question. Choice (A) nicely

describes the approach of the author. He describes recent developments in computer applications. Choice (B) is incorrect since there is no misconception mentioned. To be sure, the author answers the second question (Will computers replace humans?) in the negative. But that is not the same thing as correcting a misconception. Choice (C) is incorrect since the author describes, but does not propose, a theory. Choice (D) is incorrect, for no objections are raised. Finally, choice (E) is incorrect since the author does not focus on any particular problem and propose a solution. In general, it is possible to argue that there are elements of choices (B), (C), (D), or (E) in the passage, but it cannot be said that any one of those is the main point of the passage.

22. **The correct answer is (A).** This is a main idea question. The passage actually makes two points: Who is Josquin, and why have we never heard of him? Choice (A) correctly mentions both of these. Choice (B) is incorrect since the main focus is not to describe medieval music at all. Rather, the author focuses on Josquin, a man of the Renaissance. Choice (C) is incorrect because the author is more concerned to introduce the reader to Josquin than to place Josquin into a context. And in any event, though the author mentions some ways in which Josquin broke with his predecessors, this is not a discussion of his "influence on later composers." Choice (D) is incorrect, for the enumeration of features of Josquin's music is incidental to the task of introducing the reader to Josquin. Moreover, the author does not offer critical commentary. The mere fact that the passage praises Josquin's music does not constitute critical analysis. Finally, choice

(E) is incorrect because it fails to refer to the second major aspect of the passage: Why is Josquin not better known?

23. **The correct answer is (E).** This is an explicit idea question. Choice (A) is answered in paragraph two ("Solace me, . . ."). Choice (B) is answered in the final paragraph (sackbut). Choice (C) is answered in the second paragraph (Ockeghem). An answer to choice (D) is suggested in the final paragraph. Choice (E) must be the correct answer, since the author never makes reference to any students.

24. **The correct answer is (E).** This is an inference question. In the third paragraph, the author lists certain difficulties in reading a Renaissance score: no tempo specified, missing flats and sharps, no instrument/voice indication, and no instruction as to whether a piece is written in a major or a minor key. Since these are regarded as deficiencies of Renaissance scoring, we may infer that modern music notation contains all of these. But choice (E) overstates the case. Although modern notation provides more guidance, the author does not say that it leaves literally no room for individual interpretation.

25. **The correct answer is (B).** This is an application question. The support for choice (B) is found in paragraph 3, where the author discusses the distinction between concept and performance. The author states that music does not exist as printed notes. The notation is just a set of instructions for producing music. So the author would agree with choice (B). As for choice (A), it is conceivable that the author might endorse this statement— though it is also possible that the author would reject it. It is clear, however, that as between the statement in choice (B)

and that in choice (A), we can be sure that the author would endorse choice (B). So choice (B), rather than choice (A), must be correct. Choice (C) is incorrect because Josquin belongs to the Renaissance, not the Middle Ages. Choice (D) fails for the same reason that choice (A) fails. Finally, there is no support for the statement in choice (E).

26. **The correct answer is (D).** Here, too, we have an application question. There is some merit to each of the choices, but we are looking for the one answer that is most closely connected with the text. Since the author discusses the lack of funding as one important reason for Josquin's obscurity, an obscurity the author deplores, the argument might be used to support a proposal for funds to promote Josquin's music. That is choice (D). Choice (A) is less clearly supported by the text. To the extent that it is read as a device to promote Josquin's music, it would be less effective than choice (D) since the author states that *collegia musica* have a high turnover of students. Establishing yet another one would not do as much to bring Josquin's music to more people as choice (D). As for choices (B) and (E), these do not tie in with the idea of publicizing Josquin's music. Finally, choice (C) has some plausibility, but choice (D) has a connection with the passage that choice (C) lacks.

27. **The correct answer is (B).** This is an explicit idea question. Choices (C), (D), and (E) are mentioned in the final paragraph. Choice (A) is mentioned in the third paragraph. Choice (B) is never mentioned. The author states that musicians who read modern notation have difficulty reading Renaissance notation—not that these musicians lack talent.

28. **The correct answer is (A).** This is a tone question. The author compares Josquin to Galileo in order to praise Josquin. This must mean that the author has a very high opinion of Galileo. So choices (D) and (E) can be eliminated because they are merely neutral. Choice (B) can be eliminated because of its negative connotations. And choice (C) can be eliminated as being lukewarm, when the author is clearly enthusiastic about Josquin and therefore Galileo as well.

Section 3

1. **The correct answer is (B).** This question requires careful attention to the quantifiers in each claim. An additional expense voucher might indicate additional expenses for an already identified employee or expenses incurred by an additional employee. A claim that states only that there are "at least so many employees" and that they incurred "at least this in expenses" cannot be contradicted by a revision upward in any number. A claim that states "there were exactly so many employees" or which states "there were at most so many employees" is contradicted by the discovery of another employee. The same reasoning applies to expenses. An "at least" claim is not contradicted by an upward revision, but the other claims are. Choice (A) can be contradicted by an upward revision in the number of employees. Choice (C) can be contradicted by an upward revision in the amount of expenses claimed. Choices (D) and (E) can be contradicted on both grounds. Choice (B) cannot be contradicted by any new finding.

2. **The correct answer is (A).** The question stem contains a hidden assumption: It is a loaded question. It presupposes

that the person questioned agrees that the city is discriminating against its Hispanic residents. Choice (A) is a pretty nice parallel. The questioner assumes that the Congressman agrees that defense spending is out of hand, which may or may not be true. Choice (B) makes no such assumption. It can be answered with a simple "yes" if the chairperson plans to take a luncheon recess; otherwise a "no" will do the job. Choice (C) requires more than a "yes" or "no" answer, but it still contains no presuppositions. Since the question asks "what," the speaker may respond by saying much, little, or none at all. Choice (D) may be said to make a presupposition—Gladys is going to the store—but here the presupposition is not concealed. It is made an explicit condition of the answer. Finally, choice (E) is a little like choice (B) in that a simple "yes" or "no" can communicate the counselor's opinion. It might be objected that choice (E) presupposes that the company has an affirmative action program and that this makes it similar to the question stem. Two responses can be made. First, choice (E) is in this way like choice (D): The assumption—if there is one—is fairly explicit. Second, choice (E) does not have the same loaded tone as choice (A) does, so by comparison, choice (A) is a better choice.

3. **The correct answer is (E).** The ad is a little deceptive. It tries to create the impression that if hospitals are using Dr. John's Milk of Magnesia, people will believe it is a good product. But what the ad actually says is that Dr. John uses the same *ingredient* that hospitals use (milk of magnesia is a simple suspension of magnesium hydroxide in water). The ad is something like an ad for John's Vinegar that claims it has "acetic acid," which

is vinegar. Choices (A), (B), (C), and (D), in various ways, fall into the trap of the inviting wording, and those statements are not conclusions that can be logically inferred. Choice (E), however, is logically inferable: from 9 of 10 X use Y, you can infer that it is true that Y is used by 9 out of 10 X.

4. **The correct answer is (A).** Statements (1) and (4) combine to give us choice (A). If all wheeled conveyances that travel on the highway are polluters, and a bicycle does not travel on the highway, then a bicycle cannot be a polluter. If choice (A) is then correct, choice (B) must be incorrect because bicycles do not travel on the highways at all. Choices (C) and (D) make the same mistake. (3) must be read to say, "If I am driving, it is raining," not "If it is raining, I am driving." Choice (E) is clearly false since my car is driven on the highway. Don't make the problem harder than it is.

5. **The correct answer is (E).** Picking up on our discussion of choices (C) and (D) in the previous question, (3) must read, "If I am driving, then it is raining." Let that be: "If P, then Q." If we then had not-Q, we could deduce not-P. Choice (E) gives us not-Q by changing (4) to "It is not raining." Changing (1) or (2) or even both is not going to do the trick, for they don't touch the relationship between my driving my car and rain—they deal only with pollution and we need the car to be connected. Similarly, if we change (3) to make it deal with pollution, we have not adjusted the connection between my driving and rain, so choice (C) must be wrong. Choice (D) is the worst of all the answers. Whether or not rainwater is polluted has nothing to do with the connection between my driving and rain. Granted, there is the unstated assumption that

my car only pollutes when I drive it, but this is OK.

6. The correct answer is (E). The reasoning in the argument is representative of the fallacy of false cause. Common sense tells you that you are not necessarily safer driving at higher speeds. Moreover, the distance you are from your home does not necessarily make you more or less safe. And it will not do to engage in wild speculation, e.g., people suddenly become more attentive at speeds over 45 miles per hour. The exam is just not that subtle. Rather we should look for a fairly obvious alternative explanation, and we find it in choice (E). The real reason there are fewer fatalities at speeds over 50 miles per hour and at a distance greater than 25 miles from home is that less driving time is logged under such conditions. Most driving originates at home and proceeds at speeds set for residential areas. Choices (A), (B), and (C) all seem to make plausible statements, but they are irrelevant to the claim made in the stem paragraph. It is difficult to see how they could either weaken or strengthen the argument. Choice (D) has the merit of addressing the statistics used to support the argument, but without further information choice (D) does not weaken the argument—it merely makes an observation. To be sure, if we knew that states were notoriously bad at gathering statistics, choice (D) could weaken the argument. But that requires speculation, and we always prefer an obvious answer such as choice (E).

7. The correct answer is (D). The author states that a certain amount of rain in a given time *usually* results in mushrooms growing in his backyard. Both choices (A) and (B) are wrong for the same reason.

From the fact that there has not been the requisite minimum rainfall required for mushrooms, we would not want to conclude that there has been *no* rain at all. Choice (C) overstates the author's case and is for that reason wrong. The author specifically qualifies his claim by saying it "usually" happens this way. Thus, we would not want to say that the absence of mushrooms and fungus definitely means that the requisite amount of rain has not fallen—only that it seems likely or probable that there has not been enough rain. And choice (E) would not be supportable without some further premise about rain now. Notice that choice (D) is a safe conclusion: "probably" and "not more."

8. The correct answer is (C). Given the fairly "soft" information provided in the paragraph, any conclusion that is to be "completely justified" on the basis of that information will have to be a fairly minimal claim. We can eliminate choice (A) since the paragraph asserts something about the effect of Jack Remain's program but never claims that the Jack Remain program is unique in this respect. Choice (B) goes beyond the scope of the argument by asserting the program is effective for all ages. The paragraph actually makes only a minimal claim, namely, this is possible. Even if the program is effective only for persons 20 to 25, the claim is not false—it is true though only for that limited age group. Choice (D) overstates the case. The paragraph claims that weight loss is possible—not that it is certain. Choice (E) cannot be justified since that would be to move from the premise "weight loss is possible" to the conclusion "most people need exercise to lose weight." But the conclusion does not follow from the premise. Choice

(C), however, can be justified. If it is true, as the stem asks us to assume, that a study shows weight loss is possible, then it must be true that the program is effective for some—even if only for one person. This is all choice (C) claims: You might be one of the lucky ones.

9. **The correct answer is (D).** In essence, the advertisement attempts to shift the burden of proof to the reader. It is possible—you try it and find out whether it is possible for you. Choice (E) is incorrect since no other claims are cited. Choice (C) is incorrect since the ad is clearly an attempt to influence the reader's decision. Choice (B) should be eliminated in favor of choice (A) since the paragraph is not a logical set of premises. This leaves choice (A) as the second-best answer. And it can be argued that the paragraph does provide evidence (the study) and, further, that it does allow the reader to reach a conclusion. But what would that conclusion be? If the conclusion mentioned in choice (A) is to try or not to try the product, then choice (A) is incorrect since the ad reaches the conclusion that the reader should try it. But if the conclusion is whether or not the product works, then choice (D) is better because it more accurately describes the attempt to shift the burden of proof.

10. **The correct answer is (B).** The author's claim is self-referential—it refers to itself or includes itself in its own description. The author says that *every* action is economically motivated; therefore, we may conclude that the motivation in making such a claim and in writing a book about it is also economically motivated. The speaker in our passage says it is possible to apply the author's theory to the author's own actions. This is why

choice (B) is correct. Neither choice (A) nor choice (E) can be correct inasmuch as the author of the book claims that there are no such motivations. Ultimately, the author says, all motivations can be reduced to one, economics. Choice (C) has to be wrong, since the author of the book claims that everything done is economically motivated. The examples make it clear that even a reformer with some seemingly non-economic motive would be "pure" only on the surface, with a deeper, economic motivation for reforming. Finally, choice (D) can be rejected since it conflicts with one of the examples given by the author of the book.

11. **The correct answer is (A).** The argument makes the rather outlandish assumption that the physical characteristics of the criminal dictate the kind of crime that will be committed. But as unreasonable as that may seem in light of common sense, it *is* an assumption made by the speaker. (We did not make the assumption, the speaker did.) Choice (B) is not an assumption of the argument, since the paragraph specifically states that the killer was executed—the speaker cannot have escaped. Choice (C) does not commit the blatant error committed by choice (B), but it is still wrong. Although choice (C) might be a better explanation for the crimes now being committed than that proposed by our speaker, our speaker advances the explanation supported by choice (A), not choice (C). In fact, the speaker uses phrases such as "looks very much like" that tell us that he assumes there are two killers. As for choices (D) and (E), these may or may not be true in the real world, but they are not assumptions of the speaker's argument.

12. **The correct answer is (A).** The form of the argument can be represented using letters as follows:

    (1) All R are either O or W. (All non-Readers are non-Opinion holders or Wrong.)

    (2) All O are R.

If (2) is true, (1) might be either false or true, since it is possible that there are some who have not read the report who hold right opinions. That is, even if (2) is true and all O are R, that does not tell us anything about all the Rs, only about all the Os. The rest of the Rs might be Ws (wrong-opinion holders) or something else altogether (right-opinion holders). By this reasoning, we see that we cannot conclude that (1) is definitely true, so choice (B) must be wrong. Moreover, we have no ground for believing (1) to be more or less likely true, so choice (C) can be rejected. As for choice (D), even if we assume that all the Rs are either O or W, we are not entitled to conclude that all Os are Rs. There may be someone without an opinion who has not read the report. Finally choice (E), if it is false that all the Os (non-opinion holders) are not Rs, this tells us nothing about all Rs and their distribution among O and W.

13. **The correct answer is (A).** The fallacy in the author's argument is that he takes a group term ("the average size of women") and applies it to the individual. Choice (A) calls attention to this fallacy. The average size of women is irrelevant in the case of those women who are of sufficient size. Choice (D) concedes too much to the author. We do not have to settle for the conclusion that some women may be suitable for desk jobs. We can win the larger claim that some women may be suitable to be police officers—or at least as suitable as their male counterparts. Choices

(B), (C), and (E) are possible arguments to be used against the author's general position. We might want to claim, for example, that training or weapons will compensate for want of size, but again there is no reason even to grant the author that much. We do not even have to concede that the average size is relevant. Finally, choice (E) also gives away too much. Although the use of pistols is sometimes called "deadly force," the author's linkage of size to force specifies force as being a strength or size idea.

14. **The correct answer is (D).** We can use our capital letters to see why choice (D) is the correct answer. The structure of the stem argument is as follows:

    No S are R.

    Some S are D.

    Therefore, some D are not R.

Choice (D) shares this form:

    All pets are excluded: No P are A.

    (A = allowed)

    Some P are V.

    (Many = Some)

    Therefore, some V are not A.

Choice (A) has a very different form since it is presented as a probabilistic, not a deductive or logical, argument. Choice (B)'s conclusion goes beyond the information given in the premises. We cannot conclude that the uncle enjoys paying the bills, even though he may incur them. Choice (C) has the following form:

    Some BB are F.

    All F is WR.

    Therefore, all BB are WR.

This does not parallel our question stem for two reasons. First, our stem argument is valid, while the argument in choice (C) is not. Second, choice (D) is more nearly parallel to the stem argument than choice (C); for even if we rearrange the assumptions in choice (C) to put the "all" proposition first and the "some" proposition second, the "all's" and the "some's" of choice (C) do not parallel those of the question stem. Choice (E) does not share the stem form. First, it is not the same argument form (all, some, etc.). Second, choice (E) is clearly not a proper logical argument.

15. **The correct answer is (A).** Perhaps a little diagram is the easiest way to show this problem.

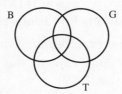

We will show all B are T by eliminating that portion of the diagram where some area of B is not also inside T:

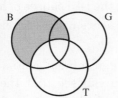

Now, let us put an x to show the existence of those Bs that are Gs:

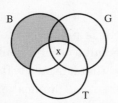

The diagram shows us that (1) is true. Since the only areas left for Bs are within the T circle, the G condition is unimportant. (2) is not inferable. Although there is some overlap of the G and T circles, there is also some non-overlap. This shows that it may be possible to be a T without also being a G. (3) is not inferable since

our diagrams are restricted to the three categories B, G, and T and say nothing about things outside of those categories. The "x" on the diagram shows that choices (D) and (E) are necessarily false.

16. **The correct answer is (C).** The stem argument has the form "If P, then Q. Q. Therefore, P." The argument is invalid. There may be other reasons that the razor is not functioning, e.g., the switch is not on, it is broken, etc. Choice (C) has this form also. John's fingerprints might have been found at the scene, yet he may not have committed the crime. Choice (A) has the form: "If P, then Q. Not Q. Therefore, not P," which not only is not parallel to the question stem, but also is valid and thus a poor parallel to the invalid original argument as well. Choice (B) has the form: "P or Q. Not P. Therefore, Q." This, too, does not parallel the stem argument, and, like choice (B), is valid. Choice (D) is invalid, but the fallacy is not the same as what we find in the stem argument. The stem argument is set up using "if, then" statements. Choice (D) does not parallel this form. Choice (E) does use "if, then" statements, but its form is: "If P, then Q. P. Therefore, P." This argument is clearly valid.

17. **The correct answer is (A).** The author's statement is self-contradictory or paradoxical. It says, in effect, "No statement is always correct," but then that statement itself must be false—since it attempts to make a claim about "always." The author's statement is inductive, that is, a generalization; but choice (E) is not as good an answer as choice (A) because it fails to pick up on the fact that the statement is internally contradictory. The statement cannot be valid, choice (D), since the author tries to pass it off as a generalization. Generalizations can be

strong or weak, well founded or ill founded, but they cannot be valid or invalid. Choice (C) is incorrect since there is nothing ambiguous or poorly defined in the argument. Finally, the argument is not circular, choice (B), because the author does not seek to establish his conclusion by assuming it. As we have noted, the statement is self-contradictory, so it could not possibly be circular.

18. **The correct answer is (B).** This item asks you to draw a conclusion from the paragraph. The best answer will be one that is well supported by the text, and this is choice (B). The initial paragraph sets up a contrast between political commitment and financial reward and indicates that Gonzalez chose political commitment over financial reward. The conclusion of the paragraph should be some consequence of this decision. Choice (B) describes a possible consequence of this decision.

Choice (A) is wrong because the paragraph implies that she did not enjoy popular acclaim. Choice (C) is incorrect because it goes beyond the scope of the selection. Although choice (C) describes an idea that is generally related to the subject matter of the paragraph, it does not flow as a conclusion from the distinction drawn in the paragraph. Choice (D) must surely be wrong, for Gonzalez's resistance to certain inducements would not be calculated to compromise the chances of those who came later. And finally, choice (E) makes the same mistake as choice (C). To be sure, this is an idea that is generally related to the subject of the initial paragraph, but this idea does not follow as a conclusion from the paragraph.

19. **The correct answer is (E).** Again, we are looking for a choice that is strongly supported by the text, and this time it is choice (E). The paragraph clearly implies a distinction between economic reward and political commitment and that the latter was the course chosen by Gonzalez. As for choices (A) and (D), these are topics that conceivably were treated by Gonzalez's films, but nothing in the paragraph requires such a conclusion. Choice (C), though possible, is not supported by the text.

20. **The correct answer is (A).** Analyze the argument into its various premises.

   ❶ Some experts maintain reductions will hurt care of the elderly and chronically ill.

   ❷ Part of recent increases in costs have helped provide service to these groups.

   ❸ But the real causes of high costs are duplication, inefficiency, inflated salaries.

Once the argument is analyzed in this way, you can see that the most likely conclusion is that contained in choice (A): Efforts to control costs will necessarily hurt the elderly and chronically ill that much.

Choice (B) is probably the second best response, but a careful reading of choice (B) shows that it is fatally flawed. Choice (B) asserts that duplication and inefficiency contribute to the rising cost of care for the elderly and the chronically ill. But the passage says (1) that recent increases in the cost of care for those groups reflect improvements in service and (2) that the factors cited inflate health-care costs in general, not just those specifically incurred by the elderly or chronically ill.

Choice (C), of course, is contradicted by the passage. Choice (D), too, is at least in tension with the passage, for the author implies that some of the increase in health-care costs for the elderly and chronically ill have come as the result of improvements in services. Finally, choice (E) goes beyond the scope of the passage. In the first place, you would need to know whether elderly and chronically ill pay their own expenses (as opposed to having them paid by the government or a third-party carrier), and the passage is silent on that question. In addition, you would need a lot more to support the conclusion that rising costs will make health care unaffordable for those groups, as opposed to just burdensome.

21. **The correct answer is (C).** The logical flaw in the argument is not that difficult to find. The argument assumes that a city that ranks below another city in any one category (in particular the crime category) cannot rank above that city in the overall category. Now the question becomes which of the choices attacks this assumption.

The best available attack is provided by choice (C). Although this choice does not state directly that the assumption just isolated is erroneous, it does provide two counterexamples to the assumption. Choices (A), (B), and (E) make assertions not inconsistent with the information provided in the paragraph about Detroit and San Francisco, and they don't attack the hidden premise we have isolated. Finally, choice (D) is somewhat like the correct answer, but it does not attack the hidden assumption in the way that choice (C) does. Notice that choice (D) describes a situation in which the city that ranks lower in the overall standings also ranks lower in other categories as well.

22. **The correct answer is (B).** This item serves as a good reminder of the importance of reading the answer choices carefully, for some of the choices here are very close. The speaker says that adults often assume that a child feels like a child but thinks like an adult. But, according to the speaker, this is wrong—the opposite is true. But what is the opposite? Children feel not like children but like adults, and children think not like adults but like children. This is the conclusion provided by Choice (B).

As for choice (A), while the speaker apparently believes that there is some connection between the emotional and mental functions of a child and those of an adult, nothing in the passage supports the conclusion that the one prefigures the other. Choice (C), too, goes beyond the scope of the paragraph. The speaker claims that there are some similarities and some differences between children and adults, but that premise will not support the conclusion that the differences are more important than the similarities. The suggestion in choice (D) seems to be contradicted by the selection, for the speaker clearly says that thought patterns change. Finally, choice (E) is surely the second best answer, for it at least has the merit of suggesting a reversal of a position. But when the speaker asserts "the opposite is true," the speaker means the opposite of the contention of many adults (specifically, that children think like adults but feel like children). The speaker does not mean that children and adults have opposite reactions to the same situations.

23. **The correct answer is (A).** Here you can use the same devices you use in solving analytical reasoning items to keep track of this information. The statements

in the initial paragraph can be summarized as follows:

$SY \rightarrow (FG \text{ or } SG)$ (Sunny implies Fishing or Swimming)

$SG \rightarrow TS$ (Swimming implies Tennis)

$\sim TS$ (Not tennis)

From this you can infer $\sim SG$. (Hector did not go swimming.) But you cannot infer from the fact that Hector did not go swimming that he did or did not go fishing; and since he might have gone fishing, it is possible that Saturday was sunny. No information is provided about Sharon's behavior when she is not playing tennis or what anyone does when it is cloudy, so neither choice (D) nor choice (E) can be deduced.

24. **The correct answer is (C).** This is a fun little item. John says the dollars should be spent right here on Earth, meaning, of course, they should be spent on practical projects rather than projects such as space exploration. Joan turned John's language around on him by pointing out that—literally—this money is spent right here on Earth (even if it is for space exploration). Notice how the question stem here guides you. It doesn't just ask you to comment on the exchange. It informs you that the exchange is characterized by a shift in meaning and then asks you to identify the critical term.

25. **The correct answer is (B).** The conclusion of the argument is "I am not impaired." The premise is "I drank wine, but I did not drink liquor." One possible assumption that could underwrite the conclusion is "It is impossible to become impaired drinking wine." This, however, is not a possible choice. But choice (B) does articulate a possible hidden assumption. The speaker means to say "I can't be

drunk, I have only been drinking wine and not liquor." (An obviously fallacious argument but for reasons not presently relevant.) This claim depends on the assumption that hard liquor impairs more than wine.

Section 4

1. **The correct answer is (B).** The proposition that you cannot argue with taste says that taste is relative. Since we are looking for an answer choice inconsistent with that proposition, we seek an answer choice that argues that taste, or aesthetic value, is absolute, or at least not relative—that there are standards of taste. Choice (B) is precisely that.

Choices (C) and (D) are just distractions, playing on the notion of taste in the physical sense and the further idea of the distasteful; but these superficial connections are not strong enough.

Choices (A), (B), and (E) are all activities in which there is some element of aesthetic judgment or appreciation. In choice (A), the holding of an exhibition, while implying some selection principle and thus some idea of a standard of taste, does not truly purport to judge aesthetics in the way that choice (B), precisely a beauty contest, does. The exhibition may be of historical or biographical interest, for example. Choice (E) also stresses more of the exhibition aspect than the judging aspect. You should not infer that all movie festivals are contests, since the word "festival" does not require this interpretation and, in fact, there are festivals at which the judging aspect is minimal or non-existent. The Cannes Film Festival, while perhaps the best known, is not the only type of movie festival there is. The questions are not tests of your knowledge of the movie industry.

2. The correct answer is (D). Note the question stem very carefully: We are to find the answer choice from which we can deduce the sample argument. You must pay very careful attention to the question stem in every problem. Choice (D) works very nicely as it gives us the argument structure: "All post-1974 students are required.... George is a post-1974 student. Therefore, George is required. . . ." Actually, the middle premise is phrased in the conditional (with an "if"), but our explanation is close enough, even if it is a bit oversimplified. Choice (A) will not suffice, for while it describes the situation before 1974, it just does not address itself to the post-1974 situation. And George is a post-1974 student. Choice (B) also fails. From the fact that all of those who took the course graduated after 1974, we cannot conclude that George was one of them (any more than we can conclude from the proposition that all airline flight attendants lived after 1900 and that Richard Nixon, who lived after 1900, was one of them). Choice (C) fails for the same reason that choice (A) fails. Choice (E) is a bit tricky because of the double negative. It makes the sentence awkward. The easiest way to handle such a sentence is to treat the double negative as an affirmative. The negative cancels the negative, just as in arithmetic a negative number times a negative number yields a positive number. So choice (E) actually says that before 1974, the course was not required. That is equivalent to choice (A) and must be wrong for the same reason.

3. The correct answer is (B). Choice (B) is the only one of the three that is completely supported by the argument. Choice (C) is easily dismissed. That there are no minnows on this side of the lake now surely does not mean that there will never be any, any more than the fact that there are no children in the park now means that there never will be any children in the park. Choice (A) is very close to choice (B) and differs only in the qualification introduced by the word "probably," but that is an important qualification. The author states specifically that bass are usually found wherever there are minnows. So where there are no bass, he expects to find no minnows. But, of course, he cannot be certain. Perhaps there are other reasons for the absence of bass: The water is too cold or too shallow or too muddy for bass, though not for minnows. So choice (A) overstates the case. The author apparently allows that you may find minnows without bass—but not usually. Choice (D) cannot be deduced from the premises since no information is provided about rivers (as opposed to lakes). And choice (E) is not inferable since the information about lakes does not preclude the possibility that largemouths are found elsewhere.

4. The correct answer is (D). Juanita wonders how Tommy knows the phone has rung if he couldn't hear it because of the shower. She overlooks the possibility that he learned the phone had rung without actually hearing it himself. Perhaps someone else lives with him who heard it; perhaps Tommy has an answering machine and later learned that the phone rang while he was in the shower; maybe the caller calls back and tells Tommy he called earlier and Tommy says "Oh, I must have been in the shower and didn't hear it." Juanita overlooks these possibilities. Choice (A) is incorrect because Juanita apparently assumes the phone does ring and that Tommy can hear it ringing. Choices (C) and (E) may or may not be true, but they do not address themselves to Juanita's statement. Choice (B) could only underlie Juanita's objection to Tommy's remarks if hearing calls were the only possible way in which Tommy could learn of the call. But as we show, there are other possibilities.

5. **The correct answer is (E).** Choice (A) is not inconsistent with the advertisement since the ad is touting the strength of the pain-reliever, not its price. Choice (C), too, can easily be seen not to be inconsistent. The ad speaks of non-prescription pain-relievers, but choice (C) brings up the irrelevant matter of prescription pain-relievers. Choice (B) is not inconsistent because RELIEF does not claim to be the one strongest pain-reliever, only that no other non-prescription pain-reliever is stronger. Choice (D) is not inconsistent because it does not talk about sales but medicine given "free of charge" in a study. Choice (E), however, directly contradicts the ad.

6. **The correct answer is (C).** Choice (C) is an assumption of the psychologist. He observed the dogs for a certain period of time and found that each time a stranger approached, they kept silent. From those observed instances, he concluded that the dogs never barked at strangers. Obviously his theory would be disproved (or at least it would have to be seriously qualified) if, when he was not watching, the dogs barked their heads off at strangers. Choice (A) is not an assumption because the speaker makes no value judgment about how dogs ought to be treated. Choice (B) is similar in that no such broad conclusion about "better adjusted" is implied. Choices (D) and (E) are simply confused readings of the speaker's thinking.

7. **The correct answer is (B).** Choice (B) would undermine the psychologist's thesis that "only a beaten dog barks." It cites instances in which the dog was not beaten and still barked at strangers. This would force the psychologist to reconsider his conclusion about the connection between beating and barking. Choice (A) is not like choice (B). It does not state the dogs were never beaten; it states only that the dogs were not beaten when they barked at strangers. It is conceivable that they were beaten at other times. If they were, then even though they might bark at strangers (and not be beaten at that moment), they would not be counter-examples to the psychologist's theory. Choice (C) is not an assumption of the psychologist, as we saw in the preceding question, so denying it does not affect the strength of his argument. The psychologist is concerned with the factual connection between beating a dog and its barking; information about the owners' feelings can hardly be relevant to the factual issue. Choice (D) is an interesting choice, but the fact that some of the dogs also barked at non-strangers doesn't address the connection between discipline and barking at strangers: so they also barked at non-strangers, so what? And choice (E) is wrong because the analysis depends not on the particular object used but rather on the notion of physical discipline.

8. **The correct answer is (B).** Here the author must assume that every effect that is part of the child's experience has been generated by a cause that was also a part of the child's experience, but that is possible only on the assumption that the cause, which is an effect itself, is the result of some previous cause. In other words, every effect flows from some ear-

lier effect. Now, admittedly, that seems to lead to a pretty absurd conclusion: Therefore, there could be no beginning of experience for the child—it must stretch back infinitely. But the question stem does not ask us to critique the argument, only to analyze it and uncover its premises. Choice (A) is wrong because the author does not say all experiences are alike, only that the one today has its roots in the one yesterday. For example, sometimes the presence of moisture in the atmosphere causes rain, sometimes snow. Choice (C) oversimplifies matters in two respects. One, while the author may agree that a child's experiences may tell us something about the parents (assuming the child is in intimate contact with them), we surely would not want to conclude that is the best way to learn about the parents. Two, the parents are not the only source of experience the child has, so the later effects would be the result of non-parental causes as well. Choice (D) is incorrect because the author need not assume that experience is cumulative. In some cases, the cause-and-effect sequence may only reiterate itself so that experience is circular rather than cumulative. Finally, choice (E) is another example of going too far—of extending a simple factual statement beyond the scope the author originally gave it. Here the author says that experience causes experience, but he never suggests that we are in a position to use this principle practically, to manipulate the input to mold the child.

9. **The correct answer is (C).** The author's claim is that we have unbounded resources, and he tries to prove this by showing that we are getting better and better at extracting those resources from the ground. But that is like saying, "I

have found a way to get the last little bit of toothpaste out of the tube; therefore, the tube will never run out." Choice (C) calls our attention to this oversight. Choice (A) does not contradict the author's claim. In fact, it seems to support it. He might suggest, "Even if we run out of fossil fuels, we still have uranium for nuclear power." Now, this is not to suggest that he would. The point is only to show that choice (A) supports rather than undermines the author's contention. Choice (B) is an attack on the author's general stance, but it does not really contradict the particular conclusion he draws. The author says, "We have enough." Choice (B) says, "It is expensive." Both could very well be true, so they cannot contradict one another. Choice (D) is similar to choice (B). Yes, you may be correct, the technology is expensive, or in this case wasteful, but it will still get us the fuel we need. Finally, choice (E) is incorrect for pretty much these same reasons. Yes, the energy will have unwanted side effects, but the author claimed only that we could get the energy. The difficulty with choices (B), (D), and (E) is that though they attack the author's general position, though they undermine his general suggestion, they do not contradict his conclusion.

Questions 10–12

10. **The correct answer is (A).**

11. **The correct answer is (D).**

12. **The correct answer is (C).** Choice (A) is circular. It is like saying, "I never tell a lie; and you must believe that because, as I have just told you, I never tell a lie." So choice (A) is the answer to question 10. Choice (E) might seem circular: Guns do not cause crimes, people do. But it is not. The author's point is that these crimes

would be committed anyway, and he explains how they would be committed. Choice (C) is an *ad hominem* attack. It rejects the conclusion of the argument not because the argument is illogical but because it comes from a particular source. Remember, as we learned in the Test Busters section, not all *ad hominem* are illegitimate. It is perfectly all right to inquire into possible biases of the source, and that is just what occurs here. So choice (C) is the answer to question 12. Choice (D) is a fairly weak argument. It takes a handful of observed instances and generalizes to a strong conclusion. But even though it may be weak, it does fit the description "generalization," so choice (D) is the answer to question 11. Choice (B) is just left over and fits none of the descriptions.

13. **The correct answer is (A).** The author places himself in opposition to the sociologists whom he cites. He claims an alternative interpretation of the evidence. In other words, the most logical continuation of the passage will be the one that explains why such sects are not a recent phenomenon even though there are no old ones around. Choice (A) does this neatly. Since the members abstain from sexual relations, they will not reproduce members and the sect will tend to die out. This explains why there are none more than 50 or 60 years old. Choice (C), if anything, supports the position of the sociologists, for it implicitly gives up trying to explain the evidence differently and also undercuts the explanation the author might have given. Choice (B) is irrelevant because intensity of religious fervor is irrelevant to the length of the sect's existence; it cannot possibly help the author explain away the evidence of the sociologists. Choice (D) is irrelevant

for another reason. The author needs to explain why the sects are all relatively young without having recourse to the thesis of the sociologists that they are a recent phenomenon. That there are other organizations that encourage sexual relations of whatever kind cannot help the author explain a phenomenon such as the Waiters. Finally, choice (E) is a distraction, picking up as it does on a minor detail. The author needs to explain the short-livedness of groups of which the Waiters is only an example.

14. **The correct answer is (E).** The conclusion of the speaker is that the checkup has no value, so anything that suggests the checkup does have value will undermine the conclusion. Choice (A) shows a possible advantage of having the checkup. It says, in effect, while the checkup is not foolproof and will not catch everything, it does catch some fairly important things. Choice (B) also gives us a possible reason for visiting our mechanic for a 5,000-mile checkup. Even if it won't keep our car in running order, it is necessary if we want to take advantage of our warranty. Finally, choice (C) also gives us a good reason to have a checkup: The mechanic will make some routine adjustments. All three of these propositions, then, mention possible advantages of having a checkup. Choice (D) weakens the argument on the theory that "A ounce of prevention is worth a pound of cure." Choice (E), however, actually seems to strengthen the argument: the policy prevents very few problems.

15. **The correct answer is (A).** Here we are looking for the most perfect analogy. Keep in mind, first, that the author opposes the move, and second, all of the features of the union-management situation, in particular that they are adversaries.

Choice (A) captures both elements. The relationship between prison administrators and inmates is adversarial, and the suggestion that inmates make decisions on security is outrageous enough that it captures also the first element. Choice (B) fails on both counts. First, the two are not on opposites of the fence; second, the senior officer is asking for advice—not deferring to the opinion of his junior officer. Choice (C) is very similar. First, the administration of the university and the student body are not necessarily adversaries; at least, although they may disagree on the best means for advancing the goals of the university, there is often agreement about those goals. Second, the administration is, as with choice (B), asking advice, not abdicating responsibility for the decision. In choice (D), we lack both elements; the mayor need not be an adversary of the state legislators (he may be seeking their assistance), nor is he giving them his authority to make decisions. Finally, choice (E) lacks both elements as well; the minister is a leader, not an adversary, who is discussing questions, not delegating authority.

16. **The correct answer is (E).** The author's reason for rejecting the notion of labor participation in management decisions is that the labor leaders first have a responsibility to the people they represent and that the responsibility would color their thinking about the needs of the corporation. His thinking is reflected in the adage (and this could easily have been worked into an LSAT-type question): No man can serve two masters. Choice (B) is incorrect since the author is referring to the labor leaders, not the rank-and-file; and he specifically mentions that the leaders are skilled administrators. Choice (D) is incorrect because

it, too, fails to respect the distinction between union leader and union member. Choice (A) is a distraction. The notion that the authority would be "symbolically undermined" is edifying but finds no support in the paragraph. In any event, it entirely misses the main point of the paragraph as we have explained it. Choice (C) also fails to observe the distinction between leader and worker, not to mention also that it is only remotely connected with the discussion.

17. **The correct answer is (E).** The question stem advises us that the inconsistency is only "seeming." Choice (E) explains it away. Of the total population, 70 percent take X and 30 percent take Y, yet only 75 percent of the population take anything at all. This means that some people took both X and Y. Choice (A) is close, but it gets no cigar. While we can infer that there must be some overlap, we cannot conclude that the 30 percent is totally contained within the 70 percent. It is possible that only 25 percent of the population take both. In that case, we would have 5 percent who take Y only, 45 percent who take X only, and 25 percent who take both X and Y. This still leaves 25 percent of the population who take neither. Choice (B) seems totally unrelated to the logic of the argument. As for choices (C) and (D), while these are possible weaknesses in any statistical argument, there is nothing to indicate that they operate here specifically.

18. **The correct answer is (A).** If (2) is true, then both independent clauses of (2) must be true. This is because a sentence that has the form "P and Q" (Eddie is tall and John is short) can be true only if both subparts are true. If either is false (Eddie is not tall or John is not short) or if both are false, then the entire sentence

makes a false claim. If the second clause of (2) is true, then (1) must also be true, for (1) is actually equivalent to the second clause in (2). That is, if "P and Q" is true, then Q must itself be true. On this basis, choices (B) and (C) can be seen to be incorrect. Choice (D) is wrong, for we can actually define the interrelationship of (1) and (2) as a matter of logic: We do not have to have recourse to a probabilistic statement; that is, it is unlikely. Choice (E) is incorrect since a statement of the form "P and Q" might be false and Q could still be true—if P is false, "P and Q" is false even though Q is true.

19. **The correct answer is (D).** Again, let us resort to the use of capital letters to make it easier to talk about the propositions. Incidentally, you may or may not find this technique useful under test conditions. Some people do, but others do not. We use it here because it makes explanation easier. Let us render the four premises as follows:

(1) All B are R.   (All Buckner are Reserve)

(2) All R are P.   (All Reserve are Priceless)

(3) No H is R.   (No Hemingway is Reserve)

(4) All R are C.   (All Reserve are Catalogue)

From this we can deduce

(5) All B are P.   (using 1 and 2)

and

(6) No H is B.   (using 1 and 3)

Since "no B is H" is equivalent to "no H is B" (there is no overlap between the two categories), choice (D) must be our correct answer. From (2), we would not want to conclude "all P are R," any more than we would go from "all station wagons are

cars" to "all cars are station wagons"; so choice (A) is not a proper inference and cannot be our answer. As for choice (B), we can show that "all B are C" (using 1 and 4) and also "all B are P" (5), so we would be wrong in concluding that "no B are not P." As for choice (C), while we know that "no H is R," we would not want to conclude that "no H is P." After all, books by Hemingway may be priceless, but the Buckner collection and the Reserve Room may just not contain any. Finally, choice (E) is not deducible from our four propositions. We cannot deduce "all C is R" from "all R is C."

20. **The correct answer is (E).** Now, it must be admitted that a liar can abuse just about any word in the English language, and so it is true that each of the five answer choices is conceivably correct. But it is important to keep in mind that you are looking for the BEST answer, which will be the one word that, more than all the others, is likely to be abused. As for choice (A), while there may be different ways of doing a random selection, we should be able to decide whether a sample was, in fact, selected fairly. Although the ad may be lying about the selection of participants in the study, we should be able to determine whether they are lying. In other words, though they may not have selected the sample randomly, they cannot escape by saying, "Oh, by random, we meant anyone who liked the Goblin." The same is true of choice (C), first. That is a fairly clear term. You add up the answers you got, and one will be at the top of the list. The same is true of choice (D), a "response" is an answer. Now, choice (B) is open to manipulation. By asking our question correctly, that is, by finagling a bit with what we mean by "handling," we

can influence the answers we get. For example, compare: "Did you find the Goblin handled well?" "Did you find the Goblin had a nice steering wheel?" "Did you find the wheel was easy to turn?" We could keep it up until we found a question that worked out to give a set of "responses" from "randomly" selected drivers who would rank the Goblin "first." Now, if the one category itself is susceptible to manipulation, imagine how much easier it will be to manipulate a "composite" category. We have only to take those individual categories in which the Goblin scored well, construct from them a "composite" category, and announce the Goblin "first" in the overall category. There is also the question of how the composite was constructed, weighted, added, averaged, etc.

21. **The correct answer is (A).** The explanation given is no explanation at all. It is like a mechanic saying to a motorist, "Your car did not get over this steep hill because it did not have enough grade climbing power." While the author may have speculated about when and how his death would occur, it cannot be said that his explanation was speculative. So choice (A) is correct, not choice (B). Of course, since the explanation is merely circular, it cannot be considered medically sound, any more than our hypothetical mechanic's answer is sound as a matter of automotive engineering, so choice (D) must be wrong. As for choice (C), while the author's announcement may be self-serving, designed to aggrandize his reputation, the explanation he gives in the announcement is not. Finally, the explanation is not self-authenticating, that is, it does not provide that standard by which its own validity is to be measured. So choice (E) can be overruled.

22. **The correct answer is (D).** It is important not to attribute more to an author than he actually says or implies. Here the author states only that Ronnie's range is narrow so he will not be an outstanding vocalist. Vocalizing is only one kind of music career, so choice (A), which speaks of professional musicians, takes us far beyond the claim the author actually makes. Choice (B) also goes beyond what the author says. He never specifies what range an outstanding vocalist needs, much less what range is required to vocalize without being outstanding. Choice (C) must be incorrect since the argument depends upon the opposite assumption. The conclusion that Ronnie will *never* be an outstanding vocalist would not follow if it were possible to expand the range. Finally, as for choice (E), the speaker makes a range one condition of success but not necessarily the only or even most important condition. It could be that most people have nice ranges but fail for other reasons—so long as those few with narrow ranges also fail. Choice (D) is an assumption since the author moves from a physical characteristic to a conclusion regarding ability.

23. **The correct answer is (C).** You should remember that there is a very important distinction between "numbers" and "percentages." For example, an increase from one murder per year to two murders per year can be described as a "whopping big 100 percent increase." The argument speaks only of percentages, so we would not want to conclude anything about the numbers underlying those percentages. Therefore, both choices (A) and (B) are incorrect. They speak of "more agents" and "more people," and those are numbers rather than percentages. Furthermore, if we would not want to draw a

conclusion about numbers from data given in percentage terms, we surely would not want to base on percentages a conclusion about efficiency or work accomplished. Thus, choices (D) and (E) are incorrect. What makes choice (C) the best answer of the five is the possibility of making percentage comparisons within each agency. Within both agencies, the number of field agents increased by a greater percentage or proportion than the non-field agents.

24. **The correct answer is (D).** Keeping in mind our comments about choices (D) and (E) in the preceding question, choice (A) must be wrong. We do not want to conclude from sheer number of employees anything about the actual work accomplished. Choices (B) and (E) are incorrect for pretty much the same reason. The question stem asks us to give an argument defending the CIA against the claim that it is overstaffed. Neither rate of pay nor appropriations has anything to do with whether or not there are too many people on the payroll. Choice (C) is the second-best answer, but it fails because it does not keep in mind the ratio of non-field agents to field agents. Our concern is not with the number of agents generally, but rather with the number of support and supervisory workers (reread the question stem). Choice (D) focuses on this nicely by explaining why the CIA should experience a faster increase (which is to say, a greater percentage increase) in the number of its supervisory personnel than the FBI.

Section 5

1. **The correct answer is (B).** This is a main idea question. The author begins by stating that a large number of auto traffic fatalities can be attributed to drivers who are intoxicated. He then reviews two approaches to controlling this problem, taxation and drunk driving laws. Neither is very successful. The author finally notes that therapy may be useful, though the extent of its value has not yet been proved. Choice (B) fairly well describes this development. Choice (A) can be eliminated since any conclusions drawn by the author from studies on drunk driving are used for the larger objective described in choice (B). Choice (C) is incorrect since, aside from suggesting possible ways to reduce the extent of the problem, the author never treats the causes of drunk driving. Choice (D) is incorrect for the same reason. Finally, choice (E) is incorrect, because the comparison between the U.S. and Britain is only a small part of the passage.

2. **The correct answer is (B).** This is an inference question. In the third paragraph, the author discusses the effect of drunk driving laws. He states that after the implementation of the Road Safety Act in Britain, motor vehicle fatalities fell considerably. On this basis, we infer that the RSA was a law aimed at drunk driving. We can eliminate choices (D) and (E) on this ground. Choice (C) can be eliminated as not warranted on the basis of this information. It is not clear whether the number of arrests increased. Equally consistent with the passage is the conclusion that the number of arrests dropped because people were no longer driving while intoxicated. Choice (C) is incorrect for a further reason, the justification for choice (B). Choices (B) and (A) are fairly close since both describe the RSA as a law aimed at drunk driving. But the last sentence of the third paragraph calls for choice (B) over choice (A). As people learned that they would not get caught for drunk driving, the law became less

effective. This suggests that the RSA made drunk driving illegal, not that it lowered the BAC required for conviction. This makes sense of the sentence "… they could drink and not be stopped." If choice (A) were correct, this sentence would have to read, "… they could drink the same amount and not be convicted."

3. **The correct answer is (A).** This is an inference question. In the first paragraph, the author states that for a person to attain a BAC of 0.1 percent, he would need to drink over five ounces of 80 proof spirits over a short period of time. The author is trying to impress on us that that is a considerable quantity of alcohol for most people to drink. Choice (A) explains why the author makes this comment. Choice (B) is incorrect and confuses the first paragraph with the second paragraph. Choice (C) is incorrect since the point of the example is that the BAC is so high that most people will not exceed it. This is not to say, however, that people will not drink and drive because of laws establishing maximum BAC levels. Rather, they can continue to drink and drive because the law allows them a considerable margin in the level of BAC. Choice (D) is a misreading of that first paragraph. Of all the very drunk drivers (BAC in excess of 0.1), only 1 percent are involved in accidents. But this does not say that most drivers involved in fatal collisions have BAC levels in excess of 0.1 percent, and that is what choice (D) says. As for choice (E), the author never states that the only way to attain a BAC of 0.1 percent is to drink five ounces of 80 proof spirits in a short time—there may be other ways of becoming intoxicated.

4. **The correct answer is (A).** This is an application question. In the second paragraph, the author states that increased taxation on alcohol would tax the heaviest drinkers most, but he notes that this would also penalize the moderate and light drinker. In other words, the remedy is not sufficiently focused on the problem. Then, in the third paragraph, the author notes that drunk driving laws are aimed at the specific problem drivers. We can infer from this discussion that the author would likely advocate drunk driving laws over taxation for the reasons just given. This reasoning is presented in answer choice (A). Choice (B) is incorrect for the reasons just given and for the further reason that the passage never suggests that taxation is likely to be more effective in solving the problem. The author never really evaluates the effectiveness of taxation in reducing drunk driving. Choice (C) is incorrect for the reason given in support of choice (A) and for the further reason that the author never raises the issue of personal liberty in conjunction with the BAC test. Choice (D) can be eliminated because the author does not discount the effectiveness of anti-drunk driving measures entirely. Even the British example gives some support to the conclusion that such laws have an effect. Choice (E) is incorrect for the author never mentions the expense or administrative feasibility of BAC tests.

5. **The correct answer is (C).** This is a question about the logical structure of the passage. In paragraph 3, the author notes that stricter enforcement of laws against drunk driving may result in a few more arrests, but a few more arrests is not likely to have much impact on the problem because the number of arrests is small compared to those who do not get caught. As a consequence, people will continue to drink and drive. The author

supports this with the British experience. Once people realize that the chances of being caught are relatively small, they will drink and drive. This is the conclusion of answer choice (C). Choice (A) is incorrect since the passage does not support the conclusion that the problem is any worse or any better in one country or the other. Choice (B) is incorrect since this is the conclusion the author is arguing against. Choice (D) is wrong because the author is not discussing the effectiveness of taxation in paragraph 3. Choice (E) is a statement the author would likely accept, but that is not the reason for introducing the British example. So answer choice (E) is true but non-responsive.

6. **The correct answer is (A).** This is an application question that asks us to examine the logical structure of the argument. In the fourth paragraph, the author argues that the effectiveness of deterrents to drunk driving will depend upon the ability of the drinker to control his consumption. But drunk driving has two aspects: drunk and driving. The author assumes that drunk driving is a function of drinking only. Otherwise, he would not suggest that control on consumption is necessary as opposed to helpful. Choice (A) attacks this assumption by pointing out that it is possible to drink to excess without driving. It is possible that stiff penalties could be effective deterrents to drunk driving if not to drinking to excess. Choice (B) is incorrect because the author himself makes this point, so this choice does not weaken the argument. Choice (C) is incorrect since the author is concerned only with the problem of fatalities caused by drunk driving. It is hardly an attack on his argument to contend that he has not solved all of the world's ills. Then choice (D) can be elimi-

nated since the author is concerned to eliminate fatalities caused by drunk driving. He takes no position on whether the drunk driver ought to be punished, only that he ought to be deterred from driving while intoxicated. Choice (E) is not a strong attack on the argument since the author does leave open the question of the value of therapy in combating drunk driving.

7. **The correct answer is (C).** This is a tone question that focuses on the final sentence of the paragraph. There the author states again that the problem is a serious one and that we must find a solution. Since he admonishes us to look for a solution, choice (C) is an excellent description. Choice (A) can be eliminated since there is no irony in the passage. Choice (B) can be eliminated since the author is concerned to find a solution. Choice (E), however, overstates the case. Concern is not indignation. Finally, choice (D) may seem plausible. The author does leave us with a project. But to acknowledge that a problem exists and that a clear solution has not yet been found is not to be indecisive. The author is decisive in his assessment of the problem.

8. **The correct answer is (D).** This is a main idea question. The author does two things in the passage: He describes the problem of increasing thermal pollution and he suggests that solar energy will solve the problem. Choice (D) neatly describes this double development. Choice (A) is incorrect, for though the author does describe the phenomenon of thermal pollution and its causes, he also proposes a solution. Choice (B) is incorrect since it fails to make reference to the fact that an important part of the passage is the description of a problem. It must be admitted that it can be argued

that choice (B) does make an attempt to describe the development of the passage, but it does not do as nicely as choice (D) does. Choice (C) is easily eliminated since no ambiguity is mentioned. Finally, choice (E) is incorrect since whatever objection the author may implicitly try to refute (opponents of solar energy), he never cites and then refutes a counterargument.

9. **The correct answer is (E).** This is an explicit idea question. Choices (A), (B), and (C) are mentioned in the second paragraph as factors contributing to thermal pollution. Choice (D) is mentioned in the third paragraph as a pressure increasing thermal pollution. Choice (E) is mentioned in the third paragraph—but not as a factor contributing to thermal pollution. Unpredictable weather patterns make it difficult to predict when the thermal pollution problem will reach the critical stage, but the patterns do not contribute to thermal pollution.

10. **The correct answer is (C).** This is an inference question. In discussing the melting of the polar ice caps, the author notes that there is a positive feedback mechanism: Since the ice caps reflect sunlight and therefore dissipate solar energy that would otherwise be absorbed by the earth, the melting of the ice caps increases the amount of energy captured by the earth, which in turn contributes to the melting of the ice caps, and so on. Choice (C) correctly describes this as intensifying the effects of thermal pollution. Choice (A) is easily eliminated since this feedback mechanism has nothing to do with a possible reduction in per capita energy consumption. Choice (B) is incorrect, for though this feedback loop increases the problem and thereby the urgency for the changeover to solar energy, the loop itself will not cause a change

in policy. Choice (D) is incorrect for the same reason. Finally, though the melting of the polar ice caps will result in flooding, this flooding is not an explanation of the feedback loop. Rather, it is the result of the general phenomenon of the melting of the ice caps.

11. **The correct answer is (A).** This is a logical detail question. Why does the author discuss energy conservation? Conservation may appear as a possible alternative to solar energy. The author argues, however, that a closer examination shows that conservation cannot avert but only postpone the crisis. In terms of tactics, the author's move is to raise a possible objection and give an answer to it—as stated in choice (A). Choice (B) is incorrect, for the refutation of a possible objection does not support the central thesis directly, only indirectly by eliminating a possible counterargument. Choice (C) is incorrect since the author never acknowledges he has fallen into any contradiction. Choice (D) is incorrect since it overstates the case. The author admits that conservation has a beneficial effect, but he denies that conservation obviates the need for solar energy. Finally, choice (E) is incorrect since the point is argumentative and not merely informational.

12. **The correct answer is (B).** This is an inference question. In the final paragraph, the author makes references to the possibility of "air-conditioning" the earth, a word placed in quotation marks, which indicates that he is using it in a non-standard way. Ordinarily, we use the word "air-condition" to mean to cool, say, a room or an entire building. Obviously, the author is not referring to some gigantic Carrier air-conditioning unit mounted, say, on top of the earth. But the general idea of removing heat seems to

be what the term means in this context. This is consonant with the passage as well. Thermal pollution is the build-up of energy, and we are showing a positive build-up because fossil fuel and other sources of energy release energy that was only stored. So this, coupled with the sun's energy that comes in each moment, gives us a positive (though not desirable) balance of energy retention over loss. The idea of air-conditioning the earth, though not feasible according to the passage, must refer to schemes to get rid of this energy, say, into outer space. This is the idea presented in choice (B). As for choice (A), redistribution of thermal energy within the earth's energy system will not solve the problem of accumulated energy, so that cannot be what proponents of "air-conditioning" have in mind. Choice (C) is a good definition of conservation but not "air-conditioning." Choice (D) is the recommendation given by the author, but that is not a response to this question. Finally, choice (E) is incorrect for the reason that burning wood is not going to cool the earth.

13. **The correct answer is (B).** This is a tone question. The author describes a very dangerous situation, but he also shows the way to solve the problem. The author does not necessarily believe that the battle for solar energy has been won; otherwise, he would not be advocating a shift to solar energy. On balance, the tone of the passage is hope or optimism, qualified by the realization that solar energy is not yet a high priority. This qualified hope is best described by choice (B). Choice (A) is incorrect since this is not the tone of the passage. Though the author may be distressed at what he perceives to be the short-sightedness of policy makers, this distress does not color

the writing in the passage. Choice (C) is totally inappropriate since the author is analytical. Choice (D) is inconsistent with the author's concern. Finally, choice (E) overstates the case. Though the author is concerned, he is not in a panic.

14. **The correct answer is (C).** This is an application question. We are looking for the most logical continuation. Since the author has urged us to adopt solar energy, an appropriate continuation would be a discussion of how to implement solar energy. And choice (C) would be a part of this discussion. Choice (B) can be eliminated since the proposal depends upon the cost and feasibility of solar energy, not on its history. Choices (A) and (E) can be eliminated since the author has explicitly asserted that only solar energy will solve the problem of thermal pollution. Finally, choice (D) is incorrect since the author need not regale us with the gory details of this situation. He has already made the point. As readers, we will want to see the practical details of his plan to avoid disaster.

15. **The correct answer is (D).** This is a main idea question. The author begins by stating that it would be useful to have a general index to measure welfare and notes that some have even suggested the GNP might be adapted for that purpose. He then proceeds to demonstrate why such an index cannot be constructed. Generally, then, the author shows the defects in a proposal for a general index of welfare, and choice (D) nicely describes this devel-opment. Choice (A) is incorrect since the author never produces any arguments for the position he is attacking. And even when the author raises points such as the suggestion that hours worked might be a measure of cost of production, he is not citing arguments

for that position; he is only mentioning the position to attack it. Choice (B) is incorrect since the author is attacking and not defending the proposal discussed. Choice (C) is easily eliminated because the author never attacks the sincerity of those he opposes. Finally, choice (E) is wrong, for the author never reviews any literature on the subject he is discussing.

16. **The correct answer is (A).** This is an inference question. We turn to the second paragraph. There the author mentions that a general index of welfare would have to include some measure of the cost of producing the output. He suggests that someone might think hours worked would do the trick. He rejects that position by noting that hours worked, as a statistic, does not take account of the quality of the worktime (e.g., long-hours versus short-hours, working conditions, satisfaction of workers). Choice (A) best describes this argument. Choice (B) is incorrect, for the author discusses environmental costs in connection with another aspect of a general index. Choice (C) is incorrect since this distinction is never used by the author. Choice (D) is incorrect since this is not mentioned as a goal of such a measure. Finally, choice (E) confuses the GNP, mentioned in the first part of the paragraph, with the index to measure real costs.

17. **The correct answer is (C).** This is an inference question that asks about the main point of the passage. The author adduces several objections to the idea of a general index of welfare. Then the final blow is delivered in the last paragraph: Even if you could devise measures for these various components of a general index, any combination or weighting of the individual measures would reflect only the judgment (personal preference)

of the weighter. For this reason alone, argues the author, the entire idea is unworkable. Choice (C) makes this point. Choices (A) and (D) can be eliminated since the author never uses cost or time as arguments against the index. Choice (B) can be eliminated on similar grounds. The author may recognize that considerable research would be needed to attempt such measures, yet he does not bother to use that as an objection. Choice (E) can be eliminated for a similar reason. The author may have some arguments against the way such statistics are gathered now, but he does not bother to make them. His argument has the structure: Even assuming there are such data, we cannot combine these statistics to get a general measure of the quality of the environment.

18. **The correct answer is (A).** This is a tone question, and the justification for choice (A) is already implicit in the discussion thus far. The author sees fatal theoretical weaknesses inherent in the idea of an index of welfare. So we might say that he regards such a notion as an unrealistic, that is, unachievable, dream. Choice (B) is incorrect because the author does not believe the idea can ever be implemented. Choices (C), (D), and (E) can be eliminated on substantially the same grounds.

19. **The correct answer is (A).** This is an explicit idea question. In the second paragraph, the author acknowledges that the GNP is a fairly accurate measure of output. He never suggests that the GNP can estimate needs, predict welfare, or measure welfare generally. So we can eliminate the remaining choices.

20. **The correct answer is (E).** This is an explicit idea question, with a thought reverser. Choices (A), (B), (C), and (D)

are all mentioned in the third paragraph as aspects of a needs index. The fourth paragraph does not treat the idea of a needs index but rather the idea of a physical environment index. That is where the author discusses the items mentioned in choice (E). So the author does mention the items covered by choice (E) but not as part of a needs index.

21. **The correct answer is (A).** This is an application question. We are looking for the most likely place for the passage. To be sure, it is possible that the passage might appear in any of the five suggested locations, but the most likely place is that suggested by choice (A). This could easily be one of a series of papers addressed to a group meeting to discuss public policy decisions. As for choice (B), it is not likely that the passage would be an introduction to a general text on statistics. It is too firmly dedicated to a particular idea, and the use of statistics is in a way subordinate to the theoretical discussion. Choice (C) is inappropriate since the discussion bears only remotely on programs to aid the poor. Choice (D) is even less likely since the passage does not discuss the foundations of government. Finally, choice (E) is to a certain extent plausible, but choice (A) is more closely connected to the content of the passage.

22. **The correct answer is (D).** This is a main idea question. The main idea of the passage is fairly clear: suggest reforms to correct the problems discussed. Choice (D) is a very good description of this development. Choice (A) is incorrect since the author himself criticizes the system. Choice (B) is incorrect since no recommendation for expanding benefits and scope is made by the author. Choice (C) overstates the case. The author limits his

indictment to unemployment compensation, even then he believes that the shortcomings of the system can be remedied. Choice (E) is incorrect because the author is discussing unemployment compensation, not government programs designed to achieve full employment generally. We may infer from the passage that unemployment compensation is not a program designed to achieve full employment, but rather a program designed to alleviate the hardship of unemployment. On balance, choice (D) is the most precise description given of the development of the passage.

23. **The correct answer is (A).** This is a logical detail question. In the second paragraph, the author introduces the example of a worker who loses surprisingly little by being unemployed. The author does this to show that unemployment encourages people to remain unemployed by reducing the net cost of unemployment. Choice (A) makes this point. Choice (B) is incorrect, for the author does not discuss the problem of employer contribution until the fourth paragraph. Choice (C) is incorrect, for this is not the reason that the author introduces the point. Choice (D) is incorrect because this topic is not taken up until the third paragraph. Finally, choice (E) is incorrect since the author analyzes the situation in a neutral fashion; there is no hint of condemnation.

24. **The correct answer is (C).** This is an explicit idea or specific detail question. Choice (C) is a recommendation made by the author in the final paragraph. Choice (A) is actually inconsistent with statements made in that paragraph, for the author proposes taxing benefits in the same way as wages. Choices (B), (D), and (E) are interesting ideas, but they are

nowhere mentioned in the passage—so they cannot possibly be answers to an explicit idea question.

25. The correct answer is (C). Here, too, we have an explicit idea question. Choices (A), (B), (D), and (E) are all mentioned in the third paragraph as ways by which an employer might reduce seasonal and cyclical fluctuations in labor needs. Choice (C), however, was not mentioned as a way to minimize unemployment. Indeed, we may infer from other information supplied by the passage that supplementary benefits actually increase unemployment.

26. The correct answer is (A). This is an application question. We are asked to apply the author's analysis of the rating system to conclusions given in the answer choices. The author is critical of the rating system because it does not place the full burden of unemployment on the employer. This is because there is a maximum contribution limit, and in the final paragraph, the author recommends the ceiling be eliminated. From these remarks, we may infer that the author believes the rating system is, in theory, sound, but that practically it needs to be adjusted. Choice (A) neatly describes this judgment. Choice (B) can be eliminated since the author implies that the system is, in principle, sound. Moreover, the author implies that the employer does have some control over the time his former employees remain out of work. The maximum limit on employer contribution allows the employer to exploit this control. As for choice (C), this is contradicted by our analysis thus far and for the further reason that the passage never suggests employee contribution should replace employer contribution. Indeed, the author implies that he regards the system as serving a useful and necessary social func-

tion. Choice (D) can be eliminated because the author never draws a distinction between contributions by large firms and contributions by small firms. Finally, choice (E) is incorrect since the experience rating system is theoretically tied to the amount drawn by employees. The difficulty is not with the theory of the system, but rather with its implementation.

27. The correct answer is (B). This is an explicit detail question. We are looking for criticisms that are made in the passage. Choice (B) is such a criticism, and it can be found in the very opening sentence. As for choice (A), the author actually states the opposite: The system allows firms of this sort to use the unemployment compensation system as a subsidy for their employees, reducing their own costs of production. As for choice (C), the author only states that employers contribute to the fund from which benefits are paid. No mention is ever made of a state contribution. Choice (D) is certainly a goal of the system, but it is not mentioned as a weakness of the system by the author. Finally, choice (E) is true—as mentioned in the final paragraph. But this is not a criticism of the system. In fact, the author views it in a positive light and as a basis for a recommendation for reform.

28. The correct answer is (A). This is a tone question. In the final paragraph, as he makes his recommendations, the author states that we must reform the system, preserving its good aspects and correcting its bad effects. Choice (A) describes this judgment. Choice (B) is incorrect since much of the discussion in the passage is an indictment of the system's economic inefficiency. Choice (C) is wrong because the author makes recommendations that, he states, will correct the wasteful effects. Choice (D) is incorrect, for the author implies that the system has usefulness. Finally, though the author criticizes the system, the objection is that the system is inefficient, not that it is outdated.

WRITING SAMPLE

Following are two responses to the Writing Sample prompt, one in favor of the first option and the other in favor of the second option. Of course, there is no "right" or "wrong" answer to a Writing Sample prompt. Rather, responses are "better" or "worse," and you'll find a discussion of how to write a good response in Chapter 8 of Part 3. For now, just note that the two responses below are serviceable: they are not great works of prose; they are not brilliant pieces of writing, but they are acceptable. And, as you'll learn in Chapter 8, that's really all you should be going for.

Sample Response for the First Option

Ashley should invest her money in a Hearty Burger franchise. A fast-food franchise would provide her with the opportunity for "hands-on" management, and the investment required would be within her reach.

First, a Hearty Burger franchise would give Ashley the opportunity to apply what she's learned in school to a real business. A fast-food restaurant is a small enough operation to permit her to supervise all aspects of the business instead of having responsibility for a narrowly defined set of duties in a large company. Additionally, even though the franchise includes advertising and other support, she would presumably be left free to make choices about hours, labor, community relations, and other exclusively local concerns. Finally, although Ashley may not have had

any formal business-school training in operating a fast-food franchise, the company's orientation and technical support should be sufficient to fill in the gaps in her knowledge.

Second, the Hearty Burger franchise is within Ashley's budget, though it would be a tight squeeze. Perhaps she could use some of the money as a down payment on the real estate she'll need and borrow additional funds from a bank. Also, the company will supply many of her restaurant needs, and that can help her cash flow during the start-up period. And the fast-food business is such that her efforts in the store can offset some of her labor costs.

The Hearty Burger franchise seems to answer the two primary concerns that Ashley has and would be the better choice.

Sample Response for the Second Option

Ashley should purchase the clothing store. A clothing store would give her a lot of opportunity to make individual decisions, and the terms of the offer of sale are attractive.

One, the clothing store offers Ashley the opportunity she's looking for to manage a business. With changing styles and tastes, clothing will present her with special challenges as she tries to anticipate shifting patterns of demand and respond to them. Additionally, Ashley still has the student perspective and so should be able to respond effectively to the tastes of the student population in the area. Essentially all of the important decisions will remain under her control.

Two, the clothing store is financially attractive. The store has been in business for 50 years, so Ashley can expect to see sales from loyal customers, money that will help her during the start-up period. Moreover, the store is already stocked, though she will probably want and need to start buying new inventory almost immediately. Of course, the plans of the building owner are a potential stumbling block, but Ashley should be able to work out an arrangement that will permit her to continue in the existing location. Perhaps she can borrow money from the bank for the purchase of the commercial co-op space, or maybe the owner will be willing to finance her purchase of the store space.

So the clothing store will be financially practical, and it will provide Ashley with the opportunity to do those things she's trained to do.

PART III

LSAT QUESTION TYPES

Logical Reasoning

OVERVIEW

- **What Logical Reasoning Tests**
- **Answering Logical Reasoning Questions**
- **What Smart Test-Takers Know**

WHAT IS LOGICAL REASONING?

As the name implies, Logical Reasoning tests your ability to think logically, and you will learn a lot about thinking logically in this chapter. The LSAT, however, does not test technical points that are taught in the typical "Introduction to Logic" college course. You would not, for example, be asked to define categorical syllogism or *petitio principii,* but you might be asked to recognize the following:

> All whales are mammals.
>
> All mammals are warm-blooded creatures.
>
> Therefore, all whales are warm-blooded creatures.

This, which technically speaking is a categorical syllogism, is a valid argument form. And you might be asked to show that you understand the following:

> Shakespeare was a better playwright than Shaw. Clearly, Shakespeare's plays are better, so the conclusion that Shakespeare was a better playwright than Shaw is unavoidable.

This, which technically speaking is a *petitio principii,* is a specious argument because it simply begs the question.

LSAT Logical Reasoning Questions

The scored portion of the LSAT contains two Logical Reasoning sections, each with 24 to 26 questions. The Logical Reasoning sections can appear as any of the exam's sections. You may receive a test form that includes more than two Logical Reasoning sections, in which case only two of the Logical Reasoning sections will be scored. The other will contain trial questions that are being tested for use in future exams. There will be no way to tell which section is the trial one, so it's important to do your best on every section.

chapter 5

What are the three "building blocks" of logical reasoning?

1. Stimulus material
2. Question stem
3. Answer choices
And each has its role to play.

Logical Reasoning questions are constructed from three elements:

Stimulus Material

Stimulus material is the "content" of the item. Stimulus material is an initial paragraph or statement that presents an argument or otherwise states a position. The stimulus material can be about almost anything, including a medical breakthrough, a moral dilemma, a scientific theory, a philosophical problem, a marketing phenomenon, and even, though very rarely, a legal issue. But you don't need any special knowledge. Everything you need to know in terms of item content is right there in the stimulus material.

Question Stem

This stem is the "question." It may come in the form of a question, or it may come in the form of an instruction. Either way, the stem tells you what to do with the stimulus material. It may ask you to do any one of the following:

- identify the conclusion of an argument
- point out a premise of an argument
- identify strengths or weaknesses in an argument
- recognize parallel reasoning
- evaluate evidence
- draw conclusions and make inferences

Answer Choices

The answer choices are the possible "responses" to the stem. One of them is the "credited" response or right answer. The wrong answers are known as "distractors" because they are carefully written to distract your attention away from the right answer. In essence, they provide the camouflage in which the test writers hide the right response.

Here are the directions for LSAT Logical Reasoning questions, together with a sample question and its explanation.

Anatomy of a Logical Reasoning Item

Directions: In this section, the questions ask you to analyze and evaluate the reasoning in short paragraphs or passages. For some questions, all of the answer choices may conceivably be answers to the question asked. You should select the *best* answer to the question; that is, an answer that does not require you to make assumptions that violate commonsense standards by being implausible, redundant, irrelevant, or inconsistent. After choosing the best answer, blacken the corresponding space on the answer sheet.

Stimulus Material

Officials of the State Industrial Safety Board notified the management of A-1 Ironworks that several employees of the plant had complained about discomfort experienced as a result of the high levels of noise of the factory operations. A-1's management responded by pointing out that the complaints came from the newest employee at the plant and that more experienced workers did not find the factory noise to be excessive. Based on this finding, management concluded that the noise was not a problem and declined to take any remedial action.

You should notice that management overlooked something: Is there another possible explanation for why complaints came from new employees and not from experienced employees?

Question Stem

Which of the following, if true, indicates a flaw in A-1's decision not to take remedial action at the plant?

The stem tells you that management has made a mistake and asks that you identify the error.

Answer Choices

(A) Because A-1 is located in an industrial park, no residences are located close enough to the plant to be affected by the noise.

A distractor. The issue is the effect of noise on employees inside the plant.

(B) The noise level at the plant varies with activity and is at the highest when the greatest number of employees are on the job.

A distractor. While this is probably true, it does not address the new employee/experienced employee distinction.

(C) The experienced employees do not feel discomfort because of significant hearing loss attributable to the high noise level.	*The credited response. Management overlooked this: Experienced employees do not complain because deafness prevents them from hearing the noise.*
(D) Issuing protective earplugs to all employees would not significantly increase the cost to A-1 of doing business.	*A distractor. If earplugs would be an effective but inexpensive remedial step, then it would make sense to issue them to employees.*
(E) The State Industrial Safety Board has no independent authority to enforce a recommendation regarding safety procedures.	*A distractor. Irrelevant to the issue at hand.*

HOW DO YOU ANSWER LOGICAL REASONING QUESTIONS?

Here's a simple, four-step plan that can help you solve Logical Reasoning questions.

Logical Reasoning: Getting It Right

1. Preview the question stem.
2. Read the stimulus material.
3. Prephrase your answer.
4. Identify the correct answer.

Let's look at these steps in more detail.

1. **Preview the question stem.** You could do a number of things with the stimulus material. You could attack the conclusion, you could defend the conclusion, you could analyze its structure, you could draw further inferences from it, you could even invent a similar argument, and there are still more things to do. You will be asked to do only one (or, occasionally, two) of these things by the stem. So previewing the stem will help you to focus your thinking.

2. **Read the stimulus material.** This is not as easy as it seems. You are going to have to read more carefully than usual. And this makes sense, since words are the tools of the lawyer's trade. The following advertisement will help to make the point. Read it carefully, because there *will* be a test.

Advertisement: Lite Cigarettes have 50 percent less nicotine and tar than regular cigarettes. Seventy-five percent of the doctors surveyed said that they would, if asked by patients, recommend a reduced tar and nicotine cigarette for patients who cannot stop smoking.

Pop Quiz

1. Does the ad say that some doctors are encouraging people to start to smoke?

2. Does the ad say that some doctors recommend Lite Cigarettes for patients who cannot stop smoking?

3. Does the ad say that most doctors would, if asked by a patient, recommend a low tar and nicotine cigarette for patients who cannot stop smoking?

Answers

1. Does the ad say that some doctors are encouraging people to start to smoke?

   No. The ad specifically says that the doctors surveyed would recommend a low tar and nicotine cigarette "for patients who cannot stop smoking." That clearly applies only to people who are already smokers.

2. Does the ad say that some doctors recommend Lite Cigarettes for patients who cannot stop smoking?

   No again. The ad specifically says that the doctors surveyed would recommend "a reduced tar and nicotine cigarette." To be sure, Lite Cigarettes apparently fall into that category, but the ad does not say that the doctors surveyed would recommend Lite Cigarettes as opposed to some other reduced tar and nicotine cigarette.

3. Does the ad say that most doctors would, if asked by patients, recommend a low tar and nicotine cigarette for patients who cannot stop smoking?

   No once again. The claim is restricted to "doctors surveyed." No information is given about how many doctors were included in the survey—perhaps only four. Nor does the ad disclose how many surveys were done. Even if the market experts had to conduct ten surveys before they found a group of four doctors to back up their claim, the ad would still be true—though, of course, potentially misleading.

The important point is this: Read carefully and pay attention to detail. This does not mean that you need to tie yourself up in paranoid knots. The LSAT is not out to get you personally. The LSAT is, however, a test that is, in part, designed to separate those who can read carefully and pay attention to detail from those who cannot. So read carefully.

❸ **Prephrase your answer.** Many LSAT problems have answers that go "click" when you find them. They fit in the same way that a well-made key fits a good lock. After you have previewed the stem and then read carefully the stimulus material, try to anticipate what the correct answer will look like. This is particularly true of

TIP

Know the common types of Logical Reasoning questions:

- Identify the conclusion
- Point out a premise
- Identify strengths or weaknesses
- Recognize parallel reasoning
- Evaluate evidence
- Draw a conclusion

questions that ask you to attack or defend an argument. (This technique does not work for questions that ask you to identify a parallel line of thinking.)

④ Identify the correct answer. If you have effectively prephrased an answer, then you should be able to identify fairly readily the correct answer. Otherwise, you will have to study the choices carefully. And, again, careful reading means very careful reading. In Logical Reasoning, each word in the answer choices counts.

Now let's look at some sample LSAT Logical Reasoning questions. As you read the explanations, think about how the solution process applies.

The governor claims that the state faces a drought and has implemented new water-use restrictions; but that's just a move to get some free publicity for his reelection campaign. So far this year, we have had 3.5 inches of rain, slightly more than the average amount of rain for the same period over the last three years.

Which of the following, if true, would most weaken the conclusion of the argument above?

(A) The governor did not declare drought emergencies in the previous three years.

(B) City officials who have the authority to mandate water-use restrictions have not done so.

(C) The snow melt that usually contributes significantly to the state's reservoirs is several inches below normal.

(D) The amount of water the state can draw from rivers that cross state boundaries is limited by federal law.

(E) Water-use restrictions are short-term measures and do little to reduce long-term water consumption.

This question stem asks you to attack the stimulus material. The argument is weak because it depends upon an invalid hidden assumption: Rainfall is the only source of water for the reservoirs. So, your prephrased answer might be "there is another source of water for the reservoirs." Choice (C) fits neatly into this prephrase.

"Channel One" is a 12-minute school news show that includes 2 minutes of commercials. The show's producers offer high schools $50,000 worth of television equipment to air the program. Many parents and teachers oppose the use of commercial television in schools, arguing that advertisements are tantamount to indoctrination. But students are already familiar with television commercials and know how to distinguish programming from advertising.

The argument assumes that

(A) the effects of an advertisement viewed in a classroom would be similar to those of the same advertisement viewed at home.

(B) many educators would be willing to allow the indoctrination of students in exchange for new equipment for their schools.

(C) television advertising is a more effective way of promoting a product to high school students than print advertising.

(D) high school students are sufficiently interested in world affairs to learn from a television news program.

(E) a television news program produced especially for high school students is an effective teaching tool.

This question stem asks you to identify a hidden assumption of the stimulus material. The argument makes the assumption that television's effect on children in the classroom will be similar to its effect on them at home. This is a questionable assumption since the teacher/pupil relationship is an authoritative one. So your prephrase might be something like "the two situations are similar," and choice (A) is a hidden assumption of the argument.

> The spate of terrorist acts against airlines and their passengers raises a new question: Should government officials be forced to disclose the fact that they have received warning of an impending terrorist attack? The answer is "yes." The government currently releases information about the health hazards of smoking, the ecological dangers of pesticides, and the health consequences of food.

The argument given relies primarily on

(A) circular reasoning.

(B) generalization.

(C) authority.

(D) analogy.

(E) causal analysis.

This question stem asks you to describe the reasoning in the stimulus material. The argument draws an analogy between two situations. So your prephrase would almost surely be "analogy." And the correct answer is (D).

"Parallel" questions can be tricky.
The stimulus for a "parallel" question will probably contain an error. Don't fall into the trap of correcting the error. Just find an answer with a similar mistake.

When it rains, my car gets wet. Since it hasn't rained recently, my car can't be wet.

Which of the following is logically most similar to the argument above?

(A) Whenever critics give a play a favorable review, people go to see it; Pinter's new play did not receive favorable reviews, so I doubt that anyone will go to see it.

(B) Whenever people go to see a play, critics give it a favorable review; people did go to see Pinter's new play, so it did get a favorable review.

(C) Whenever critics give a play a favorable review, people go to see it; Pinter's new play got favorable reviews, so people will probably go to see it.

(D) Whenever a play is given favorable reviews by the critics, people go to see it; since people are going to see Pinter's new play, it will probably get favorable reviews.

(E) Whenever critics give a play a favorable review, people go to see it; people are not going to see Pinter's new play, so it did not get favorable reviews.

This question stem asks you to parallel the stimulus material. The fallacy in the argument is confusion over necessary and sufficient causes. A sufficient cause is an event that is sufficient to guarantee some effect; a necessary cause is one that is required for some event. Choice (A) exhibits this same fallacy. (Remember that a prephrase will not be possible with this type of question.)

WHAT SMART TEST-TAKERS KNOW

Thinking Logically

Logical Reasoning stimulus material has a logical structure.

Logical Reasoning stimulus material is almost always an argument—even if it is just a single sentence. An argument is one or more statements or assertions, one of which, the conclusion, is supposed to follow from the others, the premises. Some arguments are very short and simple:

> Premise: No fish are mammals.
> Conclusion: No mammals are fish.

Others are extremely lengthy and complex, taking up entire volumes. Some arguments are good, some are bad. Scientists use arguments to justify a conclusion regarding the cause of some natural phenomenon; politicians use arguments to reach conclusions about the desirability of government policies. But even given this wide variety of structures and uses, arguments fall into one of two general categories—deductive and inductive.

A deductive argument is one in which the inference depends solely on the meanings of the terms used:

Premises:	All bats are mammals.
	All mammals are warm blooded.
Conclusion:	Therefore, all bats are warm blooded.

You know that this argument has to be correct just by looking at it. No research is necessary to show that the conclusion follows automatically from the premises.

All other arguments are termed inductive or probabilistic:

| Premises: | My car will not start; and the fuel gauge reads "empty." |
| Conclusion: | Therefore, the car is probably out of gas. |

Notice that here, unlike the deductive argument, the conclusion does not follow with certainty; it is not guaranteed. The conclusion does seem to be likely or probable, but there are some gaps in the argument. It is possible, for example, that the fuel gauge is broken, or that there is fuel in the tank and the car will not start because something else is wrong.

Locating the conclusion is the first step in evaluating an argument.

The conclusion is the main point of an argument, and locating the conclusion is the first step in evaluating the strength of any argument. In fact, some Logical Reasoning questions simply ask that you identify the conclusion or main point:

> Which of the following is the speaker's conclusion?
> Which of the following best summarizes the main point of the argument?
> The speaker is attempting to prove that . . .
> The speaker is leading to the conclusion that . . .

So, developing techniques for identifying the conclusion of the argument would be important in any case.

Conclusions, however, are important for yet another reason: You cannot begin to look for fallacies or other weaknesses in a line of reasoning, or even find the line of reasoning, until you have clearly identified the point the author wishes to prove. Any attempt to skip over this important step can only result in misunderstanding and confusion. You have surely had the experience of discussing a point for some length of time only to say finally, "Oh, now I see what you were saying, and I agree with you."

Locating the main point of an argument sometimes entails a bit of work because the logical structure of an argument is not necessarily dependent on the order in which sentences appear. To be sure, sometimes the main point of an argument is fairly easy to find. It is the last statement in the paragraph:

> Since this watch was manufactured in Switzerland, and all Swiss watches are reliable, <u>this watch must be reliable</u>.

NOTE

How important is Logical Reasoning?
It is the most important topic on the LSAT. Although many students "obsess" about Analytical Reasoning, Logical Reasoning is the "meat and potatoes" of the LSAT—accounting for just about half of all the questions.

Here the conclusion or the point of the line of reasoning is the part that is underlined. The argument also contains two premises: "this watch was manufactured in Switzerland" and "all Swiss watches are reliable." The same argument could be made, however, with the statements presented in a different order:

> <u>This watch must be reliable</u> since it was manufactured in Switzerland and all Swiss watches are reliable.

or

> <u>This watch must be reliable</u> since all Swiss watches are reliable and this watch was manufactured in Switzerland.

or

> Because this watch was manufactured in Switzerland, <u>it must be reliable</u> because all Swiss watches are reliable.

So you cannot always count on the conclusion of the argument being the last sentence of the paragraph even though sometimes it is. Therefore, it is important to know some techniques for finding the conclusion of an argument.

The conclusion of an argument can be the first sentence.

It is true that speakers often lead up to the conclusion and make it the grand finale. Sometimes, however, speakers announce in advance where they are going and then proceed to develop arguments in support of their position. So the second most common position for the conclusion of an argument is the first sentence of the stimulus material.

Key words often signal a conclusion.

The stimulus material often uses transitional words or phrases to signal a conclusion, for example, "Ms. Slote has a Masters in Education, and she has 20 years of teaching experience; <u>therefore</u>, she is a good teacher." Other words and phrases to watch include *hence, thus, so, it follows that, as a result,* and *consequently.*

Key words often signal an important premise.

TIP

**Signal words can help
you find conclusions:**

therefore

hence

thus

consequently

accordingly

so

In some arguments, the premises rather than the conclusion are signaled. Words that signal premises include *since, because,* and *if.*

> <u>Since</u> Rex has been with the company 20 years and does such a good job, he will probably receive a promotion.

or

> Rex will probably receive a promotion <u>because</u> he has been with the company 20 years and he does such a good job.

or

> <u>If</u> Rex has been with the company 20 years and has done a good job, he will probably receive a promotion.

In each of the three examples just presented, the conclusion is "Rex will probably receive a promotion" and the premise is that "he has been with the company 20 years and does a good job." Of course, many other words can signal premises.

The conclusion is the main point of an argument.

Ask what the author wants to prove. Not all arguments are broken down by the numbers. In such a case, you must use your judgment to answer the question "What is the speaker trying to prove?" For example:

> We must reduce the amount of money we spend on space exploration. Right now, the enemy is launching a massive military buildup, and we need the additional money to purchase military equipment to match the anticipated increase in the enemy's strength.

In this argument, there are no key words to announce the conclusion or the premises. Instead, you must ask yourself a series of questions:

> Is the speaker trying to prove that the enemy is beginning a military buildup?

No, because that statement is the larger argument, so it cannot be the conclusion.

> Is the main point that we must match the enemy buildup?

Again the answer is "no" because that, too, is an intermediate step on the way to some other conclusion.

> Is the speaker trying to prove that we must cut back on the budget for space exploration?

Now the answer is "yes," and that is the author's point.

Things get more complicated when an argument contains arguments within the main argument. The argument about the need for military expenditures might have included this subargument:

> We must reduce the amount of money we spend on space exploration. The enemy is now stockpiling titanium, a metal that is used in building airplanes. And each time the enemy has stockpiled titanium, it has launched a massive military buildup. So right now, the enemy is launching a massive military buildup, and we need the additional money to purchase military equipment to match the anticipated increase in the enemy's strength.

Notice that now one of the premises of the earlier argument is the conclusion of a subargument. The conclusion of the subargument is "the enemy is launching a massive military buildup," which has two explicit premises: "The enemy is now stockpiling titanium" and "a stockpiling of titanium means a military buildup."

No matter how complicated an argument gets, you can always break it down into subarguments. And if it is really complex, those subarguments can be broken down into smaller parts. Of course, the stimulus material on the LSAT cannot be overly complicated because the initial argument will not be much more than 100 or so words in length. So just keep asking yourself "What is the author trying to prove?"

LSAT conclusions are carefully worded.

Defining precisely the main point is also an essential step in evaluating an argument. Once the main point of the argument has been isolated, you must take the second step of exactly defining that point. In particular, you should be looking for three things:

1. Quantifiers
2. Qualifiers
3. The author's intention

LSAT conclusions are carefully quantified.

Quantifiers are words such as *some, none, never, always, everywhere,* and *sometimes.* For example, there is a big difference in the claims:

> All mammals live on land.
> Most mammals live on land.

The first is false; the second is true. Compare also the following:

> Women in the United States have always had the right to vote.
> Since 1920, women in the United States have had the right to vote.

Again, the first statement is false and the second is true. And compare the following:

> It is raining, and the temperature is predicted to drop below 32°F; therefore, it will surely snow.
> It is raining, and the temperature is predicted to drop below 32°F; therefore, it will probably snow.

The first is a much less cautious claim than the second, and if it failed to snow, the first claim would have been proved false, though not the second. The second statement claims only that it is probable that snow will follow, not that it definitely will. So someone could make the second claim and defend it when the snow failed to materialize by saying, "Well, I allowed for that in my original statement."

LSAT conclusions are carefully qualified.

Qualifiers play a role similar to that of quantifiers, but they are descriptive rather than numerical. As such, they are more concrete and difficult to enumerate. Just make sure that you stay alert for distinctions like this:

> In nations that have a bicameral legislature, the speed with which legislation is passed is largely a function of the strength of executive leadership.

Notice here that the author makes a claim about "nations," so it would be wrong to apply the author's reasoning to states. Further, you should not conclude that the author believes that bicameral legislatures pass different laws from those passed by unicameral legislatures. The author mentions only the "speed" with which the laws are passed, not their content.

> All passenger automobiles manufactured by Detroit auto makers since 1975 have been equipped with seat belts.

You should not conclude from this statement that all trucks have also been equipped with seat belts since the author makes a claim only about "passenger automobiles," nor should you conclude that imported cars have seat belts, for the author mentions Detroit-made cars only.

> No other major department store offers you a low price and a 75-day warranty on parts and labor on this special edition of the XL 30 color television.

The tone of the ad is designed to create a very large impression on the hearer, but the precise claim made is fairly limited. First, the ad's claim is specifically restricted to a comparison of "department" stores, and "major" department stores at that. It is possible that some non-major department store offers a similar warranty and price; also it may be that another type of retail store, say, an electronics store, makes a similar offer. Second, other stores, department or otherwise, may offer a better deal on the product, say, a low price with a three-month warranty, and still the claim would stand so long as no one else offered exactly a "75-day" warranty. Finally, the ad is restricted to a "special edition" of the television, so depending on what that means, the ad may be even more restrictive in its claim.

On the LSAT, the author's intention may be crucial.

The author's intention may also be important. You must be careful to distinguish between claims of fact and proposals of change. Do not assume that an author's claim to have found a problem means the author knows how to solve it. An author can make a claim about the cause of some event without believing that the event can be prevented or even that it ought to be prevented. For example, consider this argument:

> Because the fifth ward vote is crucial to Gordon's campaign, if Gordon fails to win over the ward leaders, he will be defeated in the election.

Find the missing link.

When an LSAT question stem asks about a premise or an assumption (the words mean the same thing), it is asking about a hidden, suppressed, or implicit (the words all mean the same thing) assumption. So look for the missing link.

You cannot conclude that the author believes Gordon should or should not be elected. The author gives only a factual analysis without endorsing or condemning either possible outcome. Also, consider this argument:

> Each year, the rotation of the Earth slows a few tenths of a second. In several million years, it will have stopped altogether, and life as we know it will no longer be able to survive on Earth.

You cannot conclude that the author wants to find a solution for the slowing of the Earth's rotation. For all we know, the author thinks the process is inevitable, or even desirable.

Premises support the conclusion.

A premise is the logical support for a conclusion. The LSAT usually refers to premises as *assumptions*, but the terminology is not important. It is important not to misunderstand the word *assumption*. Although it is related to the word *assume*, an assumption, as that term is used in logic, does not have the connotation of *surmise or guess*. Consider this argument:

> All humans are mortal.
> Socrates is a human.
> Therefore, Socrates is mortal.

The first two statements are assumptions—even though they are obviously true. You can use the words *assumption* and *premise* interchangeably.

Explicit premises are specifically stated.

In the detective novel *A Study in Scarlet* by Sir Arthur Conan Doyle, Sherlock Holmes explains to Dr. Watson that it is possible logically to deduce the existence of rivers and oceans from a single drop of water, though such a deduction would require many intermediate steps. While this may be an exaggeration, it is true that arguments can contain several links. For example:

> Because there is snow on the ground, it must have snowed last night. If it snowed last night, then the temperature must have dropped below 32°F. The temperature drops below 32°F only in the winter. So, since there is snow on the ground, it must be winter here.

Signal words can help you find premises:

since

because

given that

inasmuch as

It is easy to imagine a Holmesian chain of reasoning that strings additional links in either direction. Instead of starting with "there is snow on the ground," you could have started with "there is a snowman on the front lawn"; and instead of stopping with "it must be winter here," you could have gone on to "so it is summer in Australia." In other words, you could reason from "there is a snowman on the front lawn" to "it is summer in Australia."

Implicit premises are not stated.

In practice, arguments do not extend indefinitely in either direction. We begin reasoning at what seems to be a convenient point and stop with the conclusion we had hoped to prove: It must have snowed last night because there is snow on the ground this morning. Now, it should be obvious to you that the strength of an argument depends in a very important way on the legitimacy of its assumptions. And one of the LSAT's favorite tools for building a Logical Reasoning item is to focus upon an assumption of a special kind: the implicit premise.

Consider some sample arguments:

> Premise: My car's fuel tank is full.
> Conclusion: Therefore, my car will start.

A very effective attack on this argument can be aimed at a hidden premise—as anyone who has ever had a car fail to start can attest. The battery might be dead or a hundred other things might be wrong. This shows that the argument is not very strong. In logical terms, the argument depends upon an implicit premise:

> Premises: My car's fuel tank is full.
>   (The only reason my car might not start is lack of fuel.)
> Conclusion: Therefore, my car will start.

The statement in parentheses is a necessary part of the argument. Otherwise, the conclusion does not follow.

Implicit premises are also called *suppressed premises* (or assumptions) or *hidden premises* (or assumptions). You do not have to worry about terminology; you just have to know one when you see it:

> Premise: Edward has fewer than ten years of experience.
> Conclusion: Therefore, Edward is not qualified.
> Suppressed Premise: Only people with at least ten years of experience are
>   qualified.

> Premise: This is Tuesday.
> Conclusion: Therefore, the luncheon special is pasta.
> Suppressed Premise: Every Tuesday, the luncheon special is pasta.

> Premise: The committee did not announce its choice by 3:00.
> Conclusion: Therefore, Radu did not get the job.
> Suppressed Premise: Radu gets the job only if the announcement is made
>   by 3:00.

Many logical reasoning questions test fallacies.

A *fallacy* is a mistake in reasoning. Many LSAT questions ask you to demonstrate that you know a mistake when you see one. Of course, there are many different ways to make mistakes, so it is not possible to create an exhaustive list of fallacies. However, certain

Look for the alterna-tive causal linkage. In many items, the stimulus material is an explanation of an event or phenom-enon. You are then asked to weaken the explanation. Most often, the correct answer will be an alternative causal explanation.

fallacies come up on the LSAT fairly often. If you know what they look like, then they will be easier to spot.

Remember, however, that you do not get points for memorizing this list of fallacies. You get points for being able to apply it. So use the list as a guide as you do the practice tests in this book, but keep in mind that you will not be tested on the list itself.

Explanations often identify the wrong cause.

The mistake in reasoning that is tested most often by the LSAT is the fallacy of the false cause. An argument that commits this error attributes a causal relationship between two events where none exists or at least the relationship is misidentified. For example:

> Every time the doorbell rings, I find there is someone at the door. Therefore, it must be the case that the doorbell calls these people to my door.

Obviously, the causal link suggested here is backward. It is the presence of the person at the door that then leads to the ringing of the bell, not vice versa. A more serious example of the fallacy of the false cause is as follows:

> There were more air traffic fatalities in 1979 than there were in 1969; therefore, the airplanes used in 1979 were more dangerous than those used in 1969.

The difficulty with this argument is that it attributes the increase to a lack of safety when, in fact, it is probably attributable to an increase in air travel generally. A typical question stem and correct answer for this type of problem might be as follows:

> Which of the following, if true, most undermines the speaker's argument?
>
> (✓)   Total air miles traveled doubled from 1969 to 1979.

Analogies are often false.

A second fallacy that might appear on the LSAT is that of false analogy. This error occurs when a conclusion drawn from one situation is applied to another situation—but the two situations are not very similar. For example:

> People should have to be licensed before they are allowed to have children. After all, we require people who operate automobiles to be licensed.

In this case, the two situations—driving and having children—are so dissimilar that we would probably want to say they are not analogous at all. Having children has nothing to do with driving. An LSAT problem based upon a faulty analogy is likely to be more subtle. For example:

> The government should pay more to its diplomats who work in countries that are considered potential enemies. This is very similar to paying soldiers combat premiums if they are stationed in a war zone.

The argument here relies on an analogy between diplomats in a potentially dangerous country and soldiers in combat areas. Of course, the analogy is not perfect. No analogy can be more than an analogy. So a typical question stem and right answer for this type of problem might be as follows:

> Which of the following, if true, most weakens the argument above?
>
> (✓)   Diplomats are almost always evacuated before hostilities begin.

A generalization may be weak.

A common weakness in an inductive argument is the hasty generalization, that is, basing a large conclusion on too little data. For example:

> All four times I have visited Chicago, it has rained; therefore, Chicago probably gets very little sunshine.

The rather obvious difficulty with the argument is that it moves from a small sample—four visits—to a very broad conclusion: Chicago gets little sunshine. Of course, generalizing on the basis of a sample or limited experience can be legitimate:

> All five of the buses manufactured by Gutmann that we inspected have defective wheel mounts; therefore, some other buses manufactured by Gutmann probably have similar defects.

Admittedly, this argument is not airtight. Perhaps the other uninspected buses do not have the same defect, but this second argument is much stronger than the first. So a typical LSAT stem and correct answer might be as follows:

> Which of the following, if true, would most weaken the argument above?
>
> (✓)   The five inspected buses were prototypes built before design specifications were finalized.

Some arguments use terms ambiguously.

A fourth fallacy that the LSAT uses is that of ambiguity. Anytime there is a shifting in the meaning of terms used in an argument, the argument has committed a fallacy of ambiguity. For example:

> The shark has been around for millions of years. The City Aquarium has a shark. Therefore, the City Aquarium has at least one animal that is millions of years old.

The error of the argument is that it uses the word *shark* in two different ways. In the first occurrence, *shark* is used to mean sharks in general. In the second, *shark* refers to one individual animal. Here's another, less playful, example:

> Sin occurs only when a person fails to follow the will of God. But since God is all-powerful, what God wills must actually be. Therefore, it is impossible to deviate from the will of God, so there can be no sin in the world.

NOTE

Why do I need to know about fallacies? If you know what to look for, you're more likely to find it. This section is a checklist of common fallacies used by the LSAT.

The equivocation here is in the word *will*. The first time it is used, the author intends that the will of God is God's wish and implies that it is possible to fail to comply with those wishes. In the second instance, the author uses the word *will* in a way that implies that such deviation is not possible. The argument reaches the conclusion that there is no sin in the world only by playing on these two senses of "the will of God." So a representative question stem and correct answer might be as follows:

> The argument above uses which of the following terms in an ambiguous way?
>
> (✓)   Will

Some arguments use irrelevant evidence.

Another fallacy you might encounter in a Logical Reasoning section is an appeal to irrelevant considerations. For example, an argument that appeals to the popularity of a position to prove the position is fallacious:

> Frederick must be the best choice for chair because most people believe that he is the best person for the job.

That many people hold an opinion obviously does not guarantee its correctness. After all, many people once thought airplanes couldn't fly. A question stem for the argument above plus the correct answer might look like this:

> Which of the following, if true, most weakens the speaker's argument?
>
> (✓)   Most people erroneously believe that Frederick holds a Ph.D.

Some arguments are circular.

A circular argument (begging the question) is an argument in which the conclusion to be proved appears also as a premise. For example:

> Beethoven was the greatest composer of all time because he wrote the greatest music of any composer, and the one who composes the greatest music must be the greatest composer.

The conclusion of this argument is that Beethoven was the greatest composer of all time, but one of the premises of the argument is that he composed the greatest music, and the other premise states that that is the measure of greatness. The argument is fallacious, for there is really no argument for the conclusion at all, just a restatement of the conclusion. A typical LSAT stem and correct answer are as follows:

> The argument above is weak because
>
> (✓)   it assumes what it hopes to prove.

Ad hominem arguments attack someone personally.

Yes, *ad hominem* is a Latin phrase, and Latin is not tested on the LSAT. This phrase is just a useful shorthand for this fallacy. Any argument that is directed against the source of the claim rather than the claim itself is an *ad hominem* attack:

> Professor Peters' analysis of the economic impact of the proposed sports arena for the Blue Birds should be rejected because Professor Peters is a Red Birds fan—the most fierce rivals of the Blue Birds.

The suggestion is obviously farfetched. And a representative LSAT stem plus correct answer might look like this:

> The speaker's argument is weak because it
> (✓)   confuses a person's loyalty to a sports team with the person's ability to offer an expert economic opinion.

Making Deductions

In the previous section, we discussed some common inductive fallacies; in this section, we turn our attention to deductive reasoning. You will recall that a deductive argument is one in which the inference depends solely on the meanings of the terms used. The argument form most often associated with deductive reasoning is the *syllogism*, a term that will be familiar to anyone who has studied basic logic:

All trees are plants.
All redwoods are trees.
Therefore, all redwoods are plants.

Deductive arguments like this one hinge on the validity of positive or negative claims about all or some of a group. On the LSAT, deductive arguments come into play in questions like this:

Some lizards are carnivorous.
Some carnivores are intelligent.
Some intelligent creatures are not lizards.

If the statements above are true, which of the following could also be true?
(A) No carnivores are intelligent.
(B) No lizards are carnivores.
(C) No intelligent creatures are carnivores.
(D) No carnivores are lizards.
(E) All lizards are intelligent.

Three useful techniques for determining the validity of deductive arguments are knowing the square of opposition, using circle diagrams, and developing a logic shorthand.

Variations on direct inferences can lay out all the possibilities.

By *direct inference,* we mean a conclusion that follows from a single premise. For example, from the statement "no birds are mammals," we can conclude "no mammals are birds," since there is no individual that is a member of both the group bird and the group mammal. From "no birds are mammals," we could also reach the conclusion that "all birds are not mammals," but this is really nothing more than a grammatical restructuring of the original form, whereas the statement "no mammals are birds" is actually an inference (it is a totally new claim).

Setting aside possible variations in grammatical structure ("no B are M" = "all B are not M"; "some B are M" = "some B are not non-M"; and so on), we may organize such assertions into four groups, depending on whether they make a claim about "some" on the one hand or, on the other hand, either "all" or "no" members of groups and whether they are "affirmative" or "negative." In order to save space and also to show that our techniques are generally applicable—that is, not dependent on any particular content—we will find it convenient to use capital letters as substitutes for terms. Thus, "all birds are mammals" becomes "all B are M," which could also stand for "all bats are myopic," but nothing is lost in the translation since we are concerned with the formal relations and not the actual substantive or content relations between sentences. Using capital letters, we set up the scheme on the following page so that we have sentences that make affirmative claims about all of a group, negative claims about all of a group, affirmative claims about part of a group, and negative claims about part of a group.

(1) All S is P.
(2) No S is P.
(3) Some S is P.
(4) Some S is not P.

If **(1)** is true, then
    (2) is false.
    (3) is true.
    (4) is false.

If **(2)** is true, then
    (1) is false.
    (3) is false.
    (4) is true.

If **(3)** is true, then
    (1) undetermined.
    (2) is false.
    (4) is undetermined.

If **(4)** is true, then
    (1) is false.
    (2) is undetermined.
    (3) is undetermined.

If **(1)** is false, then
    (2) is undetermined.
    (3) is undetermined.
    (4) is true.

If **(2)** is false, then
    (1) is undetermined.
    (3) is true.
    (4) is undetermined.

If **(3)** is false, then
    (1) is false.
    (2) is true.
    (4) is true.

If **(4)** is false, then
    (1) is true.
    (2) is false.
    (3) is true.

Circle diagrams show relationships.

It is also apparent that there are interrelationships among all the statement forms. For example, if "all A are B" is true, then both "no A are B" and "some A are not B" must be false. One way of exhibiting these relationships is through the use of circle or Venn-type diagrams. (These are also used in Analytical Reasoning problems.)

Diagramming two terms. We can use a circle to mark off a "logical area." So a circle that we label "A" separates the field of the page into two spaces, A and not-A. The interior of the circle is the space where all As are located, and anything located outside the circle is not an A (it is a non-A):

Diagram 1:

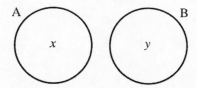

In Diagram 1, *x* is an A, but *y* is not an A; that is to say *y* is a non-A. Now, if we draw two overlapping circles, we can represent not only two groups, A and B, but also the intersection of those groups:

Diagram 2:

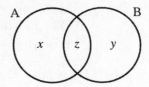

In Diagram 2, *x* is an A that is not, however, a B; *y* is a B that is not, however, an A; and *z* is something that is both A and B.

If it is true that "all A are B," then it is not possible for something to be an "A but not also a B," so we blot out that portion of our circle diagram that contains the area "A but not also B":

Diagram 3:

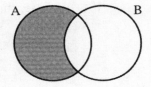

Now if it is true that "all A are B," then

> "no A are B" is false. (All the A are B.)
> "some A are B" is true. (All the A are within the B circle.)
> "some A are not B" is false. (That area is eliminated.)

If it is false that "all A are B," that might be because "no A are B":

Diagram 4:

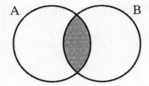

However, it might also be because "some, though not all, A are not B":

Diagram 5:

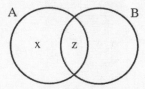

Both situations are consistent with "all A are B" being a false statement. So, if it is false that "all A are B," then

"no A are B" might be true or false. (We cannot choose between Diagram 4 and Diagram 5.)

"some A are B" might be true or false. (We have no basis for choice.)

"some A are not B" is true. (This is the case with both Diagram 4 and Diagram 5.)

If it is true that "no A are B," then there is no overlap between the two:

Diagram 6:

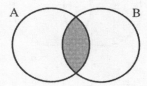

Therefore,

"all A are B" is false. (There is no overlap.)

"some A are B" is false. (There is no overlap.)

"some A are not B" is true. (That part is left open.)

But if "no A are B" is false, that might be because "all A are B":

Diagram 7:

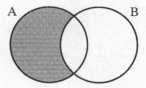

But it might equally well be because "some, though not all, A are B":

Diagram 8:

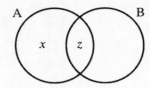

Therefore,

"all A are B" might be true or false. (There is no basis for choice.)

"some A are B" is true. (See Diagrams 7 and 8.)

"some A are not B" might be true or false. (There is no basis for choice between diagrams.)

If it is true that "some A are B,"

Diagram 9:

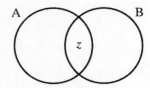

then

"all A are B" might be true or false.

"no A are B" is false. (See Diagram 9.)

"some A are not B" might be true or false.

If it is false that "some A are B," this can only be because there is no overlap between the two circles:

Diagram 10:

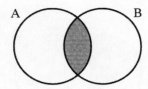

Therefore,

"all A are B" is false. (There is no overlap at all.)

"no A are B" is true. (as shown by Diagram 10)

"some A are not B" is true. (That area is left open.)

If it is true that "some A are not B,"

Diagram 11:

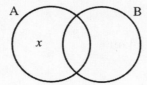

then

"all A are B" is false. (shown by the *x* in Diagram 11)

"no A are B" might be true or false. (The *x* does not close off the overlap of A and B, but, then again, we do not know that there are individuals with the characteristic A and B.)

"some A are B" might be true or false. (See the reasoning just given for ("no A are B.")

If it is false that "some A are not B,"

Diagram 12:

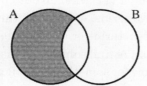

then the area of the A circle that does not overlap the B circle is empty, as shown by Diagram 12. Therefore,

"all A are B" is true. (The one is contained in the other.)

"no A are B" is false. (The one is contained in the other.)

"some A are B" is true. (In fact, all are, but see our discussion of some.)

Diagramming three terms. Technically, a syllogism is supposed to be constructed from three statements, two of which are assumptions and the third the conclusion. However, LSAT arguments of this type often include multiple statements, creating numerous possibilities for relationships. Here is an example:

All trees are plants.
All redwoods are trees.
This tree is a redwood.
Therefore, this tree is a plant.

If we analyzed this argument in a technical way, we would say it includes not one but two syllogisms—the conclusion of the first forming a premise of the second:

> All trees are plants.
> All redwoods are trees.
> Therefore, all redwoods are plants.

> All redwoods are plants.
> This tree is a redwood.
> Therefore, this tree is a plant.

Of course, a syllogism can be constructed using negative statements as well. Depending on the statements, what forms are used, and how the terms are arranged, we can construct many different syllogisms. Not all of these, however, would be valid. For example, the following syllogism is valid:

> All A are B.
> No B are C.
> Therefore, no A are C.

We can show its validity by using a variation on our circle diagrams. Because now we have three terms rather than two terms, we will use three circles to define the possible relationships. Remember that two terms or groups might be related in three ways: an A that is not a B, a B that is not an A, and something that is both A and B. When we add our third term, C, we have to allow for something that is a C but not an A or B; something that is a C and B but not an A; something that is a C and A but not a B; and something that is C, B, and A. In other words, there are seven possible combinations.

1 an A but not a B or C

2 a B but not an A or C

3 an A and B but not a C

4 a C but not an A or B

5 an A and C but not a B

6 a B and C but not an A

7 an A, B, and C

These seven possibilities can be shown on a three-circle diagram:

Diagram 13:

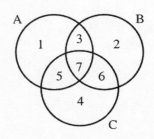

Using our three-circle diagrams, we can show the validity of the original syllogism:

> All A are B.
> No B are C.
> Therefore, no A are C.

Since our first premise states that "all A are B," we can eliminate the areas of the diagram that are within the A circle but not within the B circle. This corresponds to areas 1 and 5 in Diagram 13.

Diagram 14:

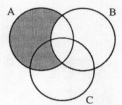

Our second premise states that "no B are C," so we must eliminate those areas, corresponding to 6 and 7 on Diagram 13, that allow that something might be a B and a C. (Notice that something that is an A, B, and C—area 7—is automatically something that is a B and a C.)

Diagram 15:

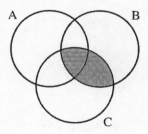

Now if we enter both premises 1 and 2 on the same diagram, we have the following:

Diagram 16:

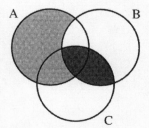

NOTE

Do you need to know "logic" to do well on this part?
No. The LSAT does not test the concepts of formal logic. (And formal language in this chapter is used just for ease of reference and will be explained.) However, an informal course in "practical reasoning" might be useful if you have not yet graduated and can fit it into your curriculum.

The conclusion of our syllogism asserts that "no A are C," and our diagram confirms this. The only area of A left open is within the B circle; all A but non-B areas have been erased.

Another example of a valid three-term syllogism is as follows:

> All A are B.
> Some C are A.
> Therefore, some C are B.

In a syllogism in which one of the propositions uses "some" and the other proposition uses "all" or "no," it is a good idea to enter the "all" or "no" information first. So we enter first "all A are B":

Diagram 17:

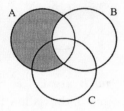

Then we enter "some C are A" by putting an *x* in the area of C and A. Since there is only one such area left, the *x* must be placed so:

Diagram 18:

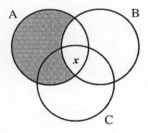

Now the diagram shows the validity of our syllogism: There is at least one C that is also a B.

An example of an invalid deductive argument is the syllogism that has the following form:

> No A are B.
> No B are C.
> Therefore, no A are C.

We can use a circle diagram to show why this syllogism is invalid. We enter the first and second premises:

Diagram 19:

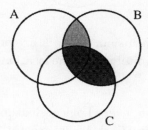

But then we observe that the overlap of A and C is still open, so our conclusion that "no A are C" is not warranted; that is, it does not definitely follow from our premises. So, too, is the following argument invalid:

> Some A are B.
> Some B are not C.
> Therefore, some A are not C.

Since there is no premise that begins with "all" or "no," we are forced to start with a premise that begins with "some." We take premise number one first—"some A are B"— but we have no way of determining whether or not the As that are Bs are also Cs. So we will leave open those possibilities:

Diagram 20:

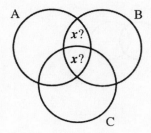

Now we add the information "some B are not C," again keeping open the possibility that something might be a B and an A or a B but not an A:

Diagram 21:

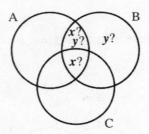

Diagram 21 shows that the conclusion, "some A are not C," does not follow from our premises because we do not definitely know the locations of our *x*s or *y*s, as indicated by the question marks.

Of course, you cannot expect that every Logical Reasoning problem on the LSAT with a form similar to the syllogism will fit this form exactly. To be sure, in the past, we have seen problems that fit the technical definition of the syllogism, but more often, LSAT problems involve more terms and more statements. Still, it is possible to adapt our circle diagram technique for use with nonstandard syllogisms:

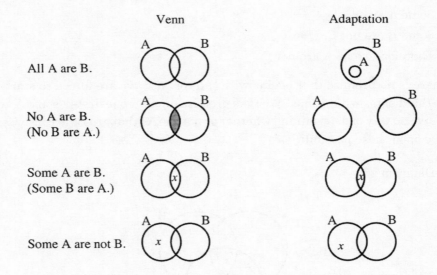

We can apply these adaptations to a nonstandard syllogism of the sort that could appear on the LSAT:

> All admirals are officers.
> No officer is not an honorable person.
> Some gentlemen are officers.
> No rogues are honorable persons.

Which of the following conclusions can be drawn from the statements above?

(A) All honorable persons are officers.

(B) No rogues are admirals.

(C) Some gentlemen are rogues.

(D) Some gentlemen are admirals.

(E) All officers are admirals.

The correct answer is (B). This can be demonstrated using diagrams.

We diagram our first statement using the adaptation:

Then we add our second statement (which is equivalent to saying "All officers are honorable persons"):

Then we add the third statement:

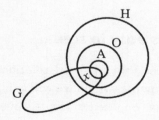

NOTE

Academic training is hazardous to your test-taking health. Look at a page of Logical Reasoning items (any such page in this book, for example). What percentage of the ink on the page is devoted to stimulus material, and what percentage is devoted to answer choices? It is at least equal, and in many cases, more space is taken up by the choices. You are used to thinking of the question as the important part of the test. For the LSAT, the answers are equally important.

Notice that in adding this statement, we leave open the question of whether all gentlemen are officers or even admirals. We know only that some gentlemen are officers, and that is the reason for the *x* entered in the space as shown. (Each spatial area is a "logical" space.) Finally, we add the fourth statement:

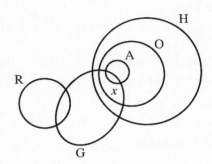

Notice that we leave open the question of whether a rogue might be a gentleman in the same way we have left open the question of whether all gentlemen are honorable.

From the diagram, we see that choices **(A)** and **(E)** commit the same error. We cannot conclude from a statement such as "all A are B" that "all B are A." The "admiral" circle is within the "officer" circle, and the "officer" circle is within the "honorable" circle. Then choices **(C)** and **(D)** commit the same error. It is possible that some gentlemen are rogues, for that is an area left open on the diagram. It is also possible that some gentlemen are admirals, but that is not necessarily true. It is true, however, as the diagram shows, that no rogues are admirals. The logical space for rogues, represented by the "R" circle, is completely outside the logical space for admirals, the "A" circle, which is completely contained within the "honorable," or "H," circle.

Let us conclude our discussion of circle diagrams by emphasizing that this is just one of many ways of solving Logical Reasoning problems. Some students remark that they find it easier to solve these problems "verbally"; that is, without the assistance of any diagram. That is fine. These diagrams are merely a suggestion. If you find them useful, then you have yet another way of attacking such problems on the exam. If you do not find them helpful, then after at least making an effort to understand how they work, you may rely on some other strategy.

Logical shorthand makes implications easy to see.

Thus far, we have treated deductive inferences that involved relationships among terms. Now we treat a group of deductive arguments, which we will call *implications*, that are based on the connections of sentences as opposed to terms. An example of an implication argument is as follows:

If John is elected president, Mary is elected vice president, and if Mary is elected vice president, Paul is elected secretary. Therefore, if John is elected president, Paul is elected secretary.

If we employ a system of logical shorthand, we can make a capital letter stand for each clause (or sentence). This shows that our argument has the following form:

If J, then M.
If M, then P.
Therefore, if J, then P.

Notice that our entire argument is phrased in the conditional. Our conclusion does not state that "Paul is elected secretary." It states rather that "*if* J, *then* P," and that entire conditional statement is the conclusion of the argument.

Another common form of implication is illustrated by the following argument:

If John is elected president, Mary is elected vice president. John is elected president. Therefore, Mary is elected vice president.

The form of the argument is as follows:

If J, then M.
J.
Therefore, M.

Notice that this argument differs from the preceding conditional argument because the second premise definitely asserts, "John is elected president." Now, since the validity of an argument is dependent only upon its form, it is clear that any argument that has this form is valid. This form of argument must not, however, be confused with the following superficially similar but invalid form:

If A, then B.
B.
Therefore, A.

The first premise asserts only that A is followed by B; it does not assert that an occurrence of situation B is necessarily preceded by an occurrence of situation A. For example, the following argument is not valid:

If an object is made of clay, it will not burn. This object will not burn. Therefore, this object is made of clay.

There are many objects that will not burn and that are not made of clay—those made of steel, for example. So any argument that has this form is invalid.

Another common form of implication that is valid is illustrated by the following argument:

> If John is elected president, then Mary is elected vice president. Mary is not elected vice president. Therefore, John is not elected president.

It has the following form:

> If J, then M.
> Not M.
> Therefore, not J.

Because the first premise states that an occurrence of situation J will be followed by an occurrence of situation M and since the second premise tells us that situation M did not occur, we can logically conclude that situation J did not occur, for if J had occurred, so, too, would M have occurred. A similar but invalid argument form is illustrated by the following argument:

> If John is elected president, then Mary is elected vice president. John is not elected president. Therefore, Mary is not elected vice president.

That this argument is invalid is demonstrated by the consideration that the first premise states only that an occurrence of J is followed by an occurrence of M. The premises do not establish that M can occur *only* if J also occurs. The first premise says, "if J, then M," not "M only if J." So any argument of the form "If A, then B. Not A. Therefore, not B" is invalid.

Not all valid implicational forms have been shown; our illustrations are intended to show the technique of substituting capital letters for sentences. This allows us to isolate the general *form* of an argument, which makes analyzing or comparing that form easier.

Devising Attack Strategies

Even though LSAT Logical Reasoning questions are worded in a wide variety of ways, there are several specific attack strategies that you can apply.

The question stem is the best starting place.

The first step in attacking a Logical Reasoning item is to read the question stem (the part to which the question mark is attached). Do this even before you read the paragraph or argument on which the question is based. The reason for this suggestion is simple. There are many different questions that could be asked about an argument: "How can it be strengthened?" "How can it be weakened?" "What are its assumptions?" "How is the argument developed?" and so on. If you read the stem first, it will guide you in what to look for as you read the argument.

The answer choices are your clues.

The differences among the answer choices can help you isolate the issues in the problem. With this in mind, here is a good plan of attack.

1 Always read every choice.

2 If possible, eliminate obviously incorrect choices.

3 Examine the remaining choices and focus on their differences.

4 Choose the best answer. Remember that the best is often not perfect and the less-than-best (incorrect) answers often have some merit.

Answering Special Question Types

Many Logical Reasoning questions are straightforward questions about how to attack and defend arguments. Some questions, however, involve special twists of thinking.

For a logical similarity question, reproduce the error.

For a question that asks, "Which of the following arguments is most similar?" remember that you are not supposed to correct the argument. You are supposed to find an answer choice with a similar structure—even if the original argument contains a fallacy. Also, be careful to notice exactly what is to be paralleled—all of an argument, one speaker, or whatever.

For a completion question, pick a conclusion.

For a question that requires you to complete a paragraph, keep in mind that you must complete the structure of the argument as a whole as well as the particular sentence. This means that an answer choice that repeats something already said is not correct. The correct answer must be the *completion* of the thought.

For an assumption question, pick a hidden premise.

When the question stem asks for the identification of assumptions, it is seeking implicit or unstated premises that—like all premises—are necessary to the argument.

For a weakening question, attack a hidden premise.

When the question stem asks for weakening ideas, it is usually a matter of attacking implicit assumptions that justify the application of the evidence to the conclusion.

ALERT!

For a parallel thinking question, a similar topic is likely to be a wrong answer. Parallel thinking questions ask you to select a line of reasoning that is similar to that in the stimulus material—warts and all. If the stimulus material is fallacious, then the correct answer choice makes the same mistake. A favorite wrong answer strategy is to toss in a choice with a similar topic, e.g., autos in the stimulus material and trucks in the choices.

EXERCISES: LOGICAL REASONING

Exercise 1

25 Questions • 35 Minutes

Directions: The following questions ask you to analyze and evaluate the reasoning in short paragraphs or passages. For some questions, all of the answer choices may conceivably be answers to the question asked. You should select the *best* answer to the question; that is, an answer that does not require you to make assumptions that violate commonsense standards by being implausible, redundant, irrelevant, or inconsistent. After choosing the best answer, circle the letter of your choice.

Example

In an extensive study of the reading habits of magazine subscribers, it was found than an average of between four and five people actually read each copy of the most popular weekly news magazine. On this basis, we estimate that the 12,000 copies of *Poets and Poetry* that are sold each month are actually read by 48,000 to 60,000 people.

The estimate above assumes that

(A) individual magazine readers generally enjoy more than one type of magazine.

(B) most of the readers of *Poets and Poetry* subscribe to the magazine.

(C) the ratio of readers to copies is the same for *Poets and Poetry* as for the weekly news magazine.

(D) the number of readers of the weekly news magazine is similar to the number of readers of *Poets and Poetry*.

(E) most readers enjoy sharing copies of their favorite magazines with friends and family members.

The correct answer is (C).

1. I.   Whenever some of the runners are leading off and all of the infielders are playing in, all of the batters attempt to bunt.

    II. Some of the runners are leading off, but some of the batters are not attempting to bunt.

    Which of the following conclusions can be deduced from the two statements given?

    (A) Some of the runners are not leading off.

    (B) Some of the batters are attempting to bunt.

    (C) None of the infielders is playing in.

    (D) All of the infielders are playing in.

    (E) Some of the infielders are not playing in.

2. The federal bankruptcy laws illustrate the folly of do-good protectionism at its most extreme. At the debtor's own request, the judge will list all of his debts; take what money the debtor has, which will be very little; and divide that small amount among his creditors. Then the judge declares that those debts are thereby satisfied, and the debtor is free from those creditors. Why, a person could take his credit card and buy a car, a stereo, and a new wardrobe and then declare himself bankrupt! In effect, he will have conned his creditors into giving him all those things for nothing.

    Which of the following adages best describes the author's attitude about a bankrupt debtor?

    (A) "A penny saved is a penny earned."

    (B) "You've made your bed, now lie in it."

    (C) "Absolute power corrupts absolutely."

    (D) "He that governs least governs best."

    (E) "Millions for defense, but not one cent for tribute."

3. MARY: All of the graduates from Midland High School go to State College.

    ANN: I don't know. Some of the students at State College come from North Hills High School.

    Ann's response shows that she has interpreted Mary's remark to mean that

    (A) most of the students from North Hills High School attend State College.

    (B) none of the students at State College are from Midland High School.

    (C) only students from Midland High School attend State College.

    (D) Midland High School is a better school than North Hills High School.

    (E) some Midland High School graduates do not attend college.

4. Total contributions by individuals to political parties were up 25 percent in this most recent presidential election over those of four years earlier. Hence, it is obvious that people are no longer as apathetic as they were, but they are taking a greater interest in politics.

    Which of the following, if true, would considerably weaken the preceding argument?

    (A) The average contribution per individual actually declined during the same four-year period.

    (B) Per capita income of the population increased by 15 percent during the four years in question.

    (C) Public leaders continue to warn citizens against the dangers of political apathy.

    (D) Contributions made by large corporations to political parties declined during the four-year period.

    (E) Fewer people voted in the most recent presidential election than in the one 4 years earlier.

exercises

5. We must do something about the rising cost of our state prisons. It now costs an average of $225 per day to maintain a prisoner in a double-occupancy cell in a state prison. Yet, in the most expensive cities in the world, one can find rooms in the finest hotels that rent for less than $175 per night.

The argument above might be criticized in all of the following ways EXCEPT

(A) it introduces an inappropriate analogy.

(B) it relies on an unwarranted appeal to authority.

(C) it fails to take account of costs that prisons have but hotels do not have.

(D) it misuses numerical data.

(E) it draws a faulty comparison.

6. Antibacterial hand soaps have been available since the 1920s, but only recently have they been mass marketed to consumers in containers bearing labels identifying them as containing an antibacterial agent. None of the antibacterial hand soaps presently available for over-the-counter use, however, truly sterilizes in the way that germ-killing scrubs used by hospitals do. So consumers wind up paying more for an enhancement that really is ineffective.

Which of the following, if true, would most weaken the argument above?

(A) Antibacterial agents are also used extensively in other products such as home cleaners for fabrics, rugs, kitchen counters, and toilet bowls.

(B) Experts generally agree that one of the most effective ways of preventing the spread of disease by personal contact or food handling is by the practice of thoroughly washing one's hands.

(C) Studies show that the agents in antibacterial hand soaps are effective in killing most germs and stopping the growth of common bacteria for as long as 6 hours.

(D) The first germ-killing body and hand soaps, which were introduced in the 1970s, did not include mention on their labels of the antibacterial agents they contained.

(E) Overuse of antibacterial agents in widely used products such as hand soaps may cause bacteria to produce strains that are resistant to the antibacterial agents.

exercises

7. The Consumer Price Index is a statistic that measures changes in prices of goods and services purchased by consumers. It is based on a "basket of goods and services" divided into seven categories such as housing, food, and transportation with each category weighted according to its relative impact on a typical budget. Although the Consumer Price Index is a useful measure of inflation, consumers themselves almost always imagine that prices are rising faster than this statistical measure.

Which of the following would help to explain the phenomenon described above?

(A) The typical consumer purchases large ticket items such as a house or a car so infrequently that even given a low rate of inflation, the price of the new purchase will be noticeably higher than that of the previous one.

(B) In recent years, advances in technology have caused the price of electronics such as computers and stereo equipment to decline even as new products are introduced that have more extensive capabilities.

(C) Because of long-term pressures in the health-care sector such as the push for higher wages for the lowest paid health-care workers, the cost of medical care has risen faster than the Consumer Price Index.

(D) The Consumer Price Index is compiled by the Bureau of Labor Statistics and is intended primarily as a measure of the effect of rising prices on a typical urban family.

(E) The prices paid for commodities such a gasoline that depend upon international market conditions are usually more volatile than those determined largely by domestic factors and tend to rise and fall sharply in the short run.

8. If college students are distracted in class, it is because they are bored. If professors are boring lecturers, it is because they are trained as researching scholars rather than as teachers. So the best way to ensure that college students will be attentive in class is to assign them professors who have been trained as teachers instead of researching scholars.

Which of the following would most weaken the argument above?

(A) Some college professors are not trained as researching scholars.

(B) College students may be bored by a subject rather than by the professor.

(C) Professors who are trained as lecturers are not distracted in class.

(D) Colleges have an obligation to ensure that students are not bored.

(E) Teachers not trained in research are almost always interesting lecturers.

9. Zora Neale Hurston, who wrote four novels, a folk opera, and nearly 100 short stories, loved a good lie. When her late-model car aroused suspicion among poor country folk whose lives she was researching, she pretended to be a bootlegger. She lied on official documents like marriage licenses, giving her age at the time of her second marriage as 31 rather than 48. Her letters sometimes seem written by different people, and her autobiography, in which she claims to have been born in Eatonville, Florida rather than Notasulga, Alabama, is full of misinformation. So, Hurston's own statements and writings are not likely to settle any of the debates over the details of her life.

   Which of the following principles best justifies the conclusion of the reasoning above?

   (A) Personal details of a writer's life can best be uncovered by studying texts produced by the author herself.

   (B) Biographical data on famous people must be confirmed by independent sources such as family and friends.

   (C) Statements made by a person who is known to tell falsehoods are not a reliable source of information.

   (D) Writers who primarily produce works of fiction cannot be trusted to portray themselves accurately.

   (E) Official documents are more authoritative sources for biographical information than personal letters.

10. Is the provincial government really as corrupt as people say? Well, I know one woman who, when her husband got his first driver's license, said that she would not permit him to drive the family car until he actually learned how to drive.

    Which of the following is the point the speaker wants to make?

    (A) The provincial government is very corrupt.

    (B) It is not difficult to learn to drive.

    (C) Governments everywhere are more or less corrupt.

    (D) A license should not be required to drive a family car.

    (E) Governmental corruption should not be tolerated.

11. The success of the new television series *Backroom* has surprised almost all the experts and critics. Unlike the main character of most other successful series, Randall is neither a good guy nor a bad guy with good qualities. Instead, he is an immature and insensitive boor concerned only with his own problems, and audiences howl with laughter as he berates and takes advantage of minor characters such as the store clerk in the first episode who is merely trying to be helpful but comes off like a total loser. Apparently, the key to the success of *Backroom* is that people had rather identify with a successful character with no redeeming social traits than any of the losers who surround him.

Which of the following can be most reliably inferred from the speaker's comments?

(A) Most successful television series feature a main character with relatively few good qualities with which the audience is able to identify.

(B) The Randall character on *Backroom* is someone whom most television viewers would like to know in real life.

(C) *Backroom's* success is likely to inspire other series that feature main characters without commendable personality traits.

(D) The greater the gap between a viewer's expectations and a television program's script, the more likely the program is to succeed.

(E) The Randall character would probably not appeal to audiences if he were featured in a series alongside other characters with admirable personality traits.

12. The Theater Arts Group plans to buy the Odeon Theater, a two-balcony house that has been boarded up for nearly fifteen years, renovate it, and offer it for rent to production companies for plays. But these old two-balcony houses have limited seating capacity, and many people do not want to sit in the second balcony. The Odeon itself can accommodate a maximum of 650 people, and a seating capacity of at least 1,500 is needed to make a production of a musical play profitable. So it seems unlikely that the plan will be successful.

Which of the following, if true, would most weaken the speaker's reasoning?

(A) Larger theaters have about 1,600 seats and only one balcony.

(B) The Odeon Theater is protected by landmark preservation laws.

(C) Musical productions that employ a full orchestra usually require removal of several rows of seats to accommodate the musicians.

(D) The current economic boom that has fueled tourism in general and theater-going in particular is coming to an end.

(E) Straight drama productions, which are less costly because they do not require an orchestra, are becoming increasingly popular with audiences.

13. Recently, a major conservationist organization announced that the spread of exotic species is the second greatest threat to biodiversity, just behind loss of habitat, and called for the Federal government to take action to ban trade in a lengthy list of exotic plants. The group explained that exotic plants cause nearly $125 billion in damage each year. But what constitutes a disaster in one ecosystem may be a mere nuisance in another or even a positive boon in a third. Lantana, for example, is a terrible pest in Hawaii but a great bedding plant in Pennsylvania.

Which of the following is most probably the conclusion that the speaker is leading up to?

(A) An annual cost of $125 billion is a small price to pay to ensure the availability of a wide array of exotic plant species.

(B) Federal legislation is generally ineffective in controlling traffic in outlawed plants.

(C) The spread of exotic plant species is unlikely to become a more serious threat to biodiversity than habitat loss.

(D) A national ban on exotic plants would prevent the sale of some species in areas where they might be valuable.

(E) Hawaii, as an ecosystem, is not typical of the conditions found in most of the other states.

14. If students find their course work too easy, then they become bored and so achieve less than their abilities would allow them to achieve. But when students find their course work too difficult, they become frustrated and give up too soon and so achieve less than their abilities would allow. Therefore, it is impossible for a teacher to assign course work in such a way that the assignment will enable students to work up to their true abilities.

Which of the following points out an error in the reasoning above?

(A) It overlooks the possibility of a third alternative.

(B) It generalizes on a limited sample of a population.

(C) It confuses an effect with a causal factor.

(D) It unfairly questions the credibility of the source.

(E) It uses a key term in an ambiguous fashion.

15. This season, 14 of the 31 teams in the National Football League will be using some variant of the West Coast offense originated by Bill Walsh. The West Coast, built around a passing attack that features precision throwing and crisp, clear passing routes, can be contrasted with the older-style "Bloody Nose" offense, originated by the Chicago Bears, that relies heavily on grinding out four or five yards per down on the ground. The reason for the popularity of the newer West Coast offense is not hard to explain. Fourteen of the 31 head coaches in the league are former assistants to Bill Walsh or former assistants to head coaches who had previously worked for Walsh.

The speaker assumes that

(A) the West Coast offense is the most effective offense ever used in the National Football League.

(B) the older-style "Bloody Nose" offense will one day be completely supplanted by the West Coast offense.

(C) a style of coaching is something that can be passed along from more experienced coaches to younger ones.

(D) a passing offense is more exciting to watch than an offense that relies primarily on gaining yards by running.

(E) younger football coaches study under Bill Walsh in order to learn a style of offense that they will later use as head coaches.

16. The outbreak of E. coli poisoning that has been traced to contaminated well water used by food vendors at the county fair has already made more than 700 people ill, and health officials expect to add another 50 or so to the list today. The virulence of this particular strain is obvious since the fair closed more than two weeks ago; yet, the number of victims continues to grow.

Which of the following, if true, would most weaken the argument?

(A) The contaminated water was used by food vendors to make frozen drinks that are consumed mainly by children.

(B) The incubation period for the disease is two to nine days, but doctor reports to health officials may be delayed by two to three weeks.

(C) The well water became contaminated when a heavy run washed manure from a cattle exhibition barn into the water supply.

(D) Many people who are infected with E. Coli and experience symptoms may not realize that they have contracted the illness and so do not see a doctor.

(E) Sixty-five of the victims of the outbreak have been hospitalized, and two have died from the poisoning.

Questions 17 and 18

The single greatest weakness of American parties is their inability to achieve cohesion in the legislature. Although there is some measure of party unity, it is not uncommon for the majority party to be unable to implement important legislation. The unity is strongest during election campaigns; after the primary elections, the losing candidates all promise their support to the party nominee. By the time Congress convenes, the unity has dissipated. This phenomenon is attributable to the fragmented nature of party politics. The national committees are no more than feudal lords who receive nominal fealty from their vassals. A member of Congress builds power upon a local base. Consequently, a member is likely to be responsive to local special interest groups. Evidence of this is seen in the differences in voting patterns between the upper and lower houses. In the Senate, where terms are longer, there is more party unity.

17. Which of the following, if true, would most strengthen the author's argument?

    (A) On 30 key issues, 18 of the 67 majority party members in the Senate voted against the party leaders.

    (B) On 30 key issues, 70 of the 305 majority party members in the House voted against the party leaders.

    (C) On 30 key issues, more than half the members of the minority party in both houses voted with the majority party against the leaders of the minority party.

    (D) Of 30 key legislative proposals introduced by the president, only 8 passed both houses.

    (E) Of 30 key legislative proposals introduced by a president whose party controlled a majority in both houses, only 4 passed both houses.

18. Which of the following, if true, would most weaken the author's argument?

    (A) Members of Congress receive funds from the national party committee.

    (B) Senators vote against the party leaders only two thirds as often as House members.

    (C) The primary duty of an officeholder is to be responsive to a local constituency rather than party leaders.

    (D) There is more unity among minority party members than among majority party members.

    (E) Much legislation is passed each session, despite party disunity.

19. ADVERTISEMENT: When you enroll with Future Careers Business Institute (FCBI), you will have access to our placement counseling service. Last year, 92 percent of our graduates who asked us to help them find jobs found them. So go to FCBI for your future!

    The answer to which of the following questions is potentially the LEAST damaging to the claim of the advertising?

    (A) How many of your graduates asked FCBI for assistance?

    (B) How many people graduated from FCBI last year?

    (C) Did those people who asked for jobs find ones in the areas for which they were trained?

    (D) Was FCBI responsible for finding the jobs, or did graduates find them independently?

    (E) Was the person reading the advertisement a paid, professional actor?

20. Either you severely punish a child who is bad or the child will grow up to be a criminal. Your child has just been bad. Therefore, you should punish the child severely.

    All EXCEPT which of the following would be an appropriate objection to the argument?

    (A) What do you consider to be a severe punishment?

    (B) What do you mean by the term "bad"?

    (C) Isn't your "either–or" premise an oversimplification?

    (D) Don't your first and second premises contradict one another?

    (E) In what way has this child been bad?

21. Studies recently published in the *Journal of the American Medical Association* say that despite the widespread belief to the contrary, girls are just as likely as boys to have the reading impairment dyslexia. The new studies examined 450 children over a four-year period, from kindergarten through third grade. The research teams found that fewer than half the students referred to them for reading problems actually had them; and although the schools identified four times as many boys as girls as being dyslexic, independent testing by the research teams revealed that the impairment appeared in both sexes with equal frequency. Yet, over the past decades, elaborate research programs have been set up to find the biological basis for the presumed gender difference in developing dyslexia.

Which of the following, if true, best explains the seeming contradiction outlined above between the new research and the conventional sex-linked view of dyslexia?

(A) Many boys who have dyslexia are not identified as suffering any learning disability.

(B) Many girls who do not have any learning impairment are incorrectly identified as having dyslexia.

(C) Earlier research was based entirely on subjects who were diagnosed by teachers as having reading problems.

(D) For years, the incidence of dyslexia has been underreported in school children of both genders.

(E) Learning disabilities are not likely to become evident until a child has reached the fourth grade.

Questions 22 and 23

We should abolish the public education system and allow schools to operate as autonomous units competing for students. Students will receive government funds in the form of vouchers that they can then "spend" at the school of their choice. This will force schools to compete for students by offering better and more varied educational services. As in private industry, only the schools that provide customer satisfaction will survive. Since schools that cannot attract students will close, we will see an overall improvement in the quality of education.

22. The argument above rests on which of the following unsupported assumptions?

(A) Maximizing student and parent satisfaction also maximizes student learning.

(B) In order to attract students, all schools will eventually have to offer essentially the same curriculum.

(C) Giving students direct financial aid encourages them to study harder.

(D) Schools should provide only educational services and not additional cocurricular or extracurricular activities.

(E) All education, both public and private, should be funded either directly or indirectly by government expenditures.

23. Which of the following, if true, would most undermine the argument above?

(A) Schools will make sure that all parents and students are thoroughly informed about the programs offered.

(B) Most students and parents will select a school based upon the convenience of its location.

(C) Students have different interests and different needs that can best be met by a variety of programs.

(D) By forcing schools to operate on a cost-effective basis, a voucher program would actually reduce total educational expenditures.

(E) Financial barriers currently limit the educational choices of students from poorer families.

24. Though I am an amateur athlete—a long-distance runner—I have no love of the Olympic Games. The original purpose was noble, but the games have become a vehicle for politics and money. For example, when the media mention the 1980 winter games at Lake Placid, they invariably show footage of a hockey game. The real story of the 1980 games—Eric Heiden's winning five gold medals in speedskating—is all but forgotten.

    The speaker above implies that

    (A) Eric Heiden was a better hockey player than speedskater.

    (B) most people would prefer to watch speedskating over hockey.

    (C) hockey produces money while speedskating does not.

    (D) only professional athletes compete in the Olympic Games.

    (E) amateur athletes are more exciting to watch than professional athletes.

25. Some judges are members of the bar. No member of the bar is a convicted felon. Therefore, some judges are not convicted felons.

    Which of the following is logically most similar to the argument developed above?

    (A) Anyone who jogs in the heat will be sick. I do not jog in the heat and will therefore likely never be sick.

    (B) People who want to avoid jury duty will not register to vote. A person may not vote until age 18. Therefore, persons under 18 are not called for jury duty.

    (C) All businesses file a tax return, but many businesses do not make enough money to pay taxes. Therefore, some businesses do not make a profit.

    (D) All non-students were excluded from the meeting, but some non-students were interested in the issues discussed. Therefore, some non-students interested in the issues are not allowed in the meeting.

    (E) The Grand Canyon is large. The Grand Canyon is in Arizona. Therefore, Arizona is large.

Exercise 2

15 Questions • 22 Minutes

Directions: The following questions ask you to analyze and evaluate the reasoning in short paragraphs or passages. For some questions, all of the answer choices may conceivably be answers to the question asked. You should select the *best* answer to the question; that is, an answer that does not require you to make assumptions that violate commonsense standards by being implausible, redundant, irrelevant, or inconsistent. After choosing the best answer, circle the letter of your choice.

Example

In an extensive study of the reading habits of magazine subscribers, it was found than an average of between four and five people actually read each copy of the most popular weekly news magazine. On this basis, we estimate that the 12,000 copies of *Poets and Poetry* that are sold each month are actually read by 48,000 to 60,000 people.

The estimate above assumes that

(A) individual magazine readers generally enjoy more than one type of magazine.

(B) most of the readers of *Poets and Poetry* subscribe to the magazine.

(C) the ratio of readers to copies is the same for *Poets and Poetry* as for the weekly news magazine.

(D) the number of readers of the weekly news magazine is similar to the number of readers of *Poets and Poetry*.

(E) most readers enjoy sharing copies of their favorite magazines with friends and family members.

The correct answer is (C).

1. The Supreme Court's recent decision is unfair. It treats non-resident aliens as a special group when it denies them some rights ordinary citizens have. This treatment is discriminatory, and we all know that discrimination is unfair.

   Which of the following arguments is most nearly similar in its reasoning to the above argument?

   (A) Doing good would be our highest duty under the moral law, and that duty would be irrational unless we had the ability to discharge it; but since a finite, sensuous creature could never discharge that duty in his lifetime, we must conclude that if there is moral law, the soul is immortal.

   (B) Required core courses are a good idea because students just entering college do not have as good an idea about what constitutes a good education as do the professional educators; therefore, students should not be left complete freedom to select course work.

   (C) This country is the most free nation on Earth, largely as a result of the fact that the founding fathers had the foresight to include a Bill of Rights in the Constitution.

   (D) Whiskey and beer do not mix well; every evening that I have drunk both whiskey and beer together, the following morning I have had a hangover.

   (E) I know that this is a beautiful painting because Picasso created only beautiful works of art, and this painting was done by Picasso.

2. Creativity must be cultivated. Artists, musicians, and writers all practice, consciously or unconsciously, interpreting the world from new and interesting viewpoints. A teacher can encourage his pupils to be creative by showing them different perspectives for viewing the significance of events in their daily lives.

   Which of the following, if true, would most undermine the author's claim?

   (A) In a well-ordered society, it is important to have some people who are not artists, musicians, or writers.

   (B) A teacher's efforts to show a pupil different perspectives may actually inhibit development of the student's own creative process.

   (C) Public education should stress practical skills, which will help a person get a good job, instead of creative thinking.

   (D) Not all pupils have the same capacity for creative thought.

   (E) Some artists, musicians, and writers "burn themselves out" at a very early age, producing a flurry of great works and then nothing after that.

3. Opponents to the mayor's plan for express bus lanes on the city's major commuter arteries objected that people could not be lured out of their automobiles in that way. The opponents were proved wrong; following implementation of the plan, bus ridership rose dramatically, and there was a corresponding drop in automobile traffic. Nonetheless, the plan failed to achieve its stated objective of reducing average commuting time.

Which of the following sentences would be the most logical continuation of this argument?

(A) The plan's opponents failed to realize that many people would take advantage of improved bus transportation.

(B) Unfortunately, politically attractive solutions do not always get results.

(C) The number of people a vehicle can transport varies directly with the size of the passenger compartment of the vehicle.

(D) Opponents cited an independent survey of city commuters showing that before the plan's adoption, only one out of every seven used commuter bus lines.

(E) With the express lanes closed to private automobile traffic, the remaining cars were forced to use too few lanes, and this created gigantic traffic tie-ups.

4. Last year, Gambia received $2.5 billion in loans from the International Third World Banking Fund, and its Gross Domestic Product grew by 5 percent. This year, Gambia has requested twice as much money from the ITWBF, and its leaders expect that Gambia's GNP will rise by a full 10 percent.

Which of the following, if true, would LEAST weaken the expectations of Gambia's leaders?

(A) The large 5 percent increase of last year is attributable to extraordinary harvests due to unusually good weather conditions.

(B) Gambia's economy is not strong enough to absorb more than $3 billion in outside capital each year.

(C) Gambia does not have sufficient heavy industry to fuel an increase in its GDP of more than 6 percent per year.

(D) A provision of the charter of the International Third World Banking Fund prohibits the fund from increasing loans to a country by more than 50 percent in a single year.

(E) A neighboring country experienced an increase of 5 percent in its Gross Domestic Product two years ago but an increase of only 3 percent in the most recent year.

5. Efficiency experts will attempt to improve the productivity of an office by analyzing production procedures into discrete work tasks. They then study the organization of those tasks and advise managers on techniques to speed production, such as rescheduling of employee breaks or relocating various equipment such as the copying machines. I have found a way to accomplish increases in efficiency with much less to do. Office workers grow increasingly productive as the temperature drops, so long as it does not fall below 68°F.

The passage leads most naturally to which of the following conclusions?

(A) Some efficiency gains will be short-term gains only.

(B) To maintain peak efficiency, an office manager must occasionally restructure office tasks.

(C) Employees are most efficient when the temperature is at 68°F.

(D) The temperature-efficiency formula is applicable to all kinds of work.

(E) Office workers will be equally efficient at 67°F and 69°F.

Questions 6–8

SPEAKER 1:   Those who oppose abortion upon demand make the foundation of their arguments the sanctity of human life, but this seeming bedrock assumption is actually as weak as shifting sand. And it is not necessary to invoke the red herring that many abortion opponents would allow that human life must sometimes be sacrificed for a great good, as in the fighting of a just war. There are counterexamples to the principle of sanctity of life that are even more embarrassing to abor-

tion opponents. It would be possible to reduce the annual number of traffic fatalities to virtually zero by passing federal legislation mandating a nationwide 15-mile-per-hour speed limit on all roads. You see, implicitly we have always been willing to trade off quantity of human life for quality.

SPEAKER 2:   The analogy my opponent draws between abortion and traffic fatalities is weak. No one would propose such a speed limit. Imagine people trying to get to and from work under such a law, or imagine them trying to visit a friend or relatives outside their own neighborhoods, or taking in a sports event or a movie. Obviously such a law would be a disaster.

6. Which of the following best characterizes Speaker 2's response to Speaker 1?

(A) His analysis of the traffic fatalities case actually supports the argument of Speaker 1.

(B) His analysis of the traffic fatalities case is an effective rebuttal of Speaker 1's argument.

(C) His response provides a strong affirmative statement of his own position.

(D) His response is totally irrelevant to the issue raised by Speaker 1.

(E) His counterargument attacks the character of Speaker 1 instead of the merits of Speaker 1's argument.

7. Which of the following represents the most logical continuation of the reasoning contained in Speaker 1's argument?

(A) Therefore, we should not have any laws on the books to protect human life.

(B) We can only conclude that Speaker 2 is also in favor of strengthening enforcement of existing traffic regulations as a means to reducing the number of traffic fatalities each year.

(C) So the strongest attack on Speaker 2's position is that he contradicts himself when he agrees that we should fight a just war even at the risk of considerable loss of human life.

(D) Even the laws against contraception are good examples of this tendency.

(E) The abortion question just makes explicit that which for so long has remained hidden from view.

8. Which of the following assumptions are made in the argument of Speaker 1?

(A) The protection of human life is not a justifiable goal of society.

(B) A human fetus should not be considered a "life" for purposes of government protections.

(C) Speed limits and other minor restrictions are an impermissible intrusion by government on human freedom.

(D) An appropriate societal decision is made in the balancing of individual lives and the quality of life.

(E) Government may legitimately protect the interests of individuals but have no authority to act on behalf of families or groups.

9. Which of the following conclusions can be deduced from the two statements below?

Some Alphas are not Gammas.

All Betas are Gammas.

(A) Some Alphas are not Betas.

(B) No Gammas are Alphas.

(C) All Gammas are Betas.

(D) All Alphas are Gammas.

(E) Some Alphas are Gammas.

10. I saw Barbara at the racetrack, and she told me that on the same horse race, she made two win bets. She said she bet $10 on Boofer Bear to win at even money and $5 on Copper Cane to win at odds of 10 to 1. After the race, she went back to the parimutuel window. So one or the other of those two horses must have won the race.

Which of the following is NOT an unstated premise of the reasoning above?

(A) The only bets Barbara made on the race were her win bets on Boofer Bear and Copper Cane.

(B) In the race in question, Boofer Bear and Copper Cane did not finish in a dead heat.

(C) Barbara did not return to the parimutuel window after the race for some reason other than cashing a winning ticket.

(D) Barbara's representation about the bets that she had placed was accurate.

(E) Barbara believed that it was more likely that Boofer Bear would win than Copper Cane.

11. Juana is dining at a Chinese restaurant. She will order either combination platter #2 or combination platter #5 but not both. If she orders combination platter #2, she will eat fried rice. If she orders combination platter #5, she will eat an egg roll. Given the statements above, which of the following must be true?

    (A) Juana will eat either fried rice or an egg roll but not both.

    (B) If Juana eats an egg roll, then she ordered combination platter #5.

    (C) If Juana does not eat an egg roll, then she ordered combination platter #2.

    (D) If Juana eats fried rice, then she ordered combination platter #2.

    (E) Anyone who orders combination platter #2 eats fried rice.

12. The harmful effects of marijuana and other drugs have been considerably overstated. Although parents and teachers have expressed much concern over the dangers that widespread usage of marijuana and other drugs pose for high school and junior high school students, a national survey of 5,000 students of ages 13 to 17 showed that fewer than 15 percent of those students thought such drug use was likely to be harmful.

    Which of the following is the strongest criticism of the author's reasoning?

    (A) The opinions of students in the age group surveyed are likely to vary with age.

    (B) Alcohol use among students of ages 13 to 17 is on the rise and is now considered by many to present greater dangers than marijuana usage.

    (C) Marijuana and other drugs may be harmful to users even though the users are not themselves aware of the danger.

    (D) A distinction must be drawn between victimless crimes and crimes in which an innocent person is likely to be involved.

    (E) The fact that a student does not think a drug is harmful does not necessarily mean he will use it.

13. AL: If an alien species ever visited Earth, it would surely be because they were looking for other intelligent species with whom they could communicate. Since we have not been contacted by aliens, we may conclude that none have ever visited this planet.

AMY: Or, perhaps, they did not think human beings intelligent.

How is Amy's response related to Al's argument?

(A) She misses Al's point entirely.

(B) She attacks Al personally rather than his reasoning.

(C) She points out that Al made an unwarranted assumption.

(D) She ignores the detailed internal development of Al's logic.

(E) She introduces a false analogy.

14. I maintain that the best way to solve our company's present financial crisis is to bring out a new line of goods. I challenge anyone who disagrees with this proposed course of action to show that it will not work.

A flaw in the preceding argument is that it

(A) employs group classifications without regard to individuals.

(B) introduces an analogy that is weak.

(C) attempts to shift the burden of proof to those who would object to the plan.

(D) fails to provide statistical evidence to show that the plan will actually succeed.

(E) relies upon a discredited economic theory.

15. If quarks are the smallest subatomic particles in the universe, then gluons are needed to hold quarks together. Since gluons are needed to hold quarks together, it follows that quarks are the smallest subatomic particles in the universe.

The logic of the above argument is most nearly paralleled by which of the following?

(A) If this library has a good French literature collection, it will contain a copy of *Les Conquerants* by Malraux. The collection does contain a copy of *Les Conquerants*; therefore, the library has a good French literature collection.

(B) If there is a man-in-the-moon, the moon must be made of green cheese for him to eat. There is a man-in-the-moon, so the moon is made of green cheese.

(C) Either helium or hydrogen is the lightest element of the periodic table. Helium is not the lightest element of the periodic table, so hydrogen must be the lightest element of the periodic table.

(D) If Susan is taller than Bob and if Bob is taller than Elaine, then if Susan is taller than Bob, Susan is also taller than Elaine.

(E) Whenever it rains, the streets get wet. The streets are not wet. Therefore, it has not rained.

ANSWER KEYS AND EXPLANATIONS

Exercise 1

1. E	6. C	11. E	16. B	21. C
2. B	7. A	12. E	17. E	22. A
3. C	8. B	13. D	18. C	23. B
4. E	9. C	14. A	19. E	24. C
5. B	10. A	15. C	20. D	25. D

1. **The correct answer is (E).** This item tests logical deduction. Statement I establishes that all batters bunt whenever two conditions are met: Some runners lead off and all infielders play in. Statement II establishes that one of the two conditions is met (some runners are leading off) but denies that all batters are bunting. This can only be because the other condition is not met: It is false that "All infielders are playing in." Recalling our discussion of direct inferences in the instructional overview, we know that this means "Some infielders are not playing in," or choice (E). We cannot conclude choice (C), that none of the infielders are playing in, only that some are not. Nor can we deduce choice (D), that all are playing in—for that is logically impossible. Then, recalling our discussion of the meaning of *some* in the instructional overview, we eliminate both choices (A) and (B). Some means "at least one" without regard to the remaining population. That some runners are leading off does not imply that some are not leading off choice (B). And that some batters are not bunting does not imply that some are bunting.

2. **The correct answer is (B).** The author's attitude toward the bankruptcy law is expressed by his choice of the terms "folly," "protectionism," and "conned." The author apparently believes that the debtor who has incurred these debts ought to bear the responsibility for them and that the government should not help the debtor get off the hook. Choice (B) properly expresses this attitude: You have created for yourself a situation by your own actions; now you must accept it. The author may share choice (A) as well, but it is not a judgment the author would make about the bankrupt, that is, a person who does not have a penny to save. Choice (C) is completely unrelated to the question at hand; the bankrupt has no power to wield. The author may believe choice (D), but the question stem asks for the author's attitude about the bankrupt debtor, not the government. Choice (D) would be appropriate to the latter, but it has no bearing on the question at hand. Finally, choice (E) would be applicable if the government were giving money to pay a ransom to terrorists or some similar situation. The assistance it provides to the bankrupt debtor is not such a program. It does not pay tribute to the debtor.

3. **The correct answer is (C).** Ann's response would be appropriate only if Mary had said, "All of the students at State College come from Midland High." That is why choice (C) is correct. Choice (D) is wrong, because they are talking about the background of the students, not the reputations of the schools. Choice (E) is

wrong, for the question is from where the students at State College come. Choice (B) is superficially relevant to the exchange, but it, too, is incorrect. Ann would not reply to this statement, had Mary made it, in the way she did reply. Rather, she would have said, "No, there are some Midland students at State College." Finally, Ann would have correctly said choice (A) only if Mary had said, "None of the students from North Hills attend State College" or "Most of the students from North Hills do not attend State College." But Ann makes neither of these responses, so we know that choice (A) cannot have been what she thought she heard Mary say.

4. **The correct answer is (E).** If you wanted to determine how politically active people are, what kind of test would you devise? You might do a survey to test political awareness; you might do a survey to find out how many hours people devote to political campaigning each week or how many hours they spend writing letters, etc.; or you might get a rough estimate by studying the voting statistics. The paragraph takes contributions as a measure of political activity. Choice (E) is correct for two reasons. First, the paragraph says nothing about individual activity. It says total contributions were up, not average or per person contributions. Second, choice (E) cites voting patterns that seem as good as or better an indicator of political activity than giving money. This second reason explains why choice (A) is wrong. Choice (A) may weaken the argument, but a stronger attack would use voting patterns. Choice (D) confuses individual and corporate contributions, so even if campaign giving were a strong indicator of activity, choice (D) would still be irrelevant. Choice (B) does not even explain why contributions

in toto rose during the four years, nor does it tell us anything about the pattern of giving by individual persons. Finally, choice (C) seems the worst of all the answers, for it hardly constitutes an attack on the author's reasoning. It seems likely that even in the face of increased political activity, public leaders would continue to warn against the dangers of political apathy.

5. **The correct answer is (B).** The chief failing of the argument is that it draws a false analogy. Since prisons are required to feed and maintain as well as house prisoners (not to mention the necessity for security), the analogy to a hotel room is weak at best. Choice (C) focuses on this specific shortcoming. Remember, in evaluating the strength of an argument from analogy it is important to look for dissimilarities that might make the analogy inappropriate. Thus, choices (A) and (E) are also good criticisms of the argument. They voice the general objection of which choice (C) is the specification. Choice (D) is also a specific objection—the argument compares two numbers that are not at all similar. So the numerical comparison is a false one. Choice (B) is not a way in which the argument can be criticized, for the author never cites any authority.

6. **The correct answer is (C).** This is a "weaken the argument" question, so the correct answer is probably a statement that attacks a hidden premise of the argument. The speaker apparently assumes that, in order to be worthwhile, an antibacterial agent must be as effective as a surgical scrub. But, of course, a hand soap could be less effective than a heavy-duty, industrial strength disinfectant and still have some value—and this is what choice (C) points out. Choice (A) is wide of

the mark, for whether the agents are or are not used in other products doesn't address the central issue, which is "effectiveness." Choice (B) too is wide of the mark. To be sure, this statement helps to prove that washing is effective, but this doesn't prove that washing with an antibacterial soap is better than washing with an ordinary soap. Choice (D) is irrelevant since effectiveness and not labeling is the issue. Finally, choice (E) is a very interesting choice; but, if anything, it is an argument against the soaps. In this case, you're looking for an argument in favor of the soaps.

7. **The correct answer is (A).** The speaker says that the CPI is a fairly accurate measure but that most people still think that prices are rising faster. That's what you have to explain: the timing of purchases gives consumers an inaccurate impression. Choices (B), (C), and (E) do point to various quirks in any general measure of prices, but none of them provides an explanation of the specific phenomenon cited by the speaker. Choice (D) is an interesting choice because it seems to suggest a possible weakness in the CPI and might be leveraged into an argument: well, if the CPI is urban-oriented, then maybe it doesn't do quite such a good job in the other regions, and maybe this creates the wrong impression. There is absolutely nothing wrong with this thinking as a matter of mental exercise, but it's wrong as a matter of test-taking strategy because it is overly speculative. After all, if those outside the urban areas get a wrong impression, it is a mistaken impression of low inflation or high inflation. You should prefer a choice like (A), which, by its terms, takes on the issue directly by giving a reason why prices seem higher than they actually are.

8. **The correct answer is (B).** The speaker's argument rests upon a hidden assumption (suppressed premise): the only reason that students would be bored is because the professor is a poor lecturer. So a good way of attacking the reasoning would be to point out that there are other reasons that students might not pay attention in class; for example, they find the subject uninteresting. As for the other choices, choice (A) implies that some professors might not be boring, but this is not an attack on the proposal advanced by the speaker: Only professors trained as teachers should be used. In other words, choice (A) does not come to grips with the logic of the reasoning; and, as a matter of test-taking tactics, the answer to a "weakening" question is almost always going to be an attack on the logic of the argument and often the denial of a hidden assumption. Choice (C) simply misses the point of the speaker's argument. The question is why students are distracted—not professors. As for choice (D), this choice, if anything, strengthens the speaker's reasoning because it seems to make necessary some kind of proposal. And finally, choice (E) also seems to strengthen the argument by suggesting that non-researchers would be interesting teachers.

9. **The correct answer is (C).** The speaker's point is that Hurston is known to have been untruthful. The problem becomes, then, how to determine which statements about her life, if any, are reliable. The speaker here concludes that this is an impossible task. Choice (A), if anything, contradicts the reasoning of the argument by stating that autobiographical writings do have a privileged status. Choice (B) is an interesting idea, but it is not relevant to the speaker's

point; that is, it doesn't help to explain why the speaker won't rely on Hurston's own statements. Choice (D) is interesting but it misses the point. The problem the speaker sees with Hurston's own statements is that she tells falsehoods when she might otherwise be expected to tell the truth. The speaker is not faulting her for writing fiction that is known by the reader to be fiction but for making false statements that might be taken to be true. And choice (E) simply picks up on a couple of details of the reasoning but doesn't address the underlying issue.

10. **The correct answer is (A).** This is one of those test problems that involves a little logical twist. The speaker is making the somewhat humorous point that the husband was able to secure a driver's license even without knowing how to drive, so the implication is that the government is corrupt.

11. **The correct answer is (E).** This is an inference question, and the correct answer to such a question may not literally be a logical inference but neither will it be wildly speculative. And that's the problem with choices (B) and (C). They may or may not be true, but there is nothing in the text of the argument to support such a deduction. Choice (E), however, is strongly implied by the text because the Randall character works only because it is set in the context of a host of minor characters who are "losers" and with whom audiences apparently will not identify, preferring the successful Randall character even though Randall is not particularly admirable. Choice (A), if anything, seems in tension with the text, for it seems more likely, given the wording, that most programs rely on a "good guy" as opposed to a "bad guy with redeeming features." And choice (D), while edifying,

just really doesn't say anything directly relevant to the issue discussed by the speaker.

12. **The correct answer is (E).** The correct answer to a "weakening" question is usually an attack on a hidden assumption of the argument. In this case, the speaker tacitly assumes that the appropriate use of a theater is the production of musicals, and choice (E) attacks this hidden premise: no, straight drama is becoming increasingly popular. Choices (A) and (B) make interesting points, but the ideas are irrelevant to the speaker's argument. Choice (C), if anything, would strengthen the speaker's argument: not only that, but when you remove the seats to accommodate the orchestra, you further reduce your gross. And so too choice (D) would be a reason for not renovating the theater.

13. **The correct answer is (D).** The stem asks you to draw a further conclusion. The speaker begins by citing the proposed ban and then uses a "But" to introduce the idea that one state's disaster is another state's boon. That suggests that the speaker is opposed to a total ban, not because such bans are ineffective but rather because they have undesirable consequences. And then the speaker gives a "for instance": lantana. So the speaker is arguing against the ban on the ground that it is too broad and would make unavailable some plants that have useful applications. Choice (A) does sound like opposition to the ban, but it doesn't take account of the particular reason the speaker gives. Choice (B) is wrong because there is nothing that suggests the speaker believes the ban would be ineffective; in fact, if anything, the speaker probably believes it would be effective, and that is why the speaker opposes it. Choice (C) is interesting in that it uses

some of the fancy language from the paragraph, but there is absolutely nothing in the paragraph to support the conclusion that the speaker believes that the spread of exotic plants is more or less dangerous than loss of habitat. As for choice (E), this is surely something the speaker would accept, but this seems to be a premise of the argument (a given) as opposed to a further conclusion.

14. **The correct answer is (A).** The speaker creates a false dilemma: either this or that. But there is a happy middle ground: just the right amount of homework.

15. **The correct answer is (C).** One important thing to remember about hidden assumption questions is that the premises you're looking for is a logical part of the argument. Usually, this means that it's going to be a fairly limited claim. So, you need to avoid the temptation to look for some very large and grand conclusion that you might like to draw from the paragraph and focus narrowly on what it said. That's why choice (C) is correct. It is not an earth-shattering revelation; it's really sort of mundane. But it is something the speaker implicitly assumes; otherwise, the argument that the West Coast offense has spread through the mentor relationship doesn't fly. Choices (A) and (B) are exactly the kind of grandiose conclusions that you need to avoid. Choice (D) may be true, but it's not logically supported by the speaker's argument. Finally, choice (E) is interesting, but you should eliminate it if you're reading carefully: "in order to." The fact that the younger coaches picked up the West Coast offense through their employment does not imply that they necessarily took those jobs "in order to" learn how to coach that offense.

16. **The correct answer is (B).** The hidden assumption of the speaker is that the residual cases that keep coming in are due to the virulence of the disease. Choice (B) attacks this assumption by suggesting another explanation: reporting lags behind the diagnosis of the illness. Choice (A) is interesting, because you might want to argue that the immune system of children is not so strong as that of adults, and thus, the sheer number of victims is not necessarily due to the virulence of the strain. The problem with choice (A) is while that is not an unintelligent argument, choice (B) is just a more powerful attack because it aims at a hidden assumption. That's the pattern that you should be looking for. Choice (C) is irrelevant, and it is difficult to see whether choice (D) would weaken or strengthen the argument. Finally, choice (E) seems to strengthen the argument.

17. **The correct answer is (E).** The author is arguing that political parties in America are weak because there is no party unity. Because of this lack of unity, the party is unable to pass legislation. Choice (E) would strengthen this contention. Choice (E) provides an example of a government dominated by a single party (control of the presidency and both houses), yet the party is unable to pass its own legislation. Choice (A) provides little, if any, support for the argument. If there are only 18 defectors out of a total of 67 party members, that does not show tremendous fragmentation. Choice (B) is even weaker by the same analysis: 70 defectors out of a total of 305 party members. Choice (C) is weak because it focuses on the minority party. Choice (D) strengthens the argument less clearly than choice (E) because there are many possible explanations for the failure; for

example, a different party controlled the legislature.

18. **The correct answer is (C).** Here we are looking for the argument that will undermine the position taken by the paragraph. Remember that the ultimate conclusion of the paragraph is that this disunity is a weakness and that this prevents legislation from being passed. One very good way of attacking this argument is to attack the value judgment upon which the conclusion is based: Is it good to pass the legislation? The author assumes that it would be better to pass the legislation. We could argue, as in choice (C), that members of the Congress should not pass legislation simply because it is proposed by the party leadership. Rather, the members should represent the views of their constituents. Then, if the legislation fails, it must be the people who did not want it. In that case, it is better not to pass the legislation. Choice (A) does not undermine the argument. That members receive funding proves nothing about unity after elections. As for choice (B), this seems to strengthen rather than weaken the argument. The author's thesis argues that there is greater unity in the Senate than in the House. Choice (D) would undermine the argument only if we had some additional information to make it relevant. Finally, choice (E) does not weaken the argument greatly. That some legislation is passed is not a denial of the argument that more should be passed.

19. **The correct answer is (E).** This advertisement is simply rife with ambiguity. The wording obviously seeks to create the impression that FCBI found jobs for its many graduates and generally does a lot of good for them. But first we should ask how many graduates FCBI had— one, two, three, a dozen, or a hundred. If it had only 12 or so, finding them jobs might have been easy; but if many people enroll at FCBI, they may not have the same success. Further, we might want to know how many people graduated compared to how many enrolled. Do people finish the program, or does FCBI just take their money and then force them out of the program? So choice (B) is certainly something we need to know in order to assess the validity of the claim. Now, how many of those who graduated came in looking for help in finding a job? Maybe most people had jobs waiting for them (only a few needed help), in which case the job placement assistance of FCBI is not so impressive. Or, perhaps the graduates were so disgusted they did not even seek assistance. So choice (A) is relevant. Choice (C) is also important. Perhaps FCBI found them jobs sweeping streets—not in business. The ad does not say what jobs FCBI helped its people find. Finally, maybe the ad is truthful—FCBI graduates found jobs—but maybe they did it on their own. So choice (D) also is a question worth asking. Choice (E), however, is the least problematic. Even if it turns out that the ad was done by a paid, professional actor, so what? That's what you'd expect for an ad.

20. **The correct answer is (D).** The argument commits several errors. One obvious point is that the first premise is very much an oversimplification. Complicated questions about punishment and child rearing are hardly ever easily reduced to "either–or" propositions. Thus, choice (C) is a good objection. Beyond that, the terms "severely punish" and "bad" are highly ambiguous. It would be legitimate to ask the speaker just what he considered to be bad behavior, choice (B), and

severe punishment, choice (A). Also, since the speaker has alleged the child has been "bad" and since the term is ambiguous, we can also demand clarification on that score, choice (E). The one objection it makes no sense to raise is choice (D). The premises have the very simple logical structure: If a child is bad and not punished, then the child becomes a criminal. Child X is bad. There is absolutely no inconsistency between those two statements.

21. **The correct answer is (C).** Notice that the question gives you some extra guidance here: There is a seeming inconsistency in the reports. On the one hand, much research suggests that dyslexia is a sex-linked problem. On the other hand, the new research suggests it is not. Of course, it is possible that the earlier research was just poorly done, but that wouldn't make a very interesting test answer, e.g., the earlier researchers just added incorrectly. Choice (C) is more representative of the kind of answer you would find on the test: The earlier research was based on data that was biased, and no one suspected that fact until now. As for the remaining choices, they hint at various weaknesses in the data on dyslexia, but they do not address the seeming contradiction that is the focus of the question stem.

22. **The correct answer is (A).** Examine each statement. Choice (A) is a hidden assumption of the argument. Under the proposed system, according to the speaker, schools will have to make the customers happy, and he concludes that this will result in improved education. Thus, a hidden assumption of the argument is the equation between "happy customers" and "improved education."

Choice (B) is not an assumption of the argument. Indeed, the speaker implies that in an effort to attract students, schools will try to differentiate themselves from each other. And as for choice (C), the speaker does not assume that there is any causal connection between "aid" and "study." The speaker expects to see a positive result because schools are doing a better job. That may prompt students to study harder, but the motivating factor then is not "direct financial aid." Choice (D) is apparently a misreading of the paragraph. While the speaker says that schools will compete in terms of "educational services," that may be broad enough to include other activities but in any event certainly does not preclude offering other activities in the mix. And as for choice (E), the speaker does not say that there should be no privately funded schools at all—only that the public schools should be funded on a different model.

23. **The correct answer is (B).** The speaker assumes that students and parents will be educated consumers. (Pardon the play on words.) If it turns out that students and parents select a school because it is nearby, then schools don't have any incentive to offer creative educational programs in order to attract students; a fundamental premise of the plan is proved incorrect. As for choice (A), this idea actually strengthens the argument for the plan: Schools will make sure that students and parents are educated consumers. Choice (C) too is consistent with the speaker's analysis: Schools will create new programs to attract customers. As for choice (D), though this idea of cost is not discussed by the speaker, reducing costs would hardly be a disadvantage of a program. Finally, choice (E) seems to

cut in favor of the program, for then the voucher plan seems calculated to ensure that everyone gets a fair opportunity to get an education.

24. **The correct answer is (C).** The speaker contrasts the Olympic sport of hockey, which gets media coverage because it generates revenues, with speedskating, which does not get media coverage. The implication here is that speedskating does not generate revenue. As for choice (A), it confuses the distinction drawn by the speaker. The speaker is contrasting two sports, not an individual's performance in two sports. Choice (B) misconstrues the logical function of the example of speedskating in the argument. Speedskating is offered as an example of a sport that receives little attention even though it produces exciting amateur performances. (In fact, the speaker implies that hockey is more popular than speedskating, at least if one uses media coverage as a standard.) Choice (D) is an interesting response because it seems at least consistent with the sentiment expressed in the paragraph: Olympic games are really not entirely amateur sports. But choice (D) overstates the case: All Olympians are professionals. (What about Heiden, whom the author mentions favorably?) Finally, choice (E) goes even further beyond the text. The speaker may or may not hold this opinion.

25. **The correct answer is (D).** Let us use our technique of substituting capital letters for categories. The sample argument can be rendered as follows:

Some J are B. (Some Judges are Bar members.)

No B are F. (No Bar members are Felons.)

Therefore, some J are not F. (Some Judges are not Felons.)

This is a perfectly valid (logical) argument. Choice (D) shares its form and validity:

Some N are I. (Some Non-students are Interested.)

No N are M. (No Non-students are Meeting-attenders.)

Therefore, some I are not M. (Some Interested Non-students are not Meeting-attenders.)

Choice (E) has the invalid argument form:

G is L.

G is A.

Therefore, A is L.

Choices (B) and (C) are both set up using more than three categories; therefore, they cannot possibly have the structure of the sample argument that uses only three categories:

Choice (B)—people, people who want to avoid jury duty, people who do not register to vote, persons under 18

Choice (C)—business, entities filing tax returns, business making enough money to pay taxes, business making a profit.

Finally, choice (A) does not parallel the sample argument since it contains the qualification "likely."

Exercise 2

1.	E	4.	E	7.	E	10.	E	13.	C
2.	B	5.	C	8.	D	11.	C	14.	C
3.	E	6.	A	9.	A	12.	C	15.	A

1.   **The correct answer is (E).** The argument given in the question stem is circular; that is, it begs the question. It tries to prove that the decision is unfair by claiming that it singles out a group, which is the same thing as discriminating, and then concludes that *since* all discrimination is unfair, so, too, is the court's decision unfair. Of course, the real issue is whether singling out this particular group is unfair. After all, we do make distinctions, e.g., adults are treated differently than children, businesses differently than persons, soldiers differently than executives. The question of fairness cannot be solved by simply noting that the decision singles out some persons. Choice (E) also is circular: It tries to prove this is a beautiful painting because all paintings of this sort are beautiful. Choice (A) is perhaps the second-best answer, but notice that it is purely hypothetical in its form: *If* this were true, *then* that would be true. As a consequence, it is not as similar to the question stem as choice (E), which is phrased in categorical assertions rather than hypothetical statements. Choice (B) moves from the premise that students are not good judges of their needs to a conclusion about the responsibility for planning course work. The conclusion and the premise are not the same, so the argument is not circular. Choice (C) is not, technically speaking, even an argument. Remember from our instructional material at the beginning of the book, an argument has premises and a conclusion. These are separate statements. Choice (C) is one long statement, not two short ones. It reads "A because B," not "A; therefore B." For example, the statement "I am late because the car broke down" is not an inference but a causal statement. In choice (D), since the premise (everything after the semicolon) is not the same as the conclusion (the statement before the semicolon), the argument is not a circular argument and so does not parallel the stem argument.

2.   **The correct answer is (B).** The author's claim depends in a very important way on the assumption that the assistance he advocates will be successful. After all, any proposed course of action that just won't work clearly ought to be rejected. Choice (B) is just this kind of argument: Whatever else you say, your proposed plan will not work; therefore, we must reject it. Choice (A) opens an entirely new line of argument. The author has said only that there is a certain connection between guidance and creativity; he never claims that everyone can or should be a professional artist. Thus, choice (A) is wrong, as is choice (E) for the same reason. Choice (C) is wrong for a similar reason. The author never suggests that all students should be professional artists; and, in fact, he may want to encourage students to be creative no matter which practical careers they may choose. Choice (E) is probably the second-best answer; it does, to a certain extent, try to attack the workability of the proposal. Unfortunately, it does not address the general connection the author says ex-

ists between training and creativity. In other words, choice (E) does not say the proposal will not work at all; it merely says it may work too well. Further, choice (E) is wrong because it does not attribute the "burnout" to the training of the sort proposed by the author.

3. **The correct answer is (E).** What we are looking for here is an intervening causal link that caused the plan to be unsuccessful. The projected train of events was (1) adopt express lanes, (2) fewer cars, and (3) faster traffic flow. Between the first and the third steps, however, something went wrong. Choice (E) alone supplies that unforeseen side effect. Since the cars backed up on too few lanes, total flow of traffic was actually slowed, not speeded up. Choice (A) is irrelevant since it does not explain what went wrong *after* the plan was adopted. Choice (B) does not even attempt to address the sequence of events that we have just outlined. Although choice (C) is probably true and was something the planners likely considered in their projections, it does not explain the plan's failure. Finally, choice (D) might have been relevant in deciding whether or not to adopt the plan, but given that the plan was adopted, choice (D) cannot explain why it then failed.

4. **The correct answer is (E).** We have all seen arguments of this sort in our daily lives, and perhaps if we have not been very careful, we have even made the same mistakes made by the leaders of Gambia. For example, last semester, which was fall, I made a lot of money selling peanuts at football games. Therefore, this spring semester, I will make even more money. Choices (A), (B), (C), and (D) point out weaknesses in the projections made by Gambia's leaders. Choice

(A): Of course, if the tremendous increase in GDP is due to some unique event (my personal income increased last semester when I inherited $2,000 from my aunt), it would be foolish to project a similar increase for a time period during which that event cannot repeat itself. Choice (B): This is a bit less obvious, but the projection is based on the assumption that Gambia will receive additional aid and will be able to put that aid to use. If they are not in a position to use that aid (I cannot work twice as many hours in the spring), they cannot expect the aid to generate increases in GDP. Finally, choice (C) also is a weakness in the leaders' projections. If there are physical limitations on the possible increases, then the leaders have made an error. Their projections are premised on the existence of physical resources that are greater than those they actually have. And choice (D) would also undermine the expectation of additional growth: Gambia won't get the whole loan. Choice (E), however, without more, won't weaken the argument, because there is no reason to believe that the experience of a neighbor is applicable to Gambia.

5. **The correct answer is (C).** The conclusion of the paragraph is so obvious that it is almost difficult to find. The author says office workers work better the cooler the temperature—provided the temperature does not drop below 68°. Therefore, we can conclude, the temperature at which workers will be most efficient will be precisely 68°. Notice that the author does not say what happens once the temperature drops below 68°, except that workers are no longer as efficient. For all we know, efficiency may drop off slowly or quickly compared with improvements in efficiency as the temperature drops to

68°. So choice (E) goes beyond the information supplied in the passage. Choice (D) also goes far beyond the scope of the author's claim. His formula is specifically applicable to *office* workers. We have no reason to believe the author would extend his formula to non-office workers. Choice (B) is probably not a conclusion the author would endorse since he claims to have found a way of achieving improvements in efficiency in a different and seemingly permanent way. Finally, choice (A) is not a conclusion the author seems likely to reach since nothing indicates that his formula yields only short-term gains that last as long as the temperature is kept constant. To be sure, the gains will not be repeatable, but then they will not be short run either.

6. **The correct answer is (A).** Speaker 2 unwittingly plays right into the hands of Speaker 1. Speaker 1 tries to show that there are many decisions regarding human life in which we allow that an increase in the quality of life justifies an increase in the danger to human life. All that Speaker 2 does is to help prove this point. He says the quality of life would suffer if we lowered the speed limits to protect human life. Given this analysis, choice (B) must be incorrect, for Speaker 2's position is completely ineffective as a rebuttal. Moreover, choice (C) must be incorrect, for his response is not a strong statement of his position. Choice (D) is incorrect, for while his response is of no value to the position he seeks to defend, it cannot be said that it is irrelevant. In fact, as we have just shown, his position is very relevant to that of Speaker 1 because it supports that position. Finally, choice (E) is not an appropriate characterization of Speaker 2's position,

for he tries, however ineptly, to attack the merits of Speaker 1's position, not the character of Speaker 1.

7. **The correct answer is (E).** Speaker 1 uses the example of traffic fatalities to show that society has always traded the quality of life for the quantity of life. Of course, he says, we do not always acknowledge that is what we are doing, but if we were honest, we would have to admit that we were making a trade-off. Thus, choice (E) is the best conclusion of the passage. Speaker 1's statement amounts to the claim that abortion is just another case in which we trade off one life to make the lives of others better. The only difference is that the life being sacrificed is specifiable and highly visible in the case of abortion, whereas in the case of highway fatalities, no one knows in advance on whom the ax will fall. Choice (A) certainly goes far beyond what Speaker 1 is advocating. If anything, he probably recognizes that sometimes the trade-off will be drawn in favor of protecting lives, and thus we need some such laws. Choice (B) must be wrong, first, because Speaker 2 claims this is not his position, and second, because Speaker 1 would prefer to show that the logical consequence of Speaker 2's response is an argument in favor of abortion. Choice (C) is not an appropriate continuation because Speaker 1 has already said this is a weak counterexample and that he has even stronger points to make. Finally, Speaker 1 might be willing to accept contraception, choice (D), as yet another example of the trade-off, but his conclusion can be much stronger than that; the conclusion of his speech ought to be that abortion is an acceptable practice—not that contraception is an acceptable practice.

8. **The correct answer is (D).** This is a very difficult question. That choice (D) is an assumption Speaker 1 makes requires careful reading. Speaker 1's attitude about the just war tips us off. He implies that this is an appropriate function of government and, further, that there are even clearer cases. Implicit in his statement is that a trade-off must be made and that it is appropriately a collective decision. Choice (A) is not an assumption of the argument. Indeed, Speaker 1 seems to assume, as we have just maintained, that the trade-off is an appropriate goal of society. Speaker 1 does not assume choice (B); if anything, he almost states that he accepts that the fetus is a life but that it may be traded off in exchange for an increase in the quality of the lives of others. Choices (C) and (E) use language related to the examples used by Speaker 1 but don't address the logical structure of the argument.

9. **The correct answer is (A).** You might attack this item using a circle diagram. To show the possible relationships of three categories, use three overlapping circles:

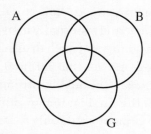

Now enter the information provided by the second statement:

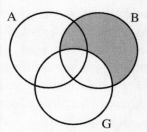

The area that is not logically possible given the second statement is shaded. Now enter the information provided by the first statement:

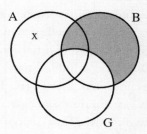

The "x" shows that there is at least one individual that is an Alpha but not a Gamma.

The diagram shows that choice (A) must be true. There is at least one individual that is an Alpha but not a Beta. Choice (B), however, is not necessarily true. The overlap between the Alpha-circle and the Gamma-circle, which represents the possibility that an individual might have both characteristics Alpha and Gamma, is left open. Choice (C) is not necessarily true for a similar reason. There is a portion of the Gamma-circle not contained in the Beta-circle, and this part represents the logical possibility that some individuals could have characteristic Gamma but not characteristic Beta. Choice (D) is shown by the diagram to be false; choice (E) is shown to be possibly but not necessarily true.

10. **The correct answer is (E).** This question asks you to identify hidden assumptions embedded in the speaker's argument. Examine each statement. Choice (A) is an assumption of the argument. Barbara told the speaker about two bets, and the speaker assumes those were the only two she made. (She could have made additional wagers.) Choice (B) is also an assumption of the argument. The speaker concludes that one or the other horse must have won, but that conclusion depends on the assumption that they did not both win. Choice (C) is also an assumption of the argument. The speaker implicitly assumes that the only reason Barbara would return to the parimutuel window is to cash a winning ticket, as opposed to placing another bet. And choice (D) is also a hidden assumption similar to choice (A). Choice (E), however, is not an assumption. Barbara could very well have believed that Copper Cane was more likely to win—indeed, she stood to win more money with that result even though her bet was smaller because of the longer odds.

11. **The correct answer is (C).** It is very important to distinguish what are called necessary conditions from what are called sufficient conditions. A necessary condition is one that must occur for a particular event to take place, e.g., oxygen is a necessary condition for a fire. A sufficient condition is one that is by itself sufficient to ensure that a certain event occurs; for example, failing the final exam of a course may be sufficient to guarantee a failing mark for the course. This distinction is the key to this item. A statement of the sort "If X, then Y" (as used here) sets up a sufficient but not a necessary connection. For example, ordering combination #2 guarantees that Juana

will eat fried rice, but that may not be the only condition on which she will eat fried rice. For all we know, combination #5 also includes fried rice. Thus, choices (A), (B), and (D) are wrong. As for choice (E), the statements that set up the problem talk specifically about Juana, not about people in general.

12. **The correct answer is (C).** If you want to determine whether or not drug use is harmful to high school students, you surely would not conduct a survey of the students themselves. This is why choice (C) is correct. That a student does not *think* a drug is harmful does not mean that it *is not* actually harmful. Choice (E) misses the point of the argument. The author is not attempting to prove that drug use is not widespread but rather that it is not dangerous. Choice (D) is part of an argument often used in debates over legalization of drugs by proponents of legalization. Here, however, it is out of place. The question is whether the drugs are harmless, that is, whether they are, in fact, victimless. Choice (D) belongs to some other part of the debate. Choice (A) sounds like the start of an argument. One might suggest that students change their minds as they get older, and eventually many acknowledge the danger of such drugs. But choice (A) does not get that far; and, even if it did, choice (C) would be stronger, for it gives us the final statement up to which that argument would only be leading. Finally, choice (B) is irrelevant. The question here is the harm of drugs, and that issue can be resolved independently of whether or not other things are harmful, such as alcohol or drag racing.

13. **The correct answer is (C).** Amy points out that Al assumes that any extraterrestrial visitors to Earth, seeking intelli-

gent life, would regard human beings here on Earth as intelligent and therefore contact us. Amy hints that we might not be intelligent enough to interest them in contacting us. This is why choice (C) is the best answer. Choice (A) is wrong. Amy does not miss Al's point: She understands it very well and criticizes it. Choice (B) is wrong since Amy is not suggesting that Al is any less intelligent than any other human being, just that the aliens might regard us all as below the level of intelligence that they are seeking. Choice (D) is more nearly correct than any other choice, save choice (C). The difficulties with it are threefold: One, there really is not all that much internal development of Al's argument, so choice (D) does not seem on target; two, in a way she does examine what internal structure there is—she notes there is a suppressed assumption that is unsound; finally, even assuming that what choice (D) says is correct, it really does not describe the point of Amy's remark nearly so well as choice (C) does. Finally, choice (E) is incorrect because Amy does not offer an analogy of any sort.

14. **The correct answer is (C).** The problem with this argument is that it contains no argument at all. Nothing is more frustrating than trying to discuss an issue with someone who will not even make an attempt to prove his case, whose only constructive argument is: "Well, that is my position; if I am wrong, you prove I am wrong." This is an illegitimate attempt to shift the burden of proof. The person who advances the argument naturally has the burden of giving some argument for it. Choice (C) points out this problem. Choice (A) is incorrect because the author uses no group classifications.

Choice (B) is incorrect because the author does not introduce any analogy. Choice (D) is a weak version of choice (C). It is true that the author does not provide statistical evidence to prove the claim, but then again, no kind of argument at all is offered to prove the claim. So if choice (D) is a legitimate objection to the paragraph (and it is), then choice (C) must be an even stronger objection. So any argument for choice (D)'s being the correct choice ultimately supports choice (C) even more strongly. The statement contained in choice (E) may or may not be correct, but the information in the passage is not sufficient to allow us to isolate the theory upon which the speaker is operating. Therefore, we cannot conclude that it is or is not discredited.

15. **The correct answer is (A).** Let us assign letters to represent the complete clauses of the sentence from which the argument is built. "If quarks . . . universe" will be represented by the letter P, the rest of the sentence by Q. The structure of the argument is therefore "If P then Q. Q. Therefore, P." The argument is obviously not logically valid. If it were, it would work for any substitutions of clauses for the letters, but we can easily think up a case in which the argument will not work: "If this truck is a fire engine, it will be painted red. This truck is painted red; therefore, it is a fire engine." Obviously, many trucks that are not fire engines could also be painted red. The argument's invalidity is not the critical point. Your task was to find the answer choice that paralleled it—and since the argument first presented was incorrect, you should have looked for the argument in the answer choice that makes the same mistake: choice (A). It has the

form: "If P, then Q. Q. Therefore, P." Choice (B) has the form: "If P, then Q. P. Therefore, Q," which is both different from our original form and valid to boot. Choice (C) has the form: "P or Q. Not P. Therefore, Q." Choice (D) has the form: "If P, then Q. If Q, then R. Therefore, if P, then R." Finally, choice (E) has the form: "If P, then Q. Not Q. Therefore, not P."

Reading
Comprehension

chapter 6

OVERVIEW
- **What Reading Comprehension Tests**
- **Answering Reading Comprehension Questions**
- **What Smart Test-Takers Know**

WHAT IS READING COMPREHENSION?

LSAT Reading Comprehension is a test of your ability to read and understand unfamiliar materials and to answer questions about them. You will be presented with passages drawn from a variety of subject areas, including humanities, ethics, philosophy, social sciences, physical sciences, and the law. The questions will ask you to analyze what is stated in the passage and to identify underlying assumptions and implications.

Reading Comprehension Questions

The scored portion of the LSAT contains one Reading Comprehension section with four reading passages, each approximately 450 words long. Each passage is followed by 5 to 8 questions for a total of 26 to 28 questions per section.

Question Format

Reading Comprehension questions follow the standard multiple-choice format with five answer choices each. All of the questions fall into one of the following six categories:

- the main idea of the passage
- specific details mentioned in the passage
- the author's attitude or tone
- the logical structure of the passage
- further inferences that might be drawn from the text
- application of the ideas in the text to new situations

Here are the directions for LSAT Reading Comprehension, along with some sample questions and explanations.

Anatomy of a Reading Comprehension Passage

Directions: Below each of the following passages, you will find questions or incomplete statements about the passage. Each statement or question is followed by lettered words or expressions. Select the word or expression that most satisfactorily completes each statement or answers each question in accordance with the meaning of the passage. After you have chosen the best answer, blacken the corresponding space on the answer sheet.

Instead of casting aside traditional values, the Meiji Restoration of 1868 dismantled feudalism and modernized the country while preserving
(5) certain traditions as the foundations for a modern Japan. The oldest tradition and basis of the entire Japanese value system was respect for and even worship of the Emperor.
(10) During the early centuries of Japanese history, the Shinto cult in which the imperial family traced its ancestry to the Sun Goddess became the people's sustaining faith. Although
(15) later subordinated to imported Buddhism and Confucianism, Shintoism was perpetuated in Ise and Izumo until the Meiji modernizers established it as a quasi-state religion.
(20)   Another enduring tradition was the hierarchical system of social relations based on feudalism and reinforced by Neo-Confucianism that had been the official ideology of the pre-
(25) modern world. Confucianism prescribed a pattern of ethical conduct between groups of people within a fixed hierarchy. Four of the five Confucian relationships were vertical,
(30) requiring loyalty and obedience from the inferior toward the superior. Only the relationship between friend and friend was horizontal, and even there the emphasis was on reciprocal
(35) duties.

(This is a much abbreviated Reading Comprehension passage, but it exhibits all of the important features that you can expect to find on the passages on your LSAT.

Summary: *The passage has a main theme that is developed with supporting arguments:*

> *The Meiji Restoration modernized Japan without repudiating traditional values. It did dismantle feudalism. But it preserved important traditions. This kind of organization is typical of LSAT reading passages.*

Note the point of the second paragraph: An important feature of Japanese society that was preserved was a hierarchical system of social relations.)

1. The author is primarily concerned with
   (A) providing a history of the rise of feudalism in Japan.
   (B) identifying the influences of Confucianism on Japanese society.
   (C) speculating on the probable development of Japanese society.
   (D) developing a history of religion in Japan.
   (E) describing some important features of the Meiji Restoration.

   This question asks about the main idea or theme of the passage. The correct answer is (E).

2. The passage mentions all of the following as being elements of Japanese society EXCEPT:
   (A) obedience to authority.
   (B) sense of duty.
   (C) respect for the Emperor.
   (D) concern for education.
   (E) loyalty to one's superior.

   This question asks about details mentioned in the passage. The correct answer is (D) because the author does not mention education.

3. It can be inferred from the passage that those who led Japan into the modern age were concerned primarily with
   (A) maintaining a stable society.
   (B) building a new industrial base.
   (C) expanding the nation's territory.
   (D) gaining new adherents of Confucianism.
   (E) creating a new middle class.

   This question asks about an idea that can be inferred from the passage. The correct answer is (A).

HOW DO YOU ANSWER READING COMPREHENSION QUESTIONS?

To answer Reading Comprehension questions, follow these steps:

READING COMPREHENSION: GETTING IT RIGHT

① Preview key sentences.

② Read for structure; ignore details.

③ Do a mental wrap-up.

④ Start with the main idea question.

⑤ Next, tackle specific detail and attitude/tone questions.

⑥ Then do logical structure questions.

⑦ Save inference and application questions for last.

Now let's look at this process in more detail.

① **Preview key sentences.** The first sentence of a paragraph is often the topic sentence. It will give you an overview of the paragraph. Previewing the first sentence of each paragraph will give you a general sense of the logical structure of the passage. You should also preview the very last sentence of the passage because it often contains the main conclusion of the passage.

② **Read for structure; ignore details.** This is an open-book test, so you do not have to memorize anything. In addition, most of the questions ask about the structure of the passage rather than specific facts. As you read, consciously ask yourself "What is the main point of the passage?" and "Why is the author introducing this idea?"

Your academic training has taught you to read for details because you know that you will be tested on them. Do not dwell on the particulars. In the first place, there are only five to eight questions, so there are not likely to be many questions about details. And in the second place, this is an open-book test, so you can refer to the passage.

③ **Do a mental wrap-up.** Before moving on to the questions, pause for just a few seconds and review in your mind what you have just read. Try to summarize in your own words the main point of the selection (think up a title for the passage) and to see in your mind's eye an outline of the passage.

④ **Start with the main idea question.** Each question set usually includes one such as

Which of the following best summarizes the main point of the passage?

The author's primary concern is to . . .

Which of the following is the best title for the passage?

ALERT!

Don't let unfamiliar topics throw you. There's no need to worry about what you know or don't know about the topic in a reading passage. The answers are all based on information in the passage, and you won't be required to draw on outside knowledge.

Regardless of form, this question asks about the overall theme or main point of the selection. Answering this question first will help you to solidify your understanding of the passage.

5 **Next, tackle specific detail and attitude/tone questions.** Most passages are followed by at least one question about a specific detail. Detail questions are easy to recognize:

> According to the passage, . . .
>
> According to the author, . . .
>
> The author mentions all of the following EXCEPT
>
> In line ##, the author says that . . .

Questions with this form are just asking about concrete details. You do not have to have a theory to answer them.

> Author's attitude or tone questions look like this:
>
> The author's attitude can best be described as . . .
>
> Which of the following best describes the tone of the passage?

Attitude/tone questions are usually fairly easy, so it makes perfect sense to do them before moving to the difficult questions.

6 **Then do logical structure questions.** Some questions ask about the overall development of the passage or about why the author introduces a specific point:

> The author develops the passage primarily by which of the following means?
>
> The author introduces the point at line ## in order to . . .

These questions focus on the logical development of the passage. If you understand the main organizing theme, then you should be able to answer them.

7 **Save inference and application questions for last.** Some questions ask you to go beyond what is explicitly stated in the passage. They often are phrased like this:

> The author implies that . . .
>
> It can be inferred that . . .
>
> The author would most likely agree with which of the following statements?

These questions are the most difficult, so save them for last.

Now let's look at a sample Reading Comprehension passage and questions about it. As you read the explanations, think about how the solution process applies.

TIP

The LSAT uses six— and only six— Reading Comprehension questions:

1. What is the main idea?
2. What did the author say?
3. Why did the author say it?
4. How does the author feel about it?
5. What is written between the lines?
6. How could you use it somewhere else?

Directions: The passage below is followed by questions based upon its content. After reading the passage, choose the best answer to each question. Answer all of the questions on the basis of what is stated or implied in the passage.

A fundamental principle of pharmacology is that all drugs have multiple actions. Actions that are desirable in the treatment of disease are considered
(5) therapeutic, while those that are undesirable or pose risks to the patient are called "effects." Adverse drug effects range from the trivial, e.g., nausea or dry mouth, to the serious, e.g., massive
(10) gastrointestinal bleeding or thromboembolism; and some drugs can be lethal. Therefore, an effective system for the detection of adverse drug effects is an important component of the health-care
(15) system of any advanced nation. Much of the research conducted on new drugs aims at identifying the conditions of use that maximize beneficial effects and minimize the risk of adverse effects. The
(20) intent of drug labeling is to reflect this body of knowledge accurately so that physicians can properly prescribe the drug; or, if it is to be sold without prescription, so that consumers can prop-
(25) erly use the drug.

The current system of drug investigation in the United States has proved very useful and accurate in identifying the common side effects associated with
(30) new prescription drugs. By the time a new drug is approved by the Food and Drug Administration, its side effects are usually well described in the package insert for physicians. The investigational
(35) process, however, cannot be counted on to detect all adverse effects because of the relatively small number of patients involved in premarketing studies and the relatively short duration of the stud-
(40) ies. Animal toxicology studies are, of course, done prior to marketing in an attempt to identify any potential for toxicity, but negative results do not guarantee the safety of a drug in humans, as
(45) evidenced by such well known examples

(In this passage, the author announces a "fundamental principle" of pharmacology. The paragraph then goes on to contrast "desirable" and "adverse" drug effects. The author emphasizes the need for an effective system of making this information available to doctors.)

(In this next paragraph, the author says that the current system of drug investigation is useful and accurate. But then the author goes on to identify some weaknesses in the system.)

as the birth deformities due to thalidomide.

(50) This recognition prompted the establishment in many countries of programs to which physicians report adverse
drug effects. The United States and other
countries also send reports to an international program operated by the World
Health Organization. These programs,
(55) however, are voluntary reporting programs and are intended to serve a limited goal: alerting a government or
private agency to adverse drug effects
detected by physicians in the course of
(60) practice. Other approaches must be used
to confirm suspected drug reactions and
to estimate incidence rates. These other
approaches include conducting retrospective control studies; for example,
(65) the studies associating endometrial cancer with estrogen use, and systematic
monitoring of hospitalized patients to
determine the incidence of acute common side effects, as typified by the Bos-
(70) ton Collaborative Drug Surveillance
Program.

Thus, the overall drug surveillance
system of the United States is composed
of a set of information bases, special
(75) studies, and monitoring programs, each
contributing in its own way to our knowledge of marketed drugs. The system is
decentralized among a number of governmental units and is not adminis-
(80) tered as a coordinated function. Still, it
would be inappropriate at this time to
attempt to unite all of the disparate
elements into a comprehensive surveillance program. Instead, the challenge is
(85) to improve each segment of the system
and to take advantage of new computer
strategies to improve coordination and
communication.

(In the next paragraph, the author claims that the system has been improved by establishing programs that keep records of reports by doctors of adverse drug consequences. But, the author notes, these reporting programs are not perfect.)

(In the final paragraph, the author summarizes by saying that the system is a composite one with many different aspects. And the last sentence summarizes the conclusion of the passage.)

TIP

The main idea of the passage is critical: Every LSAT Reading Comprehension passage is organized around a main idea. All else is supporting argument and detail. If you can say in your own words what that idea is, you are halfway to answering most of the questions.

1. The author is primarily concerned with discussing

(A) methods for testing the effects of new drugs on humans.

(B) the importance of having accurate information about the effects of drugs.

(C) procedures for determining the long-term effects of new drugs.

(D) attempts to curb the abuse of prescription drugs.

(E) the difference between the therapeutic and nontherapeutic actions of drugs.

This is a main idea question. Choice (B) correctly describes the overall point of the passage. The author starts by stating that all drugs have both good and bad effects and that correct use of a drug requires balancing the effects. For such a balancing to take place, it is essential to have good information about how the drugs work. Some of this can be obtained prior to approval of the drug, but some information will not become available until after years of use.

Choice (A) is incorrect, for the different methods for testing drugs are mentioned only as a part of the development just described. The author is not concerned with talking about how drugs are tested but rather about why it is important that they be tested. Choice (C) is incorrect for the same reason. As for choice (E), this is the starting point for the discussion—not the main point of the discussion. Finally, as for choice (D), the idea of drug abuse is not part of the passage at all.

2. The author implies that a drug with adverse side effects

(A) will not be approved for use by consumers without a doctor's prescription.

(B) must wait for approval until lengthy studies prove the effects are not permanent.

(C) should be used only if its therapeutic value outweighs its adverse effects.

(D) should be withdrawn from the marketplace pending a government investigation.

(E) could be used in foreign countries even though it is not approved for use in the United States.

This is an inference question, and the correct answer is (C). In the first paragraph, the author states that all drugs have effects and that these effects range from the unimportant to the very important. One purpose of drug labeling is to ensure that physicians (and ultimately consumers) are aware of these effects. We can infer, therefore, that drugs with side effects are used—provided the gain is worth the risks. And this is what choice (C) says.

Choice (A) seems to be contradicted by the passage. One purpose of labeling, according to the author, is to let consumers of nonprescription drugs know of possible side effects of those drugs. As for choices (B) and (D), the analysis in the preceding paragraph clearly shows that drugs are approved for use and used even though they have unwanted side effects. Finally, there is nothing in the passage to support the conclusion expressed in choice (E).

3. Which of the following can be inferred from the passage?

   (A) Drugs with serious side effects are never approved for distribution.

   (B) A centralized drug oversight function would improve public health.

   (C) Most physicians are not aware that prescription drugs have side effects.

   (D) Some rare adverse drug effects are not discovered during the limited testing.

   (E) Consumers are seldom unable to understand directions for proper use of a drug.

This is an inference question, and the correct answer is (D). Although this conclusion is not stated in so many words, the author does say that some effects are not uncovered because of the short duration of the studies. We may therefore infer that some effects do not manifest themselves for a long period.

4. The author introduces the example of thalidomide (line 47) to show that some

   (A) drugs do not have the same actions in humans that they do in animals.

   (B) drug testing procedures are ignored by careless laboratory workers.

   (C) drugs have no therapeutic value for humans.

   (D) drugs have adverse side effects as well as beneficial actions.

   (E) drugs are prescribed by physicians who have not read the manufacturer's recommendations.

This is a logical structure question, and the correct answer is (A). The example is introduced in line 40 where the author is discussing animal studies. The author says that the fact that a drug shows no dangerous effects in animals does not necessarily mean that it will not adversely affect humans and then gives the example. Thus, the example proves that a drug does not necessarily work in humans the same way it does in animals.

5. The author of the passage regards current drug investigation procedures as

   (A) important but generally ineffectual.

   (B) lackadaisical and generally in need of improvement.

   (C) necessary and generally effective.

   (D) comprehensive but generally unnecessary.

   (E) superfluous but generally harmless.

This is an author's attitude question, and the correct answer is (C). We have already determined that the author regards drug investigation procedures as necessary, so we can eliminate choices (D) and (E). And at various points in the passage, the author speaks of the current mechanism for gathering information as effective. For example, the author states that unwanted side effects are usually described in detail in the pamphlets distributed to physicians and also mentions that there is an entire discipline devoted to this area, so you can eliminate choices (A) and (B).

TIP

Most details are irrelevant.

A passage can be up to 450 words in length and can include a lot of details. However, with all the different types of questions that are asked, there can't be many devoted solely to details. Therefore, most of the details are not important.

6. It can be inferred that the estrogen studies mentioned in lines 64–66

   (A) uncovered long-term side effects of a drug that had already been approved for sale by the Food and Drug Administration.

   (B) discovered potential side effects of a drug that was still awaiting approval for sale by the Food and Drug Administration.

   (C) revealed possible new applications of a drug that had previously been approved for a different treatment.

   (D) is an example of a study that could be more efficiently conducted by a centralized authority than by volunteer reporting.

   (E) proved that the use of the drug estrogen was not associated with side effects such as thromboembolism.

This is an inference question, and the correct answer is (A). The key to this question is the word *retrospective*. This tells you that the control study mentioned was done after the drug was already in use. Choice (B) is incorrect because although the study uncovered harmful side effects, according to the passage, the drug was already in use. Choice (C) is incorrect because the paragraph in which this study is mentioned deals with methods of reporting adverse drug effects, not new applications for drugs. Choice (D) is incorrect first because the author does not mention the efficiency of the study and second because the author is not in favor of a centralized authority. In fact, in the last paragraph, the author says that it would be inappropriate at this time to attempt to unite all of the disparate elements into a comprehensive surveillance program. Finally, choice (E) is incorrect because although thromboembolism is mentioned in the passage as one of the possible harmful side effects of drugs, it is not mentioned in connection with estrogen. The use of estrogen is mentioned in connection with endometrial cancer.

7. The author is most probably leading up to a discussion of some suggestions about how to

   (A) centralize authority for drug surveillance in the United States.

   (B) centralize authority for drug surveillance among international agencies.

   (C) better coordinate the sharing of information among the drug surveillance agencies.

   (D) eliminate the availability and sale of certain drugs now on the market.

   (E) improve drug testing procedures to detect dangerous effects before drugs are approved.

This is an application question, and the correct answer is (C). In the last paragraph, the author suggests that uniting disparate elements into a comprehensive surveillance program is inappropriate at this time. This eliminates choices (A) and (B). The author suggests, however, that improvements are possible in each segment of the system and urges reliance on computers to improve coordination and communication, so choice (C) is the correct answer. Choice (D) is wrong because although the author might advocate the elimination of the availability of certain drugs, that is not what the passage is leading up to. As for choice (E), although the author acknowledges that preapproval studies are not infallible, this notion is too narrow in scope to be the next logical topic for discussion.

8. The author relies on which of the following in developing the passage?
    (A) Statistics
    (B) Analogy
    (C) Examples
    (D) Authority
    (E) Rhetorical questions

This is a logical structure question, and the correct answer is (C). The author frequently illustrates the argument's points with examples. In the first paragraph, there are examples of side effects; in the second, an example of side effects not detected by animal studies; and in the third, the Boston Collaborative Drug Surveillance Program. The author does not, however, use statistics (no numbers in this passage), analogies (no "this is like that"), authority (citing an example is not the same as appealing to an authority), or rhetorical questions.

WHAT SMART TEST–TAKERS KNOW

THE DIFFICULTY FACTOR IS MOSTLY "SMOKE AND MIRRORS."

Three features of LSAT reading passages work like "smoke and mirrors" to make the readings seem more difficult than they really are.

First, the passages will usually be on topics that are unfamiliar to you. This choice of subject matter is deliberate. The test writers go out of their way to find material that you will not have seen before, since they want to avoid giving anyone an advantage over other candidates. If you do encounter a topic you have studied before, that is an unusual stroke of luck. Rest assured, however, that everything you need to answer the questions is included in the passage itself.

Second, LSAT reading passages always start abruptly in the middle of a passage. You're given no advance warning of the topic discussed, so the passage seems to begin in the middle of nowhere. Imagine that you encounter the following as the opening sentence of a Reading Comprehension selection on your LSAT:

> Of the wide variety of opinions on which evolutionary factors were responsible for the growth of hominid intelligence, a theory currently receiving consideration is that intraspecific warfare played an important role by encouraging strategy sessions requiring a sort of verbal competition.

An appropriate reaction to this might be "What the . . . !" But in reality, the topic introduced by the sentence above is not that bizarre. Let's give the sentence a context, say a scholarly journal.

PRIMITIVE BATTLE PLANS: A NEW THEORY ABOUT THE GROWTH OF HUMAN INTELLIGENCE

Of the wide variety of opinions on which evolutionary factors were responsible for the growth of hominid intelligence, a theory currently receiving consideration is that intraspecific warfare played an important role by encouraging strategy sessions requiring a sort of verbal competition.

The title summarizes the main point of the article and alerts you to the topic that will be introduced in the opening sentence. Unfortunately, on the LSAT, you will not be shown this courtesy. The selections will start rather abruptly, in the middle of nowhere.

Third, the style of LSAT Reading Comprehension passages is dry, compact, and often tedious. To be suitable for the LSAT, the passage must not be too long or too short. So the passages, which are taken from previously published material, are carefully edited. Even when the topic of the passage is itself interesting, the selection that emerges from the editing can be deadly boring.

These three features—unusual topic, abrupt beginning, and dense style—all work to create problems for you. Many students are simply overawed by the reading selections. They begin to think "I've never even heard of this; I'll never be able to answer any questions." And when you start thinking like that, you're already beaten. Keep in mind that the passages are chosen so that you will be surprised, but remember that the selections are written so that they contain everything you need to answer the questions.

PASSAGES THAT INTEREST YOU ARE EASIER TO WORK ON.

LSAT Reading Comprehension passages are drawn from many different content areas. Although all of the information needed to answer the questions will be found in the passage, you may find one content area more comfortable to work in than another. If that is the case, start with the passage that deals with that subject. You should be able to answer the accompanying questions more quickly and easily, thus saving time for the passages you find more difficult.

DETAILS CAN BOG YOU DOWN.

If a part of a passage gets too detailed, just skip it. Bracket it mentally or draw a box around it. You do not need to have a full understanding of every single detail to appreciate the organization of the passage and to answer most of the questions.

YOU ONLY WANT TO READ THIS ONCE.

Reading the passages is very time-consuming. If you skip questions and move on to another passage, when you return to the first passage, you'll have to spend time rereading it. Since you don't want to waste these precious minutes, answer all the questions in a set before moving on. If necessary, make educated guesses.

READING COMPREHENSION QUESTIONS CALL FOR DIFFERENT LEVELS OF UNDERSTANDING.

According to the test writers, good reading involves three levels of understanding and evaluation. First, you must be able to grasp the overall idea or main point of the selection along with its general organization. Second, you must be able to subject the specific details to greater scrutiny and explain what something means and why it was introduced. Finally, you should be able to evaluate what the author has written, determining what further conclusions might be drawn and judging whether the argument is good or bad. This sequence dictates the strategy you should follow in reading the selection.

THE LSAT USES SIX—AND ONLY SIX—READING COMPREHENSION QUESTIONS.

Identify the type of question asked, and you are halfway to finding the correct answer.

1. Main idea questions ask about the central theme or main point of the passage.

2. Specific detail questions ask about details included by the author to support or to develop the main theme.

3. Inference questions ask about ideas that are not explicitly stated in the selection but are strongly implied.

4. Logical structure questions ask about the organization or the overall development of the passage.

5. Application questions ask you to take what you have learned from the passage and apply it to a new situation.

6. Attitude or tone questions ask you to identify the overall tone of the passage or the author's attitude toward something discussed in the passage.

For each of the six question types, there are special clues in the answer choices that help you tell right ones from wrong ones.

IN MAIN IDEA QUESTIONS, THE "GOLDILOCKS PRINCIPLE" APPLIES.

On a main idea question, choose an answer that refers to all of the important elements of the passage without going beyond the scope of the passage. The correct answer to a main idea question will summarize the main point of the passage. The wrong answers are too broad or too narrow. Some will be too broad and attribute too much to the author. Others will be too narrow and focus on one small element of the selection, thereby ignoring the overall point.

ALERT!

Your academic training is hazardous to your test-taking health. In college, you are rewarded for memorizing details. The LSAT penalizes for this. This is an open-book test. Do not waste time trying to understand insignificant points.

IN SOME MAIN IDEA QUESTIONS, THE ANSWER LIES IN THE FIRST WORD OF EACH CHOICE.

Some main idea questions are phrased as sentence completions. With a main idea question in sentence completion form, the first word of each choice may be all you need to pick the answer. Here's an example:

> The author's primary purpose is to
> **(A)** argue for ...
> **(B)** criticize ...
> **(C)** describe ...
> **(D)** persuade ...
> **(E)** denounce ...

Note that the first word in each choice describes the passage differently. If the selection were neutral in tone, providing nothing more than a description of some phenomenon, you could safely eliminate choices (A), (B), (D), and (E).

IN SPECIFIC DETAIL QUESTIONS, LOCATOR WORDS POINT THE WAY.

A detail question basically asks "What did the author say?" So, the correct answer to a detail question will be found right there in the passage. And there will be a word or phrase in the question stem to direct you to the appropriate part of the passage. Just find the relevant information and answer the question.

IN SPECIFIC DETAIL QUESTIONS, "SO WHAT" ANSWERS ARE WRONG.

Often wrong answer choices look like right ones because they refer to specific points in the passage. The point is right there in the passage, but it is not an answer to the question asked. So your reaction to such answer choices should be "Yes, this is mentioned, but so what?"

IN SPECIFIC DETAIL QUESTIONS, "WAY OUT" ANSWERS ARE WRONG.

Wrong answers can also refer to things never mentioned in the selection. On a detail question, eliminate answer choices referring to something not mentioned in the passage or anything going beyond the scope of the passage. One way the test writers have of preparing wrong answers is to mention things related to the general topic of the selection but not specifically discussed there. An answer to an explicit question will appear in the selection.

IN SPECIFIC DETAIL QUESTIONS, THOUGHT-REVERSERS TURN A QUESTION INSIDE-OUT.

Sometimes the test writer will use a thought-reverser. For example:

> The author mentions all of the following EXCEPT

Sometimes a detail question uses a thought-reverser. In that case, it is asking for what is *not* mentioned in the selection. Out of the five choices, four will actually appear in the selection. The fifth, and wrong, choice will not.

INFERENCE QUESTIONS CALL FOR A FURTHER CONCLUSION.

An inference question should not require a long chain of deductive reasoning. It is usually a one-step inference. For example, the selection might make a statement to the effect that "X only occurs in the presence of Y." The question might ask, "In the absence of Y, what result should be expected?" The correct answer would be "X does not occur."

LOGICAL STRUCTURE QUESTIONS ARE ALL ABOUT ORGANIZATION.

Some logical structure questions ask about the overall structure of the passage. The correct answer to this kind of question should describe in general terms the overall development of the selection.

Another kind of logical structure question asks about the logical function of specific details. For this kind of question, find the appropriate reference and determine why the author introduced the detail at just that point.

APPLICATION QUESTIONS ARE THE TOUGHEST, AND YOU MAY JUST HAVE TO GUESS.

Application questions are the most abstract and therefore the most difficult kind of question. There is no "silver bullet" for this type of question, and you may find that it is better to make a guess and just move on.

What are the topics of LSAT reading passages?
LSAT Reading Comprehension passages cover a wide variety of subjects. Your test may include passages from the humanities, physical sciences, social sciences, philosophy, ethics, or the law.

FOR ATTITUDE/TONE QUESTIONS, THE ANSWER CHOICES RUN A GAMUT.

Attitude or tone questions often have answer choices that run a gamut of judgments or emotions, from negative to positive. On this kind of question, try to create a continuum of the answer choices and locate the author's attitude or tone on that continuum. Here's an example:

The tone of the passage is best described as one of

(A) outrage.

(B) approval.

(C) objectivity.

(D) alarm.

(E) enthusiasm.

Arrange these attitudes in a line, from the most negative to the most positive:

(-) .. outrage .. alarm .. objectivity .. approval .. enthusiasm .. (+)

EXERCISES: READING COMPREHENSION

Exercise 1

24 Questions • Time—35 Minutes

Directions: Below each of the following passages you will find questions or incomplete statements about the passage. Each statement or question is followed by lettered words or expressions. Select the word or expression that most satisfactorily completes each statement or answers each question in accordance with the meaning of the passage. After you have chosen the best answer, circle the letter of your choice.

Questions 1–6

Since 1994, the International Monetary Fund (IMF) has functioned as a quasi lender of last resort to developing nations. The principles for operating as a
(5) lender of last resort were systematically expounded by Henry Thornton in 1802 and reformulated independently by Walter Bagehot in 1873: lend liberally, on good collateral, to the market, for a
(10) short term, and at a penalty rate of interest. These recommendations ensure that panic is quelled while the central bank discourages borrowing except by fundamentally solvent parties willing to
(15) pay a premium. It is generally accepted that a financial institution other than an aid institution should avoid lending at subsidized (below-market) rates of interest.
(20)   It has been a matter of debate whether the IMF honors this important principle. Contributor nations to the IMF do earn interest and can withdraw funds at any time, features that suggest the
(25) IMF is like a savings bank, but this ignores the risk involved in IMF loans. Because defaults have been rare, the IMF has not imposed costs in the sense of a nominal operating loss that would
(30) reduce the value of the contributions of the members, but a single default by a large borrower would show clearly that the IMF's status does not exclude it from the kinds of risks the private sector faces

(35) when lending to governments. Even in the absence of serious defaults, the U.S. and other contributors have, from time to time, found it necessary to make supplemental contributions to the fund.
(40)   Additionally, contributors pay an "opportunity cost." Suppose the IMF pays interest of 2 percent a year for funds it lends to other countries, but a contributor country could earn 6 percent a year
(45) lending the funds directly to the same countries. The opportunity cost of the contribution to the IMF is the difference, which amounts to 4 percent a year. Indeed, if participation in the IMF cost
(50) nothing at all, contributors would not need to supplement their positions from time to time; the IMF could instead borrow from international financial markets and lend the funds at a suitable
(55) mark-up, as banks do.
    It has been suggested that conditions imposed on loans by the IMF justify lower rates. Typically, the IMF will require that borrowing governments
(60) reduce their budget deficits and rate of money growth (inflation); eliminate monopolies, price controls, interest-rate ceilings, and subsidies; and in some cases, devalue their currencies. Often
(65) these conditions are unpopular, but setting aside the wisdom of the content of conditionality, the important question is the effect of the conditions on the

prospects of repayment. Banks, for ex- *(70)* ample, require mortgage loans to be collateralized by houses. This type of conditionality improves the prospects of repayment and enables banks to make a profit charging lower interest rates than *(75)* they otherwise could. The IMF does not require collateral. IMF conditionality therefore does not significantly improve the prospects for repayment, and conditionality does not reduce the element of *(80)* subsidy.

Giving a subsidy is undesirable because instead of making borrowers pay penalty rates of interest when they make mistakes, the IMF allows borrow- *(85)* ers to pay lower interest rates during crises than they pay to borrow from the private sector in normal, noncrisis periods. Local taxpayers rather than taxpayers in countries that are net lenders *(90)* to the IMF pay most of the cost of a crisis, so the possibility of obtaining loans from the IMF at subsidized rates of interest is not a positive inducement for a crisis; but other things being equal, subsidized *(95)* interest rates reduce the incentive to take politically painful measures that may prevent a crisis. Subsidized rates also make countries more inclined to turn to the IMF rather than the private *(100)* sector for financing. In this sense, the IMF's subsidized loans create "moral hazard" (reduced vigilance against imprudent behavior because one does not pay its full costs).

1. Which of the following best describes the development of the passage?

   (A) The author reviews two different interpretations of a set of facts and rejects one while accepting the other.

   (B) The author reviews two different interpretations of a set of facts and concludes that neither is valid.

   (C) The author outlines a list of principles and then demonstrates that the principles are outdated.

   (D) The author proposes a new economic theory and argues its advantages over the accepted theory.

   (E) The author sketches a theory and offers various objections to it without endorsing them.

2. According to the passage, opportunity cost is the difference between the

   (A) value received and the cost of pursuing a foregone opportunity

   (B) value received and savings realized by not pursuing a foregone opportunity

   (C) value received and the value that would have been received from the foregone opportunity

   (D) cost of pursuing one option and cost of pursuing a foregone alternative

   (E) cost of pursuing one option and the value that would have been received from a foregone opportunity

3. According to the passage, the IMF sometimes uses conditionality for the same purpose that a private bank requires

   (A) payment of interest

   (B) pledge of collateral

   (C) deposits from investors

   (D) proof of solvency

   (E) repayment of loans

4. The author mentions the possibility of precipitating a financial crisis in order to obtain loans on favorable terms (paragraph 5) in order to

(A) dispose of a weak argument that might otherwise cloud the analysis

(B) isolate one of the hidden assumptions of a possible counter-argument

(C) uncover a hidden contradiction in a competing line of analysis

(D) clarify the meaning of a key term used in more than one sense

(E) demonstrate that a line of reasoning leads to an absurd conclusion

5. With which of the following statements would the author of the passage most likely agree?

(A) The IMF could reduce the moral hazard attached to lending at below-market interest by exacting promises from borrowers to improve the efficiency of markets.

(B) The IMF should lend freely at below-market interest rates because any losses incurred through default can be offset by supplemental contributions from depositor nations.

(C) The IMF could minimize the danger of default of loans by requiring debtor nations to pledge collateral sufficient to secure the value of the loan.

(D) For the IMF to function as a sound financial institution, it must reform its lending practices so that it charges interest that reflects the risk attendant on its loans.

(E) It is immoral for any institution to lend funds to a borrower at interest rates below market because the subsidy encourages the borrower to assume excessive risk.

6. The passage suggests that if the IMF charged interest rates commensurable with the risks of its loans, then

(A) more borrowers would wish to obtain loans from the IMF

(B) borrowers would be more receptive to conditionality

(C) rates of default on outstanding loans would decline

(D) private lenders would relax conditions imposed on loans

(E) contributors would no longer need to make supplement contributions

Questions 7–12

Integrating defense technology with commercial technology can reduce fixed costs and result in other significant economic efficiencies by the use of common pro-
(5) cesses, labor, equipment, material, and facilities. This includes cooperation between government and private facilities in research and development, manufacturing, and maintenance operations;
(10) combined production of similar military and commercial items, including components and subsystems, side-by-side on a single production line or within a single firm or facility; and use of commercial
(15) off-the-shelf items directly within military systems. However, several factors determine the extent to which such integration is possible and the ease with which it can be accomplished. It is useful
(20) to compare the experience of the United States with its clear separation of the commercial and defense sectors with that of the People's Republic of China (PRC).
(25) In the United States, one of the biggest obstacles to integrating civil and military procurement is the body of laws governing military procurement. In large part due to past accounting and acquisi-
(30) tions scandals, myriad reporting requirements frequently deter commercially successful firms from bidding on military contracts. Additionally, the Department of Defense (DOD) demands

(35) extensive rights to technical data to ensure that production of a system continues even in the event of a serious business disruption such as bankruptcy. DOD may request not only data about the
(40) system itself but also information on proprietary manufacturing processes that commercial firms are anxious to protect. The private-public dichotomy that gives rise to these barriers has no
(45) parallel in the PRC because the state owns the bulk of the means of production in the first place.

      Additionally, the American military emphasizes high performance, even
(50) marginal improvements, regardless of cost. Not only is this additional performance not necessarily sought in commercial products (e.g., commercial jetliners have little need for an after-
(55) burner), it usually is not cost-effective. In the PRC, although operational parameters are set by the People's Liberation Army (PLA), the standards involved in actual production are set by central
(60) managers. The latter are far more versed in engineering, whereas the former have generally been capable only of setting out operational requirements without necessarily understanding the indus-
(65) trial demands involved. Thus, production standards have been the responsibility of the producers rather than the users. Consequently, in the PRC little effort is made to acquire or
(70) develop the very latest state-of-the art weapons technologies.

      Yet another obstacle to commercial-military integration involves militarily unique technologies (e.g., ballistic mis-
(75) siles and electronic warfare programming have no civilian applications). In the PRC military technologies have tended to be rendered "unique" only because certain resources have been in
(80) limited supply. That is, the PLA has priority for receiving many of the more advanced and expensive technologies and facilities, but these are in relatively short supply. It is likely, for example,
(85) that the Chinese air-defense network has a more advanced set of air-traffic

control capabilities than does the Chinese civilian air-traffic network simply because of the scarcity of such equip-
(90) ment.

      In general, the PRC appears to have been more successful in integrating military and commercial technology, but it is difficult to assess the extent
(95) to which this success is due to the relatively primitive state of technology or to political and economic conditions. It is likely a combination of both. Certainly, replicating in the United States the full
(100) degree of integration in the PRC would entail unacceptable political and economic costs. In particular, it is unlikely that the American political system would accept the ambiguity inherent in the
(105) commercial use of public facilities and, perhaps more importantly, the conflict of public appropriation of private resources.

7. The primary purpose of the passage is to

(A) compare the integration of military and commercial technology in the United States and the People's Republic of China

(B) use the Chinese political system as the basis for critiquing policies in the United States

(C) criticize the United States for failing to completely integrate military and commercial technology

(D) assess the extent to which military procurement procedures in the People's Republic of China would be useful in the United States

(E) analyze the causes of the failure of the United States to achieve a complete integration of technology between the military and commercial sectors

8. According to the passage, proprietary rights do not present a barrier to integration of commercial and military technology in the People's Republic of China because

(A) the state controls the means of production

(B) commercial and military sectors rely on similar technology

(C) military weapons are not permitted in the commercial sector

(D) the PRC does not pursue state-of-the-art weapons systems

(E) the army of the People's Republic of China does not control defense manufacturing

9. It can be inferred that an increase in the availability of high technology air traffic control equipment in the People's Republic of China would result in

(A) considerable simplification of the procurement policies for both the civilian and military components of air-traffic control

(B) less effective performance on the part of air-traffic controllers because of unfamiliarity with new technology

(C) increased waste and redundancy as the civilian and military sectors competed for the rights to develop new equipment

(D) cost savings that would be achieved by shifting technicians into lower paying positions

(E) greater disparity between the capabilities of the civilian air-traffic control system and its military counterpart

10. The passage mentions all of the following as economic efficiencies that could be achieved by the integration of commercial and military technology EXCEPT:

(A) production lines creating parts for both the commercial and military sectors

(B) manufacturing facilities producing subsystems with civilian and military uses

(C) research and development facilities working on problems of both commercial and military significance

(D) storehoused items originally manufactured for commercial use that also have military applications

(E) defense control of commercial manufacturing facilities that produce military components

11. The experience of the People's Republic of China when compared with that of the United States most strongly supports which of the following conclusions?

   (A) Advanced technologies for weapons systems are adopted more rapidly in countries with planned economies than in nations with capitalistic systems.

   (B) Uniquely military applications of advanced technology are less likely to be developed by military forces that are under the close supervision of civilian authorities.

   (C) Costs of technologically advanced acquisitions tend to be lower when procurement decisions are made by managers with engineering backgrounds.

   (D) Private firms that operate with little or no government oversight prefer to bid on government contracts rather than to produce commercial products for the private sector.

   (E) Economies that are controlled by central planners operate less efficiently than economies in which decision-making authority is widely dispersed.

12. Which of the following best states the conclusion of the passage?

   (A) Attempts at integrating commercial and military technology in the People's Republic of China have been more successful than those in the United States.

   (B) Economic and political differences would make it difficult for the United States to achieve the same integration of commercial and military technology as the People's Republic of China.

   (C) Political factors are more important determinants of a nation's ability to integrate its military and commercial technology sectors than economic considerations.

   (D) Close integration of technological breakthroughs in the civilian and military sectors frequently results in important economic advantages.

   (E) The strength of a country's military posture is in large part determined by the ability of the country's military to incorporate cutting-edge technology into its weapons systems.

Questions 13–18

Helplessness and passivity are central themes in describing human depression. Laboratory experiments with animals have uncovered a phenomenon desig-
(5) nated "learned helplessness." Dogs given inescapable shock initially show intense emotionality, but later become passive in the same situation. When the situation is changed from inescapable to es-
(10) capable shock, the dogs fail to escape even though escape is possible. Neuro-chemical changes resulting from learned helplessness produce an avoidance-escape deficit in laboratory animals.
(15)   Is the avoidance deficit caused by prior exposure to inescapable shock learned helplessness or is it simply stress-induced noradrenergic deficiency leading to a deficit in motor activation?

(20) Avoidance-escape deficit can be produced in rats by stress alone, i.e., by a brief swim in cold water. But a deficit produced by exposure to extremely traumatic events must be produced by a very

(25) different mechanism than the deficit produced by exposure to the less traumatic uncontrollable aversive events in the learned-helplessness experiments. A nonaversive parallel to the learned

(30) helplessness induced by uncontrollable shock, e.g., induced by uncontrollable food delivery, produces similar results. Moreover, studies have shown the importance of prior experience in learned

(35) helplessness. Dogs can be "immunized" against learned helplessness by prior experience with controllable shock. Rats also show a "mastery effect" after extended experience with escapable shock.

(40) They work far longer trying to escape from inescapable shock than do rats lacking this prior mastery experience. Conversely, weanling rats given inescapable shock fail to escape shock as

(45) adults. These adult rats are also poor at nonaversive discrimination learning. Certain similarities have been noted between conditions produced in animals by the learned-helplessness procedure

(50) and by the experimental neurosis paradigm. In the latter, animals are first trained on a discrimination task and are then tested with discriminative stimuli of increasing similarity. Eventually, as

(55) the discrimination becomes very difficult, animals fail to respond and begin displaying abnormal behaviors: first agitation, then lethargy.

It has been suggested that both

(60) learned helplessness and experimental neurosis involve inhibition of motivation centers and pathways by limbic forebrain inhibitory centers, especially in the septal area. The main function of

(65) this inhibition is compensatory, providing relief from anxiety or distress. In rats subjected to the learned-helplessness and experimental-neurosis paradigms, stimulation of the septum

(70) produces behavioral arrest, lack of behavioral initiation and lethargy, while rats with septal lesions do not show learned helplessness.

How analogous the model of learned

(75) helplessness and the paradigm of stress-induced neurosis are to human depression is not entirely clear. Inescapable noise or unsolvable problems have been shown to result in conditions in humans

(80) similar to those induced in laboratory animals, but an adequate model of human depression must also be able to account for the cognitive complexity of human depression.

13. The primary purpose of the passage is to

(A) propose a cure for depression in human beings.

(B) discuss research possibly relevant to depression in human beings.

(C) criticize the result of experiments that induce depression in laboratory animals.

(D) raise some questions about the propriety of using laboratory animals for research.

(E) suggest some ways in which depression in animals differs from depression in humans.

14. The author raises the question at the beginning of the second paragraph in order to

(A) prove that learned helplessness is caused by neurochemical changes.

(B) demonstrate that learned helplessness is also caused by nonaversive discrimination learning.

(C) suggest that further research is needed to determine the exact causes of learned helplessness.

(D) refute a possible objection based on an alternative explanation of the cause of learned helplessness.

(E) express doubts about the structure of the experiments that created learned helplessness in dogs.

15. It can be inferred from the passage that rats with septal lesions (line 72) do not show learned helplessness because

(A) such rats were immunized against learned helplessness by prior training.

(B) the lesions blocked communication between the limbic forebrain inhibitory centers and motivation centers.

(C) the lesions prevented the rats from understanding the inescapability of the helplessness situation.

(D) a lack of stimulation of the septal area does not necessarily result in excited behavior.

(E) lethargy and other behavior associated with learned helplessness can be induced by the neurosis paradigm.

16. It can be inferred that the most important difference between experiments inducing learned helplessness by inescapable shock and the nonaversive parallel mentioned in line 29 is that the nonaversive parallel

(A) did not use pain as a stimuli to be avoided.

(B) failed to induce learned helplessness in subject animals.

(C) reduced the extent of learned helplessness.

(D) caused a more traumatic reaction in the animals.

(E) used only rats rather than dogs as subjects.

17. The author cites the "mastery effect" primarily in order to

(A) prove the avoidance deficit caused by exposure to inescapable shock is not caused by shock per se but by the inescapability.

(B) cast doubts on the validity of models of animal depression when applied to depression in human beings.

(C) explain the neurochemical changes in the brain that cause learned helplessness.

(D) suggest that the experimental-neurosis paradigm and the learned-helplessness procedure produce similar behavior in animals.

(E) argue that learned helplessness is simply a stress-induced noradrenergic deficiency.

18. Which of the following would be the most logical continuation of the passage?

(A) An explanation of the connection between the septum and the motivation centers of the brains of rats

(B) An examination of techniques used to cure animals of learned helplessness

(C) A review of experiments designed to created stress-induced noradrenergic deficiencies in humans

(D) A proposal for an experiment to produce learned helplessness and experimental neurosis in humans

(E) An elaboration of the differences between human depression and similar animal behavior

Questions 19–24

Depletion is a natural phenomenon that characterizes the development of all non-renewable resources and oil in particular. Broadly speaking, depletion is a
(5) progressive reduction of the overall stock of a resource as the resource is produced; narrowly, the term refers to the decline of production associated with a particular field, reservoir, or well. Typically,
(10) production from a given well increases to a peak and then declines over time until some economic limit is reached and the well is shut in. If it were not for changes in prices, costs, and technology,
(15) depletion of the world's resources would resemble the simple decline curve of a single well.

Estimates of oil resources by field are routinely made by geologists and
(20) engineers, but the estimates are a "best guess" given the available data and are revised as more knowledge becomes available. There is no time frame or probability associated with estimates of
(25) total resources in place. In contrast, proved reserves of crude oil are the estimated quantities that, on a particular date, are demonstrated with reasonable certainty to be recoverable in the future
(30) from known reservoirs under existing economic and operating conditions. Generally, there is at least a 90 percent probability that, at a minimum, the estimated volume of proved reserves in
(35) the reservoir can be recovered under existing economic and operating conditions.

Each year, production is taken from proved reserves, reducing both proved
(40) reserves and the total resource. Innovative production techniques such as well recompletions, secondary and tertiary enhanced recovery techniques, and expanded production of unconventional
(45) resources have reduced net depletion rates at the well and field levels. Advanced exploration and drilling techniques, such as 3-D seismic imaging, directional drilling, and multiple wells
(50) from single boreholes, have reduced the cost of finding new pools, reduced the risk of dry holes and dry hole costs, and allowed new pools to be developed and produced more quickly. Lower explora-
(55) tion, drilling, and dry hole costs increase the return on capital by lowering costs. More rapid production of resources from a field increases the return on capital because earnings are realized sooner in
(60) the project's life, and therefore, discounted less.

Higher returns make some fields that are too expensive to develop under "normal" circumstances economically
(65) feasible, because reduced costs allow firms to make profits where they could not before. On the other hand, more rapid development and production of a field by definition increases the rate of
(70) depletion. If an operator produces a field more quickly, the rate of depletion must rise. While the rate of depletion increases with technological progress, the adverse effects of depletion are diminished, and
(75) higher levels of production can be maintained for longer periods of time. As depletion leads producers to abandon older fields and develop new ones, the process of developing domestic oil re-
(80) sources leads producers to find and develop the larger, more economical fields first. Later fields tend to be less desirable because they are farther away from existing infrastructure or smaller in size.
(85) Thus, as time progresses more effort is required to produce the same level of the resource from the same exploration area.

While the frontier for new resources is diminishing, increased innovation has,
(90) thus far, served to offset depletion at least partially, keeping production stronger than it would have been in the absence of the innovations. Technological progress is expected to continue to en-
(95) hance exploration, reduce costs, and improve production technology. But eventually, as field sizes decrease, the ultimate recovery from discovered fields will shrink. Thus, despite technological
(100) improvements, ultimate recovery from the average field of the future will be smaller than from the average field today.

19. The passage is primarily intended to

    (A) sketch a plan to prolong production of existing oil resources

    (B) warn of the consequences of overexploiting oil resources

    (C) discuss economic factors influencing oil production and depletion

    (D) describe methods of extracting oil resources more efficiently

    (E) propose alternative energy sources to replace dependence on oil

20. According to the passage, the most important difference between total oil resources and proved reserves is that proved reserves

    (A) are determined by geological principles probably to be present beneath the surface

    (B) require the use of advanced production techniques for recovery

    (C) cannot be known with certainty to exist until their existence has been verified by experts

    (D) can be produced at a cost comparable to that required for resources currently being recovered

    (E) do not presuppose the existence of advanced technologies for their extraction from the ground

21. Which of the following best explains why the author puts the word *normal* in quotation marks (paragraph 4)?

    (A) Base line conditions are not natural but are artificially defined by economic factors.

    (B) Reduced costs make oil production operations more profitable than other economic activities.

    (C) Oil is strictly a nonrenewable energy resource in spite of technological advances.

    (D) Existing oil production infrastructure eventually wears out and needs to be replaced.

    (E) Oil reserves are gradually being depleted, which makes it more and more difficult to find proved reserves.

22. The passage implies that an oil well is removed from production when

    (A) the supply of oil it produces is completely exhausted

    (B) the cost of operating the well exceeds the return

    (C) new wells have been bored to replace the capacity of the existing well

    (D) the cost of capital required to open the well has been recovered

    (E) it is no longer possible to accelerate oil production by the well

23. According to the passage, technological innovation offsets natural depletion because it

    (A) makes it profitable to locate and extract more oil resources

    (B) reduces the ratio of proved reserves to actual oil resources

    (C) replenishes oil resources even as it extracts them from the ground

    (D) permits the exploitation of more expansive oil fields with large resources

    (E) minimizes the need to invest in capital expenditures in order to produce oil

24. Which of the following would be MOST LIKELY to result in an increase in proved reserves in the United States?

(A) Increased oil production by foreign sources

(B) A significant rise in the price of crude oil

(C) A reduction in estimates of total oil resources

(D) New federal regulations requiring cleaner engines

(E) Discovery of a large field of clean-burning coal

Exercise 2

14 Questions • Time—18 Minutes

Directions: Below each of the following passages, you will find questions or incomplete statements about the passage. Each statement or question is followed by lettered words or expressions. Select the word or expression that most satisfactorily completes each statement or answers each question in accordance with the meaning of the passage. After you have chosen the best answer, circle the letter of your choice.

Questions 1–7

Like our political society, the university is under severe attack today and perhaps for the same reason; namely, that we have accomplished much of what we
(5) have set out to do in this generation, that we have done so imperfectly, and while we have been doing so, we have said a lot of things that simply are not true. For example, we have earnestly
(10) declared that full equality of opportunity in universities exists for everyone, regardless of economic circumstance, race or religion. This has never been true. When it was least true, the asser
(15) tion was not attacked. Now that it is nearly true, not only the assertion but the university itself is locked in mortal combat with the seekers of perfection. In another sense the university has failed.
(20) It has stored great quantities of knowledge; it teaches more people; and despite its failures, it teaches them better. It is in the application of this knowledge that the failure has come. Of the great
(25) branches of knowledge—the sciences, the social sciences and humanities—the sciences are applied, sometimes almost as soon as they are learned. Strenuous and occasionally successful efforts are
(30) made to apply the social sciences, but almost never are the humanities well applied. We do not use philosophy in defining our conduct. We do not use literature as a source of real and vicari
(35) ous experience to save us the trouble of living every life again in our own. The great tasks of the university in the next

generation are to search the past to form the future, to begin an earnest search for
(40) a new and relevant set of values, and to learn to use the knowledge we have for the questions that come before us. The university should use one-fourth of a student's time in his undergraduate
(45) years and organize it into courses which might be called history, and literature and philosophy, and anything else appropriate and organize these around primary problems. The difference between
(50) a primary problem and a secondary or even tertiary problem is that primary problems tend to be around for a long time, whereas the less important ones get solved. One primary problem is that
(55) of interfering with what some call human destiny and others call biological development, which is partly the result of genetic circumstance and partly the result of accidental environmental con
(60) ditions. It is anticipated that the next generation, and perhaps this one, will be able to interfere chemically with the actual development of an individual and perhaps biologically by interfering with
(65) his genes. Obviously, there are benefits both to individuals and to society from eliminating, or at least improving, mentally and physically deformed persons. On the other hand, there could be very
(70) serious consequences if this knowledge were used with premeditation to produce superior and subordinate classes, each genetically prepared to carry out a predetermined mission. This can be done,
(75) but what happens to free will and the

rights of the individual? Here we have a primary problem that will still exist when we are all dead. Of course, the traditional faculty members would say, "But

(80) the students won't learn enough to go to graduate school." And certainly they would not learn everything we are in the habit of making them learn, but they would learn some other things. Surely,

(85) in the other three-quarters of their time, they would learn what they usually do, and they might even learn to think about it by carrying new habits into their more conventional courses. The advantages

(90) would be overwhelmingly greater than the disadvantages. After all, the purpose of education is not only to impart knowledge but to teach students to use the knowledge that they either have or

(95) will find, to teach them to ask and seek answers for important questions.

1. The author suggests that the university's greatest shortcoming is its failure to

    (A) attempt to provide equal opportunity for all.

    (B) offer courses in philosophy and the humanities.

    (C) prepare students adequately for professional studies.

    (D) help students see the relevance of the humanities to real problems.

    (E) require students to include in their curricula liberal arts courses.

2. It can be inferred that the author presupposes that the reader will regard a course in literature as a course

    (A) with little or no practical value.

    (B) of interest only to academic scholars.

    (C) required by most universities for graduation.

    (D) uniquely relevant to today's primary problems.

    (E) used to teach students good writing skills.

3. Which of the following questions does the author answer in the passage?

    (A) What are some of the secondary problems faced by the past generation?

    (B) How can we improve the performance of our political society?

    (C) Has any particular educational institution tried the proposal introduced by the author?

    (D) What is a possible objection to the proposal offered in the passage?

    (E) Why is the university of today a better imparter of knowledge than the university of the past?

4. Which of the following questions would the author most likely consider a primary question?

    (A) Should Congress increase the level of social security benefits?

    (B) Is it appropriate for the state to use capital punishment?

    (C) Who is the best candidate for president in the next presidential election?

    (D) At what month can the fetus be considered medically viable outside the mother's womb?

    (E) What measures should be taken to solve the problem of world hunger?

5. With which of the following statements about the use of scientific techniques to change an individual's genetic makeup would the author LEAST likely agree?

   (A) Society has no right to use such techniques without the informed consent of the individual.

   (B) Such techniques can have a positive benefit for the individual in some cases.

   (C) Use of such techniques may be appropriate even though society, but not the individual, benefits.

   (D) The question of the use of such techniques must be placed in a philosophical as well as a scientific context.

   (E) The answers to questions about the use of such techniques will have important implications for the structure of our society.

6. The primary purpose of the passage is to

   (A) discuss a problem and propose a solution.

   (B) analyze a system and defend it.

   (C) present both sides of an issue and allow the reader to draw a conclusion.

   (D) outline a new idea and criticize it.

   (E) raise several questions and provide answers to them.

7. The development discussed in the passage is primarily a problem of

   (A) political philosophy.

   (B) educational philosophy.

   (C) scientific philosophy.

   (D) practical science.

   (E) practical politics.

Questions 8–14

The high unemployment rates of the early 1960's occasioned a spirited debate within the economics profession. One group found the primary cause of
(5) unemployment in slow growth and the solution in economic expansion. The other found the major explanation in changes that had occurred in the supply and demand for labor and stressed mea-
(10) sures for matching demand with supply.

    The expansionist school of thought, with the Council of Economic Advisers as its leading advocates, attributed the persistently high unemployment level
(15) to a slow rate of economic growth resulting from a deficiency of aggregate demand for goods and services. The majority of this school endorsed the position of the Council that tax reduction
(20) would eventually reduce the unemployment level to 4 percent of the labor force with no other assistance. At 4 percent, bottlenecks in skilled labor, middle-level manpower and professional personnel
(25) were expected to retard growth and generate wage-price pressures. To go beyond 4 percent, the interim goal of the Council, it was recognized that improved education, training and retraining and
(30) other structural measures would be required. Some expansionists insisted that the demand for goods and services was nearly satiated and that it was impossible for the private sector to absorb a
(35) significant increase in output. In their estimate, only the lower-income fifth of the population and the public sector offered sufficient outlets for the productive efforts of the potential labor force.
(40) The fact that the needs of the poor and the many unmet demands for public services held higher priority than the demands of the marketplace in the value structure of this group no doubt influ-
(45) enced their economic judgments. Those who found the major cause of unemployment in structural features were primarily labor economists, concerned professionally with efficient functioning
(50) of labor markets through programs to

develop skills and place individual workers. They maintained that increased aggregate demand was a necessary but not sufficient condition for reaching either the CEA's 4 percent target or their (55) own preferred 3 percent. This pessimism was based, in part, on the conclusion that unemployment among the young, the unskilled, minority groups and depressed geographical areas is not easily (60) attacked by increasing general demand. Further, their estimate of the numbers of potential members of the labor force who had withdrawn or not entered because of lack of employment opportunity (65) was substantially higher than that of the CEA. They also projected that increased demand would put added pressure on skills already in short supply (70) rather than employ the unemployed, and that because of technological change, which was replacing manpower, much higher levels of demand would be necessary to create the same number of jobs. (75) The structural school, too, had its hyperenthusiasts: fiscal conservatives who, as an alternative to expansionary policies, argued the not very plausible position that a job was available for every (80) person, provided only that he or she had the requisite skills or would relocate. Such extremist positions aside, there was actually considerable agreement between two main groups, though this (85) was not recognized at the time. Both realized the advisability of a tax cut to increase demand, and both needed to reduce unemployment below a point around 4 percent. In either case, the (90) policy implications differed in emphasis and not in content.

8. The primary purpose of the passage is to

(A) suggest some ways in which tools to manipulate aggregate demand and eliminate structural deficiencies can be used to reduce the level of unemployment.

(B) demonstrate that there was a good deal of agreement between the expansionist and structuralist theories on how to reduce unemployment in the 1960s.

(C) explain the way in which structural inefficiencies prevent the achievement of a low rate of unemployment without wage-price pressures.

(D) discuss the disunity within the expansionist and structuralist schools to show its relationship to the inability of the government to reduce unemployment to 4 percent.

(E) describe the role of the Council of Economic Advisers in advocating expansionist policies to reduce unemployment to 4 percent.

9. Which of the following is NOT mentioned in the passage as a possible barrier to achieving a 4 percent unemployment rate through increased aggregate demand?

   (A) Technological innovation reduces the need for workers, so larger increases in demand are needed to employ the same number of workers.

   (B) The increase in output necessary to meet an increase in aggregate demand requires skilled labor, which is already in short supply, rather than unskilled labor, which is available.

   (C) An increase in aggregate demand will not create jobs for certain subgroups of unemployed persons, such as minority groups and young and unskilled workers.

   (D) Even if the tax reduction increases aggregate demand, many unemployed workers will be unwilling to relocate to jobs located in areas where there is a shortage of labor.

   (E) An increase in the number of available jobs will encourage people not in the labor market to enter it, which in turn will keep the unemployment rate high.

10. The author's treatment of the "hyperenthusiasts" (lines 75–76) can best be described as one of

    (A) strong approval.

    (B) lighthearted appreciation.

    (C) summary dismissal.

    (D) contemptuous sarcasm.

    (E) malicious rebuke.

11. Which of the following best describes the difference between the position taken by the Council of Economic Advisers and that taken by dissenting expansionists (Paragraph 2)?

    (A) Whereas the Council of Economic Advisers emphasized the need for a tax cut to stimulate general demand, the dissenters stressed the importance of structural measures such as education and training.

    (B) Although the dissenters agreed that an increase in demand was necessary to reduce unemployment, they argued government spending to increase demand should fund programs for lower income groups and public services.

    (C) The Council of Economic Advisers set a 4 percent unemployment rate as its goal, and dissenting expansionists advocated a goal of 3 percent.

    (D) The Council of Economic Advisers rejected the contention, advanced by the dissenting expansionists, that a tax cut would help to create increased demand.

    (E) The dissenting expansionists were critical of the Council of Economic Advisers because members of the Council advocated politically conservative policies.

12. The passage contains information that helps to explain which of the following?

    (A) The fact that the economy did not expand rapidly in the early 1960s

    (B) The start of wage-price pressures as the employment rate approaches 4 percent

    (C) The harmful effects of unemployment on an individual worker

    (D) The domination of the Council of Economics by expansionists

    (E) The lack of education and training among workers in some sectors

13. Which of the following best describes the author's attitude toward the expansionists mentioned in line 31?

    (A) The author doubts the validity of their conclusions because they were not trained economists.

    (B) The author discounts the value of their judgment because it was colored by their political viewpoint.

    (C) The author refuses to evaluate the value of their contention because he lacks sufficient information.

    (D) The author accepts their viewpoint until it can be demonstrated that it is incorrect.

    (E) The author endorses the principles on which their conclusions are based but believes their proposal to be impractical.

14. It can be inferred from the passage that the hyperenthusiasts (lines 75–76) contended that

    (A) the problem of unemployment could be solved without government retraining and education programs.

    (B) the number of persons unemployed was greatly overestimated by the Council of Economic Advisers.

    (C) a goal of 3 percent unemployment could not be reached unless the government enacted retraining and education programs.

    (D) the poor had a greater need for expanded government services than the more affluent portion of the population.

    (E) fiscal policies alone were powerful enough to reduce the unemployment rate to 4 percent of the workforce.

exercises

ANSWER KEYS AND EXPLANATIONS

Exercise 1

1. A	6. E	11. C	16. A	21. A
2. C	7. A	12. B	17. A	22. B
3. B	8. A	13. B	18. E	23. A
4. A	9. E	14. D	19. C	24. B
5. D	10. E	15. B	20. D	

1. **The correct answer is (A).** This is a main idea question in the form of a question about the overall logical development of the selection. The author says that whether or not the IMF follows the accepted principles for a lender of last resort is a matter of debate. The author looks at arguments on both sides and eventually concludes that the IMF is encouraging moral hazard by lending at subsidized rates. For this reason, choices (B) and (E) have to be wrong—the author does defend one interpretation. Choice (C) is wrong because the author does not conclude that the principles are outdated, and choice (D) is wrong because the author is not proposing a new theory (rather, the author is trying to determine whether the IMF follows a long-established one).

2. **The correct answer is (C).** As the phrase "according to" signals, this is an explicit idea question. "Opportunity cost," as that phrase is used here, means the difference between value received and the value one would have received by doing something else. So if you invest $100 in bananas and make a $25 profit but could have invested the same $100 in apples and made a $30 profit, you've lost a $5 opportunity and, in this context, that is a cost you have to absorb.

3. **The correct answer is (B).** As the phrase "according to" signals, this is an explicit idea question. In paragraph four the author notes that the IMF sometimes imposes conditions on loans in the hopes of increasing the likelihood that the loan will ultimately be repaid. This is analogous to a private institution's requiring collateral. Now, ultimately, the author concludes, the practice of imposing conditions doesn't really do much good, despite the theory of the IMF. The remaining choices are all notions mentioned in other parts of the selection but not offered as analogies to collateral.

4. **The correct answer is (A).** This is a logical structure question, so you need to figure out "why" the author raises this point. The author mentions the suggestion that countries might precipitate a financial crisis in order to qualify for IMF loans on favorable terms and then quickly dismisses that idea. The strategy is to raise the possible objection and then point out that it would be foolish for the local taxpayers (people who pay taxes in the borrowing nation) to do this because of the other costs involved.

5. **The correct answer is (D).** This is a further application question. After sifting through the facts used by both sides in the debate, the author concludes that the lending practices of the IMF are not sound because loans are made at subsidized rates. The rates are lower than they would otherwise be because they do not reflect fully the risk of the loans. And

this is bad policy—like a parent who's ready to bail out a child every time the child makes a money-management mistake. Choice (A) is wrong because the author says in paragraph four that conditionality has little effect on the prospects for repayment. As for choice (B), it is true that the IMF will ask for additional funds, but this is bad policy according to the author. The IMF should be lending at rates that reflect the risk involved. As for choice (C), the author never suggests that nations could offer collateral. (What would it be? The borrowing country pledges as collateral its executive mansion and state house along with 600 miles of navigable riverway and 20 tanks.) Finally, choice (E) overstates the case. The author would allow that it is okay for an aid institution to make such loans, but then it is understood that the loan is a form of aid and not a loan the terms of which fully reflect the risk.

6. **The correct answer is (E).** This is an implied idea question. In paragraph three, the author points out that if the IMF were on a sound footing, like a well-run local bank, then the IMF would be able to cover all of its expenses and bad loans from repayments plus the appropriate interest charged. The author reasons that the fact that contributor nations keep having to make deposits shows that there is a leak somewhere—the interest charged by the IMF isn't sufficient to cover all expenses. You can infer, therefore, that if the interest rates charged by the IMF were high enough, contributor countries would not have to put more money into the system. As for the other choices, these are not supported by the selection. As for choice (A), with interest rates higher, there would likely be fewer borrowers, not more. And a similar analysis applies to choice (B): high interest rates would make the loan more difficult and give another reason to object to the conditions. As for choice (C), a higher rate would mean a greater cost for the borrower, and that could translate into defaults, but higher rates could also mean fewer bad loans in the first place. So there is just not enough information for choice (C). And as for (D), the passage says that private lenders do not, as a rule, use conditions.

7. **The correct answer is (A).** This is a main idea question, so the trick is to find the answer choice—of those that are presented—that gives the best overall description of the development of the selection. On the basis of the first word, it is possible to eliminate choice (C) because the author is not throwing stones. While there are certain criticisms implicit in the passage, it cannot be said that the main theme of the passage is criticism. Then, you'll want to eliminate choices that are too narrow, that is, that refer to part of the development but fail to capture the overall purpose of the passage. Choice (E) fails on this count. Yes, one element of the passage is to present reasons why the U.S. has not been able to integrate completely the two sectors, but that description leaves out a lot, e.g., the PRC experience. And you should eliminate choices that go beyond the scope of the selection, as choice (B) does. "Political system" is much too broad for the specific topic addressed here. And finally, you can exclude any choice that contains a misdescription, like choice (D). The author does not attempt to show that the procedures used in the PRC could be used in the U.S.; and, in fact, the passage implies that profound differences in political structures would preclude that.

And this leaves choice (A), which is a good description of the development. There is a comparison, and the comparison is the technology in the two sectors of the two countries.

8. **The correct answer is (A).** This is an explicit idea question, so the correct answer is specifically stated in the passage. In paragraph two, the author notes that the "proprietary" rights barrier has no parallel in the PRC because there is no analogous concept of proprietary rights; that is, the firms that will produce the technology are also under the control of the government. Typically, some of the wrong answers to an explicit idea question will be ideas mentioned in the passage (somewhere) that are not responsive to the question asked. Choice (C) and choice (D) are good examples. These are ideas mentioned in the passage, but they don't answer the question asked. Choice (E) is similar though perhaps more subtle. You might argue that this is one reason that technological integration has been more fully accomplished in the PRC than in the U.S., and the passage supports that idea. The problem is that choice (E) refers to a different aspect of the situation: demand for high performance weapons. Finally, choice (B) seems to be trivially true in some respects but does not respond to the question.

9. **The correct answer (E).** This is an implied idea question. We learn from the passage (in paragraph four) that even though the military is first in line for new equipment, the disparity between the technological capabilities of the civilian and the military air-traffic controllers is not so much due to the priority accorded the military as the simple lack of advanced equipment. In other words, it is not so much a conscious decision to feed the military and starve the civilian sector as it is a choice of allocating what little there is to the military. As for the wrong answers, some are more plausible than others, but all ultimately fail because there is not enough in the passage to support their conclusions. As for choice (A), what reason is there to believe that matters would be "simplified?" As for choice (B), what support is there for the idea that the technicians would not be familiar with the new equipment or trained quickly in its use? As for choice (C), this must surely be wrong because the passage implies that such competition does not take place. Finally, as for choice (D), what is there in the passage that mentions employment practices or such that would support this conclusion?

10. **The correct answer is (E).** This is an explicit idea question—with a thought-reverser. So four of the five ideas are mentioned in the selection, and you will find choice (A) through choice (D) in the first paragraph. Choice (E), however, is not mentioned. The passage does not mention defense control of production as an example of an economic efficiency.

11. **The correct answer is (C).** This is an application question (signaled by the "most strongly supports"). Remember that with such a question the credited response is not likely to be obviously right in the way that a correct answer to a specific detail item is right. Rather, the credited response to an application question is correct because, all things considered, it is the one most strongly supported by the selection. In this case, in paragraph three we learn that in the PRC military planners have responsibility for operational matters, but central planners, who tend to be engineers, have the authority for setting production stan-

dards. And in the PRC, the engineers, with their understanding of the engineering challenges presented by advanced technologies, tend to de-emphasize cutting-edge technology. And it is this type of "gee-willy-whiz-bang" technology that tends to drive up the cost of weapons systems in the U.S. Or at least you can make a pretty good argument for that interpretation. Now look at the other choices. As for choice (A), this conclusion, if anything, seems to be contradicted by the selection since the PRC is said to lag behind the U.S. in adopted new technologies for weapons. As for choice (B), the passage never offers a comparison as to which of the two countries produces more "uniquely military" applications. As for choice (D), this seems to be inconsistent with the analysis given in paragraph two: some firms don't bid on defense contracts because of the strict oversight. And as for choice (E), while the author compares the two countries in terms of technology, there is no comparison of a bottom line such as efficiency.

12. **The correct choice is (B).** This is a main idea question, and the information you need is in the final paragraph. There the passage states that although the PRC appears to have been more successful than the U.S. at achieving integration, various political and economic factors will likely prevent the U.S. from emulating the PRC model. Choice (A) is incorrect because it gives only a part of the author's findings. The passage sets out not just to compare the two countries but to determine whether the experience of the PRC is applicable to the U.S. Choice (B) is also an element of the passage, but only an element. Choice (D) is really a given so far as the argument is concerned

and not a point to be proved. And choice (E) is not supported by the selection.

13. **The correct answer is (B).** This is obviously a main idea question. The main purpose of the passage is to review the findings of some research on animal behavior and suggest that this may have implications for the study of depression in humans. Choice (B) neatly restates this. Choice (A) can be overruled since the author proposes no such cure and even notes that there are complex issues remaining to be solved. Choice (C) is incorrect since the author does not criticize any experiments. It is important to recognize that in the second paragraph, the author is not being critical of any study in which rats were immersed in cold water but rather is anticipating a possible interpretation of those results and moving to block it. So, the author's criticism is of a possible interpretation of the experiment, not the experiment itself or the results. In any event, that can in no way be interpreted as the main theme of the passage. Choice (D) is way off the mark. Though one might object to the use of animals for experimentation, that is not a burden the author has elected to carry. Finally, choice (E) is incorrect because the author mentions this only in closing, almost as a qualification on the main theme of the passage.

14. **The correct answer is (D).** This is a logical detail question. As we have just noted, the author introduces the question in the second paragraph to anticipate a possible objection: Perhaps the animal's inability to act was caused by the trauma of the shock rather than the fact that it could not escape the shock. The author then lists some experiments whose conclusions refute this alternative explanation. Choice (A) is incorrect

since the question represents an interruption of the flow of argument, not a continuation of the first paragraph. Choice (B) is incorrect and might be just a confusion of answer and question. Choice (C) can be eliminated since that is not the reason for raising the question, though it may be the overall theme of the passage. Here we cannot answer a question about a specific logical detail by referring to the main point of the text. Finally, choice (E) is incorrect since the author does not criticize the experiments but rather defends them.

15. **The correct answer is (B).** This is an inference question. We are referred by the question stem to line 72. There we find that stimulation of the septal region inhibits behavior "while rats with septal lesions do not show learned helplessness." We infer that the septum somehow sends "messages" that tell the action centers not to act. If ordinary rats learn helplessness and rats with septal lesions do not, this suggests that the communication between the two areas of the brain has been interrupted. This idea is captured by choice (B). Choice (A) is incorrect and confuses the indicated reference with the discussion of "immunized" dogs at line 35. Choice (C) seems to offer an explanation, but the text never suggests that rats have "understanding." Choice (D) is incorrect since it does not offer an explanation: Why don't rats with septal lesions learn helplessness? Finally, choice (E) is irrelevant to the question asked.

16. **The correct answer is (A).** This is an inferred idea question. The author contrasts the inescapable shock experiment with a "nonaversive parallel" in order to demonstrate that inescapability rather than trauma caused inaction in the animals. So the critical difference must be

the trauma—it is present in the shock experiments and not in the nonaversive parallels. This is further supported by the example of a nonaversive parallel, the uncontrollable delivery of food. So the relevant difference is articulated by choice (A). Choice (B) is incorrect since the author specifically states that the nonaversive parallels did succeed in inducing learned helplessness. Choice (C) is incorrect for the same reason. Choice (D) is incorrect since the value of the nonaversive parallel to the logical structure of the argument is that it was not traumatic at all. Finally, choice (E) is incorrect because even if one experiment used rats and the other dogs, that is not the defining difference between the shock experiments and the nonaversive-parallel experiments.

17. **The correct answer is (A).** This is a logical detail question, and it is related to the matters discussed above. The author raises the question in paragraph two in order to anticipate a possible objection; namely, that the shock, not the unavoidability, caused inaction. The author then offers a refutation of this position by arguing that we get the same results using similar experiments with non-aversive stimuli. Moreover, if trauma of shock caused the inaction, then we would expect to find learned helplessness induced in rats by the shock, regardless of prior experience with shock. The "mastery effect," however, contradicts this expectation. This is essentially the explanation provided in choice (A). Choice (B) is incorrect since the author does not mention this until the end of the passage. Choice (C) can be eliminated since the "mastery effect" reference is not included to support the conclusion that neurochemical changes cause the learned helplessness.

Choice (D) is incorrect, for though the author makes such an assertion, the "mastery effect" data is not adduced to support that particular assertion. Finally, choice (E) is the point against which the author is arguing when mentioning the "mastery effect" experiments.

18. **The correct answer is (E).** This is a further application question. The author closes with a disclaimer that the human cognitive makeup is more complex than that of laboratory animals, and that for this reason, the findings regarding learned helplessness and induced neurosis may or may not be applicable to humans. The author does not, however, explain what the differences are between the experimental subjects and humans. A logical continuation would be to supply the reader with this elaboration. By comparison, the other answer choices are less likely. Choice (B) is unlikely since the author begins and ends with references to human depression, and that is evidently the motivation for writing the article. Choice (C) is not supported by the text since it is nowhere indicated that any such experiments have been undertaken. Choice (D) fails for a similar reason. We cannot conclude that the author would want to test humans by similar experimentation. Finally, choice (A) is perhaps the second-best answer. Its value is that it suggests the mechanism should be studied further. But the most important question is not how the mechanism works in rats but whether that mechanism also works in humans.

19. **The correct answer is (C).** This is a main idea question. The author begins by defining "depletion." Then, in the second paragraph, the passage distinguishes two senses of reserves—the total amount remaining versus the amount recover-

able given reasonable investments. In the third paragraph, the author goes on to show how technology affects production and reserves and in the fourth paragraph points out that technological innovation has the paradoxical effect of extending reserves (because more oil can be extracted) even while using up resources faster. In the final paragraph, the author points to the obvious: continued extraction will depend on further technological innovation. So the best description is choice (C). Choice (A) is wrong because the author does not advance a plan, even though the passage does mention some technological innovations. Choice (B) is wrong because there is no "warning" tone in the passage. Choice (D) is wrong because the mention of various innovations is in the service of the larger discussion; that is, the details found in paragraph three are not the main point. And finally, choice (E) is wrong for the same reasons that (A) and (B) are wrong.

20. **The correct answer is (D).** This is an explicit idea question. According to the passage, total resources is the quantity of oil that actually exists. It's not possible to know exactly how much there is, but experts can make pretty good guesses about the amount. Some of that oil, however, is in places that are hard to get to, so it would be very expensive—though theoretically possible—to produce it. Proved reserves are that subpart of the resources that can be obtained without extraordinary effort, just by using existing technology at a comparable cost. Choice (A) represents a confused reading of paragraph two. The "probability" associated with proved reserves is the likelihood that the oil can be extracted at a reasonable cost. Choice (B) is wrong be-

cause, while proved reserves depend on available technology (that's part of the definition of whether the oil can be recovered at a reasonable cost), the fact that advanced technology makes the oil more accessible is not part of the definition of proved reserves. Choice (C) is attractive because it sounds like "proved," but "proved" in this context has a specialized meaning, as developed in the passage. And choice (E) is wrong because advanced technologies will help to define the quantity of proved reserves; for example, a break-through that reduces the cost of producing oil in otherwise inaccessible spaces increases proved reserves.

21. **The correct answer is (A).** This is a logical structure question. The author places "normal" in scare quotes because it doesn't have its usual meaning. Ordinarily, we take "normal" to mean "natural" or something like that. In this context, however, "normal" conditions are defined in part by cost considerations. For example, a technological innovation can reduce the cost of recovery making it profitable to extract a deposit that is otherwise inaccessible because unprofitable. Choice (B) is wrong because it offers a comparison between oil production and other kinds of activities, none of which are mentioned here. Choice (C) is wrong because, while true, the nonrenewability of the resource is not part of the definition of normal or baseline conditions. Choices (D) and (E) are obviously true but they don't answer the question asked.

22. **The correct answer is (B).** This is an implied idea question. The passage states that during the normal life of a well production will increase and then gradually fall off until it reaches "some economic limit" at which the well is closed. Later, the author talks about prolonging the life of a well using advanced technology, but only when the cost of the technology is acceptable. This implies that the well will be kept in production so long as it is profitable. Choice (A) is wrong because there may be oil remaining in a well or field and yet production is discontinued because it is no longer profitable. Choice (C) simply has no support in the passage; it's a nice idea (make sure you are always building new to replace the old), but the idea just isn't found in this selection about oil. Choice (D) sounds nice, too, but what it really says is that the well should be kept open even if it becomes unprofitable, and that is not what the passage implies. Finally, choice (E) uses some of the language from the passage, but it really doesn't make a statement that is meaningful in this context.

23. **The correct answer is (A).** This is a specific detail question. The last paragraph tells us that, even though total resources are declining (because oil is nonrenewable), technology makes up for the declining base by permitting the faster extraction of oil and by allowing exploitation of deposits that might otherwise be unprofitable. Choice (B) is actually an incorrect statement because innovation would increase proved reserves. Choice (C) also is incorrect since oil is not renewable—period. Choice (D) is wrong because larger fields would be the first discovered and exploited in any case; the passage makes it clear that technology is important in going after the smaller finds. And choice (E) is wrong because technology requires capital investment.

24. **The correct answer is (B).** This is an application question. The analysis of the third and fourth paragraphs shows that an increase in profitability results in an

increase in proved reserves because oil that once would not be extracted because it was unprofitable to do so becomes an economically viable product. Choice (A) would likely have the opposite result: increased production would drive down prices making production of marginal resources less attractive. Choice (C) might not affect proved reserves at all; or, if the revision were large enough, might result in a lowering of proved reserve calculations. Choices (D) and (E) could have the effect of making extraction of some oil unprofitable, thereby removing it from the "proved" category.

Exercise 2

1.	D	4.	B	7.	B	10.	C	13.	B
2.	A	5.	A	8.	B	11.	B	14.	A
3.	D	6.	A	9.	D	12.	B		

1. **The correct answer is (D).** This is a fairly easy inference question. We are asked to determine which of the problems mentioned by the author is the most important. Choice (B) can be eliminated because the author's criticism is not that such courses are not offered, nor even that such courses are not required. So we eliminate choice (E) as well. The most important shortcoming, according to the author, is that students have not been encouraged to apply the principles learned in the humanities. The support for this conclusion is to be found at the end of the second paragraph. As for choice (C), this is not mentioned by the author as a weakness in the present curriculum structure. Rather, the author anticipates that this is a possible objection to the proposal to require students to devote part of their time to the study of primary problems. Choice (A) is indeed a weakness of the university, and the author does admit that the university has not yet achieved equal opportunity for all. But this is discussed in the first paragraph, where the university's successes are outlined. Only in the second paragraph does the discussion of the university's failure begin. This indicates that the author does not regard the university's failure to achieve complete equality of opportunity as a serious problem.

2. **The correct answer is (A).** This is an inference question as well, though of a greater degree of difficulty. It seems possible to eliminate choices (C) and choice (E) as fairly implausible. The author's remarks about literature (at the end of the second paragraph), addressed to us as readers, do not suggest that we believe literature is required, nor that it is used to teach writing. As for choice (D), the author apparently presupposes that we, the readers, do not see the relevance of literature to real problems, for that it is relevant is at least part of the burden of his argument. Choice (B) is perhaps the second best answer. It may very well be that most people regard literature as something scholarly, but that does not prove that choice (B) is a presupposition of the argument. The author states that literature is a source of real and vicarious experience. What is the value of that? According to the author, it relieves us of the necessity of living everyone else's

life. The author is trying to show that literature has a real, practical value. The crucial question, then, is why the author is attempting to prove that literature has real value. The answer is, because the author presupposes that we disagree with this conclusion. There is a subtle but important difference between a presupposition that literature is scholarly and a presupposition that literature has no practical value. After all, there are many nonscholarly undertakings that may lack practical value.

3. **The correct answer is (D).** This is an explicit idea question. It is important to keep in mind that an explicit idea question is almost always answerable on the basis of information actually stated in the text. With a format of this sort, this means that the question should be readily answerable without speculation, and that this answer should be fairly complete. Choice (D) is correct because the author raises a possible objection in the final paragraph. Choice (A) is incorrect because the author never gives any such examples. Choice (B) is incorrect because the author never addresses the issue of political society. That is mentioned only as a point of reference in the introductory remarks. Choice (C) is not answered since no university is ever named. And choice (E) is incorrect since the author makes the assertion, without elaborating, that the university is a better teacher today than in the past. There is a further point to be made. It is possible to argue that choice (B) is partially answered. After all, if we improve our students' ability to pose and answer questions, is this not also a way to improve the performance of our political society? But that is clearly more attenuated than the answer we find in the question in choice (D). The

same reasoning may be applied to other incorrect answers as well. It may be possible to construct arguments in their favor, but this is a standardized exam. And there is a clear, easy answer to choice (D) in the text, indicating that this is the answer the test writer intends that you choose.

4. **The correct answer is (B).** This is an application question. The author uses the term "primary problems" to refer to questions of grave importance that are not susceptible to an easy answer. Each of the incorrect answers poses a question that can be answered with a short answer. Choice (A) can be answered with a yes or no. Choice (C) can be answered with a name. Choice (D) can be answered with a date. Choice (E) can be answered with a series of proposals. And even if the answers are not absolutely indisputable, the questions will soon become dead issues. The only problem that is likely to still be around after "we are all dead" is the one of capital punishment.

5. **The correct answer is (A).** This is an application question—with a thought-reverser. The question asks us to identify the statement with which the author would be least likely to agree. In the fourth paragraph, the author introduces an example of a primary problem. What makes this a primary problem is that there are competing arguments on both sides of the issue: There are benefits to the individual and to society, but there are dangers as well. Choice (A) is not likely to get the author's agreement since the author acknowledges that the question is an open one. The author implies that society may have such a right but points out also that the use of such measures must be studied very carefully. That same paragraph strongly suggests

that the author would accept choices (B) and (C). As for choices (D) and (E), these are strands that are woven into the text at several points.

6. **The correct answer is (A).** This is a main idea question. The author describes a problem and proposes a solution. Choice (B) is incorrect since the analysis of the system leads the author to propose a reform. Choice (C) is incorrect since the author makes a definite recommendation. Choice (D) is incorrect since the new idea the author outlines is defended in the text, not criticized. Choice (E) is incorrect since the author does not develop the passage by raising questions.

7. **The correct answer is (B).** This too is a main idea question in that the question asks, what is the general topic? Choice (B) is the best answer since the author is speaking about the university and is addressing fundamental questions of educational philosophy. Choices (A) and (C) are incorrect since politics and science are only tangentially related to the argument. Choices (D) and (E) can be eliminated on the same ground and on the additional ground that though the author wants to make education practical, the decision to do that will be a decision based on philosophical concerns.

8. **The correct answer is (B).** This is a main idea question presented in the format of a sentence completion. We are looking for the answer choice that, when added to the question stem, produces a sentence that summarizes the main thesis of the passage. Insofar as the verbs are concerned, that is, the first words of each choice, each choice seems acceptable. One could say that the author is concerned with "suggesting," "demonstrating," "explaining," "discussing," or "describing." So we must look at the fuller content of each choice. The author begins the passage by noting that there were two schools of thought on how to reduce unemployment and then proceeds to describe the main ideas of both schools of thought. Finally, the author concludes by noting that, for all of their avowed differences, both schools share considerable common ground. This development is captured very well by choice (B). Choice (A) is perhaps the second-best choice. It is true that the author does mention some economic tools that can be used to control unemployment, but the main thesis is not that such ways exist. Rather, the main thesis, as pointed out by choice (B), is that the two groups, during the 1960s, had seemingly different yet ultimately similar views on how the tools could best be used. Choice (C) is incorrect since the discussion of structural inefficiencies is only a minor part of the development. Choice (D) is incorrect because the discussion of disunity is included simply to give a more complete picture of the debate and not to show that this prevented the achievement of full employment. Finally, the CEA is mentioned as a matter of historical interest, but its role is not the central focus of the passage.

9. **The correct answer is (D).** This is an explicit idea question. Each of the incorrect answers is mentioned as a possible barrier to achieving 4 percent unemployment in the discussion of structural inefficiencies of the third paragraph. The reference is made to the effect of technological innovation, the shortage of skilled labor, the problem of minority and unskilled labor, and the reserve of workers not yet counted as being in the labor force. There is no mention, however, of the need to relocate workers to areas of

labor shortage. The only reference to relocation is in the final paragraph. Since choice (D) is never mentioned as a possible barrier to achieving the 4 percent goal, it is the correct answer.

10. **The correct answer is (C).** This is an attitude or tone question. The author refers to the position of the hyperenthusiasts as "not very plausible," which indicates the author does not endorse the position. On this ground, we can eliminate choice (A). Choice (B) can be eliminated on the same ground and on the further ground that "lighthearted" is not a good description of the tone of the passage. Choices (D) and (E), however, are overstatements. Though the author obviously rejects the position of the hyperenthusiasts, there is no evidence of so negative an attitude as those suggested by choices (D) and (E). Choice (C) describes well what the author means by mentioning the position and then not even bothering to discuss it.

11. **The correct answer is (B).** This is an explicit idea question. The needed reference is found in the second paragraph. The difference between the CEA and the dissenting expansionists grew out of the question of where to spend the money that would be used to stimulate the economy. The dissenting faction wanted to target the expansionary spending for public services and low-income groups. Choice (B) presents this difference very well. Choice (A) is incorrect and conflates the dissenting expansionists (paragraph 2) and the structuralists (paragraph 3). Choice (C) commits the same error. Choice (D) represents a misreading of the second paragraph: The CEA were expansionists. Choice (E) is incorrect since the passage does not state that the CEA were conservatives.

12. **The correct answer is (B).** This is an explicit idea question. Information that would bear on the issue raised by choice (B) is included in the third paragraph. As for choice (A), there is no such information in the passage. In the first paragraph, the author mentions that the economy failed to expand rapidly in the early 1960s but offers no explanation for that phenomenon. And choice (C) is never mentioned at any point in the text. Choice (D) is a political question that is not addressed by the passage, and choice (E) is a historical one that is not answered.

13. **The correct answer is (B).** The author mentions a dissenting group of expansionists in the closing lines of paragraph 2. The author remarks of their arguments that their commitment to certain political ideals likely interfered with their economic judgments. For this reason, the author places very little faith in their arguments. Choice (B) nicely brings out this point. Choice (A) is incorrect. The author does discount the value of their conclusions, but it is not because they were not trained as economists. As for choice (C), there is nothing that suggests that the author lacks information. Rather, it seems from the passage that the author has sufficient information to discount the position. Choice (D) is clearly in contradiction to this analysis and must be incorrect, and choice (E) can be eliminated on the same ground.

14. **The correct answer is (A).** Here we have a relatively easy inference question. The hyperenthusiasts used structuralist-type arguments to contend that jobs were already available. That being the case, the hyperenthusiasts dissented from both the positions of the expansionists and the structuralists who believed

unemployment to be a problem. We may infer, then, that the essence of the hyperenthusiasts' position was that no government action was needed at all—at least no government action of the sort being discussed by the main camps described by the author. As for choice (B), nowhere in the passage does the author state or even hint that anyone overestimated the number of people out of work.

As for choice (C), this represents a reading that confuses the hyperenthusiasts (paragraph 4) with the main-line structuralists (paragraph 3). Choice (D) is incorrect and conflates the hyperenthusiasts of the expansionary school of thought with those of the structuralist school. Finally, choice (E) is incorrect since it describes the position of the main group of expansionists.

answers

Analytical Reasoning

OVERVIEW

- **What Analytical Reasoning Tests**
- **Answering Analytical Reasoning Questions**
- **What Smart Test-Takers Know**

WHAT IS ANALYTICAL REASONING?

Analytical Reasoning problems are just logic games. For example:

> Three musicians—J, K, and L—each play exactly one instrument: the piano, the bass, or the sax—though not necessarily in that order. J, whose sister is the sax player, does not play the piano; and L is an only child.

You have to use the clues to deduce who plays which instrument.

> L does not play the sax because L is an only child (the sax player is J's sister). J cannot be the sax player because J's sister plays the sax. Since the sax player is not J or L, K plays the sax.
>
> If J does not play the sax (K plays the sax) or the piano (as we are told), then J must play the bass.
>
> Finally, since J plays the bass and K plays the sax, you can deduce that L plays the piano.

Thus, you can figure out which musician plays which instrument: J on bass, K on sax, L on piano.

> You have probably seen similar problems in logic books or in the entertainment section of a newspaper or a magazine.

In this book, you will see a variety of logical puzzles, but initial conditions and questions have some very important characteristics in common. The initial conditions establish the structure of the logical game and introduce you to the individuals involved in the puzzle as well as to the logical connections between and among those individuals.

chapter 7

NOTE

Should I try to do all of the Analytical Reasoning puzzles? Probably not. Some students should attempt all four or five of the problem sets; some students should try to do only two. The majority of students should attempt at least three of the sets.

The individuals involved in an Analytical Reasoning set are usually designated by letters or names, e.g., eight people, J, K, L, M, N, O, P, and Q, are sitting around a table. Sometimes, the individuals in the problem may be designated by some physical characteristic, e.g., six flags are displayed in a horizontal row, two red, two blue, one yellow, and one green. Further, the initial conditions always give some information about the logical relations that join the individuals to one another, e.g., J is sitting next to K, and M is not sitting next to P, or the red flags are hanging next to each other and the yellow flag is not next to the green flag.

LSAT Analytical Reasoning Questions

The scored portion of the LSAT typically includes a single Analytical Reasoning section with four to five problem sets. Each set consists of a list of conditions followed by 5–7 questions, for a total of 22–24 questions in the section.

Read over these directions for LSAT Analytical Reasoning, and examine a sample question set and explanations.

Anatomy of an Analytical Reasoning Question Set

Directions: Each group of questions is based on a set of propositions or conditions. Drawing a rough picture or diagram may help in answering some of the questions. Choose the best answer for each question and blacken the corresponding space on your answer sheet.

Six runners—J, K, L, M, N, and O—participated in a series of races with the following results:

   J always finished ahead of N but behind O.

   K always finished ahead of L but behind O.

   M always finished ahead of L but behind J.

There were no ties.

Linear ordering sets are the most common type of game used on the test. Notice that the order of finish is not completely determined, though it is possible to deduce that O always finished first.

---

1. Which of the following could be the order of finish of a race from first to last?

   (A) O, J, K, L, M, N

   (B) O, J, K, M, L, N

   (C) O, J, M, N, L, K

   (D) O, M, J, N, K, L

   (E) M, L, J, O, K, N

The correct answer is (B). Each of the other choices contradicts one or more of the initial conditions.

2. Which of the following must be true of the order of finish for all of the races?

   (A) O finished first.

   (B) J finished second.

   (C) K finished third.

   (D) N finished last.

   (E) L finished last.

The correct answer is (A). The first two conditions establish that O finished ahead of J, K, L, and N. Then, since O finished ahead of J, O also finished ahead of M.

3. For any race, which of the following is a complete and accurate listing of the runners who could have finished ahead of M?

   (A) J

   (B) J, O

   (C) J, O, K

   (D) J, O, K, N

   (E) J, O, K, N, L

The correct answer is (D). The third condition states that M finished ahead of L. So the other four runners could have finished ahead of M.

HOW DO YOU ANSWER ANALYTICAL REASONING QUESTIONS?

Here's a simple, four-step plan that can help you solve Analytical Reasoning questions.

ANALYTICAL REASONING: GETTING IT RIGHT

1   Summarize the initial conditions in a "bookkeeping" system.

2   Look for further conclusions.

3   Treat each question separately.

4   Use the answer choices to create a "feedback loop."

Now let's look at these steps in greater detail.

1 **Summarize the initial conditions in a "bookkeeping" system.** This system will include notational devices and diagramming techniques that you invent for yourself or that you adapt from those suggested in this book. You should not regard the "bookkeeping" system used in this book as the only possible system. Rather, you should regard it as a suggested system. Once you understand the system, you can take some parts of it for your own personal system, leaving behind those devices you find cumbersome or otherwise not useful.

Use these or other symbols to summarize the initial conditions:

LOGICAL CONNECTIVE	SYMBOL
and	+
or	v
not	~
if, then	⊃
same as, next to	=
not same as, not next to	≠
greater than, older, before	>
if and only if	≡
less than, younger, after	<

Be sure to double-check your summary. A mistake at this stage could be very, very costly.

Take a look at this illustration:

A chef is experimenting with eight ingredients to discover new dishes. The ingredients are J, K, L, M, N, O, P, and Q. The ingredients must be used in accordance with the following conditions:

If M is used in a dish, P and Q must also be used in that dish.

If P is used in a dish, then exactly two of the three ingredients, L, M, and N, must also be used in that dish.

L cannot be used in a dish with P.

N can be used in a dish if and only if J is also used in that dish.

K, L, and M cannot all be used in the same dish.

The information could be summarized as follows:

(1) $M \supset (P \ \& \ Q)$

(2) $P \supset (L \ \& \ M) \lor (L \ \& \ N) \lor (M \ \& \ N)$

(3) $L \neq P$

(4) $N \equiv J$

(5) $\sim (K \ \& \ L \ \& \ M)$

The "horseshoe" is used for the first statement, but the arrow could also be used. Notice also that parentheses are used as punctuation marks. If you do not set P & Q off in parentheses, the statement $M \supset P \ \& \ Q$ could be misinterpreted to read "If M is used, then P must be used; and Q must be used."

The second statement shows the logical structure of the second condition. If P is used, then either L and M must be used or L and N must be used or M and N must be used. Again, you should note the parentheses as punctuation marks.

Statement 3 uses the $\neq$, which has many other uses, to assert that L and P cannot be used together. Similarly, statement 4 uses the $\equiv$ to assert that N and J, if used, must be used together. Of course, the $\equiv$ can have many other meanings. Depending on the context in which the symbol is used, the statement "$N \equiv J$" could mean any of the following: N and J are the same age; N and J are of the same sex; N and J must ride in the same car; N and J must sit next to one another. The value of the symbol depends on the context in which it appears.

Finally, statement 5 can be read to say that it is not the case that K and L and M are used in the same dish. Of course, these are just suggestions; there are many other ways to summarize the information. Later, in the answer explanations, you will find different notational devices that will be explained as they are introduced. Remember, however, only adopt those symbols you find convenient and find substitutes for those that do not work for you.

❷ **Look for further conclusions.** The initial conditions may permit you to draw a further conclusion, and a further conclusion is often the key to one or even more questions. Here is an example:

Six students—T, U, V, X, Y, and Z—are being considered for a field trip. The final selection depends on the following restrictions:

If X is selected, then neither Y nor Z can be selected.

If T is selected, then U cannot be selected.

If U is selected, then Z must also be selected.

NOTE

What are point killers?

Point killers are Analytical Reasoning questions that will definitely take too much time. For example:

Which of the following must be true?

(A) If J is selected, then K must be selected.

(B) If J is selected, then L must be selected.

(C) If K is selected, then J must be selected.

(D) If M is selected, then N must be selected.

(E) If N is selected, then Q must be selected.

Since each answer choice includes an "if" statement, this is like five questions rolled into one. Punt.

You can deduce that certain pairs are not acceptable. For example, X and Z cannot both be selected.

3 **Treat each question separately.** Some questions provide, by stipulation, information that supplements the initial conditions, e.g., "If the traveler visits Paris on Thursday, then which city will she visit on Friday?"

Additional information provided in a question stem is to be used for that question only. In fact, different questions may ask you to make contradictory assumptions. The second question in a set may ask you to assume that the traveler visits Rome on Thursday while the third question asks you to assume that she visits Rome on Monday.

4 **Use the answer choices to create a "feedback loop."** This is a multiple-choice examination in which one and only one of the options can be correct. And an option in this section will be correct or incorrect as a matter of logic. (In this respect, this section is similar to a math test.) Thus, if your analysis of a question yields one and only one correct answer, this indicates that you have probably done the problem correctly. If your analysis produces no correct choice, then you have obviously overlooked something. On the other hand, if your analysis produces more than one seemingly correct choice, then you have made an error somewhere.

Now let's look at some sample Analytical Reasoning puzzles. As you read the explanations, think about how the solution process applies.

Linear Ordering

Over the nearly twenty years since Analytical Reasoning was introduced, the most commonly used type of problem has been the linear ordering problem. This kind of problem sets up a situation like the following:

> Seven people standing in a line.
> A dozen students in school in grades 1 through 12.
> A musical scale consisting of six notes.

Now let's solve a typical linear ordering puzzle.

> Six people, J, K, L, M, N, and O, are sitting in one row of six seats at a concert. The seats all face the stage and are numbered, facing the stage from left to right, 1 through 6, consecutively. Exactly one person is sitting in each seat.
>
> J is sitting neither in seat 1 nor in seat 6.
> N is not sitting next to L.
> N is not sitting next to K.
> O is sitting to the immediate left of N.

You would begin your attack by summarizing the initial conditions:

J ≠ (1 or 6)

N ≠ L

N ≠ K

O–N

Are there any further conclusions to be drawn? Yes and no. Yes, it would be possible to determine every possible seating arrangement given these initial conditions, but that obviously would take a lot of time. Therefore, no, there don't appear to be any further obvious conclusions, so go to the questions.

1. Which of the following seating arrangements, given in order from seat 1 to seat 6, is acceptable?
    (A) L, M, K, O, N, J
    (B) L, J, M, O, N, K
    (C) L, N, O, J, M, K
    (D) K, J, L, O, M, N
    (E) M, K, O, N, J, L

Notice that this question provides no additional information, so it must be answerable just on the basis of the initial conditions. When this is the case, use the initial conditions to eliminate choices.

The first condition states that J is seated neither in seat 1 nor in seat 6. Eliminate choice (A) because that arrangement is inconsistent with the first of the initial conditions. The second condition requires that N not sit next to L, and on that score, we can eliminate choice (C). According to the third condition, N does not sit next to K, and we eliminate choice (B). Finally, the fourth condition states that O is seated immediately to N's left, and we can eliminate choice (D). We have eliminated four of the five choices, so choice (E) must be the only arrangement that respects all of the initial conditions.

2. All of the following seating arrangements, given in order from 1 to 6, are acceptable EXCEPT
    (A) M, J, L, K, O, N
    (B) K, J, O, N, M, L
    (C) K, O, N, J, M, L
    (D) L, O, N, J, K, M
    (E) K, J, O, N, L, M

This question is the mirror image of the first, but you should use the same strategy. Each choice is consistent with the requirement that J not be seated in position 1 or 6. And choices (A) through (D) respect the second condition that N not sit next to L. In choice (E), however, N is seated next to L. Choice (E), therefore, must be the choice we are looking for, as it is NOT an acceptable arrangement.

NOTE

Are some games easier than others?
Yes. Generally speaking, linear ordering problems are the easiest. "Hybrid" sets that combine elements from different types are the most difficult. If you can see that a game has so many variables or rules that it is very difficult, save that one for last or skip it entirely.

3. If L is in seat 1 and K is in seat 5, which of the following must be true?
   (A) J is in seat 2.
   (B) M is in seat 3.
   (C) N is in seat 4.
   (D) O is in seat 4.
   (E) M is in seat 6.

This question provides additional information. When this is the case, begin by determining whether or not further conclusions can be drawn.

A diagram would be helpful. The question stem stipulates that L is in seat 1 and K in seat 5:

1	2	3	4	5	6
L				K	

Now return to the initial conditions. The first doesn't help very much, though you can conclude that J is in seat 2, 3, or 4. The second and third conditions by themselves don't operate to place any person on the diagram, but both together tell you that N must be in seat 3:

1	2	3	4	5	6
L		N		K	

And since O must be seated to N's left:

1	2	3	4	5	6
L	O	N		K	

And since J cannot sit in seat 6, you have a complete order:

1	2	3	4	5	6
L	O	N	J	K	M

So the correct answer is (E).

4. If M and O are in seats 2 and 3, respectively, which of the following must be true?
   (A) J is in seat 5.
   (B) K is in seat 3.
   (C) L is in seat 1.
   (D) L is in seat 6.
   (E) N is in seat 5.

Choice (A) is the correct answer. Begin by processing the initial information:

1	2	3	4	5	6
	M	O			

Since O is seated immediately to N's left

1	2	3	4	5	6
	M	O	N		

Since neither K nor L can sit next to N, neither can be in seat 5. This means K and L are in seats 1 and 6, though not necessarily respectively:

1	2	3	4	5	6
K/L	M	O	N		K/L

And, of course, J is in seat 5:

1	2	3	4	5	6
K/L	M	O	N	J	K/L

TIP

There are four—and only four—Analytical Reasoning questions.

1. What must be true as a matter of logic?
2. What must be false as a matter of logic?
3. What can be true or false as a matter of logic?
4. What cannot be true or false as a matter of logic?

5. If K and L are separated by exactly three seats, what is the maximum number of different arrangements in which the six people could be seated?
   - **(A)** 1
   - **(B)** 2
   - **(C)** 3
   - **(D)** 4
   - **(E)** 5

This question really asks "What could be true?" What are the possible arrangements given the additional information?

1	2	3	4	5	6
K				L	
L				K	
	K				L
	L				K

And since N cannot be seated next to either L or K, but O and N must be seated together

1	2	3	4	5	6
K	O	N		L	
L	O	N		K	
	K	O	N		L
	L	O	N		K

And J cannot sit in seats 1 or 6:

1	2	3	4	5	6
K	O	N	J	L	M
L	O	N	J	K	M
M	K	O	N	J	L
M	L	O	N	J	K

So there are only four possible arrangements given the stipulation that K and L are separated by exactly three seats. The correct answer is (D).

6. If K is in seat 2, which of the following is a complete and accurate listing of the seats that O could occupy?

(A) 1

(B) 3

(C) 3 and 4

(D) 1, 3, and 4

(E) 3, 4, and 5

As in the previous question, this question asks about logical possibilities. If K is in seat 2, then there are three possible placements for the O N pair:

1	2	3	4	5	6
	K	O	N		
	K		O	N	
	K			O	N

Are each of these possible? Yes, as you can prove to yourself by completing the three diagrams. So O could be seated in seat 3, 4, or 5. So the correct answer is (E).

Distributed Order

Another common problem type is the distributed order game. In a linear ordering problem, only one individual can occupy a position in the order. In some problem sets, however, a position in the order can accommodate more than one individual.

Six individuals, P, Q, R, S, T, and U, live in a five-story apartment building. Each person lives on one of the floors in the building.

Exactly one of the six lives on the first floor, exactly one of them lives on the fourth floor, and at least two of them live on the second floor.

Of the six people, P lives on the highest floor, and no one lives on the same floor as P.

Q does not live on the first floor or on the second floor.

Neither R nor S lives on the second floor.

When an ordering problem contains distributional restrictions, determine what consequences flow from those restrictions.

The initial conditions establish the following:

5

4 Exactly one

3

2 At least two, not Q, not R, not S

1 Exactly one, not Q

And, of course, P cannot live on floor two. (P must live on either floor four or floor five.) Since it is a requirement of the distribution that at least two persons live on floor two, we can deduce that T and U (and of the six only T and U) live on floor two:

5

4 Exactly one

3

2 Exactly two: T and U

1 Exactly one, not Q

1. All of the following must be true EXCEPT
    (A) exactly two persons live on floor two.
    (B) at most, one person lives on floor five.
    (C) at least one person lives on floor five.
    (D) at least one person lives on floor three.
    (E) P does not live on floor two.

The correct answer is (C). The diagram shows that choice (A) is necessarily true. And it has already been determined that P must be on floor four or five, so choice (E) is necessarily true. As for choice (B), this must be true: either P lives on floor five or P lives on floor four (and none of the other five lives above P). As for choice (D), either P lives on floor five, in which case the distribution of individuals is 1, 2, 1, 1, and 1 (from first to fifth) or P lives on floor four, in which case the distribution is 1, 2, 2, 1, 0 (from first to fifth). Choice (C), however, is not necessarily true, for P could live on the fourth floor.

TIP

The initial conditions are crucial. Be sure to double check your understanding of the initial conditions. A mistake at the very outset could be fatal. And, if you find that you cannot recognize answers to particular questions (the problem set is falling apart for you), go back to the initial conditions. That is probably where you took a misstep.

2. Which of the following could be true?

   (A) Either Q or R lives on the third floor.

   (B) T and U do not live on the second floor.

   (C) T and U live on the third floor.

   (D) T lives on the first floor.

   (E) U lives on the fourth floor.

The analysis above shows that choice (A) could be true. The remaining choices must be false since T and U live on the second floor.

3. If P lives on a floor directly above the floor on which R lives, which of the following must be true?

   (A) R lives on a higher floor than Q.

   (B) R and Q live on the same floor.

   (C) T and U live on different floors.

   (D) Q lives on the third floor.

   (E) S lives on the second floor.

The correct answer is (D). If R is directly beneath P, then since Q cannot be on the first floor, S must be on the first floor. This means there are two possible arrangements:

5	P	
4	R	P
3	Q	R,Q
2	T,U	T,U
1	S	S

But Q is on the third floor in both arrangements.

Selection Sets

Selection sets are also a common game. Selection sets involve choosing a subset of individuals from a larger collection.

> From a group of three faculty members, P, S, and R, four administrators, T, U, V, and W, and three students, X, Y, and Z, the president of a college must choose an ad hoc committee.
>
>   The committee will have exactly seven members.
>
>   There must be at least as many faculty members on the committee as there are students, though the number of students may be zero.
>
>   P and Z cannot both serve on the committee.

If either T or U serves on the committee, the other must also serve on the committee.

If V serves on the committee, then W must serve on the committee.

With a set like this, you begin by summarizing the information using the notational devices suggested above:

Fac. > or = Stu.

$P \neq Z$

$T = U$

$V \rightarrow W$

1. Which of the following must be true of the committee?

   (A) It cannot include more students than administrators.

   (B) It cannot include both T and W.

   (C) It cannot include all three faculty members.

   (D) It must include T and U.

   (E) It must include V and W.

The correct answer is (A). Since P and Z cannot both be on the committee and since there must be at least as many faculty members on the committee as students, the maximum number of students who could serve on the committee is two. And the maximum number of faculty members who could serve is three. This means a minimum of at least two administrators is required. Thus, choice (A) correctly notes that it is impossible to have more students than administrators on the committee. As for choices (B) and (C), the committee of seven could include all three faculty memers and all four administrators with no students. As for choices (D) and (E), a committee might consist of three faculty members and two students plus either T and U or V and W. Thus, it is not the case that either T and U or V and W must be included.

2. If the committee is to include exactly two faculty members and exactly two students, which of the following must be true?

   (A) Z is not included on the committee.

   (B) W is included on the committee.

   (C) X is included on the committee.

   (D) Y is included on the committee.

   (E) S is included on the committee.

The correct answer is (B). If four members of the committee are drawn from faculty and student body, then three must be drawn from the administration. Since T and U cannot be split up, these three must include T and U and either V or W but not both V and W. Since including V requires including W, V cannot be included; therefore, W must be included. As for choice (A), it is possible to include Z by using faculty members S and R (instead of P). As for choices (C) and (D), either X or Y could serve (with Z) or both X

TIP

Use the process of elimination. A question stem that does not include additional information is answerable solely on the basis of the initial conditions. Oftentimes, this type of question can be solved simply by comparing answer choices to the initial conditions. Eliminate those that generate a contradiction, and the last one standing is the right answer.

and Y could serve together. Finally, as for choice (E), any two of the three faculty members could be included on the committee.

3. If both V and Z are chosen for the committee, then which of the following must be true?

(A) Neither X nor W is chosen.

(B) Neither X nor Y is chosen.

(C) Both X and T are chosen.

(D) Both Y and U are chosen.

(E) V and either X or Y is chosen.

The correct answer is (B). If V is chosen, then W must also be chosen. And since Z is chosen, you need at least one faculty member. This gives a total of four people, and you need three more. If you choose another student, this requires another faculty member (for a total of six), but it isn't possible to choose only T or U. Therefore, you cannot include another student. So you must include the other faculty member and T and U. So the committee consists of V, Z, W, S, R, T, and U.

Sleepers

One of the most dangerous things that you can do is to try to guess where the LSAT will be going on the very next administration. As with clothes, Analytical Reasoning puzzles come into fashion and then go out of fashion. There are some that were very popular five years ago but that are not currently the rage. Should you ignore them? Only at your own peril. You never know when they will make a reappearance. These examples that follow fall into this group.

Greater Than, Less Than

Some problem sets rely heavily on the notions of "greater than" and "less than." In the problems, you will often be given a list of people, each of whom has more or less of a certain quality, and asked to determine how each one compares to the others in terms of that quality.

The following information is known about a group of five children:

Alice is taller than Bob and heavier than Charles.

Ed is heavier than both Diane and Alice and is shorter than Bob.

Diane is not taller than Bob and is heavier than Charles.

Charles is taller than Diane and heavier than Bob.

Use relational lines to organize clues for a "greater than/less than" set. In this case, set up two lines, one of which will represent height and the other weight:

Height ⟶   Weight ⟶

ALERT!

Asymmetrical clues.
Clues such as "If P, then Q" and "R unless T" can be deadly traps. Avoid the following:
If P, then Q. Q, therefore P. (No!)
R unless T. T, therefore R. (No!)

Enter each clue on the diagram. First, Alice is taller than Bob and heavier than Charles:

Height ——————— B   A ——————→   Weight ——————— C   A ——————→

Next, Ed is shorter than Bob and heavier than both Diane and Alice:

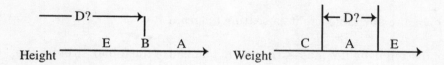

Height ——————— E   B   A ——————→   Weight ——————— C   A   E ——————→

Next, Diane is not taller than Bob and is heavier than Charles:

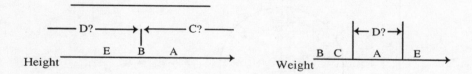

Finally, Charles is taller than Diane and heavier than Bob:

1. Which of the following CANNOT be true?
    (A) Ed is taller than Diane.
    (B) Charles is taller than Alice.
    (C) Bob is taller than Diane.
    (D) Bob weighs more than Diane.
    (E) Ed weighs more than Diane.

Our diagrams show that choices (C) and (E) are true and that choices (A) and (B) might be true. Only choice (D) cannot be true.

2. Which of the following could be true?
    (A) The tallest child is also the heaviest child.
    (B) The shortest child is also the heaviest child.
    (C) The lightest child is also the tallest child.
    (D) Charles is both taller and heavier than Alice.
    (E) Bob is both shorter and lighter than Diane.

The correct answer is (B), and you can read the information directly from the completed diagrams.

Seating Arrangements

In some problem sets, individuals are seated around a circular table.

> Eight people, F, G, H, J, K, L, M, and N, are seated in eight equally spaced chairs around a circular table.
>
> > K is sitting directly opposite M.
> >
> > M is sitting immediately to F's left.
> >
> > G is sitting next to L.
> >
> > H is sitting opposite J.

For a set based on a circular table, create a seating diagram.

The seats are not distinguishable (that is, there is not a head of the table), so enter the first clue:

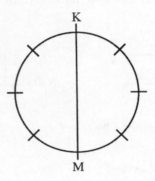

And the second clue:

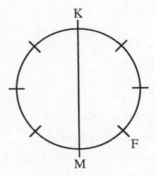

We can't enter the rest of the information without doing a little thinking. H and J are sitting opposite each other, which suggests there are the following possibilities:

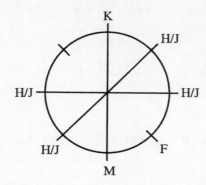

But if either H or J is seated next to F, it isn't possible to place L and G together. Therefore, either H or J is seated next to M:

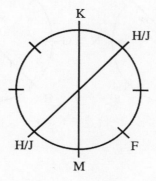

And finally:

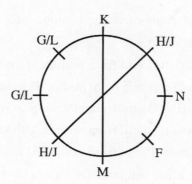

1. Which of the following must be true?

   (A) N is seated next to F.

   (B) N is seated next to H.

   (C) N is seated across from G.

   (D) F is seated across from L.

   (E) G is seated across from F.

As the diagram shows, only choice (A) makes a necessarily true statement.

2. Only one seating arrangement is possible under which of the following conditions?

    (A) G is seated next to J.

    (B) H is seated next to N.

    (C) G is seated opposite N.

    (D) G is seated opposite F.

    (E) H is seated next to K.

The correct answer is (A). If G is next to J, L is next to K, and H is next to N. So only one order is possible.

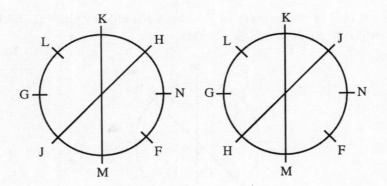

Networks

Some problem sets involve spatial or temporal connections between individuals.

> In the subway system of a certain city, passengers can go as follows:
>
> From station P to station Q.
>
> From station Q to station R and from station Q to station S.
>
> From station R to station S and from station R to station T.
>
> From station S to station U and from station S to station P.
>
> From station T to station U and from station T to station R.
>
> From station U to station P and from station U to station S.
>
> A passenger at one station can transfer for another station.

The correct approach to any network problem is to sketch the network.

From station P to station Q.

$$P \longrightarrow Q$$

From station Q to station R and from station Q to station S.

$$P \longrightarrow Q \begin{array}{c} \nearrow R \\ \searrow S \end{array}$$

From station R to station S and from station R to station T.

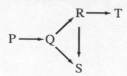

From station S to station U and from station S to station P.

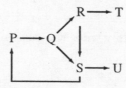

From station T to station U and from station T to station R.

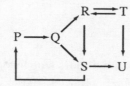

From station U to station P and from station U to station S

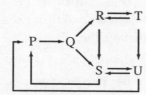

1. A passenger at station T who wishes to travel to station Q must pass through a minimum of how many other stations before finally arriving at Q?

(A) 1

(B) 2

(C) 3

(D) 4

(E) 5

Consult the network diagram. The shortest route is U to P and then on to Q. Therefore, **The correct answer is choice (B).**

2. A passenger at station U who wishes to travel through the system and return to station U before passing through any other subway station twice can choose from how many different routes?

    (A) 2

    (B) 3

    (C) 4

    (D) 5

    (E) 6

The correct answer is (C). Simply trace the possibilities with your finger:

U to P to Q to S to U

U to P to Q to R to S to U

U to P to Q to R to T to U

U to S to P to Q to R to T to U

Matrix Problems

Sometimes a problem will refer to individuals who have or lack certain characteristics, and some questions may ask which characteristics are in turn shared by which individuals.

Five people, George, Howard, Ingrid, Jean, and Kathy, work in a factory. On any given shift, a person can be assigned to one of five jobs: mechanic, truck driver, packer, weigher, or dispatcher.

George can function as mechanic, packer, or weigher.

Howard can function as either packer or weigher.

Ingrid can function as mechanic, truck driver, or dispatcher.

Jean can function as truck driver or dispatcher.

Kathy can function as truck driver or weigher.

The five workers can fill only these jobs, and only these five workers can fill these jobs.

For a problem set in which individuals do or do not share certain characteristics (and those characteristics are or are not shared by the individuals), use a matrix or table.

	M	TD	P	W	D
G					
H					
I					
J					
K					

George can function as mechanic, packer, or weigher.

	M	TD	P	W	D
G	✔		✔	✔	
H					
I					
J					
K					

Howard can function as either packer or weigher.

	M	TD	P	W	D
G	✔		✔	✔	
H			✔	✔	
I					
J					
K					

Ingrid can function as mechanic, truck driver, or dispatcher.

	M	TD	P	W	D
G	✓		✓	✓	
H			✓	✓	
I	✓	✓			✓
J					
K					

Jean can function as truck driver or dispatcher.

	M	TD	P	W	D
G	✓		✓	✓	
H			✓	✓	
I	✓	✓			✓
J		✓			✓
K					

Kathy can function as truck driver or weigher.

	M	TD	P	W	D
G	✓		✓	✓	
H			✓	✓	
I	✓	✓			✓
J		✓			✓
K		✓		✓	

1. If Jean is NOT assigned to function as dispatcher, all of the following must be true EXCEPT

   (A) George is the mechanic.

   (B) Howard is the dispatcher.

   (C) the truck driver is Jean.

   (D) the packer is Howard.

   (E) the weigher is Kathy.

The correct answer is (B). Ingrid, now Howard, would be the dispatcher. Just enter the new information into the table, and use the grid to draw further conclusions.

2. If George is assigned as mechanic, which of the following must be true?

    (A) Howard is assigned as packer.

    (B) Kathy is assigned as weigher.

    (C) Ingrid is assigned as truck driver.

    (D) Jean is assigned as dispatcher.

    (E) Howard is assigned as weigher.

The correct answer is (A). If George is assigned as mechanic, then he is not available to be packer or weigher. There is only one other person who can be the packer, and that is Howard.

Family Relationships

Barbara, an only child, is married, and she and her husband have two children, Ned and Sally.

> Ned is Paula's nephew by blood and Victor's grandson.
>
> Victor and his wife had only two children, Frank and his sister, plus four grandchildren, two boys and two girls.
>
> Wilma is Sally's grandmother.

Use the information to create a family tree.

Barbara, an only child, is married, and she and her husband have two children, Ned and Sally:

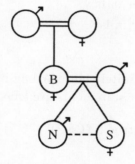

Ned is Paula's nephew by blood and Victor's grandson.

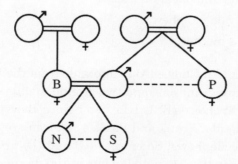

(Since Barbara is an only child, an aunt could be related by blood only by being Ned's father's sister. We don't know, however, whether Victor is Ned's paternal or maternal grandfather.)

Victor and his wife had only two children, Frank and his sister, plus four grandchildren, two boys and two girls.

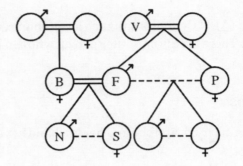

(Since Victor had two children, he could not have been Barbara's father because Barbara is an only child. So in order to be Ned's grandfather, Victor must be Ned's father's father.) It is not possible to enter the last piece of information for it is not clear whether Wilma is Barbara's mother or the mother of Frank and Paula.

1. All of the following must be true EXCEPT
    (A) Wilma is Victor's wife.
    (B) Victor is Sally's grandfather.
    (C) Victor is Barbara's father-in-law.
    (D) Paula is Barbara's sister-in-law.
    (E) Frank is Sally's father.

As we just noted, we cannot definitely place Wilma in the family tree. The diagram, however, confirms that the other statements are true. **The correct answer is (A).**

2. All of the following must be true EXCEPT
    (A) Sally is Ned's sister.
    (B) Ned has exactly two cousins.
    (C) Paula has one son and one daughter.
    (D) Barbara has only one nephew.
    (E) Wilma is Frank's mother.

The correct answer is (A). Choice (A) is inferable from the first bit of information. Then, since Victor has two grandsons and two granddaughters, Paula must have one son and one daughter, so choice (B) is true. And since Barbara has no siblings and Frank's only sibling is Paula, Frank and Paula's children are Ned's only cousins and Barbara's only nieces or nephews. So choices (C) and (D) are also true. Choice (E), however, is not necessarily true, as noted in our initial discussion of the set.

WHAT SMART TEST-TAKERS KNOW

Accept the situation at face value.

Most of the situations described by the initial conditions are common ones with which you should be familiar.

> Six people, J, K, L, M, N, and O, are standing in a single file line at a movie theater.
>
> Seven corporations, H, I, J, K, L, M, and N, have offices on four floors in the same building.
>
> Eight office workers, M, N, O, P, Q, R, S, and T, are deciding in which of three restaurants—X, Y, or Z—to eat lunch.

One reason for using familiar situations is that there is less potential for misunderstanding because there is much information implicit in a situation such as a single-file line: Each person is a separate person, each letter designates a different individual, one individual is immediately ahead of or behind another individual, and so on. Since the situations are selected for this feature, you should be careful not to "fight" with the setup. For example, there is no point in arguing that J could be standing on L's shoulders. The test writers will add an explicit clarifying note if there is any danger of a legitimate misunderstanding, e.g., each corporation has its own office.

Read the clues carefully.

Although you must accept the general situation with a fairly uncritical reading, you must be very careful in reading the particular information given about the individuals. Pay particular attention to words such as the following:

> *only, exactly, never, always, must be/can be/cannot be, some, all, no, none, entire, each, every, except, but, unless, if, more/less, before/after, immediately (before, after, etc.), possible/impossible, different/same, at least, at most.*

Be careful of asymmetrical clues.

You should be especially careful not to misinterpret conditions that are asymmetrical, e.g., if P goes on the trip, Q must also go; or S cannot eat at X restaurant unless T also eats there. In both of these examples, the dependency operates in only one direction. In the first, P depends on Q but not vice versa (Q can go on the trip without P). Similarly, in the second, S depends on T but not vice versa (S cannot eat at X restaurant without T, but T can eat there without S).

The situation will be fluid.

Often, it will be possible to draw some further inference from the initial conditions, but rarely will it be possible to determine the entire situation using just the information in the initial conditions. For example, a problem set might tell you that X must be standing third in line and that Z is two positions behind X. From this, you can deduce that Z is standing fifth in line. But the initial conditions may not fix the position of any other person in the line.

The open-ended nature of Analytical Reasoning problems will probably be very annoying. Because you will not be able to deduce a definite sequence or some similar conclusions, you will feel that you have overlooked something in the initial conditions. You haven't. The fluidity of the situation is part of the test design.

It's all a matter of logic.

Since the problem sets in this section are logical puzzles, the correct answers are determined by logical inference. And the logical status of a statement must fall into one of three categories:

1 The statement is logically deducible from the information given.

2 The statement is logically inconsistent with (contradicts) the information given.

3 The statement is neither logically deducible from the information given nor logically inconsistent with it.

NOTE

Analytical Reasoning is cut and dried.

Unlike Logical Reasoning, where there could be some argument over answers, Analytical Reasoning is cut and dried. An argument such as

If P, then Q

P

Therefore, Q

is true as a matter of logic.

The questions that can be asked fall into one of the following categories:

Which of the following must be true?

All of the following must be true EXCEPT

Which of the following could be true?

Which of the following CANNOT be true?

The logical status of each choice dictates whether it is correct or incorrect:

- The correct answer to a question asking "Which must be true?" is a statement that is logically deducible from the information given.

- The wrong answers to such a question can be statements that are inconsistent with the given information or statements that are not deducible from the information given.

- The correct answer to a question asking "All must be true EXCEPT" is either a statement that is logically inconsistent with the information given or a statement that is not deducible from the information given.

- The wrong answers to this type of question are statements that can be logically deduced from the information given.

- The correct answer to a question asking "Which can be true?" is a statement that is neither deducible from nor inconsistent with the information given.

- The correct answer to a question asking "All can be true EXCEPT" is a statement that is logically inconsistent with the information given.

Although wording may differ from problem set to problem set, every question will fall into one of these four categories. For example, a question that asks this belongs in the first category:

> If the traveler visits Paris on Wednesday, on which day must she visit Rome?

It will be possible to deduce from the information given on which day she must visit Rome. But a question that asks this belongs in the fourth category:

> If the traveler visits Paris on Wednesday, then she could visit all of the following cities on Friday EXCEPT

The correct answer will generate a logical contradiction with the given information: It will be logically impossible to visit that city on Friday. And a question that asks this belongs in the third category:

> Which of the following is a complete and accurate listing of the cities that the traveler could visit on Thursday?

The correct choice will enumerate all of the logical possibilities.

WHAT THE SMARTEST TEST-TAKERS KNOW

Breaking News on "Puzzles"

As a rule, it is probably not a good idea to try to work out all of the possibilities for an Analytical Reasoning set in order to create a master list to answer questions—for two reasons.

One, you're likely to find that there are simply too many possibilities to keep track of. Consider a problem set that requires you to put individuals into an order:

> Seven people—J, K, L, M, N, O, and P—are each going to do a solo act. The acts will follow one behind the other, and each person will perform exactly once.

As you can guess, there will probably be some additional restrictions on the order, and the questions will ask about permissible or impermissible sequences.

Now it would be possible to take the time to sketch all of the possibilities, but there are a lot of them. How many? 7 x 6 x 5 x 4 x 3 x 2 x 1—too many given the time limit.

Two, most of the possible sequences will not be relevant to the questions asked. Only a handful will actual play a role in problem solving.

So, as a rule, it's better to let the question stems be your guide. They will provide information to be used for answering questions about particular cases and guide you to the relevant possibilities.

As with every rule, however, there is an exception. And this exception has appeared on some recent test forms. If a sequencing problem has six or fewer constants to fill six or fewer positions, it may be more efficient to work out all possibilities before trying the questions.

The basis for this recommendation is mathematical and is illustrated by the following:

Five dogs—Farley, Gunther, Hans, Jerry, and Kato—will appear in a dog show. During the show, each dog will be shown exactly once, one dog at a time.

In this situation, you have 5 x 4 x 3 x 2 x 1 or 120 possibilities. That is still too many to work out comfortably within the time given; but if we add another condition:

Farley will be shown fourth.

Then we're left with only 24 possibilities, and those can be written out as follows:

	1st	2nd	3rd	4th	5th
1	G	H	J	F	K
2	G	H	K	F	J
3	G	J	H	F	K
4	G	K	H	F	J
5	G	J	K	F	H
6	G	K	J	F	H
7	H	G	J	F	K
8	H	G	K	F	J
9	J	G	H	F	K
10	K	G	H	F	J
11	J	G	K	F	H
12	K	G	J	F	H
13	H	J	G	F	K
14	H	K	G	F	J
15	J	H	G	F	K
16	K	H	G	F	J
17	J	K	G	F	H
18	K	J	G	F	H
19	H	J	K	F	G
20	H	K	J	F	G
21	J	H	K	F	G
22	K	H	J	F	G
23	J	K	H	F	G
24	K	J	H	F	G

You should be able to see how this table systematically works out all of the variations on the theme, and it does contain the answer to every possible question that could be asked about the dog show.

Of course, even 24 possibilities is a lot, but investing 3 to 4 minutes in creating the table is worthwhile because the questions can be answered very quickly:

> If Gunter is shown third, which of the following is a complete and accurate list of the positions in which Jerry could be shown if Jerry is shown after Kato?
>
> **(A)** 2
>
> **(B)** 2,3
>
> **(C)** 2,5
>
> **(D)** 2,6
>
> **(E)** 2,3,6

The correct answer is (D), as lines 14, 16, and 18 show.

And the number of possibilities is likely to be even smaller because there will probably be additional conditions such as "Hans cannot be shown first."

In light of this development, you might consider using the following strategy:

STEP ONE: Look at all four or five sets to determine whether there is a simple linear sequencing problem.

STEP TWO: If there is a simple linear sequencing set, ask:

> Does it have six or fewer positions?
>
> Does it have six or fewer individuals?
>
> Does each individual occupy exactly one position?

If the answers to these questions are "yes," then it is a simple sequencing set:

STEP THREE: WORK OUT ALL OF THE POSSIBILITIES BEFORE TRYING THE QUESTIONS.

Here's how the strategy would work:

Questions 1–4

Six athletes—two from Joplin High School, two from Kline High School, and two from Lorentz High School—run a series of races in which they finish first through last with no ties.

> No runner finishes either directly in front of or directly behind the other runner from the same high school.
>
> A runner from Joplin always finishes either first or second.
>
> Neither of the runners from Kline ever finishes last.
>
> Neither of the runners from Lorentz ever finishes third.

1. If the second and fourth place finishers in a race are from the same high school, then which of the following statements must be true?

   (A) A runner from Lorentz finishes first.

   (B) A runner from Joplin finishes second.

   (C) A runner from Lorentz finishes fourth.

   (D) A runner from Kline finishes fifth.

   (E) A runner from Joplin finishes sixth.

2. Both runners from the same high school CANNOT finish

   (A) first and third

   (B) first and fourth

   (C) second and fourth

   (D) second and sixth

   (E) third and sixth

3. If a runner from Joplin finishes third, which of the following must be true?

   (A) A runner from Joplin finishes first.

   (B) A runner from Lorentz finishes second.

   (C) A runner from Kline finishes fourth.

   (D) A runner from Lorentz finishes fifth.

   (E) A runner from Kline finishes sixth.

4. Which of the following statements must be false?

   (A) A runner from Lorentz finishes first.

   (B) A runner from Kline finishes first.

   (C) A runner from Joplin finishes second.

   (D) A runner from Kline finishes third.

   (E) A runner from Lorentz finishes fifth.

Here we have six runners, six positions, and no ties. So let's try systematically working out all of the possibilities:

A runner from Joplin always finishes first or second, and the two Joplin runners do not finish consecutively:

1st	2nd	3rd	4th	5th	6th
J		J			
J			J		
J				J	
J					J
	J		J		
	J			J	
	J				J

Neither runner from Kline finishes last, and neither runner from Lorentz finishes third:

1st	2nd	3rd	4th	5th	6th
J		J			-K
J		-L	J		-K
J		-L		J	-K
J		-L			J
	J	-L	J		-K
	J	-L		J	-K
	J	-L			J

So:

1st	2nd	3rd	4th	5th	6th
J		J			L
J	L	K	J		L
J		K		J	L
J		K			J
	J	K	J		L
	J	K		J	L
	J	K			J

Further:

1st	2nd	3rd	4th	5th	6th
J	K	J	L	K	L
J	L	K	J	K	L
J		K		J	L*
J	L	K	L	K	J
L	J	K	J	K	L
K	J	K	L	J	L
L	J	K	L	K	J

*Not possible.

Now we can turn to the answers to the questions.

1. **The correct answer is (D).** Lines 4 and 5 show orders in which runners from the same high school finish second and fourth, and in both a K appears in position 5.

2. **The correct answer is (E).** As the table shows, there is no sequence in which the third and sixth positions have the same designation.

3. **The correct answer is (A).** This is the sequence described by line 1, and position 1 is designated J.

4. **The correct answer is (E).** As the diagram shows, position 5 cannot be filled by an L.

EXERCISES: ANALYTICAL REASONING

Exercise 1

20 Questions • Time—30 Minutes

Directions: Each group of questions is based on a set of propositions or conditions. Drawing a rough picture or diagram may help in answering some of the questions. Choose the best answer for each question and circle the letter of your choice.

Questions 1–7

A candidate for public office plans to visit each of six cities—J, K, L, M, N, and O—exactly once during her campaign. Her aides are setting up the candidate's schedule according to the following restrictions:

> The candidate can visit M only after she has visited both L and N.
>
> The candidate cannot visit N before J.
>
> The second city visited by the candidate must be K.

1. Which of the following could be the order in which the candidate visits the six cities?

   (A) J, K, N, L, O, M
   (B) K, J, L, N, M, O
   (C) O, K, M, L, J, N
   (D) M, K, N, J, L, O
   (E) J, K, L, M, N, O

2. Which of the following must be true of the candidate's campaign schedule?

   (A) She visits J before L.
   (B) She visits K before M.
   (C) She visits K before J.
   (D) She visits M before J.
   (E) She visits N before L.

3. If the candidate visits O first, which of the following is a complete and accurate listing of the cities that she could visit third?

   (A) J
   (B) L
   (C) J, L
   (D) J, M
   (E) M, L

4. If the candidate visits J immediately after O and immediately before N, then she must visit L

   (A) first.
   (B) third.
   (C) fourth.
   (D) fifth.
   (E) sixth.

5. Which of the following could be true of the candidate's schedule?

   (A) She visits J first.
   (B) She visits K first.
   (C) She visits L sixth.
   (D) She visits M fourth.
   (E) She visits N sixth.

6. The candidate could visit any of the following immediately after K EXCEPT

   (A) J.

   (B) L.

   (C) M.

   (D) N.

   (E) O.

7. If the candidate visits O last, which of the following could be the first and third cities on her schedule, respectively?

   (A) J and L

   (B) J and O

   (C) L and N

   (D) L and O

   (E) N and J

Questions 8–13

At a certain restaurant, above the kitchen door there are four small lights, arranged side by side, and numbered consecutively, left to right, from one to four. The lights are used to signal waiters when orders are ready. On a certain shift, there are exactly five waiters—David, Ed, Flint, Guy, and Hank.

> To signal David, all four lights are illuminated.
>
> To signal Ed, only lights one and two are illuminated.
>
> To signal Flint, only light one is illuminated.
>
> To signal Guy, only lights two, three, and four are illuminated.
>
> To signal Hank, only lights three and four are illuminated.

8. If lights two and three are both off, then the waiter signaled is

   (A) David.

   (B) Ed.

   (C) Flint.

   (D) Guy.

   (E) Hank.

9. If lights three and four are illuminated, then which of the following is a complete and accurate listing of the waiters whose signals might be displayed?

   (A) David

   (B) Guy

   (C) David and Guy

   (D) Guy and Hank

   (E) David, Guy, and Hank

10. If light one is not illuminated, then which of the following is a complete and accurate listing of the waiters whose signals might be displayed?

    (A) Ed

    (B) Guy

    (C) Hank

    (D) Guy and Hank

    (E) Hank, Guy, and Ed

11. If light three is on and light two is off, then the waiter signaled is

    (A) David.

    (B) Ed.

    (C) Flint.

    (D) Guy.

    (E) Hank.

12. If one of the five waiters is being signaled, the lights in which of the following pairs could NOT both be off?

    (A) One and two

    (B) One and three

    (C) Two and three

    (D) Two and four

    (E) Three and four

13. If light four is on, then which of the following must be true?

    (A) Light one is on.

    (B) Light two is not on.

    (C) If light one is on, David is signaled.

    (D) If light two is not on, Flint is signaled.

    (E) If light three is not on, Ed is signaled.

Questions 14–20

A lawyer must schedule appointments with eight clients—F, G, H, I, J, K, L, and M—during one week, Monday through Friday. She must schedule two appointments for Monday, Tuesday, and Wednesday and one each for Thursday and Friday.

> She must see H on Thursday.
>
> She must see G on a day before the day on which she sees I.
>
> She must see J on a day before the day on which she sees L.
>
> She must see F on a day before the day on which she sees L.
>
> She must see K and F on the same day.

14. Which of the following is an acceptable schedule for the week's appointments?

	Mon.	Tues.	Wed.	Thurs.	Fri.
(A)	G,M	I,L	K,F	H	J
(B)	G,M	I,J	K,F	H	L
(C)	G,I	M,L	J	H	K,F
(D)	L,G	I,J	K,M	H	F
(E)	G,L	M,K	F	H,J	I

15. Which of the following CANNOT be true?

    (A) She sees M on Monday.

    (B) She sees K on Tuesday.

    (C) She sees L on Tuesday.

    (D) She sees I on Wednesday.

    (E) She sees M on Friday.

16. Which of the following is a complete and accurate listing of the clients the lawyer could see on Friday?

    (A) I, J

    (B) I, M

    (C) L, M

    (D) I, L, M

    (E) M, L, G

17. If the lawyer sees I on Tuesday, then which of the following must be true?

    (A) She sees J on Monday.

    (B) She sees M on Tuesday.

    (C) She sees K on Tuesday.

    (D) She sees M on Friday.

    (E) She sees L on Friday.

18. If the lawyer sees K on Wednesday, all of the following must be true EXCEPT

    (A) she sees I on Tuesday.

    (B) she sees L on Friday.

    (C) she sees M on Monday.

    (D) she sees G on Monday.

    (E) she sees F on Wednesday.

19. If the lawyer sees I and L on the same day, which of the following is a complete and accurate listing of the days on which she could see them?

    (A) Monday

    (B) Tuesday

    (C) Wednesday

    (D) Monday and Wednesday

    (E) Tuesday and Wednesday

20. Which of the following, if true, provides sufficient additional information to determine on which day each client will have his appointment?

    (A) M's appointment is scheduled for Monday.

    (B) G's appointment is scheduled for Monday.

    (C) G's appointment is scheduled for Tuesday.

    (D) K's appointment is two days before G's.

    (E) G's appointment is two days before I's.

Exercise 2

13 Questions • Time—20 Minutes

Directions: Each group of questions is based on a set of propositions or conditions. Drawing a rough picture or diagram may help in answering some of the questions. Choose the best answer for each question and circle the letter of your choice.

Questions 1–7

A student planning his curriculum for the upcoming semester must enroll in three courses. The available courses fall into one of five general areas: math, English, social studies, science, and fine arts.

The student must take courses from at least two different areas.

If he takes a fine arts course, he cannot take an English course.

If he takes a science course, he must take a math course; and if he takes a math course, he must take a science course.

He can take a social studies course only if he takes a fine arts course.

1. Which of the following is an acceptable schedule of courses?

   (A) One science course, one English course, and one fine arts course

   (B) One math course, one science course, and one social studies course

   (C) One math course, one social studies course, and one fine arts course

   (D) One English course, one social studies course, and one fine arts course

   (E) One math course, one science course, and one fine arts course

2. Which of the following is NOT an acceptable schedule?

   (A) Two math courses and one science course

   (B) Two science courses and one math course

   (C) Two fine arts courses and one math course

   (D) Two social studies courses and one fine arts course

   (E) One social studies course and two fine arts courses

3. Which of the following courses, when taken with one course in social studies, is an acceptable schedule?

   (A) One course in math and one in science

   (B) One course in fine arts and one course in English

   (C) Two courses in fine arts

   (D) Two courses in math

   (E) Two courses in English

4. If the student wishes to take a course in math and a course in English, then he must select his third course in the area of

   (A) English.

   (B) fine arts.

   (C) math.

   (D) science.

   (E) social studies.

5. Which of the following pairs of courses CANNOT be combined in an acceptable schedule?

    (A) A course in math and a course in fine arts

    (B) A course in science and a course in fine arts

    (C) A course in math and a course in English

    (D) A course in social studies and a course in science

    (E) A course in science and a course in English

6. If the student wishes to take a course in science, then which of the following pairs of courses would complete an acceptable schedule?

    (A) Two math courses

    (B) Two science courses

    (C) Two English courses

    (D) One science course and one English course

    (E) One math course and one social studies course

7. An acceptable schedule CANNOT include two courses in

    (A) English.

    (B) fine arts.

    (C) math.

    (D) science.

    (E) social studies.

Questions 8–13

A certain musical scale consists of exactly six notes: F, G, H, I, J, and K. The notes are arranged from lowest (the first note of the scale) to highest (the sixth note of the scale). Each note appears once and only once in the scale, and the intervals between the notes are all equal.

J is lower than K.

G is higher than F.

I is somewhere between F and G.

H is the highest note of the scale.

8. Which of the following CANNOT be true of the scale?

    (A) G is the second note.

    (B) G is the third note.

    (C) I is the second note.

    (D) I is the third note.

    (E) I is the fourth note.

9. If J is the fourth note of the scale, which of the following must be true?

    (A) F is the third note.

    (B) F is the fifth note.

    (C) I is the fourth note.

    (D) I is the second note.

    (E) G is the first note.

10. If exactly two notes separate F and I, then which of the following must be true?

    (A) F is the lowest note.

    (B) K is the fifth note.

    (C) K is higher than I.

    (D) J is somewhere between G and I.

    (E) K and J are separated by exactly one note.

11. If J is the second note, then which of the following is a complete and accurate listing of the notes that G and I, respectively, could be?

    (A) 4 and 3

    (B) 5 and 3

    (C) 5 and 4

    (D) 5 and 3 or 4 and 5

    (E) 4 and 3, 5 and 3, or 5 and 4

12. If F and I are separated by exactly one note, which of the following must be true?

    (A) G is note 4.

    (B) K is note 5.

    (C) J is lower than I.

    (D) I is lower than K.

    (E) J is between F and I.

13. If J is lower than F, then the total number of different possible orderings of the six notes, from lowest to highest, is

    (A) 1

    (B) 2

    (C) 3

    (D) 4

    (E) 5

ANSWER KEY AND EXPLANATIONS

Exercise 1

1.	A	5.	A	9.	E	13.	C	17.	E
2.	B	6.	C	10.	D	14.	B	18.	C
3.	C	7.	A	11.	E	15.	C	19.	C
4.	A	8.	C	12.	B	16.	D	20.	D

Questions 1–7

Here we have a common ordering set. Begin by summarizing the information:

$$(L + N) < M$$
$$J < N$$
$$K = 2$$

> **Note:** Since the candidate cannot visit two cities simultaneously, the condition "The candidate cannot visit N before J" is equivalent to "She must visit J before N."

1. **The correct answer is (A).** This question supplies no additional information, so just take each condition and apply it to the answer choices, eliminating those that fail to comply with any condition. The first condition requires that L and N come before M. Using this condition, we eliminate choices (C) and (E). The second condition states that J must come before N, and we eliminate choice (D). The third condition requires that K be the second city, so we eliminate choice (B). This leaves us with choice (A); and choice (A), which respects all three conditions, is a possible order.

2. **The correct answer is (B).** M must be visited after both L and N, so given that K is visited second, M could not possibly be visited earlier than fourth, which means that K comes before M. So choice (B) is correct. In fact, given that J comes

before N, and N comes before M, M must also come later than J. So M cannot be visited until L, N, J, and K have been visited, which means M is either fifth or sixth. As just noted, J must come before M, so choice (D) is necessarily false. The other three responses describe possible schedules only,

1	2	3	4	5	6
J	K	N	L	M	O

which shows that choices (A), (C), and (E) are possible. But

1	2	3	4	5	6
O	K	L	J	N	M

shows that choices (A), (C), and (E) are not necessarily true.

3. **The correct answer is (C).** Begin by entering the additional information on a diagram:

1	2	3	4	5	6
O	K				

Next, we reason that J, N, and L must all come before M, which means that M comes last:

1	2	3	4	5	6
O	K	J	N	L	M
O	K	J	L	N	M
O	K	L	J	N	M

So either J or L could be third.

4. **The correct answer is (A).** This question stipulates an order for three of the cities: O, J, and N. Given that J and N must come before M, this means that the order must be

1	2	3	4	5	6
	K	O	J	N	M

That means that L must be visited first:

1	2	3	4	5	6
L	K	O	J	N	M

5. **The correct answer is (A).** This question is a good occasion to talk about test-taking strategy. A question of this form has this peculiarity: A choice like choice (A) may not contradict any single initial condition and may still be wrong because of the way the initial conditions work together. The only way to exclude this possibility is to devise a complete order, part of which is the segment you want to test—a time-consuming process. What should you do?

The solution to the dilemma is this: Make a first run through the choices, testing them by each single initial statement. If you can eliminate all but one, then you have your correct answer. If more than one choice remains, then the key to the question is some interaction among the initial conditions, e.g., a further inference that you have overlooked. Then, and only then, try working up an entire order to test the remaining choices.

Here we are fortunate because we can find the correct choice quickly:

(A) Doesn't contradict any single condition, so go to the next choice.

(B) No. (K must be second.)

(C) No. (L must come before M.)

(D) No. (M must come after J, L, and N and therefore K as well. So M cannot be visited earlier than fifth.)

(E) No. (N must come before M, so N cannot be last.)

Thus, choice (A) must be the correct choice, so we don't have to try to construct the entire order using choice (A).

Just for reasons of completeness of explanation, however, here is a schedule in which J is the first city:

1	2	3	4	5	6
J	K	L	N	M	O

6. **The correct answer is (C).** As just noted, M cannot be earlier than fifth, so M could not immediately follow K. That the others could follow K is shown by the following schedules:

	1	2	3	4	5	6
(A)	O	L	J	J	N	M
(B)	J	K	L	N	M	O
(D)	J	K	N	L	M	O
(E)	J	K	O	N	L	M

7. **The correct answer is (A).** Start by entering the additional information on a diagram:

1	2	3	4	5	6
	K				O

Next, we have already determined that M cannot be earlier than fifth:

1	2	3	4	5	6
J	K	N	L	M	O
J	K	L	N	M	O
L	K	J	N	M	O

(A) describes the second of these possibilities. The other choices do not describe one of the three possible schedules.

Questions 8–13

This is a "characteristics" set; each waiter has a characteristic signal. Summarize the information using a table:

Lights	1	2	3	4
David	ON	ON	ON	ON
Ed	ON	ON		
Flint	ON			
Guy		ON	ON	ON
Hank			ON	ON

Whatever further conclusions you might need are already implicitly contained in the table, so go directly to the questions.

8. **The correct answer is (C).** Flint is the only waiter whose signal lights two and three are both off. For every other waiter, either two or three or both are on.

9. **The correct answer is (E).** As the table shows, if lights three and four are both on, the signal might be for David (all four on), Guy (two, three, and four on), or Hank (three and four on).

10. **The correct answer is (D).** As the table shows, if light one is off, then the signal might be for either Guy or Hank. It could not be for David, Ed, or Flint, since their signals include an illuminated light one.

11. **The correct answer is (E).** As the table shows, there are three waiters whose signals include light three: David, Guy, and Hank. For David and Guy, however, light two must be on; for Guy, it must be off. Therefore, if light three is on and light two is off, then Guy is the waiter signaled.

12. **The correct answer is (B).** Consult the table:

    (A) Lights one and two will be off if Hank is signaled.

    (B) There is no signal for which both one and three are off.

    (C) Lights two and three will be off if Flint is signaled.

    (D) Lights two and four will be off if Flint is signaled.

    (E) Lights three and four will be off if either Ed or Flint is signaled.

13. **The correct answer is (C).** As the table clearly shows, neither choice (A) nor choice (B) is necessarily true. Choice (C), however, is necessarily true, as the table shows. If four is on, then the signal might be for David, Guy, or Hank; but if one is also on, then the signal can only be for David. As for choice (D), if four is on and two is not, then it is Hank who is signaled—not Flint. As for choice (E), none of the five signals includes light four on and light three off.

Questions 14–20

This is a distributed order set, as opposed to a linear ordering set. Here, more than one individual can be placed in a given position (more than one appointment can be scheduled for certain days).

Start by summarizing the information:

H = Th.

G < I

(J + F) < L

K = F

You might notice that there is one further conclusion to be drawn. Since K and F must be scheduled for the same day and since F must come before L, we can infer that K also comes before L. Aside from that, there do not appear to be any further important inferences to be drawn, so we go to the questions.

14. **The correct answer is (B).** Since the question supplies no additional information, we just apply each condition to the answer choices, eliminating those that fail to respect one or more conditions.

The first condition states that there are two appointments for Monday, Tuesday, and Wednesday and one appointment on the other two days. On this basis, we eliminate choices (C) and (E) because it is not possible to schedule two appointments on Thursday or Friday. The second condition states that H must be seen on Thursday, and our remaining choices reflect that. Then, the next condition states that G must come on a day before that on which I has his appointment, and our remaining choices respect this condition. Next, the fourth condition states that J and F must both come before L, so we eliminate choices (A) and (D). This leaves us with choice (B) as the correct choice, and you might want quickly to confirm that choice (B) does respect that final condition: K and F are both scheduled for the same day.

15. **The correct answer is (C).** This question allows us to talk about strategy. One way of proving that a particular partial order is possible is to construct an example of a permissible order using that part. Thus, the following example proves that choice (A) is a possible order (and therefore not the correct answer to this question):

M	TU	W	TH	F
M	K	L	H	I
J	F	G		

The difficulty with this approach is that constructing an example for each choice is time-consuming. Instead of trying to construct an entire order for each choice, a better strategy is to look for an answer choice that is not possible for a specific reason, e.g., because X cannot follow Y or because Z must come before W. Here is how this strategy would apply to this question.

(A) is not likely to be correct because M is not under any specific restriction; thus, M could go almost anywhere. As for choice (B), though K is under a certain restriction, the import of that restriction is that K come earlier in the week—as choice (B) suggests. So choice (B) is probably not the correct choice. Now look at choice (C). L is under the restriction that he be scheduled later than both J and F and (as we learned above) later than K as well. This "pushes" L toward the latter part of the week. This choice, however, has L early in the week. So this choice merits some study.

The way to determine whether it is possible for L to have an appointment on Tuesday is to assume that he can and see whether that assumption is consistent with the initial conditions. If L is scheduled for Tuesday, then both J and F must be scheduled for Monday. But that can't be, as K would also have to be scheduled for Monday. This demonstrates that choice (C) cannot be true.

As for choices (D) and (E), you can construct schedules that show that they are all possible.

16. **The correct answer is (D).** One way of attacking this question would be to try to construct all of the possibilities for Friday. For example, you would reason that K cannot be seen on Friday because K must be seen on the same day as F (and only one appointment is available on Friday). The difficulty with this "direct" approach is that you must do a lot of "grinding." Here it is better to use an "indirect" approach. Look at the choices.

Since one of the choices is correct, the test writer has already done the "grinding" to find all of the possibilities for Friday. You just need to find the one choice that contains all the ones that are workable schedules.

Eliminate choice (A) because J cannot be seen on Friday. As for choice (B), I and M could be seen on Friday, because they are very "flexible." (M is under no restriction, and I is under a restriction that forces him to a day later in the week.) As for choice (C), L is under a restriction, but that restriction pushes L to a later day, so L too seems a possibility for Friday. As for choice (D), this contains I, L, and M, so it begins to look like a correct choice. As for choice (E), G cannot be scheduled for Friday, because G comes before I.

At this point, you must make a decision. Perhaps intuition tells you that choice (D) is the correct choice. You can either mark choice (D) as correct and move on to another item, or you can work out examples that prove that I, L, and M can be scheduled for Friday. Which you choose to do will depend on how much time you have left.

17. **The correct answer is (E).** Start by entering the additional information on a diagram:

M	TU	W	TH	F
	I		H	

G must come before I:

M	TU	W	TH	F
G	I		H	

K and F must be scheduled for the same day, which must now be Wednesday:

M	TU	W	TH	F
G	I	K,F	H	

L must be later in the week than F, however:

M	TU	W	TH	F
G	I	K,F	H	L

So J and M must have appointments on Monday and Tuesday, though not necessarily in that order. The diagram shows that choice (E) is necessarily true; that choices (A) and (B) are possibly, though not necessarily true; and that choices (C) and (D) are false.

18. **The correct answer is (C).** Enter the additional information on a diagram:

M	TU	W	TH	F
		K	H	

This means that F is also scheduled for Wednesday:

M	TU	W	TH	F
		K,F	H	

L must be seen sometime after F:

M	TU	W	TH	F
		K,F	H	L

Then, G must be seen before I:

M	TU	W	TH	F
G	I	K,F	H	L

M and J will be seen on Monday and Tuesday, though not necessarily in that order:

M	TU	W	TH	F	
G,J	I,M	K,F	H	L	OR
G,M	I,J	K,F	H	L	

19. **The correct answer is (C).** There are two ways of approaching this question. You can use a direct approach, in which you work with the initial conditions to track down all of the possibilities. The problem with the direct approach is that you will always worry that you haven't

gotten all the possibilities. The alternative approach is to work backward from the answer choices. Here's how this second approach works.

Does choice (A) contain all and only the possible days? No. I must follow G; therefore, I cannot be seen on Monday, and we eliminate choice (A). What about choice (B)? As for Tuesday, L must follow later in the week than J, F, and K, so L cannot be seen on Tuesday—and we eliminate choice (B). At this point, we should eliminate both choices (D) and (E), for choice (D) contains "Monday" and choice (E) contains "Tuesday." The only day on which both I and L could have appointments is Wednesday. For example:

M	TU	W	TH	F
J,G	K,F	I,L	H	M

20. **The correct answer is (D).** Here, one way or another, you are going to have to test each choice. That makes this a difficult question, but that is to be expected since it is the last one. To make the question manageable, you have to think abstractly about the individuals who are most likely to determine a certain order. As for choice (A), as we have noted, M is not under any particular restriction, so he is not likely to precipitate a fixed order. As for choices (B) and (C), G and I are under a certain restriction, but this works primarily only between the two of them. Choice (E) is a bit better than either choices (B) or (C), because it establishes that G and I are scheduled for either Monday and Wednesday, or Wednesday and Friday.

(D), however, offers even more promise. It affects not only G and I but also K and therefore F and L as well. Start with choice (D). If K has his appointment two days before G, then (given that H is already scheduled for Thursday) they must be scheduled for Monday and Wednesday or Wednesday and Friday. Here, since G must come before I, K and G must be scheduled for Monday and Wednesday:

M	TU	W	TH	F
K		G	H	

This means that F is scheduled for Monday and I for Friday:

M	TU	W	TH	F
K,F		G,L	H	I

However, L cannot be scheduled before Wednesday:

M	TU	W	TH	F
K,F		G,L	H	I

That means that J and M must be scheduled for Tuesday:

M	TU	W	TH	F
K,F	J,M	G,L	H	I

Exercise 2

1.	E	4.	D	7.	A	10.	A	13.	D
2.	C	5.	D	8.	A	11.	E		
3.	C	6.	A	9.	D	12.	C		

Questions 1–7

This is a selection set. Begin by summarizing the information:

Two different areas

$(E \supset \sim FA) + (FA \supset \sim E)$

$(S \supset M) + (M \supset S)$

$SS \supset FA$

There are no further obvious conclusions to draw, so go to the questions.

1. **The correct answer is (E).** Just test each choice by the initial conditions. First, the student must select from at least two different areas, and all of the choices pass muster on this score. Next, he cannot take courses in both English and fine arts, so we eliminate choices (A) and (D). Next, if he takes a science course, he must take a math course, and vice versa, so we eliminate choice (C). Finally, if he takes a social studies course, he must take a course in fine arts, so we eliminate choice (B). By the process of elimination, choice (E) is the correct choice.

> **Note:** Don't misread that last condition. It states only that a course in social studies must be accompanied by a course in fine arts. It is possible to take a fine arts course without taking a social studies course.

2. **The correct answer is (C).** This question is the mirror image of the first. Just test each choice by the initial conditions.

All are acceptable on the basis of the first condition (that he take courses in at least two different areas) and the second condition (English and fine arts cannot be taken together). Choice (C), however, runs afoul of the third condition, for there we have a math course without an accompanying science course. (You can check the other choices and see that they do respect the final condition.)

3. **The correct answer is (C).** If the student takes social studies, then he must take a course in fine arts. With a course in fine arts, he cannot take a course in English; and with two courses already scheduled (social studies and fine arts), he cannot take either math or science (for those must go together). His only choice, therefore, is to take another fine arts course—as choice (C) suggests—or another social studies course.

4. **The correct answer is (D).** If the student takes a course in math, he must also take a course in science, so his third course must be science.

5. **The correct answer is (D).** If you simply screen choices here by the initial conditions, it seems that all of the pairs taken in isolation are acceptable. This means that the trick to the question must be what happens to the third course. As for choices (A) and (B), math requires science and vice versa, and a schedule of math, science, and fine arts is acceptable. As for choices (C) and (E), math requires science, and a schedule of math, science, and English is acceptable. Choice

(D), however, is not acceptable; social studies requires fine arts, and science requires math, but there is not room on the schedule for both fine arts and science.

6. **The correct answer is (A).** Test each of the choices:

   (A) Science, two math (OK.)

   (B) Three science (No. Must schedule two different areas.)

   (C) Science, two English (No. Math must accompany science.)

   (D) Two science, one English (No. Math must accompany science.)

   (E) Science, math, social studies (No. Fine arts must accompany social studies.)

7. **The correct answer is (A).** Test each choice. As for choice (A), it is not possible to take two English courses. With two English courses, the student can neither take math or science (each requires the other), nor social studies (because social studies requires fine arts). It is possible to take two courses in the other areas:

   (B) Two fine arts plus one social studies

   (C) Two math plus one science

   (D) Two science plus one math

   (E) Two social studies plus one fine arts

Questions 8–13

This is a linear ordering problem. Begin by summarizing the information:

   J < K

   F < G (G is higher than F = F is lower than G.)

   F – I – G or G – I – F

   H = 6

There is one further conclusion you should probably note. Since G is higher than F and

since I is between F and G, the order for those three notes is F < I < G.

8. **The correct answer is (A).** Test each choice to learn which is possible and which is not. As for choice (A), G cannot be the second note on the scale because G must be higher than both F and I. You can grasp that the other choices are possible if you think in the following way. Imagine that F, I, and G are consecutive notes (they may be, though they don't have to be). If they are, then they could be 1, 2, and 3; or 2, 3, and 4; or even 3, 4, and 5. This will not affect the placement of J and K since in each of those arrangements, there will be two spaces left on the scale and K can be higher than J.

9. **The correct answer is (D).** Enter the additional information on a diagram:

   6   H
   5
   4   J
   3
   2
   1

Since J is lower than K:

   6   H
   5   K
   4   J
   3
   2
   1

Further, G, I, and F must be notes 3, 2, and 1:

   6   H
   5   K
   4   J
   3   G
   2   I
   1   F

10. **The correct answer is (A).** If exactly two notes separate F and I, then they must be placed as follows:

```
6    H
5    G
4    I
3
2
1    F
```

J and K are entered as follows:

```
6    H
5    G
4    I
3    K
2    J
1    F
```

The diagram shows that choice (A) is necessarily true, while the other choices are necessarily false.

11. **The correct answer is (E).** Enter the new information:

```
6    H
5
4
3
2    J
1
```

If J is second, then K must be either third, fourth, or fifth:

```
6    H    H    H
5    K
4         K
3              K
2    J    J    J
1
```

For G to be higher than I, and I higher than F, they must be entered as follows:

```
6    H    H    H
5    K    G    G
4    G    K    I
3    I    I    K
2    J    J    J
1    F    F    F
```

There are three possibilities: G and I are 4 and 3, 5 and 3, or 5 and 4.

12. **The correct answer is (C).** Start by assuming that F is the lowest note on the scale and that I is therefore the third. On that assumption, there are two positions for G:

```
6    H    H
5    G
4         G
3    I    I
2
1    F    F
```

J and K must be placed in the other two positions, with K higher than J:

```
6    H    H
5    G    K
4    K    G
3    I    I
2    J    J
1    F    F
```

Now assume that F is the second note on the scale and that I is therefore the fourth:

```
6    H
5
4    I
3
2    F
1
```

G must be higher than I:

```
6    H
5    G
4    I
3
2    F
1
```

K and J must be entered as follows:

```
6    H
5    G
4    I
3    K
2    F
1    J
```

Now try assuming that F is the third note on the scale, which would mean that I is the fifth. That is not possible, however, for G would then have to be higher than the fifth. Thus, we have accounted for all the possibilities:

```
6    H    H    H
5    G    G    K
4    I    K    G
3    K    I    I
2    F    J    J
1    J    F    F
```

Only choice (C) is necessarily true. The other choices are only possibly true.

13. **The correct answer is (D).** Again, we need to approach the question systematically. First, let us assume that J is the lowest note and that F is the second lowest. The possibilities are as follows:

```
6    H    H    H
5    G    G    K
4    I    K    G
3    K    I    I
2    F    F    F
1    J    J    J
```

That makes three possibilities. Now let's try J as the lowest note and F as the third lowest note. On this assumption, there is only one possibility:

```
6    H
5    G
4    I
3    F
2    K
1    J
```

This exhausts the possibilities. It is not possible (given the additional stipulation that J is lower than F) for J or F to be any higher on the scale. So there are exactly four possibilities.

The Writing Sample

OVERVIEW
- **The LSAT Writing Sample**
- **Handling the Writing Sample**
- **What Smart Test-Takers Know**

WHAT IS THE LSAT WRITING SAMPLE?

In addition to the three types of standardized multiple-choice questions that appear on the LSAT, the test also includes a Writing Sample. The Writing Sample is a short essay on a selected topic to be written in 30 minutes while you are in the examination room.

Writing Sample topics describe a decision that one person or a group of people must make, and you must write an argument for one of the two courses of action. The questions will not cover any topic requiring special knowledge. Paper and pens will be provided at the test center.

How Law Schools Use the Writing Sample

The Writing Sample will not be graded, but a copy of the essay will be forwarded with your score report to each school receiving your LSAT score. The point of requiring you to write an essay while in the examination room is to give a law school admissions committee a piece of writing definitely done by you and you alone. The essay gives the committee another perspective on your ability—specifically, on how well you write. The idea is that this can mitigate to some extent the severity of the artificial, multiple-choice format of the rest of the test.

Exactly what role the Writing Sample plays in the admissions process is decided by each law school. Many schools use the sample to help choose between otherwise equally qualified candidates. Very few law schools rely heavily upon the Writing Sample. Most law schools have adopted a middle-of-the-road approach. The Writing Sample will not figure heavily in the initial screening of applications, but it may be used to make decisions in difficult cases. For example, a student with marginal qualifications for a particular law school might be accepted if he or she writes a really good essay, and a student of similar background could be rejected on grounds that the Writing Sample is just not acceptable. Since no one is assured of a seat at a top law school, applicants to those schools who write a very poor essay will likely suffer.

chapter 8

LSAT Writing Sample Format

Here is a typical LSAT Writing Sample topic, along with directions for writing your essay.

Anatomy of the Writing Sample

Directions: Read the following proposals of Johnson and Smith, which were submitted to the city of Athens' Department of Urban Renewal, to renovate a decaying structure that is currently owned by the city and to operate a business in it. Then, in the space provided, write an argument in favor of the proposal that you think the Department of Urban Renewal should choose. The following considerations should guide your decision.

First come the directions. Read them now, and then you can forget about them. The point is to write an essay.

1. The Athens City Council eventually wants the ownership of the property to be transferred to the business as soon as the business is able to pay the property taxes that are in arrears.

2. The Department of Urban Renewal wants the building to be occupied by a business that will benefit the community.

Next comes the background for the situation. The criteria that should guide your decision will help you create an outline for an essay.

JOHNSON plans to operate a hardware store in the building. She will use the ground floor for retail displays and the second floor and basement for storing inventory. Johnson has $100,000 to commit to the project for purchasing inventory and for other start-up costs, plus a letter of credit from a local bank that will

Next comes a possible answer, though not necessarily the right answer. Use the details about Johnson's plan to fill in an argument patterned along the specified criteria—if this is the side that you choose.

allow her to borrow up to $150,000 for renovation. Johnson is willing to open this new business in the neighborhood because she believes that the neighborhood is about to experience a renaissance. Johnson worked for ten years as the manager of a hardware store that is part of a large chain.

SMITH plans to operate a personal financial consulting firm in the building. The firm will offer budget counseling, tax preparation, advice on completing loan applications, and help with legal documents—all for a fee. The fee will depend on the service rendered and the ability of the client to pay. Smith has $50,000 to cover the cost of renovating the building and has received a grant of $75,000 from the state's Human Resources Center to purchase computers and to cover other start-up costs. Smith's plan is initially just to renovate the ground floor and to open for business. The second floor would be renovated once the business has generated sufficient income. Smith worked for three years as a legal aid attorney and is familiar with the problems of the people in the neighborhood.

Next comes another possible answer, though again, not necessarily the right answer. Use the details about Smith's plan to fill in an argument patterned along the specified criteria—if this is the side that you choose.

HOW DO YOU HANDLE THE WRITING SAMPLE?

Here is a simple, four-step plan to help you succeed on the LSAT Writing Sample.

WRITING SAMPLE: GETTING IT RIGHT

1   Pick one side or the other—there is no right or wrong answer.
2   Make an outline.
3   Write your essay.
4   Proofread your essay.

NOTE

Organization is very important.

Perhaps the most important thing that the readers will be looking for is organization. If you create an outline and follow it, you are already halfway home.

Now let's look at each of these steps in more detail.

1   **Pick one side or the other—there is no right or wrong answer.** Pick a side—any side. There are no right or wrong answers for the Writing Sample. The technical term for the topic is "prompt." It is just an excuse for you to write an essay. You can even toss a coin to choose a side.

2   **Make an outline.** After you have selected the side of the topic you are more comfortable with, construct an outline of your position. The outline will not be very detailed. It will just be some notes to guide you as you write. In fact, since the entire exercise takes only 30 minutes, you probably cannot write more than four or five short paragraphs.

The background information always provides criteria as guidelines for making the decision. Let these criteria form the basis for the contentions in your essay. Summarize them in your own words, then build your essay around them.

3   **Write your essay.** Your essay should consist of four or five short paragraphs: introduction, first main reason, second main reason, and third main reason (if you have one), and conclusion. Each paragraph will be only two or three sentences long.

If you think that this is not "grand" enough, remember that this essay is not going to get you into law school. The objective here is to avoid writing something that is totally unacceptable.

4   **Proofread your essay.** Law school admissions officers will understand that your essay is really just a rough draft. Still, it would be better not to leave any glaring mistakes. So spend the last 3 or 4 minutes of the 30-minute session proofreading. Make any needed corrections as neatly as possible.

Now let's use the four-step process to create an essay on the following typical Writing Sample topic:

Margaret Stone will receive her Ph.D. in comparative literature in six months and wants a job teaching on the university level. After several interviews, she received job offers from two institutions, Middleburg College and Central State University. Write an essay arguing that Margaret should choose one of the two job offers. Two considerations should guide your decision:

1. Margaret wants a position that will allow her to maintain a decent standard of living. After eight years as a student, she has virtually no assets and has incurred several thousand dollars in student loans.

2. Margaret wants a position that will allow her to teach higher level courses in literature rather than the introductory course or courses designed to teach students a foreign language. In addition, she wants to earn a reputation as a scholar.

MIDDLEBURG COLLEGE is a small, liberal arts college with a student body of approximately 2,000. Although the college has a limited enrollment, its academic reputation is equal to that of many of the nation's best universities. There is no separate Comparative Literature Department at Middleburg. All literature courses are taught in various language departments. Margaret would be hired by the French Department and would be expected to teach three courses per semester: one basic French grammar course, one introduction to French literature course, and one upper-level literature course. The starting salary at Middleburg is $33,000 per year. The position is a tenure-track position, and Margaret could expect to receive tenure and a raise to $45,000 within three years.

CENTRAL STATE UNIVERSITY is a large public institution with a student body of 35,000. Margaret has been offered a position on the graduate faculty at a salary of $40,000 per year. As a member of the graduate faculty, she would offer courses of her own choosing, subject only to the approval of the Chief Executive Officer of the department. The Chief Executive Officer is a leading authority on literary criticism, and each year, the University sponsors one major and several minor conferences at which scholars from the University and other institutions present papers. The position at Central State is not considered a tenure-track position, but Margaret could hope to achieve a permanent appointment in seven or eight years if she earns a substantial academic reputation.

❶ Pick one side or the other—there is no right or wrong answer. It doesn't matter which job offer you think Margaret should choose.

❷ Make an outline. Based on the information given, you could argue that Margaret is concerned about (1) financial security and (2) professional satisfaction. Thus, your two main contentions would be as follows:

I. This job offers Margaret the financial security she wants.

II. This job offers Margaret the professional satisfaction she seeks.

Then find two or three specific points in the topic to prove each contention. Let the description of each option provide you with the subpoints needed to support your main points. For example, if you decide to argue in favor of Central State, your outline might look like this:

I. This job offers Margaret the financial security she wants.

   A. The starting salary is a generous $40,000 per year.

   B. There is the possibility of tenure if she succeeds.

TIP

Be specific.

The directions given
to readers emphasize
that a good essay
uses illustrations or
examples.

II. This job offers Margaret the professional satisfaction she seeks.

   A. She will be able to teach courses she likes.

   B. She will work with leading figures in her field.

   C. She will participate in conferences.

(You can also find equally good reasons for selecting the other job.)

 Write your essay. Now put the substance of the argument together with the formal outline given above. First, you need an introduction. An opening paragraph might be as follows:

> Margaret should accept the job offer from Central State for two reasons. First, it will give her the financial security she needs. Second, it will offer her the professional satisfaction that she seeks.

The second paragraph is the development of the first major contention. Begin the paragraph with a restatement of your first main point. Then supply the supporting details:

> First, the position at Central State provides Margaret with the income she needs to maintain a certain standard of living. The starting salary at Central State is a generous $40,000 per year. In addition, if Margaret is successful, she can expect to receive promotions after a few years, and such promotions usually carry corresponding salary increases.

The third paragraph is the development of the second major contention. Begin this paragraph with a restatement of your second main point. Then supply the supporting details:

> Second, Central State will allow Margaret to achieve her professional goals. In the first place, she will teach higher level courses and won't be required to teach the introductory courses she might find less interesting. In addition, she will be able to work with her Chief Executive Officer, who is one of the leading authorities in Margaret's field. Finally, the University itself is the center for conferences at which Margaret would meet others in her field and have an opportunity to exchange ideas.

The final paragraph should be a brief summary of the argument only a sentence or two long:

> Thus, because Central State offers better financial terms and the possibility of professional advancement, Margaret should accept its job offer.

The primary function of this paragraph is just to signal the reader that you have reached the end of your essay.

Now put all the paragraphs together. Here is how the essay would read:

> Margaret should accept the job offer from Central State for two reasons. First, it will give her the financial security she needs. Second, it will offer her the professional satisfaction that she seeks.

ALERT!

**There are
no traps here.**

The Writing Sample is
a straightforward
writing exercise. Read
the topic, do your
outline, write your
essay, and check
your work. Good luck!

First, the position at Central State provides Margaret with the income she needs to maintain a certain standard of living. The starting salary at Central State is a generous $40,000 per year. In addition, if Margaret is successful, she can expect to receive promotions after a few years, and such promotions usually carry corresponding salary increases.

Second, Central State will allow Margaret to achieve her professional goals. In the first place, she will teach higher level courses and won't be required to teach the introductory courses she might find less interesting. In addition, she will be able to work with her Chief Executive Officer, who is one of the leading authorities in Margaret's field. Finally, the University itself is the center for conferences at which Margaret would meet others in her field and have an opportunity to exchange ideas.

Thus, because Central State offers better financial terms and the possibility of professional advancement, Margaret should accept its job offer.

4 **Proofread your essay.** Read over your work to make sure that there are no glaring errors of grammar or punctuation. Incidentally, if you still doubt that this sample essay is lengthy enough, see how much time it takes you to copy it over in your own hand.

WHAT SMART TEST–TAKERS KNOW

The Writing Sample Is Not Very Important.

The Writing Sample is not as important as the other sections of the LSAT. It is important to keep in mind that law schools use the LSAT as a screening device (coupled with the grade point average). This means that the LSAT is a threshold requirement that must be met before the Writing Sample even enters the picture. Moreover, the length of the sample is such that you are not really writing a "term paper." In 30 minutes, no one is going to be able to write the definitive essay on the topic given and no one is expected to do so. This Writing Sample is just a check to see if you can write clearly and grammatically; it is not to determine whether or not you would be a great novelist.

Thinking It Through First Is the Way to Avoid Mistakes.

Many errors in writing are the result of an attempt to change structures in midsentence. Verb tenses shift, points of view get mixed up, verbs get left out, pronouns get confused, and many other things happen if the sentence is not already formed when the writing begins. For example:

> Wrong: Even if a student is somewhat distracted, they may be even better able to concentrate when their attention returns to the teacher.

This sentence contains a grammatical error. The pronoun *they*, which begins the main clause of the sentence, is plural. But it refers to *student*, which is singular. This type of error usually occurs when writers do not have the complete thought or sentence in mind when they begin to write. They lose track of what they have said and shift from the singular to the plural. The best way for you to avoid such errors is to have a good idea of what the completed sentence will say before you begin to write it down.

Subjects and Verbs Must Agree.

Everyone remembers that a verb must agree with its subject, and by and large, we all observe this rule. We tend to get into trouble when prepositional phrases or other modifiers come between the subject and its verb.

> Wrong: This distraction, which occurs in students with more limited attention spans, are easily avoided by arranging desks so that the eyes of a student is directed away from the windows.

Two errors of subject-verb agreement occur here: "distraction . . . are" and "eyes . . . is." In this sentence, a clause that includes two prepositional phrases comes between the first subject and its verb, and it is therefore likely that one of the two nouns, "students" or "spans," was mistaken for the subject when the writer chose a verb. A prepositional phrase ("of a student") comes between the second subject and its verb, and the writer has mistaken "student" for the subject of the verb and written "is."

Pronouns Must Be in the Correct Number and Case.

Many people misuse pronouns. The two most common mistakes in pronoun reference are incorrect number and incorrect case. Sometimes students use a singular pronoun where a plural pronoun is needed and vice versa (incorrect number):

> Wrong: The easiest solution is to have the teacher order each student to keep their eyes directed toward the blackboard.

In this example, the choice of the pronoun "their" is incorrect. The pronoun must refer to "student," which is singular; but "their" is plural.

Consider the next example:

> Wrong: Under this seating arrangement, all of the people in the classroom, except the class monitor and she, will face the blackboard, not the windows.

In this sentence, the use of the pronoun "she" is incorrect because it is in the wrong case. The pronoun here functions as the object of a preposition ("except"), and it should therefore be in the objective case ("her"). One sure way of avoiding errors in the use of pronouns is to avoid unnecessary pronouns.

> Better: Under this seating arrangement, all of the people in the classroom, except the class monitor and the teacher, will . . .

Modifiers Must Stay Close to Home.

As a general rule, make sure that modifiers are close to the words they are intended to modify. Be especially wary of the introductory modifier.

> Wrong: While strolling through Central Park, a severe thunderstorm required my companion and me to take shelter in the band shell.

Given the construction of the sentence, it is made to appear that the severe thunderstorm was strolling through the park. When a modifying idea starts a sentence and is set off with a comma, the modifier must be taken to modify the first noun or noun phrase after the comma. A related error to be avoided is the squinting modifier, which is placed so that it may modify either one of two things, producing ambiguity in the sentence.

> Wrong: Paul told Mary that he would wed her down by the old mill.

Did Paul tell Mary down by the old mill that he would wed her, or did Paul tell Mary that he would wed her and the wedding would take place down by the old mill?

Each Sentence Should Express Just One Thought.

Rather than trying to tack on qualifications and exceptions to an already long sentence, break it down:

Wrong: Although it might be argued that some students will be distracted by windows, but there is no proof of this presented, it is still the case that many students would benefit from the relaxing effect of open scenery, and that could even help them learn.

Better: There is no proof presented that students are distracted by windows. Even assuming some students are distracted, many other students might find the view relaxing. A relaxed student should be a better learner than one who is tense, and learning is the goal of the classroom.

The Active Voice Is Generally Best.

As mentioned, it is important to write straightforward, declarative sentences in the active voice. These sentences are easy to compose, and they express thoughts clearly. But many students imagine that the more stilted the construction, the better the writing:

Wrong: When the notice was received by me. . . .

Correct: When I received the notice. . . .

Wrong: The cake was baked by the chef to please. . . .

Correct: The chef baked the cake to please. . . .

This is not an absolute prohibition against the passive voice, but a law school admissions committee is more likely to appreciate straightforward and direct composition than needlessly complicated and imprecise sentences.

Slang Is a Turn-off.

Whatever else you do, do not allow slang to slip into your writing.

Wrong: Let the kids do their own thing. It's too heavy a trip to always have the teacher, the man, laying this guilt business on you. No windows would be a head trip. Some of the kids would wind up at the shrink's. So just lay off, and let them be themselves.

In conversation we often use expressions that are just not acceptable in formal writing. Can you dig that?

When in Doubt, It's Smart to Leave it Out.

You are in command of the Writing Sample. Unlike the other sections, in which you are forced to choose from among answers, the Writing Sample allows you to construct and write your own answer. It will be possible, to a certain extent, to "fake it": If you are not sure about the meaning or spelling of a word, find an alternative. There is absolutely no reason to expose yourself to the possibility of error when you could avoid that danger entirely by using another phrase.

Neatness Counts.

What we have tried to do in this section is reassure you that you will not be caught without anything to say. The questions will be drafted in such a way that you will be able to think of a point or two and probably more. The important thing is to express yourself clearly in order to impress upon the admissions officers that you can write, a skill every lawyer needs. Finally, although good penmanship is not a prerequisite to being a good lawyer, your writing will be read by some fairly important people. Present yourself in a way of which you can be proud. Some people have naturally beautiful handwriting, others do not. But everyone is capable of legible handwriting. It is only courteous to write clearly, so that the people who have to read your essay can do so easily. So write slowly (without sacrificing coverage), and try to use your best handwriting. Print if necessary.

Trying to Do Too Much Is a Mistake.

After you have practiced a few topics, you will have a pretty good idea of what you can hope to accomplish in the time allotted. The biggest problem for students is not going to be having too little to say but rather trying to say too much. Your little essay must be structurally complete. That is, it must have a beginning, a middle, and an end. You do not want to run out of time before you have completed your thought. Far better to write a nicely balanced and self-contained essay on the short side than a longer piece that stops in the middle of the next-to-last paragraph. Make sure you can chew what you bite off.

Legal Terminology Is Out of Place.

The LSAT is not a test of what you already know about the law, and law school admissions officers are not going to be impressed with your essay just because you flavor it with *henceforth, heretofore mentioned, above cited*, or similar terms. Such terms have no place in your essay. Your best bet is to try to write naturally, as though you were speaking to someone sitting across the table (though you should avoid slang expressions you might use in conversation).

SUMMARY

What You Must Know about LSAT Question Types

Review these pages the night before you take the LSAT. They will help you do well on your test.

- The LSAT has three question types: Logical Reasoning, Reading Comprehension, and Analytical Reasoning.

- The scored portion of the LSAT contains two 35-minute Logical Reasoning sections of 24–26 questions each. It also contains one Reading Comprehension section of 26–28 questions and one Analytical Reasoning section of 22–24 questions.

- In addition, each LSAT includes a 30-minute Writing Sample that is sent directly to the law schools you designate for scoring.

Logical Reasoning

- These steps will help you solve Logical Reasoning problems:

  1 Preview the question stem.

  2 Read the stimulus material.

  3 Prephrase your answer.

  4 Identify the correct answer.

- There are six common types of Logical Reasoning questions:

  1 Identify the conclusion.

  2 Point out a premise.

  3 Identify strengths or weaknesses.

  4 Recognize parallel reasoning.

  5 Evaluate evidence.

  6 Draw a conclusion.

- Locating the conclusion is the first step in evaluating an argument.

- Key words often signal the conclusion or an important premise.

- In Logical Reasoning questions, watch out for the seven most common logical fallacies:

  1 Wrong cause

  2 False analogy

  3 Weak generalization

④ Ambiguous terms

⑤ Irrelevant evidence

⑥ Circular argument

⑦ *Ad hominem* attack

Reading Comprehension

- These steps will help you solve Reading Comprehension questions:

  ① Preview key sentences.

  ② Read for structure; ignore details.

  ③ Do a mental wrap-up.

  ④ Start with the main idea question.

  ⑤ Next tackle specific detail and attitude/tone questions.

  ⑥ Then do logical structure questions.

  ⑦ Save inference and application questions for last.

- The LSAT uses six Reading Comprehension question types:

  ① Main idea

  ② Specific detail

  ③ Inference

  ④ Logical structure

  ⑤ Application

  ⑥ Author's attitude or tone

Analytical Reasoning

- These steps will help you solve Analytical Reasoning questions:

  ① Summarize the initial conditions in a "bookkeeping" system.

  ② Look for further conclusions.

  ③ Treat each question separately.

  ④ Use the answer choices to create a "feedback loop."

- The three most common types of Analytical Reasoning puzzles:

  ① Linear ordering

  ② Distributed order

  ③ Selection sets

Writing Sample

- These steps will help you with the Writing Sample:

  1 Pick one side or the other—there is no right or wrong answer.

  2 Make an outline.

  3 Write your essay.

  4 Proofread your essay.

- The Writing Sample is not as important as the other sections of the LSAT.

- Watch your grammar.

- Don't try to do too much.

PART IV

THREE PRACTICE TESTS

Practice Test 1

Practice Test 2

Practice Test 3

Answer Sheet

Use a No. 2 pencil only. Be sure each mark is dark and completely fills the intended oval. Completely erase any errors or stray marks. Start with number 1 for each new section. If a section has fewer than 30 questions, leave the extra answer spaces blank.

TEAR HERE

SECTION 1	SECTION 2	SECTION 3	SECTION 4	SECTION 5
1 Ⓐ Ⓑ Ⓒ Ⓓ Ⓔ	1 Ⓐ Ⓑ Ⓒ Ⓓ Ⓔ	1 Ⓐ Ⓑ Ⓒ Ⓓ Ⓔ	1 Ⓐ Ⓑ Ⓒ Ⓓ Ⓔ	1 Ⓐ Ⓑ Ⓒ Ⓓ Ⓔ
2 Ⓐ Ⓑ Ⓒ Ⓓ Ⓔ	2 Ⓐ Ⓑ Ⓒ Ⓓ Ⓔ	2 Ⓐ Ⓑ Ⓒ Ⓓ Ⓔ	2 Ⓐ Ⓑ Ⓒ Ⓓ Ⓔ	2 Ⓐ Ⓑ Ⓒ Ⓓ Ⓔ
3 Ⓐ Ⓑ Ⓒ Ⓓ Ⓔ	3 Ⓐ Ⓑ Ⓒ Ⓓ Ⓔ	3 Ⓐ Ⓑ Ⓒ Ⓓ Ⓔ	3 Ⓐ Ⓑ Ⓒ Ⓓ Ⓔ	3 Ⓐ Ⓑ Ⓒ Ⓓ Ⓔ
4 Ⓐ Ⓑ Ⓒ Ⓓ Ⓔ	4 Ⓐ Ⓑ Ⓒ Ⓓ Ⓔ	4 Ⓐ Ⓑ Ⓒ Ⓓ Ⓔ	4 Ⓐ Ⓑ Ⓒ Ⓓ Ⓔ	4 Ⓐ Ⓑ Ⓒ Ⓓ Ⓔ
5 Ⓐ Ⓑ Ⓒ Ⓓ Ⓔ	5 Ⓐ Ⓑ Ⓒ Ⓓ Ⓔ	5 Ⓐ Ⓑ Ⓒ Ⓓ Ⓔ	5 Ⓐ Ⓑ Ⓒ Ⓓ Ⓔ	5 Ⓐ Ⓑ Ⓒ Ⓓ Ⓔ
6 Ⓐ Ⓑ Ⓒ Ⓓ Ⓔ	6 Ⓐ Ⓑ Ⓒ Ⓓ Ⓔ	6 Ⓐ Ⓑ Ⓒ Ⓓ Ⓔ	6 Ⓐ Ⓑ Ⓒ Ⓓ Ⓔ	6 Ⓐ Ⓑ Ⓒ Ⓓ Ⓔ
7 Ⓐ Ⓑ Ⓒ Ⓓ Ⓔ	7 Ⓐ Ⓑ Ⓒ Ⓓ Ⓔ	7 Ⓐ Ⓑ Ⓒ Ⓓ Ⓔ	7 Ⓐ Ⓑ Ⓒ Ⓓ Ⓔ	7 Ⓐ Ⓑ Ⓒ Ⓓ Ⓔ
8 Ⓐ Ⓑ Ⓒ Ⓓ Ⓔ	8 Ⓐ Ⓑ Ⓒ Ⓓ Ⓔ	8 Ⓐ Ⓑ Ⓒ Ⓓ Ⓔ	8 Ⓐ Ⓑ Ⓒ Ⓓ Ⓔ	8 Ⓐ Ⓑ Ⓒ Ⓓ Ⓔ
9 Ⓐ Ⓑ Ⓒ Ⓓ Ⓔ	9 Ⓐ Ⓑ Ⓒ Ⓓ Ⓔ	9 Ⓐ Ⓑ Ⓒ Ⓓ Ⓔ	9 Ⓐ Ⓑ Ⓒ Ⓓ Ⓔ	9 Ⓐ Ⓑ Ⓒ Ⓓ Ⓔ
10 Ⓐ Ⓑ Ⓒ Ⓓ Ⓔ	10 Ⓐ Ⓑ Ⓒ Ⓓ Ⓔ	10 Ⓐ Ⓑ Ⓒ Ⓓ Ⓔ	10 Ⓐ Ⓑ Ⓒ Ⓓ Ⓔ	10 Ⓐ Ⓑ Ⓒ Ⓓ Ⓔ
11 Ⓐ Ⓑ Ⓒ Ⓓ Ⓔ	11 Ⓐ Ⓑ Ⓒ Ⓓ Ⓔ	11 Ⓐ Ⓑ Ⓒ Ⓓ Ⓔ	11 Ⓐ Ⓑ Ⓒ Ⓓ Ⓔ	11 Ⓐ Ⓑ Ⓒ Ⓓ Ⓔ
12 Ⓐ Ⓑ Ⓒ Ⓓ Ⓔ	12 Ⓐ Ⓑ Ⓒ Ⓓ Ⓔ	12 Ⓐ Ⓑ Ⓒ Ⓓ Ⓔ	12 Ⓐ Ⓑ Ⓒ Ⓓ Ⓔ	12 Ⓐ Ⓑ Ⓒ Ⓓ Ⓔ
13 Ⓐ Ⓑ Ⓒ Ⓓ Ⓔ	13 Ⓐ Ⓑ Ⓒ Ⓓ Ⓔ	13 Ⓐ Ⓑ Ⓒ Ⓓ Ⓔ	13 Ⓐ Ⓑ Ⓒ Ⓓ Ⓔ	13 Ⓐ Ⓑ Ⓒ Ⓓ Ⓔ
14 Ⓐ Ⓑ Ⓒ Ⓓ Ⓔ	14 Ⓐ Ⓑ Ⓒ Ⓓ Ⓔ	14 Ⓐ Ⓑ Ⓒ Ⓓ Ⓔ	14 Ⓐ Ⓑ Ⓒ Ⓓ Ⓔ	14 Ⓐ Ⓑ Ⓒ Ⓓ Ⓔ
15 Ⓐ Ⓑ Ⓒ Ⓓ Ⓔ	15 Ⓐ Ⓑ Ⓒ Ⓓ Ⓔ	15 Ⓐ Ⓑ Ⓒ Ⓓ Ⓔ	15 Ⓐ Ⓑ Ⓒ Ⓓ Ⓔ	15 Ⓐ Ⓑ Ⓒ Ⓓ Ⓔ
16 Ⓐ Ⓑ Ⓒ Ⓓ Ⓔ	16 Ⓐ Ⓑ Ⓒ Ⓓ Ⓔ	16 Ⓐ Ⓑ Ⓒ Ⓓ Ⓔ	16 Ⓐ Ⓑ Ⓒ Ⓓ Ⓔ	16 Ⓐ Ⓑ Ⓒ Ⓓ Ⓔ
17 Ⓐ Ⓑ Ⓒ Ⓓ Ⓔ	17 Ⓐ Ⓑ Ⓒ Ⓓ Ⓔ	17 Ⓐ Ⓑ Ⓒ Ⓓ Ⓔ	17 Ⓐ Ⓑ Ⓒ Ⓓ Ⓔ	17 Ⓐ Ⓑ Ⓒ Ⓓ Ⓔ
18 Ⓐ Ⓑ Ⓒ Ⓓ Ⓔ	18 Ⓐ Ⓑ Ⓒ Ⓓ Ⓔ	18 Ⓐ Ⓑ Ⓒ Ⓓ Ⓔ	18 Ⓐ Ⓑ Ⓒ Ⓓ Ⓔ	18 Ⓐ Ⓑ Ⓒ Ⓓ Ⓔ
19 Ⓐ Ⓑ Ⓒ Ⓓ Ⓔ	19 Ⓐ Ⓑ Ⓒ Ⓓ Ⓔ	19 Ⓐ Ⓑ Ⓒ Ⓓ Ⓔ	19 Ⓐ Ⓑ Ⓒ Ⓓ Ⓔ	19 Ⓐ Ⓑ Ⓒ Ⓓ Ⓔ
20 Ⓐ Ⓑ Ⓒ Ⓓ Ⓔ	20 Ⓐ Ⓑ Ⓒ Ⓓ Ⓔ	20 Ⓐ Ⓑ Ⓒ Ⓓ Ⓔ	20 Ⓐ Ⓑ Ⓒ Ⓓ Ⓔ	20 Ⓐ Ⓑ Ⓒ Ⓓ Ⓔ
21 Ⓐ Ⓑ Ⓒ Ⓓ Ⓔ	21 Ⓐ Ⓑ Ⓒ Ⓓ Ⓔ	21 Ⓐ Ⓑ Ⓒ Ⓓ Ⓔ	21 Ⓐ Ⓑ Ⓒ Ⓓ Ⓔ	21 Ⓐ Ⓑ Ⓒ Ⓓ Ⓔ
22 Ⓐ Ⓑ Ⓒ Ⓓ Ⓔ	22 Ⓐ Ⓑ Ⓒ Ⓓ Ⓔ	22 Ⓐ Ⓑ Ⓒ Ⓓ Ⓔ	22 Ⓐ Ⓑ Ⓒ Ⓓ Ⓔ	22 Ⓐ Ⓑ Ⓒ Ⓓ Ⓔ
23 Ⓐ Ⓑ Ⓒ Ⓓ Ⓔ	23 Ⓐ Ⓑ Ⓒ Ⓓ Ⓔ	23 Ⓐ Ⓑ Ⓒ Ⓓ Ⓔ	23 Ⓐ Ⓑ Ⓒ Ⓓ Ⓔ	23 Ⓐ Ⓑ Ⓒ Ⓓ Ⓔ
24 Ⓐ Ⓑ Ⓒ Ⓓ Ⓔ	24 Ⓐ Ⓑ Ⓒ Ⓓ Ⓔ	24 Ⓐ Ⓑ Ⓒ Ⓓ Ⓔ	24 Ⓐ Ⓑ Ⓒ Ⓓ Ⓔ	24 Ⓐ Ⓑ Ⓒ Ⓓ Ⓔ
25 Ⓐ Ⓑ Ⓒ Ⓓ Ⓔ	25 Ⓐ Ⓑ Ⓒ Ⓓ Ⓔ	25 Ⓐ Ⓑ Ⓒ Ⓓ Ⓔ	25 Ⓐ Ⓑ Ⓒ Ⓓ Ⓔ	25 Ⓐ Ⓑ Ⓒ Ⓓ Ⓔ
26 Ⓐ Ⓑ Ⓒ Ⓓ Ⓔ	26 Ⓐ Ⓑ Ⓒ Ⓓ Ⓔ	26 Ⓐ Ⓑ Ⓒ Ⓓ Ⓔ	26 Ⓐ Ⓑ Ⓒ Ⓓ Ⓔ	26 Ⓐ Ⓑ Ⓒ Ⓓ Ⓔ
27 Ⓐ Ⓑ Ⓒ Ⓓ Ⓔ	27 Ⓐ Ⓑ Ⓒ Ⓓ Ⓔ	27 Ⓐ Ⓑ Ⓒ Ⓓ Ⓔ	27 Ⓐ Ⓑ Ⓒ Ⓓ Ⓔ	27 Ⓐ Ⓑ Ⓒ Ⓓ Ⓔ
28 Ⓐ Ⓑ Ⓒ Ⓓ Ⓔ	28 Ⓐ Ⓑ Ⓒ Ⓓ Ⓔ	28 Ⓐ Ⓑ Ⓒ Ⓓ Ⓔ	28 Ⓐ Ⓑ Ⓒ Ⓓ Ⓔ	28 Ⓐ Ⓑ Ⓒ Ⓓ Ⓔ
29 Ⓐ Ⓑ Ⓒ Ⓓ Ⓔ	29 Ⓐ Ⓑ Ⓒ Ⓓ Ⓔ	29 Ⓐ Ⓑ Ⓒ Ⓓ Ⓔ	29 Ⓐ Ⓑ Ⓒ Ⓓ Ⓔ	29 Ⓐ Ⓑ Ⓒ Ⓓ Ⓔ
30 Ⓐ Ⓑ Ⓒ Ⓓ Ⓔ	30 Ⓐ Ⓑ Ⓒ Ⓓ Ⓔ	30 Ⓐ Ⓑ Ⓒ Ⓓ Ⓔ	30 Ⓐ Ⓑ Ⓒ Ⓓ Ⓔ	30 Ⓐ Ⓑ Ⓒ Ⓓ Ⓔ

Practice Test 1

SECTION 1

24 Questions • Time—35 Minutes

Directions: In this section, the questions ask you to analyze and evaluate the reasoning in short paragraphs or passages. For some questions, all of the answer choices may conceivably be answers to the question asked. You should select the *best* answer to the question; that is, an answer that does not require you to make assumptions that violate common sense standards by being implausible, redundant, irrelevant, or inconsistent. After you have chosen the *best* answer, blacken the corresponding space on the answer sheet.

1. There are no lower bus fares from Washington, D.C., to New York City than those of Flash Bus Line.

   Which of the following is logically inconsistent with the above advertising claim?

   (A) Long Lines Airways has a Washington, D.C., to New York City airfare that is only half of that charged by Flash.

   (B) Rapid Transit Bus Company charges the same fare for a trip from Washington, D.C., to New York City as Flash charges.

   (C) Cherokee Bus Corporation has a lower fare from New York City to Boston than Flash does.

   (D) Linea Rapida Bus Company has a New York City to Washington, D.C., fare that is less than the corresponding fare of Flash Bus Lines.

   (E) Birch Bus Lines offers a late-night fare from Washington, D.C., to New York City that is two thirds the price of the corresponding fare of Flash Bus Line.

Questions 2 and 3

Roberts is accused of a crime, and Edwards is the prosecution's key witness.

   (1) Roberts can be convicted on the basis of Edwards' testimony.

   (2) Edwards' testimony would show that Edwards participated in Roberts' wrongdoing.

   (3) The crime of which Roberts is accused can be committed only by a person acting alone.

   (4) If the jury learns that Edwards committed some wrong, they will refuse to believe any part of Edwards' testimony.

2. If propositions (1), (2), and (3) are assumed to be true and (4) false, which of the following best describes the outcome of the trial?

(A) Both Edwards and Roberts will be convicted of the crime of which Roberts is accused.

(B) Both Edwards and Roberts will be convicted of some crime other than the one with which Roberts is already charged.

(C) Roberts will be convicted, while Edwards will not be convicted.

(D) Roberts will not be convicted.

(E) Roberts will testify against Edwards.

3. If all four propositions are taken as a group, it can be pointed out that the scenario they describe is

(A) a typical situation for a prosecutor.

(B) impossible because the propositions are logically inconsistent.

(C) unfair to Edwards, whose testimony may be self-incriminatory.

(D) unfair to Roberts, who may be convicted of the crime.

(E) one that Roberts' attorney has created.

Questions 4 and 5

There is a curious, though nonetheless obvious, contradiction in the suggestion that one person ought to give up his life to save the life of the one other person who is not a more valuable member of the community. It is true that we glorify the sacrifice of the individual who throws herself in front of the attacker's bullets, saving the life of her lover at the cost of her own. But here is the _____(4): Her life is as important as his. Nothing is gained in the transaction; not from the community's viewpoint, for one life was exchanged for another equally as important; not from the heroine's viewpoint, for she is _____(5); and not from the rescued lover's perspective, for he would willingly have exchanged places.

4. **(A)** beauty of human love

(B) tragedy of life

(C) inevitability of death

(D) defining characteristic of human existence

(E) paradox of self-sacrifice

5. **(A)** dying

(B) in love

(C) dead

(D) a heroine

(E) a faithful companion

6. It is a well-documented fact that for all teenaged couples who marry, the marriages of those who do not have children in the first year of their marriage survive more than twice as long as the marriages of those teenaged couples in which the wife does give birth within the first twelve months of marriage. Therefore, many divorces could be avoided if teenagers who marry were encouraged to seek counseling on birth control as soon after marriage as possible.

The evidence regarding teenaged marriages supports the author's conclusion only if

(A) in those couples to which a child was born within the first 12 months, there is not a significant number in which the wife was pregnant at the time of marriage.

(B) the children born during the first year of marriage to those divorcing couples lived with the teenaged couple.

(C) the child born into such a marriage did not die at birth.

(D) society actually has an interest in determining whether or not people should be divorced if there are not children involved.

(E) encouraging people to stay married when they do not plan to have any children is a good idea.

7. CLARENCE: Mary is one of the most important executives at the Trendy Cola Company.

   PETER: How can that be? I know for a fact that Mary drinks only Hobart Cola.

   Peter's statement implies that

   (A) Hobart Cola is a subsidiary of Trendy Cola.

   (B) Mary is an unimportant employee of Hobart Cola.

   (C) all cola drinks taste pretty much alike.

   (D) an executive uses only that company's products.

   (E) Hobart is a better-tasting cola than Trendy.

8. ERIKA: Participation in intramural competitive sports teaches students the importance of teamwork, for no one wants to let his teammates down.

   NICHOL: That is not correct. The real reason students play hard is that such programs place a premium on winning and that no one wants to be a member of a losing team.

   Which of the following comments can most reasonably be made about the exchange between Erika and Nichol?

   (A) If fewer and fewer schools are sponsoring intramural sports programs now than a decade ago, Erika's position is undermined.

   (B) If high schools and universities provide financial assistance for the purchase of sports equipment, Nichol's assertion about the importance of winning is weakened.

   (C) If teamwork is essential to success in intramural competitive sports, Erika's position and Nichol's position are not necessarily incompatible.

   (D) Since the argument is one about motivation, it should be possible to resolve the issue by taking a survey of deans at schools that have intramural sports programs.

   (E) Since the question raised is about hidden psychological states, it is impossible to answer it.

9. Clark must have known that his sister Janet and not the governess pulled the trigger, but he silently stood by while the jury convicted the governess. Any person of clear conscience would have felt terrible for not having come forward with the information about his sister, and Clark lived with that information until his death thirty years later. Since he was an extremely happy man, however, I conclude that he must have helped Janet commit the crime.

Which of the following assumptions must underlie the author's conclusion of the last sentence?

(A) Loyalty to members of one's family is conducive to contentment.

(B) Servants are not to be treated with the same respect as members of the peerage.

(C) Clark never had a bad conscience over his silence because he was also guilty of the crime.

(D) It is better to be virtuous than happy.

(E) It is actually better to be content in life than to behave morally toward one's fellow humans.

10. Current motion pictures give children a distorted view of the world. Animated features depict animals as loyal friends, compassionate creatures, and tender souls, while "spaghetti Westerns" portray men and women as deceitful and treacherous, cruel and wanton, and hard and uncaring. Thus, children are taught to value animals more highly than other human beings.

Which of the following, if true, would weaken the author's conclusion?

(A) Children are not allowed to watch "spaghetti Westerns."

(B) The producers of animated features do not want children to regard animals as higher than human beings.

(C) Ancient fables, such as *Androcles and the Lion,* tell stories of the cooperation between humans and animals, and they usually end with a moral about human virtue.

(D) Children are more likely to choose to watch animated presentations with characters such as animals than ones with people as actors.

(E) Animals often exhibit affection, loyalty, protectiveness, and other traits that are considered desirable characteristics in humans.

11. There is something irrational about our system of laws. The criminal law punishes a person more severely for having successfully committed a crime than it does a person who fails in an attempt to commit the same crime—even though the same evil intention is present in both cases. But under the civil law, a person who attempts to defraud a potential victim but is unsuccessful is not required to pay damages.

Which of the following, if true, would most weaken the author's argument?

(A) Most persons who are imprisoned for crimes will commit another crime if they are ever released from prison.

(B) A person is morally culpable for evil thoughts as well as for evil deeds.

(C) There are more criminal laws on the books than there are civil laws on the books.

(D) A criminal trial is considerably more costly to the state than a civil trial.

(E) The goal of the criminal law is to punish the criminal, but the goal of the civil law is to compensate the victim.

12. In his most recent speech, my opponent, Governor Smith, accused me of having distorted the facts, misrepresenting his own position, suppressing information, and deliberately lying to the people.

Which of the following possible responses by this speaker would be LEAST relevant to his dispute with Governor Smith?

(A) Governor Smith would not have begun to smear me if he did not sense that his own campaign was in serious trouble.

(B) Governor Smith apparently misunderstood my characterization of his position, so I will attempt to state more clearly my understanding of it.

(C) At the time I made those remarks, certain key facts were not available, but new information uncovered by my staff does support the position I took at that time.

(D) I can only wish Governor Smith had specified those points he considered to be lies so that I could have responded to them now.

(E) With regard to the allegedly distorted facts, the source of my information is a Department of Transportation publication entitled "Safe Driving."

13. Politicians are primarily concerned with their own survival; artists are concerned with revealing truth. Of course, the difference in their reactions is readily predictable. For example, while the governmental leaders wrote laws to ensure the triumph of industrialization in Western Europe, artists painted, wrote about, and composed music in response to the horrible conditions created by the Industrial Revolution. Only later did political leaders come to see what the artists had immediately perceived and then only through a glass darkly. Experience teaches us that _____.

Which of the following represents the most logical continuation of the passage?

(A) artistic vision perceives in advance of political practice

(B) artists are utopian by nature, while governmental leaders are practical

(C) throughout history, political leaders have not been very responsive to the needs of their people

(D) the world would be a much better place to live if only artists would become kings

(E) history is the best judge of the progress of civilization

14. A parent must be constant and even-handed in the imposition of burdens and punishments and the distribution of liberties and rewards. In good times, a parent who too quickly bestows rewards creates an expectation of future rewards that it may be impossible to fulfill during bad times. In bad times, a parent who waits too long to impose the punishment gives the impression that the response was forced, and the child may interpret this as _____.

Which of the following represents the most logical continuation of the passage?

(A) a signal from the parent that the parent is no longer interested in the child's welfare

(B) a sign of weakness in the parent that can be exploited

(C) indicating a willingness on the part of the parent to bargain away liberties in exchange for the child's assuming some new responsibilities

(D) an open invitation to retaliate

(E) a symbol of the transition to adulthood

15. As dietitian for this 300-person school, I am concerned about the sudden shortage of beef. It seems that we will have to begin to serve fish as our main source of protein. Even though beef costs more per pound than fish, I expect that the price I pay for protein will rise if I continue to serve the same amount of protein using fish as I did with beef.

The speaker makes which of the following assumptions?

(A) Fish is more expensive per pound than beef.

(B) Students will soon be paying more for their meals.

(C) Cattle ranchers make greater profits than commercial fishers.

(D) Per measure of protein, fish is more expensive than beef.

(E) Cattle are more costly to raise than fish.

Questions 16 and 17

New Weight Loss Salons invites all of you who are dissatisfied with your present build to join our Exercise for Lunch Bunch. Instead of putting on even more weight by eating lunch, you actually cut down on your daily caloric intake by exercising rather than eating. Every single one of us has the potential to be slim and fit, so take the initiative and begin losing excess pounds today. Don't eat! Exercise! You'll lose weight and feel stronger, happier, and more attractive.

16. Which of the following, if true, would weaken the logic of the argument made by the advertisement?

(A) Nutritionists agree that it is permissible to skip lunch but not a good idea to skip breakfast.

(B) Most people will experience increased desire for food as a result of the exercise and will lose little weight as a result of enrolling in the program.

(C) In our society, obesity is regarded as unattractive.

(D) A person who is too thin is probably not in good health.

(E) Not everyone is dissatisfied with his or her present build or body weight.

17. A person hearing this advertisement countered, "I know some people who are not overweight and are still unhappy and unattractive." The author of the advertisement could logically and consistently reply to this objection by pointing out that he never claimed that

(A) being overweight is always caused by unhappiness.

(B) being overweight is the only cause of unhappiness and unattractiveness.

(C) unhappiness and unattractiveness can cause someone to be overweight.

(D) unhappiness necessarily leads to being overweight.

(E) unhappiness and unattractiveness are always found together.

18. Since all swans that I have encountered have been white, it follows that the swans I will see when I visit the Bronx Zoo will also be white.

Which of the following most closely parallels the reasoning of the preceding argument?

(A) Some birds are incapable of flight; therefore, swans are probably incapable of flight.

(B) Every ballet I have attended has failed to interest me; so a theatrical production that fails to interest me must be a ballet.

(C) Since all cases of severe depression I have encountered were susceptible to treatment by chlorpromazine, there must be something in the chlorpromazine that adjusts the patient's brain chemistry.

(D) Because every society has a word for justice, the concept of fair play must be inherent in the biological makeup of the human species.

(E) Since no medicine I have tried for my allergy has ever helped, this new product will probably not work either.

Questions 19–21

The blanks in the following paragraph mark deletions from the text. For each question, select the phrase that most appropriately completes the text.

Libertarians argue that laws making suicide a criminal act are both foolish and an unwarranted intrusion on individual conscience. With regard to the first, they point out that there is no penalty that the law can assess that inflicts greater injury than the crime itself. As for the second, they argue that it is no business of the state to prevent suicide, for whether it is right to take one's own life is a matter to be addressed to one's own God—the state, by the terms of the Constitution, may not interfere. Such arguments, however, seem to me to be ill-conceived. In the first place, the libertarian makes the mistaken assumption that deterrence is the only goal of the law. I maintain that the laws we have proscribing suicide are _____ (19).

By making it a crime to take any life—even one's own—we make a public announcement of our shared conviction that each person is unique and valuable. In the second place, while it must be conceded that the doctrine of the separation of church and state is a useful one, it need not be admitted that suicide is a crime _____ (20). And here we need not have recourse to the possibility that a potential suicide might, if given the opportunity, repent of the decision. Suicide inflicts a cost upon us all: the emotional cost on those close to the suicide; an economic cost in the form of the loss of production of a mature and trained member of the society that falls on us all; and a cost to humanity at large for the loss of a member of our human community. The difficulty with the libertarian position is that it is an oversimplification. It assesses the evil of _____ (21).

19. **(A)** drafted to make it more difficult to commit suicide

   (B) passed by legislators in response to pressures by religious lobbying groups

   (C) written in an effort to protect our democratic liberties, not undermine them

   (D) important because they educate all to the value of human life

   (E) outdated because they belong to a time when church and state were not so clearly divided

20. **(A)** that does not necessarily lead to more serious crimes

   (B) without victim

   (C) as well as a sin

   (D) that cannot be prevented

   (E) without motive

21. **(A)** crimes only in economic terms

   (B) suicide only from the perspective of the person who commits suicide

   (C) laws by weighing them against the evil of the liberty lost by their enforcement

   (D) the mingling of church and state without sufficient regard to the constitutional protections

   (E) suicide in monetary units without proper regard to the importance of life

22. All high-powered racing engines have stochastic fuel injection. Stochastic fuel injection is not a feature that is normally included in the engines of production-line vehicles. Passenger sedans are production-line vehicles.

   Which of the following conclusions can be drawn from these statements?

   (A) Passenger sedans do not usually have stochastic fuel injection.

   (B) Stochastic fuel injection is found only in high-powered racing cars.

   (C) Car manufacturers do not include stochastic fuel injection in passenger cars because they fear accidents.

   (D) Purchasers of passenger cars do not normally purchase stochastic fuel injection because it is expensive.

   (E) Some passenger sedans are high-powered racing vehicles.

23. During New York City's fiscal crisis of the late 1970s, governmental leaders debated whether to offer federal assistance to New York City. One economist who opposed the suggestion asked, "Are we supposed to help out New York City every time it gets into financial problems?"

   The economist's question can be criticized because it

   (A) uses ambiguous terms.

   (B) assumes everyone else agrees New York City should be helped.

   (C) appeals to emotions rather than using logic.

   (D) relies upon second-hand reports rather than first-hand accounts.

   (E) completely ignores the issue at hand.

24. Some philosophers have argued that there exist certain human or natural rights that belong to all human beings by virtue of their humanity. But a review of the laws of different societies shows that the rights accorded a person vary from society to society and even within a society over time. Since there is no right that is universally protected, there are no natural rights.

A defender of the theory that natural rights do exist might respond to this objection by arguing that

(A) some human beings do not have any natural rights.

(B) some human rights are natural while others derive from a source such as a constitution.

(C) people in one society may have natural rights that people in another society lack.

(D) all societies have some institution that protects the rights of an individual in that society.

(E) natural rights may exist even though they are not protected by some societies.

STOP

END OF SECTION 1. IF YOU HAVE ANY TIME LEFT, GO OVER YOUR WORK IN THIS SECTION ONLY. DO NOT WORK IN ANY OTHER SECTION OF THE TEST.

SECTION 2

24 Questions • Time—35 Minutes

Directions: Each group of questions is based on a set of propositions or conditions. Drawing a rough picture or diagram may help in answering some of the questions. After you have chosen the *best* answer for each question, blacken the corresponding space on your answer sheet.

Questions 1–6

A railway system consists of six stations, G, H, I, J, K, and L. Trains run only according to the following conditions:

From	G to H
From	H to G and from H to I
From	I to J
From	J to H and from J to K
From	L to G; from L to K, and from L to I
From	K to J

It is possible to transfer at a station for another train.

1. How is it possible to get from H to J?

   (A) A direct train from H to J

   (B) A train to G and transfer for a train to J

   (C) A train to L and transfer for a train to J

   (D) A train to I and transfer for a train to J

   (E) It is impossible to reach J from H.

2. Which of the following stations CANNOT be reached by a train from any of the other stations?

   (A) G

   (B) H

   (C) I

   (D) K

   (E) L

3. Which of the following is a complete and accurate listing of the stations from that it is possible to reach I with exactly one transfer?

   (A) G and H

   (B) G and J

   (C) J and K

   (D) J and L

   (E) J, G, and L

4. What is the greatest number of stations that can be visited without visiting any station more than once?

   (A) 2

   (B) 3

   (C) 4

   (D) 5

   (E) 6

5. Which of the following trips requires the greatest number of transfers?

   (A) G to I

   (B) H to K

   (C) L to H

   (D) L to I

   (E) L to K

6. If station I is closed, which of the following trips is impossible?

   (A) G to J

   (B) J to K

   (C) L to K

   (D) L to J

   (E) L to G

Questions 7–12

A travel agent is arranging tours that visit various cities: L, M, N, O, P, Q, R, S, T. Each tour must be arranged in accordance with the following restrictions:

If M is included in a tour, both Q and R must also be included.

P can be included in a tour only if O is also included.

If Q is included in a tour, M must be included along with N or T or both.

P and Q cannot both be included in a tour.

A tour cannot include O, R, and T.

A tour cannot include N, S, and R.

A tour cannot include L and R.

7. If M is included in a tour, what is the minimum number of other cities that must be included in the tour?

(A) 2

(B) 3

(C) 4

(D) 5

(E) 6

8. Which of the following cities cannot be included in a tour that includes P?

(A) M

(B) N

(C) O

(D) S

(E) R

9. Which of the following is an acceptable group of cities for a tour?

(A) M, N, O, P

(B) M, N, Q, R

(C) M, N, Q, S

(D) L, M, Q, R

(E) N, S, R, T

10. Which one city would have to be deleted from the group M, Q, O, R, T to form an acceptable tour?

(A) M

(B) Q

(C) O

(D) R

(E) T

11. Which of the following could be made into an acceptable tour by adding exactly one more city?

(A) L, O, R

(B) M, P, Q

(C) M, Q, R

(D) N, S, R

(E) R, T, P

12. Exactly how many of the cities could be used for a tour consisting of only one city?

(A) 2

(B) 3

(C) 4

(D) 5

(E) 6

Questions 13–18

A child is stringing 11 different colored beads on a string.

Of the 11, four are yellow, three are red, two are blue, and two are green.

The red beads are adjacent to one another.

The blue beads are adjacent to one another.

The green beads are not adjacent to one another.

A red bead is at one end of the string, and a green bead is at the other end.

13. If the sixth and seventh beads are blue and the tenth bead is red, which of the following must be true?

   (A) The second bead is green.

   (B) The fifth bead is yellow.

   (C) The eighth bead is green.

   (D) A green bead is next to a yellow bead.

   (E) A blue bead is next to a green bead.

14. If the four yellow beads are next to each other and if the tenth bead is yellow, which of the following beads must be blue?

   (A) Fourth

   (B) Fifth

   (C) Sixth

   (D) Seventh

   (E) Eighth

15. If each blue bead is next to a green bead and if the four yellow beads are next to each other, then which of the following is a complete and accurate listing of the beads that must be yellow?

   (A) Fourth and fifth

   (B) Fifth and sixth

   (C) Sixth and seventh

   (D) Fourth, fifth, and sixth

   (E) Fifth, sixth, and seventh

16. If the fifth and sixth beads are blue and the ninth bead is red, which of the following must be true?

   (A) One of the green beads is next to a blue bead.

   (B) One of the red beads is next to a green bead.

   (C) Each yellow bead is next to at least one other yellow bead.

   (D) The second bead is yellow.

   (E) The eighth bead is yellow.

17. If the fifth, eighth, ninth, and tenth beads are yellow, then all of the following must be true EXCEPT

   (A) the fourth bead is green.

   (B) the sixth bead is blue.

   (C) exactly one red bead is next to a green bead.

   (D) both blue beads are next to yellow beads.

   (E) the second bead is yellow.

18. If one green bead is next to a red bead and the other green bead is next to a blue bead, which of the following must be true?

   (A) The second bead is blue.

   (B) The fourth bead is green.

   (C) The fourth bead is yellow.

   (D) The seventh bead is yellow.

   (E) The eighth bead is green.

Questions 19–24

The Executive Officer of a college English department is hiring adjunct faculty members for her evening courses. She must offer exactly eight courses during the academic year, four in the fall semester and four in the spring semester. The candidates are J, K, L, M, N, and O. Each person, if hired, must teach the following:

   J must teach one course on Marlowe and one course on Joyce.

   K must teach one course on Shakespeare and one course on Keats.

   L must teach one course on Marlowe and one course on Chaucer.

   M must teach one course on Shakespeare, one course on Marlowe, and one course on Keats.

   N must teach one course on Joyce, one course on Keats, and one course on Chaucer.

   O must teach one course on Shakespeare, one course on Marlowe, and one course on Joyce.

Only one course on an author can be offered in a single semester.

19. Which of the following combinations of teachers can be hired?

(A) J, K, and N

(B) K, M, and N

(C) K, M, and O

(D) L, M, and O

(E) L, N, and O

20. If L and N are hired and if N is assigned to teach only in the spring semester, which of the following could be true?

(A) Neither M nor O will be hired.

(B) L will teach only in the spring semester.

(C) L will teach only in the fall semester.

(D) Courses on Keats and Joyce will be offered in the fall semester.

(E) Courses on Shakespeare and Marlowe will be offered in the spring semester.

21. If M and N are hired and if M will teach only one of the two semesters and N the other, which of the following must be true?

(A) J is hired.

(B) K is hired.

(C) L is hired.

(D) A course on Shakespeare will be offered in the fall semester.

(E) A course on Marlowe will be offered in the spring semester.

22. If K and N are hired, which of the following must be true?

(A) A course on Joyce is offered in one semester or the other but not both.

(B) A course on Keats is offered in one semester or the other but not both.

(C) A course on Marlowe is offered both semesters.

(D) A course on Shakespeare is offered both semesters.

(E) A course on Chaucer is offered both semeseters.

23. If L is hired and will teach both her courses in the fall semester, which of the following must be true?

(A) M and N are hired.

(B) M and O are hired.

(C) N and O are hired.

(D) A course on Joyce will be offered in the spring semester.

(E) A course on Chaucer will be offered in the spring semester.

24. If K, N, and O are hired and if N will teach all three of her courses in the fall semester, all of the following must be true EXCEPT

(A) a course on Keats will be taught in the spring semester.

(B) a course on Marlowe will be taught in the spring semester.

(C) courses on Keats and Joyce will be taught in both semesters.

(D) a course on Marlowe and a course on Shakespeare will be taught in the spring semester.

(E) a course on Shakespeare and a course on Chaucer will be taught in the spring semester.

STOP

END OF SECTION 2. IF YOU HAVE ANY TIME LEFT, GO OVER YOUR WORK IN THIS SECTION ONLY. DO NOT WORK IN ANY OTHER SECTION OF THE TEST.

SECTION 3

28 Questions • Time—35 Minutes

Directions: Below each of the following passages, you will find questions or incomplete statements about the passage. Each statement or question is followed by lettered words or expressions. Select the word or expression that most satisfactorily completes each statement or answers each question in accordance with the meaning of the passage. After you have chosen the *best* answer, blacken the corresponding space on the answer sheet.

War has escaped the battlefield and now can, with modern guidance systems on missiles, touch virtually every square yard of the earth's surface. It no longer
(5) involves only the military profession but also engulfs entire civilian populations. Nuclear weapons have made major war unthinkable. We are forced, however, to think about the unthinkable because a
(10) thermonuclear war could come by accident or miscalculation. We must accept the paradox of maintaining a capacity to fight such a war so that we will never have to do so.

(15)   War has also lost most of its utility in achieving the traditional goals of conflict. Control of territory carries with it the obligation to provide subject peoples certain administrative, health, educa-
(20) tion, and other social services; such obligations far out-weigh the benefits of control. If the ruled population is ethnically or racially different from the rulers, tensions and chronic unrest often
(25) exist that further reduce the benefits and increase the costs of domination. Large populations no longer necessarily enhance state power and, in the absence of high levels of economic development,
(30) can impose severe burdens on food supply, jobs, and the broad range of services expected of modern governments. The noneconomic security reasons for the control of territory have been progres-
(35) sively undermined by the advances of modern technology. The benefits of forcing another nation to surrender its wealth are vastly outweighed by the

benefits of persuading that nation to
(40) produce and exchange goods and services. In brief, imperialism no longer pays.

Making war has been one of the most persistent of human activities in
(45) the 80 centuries since men and women settled in cities and became thereby "civilized," but the modernization of the past 80 years has fundamentally changed the role and function of war. In pre-
(50) modernized societies, successful warfare brought significant material rewards, the most obvious of which were the stored wealth of the defeated. Equally important was human labor—control over
(55) people as slaves or levies for the victor's army—and the productive capacity of agricultural lands and mines. Successful warfare also produced psychic benefits. The removal or destruction of a
(60) threat brought a sense of security, and power gained over others created pride and national self-esteem.

Warfare was also the most complex, broad-scale, and demanding activ-
(65) ity of pre-modernized people. The challenges of leading men into battle—organizing, moving, and supporting armies—attracted the talents of the most vigorous, enterprising, intelligent, and
(70) imaginative men in the society. "Warrior" and "statesman" were usually synonymous, and the military was one of the few professions in which an able, ambitious boy of humble origin could
(75) rise to the top. In the broader cultural context, war was accepted in the

pre-modernized society as a part of the human condition, a mechanism of change, and an unavoidable, even noble, *(80)* aspect of life. The excitement and drama of war made it a vital part of literature and legends.

1. The primary purpose of the passage is to

    (A) theorize about the role of the warrior-statesman in pre-modernized society.

    (B) explain the effects of war on both modernized and pre-modernized societies.

    (C) contrast the value of war in a modernized society with its value in pre-modernized society.

    (D) discuss the political and economic circumstances that lead to war in pre-modernized societies.

    (E) examine the influence of the development of nuclear weapons on the possibility of war.

2. According to the passage, leaders of pre-modernized society considered war to be

    (A) a valid tool of national policy.

    (B) an immoral act of aggression.

    (C) economically wasteful and socially unfeasible.

    (D) restricted in scope to military participants.

    (E) necessary to spur development of unoccupied lands.

3. The author most likely places the word "civilized" in quotation marks (line 46) in order to

    (A) show dissatisfaction at not having found a better word.

    (B) acknowledge that the word was borrowed from another source.

    (C) express irony that war should be a part of civilization.

    (D) impress upon the reader the tragedy of war.

    (E) raise a question about the value of war in modernized society.

4. The author mentions all of the following as possible reasons for going to war in a pre-modernized society EXCEPT

    (A) possibility of material gain.

    (B) promoting deserving young men to higher positions.

    (C) potential for increasing the security of the nation.

    (D) desire to capture productive farming lands.

    (E) need for workers to fill certain jobs.

5. The author is primarily concerned with discussing how

    (A) political decisions are reached.

    (B) economic and social conditions have changed.

    (C) technology for making war has improved.

    (D) armed conflict has changed.

    (E) war lost its value as a policy tool.

6. Which of the following best describes the tone of the passage?

    (A) Outraged and indignant

    (B) Scientific and detached

    (C) Humorous and wry

    (D) Fearful and alarmed

    (E) Concerned and optimistic

7. With which of the following statements about a successfully completed program of nuclear disarmament would the author most likely agree?

(A) Without nuclear weapons, war in modernized society would have the same value it had in pre-modernized society.

(B) In the absence of the danger of nuclear war, national leaders could use powerful conventional weapons to make great gains from war.

(C) Eliminating nuclear weapons is likely to increase the danger of an all-out, worldwide military engagement.

(D) Even without the danger of a nuclear disaster, the costs of winning a war have made armed conflict on a large scale virtually obsolete.

(E) War is caused by aggressive instincts, so if nuclear weapons were no longer available, national leaders would use conventional weapons to reach the same end.

Although it is now possible to bring most high blood pressure under control, the causes of essential hypertension remain elusive. Understanding how hyperten-
(5) sion begins is at least partly a problem of understanding when in life it begins; and this may be very early—perhaps within the first few months. Since the beginning of the century, physicians have
(10) been aware that hypertension may run in families, but before the 1970s, studies of the familial aggregation of blood pressure treated only populations 15 years of age or older. Few studies were at-
(15) tempted in younger persons because of a prevailing notion that blood pressures in this age group were difficult to measure or unreliable and because essential hypertension was widely regarded as a
(20) disease of adults.

In 1971, a study of 700 children, ages two to fourteen, used a special blood pressure recorder that minimizes observer error and allows for standardiza-
(25) tion of blood pressure readings. Before then, it had been well established that the blood pressure of adults aggregates familially, that is, the similarities between the blood pressure of an indi-
(30) vidual and his siblings are generally too great to be explained by chance. The 1971 study showed that familial clustering was measurable in children as well, suggesting that factors responsible for
(35) essential hypertension are acquired in childhood. Additional epidemiological studies demonstrated a clear tendency for the children to retain the same blood pressure patterns, relative to their peers,
(40) four years later. Thus a child with blood pressure higher or lower than the norm would tend to remain higher or lower with increasing age.

Meanwhile, other investigators un-
(45) covered a complex of physiologic roles—including blood pressure—for a vaso-active system called the kallikrein-kinin system. Kallikreins are enzymes in the kidney and blood plasma that act on
(50) precursors called kininogens to produce vasoactive peptides called kinins. Several different kinins are produced, at least three of which are powerful blood vessel dilators. Apparently, the
(55) kallikrein-kinin system normally tends to offset the elevations in arterial pressure that result from the secretion of salt-conserving hormones such as aldosterone on the one hand and from activa-
(60) tion of the sympathetic nervous system (which tends to constrict blood vessels) on the other hand.

It is also known that urinary kallikrein excretion is abnormally low in
(65) subjects with essential hypertension. Levels of urinary kallikrein in children are inversely related to the diastolic blood pressures of both children and their mothers. Children with the lowest
(70) kallikrein levels are found in the families with the highest blood pressures. In addition, black children tend to show somewhat lower urinary kallikrein levels than white children, and blacks are
(75) more likely to have high blood pressure. There is a great deal to be learned about

the biochemistry and physiologic roles of the kallikrein-kinin system. But there is the possibility that essential hyper-
(80) tension will prove to have biochemical precursors.

8. The author is primarily concerned with

   (A) questioning the assumption behind certain experiments involving children under the age of 15.

   (B) describing new scientific findings about high blood pressure and suggesting some implications.

   (C) describing two different methods for studying the causes of high blood pressure.

   (D) revealing a discrepancy between the findings of epidemiological studies and laboratory studies on essential hypertension.

   (E) arguing that high blood pressure may be influenced by familial factors.

9. Which of the following is mentioned as a factor that initially discouraged the study of hypertension in children?

   (A) An expectation that high blood pressure in children was untreatable

   (B) Repeated unsuccessful attempts to treat hypertension in adults

   (C) The belief that blood pressure in adults aggregates familially

   (D) The belief that it was difficult or impossible to measure accurately blood pressure in children

   (E) Ignorance of important differences in the physical constitution of ethnic subgroups

10. The argument in the passage leads most naturally to which of the following conclusions?

   (A) A low output of urinary kallikrein is a likely cause of high blood pressure in children.

   (B) The kallikrein-kinin system plays an important role in the regulation of blood pressure.

   (C) Essential hypertension may have biochemical precursors that may be useful predictors even in children.

   (D) The failure of the body to produce sufficient amounts of kinins is the cause of essential hypertension.

   (E) It is now possible to predict high blood pressure by using familial aggregations and urinary kallikrein measurement.

11. The author refers to the somewhat lower urinary kallikrein levels in black children (lines 71–75) in order to

   (A) support the thesis that kallikrein levels are inversely related to blood pressure.

   (B) highlight the special health problems involved in treating populations with high concentrations of black children.

   (C) offer a causal explanation for the difference in urinary kallikrein levels between black and white children.

   (D) suggest that further study needs to be done on the problem of high blood pressure among black adults.

   (E) prove that hypertension can be treated if those persons likely to have high blood pressure can be found.

12. The author states that the kallikrein-kinin system may affect blood pressure by

 (A) directly opposing the tendency of the sympathetic nervous system to constrict blood vessels.

 (B) producing kinins that tend to dilate blood vessels.

 (C) suppressing the production of hormones such as aldosterone.

 (D) controlling the levels of kallikrein in the urine.

 (E) compensating for cross-subgroup differentials.

13. The evidence that a child with blood pressure higher or lower than the norm would tend to remain so with increasing age (lines 40–43) is introduced by the author in order to

 (A) suggest that essential hypertension may have biochemical causes.

 (B) show that high blood pressure can be detected in children under the age of 15.

 (C) provide evidence that factors affecting blood pressure are already present in children.

 (D) propose that screening of children for high blood pressure should be increased.

 (E) refute arguments that blood pressure in children cannot be measured reliably.

14. The author presents the argument primarily by

 (A) contrasting two methods of doing scientific research.

 (B) providing experimental evidence against a conclusion.

 (C) presenting new scientific findings for a conclusion.

 (D) analyzing a new theory and showing its defects.

 (E) criticizing scientific research on blood pressure done before 1971.

Many critics of the current welfare system argue that existing welfare regulations foster family instability. They maintain that those regulations, which
(5) exclude most poor husband-and-wife families from Aid to Families with Dependent Children assistance grants, contribute to the problem of family dissolution. Thus, they conclude that
(10) expanding the set of families eligible for family assistance plans or guaranteed income measures would result in a marked strengthening of the low-income family structure.
(15)   If all poor families could receive welfare, would the incidence of instability change markedly? The answer to this question depends on the relative importance of three categories of potential
(20) welfare recipients. The first is the "cheater"—the husband who is reported to have abandoned his family but in fact disappears only when the social caseworker is in the neighborhood. The sec-
(25) ond consists of a loving husband and devoted father who, sensing his own inadequacy as a provider, leaves so that his wife and children may enjoy the relative benefit provided by public assis-
(30) tance. There is very little evidence that these categories are significant.
     The third category is the unhappily married couple, who remain together out of a sense of economic responsibility
(35) for their children, because of the high costs of separation, or because of the consumption benefits of marriage. This

group is large. The formation, maintenance, and dissolution of the family is in
(40) large part a function of the relative balance between the benefits and costs of
marriage as seen by the individual members of the marriage. The major benefit
generated by the creation of a family is
(45) the expansion of the set of consumption
possibilities. The benefits from such a
partnership depend largely on the relative dissimilarity of the resources or
basic endowments each partner brings
(50) to the marriage. Persons with similar
productive capacities have less economic
"cement" holding their marriage together. Since the family performs certain functions society regards as vital, a
(55) complex network of social and legal buttresses has evolved to reinforce marriage. Much of the variation in marital
stability across income classes can be
explained by the variation in costs of
(60) dissolution imposed by society, such as
division of property, alimony, child support, and the social stigma attached to
divorce.

Marital stability is related to the
(65) costs of achieving an acceptable agreement on family consumption and production and to the prevailing social price
of instability in the marriage partners'
social-economic group. Expected AFDC
(70) income exerts pressures on family instability by reducing the cost of dissolution.
To the extent that welfare is a form of
government-subsidized alimony payments, it reduces the institutional costs
(75) of separation and guarantees a minimal
standard of living for wife and children.
So welfare opportunities are a significant determinant of family instability in
poor neighborhoods, but this is not the
(80) result of AFDC regulations that exclude
most intact families from coverage.
Rather, welfare-related instability occurs because public assistance lowers
both the benefits of marriage and the
(85) costs of its disruption by providing a
system of government-subsidized alimony payments.

15. The author is primarily concerned with
(A) interpreting the results of a survey.
(B) discussing the role of the father in low-income families.
(C) analyzing the causes of a phenomenon.
(D) recommending reforms to the welfare system.
(E) changing public attitudes toward welfare recipients.

16. Which of the following would provide the most logical continuation of the final paragraph?
(A) Paradoxically, any liberalization of AFDC eligibility restrictions is likely to intensify rather than mitigate pressures on family stability.
(B) Actually, concern for the individual recipients should not be allowed to override considerations of sound fiscal policy.
(C) In reality, there is virtually no evidence that AFDC payments have any relationship at all to problems of family instability in low-income marriages.
(D) In the final analysis, it appears that government welfare payments, to the extent that the cost of marriage is lowered, encourage the formation of low-income families.
(E) Ultimately, the problem of low-income family instability can be eliminated by reducing welfare benefits to the point where the cost of dissolution equals the cost of staying married.

17. All of the following are mentioned by the author as factors tending to perpetuate a marriage EXCEPT

   (A) the stigma attached to divorce.

   (B) the social class of the partners.

   (C) the cost of alimony and child support.

   (D) the loss of property upon divorce.

   (E) the greater consumption possibilities of married people.

18. Which of the following best summarizes the main idea of the passage?

   (A) Welfare restrictions limiting the eligibility of families for benefits do not contribute to low-income family instability.

   (B) Contrary to popular opinion, the most significant category of welfare recipients is not the "cheating" father.

   (C) The incidence of family dissolution among low-income families is directly related to the inability of families with fathers to get welfare benefits.

   (D) Very little of the divorce rate among low-income families can be attributed to fathers deserting their families so that they can qualify for welfare.

   (E) Government welfare payments are at present excessively high and must be reduced in order to slow the growing divorce rate among low-income families.

19. The tone of the passage can best be described as

   (A) confident and optimistic.

   (B) scientific and detached.

   (C) discouraged and alarmed.

   (D) polite and sensitive.

   (E) calloused and indifferent.

20. With which of the following statements about marriage would the author most likely agree?

   (A) Marriage is an institution that is largely shaped by powerful but impersonal economic and social forces.

   (B) Marriage has a greater value to persons in higher income brackets than to persons in lower income brackets.

   (C) Society has no legitimate interest in encouraging people to remain married to one another.

   (D) Marriage as an institution is no longer economically viable and will gradually give way to other forms of social organization.

   (E) The rising divorce rate across all income brackets indicates that people are more self-centered and less concerned about others than before.

21. The passage would most likely be found in a

   (A) pamphlet on civil rights.

   (B) basic economics text.

   (C) book on the history of welfare.

   (D) religious tract on the importance of marriage.

   (E) scholarly journal devoted to public policy questions

An assumption that underlies most discussions of electric facility siting is that the initial selection of a site is the responsibility of the utility concerned—
(5) subject to governmental review and approval only after the site has been chosen. This assumption must be changed so that site selection becomes a joint responsibility of the utilities and
(10) the appropriate governmental authorities from the outset. Siting decisions would be made in accordance with either of two strategies. The metropolitan strategy takes the existing distribution
(15) of population and supporting facilities as given. An attempt is then made to

choose between dispersed or concentrated siting and to locate generating facilities in accordance with some economic principle. For example, the economic objectives of least-cost construction and rapid start-up may be achieved, in part, by a metropolitan strategy that takes advantage of existing elements of social and physical infrastructure in the big cities. Under the frontier strategy, the energy park may be taken as an independent variable, subject to manipulation by policymakers as a means of achieving desired demographic or social goals, such as rural-town-city mix. Thus, population distribution is taken as a goal of national social policy, not as a given of a national energy policy. In the frontier strategy, the option of dispersed siting is irrelevant from the standpoint of community impact because there is no pre-existing community of any size.

(40)   Traditionally, the resource-endowment of a location—and especially its situation relative to the primary industry of the hinterland—has had a special importance in American history. In the early agricultural period, the most valued natural endowment was arable land with good climate and available water. America's oldest cities were mercantile outposts of such agricultural areas. Deepwater ports developed to serve the agricultural hinterlands, which produced staple commodities in demand on the world market. From the 1840s onward, the juxtaposition of coal, iron ore, and markets afforded the impetus for manufacturing growth in the northeastern United States. The American manufacturing heartland developed westwards to encompass Lake Superior iron ores, the Pennsylvania coalfields, and the Northeast's financial, entrepreneurial, and manufacturing roles. Subsequent metropolitan growth has been organized around this national core.

(65)   Against the theory of urban development, it is essential to bear in mind the unprecedented dimensions of an energy park. The existing electric power plant at Four Corners in the southwest United States—the only human artifact visible to orbiting astronauts—generates only 4 thousand megawatts electric. The smallest energy parks will concentrate five times the thermal energy represented by the Four Corners plant. An energy park, then, would seem every bit as formidable as the natural harbor conditions or coal deposits that underwrote the growth of the great cities of the past—with a crucial difference. The founders of past settlements could not choose the geographic locations of their natural advantages.

The frontier strategy implements the principle of created opportunity; and this helps explain why some environmentalists perceive the energy park idea as a threat to nature. But the problems of modern society, with or without energy parks, require ever more comprehensive planning. And energy parks are a means of advancing American social history rather than merely responding to power needs in an unplanned, *ad hoc* manner.

22. Which of the following statements best describes the main point of the passage?

(A) Government regulatory authorities should participate in electric facility site selection to further social goals.

(B) Energy parks will have a significant influence on the demographic features of the American population.

(C) Urban growth in the United States was largely the result of economic forces rather than conscientious planning.

(D) Under the frontier siting strategy for energy parks, siting decisions are influenced by the natural features of the land.

(E) America needs larger power-production facilities in urban and rural areas to meet the increased demand for energy.

23. All of the following are mentioned in the passage as characteristics of energy parks EXCEPT

   (A) energy parks will be built upon previously undeveloped sites.

   (B) energy parks will be built in areas remote from major population centers.

   (C) energy parks will produce considerably more thermal energy than existing facilities.

   (D) energy parks will be built at sites that are near fuel sources such as coal.

   (E) energy parks may have considerable effects on population distribution.

24. According to the passage, which of the following is the most important feature of the traditional process of siting decisions for electric facilities?

   (A) Sites were selected for the ability to advance social history.

   (B) Siting was viewed as a tool for achieving economic goals.

   (C) The primary responsibility for siting resided with the utility.

   (D) Decisions were made jointly by utilities and government.

   (E) Groups of affected citizens participated on advisory panels.

25. Which of the following, if true, would most seriously WEAKEN the author's position?

   (A) The first settlements in America were established in order to provide trading posts with Native Americans.

   (B) The cost of constructing an electric power plant in an urban area is not significantly greater than that for a rural area.

   (C) An energy park will be so large that it will be impossible to predict the demographic consequences of its construction.

   (D) Cities in European countries grew up in response to political pressures during the feudal period rather than economic pressures.

   (E) The United States is presently in a period of population migration that will change the rural-town-city mix.

26. With which one of the following statements would the author most likely agree?

   (A) Decisions about the locations for power plants should be left to the utilities.

   (B) Government leaders in the nineteenth century were irresponsible in not supervising urban growth more closely.

   (C) Natural features of a region such as cultivatable land and water supply are no longer important to urban growth.

   (D) Modern society is so complex that governments must take greater responsibility for decisions such as power plant siting.

   (E) The Four Corners plant should not have been built because of its mammoth size.

27. According to the passage, the most important difference between the natural advantages of early cities and the features of an energy park is

    (A) the features of an energy park will be located where the builders choose.

    (B) natural advantages are no longer as important as they once were.

    (C) natural features cannot be observed from outer space, but energy parks can.

    (D) early cities grew up close to agricultural areas, while energy parks will be located in mountains.

    (E) policy planners have learned to minimize the effects of energy parks on nature.

28. The author's attitude toward energy parks can best be described as

    (A) cautious uncertainty.

    (B) circumspect skepticism.

    (C) studied indifference.

    (D) qualified endorsement.

    (E) unrestrained enthusiasm.

STOP

END OF SECTION 3. IF YOU HAVE ANY TIME LEFT, GO OVER YOUR WORK IN THIS SECTION ONLY. DO NOT WORK IN ANY OTHER SECTION OF THE TEST.

SECTION 4

24 Questions • Time—35 Minutes

Directions: Each group of questions is based on a set of propositions or conditions. Drawing a rough picture or diagram may help in answering some of the questions. After you have chosen the *best* answer for each question, blacken the corresponding space on your answer sheet.

Questions 1–6

Six contestants, F, G, H, I, J, and K, are to be ranked first (highest) through sixth (lowest), though not necessarily in that order, at the start of a singles Ping-Pong challenge tournament.

> F is ranked above G.
> J is ranked above both H and I.
> K is ranked two places above H.
> F is ranked either third or fourth.

During the tournament, a player may challenge only the player ranked immediately above him or the player ranked two places above him.

1. Which of the following is a possible initial ranking from highest to lowest?
   - **(A)** J, H, K, F, I, G
   - **(B)** K, I, H, J, F, G
   - **(C)** K, G, H, F, J, I
   - **(D)** J, K, F, H, I, G
   - **(E)** J, K, H, F, I, G

2. If K is initially ranked first, which of the following must also be true of the initial ranking?
   - **(A)** J is ranked second.
   - **(B)** H is ranked second.
   - **(C)** F is ranked third.
   - **(D)** G is ranked fifth.
   - **(E)** I is ranked sixth.

3. If F is initially ranked third, which of the following must also be true of the initial ranking?
   - **(A)** J is ranked first.
   - **(B)** K is ranked second.
   - **(C)** G is ranked fourth.
   - **(D)** I is ranked fourth.
   - **(E)** I is ranked sixth.

4. If K is initially ranked third and if K makes the first challenge, which of the following is a complete and accurate listing of the contestants K could play in the first match?
   - **(A)** I
   - **(B)** J
   - **(C)** J and F
   - **(D)** J and I
   - **(E)** J, F, and I

5. If the first challenge of the tournament is made by F against H, all of the following must be true of the initial ranking EXCEPT
   - **(A)** K is ranked first.
   - **(B)** J is ranked second.
   - **(C)** H is ranked third.
   - **(D)** F is ranked fourth.
   - **(E)** I is ranked fifth.

6. If J makes the first challenge of the tournament against K, then which of the following must be true of the initial rankings?

(A) K is ranked first.

(B) J is ranked third.

(C) F is ranked third.

(D) H is ranked fourth.

(E) G is ranked fifth.

Questions 7–10

The supervisor of a commuter airline is scheduling pilots to fly the round trip from City X to City Y. The trip takes only two hours, and the airline has one round-trip flight in the morning and one round-trip flight in the afternoon, each day, Monday through Friday. Pilots must be scheduled in accordance with the following rules:

Only W, X, and Y can fly the morning flight.

Only V, X, and Z can fly the afternoon flight.

No pilot may fly twice on the same day.

No pilot may fly on two consecutive days.

X must fly the Wednesday morning flight.

Z must fly the Tuesday afternoon flight.

7. Which of the following must be true?

(A) W flies the Monday morning flight.

(B) X flies the Monday afternoon flight.

(C) Y flies the Tuesday morning flight.

(D) W flies the Thursday morning flight.

(E) Z flies the Thursday afternoon flight.

8. If X flies on Friday morning, which of the following must be true?

(A) X does not fly on Monday afternoon.

(B) V flies on Friday afternoon.

(C) W flies Thursday morning.

(D) Y flies Thursday morning.

(E) Neither W nor Y flies Thursday morning.

9. If X flies only one morning flight during the week, which of the following must be true?

(A) W flies exactly two days during the week.

(B) X flies exactly three days during the week.

(C) Y flies only one day during the week.

(D) Z flies Monday afternoon and Friday afternoon.

(E) X flies more times during the week than V.

10. If W is not scheduled to fly at all during the week, all of the following must be true EXCEPT

(A) X flies on Monday morning.

(B) V flies on Monday afternoon.

(C) Y flies on Thursday morning.

(D) Z flies on Friday afternoon.

(E) X flies on Friday morning.

Questions 11–15

A restaurant offers three daily specials each day of the week. The daily specials are selected from a list of dishes: P, Q, R, S, T, and U. The daily specials for the menu are selected in accordance with the following restrictions:

On any day that S is on the menu, Q must also be on the menu.

If R is on the menu one day, it cannot be included on the menu the following day.

U can be on the menu only on a day following a day on which T is on the menu.

Only one of the three specials from a given day can be offered the following day.

11. Which of the following could be the list of daily specials offered two days in a row?

   (A) S, R, and T; R, P, and Q
   (B) Q, S, and R; Q, S, and T
   (C) P, Q, and S; S, R, and T
   (D) Q, S, and P; T, U, and Q
   (E) S, Q, and R; Q, T, and P

12. If P and S are on the menu one day, which of the following must be true of the menu the following day?

   (A) U is on the menu.
   (B) S is on the menu.
   (C) T and R are on the menu.
   (D) U and T are on the menu.
   (E) U and R are on the menu.

13. If P, R, and Q are on the menu one day and P, T, and R are on the menu two days later, which daily specials must have appeared on the menu for the intervening day?

   (A) P, R, and T
   (B) P, S, and T
   (C) Q, S, and T
   (D) Q, S, and U
   (E) S, T, and U

14. If on a certain day neither Q nor T is on the menu, how many different combinations of daily specials are possible for that day?

   (A) 1
   (B) 2
   (C) 3
   (D) 4
   (E) 5

15. If Q, R, and S are on the menu one day, which specials must be offered the following day?

   (A) P, Q, and T
   (B) P, R, and T
   (C) P, R, and U
   (D) R, S, and Q
   (E) T, S, and U

Questions 16–20

The personnel director of a company is scheduling interviews for eight people—J, K, L, M, N, O, P, and Q. Each person will have one interview, and all interviews are to be held on Monday through Friday of the same week.

   At least one person will be interviewed each day.

   More than one interview will be scheduled on exactly two of the days.

   O is the only person who will be interviewed on Wednesday.

   M and N must be scheduled for interviews exactly three days after Q.

   P must be interviewed later in the week than K.

16. Which of the following CANNOT be true?

   (A) O's interview is later in the week than K's interview.
   (B) L's interview is later in the week than J's interview.
   (C) K's interview is later in the week than N's interview.
   (D) L's interview is on the same day as N's interview.
   (E) J's interview is on the same day as K's interview.

17. Which of the following must be true?

    (A) A third interview is scheduled on the same day with M and N.

    (B) Exactly three interviews will be held on one of the days.

    (C) Exactly one person will be interviewed on Monday.

    (D) Exactly two persons will be interviewed on Friday.

    (E) Q will have the only interview on Tuesday.

18. If Q and J are the only persons interviewed on Tuesday, which of the following must be true?

    (A) K's is the only interview on one of the days.

    (B) L's is the only interview on one of the days.

    (C) P's is the only interview on one of the days.

    (D) P's interview is earlier in the week than N's interview.

    (E) L's interview is earlier in the week than O's interview.

19. If M, N, and K are interviewed on the same day, which of the following must be true?

    (A) J is interviewed on Monday.

    (B) Q is interviewed on Monday.

    (C) L is interviewed on Tuesday.

    (D) J and L are interviewed on the same day.

    (E) J and Q are interviewed on the same day.

20. If L is interviewed later in the week than P, which of the following CANNOT be true?

    (A) P is the only person interviewed on one of the days.

    (B) K is the only person interviewed on one of the days.

    (C) L and Q are interviewed on the same day.

    (D) L and J are interviewed on the same day.

    (E) M and P are interviewed on the same day.

Questions 21–24

A university acting class is presenting a series of five skits using six performers, M, N, O, P, Q, and R. Each performer must perform in exactly three of the skits.

Only O and P will perform in the first skit.

R and three others will perform in the second skit.

Only N will perform in the third skit.

More people will perform in the fourth skit than in the fifth skit.

21. Which of the following must be true?

    (A) N and Q perform in the second skit.

    (B) N and R perform in the fifth skit.

    (C) Q does not perform in the fifth skit.

    (D) Exactly four people perform in the fourth skit.

    (E) Exactly five people perform in the fifth skit.

22. For which of the following pairs of performers is it true that if one appears in a skit, the other must also appear?

    (A) M and N

    (B) M and R

    (C) P and O

    (D) P and R

    (E) Q and O

23. Which of the following CANNOT be true?

(A) Neither O nor P appears in the second skit.

(B) Neither O nor P appears in the fifth skit.

(C) N and Q appear in the second skit.

(D) N appears in the second skit.

(E) O, P, and Q appear in the fifth skit.

24. If N does not appear in the fifth skit, all of the following must be true EXCEPT

(A) P appears in the second skit.

(B) N appears in the second skit.

(C) O appears in the fifth skit.

(D) P appears in the fifth skit.

(E) Q appears in the fifth skit.

STOP

END OF SECTION 4. IF YOU HAVE ANY TIME LEFT, GO OVER YOUR WORK IN THIS SECTION ONLY. DO NOT WORK IN ANY OTHER SECTION OF THE TEST.

SECTION 5

25 Questions • Time—35 Minutes

Directions: Below each of the following passages, you will find questions or incomplete statements about the passage. Each statement or question is followed by lettered words or expressions. Select the word or expression that most satisfactorily completes each statement or answers each question in accordance with the meaning of the passage. After you have chosen the *best* answer, blacken the corresponding space on the answer sheet.

1. There has been speculation that the Chairman of Global Enterprises will replace the company's CEO next week, but it would be risky for the Chairman to make such a change without first consulting formally with the Board of Directors. There have been no Board meetings recently, and no such meeting has been scheduled for the next few weeks. Therefore, the speculation regarding the change in management is probably wrong.

Which of the following principles best describes the reasoning of the speaker above?

(A) If two statements are logically inconsistent and it is known that one is false, the other statement is necessarily true.

(B) A theory may turn out to be true even though all of the available data initially suggests that the theory is false.

(C) It cannot be assumed from the fact that event E_2 follows event E_1 in time that event E_1 was therefore the cause of event E_2.

(D) A hypothesis is weakened when conditions that are normally necessary for an expected result do not exist.

(E) A cause necessary to ensure a certain outcome may not, in and of itself, be sufficient to guarantee that outcome.

2. Office supply stores and other retailers offer computer programs that will help anyone to prepare a will for themselves. The Bar Association warns that wills produced using these do-it-yourself kits might not be valid, but lawyers are simply afraid that the kits will cut into the fees that they charge. So there is no reason that a person should not create a will using a do-it-yourself kit.

The reasoning above is flawed because the speaker

(A) fails to consider the possibility that many people will still prefer to have a lawyer write their wills

(B) assumes that many lawyers do not use the same do-it-yourself programs offered by retailers to the public

(C) presents a false dichotomy in which a person must choose a lawyer or a do-it-yourself kit

(D) attempts to gain acceptance of a claim by creating apprehension about the alternative

(E) rejects a conclusion by attacking the source of the claim rather than its merits

3. CHARPENTIER: Research has demonstrated that the United States, which has the most extensive health-care industry in the world, has only the 17th lowest infant mortality rate in the world. This forces me to conclude that medical technology causes babies to die.

ADAMANTE: That is ludicrous. We know that medical care is not equally available to all. Infant mortality is more likely a function of low income than of medical technology.

Adamante attacks Charpentier's reasoning in which way?

(A) By questioning the validity of the supporting data

(B) By offering an alternative explanation of the data

(C) By suggesting that the argument is circular

(D) By defining an intermediate cause

(E) By implying that the data leads to the opposite conclusion

4. When this proposal to reduce welfare benefits is brought up for debate, we are sure to hear claims by the liberal politicians that the bill will be detrimental to poor people. These politicians fail to understand, however, that budget reductions are accompanied by tax cuts—so everyone will have more money to spend, not less.

Which of the following, if true, would undermine the author's position?

(A) Poor people tend to vote for liberal politicians who promise to raise welfare benefits.

(B) Politicians often make campaign promises that they do not fulfill.

(C) Poor people pay little or not taxes, so a tax cut would be of little advantage to them.

(D) Any tax advantage enjoyed by the poor will not be offset by cuts in services.

(E) Budget reductions when accompanied by tax cuts often stimulate economic growth.

5. Many people ask, "How effective is Painaway?" So to find out we have been checking the medicine cabinets of the apartments in this typical building. As it turns out, eight out of ten contain a bottle of Painaway. Doesn't it stand to reason that you, too, should have the most effective pain-reliever on the market?

The appeal of this advertisement would be most WEAKENED by which of the following pieces of evidence?

(A) Painaway distributed complimentary bottles of medicine to most apartments in the building two days before the advertisement was made.

(B) The actor who made the advertisement takes a pain-reliever manufactured by a competitor of Painaway.

(C) Most people want a fast, effective pain-reliever.

(D) Many people take the advice of their neighborhood druggists about pain-relievers.

(E) A government survey shows that many people take a pain-reliever before it is really needed.

Questions 6 and 7

An artist must suffer for the sake of art, say these successful entrepreneurs who attempt to pass themselves off as artists. They auction off to the highest bidder, usually a fool, the most mediocre of drawings; and then, from their well-laid tables, they have the unmitigated gall to imply that they themselves _____(6).

6. Choose the answer that best completes the paragraph.

(A) are connoisseurs of art

(B) suffer deprivation for the sake of their work

(C) are artists

(D) know art better than the art critics do

(E) do not enjoy a good meal

7. Which of the following must underlie the author's position?

(A) One must actually suffer to do great art.

(B) Financial deprivation is the only suffering an artist undergoes.

(C) Art critics have little real expertise and are consequently easily deceived.

(D) Most mediocre artists are fools.

(E) All successful entrepreneurs are fools.

Questions 8 and 9

Stock market analysts always attribute a sudden drop in the market to some domestic or international political crisis. I maintain, however, that these declines are attributable to the phases of the moon, which also cause periodic political upheavals and increases in tension in world affairs.

8. Which of the following best describes the author's method of questioning the claim of market analysts?

(A) Presenting a counterexample

(B) Presenting statistical evidence

(C) Suggesting an alternative causal linkage

(D) Appealing to generally accepted beliefs

(E) Demonstrating that market analysts' reports are unreliable

9. It can be inferred that the author is critical of the stock analysts because the author

   (A) believes that they have oversimplified the connection between political crisis and fluctuations of the market.

   (B) knows that the stock market generally shows more gains than losses.

   (C) suspects that stock analysts have a vested interest in the stock market and are therefore likely to distort their explanations.

   (D) anticipates making large profits in the market as an investor.

   (E) is worried that if the connection between political events and stock market prices becomes well known, unscrupulous investors will take advantage of the information.

10. This piece of pottery must surely date from the late Minoan period. The dress of the female figures, particularly the bare and emphasized breasts, and the activities of the people depicted, note especially the importance of the bull, are both highly suggestive of this period. These factors, when coupled with the black, semi-gloss glaze that results from firing the pot in a sealed kiln at a low temperature, make the conclusion a virtual certainty.

    Which of the following is a basic assumption made by the author of this explanation?

    (A) Black, semi-gloss glazed pottery was made only during the late Minoan period.

    (B) The bull is an animal that was important to most ancient cultures.

    (C) Throughout the long history of the Minoan people, their artisans decorated pottery with semi-nude women and bulls.

    (D) By analyzing the style and materials of any work of art, an expert can pinpoint the date of its creation.

    (E) There are key characteristics of works of art that can be shown to be typical of a particular period.

11. Most radicals who argue for violent revolution and complete overthrow of our existing society have no clear idea what will emerge from the destruction. They just assert that things are so bad now that any change would have to be a change for the better. But surely this is mistaken, for things might actually turn out to be worse.

The most effective point that can be raised against this argument is that the author says nothing about

(A) the manner in which the radicals might foment their revolution.

(B) the specific results of the revolution that would be changes for the worse.

(C) the economic arguments the radicals use to persuade people to join in their cause.

(D) the fact that most people are really satisfied with the present system so that the chance of total revolution is very small.

(E) the loss of life and property that is likely to accompany total destruction of a society.

12. At Clapboard Design, the average annual compensation, including bonuses, was $73,000 for graphic artists last year, while the average annual compensation, including bonuses, for copywriters was $48,000. Last year, the average annual compensation, including bonuses, for all employees at Clapboard Design was $40,000.

If the information provided is accurate, which of the following conclusions can be most reliably drawn?

(A) There were more graphic artists at Clapboard Design last year than copywriters.

(B) There was no graphic artist at Clapboard Design last year whose total compensation was less than the average for copywriters.

(C) At least one graphic artist at Clapboard Design received less in total compensation last year than the highest paid copywriter.

(D) The average bonus awarded to graphic artists at Clapboard Design last year was greater than the average bonus for copywriters.

(E) The total compensation for at least one employee at Clapboard Design last year was less than the average of all copywriters.

Questions 13 and 14

Having just completed Introductory Logic 9, I feel competent to instruct others in the intricacies of this wonderful discipline. Logic is concerned with correct reasoning in the form of syllogisms. A syllogism consists of three statements, of which two are premises and the third is the conclusion. Here is an example:

MAJOR PREMISE:	The American buffalo is disappearing.
MINOR PREMISE:	This animal is an American buffalo.
CONCLUSION:	Therefore, this animal is disappearing.

Once one has been indoctrinated into the mysteries of this arcane science, there is no statement he may not assert with complete confidence.

13. The reasoning of the author's example is most similar to that contained in which of the following arguments?

    (A) Any endangered species must be protected; this species is endangered; therefore, it should be protected.

    (B) All whales are mammals; this animal is a whale; therefore, this animal is a mammal.

    (C) Engaging in sexual intercourse with a person to whom one is not married is a sin; and since premarital intercourse is, by definition, without the institution of marriage, it is, therefore, a sin.

    (D) There are 60 seconds in a minute; there are 60 minutes in an hour; therefore, there are 3,600 seconds in an hour.

    (E) Wealthy people pay most of the taxes; this man is wealthy; therefore, this man pays most of the taxes.

14. The main purpose of the author's argument is to

    (A) provide instruction in logic.

    (B) supply a definition.

    (C) cast doubt on the value of formal logic.

    (D) present an argument for the protection of the American buffalo.

    (E) show the precise relationship between the premises and conclusion of his example.

Questions 15 and 16

On a recent trip to the Mediterranean, I made the acquaintance of a young man who warned me against trusting Cretans. "Everything they say is a lie," he told me, "and I should know because I come from Crete myself." I thanked the fellow for his advice but told him in light of what he had said, I had no intention of believing it.

15. Which of the following best describes the author's behavior?

    (A) It was unwarranted because the young man was merely trying to be helpful to a stranger.

    (B) It was paradoxical for in discounting the advice he implicitly relied on it.

    (C) It was understandable inasmuch as the young man, by his own admission, could not possibly be telling the truth.

    (D) It was high-handed and just the sort of thing that gives American tourists a bad name.

    (E) It was overly cautious since not everyone in a foreign country will try to take advantage of a tourist.

16. Which of the following is most nearly analogous to the warning issued by the young man?

    (A) An admission by a witness under cross-examination that he has lied

    (B) A sign put up by the Chamber of Commerce of a large city alerting visitors to the danger of pickpockets

    (C) The command of a military leader to his marching troops to do an about-face

    (D) A sentence written in chalk on a blackboard that says, "This sentence is false."

    (E) The advice of a veteran worker to a newly hired person: "You don't actually have to work hard so long as you look like you're working hard."

17. Doctors, in seeking a cure for *aphroditis melancholias,* are guided by their research into the causes of *metaeritocas polymanias* because the symptoms of the two diseases occur in populations of similar ages, manifesting symptoms in both cases of high fever, swollen glands, and lack of appetite. Moreover, the incubation period for both diseases is virtually identical. So these medical researchers are convinced that the virus responsible for *aphroditis melancholias* is very similar to that responsible for *metaeritocas polymanias.*

The conclusion of the author rests on the presupposition that

(A) *metaeritocas polymanias* is a more serious public health hazard than *aphroditis melancholias.*

(B) for every disease, modern medical science will eventually find a cure.

(C) saving human life is the single most important goal of modern technology.

(D) *aphroditis melancholias* is a disease that occurs only in human beings.

(E) diseases with similar symptoms will have similar causes.

18. Concerned about the rough waters in the harbor caused by increasing reliance on commuter ferries, the Port Authority imposed a speed limit on boat traffic because it is well known that modern ferries running at very slow speeds produce little or no wake. Paradoxically, however, during the weeks following the enactment of the speed limit, sensors installed at key monitoring points in the harbor showed that water turbulence actually increased.

Which of the following, if true, best explains the paradox described above?

(A) The sensors showed that the harbor's water is the calmest from midnight to 4:00 am when very few ferries operate.

(B) Waves produced by ferries propagate outward to the shorelines where they are reflected off bulkheads and other hard surfaces.

(C) A boat that produces less wake is operating more efficiently than one that is producing a great deal of wake.

(D) The number of ferry trips made during the period immediately following the imposition of the speed limit did not increase appreciably.

(E) At faster speeds, modern ferries ride higher, displacing less water and producing less wake than at moderate speeds.

19. A dog's nose has roughly 200 million olfactory receptors, making it an instrument of remarkable sensitivity theoretically well-suited to detective work, but dogs also return a very high rate of false positives when asked to identify people or substances. Subtle but misleading signals that a trainer can unknowingly communicate to the animal include a glance or step in a certain direction or allowing the dog to spend too much or too little time in a particular spot. A dog that works out of sight of the handler, however, cannot be influenced in these ways, so permitting it to work off-leash would eliminate the problem of false positives.

Which of the following, if true, would most weaken the reasoning above?

(A) Dogs are trained using positive reinforcements such as food treats for finding scents and so exhibit behavior calculated to earn rewards.

(B) Dogs are trained to identify basic chemicals but find it difficult to recognize these chemicals when they are included in a mixture.

(C) Handlers keep logs of all training exercises and review these records periodically for evidence that suggests they are influencing the dog.

(D) Handlers are reluctant to admit that their dogs return false positives and so usually claim that the animal reacted to a "trace" of a substance.

(E) Miniature cameras can be attached to a dog's collar to permit a handler to monitor how the dog is working even when out of sight.

20. There are over 400 species of ladybugs in North America, but more and more, the multicolored Asian lady beetle predominates. The Asian lady beetle is slightly larger than many native species, about one-third of an inch long; and it characteristically has 19 spots on its wing covers, though there may be no spots at all. A black "W" is usually found on the thorax. So if you find a ladybug without spots and with no black "W" on its thorax, it is definitely a member of a native species.

The reasoning in the argument is flawed because the argument

(A) presupposes what it is intended to prove

(B) mistakes a cause of an event for its effect

(C) fails to consider the possibility that the Asian lady beetle was introduced accidentally

(D) makes a general claim based upon examples that are not fairly representative of the larger population

(E) interprets evidence that a claim is probably true as establishing the certainty of the conclusion

21. In Entonia where the Parliament chooses the Prime Minister, anyone who supports the majority party in Parliament should also support the Prime Minister because the Prime Minister is chosen by the majority party.

The pattern of reasoning that characterizes the argument above is most closely paralleled by that which characterizes which of the following?

(A) People who enjoy watching rugby should also enjoy watching American football because American football, in its patterns of play, its rules, and its structure, derives from rugby.

(B) People who go to bed before 10:00 pm should eat dinner before 6:00 pm to ensure that the food that they've eaten is thoroughly digested before they retire for the night.

(C) People who appreciate paintings by Monet should also appreciate paintings by Renoir since both were members of the Impressionist school of painting in late nineteenth-century France.

(D) A person who is able to operate a crane can probably also operate a dredge since the mechanisms and the controls of the two machines are very similar.

(E) A person who reads a daily newspaper will have no reason to read a weekly news magazine since the magazine is just a compilation of the week's news.

22. Personal video recorders that allow viewers to skip commercials have television network executives worried that the public will stop watching commercials. However, I have noticed that people with such devices watch truly entertaining commercials two or three times because just as it is easy to fastforward past commercials, it is easy to rewind and view them again.

The statements above best support which of the following conclusions?

(A) Television executives need not be concerned that personal video recorders will result in a loss of ad revenue.

(B) People using personal video recorders may watch entertaining commercials more than once.

(C) Entertaining television commercials are more effective at promoting a product than ads that are not entertaining.

(D) Personal video recorders will someday replace traditional television sets as the primary means of viewing telecasts.

(E) Television advertising will become less effective as a means of promoting products than it has been in the past.

Questions 23 and 24

DEBORAH: The policy of legacy admissions, by which elite universities give preference to the children of the university's graduates, is unfair and should be discontinued. The policy gives an unfair advantage to exactly those applicants who don't need one: students who have one or perhaps two parents who themselves were the beneficiaries of a superb education.

ANNA: But these universities see the policy of legacy admissions as an important tool for securing alumni donations. A wealthy graduate is more likely to contribute and to contribute more generously if his or her child is a student or graduate of the university.

23. Anna's response to Deborah can best be described as

   (A) denying that legacy admissions give the children of graduates any advantage

   (B) noting that the policy, whatever its disadvantages, serves a useful purpose

   (C) suggesting that fairness is not a consideration in university admissions procedures

   (D) outlining some minor changes in the policy of legacy admissions to make it fair

   (E) challenging Deborah to define more precisely the key terms used in her argument

24. Which of the following pieces of information would be most useful in assessing the validity of Deborah's claim?

   (A) A comparison of the overall acceptance rates at schools with legacy policy with those for schools with no such policy

   (B) A comparison of the rates of acceptance for legacy applicants at schools with such a policy with overall acceptance rates at those schools

   (C) A comparison of the number of applicants who apply as legacy students at schools with such a policy with the number of applicants who claim no such affiliation

   (D) A comparison of the number of legacy applicants to schools with such policies with the last five years over the number who applied 25 years ago

   (E) A comparison of the number of legacy applicants rejected at schools with such a policy with the number of legacy applicants at those same schools

25. Every passenger who flew to St. Louis purchased an e-ticket. Therefore, some passengers who flew first class did not fly to St. Louis.

The conclusion of the argument follows logically if it is assumed that

(A) some passengers who flew first class purchased e-tickets

(B) every passenger who purchased an e-ticket flew to St. Louis

(C) some passengers who did not purchase e-tickets flew first class

(D) every passenger who purchased an e-ticket flew first class

(E) every passenger who flew first class purchased an e-ticket

STOP

END OF SECTION 5. IF YOU HAVE ANY TIME LEFT, GO OVER YOUR WORK IN THIS SECTION ONLY. DO NOT WORK IN ANY OTHER SECTION OF THE TEST.

WRITING SAMPLE

Time—30 Minutes

The Marietta Township School Board must decide which of two candidates, Paul Sellers or Francine Goode, should receive its annual Outstanding Teacher Award. Write an essay in favor of one of the two candidates. Two considerations should guide your thinking:

1 The Outstanding Teacher Award honors teaching excellence and contribution to the community and school system.

2 The Award carries with it a one-year leave of absence with pay. The Board hopes that the recipient will use this time to pursue a course of study or a project that will eventually benefit the school system and community.

PAUL SELLERS, age 55, is a social studies teacher with more than thirty years of classroom teaching experience in the school system at the junior high and high school level. For the past fifteen years, he has been coach of his school's debating team and faculty adviser to a number of clubs; and for ten consecutive years, students have voted him the outstanding teacher at their school. Last year, Sellers worked 4 hours per week without compensation tutoring disadvantaged students. Sellers says that if he receives the award, he will spend the year finishing a book about the early history of the Marietta Township.

FRANCINE GOODE, age 35, is a high school foreign languages teacher who has taught for twelve years, ten of them in the Marietta school system. She consistently receives top evaluations from her district supervisor and last year was voted Outstanding Foreign Language Teacher by the statewide conference of teachers of foreign languages. Recently, on her own time, she conducted a series of district-wide Parent Participation Seminars for parents who do not speak English. Because she speaks French, Spanish, and Italian, Francine is able to converse with parents about helping their children in school. Francine has stated that if she receives the award, she will spend the year in Europe improving her language skills. During that time, she will also compile a photographic "tour" of various cities, which she then plans to use in teaching.

ANSWER KEY

Section 1

1.	E	6.	A	11.	E	16.	B	21.	B
2.	D	7.	D	12.	A	17.	B	22.	A
3.	B	8.	C	13.	A	18.	E	23.	E
4.	E	9.	C	14.	B	19.	D	24.	E
5.	C	10.	A	15.	D	20.	B		

Section 2

1.	D	6.	A	11.	C	16.	D	21.	E
2.	E	7.	B	12.	E	17.	E	22.	D
3.	B	8.	A	13.	D	18.	D	23.	E
4.	E	9.	B	14.	B	19.	E	24.	E
5.	B	10.	C	15.	E	20.	C		

Section 3

1.	C	7.	D	13.	C	19.	B	25.	C
2.	A	8.	B	14.	C	20.	A	26.	D
3.	C	9.	D	15.	C	21.	E	27.	A
4.	B	10.	C	16.	A	22.	A	28.	E
5.	E	11.	A	17.	B	23.	D		
6.	B	12.	B	18.	A	24.	C		

Section 4

1.	D	6.	A	11.	E	16.	C	21.	E
2.	A	7.	E	12.	C	17.	B	22.	B
3.	A	8.	B	13.	C	18.	A	23.	B
4.	D	9.	A	14.	A	19.	B	24.	A
5.	E	10.	D	15.	A	20.	C		

Section 5

1.	D	6.	B	11.	B	16.	D	21.	A
2.	E	7.	B	12.	E	17.	E	22.	B
3.	B	8.	C	13.	E	18.	E	23.	B
4.	C	9.	A	14.	C	19.	A	24.	B
5.	A	10.	E	15.	B	20.	E	25.	C

EXPLANATORY ANSWERS

Section I

1. **The correct answer is (E).** This question is primarily a matter of careful reading. The phrase "no lower bus fares" must not be read to mean that Flash uniquely has the lowest fare; it means only that no one else has a fare lower than that of Flash. It is conceivable that several companies share the lowest fare. So choice (B) is not inconsistent with the claim made in the advertisement. Choice (C) is not inconsistent since it mentions the New York City to Boston route, and it is the Washington, D.C., to New York City route that is the subject of the ad's claim. Choice (A) is not inconsistent since it speaks of an air fare, and the ad's language carefully restricts the claim to bus fares. Choice (D) is a bit tricky, but the ad cites only the D.C. to New York trip—choice (D) talks about the New York to D.C. trip. So there is no contradiction. Choice (E) is fairly clearly a contradiction, and this is a good time to remind you to read all of the choices before selecting one. You might have bitten on choice (D), but when you see choice (E), you know that it is a better answer.

2. **The correct answer is (D).** We take the first three propositions together and ignore the fourth since we are to assume it is false. Roberts cannot be convicted without Edwards' testimony (1), but that testimony will show that Edwards participated in the crime (2). But if Edwards participated in the crime, Roberts cannot be convicted of it because Roberts is accused of a crime that can be committed only by a person acting alone (3). Either Edwards will testify or Edwards will not testify—that is a tautology (logically true). If Edwards testi-

fies, according to our reasoning, Roberts cannot be convicted. If Edwards does not testify, Roberts cannot be convicted (1). Either way, Roberts will not be convicted. Choice (E) cannot be correct since we have no way of knowing, as a matter of logic, whether Edwards will or will not testify. We know only that *if* Edwards does, certain consequences will follow, and *if* Edwards does not, other consequences will follow. Choice (A) can be disregarded since the crime is one that only a solo actor can commit (3). Choice (C) is incorrect because we have proven that, regardless of Edwards' course of action. Roberts cannot be convicted. Finally, choice (B) is a logical *possibility*, that is not precluded by the given information, but we cannot logically deduce it from the information given.

3. **The correct answer is (B).** Examine carefully the connection between (2) and (4). Suppose Edwards testifies. The testimony will show Edwards, too, has committed some wrong (2); but when the jury learns this, they will not believe any part of that testimony (4), that means that they will not believe Edwards committed the wrong—a contradiction. Since (2) and (4) cannot both be true at the same time, the scenario they describe is an impossible one—like saying a circle is a square. The remaining answers are all distractions. There is nothing in the information to suggest that the situation was created by Roberts' attorney, so choice (E) is incorrect. Choices (C) and (D) are value judgments that cannot be inferred from the information given and so are wrong—even if the situation is *difficult* for them, what reason is there for concluding that it is unfair? In any event, the

situation is not even difficult for Roberts, who will be acquitted (see our analysis of the preceding question). Choice (A) is wrong, and remember that the LSAT does not presuppose you have any information about the law or its workings.

4. **The correct answer is (E).** In the very first sentence, the author remarks that this is "curious" and a "contradiction," so the only correct answer choice will be one that follows up on this idea, as choice (E) does when it speaks of *paradox*. Nothing that precedes the blank suggests that the author is speaking of "beauty" or "tragedy," so choices (A) and (B) can be disregarded. As for choice (C), the passage does speak about death but not of death's inevitability; rather it dwells on death under certain circumstances that may not be inevitable. As for choice (D), while death may characterize human existence, the kind of death mentioned— self-sacrifice—is not indicated to be an inherent part of all human life.

5. **The correct answer is (C).** The author is explaining why the sacrifice is meaningless. From three different perspectives, the argument shows that it can have no value. The community does not win, because both lives were equally important. The lover who is saved does not profit, and that is shown by the fact that he would be perfectly willing to do the transaction the other way. If he has no preference (or even prefers the alternative outcome, his death), it cannot be said that he benefited from the exchange of lives. Finally, the need to prove that the action has no value to the heroine: He says she does not benefit, because she is not in a position to enjoy or savor, or whatever, her heroism. The reason for that is that she is *dead*, choice (C), not dying, choice (A), for dying would leave

open the possibility that her sacrifice would bring her joy in her last minutes, and then the author's contention that the transaction has *no* value would be weakened. Choice (D) is wrong, for it is specifically stated that she is a heroine, so it is an inappropriate *completion* of the sentence. Choices (B) and (E) may both be true, but they do not explain why the action has no value to anyone.

6. **The correct answer is (A).** The main point of the passage is that pregnancy and a child put strain on a young marriage, and so such marriages would have a higher survival rate without the strain of children. It would seem, then, that encouraging such couples not to have children would help them stay married; but that will be possible only if they have not already committed themselves, so to speak, to having a child. If the wife is already pregnant at the time of marriage, the commitment has already been made, so the advice is too late. Choices (B) and (C) are wrong for similar reasons. It is not only the continued presence of the child in the marriage that causes the stress but also the very pregnancy and birth. So choices (B) and (C) do not address themselves to the *birth* of the child, and that is the factor to which the author attributes the dissolution of the marriage. Choice (D) is wide of the mark. Whether society does or does not have such an interest, the author has shown us a causal linkage; that is, a mere fact of the matter. The author states: If this, then fewer divorces. The author may or may not believe there should be fewer divorces. Choice (E) is wrong for this reason also and for the further reason that it says "do not *plan*" to have children. The author's concern is with children during the early part of the marriage.

The author does not suggest that couples should never have children.

7. **The correct answer is (D).** Peter's surprise is over the fact that an important executive of a company would use a competitor's product, hence choice (D). Choice (B) is wrong because Peter's surprise is not that Mary is unimportant; rather, he knows Mary is important, and that is the reason for surprise. Choice (E) is irrelevant to the exchange, for Peter imagines that regardless of taste, Mary ought to consume the product she is responsible in part for producing. The same reasoning can be applied to choice (C). Finally, choice (A) is a distraction. It has legal overtones, but it is important to always keep in mind that this section, like all sections of the LSAT, tests reasoning and reading abilities—not knowledge of business or law.

8. **The correct answer is (C).** The dispute here is over the motivation to compete seriously in intramural sports. Erika claims it is a sense of responsibility to one's fellows; Nichol argues it is a desire to win. But the two may actually support one another. In what way could one possibly let one's fellows down? If the sport was not competitive, it would seem there would be no opportunity to disappoint them. So the desire to win contributes to the desire to be an effective member of the team. Nothing in the exchange presupposes anything about the structure of such programs beyond the fact that they are competitive; that is, that they have winners and losers. How many such programs exist, how they are funded, and similar questions are irrelevant, so both choices (A) and (B) are incorrect. Choice (D) is close to being correct, but it calls for a survey of *deans*. The dean is probably not in a position to describe the motiva-

tion of the *participants*. Had choice (D) specified participants, it too would have been a correct answer. Of course, only one answer can be correct on the LSAT. Finally, choice (E) must be wrong for the reason cited in explaining choice (D); it should be possible to find out about the motivation.

9. **The correct answer is (C).** Clark was unhappy if he had a clear conscience but knew, or Clark was happy if he knew but had an unclear conscience. It is not the case that Clark was unhappy, so he must have been happy. Since he knew, however, his happiness must stem from an unclear conscience. Choices (A), (D), and (E) are incorrect because they make irrelevant value judgments. As was just shown, the author's point can be analyzed as a purely logical one. Choice (B) is just distraction, playing on the connection between "governess" and "servant," which, of course, are not the same thing.

10. **The correct answer is (A).** The author's point depends upon the *assumption* that children see both animated features and "spaghetti Westerns." Obviously, if that assumption is untrue, the conclusion does not follow. It may be true that children get a distorted picture of the world from other causes, but the author has not claimed that. The author claims only that it comes from their seeing animated features and "spaghetti Westerns." Presumably the two different treatments cause the inversion of values. The intention of the producers in making the films is irrelevant since an action may have an effect not intended by the actor. Hence, choice (B) would not touch the author's point. Further, that there are other sources of information that present a proper view of the world does not prove that the problem cited by the author does

not produce an inverted view of the world. So choice (C) would not weaken his point. Choice (D) reminds us of the importance of careful reading. You might want to interpret choice (D) to say the same thing as choice (A), but then you'd have to choose choice (A) because it tells the point more forcefully and directly. Finally, choice (E) is irrelevant to the author's conclusion: children learn to value animals more than people. Of course, as an exercise in debate, you might argue that this is a good thing, but that is not what choice (E) says.

11. **The correct answer is (E).** The point of the passage is that there is a seeming contradiction in our body of laws. Sometimes a person pays for attempted misdeeds and other times does not pay for them. If there could be found a good reason for this difference, then the contradiction could be explained away. This is just what choice (E) does. It points out that the law treats the situations differently because it has different goals: Sometimes, we drive fast because we are in a hurry; other times, we drive slowly because we want to enjoy the scenery. Choice (B) would not weaken the argument, for it only intensifies the contradiction. Choice (D) makes an attempt to reconcile the seemingly conflicting positions by hinting at a possible goal of one action that is not a goal of the other. But, if anything, it intensifies the contradiction because one might infer that we should not try persons for attempted crimes because criminal trials are expensive, yet we should allow compensation for attempted frauds because civil trials are less expensive. Choices (C) and (A) are just distractions. Whether there are more of one kind of law than another on the books has nothing to do with the seeming contradiction. And whether persons are more likely to commit a second crime after they are released from prison does not speak to the issue of whether an unsuccessful attempt to commit a crime should be a crime in the first place.

12. **The correct answer is (A).** The question stem asks us to focus on the "dispute" between the two opponents. What will be relevant to it will be those items that affect the merits of the issues or perhaps those that affect the credibility of the parties. Choices (C) and (E) both mention items—facts and their source— that would be relevant to the substantive issues. Choices (B) and (D) are legitimate attempts to clarify the issues and so are relevant. Choice (A) is neither relevant to the issues nor to the credibility (e.g., where did the facts come from) of the debaters. Choice (A) is the least relevant because it is an *ad hominem* attack of the illegitimate sort.

13. **The correct answer is (A).** The point of the passage is that artists see things as they really are, while politicians see things as they want them to be. Choice (B) is wrong, for if anything, it is the politicians who see things through rose-colored glasses, while the artists see the truth of a stark reality. Choice (C) can be overruled, for the passage implies that political leaders are responsive to the needs of people—it is just that they are a little late. Moreover, the point of the passage is to draw a contrast between artists and politicians; and even if the conclusion expressed in choice (C) is arguably correct, it is not as good as choice (A), which *completes* the comparison. Choice (D) has no ground in the passage. Be careful not to move from an analysis of facts—artists saw the problems earlier than the politicians did—to a conclu-

sion of value or policy: therefore, we should turn out the politicians. The author may very well believe that as sad as these circumstances are, nothing can be done about them; for example, things are bad enough with the politicians in charge, but they would be much worse with artists running things. Choice (E) also finds no ground in the passage.

14. **The correct answer is (B).** The argument for consistency is that it avoids the danger that actions will be misinterpreted. If a parent is overly generous, a child will think the parent will always be generous, even when generosity is inappropriate. By the same token, if a parent does not draw the line until pushed to do so, the child will believe that the parent's response was forced. A parent, so goes the argument, should play it safe and leave a cushion. Choice (D) makes an attempt to capture this thought but overstates the case. The author implies only that this may show weakness, not that the child will necessarily exploit that weakness and certainly not that the child will exploit it violently. And were that thought intended, the author surely would not have used the word "retaliate," which implies a *quid pro quo*. Both choices (A) and (E) have no basis in the passage, and neither is relevant to the idea of rewards and punishments. Choice (C) does treat the general idea of the passage, but it confuses the idea of weakness with the more specific notion of willingness to bargain.

15. **The correct answer is (D).** The key phrase in this paragraph is "beef costs more per pound than fish." A careful reading would show that choice (A) is in direct contradiction to the explicit wording of the passage. Choice (B) cannot be inferred since the dietitian merely says,

"I pay." Perhaps the dietician intends to keep the price of a meal stable by cutting back in other areas. In any event, this is another example of not going beyond a mere factual analysis to generate policy recommendations (see #13) unless the question stem specifically invites such an extension; for example, which of the following courses of action would the author recommend? Choice (C) makes an unwarranted inference. From the fact that beef is more costly, one would not want to conclude that it is more profitable. Choice (E) is wrong for this reason also. Choice (D) is correct because it focuses upon the "per measure of protein" that explains why a fish meal will cost the dietitian more than a beef meal, even though fish is less expensive per pound.

16. **The correct answer is (B).** One of the most common patterns to look for with this type of question is the "surprise result," that is, an unanticipated factor that defeats the expected outcome. Choice (B) fits this pattern: you'll be so hungry from the workout that you'll eat more. (Remember that you are told to accept the soundness of each of the answer choices.) The other choices just don't have the same logical "zip." Anyway, choice (A) seems to strengthen the argument: it's okay to do what the ad suggests. And choice (C) doesn't focus on the logic of the ad—even though it probably helps to explain why the ad might be effective. Choices (D) and (E) are wrong because they address issues that are not really on the table (so to speak): the ad is addressing neither those who are already happy nor those who are overly thin.

17. **The correct answer is (B).** This question is like one of those simple conversation questions: "X: All bats are mammals. Y: Not true, whales are mammals too." In

this little exchange, Y misunderstands X to have said that "all mammals are bats." In the question, the objection must be based on a misunderstanding. The objector must think that the ad has claimed that the only cause of unhappiness, etc., is being overweight, otherwise the objector would not have offered the counterexample. Choice (A) is wrong because the ad never takes a stand on the *causes* of overweight conditions—only on a possible cure. This reasoning invalidates choices (C) and (D) as well. Choice (E) makes a similar error but about effects, not about causes. The ad does not say everyone who is unhappy is unattractive, or vice versa.

18. **The correct answer is (E).** The sample argument is a straightforward generalization: All observed S are P. X is an S. Therefore, X is P. Only choice (E) replicates this form. The reasoning in choice (A) is "Some S are P. All M are S. (All swans are birds, which is a suppressed assumption.) Therefore, all M are P." That is like saying: "Some children are not well behaved. All little girls are children. Therefore, all little girls are not well behaved." Choice (B), too, contains a suppressed premise. Its structure is "All S are P. All S are M. (All ballets are theatrical productions, which is suppressed.) Therefore, all M are P." That is like saying "All little girls are children. All little girls are human. Therefore, all humans are little girls." Choice (C) is not a generalization at all. It takes a generalization and attempts to explain it by uncovering a causal linkage. Choice (D) is simply a *non sequitur*. It moves from the universality of the *concept* of justice to the conclusion that justice is a *physical* trait of humans.

19. **The correct answer is (D).** The author is attempting to argue that laws against suicide are legitimate. The author argues against a simplistic libertarian position that says suicide hurts only the victim. The goal of the law, he argues, is not just to protect the victim from himself. A society passes such a law because it wants to underscore the importance of human life. Reading beyond the blank in the second paragraph makes clear the author's views on the value of human life. Choice (A) flies in the face of the explicit language of the passage. The author does not defend the law as being a deterrent to suicide. Choice (B) might be something the author believes, but it is not something developed in the passage. The author is not concerned here with explaining how the laws came to be on the books but is concerned only with defending them. If anything, choice (B) would be more appropriate in the context of an argument against such laws. Choice (C) also is something the author may believe, but the defense of the suicide law is not that it protects liberties—only that it serves a function and does not interfere with constitutional liberties any more than laws that prohibit doing violence to others. Choice (E) is wrong for the same reasons that choice (B) is wrong. It seems to belong more in the context of an argument against suicide laws.

20. **The correct answer is (B).** With the comments in #19 in mind, it is clear that choice (B) must be correct. The author wants to make the point that suicide is not a victimless crime; it affects a great many people—even, it is claimed, some who were never personally acquainted with the suicide. Again, reading the whole passage is helpful. Choice (A) is a joke—obviously suicide does not lead to more

serious crimes. That is like saying the death penalty is designed to rehabilitate the criminal. Choice (C) simply focuses on the superficial content of the sentence: One, it's talking about church and state, so choice (C), which mentions sin, must be correct. Choice (D) is wrong because the author is not concerned to defend the laws as deterrents to suicide, as we discussed in #19. Finally, choice (E) is irrelevant to the point that the entire community is affected by the death of any one of its members.

21. **The correct answer is (B).** This third question, too, can be answered once the comments of #19 are understood. The key word here is "oversimplification." The libertarian oversimplifies matters by imagining that the only function of the law is to protect a person from self-harm. This is oversimplified because it overlooks the fact that such laws also serve the functions of (1) underscoring the value of life and (2) protecting the community as a whole from the loss of any of its members. Choice (A) is incorrect because the libertarian does not make this error but the related one of evaluating the function of the law only from the perspective of the suicide. Choice (C) is wrong, for the author apparently shares with the libertarian the assumption that a law must not illegitimately interfere with individual liberty. The whole defense of the laws against suicide is that they have a legitimate function. Choice (D) is wrong for the same reasons that choice (C) of #20 is wrong. Finally, choice (E) is very much like choice (A).

22. **The correct answer is (A).** Choices (C) and (D) are wrong because they extrapolate without sufficient information. These are very much like choices (C) and (E) in

#15. Choice (E) contradicts the last given statement and so cannot be a conclusion of it. That would be like trying to infer "all men are mortal" from the premise that "no men are mortal." Choice (B) commits an error by moving from "all S are P" to "all P are S." Just because all racing engines have SFI does not mean that all SFIs are in racing engines. Some may be found in tractors and heavy-duty machinery.

23. **The correct answer is (E).** This is a very sticky question, but it is similar to ones that have been on the LSAT. The key here is to keep in mind that you are to pick the BEST answer, and sometimes you will not be very satisfied with any of them. Here, choice (E) is correct by default of the others. Choice (A) has some merit. After all, the economist really isn't very careful in stating the claim. The author says "here we go again" when there is no evidence that we have ever been there before. But there is no particular term the author uses that we could call ambiguous. Choice (B) is wrong because, although the economist assumes some people take that position (otherwise, against whom would the argument be directed?), the statement does not imply that the economist alone thinks differently. Choice (C) is like choice (A), a possible answer, but this interpretation requires additional information. You would have to have said to yourself, "Oh, I see that the economist is against it. He is probably saying this in an exasperated tone and in the context of a diatribe." If there were such additional information, you would be right, and choice (C) would be a good answer. But there isn't. Choice (E) does not require this additional speculation and so is truer to the given information. Choice (D) would also require

speculation. Choice (E) is not perfect, just BEST by comparison.

24. **The correct answer is (E).** The argument assumes that a right cannot exist unless it is recognized by the positive law of a society. Against this assumption, it can be argued that a right may exist even though there is no mechanism for protecting or enforcing it. That this is at least plausible has been illustrated by our own history, e.g., minority groups have often been denied rights. These rights, however, existed all the while—they were just not protected by the government. Choice (A) is incorrect, for the proponent of the theory of natural rights cannot deny that some human beings do not have them. That would contradict the very definition of natural right on which the claim is based. Choice (B) is incorrect because it is not responsive to the argument. Even if choice (B) is true, the attacker of natural rights still has the argument that there are no universally recognized rights, so there are no universal (natural) rights at all. Choice (C), like choice (A), is inconsistent with the very idea of a "natural" right. Choice (D) is incorrect because it does not respond to the attacker's claim that no one right is protected universally. Consistency or universality within one society does not amount to consistency or universality across all societies.

Section 2

Questions 1–6

This is a fairly simple "connective" set. A "connective" set is a problem set in which one event is somehow connected with another event; for example, X causes Y, or Y leads to Z. The connection can be expressed by an arrow. We begin with the first condition:

$$G \longrightarrow H$$

Adding the second condition:

$$G \rightleftarrows H \longrightarrow I$$

And the third:

$$G \rightleftarrows H \longrightarrow I \longrightarrow J$$

And the fourth:

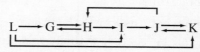

And the fifth:

$$L \longrightarrow G \rightleftarrows H \longrightarrow I \longrightarrow J \longrightarrow K$$

And the sixth:

$$L \longrightarrow G \rightleftarrows H \longrightarrow I \longrightarrow J \rightleftarrows K$$

Of course, there is no necessity that the stations be oriented in exactly this way on the page, so long as the relative connections are specified. An equivalent diagram is as follows:

Once the diagram is drawn, answering the questions is merely a matter of using the picture.

1. **The correct answer is (D).** The diagram shows that it is possible to get from H to J only via I. Choice (A) is incorrect since the direct connection between J and H runs only from J to H, not vice versa. As for choice (B), while it is possible to get from H to G, there is no connecting train between G and J. Choice (C) is incorrect because there is no train from H to L. Finally, choice (E) is incorrect for there is a route from H to J, via I.

2. **The correct answer is (E).** Notice that there are no arrows in the diagram that point toward L. This means that it is

possible only to leave L. It is not possible to arrive at L. As for choice (A), one can arrive at G from L or H. Choice (B) is incorrect since one can arrive at H from either G or J. Choice (C) is incorrect since there is a connection between H and I and between L and I. Finally, choice (D) is incorrect since K can be reached from either L or J.

3. **The correct answer is (B).** Consulting the diagram, we see that I can be reached from either H or L. H, however, can be reached from either G or J. Thus, one can go from G and J via H and reach I with only one transfer.

4. **The correct answer is (E).** All six stations can be visited, without revisiting any station, if we begin at L. The trip then proceeds L to G to H to I to J to K.

5. **The correct answer is (B).** To get to H from K, we must go via I and J, and that is a total of two transfers. As for choice (A), the trip from G to I is accomplished by transferring only at H. As for choice (C), the trip from L to H is accomplished by going via G, again requiring only one transfer. As for choice (D), though the trip from L to I would require two transfers if the L, G, H, I route is selected, note that the trip can be made directly from L to I without *any* transfers. Choice (E) is incorrect because a direct route is available from L to K.

6. **The correct answer is (A).** If I is closed, the only transfer point from H to J is closed, and that means that it is not possible to get from G to J. Choice (B) is incorrect since there is a direct link between J and K. Choice (C) is incorrect since there is a direct link between L and K. Choice (D) is incorrect since the L to K to J route remains unimpaired. Choice (E) is incorrect since there is a direct link from L to G.

Questions 7–12

This is a "selection" set; that is, we must select cities for the tours according to the restrictions set forth in the problem set. There are many different ways of summarizing the information, and each of us has our own idiosyncratic system of notational devices. There are, however, some fairly standard symbols used by logicians, and we will employ them here. We summarize the information in the following way:

❶ $M \rightarrow (Q \ \& \ R)$

❷ $P \rightarrow O$

❸ $Q \rightarrow (M \ \& \ N) \ v \ (M \ \& \ T) \ v \ (M \ \& \ N \ \& \ T)$

❹ $P \neq Q$

❺ $\sim (O \ \& \ R \ \& \ T)$

❻ $\sim (N \ \& \ S \ \& \ R)$

❼ $L \neq R$

Some clarifying remarks about this system are in order. We are using the capital-letter designation of each city to make the statement that the city will be included on the tour, e.g., "M" means "M will be included on the tour." The → stands for "if . . . then . . . "; the "&" stands for "and"; the "v" stands for "or"; the ~ stands for "not." We use parentheses as punctuation devices to avoid possible confusion. So the first condition is to be read, "If M, then both Q and R"; that is, "If M is included on the trip, then both Q and R must be included on the trip." Notice that the parentheses were necessary, for the statement

$$M \rightarrow Q \ \& \ R$$

might be misinterpreted to mean "If M is included on the tour, then Q must also be included. In addition, R must be included on the trip." That would be punctuated with parentheses as follows:

$$(M \rightarrow Q) \ \& \ R$$

As for the second condition, we note simply that if P is included, O must also be included.

As for the third condition, some students will find it easier to write this condition out rather than use the notational system. That is fine.

Statement 3 is to be read, "If Q, then M and N, or M and T, or all three," which is, of course, equivalent to the statement included in the initial conditions of the problem.

The fourth condition is similar to the second in that we use a non-standard symbol, "≠." The same information could be written as ~(P & Q) or P→~Q. This last notation is equivalent to Q→~P, for logically P→~Q is the same as Q→~P.

The fifth and sixth conditions are to be read, respectively, "It is not the case that O and R and T are included" and "It is not the case that N and S and R are included." And finally, condition seven is summarized using the "≠," which we have already discussed.

We now have the information ready for easy reference, and we turn to the individual questions.

7. **The correct answer is (B).** If M is included on the trip, we know that we must also include Q and R. And if Q is included on the trip, we must include N or T (or both, but we are looking for the minimum number of other cities). No other cities need be included. So, including M requires both Q and R plus one of the pair N and T. So a total of three *additional* cities are needed.

8. **The correct answer is (A).** By condition 4, Q cannot be included with P. Unfortunately, that is not an available answer choice, so we will have to dig a little deeper. If Q cannot be included on the tour, then we conclude that M cannot be included, for condition 1 requires that Q be included on any tour on which M is a stop.

9. **The correct answer is (B).** This question requires only that we check each of the choices against the summary of conditions. Choice (A) is not acceptable because we have M without Q. Choice (C) is not acceptable because we have M without R. Choice (D) is not acceptable because we have L with R (in violation of condition 7) and because we have Q without either N or T. Choice (E) is not acceptable because we have N, S, and R together, in violation of condition 6. The group in choice (B), however, meets all of the requirements for an acceptable tour.

10. **The correct answer is (C).** By deleting O, we have the tour M, Q, R, and T. This satisfies condition 1, since Q and R are included with M. And this satisfies condition 3 since we have M and T. No other condition is violated, so the group M, Q, R, T is acceptable. Choice (A) is incorrect, for eliminating M leaves Q in the group (without M), in violation of condition 3. Similarly, eliminating Q leaves M on the tour without Q, violating condition 1. Choice (D) is incorrect because it also violates condition 1. Choice (E) is incorrect for this would leave Q on the tour without the (M & N) or (M & T) combination required by condition 3.

11. **The correct answer is (C).** To make the group M, Q, R into an acceptable tour, we need only to add N or T. This will finally satisfy both conditions 1 and 3 without violating any other requirement. Choice (A) is incorrect, for adding another city will not remedy the violation of condition 7 (L ≠ R). Choice (B) is incorrect, because satisfying the conditions requires the addition of O (condition 2), R (condition 1), and either N or T (condition 3). Choice (D) is incorrect since the addition of another city will not correct the violation of condition 6. Finally, choice (E) is incorrect because the addition of O to satisfy condition 2 would then violate

condition 5 (O, R, and T on the same tour).

12. The correct answer is (E). Here we must test each lettered city. M cannot constitute a tour in and of itself, for condition 1 requires that Q and R be included on any tour that includes M. P, by condition 2, cannot constitute a tour of a single city. Finally, by condition 3, Q's inclusion requires more cities. The remaining cities, L, N, O, R, S, and T, however, can be used as single-city tours.

Questions 13–18

This set is a linear ordering set. At first glance, the set appears to be very complex, involving as it does the positioning of 11 items. But a closer examination shows the questions are not that difficult, since the particular restrictions considerably simplify the problem. For example, we know that a red bead is on one end, and we know further that all three red beads are together. So there are only two possible arrangements for the red beads:

```
1   2   3   4   5   6   7   8   9   10  11
R   R   R
```

or

```
                                R   R   R
```

In fact, each additional condition on the placement of the beads tends to simplify matters for us because it eliminates possible arrangements.

With a linear ordering set, we begin by summarizing the information:

Color	Number	
Blue	2	B = B
Red	3	G ≠ G
Green	2	R = R = R
Yellow	4	G or R = ends
	11	

We have made a note of the number of beads of each color, and we have summarized the particular conditions: Blue is next to blue (B = B), green is not next to green (G ≠ G), red is always next to red (R = R = R), and green or red is on each end (G or R = ends). Now we turn to the questions.

13. The correct answer is (D) From the given information and our own deductions based on the restrictions that all red be together and that one end be red and the other green, we set up the following diagram:

```
1   2   3   4   5   6   7   8   9   10  11
                B   B           R
G                   B   B           R   R   R
```

This leaves the four yellow beads and the one remaining green bead to be positioned. The only restriction on the placement of these five beads is that the green bead may not be next to the other green bead; that is, the remaining green bead cannot be in position 2. This eliminates choice (C), since the green bead might be in position 8, though it could also be in positions 3, 4, and 5. This also eliminates choice (B), since position 5 might be filled by a green bead. Choice (A) is clearly incorrect since that is the one remaining position that cannot be occupied by the other green bead. Choice (E) is incorrect since the green bead could be placed in position 3 or 4, separated from the blue beads by one or more yellow beads. We do know, however, that at least one green bead, the one in position 1, will be next to a yellow bead, for a yellow bead is needed to separate the green beads. Of course, the other green bead may also be next to a yellow bead, but that is not necessary. In any event, the fact that the green bead must be separated from the other green bead is sufficient to show the correctness of choice (D).

14. **The correct answer is (B).** The question stem stipulates

```
1  2  3  4  5  6  7  8  9 10 11
                     Y
            Y = Y = Y = Y
```

and we fill in YYYY

since the last position cannot be yellow. This then allows us to deduce

```
1  2  3  4  5  6  7  8  9 10 11
               Y  Y  Y  Y  G
```

since the three red beads are together and one of them must be on the end of the string. Then, since the two blue beads must be together, we know that only two different arrangements are possible:

```
1  2  3  4  5  6  7  8  9 10 11
R  R  R  G  B  B  Y  Y  Y  Y  G
```

or:

```
R  R  R  B  B  G  Y  Y  Y  Y  G
```

Under either arrangement, the fifth bead must be blue.

15. **The correct answer is (E).** The question stem stipulates that each blue bead be next to a green bead. Because the blue beads are next to each other, this means the blue and green beads are arranged as a bloc: GBBG. According to the stipulation in the question stem, the four yellow beads are also arranged as a bloc: YYYY. And we know from the initial presentation of restrictions that the three red beads are a bloc: RRR. The only open question is which end of the string is green and which is red. So there are only two possible arrangements:

```
1  2  3  4  5  6  7  8  9 10 11
G  B  B  G  Y  Y  Y  Y  R  R  R
```

or:

```
R  R  R  Y  Y  Y  Y  G  B  B  G
```

Under either arrangement, positions 5, 6, and 7 are occupied by yellow beads.

16. **The correct answer is (D).** The question stem stipulates

```
1  2  3  4  5  6  7  8  9 10 11
            B  B        R
```

and, given the restriction on the reds and the further restriction on the end beads, we can deduce

```
1  2  3  4  5  6  7  8  9 10 11
G           B  B        R  R  R
```

The only restriction that remains to be observed is the separation of the green beads. This means that the remaining one can occupy positions 3, 4, 7, or 8—though not 2. What is established, however, is that 2 must be yellow, not green.

17. **The correct answer is (E).** The question stem stipulates

```
1  2  3  4  5  6  7  8  9 10 11
            Y        Y  Y  Y
```

and we deduce

```
1  2  3  4  5  6  7  8  9 10 11
R  R  R     Y        Y  Y  Y  G
```

on the basis of the restrictions regarding the placement of the red beads and the colors of the end beads. Further, there is only one open pair left for the blue beads, 6 and 7, which means bead 4 will be green:

```
1  2  3  4  5  6  7  8  9 10 11
R  R  R  G  Y  B  B  Y  Y  Y  G
```

18. **The correct answer is (D).** Since we do not know on which end to place the red beads (nor the green bead), we have the possibility

```
1  2  3  4  5  6  7  8  9 10 11
R  R  R  G                 B  G
```

and its mirror image

1	2	3	4	5	6	7	8	9	10	11
G	B						G	R	R	R

We know also that the two blue beads are together, and this means the yellow beads must form a bloc:

1	2	3	4	5	6	7	8	9	10	11
R	R	R	G	Y	Y	Y	Y	B	B	G

or:

G　B　B　Y　Y　Y　Y　G　R　R　R

In either case, the seventh bead must be yellow.

Questions 19–24

The key to this set is organizing the information in such a way that it is usable. We recommend a table:

	Marlowe	Joyce	Shakespeare	Keats	Chaucer
J	YES	YES			
K			YES	YES	
L	YES				YES
M	YES		YES	YES	
N		YES		YES	YES
O	YES	YES	YES		

If you study the table, you will see that only one teacher can be chosen from the group J, K, and L. Two teachers must be chosen from the group M, N, and O. The reason for this is that the only distribution that will give the Executive Officer exactly eight assignments is to have three courses taught by each of two faculty members and two courses by a third, $3 + 3 + 2 = 8$. This is an important insight that should have occurred to you.

Further study would also show that there is a limited number of permissible combinations. Theoretically, there are nine possibilities:

M & N & → J (OK)
　　　　 → K (No, three Keatses)
　　　　 → L (OK)

M & O & → J (No, three Marlowes)
　　　　 → K (No, three Shakespeares)
　　　　 → L (No, three Marlowes)

N & O & → J (No, three Joyces)
　　　　 → K (OK)
　　　　 → L (OK)

To see this without careful study, however, requires not only powerful insight but considerable luck as well. In any event, it is not necessary to perceive this to answer the questions, for the questions will guide you to the conclusion that some groupings are not permissible.

Having done this preliminary work, we can use our chart of possibilities in explaining the answers to the individual questions.

19. **The correct answer is (E).** Choice (A) is incorrect because it generates a total of only seven courses. Choices (B), (C), and (D) are shown to be incorrect by our chart. Choice (E) is the only acceptable combination listed.

20. **The correct answer is (C).** Using the information provided in the question stem, we know

Spring

Joyce
Keats　　 } (by N)
Chaucer

and that L will teach Marlowe and Chaucer. Then our chart informs us that there are two teachers who can teach with L and N, O or M. Thus, the additional courses will be Marlowe, Joyce, and Shakespeare (by O) or Marlowe, Keats, and Shakespeare (by M). We know, therefore, that both Marlowe and

Shakespeare will be offered during the year since both O and M offer those courses. This means Marlowe must be offered in both the fall and the spring and further that L will teach Chaucer in the fall.

Fall	Spring
Marlowe (by ?)	Joyce
Chaucer (by L)	Keats ⎫
Shakes. (by ?)	Chaucer ⎬ (by N)
Joyce or Keats (by ?)	Marlowe (by ?)

From this we can see that choice (C) is correct. It is possible that L will teach Marlowe in the fall, so L *could* teach only in the fall semester. Choice (A) is incorrect as shown by our chart—either M or O must be hired with L and N. Choice (B) is incorrect since the question stipulates that N will teach only in the spring and that accounts for three of the four courses that semester. Choice (D) is incorrect since either Joyce or Keats, though not both, will be offered in the fall. Finally, choice (E) is incorrect since Shakespeare can be offered only in the fall.

21. **The correct answer is (E).** Our chart shows that if M and N are hired, either J or L can be hired. Choices (A) and (C), therefore, are possibly, though not necessarily, true. Hence, they are both incorrect answers. Choice (B) must also be incorrect, as shown by the chart. Hiring M and N, and separating their courses by semester, we have

Semester—M	Semester—N
Marlowe	Joyce
Shakes.	Keats
Keats	Chaucer

The remaining two courses will be Marlowe and Joyce (by J) or Marlowe

and Chaucer (by L). Since both J and L teach Marlowe, that will give a total of two Marlowe courses, so one of them must be offered in the spring. Choice (D) is possibly true, provided that M teaches that course in the fall, but it is not necessarily true.

22. **The correct answer is (D).** If K and N are hired, O must also be hired. This gives us a course mix of Shakespeare and Keats (by K); Joyce, Keats, and Chaucer (by N); and Marlowe, Joyce, and Shakespeare (by O). We have two courses on Shakespeare, two on Keats, and two on Joyce. So those three courses must be offered both semesters, plus a course on Marlowe one semester and one on Chaucer the other.

23. **The correct answer is (E).** If L is hired to teach only in the fall, this means Marlowe and Chaucer will be offered then. With L, it is possible to hire either M and N or N and O. We must hire N, and this means Joyce, Keats, and Chaucer will be taught. Since both L and N offer Chaucer, N must teach Chaucer in the spring. As for choice (D), this is possible but is necessarily true only if O, rather than M, is hired. Since that is not a logically necessary choice, choice (D) is merely possible.

24. **The correct answer is (E).** For this question we are told which teachers will be hired. So the course mix will be

Fall

Joyce ⎫
Keats ⎬ (by N)
Chaucer ⎭

with courses on Marlowe, Joyce, and Shakespeare (by O) and on Shakespeare and Keats (by K). Observing the restriction that the same courses may not be offered in a single semester, we have

Fall	Spring
Joyce	Joyce (by O)
Keats ⎱(by N)	Shakes. (by ?)
Chaucer ⎰	Marlowe (by O)
Shakes. (by ?)	Keats (by K)

We can see that choices (A), (B), (C), and (D) are all logically necessary. Choice (E) is our exception since Chaucer is taught only in the fall.

Section 3

1. **The correct answer is (C).** This is a main idea question, and the task is to find a choice that expresses the main thesis of the passage without being too narrow and without being overly broad and going beyond the scope of the argument. Choice (A) is too narrow since this is but a minor feature of the discussion. Choice (E) can be eliminated on the same grounds, since the possibility of nuclear destruction is but one important difference between war in a modernized society and war in a pre-modernized society. Choice (B) is an attractive choice, but it is not the main thesis of the passage. The author does indeed discuss some of the effects of war on both modernized and pre-modernized societies, but this discussion is subordinate to a larger goal: to show that because of changing circumstance (effects are different), the value of war has changed. Choice (D) is incorrect because it misses this main point, and it is incorrect for the further reason that the author discusses more than just pre-modernized societies.

2. **The correct answer is (A).** The second paragraph describes the attitude of pre-modernized society toward war: accepted, even noble, necessary. Coupled with the goals of war in pre-modernized societies, described in the first paragraph, we can infer that leaders of pre-modernized society regarded war as a valid policy tool. On this ground, we select choice (A), eliminating choices (B) and (C). As for choice (D), although this can be inferred to have been a feature of war in pre-modernized society, choice (D) is not responsive to the question: What did the leaders think of war, that is, what was their attitude? Choice (E) can be eliminated on the same ground and on the further ground that "necessity" for war was not that described in choice (E).

3. **The correct answer is (C).** The author is discussing war, a seemingly uncivilized activity. Yet, the author argues that war, at least in pre-modernized times, was the necessary result of certain economic and social forces. The use of the term "civilized" is ironic. Under other circumstances, the explanations offered by choices (A) and (B) might be plausible, but there is nothing in this text to support either of those. Choice (D), too, might under other circumstances be a reason for placing the word in quotation marks, but it does not appear that this author is attempting to affect the reader's emotions: the passage is too detached and scientific for that. Finally, choice (E) does articulate one of the author's objectives, but this is not the reason for putting the one word in quotations. The explanation for that is something more specific than an overall idea of the passage.

4. **The correct answer is (B).** This is an explicit idea question, and choices (A), (C), (D), and (E) are all mentioned at various points in the passage as reasons for going to war. Choice (B), too, is mentioned, but it is mentioned as a feature of the military establishment in pre-modernized society—not as a reason for going to war.

5. **The correct answer is (E).** This is another main idea question, and choices (B), (C), and (D) can be eliminated as too narrow. It is true the author mentions that economic and social conditions, technology, and armed conflict have all changed, but this is not the ultimate point to be proved. The author's main point is that *because* of such changes, the value of war has changed. Choice (A) is only tangentially related to the text. Though we may learn a bit about how decisions are made, in part, this is not the main burden of the argument.

6. **The correct answer is (B).** We have already mentioned that the tone of the passage is neutral—scientific and detached. Choices (A) and (D) can be eliminated as overstatements. To be sure, the author seems to deplore the destruction that might result from a nuclear war, but that concern does not rise to the status of outrage, indignation, fear, or alarm. Choice (E) is a closer call. While it is true that the author expresses concern about the ability of modernized society to survive war and while there is arguably a hint of optimism or hope, it cannot be said that these are the *defining* features of the passage. A better description of the prevailing tone is offered by choice (B). As for choice (C), the one ironic reference ("civilized") does not make the entire passage humorous.

7. **The correct answer is (D).** This is an application question, and we must take the information from the passage and apply it to a new situation. The author offers two reasons for the conclusion that war is no longer a viable policy tool: (1) the danger of worldwide destruction and (2) the costs after victory outweigh the benefits to be won. We can conclude that even in the absence of nuclear weapons,

war will still lack its traditional value, as argued by the author in the fourth paragraph. Thus, we can eliminate choices (A) and (B) on the grounds that they are contradicted by the author's thinking. Choice (E) can be eliminated for the same reason and because no such "instincts" are discussed in the text. A close look at choice (C) shows that it is not in agreement with the author's view, since the author believes that though nuclear weapons deter nuclear war, war is obsolete for other reasons as well.

8. **The correct answer is (B).** This is a main idea question. As correctly described by choice (B), the author explains the results of some studies and suggests some implications of these findings for detecting high blood pressure. Choice (E) is incorrect since it is but a minor aspect of the passage. The author notes that there is such a correlation but is not primarily concerned to prove the existence of such a relationship. Choice (C) can be eliminated because the main point is not to describe the epidemiological and clinical studies from a methodological point of view. Rather, the author is concerned with the findings of these studies. Choice (D) can be eliminated on similar grounds, for the author indicates that the two methods of study both point to the existence of a familial connection. Choice (A) can be eliminated since the author does not criticize but rather relies on these experiments.

9. **The correct answer is (D).** This is a specific detail (explicit idea) question, so the main task is to find the right part of the passage. In the last sentence of the first paragraph, the author explicitly states that a factor that initially discouraged the study of hypertension in children was the unfounded belief that it was

difficult to measure blood pressure in children. Choices (A), (B), and (E) are just not mentioned anywhere. The idea suggested by choice (C) is mentioned but in the second paragraph, so you know it can't be an answer to this question.

10. **The correct answer is (C).** This is a question that asks us to make a further application of the arguments given in the passage, and the greatest danger may be the temptation to overstate the case. This is the difficulty with choice (E). The author remarks in the closing sentences, "It may be possible." It is never asserted that it is now possible to do this. Choice (D) also overstates the case. The author states that these chemical deficiencies are associated with high blood pressure, not that such deficiencies *cause* high blood pressure. And to the extent that one wants to argue that such deficiencies *contribute* to high blood pressure (based on paragraph three), that is not sufficient to support the causal statement expressed in choice (D). As for choice (A), the author notes that the low output of urinary kallikrein is associated with high blood pressure; that is, it may be another symptom of whatever physiological disorder causes high blood pressure. But that means it is an effect of the underlying cause and not the cause itself. Finally, choice (B) can be eliminated because it is not a further conclusion of the passage. To the extent that choice (B) reiterates what is stated already (and note that it states the kallikrein-kinin system is important in determining blood pressure, not that the system *causes* high blood pressure), it is not appropriate as a further statement based on arguments presented. Choice (C) is, however, a natural extension of the argument. Remember, the author begins by noting that it is

important to determine when high blood pressure begins and suggests that it may begin as early as infancy.

11. **The correct answer is (A).** This is a logical detail question. In essence, the question stipulates that the author does introduce such evidence and then asks for what reason. In the final paragraph, the author is discussing the connection between low urinary kallikrein excretion and high blood pressure. By noting that black children often show this and noting further that blacks often have high blood pressure, the author hopes to provide further evidence in the connection. As for choice (B), though this may be an incidental effect of the reference, it cannot be said that this is the logical function of the argument in the overall development of the passage. Choice (C) is incorrect since the author is not asserting a causal connection but only a correlation. Choice (D) is incorrect for a reason similar to that which eliminates choice (B). Though this might be a further application for the point, it is not the reason the author incorporates the data into the argument of this passage. Finally, choice (E) is one of the main themes of the passage, but it does not explain why the author introduced the particular point at the particular juncture in the argument.

12. **The correct answer is (B).** This is an explicit detail question. In the third paragraph, the author discusses the operation of the kallikrein-kinin system. There it is stated that it produces chemicals that operate to dilate blood vessels. As for choices (A) and (C), the author does not state that the kallikrein-kinin system interferes directly with either the sympathetic nervous system or the production of aldosterone—only that it *offsets* the effects of those actions. As for

choice (D), the reference to kallikrein levels in urine comes in the last paragraph, the wrong place for an answer to this question. And whatever choice (E) is saying, it just doesn't answer the question.

13. **The correct answer is (C).** This is a logical detail question: Why does the author introduce this information? In the second paragraph, the author is describing new research done on children, research that suggests that the factors related to high blood pressure are already detectable in children. Choice (A) is incorrect since the author has not yet begun to discuss the biochemical research—only epidemiological surveys. Choice (B) is incorrect since it is not a correct response to the question. The author does state that such research is actually possible but does not cite the results of the study in order to prove the study was possible. Rather, the author cites the results to prove the further conclusion outlined in answer choice (C). Choice (D) is incorrect, for it is not a response to the question. To be sure, one might use the results of the study cited to support the recommendation articulated in choice (D), but that is not the author's motivation for introducing them in the argument. As for choice (E), this fails for the same reason that choice (B) fails.

14. **The correct answer is (C).** This is a logical structure question. The author develops the argument primarily by describing findings and supporting a conclusion. As for choice (A), though the author does mention two types of research, epidemiological studies and clinical studies, the author does not contrast these. Choice (B) is incorrect since the main purpose is to support a conclusion, and whatever refutation is offered in the passage (e.g., against the position that blood pressure in children cannot be measured accurately) is offered in the service of a greater point. Choice (E) must fail for a similar reason. And choice (D) fails for this reason as well: the author is supporting a position, not refuting it.

15. **The correct answer is (C).** This is a main idea question. The main point of the passage is that those who believe AFDC restrictions contribute to family dissolution are in error. It is not the restrictions on aid but the aid itself, according to the author, that contributes to low-income family dissolution. So the primary purpose of the passage is to analyze the causes of a phenomenon. Choice (A) is incorrect, for any such results are mentioned only obliquely and are only incidental to the main development. Choice (B) describes something that is integral to, but is not the main point of, the argument. As for choice (D), the author himself offers no such recommendation. While an argument for reform might use the argument in the passage for such recommendations, we cannot attribute any proposal for reform to the author. Finally, choice (E) describes what may be a result of the argument, but changing the attitude of the public, as opposed to engaging in scholarly debate, does not appear to be the objective of the text.

16. **The correct answer is (A).** As we noted above, the author argues that it is not restrictions on aid that create pressures on low-income families; it is the aid itself. We can apply this reasoning to answer this question. The analysis in the text can be used to predict that an increase in the availability of aid would tend to increase pressures on the family unit. Thus, reducing restrictions, because it would

result in an increase in aid availability, would actually tend to create more pressure for divorce. This would have the exact opposite effect predicted by those who call for welfare reforms such as eliminating restrictions. Choice (A) is nice also because of the word *paradoxically* that opens the statement, for the result would be paradoxical from the standpoint of the reformer. Choices (C) and (D) can be eliminated because they are contradicted by the analysis given in the passage. Choice (B) is eliminated because the author never addresses questions of fiscal policy. Finally, choice (E) goes too far in two respects. First, it overstates the author's case. The author does not suggest that the only factor operating in the dissolution of low-income families is welfare and therefore would not likely suggest that the problem could be entirely controlled by manipulating benefit levels. Further, it is not clear that the author advocates any particular policy. The scholarly tone of the article suggests that the author may or may not believe public policy on welfare should take into account the problem of divorce.

17. **The correct answer is (B).** This is an explicit idea question. In discussing the costs of divorce in the third paragraph (costs meaning both economic and social costs), the author mentions choices (B), (C), and (D) as encouraging people to stay married. Earlier in that same paragraph, the author mentions consumption possibilities as a factor tending to hold a marriage together. Choice (B) is never mentioned in this respect. Although the author is primarily interested in low-income family stability, it is never stated that social or economic class is a factor in perpetuating a marriage. And to the extent that one mounts an argument

to the effect that the pressures described in paragraph three (costs of divorce and greater consumption possibilities) would naturally tend to operate more powerfully for lower-income families, one is applying that reasoning to a new situation. So that argument, since it is new, cannot be a factor mentioned by the author in this passage and cannot, therefore, be an answer to the question asked.

18. **The correct answer is (A).** This is obviously a main idea question, and we have already analyzed the main point of the passage. It is nicely stated by choice (A). Choice (B) is not the main idea but only an incidental feature of the argument. Choice (C) is incorrect since this is in direct contradiction to the main point of the passage. Choice (D) fails for the same reason that choice (B) fails. Finally, choice (E) is incorrect because there is no warrant in the passage to support the conclusion that the author would make such a recommendation. The author argues in a very scholarly and neutral fashion. Given that, we cannot attribute any attitude to the author about the wisdom of welfare policy.

19. **The correct answer is (B).** As we have just noted, the scholarly treatment of the passage is best described as scientific and detached. As for choice (A), though the author may be confident in the presentation, there is no hint of optimism. Choice (C) can be eliminated for a similar reason: there is no hint of alarm or discouragement. As for choice (D), to the extent that it can be argued that the author's treatment is scholarly and therefore polite and sensitive, choice (B) is a better description of the overall tone. The defining elements of a scholarly treatment are those set forth in choice (B). Those elements suggested by choice (D)

would be merely incidental to and parasitic upon the main features of scientific neutrality and detachment. Finally, though the author's treatment is detached, it would be wrong to say that the author is callous and indifferent—any more than we would want to say that a doctor who analyzes the causes of a disease in clinical terms is therefore callous and indifferent.

20. **The correct answer is (A).** With an application question of this sort, we must be careful not to overstate the strength of the author's case. This is the reason choice (D) is incorrect. Though the author points out that there are economic pressures on families that tend to encourage divorce, it would go beyond that analysis to attribute to the author the statement in choice (D). Choice (E), too, overstates the case. Though the author prefers to analyze family stability primarily in economic terms, the text will not support the judgment that people are getting more self-centered. If anything, a rising divorce rate would be analyzed by the author in broad social and economic terms, rather than in personal terms as suggested by choice (E). Choice (B) is incorrect because it takes us too far beyond the analysis given in paragraph three. While it is conceivable that further analysis would generate the conclusion in choice (B), choice (A) is much closer to the actual text. This is not to say that choice (B) is necessarily a false statement; rather, this is to accept the structure of the question: Would the author *most likely* agree? Finally, choice (C) attributes to the author a value judgment that has no support in the text.

21. **The correct answer is (E).** This, too, is an application question and, as was just pointed out, we are looking for the most

likely source. It is not impossible that the passage was taken from a basic economics text or a book on the history of welfare. It could, conceivably, be one of several readings included in such books, but on balance, it seems more likely, given the scholarly tone and the particular subject, that choice (E) is the correct answer. It seems unlikely that this would have appeared in choices (A) or (D).

22. **The correct answer is (A).** Here we have a main idea question. The structure of the passage is first to explain that previous siting decisions have been made by regulatory agencies with only a review function exercised by government. The author then explains that in the past, the most important features affecting the demographic characteristics of the population were natural ones. Then the author argues that, given the effect siting decisions will have in the future, the government ought to take an active role in making those decisions and that the government ought to take social considerations into account in making such decisions. Given this brief synopsis of the argument, we can see that choice (A) neatly restates this thesis. Further, we can see that choice (B) constitutes only a part, not the entirety, of the argument. Choice (C), too, forms only one subpart of the whole analysis. Choice (D) can be eliminated since the author believes that future siting decisions need not be governed by only natural features. Finally, choice (E) may very well be true, but it surely is not the main point of the argument presented.

23. **The correct answer is (D).** This is an explicit idea question. Choice (A) is mentioned in the final sentence of the first paragraph along with choice (B). Choice (E) is a theme that runs generally through

that paragraph, and choice (C) is specifically mentioned in the third paragraph. Nowhere does the author suggest that proximity to fuel sources needs to be taken into the siting decision.

24. The correct answer is (C). This is a specific detail question, so the answer will be explicitly provided by the text. Your main task is to find the right part of the passage. The answer is given in the first paragraph where the author explains that, traditionally, siting decisions were made by the utilities with government relegated to a review function. Choices (A) and (B) are mentioned in the passage but as advantages of a different process, or, if you prefer, they're mentioned but in the wrong place to answer this question. Choice (D), of course, contradicts the selection; and choice (E) just is not mentioned by the author.

25. The correct answer is (C). This is a logical structure question. The author's analysis and recommendation depend on the assumption that it will be possible to predict the demographic consequences of an energy park. Without this assumption, the recommendation that the government use electric facility siting decisions to effect social goals loses much of its persuasiveness. As for choices (A) and (D), the historical explanation is in large part expository only; that is, background information that is not, strictly speaking, essential to the argument supporting the recommendation. To the extent, then, that either choices (A) or (D) does weaken the historical analysis, and that is doubtful, the damage to the overall argument would not be great. As for choices (B) and (E), these are both irrelevant, and the proof is that whether choices (B) and (E) are true or false does not affect the argument.

26. The correct answer is (D). The correct answer to this application question, is clearly supported by the concluding remarks of the passage. Choice (A) is contradicted by these remarks and must be incorrect. Choice (B) goes beyond the scope of the passage. We cannot attribute such a critical judgment (". . . were irresponsible") to the author. In fact, the passage at least implies that decisions during the nineteenth century were made in a natural (no pun intended) way. Choice (C) overstates the case. Though the author believes that siting decisions for power plants need not depend on natural features, there is no support in the text for such a broad conclusion as that given in choice (C). Finally, as for choice (E), there is no evidence that the author would make such a judgment.

27. The correct answer is (A). This is an explicit idea question, the answer to which is found at the end of the third paragraph. The most important feature of an energy park is that the place in which the massive effects will be manifested can be chosen. So, unlike the harbor, a natural feature located without regard to human desires, the energy park can be located where it will serve goals other than the production of energy. As for choice (B), even to the extent that it makes an accurate statement, the statement is not responsive to the question. This is not an important difference between the natural advantages of an early city and the created features of the energy park. A similar argument invalidates choice (D). As for choice (C), this is obviously irrelevant to the question asked. Finally, choice (E) is incorrect for two reasons. First, such a conclusion is not supported by the passage. Second, it is not a response to the question asked.

28. **The correct answer is (E).** There can be little doubt that the author is an advocate of energy parks. The criticism noted in passing in the final paragraph is simply dismissed. Thus, we can conclude that his attitude is one of wholehearted support, as indicated by choice (E). We can eliminate choice (D) because the author in no way qualifies his recommendation. Choices (A), (B), and (C) can be eliminated because of the author's positive attitude.

Section 4

Questions 1–6

This problem set is a linear ordering set with the additional complication of the challenge provision. You would probably want to summarize the information:

F > G (F above G)

J > (H & I) (J above both H and I)

K = H + 2 (K is two above H)

F = 3 or 4 (F is 3rd or 4th)

1. **The correct answer is (D).** For this question, we need check only each of the choices against the conditions. Choice (A) can be eliminated since K is not ranked two places above H. Choice (B) can be eliminated since J is not ranked above H and I and for the further reason that F is out of place. Choice (C) is not acceptable since G is ranked above F. Choice (E) is incorrect since K and H are together, not separated by another person. Only choice (D) meets all of the requirements for the initial ranking.

2. **The correct answer is (A).** For this question, we are given additional information. On the assumption that K is ranked first, we know that H must be

ranked third, which in turn places F fourth. Since J must be ranked above H, J must be ranked second. No further conclusion can be definitely drawn about the positions of G and I, so our order is:

1 2 3 4 5 6
K J H F G I

At this juncture, we check our deductions against the answer choices. Choices (B) and (C) are contradicted by the diagram. Choices (D) and (E) are possible—not necessary. Choice (A), however, makes a statement that is confirmed by the diagram.

3. **The correct answer is (A).** For this question, we assume that F is ranked third. On that assumption, there are only two positions available for K: 2 (with H in 4) and 4 (with H in 6).

1 2 3 4 5 6   1 2 3 4 5 6
  K F H   F K   H

As for the first possibility, G must be in position 5 with I in 6, or vice versa, for J must be above H, and that means J must be in first position. As for the second possibility, G must be in position 5, which forces J and I to occupy positions 1 and 2, respectively:

1 2 3 4 5 6   1 2 3 4 5 6
J K F H I G   J I F K G H

So there are a total of three possible arrangements. We are looking, however, for a statement that is necessarily true. That is choice (A), since J is ranked first in all three possibilities. Choice (B) is incorrect since it is only possible, not necessary, that K be second. Choice (C) is incorrect, for it makes a false statement. Choice (D) is incorrect for the same reason. Finally, choice (E) makes a statement that could be true, but it is not necessarily true.

4. **The correct answer is (D).** For this question, we assume that K is ranked third. This means F is fourth, H is fifth, and G must be sixth. Finally, since J must be above I, J is first, with I second.

```
1  2  3  4  5  6
J  I  K  F  H  G
```

K can challenge only the players one or two ranks above him, and those players are J and I.

5. **The correct answer is (E).** If F is able to issue a challenge to H, this can only be because F is ranked fourth with H third. It is not possible for F to be in the third position with H in the first or second. With H and F in third and fourth, respectively, we are able to deduce the following:

```
1  2  3  4  5  6
K  J  H  F  G  I
```

K must be in the first position since that is two positions above H, who is in third. Since J must be above H, this means J must be second. Now we check our answer choices. Choices (A), (B), (C), and (D) are all necessarily true, as shown by the diagram. Choice (E) is possible but is not necessary, so choice (E) is the exception and therefore our correct answer.

6. **The correct answer is (A).** We assume that J challenges K, so K must be ranked above J. But J can be ranked no lower than second, so K must be first with H in third and F in fourth:

```
1  2  3  4  5   6
K  J  H  F  G/ I
```

Checking the answer choices, we see that choice (A) is necessarily true, while choices (B), (C), and (D) are necessarily false and choice (E) only possibly true.

Questions 7–10

Although this problem set involves a temporal ordering, we render that ordering spatially:

		M	Tu	Wed	Th	F
W,Y	A.M.			X		
X						
V, Z	P.M.		Z	(V)	(Z)	

With X flying on Wednesday morning, X cannot fly Tuesday or Thursday morning, nor on Wednesday or Thursday afternoon. Further, with Z flying on Tuesday, Z is not available for Wednesday afternoon. This means V must fly Wednesday afternoon and Z Thursday afternoon.

7. **The correct answer is (E).** We were able to draw only two further conclusions from the initial conditions: V flies Wednesday afternoon and Z flies Thursday afternoon. Choices (A), (B), (C), and (D) are all possibly true; only choice (E) is necessarily true.

8. **The correct answer is (B).** We begin by processing the additional information. Since X is flying Friday morning, X cannot fly either Thursday morning or Friday afternoon. This means that either W or Y will fly on Thursday morning and that V will fly on Friday afternoon.

	M	Tu	Wed	Th	F
A.M.			X		X
P.M.		Z	V	Z	V

The diagram shows that choices (A), (C), and (D) are possibly true and that choice (E) is necessarily false. Only choice (B) is necessarily true.

9. **The correct answer is (A).** We assume that X flies only one morning flight. This does not allow us to draw any specific conclusion about a particular flight, so we are forced to look to the answer choices;

that is, we must test each choice and arrive at the correct answer by the process of elimination. Choice (A) is correct. W and Y must cover Monday, Tuesday, Thursday, and Friday. And since a pilot cannot fly on consecutive days, W must do either Monday or Tuesday and either Thursday or Friday. Choice (B) is incorrect since V could do both Monday and Friday afternoons, and then X would make only the one flight each week. Choice (C) is incorrect as shown by our analysis of choice (A)—Y also must fly two days each week. Choice (D) is incorrect, for Z cannot fly either Monday or Friday. Choice (E) is possibly, though not necessarily, true. We do not know whether Monday and Friday afternoons will go to X or V.

10. **The correct answer is (D).** We begin by processing the additional information:

	M	Tu	Wed	Th	F
A.M.	X	Y	X	Y	X
P.M.	V	Z	V	Z	V

If W does not fly at all during the week, then Y must fly on Tuesday and Thursday. This means that X must fly on Monday morning and Friday morning. Further, we must assign V to Monday and Friday afternoons. The diagram shows that choices (A), (B), (C), and (E) are all necessarily true and that choice (D) is necessarily false.

Questions 11–15

This is a selection set, and we begin by summarizing the restrictions on our selections:

S → Q (S requires Q)

R → ~R (Not two consecutive days)

T ← U (U can only follow T)

Only one carryover

11. **The correct answer is (E).** For a question such as this, which does not supply any additional information, we simply check each answer choice against the restrictions we have summarized. Choice (A) is not acceptable because R is used on two consecutive days and, further, because S appears the first day without Q. Choice (B) can be eliminated because two selections carry over from day 1 to day 2 (S and Q). Choice (C) can be eliminated because S appears on day 2 unaccompanied by Q. Choice (D) can be eliminated because U appears on day 2, but T did not appear on day 1. Only choice (E) is consistent with all of the restrictions.

12. **The correct answer is (C).** If P and S are on the menu, then Q is also on the menu for that day. As for the next day, U cannot be used since T was not offered the day before. Further, S cannot be used since S requires Q and we cannot carry over both S and Q. This leaves us with R and T to be offered along with one dish from the first day (either P or Q).

13. **The correct answer is (C).** We know that neither R nor U can be offered on the intervening day. R cannot be used on two consecutive days, and U must follow T. So we must use S and T. With S offered, we must also offer Q. So the three specials for the intervening day are S, Q, and T.

14. **The correct answer is (A).** If neither Q nor T is on the menu, this leaves us with P, R, S, and U. But S cannot be used without Q, so this leaves only P, R, and U. Hence, there is only one possible combination of specials, given the assumption that Q and T are not offered.

15. **The correct answer is (A).** On the assumption that Q, R, and S are offered on one day, R cannot be offered the following day. Nor can U be offered since T

did not appear on the preceding day. This means that both P and T will have to be included since only one of the original three can be carried over. S cannot be carried over because that would also require the carrying over of Q. Q, however, can appear without S (Q is not "dependent" on S). So the second day, the specials must be P, Q, and T.

Questions 16–20

Here we have an ordering set, but the ordering is not strictly linear. That is, rather than having a single file of items (e.g., books on a shelf), several people here could occupy the same position simultaneously, for example, three people interviewed on Thursday. We begin by summarizing the information:

M   Tu   Wed   Th   F

O

(M & N) = Q + 3 (M and N interviewed
3 days after Q)

P later than K

It does not appear possible to draw any definite conclusions about what individual will be interviewed on which day (other than O). But there are some general conclusions that are available. First, we know that Q must be interviewed on either Monday or Tuesday, with M and N coming on Thursday or Friday, respectively, for those are the only ways of observing the restriction that M and N be interviewed exactly three days after Q. Second, we can also deduce that on one day, three persons will be interviewed; on one day, two persons will be interviewed; and on the remaining three days, only one person will be interviewed. Given that Wednesday is used for only one interview and that only two days have more than one interview, a 1-1-1-2-3 arrangement (though not necessarily in that order) is the only possible distribution.

16. **The correct answer is (C).** This problem does not supply us with additional information, so we must find the correct choice using only the initial conditions. You will observe that the answer choices all make relative statements (e.g., O's interview is later in the week than K's interview) and not specific statements (e.g. K is interviewed on Thursday). The incorrect answers can all be shown to be possible by constructing examples:

M   Tu   Wed   Th   F
Q   K   O   M   P
     J   N
                  L

This, of course, is not the only possible schedule, but the diagram shows that choices (A), (B), (D), and (E) are possible. Choice (C), however, is not possible. At the latest, K could be interviewed on Thursday, since K must be followed by P. At the earliest, M and N could be interviewed on Thursday, since they are interviewed on the third day following Q's interview. So it is impossible to interview K on a day *later* in the week than that set aside for N.

17. **The correct answer is (B).** Again, we have a question that does not supply us with any more information. Our analysis regarding the distribution of interviews proves that choice (B) is necessarily true. As for the incorrect answers, using our diagram from the preceding explanation, we can prove that they are not necessarily true. As for choice (A), L can be interviewed on Tuesday with K and J, which proves that the M-N day need not be the day with three interviews. As for choice (C), we can change the diagram to have K and J on Monday and Q on Tuesday. As for choices (D) and (E), the diagram al-

ready proves these statements are not necessarily true.

18. The correct answer is (A). Here we have additional information:

M	Tu	Wed	Th	F
	Q			M
	J			N

We know that M and N must be scheduled for Friday, and we know further that a third person must be scheduled for Friday in order to meet the 1-1-1-2-3 distributional requirement. Beyond that, no further conclusions are evident, and we must turn for guidance to the choices. Choice (A) is the correct answer since P must follow K. This means that K cannot be interviewed on Friday, and we know that K cannot be interviewed on Tuesday. This means that K must be interviewed on either Monday or Thursday, days reserved for only one interview. Choices (B), (C), (D), and (E) are all possible but not necessarily true.

19. The correct answer is (B). Since P must follow K and since M and N can be interviewed only on Thursday or Friday, the stipulation that K is interviewed with M and N forces us to schedule M and N for Thursday. This requires that we schedule Q for Monday. The remaining statements are all possible, but none of them is necessarily true.

20. The correct answer is (C). If L is interviewed later in the week than P, then Thursday is the earliest available date for L (P must follow K). However, the latest date by which Q can be interviewed is Tuesday. So L and Q cannot be scheduled for the same day.

Questions 21–24

For this set we will use an information matrix:

	M	N	O	P	Q	R
1						
2						
3						
4						
5						

This allows us to keep track of which performers are used in which skits. We enter the information:

	M	N	O	P	Q	R
1	NO	NO	YES	YES	NO	NO
2						YES
3	NO	YES	NO	NO	NO	NO
4						
5						

Is there anything more to be learned? Yes. If each of the 6 performers is to appear 3 times, we need a total of 6 × 3, or 18, appearances. Thus far, we have 2 for the first performance, 4 for the second, and 1 for the third, for a total of 7. We need 11 more appearances. Skits 4 and 5 have spaces for 12 performers (6 for each performance), but we are told that fewer people are used in the fifth than in the fourth skit. So skit 5 can use a maximum of 5 people, and 4 can use a maximum of 6 people. But that is exactly the number we need, 11. So all 6 performers must appear in skit 4, and 5 out of 6 in skit 5. Thus, the distribution is 2, 4, 1, 6, and 5, for a total of 18. Now, we can enter further information on our matrix:

	M	N	O	P	Q	R	
1	NO	NO	YES	YES	NO	NO	2
2						YES	4
3	NO	YES	NO	NO	NO	NO	1
4	YES	YES	YES	YES	YES	YES	6
5							5
						Total	18

But we also know that each performer must appear three times, so we deduce the following:

	M	N	O	P	Q	R	
1	NO	NO	YES	YES	NO	NO	2
2	YES				YES	YES	4
3	NO	YES	NO	NO	NO	NO	1
4	YES	YES	YES	YES	YES	YES	6
5	YES				YES	YES	5
	3	3	3	3	3	3	18
						Totals	

For example, if M does not appear in skits 1 and 3, we know M must appear in 2, 4, and 5.

21. **The correct answer is (E).** We were able to deduce this by reflecting on the overall distributional requirements. Our chart shows that choices (A) and (B) are possibly, though not necessarily, true. Choices (C) and (D) are shown to be false by our chart.

22. **The correct answer is (B).** The chart confirms that choice (B) is the correct answer, for M and R both appear in skits 2, 4, and 5. Choice (C) is perhaps, though not necessarily, true, as shown by the chart. Choices (A), (D), and (E) are shown by the chart to be false.

23. **The correct answer is (B).** Since we need a total of five performers in the fifth skit (two in addition to M, Q, and R), at least one member of the pair, P and O, must be used. As for choice (A), it is

possible that N will be used and therefore neither P nor O. As for choices (C) and (D), the same reasoning shows that they are possible. Finally, choice (E) is possible if N appears in the second skit rather than in the fifth.

24. **The correct answer is (A).** For this question, we add the additional information to our matrix:

	M	N	O	P	Q	R
1	NO	NO	YES	YES	NO	NO
2	YES	(YES)	(NO)	(NO)	YES	YES
3	NO	YES	NO	NO	NO	NO
4	YES	YES	YES	YES	YES	YES
5	YES	(NO)	(YES)	(YES)	YES	YES
	3	3	3	3		

Section 5

1. **The correct answer is (D).** According to the speaker, a Board meeting normally precedes a shakeup in management but no such meeting has or will take place, so the shakeup is not going to occur. The other choices, in various ways, just don't describe this development. As for choice (A), although there are two competing theories discussed (shakeup v. no shakeup), these are not logically inconsistent statements. As for choice (B), this would be an apt description only if it later turned out that there was a shakeup in management even though no meeting occurred—perhaps because of special circumstance or a new policy. Then it would be correct to say, "Well, the theory that there would be a change seemed to be wrong given what we knew at the time, but now we know differently." Choice (C) cautions against the fallacy of the false cause. Just because one event follows another does not mean that the one was the cause of the other.

Finally, choice (E) talks about necessary versus sufficient causes. This is a useful distinction with which to be familiar. A necessary cause is one that is required for an event to take place: the virus is necessary for the disease to develop. But a necessary cause is not always a sufficient cause: the virus may be present but yet not cause the disease.

2. **The correct answer is (E).** The speaker rejects the position of the Bar Association that a do-it-yourself will might turn out to be invalid by attacking lawyers—the source of the claim. Choice (A) is incorrect because even though the speaker fails to mention this possibility, it is not necessarily the case that the speaker has failed to consider it; and, in any event, the fact that a proponent of a claim doesn't discuss all possible objections to the claim is not a logical weakness. Choice (B) is wrong because the speaker need not take any position on this issue. As for choice (C), while the speaker only discusses two options, the speaker doesn't claim these are the only two available. (A person might just write a will without any help at all or copy one from some other source.) And choice (D) is wrong because the alternative would be to have no will at all, an option not urged by the speaker.

3. **The correct answer is (B).** The basic move by Adamante is to offer a competing explanation for the phenomenon: Yes, the U.S. has the 17th lowest infant mortality rate, but this is due to distributional factors rather than to medical technology itself. Choice (D) is the second most attractive answer. But Adamante does not introduce any intervening variables; for example, technology allows more pregnancies that would otherwise abort to go to term, which in turn means

that weaker infants are born, and so more die. Choice (A) is incorrect since Adamante seems to accept the validity of the data and to contest the explanation. Choice (E) is incorrect for the same reason. Finally, choice (C) is incorrect since Adamante does not suggest that the first speaker has made a logical error—only a factual one.

4. **The correct answer is (C).** The speaker is arguing that the budget cuts will not ultimately be detrimental to the poor. Choice (C) attacks this conclusion directly by pointing out that they will receive little or no advantage. Choices (A) and (B) are wrong because they are irrelevant: how or why politicians are elected is not a concern of the speaker. And choices (D) and (E) both seem to strengthen the speaker's position by suggesting ways in which the poor would benefit.

5. **The correct answer is (A).** The author reasons from the premise "there are bottles of this product in the apartments" to the conclusion "therefore, these people believe the product is effective." The ad obviously wants the hearer to infer that the residents of the apartments decided themselves to purchase the product because they believed it to be effective. Choice (A) directly attacks this linkage. If it were true that the company gave away bottles of the product, this would sever that link. Choice (B) does weaken the ad but only marginally. To be sure, we might say to ourselves, "Well, a person who touts a product but does not use it is not fully to be trusted." But choice (B) does not aim at the very structure of the argument as choice (A) does. Choice (C) can hardly weaken the argument, since it appears to be a premise on which the argument itself is built. Choice (C),

therefore, actually strengthens the appeal of the advertisement. It also does not link to Painaway's effectiveness. Choice (D) seems to be irrelevant to the *appeal* of the ad. The ad is designed to *change* the hearer's mind, so the fact that someone does not now accept the conclusion of the ad is not an argument against the ability of the ad to accomplish its stated objective. Finally, choice (E) is irrelevant to the purpose of the ad for reasons very similar to these cited for choice (D).

6. **The correct answer is (B).** The author is accusing the artists of being inconsistent: they give lip service to the idea that an artist must suffer, but that they then live in material comfort—so they do not themselves suffer. Only choice (B) completes the paragraph in a way so that this inconsistency comes out. Choices (A) and (D) can be dismissed because the author is concerned with those whom he attacks as *artists*, not as connoisseurs or purchasers of art, nor as critics of art. Choice (C) is inadequate, for it does not reveal the inconsistency. The author apparently allows that these people are, after a fashion, artists but objects to is their claiming that it is necessary to suffer while they do not themselves suffer. Choice (E) is the second-best answer, but it fails, too. The difficulty with choice (E) is that the author's point is that there is a contradiction between the actions and the words of those accused: They claim to suffer, but they do not. But the claimed suffering goes beyond matters of eating and has to do with deprivation generally.

7. **The correct answer is (B).** Choice (B) is an assumption of the author because the inconsistency would disappear if, though artists were not poor, they nonetheless endured great suffering, such as

emotional pain or poor health. Choice (A) is not an assumption of the author. The author is trying to show a contradiction in another's words and actions: It is the others who insist suffering is necessary. The author never says one way or the other whether suffering is necessary to produce art—only that these others claim it is and then eat well. Choice (C) incorrectly construes the author's reference to purchasers of art. The author never mentions the role of the critic. Choices (D) and (E) both make the mistake of applying the term "fools" to a category other than "bidders."

8. **The correct answer is (C).** Take careful note of the exact position the author ascribes to the analysts: They *always* attribute a sudden drop to a crisis. The author then attacks this simple causal explanation by explaining that, though a crisis is followed by a market drop, the reason is not that the crisis causes the drop but that both are the effects of some common cause, the changing of the moon. Of course, the argument seems implausible, but our task is not to grade the argument, only to describe its structure. Choice (A) is not a proper characterization of that structure since the author never provides a specific example. Choice (B), too, is inapplicable since no statistics are produced. Choice (D) can be rejected since the author is attacking generally accepted beliefs rather than appealing to them to support a position. Finally, though the author concedes the reliability of the reports in question, he wants to draw a different conclusion from the data, choice (E).

9. **The correct answer is (A).** Given the implausibility of the author's alternative explanation, the suggestion is probably spoken tongue-in-cheek—ridiculing the

analysts for *always* attributing a drop in the market to a political crisis. But whether you took the argument in this way or as a serious attempt to explain the fluctuations of the stock market, choice (A) will be the correct answer. Choice (E) surely goes beyond the mere factual description at which the author is aiming, as does choice (D) as well. The author is concerned with the *causes* of fluctuations; nothing suggests that he or anyone else is in a position to exploit those fluctuations. Choice (C) finds no support in the paragraph, for nothing suggests that he wishes to attack the credibility of the source rather than the argument itself. Finally, choice (B) is inappropriate to the main point of the passage. Whether the market ultimately evens itself out has nothing to do with the causes of the fluctuations.

10. **The correct answer is (E).** The assumption necessary to the author's reasoning is the fairly abstract or minimal one that there is a connection—between the characteristics of a work of art and the period during that it was produced. If there were no such connection—that is, if there were not styles of art that lasted for some time but only randomly produced works unrelated to one another by medium, content, or detail—the argument would fail. Every other choice however, attributes too much to the author. Choice (D), for example, states that the expert can *pinpoint* the date of the work, but this goes far beyond the author's attempt to date generally the piece of pottery he is examining. Choice (C) says more than the author does. He mentions that the details of semi-nude women and bulls are characteristic of the *late* Minoan period, not that they generally characterize the entire history of that people.

Choice (B) also goes far beyond the details offered. The author connects the bull with a period of *Minoan* civilization—not ancient civilizations in general. Finally, choice (A) fails because, while the author apparently believes that Minoan pottery of this period was made in a certain way, it is not claimed that all such pottery came from this period. The author uses a group of characteristics in combination to date the pottery: It is the combination that is unique to the period, not each individual characteristic taken in isolation.

11. **The correct answer is (B).** The weakness in the argument is that it makes an assertion without any supporting argumentation. The author states that things might turn out to be worse but never mentions any specific way in which the result might be considered less desirable than what presently exists. As for choice (A), the author might have chosen to attack the radicals in this way, but that the author did not adopt a particular line of attack available is not nearly so severe a criticism as the expressed by choice (B)—that the line of attack finally adopted is defective or at least incomplete. The same reasoning applies to both choices (C) and (E). It is true the author might have taken the attack proposed by choice (C), but the fact that it was not chosen is not nearly so serious a weakness as that pointed out by choice (B). Choice (E) comes perhaps the closest to expressing what choice (B) says more explicitly. Choice (E) hints at the specific consequences that might occur, but it is restricted to the *transition* period. It is not really detailing the bad results that might finally come out of a revolution, only the disadvantages of undertaking the change. Finally, choice (D) describes

existing conditions, but it does not treat the question of whether there *should* be a revolution; and, in any event, to defend against the question whether there *should* be a revolution by arguing there *will not be* one would itself be weak, had the author used the argument.

12. **The correct answer is (E).** Since the average compensation for all employees was less than that for copywriters, at least one employee must have earned less than the average for the copywriters. Choice (A) cannot be inferred because the speaker provides information only about compensation, not number employed. Choice (B) and (C) are wrong for essentially the same reason: although the average for the graphic artists was greater than that for copywriters, the salary range may or may not have included the extremes described in those choices. And choice (D) cannot be inferred since the speaker talks about total compensation, including the bonuses; that is, no information is given to let you draw a conclusion about the size of the bonuses alone.

13. **The correct answer is (E).** The sample syllogism uses its terms in an ambiguous way. In the first premise, the category "American buffalo" is used to refer to the group as a whole, but in the second premise, it is used to denote a particular member of that group. In the first premise, "disappearing" refers to extinction of a group, but in the second premise, "disappearing" apparently means fading from view. Choice (E) is fraught with similar ambiguities. The argument there moves from wealthy people as a group to a particular wealthy person, an illegitimate shifting of terminology. Choice (A) is a distraction. It mentions subject matter similar to that of the question stem,

but our task is to parallel the *form* of the argument, not to find an argument on a similar topic. Choice (A), incidentally, is an unambiguous and valid argument. So, too, is choice (B), and a moment's reflection will reveal that it is very similar to choice (A). Choice (C) is not similar to choices (A) and (B), but then again it is not parallel to the question stem. Choice (C) contains circular reasoning—the very thing to be proved had to be assumed in the first place—but while circular reasoning is incorrect reasoning, it does not parallel the error committed by the question stem: ambiguity. Choice (D) is clearly a correct argument, so it cannot be parallel to the question stem that contains a fallacious argument.

14. **The correct answer is (C).** The tone of the paragraph is tongue-in-cheek. The author uses phrases such as "mysteries of this arcane science" and "wonderful discipline" but then gives a silly example of the utility of logic. Obviously, he means to be ironic. The real point he wants to make is that formal logic has little utility and that it may even lead one to make foolish errors. Choice (A) cannot be correct because the example is clearly not an illustration of correct reasoning. Choice (B) can be rejected since the author does not attempt to define the term "logic"; he only gives an example of its use. Choice (D) is a distraction. The author's particular illustration does mention the American buffalo, but he could as easily have taken another species of animal or any other group term that would lend itself to the ambiguous treatment of his syllogism. Choice (E) is incorrect since the author never examines the relationship between the premises and the conclusion. He gives the example and lets it speak for itself.

15. **The correct answer is (B).** The author's behavior is paradoxical because he is going along with the young man's paradoxical statement. He concludes the young man is lying because the young man told him so, but that depends on believing what the young man told him is true. So he accepts the content of the young man's statement in order to reject the statement. Once it is seen that there is a logical twist to this problem, the other answer choices can easily be rejected. Choice (A), of course, overlooks the paradoxical nature of the tourist's behavior. The stranger may have been trying to be helpful, but what is curious about the tourist's behavior is not that he rejected the stranger's offer of advice *but rather* that he relied on that very advice at the moment he rejected it! Choice (C) also overlooks the paradox. It is true the tourist rejects the advice, but his rejection is not *understandable;* if anything, it is self-contradictory and therefore completely incomprehensible. Choice (D) is the poorest possible choice since it makes a value judgment totally unrelated to the point of the passage. Finally, choice (E) would have been correct only if the tourist were possibly being victimized.

16. **The correct answer is (D).** As we explained in the previous question, the tourist's behavior is self-contradictory. The sentence mentioned in choice (D) is also self-contradictory. For if the sentence is taken to be true, what it asserts must be the case, so the sentence turns out to be false. On the other hand, if the sentence is taken to be false, then what it says is correct, so the sentence must be true. In other words, the sentence is true only if it is false and false only if it is true: a paradox. Choice (A) is not paradoxical. The witness *later* admits that he lied in

the first instance. Thus, though his later testimony contradicts his earlier testimony, the statements taken as a group are not paradoxical, since he is not claiming that the first and the second are true *at the same time.* Choices (B) and (C) do not have even the flavor of paradox. They are just straightforward statements. Do not be deceived by the fact that choice (C) refers to an about-face. To change directions, or even one's testimony, is not self-contradictory—see choice (A). Finally choice (E) is a straightforward, self-consistent statement. Although the worker is advised to dissemble, he does not claim that he is both telling the truth and presenting a false image at the same time.

17. **The correct answer is (E).** The author cites a series of similarities between the two diseases, and then in his last sentence, he writes, "So . . . ," indicating that the conclusion that the causes of the two diseases are similar rests upon the other similarities listed. Choice (E) correctly describes the basis of the argument. Choice (A) is incorrect, for nothing in the passage indicates that either disease is a public health hazard, much less that one disease is a greater hazard than the other. Choice (B) is unwarranted, for the author states only that the scientists are looking for a cure for *aphroditis melancholias.* The author does not state that they will be successful; and even if there is a hint of that in the argument, we surely would not want to conclude on that basis that scientists will eventually find a cure for *every* disease. Choice (C), like choice (A), is unrelated to the conclusion the author seeks to establish. All the author wants to maintain is that similarities in the symptoms suggest that scientists should look for similarities in

the causes of these diseases. The author offers no opinion of the ultimate goal of modern technology, nor does he need to do so. The argument is complete without any such addition. Choice (D) is probably the second-best answer, but it is still completely wrong. The author's argument based on the assumption that similarity of effect depends upon similarity of cause would neither gain nor lose persuasive force if choice (D) were true. After all, many diseases occur in both man and other animals, but at least choice (D) has the merit—which choices (A), (B), and (C) all lack—of trying to say something about the connection between the causes and effects of disease.

18. **The correct answer is (E).** This question asks you to explain the "paradox," and this is a fairly typical test question. Similar question stems ask for you to "account for the unexpected result" or to "explain the unusual outcome," but they are essentially asking for the same thing: Given the background, why did things turn out differently than expected? Applying that insight to this item, the stimulus material leads us to expect a decline in turbulence following the imposition of a speed limit because, after all, going slow produces less wake. Yet, the unexpected (opposite) occurred. Why? Choice (E) answers this question: the boats were operating too slowly to take advantage of the advanced designs and actually produced more, not less, wake. Now, one typical kind of wrong answer is one that mentions a fact related to the passage but that doesn't cut one way or the other, and choice (A) is such a choice. Fewer ferries operate late at night, but that doesn't explain why turbulence increased following the imposition of the speed limit. Choices (B) and (C) also fit this

pattern. Choice (D) illustrates another wrong-answer pattern: suppressing an alternative explanation. When you read the stimulus material, you might think "But maybe boat traffic increased and that accounts for the increase in turbulence." But choice (D) eliminates this possible explanation, so (D) does nothing to explain the "paradox."

19. **The correct answer is (A).** A question such as this, which asks you to weaken an argument that offers a proposal, usually is answered by a choice that highlights a hidden causal factor that will defeat the purpose. In this case, the speaker claims that working the dog off-leash will solve the problem of false positives by removing the influence of the handler, but choice (A) points out that the dog's previous training (treats for finding stuff) predisposes it to return positives in anticipation of rewards. Wrong answers tend to fall into one of three categories. Some are wrong because they simply miss the point, and these are usually fairly obviously wrong, as choice (C) here. Others cite interesting facts, like choices (B) and (D), but the facts just don't go anywhere. For example, does the "mixture" problem make it more or less likely that the dog will return false positives? And perhaps most troublesome, some choices actually strengthen the argument. This type is vexing because there is a certain logical force to the choice—but it pushes in the wrong direction. This is illustrated by choice (E). This idea does bear on the issues raised in the stimulus material, but it actually strengthens the argument by pre-empting a possible objection: Don't worry about the fact that the dog is off-leash, because we can still keep tabs on it.

20. **The correct answer is (E).** Remember that you must pay careful attention to the way in which the speaker qualifies and quantifies the claims made. In this case, words such as "usually" and "characteristically" provide support for a certain view but do not establish it definitively. In other words, the speaker overstates the case or claims too much from the evidence. Choice (A) is a description of the logical fallacy of "begging the question." This is similar to saying that the Smith Almanac predicts a hard winter, and it can't be wrong since Smith himself says that he is the leading authority on weather in the world, and the world's leading authority must be accurate. Choice (B) is a description of the fallacy of the "false cause," for example, saying that shortly after the administration announced the release of oil reserves, OPEC said it would curtail production; so it seems that OPEC retaliated for the administration's decision. (Was the release in anticipation of OPEC's actions?) Choice (D) describes the "hasty generalization": "Hello from the Eyewitness-Action-on-the-Spot News Team; we've interviewed three people leaving the poll, and all three said they voted for Johnson, so we're projecting Johnson as the winner." Finally, choice (C) doesn't address the logic of the argument.

21. **The correct answer is (A).** The initial reasoning claims that support for one institution, the majority party, entails support for another, the Prime Minister, because of a connection between the two (the one gives rise to the other). So, too, choice (A) says that appreciation for one game entails appreciation for another because the one is derived from the other. If you can imagine a diagram in which

the majority party is connected by an arrow to the Prime Minister, that might help you understand the reasoning of the stimulus material. And then you could use a similar diagram to capture the thinking of choice (A): rugby is connected by an arrow pointing to American football. Choice (C) would have two arrows leading from the Impressionist school to Monet and Renoir. Choice (D) has a similar structure: the controls might point to both machines. And choice (E) would show the week's news leading to both the newspaper and the magazine. Choice (B) simply doesn't have any similar structure.

22. **The correct answer is (B).** When you are asked to draw a conclusion from a set of statements, you want to make sure that your answer choice is the one most *strongly* supported by the information given. And that means reading critically and paying careful attention to exactly what is said. In this case, you have a speaker who says that some people using personal video recorders watch entertaining commercials a couple of times, so it's safe to conclude that such people use the machines to watch the commercials more than once. That's choice (B). Now notice how each of the other choices goes further—out on a limb, so to speak. As for choice (A), while it's a safe bet that some people will watch certain commercials extra times, if you were an executive, you would not want to conclude that your revenue stream would continue uninterrupted. After all, the people who buy the ads and pay the money might not agree. They could decide to put their money elsewhere. Or, as for choice (C), people may watch the ads but not buy the products. As for choice (D), while you're told that more and more people

are using these devices, it's a big jump to conclude that these devices will replace TV sets. And as for choice (E), you have no basis for such a conclusion.

23. **The correct answer is (B).** Anna doesn't deny the validity of Deborah's claims. Instead, she says that the legacy policy serves a useful function.

24. **The correct answer is (B).** The crux of Deborah's claim is that legacy candidates get favorable treatment. The proof of the claim would be found by comparing the acceptance rates of legacy candidates with those for all candidates. Choice (A) is interesting but wide of the mark. What is wanted is a measure of the advantage provided by the policy. A comparison between overall acceptance rates at legacy and non-legacy schools doesn't address that issue. And choice (C) is wrong because the raw number of applicants won't tell us anything about the admissions decisions—for that we need acceptance rates. Choice (D) is incorrect for the same reason: comparisons of raw numbers of any sort are just not going to be helpful, even a longitudinal study more precise than that hinted at by choice (D). And choice (E) is wrong because it provides only half the picture: the acceptance rate for legacy candidates. But we need the other part of the picture to complete the comparison: the acceptance rate for non-legacy candidates.

25. **The correct answer is (C).** Since this is a problem involving three overlapping categories, it seems a good candidate for the Venn diagram approach:

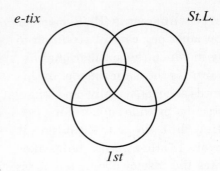

And since all of the passengers who flew to St. Louis purchased an e-ticket:

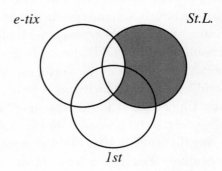

If it is assumed that some passengers who did not purchase e-tickets flew first class:

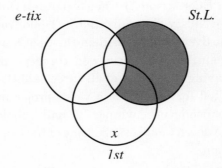

Then it follows that some passengers who flew first class did not go to St. Louis.

WRITING SAMPLE

Following are two responses to the Writing Sample prompt, one in favor of the first option and the other in favor of the second option. These responses are not necessarily Pulitzer

Prize winning essays, but remember they're not supposed to be. The objective, as developed in Chapter 8, is to write something that is serviceable. You'll notice how these responses fit the model developed in Chapter 8.

Sample Response for Option One

The Board should name Paul Sellers to receive the award. Mr. Sellers has demonstrated the teaching excellence and commitment to the community that the award is intended to honor, and he has a plan to make effective use of the sabbatical.

By any measure, Mr. Sellers is possessed of the qualities that the award is designed to honor. He has more than 30 years of teaching experience and has repeatedly been recognized for his effectiveness by the students whom he teaches. In addition, the award recognizes community service, and Mr. Sellers also qualifies on this measure. He has served as an adviser to a number of student organizations, and he has volunteered his time in other ways. These activities benefit not just the students but enrich the greater community.

Additionally, Mr. Sellers would make good use of the sabbatical that accompanies the award. He intends to finish a book about the history of the township. Importantly, this is already a work in progress and not just an idea or suggestion. A book about township history would be useful for students studying state and local history and as a way of acquainting the entire community with its local history.

While it cannot be denied that Ms. Goode also is worthy of recognition, Mr. Sellers' accomplishments simply seem weightier—he has more extensive service for more years. Also, Mr. Sellers' proposed use of the free time is more directly connected to the community of Marietta.

Sample Response for Option Two

Francine Goode should receive the Outstanding Teacher Award. She is certainly an "Outstanding" teacher who has shown the kind of commitment to students and community that the award honors, and she will make good use of the year off.

The Outstanding Teacher Award honors "teaching excellence" and "contribution to the community." Ms. Goode's teaching excellence is demonstrated by her exceptional evaluations and her selection as the Outstanding Foreign Language Teacher in the entire state. She also makes an important contribution to the community. Her unusual facility with languages gives her a unique opportunity to bring non-English speaking parents into the school and greater community. Importantly, she does this both as part of her regular teaching responsibilities and on "her own time" as a volunteer.

The award also carries with it a year off from teaching duties, a year that the Board hopes will be spent on study or some other project that will benefit the schools and community. Although Ms. Goode is already an excellent teacher, she will use her travels during the year to develop new teaching materials to engage students. Additionally, she can further improve her language skills and thereby become even more valuable in her community service.

The Outstanding Teacher Award honors excellence and service and is designed to encourage the recipient to return something to the community. Ms. Goode qualifies on both counts.

Answer Sheet

Use a No. 2 pencil only. Be sure each mark is dark and completely fills the intended oval. Completely erase any errors or stray marks. Start with number 1 for each new section. If a section has fewer than 30 questions, leave the extra answer spaces blank.

SECTION 1	SECTION 2	SECTION 3	SECTION 4	SECTION 5
1 Ⓐ Ⓑ Ⓒ Ⓓ Ⓔ	1 Ⓐ Ⓑ Ⓒ Ⓓ Ⓔ	1 Ⓐ Ⓑ Ⓒ Ⓓ Ⓔ	1 Ⓐ Ⓑ Ⓒ Ⓓ Ⓔ	1 Ⓐ Ⓑ Ⓒ Ⓓ Ⓔ
2 Ⓐ Ⓑ Ⓒ Ⓓ Ⓔ	2 Ⓐ Ⓑ Ⓒ Ⓓ Ⓔ	2 Ⓐ Ⓑ Ⓒ Ⓓ Ⓔ	2 Ⓐ Ⓑ Ⓒ Ⓓ Ⓔ	2 Ⓐ Ⓑ Ⓒ Ⓓ Ⓔ
3 Ⓐ Ⓑ Ⓒ Ⓓ Ⓔ	3 Ⓐ Ⓑ Ⓒ Ⓓ Ⓔ	3 Ⓐ Ⓑ Ⓒ Ⓓ Ⓔ	3 Ⓐ Ⓑ Ⓒ Ⓓ Ⓔ	3 Ⓐ Ⓑ Ⓒ Ⓓ Ⓔ
4 Ⓐ Ⓑ Ⓒ Ⓓ Ⓔ	4 Ⓐ Ⓑ Ⓒ Ⓓ Ⓔ	4 Ⓐ Ⓑ Ⓒ Ⓓ Ⓔ	4 Ⓐ Ⓑ Ⓒ Ⓓ Ⓔ	4 Ⓐ Ⓑ Ⓒ Ⓓ Ⓔ
5 Ⓐ Ⓑ Ⓒ Ⓓ Ⓔ	5 Ⓐ Ⓑ Ⓒ Ⓓ Ⓔ	5 Ⓐ Ⓑ Ⓒ Ⓓ Ⓔ	5 Ⓐ Ⓑ Ⓒ Ⓓ Ⓔ	5 Ⓐ Ⓑ Ⓒ Ⓓ Ⓔ
6 Ⓐ Ⓑ Ⓒ Ⓓ Ⓔ	6 Ⓐ Ⓑ Ⓒ Ⓓ Ⓔ	6 Ⓐ Ⓑ Ⓒ Ⓓ Ⓔ	6 Ⓐ Ⓑ Ⓒ Ⓓ Ⓔ	6 Ⓐ Ⓑ Ⓒ Ⓓ Ⓔ
7 Ⓐ Ⓑ Ⓒ Ⓓ Ⓔ	7 Ⓐ Ⓑ Ⓒ Ⓓ Ⓔ	7 Ⓐ Ⓑ Ⓒ Ⓓ Ⓔ	7 Ⓐ Ⓑ Ⓒ Ⓓ Ⓔ	7 Ⓐ Ⓑ Ⓒ Ⓓ Ⓔ
8 Ⓐ Ⓑ Ⓒ Ⓓ Ⓔ	8 Ⓐ Ⓑ Ⓒ Ⓓ Ⓔ	8 Ⓐ Ⓑ Ⓒ Ⓓ Ⓔ	8 Ⓐ Ⓑ Ⓒ Ⓓ Ⓔ	8 Ⓐ Ⓑ Ⓒ Ⓓ Ⓔ
9 Ⓐ Ⓑ Ⓒ Ⓓ Ⓔ	9 Ⓐ Ⓑ Ⓒ Ⓓ Ⓔ	9 Ⓐ Ⓑ Ⓒ Ⓓ Ⓔ	9 Ⓐ Ⓑ Ⓒ Ⓓ Ⓔ	9 Ⓐ Ⓑ Ⓒ Ⓓ Ⓔ
10 Ⓐ Ⓑ Ⓒ Ⓓ Ⓔ	10 Ⓐ Ⓑ Ⓒ Ⓓ Ⓔ	10 Ⓐ Ⓑ Ⓒ Ⓓ Ⓔ	10 Ⓐ Ⓑ Ⓒ Ⓓ Ⓔ	10 Ⓐ Ⓑ Ⓒ Ⓓ Ⓔ
11 Ⓐ Ⓑ Ⓒ Ⓓ Ⓔ	11 Ⓐ Ⓑ Ⓒ Ⓓ Ⓔ	11 Ⓐ Ⓑ Ⓒ Ⓓ Ⓔ	11 Ⓐ Ⓑ Ⓒ Ⓓ Ⓔ	11 Ⓐ Ⓑ Ⓒ Ⓓ Ⓔ
12 Ⓐ Ⓑ Ⓒ Ⓓ Ⓔ	12 Ⓐ Ⓑ Ⓒ Ⓓ Ⓔ	12 Ⓐ Ⓑ Ⓒ Ⓓ Ⓔ	12 Ⓐ Ⓑ Ⓒ Ⓓ Ⓔ	12 Ⓐ Ⓑ Ⓒ Ⓓ Ⓔ
13 Ⓐ Ⓑ Ⓒ Ⓓ Ⓔ	13 Ⓐ Ⓑ Ⓒ Ⓓ Ⓔ	13 Ⓐ Ⓑ Ⓒ Ⓓ Ⓔ	13 Ⓐ Ⓑ Ⓒ Ⓓ Ⓔ	13 Ⓐ Ⓑ Ⓒ Ⓓ Ⓔ
14 Ⓐ Ⓑ Ⓒ Ⓓ Ⓔ	14 Ⓐ Ⓑ Ⓒ Ⓓ Ⓔ	14 Ⓐ Ⓑ Ⓒ Ⓓ Ⓔ	14 Ⓐ Ⓑ Ⓒ Ⓓ Ⓔ	14 Ⓐ Ⓑ Ⓒ Ⓓ Ⓔ
15 Ⓐ Ⓑ Ⓒ Ⓓ Ⓔ	15 Ⓐ Ⓑ Ⓒ Ⓓ Ⓔ	15 Ⓐ Ⓑ Ⓒ Ⓓ Ⓔ	15 Ⓐ Ⓑ Ⓒ Ⓓ Ⓔ	15 Ⓐ Ⓑ Ⓒ Ⓓ Ⓔ
16 Ⓐ Ⓑ Ⓒ Ⓓ Ⓔ	16 Ⓐ Ⓑ Ⓒ Ⓓ Ⓔ	16 Ⓐ Ⓑ Ⓒ Ⓓ Ⓔ	16 Ⓐ Ⓑ Ⓒ Ⓓ Ⓔ	16 Ⓐ Ⓑ Ⓒ Ⓓ Ⓔ
17 Ⓐ Ⓑ Ⓒ Ⓓ Ⓔ	17 Ⓐ Ⓑ Ⓒ Ⓓ Ⓔ	17 Ⓐ Ⓑ Ⓒ Ⓓ Ⓔ	17 Ⓐ Ⓑ Ⓒ Ⓓ Ⓔ	17 Ⓐ Ⓑ Ⓒ Ⓓ Ⓔ
18 Ⓐ Ⓑ Ⓒ Ⓓ Ⓔ	18 Ⓐ Ⓑ Ⓒ Ⓓ Ⓔ	18 Ⓐ Ⓑ Ⓒ Ⓓ Ⓔ	18 Ⓐ Ⓑ Ⓒ Ⓓ Ⓔ	18 Ⓐ Ⓑ Ⓒ Ⓓ Ⓔ
19 Ⓐ Ⓑ Ⓒ Ⓓ Ⓔ	19 Ⓐ Ⓑ Ⓒ Ⓓ Ⓔ	19 Ⓐ Ⓑ Ⓒ Ⓓ Ⓔ	19 Ⓐ Ⓑ Ⓒ Ⓓ Ⓔ	19 Ⓐ Ⓑ Ⓒ Ⓓ Ⓔ
20 Ⓐ Ⓑ Ⓒ Ⓓ Ⓔ	20 Ⓐ Ⓑ Ⓒ Ⓓ Ⓔ	20 Ⓐ Ⓑ Ⓒ Ⓓ Ⓔ	20 Ⓐ Ⓑ Ⓒ Ⓓ Ⓔ	20 Ⓐ Ⓑ Ⓒ Ⓓ Ⓔ
21 Ⓐ Ⓑ Ⓒ Ⓓ Ⓔ	21 Ⓐ Ⓑ Ⓒ Ⓓ Ⓔ	21 Ⓐ Ⓑ Ⓒ Ⓓ Ⓔ	21 Ⓐ Ⓑ Ⓒ Ⓓ Ⓔ	21 Ⓐ Ⓑ Ⓒ Ⓓ Ⓔ
22 Ⓐ Ⓑ Ⓒ Ⓓ Ⓔ	22 Ⓐ Ⓑ Ⓒ Ⓓ Ⓔ	22 Ⓐ Ⓑ Ⓒ Ⓓ Ⓔ	22 Ⓐ Ⓑ Ⓒ Ⓓ Ⓔ	22 Ⓐ Ⓑ Ⓒ Ⓓ Ⓔ
23 Ⓐ Ⓑ Ⓒ Ⓓ Ⓔ	23 Ⓐ Ⓑ Ⓒ Ⓓ Ⓔ	23 Ⓐ Ⓑ Ⓒ Ⓓ Ⓔ	23 Ⓐ Ⓑ Ⓒ Ⓓ Ⓔ	23 Ⓐ Ⓑ Ⓒ Ⓓ Ⓔ
24 Ⓐ Ⓑ Ⓒ Ⓓ Ⓔ	24 Ⓐ Ⓑ Ⓒ Ⓓ Ⓔ	24 Ⓐ Ⓑ Ⓒ Ⓓ Ⓔ	24 Ⓐ Ⓑ Ⓒ Ⓓ Ⓔ	24 Ⓐ Ⓑ Ⓒ Ⓓ Ⓔ
25 Ⓐ Ⓑ Ⓒ Ⓓ Ⓔ	25 Ⓐ Ⓑ Ⓒ Ⓓ Ⓔ	25 Ⓐ Ⓑ Ⓒ Ⓓ Ⓔ	25 Ⓐ Ⓑ Ⓒ Ⓓ Ⓔ	25 Ⓐ Ⓑ Ⓒ Ⓓ Ⓔ
26 Ⓐ Ⓑ Ⓒ Ⓓ Ⓔ	26 Ⓐ Ⓑ Ⓒ Ⓓ Ⓔ	26 Ⓐ Ⓑ Ⓒ Ⓓ Ⓔ	26 Ⓐ Ⓑ Ⓒ Ⓓ Ⓔ	26 Ⓐ Ⓑ Ⓒ Ⓓ Ⓔ
27 Ⓐ Ⓑ Ⓒ Ⓓ Ⓔ	27 Ⓐ Ⓑ Ⓒ Ⓓ Ⓔ	27 Ⓐ Ⓑ Ⓒ Ⓓ Ⓔ	27 Ⓐ Ⓑ Ⓒ Ⓓ Ⓔ	27 Ⓐ Ⓑ Ⓒ Ⓓ Ⓔ
28 Ⓐ Ⓑ Ⓒ Ⓓ Ⓔ	28 Ⓐ Ⓑ Ⓒ Ⓓ Ⓔ	28 Ⓐ Ⓑ Ⓒ Ⓓ Ⓔ	28 Ⓐ Ⓑ Ⓒ Ⓓ Ⓔ	28 Ⓐ Ⓑ Ⓒ Ⓓ Ⓔ
29 Ⓐ Ⓑ Ⓒ Ⓓ Ⓔ	29 Ⓐ Ⓑ Ⓒ Ⓓ Ⓔ	29 Ⓐ Ⓑ Ⓒ Ⓓ Ⓔ	29 Ⓐ Ⓑ Ⓒ Ⓓ Ⓔ	29 Ⓐ Ⓑ Ⓒ Ⓓ Ⓔ
30 Ⓐ Ⓑ Ⓒ Ⓓ Ⓔ	30 Ⓐ Ⓑ Ⓒ Ⓓ Ⓔ	30 Ⓐ Ⓑ Ⓒ Ⓓ Ⓔ	30 Ⓐ Ⓑ Ⓒ Ⓓ Ⓔ	30 Ⓐ Ⓑ Ⓒ Ⓓ Ⓔ

Practice Test 2

SECTION 1

24 Questions • Time—35 Minutes

Directions: Each group of questions is based on a set of propositions or conditions. Drawing a rough picture or diagram may help in answering some of the questions. After you have chosen the *best* answer for each question, blacken the corresponding space on your answer sheet.

Questions 1–6

A genealogist has determined that M, N, P, Q, R, S, and T are the father, the mother, the aunt, the brother, the sister, the wife, and the daughter of X, but she has been unable to determine which person has which status. She does know the following:

P and Q are of the same gender.

M and N are not of the same gender.

S was born before M.

Q is not the mother of X.

1. How many of the seven people—M, N, P, Q, R, S, and T—are female?

   (A) 3
   (B) 4
   (C) 5
   (D) 6
   (E) 7

2. Which of the following must be true?

   (A) M is a female.
   (B) N is a female.
   (C) P is a female.
   (D) Q is a male.
   (E) S is a male.

3. If T is the daughter of X, which of the following must be true?

   (A) M and P are of the same gender.
   (B) M and Q are of the same gender.
   (C) P is not of the same gender as N.
   (D) R is not of the same gender as S.
   (E) S is not of the same gender as T.

4. If M and Q are sisters, all of the following must be true EXCEPT

   (A) N is a male.
   (B) M is X's mother.
   (C) Q is X's aunt.
   (D) T is X's daughter.
   (E) S is not X's brother.

5. If S is N's grandfather, then which of the following must be true?

   (A) R is N's aunt.
   (B) X is P's son.
   (C) M is X's brother.
   (D) Q is S's husband.
   (E) P is N's aunt.

6. If M is X's wife, all of the following could be true EXCEPT

(A) S is X's daughter.

(B) P is X's sister.

(C) Q is X's sister.

(D) R is X's father.

(E) N is X's brother.

Questions 7–12

Seven persons, J, K, L, M, N, O, and P, participate in a series of swimming races in which the following are always true of the results:

> K finishes ahead of L.
>
> N finishes directly behind M.
>
> Either J finishes first and O last or O finishes first and J last.

There are no ties in any race, and everyone finishes each race.

7. If exactly two swimmers finish between J and L, which of the following must be true?

(A) J finishes first.

(B) O finishes first.

(C) K finishes second.

(D) M finishes fifth.

(E) N finishes fourth.

8. Which of the following CANNOT be true?

(A) K finishes third.

(B) K finishes sixth.

(C) M finishes second.

(D) N finishes fourth.

(E) P finishes third.

9. If O and K finish so that one is directly behind the other, which of the following must be true?

(A) K finishes sixth.

(B) O finishes seventh.

(C) J finishes seventh.

(D) L finishes third.

(E) M finishes fourth.

10. If K finishes fourth, which of the following must be true?

(A) J finishes first.

(B) N finishes third.

(C) P finishes third.

(D) P finishes fifth.

(E) L finishes fifth.

11. If J finishes first and if L finishes ahead of N, in how many different orders is it possible for the other swimmers to finish?

(A) 2

(B) 3

(C) 4

(D) 5

(E) 6

12. Which of the following additional conditions makes it certain that P finishes sixth?

(A) J finishes first.

(B) K finishes second.

(C) M finishes second.

(D) N finishes third.

(E) L finishes fifth.

Questions 13–18

A group of six players, P, Q, R, S, T, and U, are participating in a challenge tournament. All matches played are challenge matches and are governed by the following rules:

> A player may challenge another player if and only if that player is ranked either one or two places above.

If a player successfully challenges the player ranked immediately above, the two players exchange ranks.

If a player successfully challenges the player two ranks above, the player who issued this challenge moves up two ranks, and both the loser of the match and the player ranked below the loser move down one rank.

If a player is unsuccessful in a challenge, that player and the player immediately below exchange ranks, unless the unsuccessful challenger was already ranked last, in which case the rankings remain unchanged.

The initial rankings from the highest (first) to the lowest (sixth) are P, Q, R, S, T, U.

Only one match is played at a time.

13. Which of the following is possible as the first match of the tournament?

(A) P challenges Q.

(B) Q challenges R.

(C) R challenges P.

(D) S challenges P.

(E) T challenges Q.

14. If S reaches first place after the first two matches of the tournament, which of the following must be ranked fourth at that point in play?

(A) P

(B) Q

(C) R

(D) T

(E) U

15. All of the following are possible rankings, from highest to lowest, after exactly two matches EXCEPT

(A) P, R, Q, T, S, U

(B) P, R, Q, S, U, T

(C) R, P, Q, U, S, T

(D) Q, P, S, R, T, U

(E) Q, P, S, R, U, T

16. If exactly two matches have been played, what is the maximum number of players whose initial ranks could have been changed?

(A) 2

(B) 3

(C) 4

(D) 5

(E) 6

17. If after a certain number of matches the players are ranked from highest to lowest in the order R, Q, P, U, S, T, what is the minimum number of matches that could have been played?

(A) 2

(B) 3

(C) 4

(D) 5

(E) 6

18. If after the initial two matches two players have improved their rankings and four players have each dropped in rank, which of the following could be the third match of the tournament?

(A) R challenges P.

(B) R challenges Q.

(C) Q challenges U.

(D) U challenges P.

(E) T challenges Q.

Questions 19–24

A farmer has three fields, 1, 2, and 3, and is deciding which crops to plant. The crops are F, G, H, I, and J.

F will grow only in fields 1 and 3, but in order for F to grow, it must be fertilized with X.

G will grow in fields 1, 2, and 3, but in order for G to grow, fertilizer X must not be used.

H will grow in fields 1, 2, and 3, but in order for H to grow in field 3, it must be fertilized with Y.

I will grow only in fields 2 and 3, but in order for I to grow in field 2, it must be sprayed with pesticide Z, and in order for I to grow in field 3, it must not be sprayed with Z.

J will grow only in field 2, but in order for J to grow, H must not be planted in the same field.

All crops are planted and harvested at the same time. More than one crop may be planted in a field.

19. It is possible to grow which of the following pairs of crops together in field 1?

(A) F and G

(B) F and J

(C) G and H

(D) J and H

(E) J and G

20. It is possible for which of the following groups of crops to grow together in field 2?

(A) F, G, and H

(B) F, H, and I

(C) G, H, and J

(D) G, I, and J

(E) H, I, and J

21. Which of the following is a complete and accurate listing of all crops that will grow alone in field 2 if the only pesticide or fertilizer used is Y?

(A) F

(B) F and H

(C) G and H

(D) G, H, and J

(E) G, H, I, and J

22. Which of the following pairs of crops will grow together in field 3 if no other crops are planted in the field and no fertilizers or pesticides are applied?

(A) F and H

(B) F and I

(C) G and H

(D) G and I

(E) H and J

23. What is the maximum number of different crops that can be planted together in field 3?

(A) 1

(B) 2

(C) 3

(D) 4

(E) 5

24. Which of the following is a complete and accurate list of the crops that will grow alone in field 2 if X is the only pesticide or fertilizer applied?

(A) H, J

(B) I, G

(C) I, H

(D) I, J

(E) J, G

STOP

END OF SECTION 1. IF YOU HAVE ANY TIME LEFT, GO OVER YOUR WORK IN THIS SECTION ONLY. DO NOT WORK IN ANY OTHER SECTION OF THE TEST.

SECTION 2

25 Questions • Time—35 Minutes

Directions: In this section, the questions ask you to analyze and evaluate the reasoning in short paragraphs or passages. For some questions, all of the answer choices may conceivably be answers to the question asked. You should select the *best* answer to the question; that is, an answer that does not require you to make assumptions that violate commonsense standards by being implausible, redundant, irrelevant, or inconsistent. After you have chosen the best answer, blacken the corresponding space on the answer sheet.

1. Children in the first three grades who attend private schools spend time each day working with a computerized reading program. Public schools have very few such programs. Tests prove, however, that public-school children are much weaker in reading skills when compared to their private-school counterparts. We conclude, therefore, that public-school children can be good readers only if they participate in a computerized reading program.

   The author's initial statements logically support the conclusion only if which of the following is also true?

   (A) All children can learn to be good readers if they are taught by a computerized reading program.

   (B) All children can learn to read at the same rate if they participate in a computerized reading program.

   (C) Better reading skills produce better students.

   (D) Computerized reading programs are the critical factor in the better reading skills of private-school students.

   (E) Public-school children can be taught better math skills.

2. Is your company going to continue to discriminate against women in its hiring and promotion policies?

   The question above might be considered unfair because it

   (A) fails to mention that other companies might have similar practices.

   (B) assumes that the interviewee agrees with the policies of the company.

   (C) reveals a bias on the part of the questioner.

   (D) contains a hidden presupposition that the responder might wish to contest.

   (E) shifts the focus of attention from the person interviewed to the company.

Questions 3 and 4

Ms. Evangeline Rose argued that money and time invested in acquiring a professional degree are totally wasted. As evidence supporting her argument, she offered the case of a man who, at considerable expense of money and time, completed his law degree and then married and lived as a house-husband, taking care of their children and working part-time at a day-care center so his wife could pursue her career.

3. Ms. Rose makes the unsupported assumption that

   (A) an education in the law is useful only in pursuing law-related activities.

   (B) what was not acceptable twenty-five years ago may very well be acceptable today.

   (C) wealth is more important than learning.

   (D) professional success is a function of the quality of one's education.

   (E) only the study of law can be considered professional study.

4. The logical reasoning of Ms. Rose's argument is closely parallelled by which of the following?

   (A) A juvenile delinquent who insists that his behavior should be attributable to the fact that his parents did not love him

   (B) A senator who votes large sums of money for military equipment but who votes against programs designed to help the poor

   (C) A conscientious objector who bases his draft resistance on the premise that there can be no moral wars

   (D) When a policeman is found guilty of murdering his wife, an opponent of police brutality who says, "That's what these people mean by law and order"

   (E) A high school senior who decides that rather than going to college, he will enroll in a vocational training program to learn to be an electrician

5. A cryptographer has intercepted an enemy message that is in code. The code is a simple substitution of numbers for letters. Which of the following would be the least helpful in breaking the code?

   (A) Knowing the frequency with which the vowels of the language are used

   (B) Knowing the frequency with which two vowels appear together in the language

   (C) Knowing the frequency with which odd numbers appear relative to even numbers in the message

   (D) Knowing the conjugation of the verb "to be" in the language on which the code is based

   (E) Knowing every word in the language that begins with the letter R

6. One way of reducing commuting time for those who work in the cities is to increase the speed at which traffic moves in the heart of the city. This can be accomplished by raising the tolls on the tunnels and bridges connecting the city with other communities. This will discourage auto traffic into the city and will encourage people to use public transportation instead.

Which of the following, if true, would LEAST weaken the argument above?

(A) Nearly all of the traffic in the center of the city is commercial traffic that will continue despite toll increases.

(B) Some people now driving alone into the city would choose to car-pool with each other rather than use public transportation.

(C) Any temporary improvement in traffic flow would be lost because the improvement itself would attract more cars.

(D) The numbers of commuters who would be deterred by the toll increases would be insignificant.

(E) The public transportation system is not able to handle any significant increase in the number of commuters using the system.

7. An independent medical research team recently did a survey at a mountain retreat founded to help heavy smokers quit or cut down on their cigarette smoking. Eighty percent of those persons smoking three packs a day or more were able to cut down to one pack a day after they began to take End-Smoke with its patented desire suppressant. Try End-Smoke to help you cut down significantly on your smoking.

Which of the following, if true, offers the strongest criticism of the advertisement?

(A) Heavy smokers may be psychologically as well as physically addicted to tobacco smoking.

(B) Of the 20 percent who failed to achieve significant results, most were addicted to other substances as well.

(C) The independent medical research team included several members who were experts in the field of nicotine addiction.

(D) A survey conducted at a mountain retreat to aid smokers may yield different results than one would expect under other circumstances.

(E) The overall percentage of the general population who smoke regularly has not declined dramatically over the past twenty years.

8. JOCKEY: Horses are the most noble of all animals. They are both loyal and brave. I knew of a farm horse that died of a broken heart shortly after its owner died.

VETERINARIAN: You're wrong. Dogs can be just as loyal and brave. I had a dog who would wait every day on the front steps for me to come home, and if I did not arrive until midnight, it would still be there.

All of the following are true of the claims of the jockey and the veterinarian EXCEPT

(A) both claims assume that loyalty and bravery are characteristics that are desirable in animals.

(B) both claims assume that the two most loyal animals are the horse and the dog.

(C) both claims assume that human qualities can be attributed to animals.

(D) both claims are supported by only a single example of animal behavior.

(E) neither claim is supported by evidence other than the opinions and observations of the speakers.

9. Rousseau assumed that human beings in the state of nature are characterized by a feeling of sympathy toward their fellow humans and other living creatures. In order to explain the existence of social ills, such as the exploitation of humans by humans, Rousseau maintained that our natural feelings are crushed under the weight of unsympathetic social institutions.

Rousseau's argument described above would be most strengthened if it could be explained how

(A) creatures naturally characterized by feelings of sympathy for all living creatures could create unsympathetic social institutions.

(B) we can restructure our social institutions so that they will foster our natural sympathies for one another.

(C) modern reformers might lead the way to a life that is not inconsistent with the ideals of the state of nature.

(D) non-exploitative conduct could arise in conditions of the state of nature.

(E) a return to the state of nature from modern society might be accomplished.

10. Every element on the periodic chart is radioactive, though the most stable elements have half-lives that are thousands and thousands of years long. When an atom decays, it splits into two or more smaller atoms. Even considering the fusion taking place inside of stars, there is only a negligible tendency for smaller atoms to transmute into larger ones. Thus, the ratio of lighter to heavier atoms in the universe is increasing at a measurable rate.

Which of the following sentences provides the most logical continuation of this paragraph?

(A) Without radioactive decay of atoms, there could be no solar combustion and no life as we know it.

(B) Therefore, it is imperative that scientists begin developing ways to reverse the trend and restore the proper balance between the lighter and the heavier elements.

(C) Consequently, it is possible to use a shifting ratio of light to heavy atoms to calculate the age of the universe.

(D) Therefore, there are now more light elements in the universe than heavy ones.

(E) As a result, the fusion taking place inside stars has to produce enough atoms of the heavy elements to offset the radioactive decay of large atoms elsewhere in the universe.

Questions 11 and 12

SPEAKER: The great majority of people in the United States have access to the best medical care available anywhere in the world.

OBJECTOR: There are thousands of poor in this country who cannot afford to pay to see a doctor.

11. Which of the following is true of the objector's comment?

(A) It uses emotionally charged words.

(B) It constitutes a hasty generalization on few examples.

(C) It is not necessarily inconsistent with the speaker's remarks.

(D) It cites statistical evidence that tends to confirm the speaker's points.

(E) It overlooks the distinction the speaker draws between a cause and its effect.

12. A possible objection to the speaker's comments would be to point to the existence of

(A) a country that has more medical assistants than the United States.

(B) a nation where medical care is provided free of charge by the government.

(C) a country in which the people are given better medical care than Americans.

(D) government hearings in the United States on the problems poor people have getting medical care.

(E) a country that has a higher hospital bed per person ratio than the United States.

13. EVERT: The newly proposed amendments to the tax code will result in a fairer tax system that puts more of the burden on the wealthy. Almost all of the projected increase in taxes will be paid by households earning $100,000 a year or more.

SCOTT: The amendments will tax individuals without regard to their wealth. Income, for tax purposes, is defined as the amount earned in any given year without regard to the accumulated assets of the taxpayer or the prospects for the future. For example, a small business taxpayer who ordinarily nets $20,000 a year but who happens, because of a single large deal, to earn $100,000 in a single year is considered just as wealthy as a taxpayer who has earned $100,000 in each of the previous 30 years.

The second speaker takes issue with the first speaker by

(A) attempting to shift the burden of proof to the first speaker

(B) accusing the first speaker of circular reasoning

(C) questioning the definition of a key term of the debate

(D) pointing out a logical contradiction in the first speaker's remarks

(E) offering expert opinion to support a conclusion

Questions 14–16

The blanks in the following paragraph indicate deletions from the text. For questions 14 and 15, select the completion that is most appropriate.

I often hear smokers insisting that they have a *right* to smoke whenever and wherever they choose, as though there are no conceivable circumstances in which the law might not legitimately prohibit smoking. This contention is obviously indefensible. Implicit in the development of the concept of a right is the notion that one person's freedom of action is circumscribed by the _____ (14). It requires nothing more than common sense to realize that there are situations in which smoking presents a clear and present danger: in a crowded theater, around flammable materials, during take-off in an airplane. No one would seriously deny that the potential harm of smoking in such circumstances more than outweighs the satisfaction a smoker would derive from smoking. Yet, this balancing is not unique to situations of potential catastrophe. It applies equally as well to situations where the potential injury is small, though in most cases, as for example a person's table manners, the injury of the offended person is so slight we automatically strike the balance in favor of the person acting. But once it is recognized that a balance of freedoms must be struck, it follows that a smoker has a *right* to smoke only when and where _____ (15).

14. **(A)** Constitution of our nation

    (B) laws passed by Congress and interpreted by the Supreme Court

    (C) interest of any other person to not be injured or inconvenienced by that action

    (D) rights of other persons not to smoke

    (E) rights of non-smoking persons not to have to be subjected to the noxious fumes of tobacco smoking

15. **(A)** the government chooses to allow smoking

 (B) the smoker finally decides to light up

 (C) the smoker's interest in smoking outweighs the interests of other persons having a smoke-free environment

 (D) the smoker can ensure that no other persons will be even slightly inconvenienced by the smoke

 (E) there are signs that explicitly state that smoking is allowed in that area

16. The author's strategy in questioning the claim that smokers have a right to smoke is to

 (A) cite facts that are not generally known.

 (B) clarify and fully define a key concept.

 (C) entertain arguments on a hypothetical case.

 (D) uncover a logical inconsistency.

 (E) probe the reliability of an empirical generalization.

17. The average selling price at auction of a painting by Renard Fox is directly proportional to the number of people who bid on the painting. Since 12 more people placed bids on Fox's "Afternoon of the Faun" than on "Teacups under Glass," the selling price of "Afternoon of the Faun" was greater than that for "Teacups under Glass."

 The reasoning of which of the following arguments is most similar to that of the argument above?

 (A) The average cost of the computers shipped by Altaric Electronics to students entering the State University is directly proportional to the conventional memory included and to the ratio of units with DVDs rather than CDs. Since the average cost of the computers shipped to entering students this year was higher than last year, more units had DVDs than CDs.

 (B) The number of computers shipped by Altaric Electronics in September is directly proportional to the number of students in the entering class at State University. Since the number of students entering State University this year was 250 more than the number last year, Altaric shipped more computers this September than last September.

 (C) The number of students in the entering class at State University is directly proportional to the number of students who have applied and to the acceptance-to-rejection ratio. For this year's entering class, the number of applicants was greater than for last year's, but the acceptance-to-rejection ratio was lower. Therefore, the number of students in this year's entering class was greater than last year's.

 (D) The average class size of courses at State University depends not only upon the number of students and the number of faculty members, but on the number of course offerings. Since the number of students and faculty this year is the same as last year but fewer courses are being offered, the average class size at State University is less this year than last.

 (E) The average salary of full professors at State University is directly proportional to the total budget of the University. Since the total budget of the University this year is 10 percent greater than the budget for last year, the total cost of salaries for full professors is higher this year than last year.

Questions 18 and 19

A study published by the Department of Education shows that children in the central cities lag far behind students in the suburbs and the rural areas in reading skills. The report blames this differential on the overcrowding in the classrooms of city schools. I maintain, however, that the real reason that city children are poorer readers than non-city children is that they do not get enough fresh air and sunshine.

18. Which of the following best describes the form of the above argument?

    (A) It attacks the credibility of the Department of Education.

    (B) It indicts the methodology of the study of the Department of Education.

    (C) It attempts to show that central city students read as well as non-city students.

    (D) It offers an alternative explanation for the differential.

    (E) It argues from analogy.

19. Which of the following would LEAST strengthen the author's point in the preceding argument?

    (A) Medical research that shows a correlation between air pollution and learning disabilities

    (B) A report by educational experts demonstrating that there is no relationship between the number of students in a classroom and a student's ability to read

    (C) A notice released by the Department of Education retracting that part of their report that mentions overcrowding as the reason for the differential

    (D) The results of a federal program that indicates that city students show significant improvement in reading skills when they spend the summer in the country

    (E) A proposal by the federal government to fund emergency programs to hire more teachers for central city schools in an attempt to reduce overcrowding in the classrooms

20. Some judges have allowed hospitals to disconnect life-support equipment of patients who have no prospects for recovery. But I say that is murder. Either we put a stop to this practice now, or we will soon have programs of euthanasia for the old and infirm as well as others who might be considered a burden. Rather than disconnecting life-support equipment, we should let nature take its course.

Which of the following objections is the LEAST effective criticism of the argument above?

    (A) It is internally inconsistent.

    (B) It employs emotionally charged terms.

    (C) It presents a false dilemma.

    (D) It oversimplifies a complex moral situation.

    (E) It fails to cite an authority for its conclusion.

21. If Paul comes to the party, Quentin leaves the party. If Quentin leaves the party, either Robert or Steve asks Alice to dance. If Alice is asked to dance by either Robert or Steve and Quentin leaves the party, Alice accepts. If Alice is asked to dance by either Robert or Steve and Quentin does not leave the party, Alice does not accept.

If Quentin does not leave the party, which of the following statements can be logically deduced from the information given?

    (A) Robert asks Alice to dance.

    (B) Steve asks Alice to dance.

    (C) Alice refuses to dance with either Robert or Steve.

    (D) Paul does not come to the party.

    (E) Alice leaves the party.

22. All students have submitted applications for admission. Some of the applications for admission have not been acted upon. Therefore, some more students will be accepted.

The logic of which of the following is most similar to that of the argument above?

(A) Some of the barrels have not yet been loaded on the truck, but all of the apples have been put into barrels. So, some more apples will be loaded onto the truck.

(B) All students who received passing marks were juniors. X received a passing mark. Therefore, X is a junior.

(C) Some chemicals will react with glass bottles but not with plastic bottles. Therefore, those chemicals should be kept in plastic bottles and not glass ones.

(D) All advertising must be approved by the Council before it is aired. This television spot for a new cola has not yet been approved by the Council. Therefore, it is not to be aired until the Council makes its decision.

(E) There are six blue marbles and three red marbles in this jar. Therefore, if I blindly pick out seven marbles, there should be two red marbles left to pick.

23. New Evergreen Gum has twice as much flavor for your money as Spring Mint Gum, and we can prove it. You see, a stick of Evergreen Gum is twice as large as a stick of Spring Mint Gum, and the more gum, the more flavor.

All but which of the following would tend to WEAKEN the argument above?

(A) A package of Spring Mint Gum contains twice as many sticks as a package of Evergreen Gum.

(B) Spring Mint Gum has more concentrated flavor than Evergreen Gum.

(C) A stick of Evergreen Gum weighs only 50 percent as much as a stick of Spring Mint Gum.

(D) A package of Evergreen Gum costs twice as much as a package of Spring Mint Gum.

(E) People surveyed indicated a preference for Evergreen Gum over Spring Mint Gum.

24. Judging from the tenor of the following statements and the apparent authoritativeness of their sources, which is the most reasonable and trustworthy?

    (A) FILM CRITIC: Beethoven is really very much overrated as a composer. His music is not really that good; it's just very well known.

    (B) SPOKESPERSON FOR A MANUFACTURER: The jury's verdict against us for $2 million is ridiculous, and we are sure that the Appeals Court will agree with us.

    (C) SENIOR CABINET OFFICER: Our administration plans to cut inefficiency, and we have already begun to discuss plans that we calculate will save the federal government nearly $50 billion a year in waste.

    (D) FRENCH WINE EXPERT: The best buy in wines in America today is the California chablis, which is comparable to the French chablis and is available at half the cost.

    (E) UNION LEADER: We plan to stay out on strike until management meets each and every one of the demands we have submitted.

25. That it is impossible to foretell the future is easily demonstrated. For if a person should foresee being injured by a mill wheel on the next day, the person would cancel the trip to the mill and remain at home in bed. Since the injury the next day by the mill wheel would not occur, it cannot in any way be said that the future has been foretold.

Which of the following best explains the weakness in this argument?

(A) The author fails to explain how one could actually change the future.

(B) The author uses the word *future* in two different ways.

(C) The author does not explain how anyone could foresee the future.

(D) The argument is internally inconsistent.

(E) The argument is circular.

STOP

END OF SECTION 2. IF YOU HAVE ANY TIME LEFT, GO OVER YOUR WORK IN THIS SECTION ONLY. DO NOT WORK IN ANY OTHER SECTION OF THE TEST.

SECTION 3

24 Questions • Time—35 Minutes

Directions: Each group of questions is based on a set of propositions or conditions. Drawing a rough picture or diagram may help in answering some of the questions. After you have chosen the *best* answer for each question and blacken the corresponding space on your answer sheet.

Questions 1–6

Six persons, J, K, L, M, N, and O, run a series of races with the following results.

O never finishes first or last.

L never finishes immediately behind either J or K.

L always finishes immediately ahead of M.

1. Which of the following, given in order from first to last, is an acceptable finishing sequence of the runners?

   (A) J, L, M, O, N, K
   (B) L, O, J, K, M, N
   (C) L, M, J, K, N, O
   (D) L, M, J, K, O, N
   (E) N, K, L, M, O, J

2. If in an acceptable finishing sequence, J and K finish first and fifth, respectively, which of the following must be true?

   (A) L finishes second.
   (B) O finishes third.
   (C) M finishes third.
   (D) N finishes third.
   (E) N finishes sixth.

3. If in an acceptable finishing sequence, L finishes second, which of the following must be true?

   (A) O must finish fourth.
   (B) N must finish fifth.
   (C) Either J or K must finish sixth.
   (D) K or O must finish fifth.
   (E) O or J must finish fourth.

4. All of the following finishing sequences, given in order from 1 to 6, are acceptable EXCEPT

   (A) J, N, L, M, O, K
   (B) J, N, O, L, M, K
   (C) L, M, J, K, O, N
   (D) N, J, L, M, O, K
   (E) N, K, O, L, M, J

5. Each of the following additional conditions determines the exact order of finish of a race for all six persons EXCEPT

   (A) J and K finish second and third, respectively.
   (B) J and K finish third and fourth, respectively.
   (C) J and K finish fourth and fifth, respectively.
   (D) L and K finish second and fourth, respectively.
   (E) J and L finish third and fifth, respectively.

6. If in an acceptable finishing sequence, exactly three runners finish between J and K, which of the following CANNOT be true?

   (A) O does not finish fourth.
   (B) Either J, K, or N finishes first.
   (C) L finishes either third or fourth.
   (D) If O finishes second, either J or K finishes last.
   (E) If O finishes third, either J or K finishes last.

Questions 7–12

Nine people, J, K, L, M, N, O, P, Q, and R, have rented a small hotel for a weekend. The hotel has five floors, numbered consecutively 1 (bottom) to 5 (top). The top floor has only one room, while floors 1 through 4 each have two rooms. Each person will occupy one and only one room for the weekend.

Q and R will occupy the rooms on the third floor.

P will stay on a lower floor than M.

K will stay on a lower floor than N.

K will stay on a lower floor than L.

J and L will occupy rooms on the same floor.

7. Which of the following CANNOT be true?

   (A) J stays on the first floor.
   (B) K stays on the first floor.
   (C) O stays on the second floor.
   (D) M stays on the fourth floor.
   (E) N stays on the fifth floor.

8. If M occupies a room on the second floor, which of the following must be true?

   (A) J stays on the fifth floor.
   (B) N stays on the fifth floor.
   (C) J stays on the fourth floor.
   (D) K stays on the second floor.
   (E) O stays on the first floor.

9. Which of the following is a complete and accurate list of the persons who could stay on the first floor?

   (A) K, O
   (B) M, N
   (C) M, O
   (D) K, M, O
   (E) K, O, P

10. If M occupies a room on the fourth floor, which of the following must be true?

    (A) J stays on the first floor.
    (B) K stays on the first floor.
    (C) O stays on the fourth floor.
    (D) O stays on the fifth floor.
    (E) N stays on the fifth floor.

11. If K and M stay in rooms on the same floor, which of the following is a complete and accurate list of the floors on which they could stay?

    (A) 1
    (B) 2
    (C) 4
    (D) 1 and 4
    (E) 2 and 4

12. Which of the following, if true, provides sufficient additional information to determine on which floor each person will stay?

    (A) P stays on the first floor.
    (B) M stays on the second floor.
    (C) K stays on the second floor.
    (D) M stays on the fourth floor.
    (E) N stays on the fifth floor.

Questions 13–18

The planning committee of an academic conference is planning a series of panels using eight professors, M, N, Q, R, S, T, U, and V. Each panel must be put together in accordance with the following conditions:

N, T, and U cannot all appear on the same panel.

M, N, and R cannot all appear on the same panel.

Q and V cannot appear on the same panel.

If V appears on a panel, at least two professors of the trio M, S, and U must also appear on the panel.

Neither R nor Q can appear on a panel unless the other also appears on the panel.

If S appears on a panel, both N and V must also appear on that panel.

13. Which of the following CANNOT appear on a panel with R?

(A) M

(B) N

(C) Q

(D) S

(E) T

14. Exactly how many of the professors can appear on a panel alone?

(A) 1

(B) 2

(C) 3

(D) 4

(E) 5

15. If S appears on a panel, that panel must consist of at least how many professors?

(A) 3

(B) 4

(C) 5

(D) 6

(E) 7

16. Which of the following is an acceptable group of professors for a panel?

(A) M, N, Q, R

(B) M, Q, R, T

(C) M, R, T, U

(D) M, S, U, V

(E) N, R, T, U

17. Which of the following groups of professors can form an acceptable panel by doing nothing more than adding one more professor to the group?

(A) M, R, T

(B) N, Q, M

(C) Q, R, S

(D) Q, R, V

(E) V, R, N

18. Of the group N, S, T, U, V, which professor will have to be removed to form an acceptable panel?

(A) N

(B) S

(C) T

(D) U

(E) V

Questions 19–24

On a certain railway route, five trains each day operate between City X and City Y: the Meteor, the Comet, the Flash, the Streak, and the Rocket. Each train consists of exactly five cars, and each car is either a deluxe-class car or a coach car.

On the Meteor, only the first, second, and fifth cars are coach.

On the Comet, only the second and third cars are coach.

On the Flash, only the second car is coach.

On the Streak, only the third and fourth cars are coach.

On the Rocket, all cars are coach.

19. On a typical day, which of the following must be true of the railway's trains operating between City X and City Y?

    (A) More deluxe cars than coach cars are used as first cars.

    (B) More deluxe cars than coach cars are used as second cars.

    (C) Every train uses a deluxe car for the fifth car.

    (D) More deluxe cars are used than coach cars.

    (E) More deluxe cars are used on the Rocket and the Streak combined than on the Flash and the Comet combined.

20. Which of the following cars cannot both be deluxe cars on the same train?

    (A) First and second

    (B) First and third

    (C) Second and third

    (D) Third and fourth

    (E) Fourth and fifth

21. To determine which train is the Streak, correct information on whether a car is deluxe or coach is needed for which car or cars?

    (A) First

    (B) Second

    (C) Third

    (D) First and fifth

    (E) Third and fifth

22. If a train has a coach car as the second car, then that train could be any train EXCEPT the

    (A) Meteor.

    (B) Comet.

    (C) Flash.

    (D) Streak.

    (E) Rocket.

23. If a train has deluxe cars as the first and third cars of the train, that train must be the

    (A) Meteor.

    (B) Comet.

    (C) Flash.

    (D) Streak.

    (E) Rocket.

24. If only one of the third, fourth, and fifth cars of a train is a deluxe car, then that train must be the

    (A) Meteor.

    (B) Comet.

    (C) Flash.

    (D) Streak.

    (E) Rocket.

STOP

END OF SECTION 3. IF YOU HAVE ANY TIME LEFT, GO OVER YOUR WORK IN THIS SECTION ONLY. DO NOT WORK IN ANY OTHER SECTION OF THE TEST.

SECTION 4

28 Questions • Time—35 Minutes

Directions: Below each of the following passages, you will find questions or incomplete statements about the passage. Each statement or question is followed by lettered words or expressions. Select the word or expression that most satisfactorily completes each statement or answers each question in accordance with the meaning of the passage. After you have chosen the *best* answer, blacken the corresponding space on the answer sheet.

Meteorite ALH84001 is a member of a family of meteorites, half of which were found in Antarctica, that are believed to have originated on Mars. Oxygen iso-
(5) topes as distinctive as fingerprints link these meteorites and clearly differentiate them from any earth rock or other kind of meteorite. Another family member, ETA79001, was discovered to con-
(10) tain gas trapped by the impact which ejected it from Mars. Analysis of the trapped gas shows that it is identical to atmosphere analyzed by the spacecraft which landed on Mars in 1976.

(15)   The rock of ALH84001 was formed 4.5 billion years ago and 3.6 billion years ago was invaded by water containing mineral salts precipitated out to form small carbonate globules with intricate
(20) chemical zoning. These carbonates are between 1 and 2 billion years old. Sixteen million years ago an object from space, possibly a small asteroid, impacted Mars and blasted off rocks. One of these
(25) rocks traveled in space until it was captured by the earth's gravity and fell on Antarctica. Carbon-14 dating shows that this rock has been on earth about 13,000 years.

(30)   The carbonate globules contain very small crystals of iron oxide (magnetite) and at least two kinds of iron sulfide (pyrrhotite and another mineral, possibly greigite). Small crystals of these min-
(35) erals are commonly formed on earth by bacteria, although they can also be formed by inorganic processes. In addition, manganese is concentrated in the

center of each carbonate globule, and
(40) most of the larger globules have rims of alternating iron-rich and magnesium-rich carbonates. The compositional variation of these carbonates is not what would be expected from high tempera-
(45) ture equilibrium crystallization but is more like low temperature crystallization. It is consistent with formation by non-equilibrium precipitation induced by microorganisms.

(50)   There are also unusually high concentrations of PAH-type hydrocarbons. These PAHs are unusually simple compared to most PAHs, including PAHs from the burning of coal, oil, or gasoline
(55) or the decay of vegetation. Other meteorites contain PAHs, but the pattern and abundances are different. Of course, PAHs can be formed by strictly inorganic reactions, and abundant PAHs
(60) were produced in the early solar system and are preserved on some asteroids and comets. Meteorites from these objects fall to earth and enable us to analyze the PAHs contained within the
(65) parent bodies. While some of these are similar to the PAHs in the Martian meteorite, all show some major differences. One reasonable interpretation of the PAHs is that they are decay products
(70) from bacteria.

    Also present are unusual, very small forms that could be the remains of microorganisms. These spherical, ovoid, and elongated objects closely resemble
(75) the morphology of known bacteria, but many of them are smaller than any

known bacteria on earth. Furthermore, microfossil forms from very old earth rocks are typically much larger than the
(80) forms that we see in the Mars meteorite. The microfossil-like forms may really be minerals and artifacts which superficially resemble small bacteria. Or perhaps lower gravity and more restricted
(85) pore space in rocks promoted the development of smaller forms of microorganisms. Or maybe such forms exist on earth in the fossil record but have not yet been found. If the small objects are
(90) microfossils, are they from Mars or from Antarctica? Studies so far of the abundant microorganisms found in the rocks, soils, and lakes near the coast of Antarctic do not show PAHs or microorganisms
(95) that closely resemble those found in the Martian meteorite.

There is considerable evidence in the Martian meteorite that must be explained by other means if we are to
(100) definitely rule out evidence of past Martian life in this meteorite. So far, we have not seen a reasonable explanation by others which can explain all of the data.

1. The main purpose of the passage is to

(A) argue that the available data support the conclusion that life once existed on Mars

(B) examine various facts to determine what thesis about ALH84001 is most strongly supported

(C) answer objections to the contention that Martian meteorites contain evidence of primitive life

(D) pose challenges to scientists who hope to prove that ALH84001 proves that life exists on Mars

(E) explore different scientific theories as to the origin of life on earth

2. According to the passage, what evidence most strongly establishes that meteorite ALH84001 originated on Mars?

(A) comparison of trapped gases and the Martian atmosphere

(B) presence of alternating iron and magnesium carbonates

(C) evidence of shapes that resemble known bacteria

(D) pattern of carbonate globules with unusual zoning

(E) discovery of unusual PAHs in unusual abundances

3. It can be inferred that discovery in Antarctica of fossils of tiny microorganisms the size of the objects noted in meteorite ALH84001 (line 17) would tend to show that the objects

(A) are the remains of bacteria that lived on Mars

(B) were produced by inorganic processes

(C) are the remains of bacteria that lived in Antarctica

(D) were present in the rock when it broke from Mars' surface

(E) are the decay products from once living organisms

4. The passage mentions all of the following as tending to prove that ALH84001 may once have contained primitive life EXCEPT:

(A) presence of objects resembling the morphology of known bacteria

(B) extraordinarily high concentrations of unusual PAHs

(C) presence of iron oxide and iron sulfide crystals

(D) unusual zonings of carbonate globules

(E) distinctive oxygen isotopes trapped in gasses

5. According to the passage, the compositional variation of the carbonate deposits (line 30) and the PAH-type hydrocarbons (line 50) both

(A) result from chemical processes more likely to occur on Mars than on Earth

(B) might be the product of an organic reaction or the product of an inorganic process

(C) tend to occur at relatively cooler temperatures than other, similar reactions

(D) are evidence of chemical processes that occurred during the formation of the Solar system

(E) are bi-products of organic processes and cannot result from inorganic reactions

6. The author mentions lower gravitation and restricted space (lines 83–86) in order to explain why

(A) bacteria on Mars might be smaller than ones found on Earth

(B) no microfossil record of bacteria has yet been found in Antarctica

(C) the spherical, ovoid, and elongated shapes in ALH84001 cannot be bacteria

(D) restricted pore space in Martian rocks were a hindrance to bacterial growth

(E) non-equilibrium precipitation is probably not the result of an organic reaction

7. With which of the following conclusions about the possibility of life on Mars would the author most likely agree?

(A) The available evidence strongly suggests that conditions on Mars make it impossible for life to have developed there.

(B) The scientific evidence is ambiguous and supports no conclusion about the possibility of life on Mars.

(C) Scientific evidence cannot, in principle, ever demonstrate that life existed on Mars.

(D) Scientific data derived from ALH84001 is consistent with the proposition that life once existed on Mars.

(E) It is as likely that life developed in a hostile environment such as Antarctica as on Mars.

Behavior is one of two general responses available to endothermic (warm-blooded) species for the regulation of body temperature, the other being in-
(5) nate (reflexive) mechanisms of heat production and heat loss. Human beings rely primarily on the first to provide a hospitable thermal microclimate for themselves, in which the transfer of
(10) heat between the body and the environment is accomplished with minimal involvement of innate mechanisms of heat production and loss. Thermoregulatory behavior anticipates hyperthermia, and
(15) the organism adjusts its behavior to avoid becoming hyperthermic: it removes layers of clothing, it goes for a cool swim, etc. The organism can also respond to changes in the temperature
(20) of the body core, as is the case during exercise; but such responses result from the direct stimulation of thermoreceptors distributed widely within the central nervous system, and the ability of
(25) these mechanisms to help the organism adjust to gross changes in its environment is limited.

Until recently it was assumed that organisms respond to microwave radia-
(30) tion in the same way that they respond to temperature changes caused by other forms of radiation. After all, the argument runs, microwaves are radiation and heat body tissues. This theory ig-
(35) nores the fact that the stimulus to a behavioral response is normally a temperature change that occurs at the surface of the organism. The thermoreceptors that prompt behavioral changes
(40) are located within the first millimeter of the skin's surface, but the energy of a microwave field may be selectively deposited in deep tissues, effectively bypassing these thermoreceptors,
(45) particularly if the field is at near-resonant frequencies. The resulting temperature profile may well be a kind of reverse thermal gradient in which the deep tissues are warmed more than
(50) those of the surface. Since the heat is not conducted outward to the surface to stimulate the appropriate receptors, the organism does not "appreciate" this stimulation in the same way that it
(55) "appreciates" heating and cooling of the skin. In theory, the internal organs of a human being or an animal could be quite literally cooked well-done before the animal even realizes that the bal-
(60) ance of its thermomicroclimate has been disturbed.

Until a few years ago, microwave irradiations at equivalent plane-wave power densities of about 100 mW/cm²
(65) were considered unequivocally to produce "thermal" effects; irradiations within the range of 10 to 100 mW/cm² might or might not produce "thermal" effects; while effects observed at power
(70) densities below 10 mW/cm² were assumed to be "nonthermal" in nature. Experiments have shown this to be an oversimplification, and a recent report suggests that fields as weak as 1 mW/
(75) cm² can be thermogenic. When the heat generated in the tissues by an imposed radio frequency (plus the heat generated by metabolism) exceeds the heat-loss capabilities of the organism, the

(80) thermoregulatory system has been compromised. Yet surprisingly, not long ago, an increase in the internal body temperature was regarded merely as "evidence" of a thermal effect.

8. The author is primarily concerned with

(A) showing that behavior is a more effective way of controlling bodily temperature than innate mechanisms

(B) criticizing researchers who will not discard their theories about the effects of microwave radiation on organisms

(C) demonstrating that effects of microwave radiation are different from those of other forms of radiation

(D) analyzing the mechanism by which an organism maintains its bodily temperature in a changing thermal environment

(E) discussing the importance of thermoreceptors in the control of the internal temperature of an organism

9. Which of the following would be the most logical topic for the author to take up in the paragraph following the final paragraph of the selection?

(A) A suggestion for new research to be done on the effects of microwaves on animals and human beings

(B) An analysis of the differences between microwave radiation and other forms of radiation

(C) A proposal that the use of microwave radiation be prohibited because it is dangerous

(D) A survey of the literature on the effects of microwave radiation on human beings

(E) A discussion of the strategies used by various species to control hyperthermia

10. The author's strategy in lines 56–61 is to

    (A) introduce a hypothetical example to dramatize a point

    (B) propose an experiment to test a scientific hypothesis

    (C) cite a case study to illustrate a general contention

    (D) produce a counter-example to disprove an opponent's theory

    (E) speculate about the probable consequences of a scientific phenomenon

11. The author implies that the proponents of the theory that microwave radiation acts on organisms in the same way as other forms of radiation based their conclusions primarily on

    (A) laboratory research

    (B) unfounded assumption

    (C) control group surveys

    (D) deductive reasoning

    (E) causal investigation

12. The tone of the passage can best be described as

    (A) genial and conversational

    (B) alarmed and disparaging

    (C) facetious and cynical

    (D) scholarly and noncommittal

    (E) analytical and concerned

13. The author is primarily concerned with

    (A) pointing out weaknesses in a popular scientific theory

    (B) developing a hypothesis to explain a scientific phenomenon

    (C) reporting on new research on the effects of microwave radiation

    (D) criticizing the research methods of earlier investigators

    (E) clarifying ambiguities in the terminology used to describe a phenomenon

14. In developing the argument, the author makes all the following points EXCEPT

    (A) behavior is the primary method by which humans regulate body temperature.

    (B) a report has shown that even microwave irradiations of a very weak power density can generate heat.

    (C) humans may remove clothing in anticipation of hyperthermia.

    (D) change of temperature at the body surface is the most common cause of thermoregulatory behavior.

    (E) new evidence supports the idea that microwave ovens are causing dangerous heat effects.

    Under existing law, a new drug may be labeled, promoted, and advertised only for those conditions in that safety and effectiveness have been dem-
    (5) onstrated and that the Food and Drug Administration (FDA) has approved, or so-called approved uses. Other uses have come to be called "unapproved uses" and cannot be legally promoted. In a real
    (10) sense, the term "unapproved" is a misnomer because it includes in one phrase two categories of marketed drugs that are very different. It is common for new research and new insights to identify
    (15) valid new uses for drugs already on the market. This is an important method of discovery in the field of therapeutics, and there are numerous examples of medical progress resulting from the ser-
    (20) endipitous observations and therapeutic innovations of physicians. Before such advances can result in new indications for inclusion in drug labeling, however, the available data must meet the legal
    (25) standard of substantial evidence derived from adequate and well-controlled clinical trials. Such evidence may require time to develop, and, without initiative on the part of the drug firm, it may not
    (30) occur at all for certain uses. However, because medical literature on new uses exists, and these uses are medically beneficial, physicians often use these drugs

for such purposes prior to FDA review or
(35) changes in labeling. This is referred to
as "unlabeled uses" of drugs. A different
problem arises when a particular use for
a drug has been examined scientifically
and has been found to be ineffective or
(40) unsafe, and yet physicians who either
are uninformed or who refuse to accept
the available scientific evidence continue
their use. Such use may have been reviewed by FDA and rejected, or, in some
(45) cases, the use may actually be warned
against in the labeling. This subset of
uses may be properly termed "disapproved uses."

      Government policy should mini-
(50) mize the extent of unlabeled uses. If
such uses are valid—and many are—it
is important that scientifically sound
evidence supporting them be generated
and that the regulatory system accom-
(55) modate them into drug labeling. Continuing rapid advances in medical care
and the complexity of drug usage, however, make it impossible for government
to keep drug labeling up to date for every
(60) conceivable situation. Thus, when a particular use of this type appears, it is also
important, and in the interest of good
medical care, that no stigma be attached
to such use by practitioners while the
(65) formal evidence is assembled between
the time of discovery and the time the
new use is included in the labeling. In
the case of disapproved uses, however, it
is proper policy to warn against these in
(70) the package insert. Whether use of a
drug for these purposes by the uninformed or intransigent physician constitutes a violation of the current Federal
Food, Drug and Cosmetic Act is a matter
(75) of debate that involves a number of technical and legal issues. Regardless of that,
the inclusion of disapproved uses in the
form of contraindications, warnings, and
other precautionary statements in pack-
(80) age inserts is an important practical
deterrent to improper use. Except for
clearly disapproved uses, however, it is
in the best interests of patient care that
physicians not be constrained by regula-
(85) tory statutes from exercising their best

judgment in prescribing a drug for both
its approved uses and any unlabeled
uses it may have.

15. The author's primary concern is to

(A) refute a theory.

(B) draw a distinction.

(C) discredit an opponent.

(D) describe a new development.

(E) condemn an error.

16. According to the passage, an unlabeled
use of a drug is any use that

(A) has been reviewed by the FDA and
specifically rejected.

(B) is medically beneficial despite the fact
that such use is prohibited by law.

(C) has medical value but has not yet
been approved by FDA for inclusion
as a labeled use.

(D) is authorized by the label approved by
the FDA on the basis of scientific
studies.

(E) is made in experiments designed to
determine whether a drug is medically beneficial.

17. It can be inferred from the passage that
the intransigent physician (line 72)

(A) continues to prescribe a drug even
though he or she knows it is not in the
best interest of the patient.

(B) refuses to use a drug for an unlabeled
purpose out of fear that he or she may
be stigmatized by its use.

(C) persists in using a drug for disapproved uses because he or she rejects
the evidence of its ineffectiveness or
dangers.

(D) experiments with new uses for tested
drugs in an attempt to find medically
beneficial uses for the drugs.

(E) is violating the Federal Food, Drug
and Cosmetic Act in using drugs for
disapproved uses.

18. All of the following are mentioned in the passage as reasons for allowing unlabeled uses of drugs EXCEPT

(A) the increased cost to the patient of buying an FDA-approved drug.

(B) the medical benefits that can accrue to the patient through unlabeled use.

(C) the time lag between initial discovery of a medical use and FDA approval of that use.

(D) the possibility that a medically beneficial use may never be clinically documented.

(E) the availability of publications to inform physicians of the existence of such uses.

19. With which of the following statements about the distinction between approved and unlabeled uses would the author most likely agree?

(A) Public policy statements have not adequately distinguished between uses already approved by the FDA and medically beneficial uses that have not yet been approved.

(B) The distinction between approved and unlabeled uses has been obscured because government regulatory agencies approve only those uses that have been clinically tested.

(C) Practicing physicians are in a better position than the FDA to distinguish between approved and unlabeled uses because they are involved in patient treatment on a regular basis.

(D) The distinction between approved and unlabeled uses should be discarded so that the patient can receive the full benefits of any drug use.

(E) The practice of unlabeled uses of drugs exists because of the time lag between the discovery of a beneficial use and the production of data needed for FDA approval.

20. The author regards the practice of using drugs for medically valid purposes before FDA approval as

(A) a necessary compromise.

(B) a dangerous policy.

(C) an illegal activity.

(D) an unqualified success.

(E) a short-term phenomenon.

21. Which of the following statements best summarizes the point of the passage?

(A) Patients have been exposed to needless medical risk because the FDA has not adequately regulated unlabeled uses as well as disapproved uses.

(B) Physicians who engage in the practice of unlabeled use make valuable contributions to medical science and should be protected from legal repercussions of such activity.

(C) Pharmaceutical firms develop and test new drugs that initially have little or no medical value but later are found to have value in unlabeled uses.

(D) Doctors prescribe drugs for disapproved purposes primarily because they fail to read manufacturers' labels or because they disagree with the clinical data about the value of drugs.

(E) The government should distinguish between unlabeled use and disapproved use of a drug, allowing the practice of unlabeled use and condemning disapproved use.

The existence of both racial and sexual discrimination in employment is well documented, and policy makers and responsible employers are particularly sen- *(5)* sitive to the plight of the black female employee on the theory that she is doubly the victim of discrimination. That there exist differences in income between whites and blacks is clear, but it *(10)* is not so clear that these differences are solely the result of racial discrimination

(15) in employment. The two groups differ in productivity, so basic economics dictates that their incomes will differ.

To obtain a true measure of the effect of racial discrimination in employment, it is necessary to adjust the gross black/white income ratio for these pro-
(20) ductivity factors. White women in urban areas have a higher educational level than black women and can be expected to receive larger incomes. Moreover, state distribution of residence is important because blacks are overrepresented in
(25) the South, where wage rates are typically lower than elsewhere and where racial differentials in income are greater. Also, blacks are overrepresented in large cities, and incomes of blacks would be
(30) greater if blacks were distributed among cities of different sizes in the same manner as whites.

After standardization for the productivity factors, the income of black
(35) urban women is estimated to be between 108 and 125 percent of the income of white women. This indicates that productivity factors more than account for the actual white/black income differen-
(40) tial for women. Despite their greater education, white women's *actual* median income is only 2 to 5 percent higher than that of black women in the North. Unlike the situation of men, the evi-
(45) dence indicates that the money income of black urban women was as great as, or greater than, that of whites of similar productivity in the North and probably in the United States as a whole. For
(50) men, however, the adjusted black/white income ratio is approximately 80 percent.

At least two possible hypotheses may explain why the adjustment for
(55) productivity more than accounts for the observed income differential for women, whereas a differential persists for men. First, there may be more discrimination against black men than against black
(60) women. The different occupational structures for men and women give some indication why this could be the case, and institutionalized considerations—

(65) for example, the effect of unionization in cutting competition—may also contribute. Second, the data are consistent with the hypothesis that the intensity of discrimination against women differs little between whites and blacks. Therefore,
(70) racial discrimination adds little to effects of existing sex discrimination.

These findings suggest that a black woman does not necessarily suffer relatively more discrimination in the labor
(75) market than does a white woman. Rather, for women, the effects of sexual discrimination are so pervasive that the effects of racial discrimination are negligible. Of course, this is not to say that
(80) the more generalized racial discrimination of which black women, like men, are victims does not disadvantage black women in their search for work. After all, one important productivity factor is
(85) level of education, and the difference between white and black women on this scale is largely the result of racial discrimination.

22. The primary purpose of the passage is to

(A) explain the reasons for the existence of income differentials between men and women.

(B) show that racial discrimination against black women in employment is less important than sexual discrimination.

(C) explore the ways in which productivity factors such as level of education influence the earning power of black workers.

(D) sketch a history of racial and sexual discrimination against black and female workers in the labor market.

(E) offer some suggestions as to how public officials and private employers can act to solve the problem of discrimination against black women.

23. According to the passage, the gross black/white income ratio is not an accurate measure of discrimination in employment because the gross ratio

    (A) fails to include large numbers of black workers who live in the large cities and in the South.

    (B) must be adjusted to reflect the longer number of hours and greater number of days worked by black employees.

    (C) represents a subjective interpretation by the statistician of the importance of factors such as educational achievement.

    (D) is not designed to take account of the effects of the long history of racial discrimination.

    (E) includes income differences attributable to real economic factors and not to discrimination.

24. Which of the following best describes the relationship between the income level for black women and that for black men?

    (A) In general, black men earn less money than black women.

    (B) On the average, black women in the South earn less money than black men in large Northern cities.

    (C) Productivity factors have a greater dollar value in the case of black women.

    (D) Black men have a higher income level than black women because black men have a higher level of education.

    (E) The difference between income levels for black and white women is less than that for black and white men.

25. Which of the following best describes the logical relationship between the two hypotheses presented in lines 58–69?

    (A) The two hypotheses may both be true since each phenomenon could contribute to the observed differential.

    (B) The two hypotheses are contradictory, and if one is proved to be correct, the other is proved incorrect.

    (C) The two hypotheses are dependent on each other, and empirical disconfirmation of the one is disconfirmation of the other.

    (D) The two hypotheses are logically connected so that proof of the first entails the truth of the second.

    (E) The two hypotheses are logically connected so that it is impossible to prove either one to be true without also proving the other to be true.

26. Which of the following best describes the tone of the passage?

    (A) Confident and overbearing

    (B) Ill-tempered and brash

    (C) Objective and critical

    (D) Tentative and inconclusive

    (E) Hopeful and optimistic

27. If the second hypothesis mentioned by the author (lines 66–69) is correct, a general lessening of discrimination against women should lead to a(n)

    (A) higher white/black income ratio for women.

    (B) lower white/black income ratio for women.

    (C) lower female/male income ratio.

    (D) increase in the productivity of women.

    (E) increase in the level of education of women.

28. The author's attitude toward racial and sexual discrimination in employment can best be described as one of

    (A) apology.

    (B) concern.

    (C) indifference.

    (D) indignation.

    (E) anxiety.

STOP

END OF SECTION 4. IF YOU HAVE ANY TIME LEFT, GO
OVER YOUR WORK IN THIS SECTION ONLY. DO NOT
WORK IN ANY OTHER SECTION OF THE TEST.

SECTION 5

24 Questions • Time—35 Minutes

Directions: Below each of the following passages, you will find questions or incomplete statements about the passage. Each statement or question is followed by lettered words or expressions. Select the word or expression that most satisfactorily completes each statement or answers each question in accordance with the meaning of the passage. After you have chosen the *best* answer, blacken the corresponding space on the answer sheet.

The following passage contains blanks that represent deleted material. For questions 1 and 2, select the most appropriate completion of the passage.

When we reflect on the structure of moral decisions, we come across cases in which we seem to be subject to mutually exclusive moral demands. But the conflict is just that, a seeming one. We must be careful to distinguish two levels of moral thinking: the *prima facie* and the critical. A *prima facie* moral principle is analogous to a workaday tool, say a(n) _____ (1). It is versatile, that is, useful in many situations, and at your fingertips, to wit, no special skill is needed to use it. Unfortunately, the value of a *prima facie* principle derives from its non-specific language, which means that in some situations, it will turn out to be an oversimplification. For example, two fairly straightforward moral rules such as "keep all promises" and "assist others in dire need," which work well enough in most cases, seem to clash in the following scenario: "I have promised a friend I will run a very important errand on his behalf (and he is relying on me); but while en route, I happen across a person in need of emergency medical assistance, which I can provide, but only at the cost of leaving my original purpose unaccomplished." The appearance of conflict arises from the choice of tools used in analyzing the situation—the two *prima facie* rules do not cut finely enough.

What is wanted, therefore, is a more refined analysis that will be applicable to the specific situation. At this, the second level of moral thinking, critical moral thinking employs a finer system of categories so that the end result is _____ (2).

1. **(A)** surgical scalpel
   (B) kitchen knife
   (C) electrical generator
   (D) tuning fork
   (E) library book

2. **(A)** not two conflicting moral judgments but rather a single consistent moral judgment
   (B) an advance for the human species over the savagery of our forebears
   (C) the improvement of medical care for the population in general
   (D) moral principles of higher levels of abstraction that are applicable to larger numbers of cases
   (E) that value judgments will no longer depend on the particulars of any given situation

3. All effective administrators are concerned about the welfare of their employees, and all administrators who are concerned about the welfare of their employees are liberal in granting time off for personal needs; therefore, all administrators who are not liberal in granting time off for their employees' personal needs are not effective administrators.

If the argument above is valid, then it must be true that

(A) no ineffective administrators are liberal in granting time off for their employees' personal needs.

(B) no ineffective administrators are concerned about the welfare of their employees.

(C) some effective administrators are not liberal in granting time off for their employees' personal needs.

(D) all effective administrators are liberal in granting time off for their employees' personal needs.

(E) all time off for personal needs is granted by effective administrators.

4. CLYDE: You shouldn't drink so much wine. Alcohol really isn't good for you.

GERRY: You're wrong about that. I have been drinking the same amount of white wine for fifteen years, and I never get drunk.

Which of the following responses would best strengthen and explain Clyde's argument?

(A) Many people who drink as much white wine as Gerry does get very drunk.

(B) Alcohol does not always make a person drunk.

(C) Getting drunk is not the only reason alcohol is not good for a person.

(D) If you keep drinking white wine, you may find in the future that you are drinking more and more.

(E) White wine is not the only drink that contains alcohol.

5. In considering the transportation needs of our sales personnel, the question of the relative cost of each of our options is very important. The initial purchase outlay required for a fleet of diesel autos is fairly high, though the operating costs for them will be low. This is the mirror image of the cost picture for a fleet of gasoline-powered cars. The only way, then, of making a valid cost comparison is on the basis of

_____ .

Which of the following best completes the above paragraph?

(A) projected operating costs for both diesel- and gasoline-powered autos

(B) the average costs of both fleets over the life of each fleet

(C) the purchase cost for both diesel- and gasoline-powered autos

(D) the present difference in the operating costs of the two fleets

(E) the relative amount of air pollution that would be created by the one type of car compared with the other

6. The Dormitory Canteen Committee decided that the prices of snacks in the Canteen vending machines were already high enough, so they told Vendo Inc., the company holding the vending machine concession for the Canteen, either to maintain prices at the then current levels or to forfeit the concession. Vendo, however, managed to thwart the intent of the Committee's instructions without actually violating the letter of those instructions.

Which of the following is probably the action taken by Vendo referred to in the above paragraph?

(A) The president of Vendo met with the University's administration, and they ordered the Committee to rescind its instructions.

(B) Vendo continued prices at the prescribed levels but reduced the size of the snacks vended in the machines.

(C) Vendo ignored the Committee's instructions and continued to raise prices.

(D) Vendo decided it could not make a fair return on its investment if it held the line on prices, so it removed its machines from the Dormitory Canteen.

(E) Representatives of Vendo met with members of the Dormitory Canteen Committee and offered them free snacks to influence other members to change the Committee's decision.

7. The president of the University tells us that a tuition increase is needed to offset rising costs. That is simply not true. Weston University is an institution approximately the same size as our own University, but the president of Weston University has announced that it will not impose a tuition increase on its students.

The author makes his point primarily by

(A) citing new evidence.

(B) proposing an alternative solution.

(C) pointing out a logical contradiction.

(D) drawing an analogy.

(E) clarifying an ambiguity.

8. Only White Bear gives you all-day deodorant protection and the unique White Bear scent.

If this advertising claim is true, which of the following CANNOT also be true?

(A) Red Flag deodorant gives you all-day deodorant protection.

(B) Open Sea deodorant is a more popular deodorant than White Bear.

(C) White Bear after-shave lotion uses the White Bear scent.

(D) All-day deodorant provides all-day protection and uses a scent with a similar chemical composition to that of White Bear.

(E) Lost Horizons deodorant contains a scent with the same chemical composition as that of White Bear and gives all-day deodorant protection.

9. Clara prefers English Literature to Introductory Physics. She likes English Literature, however, less than she likes Basic Economics. She actually finds Basic Economics preferable to any other college course, and she dislikes Physical Education more than she dislikes Introductory Physics.

All of the following statements can be inferred from the information given above EXCEPT

(A) Clara prefers Basic Economics to English Literature.

(B) Clara likes English Literature better than she likes Physical Education.

(C) Clara prefers Basic Economics to Advanced Calculus.

(D) Clara likes World History better than she likes Introductory Physics.

(E) Clara likes Physical Education less than she likes English Literature.

10. In *The Adventure of the Bruce-Partington Plans,* Sherlock Holmes explained to Dr. Watson that the body had been placed on the top of the train while the train paused at a signal.

"It seems most improbable," remarked Watson.

"We must fall back upon the old axiom," continued Holmes, "that when all other contingencies fail, whatever remains, however improbable, must be the truth."

Which of the following is the most effective criticism of the logic contained in Holmes' response to Watson?

(A) You will never be able to obtain a conviction in a court of law.

(B) You can never be sure you have accounted for all other contingencies.

(C) You will need further evidence to satisfy the police.

(D) The very idea of putting a dead body on top of a train seems preposterous.

(E) You still have to find the person responsible for putting the body on top of the train.

11. PROFESSOR: Under the rule of primogeniture, the first male child born to a man's first wife is always first in line to inherit the family estate.

STUDENT: That can't be true; the Duchess of Warburton was her father's only child by his only wife, and she inherited his entire estate.

The student has misinterpreted the professor's remark to mean which of the following?

(A) Only men can father male children.

(B) A daughter cannot be a first-born child.

(C) Only sons can inherit the family estate.

(D) Illegitimate children cannot inherit their fathers' property.

(E) A woman cannot inherit her mother's property.

Questions 12 and 13

The blanks in the following passage indicate deletions from the text. Select the completion that is most appropriate to the context.

Contemporary legal positivism depends upon the methodological assumption that a theory of law may be conceptual without, at the same time, being normative. In point of fact, this assumption is a composite principle. It makes the fairly obvious claim that a conceptual theory, which strives to be descriptive rather than normative, says what the law is—not what it ought to be. A conceptual theory must be supplemented by a normative theory, and the arguments in favor of a particular content for law are couched in terms of the results that are expected to flow from proposed legal acts. It is never a part of an argument for what the law ought to be, in the positivist's view, that to be a law it must have a certain content. While the normative argument refers ultimately to agreed-upon ends, it does not assert that these ends _____ (12). Rather, that they are accepted and acted upon is merely a contingent matter. The second part of the methodological premise is more subtle: A conceptual theory such as legal positivism does not claim that the particular description it offers is uniquely correct. Proponents of legal positivism regard their study of law as analogous to the physicists' study of the universe: They have one theory of legal institutions, _____ (13).

12. (A) must be pursued as a matter of logical necessity

(B) are not the best ends for any modern legal system

(C) would not be adopted by courts in a democratic society

(D) could be undermined by dissident elements in the community

(E) are shared by everyone

13. (A) and that is the only possible correct theory of law

(B) and someday, with sufficient work, that theory will be able to generate societal goals for us to pursue

(C) but that theory may, someday, be displaced by a better one

(D) although no theory of the physical universe is as reliable as the positivistic theory of law

(E) which is, however, strongly supported by the findings of modern science

14. The ad agency handling advertising accounts for the Super Bowl says that it expects about 120 million television viewers to tune in to the game in the United States and about 100 million more in Europe. Given that the United States is the country with the biggest interest in the game, the 220 million total seems to be considerably inflated.

All of the following, if true, would tend to strengthen the argument above EXCEPT:

(A) Outside of the United States the Super Bowl is available only on a pay subscription basis.

(B) The Super Bowl will be broadcast beginning at 6:00 pm when it is 11:00 pm in Britain and later in Europe.

(C) The football organization in charge of the Super Bowl operates an American-style football league in Europe.

(D) The World Cup soccer finals, a sporting event of major interest in Europe, attracted 12 million viewers in Britain and 90 million in Europe.

(E) Most Europeans have very little understanding of the rules and procedures of American football.

15. Chukar partridge chicks can run straight up the side of a tree by flapping their wings. The beating wings do not raise the chicks off the ground but rather serve the same purposes as spoilers on race cars: providing better traction for their feet. Feathered dinosaurs may have done something similar. They flapped their primitive wings to better run up inclines, which helped them to catch prey. Thus, the proto-wing offered a survival benefit not related to flight per se and only later did the wing-beating behavior lead to the eventual discovery of the aerial possibilities of the wings. This evolutionary path to flight is different from the two previous models, the arboreal model in which proto-birds first launched themselves from trees and the cursorial model in which they took off from the ground.

In the reasoning above, the speaker

(A) offers a third alternative to an either-or challenge

(B) provides a counter-example to refute a popular theory

(C) points out a contradiction in a competing position

(D) attacks the proponent of plan rather than its merits

(E) shifts the burden of proof to an opponent of a plan

16. As the debate on the roots of the so-called obesity epidemic among children rages, it is becoming increasingly clear that public school lunches are not one of the causes. Fully 86 percent of the school lunches prepared on any given day meet the federal nutritional guidelines.

All of the following, if true, weaken the argument EXCEPT:

(A) Children are permitted to choose their own food items from several offerings and rarely select the most nutritious items.

(B) Lunchroom administrators find it easier and less costly to heat cans of bland-tasting prepared vegetables than cook good-tasting fresh vegetables from scratch.

(C) The number of high school students taking daily physical education classes has dropped to 29 percent from 46 percent in the last ten years.

(D) School lunches feature surplus commodities high in saturated fats purchased by the government as a means of supporting farm prices.

(E) Most schools permit children to obtain lunch items from vending machines that dispense sodas and candy.

17. It is the central tenet of the ethical theory of the German Idealist thinker Immanuel Kant that a person must not be treated as a means to an end but as an end only unique unto herself or himself. Therefore, it is wrong to use animals for food or clothing, for in doing so, we reduce them to mere instrumentalities and fail to consider their uniqueness.

Which of the following, if true, is the best criticism of the speaker's use of Kant's ethical doctrine?

(A) Kant never considered the possibility that animals might be deserving of ethical treatment.

(B) The use of animals for food and clothing is offensive to many people who themselves consider animals ends and not means.

(C) Kant implies that rehabilitation is not a legitimate objective of the penal system because it treats the criminal as an end.

(D) In nature, every animal is a potential source of nourishment for other animals below it on the food chain.

(E) Kant's conclusion about treating humans as ends rests upon the assumption that humans have the ability for rational thought.

18. Recently, six Magellanic penguins taken from the wild arrived at the San Francisco Zoo. The 46 long-time resident Magellanic penguins, which had spent relatively sedentary lives of grooming and staying in burrows, began to simulate migratory behavior when they watched the new penguins swimming around the 130-by-40 foot pool. All 52 birds now swim almost all the time, resting on the artificial island in the middle of the pool only at night. Indeed, when the pool was drained for cleaning, the penguins refused to leave, walking around it instead of swimming.

Which of the following conclusions can be most reliably drawn from the information above?

(A) Migratory behavior in animals is acquired rather than innate.

(B) Animals in zoo environments rarely exhibit active behavior.

(C) Magellanic penguins in the wild spend most of their time swimming.

(D) The close quarters of a zoo environment suppresses animal migratory behavior.

(E) Animals sometimes mimic the behavior they see in other animals.

19. CARY: Last year, an outbreak of e-coli bacterial poisoning caused by contaminated drinking water at a county fair in rural, upstate New York sent hundreds of people to the hospital and caused nearly a dozen fatalities. This type of poisoning can be prevented by requiring that all sources of public drinking water be treated.

PHIL: Your suggestion is unwarranted. The number of cases of e-coli poisoning attributable to contaminated drinking water is relatively small compared to the number of cases caused by eating improperly stored or undercooked food at restaurants and other public eating places.

Phil's response to Cary is inadequate because it

(A) fails to show that Cary's suggestion would not result in advantages that more than offset any associated costs.

(B) oversimplifies a complex policy issue by quantifying public health in terms of hospital visits.

(C) provides no plan for eliminating the health risks associated with eating contaminated food in restaurants.

(D) does not provide information about the relative incidence of food poisoning contracted at restaurants versus other sources.

(E) conflates the exposure to contaminated foods from eating at restaurants with that from eating food prepared in other locations.

20. At a management training seminar, the presenter asked the class "What would you do if you made a truly horrendous error?" A class member answered, "I'd learn from my mistake." To which the presenter responded, "So what did you just learn?"

The presenter is suggesting that

(A) class members should respond directly to questions.

(B) managers do not make errors very frequently.

(C) corporations reward managers who make errors.

(D) corporate training seminars are not very productive.

(E) the class member's answer to the question was a mistake.

21. CLIFFORD: Five years ago, the Dairy Project bought the Grieg property down in Cambridge to try to show that it's possible to operate a dairy farm without purchasing feed from an outside source just by carefully monitoring the effects of grazing on pasture and rotating fields as needed. In the second year, the farm showed a profit, and it has showed a profit ever since. So it is possible to run a profitable dairy farm using just the resources available on the farm.

GENEVA: But the Grieg property has a lot of natural advantages that other farms don't. In the first place, the soil is extremely rich, so the pastures regenerate at a faster rate. In addition, the farm is about twice as large as your ordinary dairy farm, making it possible to let fields remain ungrazed for longer periods.

Which of the following best describes the exchange above?

(A) Geneva fails to point out that dairy farming, as a business, is extremely vulnerable to the uncertainties of weather and to unexpected changes in the demand for milk.

(B) Clifford's argument does not anticipate the possibility that the Dairy Project's operation might not be profitable in the next year.

(C) Geneva assumes without proof that other dairy farmers would be able to achieve the same results if their farms were configured differently.

(D) Geneva's points are irrelevant since the Dairy Project wanted only to show that techniques are feasible, not that they can be applied universally.

(E) Both Clifford and Geneva fail to consider that most diary farmers are dependent upon government subsidies to make the operation sufficiently profitable to continue in the farming business.

22. Some aromatic candles are not ginger-scented.

All Evening Balm tapers are ginger-scented.

Which of the following conclusions can be deduced from the two statements above?

(A) Some aromatic candles are not Evening Balm tapers.

(B) No ginger-scented candles are aromatic.

(C) All ginger-scented candles are Evening Balm tapers.

(D) All aromatic candles are ginger-scented.

(E) Some aromatic candles are ginger-scented.

23. A new restaurant named Frederico's just opened that will serve Northern Italian cuisine in a renovated dining room with a jazz ensemble. But because the restaurant combines eating with entertainment, it won't be able to do either function particularly well. Those who come for the food will be disappointed in their dining experience; those who come for the music won't be treated to the kind of musical performance they expect. The owners would be better advised to make the establishment a restaurant or a jazz club.

The argument above makes which of the following assumptions?

(A) There are no similarities between food service and entertainment.

(B) Jazz music is not well matched to Northern Italian cuisine.

(C) The location of the new establishment is better suited to a restaurant than a jazz club.

(D) There are no economies of scale to be achieved by combining restaurant functions.

(E) In order to be successful, a restaurant or a club must please its customers.

24. For many years, a financial analyst for a prominent newspaper would call the company from which he bought his suits when he wanted to assess where the economy was headed. If suit sales were strong, he would conclude that the economy was on a sound footing. Conversely, if sales of suits were weak, he would write that the economy was headed downward.

Which of the following, if true, provides the most support for the rule of thumb articulated above?

(A) The casual trend of the 1990s produced the worst decade of sales ever for suit manufacturers.

(B) Men's suits are classic in design and manufactured to last and so need not be replaced when the owner feels financially insecure.

(C) Women's wear is usually not affected by economic conditions because having the latest fashion has traditionally been a priority for women.

(D) Most retailers make little profit on men's suits because of the cost of alterations but do make money on other items such as shirts and ties.

(E) Few companies that manufacture men's suits survive beyond the first generation following the establishment of the company.

STOP

END OF SECTION 5. IF YOU HAVE ANY TIME LEFT, GO OVER YOUR WORK IN THIS SECTION ONLY. DO NOT WORK IN ANY OTHER SECTION OF THE TEST.

WRITING SAMPLE

Time —30 Minutes

Joyce Peterson, a French major, is graduating from college at the end of the spring term. Beginning in the fall, she will start teaching French at a high school in the South. She wants to spend her summer studying in France. Write an essay in favor of one of two summer programs, one offered by the American Institute in Paris, the other by the University of Reims. Two considerations should guide your thinking:

1 Joyce wants to improve her French accent and learn the kind of informal speech used by ordinary French people. She also wants to become as familiar as possible with the routine of French life.

2 Joyce wants to visit some of the typical attractions in France, but she also wants to avoid spending too much money on her summer studies.

The AMERICAN INSTITUTE IN PARIS is an extension of an American university that offers French language and culture study programs in Paris. It offers a six-week program in the modern French language. Students from more than twenty different countries will be enrolled in the program. Students attend classes 5 hours each day, five days a week; and all classes are taught by native speakers. The cost of the six-week program is $500, but that sum does not include room and board.

The UNIVERSITY OF REIMS is a public institution located in the small town of Reims, about 60 minutes by train from Paris, in the heart of the champagne-producing region. The University offers a four-week program in French and French literature. The classes are all taught by the faculty at the University. In addition, University students attending summer school conduct small group tutorials. Students spend an average of 6 hours a day in formal classes and another 2 hours each day in their small group tutorials. Saturdays and Sundays are free days. The fee for the program is $1,400, which includes double occupancy housing in University dormitories and two meals a day in the University cafeteria.

ANSWER KEY

Section 1

1.	C	6.	A	11.	C	16.	E	21.	D
2.	C	7.	D	12.	E	17.	B	22.	D
3.	D	8.	B	13.	C	18.	D	23.	C
4.	D	9.	C	14.	C	19.	C	24.	A
5.	C	10.	B	15.	E	20.	D		

Section 2

1.	D	6.	B	11.	C	16.	B	21.	D
2.	D	7.	D	12.	C	17.	B	22.	A
3.	A	8.	B	13.	C	18.	D	23.	E
4.	D	9.	A	14.	C	19.	E	24.	D
5.	C	10.	C	15.	C	20.	E	25.	B

Section 3

1.	D	6.	D	11.	B	16.	B	21.	B
2.	E	7.	A	12.	C	17.	A	22.	D
3.	C	8.	C	13.	D	18.	C	23.	C
4.	D	9.	E	14.	D	19.	A	24.	D
5.	E	10.	B	15.	B	20.	C		

Section 4

1.	B	7.	D	13.	A	19.	E	25.	A
2.	A	8.	C	14.	E	20.	A	26.	C
3.	C	9.	A	15.	B	21.	E	27.	A
4.	E	10.	A	16.	C	22.	B	28.	B
5.	B	11.	B	17.	C	23.	E		
6.	A	12.	E	18.	A	24.	E		

Section 5

1.	B	6.	B	11.	C	16.	C	21.	D
2.	A	7.	D	12.	A	17.	E	22.	A
3.	D	8.	E	13.	C	18.	E	23.	E
4.	C	9.	D	14.	C	19.	A	24.	B
5.	B	10.	B	15.	A	20.	E		

EXPLANATORY ANSWERS

Section I

Questions 1–6

This set is based upon family relationships. At the outset we note that of the seven people related to *X,* two are males (father, brother) and five are females (mother, aunt, sister, wife, and daughter). And we summarize the additional information:

> $P = Q$ (same gender)
>
> $M \neq N$ (not same gender)
>
> $S > M$ (born before)
>
> $Q \neq$ mother (Q is not *X*'s mother.)

There is a further deduction to be drawn. There are only two male relatives. Of the four individuals, *P, Q, M,* and *N,* three are of the same sex and one is of the opposite gender. Since there are only two males in the scheme, this means that the three of the same gender are female. So *P, Q,* and either *M* or *N* are females; either *M* or *N* is male.

1. **The correct answer is (C).** The answer to this question is evident from the analysis above.

2. **The correct answer is (C).** This question is also answerable on the basis of our previous analysis. As for choices (A) and (B), though we know that of *M* and *N* one is male and the other is female, we have no information to justify a judgment as to who is the female. Nor is there any information to support the conclusions in choices (D) and (E).

3. **The correct answer is (D).** We have established that *P* and *Q* are females and that either *M* or *N* is female. So *M* or *N* is male, and of the remaining three relatives, *S, R,* and *T,* one is male as well. If *T* is the daughter of *X,* this establishes that she is female and, further, that either *R* or *S* is the remaining male.

Choices (A), (B) and (C) are incorrect since the additional stipulation of this question does not add anything to the analysis of gender distribution above. Choice (E) is incorrect since it asserts that *S* is the male, but there is nothing to support that conclusion. Choice (D), however, is necessarily true. Of the pair *R* and *S,* one must be male and the other female, so they are not of the same gender.

4. **The correct answer is (D).** In the scheme of relations, there is only one possible pair of sisters: the mother and the aunt. It will not do to argue that *X* might have married his sister, especially when an ordinary sister relationship is available. In any event, if *M* and *Q* represent the mother and the aunt, since *Q* is not the mother, *M* must be *X*'s mother, so choices (B) and (C) are both true. Further, since *M* must be female, *N* must be male, and choice (A) is true. Then, since *M* is *X*'s mother and since *S* was born before *M, S* could not be *X*'s brother and choice (E) is true. As for choice (D), *M, Q,* and *N* (a male) are eliminated as daughters, but this still leaves several possibilities.

5. **The correct answer is (C).** There is only one available grandfather–grandchild relationship: *S* must be *X*'s father and *N* his daughter. If *N* is female, then *M* is male and must be *X*'s brother. So choice (C) is necessarily true. As for the remaining choices, choice (A) is possible though not necessary. Choice (B) is also possible since *P* might be *X*'s mother. Choice (D) is not possible since *Q* is female. Finally, choice (E) is possible since *P* is a female and might be *X*'s sister and so *N*'s aunt.

6. The correct answer is (A). Since *M* was born after *S*, if *M* is the mother of *X*'s daughter, *S* cannot be the daughter. (Again, it will not do to argue about stepdaughters, for that is clearly outside the bounds of the problem.) The remaining choices, however, are possible. As for choices (B) and (C), no restriction is placed on *P* and *Q*. And as for choice (D), *R* is not further defined. As for choice (E), we do know that *N* is male if *M* is female, and *N* could therefore be *X*'s brother.

Questions 7–12

This set is a fairly straightforward linear ordering set: Individuals are arranged in a single file from 1 to 7. We summarize the information for easy reference:

> *K* > *L* (*L* behind *K*)
>
> *M* → *N* (*N* directly behind *M*)
>
> *J*/*O* = 1/7 (*J* and *O* are first and last or vice versa.)

7. The correct answer is (D). We know that *J* finishes first or last, though we do not know which, so choices (A) and (B) are incorrect. The fourth position is the middle position of the seven. Regardless of whether *J* finishes first or last, if *L* is in position 4, *L* and *J* are separated by two swimmers. So *M* and *N* are 5 and 6. Choice (E) is not possible; choice (C) is only possible.

8. The correct answer is (B). We are given no additional information, so the question must be solvable by some general conclusions based on the initial information. We are looking for the one statement that cannot, under any circumstances, be true. Since *K* finishes ahead of *L* and since *L* cannot be in last place, *L* can finish at worst sixth, and *K* can finish at worst fifth. That the remaining statements are possible can be

proved by examples.

9. The correct answer is (C). If *O* and *K* are to finish one after the other, it must be because *O* finishes first and *K* second. Since *L* finishes after *K*, *K* and *O* cannot finish one after the other if *O* is seventh. Further, if *O* is first, *J* must be seventh.

10. The correct answer is (B). If *K* is fourth, there is only one pair of adjacent finishing positions available for the *M*–*N* pairing: second and third. So *M* finishes second and *N* third. As for *L*, we know that *L* finishes after *K*, but it is not clear whether it is *L* or *P* who finishes in fifth versus sixth position, nor is it established who finishes first and who finishes last.

11. The correct answer is (C). If *L* finishes ahead of *N*, we know that *K* finishes somewhere ahead of *M*. So we have the bloc *K* … *M*–*N* … *L*. And it is stipulated that *J* finishes first, so *O* finishes last. We have the order *J*, *K*, *L*, *M*–*N*, *O*. The only unresolved issue is where *P* goes. There are four possibilities:

$$P(?) \quad P(?) \quad P(?) \quad \quad P(?)$$
$$J \quad\quad K \quad\quad L \quad\quad M\text{--}N \quad O$$

12. The correct answer is (E). We must test each condition. As for choice (A), knowing the first and last finishers tells us nothing about the order between 2 and 6. As for choice (B), this establishes nothing about positions 3 through 6. As for choice (C), this establishes only that *N* is third and leaves open positions 4, 5, and 6. Choice (D) does tell us that *M* finishes second, but that is all. Choice (E), however, allows us to infer that *M* and *N* finish before *L* (they must be together); and we know that *K* finishes before *L*. This leaves only position 6 for *P*.

Questions 13–18

For this set, no diagram is needed since the relationships are inherent in the system of arithmetic; that is, five is one more than six, etc. You may find it useful to make a marginal note or two, for example, "challenge +1 or +2."

13. **The correct answer is (C).** The setup for this group of questions is fairly long, but once the rules of the game are understood, this question is easy. Choices (A) and (B) are incorrect, for a challenge must issue from a player of lower rank. Choices (D) and (E) are incorrect, for a challenge can be issued only to a player at most two ranks superior.

14. **The correct answer is (C).** Since *S* begins in fourth position, *S* can reach first in two plays by issuing and winning two challenges. This can be done in two ways. *S* can first challenge *Q* and then *P*, or *S* can first challenge *R* and then *P*. Either way, *R* must be in fourth position.

15. **The correct answer is (E).** This arrangement could come about only after a minimum of *three* matches: *P* versus *Q*, *S* versus *R*, and *U* versus *T*, with the challenger prevailing in each case. The other rankings are possible after only two matches:

    (A) *R* versus *Q* and *T* versus *S*

    (B) *R* versus *Q* and *U* versus *T*

    (C) *R* versus *P* and *U* versus *S*

    (D) *Q* versus *P* and *S* versus *R*

16. **The correct answer is (E).** If *U* challenges and defeats *S*, the bottom half of the ranking changes from *STU* to *UST*; and if *R* challenges and defeats *P*, the top half of the ranking changes from *PQR* to *RPQ*. So in just two matches, all 6 players could be displaced from their initial ranks.

17. **The correct answer is (B).** For *P* to be moved down to third place, at least two matches must have been played (*Q* challenging and defeating *P* and then *R* challenging and defeating *Q* or *R* challenging and defeating *P* with *Q* in turn challenging and defeating *P*). The *UST* ordering of the bottom half of the ranking could be obtained in one match, with *U* challenging and defeating *S*.

18. **The correct answer is (D).** For one player to improve and two to drop in a single match, a player must have challenged and defeated a player two ranks superior. For such challenges to have the stipulated results, it must have been player 3 challenging and defeating player 1 and player 6 challenging and defeating player 4. So the rankings at the end of two matches will be *RPQUST*. The third match could pit *U* against *P*.

Questions 19–24

The primary task here is to organize the information. And for that we will use a matrix:

	F	G	H	I	J
1	YES(X)	YES(~X)	YES	NO	NO
2	NO	YES(~X)	YES	YES(Z)	YES(~H)
3	YES(X)	YES(~X)	YES(Y)	YES(~Z)	NO

Once the information has been organized, the questions are readily answerable.

19. **The correct answer is (C).** With regard to choice (A), *F* and *G* cannot grow together (because of "X"). Choices (B), (D), and (E) are not possible because *J* does not grow in Field 1 at all.

20. **The correct answer is (D).** Since *F* does not grow at all in field 2, choices (A) and (B) can be eliminated. Then, since *J* will not grow with *H*, both choices (C) and

(E) can be eliminated. Combination *G, I,* and *J,* however, is consistent with all conditions.

21. **The correct answer is (D).** Notice that this question asks for a list of all crops that could grow *alone*. *F* cannot, since *F* simply does not grow in field 2. *G* grows in field 2 so long as *X* is not applied to the field, so *G* is part of the correct answer. *I* will not grow since it requires *Z*. Finally, *J* will grow since the question stipulates the crops will grow alone. So the correct answer consists of *G, H,* and *J.*

22. **The correct answer is (D).** Neither *F* nor *H* will grow in field 3 unless certain fertilizers or pesticides are added, so we can eliminate choices (A), (B), and (C). Choice (E) can be eliminated on the further ground that *J* simply does not grow in field 3.

23. **The correct answer is (C).** *J* does not grow in field 3, so that reduces the number of possible crops to four. But *F* and *G* cannot grow together, which further reduces the number to three. So the maximum number of crops that can be planted together is three—*F, H,* and *I* or *G, H,* and *I.*

24. **The correct answer is (A).** Consulting the chart, we see that *F* does not grow there at all. *G* will not grow in the presence of *X,* and *I* will only grow in the presence of *Z.* So only *H* and *J* will grow under the stipulated conditions.

Section 2

1. **The correct answer is (D).** The author's recommendation that public schools should have computerized reading programs depends upon the correctness of the explanation of the present deficiency in reading skills in the public schools. The contrast with private-school students shows that the author thinks the deficiency can be attributed to the lack of such a program in the public schools. So, one of the author's assumptions, and that is what the question stem is asking about, is that the differential in reading skills is a result of the availability of a computerized program in the private school system and the lack thereof in the public-school system. Choice (E) is, of course, irrelevant to the question of *reading* skills. Choice (C) tries to force the author to assume a greater burden than has been undertaken. The author claims that the reading skills of public-school children could be improved by a computerized reading program and is not concerned to argue the merits of having good reading skills. Choices (A) and (B) are wrong for the same reason. The author's claim must be interpreted to mean "of children who are able to learn, all would benefit from a computerized reading program." When the author claims that "public-school children can be good readers," this does not imply that all children can learn to be good readers nor that all can learn to read equally well.

2. **The correct answer is (D).** The question contains a hidden presupposition: that the company has discriminatory practices in the first place. This rhetorical strategy is also called a complex question or, pejoratively, a loaded question. Choice (B) is not a correct description of the question, and the questioner doesn't make such an assumption. The other choices describe features of the question but not ones that would be considered unfair, as the question stem asks.

3. **The correct answer is (A).** There are two weaknesses in Ms. Rose's argument. One will be treated in the explanation of the following question—she reaches a

very general conclusion on the basis of one example. We are concerned for the moment with the second weakness. Even if Ms. Rose had been able to cite numerous examples like the case she mentions, her argument would be weak because it overlooks the possibility that an education may be valuable even if it is not used to make a living. Importantly, Ms. Rose may be correct in her criticism of the man she mentions—we need make no judgment about that—but the assumption is nonetheless *unsupported* in that she gives no arguments to support it. Choice (B) plays on the superficial detail of the paragraph—the inversion of traditional role models. But that is not relevant to the structure of the argument; the form could have been as easily shown using a woman with a law degree who decided to become a sailor or a child who studied ballet but later decided to become a doctor. Choice (D) also is totally beside the point. Ms. Rose never commits herself to so specific a conclusion. She simply says professional education is a waste; she never claims success is related to quality of education. Choice (E) is wrong because Ms. Rose is making a general claim about professional education—the man with the law degree was used merely to illustrate her point. Choice (C) is perhaps the second-best answer, but it is still not nearly as good as choice (A). The author's objection is that the man she mentions did not use his law degree in a law-related field. She never suggests that such a degree should be used to make money. She might not have objected to his behavior if he had used the degree to work in a public interest capacity.

4. **The correct answer is (D)**. As we noted at the beginning of our discussion of question 3, there is another weakness in Ms. Rose's argument: She takes a single example and from it draws a very general conclusion. Choice (D) exemplifies this weakness. Here, too, we have a person who rests a claim on a single example, and obviously this makes the claim very weak. Choice (E) mentions education, but here education is a detail of the argument. The form of the argument—a foolish generalization—is not restricted to education. Choices (A), (B), and (C) are all wrong because they do not reflect the form of the argument, a generalization on a single example.

5. **The correct answer is (C).** To break the code, the cryptographer needs information about the language that the code conceals. Choices (A), (B), (D), and (E) all provide such information. Choice (C), however, says nothing about the underlying language. The code could even use all even or all odd numbers for the symbol substitutions without affecting the information to be encoded.

6. **The correct answer is (B).** The question is one that tests the validity or strength of a causal inference. Often such arguments can be attacked by finding intervening causal linkages, that is, variables that might interfere with the predicted result. Choice (A) cites such a variable. If the traffic problem is created by commercial traffic that will not be reduced by toll increases, then the proposed increases will not solve the problem. Choice (C), too, is such a variable. It suggests that the proposal is essentially self-defeating. Choice (D) undermines the claim by arguing that the deterrent effect of a price increase is simply not significant, so the proposal will have little, if any, effect. Choice (E) attacks the argument on a different ground. The ultimate objective of the plan is to reduce commut-

ing time. Even assuming a drop in auto traffic because some commuters use public transportation, no advantage is gained if the public transportation system cannot handle the increase in traffic. Choice (B), however, does very little to the argument. In fact, it could be argued that choice (B) is one of the predicted results of the plan: a drop in the number of autos because commuters begin to car-pool.

7. **The correct answer is (D).** The exam frequently uses arguments based on analogy, and often one that points out that two situations are not necessarily similar. That's a good way of describing this item: maybe it was the mountain retreat location rather than the medicine that was the deciding factor. Choice (A) is wrong because even granting the point, there is still a physical addiction to be addressed. Choices (B) and (E) are typical wrong answers for an item like this: interesting, but which way does this idea cut? Since neither clearly weakens the ad, neither could be the correct answer. Finally, choice (C), if anything, seems to strengthen the ad by suggesting that the study was authoritative.

8. **The correct answer is (B).** Notice that there is much common ground between the jockey and the veterinarian. The question stem asks you to uncover the areas on which they are is agreement, by asking which of the answer choices is NOT a shared assumption. Note that the exception can be an area neither has as well as an area only one has. Examine the dialogue. Both apparently assume that human emotions can be attributed to animals since they talk about them being loyal and brave choice (C), and both take those characteristics as being noble— that is, admirable choice (A). Neither speaker offers scientific evidence: each

rests content with an anecdote, choices (E) and (D). As for choice (B), though each speaker defends a choice for the first (*most* loyal), neither speaker takes a position on the second-most loyal animal. For example, the jockey might believe that horses are the most loyal animals and that goldfish are the second-most loyal animals.

9. **The correct answer is (A).** Although we do not want to argue theology, perhaps a point taken from that discipline will make this question more accessible: "If God is only good, from where does evil come?" Rousseau, at least as far as the argument is characterized here, faced a similar problem. If humans are by their very nature sympathetic, what is the source of non-sympathetic social institutions? Choice (A) poses this critical question. The remaining choices each commit the same fundamental error. Rousseau *describes* a situation. The paragraph never suggests that Rousseau proposed a *solution*. Perhaps Rousseau considered the problem of modern society irremediable.

10. **The correct answer is (C).** The last sentence of the paragraph is very important. It tells us that the proportion of light atoms in the universe is increasing (because heavy ones decay into light ones, but the reverse process does not occur) and that this trend can be measured. By extrapolation back into time on the basis of present trends, scientists can find out when it all began. Choices (B) and (E) are incorrect for the same reason. The author describes a physical phenomenon occurring on a grand scale but never hints that it will be possible to reverse it. Further, choice (E) is in direct contradiction with information given in the paragraph: The ratio is not stable because the

stars do not produce enough heavy atoms to offset the decay. Choice (D) cannot be inferred from the passage. Although the *ratio* of light to heavy atoms is increasing, we should not conclude that the ratio is greater than 1:1. And, in any event, this would not be nearly so logical a conclusion to the passage as choice (C). Finally, choice (A) is a distraction. It picks up on a minor detail in the passage and inflates that into a conclusion. Moreover, the passage clearly states that the process that keeps the stars going is fusion, not decay.

11.   **The correct answer is (C).** It is important to pay careful attention to the ways in which a speaker qualifies a claim. In this case, the speaker has said only that the *great majority* of people can get medical care—not that all can. Thus, built into the claim is the implicit concession that some people may not have access to medical care. Thus, the objector's response fails to score against the speaker. The speaker could just respond, "Yes, I realize that and that is the reason why I qualified my remarks." Choice (A) is incorrect, for the only word in the objector's statement that is the least bit emotional is "poor," and it seems rather free from emotional overtones here. It would have been a different case had the objector claimed, "There are thousands of poor and starving people who have no place to live..." Choice (D) is wrong for two reasons. First, the evidence is really not statistical; it is only numerical. Second, and more important, the evidence, if anything, cuts against the speaker's claim—not that it does any damage given the speaker's qualifications on the claim; but it surely does not strengthen the speaker's claim. Finally, inasmuch as the speaker

does not offer a cause-effect explanation, choice (E) must be wrong.

12.   **The correct answer is (C).** There are really two parts to the speaker's claim. First, he maintains that the majority of Americans can get access to the medical care in this country; and, second, that the care they have access to is the best in the world. As for the second, good medical care is a function of many variables: number and location of facilities, availability of doctors, quality of education, etc. Choices (A) and (E) may both be consistent with the speaker's claim. Even though we have fewer assistants, choice (A), than some other country, we have more doctors, and that more than makes up for the fewer assistants. Or, perhaps, we have such good preventive medicine that people do not need to go into the hospital as frequently as the citizens of other nations, choice (E). Choice (B) is wrong for a similar reason. Although it suggests there is a country in which people have greater access to the available care, it does not come to grips with the second element of the speaker's claim: that the care we get is the best. Choice (C), however, does meet both because it cites the existence of a country in which people are *given* (that is the first element) *better* (the second element) care. Choice (D) hardly tells against the speaker's claim since he has implicitly conceded that some people do not have access to the care.

13.   **The correct answer is (C).** The crux of the debate between the two speakers is what constitutes "wealthy." According to Evert, anyone who makes $100,000 per year is "wealthy." But Scott points out that annual earnings don't include accumulated assets, which are an important component of what most people would

consider "wealth." Choice (A) is incorrect. A speaker shifts the burden of proof by taking a position and challenging someone else to prove it wrong—in other words, no real argument is offered. Circular reasoning occurs when a speaker presupposes or relies upon the claim that must ultimately be proved in order to prove the claim: Fairies must exist because they are invisible creatures; and since no one has ever seen a fairy, they must exist because it is in their nature not be observed. A logical contradiction is an inconsistency. For example, opponents of capital punishment sometimes suggest that defenders of the death penalty who argue that execution is justified for murder as a matter of respect for the sanctity of life have fallen into a contradiction because they call for the death of someone to protect the "sanctity of life." An expert opinion would be just what the phrase suggests.

14. **The correct answer is (C).** Note the word *right* is italicized in the first sentence of the paragraph. The author is saying that this idea of a right can be only understood as the outcome of a balancing of demands. The smoker has an interest in smoking; the non-smoker has an interest in being free from smoke; so the question of which one actually has a *right* to have that *interest* protected depends upon which of those interests is considered to be more important. In some cases, the balance is easily struck; in other cases, it is difficult; but in all cases, the weighing, implicitly or explicitly, occurs. Choice (C) captures the essence of this thought. In the case of smoking, the interests of both parties must be taken into account. Choice (A) is a distraction. It is true the passage treats "rights," and

it is also true that our Constitution protects our rights; but the connection suggested by choice (A) is a spurious one. It fails to address itself to the logic of the author's argument. The same objections can be leveled against choice (B). The wording of choice (D) makes it wrong. The passage is concerned with the demands of the nonsmoker *to be free from* the smoke of others, not with whether someone chooses to smoke. Choice (E) is premature. At this juncture, the author is laying the foundation for the argument and is speaking about rights in general. The author reaches the conclusion with regard to smoking only at the end of the paragraph. (See discussion of the following question.) Choice (E) is wrong also because it mentions the "rights" of non-smoking persons. The whole question the author is addressing is whether the non-smoking person has a *right* as opposed to an interest or a mere claim.

15. **The correct answer is (C).** Here is where the author makes the general discussion of the balancing of interests to determine rights specifically applicable to the question of smoking. A smoker will have a *right* to smoke when and where that interest outweighs the interests of those who object, and choice (C) provides a pretty clear statement of this conclusion. Choice (A) overstates the author's case. While it may be true that ultimately it will be some branch of the government that strikes the balance of interests, the phrase "chooses to allow" does not do justice to the author's concept of the balancing. The government is not simply choosing; it is weighing. Of course, since the balance may or may not be struck in favor of the smoker, choice (B) is incorrect. Choice (E) confuses the problem of enforcement with the process of

balancing. The passage leads to the conclusion that the balance must be struck. How that decision is later enforced is a practical matter the author is not concerned to discuss in this passage. Finally, choice (D), like choice (A), overstates the case. The smoker has an interest in being allowed to smoke, just as much as the non-smoker has an interest in being free from the smoke. A balance must be struck by giving proper weight to both. The author never suggests that the interest of the smokers can be completely overridden. Thus, for example, a smoker may have a more powerful interest in smoking than a non-smoker has in being free from smoke, if the non-smoker can—at some smaller cost—be protected from the smoke.

16. **The correct answer is (B).** The whole passage is to clear up a misunderstanding about the concept of a *right*. The author explains that the term is misused since most people fail to realize that the right is not absolute, but is qualified by the interests and claims of other persons. While it is true that this is not generally known, choice (A) is incorrect because the author's *strategy* in argument is to clarify that term, not merely to bring up facts to support a contention that is already well defined. Choice (C) also fails to describe the author's strategy. It is true that the author mentions hypothetical cases, but that is a detail, not the principal strategy. As for choice (D), though the author argues that smokers who claim an unqualified right to smoke are wrong, the author does not argue that they have fallen into contradiction. Finally, although the author argues that the general claim of smokers is ill-founded, the general claim under attack (smokers have a right to smoke) is

not an induction based on *empirical* evidence. A person who makes such a claim is not generalizing on observed instances (All swans I have seen are white…) but rather is making a conceptual claim.

17. **The correct answer is (B).** The stimulus material describes a situation in which a certain event (selling price) is contingent upon a single factor (number of bidders) and then compares two outcomes (two paintings) by contrasting two factors (bidders on two paintings). Similarly, choice (B) describes a situation in which a certain event (number shipped) is contingent upon a single factor (number of students) and then compares two outcomes (sales this year and last) by contrasting two factors (students last year and students this year).

18. **The correct answer is (D).** The author's argument is admittedly not a very persuasive one, but the question stem does not ask us to comment on its relative strength. Rather, we are asked to identify the form of argumentation. Here the author suggests an alternative explanation, albeit a somewhat outlandish one. Thus, choice (D) is correct. Choice (E) is incorrect because the claim about fresh air and the country is introduced as a causal explanation, not an analogy to the city. Choice (C) is wrong, for the author accepts the differential described by the report and just tries to explain the existence of the differential in another way. By the same token, we can reject both choices (A) and (B) since the author takes the report's conclusion as a starting point. Although the argument attacks the explanation provided by the *report* published by the Department of Education, it does not attack the *credibility* of the *department* itself. Further, though it dis-

agrees with the *conclusion* drawn by the report, it does not attack the way in which the *study* itself was *conducted*. Rather, it disagrees with the interpretation of the data gathered.

19. **The correct answer is (E).** The question stem asks us to find the one item that will not strengthen the author's argument. That is choice (E). Remember, the author's argument is an attempt (to be sure, a weak one) to develop an alternative causal explanation. Choice (A) would provide some evidence that the author's claim—which at first glance seems a bit far-fetched—actually has some empirical foundation. While choice (B) does not add any strength to the author's own explanation of the phenomenon being studied, it does strengthen the author's overall position by undermining the explanation given in the report. Choice (C) strengthens the author's position for the same reason that choice (B) does: It weakens the position that is attacked. Choice (D) strengthens the argument in the same way that choice (A) does, by providing some empirical support for the otherwise seemingly far-fetched explanation.

20. **The correct answer is (E).** Perhaps the most obvious weakness in the argument is that it oversimplifies matters. It is like the domino theory arguments adduced to support the war in Vietnam: Either we fight Communism now, or it will take us over. The author argues, in effect: Either we put a stop to this now, or there will be no stopping it. Like the proponents of the domino theory, the author ignores the many intermediate positions one might take. Choice (C) is one way of describing this shortcoming: The dilemma posed by the author is a

false one because it overlooks positions between the two extremes. Choice (B) is also a weakness of the argument: "Cold-blooded murder" is obviously a phrase calculated to excite negative feelings. Finally, the whole argument is also internally inconsistent. The conclusion is that we should allow nature to take its course. How? By prolonging life with artificial means. But the failure of an argument to cite an authority is not necessarily a weakness. To be sure, the argument is subject to criticism; but, in general, unless the argument is one that requires an authority (say, for some key detail), the failure to cite an authority is not a defect.

21. **The correct answer is (D).** We can summarize the information, using capital letters to represent each statement:

> If *P*, then *Q*.
>
> If *Q*, then *R* or *S*.
>
> If *R* or *S* and if *Q*, then *A*.
>
> If *R* or *S* and if not-*Q*, then not-*A*.

P represents "Paul comes to the party," *Q* represents "Quentin leaves the party," *R* represents "Robert asks Alice to dance," *S* represents "Steve asks Alice to dance," (and conversely *R* represents "Alice is asked by Robert to dance" and *S* represents "Alice is asked by Steve to dance"), and *A* represents Alice accepts. If we have not-*Q*, then we can deduce not-*P* from the first statement; thus, we have choice (D). Choices (A), (B), and (C) are incorrect since there is no necessity that Robert or Steve ask Alice to dance. Choice (E) is incorrect since this statement is different from our other statements and must be assigned a different letter, perhaps *X*. Notice that "Alice will accept . . ." tells us nothing about whether Alice leaves the party.

22. **The correct answer is (A).** The question stem has the following form:

> All *S* are *AP*. (All Students are Applicants.)
>
> Some AP are *AC*. (Some Applicants are Accepted.)
>
> Some *more S* are *AC*. (Some more Students are Accepted.)

Notice that choice (A) preserves very nicely the parallel in the conclusion because it uses the word "more." Thus, the error made in the stem argument (that some *more* students will be *accepted*) is preserved in choice (A): *more* apples will be *loaded*. Choice (B) has a valid argument form (All *S* are *J*; *X* is an *S*; therefore, *X* is a *J*), so it is not parallel to the sample argument. Choice (C) is not similar for at least two reasons. First, its conclusion is a recommendation ("should"), not a factual claim. Second, choice (C) uses one premise, not two premises as the sample argument does. Choice (D) would have been parallel to the sample argument only if the sample had the conclusion "some more applications must be acted upon." Finally, choice (E) contains an argument that is fallacious, but the fallacy is not similar to that of the question stem.

23. **The correct answer is (E).** The advertisement employs the term "more" in an ambiguous manner. In the context, one might expect the phrase "more flavor" to mean "more highly concentrated flavor," that is, "more flavor per unit weight." What the ad actually says, however, is that the sticks of Evergreen are *larger*, so if they are larger, there must be more *total* flavor. As for choice (A), it is possible to beat the ad at its own game: Want more flavor? Chew more sticks? As for choice (B), more highly concentrated favor means more flavor per stick, so

size is not important. As for choice (C), a bigger stick doesn't necessarily mean more flavor. And choice (D), of course, cuts to the heart of the claim: money or value. Choice (E), however, if anything, would add to the appeal of the ad: Do what most people do.

24. **The correct answer is (D).** Again, we remind ourselves that we are looking for the most reliable statement. Even the most reliable, however, will not necessarily be perfectly reliable. Here, choice (D) is fairly trustworthy. We note that the speaker is an expert and so is qualified to speak about wines. In choice (A), the speaker is making a judgment about something outside the expertise of a film critic. Also, in choice (D), there is no hint of self-interest—if anything, the speaker is admitting against a possible self-interest that American chablis is a better buy than French chablis. By comparison, choices (B) and (C), which smack of a self-serving bias, are not so trustworthy. Finally, choice (E) sounds like a statement made for dramatic effect and so is not to be taken at face value.

25. **The correct answer is (B).** The weakness in the argument is the fallacy of ambiguity. It uses the term "future" in two different ways. In the first instance, it uses the word "future" to mean that which is fixed and definite, that which must occur. But then comes the shift. The author subtly changes usage so that "future" denotes events that might, though not necessarily will, come to pass. As for choice (A), the author gives a good example of how one might very well be able to change the future. As for choice (C), the author is concerned to refute the idea of foreseeing future events, so it is not surprising that there is no attempt to explain the mechanism by which such

foresight is achieved. Choices (D) and (E) are incorrect because the fallacy is that of ambiguity, not of internal inconsistency (self-contradiction) nor circular reasoning (begging the question).

Section 3

Questions 1–6

This is a linear ordering set. We begin by summarizing the information for easy reference:

$O \ne$ 1st or 6th

$L \ne J$
$L \ne K$ } (We know that $L > M$, so this means L cannot be
$L \to M$ next to J or K in the line.)

1. **The correct answer is (D).** For this question, we simply check each choice against the initial conditions. On the ground that O does not finish first or last, we eliminate choice (C). On the ground that L cannot be next in line to either J or K, we eliminate choices (A) and (E). Finally, since L must finish immediately ahead of M, we eliminate choice (B). Only choice (D) satisfies all of the restrictions.

2. **The correct answer is (E).** We begin by processing the additional information:

   1 2 3 4 5 6
   J   *K*

   This places the L–M combination in positions 3 and 4, respectively (to avoid the J–L conflict). And O must be in position 2, with N in position 6:

   1 2 3 4 5 6
   J O L M K N

   This shows that only choice (E) is true.

3. **The correct answer is (C).** We begin by processing the additional information:

   1 2 3 4 5 6
   N L M

We put N in first because J, K, and O cannot be there. We know further that either J or K must be sixth, since O cannot finish last. But there are four possible arrangements using these restrictions:

1 2 3 4 5 6
N L M O J K
N L M O K J
N L M K O J
N L M J O K

4. **The correct answer is (D).** For this question, we test each arrangement against the initial conditions. We know that four of the five will be acceptable and that only one will not be acceptable. The exception is the correct choice. Choice (D) is not acceptable since we have the impermissible arrangement of J in second and L in third.

5. **The correct answer is (E).** For this question, we must treat each statement as providing additional information. As for choice (A), we get:

   1 2 3 4 5 6
   N J K O L M

   With J and K in 2 and 3, respectively, we must put L in 5 and therefore M in 6. But O must then be in 4, with N in 1. So there is only one possible arrangement using this information. As for choice (B), we have:

   1 2 3 4 5 6
   L M J K O N

   With K in 4, we must put the L–M combination in 1 and 2. This means that N finishes last with O in position 5. So, again, the statement guarantees only one arrangement. As for choice (C):

   1 2 3 4 5 6
   L M O J K N

With J and K in 4 and 5, L and M must be in 1 and 2 or 2 and 3. But they cannot be in 2 and 3, for this would require O to be first or last. So L and M must be in 1 and 2, N must be in 6, and O must be in 3.

As for choice (D):

```
1  2  3  4  5  6
   L     K
```

We can put M in fifth:

```
1  2  3  4  5  6
   L  M     K
```

And O is neither first nor sixth:

```
1  2  3  4  5  6
   L  M  K  O
```

And with J not next to L:

```
1  2  3  4  5  6
N  L  M  K  O  J
```

Now for choice (E):

```
1  2  3  4  5  6
   J     L
```

And we can put M on the diagram:

```
1  2  3  4  5  6
   J     L  M
```

But that's as far as we can go. O could be second or fourth, K first or second, with N in the remaining position.

6. **The correct answer is (D).** For J and K to be separated by exactly three runners, they must finish in 1 and 5 or 2 and 6, though not necessarily in that order. We test each:

```
   1    2   3   4   5    6
J/K  O   L   M  J/K  N
```

With either J or K in 1, L and M must be in 3 and 4, with O in 2 and N in 6.

```
   1     2   3   4    5    6
 N  J/K  O   L   M  J/K
```

With J or K in 2, L and M must be in 4 and 5 with N in 1 and O in 3. Now we are

looking for the answer choice that *cannot* be true. Choice (A) is true since O does not finish fourth. Choice (B) is true since only J, K, or N can finish last. Choice (C) is true since L finishes either third or fourth. Choice (E) is true since O in third means that either J or K is last. Choice (D) is not true, however: When O is second, N is sixth.

Questions 7–12

Here we have an ordering set that is not strictly linear; that is, the individuals are not aligned in a single file. We begin by summarizing the information:

$$(Q \,\&\, R) = 3$$
$$P < M$$
$$K < N$$
$$K < L$$
$$J = L$$

A moment's study will lead us to one or two further conclusions. If K is lower than L, then, of course, K cannot occupy the top floor. Further, since J and L occupy the same floor and since the fifth floor has only one room, J and L cannot occupy a floor higher than the fourth floor, which means that K cannot occupy a floor higher than the second floor. (Remember that Q and R must occupy the third floor.) With these preliminary conclusions in mind, we can turn to the questions.

7. **The correct answer is (A).** Since K must stay below J, J cannot occupy the first floor. Choice (A), as the exception, must be the correct answer. The other choices could be true, as illustrated by the diagram:

```
5 M/N        5 O
4 J L        4 M N
3 Q R   or   3 Q R
2 O          2 J L
1 K P        1 K P
```

8. **The correct answer is (C).** We begin by processing the additional information. With *M* entered on the second floor, we deduce:

5

4   *J L*

3   *Q R*

2   *M*

1   *P*

With *M* on the second floor, *P* must be on the first floor. Then, with floors 1, 2, and 3 occupied, *J* and *L* must occupy floor 4 because the fifth floor has only one room. This seems as far as we can go. We know that *K* must occupy either 2 or 1, but that is not very helpful. So we look to the choices. We see that choice (A) is definitely incorrect, since choice (C) is proved by the diagram. Choice (B) is possibly, though not necessarily, true. As we just noted, choice (D) is also only possible. Finally, choice (E) is also just a possibility, since *O* might also be on floor 5 or 2.

9. **The correct answer is (E).** We have the list of people, *J, K, L, M, N, O, P, Q, R*, and we eliminate people as first-floor occupants as follows. *Q* and *R* must occupy the third floor. *J* and *L* occupy a floor together above that of *K*. *M* occupies a floor above *P* and so cannot occupy floor 1. And the same reasoning applies to *N*. So we eliminate *J, L, M, N, Q*, and *R*, leaving *K, O*, and *P*.

10. **The correct answer is (B).** We begin by assimilating the additional information. With *M* on floor 4, we have:

5

4   *M*

3   *Q* and *R*

2   *J* and *L*

1   *K* and *P*

With *M* on 4, we must put *J* and *L* on 2, for that is the only floor above floor 1 that remains open and has two rooms. Then, *K* must be on 1 (below *L*) and *P* must be on 1 (to be below *M*). As for *N* and *O*, they must occupy floors 4 and 5, though not necessarily in that order.

11. **The correct answer is (B).** We know that *K* and *M*, if they are together, cannot occupy floor 3 (because of *Q* and *R*) nor floor 5 (which has only one room). Nor can *M* occupy floor 1. *K* must be below *J* and *L*, so it cannot occupy 4. The only floor for *K* and *M* together is 2.

12. **The correct answer is (C).** The additional information provided in choice (C) proves the following:

5   *N*

4   *J* and *L*

3   *Q* and *R*

2   *K* and *M*

1   *P* and *O*

With *K* on 2, *J* and *L* must be on 4 (since *L* must be above K). Then, since *K* is lower than *N, N* must occupy 5. Next, since *P* < *M, P* must occupy 1 and *M* must occupy 2. And this leaves only *O* to occupy the other room on 1. The other answers will not do the trick. As for choice (A), putting *P* on 1 does not force *J* and *L* onto a floor. They might occupy either 2 or 4. As for choice (B), putting *M* on 2 means that *J* and *L* will occupy 4 and that *P* will occupy 1, but this leaves several individuals unplaced. As for choice (D), see Question 10, above. Finally, placing *N* on the top floor does not place *J* and *K*, and that is critical to fixing a definite order.

Questions 13–18

Here we have a selection problem, and we begin by using a notational system to summarize the information:

(1) ~(N & T & U)

(2) ~(M & N & R)

(3) Q ≠ V

(4) V ⊃ [(M & S) v (M & U) v (S & U) v (M & S & U)]

(5) R = Q

(6) S ⊃ (N & V)

Perhaps (4) requires some clarification. The statement given in the problem structure is logically equivalent to the following: If V is selected, then either (a) M and S are selected or (b) M and U are selected, or (c) S and U are selected, or (d) all three are selected.

13. **The correct answer is (D).** If R appears, then Q must appear (5). And if Q appears, then V cannot appear (3). But if V does not appear, then S cannot appear (6). So choice (D) is the correct answer. As for the remaining choices, we could have:

    (A) R, Q, and M

    (B) R, Q, and N

    (C) R and Q

    (E) R, Q, and T

14. **The correct answer is (D).** There are four professors who must be accompanied by other professors: V (4), R and Q (5), and S (6). Every other professor, M, N, T, and U, can appear without the necessity of including any other professor.

15. **The correct answer is (B).** If S appears, then both N and V must also appear (6). And if V appears, then two of the three, M, S, and U, must appear. Since S is already included (by stipulation), we need choose only one of the pair M and U. Thus, at minimum, we have S, N, V, and either M or U, for a total of four.

16. **The correct answer is (B).** We handle this question by the process of elimination, checking each of the available choices against the restrictions established in the initial set of conditions. Choice (A) can be eliminated because it violates (2). Choice (C) violates (5) since Q is not there to accompany R. Choice (D) can be eliminated because we have S without N, in violation of (6). And choice (E) violates (5) because we have R without Q.

17. **The correct answer is (A).** This question, too, is solved in a manner similar to that used for the preceding question. But here we must check each choice against the initial conditions in an effort to add exactly one more professor to obtain a permissible grouping. Choice (A) can be turned into an acceptable grouping just by adding Q: M, R, T, and Q. Choice (B) can be eliminated since Q requires R (5), but N, M, and R cannot appear together (2). Choice (C) can be eliminated since S will require the addition of both N and V (6), two professors, not just one. Choice (D) can be eliminated since V requires the addition of two out of three from the trio M, S, and U (4). Finally, choice (E) is incorrect since R requires Q (5) and V requires other professors (4).

18. **The correct answer is (C).** Removing T from the group eliminates the violation of (1), without violating any other restriction. As for choice (A), removing N eliminates the violation of (1), but this places the group in violation of (6) (S without N). As for choice (D), removing U corrects the violation of (1), but the resulting group violates (4) because V is included without two out of three from the group M, S, or U. Finally, eliminating V runs afoul of (5).

Questions 19–24

With a set such as this, the main task is organizing the information. We will use a matrix:

Cars

	1	2	3	4	5
Meteor	C	C	D	D	C
Comet	D	C	C	D	D
Flash	D	C	D	D	D
Streak	D	D	C	C	D
Rocket	C	C	C	C	C

D = Deluxe   C = Coach

19. **The correct answer is (A).** This is seen to be true by our matrix. Three of the five trains use deluxe cars in the first position. The matrix shows that choice (B) is false since the ratio of deluxe to coach here is only one to four. Choice (C) is also seen to be false since the Meteor and the Rocket have coach cars in the fifth position. Choice (D) is proved false by a quick count. In a typical day, 12 deluxe cars and 13 coach cars are used. Finally, choice (E) is incorrect since the Rocket and the Streak together use only three deluxe cars, while the Flash and the Comet use seven deluxe cars.

20. **The correct answer is (C).** No train has deluxe cars in positions 2 and 3. As for choice (A), the Streak has deluxe cars first and second. As for choice (B), the Flash has deluxe cars first and third. As for choice (D), the Flash has deluxe cars third and fourth. And as for choice (E), the Flash also has deluxe cars fourth and fifth.

21. **The correct answer is (B).** If we know correctly that the second car of a train is a deluxe car, this establishes that train as the Streak—as shown by the matrix. As for choice (A), knowing the first car to be deluxe does not distinguish the Streak from the Comet or the Flash. As for choice (C), knowing the third car to be a coach car leaves open the possibility that the train might be the Comet, the Streak, or the Rocket. As for choice (D), although the Streak has deluxe as its first and fifth cars, this is also true of the Comet and the Flash. Finally, as for choice (E), the Streak has coach and deluxe in places 3 and 5, but this is also true of the Comet.

22. **The correct answer is (D).** As the matrix shows, the Meteor, the Comet, the Flash, and the Rocket all have coach cars as the second car. Only the Streak has a deluxe car in the second position.

23. **The correct answer is (C).** A quick look at the matrix shows that only one train, the Flash, has deluxe cars as the first and third cars of the train.

24. **The correct answer is (D).** Again, a quick glance at the matrix gives us the needed information. For the Streak, of the last three cars, only the fifth is a deluxe car. For the Meteor, two of the three last cars are deluxe cars. The same is true for the Comet. For the Flash, the last three cars are all deluxe cars, while for the Rocket, none of the last three cars is a deluxe car.

Section 4

1. **The correct answer is (B).** One of the striking features about the passage is that the author doesn't first produce a contention and then offer facts to support it. Rather, the author's method is to produce the facts and then ask what conclusions might be drawn. And that is the description offered by choice (B). Choice (A) is wrong for this reason, to wit, the author is not arguing for a single conclusion but rather working toward a conclusion by exploring data. Choice (C) is wrong for the same reason. To be sure, the

author does answer some objections along the way, but that is not the main purpose. As for choice (D), while the final paragraph does seem to be a sort of challenge, there is a lot more going on the passage than (D) suggests. And finally, choice (E) just misses the point entirely.

2. **The correct answer is (A).** This is an explicit idea question. How do we know the meteor is from Mars? Oxygen isotopes found in the group of meteorites match the analysis of the Martian atmosphere. The other choices all mention ideas from the passage but each proves something different. The other choices may be evidence of microorganisms, but not where they originated.

3. **The correct answer is (C).** In paragraph five, the author notes that odd shapes seems to be microfossils of bacteria but cannot rule out the possibility that the bacteria were introduced after the rock left Mars, that is, while it lay in Antarctica. Finding microfossils in Antarctica would tend to prove that the bacteria originated on earth.

4. **The correct answer is (E).** This is an explicit idea question. All of the ideas given are mentioned in the passage, but choices (A), (B), (C), and (D) all provide evidence that ALH84001 may shows signs of life. As for choice (A), the shapes that resemble bacteria suggest that bacteria once lived in the rock. As for choice (B), the PAHs, while possibly produced by inorganic processes, might have been produced by living matter. As for choices (C) and (D), the odd deposits suggest checmical processes. Choice (E), however, suggests only that that the rock came from Mars, not that it contains signs of extinct life.

5. **The correct answer is (B).** This an explicit idea question, and the passage specifically states that the carbonate deposits might have come from inorganic processes but seem more likely to have been deposited by a microorganism. Similarly, the PAHs are different from the biproducts of ordinary combustion but, admits the author, might conceivably be the result of inorganic reactions.

6. **The correct answer is (A).** This is a logical structure question that asks about the connection between the two ideas mentioned in the stem and the larger argument. Why does the author mention gravitation and space? Well, there are some shapes in the meteorite that seem to be bacteria or at least they have the right shape, but they're very, very small compared to any bacteria we actually know. So the author suggests that the unique conditions on Mars (weaker gravitational field) and the conditions in the rock (small spaces) might mean that the bacteria would be small.

7. **The correct answer is (D).** This is an application question. The author seems to incline toward the view that the scientific evidence is at least consistent with the possibility of life on Mars even if the passage does not affirmatively support the conclusion that life once existed on Mars. Of course, the author doesn't go so far as to say that the data prove the existence of life on Mars, but, on balance, that would seem to be the author's view.

8. **The correct answer is (C).** This is a main idea question. Choice (A) describes a point made in the selection (in the last sentence in the first paragraph), but that idea is not the overall or main point of the selection. The idea suggested by choice (B) is certainly one that is consistent with the overall tone of the passage, but again, the idea is not the main point of the selection. The author is not just con-

cerned with criticizing those who won't abandon their theories; he is more concerned with demonstrating that those theories are in fact wrong. And this is the idea mentioned by choice (C): the main point of the passage is that the popular theories are incorrect. Choices (D) and (E) are like choice (A). They mention ideas covered in the passage, but neither describes the main point of the passage.

9. **The correct answer is (A).** This is a further application question. Since the last paragraph deals with a recent report suggesting that previous assumptions about microwaves were incorrect, the author would probably go on to talk about the need for more research. Choice (B) is incorrect because the author is dealing with microwave radiation and there would be no reason at this point to compare it to other forms of radiation. Besides, the author made the comparison earlier in the passage. Choice (C) is incorrect because it overstates the case. There is no evidence to suggest that microwave radiation is so dangerous that it should be prohibited—just understood and regulated. Choice (D) is incorrect because clearly the author is concerned with new information about microwave radiation. He has already suggested that what we now believe is erroneous. Finally, choice (E) is incorrect because a discussion of the strategies used by various species to control hyperthermia would not follow logically from his remarks that microwave radiation has not been correctly understood. In any event, the discussion of such strategies early in the passage is intended to set the stage for the main point of the selection.

10. **The correct answer is (A).** In the lines indicated, the author states that it is possible that an organism could be cooked by microwave radiation (because the radiation penetrates into the core) before it even realizes its temperature is rising. The verb tense clearly indicates that the author is introducing a hypothetical possibility. Given the shocking nature of the example, we should conclude that he has introduced it to dramatize a point.

11. **The correct answer is (B).** In the first sentence of the second paragraph the author remarks that proponents of the generally accepted theory (which treats microwave radiation like other radiation) simply assumed that one type of radiation would have the same thermal effect as other types of radiation. Then the author goes on to demonstrate that this assumption is wrong. Thus, (B) is the best description of the error identified by the author. Certainly, there is no suggestion that the proponents of the accepted theory did special laboratory research, control group surveys, or causal investigation. As for choice (D), while the proponents of the accepted theory may have used deductive reasoning to reach their conclusion, this would not have been the main basis for their conclusions. (Note the wording of the question stem.)

12. **The correct answer is (E).** This is a tone question. The author gives facts and analyzes or discusses a problem, so the tone could be called scholarly or analytical. The author is clearly concerned that other scientists made an error in their assessment of the effects of microwave radiation. Choice (A) is incorrect because the tone is not conversational at all, but expository. Choice (B) is incorrect because although the author seems disturbed by the ignorance of the scientists, he is never disparaging. He is also never facetious or cynical, choice (C). Choice

(D) is close because the tone is scholarly, but (E) is the best choice because the author is more "concerned" than he is "noncommittal."

13. **The correct answer is (A).** This is a main idea question. The passage explains why microwave radiation is not like other radiation and why it is therefore dangerous to warm-blooded species. Since it was until recently assumed that microwave radiation was like other radiation, the author is concerned with pointing out the weaknesses of this theory.

14. **The correct answer is (E).** This is an explicit idea question. Choice (A) is mentioned in the first paragraph, choice (B) is mentioned in the third paragraph, choice (C) is mentioned in the first paragraph, and choice (D) is mentioned in the second paragraph. Nowhere, however, does the author mention the dangers of microwave ovens.

15. **The correct answer is (B).** This is a main idea question. In the very first paragraph, the author presents the distinction between unlabeled and prohibited uses and then proceeds to develop the important implications of the distinction. Choice (B) correctly describes this form of argument. Choice (A) must be incorrect since no theory is cited for refutation. Choice (C) is incorrect since no opponent is mentioned. Choice (D) can be eliminated since there is no evidence that the practice of unlabeled uses is a recent development. Choice (E) can be eliminated for either of two reasons. First, if one interprets "error" here to mean the practice of forbidden uses, then that is not the main point of the argument. Or if one interprets "error" to mean the conflating of unlabeled with prohibited uses, then choice (E) is eliminated because "condemn" is inappropriate. The

author may wish to correct a misconception, but that is not the wording of choice (E). Moreover, the method he uses to accomplish that end is drawing a distinction. Thus, choice (B) stands as correct.

16. **The correct answer is (C).** This is an explicit idea question. The reference we need is to be found in paragraph 1. There the author explains that he uses the term "unlabeled use" to refer to any medically valuable use of an already approved drug that has not yet been specifically recognized by the FDA. Choice (A) is incorrect because this is a prohibited use, as that term is used in the text. Choice (B) is incorrect because an unlabeled use is one that was not considered when the drug was originally labeled. It is one discovered later, not one proposed, tested, and rejected. Choice (D) is incorrect because the author would term this use a labeled use. Finally, choice (E) is incorrect since this refers to research designed to determine whether a drug has labeled uses because it meets the legal standard of substantial evidence of such uses.

17. **The correct answer is (C).** This is an inference question that requires that we collate information from two parts of the passage. In paragraph 2, the author refers to physicians who persist in prohibited uses for one of two reasons: ignorance or refusal to accept evidence. Then, in paragraph 3, the author refers to physicians who use drugs in violation of labeling instructions as either uninformed or intransigent. The parallelism here tells us that the intransigent physician is the one who rejects the evidence that the drug is ineffective. This is neatly captured by choice (C). Choice (A) is incorrect since the intransigent physician prescribes the drug in violation of the labeling provision because he or she be-

lieves that the drug is effective. Choice (B) is incorrect, for this would be a physician who is anything but intransigent. As for choice (D), an intransigent physician might take such actions, but this is not the defining characteristic of an intransigent physician. Finally, choice (E) can be eliminated since the author specifically expresses reservations as to whether such behavior is illegal.

18. **The correct answer is (A).** This is an explicit idea question. The danger that a medical benefit might be otherwise denied a patient during the period between the discovery of a new use and its approval is mentioned in paragraph 3 as a reason for allowing unlabeled uses. So both choices (B) and (C) receive explicit mention. Choice (D) is mentioned in paragraph 1: The use may never be researched. Finally, choice (E) is also mentioned in that paragraph as a further justification for the practice. Choice (A) is incorrect since the author never relates cost to unlabeled uses.

19. **The correct answer is (E).** This is an application question, and we must find the statement that is most likely to be acceptable to the author. Choice (E) would likely be embraced by the author since he explains in the first paragraph that unlabeled uses are created by the time lag between the discovery of the use and the accumulation of data needed to prove that use. Choice (A) is an attractive answer, but it fails upon careful reading. The distinction referred to there is that between approved and unlabeled uses. The distinction that the author attempts to draw is between two types of unapproved uses: unlabeled and prohibited. This is the distinction that has been blurred, says the author, not the distinction between approved and unlabeled.

Choice (B) is incorrect for the same reason. The blurred distinction is between unlabeled and prohibited uses (both types of unapproved uses), not between approved and unlabeled uses. Choice (C) is incorrect since the distinction between unlabeled and approved uses is a matter of practice, not categorization. The unlabeled use exists because a physician uses the drug in a beneficial but not yet approved way, not because the physician or government decides that the use is unlabeled versus approved. Choice (D) is incorrect since the author calls for caution in unlabeled use in the final paragraph.

20. **The correct answer is (A).** This is an attitude question. In our discussion of Question 18, above, we mentioned several points in the passage that argue for the value of unlabeled uses. But the author's support for this practice is not unqualified. He does recognize the value of FDA regulation. His attitude toward the practice is one of acceptance, as suggested by choice (A). Choice (B) is incorrect because the author argues for the practice, given the strictness of the FDA regulations. Choice (C) is incorrect since the author does not imply that unlabeled use is illegal (as opposed to the disapproved use). Choice (D) is incorrect because it overstates the case. Though the author sees the value of unlabeled uses, the practice receives only a qualified endorsement. Finally, choice (E) must be incorrect because the author sees unlabeled use as a practice inherent in the regulatory framework.

21. **The correct answer is (E).** This is a main idea question, and the main idea of this passage, already discussed at some length, is neatly summarized by choice (E). Choice (B) is surely the second-best answer, but choice (B) must fail by com-

parison to choice (E) because choice (B) is too narrow. To be sure, one point the author makes is that the physician who prescribes unlabeled uses should not be subject to legal liability, but that is only part of the argument. That recommendation depends upon the distinction between the two types of unapproved uses. Choice (E) makes reference to this additional point. Notice also that in a way choice (B) is included in choice (E), so it is broad enough to describe the overall point of the author. Choice (A) is incorrect since the author is cautioning against overzealous enforcement of laws against unlabeled uses. Choice (C) is incorrect because it is never mentioned in the passage. Finally, choice (D) is incorrect, for this is at best a minor part of the argument.

22. **The correct answer is (B).** This is a main idea question. The author begins by acknowledging that there exists an actual differential between the earnings of whites and blacks, but then the author moves quickly to block the automatic presupposition that this is attributable to "racial discrimination in employment." The author then examines the effect of various productivity variables on the differentials between black and white men and between black and white women, with particular emphasis on the latter. The conclusion of the argument is that there is little difference in the adjusted earnings of black and white women, and the reason for this is the overpowering influence of *sexual* discrimination. Choice (B) captures this analysis. Choice (A) is incorrect since the author's primary focus is the black woman. He studies workers who are both black and female by comparing them with white female work-

ers. The differentials between men and women generally are only incidentally related to this analysis. Choice (C) fails because this is a subordinate level of argumentation. To be sure, the author does introduce productivity factors to adjust actual earnings, but that is so he can better evaluate the effects of discrimination. Choice (D) is incorrect since no history is offered aside from casual references to distribution of workers. Finally, choice (E) is incorrect since the author makes no such recommendations.

23. **The correct answer is (E).** This is an explicit idea question, the answer to which is found in paragraphs 1 and 2. There the author states that the actual ratio is not an accurate measure of discrimination in *employment* because it fails to take account of productivity factors. Choice (A) is incorrect because of the word "include"—the gross ratio fails to *adjust* for distribution. Choice (B) is not mentioned and so cannot be an answer to a question that begins with the phrase "According to the passage …" Choice (C), too, is never mentioned in the passage, and so it fails for the same reason, as does choice (D).

24. **The correct answer is (E).** This is an explicit detail question, and our needed reference is the third paragraph. That paragraph gives us comparisons or ratios of earnings by black men to earnings by white men and of earnings by black women to earnings by white women. Notice that the comparisons are relative. We never get actual dollar amounts, nor do we get comparisons between women and men. Choice (E) recognizes that the only conclusion that can be drawn on that basis is that the differential between black and white women is less

than the differential between black and white men. The first is a difference of only 2 to 5 percent (before adjustment for productivity factors), while the second is about 20 percent (before adjustment). Choices (A), (C), and (D) can be eliminated on the ground that no such male/female comparison is possible. Choice (B) can be eliminated since no such information is supplied.

25. **The correct answer is (A).** This is a logical structure question. The author states that there are two explanations to be considered: (1) black men are found in jobs characterized by greater discrimination, and (2) sexual discrimination renders insignificant the racial discrimination against black women. But each of these could be true since both could contribute to the phenomenon being studied. There is only an empirical, not a logical, connection between the two; that is, the extent to which each does have explanatory power is a matter of fact. On this ground, we can eliminate every other answer choice.

26. **The correct answer is (C).** This is a tone question, and the best description of the treatment of the subject matter is provided by choice (C). Choice (A) can be eliminated, for the treatment, while confident, is not offensive. Choice (B) can be eliminated for the same reason. Choice (D) is incorrect since there is nothing tentative or inconclusive about the treatment. To acknowledge that one is unable to determine which of two competing theories is preferable is not to be inconclusive or tentative. Finally, though some readers may find in the author's discussion reason for hope or optimism, we cannot say that the author himself shows us these attitudes.

27. **The correct answer is (A).** This is an application question. What would happen if sexual discrimination against women were no longer a factor? On the assumption that the second hypothesis is correct, racial discrimination for women is not a significant factor because it is overpowered by sexual discrimination. The author acknowledges the existence of racial discrimination, so elimination of the sexual discrimination should result in the manifestation of increased racial discrimination against black women (on the assumption that the second theory is correct). The result should be a greater disparity between white and black female workers, with white female workers enjoying the higher end of the ratio. This is articulated by choice (A). Choice (B) is contradicted by this analysis and must be incorrect. Choice (C) is inconsistent with the stipulation in the question stem. Finally, there is nothing to suggest that choices (D) or (E) would occur.

28. **The correct answer is (B).** This is a tone question. Notice that this question asks not about the tone of the presentation but about the author's attitude toward a particular subject. We must take our cue from the first paragraph, where the author refers to the efforts of "responsible employers." This indicates that the author is sympathetic to the situation of workers who are victims of discrimination. Choice (B) is the best way of describing this attitude. Choice (E) is much too strong, for concern is not anxiety. Further, choice (C) is much too weak, for the reference to "responsible employers" indicates the author is not indifferent. Choice (D), like choice (E), overstates the case. Finally, choice (A) is incorrect since the author offers no apology.

Section 5

1. **The correct answer is (B).** This is essentially an analogy question. Argument from analogy is an important form of argument, and the LSAT has many different ways of determining whether or not a student can use that argumentative technique. In this question, we are looking for the tool that is most analogous to a rule-of-thumb moral principle. Our task is made easier by the string of adjectives that follows the blank. We need a tool that is useful in many situations, which rules out a tuning fork, choice (D), and an electrical generator, choice (C), both of which have highly specialized functions. Moreover, we need a tool that requires no special training, so we can eliminate choice (A). Finally, although a library book requires no special training, it has only one use—to be read. Though the knowledge it contains may be generally useful, the book itself, *qua* book, has only one use.

2. **The correct answer is (A).** The point of the passage is that a moral decision sometimes seems difficult because we are using moral principles that are too general. They work most of the time, but sometimes they are too abstract, and as a result, two or more of them give contradictory results. Choices (D) and (E) are wrong, then, for they confuse the value of abstract and particular principles. When a conflict arises, we need principles that are more specific, not more abstract, choice (D) and particularly choice (E). Choice (C) is a distraction; the medical character of the example was purely fortuitous and irrelevant to the author's point about moral reasoning. Choice (B) is edifying but hardly a logical completion of the paragraph. The author is not trying to explain advances in moral rea-

soning; he is explaining two different levels of moral reasoning available to us now.

3. **The correct answer is (D).** Let us use letters to represent the categories. "All effective administrators" will be *A*. "Concerned about welfare" will be *W*. "Are liberal" will be *L*. The three propositions can now be represented as follows:

   ❶ All *A* are *W*.

   ❷ All *W* are *L*.

   ❸ All non-*L* are not *A*.

   Proposition #3 is equivalent to "all A are not non-*L*," and that is in turn equivalent to "all *A* are *L*." Thus, choice (D) follows fairly directly as a matter of logic. Choice (A) is incorrect, for while we know that "all *A* are *L*," we would not want to conclude that "No *L* are *A*"—there might be some ineffective administrators who grant time off. They could be ineffective for other reasons. Choice (B) is incorrect for the same reason. Even though all effective administrators are concerned about their employees' welfare, this does not mean that an ineffective administrator could not be concerned. He might be concerned but ineffective for another reason. Choice (C) is clearly false given our propositions; we know that all effective administrators are liberal. Finally, choice (E) is not inferable. Just because all effective administrators grant time off does not mean that all the time granted off is granted by effective administrators.

4. **The correct answer is (C).** The weakness in Gerry's argument is that he assumes, incorrectly, that getting drunk is the only harm Clyde has in mind. Clyde could respond very effectively by pointing to some other harms of alcohol. Choice (A) would not be a good response for Clyde since he is concerned with Gerry's

welfare. The fact that other people get drunk when Gerry does not is hardly a reason for Gerry to stop drinking. Choice (B) is also incorrect. That other people do or do not get drunk is not going to strengthen Clyde's argument against Gerry. He needs an argument that will impress Clyde, who apparently does not get drunk. Choice (D) is perhaps the second-best answer, but the explicit wording of the paragraph makes it unacceptable. Gerry has been drinking the same quantity for fifteen years. Now, admittedly, it is possible he will begin to drink more heavily, but that *possibility* would not be nearly so strong a point in Clyde's favor as the *present* existence of harm (other than inebriation). Finally, choice (E) is irrelevant, since it is white wine that Gerry does drink.

5. **The correct answer is (B).** The point of the passage is that a meaningful comparison between the two systems is going to be difficult since the one is cheap in the short run but expensive in the long run, while the other is expensive in the short run and cheap in the long run. The only appropriate way of doing the cost comparison is by taking account of both costs—which is what choice (B) does. To take just the long-run costs would be to ignore the short-run costs involved, so choice (A) is wrong; and taking the short-run costs while ignoring the long-run costs is no better, so choice (C) is wrong. If choice (A) is wrong, then choice (D) also has to be wrong, and the more so because it is not even projecting operating costs. Finally, choice (E) is a distraction—the connection between diesel fuel and air pollution is irrelevant in a paragraph that is concerned with a cost comparison.

6. **The correct answer is (B).** One way of "making more money" other than raising the price of a product is to lower the size or quality of the product. This is what Vendo must have done. By doing so, they accomplished the equivalent of a price increase without actually raising the price. Choice (C) contradicts the paragraph that states that Vendo did not violate the letter of the instructions—that is, the literal meaning—though they did violate the intention. Choice (D) also contradicts the paragraph. Had Vendo forfeited the franchise, that would have been within the letter of the "either-or" wording of the instructions. Choices (A) and (E) require much speculation beyond the information given, and you should not indulge yourself in imaginative thinking when there is an obvious answer such as choice (B) available.

7. **The correct answer is (D).** The author's argument seems fairly weak. He introduces the example of the second university without explaining why we should consider that case similar to the one we are arguing about (except for size). This shows that the author is introducing an analogy—though not a very strong one. Choice (A) is perhaps the second-best answer. But it would be correct only if there were a *contention* that the author had introduced new evidence in support of the argument. He does not articulate a contention and then adduce evidence for it. Choice (B) is wrong because the author really has no solution to the problem—he wants to argue the problem does not exist. Finally, choices (C) and (E) must be wrong because the author never mentions a logical contradiction nor does he point to any ambiguity in his opponent's argument.

8. **The correct answer is (E).** Another deodorant might also give all-day protection. The ad claims that White Bear is the only deodorant that gives you *both* protection and scent—a vacuous enough claim since White Bear is probably the only deodorant with the White Bear scent. Of course, choice (C) is not affected by this point, since the White Bear Company may put its unique scent into many of its products. Choice (B) is also not inconsistent with the ad—that another product is more popular does not say that it has the features the ad claims for the White Bear deodorant. Choice (D) is not inconsistent because the chemical composition is merely "similar." But choice (E) is inconsistent: it's the same protection and the same scent.

9. **The correct answer is (D).** The easiest way to set this problem up is to draw a relational line:

PE   IP   EL   BE

Dislikes ——————————————→ Likes

We note that Clara likes Basic Economics better than anything else, which means she must like it better than Advanced Calculus. So even though Advanced Calculus does not appear on our line, since we know that Basic Economics is the maximum, Clara must like Advanced Calculus less than Basic Economics. So choice (C) can be inferred. But we do not know where World History ranks on the preference line, and since Introductory Physics is not a maximal or a minimal value, we can make no judgment regarding it and an unplaced course. Quick reference to the line will show that choices (A), (B), and (E) are inferable.

10. **The correct answer is (B).** We have seen examples before of the form of argument Holmes has in mind: "*P* or *Q*; not-*P*;

therefore, *Q*." Here, however, the first premise of Holmes' argument is more complex: "*P* or *Q* or *R* ... *S*," with as many possibilities as he can conceive. He eliminates them one by one until no single possibility is left. The logic of the argument is perfect, but the weakness in the form is that it is impossible to guarantee that all contingencies have been taken into account. Maybe one was overlooked. Thus, choice (B) is the correct answer. Choices (A), (C), and (E) are wrong for the same reason. Holmes' method is designed to answer a particular question—in this case, "Where did the body come from?" Perhaps the next step is to apply the method to the question of the identity of the murderer, as choice (E) suggests, but at this juncture, he is concerned with the preliminary matter of how the murder was committed. In any event, it would be wrong to assail the logic of Holmes' deduction by complaining that it does not prove enough. Since choices (A) and (C) are even more removed from the particular question raised, they, too, must be wrong. Finally, choice (D) is nothing more than a reiteration of Watson's original comment, and Holmes has already responded to it.

11. **The correct answer is (C).** Notice that the student responds to the professor's comment by saying, "That can't be true," and then uses the Duchess of Warburton as a counterexample. The Duchess would only be a counterexample to the professor's statement had the professor said that women cannot inherit the estates of their families. Thus, choice (C) must capture the student's misinterpretation of the professor's statement. What has misled the student is that he has attributed too much to the professor. The professor has cited the general rule of

primogeniture—the eldest male child inherits—but he has not discussed the special problems that arise when no male child is born. In those cases, presumably a non-male child will have to inherit. Choice (E) incorrectly refers to inheriting from a mother in discussing a case in which the woman inherited her father's estate. Choice (D) is wrong, for the student specifically mentions the conditions that make a child legitimate: born to the wife of her father. Choice (A) was inserted as a bit of levity: Of course, only men can *father* children of either sex. Finally, firstborn or not, a daughter cannot inherit as long as there is any male child to inherit, so choice (B) must be incorrect.

12. **The correct answer is (A).** The ends of law, according to legal positivism, are to be agreed upon—"accepted as a contingent matter." They are values that the community adopts; they are not handed down by God, nor are they dictated by logic. Choice (B) actually reverses the point. The legal positivist probably would say he does not claim these ends are the best for all modern legal systems. He does not want to commit himself to anything beyond a mere factual description of things as they are. The normative theory ultimately reduces to a question of practical politics—whatever succeeds. Choice (C) can be rejected because the question raised by the normative theory is what values the law ought to generally embody, not just what values the courts ought to promote. Choice (D) is incorrect because while it is perhaps true, it does not address itself to the *status* of the normative values: Are they universally held and dictated by logic? Are they given by God? etc. Choice (E) is similar to choice (D) in that it may be true simply as

a matter of fact, but, again, choice (E) does not address itself to the status of the values. It is true that the values are those the community chooses, but that such status is *selected* rather than dictated is not undermined because there is not complete agreement on the values. Whatever values are selected will be chosen by more or less unanimous agreement.

13. **The correct answer is (C).** The analogy to physical theory is highly suggestive. The physicist advances a theory that represents an improvement on existing theories, but he is aware that tomorrow another theory may be proposed that is more correct than his. So the legal positivist advances a descriptive theory—that is, a description of existing legal institutions—but new information or advances in theory may displace that theory. Choice (A) is directly contrary to the legal positivist's position that no one theory is uniquely correct. Choice (B) ignores the radical and complete divorce of description and normative recommendation upon which the legal positivist insists. Choice (D) just confuses the point of the analogy to physics. The author introduces the analogy to explain how the legal positivist views his theory—in the same way the physicist views his—not to compare the reliability of physics with jurisprudence. Choice (E) makes a mistake similar to that committed by choice (D).

14. **The correct answer is (C).** Choices (A), (B), (D), and (E) all give reasons why people outside the U.S. wouldn't be watching the Super Bowl: it costs money; it comes on too late; even soccer doesn't attract that many; and people outside of the U.S. don't know the game. Choice (C), however, is a reason to expect some interest in the game.

15. **The correct answer is (A).** The speaker says that there are two established theories: the arboreal model and the cursorial model. The newly discovered evidence supports a third explanation. As for choice (B), though the speaker does provide evidence, it is not adduced as a counterexample to a claim. As for choice (C), there is a new theory, but the speaker does not suggest that the existing theories are self-contradictory. And choices (D) and (E) are surely the weakest responses because there is nothing in the paragraph to support such conclusions.

16. **The correct answer is (C).** The conclusion of the argument is, in essence, that school lunches are healthful or at least not harmful. Choices (A), (B), (D), and (E) all contradict this conclusion. Choice (C), however, does not, and that is why it is correct. In fact, like so many right answers to this type of question (weakening), choice (C) seems to strengthen the argument: the obesity epidemic is partly caused by a decline in physical activity. So be particularly alert for choices like choice (C) that are, in fact, relevant but cut in the wrong direction.

17. **The correct answer is (E).** The speaker relies on a key element of Kant's ethical theory to reach a conclusion about the ethical treatment of animals. But is the theory applicable to animals? Choice (E) answers that question by saying that the theory, taken on its own terms, applies only to people. Choice (A) is perhaps the third-best answer, for it can be read to suggest that Kant's failure to consider the possibility somehow vitiates the use made of the theory by the speaker. But the fact that the original proponent did not see all possible implications of a theory doesn't mean that the theory itself does not have those implications. Choice (B) is a fairly weak answer, unless you try to read it as saying those who use animals for food and clothing are behaving unethically because they give offense to others, but that seems a fairly attenuated reading. Choice (C) is pretty obviously irrelevant to the question of whether the argument can be applied to animals. And choice (D) may be the second-best answer, because it suggests, at least, that animals don't think—they just eat. But to the extent that you want to use choice (D) to make that kind of argument (and there's nothing wrong with making a creative argument in school), in the testing environment, you should quickly see that choice (E) is the better, more direct route to the same conclusion.

18. **The correct answer is (E).** Remember that the correct answer to a question stem that asks for a further conclusion is likely to be the "safest" response available, that is, the answer that is most limited. And that is why choice (E) is correct. Choice (E) says only that animals sometimes mimic the behavior they see. By contrast, the other choices make very ambitious claims. Choice (A), for example, seems to use the limited evidence provided to build an entire theory of animal behavior, and choice (C) draws a conclusion about penguins in the wild based upon their behavior in a zoo.

19. **The correct answer is (A).** This item asks you to describe the exchange between the two speakers, and the most striking thing about Phil's response is that it is tantamount to saying, Well, you've solved one problem, but there are other problems that you haven't solved. Ordinarily, we require the opponent of a policy suggestion to show that the policy would cost too much to implement or result in other disadvantages that out-

weigh the benefits. As for choice (B), given the topic, it would seem fair to measure health in terms of the reported incidence of illness; and, in any event, Cary first proposes, at least implicitly, this as an appropriate measure. Choice (C) is perhaps the second-most attractive answer because it is true that Phil fails to offer a plan to solve his problem, but neither does Cary. So while in the real world, you would press Phil on this issue, in the testing environment, choice (A) is a better answer because it addresses the *exchange* between the two speakers. Choice (D) is an accurate description of Phil's response, but remember that the stem asks for a *weakness* in that response. And choice (E), like choice (D), is arguably true, but it is not clear that this is a weaknesses of the response.

20. **The correct answer is (E).** This is one of those test items that turns on a cute little twist of reasoning, and once you've found that insight, the answer is clear. The leader's response is meant to say that it is a mistake to admit a mistake— and that's choice (E).

21. **The correct answer is (D).** This item asks you to describe the exchange. Clifford reports on an experiment to test a proposition about dairy farming; Geneva argues that the result should be discounted because the conditions were unique. But Geneva's response is not really relevant because the project was an experiment designed to test the proposition. Choices (A), (B), and (E) contain suggestions that are probably true about dairy farming, but as statements, they don't describe the exchange. And choice (C) is wrong because Geneva does not necessarily believe that just any farmer (as opposed to the Dairy Project, whatever that might be) could achieve the same result given a similar setting.

22. **The correct answer is (A).** You might attack this item using a circle diagram. To show the possible relationships of three categories, use three overlapping circles:

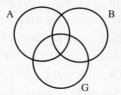

Now enter the information provided by the second statement:

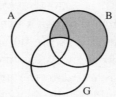

The area that is not logically possible given the second statement is shaded. Now enter the information provided by the first statement:

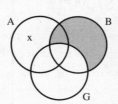

23. **The correct answer is (E).** This item asks you to identify a hidden assumption of the argument. The speaker says that neither set of customers will be entirely pleased and that the owners should reconsider their plans. The hidden assumption, perhaps obvious but nonetheless unstated, is that pleasing customers is good business. Choice (A) has some flavor of this idea but states the case too strongly. Choice (B) is pretty much a non-answer, since the particular type of cooking is not relevant. Choice (C) is a judgment not made by the speaker. And choice (D), like choice (A), overstates the case.

24. **The correct answer is (B).** This is a somewhat unusual question in that the stimulus material involves a cute—and peculiar—twist of reasoning: Why would the analyst use sales of men's suits to assess the economy? Choice (B) provides the answer: sales of men's suits are correlated not so much with fashion trends as with underlying financial cycles. Choice (A), if anything, weakens the argument by suggesting the lack of such a correlation. Choice (C), because it talks about women's fashion, is irrelevant. Choice (D) is somewhat related to the general topic but nonetheless irrelevant since the issue is the tie between suits and the economy. And to make choice (E) directly relevant to the argument provided would require a lot of backing and filling—a sure sign that it is not the correct answer to a test question.

WRITING SAMPLE

Following are two responses to the Writing Sample prompt, one in favor of the first option and the other in favor of the second option. These responses are not necessarily Pulitzer Prize winning essays, but remember, they're not supposed to be. The objective, as developed in Chapter 8, is to write something that is serviceable. You'll notice how these responses fit the model developed in Chapter 8.

Sample Response for Option One

Given her objectives, Joyce should enroll in the program at the American Institute in Paris. The program will give her the chance to improve her French and to learn about the routine of French daily life. Additionally, it will leave her free to visit some of the important points of interest in the country at a reasonable cost.

First, the Institute of Paris provides a program based in Paris, the heart of French culture. There Joyce can refine her accent and converse with people who live in a typical urban environment, including students from around the world. Additionally, the curriculum emphasizes French culture as well as language skills, and all of the classes are taught by native speakers.

In addition, the cost of the program is reasonable—only $500 for a full six weeks. The difference between that figure and the $1,400 for the program at the University of Reims will leave her $150 per week for living expenses, and she can probably find a youth hostel or similar accommodation in that range.

To be sure, the total cost of the Paris-based program is likely to be greater, but then that is largely a function of the greater cost-of-living of an urban area. Moreover, since she will already be based in Paris, many museums, historical sites, and cultural activities will be accessible by walking or public transportation, inexpensive modes of travel.

Of course, there is much to be said for a program based at a French university in the countryside. In this case, however, it seems that the Paris-based American Institute better suits Joyce's needs.

Sample Response for Option Two

Joyce should choose the summer program offered by the University of Reims. The intense program of study will give her ample opportunity to improve her language skills, and the location and cost will make it possible to enrich her studies by visiting various sites of interest.

It should be noted first that the program at Reims is an intensive learning experience. It is four weeks of study of French and French literature, and all of the classes are taught by University faculty. These classes are then supplemented by small group sessions led by French university students. The total time devoted to study is 8 hours per day, five days a week for the four weeks.

Second, the location and cost of the program at Reims are attractive. The $1,400 tuition includes housing and meals. Perhaps the student dormitory and cafeteria do not provide deluxe accommodations, but they should be serviceable. Furthermore, Reims is just a short train ride from Paris, so Joyce will be able to see not only a portion of the French countryside but a lot of the capital as well. Weekends are left open for exactly this type of travel.

There is no doubt that a summer stay in Paris would be exciting, but the cost of the American Institute is substantially higher. By the time Joyce includes the cost of housing and meals, it could run to $4,000 or $5,000, triple the cost of the program at Reims. Aside from the convenience of being physically situated in Paris, there seems to be little that Joyce could not just as well obtain by staying at Reims.

Answer Sheet

Use a No. 2 pencil only. Be sure each mark is dark and completely fills the intended oval. Completely erase any errors or stray marks. Start with number 1 for each new section. If a section has fewer than 30 questions, leave the extra answer spaces blank.

SECTION 1	SECTION 2	SECTION 3	SECTION 4	SECTION 5
1 Ⓐ Ⓑ Ⓒ Ⓓ Ⓔ	1 Ⓐ Ⓑ Ⓒ Ⓓ Ⓔ	1 Ⓐ Ⓑ Ⓒ Ⓓ Ⓔ	1 Ⓐ Ⓑ Ⓒ Ⓓ Ⓔ	1 Ⓐ Ⓑ Ⓒ Ⓓ Ⓔ
2 Ⓐ Ⓑ Ⓒ Ⓓ Ⓔ	2 Ⓐ Ⓑ Ⓒ Ⓓ Ⓔ	2 Ⓐ Ⓑ Ⓒ Ⓓ Ⓔ	2 Ⓐ Ⓑ Ⓒ Ⓓ Ⓔ	2 Ⓐ Ⓑ Ⓒ Ⓓ Ⓔ
3 Ⓐ Ⓑ Ⓒ Ⓓ Ⓔ	3 Ⓐ Ⓑ Ⓒ Ⓓ Ⓔ	3 Ⓐ Ⓑ Ⓒ Ⓓ Ⓔ	3 Ⓐ Ⓑ Ⓒ Ⓓ Ⓔ	3 Ⓐ Ⓑ Ⓒ Ⓓ Ⓔ
4 Ⓐ Ⓑ Ⓒ Ⓓ Ⓔ	4 Ⓐ Ⓑ Ⓒ Ⓓ Ⓔ	4 Ⓐ Ⓑ Ⓒ Ⓓ Ⓔ	4 Ⓐ Ⓑ Ⓒ Ⓓ Ⓔ	4 Ⓐ Ⓑ Ⓒ Ⓓ Ⓔ
5 Ⓐ Ⓑ Ⓒ Ⓓ Ⓔ	5 Ⓐ Ⓑ Ⓒ Ⓓ Ⓔ	5 Ⓐ Ⓑ Ⓒ Ⓓ Ⓔ	5 Ⓐ Ⓑ Ⓒ Ⓓ Ⓔ	5 Ⓐ Ⓑ Ⓒ Ⓓ Ⓔ
6 Ⓐ Ⓑ Ⓒ Ⓓ Ⓔ	6 Ⓐ Ⓑ Ⓒ Ⓓ Ⓔ	6 Ⓐ Ⓑ Ⓒ Ⓓ Ⓔ	6 Ⓐ Ⓑ Ⓒ Ⓓ Ⓔ	6 Ⓐ Ⓑ Ⓒ Ⓓ Ⓔ
7 Ⓐ Ⓑ Ⓒ Ⓓ Ⓔ	7 Ⓐ Ⓑ Ⓒ Ⓓ Ⓔ	7 Ⓐ Ⓑ Ⓒ Ⓓ Ⓔ	7 Ⓐ Ⓑ Ⓒ Ⓓ Ⓔ	7 Ⓐ Ⓑ Ⓒ Ⓓ Ⓔ
8 Ⓐ Ⓑ Ⓒ Ⓓ Ⓔ	8 Ⓐ Ⓑ Ⓒ Ⓓ Ⓔ	8 Ⓐ Ⓑ Ⓒ Ⓓ Ⓔ	8 Ⓐ Ⓑ Ⓒ Ⓓ Ⓔ	8 Ⓐ Ⓑ Ⓒ Ⓓ Ⓔ
9 Ⓐ Ⓑ Ⓒ Ⓓ Ⓔ	9 Ⓐ Ⓑ Ⓒ Ⓓ Ⓔ	9 Ⓐ Ⓑ Ⓒ Ⓓ Ⓔ	9 Ⓐ Ⓑ Ⓒ Ⓓ Ⓔ	9 Ⓐ Ⓑ Ⓒ Ⓓ Ⓔ
10 Ⓐ Ⓑ Ⓒ Ⓓ Ⓔ	10 Ⓐ Ⓑ Ⓒ Ⓓ Ⓔ	10 Ⓐ Ⓑ Ⓒ Ⓓ Ⓔ	10 Ⓐ Ⓑ Ⓒ Ⓓ Ⓔ	10 Ⓐ Ⓑ Ⓒ Ⓓ Ⓔ
11 Ⓐ Ⓑ Ⓒ Ⓓ Ⓔ	11 Ⓐ Ⓑ Ⓒ Ⓓ Ⓔ	11 Ⓐ Ⓑ Ⓒ Ⓓ Ⓔ	11 Ⓐ Ⓑ Ⓒ Ⓓ Ⓔ	11 Ⓐ Ⓑ Ⓒ Ⓓ Ⓔ
12 Ⓐ Ⓑ Ⓒ Ⓓ Ⓔ	12 Ⓐ Ⓑ Ⓒ Ⓓ Ⓔ	12 Ⓐ Ⓑ Ⓒ Ⓓ Ⓔ	12 Ⓐ Ⓑ Ⓒ Ⓓ Ⓔ	12 Ⓐ Ⓑ Ⓒ Ⓓ Ⓔ
13 Ⓐ Ⓑ Ⓒ Ⓓ Ⓔ	13 Ⓐ Ⓑ Ⓒ Ⓓ Ⓔ	13 Ⓐ Ⓑ Ⓒ Ⓓ Ⓔ	13 Ⓐ Ⓑ Ⓒ Ⓓ Ⓔ	13 Ⓐ Ⓑ Ⓒ Ⓓ Ⓔ
14 Ⓐ Ⓑ Ⓒ Ⓓ Ⓔ	14 Ⓐ Ⓑ Ⓒ Ⓓ Ⓔ	14 Ⓐ Ⓑ Ⓒ Ⓓ Ⓔ	14 Ⓐ Ⓑ Ⓒ Ⓓ Ⓔ	14 Ⓐ Ⓑ Ⓒ Ⓓ Ⓔ
15 Ⓐ Ⓑ Ⓒ Ⓓ Ⓔ	15 Ⓐ Ⓑ Ⓒ Ⓓ Ⓔ	15 Ⓐ Ⓑ Ⓒ Ⓓ Ⓔ	15 Ⓐ Ⓑ Ⓒ Ⓓ Ⓔ	15 Ⓐ Ⓑ Ⓒ Ⓓ Ⓔ
16 Ⓐ Ⓑ Ⓒ Ⓓ Ⓔ	16 Ⓐ Ⓑ Ⓒ Ⓓ Ⓔ	16 Ⓐ Ⓑ Ⓒ Ⓓ Ⓔ	16 Ⓐ Ⓑ Ⓒ Ⓓ Ⓔ	16 Ⓐ Ⓑ Ⓒ Ⓓ Ⓔ
17 Ⓐ Ⓑ Ⓒ Ⓓ Ⓔ	17 Ⓐ Ⓑ Ⓒ Ⓓ Ⓔ	17 Ⓐ Ⓑ Ⓒ Ⓓ Ⓔ	17 Ⓐ Ⓑ Ⓒ Ⓓ Ⓔ	17 Ⓐ Ⓑ Ⓒ Ⓓ Ⓔ
18 Ⓐ Ⓑ Ⓒ Ⓓ Ⓔ	18 Ⓐ Ⓑ Ⓒ Ⓓ Ⓔ	18 Ⓐ Ⓑ Ⓒ Ⓓ Ⓔ	18 Ⓐ Ⓑ Ⓒ Ⓓ Ⓔ	18 Ⓐ Ⓑ Ⓒ Ⓓ Ⓔ
19 Ⓐ Ⓑ Ⓒ Ⓓ Ⓔ	19 Ⓐ Ⓑ Ⓒ Ⓓ Ⓔ	19 Ⓐ Ⓑ Ⓒ Ⓓ Ⓔ	19 Ⓐ Ⓑ Ⓒ Ⓓ Ⓔ	19 Ⓐ Ⓑ Ⓒ Ⓓ Ⓔ
20 Ⓐ Ⓑ Ⓒ Ⓓ Ⓔ	20 Ⓐ Ⓑ Ⓒ Ⓓ Ⓔ	20 Ⓐ Ⓑ Ⓒ Ⓓ Ⓔ	20 Ⓐ Ⓑ Ⓒ Ⓓ Ⓔ	20 Ⓐ Ⓑ Ⓒ Ⓓ Ⓔ
21 Ⓐ Ⓑ Ⓒ Ⓓ Ⓔ	21 Ⓐ Ⓑ Ⓒ Ⓓ Ⓔ	21 Ⓐ Ⓑ Ⓒ Ⓓ Ⓔ	21 Ⓐ Ⓑ Ⓒ Ⓓ Ⓔ	21 Ⓐ Ⓑ Ⓒ Ⓓ Ⓔ
22 Ⓐ Ⓑ Ⓒ Ⓓ Ⓔ	22 Ⓐ Ⓑ Ⓒ Ⓓ Ⓔ	22 Ⓐ Ⓑ Ⓒ Ⓓ Ⓔ	22 Ⓐ Ⓑ Ⓒ Ⓓ Ⓔ	22 Ⓐ Ⓑ Ⓒ Ⓓ Ⓔ
23 Ⓐ Ⓑ Ⓒ Ⓓ Ⓔ	23 Ⓐ Ⓑ Ⓒ Ⓓ Ⓔ	23 Ⓐ Ⓑ Ⓒ Ⓓ Ⓔ	23 Ⓐ Ⓑ Ⓒ Ⓓ Ⓔ	23 Ⓐ Ⓑ Ⓒ Ⓓ Ⓔ
24 Ⓐ Ⓑ Ⓒ Ⓓ Ⓔ	24 Ⓐ Ⓑ Ⓒ Ⓓ Ⓔ	24 Ⓐ Ⓑ Ⓒ Ⓓ Ⓔ	24 Ⓐ Ⓑ Ⓒ Ⓓ Ⓔ	24 Ⓐ Ⓑ Ⓒ Ⓓ Ⓔ
25 Ⓐ Ⓑ Ⓒ Ⓓ Ⓔ	25 Ⓐ Ⓑ Ⓒ Ⓓ Ⓔ	25 Ⓐ Ⓑ Ⓒ Ⓓ Ⓔ	25 Ⓐ Ⓑ Ⓒ Ⓓ Ⓔ	25 Ⓐ Ⓑ Ⓒ Ⓓ Ⓔ
26 Ⓐ Ⓑ Ⓒ Ⓓ Ⓔ	26 Ⓐ Ⓑ Ⓒ Ⓓ Ⓔ	26 Ⓐ Ⓑ Ⓒ Ⓓ Ⓔ	26 Ⓐ Ⓑ Ⓒ Ⓓ Ⓔ	26 Ⓐ Ⓑ Ⓒ Ⓓ Ⓔ
27 Ⓐ Ⓑ Ⓒ Ⓓ Ⓔ	27 Ⓐ Ⓑ Ⓒ Ⓓ Ⓔ	27 Ⓐ Ⓑ Ⓒ Ⓓ Ⓔ	27 Ⓐ Ⓑ Ⓒ Ⓓ Ⓔ	27 Ⓐ Ⓑ Ⓒ Ⓓ Ⓔ
28 Ⓐ Ⓑ Ⓒ Ⓓ Ⓔ	28 Ⓐ Ⓑ Ⓒ Ⓓ Ⓔ	28 Ⓐ Ⓑ Ⓒ Ⓓ Ⓔ	28 Ⓐ Ⓑ Ⓒ Ⓓ Ⓔ	28 Ⓐ Ⓑ Ⓒ Ⓓ Ⓔ
29 Ⓐ Ⓑ Ⓒ Ⓓ Ⓔ	29 Ⓐ Ⓑ Ⓒ Ⓓ Ⓔ	29 Ⓐ Ⓑ Ⓒ Ⓓ Ⓔ	29 Ⓐ Ⓑ Ⓒ Ⓓ Ⓔ	29 Ⓐ Ⓑ Ⓒ Ⓓ Ⓔ
30 Ⓐ Ⓑ Ⓒ Ⓓ Ⓔ	30 Ⓐ Ⓑ Ⓒ Ⓓ Ⓔ	30 Ⓐ Ⓑ Ⓒ Ⓓ Ⓔ	30 Ⓐ Ⓑ Ⓒ Ⓓ Ⓔ	30 Ⓐ Ⓑ Ⓒ Ⓓ Ⓔ

Practice Test 3

SECTION 1

28 Questions • Time—35 Minutes

Directions: Below each of the following passages, you will find questions or incomplete statements about the passage. Each statement or question is followed by lettered words or expressions. Select the word or expression that most satisfactorily completes each statement or answers each question in accordance with the meaning of the passage. After you have chosen the *best* answer, blacken the corresponding space on the answer sheet.

When we are speaking casually, we call *Nineteen Eighty-Four* a novel, but in a more exacting context we call it a political fable. This requirement is not re- (5) futed by the fact that the book is preoccupied with an individual, Winston Smith, who suffers from a varicose ulcer, nor by the fact that it takes account of other individuals, including Julia, Mr. (10) Charrington, Mrs. Parsons, Syme, and O'Brien. The figures claim our attention, but they exist mainly in their relation to the political system that determines them. It would indeed be possible (15) to think of them as figures in a novel, though in that case they would have to be imagined in a far more diverse set of relations. They would no longer inhabit or sustain a fable, because a fable is a (20) narrative relieved of much contingent detail so that it may stand forth in an unusual degree of clarity and simplicity. A fable is a structure of types, each of them deliberately simplified lest a sense (25) of difference and heterogeneity reduce the force of the typical. Let us say, then, that *Nineteen Eighty-Four* is a political fable, projected into a near future and incorporating historical references (30) mainly to document a canceled past.

Since a fable is predicated upon a typology, it must be written from a certain distance. The author cannot afford the sense of familiarity which is induced (35) by detail and differentiation. A fable, in this respect, asks to be compared to a caricature, not to a photograph. It follows that in a political fable there is bound to be some tension between a (40) political sense, which deals in the multiplicity of social and personal life, and a sense of fable, which is committed to simplicity of form and feature. If the political sense were to prevail, the nar- (45) rative would be drawn away from fable into the novel, at some cost to its simplicity. If the sense of fable were to prevail, the fabulist would station himself at such a distance from any imaginary con- (50) ditions in the case that his narrative would appear unmediated, free or bereft of conditions. The risk in that procedure would be considerable: a reader might feel that the fabulist has lost interest in (55) the variety of human life and fallen back upon an unconditioned sense of its types, that he has become less interested in lives than in a particular idea of life. The risk is greater still if the fabulist projects (60) his narrative into the future: the reader can't question by appealing to the conditions of life he already knows. He is asked to believe that the future is another country and that "they just do (65) things differently there."

In a powerful fable the reader's feeling is likely to be mostly fear: he is afraid that the fabulist's vision of any life that is likely to arise may be accu-
(70) rate and will be verified in the event. The fabulist's feeling may be more various. Such a fable as *Nineteen Eighty-Four* might arise from disgust, despair, or world-weariness induced by evidence
(75) that nothing, despite one's best efforts, has changed and that it is too late now to hope for the change one wants.

1. In drawing an analogy between a fable and a caricature (lines 35–37), the author would most likely regard which of the following pairs of ideas as also analogous?

   (A) The subject of a caricature and the topic of a fable

   (B) The subject of a caricature and the main character in *Nineteen Eighty-Four*

   (C) The subject of a fable and the artist who draws the caricature

   (D) The artist who draws the caricature and a novelist

   (E) The minor characters in a fable and a photographer

2. Which of the following would be the most appropriate title for the passage?

   (A) A Critical Study of the Use of Characters in *Nineteen Eighty-Four*

   (B) *Nineteen Eighty-Four*: Political Fable Rather Than Novel

   (C) *Nineteen Eighty-Four*: Reflections on the Relationship of the Individual to Society

   (D) The Use of Typology in the Literature of Political Fables

   (E) Distinguishing a Political Fable from a Novel

3. Which of the following best explains why the author mentions that Winston Smith suffers from a varicose ulcer?

   (A) To demonstrate that a political fable must emphasize type over detail

   (B) To show that Winston Smith has some characteristics that distinguish him as an individual

   (C) To argue that Winston Smith is no more important than any other character in *Nineteen Eighty-Four*

   (D) To illustrate one of the features of the political situation described in *Nineteen Eighty-Four*

   (E) To suggest that *Nineteen Eighty-Four* is too realistic to be considered a work of fiction

4. The "tension" that the author mentions in line 39 refers to the

   (A) necessity of striking a balance between the need to describe a political situation in simple terms and the need to make the description realistic

   (B) reaction the reader feels because he is drawn to the characters of the fable as individuals but repulsed by the political situation

   (C) delicate task faced by a literary critic who must interpret the text of a work while attempting to describe accurately the intentions of the author

   (D) danger that too realistic a description of a key character will make the reader feel that the fable is actually a description of his own situation

   (E) conflict of aspirations and interests between characters that an author creates to motivate the action of the narrative

5. The author's attitude toward *Nineteen Eighty-Four* can best be described as

(A) condescending

(B) laudatory

(C) disparaging

(D) scholarly

(E) ironic

6. The author uses the phrase "another country" to describe a political fable in which

(A) political events described in a fable occur in a place other than the country of national origin of the author

(B) a lack of detail makes it difficult for a reader to see the connection between his own situation and the one described in the book

(C) too many minor characters create the impression of complete disorganization, leading the reader to believe he is in a foreign country

(D) the author has allowed his personal political convictions to infect his description of the political situation

(E) an overabundance of detail prevents the reader from appreciating the real possibility that such a political situation could develop

7. The author's primary concern is to

(A) define and clarify a concept

(B) point out a logical inconsistency

(C) trace the connection between a cause and an effect

(D) illustrate a general statement with examples

(E) outline a proposal for future action

In the art of the Middle Ages, we never encounter the personality of the artist as an individual; rather, it is diffused through the artistic genius of centuries
(5) embodied in the rules of religious art. Art of the Middle Ages is first a sacred script, the symbols and meanings of which were well settled. The circular halo placed vertically behind the head
(10) signifies sainthood, while the halo impressed with a cross signifies divinity. By bare feet, we recognize God, the angels, Jesus Christ, and the apostles, but for an artist to have depicted the Virgin
(15) Mary with bare feet would have been tantamount to heresy. Several concentric, wavy lines represent the sky, while parallel lines represent water or the sea. A tree, which is to say a single stalk with
(20) two or three stylized leaves, informs us that the scene is laid on earth. A tower with a window indicates a village; and should an angel be watching from the battlements, that city is thereby identi-
(25) fied as Jerusalem. Saint Peter is always depicted with curly hair, a short beard, and a tonsure, while Saint Paul has always a bald head and a long beard.

A second characteristic of this ico-
(30) nography is obedience to a sacred mathematics. "The Divine Wisdom," wrote Saint Augustine, "reveals itself everywhere in numbers," a doctrine attributable to the neo-Platonists who revived
(35) the genius of Pythagoras. Twelve is the master number of the Church and is the product of three, the number of the Trinity, and four, the number of material elements. The number seven, the most
(40) mysterious of all numbers, is the sum of four and three. There are the seven ages of man, seven virtues, seven planets. In the final analysis, the seven-tone scale of Gregorian music is the sensible em-
(45) bodiment of the order of the universe. Numbers require also a symmetry. At Chartres, a stained glass window shows the four prophets Isaac, Ezekiel, Daniel, and Jeremiah carrying on their shoul-
(50) ders the four evangelists Matthew, Mark, Luke, and John.

A third characteristic of this art is to be a symbolic language, showing us one thing and in inviting us to see an-
(55) other. In this respect, the artist was called upon to imitate God, who had hidden a profound meaning behind the literal, and who wished nature itself to be a moral lesson to man. Thus, every
(60) painting is an allegory. In a scene of the

final judgment, we see the foolish vir-
gins at the left hand of Jesus and the
wise at his right, and we understand
that this symbolizes those who are lost
(65) and those who are saved. Even seemingly insignificant details carry hidden
meaning: The lion in a stained glass
window is the figure of the Resurrection.

These, then, are the defining char-
(70) acteristics of the art of the Middle Ages,
a system within which even the most
mediocre talent was elevated by the genius of the centuries. The artists of the
early Renaissance broke with tradition
(75) at their own peril. When they are not
outstanding, they are scarcely able to
avoid insignificance and banality in their
religious works; and even when they are
great, they are no more than the equals
(80) of the old masters who passively followed the sacred rules.

8. The primary purpose of the passage is to

   (A) theorize about the immediate influences on art of the Middle Ages.

   (B) explain why artists of the Middle Ages
   followed the rules of a sacred script.

   (C) discuss some of the important features of art of the Middle Ages.

   (D) contrast the art of the Middle Ages
   with that of the Renaissance.

   (E) explain why the Middle Ages had a
   passion for order and numbers.

9. It can be inferred that a painting done in
   the Middle Ages is most likely to contain

   (A) elements representing the numbers 3
   and 4.

   (B) a moral lesson hidden behind the literal figures.

   (C) highly stylized buildings and trees.

   (D) figures with halos and bare feet.

   (E) a signature of the artist and the date
   of execution.

10. Which of the following best describes the
    attitude of the author toward art of the
    Middle Ages?

    (A) The author understands it and ad-
    mires it.

    (B) The author regards it as the greatest
    art of all time.

    (C) The author prefers music of the pe-
    riod to its painting.

    (D) The author realizes the constraints
    placed on the artist and is disap-
    pointed that individuality is never
    evident.

    (E) The author regards it generally as
    inferior to the works produced during
    the period preceding it.

11. The author refers to Saint Augustine in
    order to

    (A) refute a possible objection.

    (B) ridicule a position.

    (C) present a suggestive analogy.

    (D) avoid a contradiction.

    (E) provide proof by illustration.

12. All of the following are mentioned in the
    passage as elements of the sacred script
    EXCEPT

    (A) abstract symbols such as lines to rep-
    resent physical features.

    (B) symbols such as halos and crosses.

    (C) clothing used to characterize indi-
    viduals.

    (D) symmetrical juxtaposition of figures.

    (E) use of figures to identify locations.

13. The passage would most likely be found
in a

   (A) sociological analysis of the Middle
   Ages.

   (B) treatise on the influence of the Church
   in the Middle Ages.

   (C) scholarly analysis of art in the Middle
   Ages.

   (D) preface to a biography of Saint
   Augustine.

   (E) pamphlet discussing religious beliefs.

14. By the phrase "diffused through the artistic genius of centuries," the author most
likely means

   (A) the individual artists of the Middle
   Ages did not have serious talent.

   (B) great works of art from the Middle
   Ages have survived until now.

   (C) an artist who faithfully followed the
   rules of religious art was not recognized while still alive.

   (D) the rules of religious art, developed
   over time, left little freedom for the
   artist.

   (E) religious art has greater value than
   the secular art of the Renaissance.

The most damning thing that can be
said about the world's best-endowed and
richest country is that it is not only not
the leader in health status, but that it is
(5) so low in the ranks of the nations. The
United States ranks 18th among nations of the world in male life expectancy
at birth, 9th in female life expectancy at
birth, and 12th in infant mortality. More
(10) importantly, huge variations are evident in health status in the United States
from one place to the next and from one
group to the next.

   The forces that affect health can be
(15) aggregated into four groupings that lend
themselves to analysis of all health problems. Clearly the largest aggregate of
forces resides in the person's environment. Behavior, in part derived from
(20) experiences with the environment, is

the next greatest force affecting health.
Medical care services, treated as separate from other environmental factors
because of the special interest we have
(25) in them, make a modest contribution to
health status. Finally, the contributions
of heredity to health are difficult to judge.
We are templated at conception as to our
basic weaknesses and strengths; but
(30) many hereditary attributes never become manifest because of environmental and behavioral forces that act before
the genetic forces come to maturity, and
other hereditary attributes are increas-
(35) ingly being palliated by medical care.

   No other country spends what we
do per capita for medical care. The care
available is among the best technically,
even if used too lavishly and thus dan-
(40) gerously, but none of the countries that
stand above us in health status have
such a high proportion of medically dis-
enfranchised persons. Given the evidence that medical care is not that valu-
(45) able and access to care not that bad, it
seems most unlikely that our bad showing is caused by the significant proportion who are poorly served. Other hypotheses have greater explanatory
(50) power: excessive poverty, both actual
and relative, and excessive affluence.

   Excessive poverty is probably more
prevalent in the U.S. than in any of the
countries that have a better infant mor-
(55) tality rate and female life expectancy at
birth. This is probably true also for all
but four or five of the countries with a
longer male life expectancy. In the notably poor countries that exceed us in male
(60) survival, difficult living conditions are a
more accepted way of life and in several
of them, a good basic diet, basic medical
care and basic education, and lifelong
employment opportunities are an every-
(65) day fact of life. In the U.S., a national
unemployment level of 10 percent may
be 40 percent in the ghetto while less
than 4 percent elsewhere. The countries
that have surpassed us in health do not
(70) have such severe or entrenched problems. Nor are such a high proportion of
their people involved in them.

Excessive affluence is not so obvious a cause of ill health, but, at least
(75) until recently, few other nations could
afford such unhealthful ways of living.
Excessive intake of animal protein and
fats, dangerous imbibing of alcohol and
use of tobacco and drugs (prescribed and
(80) proscribed), and dangerous recreational
sports and driving habits are all possible
only because of affluence. Our heritage,
desires, opportunities, and our ma-
chismo, combined with the relatively
(85) low cost of bad foods and speedy vehicles, make us particularly vulnerable
to our affluence. And those who are not
affluent try harder. Our unacceptable
health status, then, will not be improved
(90) appreciably by expanded medical resources nor by their redistribution so
much as by a general attempt to improve
the quality of life for all.

15. Which of the following would be the most
logical continuation of the passage?

(A) Suggestions for specific proposals to
improve the quality of life in America

(B) A listing of the most common causes
of death among male and female
adults

(C) An explanation of the causes of poverty in America, both absolute and
relative

(D) A proposal to ensure that residents of
central cities receive more and better
medical care

(E) A study of the overcrowding in urban
hospitals serving primarily the poor

16. All of the following are mentioned in the
passage as factors affecting the health of
the population EXCEPT

(A) the availability of medical care services.

(B) the genetic endowment of individuals.

(C) overall environmental factors.

(D) the nation's relative position in health
status.

(E) an individual's own behavior.

17. The author is primarily concerned with

(A) condemning the U.S. for its failure to
provide better medical care to the
poor.

(B) evaluating the relative significance
of factors contributing to the poor
health status in the U.S.

(C) providing information that the reader
can use to improve his or her personal
health.

(D) comparing the general health of the
U.S. population with world averages.

(E) advocating specific measures designed to improve the health of the
U.S. population.

18. The passage best supports which of the following conclusions about the relationship between per capita expenditures for medical care and the health of a population?

(A) The per capita expenditure for medical care has relatively little effect on the total amount of medical care available to a population.

(B) The genetic makeup of a population is a more powerful determinant of the health of a population than the per capita expenditure for medical care.

(C) A population may have very high per capita expenditures for medical care and yet have a lower health status than other populations with lower per capita expenditures.

(D) The higher the per capita expenditure on medical care, the more advanced is the medical technology; and the more advanced the technology, the better is the health of the population.

(E) Per capita outlays for medical care devoted to adults are likely to have a greater effect on the status of the population than outlays devoted to infants.

19. The author refers to the excessive intake of alcohol, tobacco, and drug use in order to

(A) show that some health problems cannot be attacked by better medical care.

(B) demonstrate that use of tobacco and intoxicants is detrimental to health.

(C) cite examples of individual behavior that have adverse consequences for health status.

(D) refute the contention that poor health is related to access to medical care.

(E) illustrate ways in which affluence may contribute to poor health status.

20. The passage provides information to answer which of the following questions?

(A) What is the most powerful influence on the health status of a population?

(B) Which nation in the world leads in health status?

(C) Is the life expectancy of males in the U.S. longer than that of females?

(D) What are the most important genetic factors influencing the health of an individual?

(E) How can the U.S. reduce the incidence of unemployment in the ghetto?

21. In discussing the forces that influence health, the author implies that medical care services are

(A) the least important of all.

(B) a special aspect of an individual's environment.

(C) a function of an individual's behavior pattern.

(D) becoming less important as technology improves.

(E) too expensive for most people.

Nitroglycerin has long been famous for its relief of angina attacks but ruled out for heart attacks on the theory that it harmfully lowers blood pressure and
(5) increases heart rate. A heart attack, unlike an angina attack, always involves some localized, fairly rapid heart muscle death, or myocardial infarction. This acute emergency happens when the ar-
(10) teriosclerotic occlusive process in one of the coronary arterial branches culminates so suddenly and completely that the local myocardium—the muscle area that was fed by the occluded coronary—
(15) stops contracting and dies over a period of hours, to be replaced over a period of weeks by a scar, or "healed infarct."

In experiments with dogs, it was discovered that administration of nitro-
(20) glycerin during the acute stage of myocardial infarction consistently reduced

the extent of myocardial injury, provided that the dogs' heart rate and blood pressure were maintained in the normal (25) range. Soon after, scientists made a preliminary confirmation of the clinical applicability of nitroglycerin in acute heart attacks in human patients. Five of twelve human subjects developed some degree (30) of congestive heart failure. Curiously, the nitroglycerin alone was enough to reduce the magnitude of injury in these five patients, but the other seven patients, whose heart attacks were not (35) complicated by any congestive heart failure, were not consistently helped by the nitroglycerin until another drug, phenylephrine, was added to abolish the nitroglycerin-induced drop in blood pres-(40) sure. One explanation for this is that the reflex responses in heart rate, mediated through the autonomic nervous system, are so blunted in congestive heart failure that a fall in blood pressure prompts (45) less of the cardiac acceleration that otherwise worsens the damage of acute myocardial infarction.

It appears that the size of the infarct that would otherwise result from a (50) coronary occlusion might be greatly reduced, and vitally needed heart muscle thus saved, by the actions of certain drugs and other measures taken during the acute phase of the heart attack. This (55) is because the size of the myocardial infarct is not really determined at the moment of the coronary occlusion as previously thought. The fate of the stricken myocardial segment remains (60) largely undetermined, hanging on the balance of myocardial oxygen supply and demand that can be favorably influenced for many hours after the coronary occlusion. So it is possible to reduce the (65) myocardial injury during acute human heart attacks by means of nitroglycerin, either alone or in combination with phenylephrine.

Other drugs are also being tested (70) to reduce myocardial infarct size, particularly drugs presumed to affect myocardial oxygen supply and demand, including not only vessel dilators such as

nitroglycerin but also antihypertensives (75) that block the sympathetic nerve reflexes that increase heart rate and work in response to exertion and stress. Such measures are still experimental, and there is no proof of benefit with regard to (80) the great complications of heart attack such as cardiogenic shock, angina, or mortality. But the drugs for reducing infarct size now hold center stage in experimental frameworks.

22. According to the passage, the primary difference between a heart attack and an angina attack is that a heart attack

   (A) involves an acceleration of the heartbeat.

   (B) cannot be treated with nitroglycerin.

   (C) generally results in congestive heart failure.

   (D) takes place within a relatively short period of time.

   (E) always results in damage to muscle tissue of the heart.

23. In the study referred to in lines 25–28, the patients who developed congestive heart failure did not experience cardiac acceleration because

   (A) the nitroglycerin was not administered soon enough after the onset of the heart attack.

   (B) the severity of the heart attack blocked the autonomic response to the nitroglycerin-induced drop in blood pressure.

   (C) administering phenylephrine mitigated the severity of the drop in blood pressure caused by nitroglycerin.

   (D) doctors were able to maintain blood pressure, and thus indirectly pulse rate, in those patients.

   (E) those patients did not experience a drop in blood pressure as a result of the heart attack.

24. The passage provides information to answer all of the following questions EXCEPT

(A) What are some of the physiological manifestations of a heart attack?

(B) What determines the size of a myocardial infarct following a heart attack?

(C) What effect does nitroglycerin have when administered to a patient experiencing a heart attack?

(D) What are the most important causes of heart attacks?

(E) What is the physiological effect of phenylephrine?

25. It can be inferred from the passage that nitroglycerin is of value in treating heart attacks because it

(A) lowers the blood pressure.

(B) stimulates healing of an infarct.

(C) causes cardiac acceleration.

(D) dilates blood vessels.

(E) counteracts hypertension.

26. The author's attitude toward the use of nitroglycerin and other drugs to treat heart attack can best be described as one of

(A) concern.

(B) resignation.

(C) anxiety.

(D) disinterest.

(E) optimism.

27. It can be inferred that the phenylephrine is administered in conjunction with nitroglycerin during a heart attack in order to

(A) prevent the cardiac acceleration caused by a drop in blood pressure.

(B) block sympathetic nerve reflexes that increase the pulse rate.

(C) blunt the autonomic nervous system, which accelerates the pulse rate.

(D) reduce the size of a myocardial infarct by increasing oxygen supply.

(E) prevent arteriosclerotic occlusion in the coronary arterial branches.

28. The author is primarily concerned with

(A) explaining a predicament.

(B) evaluating a study.

(C) outlining a proposal.

(D) countering an argument.

(E) discussing a treatment.

STOP

END OF SECTION 1. IF YOU HAVE ANY TIME LEFT, GO OVER YOUR WORK IN THIS SECTION ONLY. DO NOT WORK IN ANY OTHER SECTION OF THE TEST.

SECTION 2

24 Questions • Time—35 Minutes

Directions: Each group of questions is based on a set of propositions or conditions. Drawing a rough picture or diagram may help in answering some of the questions. After you have chosen the *best* answer for each question, blacken the corresponding space on your answer sheet.

Questions 1–6

Ten pennants are to be hung side by side on a rope that will then be stretched parallel to the ground between two poles. The positions are numbered consecutively 1 through 10, starting at the left.

There are two green, two blue, three red, and three yellow pennants.

The two green pennants are next to each other.

The two blue pennants are not next to each other.

The three red pennants are next to each other.

A blue pennant is at one end of the rope, and a red pennant is at the other.

1. If the fourth and fifth pennants are green and if the ninth pennant is red, which of the following must be true?

   (A) A blue pennant is next to a green pennant.

   (B) A blue pennant is next to a red pennant.

   (C) Each blue pennant is next to a yellow pennant.

   (D) The sixth pennant is a blue pennant.

   (E) The sixth pennant is a yellow pennant.

2. If a blue pennant is in position 7 and a yellow pennant in position 8, which of the following positions must be a green pennant?

   (A) 3

   (B) 4

   (C) 5

   (D) 6

   (E) 7

3. If each blue pennant is next to a green pennant, then which of the following pennants must be yellow?

   (A) Fifth and sixth

   (B) Fifth, sixth, and seventh

   (C) Fourth, fifth, and sixth

   (D) Fourth, sixth, and seventh

   (E) Fourth, fifth, sixth, and seventh

4. If a yellow pennant is in position 9 and the yellow pennants are next to each other, which of the following must be true?

   (A) A blue pennant is in position 1.

   (B) A green pennant is in position 3.

   (C) A green pennant is in position 4.

   (D) A yellow pennant is in position 5.

   (E) A green pennant is in position 5.

5. If yellow pennants are in positions 3 and 5, all of the following must be true EXCEPT

(A) a yellow pennant is in position 4.

(B) a green pennant is in position 6.

(C) a green pennant is in position 7.

(D) each blue pennant is next to at least one yellow pennant.

(E) exactly one yellow pennant is not next to another yellow pennant.

6. If one green pennant is next to a blue pennant and the other green pennant is next to a red pennant, which of the following must be true?

(A) The first pennant is a red pennant.

(B) The first pennant is a blue pennant.

(C) The third pennant is a red pennant.

(D) A yellow pennant is flanked by blue pennants.

(E) A yellow pennant is flanked by yellow pennants.

Questions 7–12

A winery is conducting a tasting of seven wines: *J, K, L, M, N, O,* and *P.* Each wine will be tasted in succession according to the following conditions:

J must be tasted either third or seventh.

If *J* is tasted seventh, then *N* must be tasted fourth; otherwise, *N* is not tasted fourth.

If *J* is tasted seventh, then *L* is tasted sixth.

If *J* is tasted third, then *O* is tasted sixth.

N must be the third wine tasted after *K.*

7. If *L* is tasted fourth, which wine must be tasted third?

(A) *J*

(B) *K*

(C) *M*

(D) *N*

(E) *O*

8. If *M* is tasted immediately following *L,* which of the following must be true?

(A) *K* is tasted first.

(B) *L* is tasted second.

(C) *M* is tasted third.

(D) *P* is tasted fourth.

(E) *P* is tasted fifth.

9. *M* CANNOT be which wine in the tasting sequence?

(A) Second

(B) Third

(C) Fourth

(D) Fifth

(E) Sixth

10. Which of the following must be true?

(A) *J* is tasted earlier than *K.*

(B) *J* is tasted earlier than *L.*

(C) *K* is tasted earlier than *L.*

(D) *K* is tasted earlier than *O.*

(E) *M* is tasted earlier than *O.*

11. If *P* is tasted earlier than *N* but later than *O,* which of the following must be true?

(A) *O* is tasted first.

(B) *L* is tasted third.

(C) *O* is tasted third.

(D) *M* is tasted fifth.

(E) *P* is tasted fifth.

12. If *M* is the second wine tasted after *P,* in how many different orders can the wines be tasted?

(A) 1

(B) 2

(C) 3

(D) 4

(E) 5

Questions 13–18

The principal of a high school is selecting a committee of students to attend an annual student leadership conference. The students eligible for selection are P, Q, R, S, T, U, and V. The committee must be selected in accordance with the following considerations:

If V is selected, R must be selected.

If both R and Q are selected, then P cannot be selected.

If both Q and P are selected, then T cannot be selected.

If P is selected, then either S or U must be selected; but S and U cannot both be selected.

Either S or T must be selected, but S and T cannot both be selected.

13. If neither S nor U is selected, what is the largest number of students who can be selected for the conference?

(A) 2

(B) 3

(C) 4

(D) 5

(E) 6

14. If both P and V are selected, what is the smallest number of students who can be selected for the conference?

(A) 3

(B) 4

(C) 5

(D) 6

(E) 7

15. If both P and U are selected, which of the following must be true?

(A) Q must be selected.

(B) S must be selected.

(C) T must be selected.

(D) R cannot be selected.

(E) V cannot be selected.

16. Which of the following is an acceptable delegation to the conference if only three students are selected?

(A) P, Q, and S

(B) P, Q, and T

(C) P, R, and V

(D) R, S, and T

(E) R, S, and U

17. If both P and T are chosen, which of the following CANNOT be true?

(A) The committee consists of three students.

(B) The committee consists of four students.

(C) The committee consists of five students.

(D) U is not chosen.

(E) V is not chosen.

18. If U and three other students are selected, which of the following groups can accompany U?

(A) P, Q, and T

(B) P, R, and T

(C) P, Q, and V

(D) P, V, and S

(E) R, S, and V

Questions 19–24

A musical scale contains seven notes—J, K, L, M, N, O, and Q—ranked from first (lowest) to seventh (highest), though not necessarily in that order.

The first note of the scale is O, and the last note of the scale is Q.

L is lower than M.

N is lower than J.

K is somewhere between J and M on the scale.

19. If *N* is the fifth note on the scale, which of the following must be true?

    (A) *J* is the sixth note, and *M* is the fourth note.

    (B) *K* is the fourth note, and *L* is the third note.

    (C) *M* is the third note, and *L* is the second note.

    (D) *M* is the fourth note, and *L* is the third note.

    (E) *L* is the fourth note, and *J* is the second note.

20. If *M* is the sixth note, then which of the following is a complete and accurate listing of the positions that could be occupied by *J* and *N*, respectively?

    (A) Fifth and third

    (B) Fourth and third

    (C) Third and second

    (D) Fourth and third or third and second

    (E) Third and second or fifth and third

21. If there are exactly two notes on the scale between *K* and *N*, which of the following must be true?

    (A) *K* is the fifth note on the scale.

    (B) *L* is between *J* and *K* on the scale.

    (C) *M* is the sixth note on the scale.

    (D) *M* is above *J* on the scale.

    (E) *L* and *M* are separated by exactly one note on the scale.

22. Which of the following CANNOT be true?

    (A) *J* is the fourth note on the scale.

    (B) *J* is the third note on the scale.

    (C) *K* is the third note on the scale.

    (D) *K* is the fourth note on the scale.

    (E) *K* is the fifth note on the scale.

23. If *N* and *O* are separated by exactly two notes, which of the following must be true?

    (A) *J* is the sixth note on the scale.

    (B) *L* is the fifth note on the scale.

    (C) *K* is below *M* on the scale.

    (D) *K* is between *N* and *O* on the scale.

    (E) *M* is above *N* on the scale.

24. If *N* is one note above *L* on the scale, what is the number of logically possible orderings of all seven notes from the bottom of the scale to the top of the scale?

    (A) 1

    (B) 2

    (C) 3

    (D) 4

    (E) 5

STOP

END OF SECTION 2. IF YOU HAVE ANY TIME LEFT, GO OVER YOUR WORK IN THIS SECTION ONLY. DO NOT WORK IN ANY OTHER SECTION OF THE TEST.

SECTION 3

24 Questions • Time—35 Minutes

Directions: In this section, the questions ask you to analyze and evaluate the reasoning in short paragraphs or passages. For some questions, all of the answer choices may conceivably be answers to the question asked. You should select the *best* answer to the question; that is, an answer that does not require you to make assumptions that violate commonsense standards by being implausible, redundant, irrelevant, or inconsistent. After you have chosen the *best* answer, blacken the corresponding space on the answer sheet.

Questions 1 and 2

On his trip to the People's Republic of China, a young U.S. diplomat of very subordinate rank embarrassed himself by asking a Chinese official how it was that Orientals managed to be so inscrutable. The Chinese official smiled and then gently responded that he preferred to think of the inscrutability of his race in terms of a want of perspicacity in Occidentals.

1. Which of the following best describes the point of the comment made by the Chinese official?

   (A) It is not merely the Chinese but all Oriental people who are inscrutable.

   (B) Most Americans fail to understand Chinese culture.

   (C) What one fails to perceive may be attributable to carelessness in observation rather than obscurity inherent in the object.

   (D) Since the resumption of diplomatic relations between the United States and Communist China, many older Chinese civil servants have grown to distrust the Americans.

   (E) If the West and the East are ever to truly understand one another, there will have to be considerable cultural exchange between the two.

2. Which of the following best characterizes the attitude and response of the Chinese official?

   (A) Angry
   (B) Fearful
   (C) Emotional
   (D) Indifferent
   (E) Compassionate

3. People waste a surprising amount of money on gadgets and doodads that they hardly ever use. For example, my brother spent $25 on an electric ice-cream maker two years ago, but he has used it on only three occasions. Yet, he insists that regardless of the number of times he actually uses the ice-cream maker, the investment was a good one because _____.

Which of the following best completes the thought of the paragraph?

(A) the price of ice cream will go up in the future

(B) he has purchased the ice-cream maker for the convenience of having it available if and when he needs it

(C) in a society that is oriented toward consumer goods, one should take every opportunity to acquire things

(D) today $25 is not worth what it was two years ago on account of the inflation rate

(E) by using it so infrequently, he has conserved a considerable amount of electrical energy

4. A poet was once asked to interpret a particularly obscure passage in one of his poems. He responded, "When I wrote that verse, only God and I knew the meaning of that passage. Now, only God knows."

What is the point of the poet's response?

(A) God is infinitely wiser than humans.

(B) Most humans are unable to understand poetry.

(C) Poets rarely know the source of their own creative inspiration.

(D) A great poem is inspired by the muse.

(E) He has forgotten what he had originally meant by the verse.

5. A recent survey by the economics department of an Ivy League university revealed that increases in the salaries of preachers are accompanied by increases in the nationwide average of rum consumption. From 1965 to 1970, preachers' salaries increased on the average of 15 percent and rum sales grew by 14.5 percent. From 1970 to 1975, average preachers' salaries rose by 17 percent and rum sales by 17.5 percent. From 1975 to 1980, rum sales expanded by only 8 percent and average preachers' salaries also grew by only 8 percent.

Which of the following is the most likely explanation for the findings cited in the paragraph?

(A) When preachers have more disposable income, they tend to allocate that extra money to alcohol.

(B) When preachers are paid more, they preach longer; and longer sermons tend to drive people to drink.

(C) Since there were more preachers in the country, there were also more people; and a larger population will consume greater quantities of liquor.

(D) The general standard of living increased from 1965 to 1980, which accounts for both the increase in rum consumption and preachers' average salaries.

(E) A consortium of rum importers carefully limited the increases in imports of rum during the test period cited.

6. Since all four-door automobiles I have repaired have eight-cylinder engines, all four-door automobiles must have eight-cylinder engines.

The author argues on the basis of

(A) special training.

(B) generalization.

(C) syllogism.

(D) ambiguity.

(E) deduction.

7. Two people, one living in Los Angeles, the other living in New York City, carried on a lengthy correspondence by mail. The subject of the exchange was a dispute over certain personality traits of Winston Churchill. After some two dozen letters, the Los Angeles resident received the following note from the New York City correspondent: "It seems you were right all along. Yesterday I met someone who actually knew Sir Winston, and he confirmed your opinion."

The two people could have been arguing on the basis of all of the following EXCEPT

(A) published biographical information.

(B) old news film footage.

(C) direct personal acquaintance.

(D) assumption.

(E) third-party reports.

8. The protection of the right of property by the Constitution is tenuous at best. It is true that the Fifth Amendment states that the government may not take private property for public use without compensation, but it is the government that defines private property.

Which of the following is most likely the point the author is leading up to?

(A) Individual rights that are protected by the Supreme Court are secure against government encroachment.

(B) Private property is neither more nor less than that which the government says is private property.

(C) The government has no authority to deprive an individual of his liberty.

(D) No government that acts arbitrarily can be justified.

(E) The keystone of American democracy is the Constitution.

9. *Daily Post* newspaper reporter Roger Nightengale let it be known that Andrea Johnson, the key figure in his award-winning series of articles on prostitution and drug abuse, was a composite of many persons and not a single, real person, and so he was the subject of much criticism by fellow journalists for having failed to disclose that information when the articles were first published. But these were the same critics who voted Nightengale a prize for his magazine serial *General*, which was a much dramatized and fictionalized account of a Korean War military leader whose character was obviously patterned closely after that of Douglas MacArthur.

In which of the following ways might the critics mentioned in the paragraph argue that they were NOT inconsistent in their treatment of Nightengale's works?

(A) Fictionalization is an accepted journalistic technique for reporting on sensitive subject matter such as prostitution.

(B) Critic disapproval is one of the most important ways members of the writing community have for ensuring that reporting is accurate and to the point.

(C) Newspaper reporters usually promise confidentiality to their sources and have an obligation to protect their identities.

(D) There is a critical difference between dramatizing events in a piece of fiction and presenting distortions of the truth as actual fact.

(E) Well-known personalities are public figures who personal lives are acceptable material for journalistic investigations.

10. Why pay outrageously high prices for imported sparkling water when there is now an inexpensive water carbonated and bottled here in the United States at its source—Cold Springs, Vermont. Neither you nor your guests will taste the difference, but if you would be embarrassed if it were learned that you were serving a domestic sparkling water, then serve Cold Springs Water—but serve it in a leaded crystal decanter.

The advertisement rests on which of the following assumptions?

(A) It is not difficult to distinguish Cold Springs Water from imported competitors on the basis of taste.

(B) Most sparkling waters are bottled at the source, but additional carbonation is added to make them more active.

(C) Import restriction and customs duties that are passed on to consumers artificially inflate the price of imported waters.

(D) Sparkling waters taste best when they are decanted from their bottles into another container for service.

(E) Some people may purchase an imported sparkling water over a domestic one as a status symbol.

11. Choose the best completion of the following paragraph.

Parochial education serves the dual functions of education and religious instruction, and church leaders are justifiably concerned to impart important religious values regarding relationships between the sexes. Thus, when the administrators of a parochial school system segregate boys and girls in separate institutions, they believe they are helping to keep the children pure by removing them from a source of temptation. If the administrators realized, however, that children would be more likely to develop the very attitudes they seek to engender in the company of the opposite sex, they would

_____.

(A) put an end to all parochial education

(B) no longer insist upon separate schools for boys and girls

(C) abolish all racial discrimination in the religious schools

(D) stop teaching foolish religious tripe and concentrate instead on secular educational programs

(E) reinforce their policies of isolating the sexes in separate programs

12. Professor Branch, who is chair of the sociology department, claims she saw a flying saucer the other night. But since she is a sociologist instead of a physicist, she cannot possibly be acquainted with the most recent writings of our finest scientists that tend to discount such sightings, so we can conclude her report is unreliable.

Which of the following would be the most appropriate criticism of the author's analysis?

(A) The author makes an irrelevant attack on Professor Branch's credentials.

(B) The author may not be a physicist and therefore may not be familiar with the writings he cites.

(C) Even the U.S. Air Force cannot explain all of the sightings of UFOs that are reported to them each year.

(D) A sociologist is sufficiently well educated that she can probably read and understand scientific literature in a field other than her own.

(E) It is impossible to get complete agreement on matters such as the possibility of life on other planets.

13. INQUISITOR: Are you in league with the devil?

VICTIM: Yes.

INQUISITOR: Then you must be lying, for those in league with the "Evil One" never tell the truth. So you are not in league with the devil.

The inquisitor's behavior can be described as paradoxical because he

(A) charged the victim with being in league with the devil but later recanted.

(B) relies on the victim's answer to reject the victim's response.

(C) acts in accordance with religious law but accuses the victim of violating that law.

(D) questions the victim about possible ties with the devil but does not really believe there is a devil.

(E) asked the question in the first place but then refused to accept the answer that the victim gave.

14. "Whom did you pass on the road?" the King went on, holding his hand out to the messenger for some hay.

"Nobody," said the messenger.

"Quite right," said the King. "This young lady saw him, too. So, of course, Nobody walks slower than you."

The King's response shows that he believes

(A) the messenger is a very good messenger.

(B) "Nobody" is a person who might be seen.

(C) the young lady's eyesight is better than the messenger's.

(D) the messenger is not telling him the truth.

(E) there was no person actually seen by the messenger on the road.

15. An experienced attorney agreed to take on a law clerk and train her for admission to the bar. According to their agreement, the fee for the training would be due and payable at the time that the new attorney won her first case. After receiving the training, the new attorney decided not to practice law, and the experienced attorney, tired of waiting for payment, sued for the fee. The new attorney represented herself and claimed that the fee was not owed since she had not won her first case.

Which of the following conclusions can be logically inferred from the information above?

(A) If the younger attorney wins, the fee is then due.

(B) If the younger attorney wins, the fee is never payable.

(C) If the younger attorney wins, the fee was due before the suit was filed.

(D) If the suit is withdrawn, the fee is never payable.

(E) If the suit is withdrawn, the fee was due before the suit was filed.

16. In the new car market, purchasing decisions are often based on emotion rather than rationality. Consumers buy a bewildering array of packages that include secure child seats, antilock brakes, side airbags, and other safety features, while also choosing expensive options such as entertainment systems and extra-powerful engines. It is rare for consumers in similar circumstances to buy identical new car packages.

The reasoning above presupposes that

(A) automotive safety features are more important than other options

(B) consumers buy cars with options packages already on dealer lots

(C) different consumers cannot rationally reach different decisions

(D) safety features on cars are more expensive than other options

(E) reliability is not an important factor in the decision to buy a new car

17. BILL:　The heating, ventilation and air conditioning (HVAC) controls in our office building are completely fake, intended to fool us into thinking that we are exercising control over office weather conditions. Remove the device from the wall, and you'll probably find that it doesn't even have a wire attached, or if it does have a wire attached, the other end dangles uselessly in the dead space behind the wall.

RICHARD:　But we did an experiment. We found that when we were uncomfortably warm and we adjusted the thermostat, a few minutes later, cooler air began to circulate. Or if we were uncomfortably cool and adjusted the thermostat accordingly, a few minutes later, warmer air began to circulate.

Which of the following, if true, best reconciles the conflicting opinions of Bill and Richard?

(A) People have different tolerances for temperature extremes, so conditions that some perceive as too warm or too cool will be regarded as comfortable by others.

(B) In order to conserve energy, temperature settings in office buildings are normally reduced during the night, and it takes about an hour's operation for the HVAC system to return the temperature to normal.

(C) The windows in modern office buildings are covered with a glaze that reflects sunlight, thereby reducing the penetration of the infrared rays that account for most of the heat buildup in offices.

(D) The working thermostat for the HVAC system is usually placed in a locked plastic or glass box to which only an office manager or other supervisory person has access.

(E) Real HVAC controls are set to conserve energy and so do not activate the heating or cooling system until conditions have become too warm or too cool for most occupants.

18. Copyright protection lasts for a fixed term of years following the death of the work's creator, after which anyone is free to reprint or otherwise copy a work without the permission of or the need to pay compensation to the heirs of the creator of the work. However, the protection of property rights is essential to a democracy. A copyrighted work such as a symphony or a novel has value, so it's property that should be protected by law. Therefore, copyright should be in perpetuity and not just for a limited time.

The reasoning above can be criticized because it

(A) fails to provide examples of named works that are protected by copyright

(B) presumes without argument that creative works are property

(C) attempts to discredit the source of an argument rather than address its merits

(D) reaches a general conclusion based upon an unrepresentative sampling

(E) ignores the possibility that some works are more valuable than others

19. If the artifacts include armaments, then the recently uncovered ruins are remnants of a fortress built by the Etonians. If the artifacts include writing utensils, then the ruins are remnants of a trading center built by the Heratians. The artifacts must include either armaments or writing utensils.

Which of the following can be deduced from the statements above?

(A) The Etonians built only fortresses while the Heratians built only trading centers.

(B) The remnants of any fortress built by the Etonians would include armaments among the artifacts.

(C) The remnants of any trading center built by the Heratians would not include armaments among the artifacts.

(D) If the artifacts do not include writing utensils, then the ruins are remnants of a fortress built by the Etonians.

(E) If the artifacts do not include armaments, then the ruins are remnants of a fortress built by someone other than the Etonians.

20. In determining what organisms may morally be used for food, vegetarians are often guided by the principle of "capacity for suffering." If the organism has the capacity for suffering, then it is not morally acceptable to use it for food. Given this rule of thumb, plants are acceptable because they lack even the rudiments of a central nervous system.

The reasoning above depends on which of the following assumptions?

(A) All animals, even the most primitive, have a central nervous system.

(B) Only organisms with a central nervous system have the capacity for suffering.

(C) Primitive animals such as mollusks lack a functioning central nervous system.

(D) Any organism with a central nervous system has the capacity for suffering.

(E) Only organisms that have the capacity for suffering should not be eaten.

21. In the earliest stages of the common law, a party could have a case heard by a judge only upon the payment of a fee to the court and then only if the case fit within one of the forms for which there existed a writ. At first, the number of such formalized cases of action was very small, but judges invented new forms that brought more cases and greater revenues.

Which of the following conclusions is most strongly suggested by the paragraph above?

(A) Early judges often decided cases in an arbitrary and haphazard manner.

(B) In most early cases, the plaintiff rather than the defendant prevailed.

(C) The judiciary at first had greater power than either the legislature or the executive.

(D) One of the motivating forces for the early expansion in judicial power was economic considerations.

(E) The first common law decisions were inconsistent with one another and did not form a coherent body of law.

22. If Martin introduces an amendment to Evans' bill, then Johnson and Lloyd will both vote the same way. If Evans speaks against Lloyd's position, Johnson will defend anyone voting with him. Martin will introduce an amendment to Evans' bill only if Evans speaks against Johnson's position.

If the above statements are true, each of the following can be true EXCEPT

(A) if Evans speaks against Johnson's position, Lloyd will not vote with Johnson.

(B) if Martin introduces an amendment to Evans' bill, then Evans has spoken against Johnson's position.

(C) if Evans speaks against Johnson's position, Martin will not introduce an amendment to Evans' bill.

(D) if Martin introduces an amendment to Evans' bill, then either Johnson will not vote with Lloyd or Evans did not speak against Johnson's position.

(E) if either Evans did not speak against Lloyd's position or Martin did not introduce an amendment to Evans' bill, then either Johnson did not defend Lloyd or Martin spoke against Johnson's position.

23. Once at a conference on the philosophy of language, a professor delivered a lengthy and tiresome address, the central thesis of which was that "yes" and related slang words such as "yeah" can be used only to show agreement with a proposition. At the end of the paper, a listener in the back of the auditorium stood up and shouted in a sarcastic voice, "Oh, yeah?" This constituted a complete refutation of the paper.

The listener argued against the paper by

(A) offering a counterexample.

(B) pointing out an inconsistency.

(C) presenting an analogy.

(D) attacking the speaker's character.

(E) citing additional evidence.

24. If military aid to Latin American countries is to be stopped because it creates instability in the region, then all foreign aid must be stopped.

Which of the following is most like the argument above in its logical structure?

(A) If a war in Central America is to be condemned because all killing is immoral, then all war must be condemned.

(B) If charitable donations are obligatory for those who are rich, then it is certain that the poor will be provided for.

(C) If the fascist government in Chile is to be overthrown because it violates the rights of the people, then all government must be overthrown.

(D) If a proposed weapons system is to be rejected because there are insufficient funds to pay for it, then the system must be purchased when the funds are available.

(E) If a sociological theory is widely accepted but later proven wrong by facts, then a new theory should be proposed that takes account of the additional data.

STOP

END OF SECTION 3. IF YOU HAVE ANY TIME LEFT, GO OVER YOUR WORK IN THIS SECTION ONLY. DO NOT WORK IN ANY OTHER SECTION OF THE TEST.

SECTION 4

28 Questions • Time—35 Minutes

Directions: Below each of the following passages, you will find questions or incomplete statements about the passage. Each statement or question is followed by lettered words or expressions. Select the word or expression that most satisfactorily completes each statement or answers each question in accordance with the meaning of the passage. After you have chosen the *best* answer, blacken the corresponding space on the answer sheet.

Desertification in the arid United States is flagrant. Groundwater supplies beneath vast stretches of land are dropping precipitously. Whole river systems
(5) have dried up; others are choked with sediment washed from denuded land. Hundreds of thousands of acres of previously irrigated cropland have been abandoned to wind or weeds. Several million
(10) acres of natural grassland are eroding at unnaturally high rates as a result of cultivation or overgrazing. All told, about 225 million acres of land are undergoing severe desertification.
(15)   Federal subsidies encourage the exploitation of arid land resources. Low-interest loans for irrigation and other water delivery systems encourage farmers, industry, and municipalities
(20) to mine groundwater. Federal disaster relief and commodity programs encourage arid-land farmers to plow up natural grassland to plant crops such as wheat and, especially, cotton. Federal
(25) grazing fees that are well below the free market price encourage overgrazing of the commons. The market, too, provides powerful incentives to exploit arid land resources beyond their carrying
(30) capacity. When commodity prices are high relative to the farmer's or rancher's operating costs, the return on a production-enhancing investment is invariably greater than the return on a
(35) conservation investment. And when commodity prices are relatively low, arid land ranchers and farmers often have to

use all their available financial resources to stay solvent.
(40)   The incentives to exploit arid land resources are greater today than ever. The government is now offering huge new subsidies to produce synfuel from coal or oil shale as well as alcohol fuel
(45) from crops. Moreover, commodity prices are on the rise; and they will provide farmers and agribusiness with powerful incentives to overexploit arid land resources. The existing federal govern-
(50) ment cost-share programs designed to help finance the conservation of soil, water, and vegetation pale in comparison to such incentives.
      In the final analysis, when viewed
(55) in the national perspective, the effects on agriculture are the most troublesome aspect of desertification in the United States. For it comes at a time when we are losing over a million acres of
(60) rain-watered crop and pasture land per year to "higher uses"—shopping centers, industrial parks, housing developments, and waste dumps—heedless of the economic need of the United States
(65) to export agricultural products or of the world's need for U.S. food and fiber. Today the arid West accounts for 20 percent of the nation's total agricultural output. If the United States is, as it
(70) appears, well on its way toward over-drawing the arid land resources, then the policy choice is simply to pay now for the appropriate remedies or pay for more later, when productive benefits from arid
(75) land resources have been both realized and largely terminated.

1. The author is primarily concerned with
   (A) discussing a solution.
   (B) describing a problem.
   (C) replying to a detractor.
   (D) finding a contradiction.
   (E) defining a term.

2. The passage mentions all of the following as effects of desertification EXCEPT
   (A) increased sediment in rivers.
   (B) erosion of land.
   (C) overcultivation of arid land.
   (D) decreasing groundwater supplies.
   (E) loss of land to wind or weeds.

3. The author most likely encloses the phrase "higher uses" (line 61) in quotation marks in order to
   (A) alert the reader to the fact that the term is very important.
   (B) minimize the importance of desertification in non-arid land.
   (C) voice support for expansion of such programs.
   (D) express concern over the extent of desertification.
   (E) indicate disagreement that such uses are more important.

4. The passages mentions all of the following as economic factors tending to contribute to desertification EXCEPT
   (A) price incentives for farmers to use arid lands to produce certain commodities.
   (B) artifically low government fees for use of public grazing lands.
   (C) government subsidies for fuels that are manufactured from a variety of crops.
   (D) worldwide demand for the food and fiber produced in the United States.
   (E) lack of effective government financial incentives to conserve soil, water, and vegetation.

5. According to the passage, the most serious long-term effect of desertification would be the reduced ability of
   (A) the United States to continue to export agricultural products.
   (B) municipalities to supply water to meet the needs of residents.
   (C) farmers to cover their expenses.
   (D) the United States to meet the food needs of its own people.
   (E) the United States to produce sufficient fuel for energy from domestic sources.

6. The passage leads most logically to discussion of a proposal for
   (A) reduced agricultural output in the United States.
   (B) direct government aid to farmers affected by desertification.
   (C) curtailing the conversion of land to shopping centers and housing.
   (D) government assistance to develop improved farming methods to increase exploitation of arid land.
   (E) increased government assistance to finance the conservation of arid land.

7. The author's attitude toward desertification can best be described as one of
   (A) alarm.
   (B) optimism.
   (C) understanding.
   (D) conciliation.
   (E) concern.

The need for solar electricity is clear. It is safe, ecologically sound, efficient, continuously available, and it has no moving parts. The basic problem with the
(5) use of solar photovoltaic devices is economics, but until recently very little progress had been made toward the development of low-cost photovoltaic devices. The larger part of research funds
(10) has been devoted to the study of

single-crystal silicon solar cells, despite the evidence, including that of the leading manufacturers of crystalline silicon, that this technique holds little promise.
(15) The reason for this pattern is understandable and historical. Crystalline silicon is the active element in the very successful semiconductor industry, and virtually all of the solid state devices
(20) contain silicon transistors and diodes. Crystalline silicon, however, is particularly unsuitable to terrestrial solar cells.

Crystalline silicon solar cells work well and are successfully used in the
(25) space program, where cost is not an issue. While single crystal silicon has been proven in extraterrestrial use with efficiencies as high as 18 percent, and other more expensive and scarce mate-
(30) rials such as gallium arsenide can have even higher efficiencies, costs must be reduced by a factor of more than 100 to make them practical for commercial uses. Beside the fact that the starting crystal-
(35) line silicon is expensive, 95 percent of it is wasted and does not appear in the final device. Recently, there have been some imaginative attempts to make polycrystalline and ribbon silicon that are
(40) lower in cost than high-quality single crystals; but to date the efficiencies of these apparently lower-cost arrays have been unacceptably small. Moreover, these materials are cheaper only be-
(45) cause of the introduction of disordering in crystalline semiconductors, and disorder degrades the efficiency of crystalline solar cells.

This dilemma can be avoided by
(50) preparing completely disordered or amorphous materials. Amorphous materials have disordered atomic structure as compared to crystalline materials: that is, they have only short-range
(55) order rather than the long-range periodicity of crystals. The advantages of amorphous solar cells are impressive. Whereas crystals can be grown as wafers about four inches in diameter, amor-
(60) phous materials can be grown over large areas in a single process. Whereas crystalline silicon must be made 200 mi-

crons thick to absorb a sufficient amount of sunlight for efficient energy conver-
(65) sion, only 1 micron of the proper amorphous materials is necessary. Crystalline silicon solar cells cost in excess of $100 per square foot, but amorphous films can be created at a cost of about
(70) 50¢ per square foot.

Although many scientists were aware of the very low cost of amorphous solar cells, they felt that they could never be manufactured with the efficiencies
(75) necessary to contribute significantly to the demand for electric power. This was based on a misconception about the feature that determines efficiency. For example, it is not the conductivity of the
(80) material in the dark which is relevant, but only the photoconductivity, that is, the conductivity in the presence of sunlight. Already, solar cells with efficiencies well above 6 percent have been
(85) developed using amorphous materials, and further research will doubtless find even less costly amorphous materials with higher efficiencies.

8. The author is primarily concerned with

(A) discussing the importance of solar energy.

(B) explaining the functioning of solar cells.

(C) presenting a history of research on energy sources.

(D) describing a possible solution to the problem of the cost of photovoltaic cells.

(E) advocating increased government funding for research on alternative energy sources.

9. According to the passage, which of the following encouraged use of silicon solar cells in the space program?

(A) Plentiful supplies of materials such as gallium arsenide

(B) Difficulties encountered in laboratory experiments with ribbon silicon

(C) Low cost of silicon cells compared with ones made of other materials

(D) Relatively high efficiency of extraterrestrial silicon solar cells

(E) Highly disordered atomic structure of the materials used in the cells

10. The author mentions recent attempts to make polycrystalline and ribbon silicon (lines 38–43) primarily in order to

(A) minimize the importance of recent improvements in silicon solar cells.

(B) demonstrate the superiority of amorphous materials over crystalline silicon.

(C) explain why silicon solar cells have been the center of research.

(D) contrast crystalline silicon with polycrystalline and ribbon silicon.

(E) inform the reader that an alternative type of solar cell exists.

11. Which of the following pairs of terms does the author regard as most nearly synonymous?

(A) Solar and extraterrestrial

(B) Photovoltaic devices and solar cells

(C) Crystalline silicon and amorphous materials

(D) Amorphous materials and higher efficiencies

(E) Wafers and crystals

12. The material in the passage could best be used in an argument for

(A) discontinuing the space program.

(B) increased funding for research on amorphous materials.

(C) further study of the history of silicon crystals.

(D) increased reliance on solar energy.

(E) training more scientists to study energy problems.

13. All of the following are mentioned in the passage as advantages of amorphous materials over silicon cells EXCEPT

(A) the minimal trade-off required between cost of production and efficiency.

(B) the relative thinness of amorphous materials needed for acceptable efficiency.

(C) the cost per unit area of manufacturing amorphous materials.

(D) the possibility of manufacturing large wafers in a single process.

(E) the historical commitment of the semiconductor industry to a particular material.

14. The tone of the passage can best be described as

(A) analytical and optimistic.

(B) biased and unprofessional.

(C) critical and discouraged.

(D) tentative and inconclusive.

(E) concerned and conciliatory.

According to legend, Aesculapius bore two daughters, Panacea and Hyegeia, who gave rise to dynasties of healers and hygienists. The schism remains today,
(5) in clinical training and in practice; and because of the imperative nature of medical care and the subtlety of health care, the former has tended to dominate. Preventive medicine has as its primary ob-
(10) jective the maintenance and promotion

of health. It accomplishes this by controlling or manipulating environmental factors that affect health and disease. For example, in some areas presently (15) there is serious suffering and substantial economic loss because of the failure to introduce controlled fluoridation of public water supplies. In addition, preventive medicine applies prophylactic (20) measures against disease by such actions as immunization and specific nutritional measures. Third, it attempts to motivate people to adopt healthful lifestyles through education.

(25)   For the most part, curative medicine has as its primary objective the removal of disease from the patient. It provides diagnostic techniques to identify the presence and nature of the dis-(30) ease process. While these may be applied on a mass basis in an attempt to "screen" out persons with preclinical disease, they are usually applied after the patient appears with a complaint. Sec-(35) ond, it applies treatment to the sick patient. In every case, this is, or should be, individualized according to the particular need of each patient. Third, it utilizes rehabilitation methodologies to (40) return the treated patient to the best possible level of functioning.

     While it is true that both preventive medicine and curative medicine require cadres of similarly trained person-(45) nel such as planners, administrators, and educators, the underlying delivery systems depend upon quite distinctive professional personnel. The requirements for curative medicine call for clini-(50) cally trained individuals who deal with patients on a one-to-one basis and whose training is based primarily on an understanding of the biological, pathological, and psychological processes that deter-(55) mine an individual's health and disease status. The locus for this training is the laboratory and clinic. Preventive medicine, on the other hand, calls for a very broad spectrum of professional person-(60) nel, few of whom require clinical expertise. Since their actions apply either to environmental situations or to popula-

tion groups, their training takes place in a different type of laboratory or in a (65) community not necessarily associated with the clinical locus.

     The economic differences between preventive medicine and curative medicine have been extensively discussed, (70) perhaps most convincingly by Winslow in the monograph *The Cost of Sickness and the Price of Health*. Sickness is almost always a negative, nonproductive, and harmful state. All resources ex-(75) pended to deal with sickness are, therefore, fundamentally economically unproductive. Health, on the other hand, has a very high value in our culture. To the extent that healthy members of the (80) population are replaced by sick members, the economy is doubly burdened. Nevertheless, the per capita cost of preventive measures for specific diseases is generally far lower than the per capita (85) cost of curative medicine applied to treatment of the same disease. Prominent examples are dental caries, poliomyelitis, and phenylketonuria.

     There is an imperative need to pro-(90) vide care for the sick person within a single medical care system, but there is no overriding reason why a linkage is necessary between the two components of a health-care system, prevention and (95) treatment. A national health and medical care program composed of semiautonomous systems for personal health care and medical care would have the advantage of clarifying objectives and (100) strategies and of permitting a more equitable division of resources between prevention and cure.

15. The author is primarily concerned to

   (A) refute a counterargument.

   (B) draw a distinction.

   (C) discuss a dilemma.

   (D) isolate causes.

   (E) describe new research.

16. Which of the following points about the nature of medical practice is NOT made by the author?

    (A) Curative medicine is aimed primarily at people who are already ill, while preventive medicine is aimed at healthy people.

    (B) Curative medicine is focused on an individual patient, while preventive medicine is applied to larger populations.

    (C) The per capita cost of curative medicine is generally much higher than the per capita cost of preventive medicine.

    (D) Both preventive care and curative care trace origins to classical legend and the dynasties of hygienists and healers.

    (E) Because of the urgency involved in treating disease, curative medicine is logically prior to preventive care.

17. It can be inferred that the author regards a program of controlled fluoridation of public water supplies as

    (A) an unnecessary government program that wastes economic resources.

    (B) a potentially valuable strategy of preventive medicine.

    (C) a government policy that has relatively little effect on the health of a population.

    (D) an important element of curative medicine.

    (E) an experimental program, the health value of which has not been proved.

18. Which of the following best explains the author's use of the phrase "doubly burdened" (lines 80–81)?

    (A) A person who is ill not only does not contribute to production, but medical treatment consumes economic resources.

    (B) The per capita cost of preventive measures is only one half of the per capita cost of treatment.

    (C) The division between preventive medicine and curative medicine requires duplication of administrative expenses.

    (D) The individual who is ill must be rehabilitated after the cure has been successful.

    (E) The person who is ill uses economic resources that could be used to finance prevention rather than treatment programs.

19. It can be inferred that the author regards Winslow's monograph (lines 70–73) as

    (A) ill conceived.

    (B) incomplete.

    (C) authoritative.

    (D) well organized.

    (E) highly original.

20. The author cites dental caries, poliomyelitis, and phenylketonuria in order to prove that

    (A) some diseases can be treated by preventive medicine.

    (B) some diseases have serious consequences if not treated.

    (C) preventive medicine need not be linked to treatment.

    (D) the cost of preventing some diseases is less than the cost for treatment.

    (E) less money is allocated to prevention of some diseases than to treating them.

21. The main reason the author advocates separating authority for preventive medicine from that for curative medicine is

(A) the urgency of treatment encourages administrators to devote more resources to treatment than to prevention.

(B) the cost of treating a disease is often much greater than the cost of programs to prevent the disease.

(C) the professionals who administer preventive health-care programs must be more highly trained than ordinary doctors.

(D) curative medicine deals primarily with individuals who are ill, while preventive medicine is applied to healthy people.

(E) preventive medicine is a relatively recent development, while curative medicine has a long history.

From the time they were first proposed, the 1962 Amendments to the Food, Drug and Cosmetic Act have been the subject of controversy among some elements of
(5) the health community and the pharmaceutical industry. The Amendments added a new requirement for Food and Drug Administration approval of any new drug: The drug must be demon-
(10) strated to be effective by substantial evidence consisting of adequate and well-controlled investigations. To meet this effectiveness requirement, a pharmaceutical company must spend consid-
(15) erable time and effort in clinical research before it can market a new product in the United States. Only then can it begin to recoup its investment. Critics of the requirement argue that the added
(20) expense of the research to establish effectiveness is reflected in higher drug costs, decreased profits, or both, and that this has resulted in a "drug lag."

The term "drug lag" has been used
(25) in several different ways. It has been argued that the research required to prove effectiveness creates a lag between the time when a drug could theoretically

be marketed without proving effective-
(30) ness and the time when it is actually marketed. "Drug lag" has also been used to refer to the difference between the number of new drugs introduced annually before 1962 and the number of new
(35) drugs introduced each year after that date. It is also argued that the Amendments resulted in a lag between the time when the new drugs are available in other countries and the time when the
(40) same drugs are available in the United States. And "drug lag" has also been used to refer to a difference in the number of new drugs introduced per year in other advanced nations and the number
(45) introduced in the same year in the United States.

Some critics have used "drug lag" arguments in an attempt to prove that the 1962 Amendments have actually
(50) reduced the quality of health care in the United States and that, on balance, they have done more harm than good. These critics recommend that the effectiveness requirements be drastically modi-
(55) fied or even scrapped. Most of the specific claims of the "drug lag" theoreticians, however, have been refuted. The drop in new drugs approved annually, for example, began at least as early as
(60) 1959, perhaps five years before the new law was fully effective. In most instances, when a new drug was available in a foreign country but not in the United States, other effective drugs for the con-
(65) dition were available in the country and sometimes not available in the foreign country used for comparison. Further, although the number of new chemical entities introduced annually dropped
(70) from more than 50 in 1959 to about 12 to 18 in the 1960s and 1970s, the number of these that can be termed important— some of them of "breakthrough" caliber—has remained reasonably close
(75) to 5 or 6 per year. Few, if any, specific examples have actually been offered to show how the effectiveness requirements have done significant harm to the health of Americans. The require-
(80) ment does ensure that a patient ex-

posed to a drug has the likelihood of benefiting from it, an assessment that is most important, considering the possibility, always present, that adverse (85) effects will be discovered later.

22. The author is primarily concerned with

(A) outlining a proposal.

(B) evaluating studies.

(C) posing a question.

(D) countering arguments.

(E) discussing a law.

23. The passage states that the phrase "drug lag" has been used to refer to all of the following situations EXCEPT

(A) a lag between the time when a new drug becomes available in a foreign country and its availability in the United States.

(B) the time period between which a new drug would be marketed if no effectiveness research were required and the time it is actually marketed.

(C) the increased cost of drugs to the consumer and the decreased profit margins of the pharmaceutical industry.

(D) the difference between the number of drugs introduced annually before 1962 and the number introduced after 1962.

(E) the difference between the number of new drugs introduced in a foreign country and the number introduced in the United States.

24. The author would most likely agree with which of the following statements?

(A) Whatever "drug lag" may exist because of the 1962 Amendments is justified by the benefit of effectiveness studies.

(B) The 1962 Amendments have been beneficial in detecting adverse effects of new drugs before they are released on the market.

(C) Because of the requirement of effectiveness studies, drug consumers in the United States pay higher prices than consumers in foreign countries.

(D) The United States should limit the number of new drugs that can be introduced into this country from foreign countries.

(E) Effectiveness studies do not require a significant investment of time or money on the part of the pharmaceutical industry.

25. The author points out the drop in new drugs approved annually before 1959 in order to

(A) draw an analogy between two situations.

(B) suggest an alternative causal explanation.

(C) attack the credibility of an opponent.

(D) justify the introduction of statistics.

(E) show an opponent misquoted statistics.

26. The author implies that the non-availability of a drug in the United States and its availability in a foreign country is not necessarily proof of a drug lag because this comparison fails to take into account

    (A) the number of new drugs introduced annually before 1959.

    (B) the amount of research done on the effectiveness of drugs in the United States.

    (C) the possible availability of another drug to treat the same condition.

    (D) the seriousness of possible unwanted side effects from untested drugs.

    (E) the length of time needed to accumulate effectiveness research.

27. The author attempts to respond to the claim that the number of new chemical entities introduced annually since the Amendments has dropped by

    (A) denying that the total number of new chemical entities has actually dropped.

    (B) analyzing the economic factors responsible for the drop.

    (C) refining terminology to distinguish important from non-important chemical entities.

    (D) proposing that further studies be done to determine the effectiveness of new chemical entities.

    (E) listing the myriad uses to which each new chemical entity can be put.

28. The comparisons made by proponents of the "drug lag" theory between the availability of drugs in foreign countries and their availability in the United States logically depend upon which of the following presuppositions?

    (A) The Food and Drug Administration is less efficient than its governmental counterparts in other countries around the world.

    (B) On balance, more important new drug therapies are developed in other countries than in the United States.

    (C) New drugs in foreign countries are subject to a more rigorous testing requirement than new drugs in the United States.

    (D) The pharmaceutical industry in the foreign country is roughly as sophisticated as that in the United States.

    (E) The pharmaceutical industry in the foreign country is more profitable than that of the United States.

STOP

END OF SECTION 4. IF YOU HAVE ANY TIME LEFT, GO OVER YOUR WORK IN THIS SECTION ONLY. DO NOT WORK IN ANY OTHER SECTION OF THE TEST.

practice test

SECTION 5

25 Questions • Time—35 Minutes

Directions. Below each of the following passages, you will find questions or incomplete statements about the passage. Each statement or question is followed by lettered words or expressions. Select the word or expression that most satisfactorily completes each statement or answers each question in accordance with the meaning of the passage. After you have chosen the *best* answer, blacken the corresponding space on the answer sheet.

1. Senator Allen has admitted to having an illicit affair and lying to her husband about it. Although the affair ended several years ago and Allen and her husband are now reconciled, this episode should disqualify Allen from seeking higher office. How could world leaders be expected to negotiate with a president who has admitted lying to her spouse?

   Which of the following assumptions underlies the argument above?

   (A) A president who has committed adultery might be subject to blackmail or other pressures.

   (B) Many voters would not vote for Allen because she admitted to having an affair.

   (C) The personal life of a political leader may affect that leader's ability to make correct decisions.

   (D) A person who would tell an untruth in a personal situation is likely to tell a lie in public.

   (E) A public leader has an extraordinary obligation to set an example of high moral standards.

Questions 2 and 3

   (A) The safety of the new drug Zorapan has yet to be clearly demonstrated. Only one study of its effects has been conducted, and the results were inconclusive.

   (B) George is unlikely to make a good class president. He is hot-tempered and extremely critical of all those around him.

   (C) Mayor Warren favors the new zoning law for one reason only: Her husband is a building contractor who stands to profit from the increased construction the law will encourage.

   (D) It's almost impossible to get good repair service nowadays. I brought my camera to the local camera shop for repair, and it still doesn't work properly.

   (E) Helen probably got her interest in medicine from her family. Both of her parents, as well as two of her uncles, are physicians.

2. Which of the arguments above is a generalization that could be criticized because it is based upon a limited sampling?

3. Which of the arguments above attempts to discredit an opponent rather than attack the merits of a position?

4. Conservatives often boast of the freedoms that U.S. citizens enjoy, yet how much freedom do they really have? Housing, medical care, and other basic needs are increasingly costly, and no one is guaranteed a job. It is the people living in socialist nations who enjoy true freedom since they are free from the fear that the constant threat of poverty brings.

The persuasive force of the argument above depends largely upon the ambiguous use of which of the following pairs of terms?

(A) Basic needs and job

(B) Poverty and fear

(C) Free and freedom

(D) Guarantee and poverty

(E) Spokespeople and people

5. French painting during the first half of the nineteenth century was characterized by a lack of imagination. The Ecole des Beaux Arts, the quasi-governmental agency that controlled the dissemination of lucrative government scholarships and commissions, effectively stifled creativity. A student who hoped to achieve any fame or financial success was well advised to paint in the style of the Ecole. It is a small wonder then that the Impressionist painters initially earned only the scorn of their colleagues and empty bellies for their efforts.

The passage above implies that

(A) Impressionist painters did not paint in the style of the Ecole des Beaux Arts.

(B) the Impressionist painters eventually gained control of the Ecole des Beaux Arts.

(C) the Ecole des Beaux Arts promulgated rules defining the permissible subject matter of paintings.

(D) the Ecole des Beaux Arts determined licensing standards for those who wanted to become professional artists.

(E) French painting during the second half of the nineteenth century was less creative than during the first half of the nineteenth century.

6. TEACHER: Some students have received passing marks on the test, but you were not one of them.

STUDENT: I sure hate to tell my parents that I failed a test.

TEACHER: That is not yet necessary.

Which of the following, if true, best explains the teacher's second remark?

(A) The student should lie to the parents about the mark.

(B) One low test mark will not result in a failing mark for the course.

(C) The student should wait for an opportune time to tell the parents.

(D) The teacher has not finished grading the test papers.

(E) The student will have to take other exams before the course is over.

7. Most arguments in favor of legalizing marijuana focus attention on the lack of evidence of harmful effects of the drug. The purpose of such contentions is to neutralize the negative effect of arguments supporting prohibition because of a supposed correlation between the use of marijuana and violent antisocial behavior. Thus far, the burden of constructive argumentation has been borne by the doctrine of individual rights. "Liberty" has been the rallying cry of those who favor legalization. No serious proponent of legislative change has yet advanced the obvious proposition that the sale of marijuana should be legal because smoking marijuana is pleasurable.

The author of the paragraph implies that

(A) smoking marijuana can, in some cases, lead to criminal behavior.

(B) the sale of marijuana is illegal because the smoking of marijuana is pleasurable.

(C) the fact that an activity is pleasurable is a reason for allowing people to engage in it.

(D) advocates of the legalization of marijuana are not really concerned about individual liberty.

(E) opponents of the legalization of marijuana deny that smoking marijuana is a pleasurable activity.

8. DAVID: Every painting by Kissandra should be displayed in the National Art Museum.

   MARAT: I disagree. I have seen some very fine works by Electra and Bluesina that should be displayed in the Museum.

   Marat's response indicates that he has understood David to mean that

   (A) paintings by Electra and Bluesina should be displayed in the Museum.

   (B) only Kissandra's paintings should be displayed in the Museum.

   (C) every painting by Kissandra should be displayed in the Museum.

   (D) not every Kissandra painting should be displayed in the Museum.

   (E) Kissandra's paintings should only be displayed in the Museum.

Questions 9 and 10

Paul is older than Sally.

Sally is older than Fred.

Mike is older than Paul.

Ralph is younger than Mike but older than Fred.

9. If the statements above are true, which of the following must also be true?

   (A) Ralph is the oldest.

   (B) Paul is the second oldest.

   (C) Sally is the youngest.

   (D) Fred is the youngest.

   (E) Ralph is older than Paul.

10. If a sixth person, Chuck, is younger than Ralph, all of the following could be true EXCEPT

   (A) Chuck is younger than Sally.

   (B) Chuck is older than Sally.

   (C) Fred is younger than Chuck.

   (D) Chuck is younger than Fred.

   (E) Mike is younger than Chuck.

11. CHARLOTTE: I don't see any good reason for lending you the money you want.

   CATHY: By your own admission, there is a good reason for lending me the money— even though you can't see it. Therefore, you should lend me the money.

   The exchange above is characterized by

   (A) a hasty generalization.

   (B) the ambiguous use of language.

   (C) an attack on someone's character.

   (D) a reliance on authority.

   (E) circular reasoning.

12. The earliest vaccines used whole dead viruses or weakened live ones to stimulate the body's immune system. Unfortunately, in a small number of cases, the vaccines caused very serious allergic reactions and in some cases even the disease itself. Vaccines being developed today are much safer because they use only a specific subunit of the viral protein chain.

   Which of the following conclusions is best supported by the paragraph above?

   (A) The body's immune system responds to a particular part of a virus rather than the virus as a whole.

   (B) The body's immune system is more likely to react to a whole dead virus than a part of a live one.

   (C) Reactions to weakened live viruses are more predictable than reactions to whole dead viruses.

   (D) A vaccine manufactured from a subunit of a virus is more likely to trigger than to prevent a disease.

   (E) The body reacts to a subpart of a virus in the same way it reacts to the virus as a whole.

13. AURORA: Tony, who just bought a new Hugo Hatchback, test drove both the Hugo Hatchback and a Ouigo Hatchback. Standard equipment on the Hugo includes factory air conditioning. So Tony must have bought the Hugo because air conditioning comes as standard equipment on the Hugo.

ANTHONY: But Tony bought an entire car —not just an air conditioner. He might very well have bought the Hugo even if it were not equipped with air conditioning.

Which of the following, if true, would be the most effective attack on Anthony's conclusion?

(A) The Ouigo, which does not offer air conditioning as an option, is otherwise almost identical to the Hugo.

(B) The Ouigo, which does not offer air conditioning, is markedly inferior to the Hugo.

(C) The Ouigo, which does not offer air conditioning, is markedly superior to the Hugo.

(D) The Ouigo is imported from abroad, while the Hugo is manufactured by a foreign firm in this country.

(E) Both the Hugo and the Ouigo offer power steering and power brakes as standard equipment.

14. Ethical vegetarians argue that it is wrong to rank humans above other animal species. But what then is the rationale for ranking any animal species above plants? If a human being is on a par with a lobster, then perhaps a lobster is on a par with a spear of broccoli. So a spear of broccoli is really the equal of a human being. Why not try to protect vegetables against the animals that would eat them? Maybe we should stop eating altogether to protest the brutal rule of nature that requires living things to eat other living things in order to stay alive.

The speaker above argues primarily by

(A) accusing ethical vegetarians of being insincere in their convictions.

(B) suggesting that the argument for ethical vegetarianism leads to absurd conclusions.

(C) citing scientific evidence that contradicts the claim of the ethical vegetarian.

(D) calling on commonly accepted opinions regarding ethical vegetarianism.

(E) attempting to reconcile two seemingly inconsistent ethical positions.

15. Recently there has been a surge in the number of births per year in the United States, and many fear that a new baby boom is under way that will strain our social institutions just as the baby boom of the middle of this century did. These fears, however, are unfounded. The recent rise in births is attributable to the fact that the original baby boomers are now potential parents.

Which of the following is an unstated assumption of the argument above?

(A) Baby boomers who become parents begin their families at the same age as their parents did.

(B) The average number of children per family in the United States will decrease drastically.

(C) Baby boomers who are now becoming mothers are having babies at a much lower rate than their mothers.

(D) A third baby boom will occur thirty years after this one is over.

(E) Any increase in the population of the United States above current levels is undesirable.

16. U.S. chemical manufacturers currently export numerous chemicals used in agriculture that are banned here. Now Congress wants to prevent the companies from exporting chemicals. Yet, foreign governments are willing to allow the continued use of the chemicals and may have very good reasons for doing so. It seems to me wrong for the government of this country to substitute its judgment for that of another country about what is best for its citizenry. Therefore, the proposed ban should be voted down.

Which of the following, if true, would most WEAKEN the argument above?

(A) The chemicals that are the subject of the proposed ban greatly enhance agricultural productivity.

(B) The chemicals that are the subject of the proposed ban contaminate produce that is imported into the United States.

(C) The chemicals that are the subject of the proposed ban account for a very small part of the sales of the chemical companies that would be affected.

(D) The U.S. chemical companies that would be affected by the ban are the only ones with the technology to produce the chemicals that would be banned.

(E) Some foreign governments already prohibit the importation and the use of the chemicals that would be the subject of the ban.

17. Yes, it is true that a regular jar of Fulghum's Instant Coffee costs 50 percent more than a regular jar of the leading brand of instant coffee, but Fulghum's is still cheaper to use.

Which of the following, if true, best explains the seeming contradiction in the statement above?

(A) More than twice as many people use the leading brand of instant coffee as use Fulghum's.

(B) A regular jar of Fulghum's instant coffee will make twice as many cups as a regular jar of the leading brand.

(C) The regular jar of Fulghum's and the regular jar of the leading brand both contain 8 ounces of instant coffee.

(D) Both Fulghum's and the leading brand used to charge the same price for a regular jar, but the leading brand reduced its price by one third.

(E) In a taste survey using coffee prepared according to the instructions on the label of each brand's jar, coffee drinkers were unable to distinguish one brand from the other.

18. All employees who will be promoted by the company will receive higher salaries. Some of the employees who will be promoted by the company are highly skilled, others are merely competent, and still others are bunglers.

If the statements above are true, which of the following statements must also be true?

(A) Some of those who are promoted by the company do not receive higher salaries.

(B) Some of those who are not promoted by the company receive higher salaries.

(C) Both highly skilled employees and bunglers will receive higher salaries.

(D) All employees who receive higher salaries will be given promotions.

(E) No employee who receives a higher salary is a bungler.

19. It is often thought that crime in large metropolitan areas is much worse now than ever before. In fact, other periods of history have been far more violent. In his police history, James Richardson reports that in New York City between 1814 and 1834, the number of complaints at the police courts quadrupled while the population of the city little more than doubled. This increase in crime during a short period is simply unimaginable today.

The argument above depends upon all of the following assumptions EXCEPT

(A) a useful measure of the prevalence of violence in a society is the number of reported crimes.

(B) the experience of New York City with crime was representative of metropolitan areas of the time.

(C) the crimes that were committed between 1814 and 1834 were more serious than those committed today.

(D) the statistics used and reported by Richardson accurately describe the situation in New York City.

(E) the number of crimes that are reported can be expected to rise with an increase in population.

20. A country-western song tells of a man trying to impress a woman he has just met. After telling her a lot about himself, he finally says, "I want you so badly I would lie to you. And that's the truth."

Which of the following conclusions about the man in the song can be most reliably drawn?

(A) He is definitely lying.

(B) He is definitely telling the truth.

(C) He might or might not be telling the truth.

(D) He is contradicting himself.

(E) It is logically impossible to make such a statement.

21. There are at least three spies at a diplomatic reception. At least one spy knows the true identity of every other spy at the reception. At most, two spies know each other's true identities.

Which of the following is inconsistent with the information provided above?

(A) Four spies are at the reception.

(B) No spies at the reception know each other's true identities.

(C) Exactly one spy at the reception knows the true identities of every other spy at the reception.

(D) The true identity of one spy at the reception is known by every other spy at the reception.

(E) If a spy knows the true identity of another spy, that second spy in turn knows the true identity of the first.

22. A member of the University Council, who asked not to be identified, confirmed last week that without the support of the head of the faculty union, the proposed budget cuts would be defeated. Since the budget cuts were approved by the University Council, the head of the union must have supported the budget cut proposal.

The logic of which of the following is most similar to the logic of the argument above?

(A) The mechanic told us to replace the ignition module before we left for our vacation trip. Now the car won't start, so the ignition module must have gone bad.

(B) The medical book states that a high fever and chills are symptoms associated with severe sun poisoning. The patient, however, has not recently been exposed to the sun, so she cannot have a high fever or chills.

(C) The rules enacted by the Board of Bar Examiners state that a person cannot practice law in this state without first having passed the bar examination. Claudia is a licensed attorney in this state. Therefore, Claudia must have passed the bar examination.

(D) According to the rules of the American Kennel Club, a show dog cannot be declared a champion until it has accumulated 15 points at various shows. My 3-year-old Akita has already won 12 points, so he will probably become a champion.

(E) According to the company's work rules, a worker who is absent more than twelve days during a year can be terminated. Since Peter was fired last week, he must have been absent more than twelve days last year.

23. Chrysler Corporation's advertising campaigns often appeal to the chauvinism of American buyers. In the mid-1980s, it appealed explicitly to patriotic feelings with its "Born in the U.S.A." campaign. More recently, Chrysler calls its cars the "Americans that beat the Hondas." But when it came time for Chrysler to buy metal stamping presses, it bought Japanese models rather than American models. In addition, for years, Chrysler has sold under its own brand name a significant number of cars and trucks made in Japan by Mitsubishi.

The primary purpose of the speaker above is to

(A) prove that Chrysler cars are really not better than Japanese-made cars.

(B) suggest that Chrysler sever its ties with Japanese manufacturers.

(C) cast doubt on the credibility of the Chrysler corporation.

(D) encourage people to buy Japanese cars rather than Chrysler cars.

(E) discourage consumers from purchasing Japanese products in lieu of American products.

24. There is no theoretical objection to enforcing all verbal agreements. In practice, however, certain agreements—such as those for the conveyance of land and those for the sale of goods, the value of which exceeds a certain dollar amount—must be in writing to be enforceable. When a judge refuses to rule in favor of a plaintiff in a suit brought on a contract that must be in writing but is not, the judge does not deny the existence of a contract. Rather, the court refuses to recognize the agreement, if any, because it was not properly formalized.

The argument above is primarily concerned with the distinction between

(A) a court and a judge.

(B) plaintiffs and defendants.

(C) buyers and sellers.

(D) an agreement and the written record of the agreement.

(E) a contract for the sale of land and a contract for the sale of goods.

25. ALAN: The economy is definitely not entering a recession. Last month, according to the Bureau of Labor Statistics, the number of persons drawing unemployment benefits declined by 0.1 percent.

DICK: That just proves how bad the down turn really is. Virtually all of those who stopped drawing benefits did so because they had exhausted their benefits.

The speakers

(A) accept the accuracy of the government's report and reach similar conclusions.

(B) accept the accuracy of the government's report but interpret it differently.

(C) question the accuracy of the government's report and interpret it differently.

(D) question the accuracy of the government's report and reach different conclusions.

(E) disagree over the accuracy of the government's report and reach different conclusions.

STOP

END OF SECTION 5. IF YOU HAVE ANY TIME LEFT, GO OVER YOUR WORK IN THIS SECTION ONLY. DO NOT WORK IN ANY OTHER SECTION OF THE TEST.

WRITING SAMPLE

Time—30 minutes

The Board of Trustees of State University has recently received an anonymous gift to the university in the amount of $100,000 for the construction of a memorial dedicated to students and graduates of the university who lost their lives in the service of their country. The board is considering proposals by Ann Gerson and Phil Maxwell. Write an argument in favor of one of the two proposals. The following criteria should be taken into consideration:

❶ The $100,000 must be spent on a memorial, but the board would like the memorial to have some additional function.

❷ The board wants a memorial that will assist students in understanding and appreciating the sacrifice made by others.

ANN GERSON is an artist with a substantial national reputation but no particular ties to the university. Many of her sculptures, such as the Plaza Fountain she designed for the Federal Government Center, combine function and art. Ann proposes to build an "oasis" in the center of the campus: a fountain surrounded by greenery and marble benches. The center of the fountain will be a shrouded figure sculpted from stone that is intended to symbolize death, and on the containing wall of the fountain will be engraved the names of university students and graduates who died and the dates and places of their deaths.

PHIL MAXWELL, a graduate of State University, is a local architect who paints and sculpts as a hobby. Several of Phil's paintings are on display in the university museum in the special wing devoted to student alumni work. In addition, Phil teaches a course in the History of Architecture in the university's continuing education division. Phil proposes a simple memorial, a wall on which will be inscribed the names of the students and graduates who died, the dates of their actual or intended graduation, and brief personal notes to be supplied by relatives such as major area of study, career plans, or outside interests. Phil has designed the wall so that it can be the outside wall of the main entrance of the new student union now being planned for the university.

ANSWER KEY

Section 1

1.	A	7.	A	13.	C	19.	E
2.	B	8.	C	14.	D	20.	A
3.	B	9.	B	15.	A	21.	B
4.	A	10.	A	16.	D	22.	E
5.	D	11.	E	17.	B	23.	B
6.	B	12.	D	18.	C	24.	D

25.	D
26.	E
27.	A
28.	E

Section 2

1.	C	6.	E	11.	D	16.	A
2.	C	7.	A	12.	A	17.	D
3.	A	8.	E	13.	C	18.	B
4.	E	9.	E	14.	B	19.	C
5.	A	10.	D	15.	C	20.	D

21.	A
22.	C
23.	A
24.	B

Section 3

1.	C	6.	B	11.	B	16.	C
2.	E	7.	C	12.	A	17.	E
3.	B	8.	B	13.	B	18.	B
4.	E	9.	D	14.	B	19.	D
5.	D	10.	E	15.	A	20.	B

21.	D
22.	D
23.	A
24.	C

Section 4

1.	B	7.	E	13.	E	19.	C
2.	C	8.	D	14.	A	20.	D
3.	E	9.	D	15.	B	21.	A
4.	D	10.	A	16.	E	22.	D
5.	A	11.	B	17.	B	23.	C
6.	E	12.	B	18.	A	24.	A

25.	B
26.	C
27.	C
28.	D

Section 5

1.	D	6.	D	11.	B	16.	B
2.	D	7.	C	12.	A	17.	B
3.	C	8.	B	13.	A	18.	C
4.	C	9.	D	14.	B	19.	C
5.	A	10.	E	15.	C	20.	C

21.	E
22.	C
23.	C
24.	D
25.	B

EXPLANATORY ANSWERS

Section 1

1. **The correct answer is (A).** This is an implied idea question. The author draws an analogy between a political fable and a caricature because the political fable emphasizes certain points over others; it paints with a very broad brush, dealing in types rather than characters. Similarly, a caricature emphasizes certain personal characteristics over others. Thus, this is the analogy: society:political fable::person:caricature.

2. **The correct answer is (B).** This is a main idea question of the variation "pick the best title." The author begins by announcing that *Nineteen Eighty-Four* is not a novel in the strict sense of that term but really a political fable. Choice (B) echoes the author's statement of his own purpose. Choice (A) is incorrect because it is too narrow. The author barely mentions in passing some of the characters in the book. Choice (C) also is too narrow. Although it is true that the author does state that one of the characteristics of a political fable is that characters are defined in relation to their society, that is but one of many points made in the selection. Choice (D) suffers from the same defect. There are several other points made by the author in the passage. In addition, choice (D) is in a sense too broad, for the author takes as the focus for his discussion the particular work *Nineteen Eighty-Four*—not political fables in general. Finally, choice (E) suffers from both of the ills that afflict choice (D). Choice (E) is both too narrow because the distinction between novel and political fable is but one part of the discussion and too broad because it fails to acknowledge that the author has chosen to focus on a particular work.

3. **The correct answer is (B).** This is a logical detail question. Why does the author mention this characteristic of Winston Smith? The answer to this question doesn't become clear until you have read the entire selection. One important feature of a political fable is that characters are reduced to mere types. They don't have the idiosyncrasies that they would have in a novel. The function of that part of the first sentence which begins, "a requirement not refuted...." is to preempt an objection to this claim: Winston Smith is described in some detail. So the author mentions this to let the audience know that he is aware that Winston Smith is described in some detail and to insist that this makes no difference to his argument. Given this analysis, choice (A) must be incorrect. Small details like an ulcer would not be characteristic of a type but of an individual. Choice (C) simply represents a confused reading of that section of the passage. The author implies there that Winston Smith is the main character of the work. As for choices (D) and (E), though these echo some of the ideas developed in the selection, they are not responsive to the question.

4. **The correct answer is (A).** The tension the author describes is between the political sense of a political fable (the political element which must be conveyed by talking about individual people in their social situation) and the sense of fable (which must rely on type). The passage then states that the author faces a difficult task. If he errs on the side of the political sense, the value of the work as a

fable is lost; if he errs on the side of the fable, the reader can't identify with the situation described. This dilemma is described by choice (A). Choice (B) does refer to ideas mentioned in the text, but choice (B) is not responsive to the question. Choice (C) describes a "tension" that might exist in other situations, but this is not the situation the author describes. Choice (D) is contradicted by our analysis above, for the danger is that the reader won't find the situation realistic enough. Finally, though choice (E) does echo the idea of "tension," this is not the kind of tension the author is discussing.

5. **The correct answer is (D).** This is an author's attitude question. The tone of the passage is neutral. The author makes neither positive nor negative comments about the particular work, *Nineteen Eighty-Four.* So the best description is scholarly.

6. **The correct answer is (B).** This specific detail question asks that you show an understanding of the meaning of a particular part of the selection. Our analysis above will help us here. The dilemma faced by the political fabulist is the danger of too much versus too little detail. In discussing this dilemma, the author says that too little detail will leave the reader without a sense of connection to life. The author continues to say that this is particularly true if the writer projects his narrative into the future. Then the reader may conclude that the situation described by the fable is completely alien to him— just a foreign country with strange customs, meaning that he can't understand why anyone does anything so their actions are really not connected with his. Choice (B) summarizes this idea. Choice (A) is incorrect because the author does not mean that the action literally takes

place in another country but that the reader feels no connection with the situation. As for choice (C), it is the lack of detail (e.g., interacting characters) that creates the problem mentioned in this reference. Choice (D) finds no support in the passage; and, indeed, the political fabulist is actually presenting his own political vision. Finally, as for choice (E), it is the lack of detail, not the overabundance of detail, that creates the "foreign country" problem.

7. **The correct answer is (A).** This is a logical structure question that asks about the overall development of the selection. As we have seen, the author is concerned with discussing the elements of a political fable, and this development is described by choice (A). Choices (B) and (C) are incorrect because the author doesn't mention a logical inconsistency or a cause-and-effect connection. As for choice (D), to the extent that the author does introduce examples (the characters of the book), this is not the main concern of the selection. Finally, though the selection discusses a political fable that projects its situation into the future, the author doesn't introduce any proposals for future action himself.

8. **The correct answer is (C).** This is obviously a main idea question. The author discusses three important characteristics of art of the Middle Ages—the sacred script, the sacred mathematics, and sacred symbolic language. At the close of his remarks, the author mentions in passing the Renaissance, primarily as a way of praising the art of the Middle Ages. Choice (C) does a fair job of describing this development. Choice (A) can be eliminated because the discussion focuses upon the art of the Middle Ages, not upon the art preceding the Middle Ages. And to

the extent that the author does mention what might be called influences, e.g., the revival of certain views of Pythagoras, this is done in passing. They do not constitute the focus of the passage. Choice (D) is incorrect for the same sort of reason. The reference in closing to the art of the Renaissance cannot be considered the overall theme of the passage. Finally, choices (B) and (E) are incorrect because the author never takes on the "why."

9. **The correct answer is (B).** This is an inference question. In essence, the question is asking which of the five features listed was most likely to be found in a painting. Choice (E) can be eliminated since that is inconsistent with the concept of the artist who recedes into the background of the sacred rules. As for choice (A), the author's only example of numbers was their use in music. This does not lead us to conclude that numbers might not be important in painting as well, but we cannot conclude, on the other hand, that every painting was likely to use the numbers 3 and 4. Choices (C) and (D) are mentioned as characteristics of certain subjects. But the author does not imply that the subjects were treated in every painting. Choice (B), however, has the specific support of paragraph 3. There the author states that "Every painting is an allegory." So, though the specific content of paintings of the period would vary from work to work, the overarching idea of a literal and hidden meaning pervaded the work of the period.

10. **The correct answer is (A).** The tone of the passage is clearly one of appreciation—both in the sense that the author understands and in the sense that the author admires. This is further supported by the contrast between art of the Middle Ages and religious art of the Renaissance at the end of the passage. Choice (B) overstates the case. The author is only discussing the one period, with only casual reference to the period following it. We cannot conclude from the fact that the author discusses art of the Middle Ages in this text that the author considers this art the greatest of all art. Choice (C) cannot be deduced from the passage: the reference to music will not support such a judgment. Choice (D) is inconsistent with the author's opening and closing remarks. Finally, choice (E) too must be incorrect given the general approving treatment of the passage.

11. **The correct answer is (E).** This is a question about a logical detail: Why does the author quote Saint Augustine? At that point, the author has just asserted that the art of the Middle Ages also is characterized by a passion for numbers. Then the author quotes a statement from Augustine that makes that very point. The reason for the quotation must be to give an example of the general attitude toward numbers. Choice (E) describes this move. Choice (A) is incorrect since no objection is mentioned. Choice (B) is incorrect for the same reason and for the further reason that "ridicule" is inconsistent with the tone of the passage. Choice (C) is incorrect because the author is not attempting to demonstrate the similarities between two things. Finally, choice (D) is incorrect since it does not appear that the author is in any danger of falling into a contradiction.

12. **The correct answer is (D).** This is an explicit idea question. Each of the incorrect answers is mentioned in paragraph 1 as an element of the sacred script. As for choice (A), lines may be used to represent water or the sky. As for choice (B),

these indicate sainthood or divinity. As for choice (C), shoes are mentioned as an identifying characteristic. And choice (E) also is mentioned (a tree represents earth). Choice (D), however, is not mentioned as an element of the sacred script. Symmetry is discussed in conjunction with numbers, and that has to do with another characteristic altogether.

13. **The correct answer is (C).** This is an application question. Of course, we do not know where the passage actually appeared, and the task is to pick the most likely source. We stress this because it is always possible to make an argument for any of the answer choices to a question of this sort. But the fact that a justification is possible does not make that choice correct; the strongest possible justification makes the choice correct. Choice (C) is the most likely source. The passage focuses on art and is scholarly in tone. Choice (A) can be eliminated, for the passage casts no light on social conditions of the period. Choice (B) can be eliminated for a similar reason. The author treats art in and of itself—not as a social force. And we certainly cannot conclude that by discussing religious art, the author wants to discuss the church. Choice (D) is incorrect because the reference to Saint Augustine is incidental and illustrative only. Choice (E) is incorrect because it is inconsistent with the scholarly and objective tone of the passage.

14. **The correct answer is (D).** This is an inferred idea question, one asking for an interpretation of a phrase. The idea of the first paragraph is that the rules of art in the Middle Ages placed constraints on the artist so that the artistic effort had to be made within certain conventions. As a result, painting was not individualistic.

This is most clearly expressed by choice (D). Choice (A) is incorrect since the author is saying that the artist's talent just did not show as individual talent. Choice (B) is incorrect, for though this is a true statement, it is not a response to the question. Choice (C) is perhaps the second-best answer because it at least hints at what choice (D) says more clearly. But the author does not mean to say the artist was not recognized while still alive. That may or may not have been the case. What the author means to say is that we do not now see the personality of the artist. Finally, choice (E) is just a confused reading of a part of the passage not relevant here.

15. **The correct answer is (A).** This is an application. As we have noted before, application questions tend to be difficult because the correct answer can be understood as correct only in context. With an explicit idea question, for example, an answer can be understood as right or wrong—either the author said it or did not. With a question such as this, the *most logical continuation* depends upon the choices available. Here the best answer is choice (A). The author concludes the discussion of the causes of our poor showing on the health status index by asserting that the best way to improve this showing is a general improvement in the quality of life. This is an intriguing suggestion and an appropriate follow-up would be a list of proposals that might accomplish this. As for choice (B), this could be part of such a discussion, but a listing of the most common causes of death would not, in and of itself, represent an extension of the development of the argument. Choice (C), too, has some merit. The author might want to talk about the causes of poverty as a way of

learning how to improve the quality of life by eliminating the causes. But this argument actually cuts in favor of choice (A), for the justification for choice (C) then depends on choice (A)—that is, it depends on the assumption that the author should discuss the idea raised in choice (A). Choice (D) is incorrect because the author specifically states in the closing remarks that redistribution of medical resources is not a high priority. Choice (E) can be eliminated on the same ground.

16. **The correct answer is (D).** This is an explicit idea question, and we find mention of choices (A), (B), (C), and (E) in the second paragraph. Choice (D), too, is mentioned, but it is not a factor "affecting the health of the population." It is a measure of, or an effect of, the health of the population, not a factor causing it.

17. **The correct answer is (B).** This is a main idea question. Choice (A) can be eliminated because the author actually minimizes the importance of medical care as a factor affecting the health of a population. Choice (C) can be eliminated because this is not the author's objective. To be sure, the information supplied in the passage might be used by a person to live more healthfully, but that is not why the author wrote the passage. Choice (D) is incorrect because this is a small part of the argument, a part that is used to advance the major objective outlined in choice (B). Finally, choice (E) is incorrect since the author leaves us with a pregnant suggestion but no specific recommendations. Choice (B), however, describes the development of the passage. The author wishes to explain the causes of the poor health status of the U.S. It is not, the author argues, lack of medical care or even poor distribution of medical care, hypotheses that, we can infer from the text, are often proposed. The author then goes on to give two alternative explanations: affluence and poverty.

18. **The correct answer is (C).** This is an application question. Choice (C) is strongly supported by the text. In paragraph 3, the author specifically states that we have the highest per capita expenditure for medical care in the world. Yet, as noted in the first paragraph, we rank rather low in terms of health. Choice (A) is not supported by the arguments given in the passage. Though medical care may not be the most important determinant of health, the author never suggests that expenditure is not correlated with overall availability. Choice (B) is incorrect and specifically contradicted by the second paragraph, where the author states that genetic problems may be covered over by medical care. Choice (D) is incorrect since the author minimizes the importance of technology in improving health. Finally, choice (E) is simply not supported by any data or argument given in the passage.

19. **The correct answer is (E).** This is a logical detail question. The author refers to excess consumption to illustrate the way in which affluence, one of his two hypotheses, could undermine an individual's health. As for choice (A), while it is true that such problems may not be susceptible to medical treatment, the author does not introduce them to prove that. They are introduced at the particular point in the argument to prove that affluence can undermine health. Choice (B) is incorrect for a similar reason. The author does not introduce the examples to prove that drinking and smoking are unhealthful activities. The

passage presupposes readers know that already. Then, on the assumption that the reader already believes that, the author can say, "See, affluence causes smoking and drinking—which we all know to be bad." Choice (C) must fail for the same reason. Finally, choice (D) is incorrect since this is not the reason for introducing the examples. Although it is argued that medical care and health are not as tightly linked as some people might think, this is not the point the author is working on when the examples of smoking and drinking are introduced. With a logical detail question of this sort, we must be careful to select an answer that explains why the author makes a certain move at the particular juncture in the argument. Neither general reference to the overall idea of the passage (e.g., to prove the main point) nor a reference to a collateral argument will do the trick.

20. **The correct answer is (A).** The answer to the question posed in choice (A) is explicitly provided in the second paragraph: environment. As for choice (B), though some information is given about the health status of the U.S., no other country is mentioned by name. As for choice (C), though some statistics are given about life expectancies in the U.S., no comparison of male and female life expectancies is given. As for choice (D), though genetic factors are mentioned generally in paragraph 2, no such factors are ever specified. Finally, the author offers no recommendations, so choice (E) must be incorrect.

21. **The correct answer is (B).** This is an inferred idea based on a specific reference. In the second paragraph, the author lists four groups of factors that influence health. In referring to medical

services, the author says they are treated separately from environmental factors because of our special interest in them. This implies that the author would actually consider them to be just another, although important, factor in the environment. As for choice (A), the least important group of factors is specifically stated to be genetic factors. As for choice (C), there is no support for such a conclusion in that paragraph. The same reason allows us to eliminate both choices (D) and (E).

22. **The correct answer is (E).** This is an explicit idea question. The answer can be found in the first paragraph, where the author notes that a heart attack is unlike an angina attack because the heart attack always involves the death of heart muscle. As for choice (A), although a heart attack may involve acceleration of the heartbeat, this is not what distinguishes it from angina. Choice (B) is incorrect since the author describes the way in which nitroglycerin may be used to treat heart attack. Choice (C) is incorrect both because this is not a statement that can be justified by the text (generally?) and because it is not the defining characteristic of a heart attack. Finally, choice (D) is incorrect, for though the heart attack involves rapid muscle death, it is the death of tissue and not the length of time of the attack that is the distinguishing feature.

23. **The correct answer is (B).** This, too, is an explicit idea question, but it is more difficult than the preceding question. The author cites the "curious" result that the nitroglycerin helped the most seriously stricken patients but did not help the less seriously stricken patients. The author explains that in the more seriously stricken patients, the ordinary

autonomic response to a drop in blood pressure, which would be a faster heart rate, did not occur. Apparently, the congestive heart failure effectively blocked this reaction. Consequently, the drop in blood pressure caused by the nitroglycerin did not invite the normal increase in heart rate. This explanation is presented by choice (B). Choice (A) is incorrect since no mention is made of any delay in administering drugs. Choice (C) is incorrect since phenylephrine was not available to the 12 patients at the time of the study. Phenylephrine was later used to counter the drop in blood pressure caused by nitroglycerin. Choice (D) is incorrect since the passage states that blood pressure did drop in those patients with congestive heart failure. The difference between those patients and the less seriously stricken ones was that the drop in blood pressure did not cause an increase in heart rate. For the same reason, choice (E) must also be eliminated.

24. **The correct answer is (D).** This is an explicit idea question. As for choice (A), several results of heart attack are mentioned at various points in the text. The answer to the question in choice (B) is explicitly provided in the third paragraph. As for choice (C), the author mentions the effect of nitroglycerin at various points; that is, it dilates blood vessels and reduces blood pressure. Finally, the question in choice (E) is answered in the second paragraph. Choice (D), however, is not answered in the passage. Though the author discusses the effects of heart attack, the passage does not discuss the causes of heart attack.

25. **The correct answer is (D).** The answer to this inference question can be found in the final paragraph. There the author states that research is being done

on drugs that affect myocardial oxygen supply and demand "including . . . vessel dilators such as nitroglycerin . . ." From this, we can infer that nitroglycerin dilates blood vessels and this somehow affects the oxygen balance in the heart muscle. This is the value of the drug. Choice (A) is incorrect because the lowering of blood pressure is an unwanted side effect of nitroglycerin, not its medical value. Choice (B) is incorrect since the value of nitroglycerin is to prevent damage, not to aid in healing. Choice (C) is incorrect for the same reason that choice (A) is incorrect. Finally, choice (E) is incorrect because nitroglycerin is mentioned as a vessel dilator in the final paragraph, not a drug that counters hypertension.

26. **The correct answer is (E).** This is a tone question. The author's attitude is best studied in the final paragraph. Having described the possibility of treating heart attack with nitroglycerin, the author adds the disclaimer that there is no proof yet of the value of the treatment in very serious cases. From this, we may infer, however, that the author believes it has some value in less serious cases. Moreover, since the passage refers to research being done, the author apparently believes that the treatment may prove to have value in other cases as well. This attitude is best described as one of optimism. Since the passage has, on balance, a positive tone, we can eliminate choices (B), (C), and (D). As for choice (A), though the author may be concerned about the treatment of heart attacks, the overall tone of the discussion is not concern or worry but rather hope or optimism.

27. **The correct answer is (A).** This is an inference question, the answer to which

is found in the second paragraph. There it is stated that phenylephrine is used to maintain blood pressure: but that simple statement is not enough to answer the question. We must dig deeper. Why is it important to maintain blood pressure? The final sentence of the paragraph states that a drop in blood pressure causes the heart to speed up. It is this increase in heart rate that "worsens the damage." So the value of phenylephrine is that it prevents cardiac acceleration by maintaining blood pressure. This is the explanation given in choice (A). As for choices (B) and (C), these answers make essentially the same statement using language drawn from different parts of the passage. But they describe something other than the effect of phenylephrine. Choice (D) is incorrect since the phenylephrine has a particular use that complements nitroglycerin. Although the effect of both drugs taken together may be something like that described in choice (D), this is not an answer to the question asked. Finally, choice (E) is just language taken from the first paragraph and is not an answer to the question asked.

28. **The correct answer is (E).** This is a main idea question. The best way of describing the development of the passage is given in choice (E). The author is discussing a treatment for heart attack. As for choice (A), the only suggestion of a predicament is contained in paragraph 1: Nitroglycerin has beneficial effects, but it also lowers blood pressure. But once that has been stated, the author proceeds to explain how the dilemma has been resolved. So the passage, if anything, explains not a predicament but how a predicament has been solved. As for choice (B), though the author does

evaluate the results of a study, that evaluation is incidental to the larger goals of describing a treatment. As for choice (C), though we, the readers, may see implicit in the treatment some sort of proposal, it cannot be said that the author's intention is to outline a proposal. Finally, choice (D) is the least effective choice since there is no argument presented.

Section 2

Questions 1–6

Here we have a linear ordering problem involving ten individuals. Since the number of individuals is so large, we will probably do better to sketch a diagram for each problem; after all, the diagram is nothing more than a series of positions numbered 1 through 10. We should also summarize the particular restrictions placed on each color pennant:

2 Green, 2 Blue, 3 Red, 3 Yellow

$G = G$ (Greens are next to each other.)

$B \neq B$ (Blues are not next to each other.)

$R = R = R$ (Reds are next to each other.)

$B/R =$ ends (Blue at one end; red at the other.)

1. **The correct answer is (C).** We begin by entering the additional information:

1 2 3 4 5 6 7 8 9 10
            G G R

And since the red pennants are together and one of the pennants on the end is red and the other blue, we know:

1 2 3 4 5 6 7 8 9 10
B G G R R R

The only condition remaining to be observed is to separate the blue pennants. This means the remaining blue pennant can be placed in positions 3, 6, and 7 and that yellow pennants will fill the remaining places. Now we turn to the answer choices. Choices (A), (B), (D), and (E) are all incorrect since the other blue pennant can occupy positions 3 or 6 or 7 though precisely which is not determined. In any event, no matter which position the remaining blue pennant occupies, position 2 will be occupied by a yellow pennant, so both blue pennants will be next to yellow pennants.

2. **The correct answer is (C).** We enter the additional information on a diagram:

1 2 3 4 5 6 7 8 9 10
       B *Y*

Then, since the red pennants are together, with one on one end and a blue pennant on the other end, we deduce:

1 2 3 4 5 6 7 8 9 10
R *R* *R*   *B* *Y*   *B*

We now must place two yellow and two green pennants; since the green pennants must go next to each other, they must occupy positions 4 and 5, or 5 and 6:

    1 2 3 4 5 6 7 8 9 10
    R *R* *R* *G* *G* *Y* *B* *Y* *Y* *B*
or *R* *R* *R* *Y* *G* *G* *B* *Y* *Y* *B*

We can see from the diagram that position 5 is necessarily occupied by a green pennant.

3. **The correct answer is (A).** We begin by entering the additional information on a diagram:

    1 2 3 4 5 6 7 8 9 10
    B *G* *G* *B* *Y* *Y* *Y* *R* *R* *R*
or *R* *R* *R* *Y* *Y* *Y* *B* *G* *G* *B*

There are only two possible arrangements given all of the restrictions. Since the question stem stipulates that the blue pennants are next to green pennants, we know those four pennants form

a bloc, *BGGB*, at one end or the other. Further, at the opposite end will be the bloc *RRR*, which means that the yellow pennants will be adjacent to each other. It is not determined from the information at which end the blue pennants will be and at which end the red pennants will be. But we can see that under either scenario, both the fifth and sixth positions are occupied by yellow pennants.

4. **The correct answer is (E).** We begin by entering the additional information on a diagram:

1 2 3 4 5 6 7 8 9 10
                   Y

So, we deduce

1 2 3 4 5 6 7 8 9 10
R *R* *R*   *Y* *Y* *Y* *B*

for we know that the three red pennants are in a row at one end or the other and that a blue pennant occupies the other end. The only pennants left to place are the two green pennants, which must be next to each other, and the remaining blue pennant:

    1 2 3 4 5 6 7 8 9 10
    R *R* *R* *G* *G* *B* *Y* *Y* *Y* *B*
or *R* *R* *R* *B* *G* *G* *Y* *Y* *Y* *B*

Then we look to the answer choices. We can see that choices (A), (B), and (D) are false. Further, choice (C) is only possibly true. Under either scenario, however, choice (E) is necessarily true.

5. **The correct answer is (A).** We enter the additional information on a diagram:

1 2 3 4 5 6 7 8 9 10
    Y   *Y*

So we know:

1 2 3 4 5 6 7 8 9 10
B   *Y*   *Y*   *R* *R* *R*

given the restrictions on the red pennants and the end pennants. Now we may also deduce:

```
1   2   3   4   5   6   7   8   9   10
B   Y   Y   B   Y   G   G   R   R
```

because position 2 may not be blue and position 6 and 7 must be green. Now we can see that choices (B), (C), (D), and (E) are necessarily true and that choice (A) is necessarily false.

6. **The correct answer is (E).** Given the restriction that one end pennant is blue and that at the other end we have three red pennants, we can deduce the following since the question stem stipulates that one green pennant is next to a blue pennant and the other next to a red pennant:

```
     1   2   3   4   5   6   7   8   9   10
     R   R   R   G   G   B   Y   Y   Y   B
or   B   Y   Y   Y   B   G   G   R   R
```

So there are only two possible arrangements given the stipulation of the question stem. We can see that choices (A) and (B) are possibly, though not necessarily, true. Choice (D) is impossible. Choice (E) is, as the diagram proves, necessarily true.

Questions 7–12

This set is an ordering set with a twist: There are two main orders, depending on whether J is tasted third or seventh. We begin then with the following:

```
     1   2   3   4   5   6   7
                 J
or                           J
```

Then we enter the second condition:

```
     1   2   3   4   5   6   7
                 J   (~N)
or           N               J
```

Then comes the third condition:

```
     1   2   3   4   5   6   7
                 J   (~N)
or           N           L   J
```

And the fourth condition:

```
     1   2   3   4   5   6   7
                 J   (~N)
                             O
or           N           L   J
```

and finally:

```
     1   2   3   4   5   6   7
    (~K)         J   (~N)     O
or       K   N           L   J
```

7. **The correct answer is (A).** L can only be tasted fourth if we use the upper order. In that case, it will be J that is tasted third.

8. **The correct answer is (E).** For M to follow L, we cannot use the lower arrangement, for there L is already scheduled as the sixth wine followed immediately by J. We must therefore use the upper arrangement. The key to the solution is to see that there is a further conclusion to be drawn about the scheduling of K and N. Our original diagram shows positions 1 and 4, 2 and 5, and 4 and 7 as open and available for the K --- N schedule. A closer look shows that we can eliminate the 1–4 arrangement, because N cannot be the fourth wine tasted in that sequence. So K and N are either 2 and 5, or 4 and 7, respectively. If, however, M must be tasted immediately following the tasting of L, then K cannot be in position 2. Only if K and N are in positions 4 and 7 can we put L and M together in sequence. So the entire sequence is:

```
1   2   3   4   5   6   7
L   M   J   K   P   O   N
```

The only position left for P is fifth, and choice (E) is necessarily true. The other choices are necessarily false.

9. **The correct answer is (E).** M is under no particular restriction with regard to another wine, so M can be inserted in any open position. Positions 1, 2, and 4 are open under the first order. Positions 2, 3, and 5 are open under the second order. So depending on when J is tasted, M could be tasted second, third, fourth, or fifth. M cannot be tasted sixth, however, since either O or L is tasted sixth (depending on when J is tasted).

10. **The correct answer is (D).** This question must be answered on the basis of the information provided in the initial set of conditions. In spite of the fact that these conditions leave considerable flexibility in the scheduling of wines, it is necessarily true that K will be tasted earlier than O. In the second possible order, K is tasted first and necessarily ahead of every other wine. In the first order, K must be tasted either second or fourth (so that N can follow as the third wine after K). So choice (D) is the correct answer. Choice (A) is incorrect because K could be tasted second under the first arrangement. Choice (B) is incorrect since the second arrangement places L before J. Choice (C) is incorrect since K could follow L under the first arrangement. Finally, choice (E) is incorrect since M is under no restriction and could be tasted in every position except sixth (see explanation for question 9).

11. **The correct answer is (D).** In order for P to be tasted earlier than N and yet later than O, we must use the second possible sequence, placing O in the second tasting position and P in the third. This means that M will be tasted fifth:

1	2	3	4	5	6	7
K	O	P	N	M	L	J

Choice (D) is proved by the diagram to be true, while the other choices are shown by the diagram to be false.

12. **The correct answer is (A).** If M is to be the second wine after P, the first arrangement cannot be used. Under the first arrangement, M and P would have to be tasted second and fourth or fifth and seventh, but K must be second or fourth and N fifth or seventh. Under the second arrangement, one sequence is possible: K, O, P, N, M, L, J.

Questions 13–18

This is a selection set, and we begin by setting up the information in more usable form:

(1) $V \to R$

(2) $(R \ \& \ Q) \to {\sim}P$

(3) $(Q \ \& \ P) \to {\sim}T$

(4a) $P \to (S \lor U)$

(4b) ${\sim}(S \ \& \ U)$

(5a) $(S \lor T)$

(5b) ${\sim}(S \ \& \ T)$

The numbered statements (1) through (5b) correspond to the five conditions given in the set. We have broken the fourth and fifth conditions down into two statements because each of those conditions is actually two conditions. So (4a) corresponds to "If P is selected, then either S or U must be selected," and (4b) corresponds to "S and U cannot both be selected." (5) is treated in similar fashion.

13. **The correct answer is (C).** If neither S nor U is selected, then we know by (5a) that T is selected and by (4a) that P is not selected. Thus far we have eliminated S and U (by stipulation) and P, and we have selected T, which leaves Q, R, and V for consideration. Since P is not selected,

we may include both R and Q without violating (2). And having chosen R, we may include V without violating (1). So, on the assumption that neither S nor U is selected, the largest delegation would consist of T, R, Q, and V.

14. **The correct answer is (B).** If V is selected, then by (1), R must also be selected. Further, if P is selected, by (4a), either S or U must be selected. But we also have (5a), and either S or T must be selected. Since we have both (S or U) and (S or T), we will minimize the number selected if we choose S rather than U or T. So the smallest delegation that includes both P and V will also include R and S.

15. **The correct answer is (C).** If P is selected, then by (4a), either S or U must be selected. Since by (4b), we cannot choose both S and U, S cannot be selected. But we know by (5a) that either S or T must be chosen, so we must pick T. As for the incorrect answers, this reasoning eliminates choice (B) as definitely false. As for choice (A), we cannot choose Q, for to choose Q along with P would mean we could not select T [by (3)]. But we have already learned that we must choose T because S cannot be chosen. As for choices (D) and (E), it is possible to choose R or V and R: since Q cannot be selected [see rejection of choice (A)], this effectively isolates R and V from the other students by breaking the only connection with R and V, which is (2).

16. **The correct answer is (A).** P, Q, and S are a possible three-student delegation. Selecting P requires that we have either S or U (4a), and that condition is satisfied by including S. Having P and Q together means only that we may not have T (3), but that can be avoided if we choose S to satisfy (5a). As for choice (B), P, Q, and T

are not a possible delegation, since Q and P together require that T not be chosen, by (3). As for choice (C), P, R, and V are not acceptable because, by (5a), we must have either S or T. As for choice (D), R, S, and T are not permissible because this violates (5b). Finally, choice (E) is incorrect since the group R, S, and U violates (4b).

17. **The correct answer is (D).** If P is selected, then either S or U must also be selected, by (4a). But if T is chosen, then S cannot be chosen, by (5b), which means that U must be chosen. So it is not possible that U is not chosen. Then, since T and P are chosen, we cannot choose Q, by (3). R and/or V may be chosen, so the committee could consist of 3, 4, or 5 students.

18. **The correct answer is (B).** P, R, and T accompanied by U will satisfy all of the requirements. Choosing T satisfies (5a). Then, P and U together satisfy (4a). We do not have S, so both (4b) and (5b) are respected. And since we do not have Q, (2) and (3) are satisfied. Finally, without V, we have no problem with (1). As for choice (A), P and Q cannot accompany T; that is a violation of (3). As for choice (C), V must be accompanied by R, by (1); and choice (D) can be eliminated on the same ground. Finally, as for choice (E), S and U violates (4b).

Questions 19–24

For this ordering set, the order is so highly underdetermined that a single overall diagram is not likely to be of much assistance. Instead, for each problem, we will simply sketch the scale using dashes and numbers. To conserve space, we will render the scale horizontally

$\underline{1}$ $\underline{2}$ $\underline{3}$ $\underline{4}$ $\underline{5}$ $\underline{6}$ $\underline{7}$

though a more intuitive approach would use a vertical arrangement

$$7$$
$$6$$
$$5$$
$$4$$
$$3$$
$$2$$
$$1$$

We know

$$L < M$$
$$N < J$$
$$J < K < M \text{ or } M < K < J$$

We can effectively ignore O and Q since they are placed in positions 1 and 7 and will not change.

19. **The correct answer is (C).** With N as the fifth note, we know that J, in order to be higher than N, must be the sixth note. Then, to keep M higher than L while keeping K between M and J, we must have the order

1	2	3	4	5	6	7
O	L	M	K	N	J	Q

which demonstrates that choice (C) is necessarily true, while each other choice is clearly false.

20. **The correct answer is (D).** If M is the sixth note, then J can be no higher than the fourth note, for K must come between J and M. Further, K could be no lower than the third since N must be below J. So we have the following:

1	2	3	4	5	6	7
O	N	J	K	L	M	Q

or

1	2	3	4	5	6	7
O	L	N	J	K	M	Q

These are not the only possible arrangements with M as note 6, but this does prove that J and N can be third and

second, respectively, and fourth and third, respectively.

21. **The correct answer is (A).** For K and N to be separated by two notes, they must occupy positions 2 and 5 or 3 and 6. Ignoring the other restrictions we would have four possibilities:

1	2	3	4	5	6	7
O	N			K		Q
O		N			K	Q
O	K			N		Q
O		K			N	Q

The second and third possibilities are not permissible because K could not be between J and M. The fourth also can be eliminated since N must be lower than M. Only the first is possible, and this proves that K must be the fifth note on the scale. As for choice (B), though L might be between J and K:

1	2	3	4	5	6	7
O	N	J	L	K	M	Q

it is not necessarily true that L is between J and K:

1	2	3	4	5	6	7
O	N	L	J	K	M	Q

As for choice (C), we have just seen it is possible for M to be the sixth note, but that is not necessarily the case:

1	2	3	4	5	6	7
O	N	L	M	K	J	Q

As for choice (D), our diagrams show this is possibly, though not necessarily, the case. Similarly, choice (E) is incorrect since the diagrams show that L and M may or may not be separated by exactly one note.

22. **The correct answer is (C).** Since K must be between J and M, either J or M must be lower on the scale than K. In addition, some other note must be lower

than whichever note is lower than *K*; that is, if *J* is lower than *K*, then *N* is lower than *K* as well, and if *M* is lower than *K*, then *L* is lower than *K* as well. This means that *K* can be no lower than the fourth note. The other choices are possibilities:

Choices (A) and (E)	Choices (B) and (D)
1 2 3 4 5 6 7	1 2 3 4 5 6 7
O N L J K M Q	O N J K L M Q

23. **The correct answer is (A).** If *N* is separated by two notes from *O,* then *N* must be note 4; and we know *J* must be above *N*. Since *K* can be no lower than fourth, this means *K* must be note 5, and *J* note 6, leaving *L* and *M* as 2 and 3, respectively.

1 2 3 4 5 6 7

O L M N K J Q

The diagram confirms that choice (A) is necessarily true, while each of the other choices is necessarily false.

24. **The correct answer is (B).** If *L* and *N* are together, they must be notes 2 and 3, respectively, for both *J* and *M* must be higher than *L* and *N,* and *K* must be between *J* and *M* on the scale. This means that *J, K,* and *M* are notes 4, 5, and 6, though not necessarily in that order. So we have two possibilities:

1 2 3 4 5 6 7

O L N J K M Q

or O L N M K J Q

Section 3

1. **The correct answer is (C).** The point of the Chinese official's comment is that the Chinese may appear to some Westerners to be "inscrutable" because those Westerners simply do not pay very careful attention to what is directly before them. Thus, choice (C) is the best answer. Choice (A) is misleading. The Chinese official refers to Occidentals in general, but he never mentions Orientals in general. Even so, choice (A) misses the main point of the anecdote. Choice (B) is better than choice (A) since it is at least generally related to the point of the Chinese official, but the precise point is not that Americans (rather than Occidentals) fail to understand Chinese culture but rather that they suffer from a more specific myopia: They find they are not able to penetrate the motivations of the Chinese. In any event, the point of the passage is not just that there is such a failure, but also that such failure is attributable to the lack of insight of Westerners—not any real inscrutability of the Chinese. Choice (E) mentions the problem of understanding, but the difficulty described in the passage is one way only. Nowhere is it suggested that the Chinese have difficulty in understanding Westerners. Finally, choice (D) would be correct only if the passage had contained some key word to qualify the official's response, such as *hesitatingly* or *cautiously.*

2. **The correct answer is (E).** Once it is seen that the passage is humorous, this question is fairly easy. The official "smiles," and he "gently" responds. Further, the scenario is set by the first sentence: a *junior* official *embarrassed* himself. This shows the situation is uncomfortable for the American, but it is not a serious international incident. And the Chinese official's response is kind— not angry, choice (A); not fearful, choice (B); and not indifferent, choice (D). Choice (C) requires an assumption of malice on the part of the Chinese official. By comparison, "compassion" better fits the description of the official's action—smiling and gentle.

3. **The correct answer is (B).** Here the problem is to make sense out of the brother's claim that a device he rarely used and may never use again is still a good investment. It is not land, a work of art, or some similar thing, so it does not appear as though it will appreciate in value. The advantage, then, of owning must come from merely being able to possess it. Thus, choice (B), which cites the convenience of having the item to use if and when he should decide to do so, is best. Choice (A) can be disregarded because the brother regards the investment as a good one *even if* he never again uses the device. To save money on ice cream, he would have to use it. Choice (C) is highly suggestive—is the brother saying that it is a good idea to have things around in case one needs them? If so, then choice (C) sounds a bit like choice (B). But choice (C) is not nearly so direct as choice (B), and it requires some work to make it into choice (B). Choice (D) is wrong because saving money by having purchased earlier would be worthwhile only if the item is actually needed. After all, a great deal you made by buying a ton of hay is not a great deal just because the price of hay is going up—you need an elephant (or a horse, or a plan to resell, or something) to make it worthwhile. Just buying hay because it's a "bargain" is no bargain at all. Choice (E) is fairly silly. It is like saying, "The bad news is you are to be executed tomorrow morning; the good news is you would have had liver for lunch." Or perhaps closer to this example would be, "The bad news is that someone stole your car; the good news is that the price of gasoline went up by 25¢ a gallon this morning." The point is that you will avoid some trivial injury or cost at the expense of something more serious.

4. **The correct answer is (E).** Again, the passage is somewhat lighthearted. The poet is saying that the poem is obscure: When he wrote it, only he and the Almighty could understand it, and now (it is so difficult) even he has forgotten the point of the verse. Choice (A) is somewhat attractive because the passage does state that God knows what people do not. Of course, once one understands the point of the passage, choice (A) can be discarded. Even so, there is something about choice (A) that lets you know it is wrong— "infinitely." One might infer from the poet's comments that people are not as wise as God, but it is not possible to conclude, on the basis of the one example, that God is infinitely wiser than people. Choice (B) is also attractive, for the poet is saying that it is difficult to understand this particular poem. But choice (B) is wrong because he is not saying that people cannot understand poetry in general. Choices (C) and (D) are distractions. They play on the term "God" in the paragraph. The poet cites God as the one who understands the verse—not the one who inspired it.

5. **The correct answer is (D).** Here we have one final humorous passage. Now this should not lead you to conclude that *many* LSAT paragraphs are amusing— to generalize to that conclusion on the basis of three examples would be a fallacy in and of itself—but taken individually, each is reflective of the LSAT. And even if the LSAT does not string together three or four in a row, we hope that you have found them diverting. After all, study for this test is not the most enjoyable pastime available to human beings. But back to the task at hand . . . . You must always be careful of naked correlations. Sufficient research would prob-

ably turn up some sort of correlation between the length of movies and the number of potatoes produced by Idaho, but such a correlation is obviously worthless. Here, too, the two numbers are completely unrelated to one another at any concrete cause-and-effect level. What joins them is the very general movement of the economy. The standard of living increases; so, too, does the average salary of a preacher, the number of vacations taken by factory workers, the consumption of beef, the number of color televisions, and the consumption of rum. Choice (D) correctly points out that these two are probably connected only this way. Choice (A) is incorrect for it is inconceivable that preachers, a small portion of the population, could account for so large an increase in rum consumption. Choice (B) is wildly implausible. Choice (C), however, is more likely. It strives for that level of generality of correlation achieved by choice (D). The difficulty with choice (C) is that it focuses upon *total* preachers, not the *average* preacher; and the passage correlated not *total* income for preachers with rum consumption but rather *average* income for preachers with consumption of rum. Choice (E) might be arguable if only one period had been used, but the paragraph cites three different times during which this correlation took place.

6. **The correct answer is (B).** This is a relatively easy question. The argument is similar to "All observed instances of *S* are *P*; therefore, all *S* must be *P*." (All swans I have seen are white; therefore, all swans must be white.) There is little to suggest the author is a mechanic or a factory worker in an automobile plant; therefore, choice (A) is incorrect—and would be so even if the author were an expert because the argument does not require expertise. A syllogism is a formal logical structure such as "All *S* are *M*; all *M* are *P*; therefore, all *S* are *P*," and the argument about automobiles does not fit this structure—so choice (C) is wrong. By the same token, choice (E) is wrong since the author generalizes. The author does not deduce, as by logic, anything. Finally, choice (D) is incorrect because the argument is not ambiguous, and one could hardly argue on the basis of ambiguity anyway, especially on the LSAT.

7. **The correct answer is (C).** The key phrase here—and the problem is really just a question of careful reading—is "who actually knew." This reveals that neither of the two knew the person whom they were discussing. There are many ways, however, of debating about the character of people with whom one is not directly acquainted. We often argue about the character of Napoleon or even fictional characters such as David Copperfield. When we do, we are arguing on the basis of indirect information. Perhaps we have read a biography of Napoleon, choice (A), or maybe we have seen a news film of Churchill, choice (B). We may have heard from a friend, or a friend of a friend, that so and so does such and such, choice (E). Finally, sometimes we just make more or less educated guesses, choice (D). At any event, the two people described in the paragraph could have done all of these things. What they could not have done—since they finally resolved the problem by finding someone who actually knew Churchill—was to have argued on the basis of their own personal knowledge.

8. **The correct answer is (B).** Here we have a question that asks us to draw a conclusion from a set of premises. The

author points out that the Constitution provides that the government may not take private property. The irony, according to the author, is that government itself defines what it will classify as private property. We might draw an analogy to a sharing practice among children: You divide the cake, and I will choose which piece I want. The idea behind this wisdom is that this ensures fairness to both parties. The author would say that the Constitution is set up so that the government not only divides (defines property), but it chooses (takes what and when it wants). Choice (A) is contradicted by this analysis. Choice (C) is wide of the mark since the author is discussing property rather than liberty. While the two notions are closely connected in the Constitution, this connection is beyond the scope of this argument. Choice (D) is also beyond the scope of the argument. It makes a broad and unqualified claim that is not supported by the text. Choice (E) is really vacuous and, to the extent that we try to give it content, it must fail for the same reason as choice (A).

9. **The correct answer is (D).** The insight required to solve this problem is that the apparent contradiction can be resolved by observing that the two cases are essentially different. The one is supposed to be a factual story; the other is a fictional account. Choice (B) misses the point of the problem: the task is to reconcile the seemingly conflicting positions of the critics, not to explain what role critics fill. Choices (A), (C), and (E) are possibilities. For example, you might argue any one of this points in defense of the journalist—but that's not what the question stem asks for. You're supposed to explain the seeming inconsistency in

the position of the critics. And in the testing environment, to the extent that you want to argue that one or more of these choices might help to make an argument to support choice (D), then you'd have to choose choice (D) as the better answer just because it makes the point the most directly.

10. **The correct answer is (E).** The main point of the advertisement is that you should not hesitate to buy Cold Springs Water even though it is not imported. Choice (A) would weaken the appeal of the ad: if your guests can taste the difference, then the subterfuge (even though introduced only as a dramatic device) would not be effective. As for choice (B), while it may be true that even "naturally carbonated" waters are further carbonated at the time of bottling, this idea is not relevant. Choice (C) has some merit in the real world, but it is not an assumption of this speaker: why the imports are more costly is not relevant. And choice (D) is wrong because the subterfuge suggestion is not to be taken literally but only as a suggestion to make the point dramatically. Choice (E) is an assumption of the argument: status counts.

11. **The correct answer is (B).** Careful reading of the paragraph shows that the author's attitude toward parochial education is that insistence on instruction in religious values is *justifiable*; the author disagrees, however, on the question of how best to inculcate those values. The author believes that the proper attitude toward relations between the sexes could best be learned by children in the company of the other sex. Thus, choice (E) is diametrically opposite to the policy the author would recommend. Choices (A) and (D) must be wrong because the passage clearly indicates that the author

supports parochial schools and the religious instruction they provide. Choice (C) is a distraction. It plays on the association of segregation and racial discrimination. Racial segregation is not the only form of segregation. The word *segregation* means generally to separate or to keep separate.

12. **The correct answer is (A).** In this story, the identity of the person who reports the incident is irrelevant. So long as it is not someone with a special infirmity (very poor eyesight, for example) or poor credibility (an inveterate liar), the person is quite capable of reporting what she saw—or what she thought she saw. The most serious weakness of the analysis presented is that it attacks Professor Branch's credentials. To be sure, one might want to question the accuracy of the report: At what time did it occur? What were the lighting conditions? Had the observer been drinking? But these can be asked independently of attacking the qualifications of the source. Thus, choice (D) must be wrong, for special credentials are just not needed in this case, so the wrong way to defend Professor Branch is to defend those. By the same token, it makes no sense to defend Branch by launching a counter–*ad hominem* attack on her attacker, so choice (B) is incorrect. Choices (C) and (E) may or may not be true, but they are surely irrelevant to the question of whether or not this particular sighting is to be trusted.

13. **The correct answer is (B).** The inquisitor's behavior is paradoxical— that is, internally inconsistent or contradictory. The victim tells him that he is in league with the devil, so the inquisitor refuses to believe him because those in league with the devil never tell the truth. In other words, the inquisitor refuses to believe the victim because he accepts the testimony of the victim. Thus, choice (B) is correct. Choice (A) is incorrect because the inquisitor does not *withdraw* anything he has said; in fact, he lets everything he has said stand, and that is how he manages to contradict himself. Choice (E) is a bit more plausible, but it is incomplete. In a certain sense, the inquisitor does not accept the answer, but the real point of the passage is that his basis for *not* accepting the answer is that he *does* accept the answer: He believes the victim when he says he is in league with the devil. Choices (C) and (D) find no support in the paragraph. Nothing suggests that the inquisitor is violating any religious law, and nothing indicates that the inquisitor does not himself believe in the devil.

14. **The correct answer is (B).** The key here is that the word "nobody" is used in a cleverly ambiguous way; and, as many of you probably know, the "young lady" in the story is Lewis Carroll's Alice. This is fairly representative of his wordplay. Choice (E) must be incorrect since it misses completely the little play on words: "I saw Nobody," encouraging a response such as "Oh, is he a handsome man?" Choice (D) is beside the point, for the King is not interested in the messenger's veracity. He may be interested in his reliability, choice (A); but, if anything, we should conclude the King finds the messenger unreliable since "nobody walks slower" than the messenger. Choice (C) is wrong because the question is not a matter of eyesight. The King does not say, "If you had better eyes, you might have seen Nobody."

15. **The correct answer is (A).** This is an exercise in logic. The story told by the

stimulus material has the flavor of a paradox ("This sentence is false."), but in actuality, it does not present such a logical problem. Rather, the fee is not due until the younger attorney wins her first case, so the suit that is pending should be decided for the younger attorney. But once that judgment has been entered, then the younger attorney has won her first case and the fee does become due—but not before.

16. **The correct answer is (C).** Remember that it is important to find the conclusion of an argument. Sometimes the conclusion will be the last sentence of the paragraph, but that is not the case here. And sometimes you'll get help from a transitional word or phrase such as "therefore," "so," or "it follows." Again, no such luck here. Instead, you'll have to examine each idea in the paragraph to ask whether it is the main point the speaker hopes to prove, and the conclusion of this argument is found, unsignalled, in the very first sentence: consumers are not rational. And the proof of this conclusion is that consumers reach different decisions. But that presupposes that rationality would require consumers to reach substantially similar decisions—as choice (C) points out. If this item had been developed as a "weakening" question rather than a "presupposes" question, then the correct answer might have been worded: It is possible for rational consumers to weigh variables differently and arrive at different, though equally rational, decisions.

17. **The correct answer is (E).** The task here is to reconcile the two options expressed (like a "paradox" question). Richard's opinion that the experiment shows that manipulating controls is followed by actual changes in climate conditions seems inconsistent with Bill's opinion that manipulating the thermostat is ineffective because the device is a fake. But Richard is really only reporting that event e^1 (adjusting the thermostat) is following by event e^2 (a change in climate). That could be true without a causal connection—as choice (E) suggests: people get uncomfortable and start to manipulate the fake thermostat just about the time that real control is going to kick in anyway.

18. **The correct answer is (B).** The problem with the argument is that it is circular. The speaker notes that a creative work has no value apart from that afforded by copyright protection and then concludes, based upon the fact that copyright protection gives the work value, that the work is valuable property that requires protection. As for choice (A), while the speaker doesn't provide examples, this is not a weakness of the argument. The listener can understand the argument as it is presented, and the persuasive force would not be greatly increased by mentioning a particular song or book. Choice (C) is wrong since the speaker does not attack another person. (That would be an *ad hominem* argument or attack.) Choice (D) is wrong because the argument is not a generalization. And choice (E) is wrong for the same reason that choice (A) is wrong. While it is true that this is not considered by the speaker, nothing seems to turn on this consideration.

19. **The correct answer is (D).** The argument has the structure:

    If *A*, then *E*.

    If *WU*, then *H*.

    Either *A* or *WU*.

So it can be deduced:

    If not *WU*, then *A*.

    A.

    Therefore *E*.

The problem with the other choices is that they go beyond what is stated. Take choice (A) for example. The statements refer to a particular set of ruins. You cannot infer that these statements apply to all possible ruins. Thus, it is possible that the Etonians built trading centers, but, given the unique characteristics of this particular group of ruins, it is known that armaments would prove that Etonians built them as a fortress.

20. **The correct answer is (B).** The rule of thumb is based upon the assumption that a central nervous system is a necessary condition of the capacity for suffering: if the organism lacks a central nervous system, then it lacks the capacity for suffering. It's instructive to contrast choice (B) with choice (D). Choice (D) says that a central nervous system is a sufficient condition of the capacity for suffering but leaves open the logical possibility that other conditions may be the basis for a capacity for suffering.

21. **The correct answer is (D).** The author explains that the expansion of judicial power by increasing the number of causes of action had the effect of filling the judicial coffers. A natural conclusion to be drawn from this information is that the desire for economic gain fueled the expansion. Choice (A) is not supported by the text since the judges may have made good decisions—even though they were paid to make them. Choice (E) is incorrect for the same reason. Choice (C) is not supported by the text since no mention is made of the other two bodies (even assuming they existed at the time the au-

thor is describing). Choice (B) is also incorrect because there is nothing in the text to support such a conclusion.

22. **The correct answer is (D).** As we did in question 20, let us use letters to represent the form of the argument. The first sentence is our old friend: "If *P,* then *Q*." Now we must be careful not to use the same letter to stand for a different statement. No part of the second sentence is also a part of the first one, so we must use a new set of letters: "If *R,* then *S*." Do not be confused by the internal structure of the sentences. Though the second clause of the first sentence speaks about Johnson and Lloyd voting the same way, the second clause of the second sentence speaks about Johnson's defending someone. So the two statements are different ideas and require different letters. The first clause of the third sentence is the same idea as the first clause of the first sentence, so we use letter *P* again, but the second clause is different, *T*. The third sentence uses the phrase "only if," "*P* only if *T*," which can also be written "If *P,* then *T*." Our three sentences are translated as follows:

❶ If *P,* then *Q*.

❷ If *R,* then *S*.

❸ If *P,* then *T*.

Now we can find which of the answers cannot be true.

Choice (A) "If *R,* then not *Q*." That is a possibility. While it cannot be deduced from our three assumptions, nothing in the three assumptions precludes it. So choice (A) could be true.

Choice (B) "If *P,* then *T*." This is true, a restatement of the final assumption.

Choice (C) "If *T,* then not-P." This is possibly true. Sentence 3 tells us, "If *P,* then *T*," which is the same thing as "if not-*T*, then not-*P*"; but it does not dictate consequences when the antecedent clause (the if-clause) is *T*.

Choice (D) "If *P,* then either not-*Q* or not-*T*." This must be false, since sentences 1 and 3 together tell us that from *P* must follow both *Q* and *T*.

Choice (E) "If not-*T* or not-*P*, then either not-*S* or *U*." We have to add a new letter: U. In any event, this is possible for the reasons mentioned in choice (C).

23. **The correct answer is (A).** The listener's comment constitutes a counterexample. It shows by sarcasm that "yeah" can be used to show disagreement. Obviously, the listener does not point out an inconsistency within the speaker's address (even though the listener's remark is inconsistent with the speaker's position). There is no analogy developed by the listener, whose remark is very brief, so choice (C) is incorrect. The argument is directed against the speaker's contention, not character, so choice (D) is incorrect. Finally, though the listener's comment is high evidence that the speaker is wrong, the comment itself does not cite evidence, so choice (E) is incorrect.

24. **The correct answer is (C).** The argument in the question stem commits the fallacy of hasty generalization in two respects. It reasons from *military* aid to *Latin America* (a particular type of aid to a certain region) to the general conclusion that *all* aid must be stopped, regardless of type or of recipient. Choice (C) parallels this. From a particular conclusion about one form of government in one country, it moves to a general conclusion about all government—regardless of form or of society. Although choices (A), (B), and (D) have superficial similarities of

content (war, donation, military), the logical structures of these arguments differ from that of the stem paragraph. Choice (A) is a valid argument: Given anything that is a war, if any war is to be condemned, then all wars are to be condemned. Choice (B) is not a valid argument but a nonsequitur. It does not follow that an obligation on one party guarantees a benefit to any other. For example, there may not be enough rich to provide for all the poor. Choice (D) is also a nonsequitur. That we reject a system now because we lack the money to buy it does not imply we should buy it when we have funds. Finally, choice (E) is not really an argument but only a statement. Not all "If . . . , then . . . " statements mean "*P*, therefore *Q*." For example, "If you do not do the assignment, you will fail the course" is not an argument with a premise and a conclusion but a single statement that describes a causal relation.

Section 4

1. **The correct answer is (B).** This is a main idea question. The author's primary concern is to discuss the problem of desertification. So choice (B) is correct. A natural extension of the discussion would be a proposal to slow the process of desertification, but that is not included in the passage as written, so choice (A) must be incorrect. Choices (C), (D), and (E) are each incorrect because we find no elements in the passage to support those choices. Even admitting that the author intends to define, implicitly, the term "desertification," that is surely not the main point of the passage. The author also dwells at length on the causes of the problem.

2. **The correct answer is (C).** This is an explicit idea question. In the first para-

graph, the author mentions choices (A), (B), (D), and (E) as features of desertification. Choice (C), however, is one of the *causes* of desertification mentioned in the second paragraph.

3. **The correct answer is (E).** This is an inference question. The author places the phrase "higher uses" in quotation marks. In essence, this is similar to prefacing the phrase with the disclaimer "so-called." This impression is reinforced by the final entry in the list of examples of "higher uses": waste dumps. This is not to say that the author would argue that such uses are not important. Rather, this is to say that the author does not believe that those uses are more important than agricultural uses. Choice (A) is incorrect since this term is no more important than other terms used in the passage. Choice (B) is incorrect since the author is talking about the conversion of non-arid land to higher uses. Choice (C) is incorrect since the author is clearly opposed to such expansion. Finally, choice (D) is a sentiment expressed in the passage, but that is not the reason for placing this phrase in quotation marks.

4. **The correct answer is (D).** This is a specific detail (explicit idea) question with a thought-reverser. The author mentions world demand for U.S. products in the final paragraph, but "mention" alone does not make this a correct answer to the question. The right answer to a specific detail question must not only be mentioned; it must also answer the question asked. In this case, global need is mentioned as a reason to avoid desertification (feeding people is important) and not as a cause. The other choices are mentioned as causes: choices (A) and (B) in paragraph two; choices (C) and (E) in paragraph three.

5. **The correct answer is (A).** This is an explicit idea question, and the answer is found in the last paragraph. There the author states that the most serious long-term effect of desertification will be on the U.S.'s ability to export agricultural products. This will be harmful to the U.S. economically and to the rest of the world in terms of meeting the demand for food and fiber. As for choices (B) and (C), though these are plausible as effects of desertification, the author does not mention them specifically, and he certainly does not describe them as the most serious effects of desertification. Choice (D) is incorrect because the author's concern is over the ability of the U.S. to continue to export agricultural products, not the ability of the U.S. to meet domestic demand. Finally, choice (E) fails for the same reason that choices (B) and (C) are incorrect. Though it might arguably be one result of desertification (and that is an issue we need not address), the author never mentions it as a possible effect.

6. **The correct answer is (E).** This is an application question. In the passage, the author indicates that government programs that encourage exploitation of arid land are in large measure responsible for the rapid rate of desertification. A natural extension of the discussion would be a proposal for government spending to conserve arid lands. And this receives specific support in the third paragraph, where the author mentions that government conservation incentives are inadequate. With regard to choice (A), the author seems to believe that it is necessary for the U.S. to continue to export agricultural products to meet the world demand; the author favors conserving arid land while meeting this demand.

Choice (B) is surely incorrect, for the author argues that aid to farmers is one cause of the rapid rate of desertification. Choice (D) is incorrect for the same reason. As for choice (C), the conversion of land to "higher uses" is mentioned as a factor complicating the process of desertification. It is not a cause of desertification. The most natural extension of the passage would be a discussion of how to combat desertification.

7. **The correct answer is (E).** This is a tone question. We can surely eliminate choices (B), (C), and (D) as not expressing the appropriate element of worry. Then, between choices (A) and (E), choice (A) overstates the case. The author says we solve the problem now or we solve it later (at a higher cost). But that is an expression of concern, not alarm.

8. **The correct answer is (D).** This is a main idea question. The author begins by noting that solar energy is very important and, further, that the problem of the cost of solar cells, apparently an important part of solar energy technology, has not yet been solved. The author then discusses research on solar cells and the difficulties with silicon cells. In the third paragraph, the author states that there is a solution to this problem: amorphous materials. So the overall objective of the passage is to present amorphous material as a possible solution to the problem of cost. This is neatly summarized by choice (D). Choice (A) is incorrect since the author discusses the importance of solar energy only by way of introduction. Choice (B) is incorrect because the author never explains how solar cells work. Choice (C) is incorrect because the only reference to history is included to explain the bias in favor of silicon solar cells. Choice (E) is incorrect because the au-

thor never mentions such funding. To be sure, the arguments contained in the passage might be very useful in making the further point suggested by choice (E), but then that is to admit that choice (E) is not the main point of the passage as written.

9. **The correct answer is (D).** This is a specific detail (explicit idea) question. In paragraph two, the author specifically states that single crystal silicon is relatively efficient, even though expensive, and for that reason is used in the space program. Choices (A) and (C) are inconsistent with the passage, because gallium arsenide is said to be scarce and silicon cells are said to be expensive. Choice (B) is wrong because ribbon silicon can be produced, but it is not very efficient. And choice (E) is wrong because silicon is highly structured; the amorphous materials are not discussed until the next paragraph.

10. **The correct answer is (A).** This is a logical structure question: Why does the author mention polycrystalline and ribbon silicon? In a way, the mention of these techniques could undermine the case for amorphous materials, since these are recent developments in crystalline substances that improve silicon solar cells. The author surely does not intend to weaken the argument. The logical move is to acknowledge the existence of a possible objection and to attempt to demonstrate that it is not really a very important objection. This is described by choice (A). Choice (B) is incorrect, for though this is the general idea of the passage, choice (B) is not a proper response to the question asked. Choice (C) is a point raised in the passage, but this is not the reason for the reference to polycrystalline and ribbon silicon. Choice (D) is incorrect be-

cause the author never elaborates on the distinction between crystalline silicon and other forms of silicon. The author only mentions that the latter are further developments on crystalline silicon. As for choice (E), though we infer from the mention of polycrystalline and ribbon silicon that other forms of solar cells exist, this is not the reason the author has introduced them into the discussion.

11. **The correct answer is (B).** This is an inference question. In the first paragraph, the author mentions that the basic problem with solar energy is the economics of solar photovoltaic devices. The rest of the passage discusses solar cells. We may infer from the juxtaposition of these terms that the author uses them synonymously. In any event, none of the other pairs are used interchangeably. As for choice (A), from the passage we may infer that "extraterrestrial" refers to space and that "solar" refers to the sun. As for choice (C), these terms are used as opposites. As for choice (D), though the author claims that amorphous materials are more efficient than silicon materials, the passage does not equate amorphous materials and efficiency. Finally, choice (E) is incorrect since a wafer is apparently a big crystal of silicon. But that means the terms are not used interchangeably.

12. **The correct answer is (B).** This is a further application question. We noted earlier, in question 8, that though the author does not specifically advocate greater funding for research on amorphous materials, the passage might be used in such an argument. Since there is a historical bias in favor of silicon cells and since such cells have been the focus of most research, and amorphous materials offer an alternative, the natural conclusion is that further research should

be done on amorphous materials. This is choice (B). Choice (A) must be incorrect since the author never condemns the space program. The author only notes that silicon cells were appropriate for the space program since cost was no object. Choice (C) must be incorrect since the author advocates amorphous materials as opposed to silicon crystals for solar cells. Choice (D) has some merit. To the extent that the entire passage advocates further research for solar energy, it could be used for the purpose suggested by choice (D). With an application question, however, the task is to find the answer choice most closely tied to the text, and that is choice (B). Logically, then, there is nothing "wrong" with choice (D); it is just that it is not so closely related to the passage as choice (B). Finally, choice (E) is incorrect for the same reason: One could conceivably use the passage in the service of this goal, but choice (B) is a more obvious choice.

13. **The correct answer is (E).** This is a specific detail question. Choices (A), (B), (C), and (D) are all mentioned in paragraph three. Choice (E) is mentioned in paragraph one but not as an advantage of amorphous materials. Rather, the commitment of the semiconductor industry to silicon-based technology was a historical factor, helping to explain the rather late development of other, better technologies.

14. **The correct answer is (A).** This is a tone question. The tone of the passage is clearly analytical. The final paragraph is the warrant for the "optimistic" part of choice (A). The author implies that the problem of the cost of solar cells can be solved by further research on amorphous materials. Choice (B) is incorrect since though the passage advocates a position,

it cannot be termed biased. Choice (C) is correct insofar as the passage is critical, but the author does not seem to be discouraged. Choice (D) is incorrect because the passage is argumentative and the author seems to be confident. Finally, choice (E) is correct in that it states that the author is concerned, but there is nothing mentioned in the passage about which the author could be conciliatory.

15. **The correct answer is (B).** This is a main idea question. The author draws a distinction between preventive health care and curative health care. Using this distinction, the text suggests that there should be established separate authorities for each. So the primary method of developing the argument is the drawing of a distinction, as correctly stated by choice (B). Choice (A) is incorrect since the author does not cite any counterarguments to the position. Choice (C) is incorrect, for a dilemma is a "damned if you do and damned if you don't" argument. To draw a distinction is not necessarily to set up a dilemma. Choice (D) is incorrect, for whatever causes of poor health are discussed in the passage are not the main focus of the discussion. Choice (E) is incorrect for a similar reason. Whatever new research we may try to read into the passage, such as the Winslow monograph, is surely not the main point of the passage.

16. **The correct answer is (E).** This is an explicit idea question. In the first sentence of the second paragraph, the author notes that treatment is aimed at a patient already ill, but we have been told in the first paragraph that preventive care is just that, aimed at people who are healthy in order to keep them that way. So choice (A) is mentioned in the passage. Choice (B) is supported by the first

two paragraphs, particularly the sentence of the second paragraph that reads, "While these may be applied on a mass basis . . ., they are usually applied after the patient appears with a complaint," thus distinguishing preventive care from curative care. As for choice (C), per capita differences in cost are discussed in paragraph four. And as for choice (D), the historical roots of the distinction are discussed in the first paragraph. Choice (E), however, is not mentioned. In fact, choice (E) seems to be inconsistent with the author's point in that the author emphasizes the importance of and advantages to preventive care.

17. **The correct answer is (B).** This is an inference question. In the first paragraph, the author is discussing the basic strategy of preventive medicine. The text then states that in some areas, there is needless suffering and economic harm due to the failure of authorities to implement controlled fluoridation. The development of the argument leads us to conclude that the author regards the failure of the authorities to fluoridate water as a failure to implement a preventive health-care program. Choice (B) explains this reasoning. Choice (A) is incorrect since the author holds a positive attitude about fluoridation. Choice (C) is incorrect because the author cites the failure to fluoridate as an example of a failure to adopt a potentially valuable preventive strategy. Choice (D) is incorrect because fluoridation is a preventive, rather than a treatment, strategy. Finally, choice (E) is incorrect since the author recommends the fluoridation of water as a valuable preventive strategy.

18. **The correct answer is (A).** This is an inference question. In paragraph 4, the author remarks that expenditure of re-

sources on treatment is an expenditure that is lost, that is, produces nothing positive (eliminating the negative is not regarded as producing a positive result). Then, the sick person is also not contributing anything positive during the illness. So the economy is doubly disadvantaged because of the burden on or drain on resources to cure an ill person and because production is lost. Choice (A) neatly captures this idea. Choice (B) is incorrect because the author never quantifies the cost difference between the two types of care. The text says only that prevention is less costly than treatment. Choice (C) is incorrect because the author eventually will support such a division on the ground that the two activities are sufficiently dissimilar to warrant a division of authority. Choice (D) is incorrect since both rehabilitation and cure belong to curative medicine, so that will not explain why the economy is doubly burdened. Finally, choice (E) is attractive because it is at least consistent with the general theme of the passage. But choice (E) is not responsive to the question. It does not explain why the economy is doubly burdened by the person who requires treatment.

19. **The correct answer is (C).** This is an attitude, or tone, question. Two clues support choice (C). First, the author refers to the monograph and then continues to make points made by Winslow. This indicates the author agrees with Winslow. Second, the author refers to the analysis by Winslow as "convincing." Choices (A) and (B) can be eliminated because of the negative connotations associated with both terms. Choice (D) can be eliminated because style is not relevant to the point under discussion. Finally, choice (E) is the second best answer.

We eliminate choice (E) because the author states that the economics of prevention have been widely discussed, indicating that the uniqueness of Winslow's contribution is not necessarily originality. Further, the reference to the persuasiveness of Winslow's analysis makes choice (C) a better descriptive phrase to apply to the author's attitude than choice (E).

20. **The correct answer is (D).** This is a logical detail question. The author introduces these three diseases in the paragraph discussing the economics of prevention and following the statement that the cost of prevention is less than the cost of treatment when averaged out on a per capita basis. Choice (D) makes this point. Choice (A) is incorrect, for while this is a statement the author would surely accept, it is not the reason for introducing the examples. Choice (B) is incorrect for a similar reason. This may very well be true, but it is not an answer to the question. Choice (C) must be wrong, for though this is one of the main points of the discussion, it will not answer this particular question. Finally, choice (E) is also a statement that the author could accept, but it is not responsive to the question.

21. **The correct answer is (A).** This is a question about the logical structure of the argument. The author mentions several differences between preventive and curative medicines: cost, personnel, persons addressed. But these differences are not compelling reasons for creating a division of authority. The need to separate authority for the two strategies is discussed in the first and last paragraphs. The value of the division will be to clarify objectives and redress the inequitable division of resources. These are prob-

lems, so says the first paragraph, because "the imperative nature of medical care" will allow it to dominate health care. In other words, the urgency of treatment attracts attention. This is the explanation provided in choice (A). And for this reason, it is not cost, choice (B); personnel, choice (C); or persons addressed, choice (D) that is the important difference. Finally, choice (E) is directly contradicted by the opening sentences of the passage.

22. **The correct answer is (D).** This is a main idea question. The author cites several arguments in favor of the "drug lag" theory, then offers refutations of at least some of them. The author concludes that the arguments for "drug lag" are not conclusive and that, contrary to the view of the "drug lag" theoreticians, the 1962 Amendments are not, on balance, harmful. The main technique of development is refutation of arguments cited. Choice (D) is therefore the best answer to this question. Choice (A) can be eliminated since the author does not outline a proposal. Discussing the effectiveness of some past action is not outlining a proposal. Choice (B) has some merit because the author does analyze the evidence presented by the "drug lag" theoreticians. This analysis, however, is not the final objective of the passage. It is presented in order to further the goal of refuting the general position of that group. Choice (C) is incorrect since the author poses no question and indeed seems to answer any question that might be implicit in the passage regarding the value of the Amendments. Choice (E) has some merit since the focus of the passage is a law. But the intent of the author is not to discuss the law per se. Rather, the intent of the passage is to refute objections to the law. On balance, choice (D) more

precisely describes the main idea than the other choices.

23. **The correct answer is (C).** Choices (A), (B), (D), and (E) are all mentioned as "drug lag" arguments in the second paragraph. As for choice (C), the argument that effectiveness studies cost money is mentioned in the first paragraph. But "drug lag" results from the time and cost of effectiveness studies. "Drug lag" is not the increased cost itself.

24. **The correct answer is (A).** This is an application question. Support for choice (A) is found in the closing sentences of the passage. In the final paragraph, the author insists that there are few, if any, examples of harm done by the requirements of effectiveness studies. Then the author says that we are at least assured that the drug, which might actually prove harmful, does have some benefit. The qualified nature of the claim suggests that the author would acknowledge that some "drug lag" does exist but that, on balance, it is justified. This thought is captured by choice (A). Choice (B) is incorrect because the author never states the effectiveness studies are designed to determine whether the drug has unwanted effects. Apparently, effectiveness studies, as the name implies, are designed to test the value of the drug. This is not to say that such studies may not, in fact, uncover unwanted side effects, but given the information in the passage, choice (B) is a more tenuous inference than choice (A). Choice (C) is incorrect for two reasons. First, the passage never states that the cost of drugs is higher in the United States than in other countries. The passage states only that the proponents of the "drug lag" theory argue that the effectiveness study requirement increases the cost of drugs here.

That makes no comparison with a foreign country. Second, the author seems to discount the significance of the increased cost. Choice (D) is incorrect because there is no basis for such a recommendation in the passage. Finally, choice (E) is incorrect because the passage never states that the studies do not cost money or time. The author only doubts whether the cost or time create profit pressures serious enough to cause "drug lag."

25. **The correct answer is (B).** This is a logical structure question. In the final paragraph, the author states that the drop in new drugs introduced annually began before the Amendments took effect. The author does not deny that the drop occurred but rather points out that it predated the supposed cause. In other words, the author is suggesting that there must be some other reason for the drop. Choice (B) correctly describes the author's logical move. Choice (E) is directly contradicted by this analysis. The author does not deny that there was a drop in the number of new drugs introduced every year. As for choice (A), the author does not point to any similarity between two situations. The text says only that the situation being studied existed even before the Amendments took effect. Choice (C) is incorrect because the author never questions the credibility of an opponent, only the value of the opponent's arguments. Finally, choice (D) is incorrect because the author's use of statistics is not an attempt to justify the use of those statistics. The statistics are used to prove some further conclusion.

26. **The correct answer is (C).** This is a logical structure question. In the second paragraph, the author cites, as one argument for the existence of "drug lag," the non-availability in the U.S. of a drug that is available in a foreign country. In the third paragraph, the author offers a refutation of this argument. The simple availability–non-availability comparison is not valid because consumers may not suffer from the non-availability of that particular drug if another drug is available to treat the same condition. Choice (C) correctly describes the structure of this argument. The remaining answer choices are in various ways related to the overall argument of the passage, but they are not answers to this particular question.

27. **The correct answer is (C).** Again, we have a logical structure question. We have already noted that the author does not deny that fewer drugs were introduced each year after the Amendments than before the Amendments but does offer that the total number of new chemical entities is not necessarily a measure of the value of new drugs introduced. By redefining terms so that we speak not just of new chemical entities but of unimportant, important, and breakthrough chemical entities, the author minimizes the significance of the argument. The relevant comparison, the author claims, is between important and breakthrough chemical entities, not total new chemical entities introduced. Choice (C) correctly points out that the essence of this logical move is redefining terminology. Choice (A) is incorrect because the author does not deny that the total number had dropped. Choice (B) is incorrect because the author does not explain why that number has dropped. Choice (D) is incorrect because the author makes no such proposal. Finally, choice (E) is only remotely related to the correct answer. While it may be true that an important or breakthrough chemical has many more

uses than an unimportant chemical entity, the author does not list the uses of any chemical.

28. The correct answer is (D). This is an application question. What are the logical underpinnings of the comparison? Notice that the author's description of the arguments under attack includes reference to "advanced" nations. Apparently, the proponents of the "drug lag" theory realize that a comparison between the United States and a non-advanced country would not be relevant. They want a situation in which the only important difference is the strictness of the laws on new drugs. For this reason, choice (D) is a presupposition of the argument.

Section 5

1. The correct answer is (D). This item, too, asks you to identify a hidden assumption. First, find the conclusion of the argument. It is contained in the rhetorical question at the end of the paragraph, a question that should be read to assert affirmatively "World leaders would not trust someone who has admitted lying to her spouse." That conclusion rests upon the hidden assumption that a person who would lie to her or his spouse about an affair would also lie to world leaders.

2. The correct answer is (D). The only paragraph containing an argument that makes a generalization is choice (D). The speaker makes a claim about cameras in general based upon the one incident.

3. The correct answer is (C). The only paragraph containing an argument directed toward an opponent instead of the merits of the argument is choice (C). There the speaker attacks the Mayor by alleging that the Mayor is biased by a financial interest in the issue.

4. The correct answer is (C). The speaker uses the word "free" in two different ways. In the first occurrence of the word, it means "liberty"—a general term—meaning freedom from governmental or other constraint. The second occurrence is the use we reserve for being free of some particular problem, e.g., free or rid of a problem.

5. The correct answer is (A). The author states that the Ecole was a quasi-governmental agency that controlled the distribution of government money for artists. Since the Impressionist painters were scorned and received no money (only empty bellies) for their efforts, we can infer that they did not paint in the accepted style. Choice (B) goes beyond the scope of what is specifically stated in the initial paragraph. Although you can infer that the Impressionists rejected the standards of the Ecole and further that they were ultimately successful (note the word "initially," which qualifies their lack of success), you cannot infer that they gained control over the Ecole. Choices (C) and (D) also go beyond the scope of the initial paragraph. According to the author, the Ecole exercised its control by the ways in which it distributed money. The passage does not suggest that the Ecole exercised any direct control. Finally, choice (E) too goes beyond what can be legitimately inferred from the initial paragraph. In fact, if anything can be inferred from the selection about the state of painting in France in the second half of the nineteenth century, it is that it was more creative than the art of the first half of the century, for you might reasonably infer that the Impressionists constituted a new creative force.

6. The correct answer is (D). The task here is to explain why the teacher makes the second remark. Choice (D) provides the best explanation. The teacher's first remark says only that the student being addressed is not one of the students who has passed the test. You cannot infer from that remark that the student in the conversation has not passed the test. It is possible that his paper has not yet been graded. (Consider a similar situation: You look into a classroom through a door that is slightly ajar and see three students, all of whom are girls. You then say "Some of the students in this class are girls"—obviously a true statement. If you later open the door completely and see only female students in the classroom, you can say "All of the students in this class are girls"—also a true statement. But your first statement is not thereby rendered false. It remains true as well.) The other choices fail to explain why the teacher would say, "You don't yet need to tell your parents that you failed the test."

7. **The correct answer is (C).** The author notes that arguments in favor of legalizing marijuana have generally fallen into two categories: those that assert that there is no evidence that marijuana is dangerous and those that assert that laws proscribing the use of marijuana infringe on an individual's liberty. The arguments of the first sort are designed to show that there is no good reason to have laws against marijuana, while arguments of the second sort are intended to show that there is a reason to legalize marijuana. At this point, the author says that there is yet another reason to legalize marijuana: smoking marijuana is pleasurable. Thus, the author implies that the fact that an activity is pleasurable is a reason that might be given for allowing people to engage in it. Choice (A) is not inferable from the paragraph. In fact, the author states that there is no

evidence to prove such a contention. Choice (B) represents a possible misreading of the paragraph. The author does not state that marijuana is illegal because it is pleasurable but that it should be legal because it is pleasurable. As for choice (D), the author states that arguments based on claims of individual liberty are not the only ones that could be advanced for the legalization of marijuana, not that those who use such arguments are insincere. Finally, as for choice (E), opponents of marijuana might not deny that the drug has a pleasurable effect, but they would insist that people are not entitled to that pleasurable effect because the use of marijuana leads to ill effects as well, such as antisocial behavior.

8. **The correct answer is (B).** A neat way to attack problems like this (in which a second speaker evidently misconstrues the remark of a first speaker) is to put each answer choice into the mouth of the first speaker. The correct choice will be the one that creates a meaningful exchange between the two speakers:

Choice (A)

DAVID: Paintings by Electra and Bluesina should be displayed in the Museum.

MARAT: I disagree. I have seen some very fine works by Electra and Bluesina that should be displayed in the Museum.

Choice (B)

DAVID: Only Kissandra's paintings should be displayed in the Museum.

MARAT: I disagree. I have seen some very fine works by Electra and Bluesina that should be displayed in the Museum.

Choice (C)

DAVID: Every painting by Kissandra should be displayed in the Museum.

MARAT: I disagree. I have seen some very fine works by Electra and Bluesina that should be displayed in the Museum.

Choice (D)

DAVID: Not every Kissandra painting should be displayed in the Museum.

MARAT: I disagree. I have seen some very fine works by Electra and Bluesina that should be displayed in the Museum.

Choice (E)

DAVID: Kissandra's paintings should be displayed only in the Museum.

MARAT: I disagree. I have seen some very fine works by Electra and Bluesina that should be displayed in the Museum.

Questions 9 and 10

9. **The correct answer is (D).** A diagram makes it easy to keep track of the relationships:

Younger————————> Older

Paul is older than Sally:

$S \quad P$

————————>

Sally is older than Fred:

$F \quad S \quad P$

————————>

Mike is older than Paul:

$F \quad S \quad P \quad M$

————————>

Ralph is younger than Mike but older than Fred:

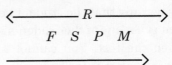

As the diagram shows, only choice (D) is necessarily true.

10. **The correct answer is (E).** Since Chuck is younger than Ralph and Ralph is younger than Mike, Chuck must be younger than Mike.

11. **The correct answer is (B).** Cathy's response exploits an ambiguity in the way that the word "see" is used in English. When Charlotte says that she doesn't "see" any good reason to lend Cathy money, she doesn't mean that there is such a reason but she cannot see it. Rather, she means that there is no reason to lend Cathy money.

12. **The correct answer is (A).** This item asks you to draw a further conclusion. The speaker explains that older vaccines were more dangerous than newer ones because they used entire viruses, whereas newer vaccines use only part of the virus. Although the newer vaccines use only a part of the virus, they are still effective in stimulating the body's immune system. We are entitled to conclude, therefore, that it is a specific subunit of the virus that makes the vaccine effective. As for the wrong answers, choices (B) and (C) can be eliminated because the speaker contrasts old and new vaccines, not the two different older methods of creating vaccines using entire viruses. Choice (D) is contradicted by the passage, for the speaker notes that the newer vaccines are safer. Finally, choice (E) is perhaps the second-best response. But choice (E) overstates the speaker's position. The body does not react to a subpart of the

virus in exactly the same way as it reacts to the whole virus. Rather, the immune system reacts to the subpart (as thought it were embedded in a whole virus), but the body as a whole is not at risk as it would be if the vaccine used whole viruses.

13. **The correct answer is (A).** Here we are asked to weaken the second speaker's position. Anthony maintains that air conditioning was not the feature that prompted Tony to buy his car. Choice (A) weakens this by stating that of two very similar vehicles, Tony chose the one with air conditioning. Choice (B) seems to strengthen rather than weaken Anthony's argument: the Ouigo is, on the whole, inferior to the Hugo. Choice (C) seems to strengthen the first speaker's position by implying that it was the air conditioning that made the difference in Tony's choice. As for choice (D), without further information, this idea does not bear on the debate. (Does Tony like or dislike imports?) Finally, as for choice (E), though this statement establishes that Tony did not make his decision based on these two items of equipment, it doesn't help us decide whether Tony made his decision based on air conditioning.

14. **The correct answer is (B).** The stem here asks that you describe the argument. The best description is provided by choice (B). The speaker argues that the logical extension of the ethical vegetarian's argument leads to conclusions such as a human being is equal to a spear of broccoli and we should stop eating altogether. I am not saying that the argument succeeds—only that choice (B) is the best description of the argument. As for choice (A), there simply is no such insinuation in the speaker's argument: the speaker does not say, for example,

that the vegetarians continue to wear leather clothing. As for choices (C) and (D), the speaker doesn't cite any scientific evidence and doesn't mention any commonly accepted opinions. As for choice (E), though the speaker's own position seems irreconcilable with that of the ethical vegetarians, the speaker is not attempting to reconcile the two positions.

15. **The correct answer is (C).** The hidden assumption in this argument is not that easy to spot, and it may become clear to you only after you have studied the answer choices. The speaker concludes that the recent surge in births is not a serious problem. But why shouldn't we expect an echo of the earlier baby boom? There must be a crucial difference between the recent surge in births and the true baby boom of the 50s. Choice (C) highlights that difference. As for choice (A), this idea suggests that the speaker might be wrong: there is no reason for concern since the new parents are in a position to have the same number of offspring as their parents. Choice (B) overstates the speaker's position. The speaker is saying only that there is no reason to fear a sudden population explosion, not that the population will decline. Choice (D) seems to be inconsistent with the speaker's position. The speaker is arguing that we should not expect a recurring cycle of baby booms. Finally, choice (E) imputes a value judgment to the speaker that has no support in the factual statements of the paragraph.

16. **The correct answer is (B).** The speaker's argument rests on a hidden assumption that the Congress is acting to protect citizens of other countries and not citizens of the United States. Choice (B) attacks this hidden premise. As for choice (A), this idea can only strengthen

the speaker's position: the ban is unfair because other countries may need these very effective chemicals. Choice (C) too seems to cut in the speaker's favor; and the chemical companies won't be harmed. And so too choice (D) seems to pre-empt a possible objection to the speaker's position: foreign companies will simply fill the void. About the best justification for choice (E) is that it shows that the Congress doesn't need to enact a ban. But that is too strong a conclusion to rest on a statement that clearly says "some" (not "all") foreign governments have already banned the chemicals.

17. **The correct answer is (B).** The explanation for the seeming contradiction, given by choice (B), is that Fulghum's instant coffee is more concentrated than the leading brand. For this reason, Fulghum's is actually cheaper to use. As for choice (A), the number of people who use one brand or the other doesn't bear on the issue of cost. As for choice (C), this reinforces the seem-ing contradiction by eliminating a possible explanation, namely, Fulgum's regular jar is larger. As for choice (D), this is irrelevant since the ad specifically states that Fulghum's costs more. And as for choice (E), the taste test is irrelevant to the issue of cost.

18. **The correct answer is (C).** This item asks for a further conclusion. Since some of the employees who will be promoted are highly skilled and others bunglers and since all will receive higher salaries, we can infer that both highly skilled employees and bunglers will receive higher salaries. Choice (A) is directly contradicted by the first statement of the paragraph. Choice (B) is not inconsistent with the statements of the stimulus paragraph, but choice (B) cannot be inferred

from those statements. Choice (D) makes the following mistake: All S are P, therefore all P are S. Finally, choice (E) is inconsistent with the initial paragraph, for we know that some bunglers will be promoted and will therefore receive higher salaries.

19. **The correct answer is (C).** This question asks you to identify assumptions of the argument. First, choice (C) is not an assumption. Perhaps the speaker thinks that the seriousness of the crimes was equivalent for the two periods, but nothing commits the speaker to the idea that things were worse in the "old days." Choice (A) is a presupposition: since the speaker makes a descriptive judgment about whether a society is more or less violent, the speaker evidently thinks that the number of reported crimes is a good indicator of that characteristic. And choice (B) is an assumption since the speaker reaches a general conclusion about "large metropolitan areas" based upon the New York City experience. And choice (D) is an assumption since the Richardson data are the basis for the argument. And choice (E), while a little harder to detect, is also an assumption, because the speaker regards the increase in New York City as out of line; therefore, the speaker believes there is a correlation between population and crime.

20. **The correct answer is (C).** What sort of judgment can you make about a statement coming from a person who is a self-confessed liar? You can't confidently accept the statement, yet you can't know for certain that it is a lie. Choice (C) describes the appropriate conclusion. Choices (A) and (B) are wrong for the reason just given. As for choice (D), the language quoted here is not the same as

the well-known Liar Paradox: This sentence is false. That sentence is paradoxical because if what it says is true, then it is false, and conversely if what it says is false, then it is true. As for choice (E), we know that it is logically possible to make such a statement—it's right there on the page.

21. **The correct answer is (E).** This item is primarily a problem in careful reading. Since there are at least three spies at the reception, choice (E) cannot be true. Assume that there are exactly three spies at the reception, X, Y, and Z, and further that X knows the true identities of both Y and Z. If choice (E) is also true, then both Y and Z would know the true identity of X. But then three spies would know each other's true identities—in violation of the final statement of the initial paragraph. As for choice (A), the first statement of the initial paragraph says that there are "at least" three spies at the reception, so there could be more. As for choice (B), the final statement says that "at most" two spies know each other's true identities, so there could be fewer. As for choice (C), the second statement says "at least" one spy has this knowledge, so there could be exactly one. And as for choice (D), this statement could be true so long as the spy whose identity is known doesn't know the true identity of more than one other spy.

22. **The correct answer is (C).** One way of analyzing this item is to use capital letters to represent the logical form of the stimulus argument:

If S, then P.

Not P, therefore not S.

Where S = "no union support," and "P = "defeated." Then the "not P" of the second line indicates "not not defeated" or

"passed," and "not S" indicates "not no union support" or more directly "union support." The argument of choice (C) also has this form:

If S, then P.

Not P, therefore not S.

Where S = not having passed bar, and P = cannot practice law. Then, the "not P" of the second line indicates "not cannot practice" or more directly "can practice," and "not S" means "not not having passed bar" or more directly "passed bar." Choices (A), (B), and (E) present invalid arguments, so they do not parallel the form of the stimulus material. As for choice (A), there may be many other reasons the car won't start. Similarly for choice (B), a person can have the symptoms described without ever having been in the sun. And as for choice (E), there are many other reasons that Peter might have been fired. As for choice (D), this is a probabilistic argument that looks toward the future.

23. **The correct answer is (C).** The speaker here is pointing out an inconsistency of the policies of the corporation: their ads say "Buy American," but they buy Japanese. Choice (C) correctly describes this fact. Every other answer choice overstates the speaker's case. It is not clear what lesson should be drawn from the paragraph—except that the Chrysler corporation is not consistent in its policies.

24. **The correct answer is (D).** The speaker draws a distinction between the underlying agreement between the parties and the written document that commemorates that agreement. According to the paragraph, there are times when an agreement may exist but be unenforceable because it has not been reduced to writing. This is the distinction highlighted by choice (D).

25. The correct answer is (B). Both parties to the debate here apparently agree that the government has correctly gathered the statistics mentioned, but Dick uses the data to reach a conclusion directly opposite to that reached by Alan. Choice (B) best describes this exchange. As for choice (A), the two reach different conclusions. As for the remaining choices, both speakers accept and use as evidence the data mentioned.

Writing Sample

Following are two responses to the Writing Sample prompt, one in favor of the first option and the other in favor of the second option. These responses are not necessarily Pulitzer Prize winning essays, but remember they're not supposed to be. The objective, as developed in Chapter 8, is to write something that is serviceable. You'll notice how these responses fit the model developed in Chapter 8.

Sample Response for Option One

The Board of Trustees should award the contract for the memorial to Ann Gerson for two important reasons. One, from an artistic standpoint, Ms. Gerson's proposal is better calculated to have the intended effect on viewers. Two, the "oasis" approach will give the sculpture additional functionality.

First, Ms. Gerson's shrouded figure, symbolizing death, will make a powerful, though not overly dramatic, statement about the sacrifice of the university's students and graduates. This statement will be enhanced by the containing wall, which will personalize the artistic message by providing information about individuals. Additionally, by positioning the grouping at the center of the campus, Ms. Gerson announces the central impor-

tance of sacrifice in human life and says, in effect, that these individuals remain forever at the "heart" of the school.

Second, Ms. Gerson's oasis provides the additional functionality that the Board wants. The benches and greenery are likely to attract students who want to study quietly or to think reflectively—critical university functions. Plus, the memorial will be located at the center of the campus where it will be convenient for students and faculty to stop for a few minutes or even longer.

It must be allowed that Ms. Gerson does not have the close connections to the University that Mr. Maxwell has, but that doesn't seem to be important to the Board's thinking. In any case, the task is to create a memorial, and death is a universal artistic theme, not one that is the exclusive province of a teacher at a particular school.

Sample Response for Option Two

Mr. Maxwell's proposed memorial wall better meets the criteria set down by the Board. First, the idea of a memorial wall is familiar and will serve the function of encouraging students to think about the sacrifices of those who died. Second, the memorial wall will literally merge form and function, substance and style.

In the first place, the idea of a memorial wall is not a new one. Perhaps the most famous exemplar is the Vietnam Veteran's Memorial on the National Mall. A memorial wall is a concept that is both familiar and effective. Additionally, Mr. Maxwell's intention to add personal information to the usual "data" will make this wall particularly appropriate for its university setting. What better way of reminding current students that these were actual living people who died in the prime of their lives than to mention their unfulfilled goals and aspirations?

Second, Mr. Maxwell's wall will quite literally unite form and function, as the Board hopes. The wall will be integrated structurally into the new student union. Moreover, that merger is highly symbolic because the student union is often seen as the focus of campus life. At the risk of sounding overly dramatic, the inter-play between campus life and sacrifice of death has to challenge the imagination.

Finally, Mr. Maxwell is a member of the university community; Ms. Gerson is not. Though the Board does not raise this issue, it is not unreasonable to think that someone who lives and teaches at the university will have a better understanding as to how the unique physical and emotional spaces of the university can be brought together.

answers

PART V
APPENDICES

Creating Your Law School Application

In order to create the most effective application you can, you must understand and appreciate the goals of the process by which some applicants are selected for legal study (and others not) as a social and economic process. With this knowledge, you can intelligently craft an application that is consistent with the workings of these processes—one that has the maximum chance of success.

Application success is no accident. You must have a plan. Your completed application must hang together as a coherent whole. Your GPA, your LSAT score, and your application form the core of this whole. Your personal statement should incorporate some of the most important themes from the application itself and weave them into a story or an argument for why you should be accepted. Plus, your letters should come from people who know you well enough to echo some of the points contained in both the core and your personal statement.

UNDERSTANDING THE APPLICATION PROCESS

If you're like most candidates, at the outset, you think of the application process as taking a test, answering a few questions about your educational background and employment history, writing a personal statement, and arranging for a couple of recommendations. After which, you put everything into an envelope (with a check) and then wait for an answer. The application process is much, much more than this. The cost of the application process routinely exceeds $1,000. The fees that you pay to the Law School Admissions Services to take the Law School Admission Test and for score and grade reports could be as much as $200. Further, the application fees charged by schools run between $50 and $75. Assuming that you apply to ten schools, you could easily spend $750 on application fees. In addition, you will probably spend at least $100 on administrative details such as document preparation, copying, postage, and long distance telephone calls. Add another $300 or so for test preparation for the LSAT, and you have already committed more than $1,000.

The total cost of a legal education can be more than $150,000. Concerned? You'd be crazy not to be. For further guidance, you might want to consult *Looking at Law School: A Student Guide from the Society of American Law Teachers*, 4th Ed., Stephen Gillers, Ed. (Meridian Books, 1997). NYU Law School Professor

Stephen Gillers, whom you may have seen on television, wrote a chapter entitled "Making the Decision to go to Law School." It is particularly helpful on this issue. The Preface is by the late William J. Brennan, Jr., a former Associate Justice of the United States Supreme Court.

Don't let those numbers frighten you. They are not intended to dissuade you from pursuing a legal education but rather to dramatize a point. The decision to apply to law school has significant financial implications for you as an individual (and probably for your family).

To create the most powerful application possible given your GPA, test score, and background, you need to be aware of the criteria the law school will use when it reviews your application. That way, you can craft an application that, in its every detail, answers to the concerns of the admission committee.

The Business of Education

A law school, like any educational institution, is a corporate individual, and its admissions decisions reflect financial and social policies adopted by the corporation. Consider first some of the financial implications for a law school to accept or reject an applicant. The law school has to be run as a business. It has employees, it owns or rents property, it operates a library, it buys furniture and office equipment, it pays utility bills, and so on. A large part of those expenses are paid using student tuition. A law school, therefore, is dependent on a steady flow of tuition money. So admissions decisions must be made in the context of budgetary constraints. A law school simply cannot afford to have large numbers of students dropping out of school.

So one concern of a law school admissions officer is to ensure that those applicants who are accepted are committed to completing the course of study. In addition—though this may not be an explicit concern—law schools rely heavily on alumni donations. So it would not be surprising to learn that an applicant who shows considerable professional promise would be considered favorably. And a school that graduates successful lawyers gets a reputation for being a good school and such a reputation in turn tends to attract highly qualified applicants.

Financial considerations are only one aspect of the admissions decision. Law schools also have a sense of the social responsibility they bear as educators of lawyers—one of the most influential groups of people in our society. They meet this responsibility in some fairly obvious ways, such as actively seeking applications from groups who are underrepresented in the practice of law and by establishing programs to train lawyers for positions of special need.

The Competition

About 100,000 people start the admission process each year, but there are fewer than 50,000 seats. The admissions process, then, is the interface between two perspectives. The process is designed to match individuals and institutions who can mutually satisfy each other's needs. This matching function, however, is somewhat skewed. For decades, there have been more people interested in pursuing law as a career than there are seats available at accredited law schools. In recent times, there have been about two applicants for each available seat. As a consequence, applicants are competing for law school seats. Given the mismatch between the number of seats and the number of applicants, the application process is turned into a competition. You will have to compete against others for a law school seat (or at least for a seat at the law school of your choice). To do this, you must make yourself attractive to a law school. You must persuade the admissions committee that you will help them satisfy their economic and social needs. And that thought must guide you as you create your application.

Finally, tell them what they want to hear. Law schools want students who have the ability to handle the curriculum and the motivation to study hard and who will be interesting additions to the law school. Everything that goes into your application should bear on one of these points.

Behind Closed Doors: An Inside Look at the Admissions Process

What goes on behind the closed doors of the admissions office? Well, the first thing that you should know about the law school admissions process is that there is no one admissions process. Rather, each law school has its own individual admissions process, and its process differs somewhat from that of every other law school in the country.

At some schools, the decisions are made by faculty committees. At such schools, decisions may be made by majority vote, or unanimous agreement may be required before an acceptance is extended to an applicant. At other schools, the decisions may be made by a single professional admissions officer or officers who may not themselves be lawyers or by a dean of admissions who is a lawyer but not a faculty member. At other schools, decisions may be made by a committee with members drawn from both administration and faculty. And at some schools, students themselves may have some input into admissions decisions.

The LSAT/GPA Factors and the "Admissions Index"

Despite the variety of formal structures, one generalization is possible: Every law school relies to some extent on the applicant's Grade Point Average (GPA) and LSAT score, but there are few (if any) law schools that rely only on these quantitative factors. What does this statement mean for you? First, it says that every law school uses the GPA and the LSAT score. The exact use of these numbers varies from school to school, but many use a formula that combines the two together into an index. The formula is designed to weight the two numbers approximately equally to give admissions officers some idea of how one applicant stacks up against other applicants.

You've heard it said before, but it really is true: the two most important factors in your application are your GPA and your LSAT score. While law school admissions officers often say that they prefer to minimize the importance of the objective measures (and won't say exactly how much each is worth), an application with numbers that are too low will be rejected—whether there is a formal or just an informal cutoff.

The LSAT is now scored on a scale from 120 (the minimum) to 180 (the maximum). You may notice that the 20 and the 80 are reminiscent of the 200 and 800 scale of the SAT, and this is not accidental. Originally, the LSAT was scored on a scale ranging from 200 to 800. In 1991, the present scale was adopted so that it wouldn't look exactly like the SAT scale but could still be used in formulas combining test score with GPA.

The 20-to-80 point scale has a special relation to the 0-to-4 grading system used by most colleges: 80 is 20 times 4. This permits the use of a formula to combine the two measures. For example:

$$\text{Index} = (\text{LSAT} - 100) + (20 \times \text{GPA})$$

This formula combines the two numbers to create an index. Let's use some numbers, say a GPA of 3.5 and an LSAT score of 170:

$$I = (\text{LSAT} - 100) + (20 \times \text{GPA})$$
$$I = (170 - 100) + (20 \times 3.5) = 140$$

Thus, the Index for this particular applicant is a 140—an artificial number but one that will make sense to the admissions committee because all other applications at their school are classified in the same manner.

Another Index formula might generate a number with a more familiar look.

$$\text{Index} = \frac{(\text{LSAT} - \frac{100}{20}) + \text{GPA}}{2}$$

An LSAT score of 170 and a GPA of 3.5 would generate the value 3.5 using this formula, and the 3.5 is a fairly intuitive number: this applicant is a B+/A– student.

What does the Index do? That varies from school to school. Some schools have a fairly mechanical admissions process that emphasizes the Index. The school may set a minimum Index below which applications receive little or no attention because they are probably going to be rejected anyway. Such schools may also have a second, higher minimum that triggers an automatic acceptance (unless the application shows some glaring weakness, e.g., the applicant is a three-time felon). At the opposite extreme are schools that minimize the importance of the "numbers." These schools may not even calculate an Index. Such schools have a very flexible admissions process.

Most schools fall somewhere in between these extremes. Many schools use the Index as a screening device to determine how much attention will be given to an application. Applications with very low Indices will receive little attention. The schools reason that unless there is something obvious and compelling in the application to offset the low numbers, then the applicant will be rejected. Applications with very high Indices will also receive little attention. The reasoning is that unless there is something obvious and compelling in the application to reject it, it should be accepted. On this theory, the applications with Indices in the middle receive the greatest attention. These are applications from candidates who are at least competitive for the school but who do not command an automatic acceptance. It is in this pool that competition is the most severe.

Here is a table that illustrates what happens at most law schools. (Law schools are notoriously edgy about releasing this kind information, so the table is a composite based on data from several schools.):

ADMISSIONS CHANCES

	LSAT (Percentile Rankings)			
	61–70	71–80	81–90	90+
G 3.75+	2/19	40/101	102/116	72/79
P 3.50–3.74	6/112	75/275	301/361	120/129
A Below 3.50	10/160	90/601	375/666	201/250

(The number to the right of the slash shows the number of applicants; the number to the left of the slash shows the number of applicants accepted.)

In the category in the upper right hand corner are candidates with scores above the 90th percentile and GPAs above 3.75. The table shows that 72 of the 79 were accepted and seven rejected.

Interestingly, the table also shows that some candidates with higher Indexes were rejected in favor of candidates with lower numbers. For example, of those candidates with scores between the 81st and 90th percentiles, 74 more candidates were accepted with a GPA below 3.50 than the higher GPA between 3.5 and 3.74. Why would a law school reject an applicant with higher numbers for one with lower numbers? Because of the unquantifiable factors such as motivation, commitment, leadership, experience, and so on. (More information on the role of these factors and how you can demonstrate that you have them is given later in this chapter.)

As you prepare your applications, you are, of course, saddled with your GPA and your LSAT score. There is nothing you can do to change those factors. This means that you have to work hard to craft an application that presents your credentials in the best light.

Want to know more about your chances for success at a particular law school? Consult the *Official American Bar Association Guide to Approved Law Schools*, American Bar Association (Macmillan General Reference, 1998). The American Bar Association is the professional association for lawyers in the United States. And their committee on legal education is responsible for deciding which law schools will receive accreditation. This book is filled with admissions data on every ABA-accredited law school, and it will give you a good idea of what your chances are at particular schools.

ROLLING AND EARLY ADMISSIONS

Rolling admissions is a device used by many law schools that regulates the release of acceptances. A typical law school application season opens in October and closes in February or perhaps March. Applications will be received throughout the application season, and decisions are made on an ongoing basis. Rather than saving all applications until the deadline for applications is past and then making decisions, rolling admissions allows law schools to notify applicants on an ongoing basis.

Law schools begin the rolling admission process by creating a target profile of the entering class. Based on its admissions history, a law school will estimate what it thinks will be the range of LSAT scores and the range of GPAs of the students it will accept for the upcoming year. Then, as it receives applications (say, month by month), the school will act on them. Students with very strong applications compared with the target group will receive acceptances, and students with weak applications receive rejections. Applications that are neither weak nor strong are carried over—though these applicants receive no notification that the application is still pending.

The rolling admissions process has advantages for both the law school and the applicant. From the applicant's point of view, the earlier the notification of the disposition of an application, the better. That is, you know whether you were accepted or rejected and can go on from there. From the law school's viewpoint, the entering class (and the stability of the budget) begin to take shape as early as possible.

The rolling admissions process is also a tool you can use to your advantage: Apply early. Obviously, schools have greater flexibility earlier in the admission season than later. There are more seats available earlier in the year. That is not to say that if you apply late in the season, you will be rejected. In fact, it is impossible to quantify exactly the advantage that applications received earlier rather than later enjoy. Still, if you want to maximize your chances of acceptance, apply early!

The same advice applies for schools that offer early admission. Early admission procedures require applications by a certain date early in the application season and guarantee you a decision by a certain date. Early admission procedures may be restrictive or non-restrictive. A restrictive procedure requires the applicant to agree that if an offer of admission is extended then the candidate will withdraw applications from all other schools and decline any other offers of admission. In other words, applying for the early decision commits you to attending that law school if you are accepted. Other early admission procedures do not require such a commitment.

For more information on early admissions and other special features, visit law school web sites. For example, check out www.law.nyu.edu/, home page of the New York University (NYU) Law School. The Law School's tax, corporate, and clinical programs are unsurpassed. Plus, the Root-Tilden-Snow Scholars is a premier program for public interest law. And the law school, which has students and faculty members from around the world, is noted for is global orientation.

DECIDING WHERE TO APPLY

Given the financial commitment that you will be making, one of the obvious questions on your mind will be "Where should I apply?"

Let's assume that you have the resources to apply to ten schools and that you have an above average GPA and LSAT score. Depending on the exact numbers, you may very well have a chance at one of the top law schools. But those are your long shot schools. You are almost a sure thing at many schools. And there is a long list of schools in the middle at which your application will almost surely receive serious consideration but is not guaranteed for acceptance. Given these considerations, you should select two or perhaps three long shot schools. As the term *long shot* implies, the odds of your being accepted at these schools are not very good, but the potential pay-off justifies the gamble.

On the other hand, you should also select one or two sure thing schools. To do this, you may have to apply to a school in your geographical area that doesn't enjoy a particularly good reputation or to a school that is located in another part of the country. The rest of your applications should go to your good bet schools—schools for which the chances for acceptance are 40 percent to 75 percent.

Hedge your application bets. Given your LSAT score and GPA, classify schools on your list as "sure things" (odds of acceptance are better than 4 out of 5), "long shots" (odds are worse than 1 out of 5), and "solid favorites" (odds are 2 out of 5 to 4 out of 5). Put most of your "money" on the solid favorites with lesser amounts on sure things and long shots. (The exact proportions will depend on your personal risk-taking preferences.)

This strategy of "stacking" your applications will maximize your chances of acceptance at a school you want while minimizing the chance that you won't get in to any school. Of course, the way the strategy gets implemented will vary from person to person. For people who are lucky enough to have a high GPA and a top LSAT score, the middle- and bottom- tier schools collapse into a single tier. And at the other extreme, those who are unlucky enough to have a GPA and LSAT score that are below what most schools accept will have to work with the second and third tiers.

As you prepare to implement your strategy, make a realistic assessment of your chances. Candidates unfortunately tend to overestimate the importance of what they believe to be their own interesting or unique factors. It is not unusual to hear candidates make statements such as "Well sure my GPA is a little low, but I had to work part-time while I was in school" and "I know my LSAT score is not that good, but I was a member of the University Senate." These are valid points and are usually taken into consideration by admissions officers. But the question is how much weight they will be given, for they (or some similar point) are true of most of the people who are applying to law school.

Be realistic. If you are thinking of applying to Yale Law School and you have a 3.25 GPA and an LSAT score of 75th percentile, then there had better be something really special in your background (such as the Nobel Peace Prize) because in some years, Yale has a hundred-plus applicants with such numbers and accepts none.

WHICH LAW SCHOOL IS THE BEST?

A question related to the "Where should I apply?" question is "What are the top law schools in the country?" Since there is no single criterion for "best law school" that would be accepted by everyone, it is arguable that this question simply cannot be given a meaningful answer. But even though no unequivocal answer can be given, it is possible to get an approximate answer. The following list is reprinted from *The Best Law Schools*, Thomas H. Martinson (ARCO Books, 1993). It presents the author's view of the top 25 law schools as ranked by selectivity, reputation, and placement success:

1. Yale	7. Michigan	13. Vandy	19. Wm & Mary
2. Chicago	8. Berkeley	14. Cornell	20. Wash & Lee
3. Harvard	9. Virginia	15. So. Cal.	21. Washington
4. Stanford	10. N'western	16. G'town	22. North Carolina
5. NYU	11. Penn	17. Davis	23. Minnesota
6. Columbia	12. Duke	18. Fordham	24. Texas
			25. Notre Dame

Another way of evaluating law schools is to think of them as falling into one of three groups: national schools, regional schools, and local schools. National schools are those with substantial academic reputations, such as those listed above. Regional schools have a substantial regional reputation but are not known nationally as "top" schools. Local schools are those whose educational mission is the training of practitioners for a particular jurisdiction. If your goal is a partnership track position with a top law firm in a big city, then you should aim for a "national" school. On the other hand, if you plan to go into practice with your mother's three-person firm, then (aside from the educational challenge) it really doesn't matter much where you go to school. And don't forget, many law school admissions officers say that there are 20 schools in the top 10.

CRAFTING YOUR APPLICATION

To maximize your chances of success, you must create an application that satisfies the needs of the school to which you are applying. This does not mean that you create an application out of whole cloth, but it does mean that you organize and present your experiences in a way that depicts you in the most favorable light.

Answering the "Short Answer" Application Questions

Most of the questions you will be asked need only short answers; for example, "Did you work while you were in school?", "What clubs did you join?", and "What honors or awards did you receive?" You don't have much room to maneuver here. But you should try to communicate as much information as possible in your short answers. Compare the following pairs of descriptions:

Good	Member of the College Orchestra
Better	Second Violinist of the College Orchestra
Good	Played Intramural Volleyball
Better	Co-captain of the Phi Kappa Volleyball Team
Good	Member of the AD's CSL
Better	One of three members on the Associate Dean's Committee on Student Life
Good	Worked at Billy's Burger Barn
Better	Assistant Manager at Billy's Burger Barn (25 hours/week)

In addition to the short answer questions, most applications invite you to make a personal statement. Some applications ask for very little; for example, "In a paragraph, explain to us why you want to go to law school." Other applications are open-ended: "On a separate sheet of paper, tell us anything else you think we ought to know about you." The point of the question is to give you the opportunity to give the admissions committee any information that might not be available from the LSAT score, GPA, and short-answer questions.

Before filling out any applications, sit down and make a list of all of your accomplishments. Include everything. Then prioritize the list. Keep only the ones that are likely to be meaningful to a law school admission committee.

Writing an Effective Personal Statement

For two reasons, you should consider the personal statement to be the most important part of your application. First, the personal statement should be your argument to the admissions committee for your acceptance. It should give the reasons to accept you. Second, the personal statement is the one aspect of the application over which you can exercise any real control. Your GPA is already settled. Your work experience was accumulated over years; your LSAT has been scored. Those are aspects of the application that cannot easily be manipulated. The personal statement, however, is under your control. For an in-depth review "before and after" versions of some sample personal statements, see Appendix B, *Workshop: Personal Statements.*

What should go into a personal statement? Arguments that interpret your academic, employment, and personal history in such a way as to indicate that you have the ability to do law school studies and that you are committed to studying and later to practicing law. Importantly, the personal statement must not be a simple restatement of facts already in the application.

Imagine, for example, a personal statement that reads as follows:

> *I went to State University where I got a 3.5 GPA. I was a member of the Associate Dean's Committee on Student Life, and I worked as the assistant manager on the night shift at Billy's Burger Barn. Then I took the LSAT and got a 160. I know I will make a really good lawyer and will enjoy the job.*

Not very interesting. Furthermore, all of that information is already included in the answers to the standard questions on the application. There is no point in simply repeating it.

Instead, your personal statement should interpret the facts of your life to make them reasons why you should be accepted into law school. Let's start with the GPA. Try to bring out facts that suggest that the GPA is really better than it looks:

- Did you have one particularly bad semester during which you took Physics, Calculus, and Latin that pulled your average down?

- Was there a death in the family or some other difficult time that interfered with your studies?

- How many hours did you work in an average week?

- What extracurricular or family commitments took time away from your studies?

- Did you follow an unusual course of study such as an honors program or a double major?

- Was your major a particularly challenging one?

- Did you participate in any unusual courses such as field research?

These are the points that the admissions committee wants to hear. For example:

> *The committee will see that my final GPA is 3.5. I should point out that the average would have been higher had I not had to work 20 hours each week to finance my education. In addition, my grades in the first semester of my junior year were disappointing because my grandmother, who lived with my family and with whom I was very close, died. Finally, in order to fulfill the requirements for the honors program, I wrote a 50-page honors thesis on the economics of the Dutch fishing industry of the eighteenth century. I have included with this application a copy of the introduction to this paper.*

You should take the same approach to your work experience. For example:

> *During my junior and senior years in college, I worked an average of 20 hours per week at Billy's Burger Barn as the manager on the night shift. I reported to work at midnight and got off at four a.m. As night manager, I supervised eight other employees and was responsible for making emergency repairs on kitchen equipment. For example, once I was able to keep the deep fryer in operation by using a length of telephone cable to repair a faulty thermostat. The night manager was also responsible for maintaining order. It's no easy job to convince intoxicated students who become too rowdy to leave without calling the police. And we were robbed at gunpoint not once but twice.*

Of course, if you have considerable work experience, e.g., if you graduated from college several years ago, you will want to go into your experience in more detail than student work experience merits.

Can you say anything about the LSAT? Probably not much. The LSAT score is not usually open to interpretation, but there are some exceptions. One such exception is a history of poor scores on standardized exams. Consider the following:

> *I believe that my LSAT score of 160 understates my real ability, for I have never had much success on aptitude tests. My SAT score was only 925. Yet, I finished college with a 3.6 GPA.*

Or

> *The committee will see that I have two LSAT scores, 131 and 160. During the first test, I had the flu and a fever and simply could not concentrate.*

These are the two most common excuses for a disappointing LSAT score.

Finally, you must also persuade the admissions committee that you are serious about studying law. It won't do to write "I really like those old Matlock reruns." You must be able to show the committee something in your background that explains why you want to go to law school. Also, it will help your case if you can suggest what you might do with a law degree. For example:

> *As a chemistry major, I joined the Student Environmental Association. Working with private lawyers, we provided evidence in court that ultimately forced the University to stop polluting the Ten Mile Run Creek. From this experience, I learned how the law helps to protect our environment. I plan to make environmental law my area of study, and I hope to work for the government or a private agency to protect the environment.*

A word of warning. Your career objectives have to be believable. It won't do to write "I plan to fight for truth, justice, and the American way." That's much too abstract. Nor are law school admissions officers interested in a general discourse on the advantages of democracy or the hardship of poverty. And any statement about motivation must be credible. If you write "I want to defend the poor and help the needy," then there better be something in your experience that makes this believable. For example:

> *As a member of the Volunteers for the Needy, I work 5 hours each week cooking in our neighborhood soup kitchen. In addition, I telephone local businesses trying to find jobs for the people we help. I have learned that many people who need our help are victims of rigid government standards or unfair landlord or employer practices. As a lawyer, I would be able to help attack the causes of some poverty.*

With regard to motivation, don't imagine that there is a preferred political position that you should adopt. Law school admissions officers span the political spectrum. To be sure, some are political liberals, but there are also conservatives. You don't have to make up a " tear jerker" to get accepted.

Finally, you may also wish to include in your personal statement information that shows that you have something that will help the school create a diverse student body. This additional information can be something dramatic:

> *One morning, a patron choked on a burger and lost consciousness. I used the Heimlich maneuver to dislodge the food and performed CPR until a team of paramedics arrived. The patron recovered fully in large part, according to her doctors, because of my first aid.*

Or the information may not be dramatic:

> *My parents are Armenian immigrants, so I am fluent in Armenian as well as English. I would enjoy meeting others who share an interest in the politics, legal developments, and culture of that part of the world.*

Don't overestimate the value of this kind of information. It is, so to speak, the icing on the cake. It makes you a more interesting individual and might tip the scale in your favor when all other things are equal. It will not, however, get you an acceptance at a school for which you are not otherwise competitive in terms of LSAT and GPA.

Organizing Your Argument

Your personal statement represents your "case" in that it presents your arguments for why you should be accepted. When you marshal your arguments for acceptance, you need to present them in an organized fashion. There is no single preferred format, but you might start with the following outline:

I.   I have the ability.
    A. My college studies were good.
       i. I had one bad semester.
       ii. I was in the honors program.
       iii. I wrote a thesis.
    B. My work experience is good.
       i. I was promoted to VP of my firm.
       ii. I worked while in college.
II. I want to become a lawyer.
    A. I worked with lawyers on the pollution problem.
    B. I would become a specialist in environmental law.
III. There is something interesting about me.

You should create your outline, using all the arguments you can think of. Then you must begin to edit. For most people, the final document should not be more than a page to a page and a half—typed of course! During the editing process, you should strive for an economy of language so that you can convey as much information as possible. In addition, you will be forced to make considered judgments about the relative importance of various points. You will be forced to delete those ideas that aren't really that compelling. To obtain a really good personal statement, it may be necessary to reduce five or six pages to a single page, and the process may require more than 20 drafts.

If your numbers (LSAT and GPA) are in the ballpark, then your personal statement is likely to be the most important part of the application. It will never be perfect, but make it as much so as possible. Ask professors, friends, and co-workers to read it and to comment on it. You might even want to consult a professional adviser to help to construct the application.

Finally, the prose you use should be your own natural style of writing. Don't try something cute. Admissions officers detest essays that try to look like legal briefs and refer to the "evidence" and "reasonable doubt."

Letters of Recommendation

Perhaps the best advice about so-called letters of recommendation is to think of them as evaluations rather than recommendations. Indeed, many admissions officers refer to letter-writers as evaluators. These letters can be very important factors in an application, so you need to choose their authors carefully.

Too many applicants choose evaluators because they think they need character witnesses (the applicant is honest and trustworthy) or endorsements from powerful people (Judge So-and-So). But admissions officers are not really interested in either of those qualities in an evaluator. Instead, they want to hear from someone who knows you well and who can detail the characteristics that you have that would make you a good law student—to wit, the ability to do the curriculum and the motivation to work hard.

First of all, most schools require a letter from the dean of students (or some similar functionary) at your college. Even if you never met the dean, you have to get this letter if the law school to which you're applying requires it. But law schools don't really expect the dean to have much to say. The requirement is in essence an inquiry to the college about your behavior. It is intended to evoke any information about disciplinary problems that might not otherwise surface. So the best letter from a dean, and the one that most people get, is just a statement to the effect that there is nothing to say about you.

In addition to the dean's letter, most law schools require or at least permit you to submit two or three letters of evaluation from other sources. Who should write these? First, let's dispose of a common misunderstanding. A letter of evaluation does not have to come from a famous person. How effective is the following letter?

> *William Hardy, Chief Judge*
> *State Superior Court*
>
> *To the Admissions Committee:*
>
> *I am recommending Paul Roberts for law school. His mother appears frequently in my court and is a very fine attorney. If Paul is anything like his mother, he too will be a fine lawyer.*
>
> *Sincerely,*
>
> *William Hardy*

The letterhead holds out great promise, but then the letter itself is worthless. It is obvious that the letter-writer doesn't really have any basis for the conclusion that the candidate will make a good lawyer.

The best letters of evaluation will come from people who know you very well, e.g., a professor with whom you took several courses, your immediate supervisor at work, or a business associate with whom you have worked closely. A good evaluation will incorporate the personal knowledge into the letter and will make references to specific events and activities. For example:

Mary P. Weiss
White, Weiss, and Blanche

To the Admissions Committee:

White, Weiss, and Blanche is a consulting firm that advises businesses on environmental matters. Paul Roberts has worked for us for the past two summers. His work is outstanding, and he is an intelligent and genial person.

Last summer, as my assistant, Paul wrote a 25-page report that outlined a way of altering a client's exhaust stack to reduce sulfur emissions. The report was organized so that it was easy to follow and written in a style that was clear and easy to understand. In addition, Paul made the live presentation during a meeting with the client's board of directors, engineers, and lawyers. He was confident and handled some very difficult questions in an easy manner. I should note that we have used Paul's innovation in several other plants.

Finally, I would note that Paul made an important contribution to our company softball team. The team finished in last place, but Paul played in every game. His batting average wasn't anything to brag about, but his enthusiasm more than made up for it.

Sincerely,

Mary Weiss

To get a letter such as this, you will have to ask someone who knows you well. It may also help to provide them with some "suggestions" about what should go into the letter. So if you have not been in recent contact, send a resume with a cover letter reminding them of some of the important points that you might want them to mention.

SOME FINAL THOUGHTS ON THE LAW SCHOOL APPLICATION PROCESS

You are about to make a huge investment in your future. The cost of applying to law school is virtually nothing when compared to the cost of a legal education. And the cost of a legal education is minuscule when compared with your earnings potential over a lifetime—depending on where you get in. More importantly, it is your life—your time needed to complete applications, three years in law school, and a career. So explore all options and maximize your opportunities.

Workshop: The Personal Statement

This part gives you a look at the "before" and "after" of two personal statements. The case studies used are composites, suitably sanitized, that have been created from two or more actual files in order to illustrate a wider range of points. For each case study, there is a summary of the candidate's credentials, a first version of the personal statement, a critique of the first version, and an "improved version" of the personal statement. The "improved version" should not be taken as a final version. Even the "improved version" needs further work, but the work becomes a matter of careful attention to detail rather than a major reorganization.

CASE STUDY 1: J.V.

J.V. was 27 when she decided to apply to law school. At the time, she was a civil service worker for a government agency. She realized that while she enjoyed considerable job security, that job security also meant a fairly tedious day-to-day routine and a plodding career track. She took the LSAT and got a 174 and the GMAT and got a 510. She decided to apply to law school. Her undergraduate grade point average was 3.7. After considering her options, she selected six schools—three Ivy League schools, two "second tier" schools, and one local school at which admission was all but assured.

RESUME OF J. V. PERSONAL INFORMATION

Address: 355 West Oak Street

Anywhere, USA

Telephone: 555-1212 (Day); 555-2323 (Evening)

Educational Background

M.A., State University, French Literature, 1994

Thesis: Deconstructing the Sartre–de Beauvoir Correspondence

Activities: University Graduate Student Council

French Literature & Philosophy Forum

B.A., State College, Romance Languages, 1993 (Honors)

Activities: Junior Year Abroad, Paris

University Choral Society

Italian-American Caucus

Employment History

1994–Present: Social Security Administration

Supervise 25 claims agents; responsibility for reviewing claimant ap
peals for benefits.

1993–1994: State University, French Dept.

Adjunct Professor

Other Interests

Music (Opera and Piano)

Travel

Personal Statement

WHY I WANT TO GO TO LAW SCHOOL

The decision to apply to law school represents the third and final important reorientation in my life. I came to college certain that I would want to pursue a teaching career and entered the School of Education. After a semester, I realized that I did not want to teach on the elementary or even secondary level, so I transferred to the College of Arts and Sciences to study languages and become a college teacher. After graduation, I took a Masters in French while I taught on the college level. During that year, I realized that even college teaching was not for me. At the end of that time, I took a job with the Federal Government.

While with the Federal Government, I have received several promotions. In my present capacity, I am a Supervisor for the Social Security Administration. I have the responsibility for supervising 25 Claims Agents. This means that I supervise their day-to-day activities (assigning cases and monitoring progress) and handle crisis situations (such as labor union grievances). One of my most important duties is to review the appeals of people whose claims for benefits have been denied. In order to do this, I have to have a detailed knowledge of the regulations governing the eligibility of claimants. I believe that my experience with our procedures is good training for practicing law.

Finally, I would add that my outside interests include both travel and music. Over the past five years, I have visited Mexico, Peru, Spain, and Israel. I have studied piano since I was a small child, and I been involved with several opera workshops.

One of the most common mistakes made by applicants is to write a personal statement that "moves across the surface," and that is the main weakness of this statement. For example, paragraph one simply repeats a chronology that will be available to the reader elsewhere in the application. (Just as it is available in the resume.) It simply reiterates "what" happened without addressing the "why" of the events. What is the significance of the transfer from the School of Education to the College of Arts and Sciences? And if it doesn't have any significance (from the perspective of an admissions officer), then it doesn't belong in the personal statement.

Next, why explain the move from academia to government service? On its face, the move looks like the applicant taught for a year while doing an M.A. and then moved on to the "real world." Unless there is something more to the event than that, it speaks for itself and doesn't need to be addressed in the personal statement—particularly since it happened so long ago.

The second paragraph likewise "moves across the surface." Much of the information provided there will already have been included in the "Q and A" part of the application. As you can see, the second paragraph really does not add anything to this. The last part of the second paragraph attempts to explain the significance that the employment experience has in terms of a law school application. This part should be expanded, and more detail should be included.

The third paragraph is a good idea, but its treatment is too cursory. How much time did the applicant spend in the places mentioned? If just a week or two, then this travel probably won't mean much to a law school admissions officer. In addition, the effectiveness of the discussion about musical talent would be considerably enhanced with some more detail.

As it turns out, further discussion with this applicant revealed some important information that was not apparent from the resume (and likely would not have shown up in the "Q and A" part of the application). After reworking, the applicant's statement has much greater impact. Here's the revised version of J. V.'s personal statement:

WHY I WANT TO GO TO LAW SCHOOL

My decision to apply to law school was made after careful reflection. My present employment affords me a comfortable standard of living and considerable job security, but the position no longer offers the challenges and variety that it once did. To be sure, there are occasional surprises. A few months ago, for example, a male employee filed a grievance claiming that he was the victim of sexual harassment in the workplace. (He alleged that two female co-workers had made suggestive remarks about parts of his anatomy.) As it turns out, what really happened was that a male co-worker reported to the complainant that such remarks had been made. Since they were not made directly to the complainant, there was no ground under our rules for any action. (And the comments of the male co-worker were not, in and of themselves, sexual harassment.) By and large, however, the supervisory duties are fairly routine.

Sometimes appeals claims offer a surprise. Last year, for example, a claimant appeared at a hearing accompanied by an adviser/translator. The adviser/translator would translate my questions (stated in English) into Spanish. What the adviser/translator did not realize is that I am fluent in Spanish, and I knew that throughout the hearing that the adviser/translator was instructing the claimant on how to fabricate a claim. At the end of the hearing, both claimant and adviser/translator were flabbergasted when I told them in Spanish that they were both being charged with attempted fraud. By and large, however, even the appeals on denied claims are usually fairly routine.

What I would hope to find in law school and later in the practice of law is more of the very best moments of the position I currently have. Even though I know that every occupation has its tedium, I expect that the practice of law would offer greater variety and challenge. While I hear 30 to 40 cases each month, most of these are similar in their details. Even those that present unusual facts are resolved by reference to a fairly compact body of regulations. I look forward with anticipation to the opportunity to handle cases with variety and surprises and to the need to address a much wider range of legal concepts.

I am confident in my ability to handle the law school curriculum. My college transcript shows that I graduated with "General Honors" (top 15 percent), but it does not show that my studies made me fluent in French and Italian (as well as Spanish). I anticipate that studying law will be like learning yet another "foreign" language—vocabulary, syntax, logic, etc. While a graduate student, I was a member of the French Literature & Philosophy Forum. During that academic year, three of the featured speakers were law professors who discussed the application of literary analysis to legal texts. For one of my courses, I wrote a paper entitled "Con-text-ualizing the Law." (I have enclosed a copy for the Committee's review.)

Finally, in addition to my experience in a government agency and my academic perspective, I think that I can add something to the law school on a personal level. I have studied voice for nearly ten years. I am a Mezzo-Soprano, and I have participated in several opera workshops. Most recently, I sang the role of Dorabella in Mozart's **Cosi Fan Tutte** with the Northern State Regional Opera Company. This was a particularly satisfying experience because, unlike most workshop productions, this one was done with an orchestra instead of just piano, and the orchestra included several well-known members of the City Orchestra.

In addition to eliminating the weaknesses mentioned, the revised version contains a couple of very nice features. The additional details—the name of the paper, the role of Dorabella, the importance of the orchestra—all make the revised version more readable as well as more credible. Also, the anecdote that illustrates the use of Spanish is a nice touch. It's an interesting story, in and of itself. In fact, don't underestimate the importance of holding the reader's attention. Admissions officers may be reading a dozen or more personal statements an hour and hundreds in just a few weeks. You need something that will make yours stand out.

CASE STUDY 2: P.D.

P.D. was 20 and a junior in college when he decided on a career in law. He took the LSAT in the spring of his junior year and scored 148. He took the exam a second time in the fall of his senior year and scored 162. His GPA through the first six semesters was 3.4. In order to maximize his options, P.D. decided to apply to ten schools—only one top-tier school, two second-tier schools, and seven schools with various distinguishing features. (The following application document was completed in the fall of P.D.'s senior year, so some information was not yet available.)

APPLICATION FOR ADMISSION

Educational Background

List the official names of all colleges, universities, and other postsecondary institutions attended, including those for summer session or evening class. Complete an LSDAS (Law School Data Assembly Service) report. Send any transcripts not a part of that report directly to the law school.

Institution	Dates	Major	Degree	Date
Loyola U.	94–	History	A.B.	NA
Kramer CC	Sum '93	NA	NA	NA

List Academic Honors and other Awards Received

Dean's List (2 Semesters)

Honorable Mention, Robertson Prize in History

APPLICATION FOR ADMISSION (PAGE 2)

Employment History

Loyola U., Public Relations, Summer '96, 40 hours per week

City News, Account Rep., Summer '95, 40 hours per week

TV Cable Co., Installer, Summer '94, 40 hours per week

City News, Carrier, Spring '96, 15 hours per week

City News, Carrier, Spring '95, 10 hours per week

Personal Statement

Staple to this page a typed, signed personal statement that tells us why you want to pursue a legal education. Please discuss personal and professional goals that are important to you. You should consider this an opportunity to introduce yourself to us.

PERSONAL STATEMENT

I want to take this opportunity to introduce myself to the Admissions Committee. I will graduate from Loyola University next spring with a major in history. I hope to become a lawyer. I want to become a lawyer because I am vitally concerned with the important problems that face us as a society. These include issues such as the environment, ethics in government, and social injustice. As a lawyer, I know that I will be in a position to address these important matters.

If the Committee reviews my record, they will see that I have a strong academic background. Through my first six semesters, I have a 3.4 GPA, and

I expect to do better during the next two semesters. I have taken the LSAT twice because I did not do very well the first time (scoring only 148), but the second time I got a 162. I have been on the Dean's List twice, and my paper on the Federalist Papers received "Honorable Mention" in the History Department's Robertson Competition. I would point out that I achieved these accomplishments while working part-time. I even took courses at the community college during the summer.

My employment also demonstrates that I have the ability to do well in law school. While it is true that my first summer in college I worked as a laborer for TV Cable installing cable, my second summer I was an Account Representative for the City News. In that capacity, I dealt with people on a daily basis and had to think on my feet. After that I worked for the University in its Public Relations Office.

As a member of the Student Government, I was exposed to the legislative process. I was able to observe first hand the give and take that goes into the formation of laws. Plus I was a member of the Demosthenes Club and a member of an intramural basketball team.

The problem that P.D. faces—and it is one faced by thousands of candidates who are applying for admission directly out of college—is that it may be difficult to articulate specific reasons why one wants to become a lawyer. To be sure, many undergraduates may have fairly settled career goals; and if you are one of them, you should not hesitate to state your goals. Other students, however, may have only the vaguest idea of why they want to become lawyers; and if you are one of them, you should not overstate your case. Instead, you should address the issue in general terms and let your record speak for you. Let's walk through some of the weaknesses in P.D.'s personal statement.

There is nothing particularly wrong with the first paragraph. There may be better ways of beginning this type of essay, but certainly it cannot be said that this style is completely inappropriate.

The second paragraph, however, is almost completely a waste of ink. P.D. expects the reader to believe that he wants to go to law school because he wants, in essence, to "reform the world." Is there any evidence in P.D.'s background to suggest that this is a real commitment? Is a member of student government necessarily a social reformer? Is a member of an intramural basketball league? An account representative for a newspaper? No. Without some further evidence of a real and long-standing commitment to social reform, this sort of language seems contrived and will likely fall on deaf ears.

The next paragraph is also pretty much useless. The explanation regarding the LSAT score is typical of many personal statements: "I didn't do well the first time I took the test, so I took it again." Since the LSAS reports multiple scores to the law schools, that much will be obvious! If you are going to address the fact that you have taken the LSAT more than once, then you must be prepared with an explanation: "The first time I took the LSAT I got a 148, but I was very ill with the flu that day. My second test, taken when I felt well, is a better indicator of my ability."

The last part of the essay has the merit of mentioning the title of the paper that earned P.D. the "Honorable Mention." This is something that is probably not covered elsewhere in the application and so should be expanded upon. It might even be a good idea to include a copy of the paper or at least the introduction. One would not expect that an Admissions Committee would read it as thoroughly as a professor would, but one might hope that an admissions officer might say "Mmmmm, I don't have time to read all of this, but it does look like a good piece of work." The third and fourth paragraphs also don't say very much beyond what is already evident in the rest of the application. It is important to explain to an admissions officer the significance of events and accomplishments.

As for the entry about intramural basketball, P.D. was twice a member of the Intramural Allstars; and at this college, each spring the Intramural Allstars play an exhibition game in the arena against members of the college's varsity basketball team. This experience obviously does not qualify P.D. to practice law, but it is an experience that few other law school applicants will have had—and it may count for something.

With these points in mind, P.D. can revise his personal statement to carry much more impact:

PERSONAL STATEMENT

I want to take this opportunity to introduce myself to the Admissions Committee and to provide you with some information that is not included in other parts of my application. I want to discuss further both the issue of my ability to succeed in law school and my reasons for wanting to become a lawyer.

First, my GPA alone does not describe the full extent of my academic ability. It is lower than it otherwise would have been because my performance in my freshman year was not particularly good. In addition, it was financially necessary for me to work the past two spring semesters, and you will observe that my grades during the spring semesters are lower than those of the fall semesters. Finally, I devoted considerable time to extracurricular activities.

As for the LSAT, the first time I took the exam, I was sick with the flu and obviously did not do as well as I could. My second score is a better measure of my real ability.

Setting aside the considerations above, if the Admissions Committee is looking for a good example of my ability, you should look at my paper "Implicit Religious Convictions in the Federalist Papers." I wrote this paper for

Professor M.V., a notoriously hard grader, who not only gave it an "A" but also encouraged me to enter it in the Robertson Competition. The Robertson Competition is sponsored by the History Department each year as part of its Colloquium on American History and is open to both graduate and undergraduate students. Twelve students read papers to a panel of distinguished historians from universities across the nation. One paper receives the "Robertson Award," and two others receive "Honorable Mention." I have enclosed a copy of this paper.

I have decided on a career in law because I enjoy doing those things that I have seen lawyers do. The Demosthenes Club is a debating society with 35 active members. We meet for 3 hours every other week to debate a topic such as "Capital Punishment" or "U.S. Military Commitments." The schedule allows members time to do some additional background research on announced topics. I particularly enjoy playing "Devil's Advocate" during the debates, offering counterexamples or pointing out inconsistencies in the arguments of others. In addition, I enjoy writing, and my work in the University's Public Relations Office has been particularly helpful in this regard. A press release has to be carefully crafted because it usually deals with a complex situation that must be described in terms that those not familiar with its details can grasp.

Finally, I noted in your Bulletin that the Law School sponsors an intramural basketball league. In high school, I dreamed of playing college basketball; and, in a way, I fulfilled this dream. Each year, the Intramural Allstars play members of the Varsity in an exhibition game in the Arena, and I was selected to play for the Allstars twice. Thus, I have had the privilege of being soundly defeated by some of the best in college basketball.

You'll notice that the revised statement answers all of the objections that were raised in response to the first version. Beyond that, the revised version is an improvement in a couple of other ways. First, the mention of the paper (as recommended) drives the point home: It's an impressive title suggesting critical analysis and research. The further detail about the debating society is also useful since it hints at skills a lawyer ought to have. Finally, the mention of the basketball game is good fun. And the self-deprecating tone of that paragraph, because it is in good humor, avoids the danger of sounding like a boast.

Ask the Experts

Here are 50 Frequently Asked Questions (FAQs) about applying to law school. You will find answers to these questions below. You can use the list of questions to reference answers on topics that are of interest to you, or you can read through the answers to all 50 FAQs. The topics are arranged in a logical order so that the list, when read in its entirety, tells a more complete story.

1. Is it difficult to get into law school?
2. Who makes the admissions decisions?
3. How are admissions decisions made?
4. What factors do law schools take into consideration?
5. Do law schools have formal LSAT and GPA cutoffs?
6. Does every applicant have a chance at every school?
7. Why do law schools use GPAs and the LSAT scores?
8. What about the quality of my undergraduate school?
9. Are law schools interested in leadership ability?
10. Are other indicators considered?
11. Why are law schools interested in other indicators?
12. Should I say that I want to "serve justice" or "save the world"?
13. How do I demonstrate motivation?
14. Is it necessary to be a law major?
15. Does a law major have an advantage?
16. How can I determine my chances of being accepted?
17. Can other indicators offset a low GPA or a low LSAT score?
18. What if I have a good LSAT score but a low GPA?
19. What if I have a good GPA but a low LSAT score?
20. What if I have a low GPA and a low LSAT score?
21. How can I assess my non-numerical indicators?
22. Is it important to attend an ABA-accredited law school?
23. What about new schools that have not yet been accredited?
24. What about state-accredited schools?
25. Can I become a lawyer by clerking?
26. Are any other factors taken into consideration?
27. Do law schools give special consideration to members of minority groups?
28. Why do law schools have special procedures?
29. What other characteristics might be important?
30. What are the top law schools?
31. Are there jobs for lawyers?
32. Do graduates of top law schools have better job prospects?
33. Should I go to school in the state where I want to practice?

34. Do law schools offer specialties in certain fields?

35. To how many law schools should I apply?

36. When should I take the LSAT?

37. Can I take the LSAT for practice?

38. How do law schools treat multiple LSAT scores?

39. Is it wise to take the test a second time?

40. Do I have to say if I am applying for financial aid?

41. What should be included in the personal statement?

42. Is the personal statement really important?

43. What if a school does not require a personal statement?

44. Should I send other supporting information?

45. Why do law schools ask for letters of recommendation?

46. Should my recommendations come from judges and lawyers?

47. What if I have been out of school for some time?

48. What about a personal interview?

49. What else can I do to maximize my chances?

50. Where can I get more information?

JUST THE FAQS

1. Is it difficult to get into law school?

In a typical year, about 100,000 people start the law school application process, but there are fewer than 50,000 places for entering students in the 175+ law schools that are accredited by the American Bar Association. So the chance of getting into law school is less than one out of two. However, law school seats are not assigned by lottery, so the chance of getting into a certain law school depends on your qualifications, the level of competition for seats at that law school, the time you invest in preparing for the LSAT, and the effort you spend on your application.

If you want to know more about your chances for success at a particular law school? Consult the *Official American Bar Association Guide to Approved Law Schools*, American Bar Association Law Schools (Macmillan General Reference, 1998). This book has admissions data on every ABA-accredited law school, and it will give you a pretty good idea of what your chances are at particular schools.

2. Who makes the admissions decisions?

Each law school has an admissions committee of one or more people who are responsible for reviewing and acting on applications for admission. At some schools, the authority is given to a group of faculty members; at others, it is given to a dean or to professional admissions officers; at still others, students are included in the deliberations. Of course, there are many variations on these practices.

3. How are admissions decisions made?

The mechanics of the decision-making process vary from school to school. For example, at one school, applications are assigned an index that is calculated by mathematical formula to produce a weighted average of the GPA and the LSAT score. The dean of admissions, acting alone, has the authority to accept applications with very high indexes and to reject those with very low indexes. All other applications must be referred to the admissions committee as a whole for debate and a vote. At another school, applications are distributed for reading to committee members, who must then make a recommendation to the committee as a whole for debate and a vote. At a third school, the dean of admissions acts as the committee. The dean reads each application in its entirety before looking at the LSAT score. The LSAT score is then used to confirm or disconfirm the dean's impression of the applicant based on all other factors. Ultimately, however, even though the mechanics are interesting, they are not terribly important because you cannot control them. The best you can do is submit a well-prepared application and hope for the best.

For more detailed information on the law school admissions process, you can consult *Getting Into Law School Today,* Thomas H. Martinson and David P. Waldherr (ARCO/Thomson Learning, 1998).

4. What factors do law schools take into consideration?

Typically, a law school will say that its admissions committee takes into account "all relevant factors," including the applicant's GPA (undergraduate Grade Point Average) and LSAT score. However, you should distinguish between what might be called "factors" and what might be called "indicators." By far, the two most important factors in the admissions process are ability and motivation. On the one hand, the committee has to be convinced that you have sufficient intellectual ability to handle the curriculum; on the other hand, the committee needs to know that you are seriously committed to completing the curriculum. Intellectual talent without proper discipline or dedication is not likely to ensure successful completion of the curriculum. Similarly, great aspirations without intellectual ability will get a student nowhere. The LSAT score and GPA are indicators of these factors. The LSAT score is designed to measure intellectual ability; the GPA provides information about both intellectual ability and motivation. Thus, the two most important factors in the admissions process are ability and motivation, and the two most important indicators of those factors are the GPA and the LSAT score.

5. Do law schools have formal LSAT and GPA cutoffs?

Although the LSAT score and the GPA are the two most important indicators, law schools are reluctant to say that they use a mechanical device, like a cutoff, to reject applications. And the school mentioned earlier that uses an index does so only to sort applications, not to make final decisions on them. Other schools, however, may specifically announce that applicants with numbers below certain minimal are "not likely" to be accepted.

6. Does every applicant have a chance at every school?

Not necessarily. At most law schools, it is possible to find students whose LSAT score or GPA or both are markedly below the medians of the student body, but such students are the exceptions. For most applicants, the probability of acceptance is largely a function of the GPA and LSAT score. Furthermore, even though a school does not have a formal cutoff for applications, it may have a *de facto* cutoff. One school, for example, states that applicants with an LSAT score below the 90th percentile or a GPA below 3.0 are rarely accepted, though there are exceptions. This statement implies that there is an informal minimum LSAT score and an informal minimum GPA, and applications with numbers below these minimums don't receive serious consideration. Be realistic, but don't underestimate your chances.

7. Why do law schools use GPAs and the LSAT scores?

The GPA plays an important part in the admissions process because virtually every applicant has one. The GPA is a readily available yardstick of intellectual ability and motivation by which most applicants can be compared. Law schools recognize, however, that grading practices vary from school to school, and that the variation can be significant. The LSAT was designed as another measure of ability, one that tests all applicants in a uniform way. Taken together, the GPA and the LSAT score are, statistically speaking, relatively accurate in predicting success in the first year of law school.

8. What about the quality of my undergraduate school?

Some admissions offices actually keep records on how students from different colleges and universities perform at the law school and use this information to judge the GPAs of applicants from schools for which they have records. Other admissions officers may make a subjective judgment about the quality of the GPA.

9. Are law schools interested in leadership ability?

To a certain extent, yes, because many lawyers wind up in positions of leadership. But you should not overestimate the importance of leadership ability as a factor in the admissions process. Law schools are primarily looking for evidence of academic ability and commitment.

10. Are other indicators considered?

Absolutely! Other indicators that might be considered relevant are graduate study, employment experience, extracurricular activities, community service work, family background, or interesting accomplishments of any kind, such as mastery of a second language, success in athletic competition, or musical talent.

11. Why are law schools interested in other indicators?

GPA and LSAT scores are not the only measures of ability. Law schools also want to know about other accomplishments. For example, an applicant who earned a mediocre GPA while working full-time as an undergraduate might have as much academic promise as an applicant with a very high GPA who had the luxury of devoting every waking hour to studying. Also, schools recognize that the LSAT is not a perfect measure. An applicant with a low-to-average LSAT score may have demonstrated considerable ability in business or in a profession. Motivation is important too. A law student with perhaps less ability but a greater measure of motivation might very well outperform a law student with more raw talent but less motivation. For this reason, law schools take commitment and motivation into consideration.

12. Should I say that I want to "serve justice" or "save the world"?

As a factor in the law school admissions process, motivation doesn't necessarily mean having a specific post-law school goal. To be sure, a few people enter law school with specific career objectives in mind, and these individuals often already have specialized training or experience (e.g., a social worker who wants to practice family law or an engineer who wants to practice patent law). The great majority of first-year law students have no idea what position they will fill after graduation. It is not necessary to express some lofty aspiration such as the desire to serve justice. In fact, unless you can point to specific experiences to show that such a claim is sincere (e.g., a community organizer who wants to use a law degree for social change), expressions of noble purpose are likely to seem contrived and unconvincing.

13. How do I demonstrate motivation?

Only a small percentage of candidates can demonstrate their motivation by showing that the study of law is the natural extension of the work they have been doing and leads to a particular type of practice. Most applicants indicate their motivation by previous success as a student or by success in a career. For such an applicant, a thoughtful explanation about the decision to become a lawyer may also show motivation.

14. Is it necessary to be a law major?

No. Law schools are interested in candidates who have studied a rigorous and broad-based liberal arts curriculum. It is not important whether an applicant's major was history, political science, economics, or chemistry, so long as the transcript shows a variety of challenging courses that would help to develop analytical skills and writing ability.

15. Does a law major have an advantage?

No. Undergraduate law courses teach about the law; they do not teach the practice of law. The law school curriculum is designed not just to familiarize students with important legal principles but also to teach them how to think like lawyers; that is, how to interpret legal principles and how to apply them in different situations. In fact, an undergraduate transcript that shows too many "criminal procedure" or "business law" courses may be viewed as weak. It may not exhibit the range of courses desired by the law school, and it may raise suspicion about the broadness and rigor of the undergraduate liberal arts curriculum.

16. How can I determine my chances of being accepted?

Admissions bulletins of law schools include information about the median or average GPA and LSAT score of the student body. Using that information, you can at least determine whether your numbers are above or below those that are typically accepted at that school. You should also consult the ABA publication mentioned above.

17. Can other indicators offset a low GPA or a low LSAT score?

In many cases, the answer is "yes," but the mitigating power of alternative indicators depends on the weakness of the GPA or LSAT score. For example, a law school admissions committee might be willing to forgive a business executive for a 2.9 GPA earned several years earlier but not for a 2.3 GPA. Or, in another example, a candidate who has earned a Ph.D. in economics might be forgiven for having an LSAT score in the 50th percentile but not in the 20th percentile.

18. What if I have a good LSAT score but a low GPA?

Law school admissions officers are aware that the GPA is an average or a summary of an applicant's college grades, and they are on the alert for anomalies or trends that would help them better to understand the significance of the average. For example, a single poor semester that depresses an otherwise respectable GPA may be forgiven, or a rising trend in grades from the first through the senior year might create a favorable impression.

19. What if I have a good GPA but a low LSAT?

If there is any reason for a poor LSAT score, you should make the admissions committee aware of it. If, for example, you took the LSAT when you were ill and did not do very well but later performed better, you should make sure the committee knows this. More generally, if you have a history of poor performances on standardized exams and yet have done very well in school, this too could be important and should be called to the committee's attention.

20. What if I have a low GPA and a low LSAT score?

In that case, you might want to consider very seriously the wisdom of investing money in an application fee for that school. Unless there is something extraordinary in the personal background to overcome those two disadvantages, you may simply be wasting money. The greater the difference between the median scores accepted and yours, the worse your chances are for acceptance.

21. How can I assess my non-numerical indicators?

The GPA and LSAT scores are the most important indicators in the law school admissions process. Other significant achievements are also important, but you have to interpret them not only in light of your own background but also in light of the backgrounds of those against whom you will be competing. Most of the people who are successful in applying to law school not only have good LSAT scores and GPAs, but they also have some additional dimension: extracurricular activities, employment experience, unusual personal history, special talent, or other achievements. This is the rule, not the exception. So as you measure your own numerical credentials against the standard published by a particular law school, keep in mind that most of the people who applied to that school had other significant achievements as well. Nevertheless, don't underestimate yourself. Be sure to include those factors that make you an individual.

22. Is it important to attend an ABA-accredited law school?

Each state and the District of Columbia regulate admission to the practice of law. One requirement for admission to the bar is a degree from an approved school. Most jurisdictions defer to the American Bar Association and accept degrees only from those schools that are accredited by its Section of Legal Education and Admissions to the Bar. In those jurisdictions, a degree from a school not on the list of accredited law schools will not qualify its holder to practice law.

23. What about new schools that have not yet been accredited?

A newly opened law school is not eligible to apply for full accreditation with the ABA. Instead, it can apply for provisional accreditation, which will mature into full accreditation if and when the school is fully operational and meets all ABA standards. At that time, its graduates, including those of earlier classes, receive the official ABA stamp of approval and are eligible to apply for admission to the bar in those jurisdictions that require degrees from ABA-accredited schools.

24. What about state-accredited schools?

A few states, notably California, accredit law schools that do not also have ABA accreditation and permit their graduates to apply for admission to the practice of law. Such schools offer an alternative route to the bar, but there are some serious drawbacks:

first, the bar-pass rate of the graduates of state-accredited schools is not very encouraging; and second, jurisdictions that require a degree from an ABA-accredited law school do not recognize degrees from state-accredited schools.

25. Can I become a lawyer by clerking?

Not any longer. Although there may be an exception or two buried in the fine print of the regulations governing admission to the bar in some states, for all practical purposes, the clerkship route to the bar has been eliminated. Of course, many law students do clerkships with lawyers, government agencies, and judges; but the clerkship is in addition to their formal studies—not a substitute for it.

26. Are any other factors taken into consideration?

Yes. Law schools want to assemble student bodies that include individuals from many different backgrounds, so diversity becomes a factor in admissions decisions. Given applicants with very similar indicators, those whose backgrounds suggest they are in a position to make a unique contribution to the law school stand a better chance of acceptance.

27. Do law schools give special consideration to members of minority groups?

Yes. At some schools, special consideration may simply mean reading applications of members of minority groups with heightened sensitivity; at other schools, formal procedures have been established for handling applications of members of minority groups. At one school, for example, all applications are reviewed by at least one member of the admissions committee, and that reader must make a recommendation to the committee as a whole. Applications from individuals who claim an ethnic or minority group status are reviewed by two readers, each of whom must make an independent recommendation to the committee as a whole. As you probably are aware, however, courts have been asked to review the constitutionality of such procedures.

28. Why do law schools have special procedures?

These special procedures consider three facts: one, members of certain ethnic and minority groups have traditionally been underrepresented in law schools; two, the indicators of ability and motivation may be different for individuals who come from backgrounds that are not like those of members of the majority; and three, individuals who come from different backgrounds can make different contributions to the law school. Again, however, whether these justifications will survive scrutiny by the courts is an open issue.

29. What other characteristics might be important?

Virtually anything imaginable. At those law schools that receive many more applications from qualified candidates than there are positions available, the diversity factor takes on even more importance. Indeed, it is a source of pride for an admissions officer to be able to point to someone with an unusual background (e.g., a nightclub singer, a jet pilot, a forest ranger).

30. What are the top law schools?

There is no single authoritative ranking of law schools, and the American Bar Association specifically declines to attempt one. As you look at schools, you will probably want to consider several quantitative factors, such as the percent of applicants accepted, the median LSAT and GPA of the student body, or the average starting salary of graduates. Any list of the top 10 law schools would surely include the University of Chicago, Columbia, Harvard, New York University, Stanford, and Yale. In addition to those schools, you probably find the remaining positions in the top ten list filled by four of the following: University of California at Berkeley, Cornell, Duke, Georgetown, the University of Michigan, Northwestern, the University of Pennsylvania, and the University of Virginia. A list of the top 25 would probably also include several if not all of the following: Boston College, UCLA, the University of California at Davis, Fordham University, George Washington, the University of Minnesota, the University of North Carolina at Chapel Hill, Notre Dame, the University of Southern California, the University of Texas, William and Mary, and Vanderbilt.

31. Are there jobs for lawyers?

Yes. In fact, a lawyer is never really unemployed if you consider that as a member of the bar, a lawyer is licensed to do legal work and collect a fee for it. Seriously, the job market for lawyers seems to be cyclical. But if you really, really want to practice law, once you are admitted to the bar, you are an attorney and will always have a job (even if you have to "hustle" to pay the bills).

32. Do graduates of top law schools have better job prospects?

In general, yes. The average starting salary of graduates of top law schools tends to be higher than those of other schools, but it is important to keep in mind that an average is just that. A person's standing in a graduating class is also a very important determinant of employment possibilities.

33. Should I go to school in the state where I want to practice?

Not necessarily. A degree from any ABA-accredited school is good in every jurisdiction, so it is not necessary to attend school in the state in which you plan to practice. There may, however, be some practical advantages to doing so. First, professors at some law schools may be more familiar with the law of the jurisdiction in which they teach than professors elsewhere, and this may translate into an advantage on the bar exam. Second, access to part-time and summer employment may in part depend on where a person lives while in school, and this may affect your finding full-time employment after graduation.

34. Do law schools offer specialties in certain fields?

Not really, or at least not in the same way that graduate programs are organized departmentally (e.g., history, philosophy, economics, and English). In fact, the first-year law school curriculum is remarkably uniform across the country. It almost always includes a mix of contracts, civil procedure, criminal law, property, torts, and a seminar on legal research and writing, with perhaps an elective or two. And every law school offers standard upper-division courses such as taxation, constitutional law, accounting, business organizations, and so on. Some law schools offer additional courses in areas such as "entertainment law" or "sports law"; but those additional courses do not really create specialists. For most applicants, it would probably be a mistake to choose one school over another because it offers a "specialization." For more information about law school curriculum, you might want to consult *Looking at Law School: A Student Guide from the Society of Law School Teachers,* 4th Ed., Stephen Gillers, Ed. (Meridian Books, 1997). It is edited by Stephen Gillers, a professor at New York University (NYU) Law School, with a preface by the late Supreme Court Justice William J. Brennan, Jr. It includes Part One: Deciding to Go to Law School, Part Two: The Law School Experience, Part Three: First-year and Required Courses, and Part Four: Special Courses and Course Selection.

35. To how many law schools should I apply?

To apply to every law school that seems interesting would be prohibitively expensive for most people. Instead, you must decide how many schools you can afford to apply to, say 10. For a candidate with average indicators, this means selecting a mix of schools that will maximize the chances of acceptance while offering the richest variety of options. The mix should include one or two "safe" schools at which acceptance appears to be certain. And it can include two or three "reach" school—perhaps top schools at which the chance of admission is less than 15 percent. The rest of the applications should go to schools where the chance for admission is solid. Of course, the application of this strategy will vary from candidate to candidate. For those with super indicators, even top schools are safe. For those with relatively low indicators, there are no safe schools.

36. When should I take the LSAT?

At least fifteen months before you plan to enter law school. The LSAT is given four times each year, usually in October, December, February, and June. Law schools begin accepting applications in October for the class that will enter the following year. So if you take the LSAT in February or June, you will have your score and be ready to file a completed application early in the application season.

37. Can I take the LSAT for practice?

Yes, but don't! You can take the LSAT as many times as you care to, but multiple scores are reported to the law schools that you designate to receive your scores whether or not you want them reported. Obviously, you don't want a practice score reported along with a "real" score. You can easily find plenty of material for practice without registering to take an actual LSAT.

38. How do law schools treat multiple LSAT scores?

Many use the average of the scores. Others may discount a low score if the candidate can explain that it is not a true measure of his or her ability. And some will discount a previous, lower score if a later score is significantly better.

39. Is it wise to take the test a second time?

As noted above, when a law school receives your LSAT report, it receives all of your recent scores. So the decision to retake the LSAT must be viewed in that light. Each year, 20,000 or so candidates take a second LSAT. On average, the results are not very encouraging. Some candidates improve, some candidates lose ground, and many candidates simply repeat their previous performance. Unless you have reason to believe that your score will improve (you were sick or exceptionally unnerved the first time), then it might be better to stick with the first score. Or if you were not adequately prepared the first time, then there is reason to believe that you will improve on a second attempt. Our advice is "Do it once, do it right, and don't do it again." So be prepared the first time.

40. Do I have to say if I am applying for financial aid?

If the question is asked, then you should answer truthfully. In any event, most schools make it quite clear that the application process is "need blind," meaning that your need to apply for financial aid will not affect the admissions decision. Most students need some form of assistance to finance their legal education.

41. What should be included in the personal statement?

Basically, the personal statement is your opportunity to add any information to your application that is not already covered in your responses to the questions on the standardized application form. And it is a golden opportunity! You can explain why you got that failing grade in Russian, discuss what you accomplished as a member of the university senate, or describe your re-sponsibilities in your position of employment. Do not, however, simply repeat what is already contained in your application form. Rather, present information that you believe will help the committee get to know you better.

42. Is the personal statement really important?

From the standpoint of the applicant, the answer is an unqualified "yes." Not only does the personal statement offer you the opportunity to contribute something to the admissions process, but it is also the only such opportunity you have, so you will want to make the most of it. Also, law school admissions officers frequently stress that a thoughtful and well-written personal statement can greatly improve a candidate's chance for admission. As you write your personal statement, keep in mind the three factors that were discussed above: ability, motivation, and diversity. Select content for the personal statement that bears on one or more of these issues.

43. What if a school does not require a personal statement?

Send one anyway. It may be that some law schools do not require a personal statement simply because most of the personal statements they receive are neither thoughtful nor well written and so contribute nothing to the decision-making process. A good personal statement, even though not required, might very well make a favorable impression. And, in any event, no law school is going to reject you because you made the extra effort.

44. Should I send other supporting information?

Yes, but be selective. The introductory chapter to a thesis or a major term paper would provide an admissions officer with information about the author's analytical ability and writing skills. A videotape of a news program would provide an admissions committee with the opportunity to see firsthand the quality of the work done by a candidate who is a broadcast journalist. A photograph taken by an amateur photographer might catch the committee's fancy as it attempts to create a diverse student body. As you try to decide what you should include in the application, keep three important points in mind. One, any exhibit must bear on one of the three important factors: ability, motivation, or diversity. Two, do not overwhelm the committee by submitting a little of this and a little of that. Submitting a lot of extra material, no matter how impressive you think it is, will have a negative rather than a positive effect. Three, make it very clear that the additional material is just that, additional, and that the committee is welcome to review it if they wish—or to ignore and discard it. "Stunts" are risky. Sometimes they work; sometimes they don't work. One candidate submitted the application by inserting it into the arms of a full-size cardboard cutout of a human being with a photograph of her own face carefully trimmed to fit the cutout and a dialogue bubble saying "I'm a real person." It worked. Another submitted a collage of newspaper headlines reporting various injustices with a note attached saying "I want to fix this." It didn't work. Still another candidate pitched a tent in a public park opposite the law school and called the dean of admission on a cell phone to say "Look out your window; I'm here, and I'm not leaving until you accept me" and waved to the dean. It worked.

45. Why do law schools ask for letters of recommendation?

Law schools hope that letters of recommendation will provide them with information about applicants that will help them to make better decisions. A written evaluation of an applicant's ability and motivation gives an admissions committee another perspective.

46. Should my recommendations come from judges and lawyers?

Probably not. In fact, most law school applications specify that letters of recommendation should come from college professors. You should solicit a letter of recommendation from a judge or a lawyer only if the person knows your work well and can make a meaningful evaluation of your qualifications to study law—not just because you happen to know someone who is in the legal profession. A letter of evaluation from a prominent member of the profession is not wrong per se; it's just that a "Star Search" approach is probably not going to yield the best results.

47. What if I have been out of school for some time?

Law schools recognize that it will be difficult if not impossible for some applicants to secure academic recommendations. In such cases, letters from colleagues or employers may be substituted.

48. What about a personal interview?

At most law schools, evaluative interviews are not a part of the review process. Most schools feel that the written application, including the personal statement and letters of recommendation, provides an accurate picture of a candidate. Further, granting evaluative interviews might unfairly disadvantage candidates who cannot afford to travel to them. A few schools do use evaluative interviews. One school, for example, invites candidates whose applications are bordering on acceptance to meet with the admissions committee in order to help the committee reach final decisions on those applications. Of course, most schools will welcome a visit from an applicant who wants to learn more about the school, but that visit does not usually include an evaluative interview. One dean who does grant interviews explains that most don't make any difference. In a very few cases, the dean concludes that the applicant should be accepted (and probably would have been, anyway); in a few more cases, the dean decides that the candidate is just not right for the law school; and in the great majority of cases, the dean just sends the file on to the committee with no comment.

49. What else can I do to maximize my chances of acceptance?

One, as you prepare the application, keep firmly in mind the three factors discussed above: ability, motivation, and diversity. Your responses to the application questionnaire, the content of your personal statement, your choice of recommenders—in short, every aspect of the application—should be guided by those three criteria. Too many applicants go astray because they don't understand or have forgotten what factors are important in the admissions process. Two, present a professional image in every respect. All parts of the application should be typed (preferably using a word processor) and, if need be, clearly identified. Make sure that you read carefully all of the directions and abide by them. Finally, pay careful attention to detail and follow up on every procedure (e.g., proofread the application several times and call to make sure that letters of recommendation have been sent). Also, be sure you follow through. We know of an undergraduate who wrongly assumed that the canceled check to the university in payment for the transmittal of a transcript to LSDAS meant that the transcript was actually sent only to receive a note from Harvard Law School to the effect "We wanted to accept you but can't because Law Services never received your grades and the deadline has passed." The story did have a happy ending because the student, acting in a most lawyerly manner, threatened to sue the Registrar and university unless a letter of apology was sent to Harvard Law School. Upon receipt of the letter and later the processed transcript from LSDAS, the student was accepted.

50. Where can I get more information?

For further information about the law school admissions process and for detailed instructions on how to get admitted to the law school of your choice, consult the publications mentioned above. Also, request catalogues from the schools you're interesting in and visit their Web sites.

NOTES

NOTES

NOTES

NOTES

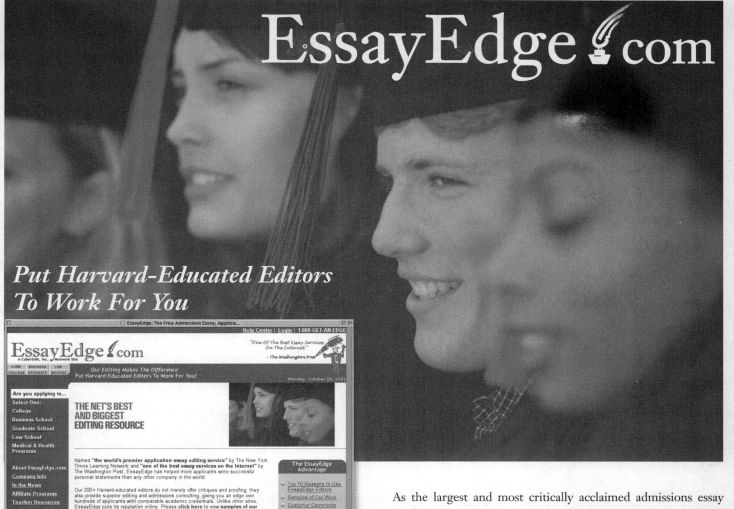

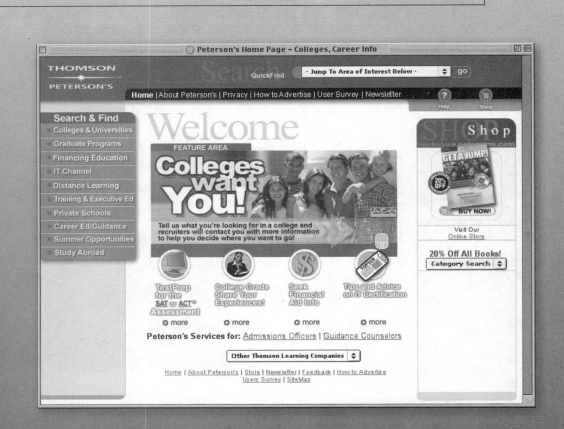